# PREHISTORIC MOURNE

Inspiration for Newgrange

# PREHISTORIC MOURNE

## Inspiration for Newgrange

Written and illustrated by
## Nicholas Russell

Ballaghbeg Books

First published 2015
by Ballaghbeg Books, Newcastle
Email: russelltollymore@gmail.com

Text © Nicholas Russell and Ballaghbeg Books
Photographs © Nicholas Russell
Photographs on pages 360, 372/3, 387, 389, 409,
416, 418, and 467 supplied by Photographic Unit,
National Monuments Service.
Maps on page viii reproduced from the OSNI
with the permission of the Controller of HMSO
© Crown copyright, date 25th February 1955.

All rights reserved. No part of this publication
may be reproduced, stored in a retrieval system,
or transmitted in any form or by any means,
electronic, mechanical, photocopying, recording
or otherwise, without prior permission in writing
of the copyright holders and publishers.

ISBN 978-0-9557922-4-3  HB

Under the Copyright and Related Rights Act 2000, legal deposits of this work
have been made with British Library, Bodlelian Library, Cambridge University,
National Library of Scotland, and the National Library of Wales at Aberystwyth.

In Ireland copies have been sent to Trinity College Library, Dublin, National
Library of Ireland, Dublin City University, NUI Galway, NUI Maynooth, UCD,
University College Cork, the University of Limerick and the Royal Irish Academy
Library, Dawson Street, Dublin.

In Northern Ireland copies have been sent to Queens University, Linenhall
Library, Belfast City Library, the Down Museum, and the Local Studies History
Archive at Downpatrick Library.

Internationally a copy has been lodged with the United States Copyright Office
at the Library of Congress.

Printed by Gráficas Castuera, Navarra, Spain

*Frontispiece*: The Devil's Coachroad megalith of Slievenaglogh, Trassey
*This page*: Summit of Drinnahilly
*Page vi & vii*: Slieve Lamagan from Upper Cove
*Page x:* Three Spear Stones on Meelmore overlooking the Silent Valley

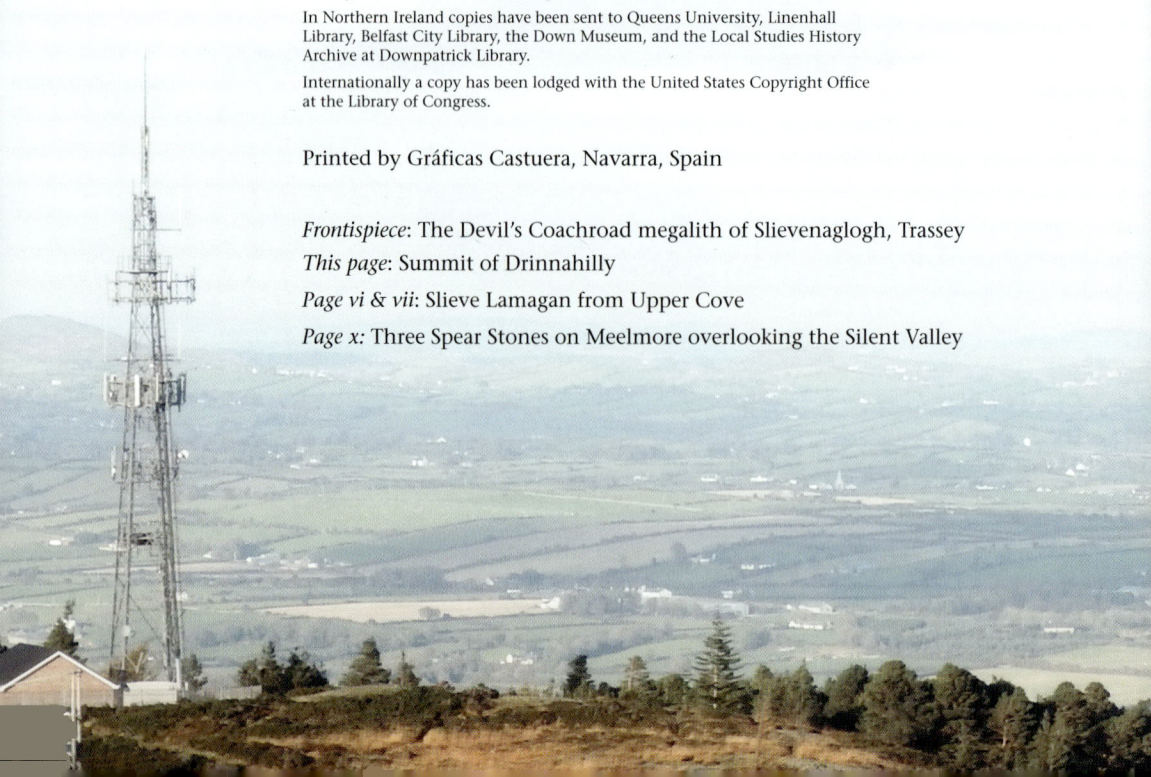

# CONTENTS

| | |
|---|---|
| A good place to live | 1 |
| Mourne: The Mountains of Sex | 32 |
| The Face Stones of Mourne | 140 |
| Spear and Phallic Stones of Mourne | 168 |
| Vagina Stones | 218 |
| Begetting Stones | 248 |
| Slidderyford Dolmen | 270 |
| Bloody Bridge Valley and the Spear of Abundance | 288 |
| Chimney Rock | 320 |
| Upper and Lower Cove | 342 |
| Newgrange and Mourne | 360 |
| Slieve Bearnagh | 392 |
| Slieve Bignian and Vicinity | 420 |
| The Coming of Christianity | 486 |
| | |
| Notes | 522 |
| Bibliography | 550 |
| Index | 559 |

Dedicated with all the thanks of my heart to family, friends and colleagues who offered many special prayers, gave much love and generously extended all possible support and encouragement while this book was being written.

# A GOOD PLACE TO LIVE

The treasure of the early settlers of Mourne is still to be found on the mountains. Undisturbed by the vicissitudes of Irish history the stones the early settlers moved, the megaliths they erected, the art they shaped and the designs they carved are there high in the hills for the discerning eye. The influence of prehistoric Mourne was felt throughout Ireland and was to be an inspiration to the builders of the great Neolithic tomb of Newgrange. In this chapter we see many of the animals that were important to early man rendered in stone. It would have taken much time and effort to fashion these sculptures and they constitute a cultural heritage beyond price not only for Mourne but for all mankind.

About the year 2010, Paddy Hardy, a well-pointer from the Middle Tollymore Road, was working on a building site at the edge of Newcastle on the Dundrum Road. Paddy's job involved drilling bore holes and lowering the water levels to improve building foundations. He recalled what happened on the site near the caravan parks. A bore-hole started gushing water and as it did so, hundreds of little black balls skittered and danced across the yard in the flowing water. The bore hole was a deep one but when Paddy examined a handful of the little black balls he found they were hazelnuts that had been preserved in the oxygen free environment of bog water. Hundreds of hazelnuts flowed out of the hole meeting the sun for the first time in thousands of years. The presence of the nuts in such abundance showed that this important food source had been available from the earliest times. Calculations show that half a ton of hazelnuts could have been gathered by early settlers from a single hectare and it is likely that the autumn crop was stored to provide for the winter. It has been proved that hazelnuts buried in the ground in a well-sealed container remain safe from frosts and pests. Large quantities of hazelnut shells were found at Mount Sandel giving them great dietary importance in the Irish Mesolithic.[1] 'These, gram for gram are seven times richer in fat, five times richer in carbohydrates, four times richer in calcium and five times richer in vitamin B, than eggs.'[2] It was the carbon dating of charred hazelnut shells found at Mount Sandel near Coleraine that demonstrated that people were living in Ireland between 7000 and 6500 BC, much earlier than expected.[3] When excavations were carried out at Murlough in 1950-51, A.E.P. Collins recorded 'a quantity of carbonised hazel nut shells and a few fragments of burnt bone' in a system of post-holes and shallow pits.[4] Years earlier, before the war, Rev Lindsay Hewson noted other nuts found in the same vicinity. 'The remains of fire were pretty frequent in this area and I was able to observe the presence of beech nuts, which I believe could hardly have been there save as carried from a distance either with the firewood or for human consumption.'[5]

A boar's head has been wonderfully rendered on this huge megalith on the west slope of Chimney Rock mountain.

Prehistoric Mourne: Inspiration for Newgrange

Recently while passing by the closed technical college at the top of Bryansford Avenue I couldn't help noticing a rich crop of rose-hips growing on the bushes alongside the fence. Rose-hips contain twenty times as much vitamin C as oranges and were used in desserts in the Middle Ages. When we gathered the hips as youngsters however, the intention was to use the fine hairs inside the fruit as an itching powder.

To the hazelnuts and beech nut would be added haws, blaeberries and blackberries. Fungi, roots, leaves, stems, flowers, nuts, seeds, berries and fruits would also have been harvested by early man to provide a diet with plentiful vitamins and minerals. Even a hundred years ago such collecting often formed an important part of a farmer's effort and income. In 1910 a Ballylough man, Charles Flinn, together with his family, gathered in the district and marketed in Belfast 11½ cwt of blackberries – that's 584 kilos of blackberries.[6] For this effort they then earned just over £5. Blaeberries, also known as bilberries or fraochóga, fraughans, heatherberries, hurs, hurts, mulberries, whortleberry and whorts, were enjoyed on the mountains on the last Sunday of July or the first Sunday of August. The eastern flank of Chimney Rock mountain is also known as Blaeberry Mountain. The southern flank is known at Spence's Mountain. Here the mountain slopes

Long Mountain otherwise known as Blaeberry Mountain.

descend to the lowland. The Place-names project of QUB has undertaken much research to establish that the surname Spence can be connected with this part of the Mournes as far back as the middle of the 17th century.[7] However I believe the origin of the name lies in the Irish *Spíonadh* meaning 'the act of pulling, plucking'. From the plucking of the blaeberries the mountain could be associated with a place of food, a 'spence', in Irish *Speansa*. Spence is an early word for a pantry or a cellar. The old French word *despense* meaning 'to distribute' conveys the idea that it was from the pantry or cellar that supplies of food were given out. Collecting these small sweet berries in season was an important addition to the diet of Mourne and the first Sunday of August was the happy festival day for such gathering.[8]

The early settlers most likely arrived by boat and would have been good fishermen. There are numerous stones on the mountains that have received the attention of man and very many of these appear to be representations of fish. Based on the megaliths that are marvellous depictions of sea life (and the shady valley of Pollaphuca so suggestive of the dark ocean is rich in such stones), I would

This phallic projection on the Leestone Rock, perhaps representing a seal with a nearby stone its pup, gave the stone its name in Irish – *Lia Stáin* – 'great stone of stiffness'. The projecting rock points towards winter solstice sunrise on the horizon.

even make bold to say they were incredible fishermen, ranging far and hunting species apparently no longer found in these waters. The Leestone Rock at Kilkeel is a fertility megalith that a fisherman would be proud of. An impudent projection with a face, perhaps that of a seal, points assertively seawards to where the sun rises at the winter solstice while the other end of the huge stone, which looks to the sunset at the summer solstice, shows a well executed face of a grouper fish. The Leestone name is said by some to be of English origin but it is just an imitation of the sound of the Irish *Lia Stáin* meaning 'great stone of (sexual) stiffness'. We will look further at the animation of stones but fish was an incredibly rich local resource and would have been a crucial part of the early diet. Up until the early 20th century when the steam trawlers scoured the floor of Dundrum Bay with their trammel nets, the Bay was a place of unbelievable fecundity. Walter Harris mentioned how the largess of the sea was a boon to the poor. 'The coast affords plenty and variety of sea fish, and such quantities of sand eels have sometimes been taken on it, particularly in the late season of scarcity, that the poor carried them away in sack fulls.'[9] Lewis's *Topographical Dictionary of Ireland* published in 1837 stated; 'The ground immediately outside the large Bay is said to be one of the best fishing grounds in the British seas, affording always in their respective seasons large supplies of excellent haddock, cod, whiting, plaice, sole and turbot'. Giving evidence at an inquiry into trawling in Dundrum Bay, line fisherman James Murphy, on oath, mentioned that he had hooked a plaice over 2ft long.[10] People could remember that before plaice nets were introduced in the Bay about 1875 it was a common occurrence to see turbot caught weighing 15 and 20lbs and upwards, besides splendid specimens of sole, brill and plaice; in fact, all classes of fish exceptionally large and choice.[11] Such were the heavy takings of whiting in February 1907 that fishermen who had invested in smacks knew they had made a good investment. As for the good old herring, 127,000 tons were landed in Co Down during the 1908 season valued at £56,721.[12]

To the richness of the sea should also be added the shellfish. Oysters are now grown commercially in Dundrum Bay. Although now rare in the wild they were until relatively recently extremely common and were favoured as an abundant food source. We can be sure the early settlers also looked for cockles, razor-shells, winkles and crabs. If you have ever lifted a stone to whack a limpet free from its suction grip you are only following what others have done for thousands of years. The tough muscle of the limpet's foot however makes it a very hard food to eat and it really would likely only have been used as an emergency food source. The usual practice with limpets was to soak and soften them in water for at least a week and then use them as fish-bait. Clay lined stone boxes in the houses at Skara Brae are thought to have been used for this purpose.[13] Limpets together with sand eels that were dug up from the mud flats at Murlough were used locally as bait by

The face of a large grouper fish looks out from the Leestone Rock.

Little is more. Can you visualise a claw on this stone crustacean?
It is to be found in Pollaphuca valley.

line-fishermen until the start of the twentieth century. Watching foreign nationals gathering bags of periwinkles and whelks at low tide at Leestone beach a few years ago was a reminder that this unloved food source is still prized by many on the continent and would have been a reliable addition to the diet in ancient times. You can find winkles everywhere on a rocky shore between high and low tide-marks. They may be unloved now but a century ago the collection of periwinkles was important enough to warrant inclusion in the 1906 official fishery returns for the Newcastle division made by the coastguard. The same returns that valued the periwinkles at £44 for that season also valued lobsters captured at £631 and crabs at £23.

It is a great pity that the noble fish associated in Celtic mythology with wisdom is no longer to be found in the Shimna river. A century ago the picture was different. When the Banbridge and Portadown Joint Waterworks Board sought by act of parliament to abstract water from the Shimna for their urban districts, evidence had to be given before the select committee of the House of Commons. In the course of proceedings, Colonel Jocelyn, brother to and representing Lord Roden, said that there had been so much netting that it had prevented the salmon from coming up the river. However, the river was full of salmon in the winter.[14] The returning salmon were so familiar to fishermen of earlier generations that the sea chasm south of Newcastle known as Maggie's Leap derived its name from the fish. The fishermen had a couple of names for the area. One old name for the place in Irish was *Coiscéim na Caillí* meaning 'the footstep of the cormorant' but there was also another Irish name *maighre liopaí*. Maggie's Leap is a mnemonic from the Irish *maighre liopaí* which means 'big lipped salmon'; the name is metaphorical, comparing the long narrow sea chasm to the mature salmon swimming with its mouth cracked open.[15] The salmon would have run late in the Shimna. There used to be a few in June but the main run began with the first flood after the middle of July and continued well into November.[16] In April or May, young elvers would start arriving from the ocean and enter freshwater in enormous numbers. As a youngster, and long before the weir was built across the Shimna, great fun was to be had turning over stones behind Whiteside's garage, now the present library, and trying to catch the young eels as they wriggled and squirmed.

A most magnificent work of ancient art in Pollaphuca valley. Note the rough chop marks where stone has been removed at the side and front to change this block into a sublime rendering of an attacking octopus.

Sculpture at its best. The unmistakeable and glorious proboscis on this rearing adult bull Elephant Seal put this megalith in a very special class. Carved in granite probably thousands of years ago, it is to be found on the South Tor of Slieve Bearnagh.

The addition of eyes to this stone at Douglas Crag changes it into quite a realistic seal.

The slopes under Spellack cliff in the Trassey valley are particularly rich in face stones. Here, with the addition of a couple of eyes, a stone has been transformed into a well fed seal pup.

Sea mammals were another source of food. Seals still haul themselves out onto the shore at Ballykinlar to rest undisturbed. Millennia ago we can imagine many more rested all along the miles of shore-line. The stone elephant seal in an aggressive stance on the south tor of Slieve Bearnagh bespeaks the importance of this animal to the ancients. Perhaps this species was early hunted to extinction because it is no longer found in northern Atlantic waters. Whales too, when they were washed ashore would have been a bonanza of food. Large fish, like sharks and whales, make an impression on watchers even today. Should we be surprised that particularly large specimens of fish were held in awe long ago? The northern orthostat at Slidderyford dolmen could reasonably be construed as a rising basking shark. The tomb monument on the slopes of Slieve Thomas is undoubtedly that of a breeching whale and sun marker stones on the western slopes of the Spinkwee valley could be looked upon as sharks so realistic are the outlines. In Pollaphuca valley is a remarkable stone which has been shaped as a basking shark complete with open mouth. Such resemblances on many stones throughout Mourne are not a co-incidence but are the deliberate choice of early man, possibly to honour that particular animal or encourage its fertility.

At the foot of Leganabruchan this megalith with its block shaped front is a magnificent representation of a Sperm Whale complete with calf.[17]

In centuries past, the fishermen of Newcastle referred to the hill west of Newcastle as a whale. Nowadays this hill, which is part of Tollymore forest park, is locally called 'The Drinns' although, as we shall see in another chapter, this name strictly belongs to the south side of the hill (OS J343314) overlooking the high marsh of Curragh Ard. From out in Dundrum Bay the profile of the hill, with its dip resembling a blowhole, reminded the fishermen of a whale breaking the surface of the ocean. The only remnant of the lost name is Parnell's View. Some have previously sought to explain this by reference to distinguished visitors of the same name to Tollymore Park[18]. However, the name derives from Irish where *Parn Eile* means 'another whale'. The name was probably discontinued with the coming of English. The 'whale' part of the name would often be eclipsed, as in *Tulaigh na bParn eile* (hill of the other whale), but as this sounded the same as 'barn' in English it was too open to confusion as a building for storing hay, grain or livestock instead of a whale and so the name scarcely made the transition from Irish to English.

This beautiful rendition of a feeding basking shark with its mouth typically open is found in Pollaphuca valley. Note the lines on the right side of the mouth showing where the stone has been spalled off in the creation of this work of art

The tip of the granite orthostat at Slidderyford bears a remarkable resemblance to the open mouth of a basking shark.

This megalith with its closed eye is an astute interpretation of a whale's head emerging from the ocean. It is found on the lower slopes of Leganabruchan close to the Sperm whale megalith.

In thinking of the food sources that could be exploited locally thousands of years ago the Shimna river names are of significance; Shimna means the river of bulrushes and in old maps the Shimna was known as Hanolock. Hanolock derives from the Irish as in the phrase *ag tarraing na hanálach* which conveys the sense of taking one's time and slowly drawing one's breath particularly in dying when there are long pauses between the breaths. It is a magnificent metaphor for the tide going in and out of the Shimna. Originally the whole area behind Main Street and out to the Bryansford Road and beyond would have been a large tidal swamp fed not only by the ocean but by the waters of the Burren, Shimna and Tullybrannigan rivers. This large area would have taken a long time to fill and drain and was probably so slow in doing so that the exiting waters would be meeting the next incoming tide. The whole area with pools, islands, swaths of bulrushes and probably some mud flats would have been a very attractive habitat for eels and overwintering geese, duck and whooper swans, just like the inner

This hill to the west of Newcastle is known today to the locals as The Drinns. To the fishermen of old this hill, when seen from far out on Dundrum Bay and likely without its present covering of trees, resembled a whale and was referred to by them as *Parn Eile*, 'the other whale'. The only remnant of the name today is the vista location called Parnell's View.

A breaching humpback whale. Erecting this massive stone (it measures 18 feet in height alone for the part above ground) would have been an immense technical challenge on the steep sided slope of Thomas. It was probably this work that gave the mountain its name in Irish, Tuama, meaning 'tomb', and which was later changed to Thomas by newly arriving settlers from England and Scotland. If you are on the main path en route to Slieve Donard, the stone can be clearly seen in profile on Slieve Thomas by looking left from the area of the Ice House.

Another view of the breaching whale megalith on the slopes of Slieve Thomas taken at summer solstice dawn. The two water bottles placed for scale at the base of the huge stone are hardly discernable. This important megalith may be more sophisticated than imagined. The stones on the left have likely been carefully positioned to act as a gnomon so that the shadow cast at dawn on the spring equinox would coincide with chip marks on the face of the megalith showing the early farmers that the time for planting their crops had come.

The stone of the two mating frogs on the Glen River is a true artistic treasure of ancient Mourne. An awareness of the artistic intention may only come from first looking at the stone from various angles, noting the chipped indentations to simulate eyes.

marsh of Dundrum Bay today. There had also been a large swampy area at the foot of the Glen river until the river was diverted in the 19th century to a more direct path to the sea as a relief scheme. This swampy area, not being as saline as the Shimna was, would have supported another food source namely an almost inexhaustible supply of frogs.

For a lifetime I have passed the huge rock in the middle of the Glen river just up-stream from the Donard Lodge bridge without thinking about it. Only recently did I realise that this is a fertility megalith deliberately placed here. Look carefully at this masterpiece of ancient impressionism. The slits that hint of eyes, the simple point to intimate a chin and just enough surplus stone knocked away to suggest the hidden forms and you realise that you are looking at two mating frogs. The smaller male frog clings to the back of the larger female until she lays her eggs and he then fertilises them. It was the sharp, spear shaped, part of the stone that was pointing, I suspected, either to summer solstice sunrise or to where the sun would rise at the frogs breeding season, that made me look at the rock more carefully.

This stone frog in Glen Fofanny valley points to where the winter solstice sun will rise.

This megalith has been wedged into position at the one part of the river where, long before the Annesleys built their bridge in 1835, people could safely cross and the site offered a commanding viewpoint down to the fresh water habitat of the frogs. Locals always named Donard bridge as 'first'. Originally I could only imagine that it enjoyed this primacy as it was the first bridge across the river *inside the demesne*. This was to make a distinction from the original main road bridge leading to Kilkeel which existed earlier at the mouth of the Glen river and was known as Patton's bridge until it was washed away by flood waters in 1968. The name 'first' comes however from the Irish *foisteán* meaning a terrace or a bench and refers to the relatively flat stretch of rock at this part of the river just above Annesley's bridge. It was this terrace that allowed early man to manoeuvre the monument into its fittingly wet location. If you have to work with your imagination to perceive the intention of the ancients then so much the better. The very paucity of design conveying so much without fuss or elaboration of detail yet still having the gist of the frogs, one on top of the other, makes this a true artistic treasure of ancient Mourne. We are particularly fortunate that this megalith is probably the most easily accessible of all.

A beautifully observed and magnificently executed sculpture of a howling wolf carefully placed to catch the light of summer solstice dawn. The length and slimness of the stone show it to be of phallic import. This artwork is truly treasure in stone.

This delicate little head of a shrew is to be found on Slieve Muck.

The right end of this important megalith shows a sleeping head but there is no mistaking the profile of a little boar on the left.

With its sleeping eye, this long tapering megalith on the southern slopes of Slieve Meelmore is quite suggestive of a deer's head.

Judging from the animals depicted, this rock platform on the Chimney Rock side of the col at the head of the Bloody Bridge valley must have been of importance to the ancients. It was probably used for ritual at the vigil of the summer solstice sunrise and compliments the other platform, much higher up, on the south facing slope of Slieve Donard which would have been used for the winter solstice. From the left at the back of the platform we have the lovely carving of a dog (or would that be a wolf's head?) being groomed by a large tongue behind it and on the right the sculpture of a pig. Other stones below the platform have been 'animated' with a simple eye and a mouth.

Besides the foraging and gathering there was always hunting to provide food. Archaeologist Rachel Maclean listed the fourteen species of mammals that we can be reasonably certain were present during the Mesolithic; the Irish hare, the Irish stoat, the pygmy shrew, the red squirrel, the fox, the badger, the otter, the pine marten, the red deer, the wild pig, the wolf, the brown bear, the wild cat and the lynx.[19] Of these species it usually was only the wild pig and the red deer that were hunted for meat. Pigs even left us the place-name Carrowmurwaghnemucklagh which is part of the townland of Tollymore. The pigs would have done well in an area where, as we mentioned earlier, hazelnuts flourished.[20] The unusual name is from the Irish *'Ceathrú muirbheach na muclach'* meaning 'the quarter of the level stretch of the droves of pigs'. Wild boars are really good breeders and can increase in numbers quite rapidly. Sows can have litters of up to twelve piglets and populations have the ability to double or triple each year. The boars can also grow to impressive sizes. One that was shot in 2012 at the Forest of Dean weighed

*This megalith of a pig is found towards the northern end of Slieve Muck and probably contributed to the mountain being so called – 'Pig Mountain'.*

167kg (368lb)[21]. Slieve Muck in the Mournes is 'pig mountain' and probably owes its name both to the distinctive cliff edge, like a boar's spine, which runs the length of the mountain top and to this distinctively piggy megalith found on the north eastern slope.[22] This is only one of a number of megaliths depicting pigs and demonstrates their importance in the early economy. The spear, the symbol of hunting, is widespread among the megaliths of Mourne. There is no mistaking 'spear stones' with their pointed termini. Not only was the weapon a symbol of male power but, by extension came to represent male sexual prowess.

One further habitat that was an important food source would have been the sea cliffs south of Newcastle. I am very conscious how the numbers of seabirds seem to have declined very significantly even in my lifetime. When the tide was out in the 1950's it was a common sight to see thousands of gulls roosting on the stony shore at the mouth of the Shimna river in what was a great white carpet. It was a part of growing up to be familiar with the early morning screeching of herring gulls as they landed on the roofs of the houses in the town. Today all is very quiet by comparison and something unique has been lost. It was on the cliffs south of Newcastle harbour that the gulls made their nests and laid their eggs. Such were the numbers of gulls that the practise of collecting their eggs in springtime centuries ago made hardly a dent in their numbers. The story of Maggie at Maggie's Leap gives a clue to how the eggs were collected. Maggie was described as 'going to market with a basket of eggs on her head' when she leaped the gorge. In times past, those who were collecting sea bird eggs needed both their hands free for climbing the cliff. Eggs that were put in pockets in clothes were liable to be crushed against the rocks so it was the practice to tie a basket onto the head in which to save what was gathered.[23] Not only eggs were collected but probably later the birds as well. The guga hunt endures in Scotland where 2,000 gannets are still harvested by traditional means. Men would wait until the moment the young chicks had put on sufficient weight yet were still unable to fly and then climbed the cliffs to take the birds off the nests. Guga meat is considered by some to be a delicacy although it is grey, strong tasting and salty. An important seagull megalith on the slopes of Meelmore suggests the birds were a food source in Mourne as well.

Mention has been made of overwintering geese, duck and whooper swans. A mirror stone at the col of the Hare's Gap is undoubtedly the image of a whooper swan. Swans, mallards, barnacle geese and indeed any wintering bird would have been eaten by early man just as we have our turkey at Christmas. A word of explanation about the term 'mirror stone.' Such stones are distinctive in having a large flat area presented towards the rising sun like a mirror. The reason for this is now long lost but perhaps we can surmise a faith that wanted to capture as much light of the new rising sun as possible in the belief that it brought fresh life and fertility to whatever it touched.

The stones depicted so far relate to a hunting and foraging lifestyle as would have been prevalent during the Mesolithic or middle stone age period. Carbon dating has established human occupation at the coastal site of Mount Sandel, Coleraine, at around 7,000BC, making it the oldest archaeological site in Ireland. It is not unreasonable to imagine that early man was also exploiting the food resources around the coast of Mourne about the same time. The Mesolithic in Ireland is thus seen as extending from 7,000BC to 4,000BC when the Neolithic way of life brought about a transition to farming and herding. The presence of the numerous animal megaliths around Mourne suggest not only a successful lifestyle but a permanency of settlement and a higher Mesolithic population than perhaps previously hitherto imagined. Hopefully archaeological excavations in Mourne in the future may determine a time frame for the animal megaliths. Not all these animal megaliths are suggestive of an early origin in the time of hunter gatherers.

On the summit of Chimney Rock mountain can be seen a stone evocative of a ram's head and also a small stone shaped as a young animal. This last could easily be imagined as a lamb or a dropped calf. The presence also of the image of a stone calf or heifer on the western slopes of Chimney Rock mountain bespeaks the interest of herding people, namely the early farmers of the Neolithic. The valleys of Mourne would have been of vital importance for summer pasturage

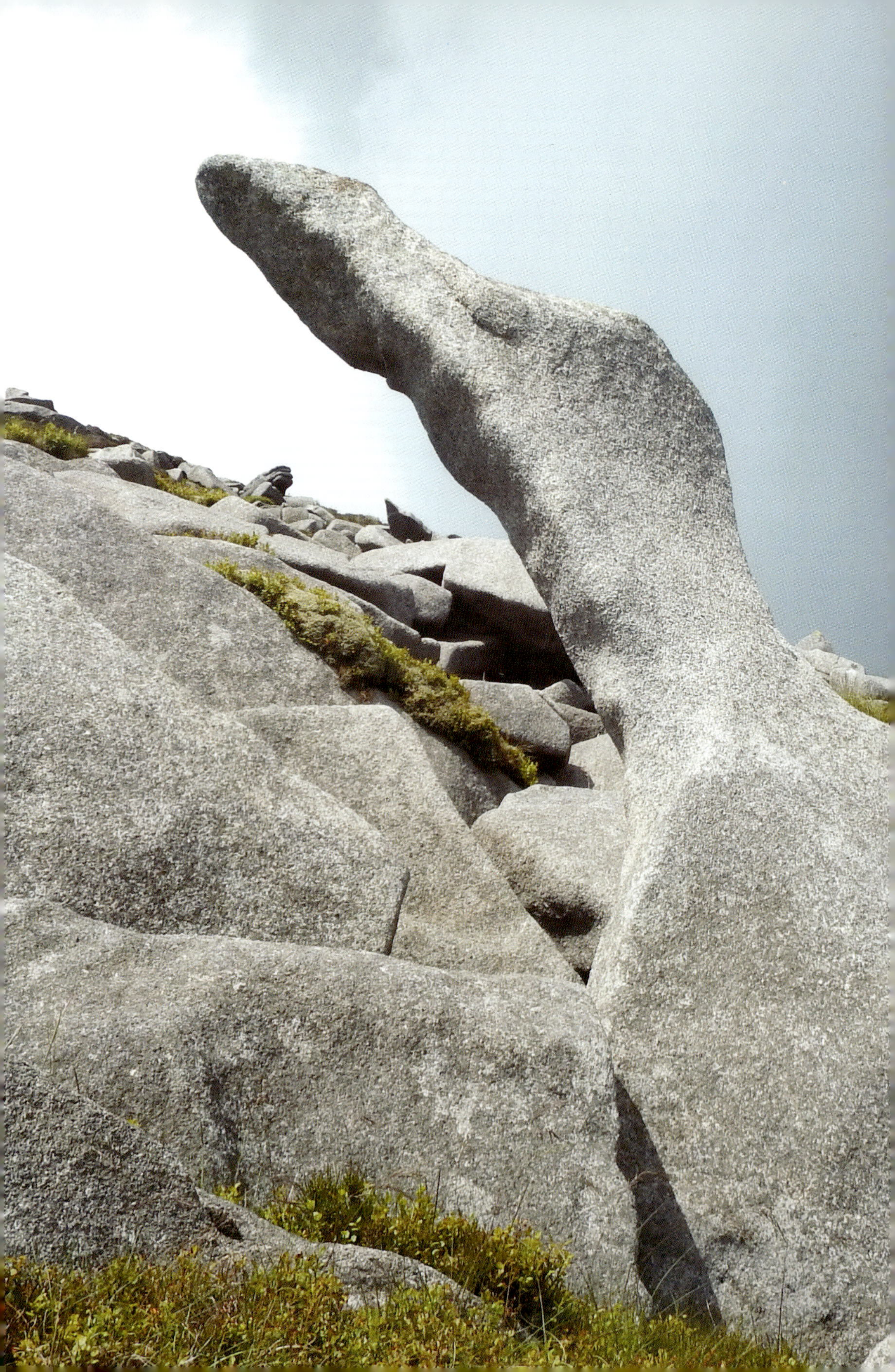

A large megalith on the flank of Slieve Meelmore overlooking the Silent Valley has been rendered as a rather phallic seagull's head with a face on either side. This is a particularly fine and important piece of ancient sculpture.

*When next at the col of the Hare's Gap, stop to admire this sculpture of the head of a whooper swan. The flat area – I call this a mirror stone – is oriented towards the winter solstice sunrise.*

thus sparing the lowlands for winter fodder. It was the Neolithic farmers who started growing crops such as wheat and with the cereals came mice and rats. By far and away my favourite megaliths must be a pair of stones high on the south facing slope of Slieve Donard. I call them 'Tom and Jerry' after the cartoon characters for they unmistakeably resemble a mouse with large ears, its nose anxiously in the air, and a cat sitting upright. The stones are propped up about fifty metres apart where they can warily keep eye on each other. No-one can say that the Neolithic people did not have a sense of humour.

With the wide range of habitats available locally, our area at the foot of Mourne would have been very attractive to early man. There were the sea-cliffs for birds and eggs; the waters of Dundrum Bay rich in crabs and fish; the rocky shores for rock clinging shell-fish; the sandy shores for seals, cockles, razor-shells and the occasional stranded whale; the forest fringe for hazelnuts, seeds, berries and fruits; the forests and mountains for hunting pigs and deer; the fresh water rivers for salmon, eels and frogs; the estuarine mudflats for fish bait and over-wintering wild fowl and the heath for grouse and ground nesting birds. Man had access to a plant-rich diet, supplemented by molluscs, crustaceans, fungi, fish, frogs, fowl and herbivores. The foot of the Mournes was indeed a very good place to live.

*A stone of a young lamb or a new born calf perhaps shaped by an early farmer hoping for increased fertility in his herds or maybe by way of thanksgiving*

This stone shaped like a ram's head is to be found on one of the boulder clump peaks of Chimney Rock mountain.

On the south west slope of Chimney Rock is this large stone shaped like a cow or calf and as such would have been erected by people whose livelihood was animal husbandry.

The nervous mouse with its big ears and nose high, keeps an anxious eye on the 'cat' a little further down the slope.

The cat and mouse monuments, 'Tom and Jerry', are high on Donard's southern slopes. Crossone mountain is in the background.

With stones firmly wedging it in place, this substantial stone cat sits calmly overlooking the Bloody Bridge valley and doubtlessly watching the nearby mouse out of the corner of its eye.

This stone turtle with a rather large carapace is found on the slopes of Slieve Lamagan above the Blue Lough; the 'head' faces towards the fertility fissure of Ben Crom. The Harleck leatherback turtle stranded in Wales in 1989 weighed 916 kilos. Note the numerous tiny outlines of megaliths, skylined on Douglas Crag, seen on the right in the middle distance.

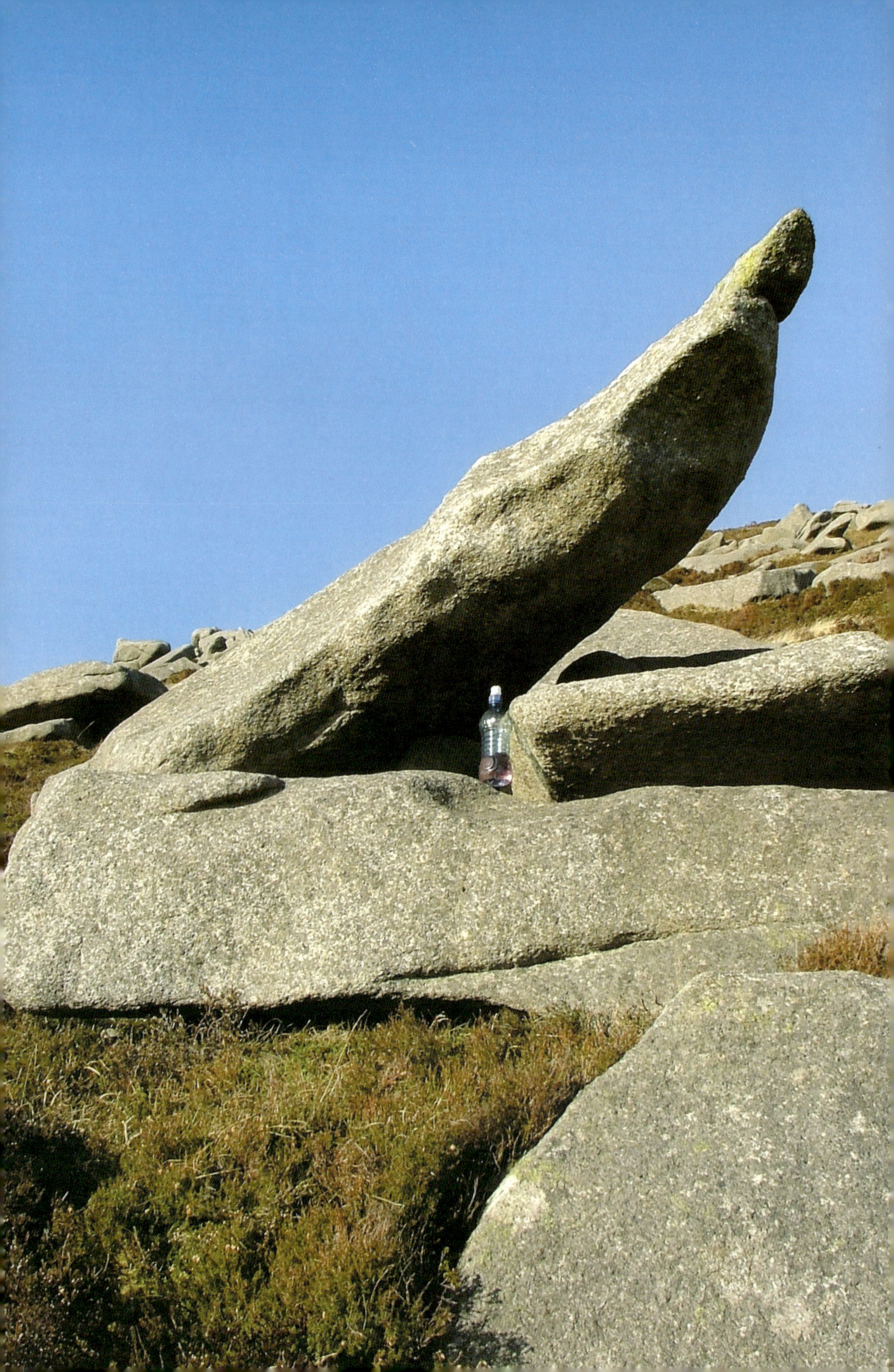

# MOURNE:
# THE MOUNTAINS OF SEX

On 21st April 1834 the Irish scholar John O'Donovan wrote to the headquarters of the Ordnance Survey from Castlewellan: 'It will puzzle me to ascertain the correct names of the Mourne mountains, and of others in this neighbourhood.'[1] John O'Donovan was in a rush when he came to Mourne. He had spent too long in the Rathfriland district and finally left there to go to Castlewellan on Friday morning 19th April 1834. Four days he spent in this district in his quest to ascertain the correct version of townlands, mountains, parishes, rivers, villages, etc., and one of these days was spent climbing Slieve Donard. He then moved on to Downpatrick. O'Donovan was vexed that the name books on which he relied to help him decide the proper names seemed to be missing many names of Mourne.

> 'Those who have surveyed the land,' he said, 'and who therefore know every name that must appear on the face of the map should have furnished me with a perfect list of all the mountains, hills, Trig. Stations, rivers, streams, forts, rocks, & c, in each parish, because I have no plan of any parish, and it is hard for any inhabitant to recollect all these names, without some such help.'[2]

It would seem that Mourne would cause problems even to the very end. O'Donovan walked from Downpatrick to Donaghadee and back again through the Ards and Lecale, hurting his left foot in the process. Then he returned to Newry from where he wrote:

> 'The names of the Mourne Mountains are very curious, but as Mr James has not his plans yet finished I cannot possibly know what names I am to get. He has furnished me with as perfect a list of them as he could with a plan of their relative situation but I find that every shoulder on them bears a distinct appellation. Mr James shewed me the Boundary Surveyor's Sketch map of the Barony but the names of half the Mts are not given.
>
> I shall obtain as many names as I can with their situations, but it is possible and very probable that I may omit some, but I expect to get the names of the most remarkable features, as well valleys as mountains.'[3]

We may imagine that his success was rather limited as four days later he admitted:

> 'I have now settled the orthography of the whole Co. except the Names of the Mourne Mountains.'[4]

In the years since O'Donovan collected the local names there have been four further examinations of our place-names each giving English explanations. Canon

High on the south facing slope of Slieve Donard is this phallic representation of the long nose of a pygmy shrew, the only shrew native to Ireland. As well as its 'phallic nose' the little animal was an ideal fertility symbol; a female could have between two to eight young per litter and up to five litters a year.

Prehistoric Mourne: Inspiration for Newgrange

Henry William Lett, read a paper on *Names of Places in the Mountains of Mourne* to the Royal Irish Academy in 1906.[5] He formed his list by taking all the names given on the 6 inch to 1 mile maps of the Ordnance Survey of County Down and collating them with O'Donovan's map and manuscripts, Williamson's map of County Down and other sources. In 1950 two scholars again looked at Mourne place-names. Fr Bernard Mooney produced his now scarce *The Place-names of Rostrevor* and professor Evans looked at place-name meanings in an appendix of his classic work, *Mourne Country*. Latterly in 1993, the institute of Irish studies at Queen's gathered, interpreted and published a wealth of invaluable information about Mourne in their Northern Ireland place-name project.

All these efforts were lacking in one decisive respect, namely an awareness of how the old pagan religion had crucially influenced the names of Mourne. This was why O'Donovan thought the names were 'very curious'. Without an awareness of the significance of the old religion many of our mountain names would always seem peculiar, odd, strange, unusual, intriguing and even bizarre and weird. A number have been mis-translated because the correct version did not otherwise seem to make sense. Many names missed receiving close attention

Slievenamiskan on the left projected a huge phallic like shadow across the former floor of Spelga valley at summer solstice sunset. This 'huge dagger' of a shadow was in Irish *Déar-Meadóg* and and became the now obsolete Deers' Meadow.

because they were thought to be of recent or English origin whereas they really were the sound of the old Irish in an English skin, a mnemonic.[6] With the arrival of colonists from England and Scotland who were unfamiliar with Irish, some names went from Irish to English and then were translated back into Irish again but now with a different meaning. The site of Spelga Dam likely began with the name *Déar-Meadóg,* then was changed to the mnemonic 'Deers' Meadow' only for this in turn to be re-translated back into Irish for O'Donovan by local man John McLindon in 1834 as *Léuna na bh-fiadh,* 'meadow of the deer'. The original name *Déar-Meadóg*[7] was not recorded in written records; it means 'huge dagger'. However, the phenomenon that gave rise to the name, namely the huge shadow, with phallic import, cast across the meadow by Slievenamiskan at summer solstice sunset, still endures. One can hardly blame John McLindon, from the Clonduff area, in his sincere but erroneous effort to help O'Donovan as the *Déar-Meadóg* shadow was so transient, would appear briefly for a few days either side of the solstice and was further subject to the vagaries of the weather for its existence. The other form of the name for the Deers' Meadow mentioned in Walter Harris's history of County Down, namely 'King's Meadow', supposedly 'because people had their grazing in it free'[8], comes from the Irish *Caoin Meadóg*. This means variously 'gentle, pleasing, smooth or delicate dagger'; again all are references to the shadow dagger that had no sharpness. Nowadays if we were to describe the dagger outline we might use the painting term *sfumato* which Leonardo da Vinci used in his painting of the Mona Lisa and which he described as 'without lines or borders, in the manner of smoke'.

As O'Donovan was discovering in his travels, finding native speakers of Irish was difficult enough. In the matter of the old religion, finding those with even a tiny residual knowledge prepared to court the ire of the church in even talking about it would likely have been utterly impossible outside of Mourne[9]. The truth is that Christianity had so successfully replaced or overlaid the old religion that the original reason behind many names was lost. To this should also be added the unimaginable loss sustained when the vast store of ancient Gaelic lore, with its information on local and regional life, disappeared under the triple hammer blows of the famine, the passing of the Gaelic language and the haemorrhage of emigration.

## Beanna Boirche

*Beanna Boirche* is the old name for Mourne, being found in the early seventh century Annals of Ulster and the eighth century Annals of the Four Masters. This name was translated by the place-names project as 'the peaks of the peak district' but it must have been with some reservation as a note was made that it was 'obviously a tautological name'. In 'the lore of famous places', *Dindshenchas* in Irish, *Boirche* was personified as a shepherd or cowherd. QUB place-names,

Rounded mountain tops, long impertinent shadows and megaliths such as this, gave Mourne its meaning of 'the mountains of very many sexual swellings'. This monument is on the west slope of Chimney Rock and probably marks a spot where the setting winter solstice sun connected with a distant tor on Slieve Bignian in a perceived act of fertility.

however, would state that *'Beanna Boirche* is not derived from a personal name' but was applied to the district as a whole.

*Beanna Boirche* is one of the local names that, as mentioned earlier, have been mis-translated because the correct version did not otherwise seem to make sense. So what does *Beanna Boirche* mean? A tiny Irish lesson is necessary for a moment. The first word is straight forward. *Beanna,* (genitive *beinne, binne, beanna);* (plural *beanna*), means 'a point, a peak; a mountain peak; a headland; a cliff; a pinnacle; a crest; a top'[10]. For the second word, the Irish-English dictionary of Rev Patrick Dinneen translates *Boirrche* as 'a swelling; a growing; an inflation through anger, a fit of anger; roughness of weather;' So we can arrive at a translation 'the peaks of swellings'. If one didn't know about the importance of the old religion you could hardly be surprised that *Beanna Boirche,* 'the peaks of swellings' didn't appear too sensible. That was why it was 'improved on' and made more logical, if somewhat repetitious, by the translation 'peaks of the peak district'. But 'the peaks of swellings' it is. To make it quite clear what the real meaning is we would say 'the peaks of (sexual) swellings'. To make life more interesting a case can be made that the name Mourne comes from a similar root and means the same thing. The sexual swellings that gave rise to *Beanna Boirche* will be examined in the coming pages as we look at the meaning of many Mourne place-names and in the coming chapters as we look at the wide proliferation of phallic spear stones, vagina stones and stones that imitate copulation. These last I refer to as *gein* stones, from the Irish *gein* meaning 'the act of begetting'.

## The Meaning of 'Mourne'

The name of Mourne has been thought until now to have derived from the tribal name of Mughdhorna. A branch of a Monaghan tribe, being under pressure, 'sought for themselves another settlement, namely, this Mugharna, which they subdued by force of arms, and called after the name of their former inheritance.'[11] The place-names project of QUB has done us a great service by collating all known names that refer to the mountains so that the development of these names can be followed. The various listings of the tribal name *Mughdhorna* are carefully set forth and the most significant usage is probably that by John O'Donovan who titled his map of the Mournes as *Sléibhte Múghdhorn*. There is plenty to argue about at how the present name of Mourne was arrived at besides a possible genesis in county Monaghan. Because the enduring influence of the old pagan religion was not previously realised, two new interpretations of the derivation of the name Mourne can now be offered. It should not be automatically presumed therefore that one of the explanations has to be wrong. Let us remember what John O'Donovan said of the mountains: 'I find that every *shoulder* on them bears a distinct appellation'. Multiple names were common in the past and sometimes overlapped. In its short duration even Newcastle has been known variously as Caisleán Nua, Donomawe (from *Dún na mBáid*, 'Fort of the boats') and Shyleke.[12]

In the first explanation of the derivation of Mourne we look to the Irish word *Borr*, (genitive *buirr*), (plural *borra*), meaning 'a bunch, **a lump**; pride'. This is close to the same root as *Boirrche* meaning 'swelling'. Originally this word would have been part of a longer title causing it to be eclipsed. Eclipse, as the name suggests, involves, in Irish, adding to the beginning of a word a consonant which replaces the sound of the original consonant. This arises where we have a noun plus the definite article *na*, plus the genitive plural. Without making a whole lesson on grammar, in certain usages the first letter [B] has the letter [m] added in front of it. The sound of [m] is heard but the sound of [B] is not; the letter [B] is eclipsed. This will have implications for our word mentioned above, the plural *borra* meaning 'lumps'. Looking next at Dinneen's dictionary we see that adding -*ne*, or -*na* to the end of a word gives it a strong collective sense. By way of example, the Irish word for a 'drop' is *bann*; but *bain* plus -*ne* gives us the Irish word *bainne* meaning 'milk'. The single drop has grown exponentially. The word Mourne is the telescoped remnant of a longer phrase that invoked eclipse and used the collective suffix –*na*.

37

'The mountains of very many (sexual) lumps, or swellings', is in Irish
*Sléibhte na mBorra-na*

In the word *mBorra-na* we remember that the [B] sound is not heard, only [m]; this would leave us with M_orra-na. The start of the phrase *Sléibhte na* has been dropped and all we are left with is the shorthand *mBorra-na*, which with usage has become our familiar Mourne. On account of its affinity with *Beanna Boirche*, this explanation has a merit not easily dismissed. The real proof of the pudding is the recognition of the 'very many sexual lumps' and in this respect the mountains certainly live up to their name. The topography supports this interpretation from the Irish and the photographs here will hopefully raise an awareness of the many megaliths erected to mark an interaction between the hills, mountain tops/sexual lumps and the fertilising sun.

The use of the word 'lumps' or 'swellings' in Irish instead of more explicit sexual terms is an understandable euphemism in light of the ascendancy of Christianity. Even these terms of 'lumps' or 'swellings' may have been too impertinent for the new religion and a morphing from *Sléibhte na mBorra-na* to *Sléibhte na mBúir-na* would be not unreasonable. This is the second and preferred explanation of a possible derivation of the name Mourne.

'The mountains of very many roars,' is in Irish
*Sléibhte na mBúir-na*

The operative Irish word is *Búir* meaning 'a shout, a cry; a roaring, a bellow'. Like the first explanation and because the word begins with [B] and follows on after the definite article *na*, it has been eclipsed with [m]. *Búir* has likewise had the collective suffix –*na* added. Again the sheer number of huge megaliths on the mountains guarantee that in millennia past the mountains echoed with strained shouts and commands as men sweated with extreme exertion to manoeuvre massive stones into place. Many stones have been dragged from elsewhere to mark positions on the hills deemed to be sacred fertility spots.

The 'shelter' stones at the head of the Ben Crom Reservoir (Map reference: J325274) are a case in point. I have known men who indeed sheltered under the rocks and they have told me it wasn't much of a shelter being too damp. But then it never was intended to be a 'shelter' in the English sense of the word. The stones that make up the 'shelter' have been brought specially to this place by the ancients to mark where the winter solstice sun is finally 'born' from the pregnant bulge that is Slieve Lamagan. A number of the 'shelter' stones are mounted up in the act of copulation and the points of these stones are carefully directed to the summit of the swollen womb. The sun's appearance finally takes place around 12.35pm, nearly four hours after initial sunrise. An incredible amount of effort has been expended by the ancients in marking the importance of this fertility site. A rough guess of the weight of the eight or more stones that comprise the monument would likely be in the range of hundreds of tons. The anchor slab alone, lying as it does in the grass of the slope, could easily be overlooked yet it

*The Shelter Stones on the hill at the head of the Ben Crom reservoir have been brought here at great effort to mark the emergence (circa 12.35pm) of the winter solstice sun from the swollen womb of Slieve Lamagan. The name 'shelter' comes from the Irish* seolta *meaning 'conveyed'.*

has been placed there to stop the other stones sliding downhill. It is a truly massive stone that would have required commensurate effort. The name 'shelter' is only a mnemonic for the Irish *seolta* meaning 'conveyed'. The Irish word *seoltóir* likewise reflects that the stones were transferred here from another site. *Seoltóir* is the Irish for 'a sailor, a voyager, a navigator'. Given the size of the stones, even moving them a short distance would have been a herculean effort. The more one recognises the vast number of stones across the hillsides that have been moved by the hand of men then 'The mountains of very many roars', *Sléibhte na mBúir-na*, is a wonderfully appropriate origin for the name of Mourne. Remember that the 'B' of *Búir* has been eclipsed so we are left with *m_úir-na*. This accords with present usage as for instance Newry and Mourne District Council which is rendered *Comhairle an Iúir agus Mhúrn;* or, 'visit Newry and Mourne' is given as visit *'an tIúr agus Múrna'*.[13] Shall we say 'Three cheers, or roars, for Mourne'?

### Slievenamaddy

For over a century the true and lovely name behind this mountain above Newcastle has lain hidden. Slievenamaddy does not seem to have been brought

Ben Crom, on the far right, broods over the waters of the reservoir.

to the attention of O'Donovan and it was left to Canon Henry Lett to sadly misattribute the derivation of the name to the Irish *Sliabh na madadh* meaning 'the mountain of dogs, or, foxes'. It is possible that, with the strong Victorian mores prevailing at that time, the good gentleman would have baulked at rendering the real meaning had he known it. Slievenamaddy would be one of the 'swellings' behind the name *Beanna Boirche*. It is by no means unique for, as we shall see later, Doan, Carn, Slieve Lamagan, Drinnahilly, the three Rocky mountains, Ben Crom, Slieve Bearnagh, the Castles, Slievedermot, Slievemartin and others, have also all been misunderstood and originally had names related to fertility.

Slievenamaddy is mentioned here because we have just been dealing with grammatical eclipse and the true meaning of this mountain lies behind the eclipsed word *Báidh*, (gen) *báidhe*, meaning 'love, friendship'. As mentioned for the name of Mourne, in certain usages the first letter *'B'* has the letter *'m'* added in front of it. The sound of *'m'* is heard but the sound of *'B'* is not; the letter *'B'* is eclipsed. This has also happened here. The true rendering of Slievenamaddy in Irish should be *Sliabh na mBáidh*, which gives us the lovely name of 'the mountain of loves'. Look again at this mountain with a gully running down the side. The ancients saw it and thought of a vagina. The Romans would have

40

MOURNE: THE MOUNTAINS OF SEX

is the spot known as Diamond Rocks. By pure co-incidence this locality is, in the words of Professor Estyn Evans, 'specially rich in 'diamonds' and 'drusy cavities'. Before giving an explanation of the Irish behind Diamond Rocks we must hear about the remarkable geology of the area as recorded in *Mourne Country*.

'It is interesting that these localities, Slieve Binnian and Slieve Corragh, are specially rich in 'diamonds' and 'drusy cavities'. Both terms need some explanation. The cavities in which the so-called diamonds occur are holes and veins, known to the granite workers as 'pummy holes' and 'diamond races' where mineral infillings have had room to form crystals. These are the 'diamonds' from which the Diamond Rocks are named. The commonest crystals are of smoky quartz, some of them attaining a length of several inches, but the careful seeker may also find small crystals of beryl, topaz, orthoclase, fluor-spar, tourmaline, haematite, chrysoberyl and peridot. Some of the stone men made large collections of diamonds and used to act as guides to interested collectors. The best known locality, the 'Diamond Rocks' is near

Pierced stones, which are found throughout the Mournes, carried obvious sexual connotations. This example is to be found near the wall at the Hare's Gap. Someone, millennia ago, has taken great care to pierce this stone while keeping the crystals intact. This stone may also have been carefully positioned to allow the evening solstice sun enter the spear shaped opening on the far side and light the crystal.[18]

the margin of the Annalong (quartzose) granite west of Slieve Corragh. Another good hunting ground is on the eastern slope of Donard in line with the Crossone ridge. Both veins and holes are regarded by Richey as marginal features, but they occur frequently in the interior exposures also, especially in the Annalong granites. The mineralised veins nearly always follow the direction of the rede-joints, from N.N.E to S.S.W.'[17]

It is a telling remark that 'some of the stone men made large collections of diamonds and used to act as guides to interested collectors'. I have a distinct impression that the scramble of the collectors to acquire specimens must have been looked on with askance by other stone men. The name 'drusy' comes from the Irish *drúiseach* meaning 'adulterous, lustful'. There probably was a lot of greed and avarice involved in the amassing of such crystal collections. The term diamond 'races' is likewise derived from the Irish and perhaps here with a tinge of scorn. Like a stone-man acting as a guide to collectors, the word *rias* in Irish was used to denote 'feudal service', 'rendering tribute to a chief' or 'the act of serving'. Pummy holes are likely derived either from the Irish *fúm* meaning 'below, beneath' or more likely as a corrupted contraction of *fuamamhlacht*. *Fuamamhlacht* was the process of going round tapping the rocks to sound their acoustic qualities and making a judgment from the resonance if there was likely to be a cavity, hopefully with crystals, underneath.[19]

The name Diamond Rocks has not come from the discovery of nearby quartz crystals but more likely the other way round, that the crystals have been expansively called 'diamonds' because of the old pre-existing name. We can thank the discovery of crystals in the vicinity for having preserved the old name which probably would otherwise have been lost. The old name, of course, was in Irish and the present rendering is a mnemonic in English; the old name had nothing to do with precious stones of pure carbon. Diamond Rocks is a remnant of (*Sliabh*) *Tí an Bhunaidh Roc,* meaning '(Mountain of the) Place of Origin Hollow'.

A gigantic megalith marks the Place of Origin Hollow, the source of the Kilkeel river. From this spot on the winter solstice, the sun could be seen setting on the phallic summit of Doan. This was the explosive moment of solar ejaculation; this was the moment of exceptional fertility and this phenomenon deservedly earned the site of the megalith 'the place of origin hollow'. We can only stand in awe of the men who dared to manoeuvre such a huge boulder on such a steep slope. Its pitted surface was probably once rich with quartz crystals but these have all now been removed. A farmer told me that it was a common occurrence in decades past for couples down on holidays to take a bit of crystal from the rock back to Belfast with them to have made into engagement rings. Some lingering folk memory may still have endured at that time that this particular stone was associated with fertility. Such memories would have only encouraged lovers to remove bits as talismans and souvenirs. This megalith seems so naturally ensconced on the hillside above the Brandy Pad that one could be forgiven for overlooking the truly astonishing exertions necessarily involved with a stone of such size. Considering the difficulties involved in dragging this boulder from its original site, to its further man-handling and risk of sudden uncontrollable downhill momentum, the successful placing of this megalith on the particularly steep slope of Slievenaglogh is an enduring testimony to the engineering skill of the ancients. We ponder on the enormous effort of muscle and sweat that was undoubtedly exerted, on the sophisticated and organised nature of their society that could undertake a project of this size and on the importance of the sun and fertility in their belief system. The stone has also been animated with the addition of huge sleeping eyes. There is a different face on either side of the megalith. The stone has thus been imbued with power by the ancients, who sought to impart a spirit of life to the inanimate. The securing of this huge rock on such an awkward slope is a truly remarkable achievement and this boulder must rank as one of the most important megaliths of Mourne.

## Carn Mountain

When John O'Donovan collected the name form *Sliabh an Chairn* from John McLindon in 1834 he was only receiving a truncated remnant of a name. The Ulster maps of Lythe and Mercator fortunately preserved the fuller name of Carnestella. The Place-names project of Queens could hardly be faulted for stating 'there is an element of doubt concerning the 16th century map forms' because even with an awareness of the importance of the old pagan religion behind the origin of many Mourne names, this, in itself, was still not enough to understand the significance of the name. First an examination of Carnestella. This name is derived from the Irish *Cairn na steille*; *steille* is the genitive of *steall,* meaning 'a splash, dash or squirt of water, a quantity of fluid'. The verb form of the word, namely *steallaim*, was delicately translated by the reverend Dinneen as 'I spurt, squirt, splash, pour violently'. A sexual ejaculation is being referred to and *Cairn na steille* is 'the cairn of ejaculation'. John O'Donovan explained, erroneously but not unreasonably, that the Cairn part of the name was derived from 'a cairn of stones on its summit' though as the photo shows there is no cairn of significance. The name does not rest with any summit stones but with a distinctive phallic shadow cast onto the side of Carn on a winter's evening by adjacent Slieve Muck. The shadow resembled the hump of a cairn but was also looked on as phallic especially as the sun declined and the shadow lengthened and was deemed to achieve sexual climax. It is a pity we are now left with only a bland eviscerated vestige of the original name.

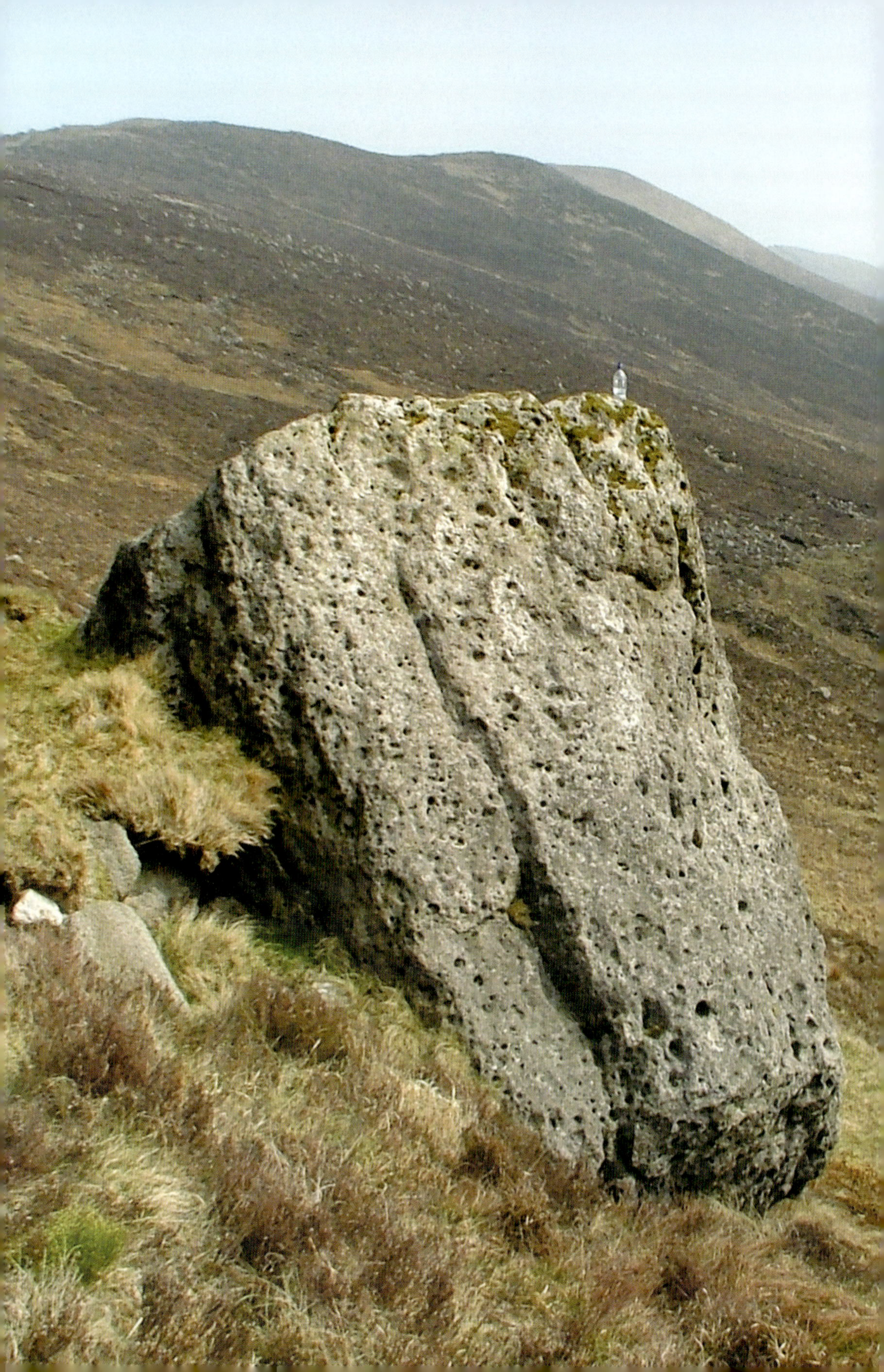

This megalith above the Brandy Pad is Diamond Rock, from the Irish *Tí an Bhunaidh Roc*, meaning 'Place of Origin Hollow'. It is a 'face stone'; note the closed sleeping eye and the long line representing a mouth. Another face is depicted on the other side. The immense size of the stone may be gauged from the water bottle on the top. The megalith marks the fertility event at winter solstice sunset when, from this location, the sun touches the top of Doan in a moment of solar ejaculation. To give added significance to this site it is also the start of the Kilkeel river which was called in Irish *An Úrach* meaning 'the newness'.

*The dawn summer solstice shadow of Rocky mountain (OS J2325) stretched down the 'vaginal' valley between Crotlieve and Tievedockaragh. The notional tight fit of the huge phallic shadow gave Tievedockaragh its name of 'painful slope'.*

The second Rocky mountain at J2325 overlooks the Rostrevor Road and the area previously known as *Cluain Daimh*, the 'meadow of the ox'. This is also the area of the ruined church of Clonduff (J229295). The body of folklore associated with the church recorded by John O'Donovan, Prof Evans and the Place-names project, is interesting as a remnant of the struggle between the old and the new religions. A great pity it is that we do not know more about the stories heard by O'Donovan when he visited Clonduff in April 1834.

> 'I travelled a great deal yesterday to get the names of the mountains of Clonduff, and had to return by moon-light to Rathfriland where I arrived about 11 o'clock. It was a most glorious night! The peaks of the blue mountains of Clonduff illumined by the silvery beams of the moon, and the deep glens between them rendered gloomy and (dismally) dark by the shadows of the mountains – haunts of goblins and other beings of the imagination – had a most sublime effect upon my fancy, the picture being rendered more vivid by the legends heard during the day.'[20]

Whatever the legends were we will never know for he added, 'I can not spare time to write.' Fortunately professor Evans recorded a tale about Clonduff chapel.

'The time they were building Clonduff Chapel long ago a bull used to come every night and knock down all they built the day before, till at last the priest took his stick and beat the bull off and chased him half a mile away. And then the priest stuck his stick in the ground and said: 'You'll hardly come back past that! And back the bull never come, and the stick took root and grew into the fairy thorns.'[21]

In telling this tale more attention was paid to the superstitions surrounding fairy thorns. In all the talk about bad luck attending anyone who dared to destroy a fairy thorn, no good explanation seems to have been given for the bad luck beyond the displeasure *of na daoine maithe*, 'the good people', the 'gentry', the fairies. The reason for not cutting the thorn bush goes back beyond the fairies, back to the time of the old fertility religion. Simply put, the thorn, hard, stiff and occasionally piercing, was the very epitome of the phallus. For all its sharp unpleasantness, the thorn symbolised sexual urgency, potency and strength. To destroy the thorn was to destroy fertility. To destroy fertility was to bring down a curse on one's clan, one's cattle and one's crops. It was unthinkable. Farmers who endure the obvious inconvenience of leaving a thorn tree growing in the middle of a field deserve admiration. Sometimes a brave face is put on the existence of old thorns. 'Sure it will give the cattle something to scratch against'. Such practices,

Clonduff chapel as it is today.

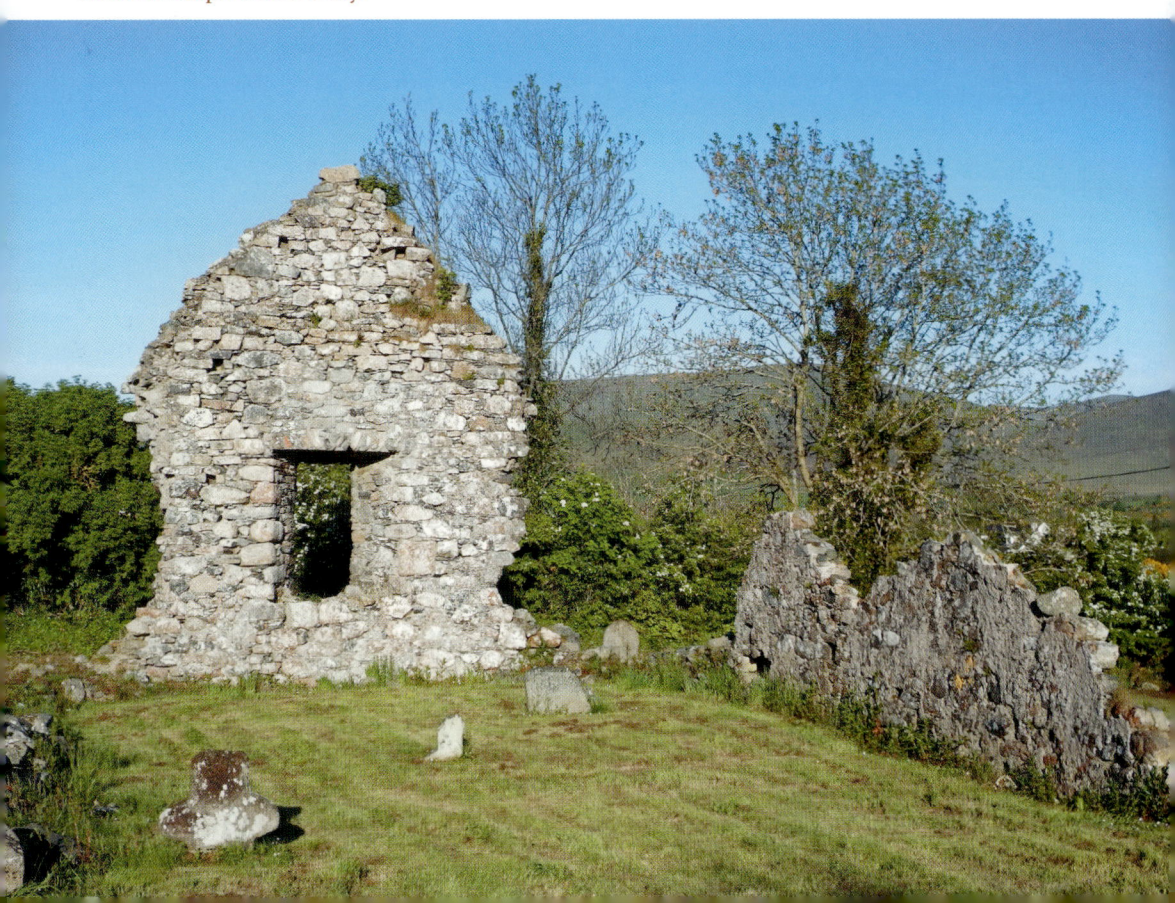

PREHISTORIC MOURNE: INSPIRATION FOR NEWGRANGE

A fairy thorn has been allowed to grow peacefully in the middle of this field in the Mournes. In the background to the left is Cock mountain and on the right is Cock and Hen mountain.

however, should not be scorned, belittled, thought eccentric or old-fashioned. It is an unspoken, unrecognised, intangible cultural treasure to have farmers still holding on to many old practices; this is not to suggest in the least any acceptance or approval thereby of the thorn's phallic symbolism. Removing an inconvenient thorn tree with a JCB is all too easy nowadays. But life around Ulster would be immeasurable poorer were we to lose these ethereal assets. A lone thorn tree in a field is more than just a tourist attraction. It is not something insignificant or quaint; leaving it to grow is a powerful statement of continuity and respect for the values of our forefathers. Leaving these thorns to grow, when the clamour all around is for efficiency and progress, commands at least a grudging respect.

Along with isolated thorn trees, another surviving relic of the former pervasiveness of the ancient fertility religion was the erection of the round fertility gates at the entrance to farm fields. These gates, with their conical tops surmounted by a stone 'nipple', once so ubiquitous throughout Ulster, represented the female breasts and no doubt were built with the hope that the

The builders of the Mourne Wall finished the section coming down from Rocky Mountain with a creative flourish of a stone breast complete with ample nipple.

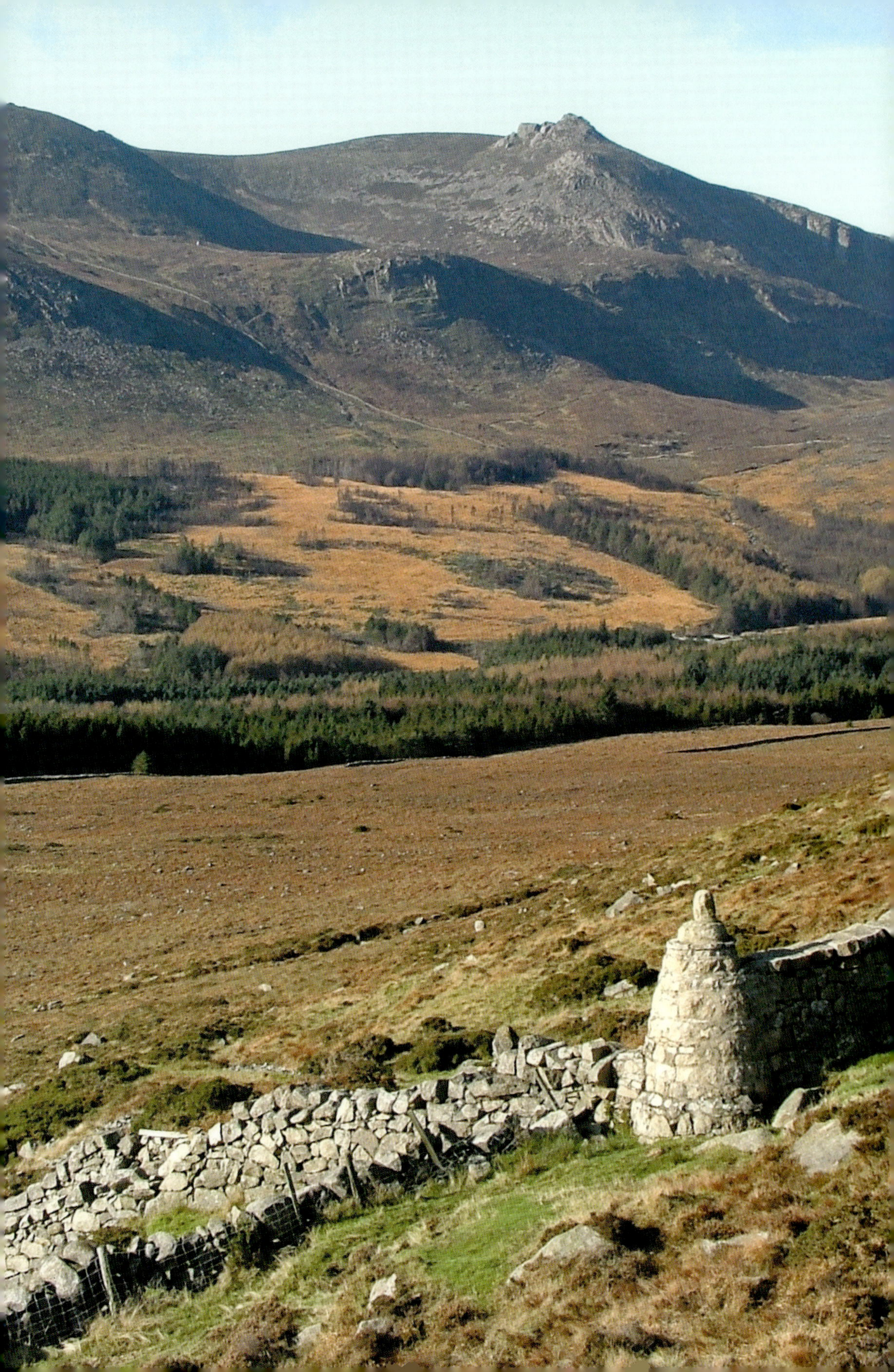

*These beautiful traditional farm gates on the Tullyree Road that once were so common throughout Ulster, were remnants of the ancient fertility religion. The gates represented the female breasts and the hope that lushness and fecundity would bless all crops and animals in the field.*

same fruitfulness and abundance would extend to all crops and livestock in the field. I remember one time being impressed at the perfection of the nipples a farmer had achieved in the building of his traditional gates. On closer examination I found that he had used the round finials of an old brass bed and painted them with whitewash[22]. These time-honoured entrances have sadly greatly disappeared since the 2nd World War as the increasingly larger size of farming machinery necessitated the replacement of the old gates with something wider.

Despite our thoughts about retention of disappearing isolated thorns, this was not the main point of the tale of Clonduff chapel. What we have is a parable about the contest between the old fertility religion, symbolised by the horned bull, and Christianity. The horned bull is an allegory for the phallic solstice shadows cast by the surrounding mountains, particularly Cock and Rocky mountain, across *Cluain Daimh*, the 'meadow of the ox'. It would seem that the site of old Clonduff chapel was of pagan significance. Perhaps there was more than reluctance to surrender the site but actual resistance with pagan believers

These old fertility gates surmounted with water rolled granite nipples are to be found on the Moyad Road. The entrance into the field is only eight feet wide which was the usual size in the days of horse and cart but now many of these old pillars have sadly been removed to permit the entrance of larger farming machinery.

initially tumbling the early chapel walls. One reason for the importance of Clonduff to the pagans was that it was from here that the sun could finally be seen rising from behind the summit of Cock mountain on winter solstice morning. The twin peaks of Cock mountain became the shadow horns of the bull cast across the plain below giving it its name of *Cluain Daimh*, the 'meadow of the ox'. The shadow of Rocky mountain passes over the area just under Hen mountain at winter solstice sunset and in the opposite direction on the same day there is even a megalith on Rocky's lower southern slopes just above the track to Pierces Castle that marks where the sun sets into a fertility notch on the distant Cooley mountains as seen down through the valley of the Newtown Road towards Rostrevor. The main 'reaching' of this particular Rocky mountain, however, is done at summer solstice dawn when the mountain's phallic shadow enters the vaginal valley between Crotlieve and Tievedockaragh. Indeed, I would respectfully suggest that O'Donovan's informant, John McLindon was unaware of the pagan origins of the name when he proposed that Tievedockaragh was derived from the slope being difficult to climb. Steep the slope most certainly is but the Irish

*The top of Rocky mountain is on the left as seen here from the Quarter Road on an early November morning. In the foreground is Round Seefin Hill and behind it with the Mourne wall going up its slope is Long Seefin.*

adjective *Dochrach* also has the meaning 'grievous, hurtful, injurious' and the name refers rather to perceived vaginal injury at summer solstice dawn when the mighty phallic shadow of Rocky mountain squeezed its way into the valley.

The third Rocky mountain overlooks the Annalong valley at J3425. Recalling that this mountain name is derived from *Roicheadh*, meaning 'reaching', Rocky's winter solstice dawn shadow reaches across the Annalong valley towards Cove mountain and then, as the sun moves round, right up the Annalong valley itself. In the vicinity, solstice phallic shadows have given us the name Lamagan Slabs. On the map of Mourne there are only two named slabs and four named buttresses; these are Lamagan Slabs and Bearnagh Slabs and then Blue Lough Buttress, Annalong Buttress, Pigeon Rock left hand buttress and Pigeon Rock right hand buttress. Nowadays these terms are associated with climbing but originally they came from phallic shadows cast at the time of solstice. The names come from Irish, not climbing. The term Slab as used for Lamagan and Bearnagh has come from the Irish *Sleabhac*, meaning 'a horn'. In the case of Slieve Lamagan, note that on the OS map the name Lamagan Slabs is placed on the south face of the mountain, across from Bignian, and not where the climbing is done on the east. The horn of Lamagan is the shadow of Bignian's north tor passing over Lamagan at winter solstice sunset. In the case of Slieve Bearnagh, the horn is the phallic shadow cast high onto the flank of Bearnagh at summer solstice dawn by the shoulder of Spellack[23].

Blue Lough Buttress, Annalong Buttress and Pigeon Rock Buttresses are from the eclipsed word *bPutraisc* and again refer to phallic shadows. It once would have been a familiar term to a farmer walking behind his plough. *Putraisc* was the Irish for the chains connecting the plough to the horses. The phrase, 'the shadow of the chains' would be *scáth na bputraisc*. The start of the phrase has been lost in the change to English and only the mnemonic 'buttress' is left to remind us of the eclipsed Irish *bPutraisc*. The idea of the chain casting its shadow on the ground has been transferred to the early morning winter shadows cast by Annalong Buttress at the head of the Annalong valley and also by the shoulder of Blue Lough Buttress in the direction of Ben Crom.[24] In the case of Pigeon Rock the phallic shadows are supplied by the end of Slieve Muck. As mentioned in the notes of chapter one, the phallic megalithic stones at the southern end of Slieve Muck catch the winter solstice sun and together with the stepped shoulder of the

Annalong Buttress at 10.55am on 3rd November, showing the disappearing phallic shadows that were evocative of chains on a plough. Earlier the shadows would have been much longer.

Taken at 11.30am on 3rd November when this phallic shadow is retreating from the Annalong valley. The lower sun at winter solstice would greatly extend its reach and potency.

3.05pm on 2nd December and the declining sun casts the phallic shadow horn of Bignian's north tor onto Slieve Lamagan. This perceived phallic interest led to Lamagan's name in Irish, *Lab an Geine*, 'considerable lump of a woman' and the horn (*Sleabhac* in Irish) gave us the mnemonic 'Lamagan Slabs'.

MOURNE: THE MOUNTAINS OF SEX

mountain cast a potent and symbolically fertilising shadow into the notional vagina of the White Water valley the route of B27, the Moyad Road. It is this phallic shadow, once referred to as *bPutraisc*, that has left us the right hand buttress and the left hand buttress. When next driving on B27 look for the large stones down on the valley floor. These are megaliths that have been deliberately placed by the ancients to delimit the solstice shadow cast by the edge of Slieve Muck. The association of shadows with male genitalia in Irish is obviously very old. Note the similarity between the Irish *scáth* meaning 'shadow' and the Irish *scáthachán* meaning 'the private parts of the body'.

### Crocknafeola hill

While mentioning the buttresses of Pigeon Rock Mountain we should refer to nearby Crocknafeola Hill (J2722). Place-names project advise us that Crocknafeola is from the Irish *Cnoc na Feola* meaning 'hill of meat'. This translation was nevertheless a source of mystification. As the project writers noted: 'How it earned such a name is difficult to say. It is possible that meat was once stored or preserved here, or even that it was grazing ground specifically used for the production of meat.[25]' It is proposed instead that while the 'meat' referred to in *Cnoc na Feola*

10.15am on 2nd December and the twin phallic shadows of Blue Lough Buttress are starting to form. These shadows were reminiscent of ploughing chains (*bPutraisce*) and gave us the mnemonic 'Blue Lough Buttress'. Closer to solstice these shadows stretch out quite extensively over towards Ben Crom. Large stones (not shown) on the valley floor probably mark the extent of the shadows' reach.

seemed to again enter the mountain as if in copulation. A further sign of the importance of *Bean Crom* in the ancient religion is evidenced by the huge megalith on the col between Bignian and Lamagan, the point of which, with phallic intent, is directed unambiguously at the fissure. As if this was not enough, you do not have to look far at the side of Slieve Lamagan to see that other stones, many of quite significant size, have likewise been man-handled so as to intentionally point into the fissure. The ancients paid *Bean Crom* a lot of attention.

## Drinneevar, Millstone and Thomas Mountain

The origin of Drinneevar may long ago have resembled something like *Droinn na fearta,* 'the ridge of the grave'. The present name however is from the Irish *Droinn eibhir,* 'Ridge of Granite' which is rather ironic as this part of the mountain is composed of the shale that once overlaid the granite. The name came about when a quarry was opened behind the ridge-line to provide stone for what is now the old quay at the harbour.[27] A special road to bring down the granite was constructed in a diagonal across the face of the ridge and this is still the most pleasant way to access the top of the ridge. Considering that parliament voted funds for the quay in 1807 and presuming that local labour was used at the

*This long, suggestively phallic, granite megalith under the cairn of Drinneevar is oriented on the line of winter solstice sunrise and summer solstice sunset.*

quarry, in the construction of the access road and for the transportation of the granite, the inference is that Irish was still the primary language of many locals at the start of the 19th century and that *Droinn eibhir* is, relatively speaking, a very recent name. Beyond a closeness of sound that would have facilitated a transition from one name to another there is no documentary evidence to support an earlier version of *Droinn na fearta*, 'the ridge of the grave' which must remain speculative. Nevertheless, Thomas mountain gets its name from a tomb,[28] and likewise a large stone of priapic import found below the cairn on the ridge of Drinneevar would appear to be the location of a grave. Another interesting fertility stone on the ridge is a low pierced granite boulder on top of shale bedrock. The implication of the bedrock being shale is that the granite stone was specially brought here. Someone has spent a lot of time piercing this stone so that the two holes joined up and that the top hole could act as a funnel. Rainwater falling on top of the stone now weeps through and comes out at the side. It is a simple but very effective and suggestive representation of fertility; the boulder may be small but this is gynaecomorphism at its best.

This is an important fertility stone on Drinneevar ridge. I poured water into the top hole to show the symbolism of the pierced stone at work.

Speaking of Irish being the primary language of many locals at the start of the 19th century, there is evidence that Irish even survived as a spoken language among the older residents in Glasdrumman at least up until the 1950's. My stone cutting relations who lived high on the hillside, the McCartans of Moneydarraghmore, were all bi-lingual. Local schoolteacher and author, Arthur Doran, recalled Irish being spoken in the area in the 1940s and 1950s. The most common occasion to hear the Irish was after Sunday Mass when the old folk would catch up on all the gossip. Another place where Irish was heard was on the GAA pitches of Mourne. John Fagan who was born in Newcastle in the late 1860's was still alive and near ninety years old when he gave his reminiscences about the time he played for the once famous Newcastle Clannabarcaigh Hurling team.[29] The name was from the Irish *Clann na Bárcaighe*, which, with a nod to the harbour, meant 'the tribe of the very many boats'. John, being a great Gaelic scholar, unsurprisingly gave his advice to the players of 1954 in Irish. It was

*An Chathaoir Mhór*, 'The Big Chair': This megalith above the quarry at the foot of Thomas mountain once gave the name to Newcastle. In Elizabethan times the village of Newcastle was known as Shyleke, from the Irish *sithe leacht*, 'the hill of the monument'.

*'Is fearr Gaedhilg bhriste na Bearla cliste'*, 'It is better to have broken Irish than good English'. The use of Irish on the pitch was also tactical as the opposing team would not know your intentions. One Glasdrumman player recalled various Irish shouts being used in games one of which was a call for a low pass; the shout would go out, *'Barr a Drúchta'*, 'above the top of the dew'.

My favourite story of the endurance of Irish in the locality was of the Irish speaker Hugh Cromwell, a shepherd, who trained his dogs in Irish. One day while working a dog he caused great mystification to some American tourists who thought he was abusing the animal by calling it 'trash'. The dog was herding the sheep in good order and seemed to be doing everything right and the insult didn't seem right to them. Only later when they voiced their vexation to a neighbour did they learn that the shepherd was calling out in Irish *'Tar Arais'*, 'Come Back!'[30]

Slieve Thomas is a mnemonic from the Irish *Tuama* 'a tomb, a sepulchre, a grave'. In our earlier work, *Slieve Donard's Domain,* a chapter was devoted to the likely burial monument *An Chathaoir Mhór*, 'the big chair', above Donard quarry. Besides the breaching whale megalith featured in the first chapter, many other promising burial sites can be found on the slopes by the discerning searcher,

*Propped up at the back by a shale boulder, this granite megalith on the front of Thomas mountain points towards the breast-like summit of Drinnahilly. Of particular interest is the tiny little phallic horn carved on the apex of the stone.*

including a granite megalith pointing towards the summit of Drinnahilly on which a tiny little phallic horn has been carved at the front. Of particular interest is what appears to be a stone lined grave at the back of Thomas mountain. First a recap from part of the letter of John O'Donovan after he climbed Slieve Donard on 23rd April 1834; of importance are his remarks on the terrain at the top of Amy's River.[31]

'This stream is said to divide the Millstone Mt from Thomas Mt, two very high mountains situated at the base of S. Donard to the N.E. & N. and originally considered a part of it, before these mountains received separate names. When you arrive at the source of this stream, you turn towards the west a little above the summit of Thomas' Mt where the ground though rugged and full of holes becomes comparatively level. This is called (*The top of the Hill*) by the country people, who do not include it in the Millstone Mt, Thomas's Mt, or Slieve Donard. From this place *Donard* is seen towering majestically and awfully above the neighbouring mountains…'[32]

That the country people had a special name for a particular part of the mountain and pointedly excluded other parts, is of significance. The name that O'Donovan

67

This fertility stone, perhaps a burial site, has been secured in an upright position on the upper reaches of Thomas Mountain. The beauty of the panorama below doubtlessly encouraged many burials on the front of the mountains. Best access is by a diagonal line up through the heather on the Millstone mountain side of Thomas following what is probably the remains of an ancient path.

has preserved by his letter, 'The top of the Hill', is probably another mnemonic from the Irish, namely *Top na h-Aille,* which would mean 'The Torch of Stone'. This stone structure is high enough on the hillside to receive the light of the summer and winter solstice dawns. The parallel lines of inclined stones would have been evocative of a burning brand when lit by the sun.[33] The name, of course, is metaphorical as the stones would not be a grate for a vigil fire but are more than likely a lined grave constructed on this auspicious location. We will meet later with bowl receptacles for vigil fire on the summits of Slieve Bignian, Slieve Bearnagh and Chimney Rock.

I earlier described Millstone mountain as an open air museum to the manufacture of millstones.[34] Stones selected for grinding are scattered across the mountain-side at all stages of preparation. Yet long before this mountain received its English name it would have had an Irish name. Just as Slieve Thomas is a mnemonic of the Irish *Tuama,* so a case can be made that Millstone mountain, appropriate as the name is, is also a mnemonic of the original Irish. Although it is not attested in written sources, I believe the name Millstone mountain, before the hillside was quarried for actual millstones, was derived from the Irish *Mí-Ail tón,* meaning the 'lower evil stone'. My eye is on a huge stone in the upper reaches of Amy's River valley as a prime contender for the origin of the name. This stone, weighing certainly many tens of tons, has been raised up and a chock stone put underneath. There is a hump to the top of the stone and taken together with the tapering end, the whole gives the uncomfortable resemblance of a shark. Apart from its phallic import, this added shark-like simulation would have been further justification for naming it *Mí-Ail*, 'evil stone'. The phallic import comes not only from the shape but also from having the 'business end' oriented to the breast-like summit of Slieve Donard. I have also found an upright phallic stone further up the hillside which would therefore be its partner as the 'higher evil stone', *Mí-Ail Ard.*

Another, if less likely, explanation for the origin of Millstone mountain can be given, namely that it has come from the Irish *Mí-Áil tonn,* meaning 'evil pleasure surface'. First it is necessary to recall that when professor Michael O'Kelly uncovered the roof of the entrance passage-way during the restoration of Newgrange, it was found that channels had been cut into the upper surfaces of the rock to drain water away to the side and keep the passage dry. This was a detail of

These parallel lines of stones that gave the area the name 'Top of the Hill' are so placed as to catch the dawn light of both solstices. The name is originally derived from the Irish *Top na h-Aille*, meaning 'Torch of Stone'. A similar smaller grave can be seen behind it.

'This chocked fertility megalith has one point set towards the summit of Millstone mountain and another towards the 'Top of the Hill' area. The stone is the worthy candidate for the name *Mí-Ail tón*, the 'lower evil stone', which eventually morphed into the present name of Millstone mountain.

sophistication that was entirely unexpected. Here in Mourne the same idea has been employed in reverse. In the vicinity of the megalith that is pointed at Donard's summit there is a large bare rock surface and a long shallow depression appears to have been mauled into the surface with the express intention of gathering rain water. I paced out a length of channel in this locality at over twelve metres. In the upper reaches the channel is really a very shallow runnel and easily missed but towards the end the groove deepens and divides. It is probably no accident that the divided channel gives the impression of a small animal suckling. The purpose of the channel appears to be the gathering of water from the surrounding hillside and funnelling it to drip over the point of the rock as if it were a permanent ejaculation, or at least permanent in wet weather. I have found other rocks to have similar grooves or depressions near their point in which rain water would either flow or gather, thus imparting exceptional symbolic fertility to the stone. I still favour the origin of Millstone mountain beginning with *Mí-Ail tón,* 'the lower evil stone' but as we wish to show in a later chapter that Mourne

MOURNE: THE MOUNTAINS OF SEX

had a profound influence on the conception of the world heritage passage grave of Newgrange, it is good to be aware that the grooving of stones to direct water for a suggestive purpose was prevalent and I would even say fairly widespread in Mourne from the earliest times.

## The Black Stairs, Eagle Rock and the Glen River Valley

The Black Stairs always reminds me of the record time of 16 minutes 42 seconds from the top of Slieve Donard to Newcastle Centre, set by Stephen Cunningham in the 2010 Slieve Donard Race. Before the Glen River Valley became the most popular access route to the top of Slieve Donard, ancient man was marking the valley with megaliths. A number of large boulders below the Black Stairs that rest on top of numerous smaller stones probably mark burial sites. These large stones invariably point towards the summer solstice sunrise. Picking this location for a burial by the ancients could also have been determined by the potent fertility symbolism of the Black Stairs demonstrated after severe rainstorms on the hills. The name, while quite appropriate for this waterfall on the shoulder of Slieve Thomas, is nevertheless a mnemonic of the Irish and is subtly sexual in its meaning. Black Stairs comes from the Irish *Bleacht Starr* and means the 'milk rush'.

Numerous stones throughout Mourne have been channelled to direct water in imitation of fertility functions. Here, between the two channels, the shape of a young animal has been created in the act of suckling.

The Irish behind the Black Stairs, *Bleacht Starr*, is best appreciated when the waterfall is in spate after heavy rain. With overtones of ejaculation, *Bleacht Starr* means 'milk rush'.

The dawn sunlight on 6th June illumines this chocked megalith below the Black Stairs. The diagonal stripe at the side, caused by an infusion in the rock, is used here and in many other stones to point towards other parts of the landscape, usually a rounded summit, that have been interpreted sexually.

The point of this propped spear shaped stone is directed towards the summer solstice sunrise.

This fissure on the cliff face of Eagle rock has been treated as a vagina and has received particular attention from the ancients. We can only wonder at the efforts and skills involved; an upright phallic spear stone has somehow been lowered down the cliff and with precision and great delicacy been wedged upright in the fissure. At the top of the fissure further stones have been placed across the gap.

The construction of this cluster of megaliths on the steep slope of Slieve Commedagh has involved nearly two dozen huge stones each of many tons weight.

Prehistoric Mourne: Inspiration for Newgrange

accompanying wedging stones have somehow been lowered down the sheer cliff-face of Eagle Rock and placed with precision in the middle of the natural fissure so that the priapic point faces upwards. The symbolism of intercourse was further achieved by the evening shadow of these stones penetrating the fissure. The cleft was changed into a figurative vagina complete with a rocky phallus and could now be justifiably referred to as 'notch of pleasure'. The effort involved in this undertaking is really quite exceptional. At the top of the fissure further large stones have been wedged across the gap and these in turn are surmounted by a large face stone pointing towards the col. Remnants of climbing ropes are still tied round the middle of this long priapic megalith as it made a good belay point for climbers ascending the cliff. Coming down to this place from the top of Donard is exceedingly dangerous, the more so as one approaches the edge of the sheer cliff. It is far safer and strongly recommended that you bring a good pair of binoculars to view the fissure with its inserted rocks from the valley below.

The location of these fertility stones high on the flank of Eagle's sheer cliffs – and Commedagh has a generous quota of sensational megaliths as well – has

Note the counter-balancing stones at the back placed to prevent this megalith toppling down the steep flank of Commedagh. But how these stones were manipulated on such a dangerous slope is an incredible marvel indeed.

*Slieve Donard corrie as seen from Slievenamaddy. Look at the very middle of the photo at the little pinprick of light. Incredibly the ancients seem to have erected a megalith on this awful slope at the spot where summer solstice sunrise would be seen emerging from the top of Slieve Thomas.*

made me wonder how many men died in the placement of these stones. These megaliths, however, do not need any possible embellishment of a gory nature, for the sheer size of the stones combined with their almost hopelessly difficult location has made the mind-blowing exertions of the ancients embellishment enough. No challenge seemed too difficult, no location was regarded as impossible. Huge stones have been moved on very steep slopes and in places fraught with tremendous danger. A later chapter of photographs is devoted to vagina stones, showing that the transformation of gaps and crevices into symbolic acts of fertility is actually a practice common in Mourne.

Having moved with the greatest trepidation over the steep slopes of Commedagh in the search for stones erected by the hand of man, may I again give warning least anyone else would follow my foolhardiness. The dangers are very real. Leave the precipitous sides of the valley to the sheep or experienced climbers. Make it easy for yourself. Bring binoculars and prop yourself against a rock and gaze in awe at the number of pointed stones on either height of the valley that have been deliberately raised into provocatively suggestive sexual positions. The flank of Slieve Commedagh from the back of the Glen river valley to Pulgarve is

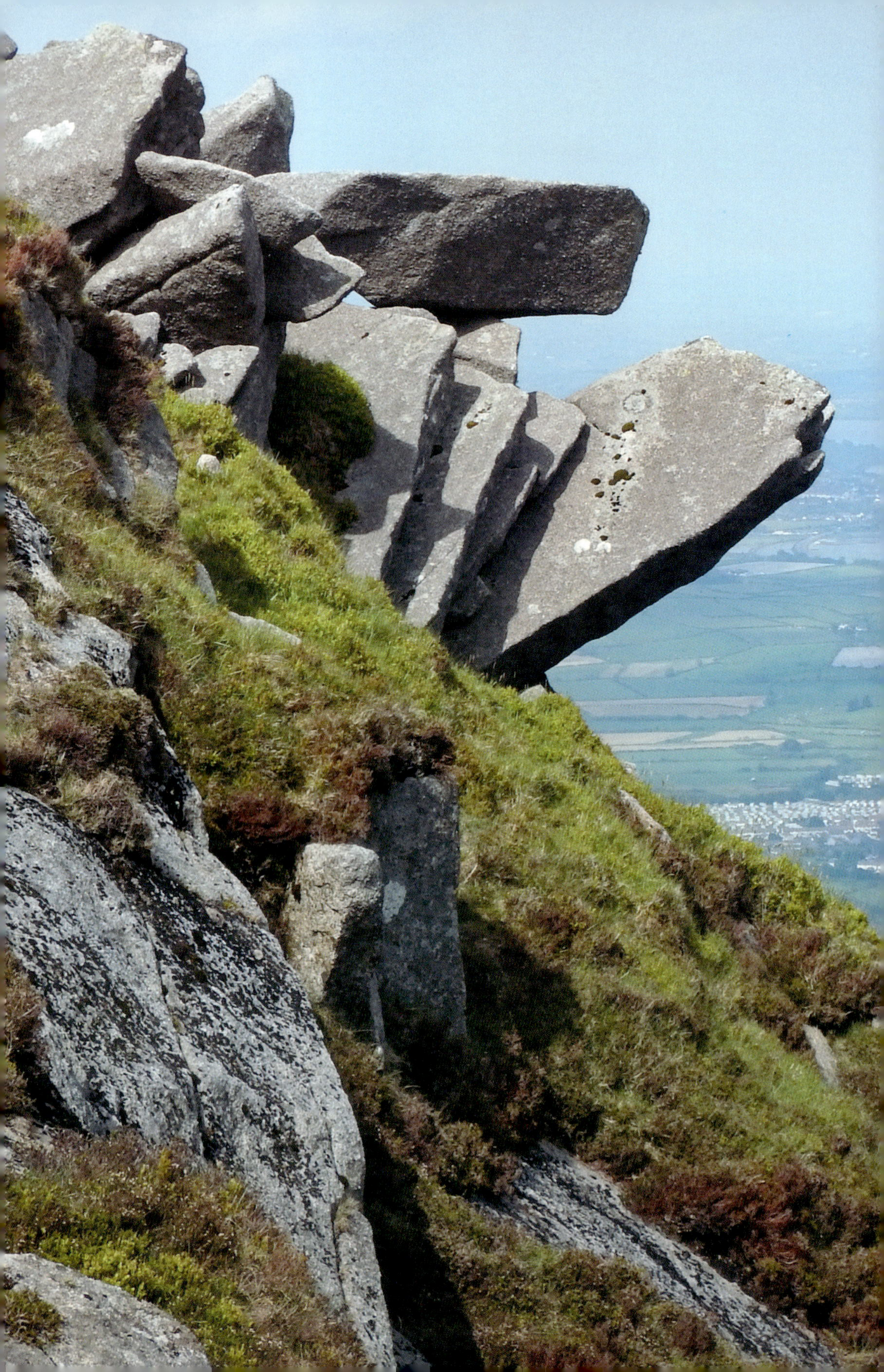

A marvel of ancient engineering; the large prominent phallic stone to the left must alone weigh nearly twenty tons yet somehow it and the other wedging stones have been moved on this very steep slope of Slieve Commedagh and arranged to point towards Slieve Donard's summit.

exceptional for the size and number of megaliths raised on such steep slopes. We should remember also that these raised stones usually required anchor blocks at the base to stop them shifting on the steep incline, with perhaps wedge stones at the side and invariably judicious counter-balance stones at the top and back to prevent the megalith toppling. The number of stones moved therefore in the creation of even a modestly sized phallic projection could be quite substantial. The scree slopes below Slieve Commedagh also contain a surprising number of face stones, which we treat with in the coming chapter, together with priapic stones pointing towards the summit of Eagle or Slieve Donard. It was also discovered by chance that one of the large stones on the valley floor marked a raised spot on the skyline of Slieve Commedagh where the sun disappeared on the afternoon of summer solstice. This discovery, taken in conjunction with the enormous exertions made on the heights above, makes one bold enough to predict that most of the larger stones along the length of the Glen river valley, if fully examined in regard to the circuit of the sun at solstice, will be found not to be random falls but deliberate placements marking fertility junctions between sun and parts of the valley skyline. The challenge now would be to recover a fraction of the intimate knowledge our ancestors had acquired through long observations.

Limitations of space unfortunately preclude an examination of the whole Mournes as the 'mountains of sex' mentioned at the head of the chapter. Nevertheless, a quick look at the other Eagle Mountain north-west of Attical (J2423) is in order. The name, Eagle, seems to have yo-yoed between the two languages of Irish and English after the fashion of Deers' Meadow mentioned earlier. The original Irish *Eag Áil*, changed to the English mnemonic 'Eagle' and then back into the Irish *Sliabh an Iolair*, 'mountain of the eagle', at the time of the ordnance survey. That the early pagan fertility religion lies behind the name can be seen from other place-names in the vicinity. The starting point would be Slievemageogh (J2621) and the phallic shadow that this mountain casts into the steep sided valley of the Windy Gap river on the morning of winter solstice. Slievemageogh is from the Irish *Sliabh maigh-eo*, 'Big Brooch Mountain'. The brooch, of course, with its long sharp pin, is only a sexual euphemism for the phallus. The place-name 'Great Gully' at J2522 derives from the solstice shadow of the shoulder of Slievemageogh cast across the Windy Gap valley. It comes from *(Tí an) Chreatha Gualann*, '(Place of the) shivering mountain shoulder'. *Crioth*, (genitive *Creatha*), stands for 'quaking, shivering, trembling, quivering' and refers to the transient, shifting shadow, constantly moving in relation to the changing sun. The Irish *Creatha* has morphed into the English 'great'. *Guala*, (genitive *gualann*), means 'a shoulder, a mountain-shoulder or bluff'. It has been rendered in English on the basis of proximity of sound as 'gully'. As the sun rises, the shadow of Slievemageogh slides further up the valley towards a place marked on the map as 'The Slates' at J249231. The sexual dimension of this shadow is quite

Sunlit Slievemageogh, 'Big Broach Mountain', as seen from the Banns Road. The winter solstice shadow of this mountain was of such priapic proportions it was responsible for 'the slates' at OS J2423, from the Irish *Slaite*, a euphemism for the rampant aroused male sexual organ.

explicit in the Irish. In English 'the slates' makes no real sense as it calls to mind roofing tiles but 'the slates' is only another mnemonic, a copy of the sound of the Irish. 'The Slates' comes from the Irish *Slat* (genitive *Slaite*) which, in amongst its various meanings, Rev Dinneen diffidently tells us is one that is obscene but means the erect penis. The same Irish word lies behind the name of Slievenaslat at Castlewellan which we will examine later. The shadow 'pin' of Slievemageogh penetrates the valley; the shadow slides up between the steep valley sides or the 'legs' of Eagle Mountain and Slievemageogh.

The sexual interpretation of the landscape does not end with this valley but, controversially, extends to the name of Attical, (J2719). The location of Attical provides views up the length of the steep Windy Gap valley, the White Water valley and the Yellow Water valley. First we mention that *Col,* (genitive *Cuil* and *Cola*), in Irish is rendered in Dinneen's dictionary as 'sin, lust, incest, wickedness…'. *Aith* or *Ath* in Irish can represent the intensive prefix meaning 'very'. To follow the sexual interpretation of the landscape to its logical conclusion, one could postulate that, from its unique position, the name of the

*The Glen River may get its name from the Irish* Glan, *meaning 'clean, pure, clear'. (But see opposite). It is a contraction of a longer earlier name* Abha h-Éarmaidheacht Glan, *'the pure frolicking river' which became for a while 'hermit's glen', a name now long redundant.*

locality of Attical derives from being able to 'look up the legs' of these valleys and thus gave rise to the Irish name *Aith Tí Cuil,* meaning 'the very place of lust'.[35]

To return to the Eagle Rock of Slieve Donard and to the Glen River valley, the summer solstice sunrise brings about a phallic shadow from the shoulder of Eagle Rock after the fashion of 'the slates/*Slat-Slaite*'. The sun also shines clear up the valley and into the cragged, ragged and rocky gully at the western side of the head of the valley. This gully, with its numerous phallic-like tors of granite, is as impressive today as it probably was to the ancients millennia ago. If we may have a moment for semantics, it is important to mention that locals always refer to the valley between Slieve Thomas and Slievenamaddy, taken by many as the route to the top of Slieve Donard, as 'the Glen River'. It is never 'The Glen', 'The Donard Valley' or 'The Glen Valley' but always 'the Glen River'. Such distinctions might seem trivial or petty until we search for the likely Irish origins of the name. Because of the spectacular gully at the head of the valley and the proximity of Eagle's huge phallic shadow at summer solstice dawn, I believe that the name 'Glen River' has its origin in the Irish *Gleann Réabóra*, 'Valley of the Violator'. The ancients looked at the large open gully at the head of the valley and envisaged a

MOURNE: THE MOUNTAINS OF SEX

torn and wounded vagina. The phallic shadow from the shoulder of Eagle Rock does not reach to this gully at the moment of summer solstice dawn although it moves closer to the gully as the sun rises and begins its journey. The size and proximity of the shadow to the vaginal gully were probably enough to impute violation by rape.

The river itself received the following description from the great Irish naturalist, Robert Lloyd Praeger, at the end of the nineteenth century when Lady Annesley's demesne was a show-piece garden for tourists and residents:

'The Glen river, which rises in the deep valley between Slieve Donard and Slieve Commedagh, comes foaming down the mountain-side in a continuous series of beautiful cascades. Its banks have been planted with rhododendrons and pines, bridges have been thrown across the torrent, and seats set to command the prettiest views. The place is deservedly one of the favourite spots in the country. Fanciful names have been bestowed on the cascades, etc., and the gorge itself is called the Hermit's Glen, apparently out of

This is the phallic shadow from the shoulder of Eagle Rock as observed at 5.11am on 14th June. The proximity of this potent shadow to the wide gully at the back of the valley is likely responsible for an early Irish name *Glenn Réabóra*, 'Valley of the Violator', which has now changed into the innocent, innocuous Glen River. In the middle foreground is the important mirror stone and a little further up on the right alongside the path is the great face stone featured in the following chapter.

*The ancients regarded this steep gully at the head of the Glen River valley as a rent and torn vagina. It is not recommended to enter this gully as sliding scree, even in dry weather, make walking here treacherous.*

compliment to St. Domangard. Visitors who prefer nature unadorned by art need only push further up the hill, where, amid a wild tangle of gorse, heather, bog myrtle, and pines, the stream leaps over rugged ledges of slaty rock, or lies darkling in deep pools where the polished banded grit shows like green marble through the clear water.'[36]

Of importance to us is the name Praeger preserved, namely 'the Hermit's Glen'. Rather than the name being a compliment to St Donard, it is more likely to be a part Anglicisation of the original Irish, and probably derives from (*Abha*) *h-Éarmaidheacht Glan*, 'the pure frolicking (river)'. The Irish *Éarmaidheacht* is often used in the sense of controlling a sprightly spirited horse and frolicking is a worthy description for this uninhibited, brawling, crystal clear river.

At the head of the Glen River valley and before one starts the steep climb, is an exceptional 'mirror stone'. This term it used to describe megaliths that have been arranged to present a large flat area towards the rising sun. Already illustrated in the first chapter have been the similar examples of the breaching whale stone

The flat surface of the mirror stone receives the dawn light, here at 5.33am on 14th June, close to the summer solstice. The stone is beside the path to Slieve Donard at the head of the Glen River Valley. Note the long hammered line on the side of the stone which both points towards the col where the winter sun first appears and imparts to the stone the suggestion of a sleeping eye. The great size of this stone marks it as one of the important megaliths of Mourne.

on the slopes of Slieve Thomas and the whooper swan stone at the Hare's Gap. The first of these stones faces the summer solstice sunrise and the second faces the winter solstice sunrise. This mirror stone marks where the sun at summer solstice dawn can be seen rising in symbolic birth out of a swelling of the ground further down the valley. The sheer size of the stone is enough to show the importance of the spot to the fertility conscious people of old.[37] The stone is right beside the path up to the top of Donard and is unfortunately by-passed by thousands unaware of its ancient significance. Note the long groove hammered along the Donard side of the stone that points towards the col. This line could also be seen as part of the animation of the stone; it is suggestive of a closed sleeping eye. The best respect that could be paid to the stone, not to mention our multitude of annual visitors en route to Donard, would be the removal of the tasteless graffiti, the covered remnants of which still besmirch the stone surface even after forty years.

Another view of the mirror stone and its companion showing the swelling of ground a little further down the valley. The ancients regarded the swelling (*Boirrche*) as a vagina and marked with this huge megalith the spot where the sun could be seen being born out of the earth at summer solstice dawn.

## Craignagore

Craignagore, on the wooded slopes of Slievenamaddy, was not treated in Place-names of Mourne. The present prevailing explanation proposes the Irish *Craig na Gabhair*, meaning 'the rock of the goats'. The first difficult with this is that it should properly be rendered as *Craig na nGabhair*. This, incidentally, could also mean a stash of smuggled goods but Craignagore was not exactly on the smuggling trail and this explanation has never had any traction. The origin of the name, like so many others in Mourne, lies with the old pagan religion. Few have probably ever visited this rock as it is off the beaten track and presently buried in a forest plantation. The important part is where a small rock platform, a couple of feet high, juts out from a rock face and overlooks a relatively flat area on this otherwise steep slope. It is easy to bandy terms like 'ritual platform' but this location deserves consideration. The two most important aspects of the location are the front of the platform which has been carefully shaped as a spear point, a symbol of male power and, by extension, of male virility. It is this feature that has given the place its

MOURNE: THE MOUNTAINS OF SEX

name, *Craig na gCuirre,* 'the rock of the projection'.[38] Secondly, although the existing trees made confirmation difficult, the spear point of this platform appears to be quite deliberately aligned with the summer solstice sunrise. If we were to imagine pagan fertility practices taking place here at the solstice dawn, the slightly sloping area in front of the platform would easily accommodate a gathering. Should the present trees around the rock be removed in the future, a most breathtaking panorama awaits.

### Drinnahilly and The Drinns

A later chapter will discuss the profound influence that Mourne had on the great passage tomb of Newgrange. Conjunctions of earth and sun at the solstices made this next part of Mourne, namely from Drinnahilly westwards to Spinkwee hill and from Slievenabrock to the Drinns, one of great importance to the ancients. The three symbols of 'double diamonds' on the left side of the K1 entrance stone of Newgrange relate to this area. The symbols represent the rising sun in the act of fertility. Depending, most importantly, on where the observer was standing on

The front of this small rock platform has been shaped into a spear point directed towards summer solstice sunrise. This is Craignagore, 'the rock of the projection'. Behind it, even though covered in moss, the back wall has the semblance of a beastly face.

This classic example of a spear stone, symbol of male power, is found up behind the Water Works pump house at Tullybrannigan, at the entrance to Curragh Ard marsh. The supremely well defined tip of the stone points towards summer solstice sunrise. Achieving such a perfect point with this rock would have been particularly challenging given the difficulty of controlling the breaking of shale rock on account of its propensity to shatter.

the solstice mornings, we would anticipate that these three events at winter solstice would be the appearance of the sun at the top of Drinnahilly, the emergence of the sun from the notch between Drinnahilly and Shanslieve at the same solstice and the appearance of the sun at the tip of Slieve Thomas, the edge of which can just be seen from near the base of Slievenabrock. The abundant megaliths that mark the area and the meanings behind the place-names confirm the fertility significance of the locality, yet much mystery remains despite examination of the terrain. If we are blessed with good weather at some future dawn of a winter solstice, a fortunate early morning walker around Curragh Ard valley may enjoy making further discoveries as to why large shale stones have been placed where they are, especially along the Slievenabrock side of the valley. It is tantalising to think that stones, by their very position, may hold much hidden knowledge from thousands of years ago, information about the passage of the sun that was precious to our ancient ancestors; messages that they left for us. It would have been a hardy and physically robust people who moved so many large stones. The title of Clanbrassil, the lands of which stretch even to Lough Neagh, honours these people of millennia past; the name is from the Irish *Clann Bras Aille*, meaning 'the strong tribe of the stones'.[39]

MOURNE: THE MOUNTAINS OF SEX

The reason why Drinnahilly and the area west of it was an important fertility area has unfortunately been obscured by a misunderstanding of the meaning of local names. Based on the information gathered by the ordnance survey in 1834, Drinnahilly had been interpreted as from the Irish *Droinn an Choiligh,* meaning 'hill or ridge of the cock'.[40] When the importance of the ancient fertility religion is taken into account, a completely different meaning is possible. Instead of *Droinn an Choiligh* we look to the Irish *Droinn an Choillidhe*, 'the hill of the polluter'. This name came about because of the way the phallic shadow of Drinnahilly stretched out up the valley of Curragh Ard and particularly over to the side of the Drinns at winter solstice dawn. The name of the Drinns was presumed to come from the Irish *Dronn* meaning 'a hump or a ridge'. This name would answer to the topography but the Place-names project acknowledged a difficulty; there was no satisfactory way to explain why there was an [S] sound at the end of the name Drinns. If the name had been plural in the original Irish it could not have been anglicized as 'The Drinns'. The explanation to reconcile the final [S] sound of the Drinns lies again with the old pagan religion that sexualised the landscape. We look, not to the Irish of *Dronn*, 'a hill' but to the Irish *Droinnse* meaning 'a drench'. The site where the phallic shadow of Drinnahilly was

At winter solstice the phallic shadow of Drinnahilly (*Droinn an Choillidhe*, 'the hill of the polluter'), the forested hill in the background, reached across Curragh Ard valley to climax at this quarry site. The name Drinns is from the Irish *Droinnse* meaning drench.

The granite fertility stone, bottom left, at the Drinns shale quarry has been left pointing towards Drinnahilly. Note how the stone has been animated by being chopped on either side to provide the semblance of eyes.

perceived to ejaculate and 'drench' the Tollymore hillside with notional solar sperm is marked by a quarry. The quarrymen throughout Mourne seem to have exercised a strong preference for opening quarries at locations 'blessed' with solar fertility. The moment of fertility would be achieved when the rising sun appeared at the top of Drinnahilly. The 'hill of the polluter', already imagined as an erect phallus, was now believed to reach sexual climax and 'stain' the hillside across the valley at the quarry site.

That part of the Tollymore Park walk along the Curragh Ard valley is most pleasant. It can be conveniently accessed from the Tullybrannigan Road though many start from the shepherd's lodge area and cross the valley from the water commissioners' pump station. If you are walking up the Curragh Ard valley outside the forest park and want to avoid boggy conditions underfoot, then this is best done on the north side following the beautifully constructed estate boundary wall rather than along the flank of Slievenabrock where the water draining off the slopes leaves the ground slippy and generally disagreeable. Inside the forest park the walk is part of the Mourne and Ulster way. It is while on this trail that you come to the shale quarry. One thing to look for at the quarry is the fertility stone at the side. The quarry is of shale rock but the fertility site had been marked by the ancients with a boulder of granite probably weighting a couple of tons. The fact that the shale rock has been quarried behind the fertility stone gives me to believe that in order to protect the stone and not bring bad luck on their work by damaging it, the quarrymen moved the megalith from its original position to this west side of their quarrying operations. The stone still points towards Drinnahilly summit. A careful look shows this rock is also a face stone as the sides have been chopped to provide it with shadow eyes and a little pointy nose thus bestowing a semblance of life befitting a marker of the sun's fecundity. Further westward along the forest road another larger moss covered face stone looking towards Drinnahilly can be seen down off the road among the trees.

## Slievenaslat, Tullynasoo and a look at Slieve Croob

We take a quick digression a few miles north to the main hill of Castlewellan, Slievenaslat (OS J3337), on the slopes of which William Richard, 4th Earl Annesley built his castle. The origin of Slievenaslat's name is close to that of Drinnahilly. Slievenaslat is from the Irish *Sliabh na Slaite*, which, until now, has been literally translated as 'mountain of the willows'. The common understanding of *Slat* (genitive *Slaite*) is of 'a rod, switch or slender branch (especially of willow, palm, etc.)'. Coming closer to the real significance is 'any long member in framework', be it in wickerwork, boatbuilding, measuring or a fishing rod. In his dictionary, Rev Pádraig Dinneen made an indirect reference to the true meaning. He considered the translation to be of such a delicate nature that he only obliquely referred to it in Latin saying that there was a meaning '*sensu obscoeno*', namely 'of an obscene sense'. *Slat*, the reverend gentleman was saying, was used as a euphemism for the rampant aroused male sexual organ. Slievenaslat had its name from the phallic shape of the denuded top of the hill and also its solstice shadow, giving it the meaning of 'the mountain of the penis'.[41] The solstice shadows of Slievenaslat and its companion hills in Annesley's demesne influenced place-names to their north. On a winter's morning the line of hills from Clarkill to Ballymagreehan presented a 'grey ridge' or Liatriom to the land lying to the north and gave this name to Leitrim village. Bighouse Bog (OS J3037) near Dolly's Brae which would receive a hill shadow from the demesne is only a mnemonic for the Irish *Biach Uais* meaning 'lofty penis'. Backaderry would be from the Irish *Biach an deoraidh* meaning 'the erect penis of the wanderer', a reference to the hill shadow shifting with the movement of the sun. Ballymagreehan would seem to have thrown a substantial shadow as this name is derived from the Irish *Baile magh-roicheadh*, 'townland of great reaching'. A shadow from either Altnadua or Ballymagreehan hill stretched over to Carrownaforling (OS J3036) on the slopes of Tullynasoo mountain at winter solstice dawn 'raping' this part of the

The Castle of William Richard, 4th Earl Annesley, built on the slopes of Slievenaslat. The hill's long shadow at winter solstice earned Slievenaslat the risqué name of 'mountain of the penis'.

countryside; Carrownaforling is from the Irish '*Ceathrú na Forlainn*', meaning 'the quarter of rapes'. *Forlann* (genitive *Forlainn*) means 'excess, force majeure, violence; acute pain'. The name of Tullynasoo is presently translated as from *Tulaigh na Sú*, meaning 'mound or hill of the berries' but, on account of the solstice sexual shadow of Altnadua, perhaps *Tulaigh na Suib*, with the meaning of 'hill of excitement' would be preferable. Two different meanings but in Irish more a matter of interpretation; the plural of 'berries' in Irish is *Subha* but the same word can also refer to 'gladness and joy' which in the case of Tullynasoo has been given a sexual connotation. Mourne, 'the mountains of sex', certainly extends to the Castlewellan area.

**Slieve Croob:** According to the place-names project, the name of Slieve Croob comes from the Irish *Sliabh Crúibe*, 'mountain of the hoof'. Continuing, it states, 'the name suggests an association with cattle and no doubt has mythological connotations'. It is important to note that the Irish name is for a single hoof. The name has come not from cattle but from the shape cast by the mountain's shadow at winter solstice. The top of Slieve Croob is 534 metres but it has a lesser peak nearby and between them they cast a shadow like a cloven hoof which is why the name is singular. Earlier names like *Eirrgi Echbél ó Brí Eirgi* found around the twelfth century in the *Táin Bó Cúailnge Recension 1*, derive from the Irish *Éirghe*, 'the act of rising, arising, getting up...' and with phallic overtones refers to the strengthening shadow as the sun rises. Likewise a later name for Slieve Croob that has been a source of mystification, namely Mollogh Scroby, found in Boazio's Map of 1599, can be explained as the gradual shifting of the mountain's shadow. Interestingly Dinneen's Irish dictionary gives a translation of 'stateliness of movement' for the Irish *moille* which is normally understood as 'slowness'. Scroby is from the Irish *Scríobadh*, 'the act of scratching, scraping'. Mollogh Scroby was the name for the slow, gradual, stately passing of the mountain's shadow 'scraping' over the countryside at the solstice. Slieve Croob is best understood then as the mountain of the hoof shaped shadow.

## Tullybrannigan

The place-names project suggested that this name came from the Irish *Tulaigh Uí Bhranagáin* where the surname *Ó Branagáin* was anglicized as Branigan, but they concluded that 'the subject requires further investigation'.[42] The name Tullybrannigan is applied to a large part of the built up area of Newcastle west of the Bryansford Road through which the river of the same name flows. Rather than coming from a surname, Tullybrannigan derives from a feature high on the north facing slopes of Slievenabrock overlooking Curragh Ard (from the Irish *Currach Ard*, 'high marsh') from which the Tullybrannigan river emerges.[43] A quick look at a couple of Irish words will help our understanding of the name. The first word is *Brannda*; this was a term used by fishermen to describe a reef of rocks under the sea surface partly or sometimes visible.[44] It is applied here to a high rock face, about four metres in height, on Slievenabrock which has grass below and above it. Like a shallow submerged reef, the feature is not easily seen as it faces towards the summer solstice sunrise and is usually in shade most of the time. The second Irish word is the Irish for 'head', namely *Ceann*, (genitive *Cinn*). The full origin of Tullybrannigan is *Tulach Brannda an Chinn*, literally 'The hill reef of the head'. The 'head' is a resemblance to a face which, as mentioned, looks out towards summer solstice sunrise. The sharp angular features of the face, especially the sunken shadow eyes, are not the product of natural erosion. Representations of the human face, however rough, are rare in Mourne. The following chapter will illustrate a multitude of 'face stones' but these are all of notional beasts, sometimes fierce, sometimes shown as sleeping, but none of human resemblance.

## The Pot of Legawherry, Slievenabrock and Spinkwee

Depending on where an observer was standing in Curragh Ard valley to greet the winter solstice dawn, it would have been possible to imagine the sun in fertility mode as it touched the side of Slievenabrock. The name of this mountain was

*The circle marks the location, on the slope of Slievenabrock, of the face on the rock that gave the area the name of Tullybrannigan.*

thought to come from the Irish *Sliabh na mBroc,* meaning 'mountain of the badgers'.[45] The name doesn't seem to have been recorded by the ordnance survey in 1834. As Place-names project point out, the grammatical eclipse of *Broc* with the letter [m] has been set aside. If it was to be 'mountain of the badgers' one would expect the Irish to be *Sliabh na mBroc* without the [B] sound, leaving us with *m_roc*. There is no satisfactory reconciliation for the absence of the eclipse. Two other possible meanings might be considered. *Broc* is Irish could also stand for 'filth or refuse' and could give us 'mountain of filth'. Secondly, it is possible that Christian sensitivities brought about a subtle if somewhat ungrammatical word change. Slievenabrock may once have had its origins in the Irish *Sliabh na mBrúchta*, 'mountain of the ejaculation' and this was amended to a less embarrassing *Sliabh na (m)Broc*. Whether as 'mountain of filth' or possibly one time as 'mountain of the ejaculation', Slievenabrock would have earned its infamous name on account of the phallic shadow it cast at summer solstice dawn across the Cascade valley into the 'vagina' of the corrie on the east side of Slieve Corragh mountain. Incidentally the nearby Cascade river receives its name, not from some waterfall or tumbling water, but rather from the multitude of twists and turns the river makes on its way down the valley. Cascade is from the Irish *Cas-Céad*, 'hundred twists'.

The resemblance of a face on this rock high on Slievenabrock is the origin of Tullybrannigan; the name is from the Irish *Tulach Brannda an Chinn*, literally 'The hill reef of the head'.

**Legawherry:** The beautiful corrie of Legawherry is one of the quiet and relatively undisturbed areas of Mourne. I have memories of making my way there through deep snow at the start of 1970 to assist members of an Ulster climbing expedition to the Hindu Kush. The expedition members realised that the steep corrie walls retained the snow and provided the rare opportunity to get some home based experience in ice climbing techniques using crampons and ice axes. Earlier explanations of the derivation of the name of the Pot of Legawherry unfortunately dismissed the first part of the name 'Pot' as an English prefix whereas it is an integral part of the original Irish. The name of Pot of Legawherry is from the Irish *Pota Leaghtha an Choirigh*, 'The pot or hollow of the disappearing sinner'. The Irish *Leaghadh*, (genitive *Leaghtha*) refers to the transient nature of the phallic evening shadow which quickly changes as the sun sets and is usually translated as 'the act of melting, thawing, dissolving, wasting away, dissipating'. The lower western shoulder of the corrie generates the phallic shadow that enters the Pot of Legawherry towards summer solstice sunset.

At summer solstice dawn the corrie of Legawherry is masked by Shan Slieve and remains in complete shade. We have already mentioned how the Great Gully (J253221) at Eagle Mountain likewise derived from the notion of a fleeting,

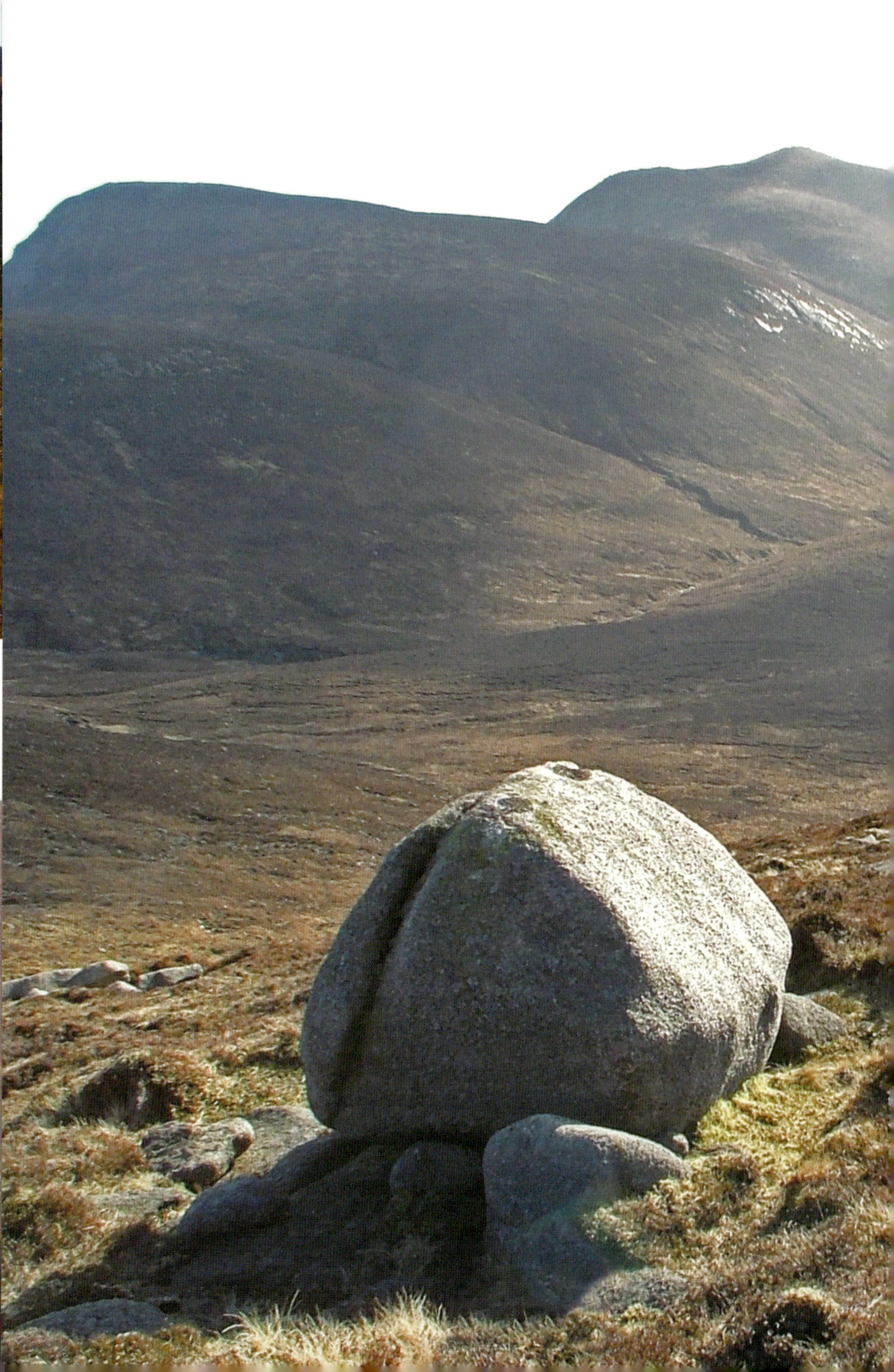

This fertility megalith on Slieve Corragh enjoys a beautiful view down the valley of the Ben Crom reservoir. The name of the mountain possibly comes from the Irish (*Cloch an*) *Corr-Àigh*, meaning '(Stone of) round good luck'. But look for the nearby flatter rock to the east of this boulder which has an important round pierced fertility hole that is also a contender for giving the mountain its name.

The sunny pointed stone, *Splinnc Buidhe* in Irish is the origin of the name Spinkwee. Great effort was involved in bringing this boulder here for the nearest granite outcrop is far up the Legawherry valley.

and exceedingly dangerous. This real danger only magnifies the awe at the determined labours and palpable skill of the ancients who nevertheless persevered in manipulating these huge stones despite the frightening hazards of such a precarious space. Safer of access is the rounded, suggestively egg shaped megalith on the nearby slopes of Slieve Corragh with a wonderful view down the Ben Crom reservoir valley.[46] There are numerous other isolated stones on the slopes and across the Cascade valley floor below which we can only guess are markers recording the reach and progress of the sun around the valley. The intimate knowledge of this part of the Mourne landscape at solstice dawn, garnered by the ancients perhaps over hundreds of years, has been lost. Hopefully, either through technology or by careful observation, the secrets of the valley may yet be again revealed.

**Spinkwee:** At the end of Cascade river valley is the rounded shape of Spinkwee Hill. The name is from the Irish *Spinnc Buidhe,* meaning 'sunny pointed stone' and refers to the highest massive granite megalith on the upper eastward slope[47]. At nearly twenty feet long and six feet high, this is a massive stone weighing many tens of tons. Considering that Spinkwee Hill is composed of shale

*One of the many standing stones in Cascade river valley that have yet to reveal their secrets. In the background, with its skylined megaliths, is the breast-like shape of Spinkwee Hill.*

and that the nearest source of granite is much further up the valley, tremendous effort has been involved in dragging this megalith to its present site. There are actually four megaliths on the eastern slope of Spinkwee hill two of which are truly enormous. The *Spinnc Buidhe* and the lower large stone mark the sun rising from between the Drinns hills at dawn on the summer solstice and on the Spinkwee megalith the lower point of the stone is directed emphatically towards the 'cleavage' of these hills. At the end of the summer solstice day, the sun sank down behind the summit of the distinctly breast-like hill of Spinkwee and the upper phallic point of the stone was directed to where the sun could be seen descending on the rounded breast-like swelling of the summit. Spinkwee hill is composed of shale as are the immediate hills. These huge lumps of granite have been thoughtfully selected and placed with utmost care to mark spots of unique solar fecundity. After such immense effort in bringing the stones to these locations it is no surprise that the megaliths mark more than one important sun fertility event. The 'mouth' of the largest lower stone, which I fondly regard as 'Pac-man' after the classic 1980's video game, has also been carefully aligned on the summit of Shan Slieve. It is surmised that from this spot the winter solstice sun also appears at the top of Shan Slieve in a potent fertility moment.

PREHISTORIC MOURNE: INSPIRATION FOR NEWGRANGE

This huge megalith on the lower slopes of Spinkwee Hill, the Pac-man stone, has its open mouth carefully aligned with the summit of Shan Slieve.

There are other megaliths on the slopes of Spinkwee and along the Cascade valley to remind us that the ancients had recorded in stone their long standing observations of the interaction between sun and landscape at the solstices. As is the case with most of the megaliths, the knowledge behind them has been lost. To chasten us even further, one of the larger stones on the other side of Spinkwee has been split by granite-men with plug and feathers. While this particular split stone has been left in situ, the damage done is a reminder that other significant stones from the locality may very well have been split up and removed. We can only trust now that our hope of understanding why the stones were first placed here on the hill may not be irretrievably lost.

**Luke's Mountain and Clonachullion/Clanawhillan**

**Luke's Mountain:** A re-examination of the origin of the name of Luke's mountain is personally very instructive. Prompted by the realisation that Thomas mountain was a mnemonic of the Irish *Tuama*, similar sounding words in Irish had been earlier examined for Luke's mountain and the following had been written:

MOURNE: THE MOUNTAINS OF SEX

'In their present form these names are indeed comparatively recent. We all have been diverted by the assumption that the names for these mountains were derived from actual people, Thomas or Luke, whose details had been lost in history. The names of these mountains however, have been transposed, like Lindsay's Leap, from the original Irish into English sound-a-likes. Luke's mountain could be a phonetic simulation of *luachair,* meaning rushes, or possibly from *lóiche* meaning 'light', or *luigín* meaning 'a little hollow', referring to the depression on the summit of the hill which are usually water filled small ponds.'[48]

The terrain had been walked, features examined, and finally these three suggestions had been made. Not one of them was correct despite having taken as much care as possible to find a solution. The realisation of one's errors with this name only heightens one's respect for the men of the ordnance survey in 1834 or for the diligent efforts of the Place-names project of Queen's university. We all laboured, but without the key. The solution, as mentioned earlier, was to be found in the ancient religion of Mourne; the worship of the sun and fertility, expressed in terms of human sexuality, what we have referred to as the gynaecomorphic interpretation of the landscape.

Luke's mountain can be seen in the middle distance. The track of the setting solstice sun into the [V] shaped notch (not shown) between the shoulder of Slievenaglogh and Slieve Bearnagh would diagonally bisect the faint turf trail that rises from left to right across the hill.

Snowy Clanawhillan hill is marked on the maps as Clonachullion. Slieve Meelmore is to the left and below it the great cliff of Spellack.

The secret behind the name of Luke's mountain is found in the Irish *Luighe na Gréine* meaning 'sunset'. The operative word is the Irish *Luighe* which is translated variously as 'act of lying down, reclining, declining, setting' and it is from this Irish word we have inherited the close sounding English approximation 'Luke'. The name comes, not from any feature on the mountain but from the unique spectacle seen from the slopes of Luke's mountain at the end of the winter solstice. Starting at two huge megaliths at the bottom of the hill an observer can witness the sun setting into the [V] shaped notch, a notional vagina, formed on the nearby horizon between Slievenaglogh and Slieve Bearnagh. As the sun sets into the notch, this potently symbolic sexual union between sun and earth can be witnessed along an ascending line across the slope of Luke's mountain. I like to think of Luke's mountain now as *Luighe* or 'sunset mountain'.[49]

**Clanawhillan:** I have heard many an argument about the pronunciation of the hill marked on the map of Mourne at J3129 as Clonachullion. Decades ago, Master McClean, the principal of Ballymoney primary school at Kilcoo, would tell his pupils that the name was Clonachullion yet others would swear that the name was Clanawhillan and that the map was wrong. Both are right as we have here two names of Irish origin for the same area.

106

Clanawhillan, which I personally find to be of more common usage, has its name from the former village or clachan on the south east side of the hill. The ruins of the houses cannot be seen from the main Bryansford to Hilltown road. The name is a contraction of the Irish *Clochán an buidhe lán,* meaning 'village of the full sun'. The name of Clonachullion on the other hand is another reference to the [V] shaped notch between Slievenaglogh and Slieve Bearnagh into which the solstice sun sets. The name comes from the Irish *Cluain na h-Uilleann,* meaning 'meadow of the notch or angle'. In Irish *Uille,* (genitive *Uilleann*) literally means 'elbow'. The same word lies behind Newell's Cross (J2414) roughly half-way between Killowen and Kilkeel, where the original Irish once referred to the angle of the road junction.[50]

**Spellack:** Walkers up the Trassey track behind Clanawhillan must pass under the imposing bulk of Spellack cliff. Mention has already been made of the numerous megaliths to be found in the vicinity. The area has certainly been important to the ancients. The Irish name *Spealag,* meaning 'pointed rock', well describes this cliff that resembles a broad spear head[51]. The evidence that human sacrifice took place in Mourne will be looked at later and although such happenings cannot be proved for this location, the possibility of a subtle name

Brown topped Clonachullion Hill as seen from the Brandy Pad at the end of the Trassey valley.

Clanawhillan Hill, seen here from Luke's mountain, is from the Irish *Clochán an buidhe lán*, meaning 'village of the full sun'. The village is sheltered behind the trees. Note the walled enclosure above the houses for the potatoes. The high wall would have been necessary to protect crops from wind and livestock.

change under the influence of Christianity must be considered. People may have been thrown from the spear shaped summit when it was lit by the full light of summer solstice dawn. There is an ominous proximity and similarity between *Spealag* and *Spealadh*, but the later means 'the act of shedding, flinging to waste, scattering, a falling away...'. Human sacrifice?

**Pollaphuca Hollow, Slieve Meelmore and the Trassey Valley**

Pollaphuca Hollow under the shadow of Slieve Bearnagh has certainly received attention from ancient man. Stunning and important megaliths are to be found the length of the valley. On the map, only the name Pollaphuca is recorded, but local usage still preserves a fuller version of Pollaphuca Hollow. In the Irish more than one interpretation is possible and the likelihood is that the two distinct names refer to two different megaliths. Place-names of Northern Ireland record Pollaphuca as coming from the Irish *Poll an Phúca*, meaning 'hole of the goblin'. For those familiar with the valley, this name is instantly recognisable as the small,

Spellack mountain, seen here at 5.50am on 30th May, receives full sun at dawn of summer solstice. The present name *Spealag* (pointed rock), may hide an earlier dark secret of human sacrifice with victims possibly thrown from the summit. We can only wonder if an earlier but similar Irish name of *Spealadh* was expunged on account of its pagan past. *Spealadh* means 'flinging to waste, scattering, falling away.'

low recess under a truly massive capstone. It could even be argued that the support stone to the right of the entrance is a depiction of the sprite. Certainly a nicely rounded eyeball has been carved into the stone. The cave, if we can call it that for it is really an unprepossessing recess, is not hard to find as this monument lies along the old quarry road under the slopes of Slieve Bearnagh. Indeed the quarry, which is just a few metres on past the megalith, was probably opened because the quarrymen looked on this as a lucky location. One look at the really mucky floor under the stone will surely deter the slightest thought of crawling in. The enormity of effort required in the moving of the huge slab implies that the location was regarded as a fertility spot of great importance, possibly combining more than one significant union between sun and earth at the solstices. The opening of the cave is a symbolic vagina intended for the entry of the summer solstice sun appearing at Slievenaglogh summit in a moment of solar ejaculation. The sun's rays enter and impregnate the womb of the cave ensuring fertility for the earth for the coming year. The top of the rock sports twenty-seven jumper holes where the

*The Hole of the Puca or goblin lies under a huge capstone weighing many tens of tons. The capstone shows the gouge where the granite-men broke off the apex, presumably to protect themselves by breaking the imagined power of the stone.*

granite men tried to split the capstone. They only partly succeeded for two sections of the front part of the capstone broke off but the back of the capstone remained intact. After all that effort, the fact that the granite-men left the detached blocks behind bespeaks exertion inspired more by superstition than any desire to commercially exploit the granite. It would be no surprise that the granite men were so wary, even frightened, of the goblin that to protect themselves they decided to break off the pointed apex of the stone and rob the capstone of its fertility potency thereby ruining the goblin's power. The freed granite blocks would have made good kerbstones but they lie unused where they fell.

When the early tribe of Ireland, the Tuatha Dé Danann, were vanquished, they were said to have retreated to holes underground such as this cave. Another such cave with its entrance towards first light of summer solstice can be found at a huge megalith (I fancifully called it 'The Hotel' on account of the space underneath) under the north tor of Slieve Bearnagh and illustrated on page 400. These places were widely believed to be the home of the fairies and I am probably not the only local who, over the years, was aware that this dark valley of Pollaphuca seemed to possess a lingering sense of awe and scarcely subdued dread.

This is the Goblin face-stone with its carefully crafted eyeball. To the left is one of the rejected granite blocks that were removed from the capstone.

As youngsters we probably had been severely told, 'Don't you dare go there!' As this megalith was regarded as the home of the fairies or *Sídhe*, the monument gave its name to the river that flowed across the entrance to the valley. The name Trassey is only a contraction of the Irish *Trasna Sídhe*, 'across the abode of the fairies'. There are some who cautiously believe even yet that it is risky to use the term 'fairies'. 'Appellations such as *na daoine maithe*, 'the good people', *na daoine uaisle*, 'the gentry', or *Bunadh na gcnoc*, 'the people of the hills', are preferable'.[52]

The other name of the valley favoured by the locals is Pollaphuca Hollow. This is part Irish and part mnemonic and comes from *Polla an Phúca Oilc*, meaning 'the pillar of the malevolent goblin'. When looked for from the path across the valley, this 'pillar' is not particularly easy to see against the mountain background. It is three/four hundred metres to the right of the great Meelmore megalith featured here in a double page photograph, higher up and on the left side of a boulder scree. The megalith is undoubtedly intended as an erect phallus and must have been so placed to mark a particularly important fertility site.[53] The climb up to the megalith to photograph it was fraught and especially steep. The effort begged the question, 'how did the ancients manoeuvre and control this stone of

111

*The rucksack and water bottle are positively tiny on top of the massive slab covering the hole of the goblin. The shoulder of Spellack is in the background.*

many tons on such a steep slope'? The incline on the side of Slieve Meelmore is much more acute than the slope on which the huge Diamond Rock was settled. The raising of the stone erection is a work of consummate skill and a lasting tribute to the dedication, efforts and perseverance of its makers. Such praise is not an endorsement of the stone or the creed that raised it. We recall the words of Deuteronomy 16:21-22,

'Do not set up any Asherah pole beside the altar you build to the Lord your God, and do not erect a sacred stone, for these the Lord your God hates.'

The triumph of Christianity and its acceptance on this island has already settled the question about the appropriateness of phallic stones. The fertility culture and the context of its time have passed. But the legacy of the stones left behind is now part of our culture and there is no shame in accepting ownership of them. We mentioned earlier that 'stunning and important megaliths are to be found the length of the valley'. This 'pillar of the malevolent goblin' is certainly one of them.

An observation must be made on the Irish *Olc* that was later transformed by usage into the English word 'hollow'; the fullness of meanings given in Fr Dinneen's dictionary are: 'evil, an evil thing, wickedness, vice, misfortune, damage, mischief; rage, fury, rabies; spite, malevolence'. The megalith bears within itself the reason for the description of 'malevolent'. In the following chapter we hope to illustrate many of the 'face stones' of Mourne. The addition of an eye and a mouth on the side of stones brought them to life and although we cannot know why the ancients indulged in this widespread practise it seems to have been important to them to imbue stones with a living essence, a spirit reflected in this case in the faces. Readers are invited to look closely sideways at the phallic pillar and it will be seen that beastly heads may be discerned, having slits for eyes and mouth, when viewed either from the left or the right. It was not unusual for stones to be given multiple heads depending on one's viewpoint. There is nothing kindly about these faces and there was no difficulty in selecting the word 'malevolent' as part of the translation. The sinister aura of these 'faces' is made all the more baleful by their intangible nature in that they bear no resemblance to any recognisable animal. The most disturbingly evil stone 'face' I have found is on the floor of the ritual platform on the upper slopes of Slieve Donard, of which more later. This last mentioned face can only be seen when

The pillar of the malevolent goblin on the side of Meelmore is quite a sexually explicit megalith. The trekking poles placed for scale against the monument are insignificant and we can only wonder at how such a huge stone was moved around on such a steep hillside. Turn the page sideward, left and right, to see the subtly evil 'faces' imparted to the stone. The dangers and incredible efforts involved in raising this really big stone secures its place among the most important megaliths of Mourne.

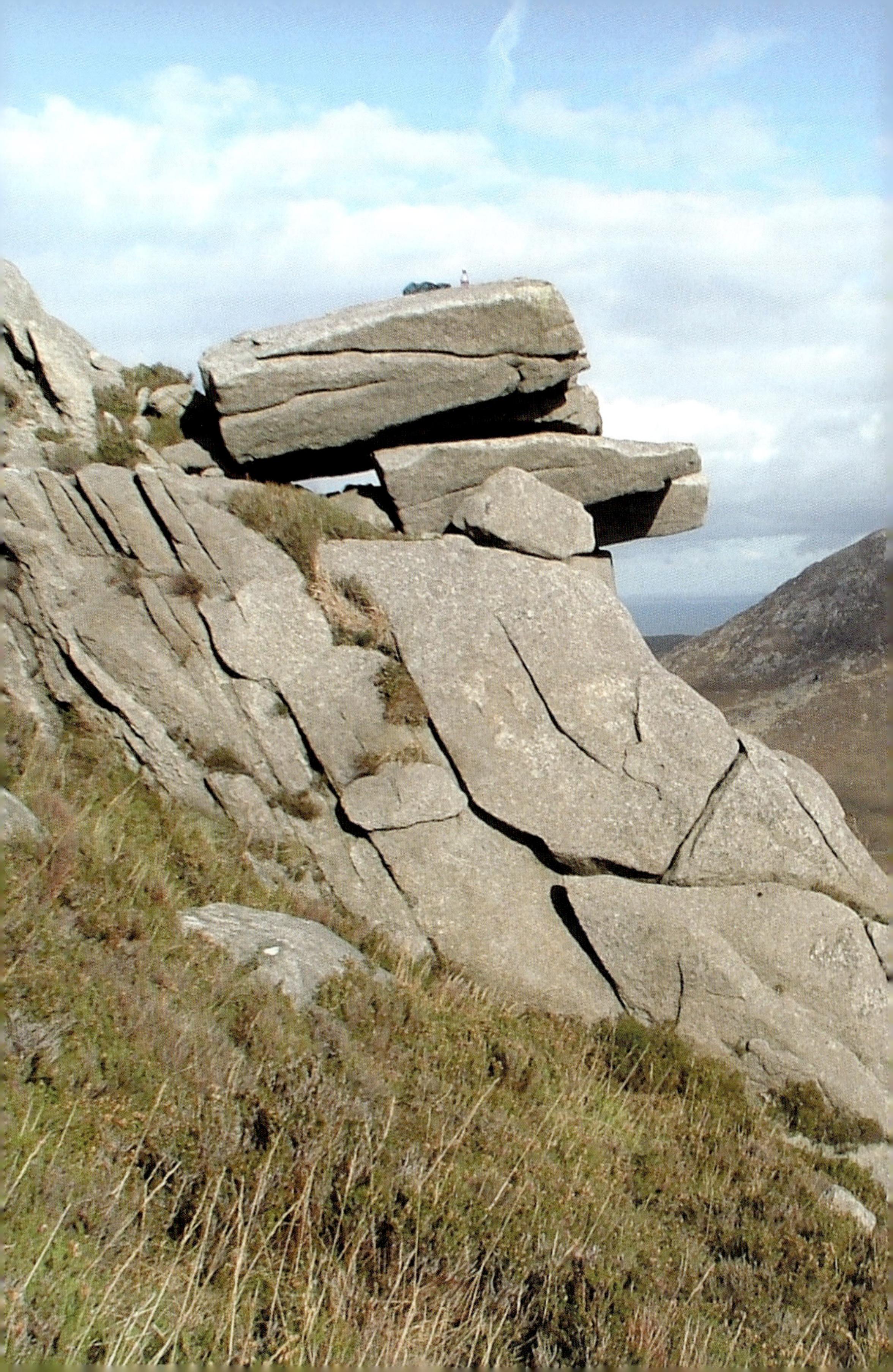

This huge megalith of copulation is to be found on the slopes of Meelmore in Pollaphuca valley. It probably marks where the sun touches Slieve Bearnagh at winter solstice. The distant cliffs of Slievenaglogh on the right are the location for the other great fertility megalith featured on the cover and title page.

looking down from the height of the rocks behind the platform. The Annals of Ulster, 1096, record that the province of *Ulaidh*, from which we derive the present name of Ulster, was associated with witchcraft in the folk imagination. There seems to be little doubt that, in their fertility rituals, the ancients must have connected with the very spirit of profound evil, perhaps, one shudders to think, an incarnate presence of the devil himself that they tried to sustain on such stones as *Polla an Phúca Oilc*. That we can look now on such menacing stones with equanimity I personally ascribe to the prayers and sacrifices of St Donard whose early name in Irish, *domangard,* was a compound of *Domhain Gárda* meaning 'the guard or protector of the world'.[54]

**Meelmore**: The ordnance survey of 1834 recorded the name versions of Slieve Meel-more, *Sliabh Míol Mór*, Sleivemanmore and Slaimonmore. This last name was described by Place-names project as 'particularly curious'. It is possible we have at least three different names here rather than different versions of a single core name. A sexual construct was certainly put on Meelmore. This sexual interpretation of the landscape would account for two of the names, Sleivemanmore and Slaimonmore. Sleivemanmore may well be a truncation of *Sliabh na mBan Mór*, 'mountain of the great woman', which was really an indirect way of saying the mountain was a great vulva. The second name of Slaimonmore is thought to come from the Irish *Slaimín Mór* which retained the idea of the mountain being a vulva and introduced the idea of sexual wantonness. *Slaimín* means 'a sexually promiscuous woman'. There is a case, however tenuous, for claiming that the name of *Sliabh Míol Mór*, with the rather incongruous translation given by the ordnance survey of 'great mountain of the ants', could be justified if re-translated as 'great mountain of the beasts' on account of the many face stones surrounding the mountain. My preference however, to explain the names of both Meelbeg and Meelmore would be with *Sliabh Maol Mór*. *Maol* normally means 'bald' but in this context it gives us 'great blunt mountain'. It is the topography that supplies the answer. Meelmore has the great blunt end of Spellack cliff and Meelbeg likewise has a blunt projection or angular ledge high on its side looking out over to Slieve Lamagan. *Sliabh Maol Beag* would give us 'little blunt mountain'. It should be no surprise that Meelmore, along with its erstwhile sexual names, has spectacular sexual megaliths. The larger of these megaliths, illustrated overleaf, is about halfway up Pollaphuca valley and is sited on a promontory that itself is phallic. The muscle power of oxen could not have been used on the steep slopes so, incredibly, this monument would have been secured in place by human strength alone. More than human strength is the whole sequence of sourcing the stone, bringing it to this outcrop, manoeuvring the lower stone out over the edge without going beyond the point of balance and then bringing into position the larger and immensely heavier top stone and positioning it onto its lower companion without dislodging or pushing it over the edge or knocking it askew from its alignment. Further, the flat surface atop the

MOURNE: THE MOUNTAINS OF SEX

The great compound megalith on the flank of Meelmore, shown in detail on the previous double page, has itself been placed on a promontory of phallic significance.

*A contented looking face adorns the top surface of the great megalith on the flank of Meelmore.*

formidable upper stone has been decorated with a face. I mark this megalith among the great accomplishments of Mourne. The cover photograph for this book featuring a similar style of megalith involving multiple stones projected out over a void is found across the Trassey valley atop the cliff face of Slievenaglogh.

The south-east flank of Meelmore beyond the Mourne wall is truly festooned with spear stones and megaliths to the extent that I first imagined virtually every stone on the mountain-side had been moved in some way or other by the ancients. Pass up Pollaphuca valley and over the Mourne wall, then angle southwards up the side of Meelmore. Stones are in profusion; many have been arranged in an angled phallic fashion, many point towards the distant peaks of Bignian, Bearnagh or Doan and many others have been adorned with eyes. One of the most astounding creations is a megalith bird and beside it a phallic spear stone of daunting dimensions that points towards Doan. It is such a large construction that there is no difficulty in seeing the great spear shape on the hillside a few hundred metres uphill from the Mourne wall stile.

**From The Hare's Gap to Slieve Bearnagh Quarry**

The Hare's Gap is one of the main entrances into the heart of Mourne. The ancients marked the area with its share of monuments. One of the most

MOURNE: THE MOUNTAINS OF SEX

prominent fertility stones is the likely source for the name of the Hare's Gap. Coming up the Trassey valley you will see a conspicuous pointed rock projecting from the right-hand shoulder of the col. This phallic rock seems to have been particularly important to the ancients as it was high enough to receive the first light of the winter solstice sunrise. At the other turn of the year, the summer solstice sunset, the reverse side of the stone is illuminated as illustrated in the photograph. Because of a variety of possible interpretations, the unravelling of the origins of the place-name is uncertain. Estyn Evans believed the name came from an O'Hare family who farmed nearby at Clonachullion while Queens Place-names project favoured the name coming from the name of the animal. The working assumption here is that the name, like so many others of Mourne, is a mnemonic of the original Irish and a remnant of it as well. The Irish word for a mountain pass is *Bealach*. The narrow route between the mountain and the sea followed by the main road from Newcastle to Kilkeel, just south of Newcastle harbour, is called the Ballagh. The Irish word for a block is *Ceap* which is now rendered as the English word 'gap'. Nothing is ever certain when working with

This photo of the phallic rock at the side of the Hare's Gap col was taken at 9.32pm on 17th June. The rock is lit on alternate sides; firstly at dawn of winter solstice and also as seen here by the declining sun near summer solstice. The name comes from the Irish *(Bealach na) h-Éirí Cheap*, 'the pass of the rising (becoming tumescent) block'.

This projecting megalith under the cliffs of Slievenaglogh may seem small and insignificant but there are at least thirty other large stones used in this construction. The anchor stone, seen here at the bottom, is of monstrous proportions and it has a comfortable shelter below it. This construction marks where the declining winter solstice sun sets into the 'womb' of the distant [V] shaped notch formed between the shoulder of Slieve Bearnagh and Cove Mountain.

mnemonics but the closer they can be reconciled with existing topography the better. In this particular case account is also taken of the local propensity in Mourne to unashamedly continue using pagan names denoting fertility features. Looking to the projecting phallic rock at the side of the col, it is proposed that the name of the Hare's Gap has come down to us from the remnant of the Irish 'the pass of the rising (becoming tumescent) block', (*Bealach na*) *h-Éirí Cheap*.[55] The pointed or phallic nature of the rock is most pronounced when seen from underneath. The south side of the stone has also been decorated low down with a simple sleeping eye chopped into the rock making it a 'face stone', a phenomenon we will look at in the following chapter.

**Brandy Pad:** Smugglers who had collected their contraband from the Mourne shore and were en route inland, used the Brandy Pad which, on passing through the Hare's Gap, followed the slope under the shoulder of Slieve Bearnagh avoiding the boulder field at the steep head of the Trassey valley. The present rendering in English of Brandy Pad would have us believe that the name derived from the most popular spirituous commodity trafficked along this mountain trail even though quite a variety of other items were carried including tea, silk and tobacco.[56] The name of the Brandy Pad is a mnemonic. It comes, not from the Brandy spirit but from the Irish (*Bóthar na*) *bPránnaidhe Pead*. The Irish *Pead* means 'a pony' but the sound has morphed into the English 'pad', a path or trail; *bPránnaidhe*, which was later rendered as Brandy, is the eclipsed version of *Pránnaidhe,* a word usually used to describe 'a large fat cat'. We should again remember that with eclipse the [*P*] sound is not heard only the [*b*]. In this context *Pránnaidhe* was applied to the load carried by the pony. The meaning of the Irish (*Bóthar na*) *bPránnaidhe Pead* is (the trail of) 'the well packed ponies'.

If you are on the start of the Brandy Pad on the Trassey side of the Mourne Wall, look for the marvellous megalithic mirror stone not far below the trail. It is tempting to describe these various monuments as burial sites, and most likely they were, but we are unlikely to ever know. Besides, bones would not last long in the acidic mountain soil and nothing could realistically be expected to survive after thousands of years. Again we can only marvel at the effort involved in the preparation of this site. A huge anchor stone has been placed on the slope to allow the megalith and its surrounding wedge stones to remain in place. The back of the stone, not seen in the photograph, is beautifully flat and faces towards the Mourne Wall as if to absorb as much as possible of the first light of the winter solstice sun rising out from the middle of the col; in fertility terms this was the sun being born anew out of the vaginal notch of the Hare's Gap. On the other side of the Mourne Wall is another mirror stone carefully shaped as the head of a whooper swan which was illustrated on page 26. This stone too, faces towards the rising sun of the winter solstice.

Continuing down the Brandy Pad towards Bearnagh quarry you will come to a wide [V] shaped recess in the rock wall. Readers are invited to examine the back wall of this niche and to form their own conclusions as to whether or not the ancients have imparted the suggestion of a phallus in relief on the back wall in simulation of intercourse in this fancied vagina. The position of this notch means that it would only receive the sun's light in the early morning around the time of the summer solstice. The remarkably smoothed lower right-hand wall of this cleft with a single part like a flexed arm left in mysterious relief is challenging to explain. We can only wonder, for instance, why the whole wall was chipped back to put this 'flexed arm' in relief. Perhaps only this outer part of the rock face was lit by winter solstice sun and the relief acts like a sundial gnomon? This recess into the shoulder of Slieve Bearnagh would bear further observation to reveal more secrets of the ancients.

High on the hill-side, above where the Brandy Pad makes its descent to the valley floor and where the shoulder of Slieve Bearnagh turns into Pollaphuca Hollow valley, there is an awe-inspiring construction that I refer to as the Bearnagh quarry megalith. One is left stunned at the effort that would have been

# Prehistoric Mourne: Inspiration for Newgrange

The evening sun warms this megalith under the Brandy Pad near the col of the Hare's Gap. Note the huge anchor slab on the slope which wedges the megalith upright and keeps it in place.

required to build this intricate assembly of boulders on such a dangerously steep slope, commanding a wonderful view of the entire valley below. Again, lest it be overlooked because it lies flat on the slope, attention is drawn to the absolutely huge anchor slab below the primary stone without which nothing could have been secured in position. Such would have been the immensity of effort entailed in marking this fertility location, one suspects that it is dual purpose. It is one of the great frustrations of finding such incredible monuments that they cannot presently be accompanied by a conclusive rational for their construction. For the moment it has to be enough to rest in plain astonishment at the planning, proficiency and physical power involved in their creation.

Later generations will certainly look at the quarry and marvel at the work of the quarrymen and the volume of stone removed, much of it before the advent of power tools. When granite could have been extracted much more easily further down the valley and saving enormously on the effort of transportation, the question has to be asked what was so special about this quarry location to warrant all the extra effort? Insufficient observations proscribe emphatic declarations

One of the mysteries of Mourne; why was the rest of the wall of stone chipped away to leave this apparently phallic part in relief?

about the reason for erecting this megalith on a most difficult and challenging slope but the following explanation is recorded that others may later verify its possibility. When in doubt pay particular attention to the point of the spear. There is indeed a pronounced point on this megalith pointing towards where the sun should rise on the summer solstice. On the horizon, as seen from this location, there is a distinct notch between Slieve Croob, 534 metres, and Slievenisky, 446 metres. The likelihood is that the summer solstice sun can be observed here rising, as it were, from the womb of the earth. It would be no surprise then that the quarry site was chosen thereby on account of such potent fertility associations and attendant good luck rather than the granite per se. There is good reason to associate the quarry with the megalith because if you look carefully at the hillside before getting too close, you will notice that the quarrymen of old started to quarry the hill high on the left-hand side beside the megalith. They then stopped and changed to the right-hand side of the megalith where the much bigger quarry developed, but never at any time did they disturb the monument itself. A similar situation prevailed at the Ballagh quarry up behind Drinneevar where the fertility

*High above the Trassey Valley enormous energy has been expended in erecting this assembly of massive stones marking sunrise of the summer solstice over beyond Slievenaglogh.*

monument, illustrated on pages 266 and 267, ended in isolation as the men quarried around it. Despite all the aforegoing excitement about this one wonderful megalith there are many other great megalithic stones in the vicinity including up and behind the quarry. There is just so much to see and no room to write about them.

### Kinnahalla, Spaltha, Spelga and Slievenamiskan

**Kinnahalla:** To understand the meaning of Kinnahalla one must start with the topography. Visitors driving along the Bryansford to Hilltown road, or perhaps coming down from the Spelga Pass would hardly give the long low hill of Kinnahalla a second look. Other nearby mountains like Cock and Hen are much more noticeable and dramatic. Kinnahalla is smooth and gently rounded and a closer look reveals that the long low hill actually has two tops, reaching 296 metres and 271 metres respectively. The present designation of Kinnahalla is apparently a macaronic, the term given to a mix of Irish and English. In submitting the name Kinnahalla to redaction we surmise that originally this hill

*The Bearnagh quarry megalith as seen from below: note the massive anchor slab on the right of the picture securing everything on the steep hillside. Manoeuvring such colossal stones in this dangerous location still remains an amazing feat.*

124

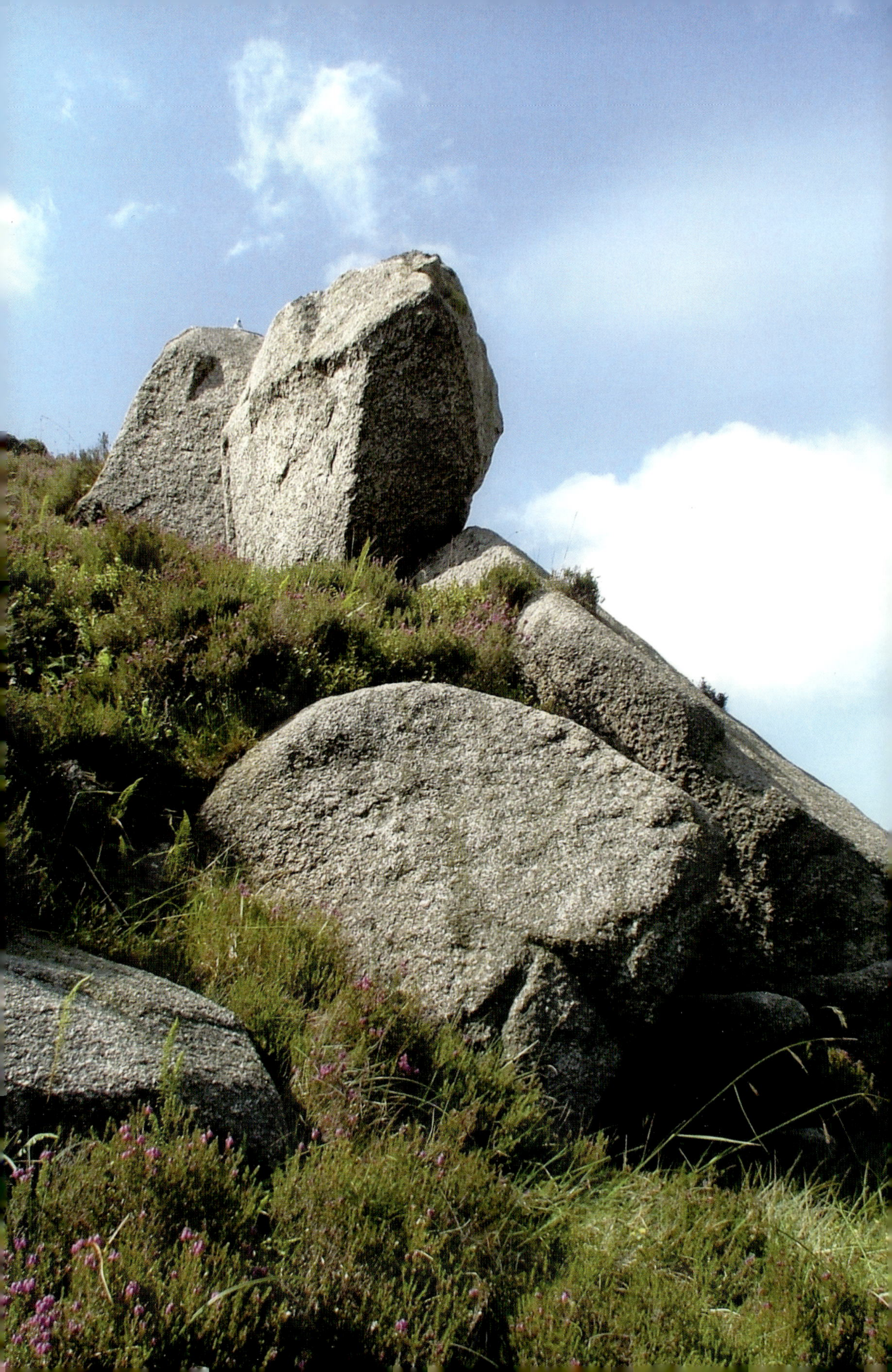

*The two gentle undulating tops of Kinnahalla are on the right. Kinnahalla is from the Irish* Cion an h-Ala, *'the sin or passion of the swan'.*

with two tops had the Irish name of *Cion an Sabhán*, 'the sin or passion of the peg'. A *sabhán* was the term for a notched or [V] shaped piece of wood used as a long pin to bolt or secure the movable bottom of panniers. This descriptive term of *Sabhán* used for the two hills was at some stage changed from Irish to the similar sounding English 'swan'. From 'swan' the name was literally translated back again into Irish as *Cion an h-Ala*, 'the sin or passion of the swan'. When the ordnance survey collected the name *Cionn S(h)alach*, 'dirty head/summit', in 1834 they at least preserved the reason for the original name, namely the phallic and therefore 'passionate' shadows cast by the hill at summer solstice sunset. The declining summer solstice sun greatly extended these otherwise insignificant hill curves across the landscape until the shadows took on more emphatic phallic shapes. The early Christians, unsurprisingly, branded the fertility shadows as evil and so the mountain got the name of 'dirty head'; this was the 'sin of the swan' or would that be 'the peg'. Nevertheless, the shadows were of great local significance and influenced surrounding names which is why we treat these names together.

**Spaltha and Glenaveagh:** When Place-names of Northern Ireland treated of Spaltha mountain to the south of Lugagour the following was stated:

> 'The verb *spall* 'scorch, shrivel, parch' (Ó *Dónaill*) is well attested and *spallta*, the past participle of this verb, is used adjectivally in the sense of 'burned, dried up, parched' (*Dinneen*).'

Dinneen also has the participial adjective *Spalptha* meaning 'dried up'. To avoid any misunderstanding it should be said that the name (*Sliabh*) *Spalptha* has nothing to do with desiccated pasturage as this part of the Mournes receives the same rain and is just as green in season as the surrounding hills. The explanation of the name lies with the solstice phallic shadow of Kinnahalla notionally waiting for its sexual entry into the declivity formed by the youthful Glenaveagh Stream. As it moved clockwise the phallic shadow of the sun really only touches the lower slopes of Spaltha. The slopes of Spaltha mountain were fancied as safe or 'dry' from the solar semen as the shadow bided its time before reaching the little valley of Glenaveagh. The name Glenaveagh takes its name from the phallic shadow of Kinnahalla, being derived from the Irish *Glan na Fé*, 'the valley of the rod'. The declivity is also called 'Lugaveagh' by the locals, meaning 'hollow of the rod'.

**Spelga:** The sun moved closer to its setting and the solstice shadow now moved up the slopes of Spelga. Place-names of Northern Ireland inform us that Spelga derives from *Speilgeach*, '(place) abounding in pointed rocks'. In an earlier work, and thinking of the summer herding that took place in the area, I had

This little mountain-side hollow is the source of Glenaveagh Stream. The shadow of Kinnahalla hill will reach up towards this hollow at summer solstice sunset.

thought instead 'it is a corruption of the plural *speileacha,* 'herds of cattle'.[57] This explanation was influenced by the long standing practice of transhumance in the area when herds of cattle were brought to the Spelga valley for the summer grazing. It was this practice that gave the name to Butter mountain from the Irish *Bothach,* 'full of booths, tents, huts'.[58] Nevertheless, Spelga has plenty of rocks on the slope overlooking the dam and the gorge, as well as on its western slopes overlooking Kinnahalla.

A number of reasons for the derivation of Spelga are feasible. One explanation could be if *speilgeach,* the 'place abounding in pointed rocks', was interpreted metaphorically with the many 'pointed rocks' being understood as the area's many pointed phallic shadows. Another explanation would be to understand the 'pointed rocks' not as random jagged stones but rather as 'pointing rocks'. The slopes above Spelga Pass are rich in megaliths. Looking south from the upper slopes of Spelga you see the summits of Slievenamiskan, Cock mountain, Rocky mountain and the Cock and Hen. Many of the spear stones on the slopes have been deliberately arranged to point to the tops of one or other of these mountains. One particular monument is of particular importance on account of its size and intention. On the higher slopes there is a huge pointed rock. It cannot be called a megalith as the whole monument has been prepared from the living rock face. With distinctive notches for an eye and mouth, this rock can be regarded as a face stone. The ancients have spent much time here for it is from this location that the winter solstice sun can be seen rising from the top of distant Slieve Muck. A vertical groove on the business end of the point – not seen in the photograph – represents the penis meatus groove and confirms the rock's phallic credentials.

Yet perhaps the best reconciliation of the name Spelga with the landscape would come from recognising it as a contraction of the Irish *Spealadh Ga,* 'the declining spear'. *Spealadh* means 'the act of shedding, flinging to waste, scattering abroad; a falling away in health or appearance, decline.' The sun was setting and the summer solstice shadow cast by Kinnahalla was about to disappear. Among the various meanings for the Irish *Ga* we have 'a javelin, a small spear, dart or arrow; a shaft or ray of light;' and notably. '*membrum virile*'. The reverend Dinneen was always quick to spare the sensitivities of his readers by rendering in Latin indelicate matters arising in his translations. '*Membrum virile*' is, of course, the erect male penis. 'The declining spear' referred to the passing of the phallic shadow of Kinnahalla over the slopes of Spelga hill and on towards its demise on the slope of Slievenamiskan.

**Spelga Pass:** I am following common English usage and local understanding when I refer to the gorge down which the River Bann flows from the Spelga reservoir as Spelga Pass. When next you look at a map of the Mournes note however that the name Spelga Pass refers to a part of the northern slope of Slievenamiskan at OS J257278 and not the gorge down which passes the B27, Kilkeel Road. The Irish name would have been *Spealadh Ga Páis* and is totally

This hillside of Spelga is rich in stones deliberately arranged to point to the summits of distant mountains. The circled rock on the upper slope is one of the many megaliths along the rock outcrop across the upper part of the hill. This stone is a phallic creation complete with an eye, mouth and penile meatus groove carved into it; it indicates where the winter solstice sun can be seen rising from the summit of distant Slieve Muck. It is one of the more important monuments of Mourne.

different in meaning from the English. *Páis* in Irish does not mean a pass, gorge or defile but rather in this context, 'death'[59]. Spelga Pass originally referred to the spot reached on Slievenamiskan by Kinnahalla's summer solstice shadow at the moment of sunset when the shadow finally terminated and died. *Spealadh Ga Páis* means 'death of the declining spear'.

**Slievenamiskan:** Earlier we mentioned how a huge shadow, with phallic import, would be cast across the former Spelga meadow, now the reservoir, at summer solstice sunset by the outline of Slievenamiskan. It was the phallic shadow that gave Slievenamiskan its name. However, the present prevailing understanding is that the name derives from *Sliabh Meascáin,* meaning 'mountain of the *meascán* of butter', a *meascán* being a lump or ball of butter. There is a very important observation made by Place-names project in regard to Slievenamiskan:

'The curious thing about this name is that there is no support for the article *na* either in the historical forms or in the current local pronunciation …

This photograph was taken at 9.35pm on 19th June on the Kinnahalla road near its junction with the Kilkeel road and shows the progress of the phallic shadow of Kinnahalla hill up into the gorge of Spelga Pass. Spelga mountain is on the left and Slievenamiskan on the right. The dimple in the middle of the picture is the horse-shoe bend. In another ten minutes it will be completely in shade as the sun continues to set and the shadow lengthens.

Slievenamiskan is derived from the Irish *Sliabh mí-scian*, meaning 'evil dagger mountain' after the long phallic shadow it cast across the former Spelga meadow at summer solstice sunset.

The Irish forms, which O'Donovan obtained in the locality, suggest that Slievenamiskan derives its name, not from a number of *meascáns*, but from one *meascán*: Irish *Sliabh Meascáin*.'[60]

The importance of this is the support it gives to a singular event. A single lump of butter giving its name to a mountain must have seemed so improbable that logic called for it to be made plural by the introduction of *na*. The present proposed amendment is that the original Irish was *Sliabh mí-scian,* meaning 'evil dagger mountain'. Along with the sound, this reconciles with an historical form of singularity. A variation for the name of the shadow was *Déar-Meadóg*, meaning 'huge dagger', from which came the now obsolete name form of Deers' Meadow.[61]

**Cock Mountain, Hen Mountain also called the 'Cock and Hen'**

**Cock Mountain:** This was recorded by the ordnance survey as *Sliabh a choiligh*, the translation being 'mountain of the cock'. The top of the mountain however has two crests. They are not as dramatic as the summits of the lower 'Cock and Hen' but they are relatively close in height and as a pair would have earned the mountain the fertility name of *Sliabh na Cíocha*, 'the mountain of the breasts'. Cock mountain appears to be a weak and tenuous mnemonic of *Cíoch* meaning

Photograph taken at 9.00pm on 19th June as sheep graze on Spaltha pastures; note the length of their shadows. Beyond are the still sun-lit slopes of Spelga; then shaded by clouds, the shoulder of Slievenamiskan and the dark brooding head of Cock Mountain.

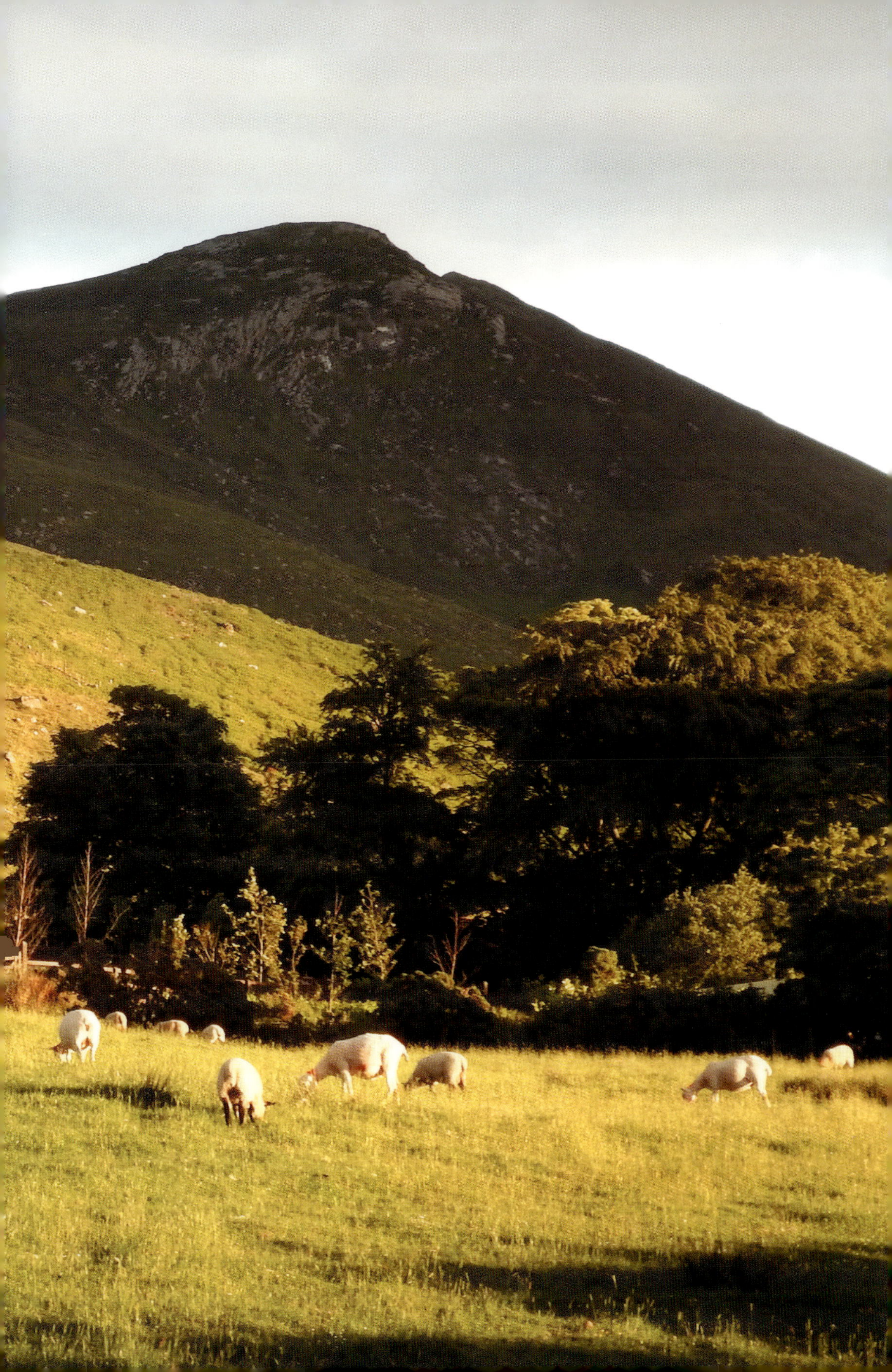

*With its two crests, this mountain would have had the Irish name of Sliabh na Cíocha, 'the mountain of the breasts'. The Irish Cíocha would be changed into the English mnemonic 'Cock mountain'.*

'a breast' [*Cíoch* sounds like *key-och*]. The transition from Irish 'Key-och' to English 'Cock' probably owes more to farmyard affinity of cocks and hens than to the sound of the Irish.

**Hen Mountain:** Hen (J2427) is easily seen from the Bryansford and Sandbank Roads outside Hilltown. For the ancients, who looked at the landscape in sexual and gynaecomorphic terms, it would have been straightforward to view the distinctive tors on Hen mountain as nipples on breasts. Thus the early name was likely *Sliabh na h-Áine*, 'The Mountain of Pleasure'. The coming of new English speaking settlers saw the transformation of *Sliabh na h-Áine* to the phonetically close substitute of 'Hen'. For Christians it was preferable to imagine the summit tors as the crest on a hen's head instead of indelicate references to the female swellings. Another word for hen in Irish is *Cearc* (genitive *circe*) and this is the likely source of other early names such as *circe Boirche* (Rennes Dindsenchas), or, *ceirce Boirche* (The metrical Dindsenchas), giving us '(the mountain of the) swelling hen'.[62]

A comment is necessary on the combined name of Cock and Hen as I am perplexed that it is only shown on present OS maps as 'Hen mountain'. I wonder

MOURNE: THE MOUNTAINS OF SEX

if there are others like myself who had Hen mountain pointed out to them in decades past as the Cock and Hen? The name is applied to a single mountain and not two. It is always possible that the ordnance survey officers back in 1834, on hearing the name, misunderstood and divided the Cock and Hen between two mountains rather than one. I am trusting however to my recollections of almost sixty years when the mountains were named to me on every bus journey to the great weekly market at Newry. As a single name applied to Hen mountain, 'Cock and Hen' could certainly be viewed as a mnemonic of the Irish *Cíocha h-Áine*, 'breasts of pleasure'.

**Crenville, Slievedermot, Cloghmore and Slievemartin**

Many historians now accept that 'every piece of legend, every piece of folklore is based on some fact, however garbled'.[63] Back over sixty years ago when Fr Bernard Mooney researched the meaning of Crenville mountain (J2018), which is adjacent to Slievedermot overlooking the Kilbroney River valley, an old woman told him that according to local legend this mountain took its name from a mysterious tree that had a way of disappearing and reappearing as if by magic.[64] The name

Cock and Hen mountain, seen here on the right, is probably a mnemonic of the Irish fertility name *Cíocha h-Áine*, 'breasts of pleasure'. Cock mountain is on the left background.

was therefore presumed to derive from the Irish *Crann-bhile,* meaning 'sacred or historic tree'. The old woman's version of the legend was, however, garbled. Nevertheless, she was, without realising it, the custodian of the dying remnant of sun worship folklore. It was the sun's shadow and not a tree that had a way of disappearing and reappearing as if by magic. The confusion arose from a reasonable similarity in sound between the Irish for tree, *Crann,* and the Irish for sun, *Grian* (genitive *Gréine*). Crenville is from the Irish (*Sliabh na*) *Gréine Buille,* 'mountain of the sun's cast'. Dawn of winter solstice sees Crenville's great obscuring shadow cover much of the Kilbroney river valley but as the sun rises it is Slievedermot (J1918) that demonstrates its fertility name. Slievedermot is from the Irish *Sliabh Dear Moth,* meaning 'huge penis'. The name comes from the monstrous phallic shadow cast 'up the legs' of the Kilbroney valley. The building of St Bronagh's chapel in the valley below claimed the area for Christianity but significantly the chapel is not touched by Slievedermot's phallic winter shadow.[65]

At an elevation of 957 feet above Rostrevor is the magnificent stone of Cloghmore, from the Irish *Cloch Mór* meaning 'great stone'. It was a very popular tourist destination in Victorian times and later was featured in Robert Lloyd Praeger's *Official Tourist Guide to County Down and the Mourne Mountains*. The stone suffered terribly at the hands of many visitors who, unaware of the cultural heritage they were defacing, vandalised the stone by chiselling their names into the rock. This great granite boulder of over twenty tons sits on a bedrock of shale and from this fact it has always been regarded as a glacial erratic. Geologists and Praeger attributed the stone's present position to the action of ice during the glacial period, believing that the stone was deposited where it now rests as the ice melted. Praeger remarks that the composition of the stone proves that it came from the northward, from the neighbourhood of Newry and that such was the general ice-flow from that direction.[66] The relatively rounded and smooth surface of the rock would certainly indicate abrasion by ice but this great stone is more than an erratic, it is a megalith of wonderful significance; a treasure. It is a fertility stone, a work of art, a face stone and a sun pointing marker. The final resting place of this megalith has been precisely and quite deliberately determined by man, not ice. What a pity, after all the millennia the stone has rested here, it has finally been despoiled over the recent decades by trivial memory seeking.

Great disservice has been done to the ancients by not crediting them for placing the stone where it is. This fact alone serves as a humbling reminder of the immense wealth of knowledge about the mountains that has been lost. There are a number of angled points on the Cloghmore rock and the most prominent and important is the one that points towards the summit of Slievemartin. This is the raison d'être for the stone's location. Cloghmore is a fertility stone as it marks the spot where the summer solstice sun could be seen rising from the top of Slievemartin in a great symbolic act of ejaculation bringing with it fruitfulness, productiveness and, it was probably believed, the promise of fecundity to families,

*The remains of St Bronagh's chapel at Kilbroney, Rostrevor. In the background is Slievedermot, (from the Irish* Sliabh Dear Moth, *'huge penis') which casts its phallic winter solstice shadow 'up the legs' of the Kilbroney valley. The shadow does not impinge on the sacred site.*

animals and crops. Slievemartin is not named after some forgotten hero called Martin. The name has probably devolved into Martin from the Irish *Marthain*, meaning 'a charm or spell', or indeed, *Marthain* with the sense of 'act of living, being alive'. But both of these words themselves reflect the earliest origins, for spells and incantations for health and well-being were probably all part of first fertility rituals. The name of Slievemartin is a contraction of *Sliabh na mBáirr Teine*, 'mountain of the tip of fire'.

It would be no surprise that the immense effort involved in bringing such a mighty stone to this special location would be justified by more than one reason. At the other end of the year, the winter solstice dawn was initially masked from Cloghmore by the shoulder of Ballynagelty (OS J1916). The name of Ballynagelty was not treated by Place-names of N.I. project but Praeger, in his guide, gave the unfortunate interpretation of *Baile na ngealtaigh*, 'the town of the madmen'.[67] The proper rendering in Irish of Ballynagelty should be *Baile na Ceilte*, meaning 'the place of concealment'. It was this hill that obscured the first appearance of the solstice sun at the moment of dawn from Cloghmore. The Point Park (Irish *poinnte*) below Ballynagelty would have been the location where an observer at Cloghmore would have seen the birth of the new sun emerging from the

*The point of the great fertility megalith of Cloghmore points towards the summit of Slievemartin from where the sun can be seen rising from the summit at summer solstice. Note the large circular hooded eye on the side of the stone. This faces towards where the winter solstice sun appears from Ballynagelty.*

symbolically suggestive swelling of the hillside. Also in the vicinity is Fiddlers Green (OS J17718) which has given its name to the now famous and well established annual international festival of music and fun at Rostrevor. The name, like so many others, is a mnemonic from the Irish, in this case *Fiadh-Léar Gréine,* 'great sight of the sun'. The presumption is that, unlike Ballynagelty, there was no difficulty in seeing the new winter solstice sun from this location. Verification, however, has not been sought on account of the present surrounding forest.

Despite the ravages of the chisellers, Cloghmore remains a tremendous work of art for it is a great face stone. It is also a good introduction to the following chapter which will look at a variety of these stones throughout Mourne. A face stone, as the name implies, is a rock or boulder, usually of a fairly large size and appropriate profile, on which the impression of a beast's face has been imparted by removing selective parts of the rock so as to give the strong suggestion of an eye and a mouth, these features often being convincingly enhanced by the shadow of the sun. Quite why the ancients decided to do this remains unknown but imbuing stones with the impression of life, and especially strong, formidable

# Mourne: The Mountains of Sex

life-forms at that, certainly created a great feeling of intense power, dominance and energy. The side of Cloghmore that faces towards the winter solstice sun has, to this man's eyes, been shaped to suggest the head of a humpback whale. On the left of the stone is a large circular hooded eye and to the right the lines incised into the rock near the point are evocative of the humpback whale's great hinged mouth. The large circular stone eye motif would seem to faintly appear again high on the rock face of Slieve Bignian where the Mourne wall butts up against the summit tor. The zig-zag pattern of the eye-lid however is really only noticeable in the mornings.

Walk round Cloghmore so as to face towards Slievemartin and the profile of the great boulder changes completely. Others will hopefully later check the assumption that the muzzle is orientated towards the setting summer solstice sun and, if so, verify whether the sun can be seen setting on the distant Cooley mountains in true fertility fashion, perhaps symbolically into a notch between hills or onto the top of a hill. There is surely much more waiting to be revealed about Cloghmore, about its environs and the megaliths on the slopes on the far side of Kilbroney valley.

Cloghmore stone takes on the aspect of a great animal muzzle as it faces towards the location of the summer solstice sunset. In the background is Slievemartin from the Irish *Sliabh na mBáirr Teine*, 'mountain of the tip of fire'. Cloghmore marks where the sun appears at summer solstice dawn from the top of the mountain in a great notional moment of solar ejaculation.

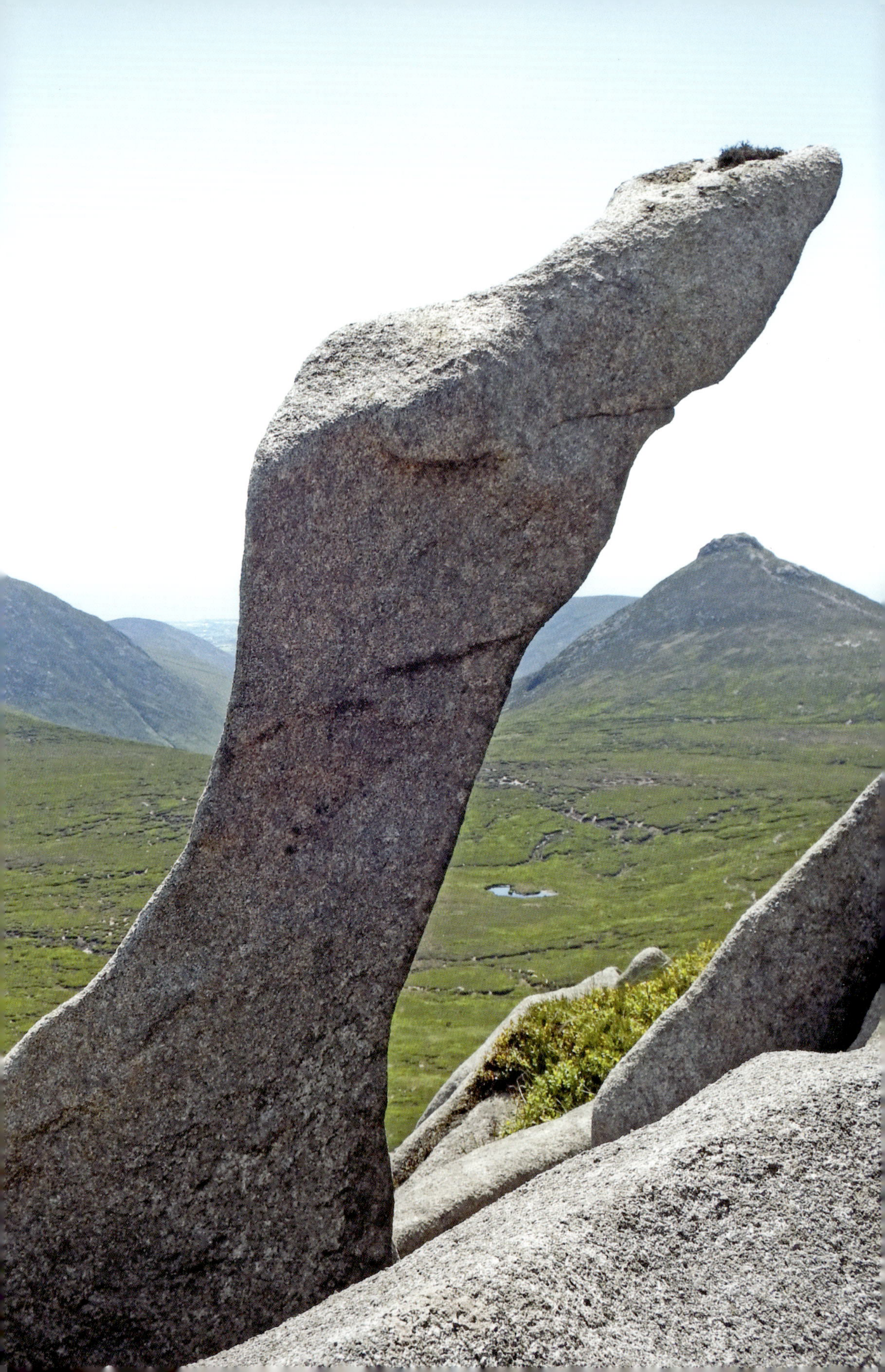

# THE FACE STONES OF MOURNE

The credit for first recognising the faces of Mourne must go to Newcastle man W.H. Carson. In an appendix to his book, *The Dam Builders; The story of the men who built the Silent Valley Reservoir,* he included photographs of three stone faces above the Silent Valley. Certainly, were it not for pressure of space, he could easily have included more. When *The Dam Builders* was first published in 1981 the faces were unfortunately treated as an interesting oddity. Three photographs were not apparently enough to alert us to this treasure trove of early art.[1] The purpose of this chapter, comprised exclusively of photographs showing face stones, is to show that this phenomenon is not an accident of nature but is deliberate, widespread and an art form worthy of serious appreciation and celebration.

The Mournes are indeed a treasure trove of the art of early man. With deceptive simplicity stones all across the hills have been brought to life by the addition of an eye and a mouth. The bigger the stone the more likely it will be found to have been given lines evocative of a face. Men have even dangled on ropes over cliffs to gouge recesses into rocks that the sun, filling them with shadow, would create faces on a grand scale. A case can be made that the whole south face of Slieve Lamagan, when viewed from Bignian in the morning, could be viewed as a boar because of the strategic creation of a shadow area high on the mountain-side. The north tor of Slieve Bearnagh, when viewed from Meelmore, has, most certainly, been shaped into a boar's head. Bignian too has been generously decorated with face stones. The ancients thought in broad dimensions and acted on them.

Frequently the transformation of a boulder has been achieved by whacking the stone with an axe to impart a simple line. Sometimes a stone maul has been used to make an eye by hammering a hollow into the stone. Often we have a drooped eyelid suggesting that a stone is asleep. Rocks on the Brandy Pad and in Pollaphuca valley have received special attention and been carefully chiselled with very realistic eyes. Large stones will often have a number of shadow eyes allowing for various interpretations and it is not uncommon to have three or four possible faces on the same boulder. We are not talking about real identifiable faces but beastly representations, many of which are peaceful and tranquil but many others are grim and undoubtedly of malign intent. The skill of the ancients has seen them magically change inert lumps of granite to vibrant sculptures. Anyone who walks in the Mournes will have passed many of these stones. They hide in plain view, overlooked by their commonness and by a previous presumption that

The south-east flank of Slieve Meelmore has this treasure in stone of an amazing bird's head.

the marks on the stones were accidents of nature, or weathering and thus meaningless. An awareness of these treasures and the joy of discovering them will add immensely to the pleasure of walkers and visitors.

Hammering granite is a dangerous occupation; sharp chips of stone frequently spall off when the granite is struck stinging hands and face. Nowadays workers wear protective goggles but in the past the great hazard was a blinding stone into the eye and many unfortunately suffered this fate. The working with great stones is an occupation fraught with peril and many a man has been caught unawares by the sudden shift of the huge weights and been crushed in hand or leg. Such accidents undoubtedly happened regularly in Mourne in ancient times. A folklore snippet about the ancient people, the Fir Bolg, was previously thought to be a disparaging remark about a supposedly inferior conquered people but it can now be considered a fair comment on the tribe who, because they single-mindedly erected great megaliths in profusion throughout Mourne, must have suffered incredible injuries in the process. We are told that they were:

'...hideous to behold, with single legs, single hands and single eyes...'[2]

This catalogue of injuries sustained by the people would be consistent with frequent manipulation of huge stones of granite. One of the great chiefs of the Formorians, or Fir Bolg, was Balor best known as the giant with the evil eye. Although the figure is shrouded in myth, could we imagine him as a man who lost an eye while working with granite, became an overseer of the granite and megalith workers and eventually the local Fir Bolg tribal leader? The name Balor could be derived from the Irish *Ball Óir*, 'golden limb' and indeed one could imagine the king of a wealthy tribe wearing gold torcs on his arms. Alternatively, *Ball Óir* could be translated as 'golden spot or location'.[3] There is a gigantic megalith near the summit tor of Chimney Rock, one face of which can be construed as a figure with a blinded eye. As a possible burial place, this megalith would certainly mark the grave of an important individual. Another side of this same megalith, illustrated at the start of the first chapter, depicts the head of a boar. This is certainly a noteworthy stone and the importance of the location has been further endorsed by two other large megaliths in a line below it. Musings about who might be buried in such a prestigious spot would be in the mists of time but there is no doubt about the enormous effort expended in erecting and decorating this huge stone. Mourne climbers, unaware of the stone's possible significance, look to it as a place for some testing bouldering and three climbs are now recorded up the sides.[4] When you get used to looking for eyes and mouths on rocks you quickly realise how productively busy the ancients have been. The following photographs are only a very small sample of what is to be found locally[5].

*This important megalith on Chimney Rock, previously illustrated opposite page one, is part of the 'Lamagan Line'. The face could be construed as a man with a blinded eye. The nose points to summer solstice sunset over at Slieve Corragh.*

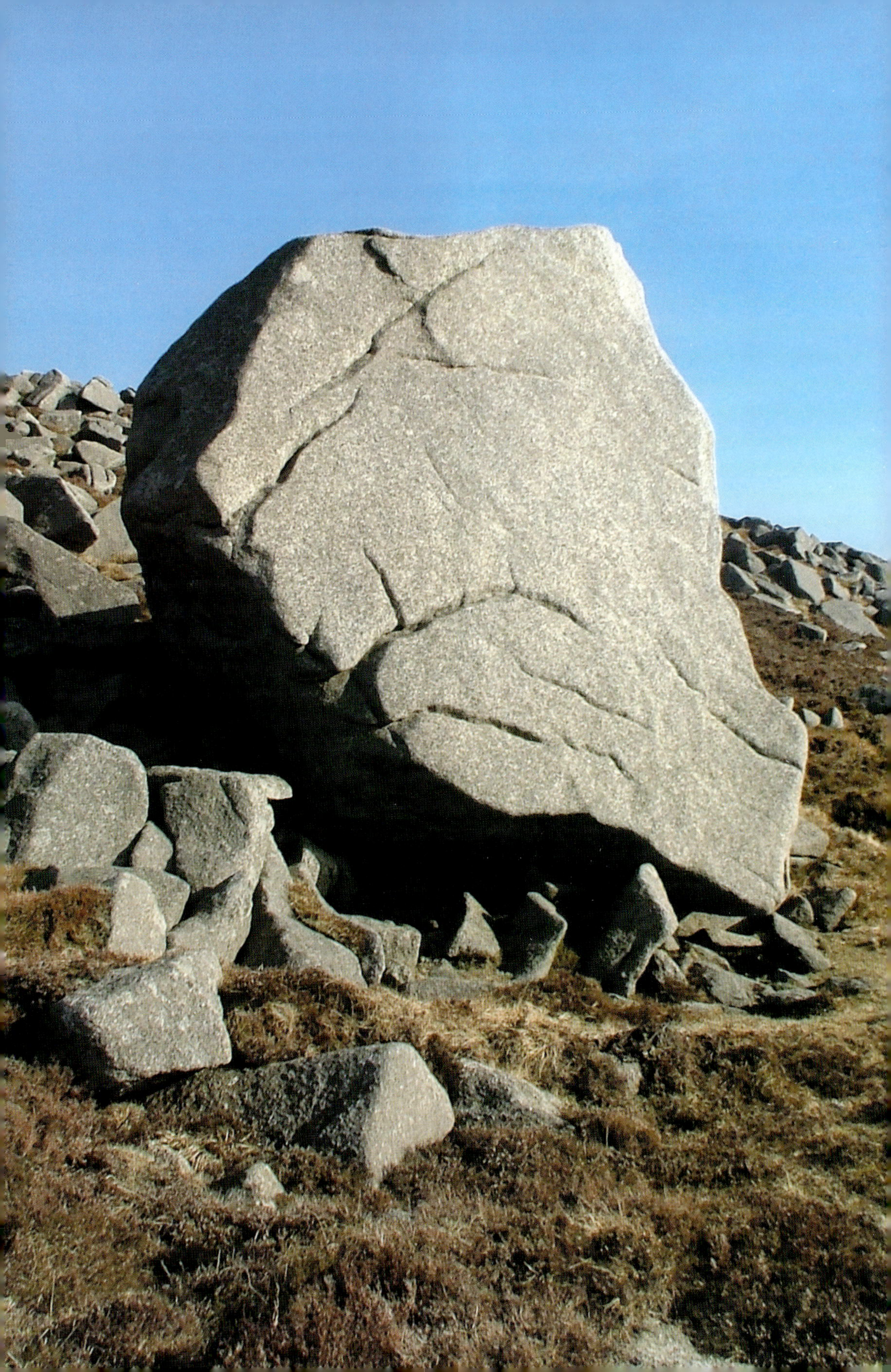

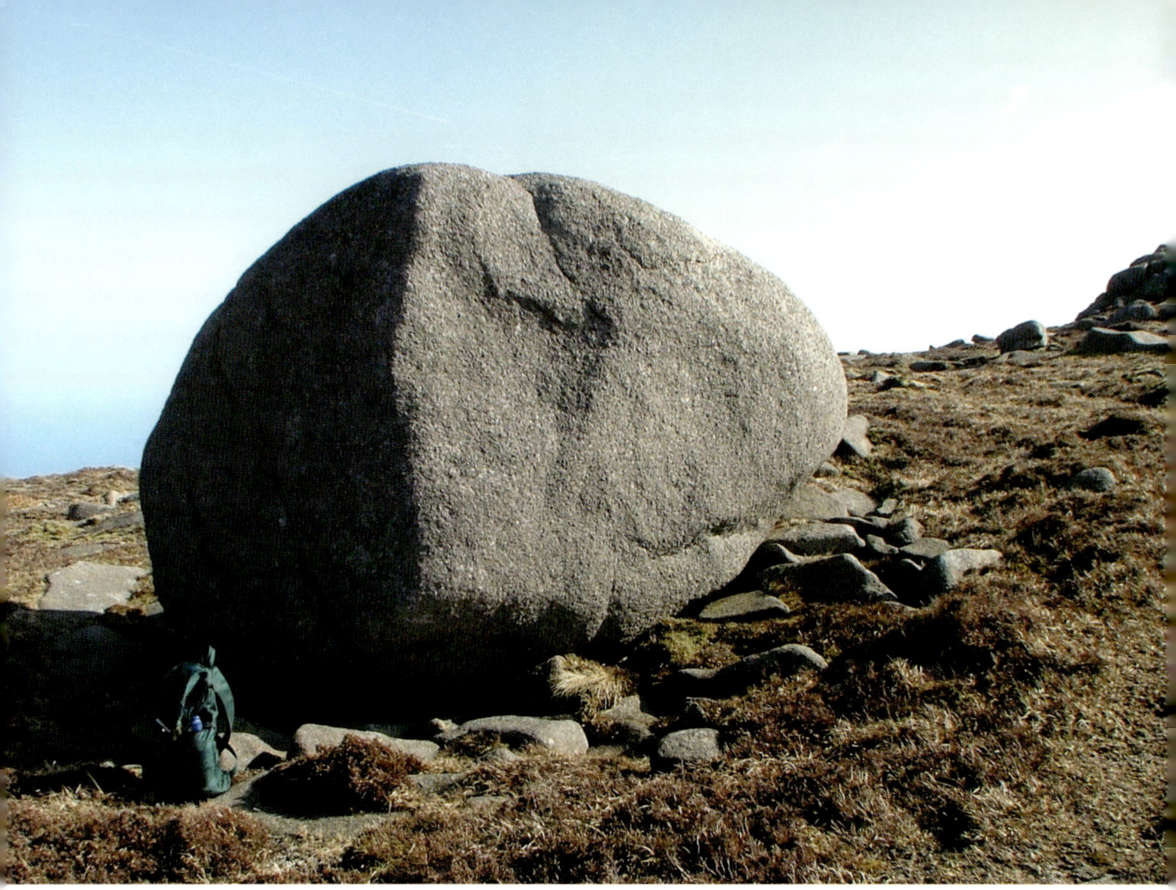

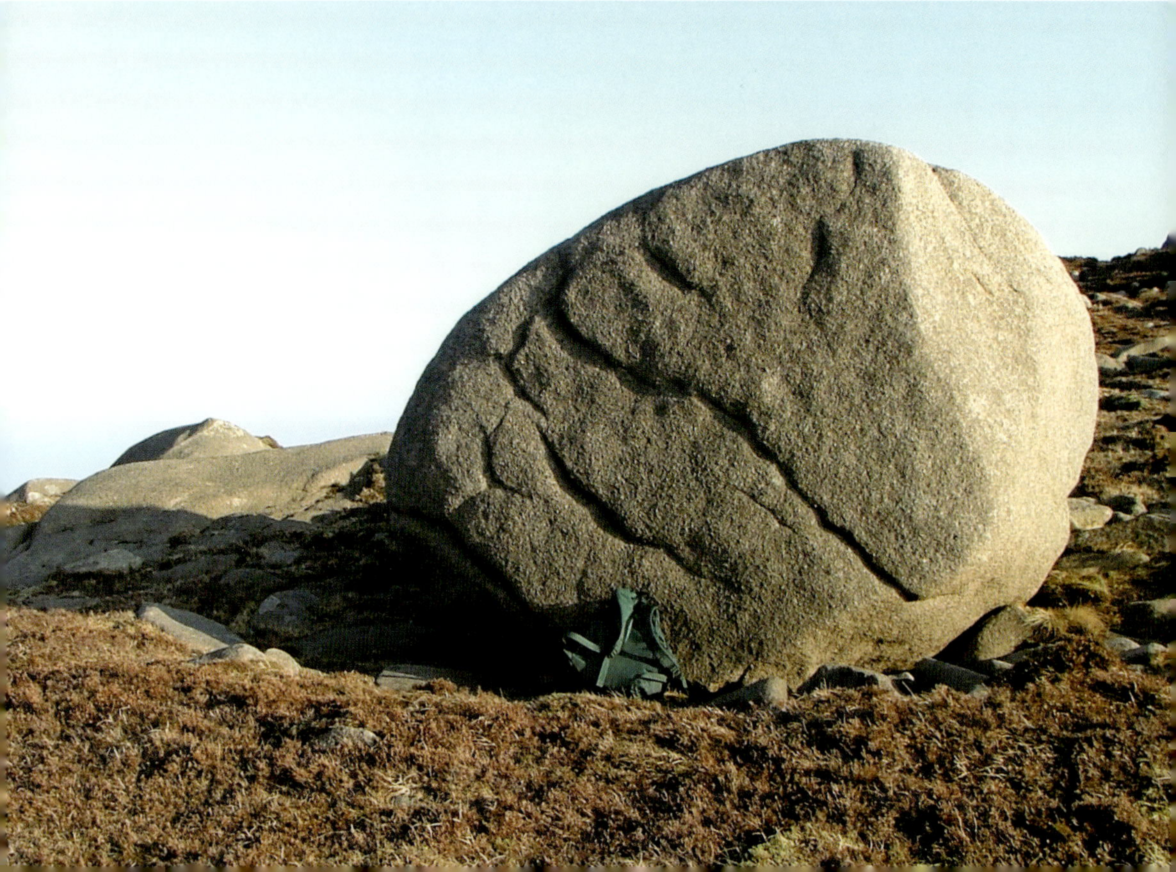

Top left: A benign face is found on this boulder on the western top of Chimney Rock near the great horizontal summit tor. The nose points over to Bignian to where the winter solstice sun sets.

Bottom left: This is the same boulder over four hours later when the sun has moved round lighting another side. A different face is now revealed complete with a boar's head across the middle. Because of its fecundity, the boar was a great symbol of fertility for the ancients. This boulder is a reminder of the tale of the Otherworld in *Togail Bruidne Da Derga* where the lord of the feast was sometimes represented as a man carrying a pig on his shoulder. The chance discovery of significant additional meaning for this boulder, revealed by the passing of the sun, is an reminder of how new insights, often of a most important nature, can be found at the same place at different times and seasons.

Above: This mighty chocked face stone, perhaps a burial site, is on the north bank of the Bloody Bridge river and points towards the horizon where the winter solstice sun rises.

The bottle marks where one edge on this face stone under Crossone mountain points towards the crest of Chimney Rock; the nose looks to Leganabruchan and the summer solstice sun.

This large face stone on the north-east side of Chimney Rock appears to enjoy a peaceful sleep.

Look again at this delightful face stone above Lynn's quarry on Millstone Mountain and you will see the chocked stone has been crafted into a frog facing towards winter solstice sunrise.

Lying beside the main path to Slieve Donard by the Glen River valley, this important face stone megalith is a marker tracing the sun's circuit around the upper valley. Many thousands pass through this landscape unaware of the rich heritage of the ancient pagan past all around.

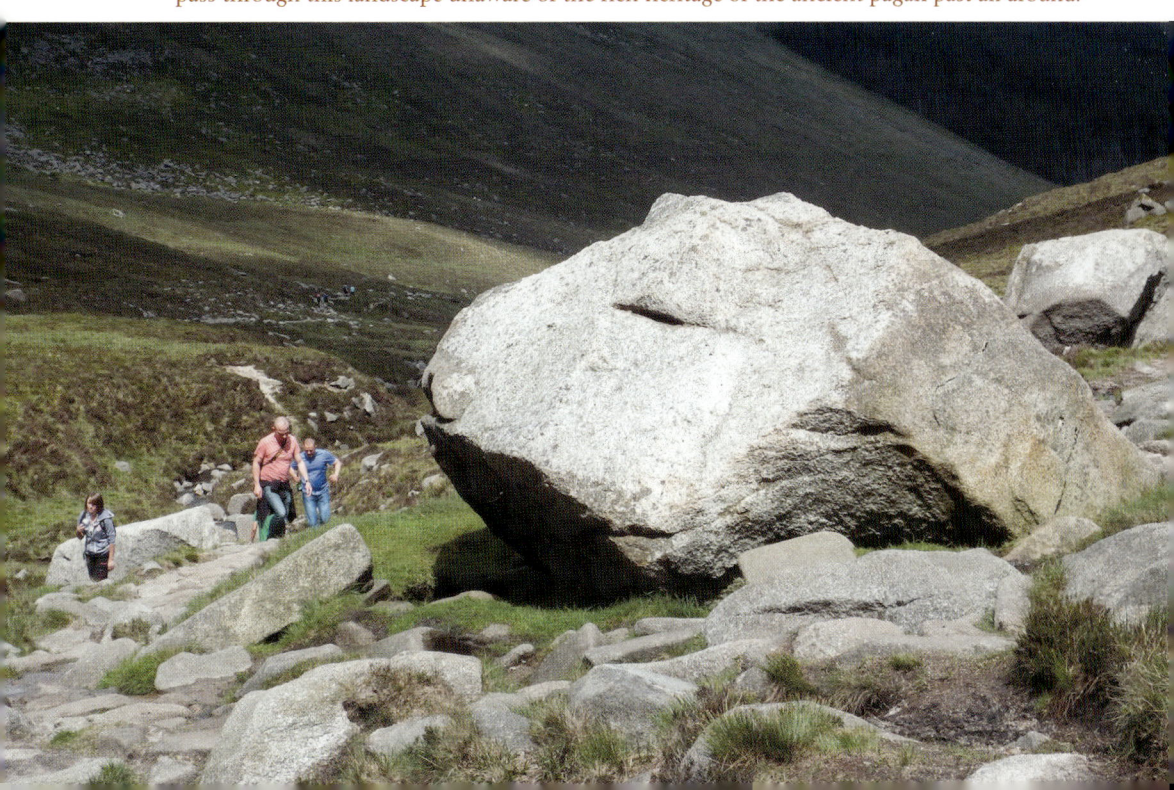

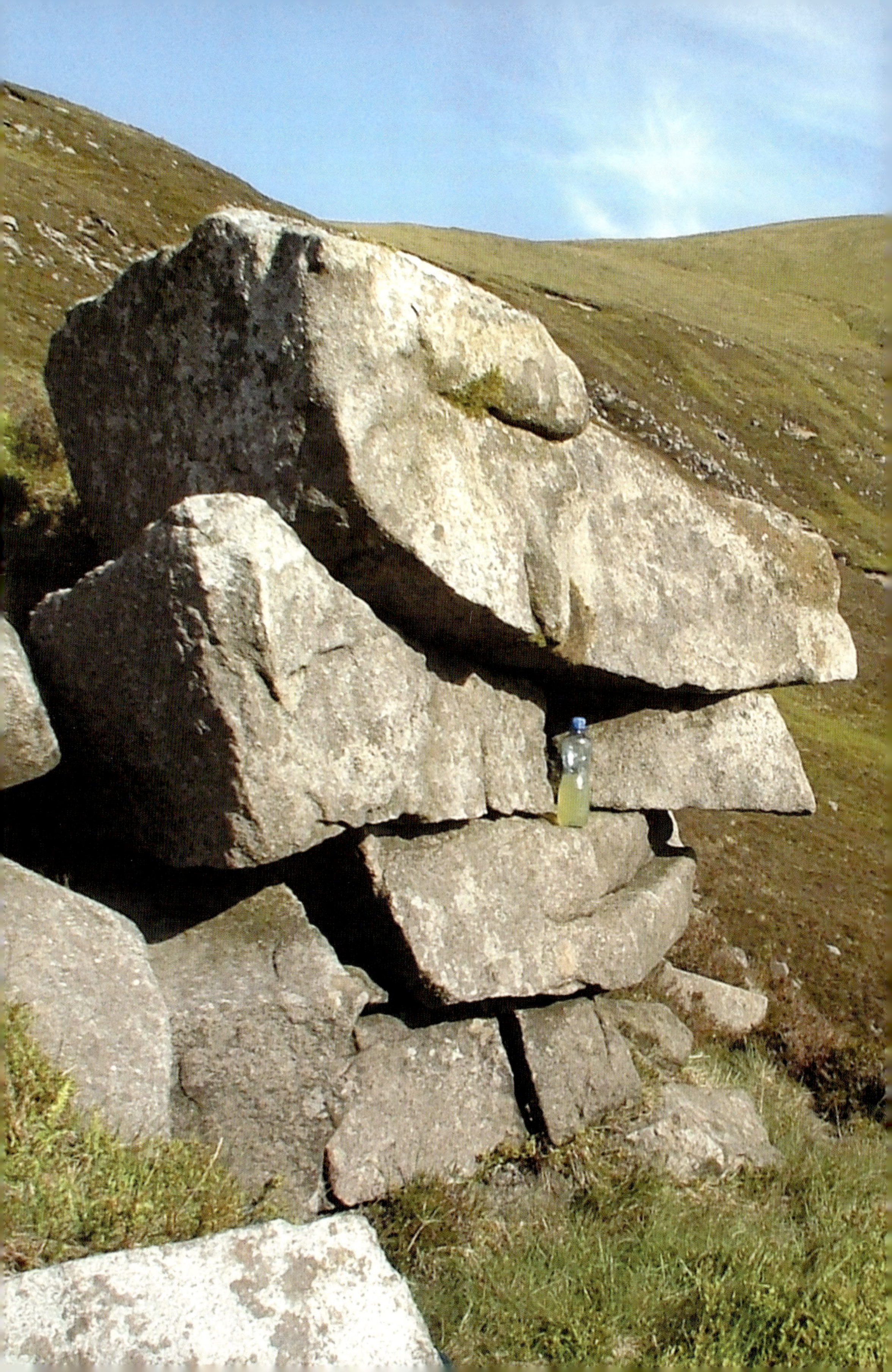

This grim muzzle stone in the middle of the col between Donard and Commedagh stands watch over the Glen River valley, a major pass into Mourne. The construction of this imposing stack of stones weighing quite some tons at the edge of a precipitous cliff is an awesome achievement. The fierce aspect on the face was no doubt intended as a warning to any intruders coming up the Glen River valley.

This sleeping giant is on the south facing upper slopes of Slieve Donard. It is just one of many face stones in this locality.

The eye on this stone, also on Slieve Donard, may be closed and deemed to be resting but the ancient artist has still managed to imbue it with lurking menace.

The face on this megalith is fairly emphatic and is not unlike a blood-hound. It is found on the west facing slope of Luke's Mountain. Note how the ancients have made clever use of the infusion line in the stone; it is a reminder of the setting of the winter solstice sun into the notch between Slievenaglogh and Slieve Bearnagh witnessed along a diagonal line up the mountain slope

There are very many face stones under Spellack hill and even on Spellack cliff face itself. This large contented looking face stone which faces towards Spellack is included because many will have inadvertently walked past it. It is right beside the Trassey path. As a size guide the trekking poles are 117cm. in length.

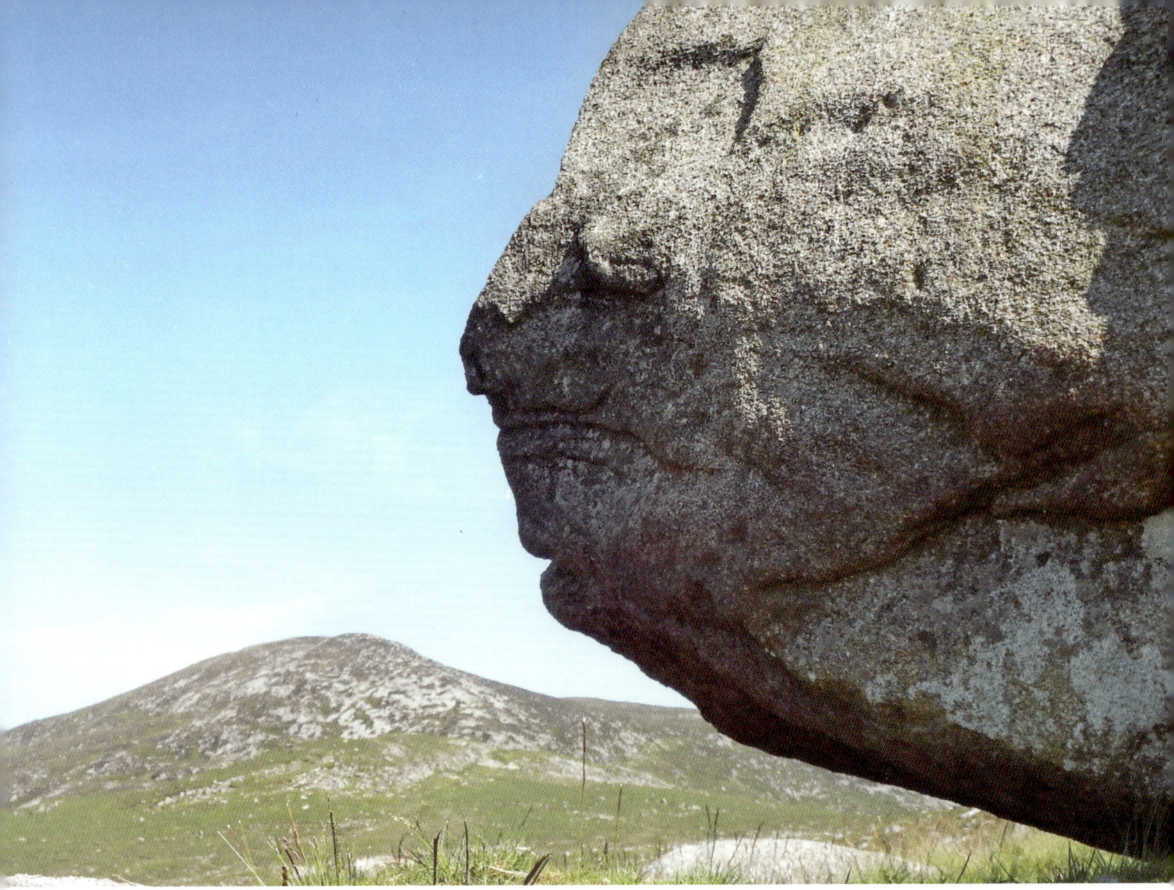

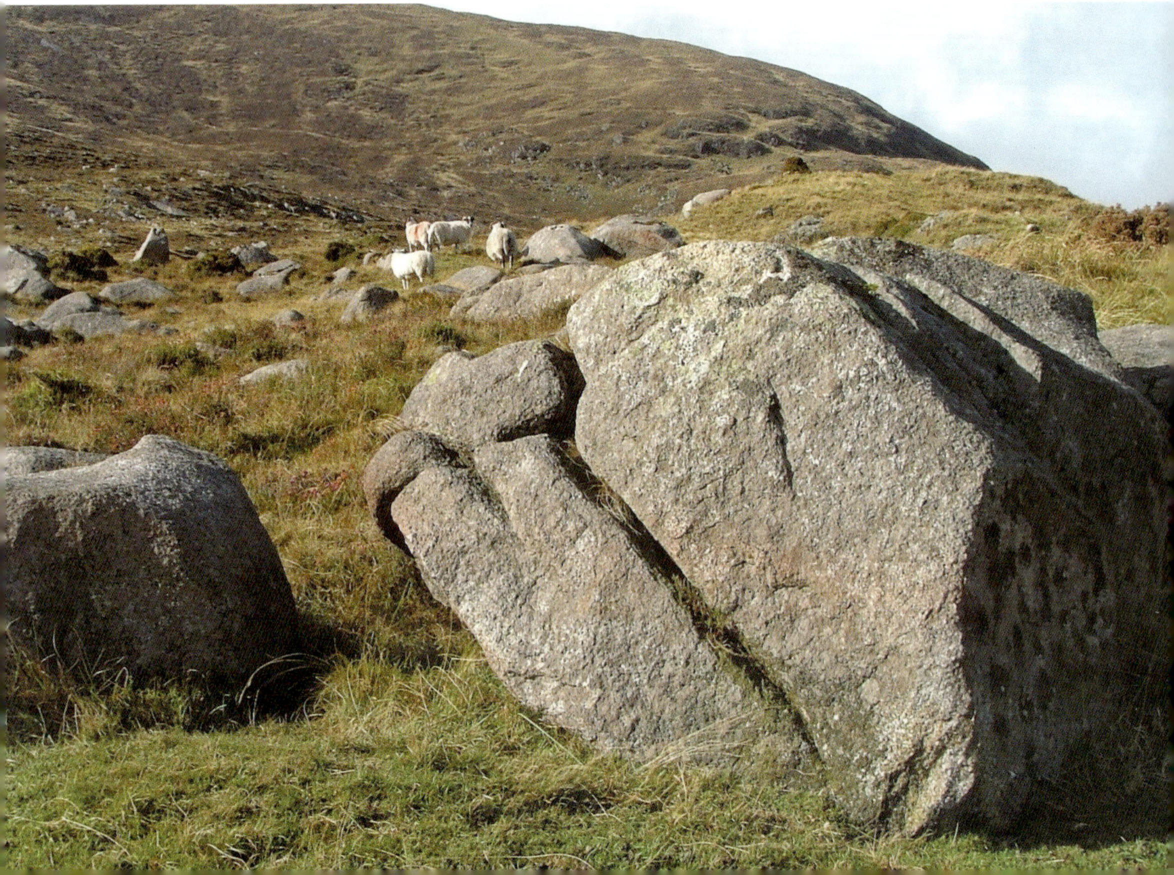

Top left: Look for the largest stone in the boulder field west of Trassey sheepfolds and you will find this face on the corner. The shoulder of Slievenaglogh is in the background.

Bottom left: This face stone is found under the northern slopes of Spellack, near the Trassey river sheepfolds. This area is profusely strewn with boulders most of which seem to have received attention from the hand of man. The Mourne Way/Ulster Way passes nearby along the boundary wall en-route towards Fofanny Dam. If passing this way, it is worth a detour among the stones to see how many faces you can find.

Above: This is the great granite megalith, the *Spinnc Buidhe*, meaning 'sunny pointed stone' from which Spinkwee hill gets its name. From this angle the stone is not unlike a sheep's head. The notched eye is obvious but there is another sleeping eye lower down where present day sheep have rubbed their red marking dye along the flank of the stone. A third eye, meant to be viewed from further upslope, is present just above and to the right of the water bottle. The nose of this stone points to where the summer solstice sun rises from between the two hills of The Drinns. Spinkwee Hill is composed of shale so this huge granite megalith has been dragged here from quite some distance.

Above: A monstrous face megalith found under the shoulder of Slieve Meelmore. It looks to where the summer solstice sun rises from the top of Clanawhillan hill. Two small quarries in the upper background were probably opened there for the same reason; it was regarded as a 'lucky' fertility site.

Top right: A sleeping face rears out of the ground in the boulder field under Meelmore, not far from the Trassey sheepfolds. In the background are the two summit dimples, construed as breasts, which gave Slievenaman its name in Irish, *Sliabh na mBan*, 'mountain of the woman'.

Bottom right: Those who enter the Annalong valley by the Carrick Little track and follow the wall up to Slieve Bignian will find this huge spear and face stone on the right hand tor at the top. The point of the spear is directed towards the top of Chimney Rock.

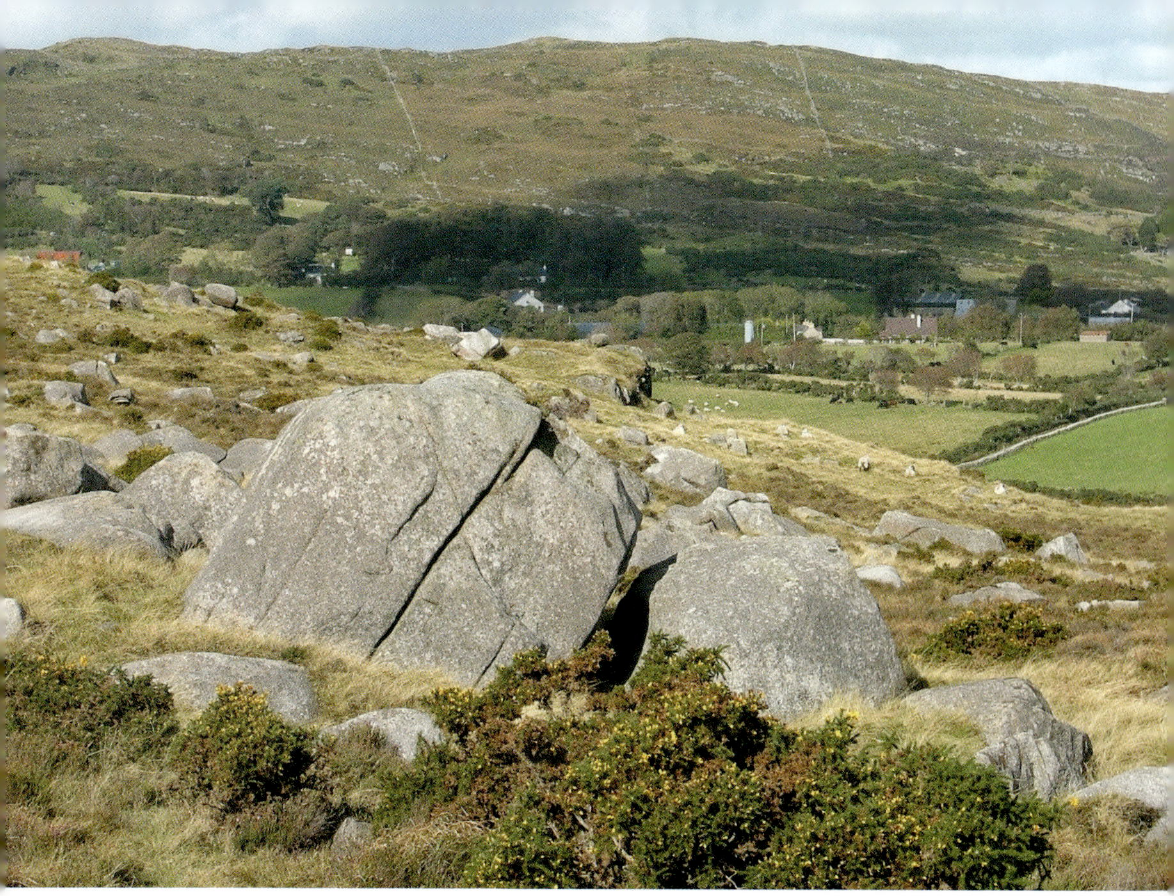

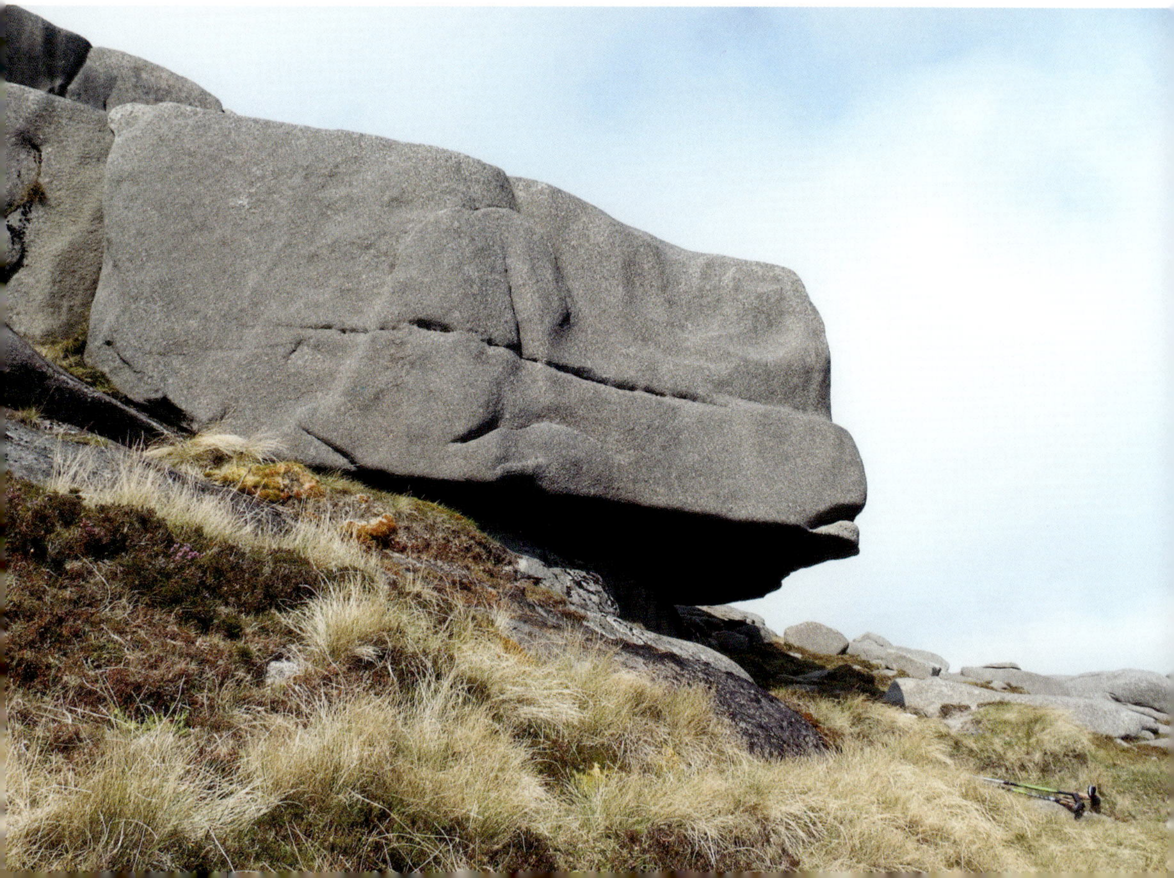

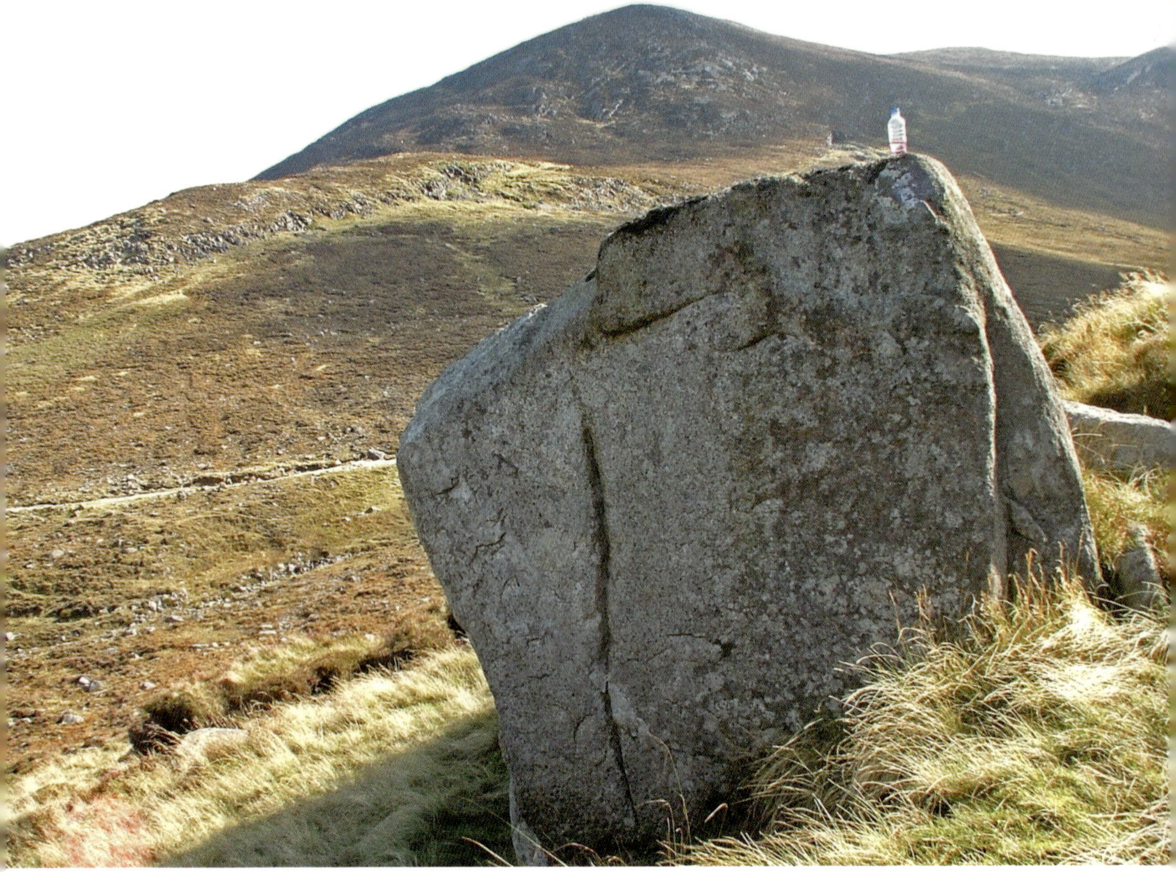

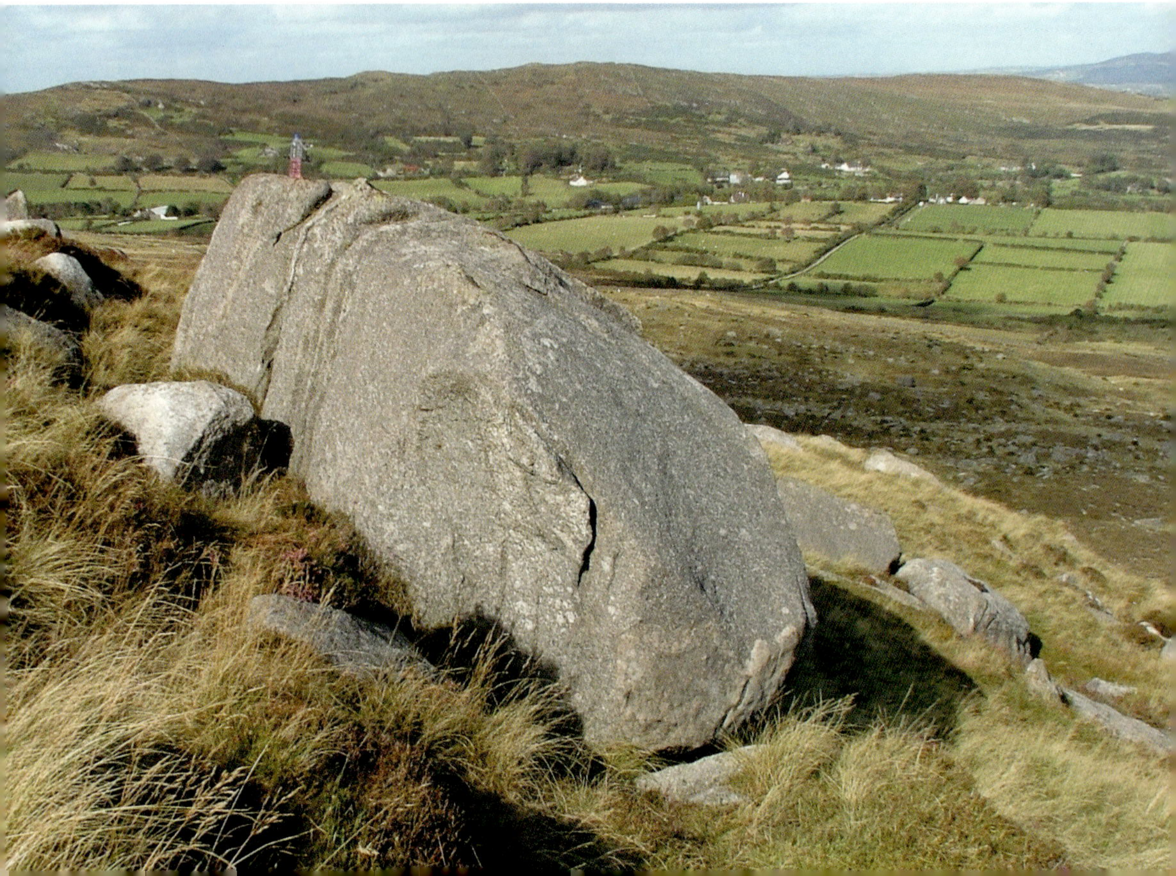

Top left: An imposing face; but this is only the back end of a very substantial megalith under Spellack. This stone is really aligned on the far shoulder summit of Slievenaglogh. The presumption is that the megalith marks the location where the winter solstice sun can be seen rising from the distant summit in a symbolic moment of phallic ejaculation.

Bottom left: The same stone from another angle and showing more eyes. On top the water bottle is positively tiny yet despite this megalith's massive size it has been precisely focused on distant Slievenaglogh. From the Trassey track under Spellack this megalith is seen as a massive skyline stone to the right of Spellack. The middle of the stone has an infused streak beloved by the ancients apparently as a symbol of the fertility union of two opposites. The streak has been used as a pointer towards summer solstice sunrise. The stone's phallic shape has also been emphasised by the addition of a meatus groove low at the front and the further ingenious exploitation of a lighter coloured infused rock around the groove symbolically denoting a seminal discharge. From its size, faces, position, orientation and inspired use of coloured rock intrusions, this complex imaginative megalith is up there among the important monuments of Mourne.

Above: A face stone emerges from the slopes under Spellack. The chin may face towards the ridge of Slievenaglogh but the mouth is cleverly opened along a line towards summer solstice sunrise on the horizon.

157

Above: On Slieve Bearnagh's north tor this formidable reptilian stone dominates its neighbour. These slopes have many large boulders that have been given the face treatment.

Top right: The very end of the tor itself has been animated with a large closed eye and a distinctive mouth. Such is the height of the eye above ground that timber ladders or ropes would have had to be brought uphill to gain access to this part of the rock-face. On the other side of the Mourne wall the further outcrop of rock has had numerous faces applied.

Bottom right: Another of the large faced boulders on the north tor slopes of Slieve Bearnagh. It faces towards where the sun rises at the winter solstice on Chimney Rock mountain.

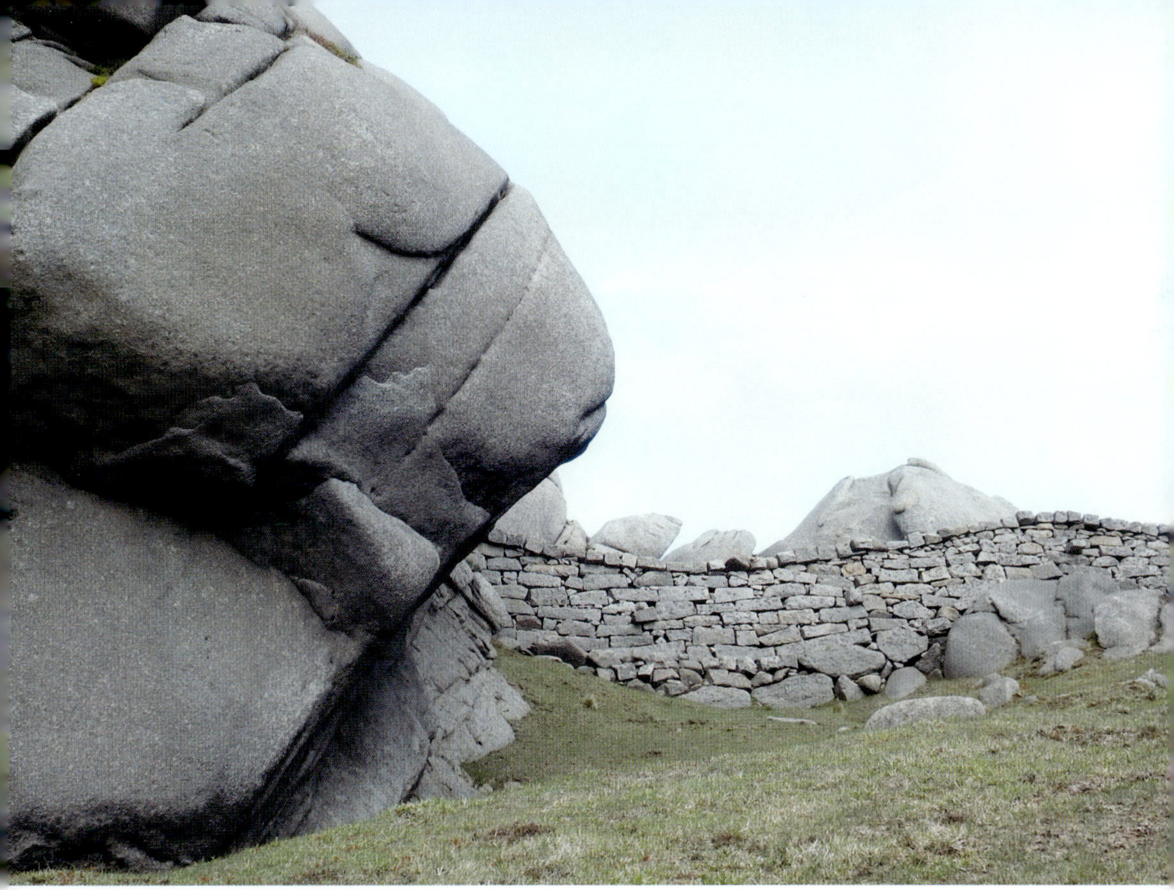

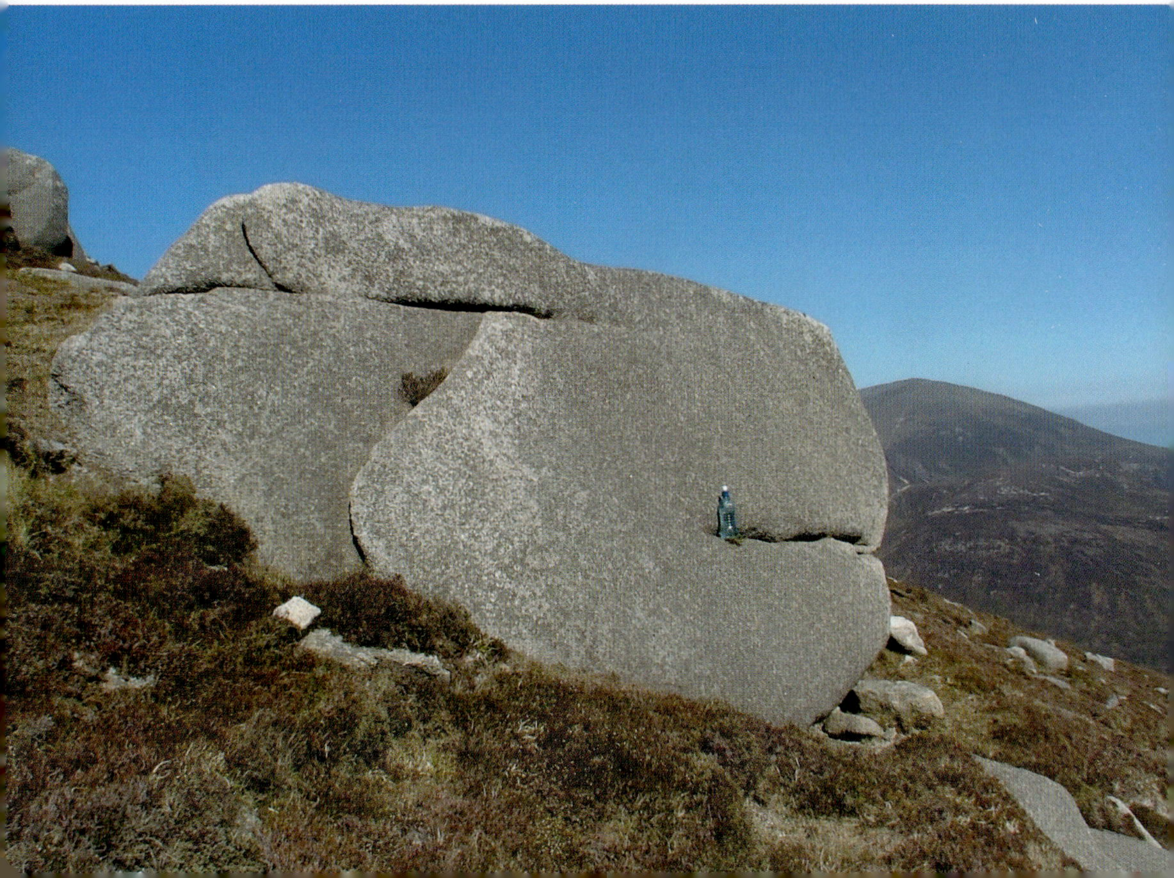

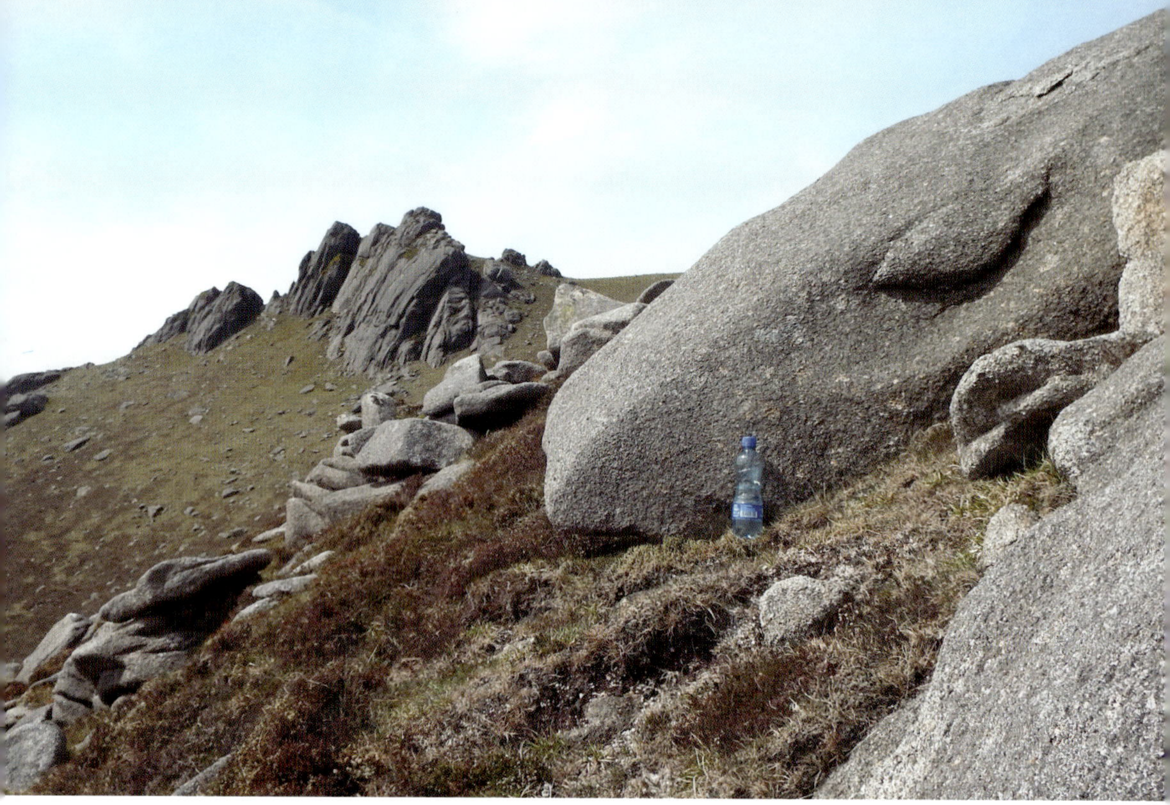

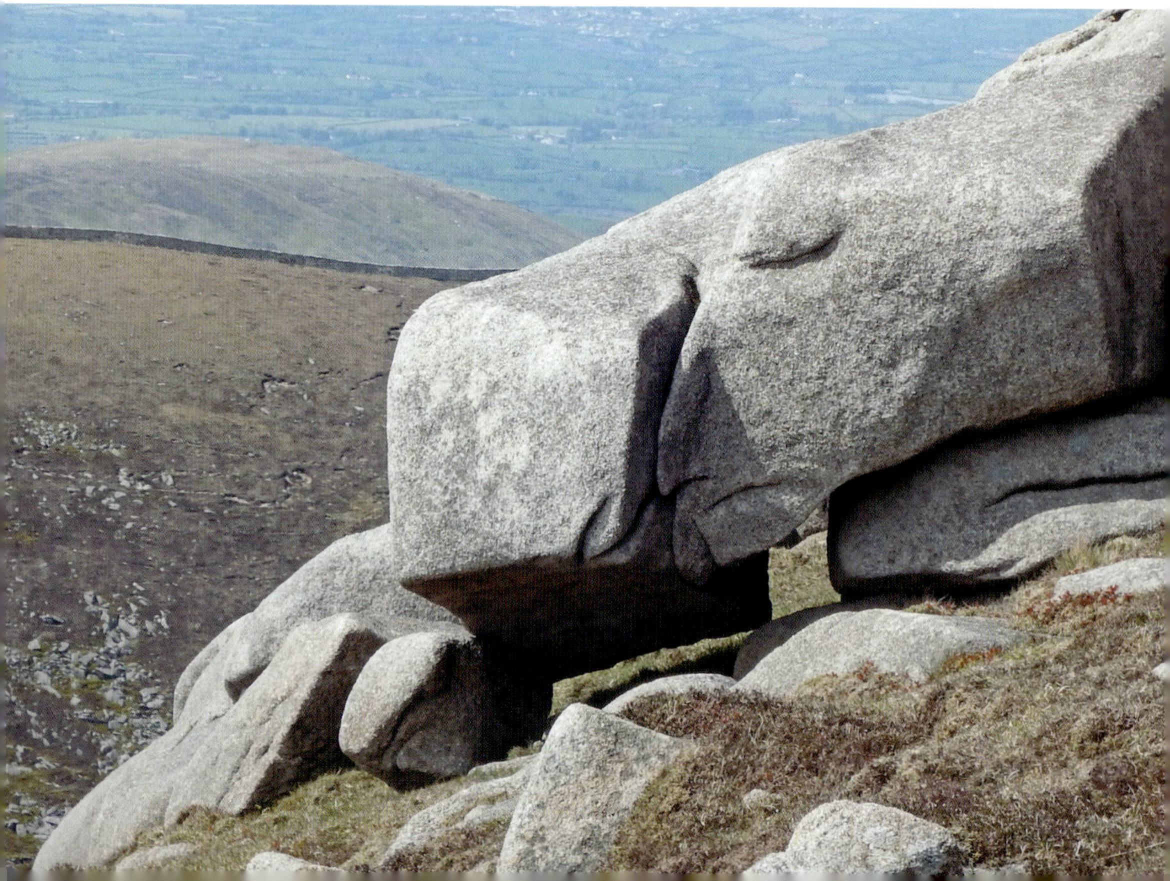

Top left: This relatively small face on Slieve Bearnagh has been chosen on account of the work on the eye and the very effective use made of shadow to enhance it.

Bottom left: Here, on the south facing slope of Bearnagh's south tor, a face is shown giving a lick; though whether is it grooming or stimulation depends on one's interpretation of the object stone.

Above: This face stone on Slieve Bearnagh's south tor has its tongue out to give a lick.

This muzzle face is found at the Hare's Gap. It is lit by the early winter solstice sun and the angle of the point at the back of the head points to winter solstice sunset.

This megalith on top of Slieve Beg has a distinctly feline look. Note the other megalith in the background.

THE FACE STONES OF MOURNE

Hundreds pass by this megalith on the Brandy Pad. It has toppled from its original position but the carefully worked eye is now very accessible and the workmanship is worth having a look at close-up.

163

It is the wonderful eye that steals the show on this megalith found above the path under Bearnagh slabs towards the end of Pollaphuca valley. Look again at the bottom part of the stone to realise it is nuzzling up underneath. Enough is suggested yet still left ambiguous to make this a very clever little masterpiece on sexuality.

This megalith overlooking the gorge of Spelga Dam is not unlike a sheep's head. Look again at the left side and it becomes a young sleeping pig.

This substantial megalith sporting a bent nose is found on upper Cove. This is one of a number of quite large megaliths that mark the appearance of the winter solstice sun on distant mountain tops. It is reasonable to expect that this stone further marks the setting of the sun on one or other of the Back Castles of Bignian in a moment of symbolical fertility ejaculation.

The water bottle is tiny on this long face-stone megalith on Upper Cove. The nose of the stone is directed towards Slieve Donard.

A detail of the marvellous canine head from the Chimney Rock ritual platform shown on page 21.

A cauliflower nose adorns this delightful little face on the slopes of Slieve Bearnagh.

These two face stones lie side by side on Ben Crom.

This contented looking face-stone is found under Upper Cove cliff face. Walkers will have no difficulty finding many other face-stones in the surrounding boulder field.

This spear stone is prominent enough to be easily found on the lower Donard slopes at the 'Top of the Hill' col between Millstone and Donard (See illustration on page 69). A representation of a beastly face is to be found underneath the stone.

A view of the same spear pointed stone from the top side showing how the main point has been directed to the breast-like summit of Millstone mountain.

The scramble from the Glen River path up to this marvellous spear stone on the slopes of Eagle was very rewarding. Each 'layer' at the right side of the stone could be said to have a little face of its own. The ancients erected this emphatically pointed stone over a vigorous spring, itself a symbol of fertility. The top point of the stone, directed towards Slieve Commedagh, is a fusion of shale and granite, a union of opposites and a further representation of fertility.

Hammered out of the rock surface is a profile of the Mourne Mountains as would be seen from around Murlough or Dundrum. This very important work of art is probably many thousands of years old and has to be the earliest depiction of the Mournes sweeping down to the sea. The five prominent expanding crescents on the left are a likely representation of the growing light of a rising winter solstice sun.

The artist would certainly have been facing towards that part of the horizon as he hammered out the rock. To find this creation, start at the lower cairn on the top of Millstone mountain (the one overlooking the town of Newcastle) and, taking a line between the Rock swimming pool and the harbour, go downhill for approximately forty paces.

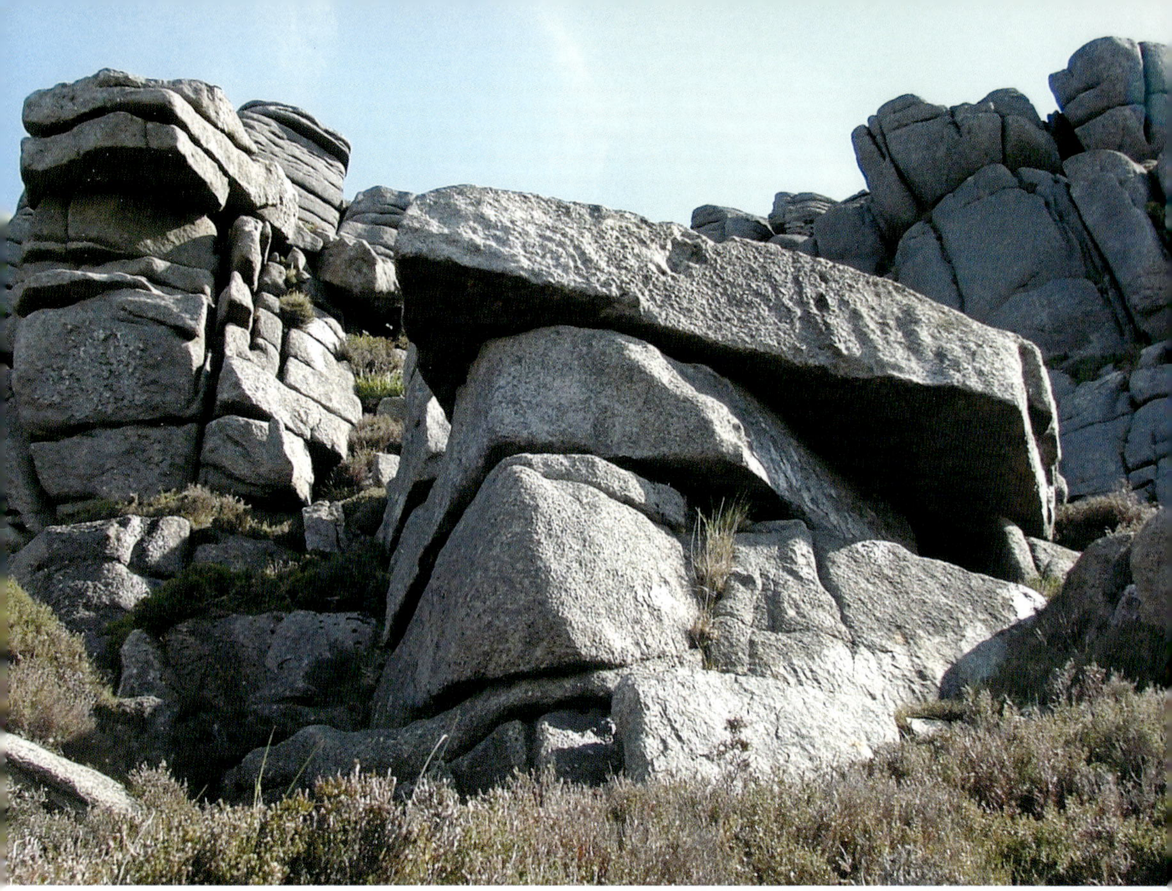

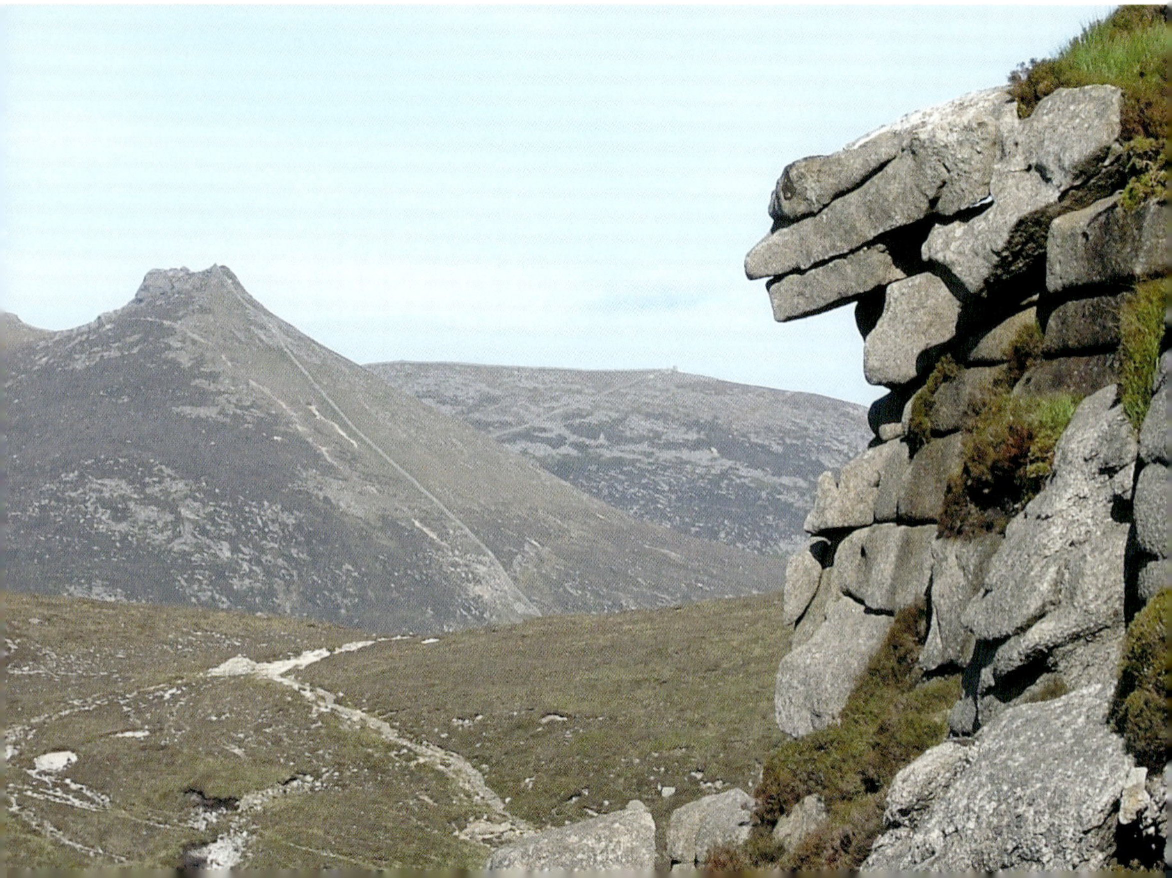

Top left: This impressive large spear stone is found at the Castles above the Brandy Pad but near the Donard, Slieve Commedagh col. The spear point is directed to the Devil's Coachroad. Numerous hammered cup marks were found on the flat stone surface. On the top left of the photo is a large projecting spear and face stone, shown more prominently in profile below. To enhance its phallic credentials the apex of the bottom stone has been given a 'pee point' notch.

Bottom left: Another view of the projecting stone at the Castles. The north tor of Slieve Bearnagh is in the left background with Meelmore in the middle background. It is likely the cliff was undercut to accentuate the jutting out and hence the phallic nature of the stone.

Above: Like many phallic spear stones, this megalith projects out over a void, in this case the gully at the end of the Glen River valley.

Overlooking the Silent Valley, this monstrous megalith with a great hammered hollow of an eye, is found near the southern end of Slieve Bignian.

The same stone as seen from the bottom has been given a large meatus groove transforming this long megalith into a penile shaft. The top end of the stone is directed towards a weeping fissure on a higher rock face on one of Bignian's tors making the fissure into a symbolic vagina.

Like a turtle looking out from its shell, this impertinent phallic stone is found on the seaward slopes of Leganabruchan. The ridge of Drinneevar is in the background. The apex of the stone, of course, is directed to the horizon and the place of winter solstice sunrise.

Out of all the many hundreds of megaliths of Mourne, this is one of the few for which we know the original Irish name. This commanding stone was called *an nAb*, 'the abbot' from its similarity to a monk with his cowl over his head and for a while gave its name to that part of Leganabruchan hillside as 'The Nab' (mentioned by E.E. Evans in *Mourne Country*, page 173). The profile of this stone is clearly visible from the start of the granite trail on the other side of Bloody Bridge valley.

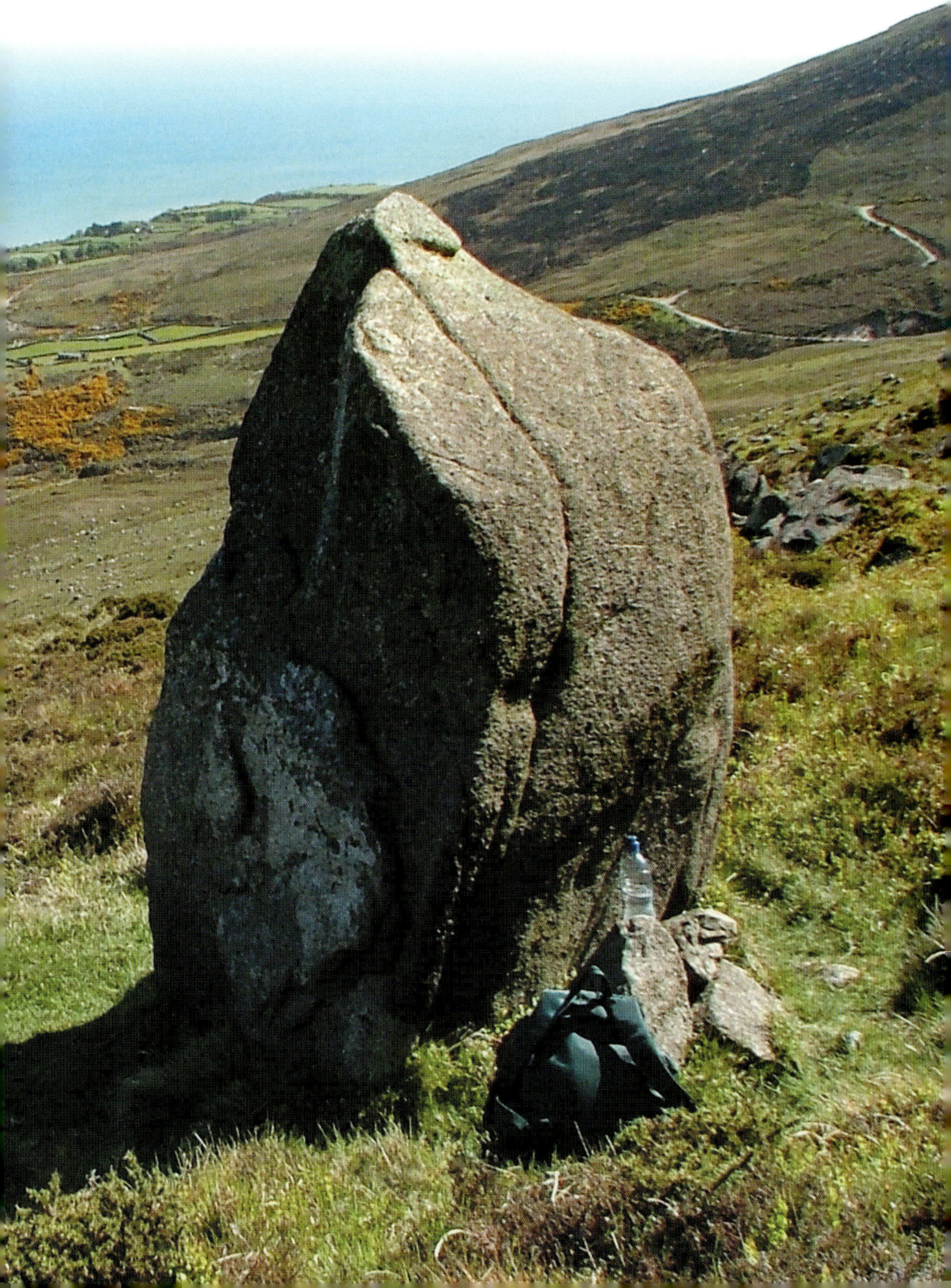

Above: The two side stones that were meant to represent a vagina are shown as having been penetrated by a disproportionately large phallic spear stone. This creation will be found at the eastern end of Chimney Rock mountain.

Top right: This large spear stone reminded me of Concorde; and indeed, if you get to look closely at it yourself you will find this megalith has been subtly decorated with a bird-like beak and head. It is to be found on the south-west slopes of Chimney Rock facing towards Slieve Bignian and likely marks a fertility event where the winter solstice sun sets on one of Bignian's rock outcrops. Incidentally this part of the mountain is treacherously dangerous underfoot with heather hiding many ankle breaking holes between rocks.

Bottom right: A rare sighting in the Mournes of Ireland's only native reptile, the common or viviparous lizard, the inspiration for the large megalith featured overleaf and found on the south western slopes of Chimney Rock. These small reptiles (they only measure about 10-16cm) hibernate from October to March. The female does not lay eggs but between three and eleven babies develop inside the mother's body and they are born fully formed and independent. Despite the name, common lizards are not often seen as they usually skitter quickly away when you approach. I have only caught a brief glimpse of three in my time and this one obligingly froze while I photographed it on a sunny September day on the lower slopes of Rocky mountain near the Hares Castle.

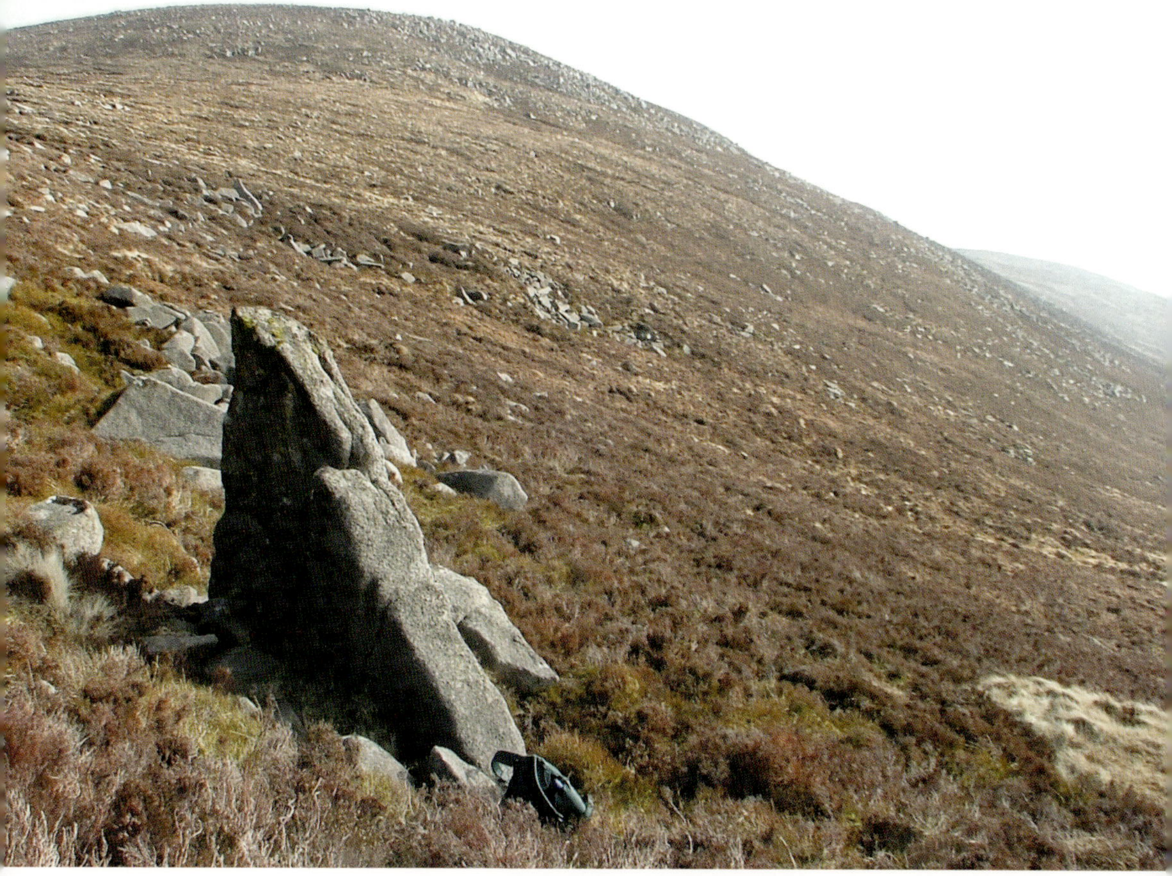

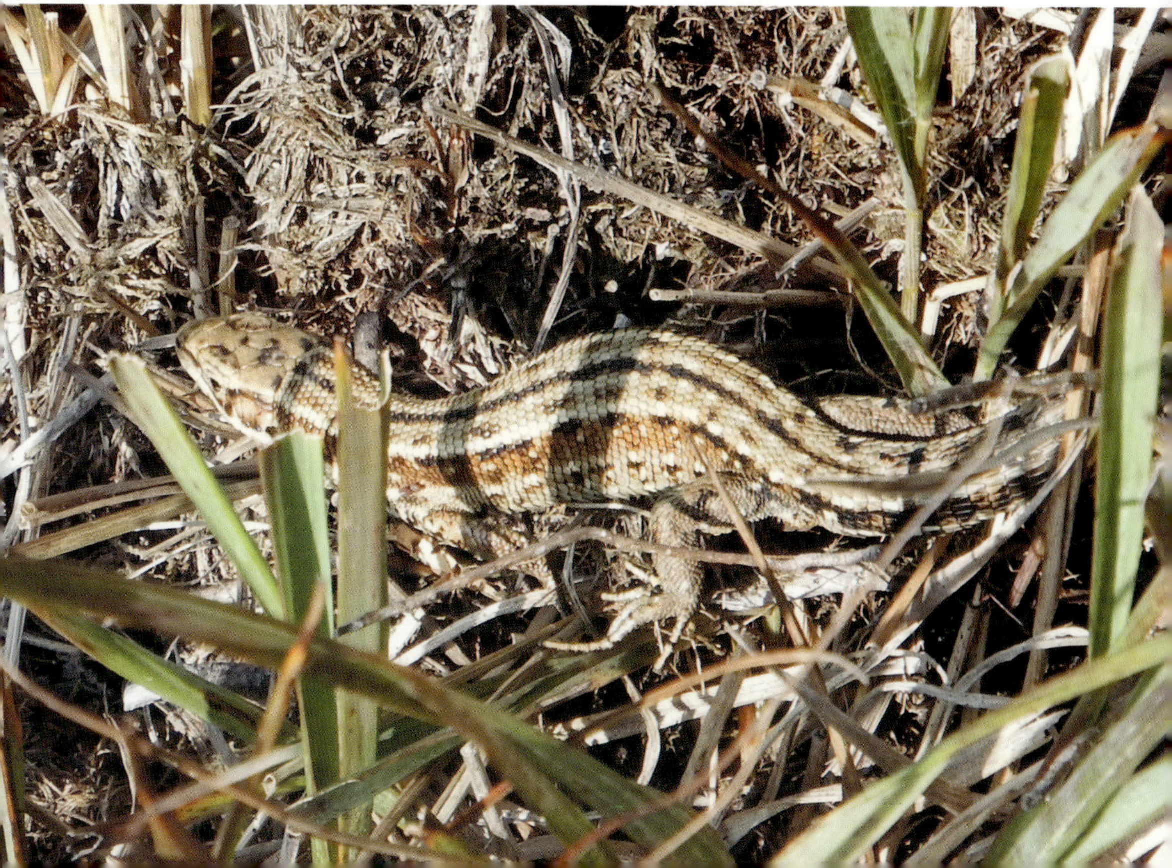

Supported on Chimney Rock's southern slopes by a massive anchor stone, this great megalith commands magnificent views. The profile from this angle has a fair resemblance to a common or viviparous lizard. When viewed from down-slope this same stone reveals the face of a man with a curled and broken nose. The size of this monument, the sculpture it reveals and the association of the lizard with fertility, mark this monument as a treasure of Mourne.

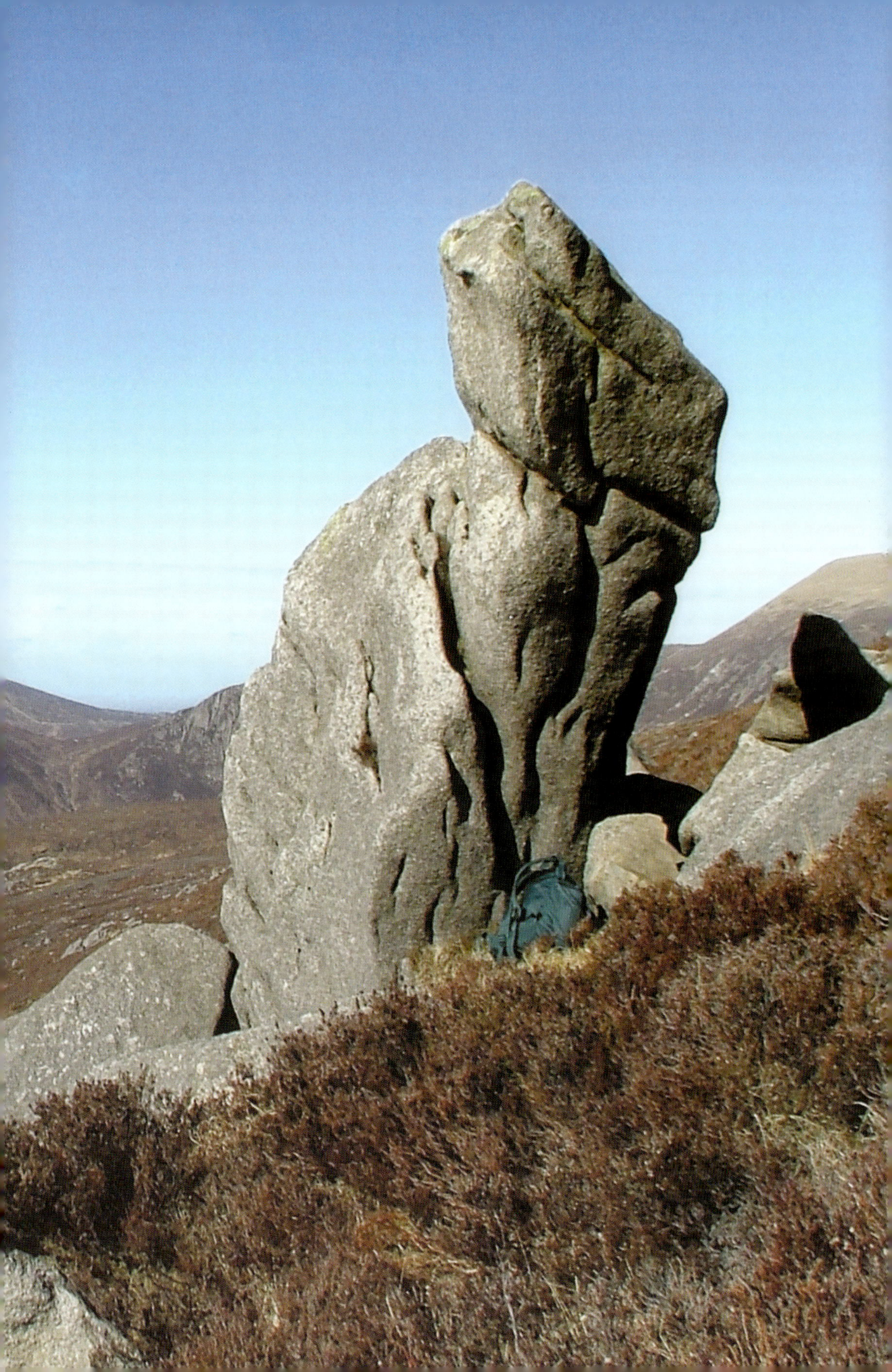

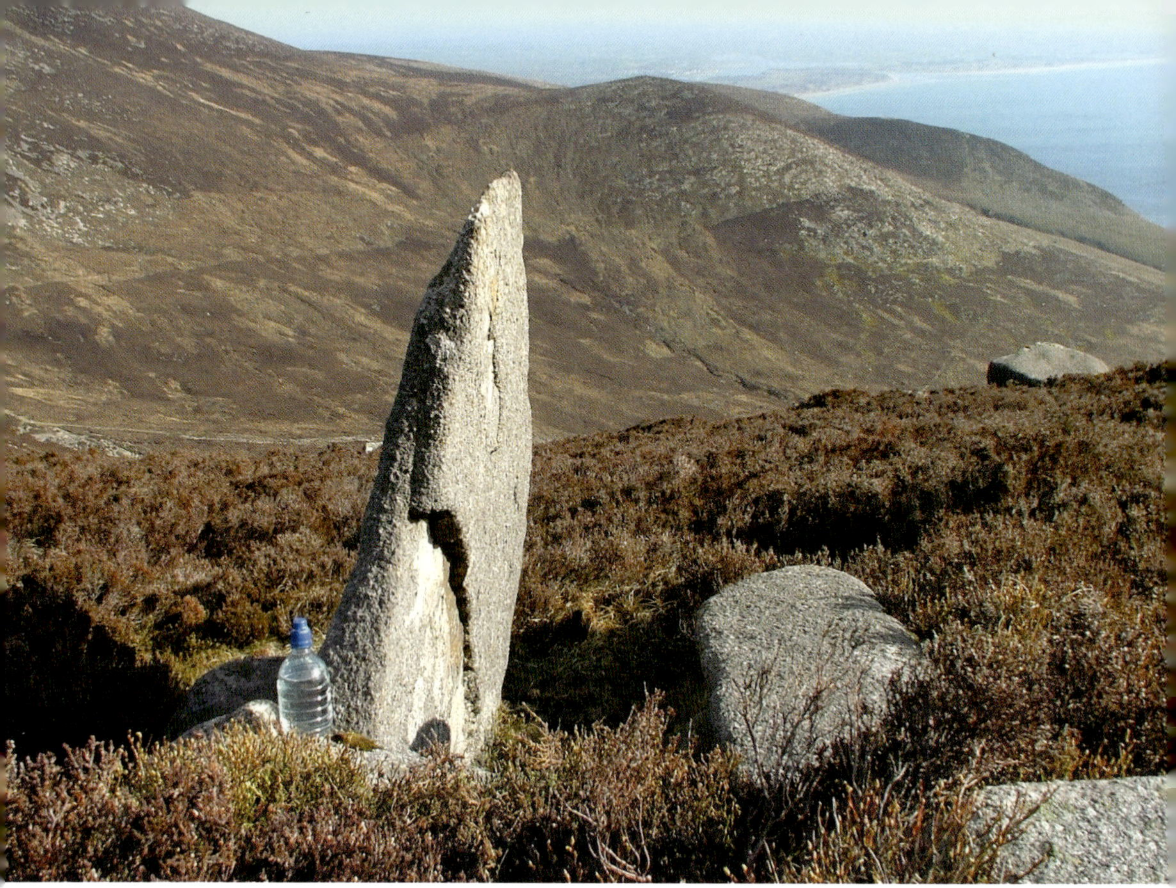

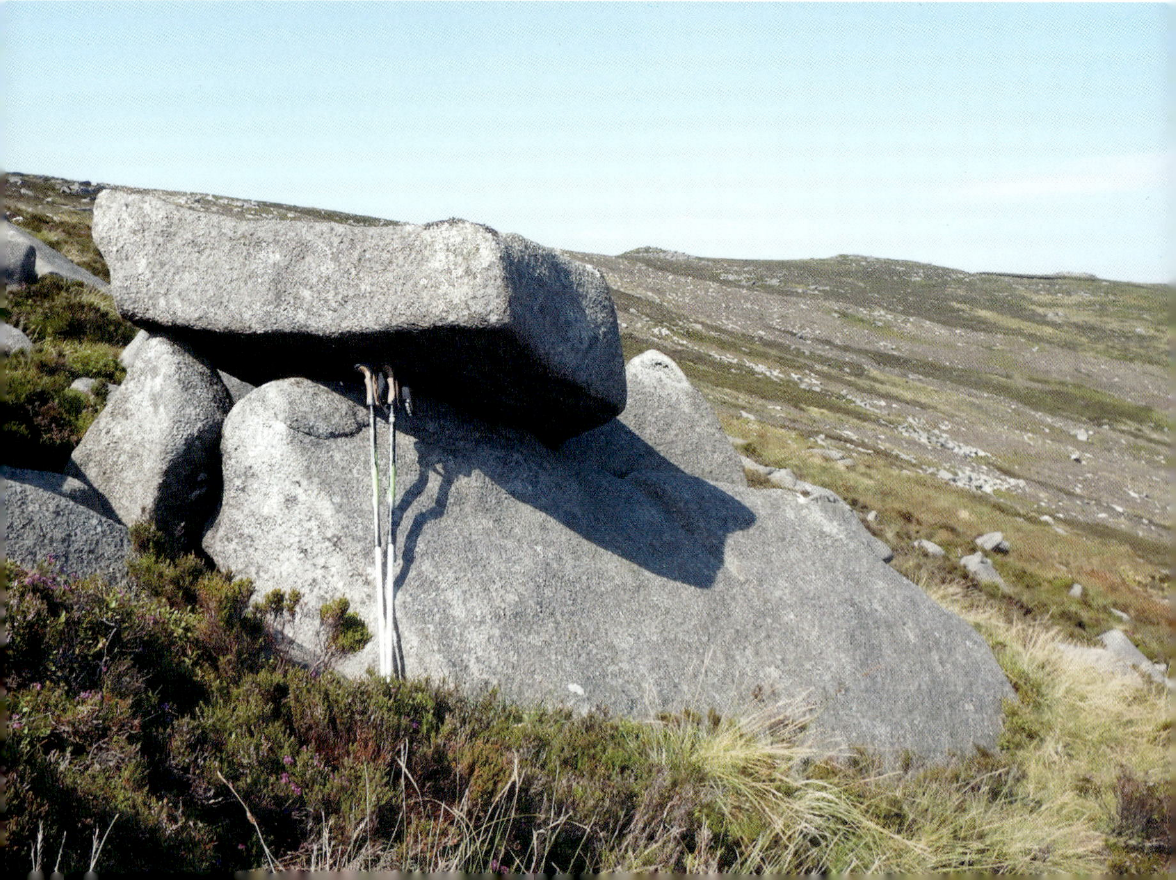

Top left: This upright sliver of a stone boldly proclaims its phallic intent. Like most of the fertility stones on the northern side of Chimney Rock it is directed towards summer solstice sunrise.

Above: The same sliver stone when viewed from the side reveals an image of a Mastiff or an Irish Wolfhound. The name of the dog comes from its purpose as a hunter of wolves which once roamed the Mournes. Such a large dog would have been an indispensable helper and guard for early stockmen.

Bottom left: The three points on this substantial spear stone point to the summit of Chimney Rock, to summer solstice sunrise and to Slieve Donard summit. It also rests on a simple yet discernable snout of a face stone.

Above: In an area rich in arranged stones this spear megalith on the eastern slopes of Chimney Rock is one of the mountain's larger ornaments. Beside it to the left is a phallic stone placed in such a way that, in a vaginal arrangement, the early winter solstice light will cast the shadow of the phallus into the cavity under the spear stone.

Top right: Truly the most delightful and unambiguous of spear stones. It points to where the winter solstice sun disappears on the summit of Chimney Rock. In the background is present Slievenagarragh or what I believe should properly have been named Gleasdromainn hill. Notice the barbs on either side of the stone, how it is notched at the back and the round animating eye hammered into the rock at the side.

Bottom right: This spear stone, with a bird-like beak, on the north facing slope of Chimney rock has been carefully wedged upright to evoke a phallus and it is representative of many such fertility stones across the slopes of Mourne though not all so up-standing.

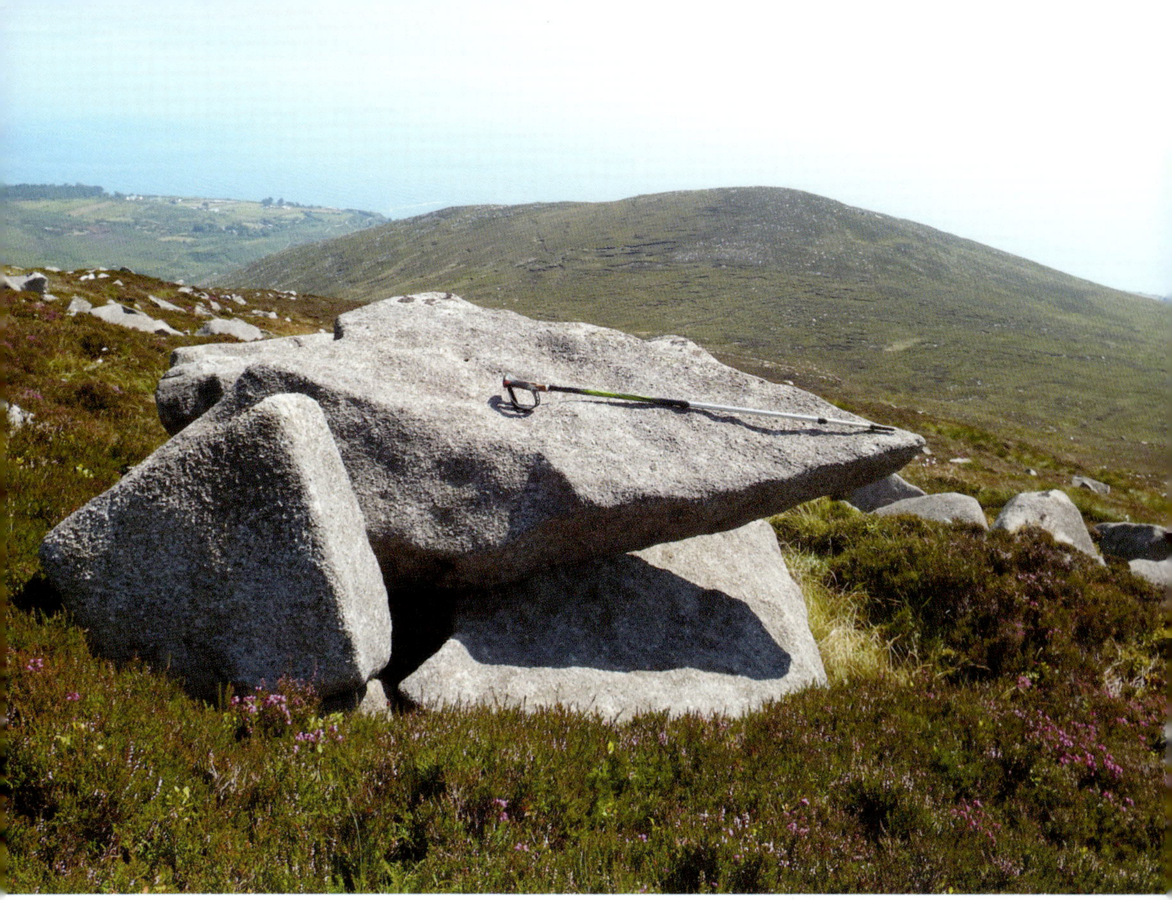

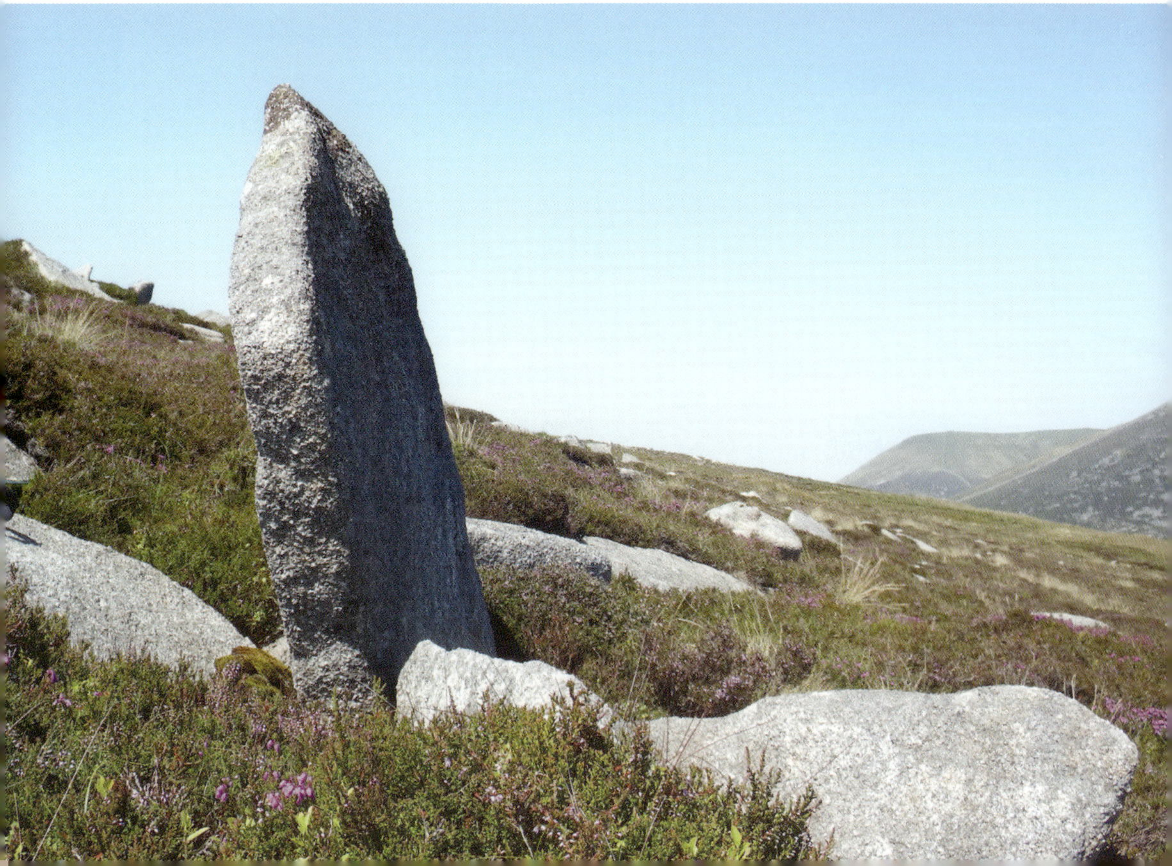

The stone testicles, or would that be breasts, atop the lower phallic erection on Ben Crom make these fertility stones with a difference.

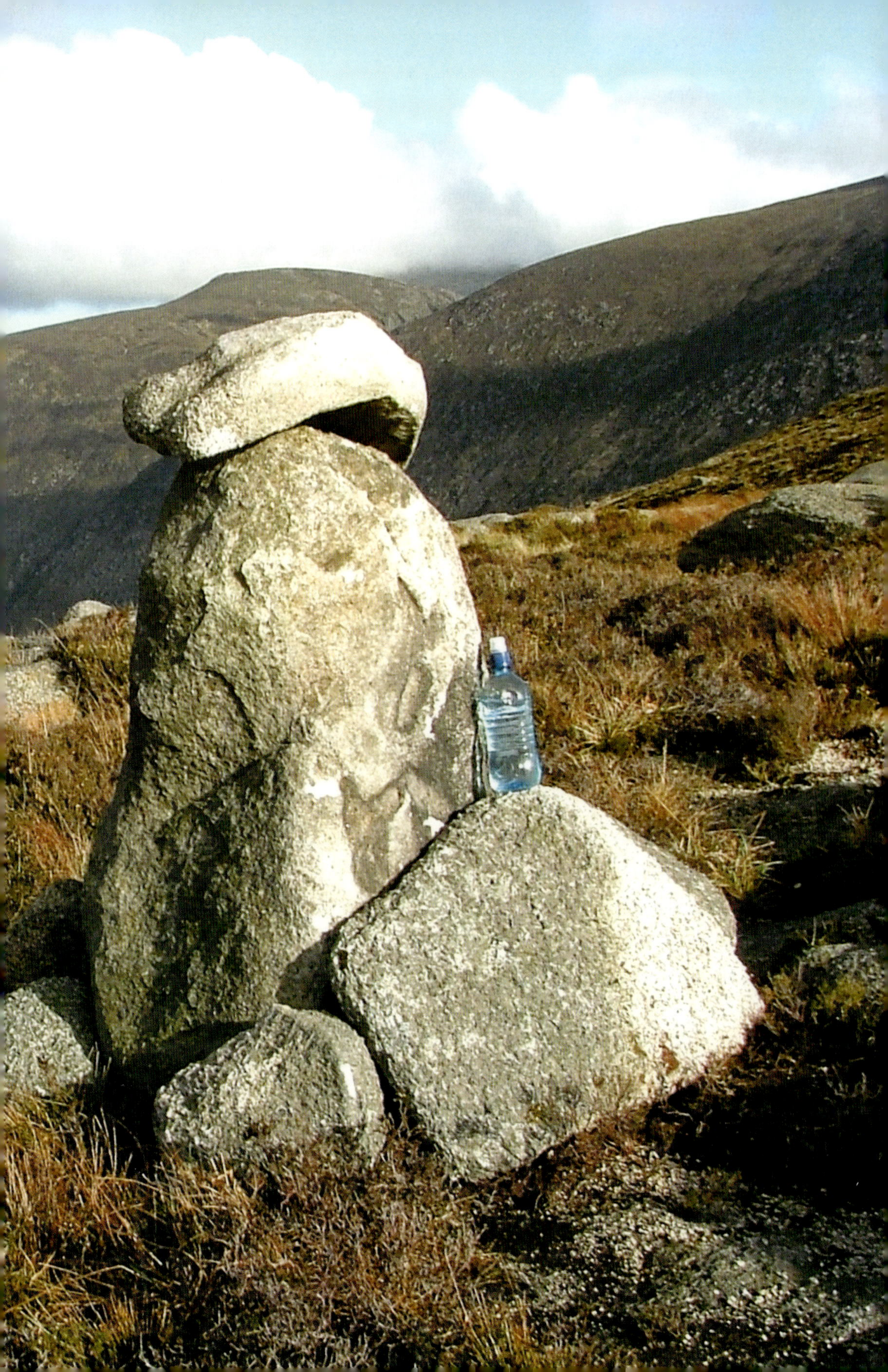

The corner of the cliff face has been undercut to create this great spear point. We also have a close-up view of the fresher golden white granite face that earned this part of the cliff the Irish name *Snab Bán*, the origin of the Walter Harris's 'Slieve Snavan'.

## Spear and phallic stones of Mourne

The projecting of a spear point rock out over a void for dramatic effect is frequently employed in Mourne. Here on the side of Cove cliff, despite the dangers entailed, the ancients have pushed a goodly portion of a mighty spear stone out into space. It points over to Chimney Rock mountain.

Ordnance Survey maps. 'Knockgoran' from its position, is probably Slieve Donard; while due west of it is 'Gedic' and more west still is 'Bennyng gr'; while north of this last is placed 'The top of ye mountain fote', in which the 'Banna flu' rises....

On a map of Ulster by Joann Jansson, the Mournes are designated as 'The Mountayn of Mourne' and what is termed 'The Bishop's Seat' is marked as a church situated just south of 'The Passe', which is figured as a wood.'[9]

Whatever its position on Mercator's map, it is inconceivable, as Canon Lett maintains, that Slieve Donard, the greatest mountain of Mourne should carry a name such as Knockgoran. In Irish Knockgoran would be *Cnoc Goráin*, 'Height of the pimple'. The answer instead lies with a great boulder placed by the ancients on the edge of the height overlooking the Annalong valley and south of Slieve Donard. From down in the valley the boulder appears as no more than a pimple on the skyline. The stone itself marks where the summer solstice sun rises from the notch between Slieve Donard and Commedagh and possibly also where the winter solstice sun touches the top of Rocky mountain. A fusion line right across the stone has been aligned with the phallic summit of Slieve Bignian's north tor. Slightly down slope from this megalith is to be found an impertinent phallic stone, not unlike a pygmy shrew with its nose high sniffing the air.

**Gedic:**

'Due west of (Knockgoran) is 'Gedic'', stated the Canon. This, as it turns out, is a lovely alternative name for the white cliff face of Slieve Snavan, part of Cove cliff, mentioned above. The name is from the Irish *Geadach* (genitive: *Geadaighe*) which means, 'having a white star on the forehead (as a horse)'.

**Bishop's Seat:**

'The Pass' of Jansson's map is the Bloody Bridge valley and in Harris's map this area was also marked as wood. Of particular interest is the preservation of the name 'Bishop's Seat'. In English it would have seemed reasonable to assume that the name belonged to the little church of St Mary's at Ballaghanery. The church, however, was too remote and too small for such a title. The name belongs across the road in the valley of the Bloody Bridge river. Bishop's Seat is a mnemonic of the Irish (*Bealach na*) *bPis óibhéala seata,* meaning (Pass of the) 'wide open vulva of the harlot'. The name reflects the distaste of Christianity for the great centre of paganism that the Bloody Bridge valley originally was. How such an interesting name came about we will look at in 'The Spear of Abundance' chapter.

Overlooking the Annalong valley, this spear stone on the cliff edge of Cove has been arranged to point towards the summit of Slieve Donard.

This view from underneath a spear stone above the path leading to Upper Cove belies its truly gigantic size. It points to where winter solstice sun arises between distant Chimney Rock summit and Rocky mountain. Note how a little meatus groove has been added to the point of the spear to emphasise its phallic purpose.

This important megalith, sky-lined on the heights above the Annalong valley, seemed like a pimple when viewed from below and earned this part of the Mournes the Irish name *Cnoc Goráin*, 'Height of the pimple'

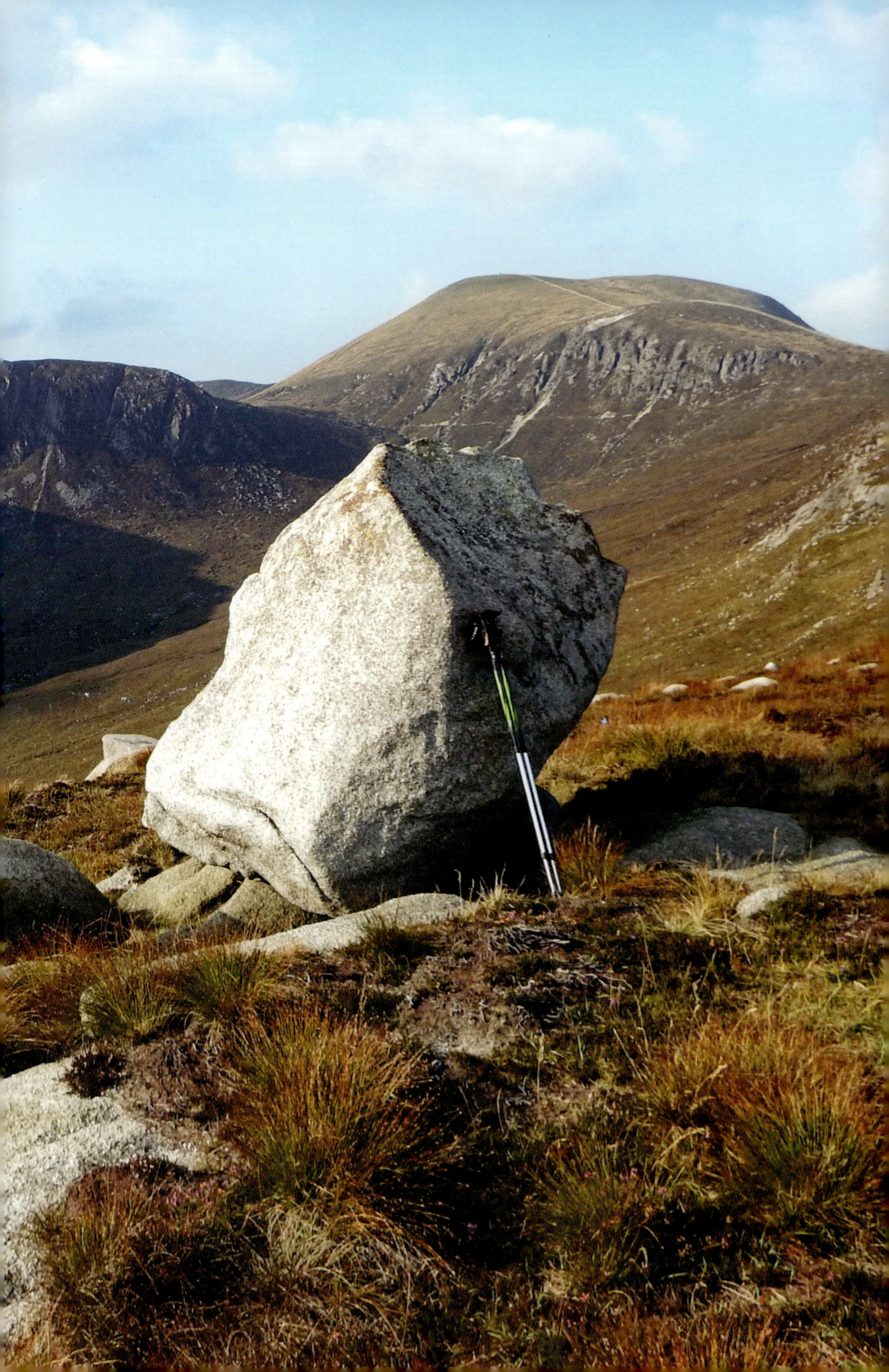

PREHISTORIC MOURNE: INSPIRATION FOR NEWGRANGE

A granite finger has been arranged on the Cove cliff top so that the winter solstice sun setting behind Slieve Bignian will cast the shadow of the phallic point into this south facing gully on Cove.

An emphatic spear point has been carved out of the solid rock on the side of Cove Mountain so that the early winter solstice sun would cast the phallic fertility shadow into the vaginal crevice on the right. This photo was taken at 11.40am on 3rd November so the shadow phenomenon is not illustrated here.

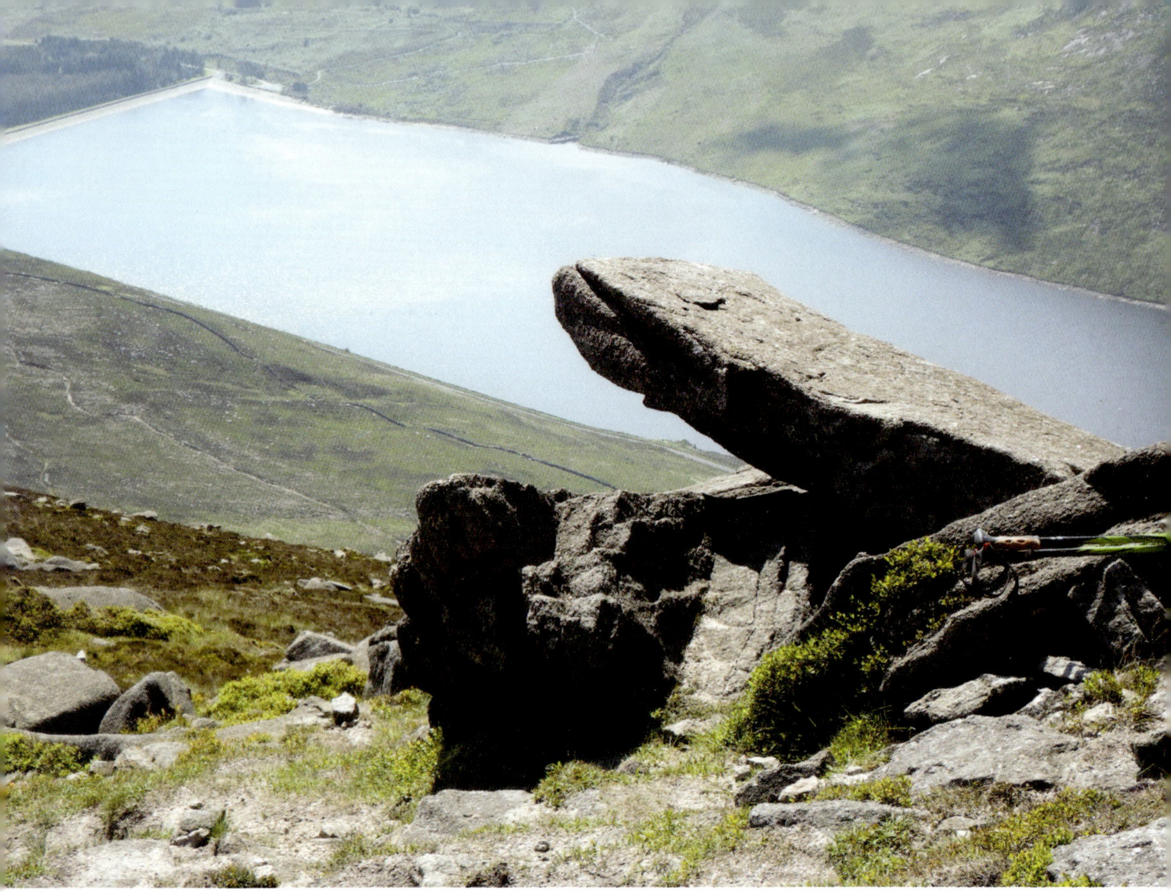

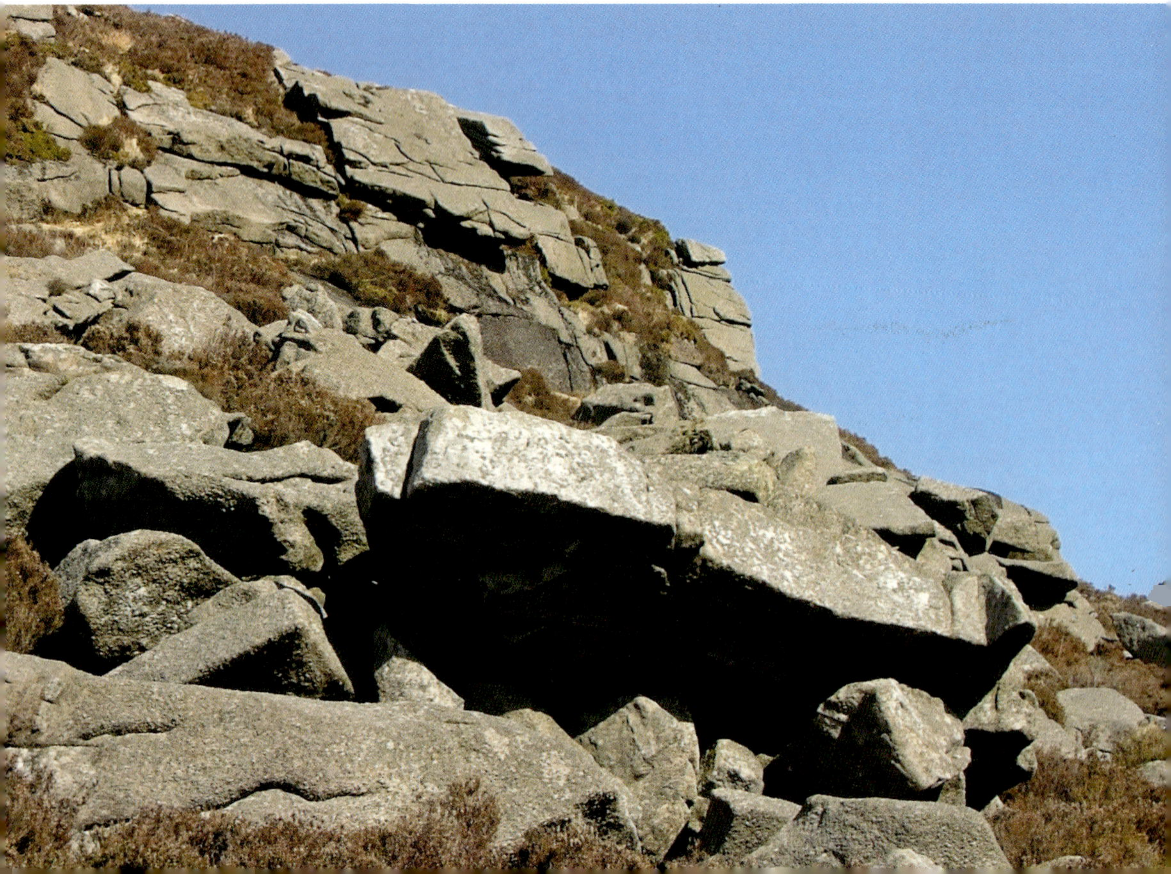

Top left: High on the slopes of Slieve Bignian overlooking the Silent Valley reservoir is this impressive spear and face stone. This stone has been stood on by many ramblers over the years striking photogenic poses against the scenic background; doubtlessly they would have been unaware that the phallic stone catwalk is the work of ancient man.

Bottom left: Another substantial spear stone, this time on the southern slope of Slieve Lamagan. The very pronounced meatus groove at the stone's tip points to the 'vaginal' fissure on nearby Ben Crom. At the back of the megalith is another small point directed to the phallic north tor of Slieve Bignian: likewise the spear stone on the bottom left. Above, at the corner of the cliff, a monstrous stone has been positioned towards winter solstice sunrise as too has another huge spear arrangement behind it at top middle.

Above: High above the Blue Lough is to be found this marvellous rendering of a razor-shell mollusc with its siphon portrayed with phallic intent. Like a multitude of other megaliths on Lamagan's south slope, the siphon points to the decidedly phallic tip of Bignian's north tor.

Above: This spear stone, with a delightful little mouth at the front, is one of many megaliths on the south slope of Lamagan. The stone is not unlike a turtle. It points towards the phallic north tor of Slieve Bignian which, because it casts its shadow over the southern flank of Slieve Lamagan, apparently influenced the name of that mountain. Slieve Lamagan (local pronunciation *Lavigan*), in a classic case of gynaecomorphic interpretation of the landscape, was regarded by the ancients as a monstrously swollen vulva and being construed in sexual terms got its name from the Irish *Sliabh Lab a Geine*, 'Mountain of the considerable lump of a woman'; the 'lump', of course, being the vulva. The name has nothing to do with the Irish *Lámhacán*, 'creeping on hands and feet', which was erroneously suggested by Walter Harris in 1744.

Top right: The spear stone atop the pillar on the side of Douglas Crag cliff points, with phallic intent, into a fissure (not in the photograph). The question must be how such a heavy stone was turned round and manipulated in such a challenging location.

Bottom right: The well defined point on this megalith on the slopes of Slieve Muck looks to the 'breast' of distant Slievenaglogh.

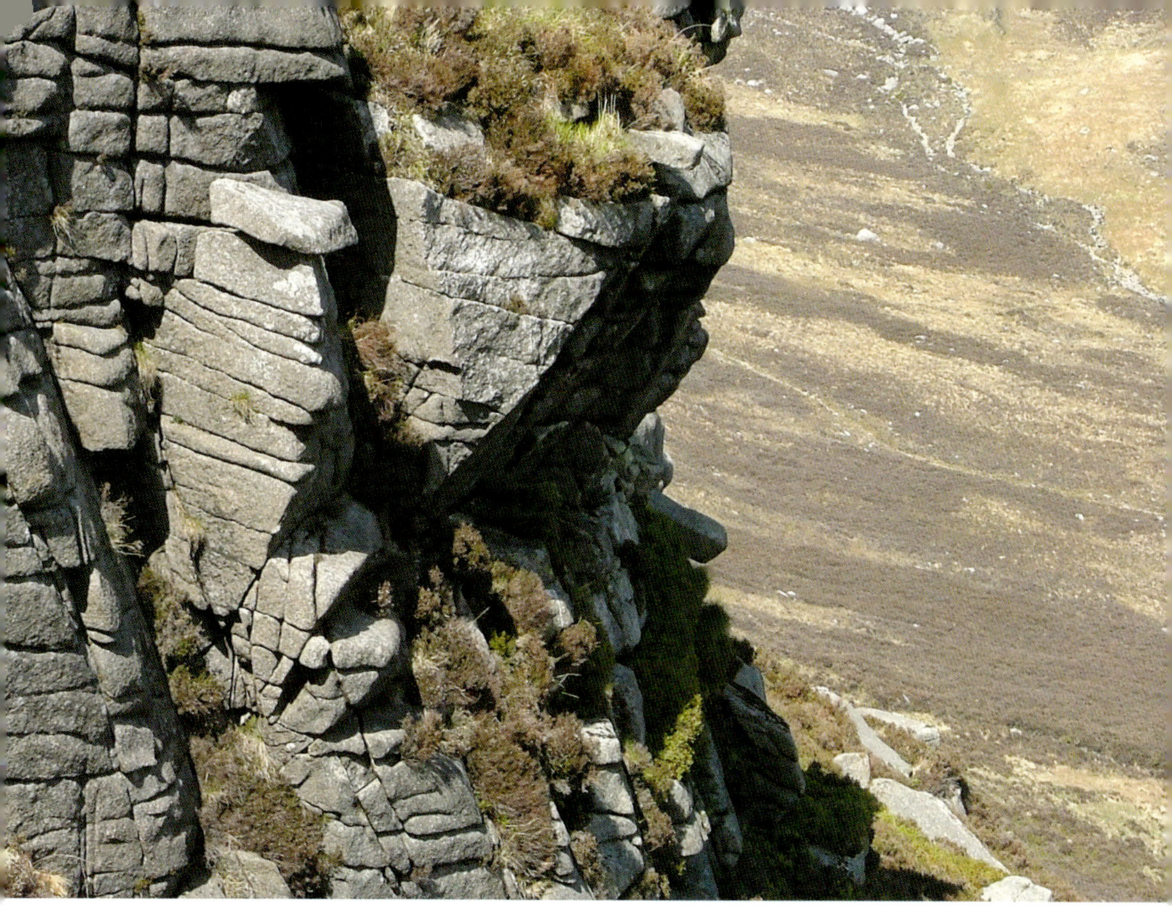

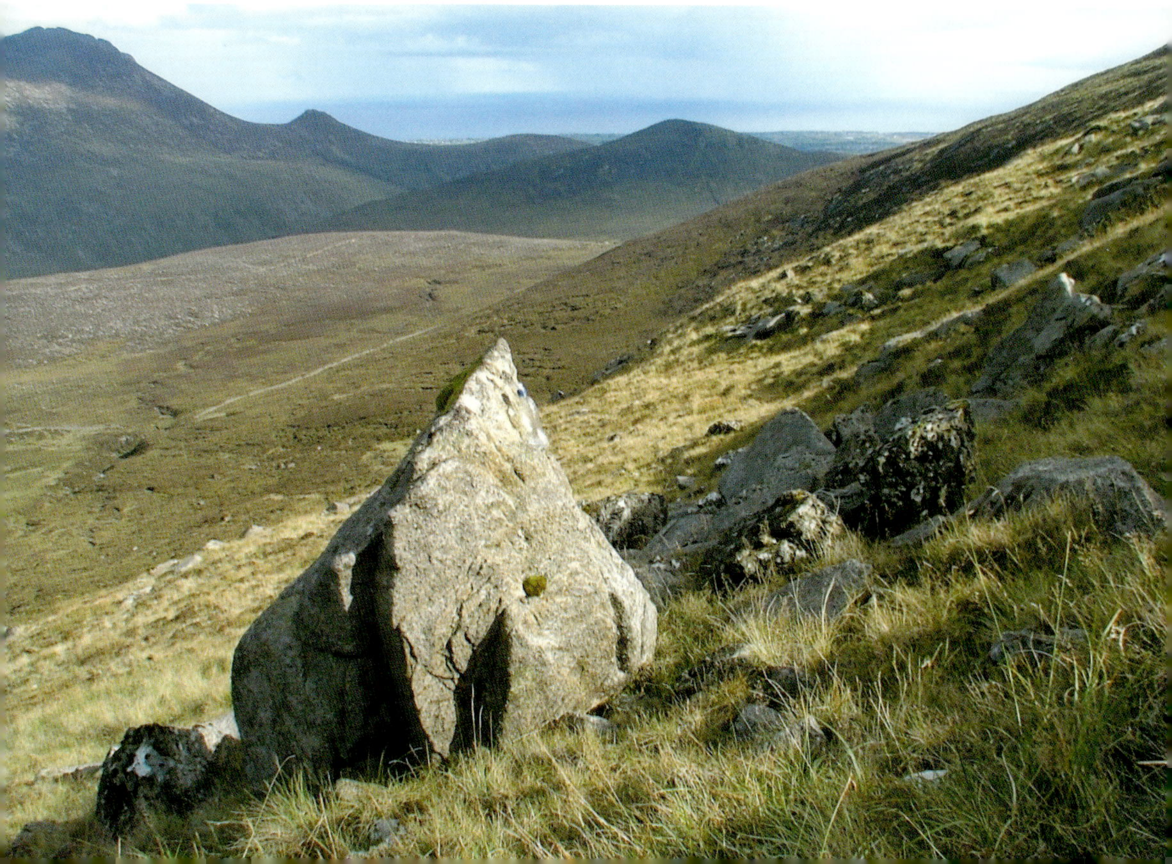

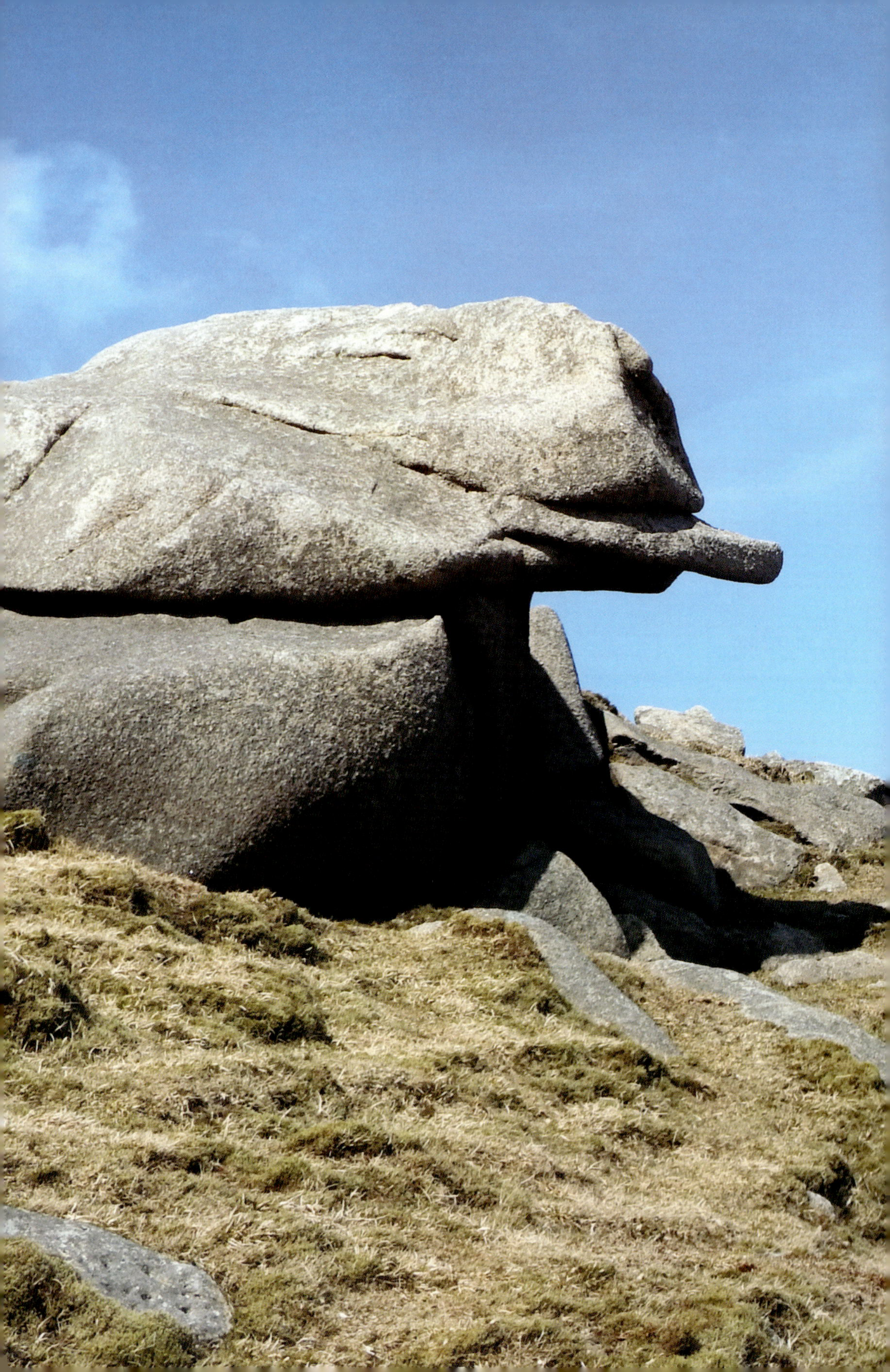

Somewhere on a Mourne hillside is this large monument of fellatio.

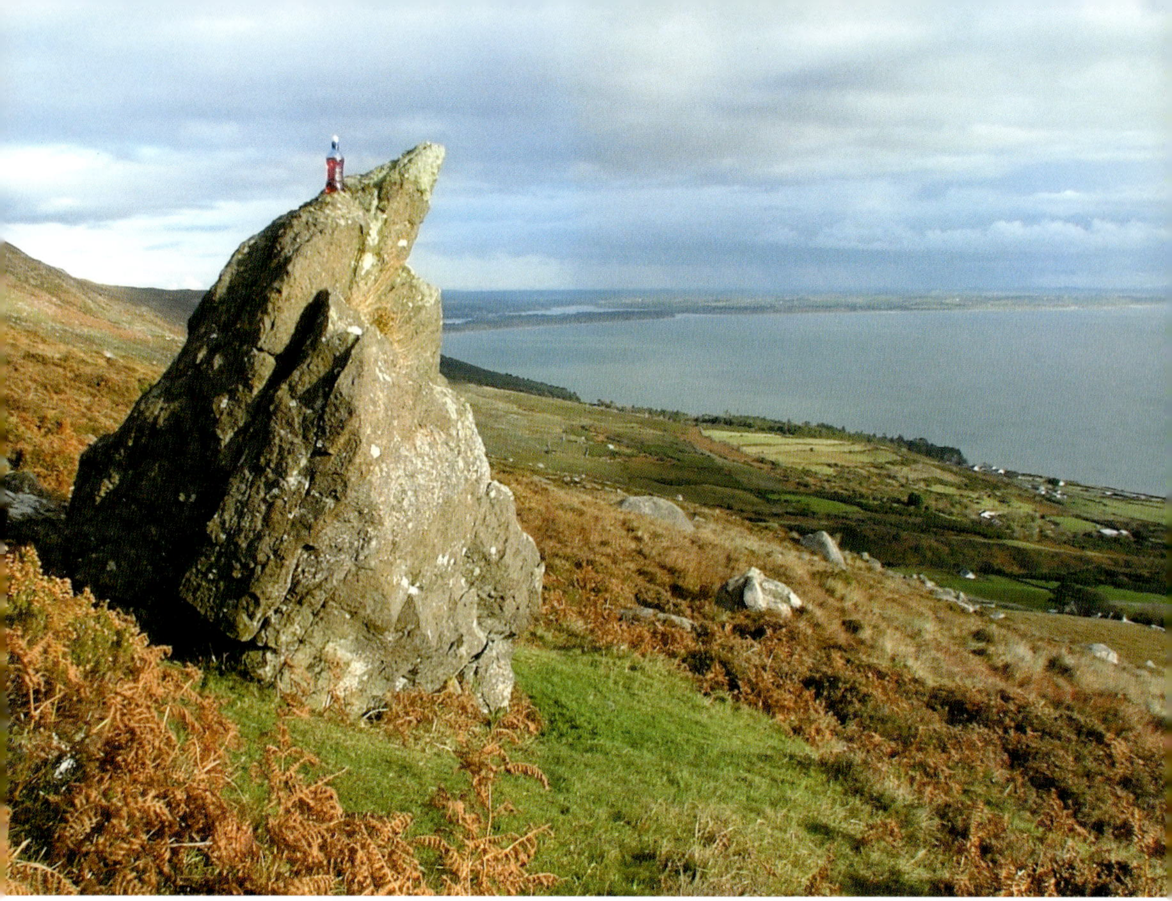

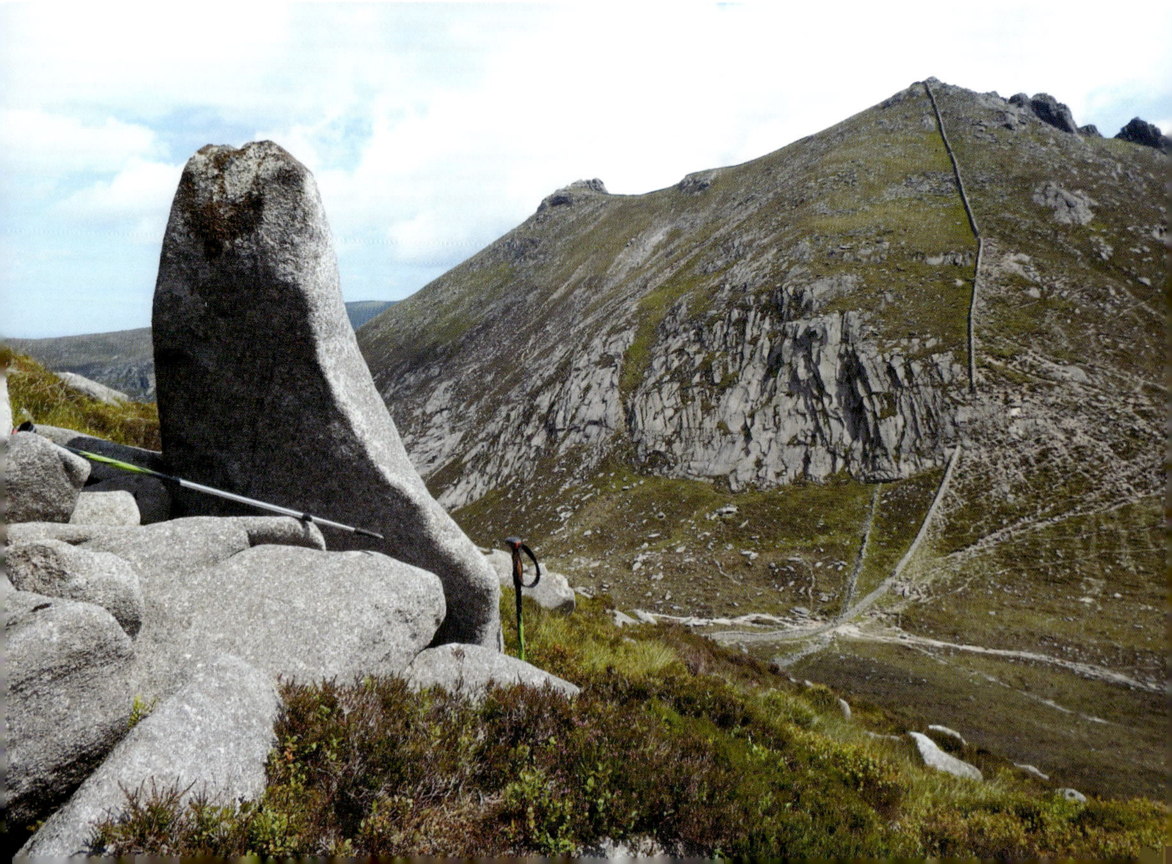

Top left: High on Slievenagarragh (what I regard as Gleasdromainn Hill) is this great stone with its beak-like point quite evocative of a fledgling. Collecting plump young seabirds from their cliff top nests before they learned to fly was likely part of the ancients' diet. The tip of the stone, as expected, points out across the sea towards the horizon where the winter solstice sun appears.

Bottom left: One of many of the phallic rocks on this part of Slieve Meelmore. Note the little meatus groove (pee point) at the top of the stone. In the background is Slieve Bearnagh and below is the col stile at the end of Pollaphuca Valley.

Above: The angle of the photograph is deceiving for this striking phallic stone on the slopes of Slieve Meelmore measures at least three and a half lengths of the trekking pole. The stone is an impressive 14' long by 6.5' wide and the counter-balance stone behind it is even bigger. The point of this megalith looks to the summit of Doan. The sheer size of this megalith makes it stand out from among a host of other arranged stones on this hillside and it is easily enough spotted from the stile at the col below. Adjacent to it is the magnificent bird sculpture featured on pages 24 and 25. I found it worth the climb for the scenic views alone.

Above: An impudent phallic stone on the slope of Slieve Bearnagh's north tor.

Top right: A view of the quite explicit phallic front of Puca's Pillar high on the steep slope of Meelmore in Pollaphuca valley, a profile of which has already featured on page 113. It was this stone that gave the valley its second name of Pollaphuca Hollow, from the Irish *Polla an Phúca Oilc*, meaning 'the pillar of the malevolent goblin'. Rather than attempting to climb the slope, stay on the regular path under Bearnagh slabs and use binoculars to find and study this overtly sexual stone high across the valley on the side of Meelmore. Such was the steepness of the slope that I was slipping when taking the photograph and it is actually quite askew. That little difficulty only highlighted the question, 'how was it possible to manoeuvre this very substantial monument on such a steep slope?' The stone may be malevolent but the brute engineering that raised it is a demonstation of absolute skill and ability.

Bottom right: One of the great treasures of Mourne. Project a line seaward along the top of the stone to find the winter solstice sunrise point. Look at the insignificant size of the blue water bottle at the bottom. While taking this photograph the bottle fell from its perch down into the rocks below the stone and when I climbed down to retrieve it I still could not see the bottom of the megalith and realised this is a monstrous piece of granite supported in place by a multitude of other sizeable stones. It is to be found on the seaward side of Slieve Bearnagh's south tor.

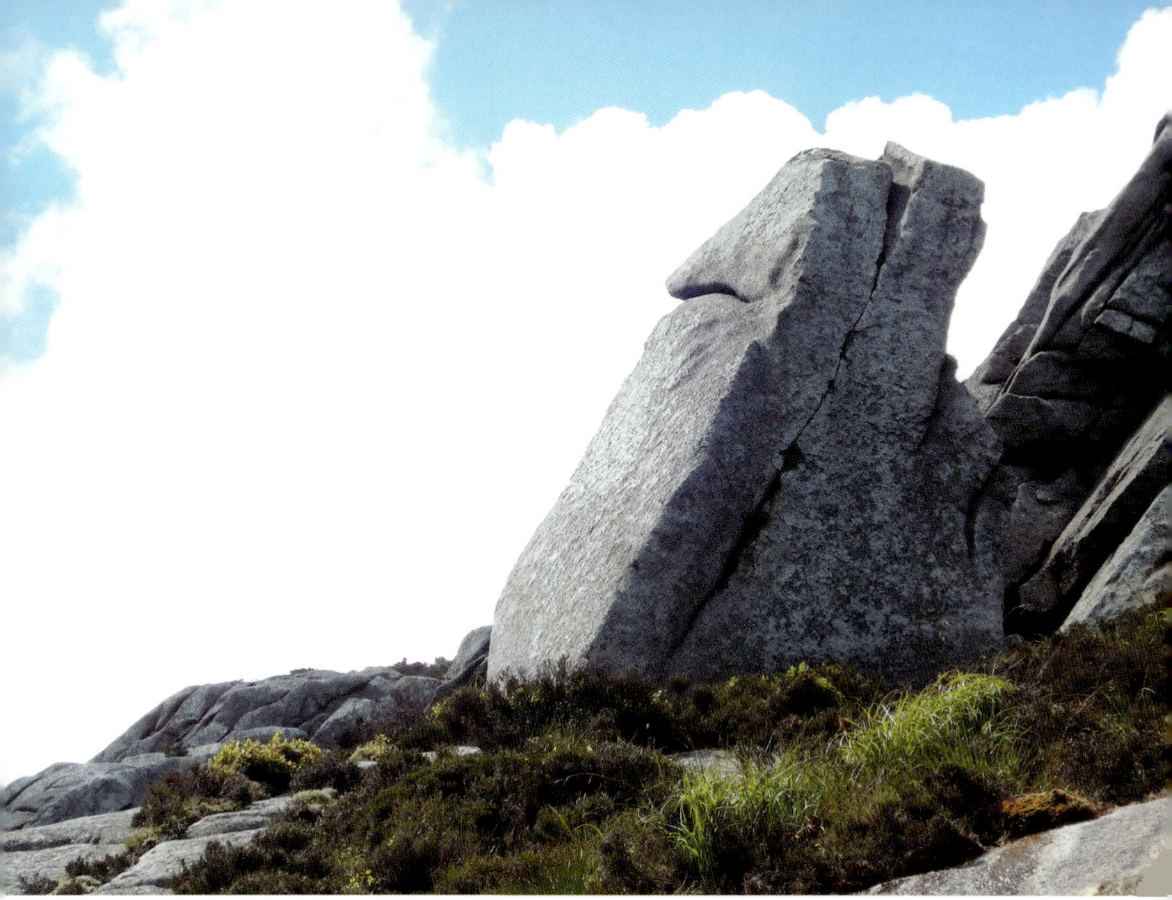

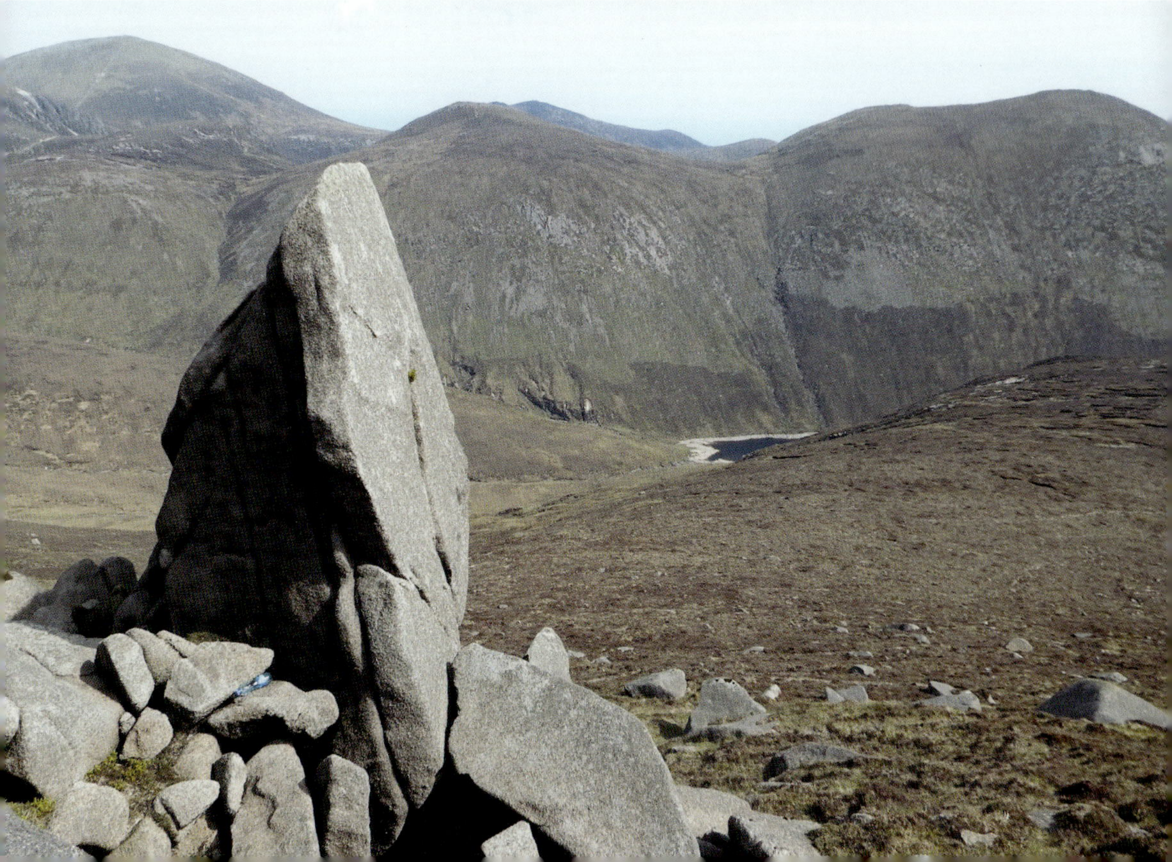

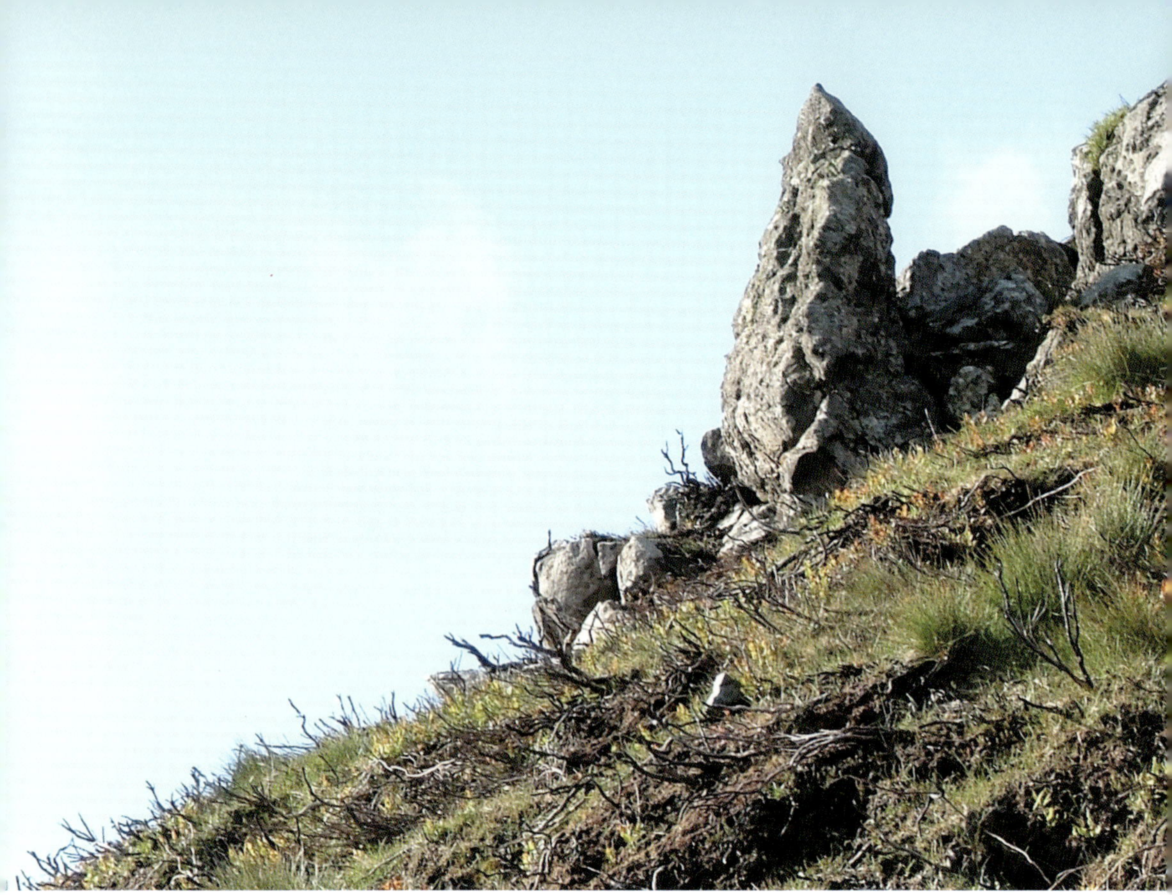

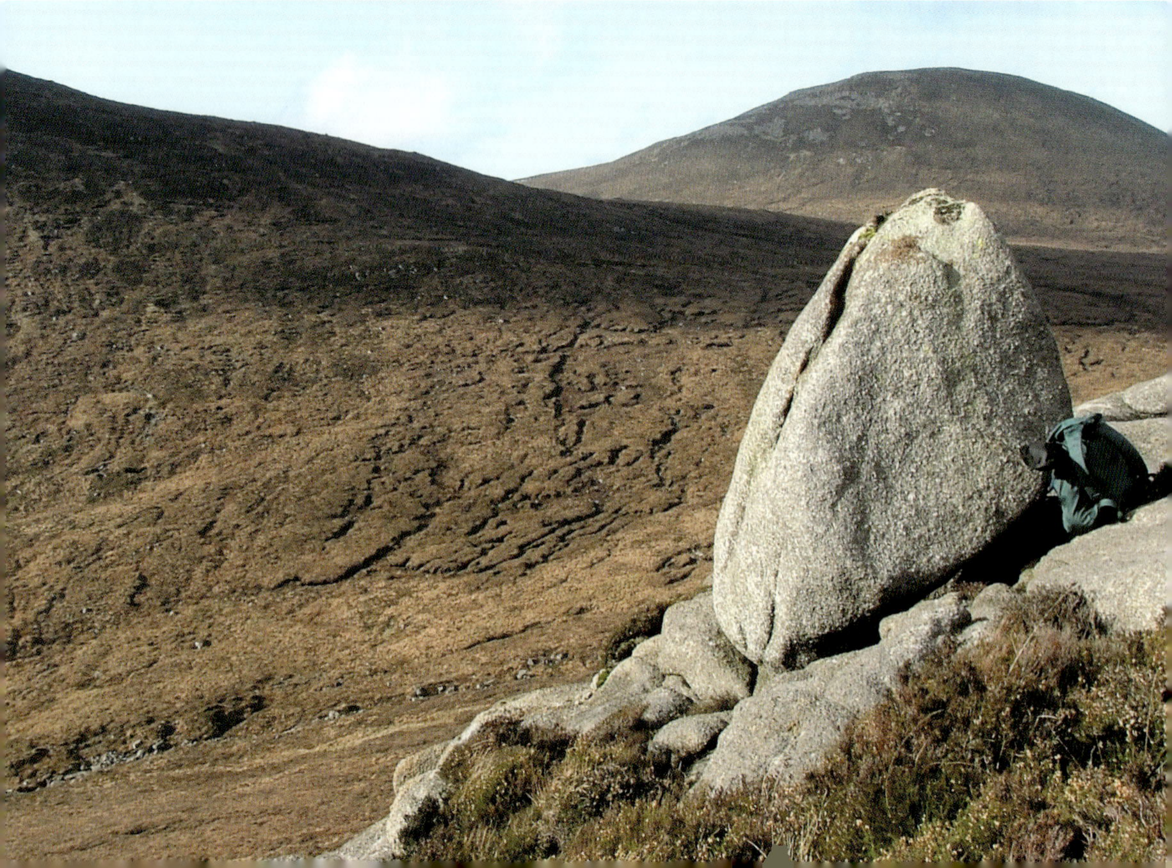

Top left: A scaldy bird? This stone, high on the slope of Slieve Thomas, has already featured on page 68. From this angle below it could well be construed as a plump young bird upright in the nest. The white rock found on the tip of the stone is likely meant to symbolise a seminal discharge. The ancients were also very partial to these fusions of different rock in the same stone, seeing in them an allegory of the union of male and female.

Bottom left: A phallic face stone with substantial meatus groove is to be found on the heights of Ben Crom. From this vantage point the cheeky stone can 'look up the legs' of the Silent Valley, ie. imagine the steep sides of the valley below as a woman's legs.

Above: These phallic stones on Ben Crom must have been balancing for thousands of years. Note the 'sad' face on the bottom stone.

The famous phallic Longstone near Annalong is both a face stone and solstice marker. The right-hand side of this stone is sharply defined like a spear head and points out to sea towards winter solstice sun-rise. The effect is unfortunately spoiled by the presence now of a house across the road obscuring the sight.

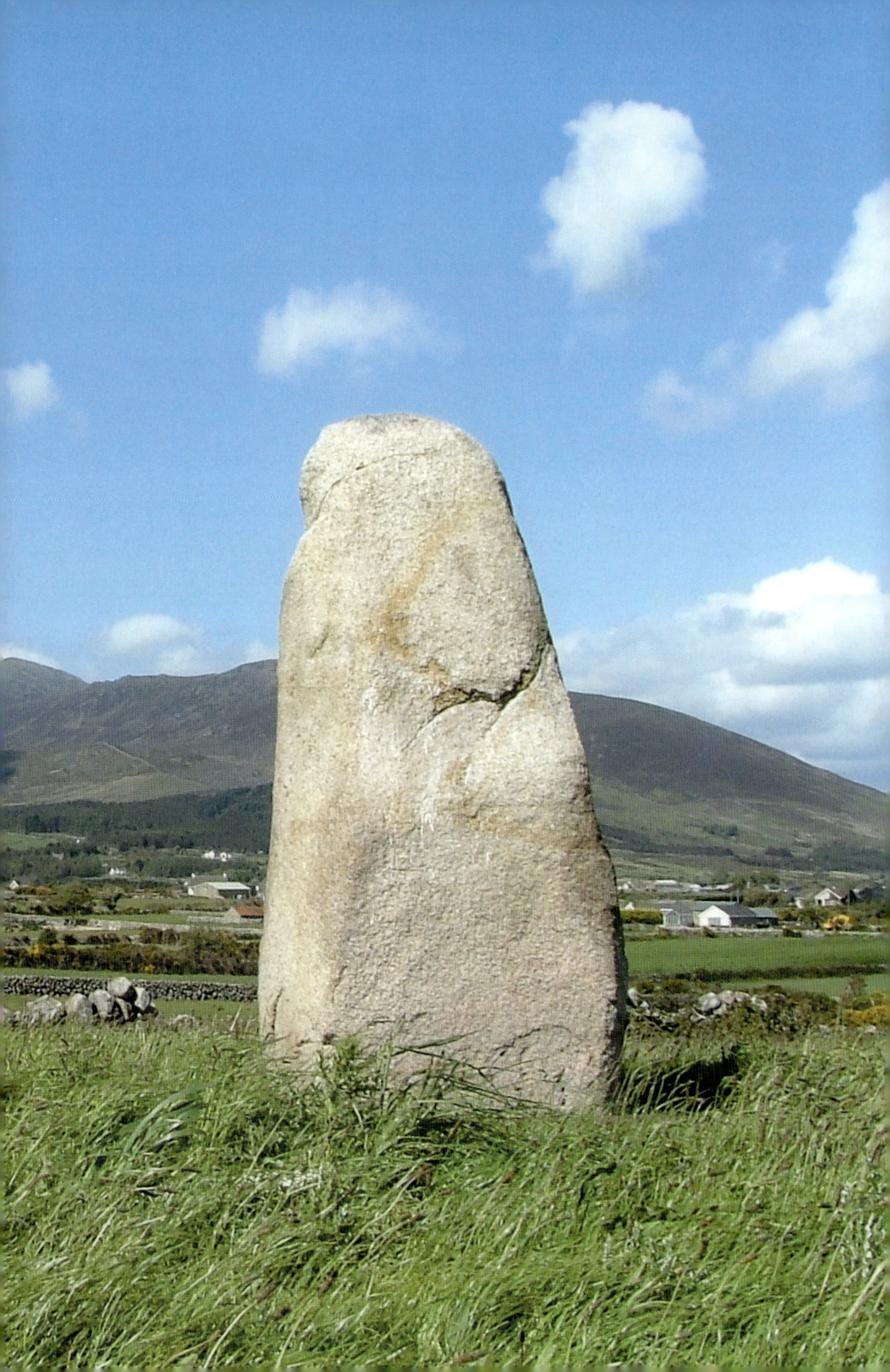

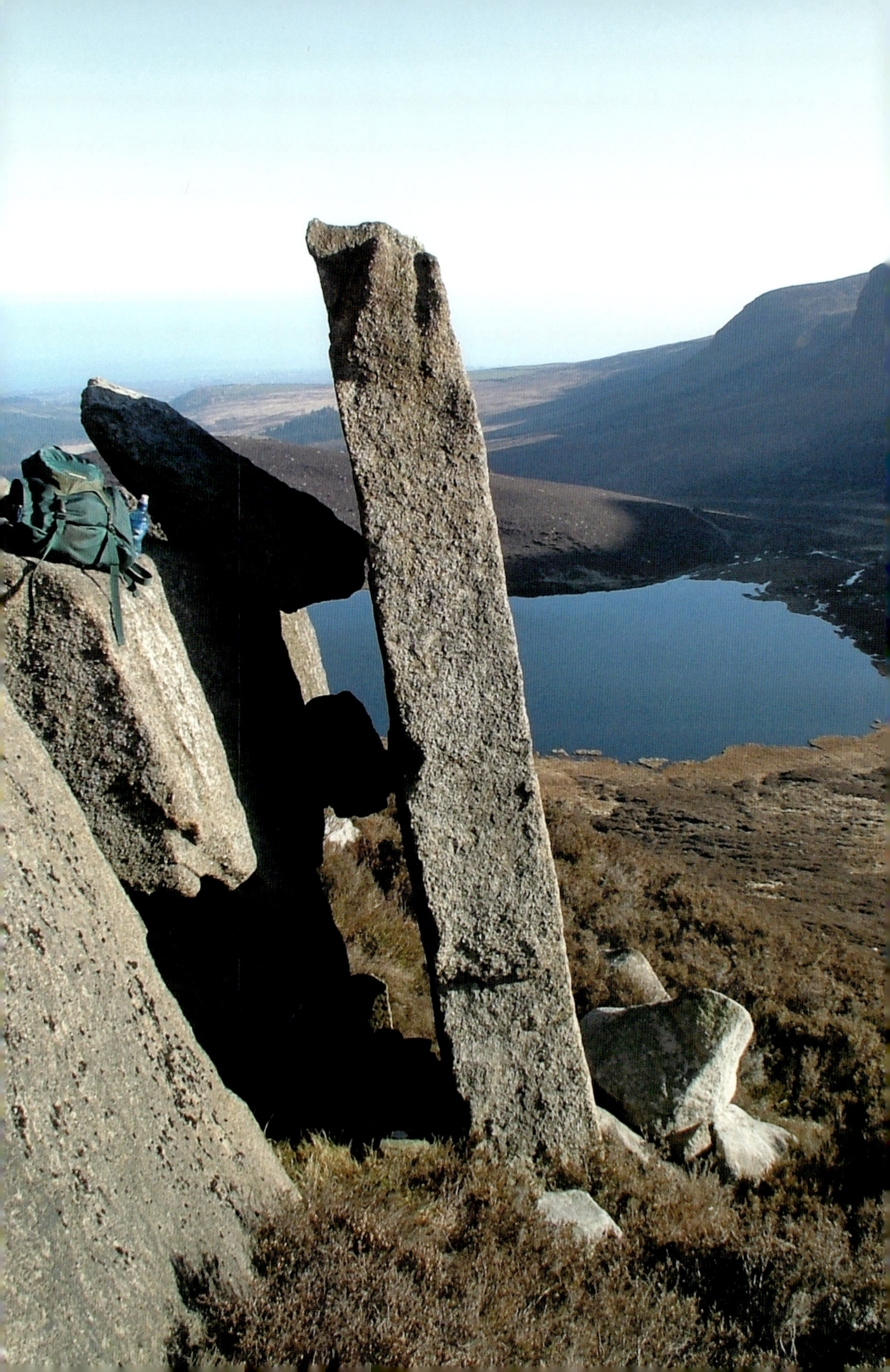

# VAGINA STONES

Slieve Donard was a magnificent landmark for sailors out on the Irish Sea during millennia past. In dealing with earlier names for Slieve Donard, we had previously written:

'Sight of our majestic mountain would have been welcomed as an indication of a good place to make landfall. Generally speaking the coast of Mourne and, for that matter, the coast of the Ards peninsula, is rocky. Dundrum Bay with its miles of sandy beach made a wonderful landing place and boats could be hauled up the shore. I believe the name Slángha was conferred on the mountain by sailors and is a surviving amalgam of *Slán,* meaning 'safe', and *gaoth* meaning 'an inlet of the sea'. *Slán gaoth,* with the elision of 'th', merged into Slángha. Slieve Donard earned its earlier name of Slieve Slángha for being a guiding beacon to the safe landing place of Dundrum Bay.'[1]

We know that Mesolithic man was established at Mount Sandel, Coleraine, nine thousand year ago and Mourne with its favourable living conditions and wide range of habitats would also have been an attractive place for early man to settle. Various waves of settlers would come to Ireland after the ice melted and among those that deserve special attention are the *Fir-Bolg*, not least because the *Annals of the Four Masters* under the age of the world 2533, tell us that the first *Fir-Bolg* king, Slainge son of Partholan[2], died in this year and was interred in the cairn of Sliabh Slángha,[3] otherwise Slieve Donard.

The name of the *Fir-Bolg*, who made Mourne their home, has been sadly misunderstood. We hear of them in the 12th century book the *Leabhar Gabhála* – 'The Book of Invasions', a highly mythologised version of Ireland's early history which tells of the *Fir-Bolg* as among the first arrivals in Ireland. It was the Celtic scholar Whitley Stokes (1830-1909) and later Sir John Rhys (1840-1915), the first professor of Celtic at Oxford, who made the suggestion that the *Fir-Bolg* got their name because they wore breeches. Others concluded that *Fir-Bolg* meant 'men of the bags or sacks' either because of their propensity to steal farmers' stores, or, because as slaves their servitude involved carrying bags of soil. More recently it was claimed that *Fir-Bolg* meant 'bog men'.[4] The great Irish scholar of place-names, P.W. Joyce, also interpreted *Bolg* as meaning 'sacks or bags', though his remarks showed that he accepted this explanation only for want of a more intelligible alternative.[5] After seeing the multitude of stones in Mourne that have been constructed with phallic import or in imitation of vaginas, we would contend that the intelligible alternative for *Fir-Bolg* should be 'womb men'.

In a symbolical act of intercourse, this spear slab on the south facing slopes of Slieve Lamagan has been staged so that the fertility bringing winter solstice sunrise would shine into the gap between the slab and the rock-face as if it was penetrating a vagina. The middle stone that is jammed in place represents the male insertion.

That confusion has reigned for so long arises from the multitude of interpretations possible for the Irish word *Bolg*. The various meanings mentioned by Dinneen are as follows: 'the abdomen, the belly, stomach; womb; appetite; heart, mind; a bag, pouch, pocket, receptacle, repertoire; a harp case; bellows; a ship's hold; sound-box; a small bell; a husk; a bladder; a pimple, a blister, a bubble; a bulge, a swell (on the sea); midst, centre'. There was certainly a lot to choose from. To the early scholars a designation of 'womb men' would have seemed a contradiction in terms and nonsensical which made them look to other explanations. In an earlier work we mentioned how *Bolg* already had a place in local place-names:

> 'Maghera is a site of great antiquity. The earliest remains are of the rath which is obscured by the growth of trees and bushes. It was strategically located near the Carrigs river and one of its tributaries, to give a measure of protection from raiders and as a safeguard against the cattle either straying or being stolen. From this ancient fort the place took its name, *Rath Murbholg*, or the fort of the belly of the sea. The aptness of this description can certainly be seen from Slieve Donard. Looking down at the great sweep of Dundrum bay the sea can easily be imagined as a big paunch.'[6]

The preoccupation of the *Fir Bolg* with fertility, be it for their harvests, livestock and especially their families, brought about assiduous and permanent works of procreation in stone and it is the frequency of these stone creations that makes the designation of *Fir Bolg* as 'womb men' well deserved. These are probably the same people that the Egyptian geographer, Ptolemy, referred to in his 2nd century *Geographia*, as the *Volunti*, a name which is only a Romanised modification of *Bolgii*, 'womb people'. Remember there is no letter [v] in Irish, but, depending on usage, lenition of the Irish [b] yields a [v] sound. An instance given early is the mountain above Kilbroney, Rostrevor, where the Irish name (*Sliabh na*) *Gréine Buille*, '(mountain of the) sun's cast' is now known as Crenville (OS 2018).

Mention was made earlier how the name of Mourne derived from (*Sléibhte na*) *mBúir-na*, 'The mountains of very many roars.' By the time the Vikings came to these shores the people they encountered here were known as the *Ulaidh*. It is generally accepted that 'Ulster' is a compound of the name of those people plus the Norse suffix for 'place', namely '*staôr*'. However, looking at the derivation of *Ulaidh*, a case can be made that they were continuing the work of their megalith making predecessors, the *Fir Bolg*, and that their name comes from the Irish *Uaill-Áidh*, 'screams of prosperity'. Screams, shouts and roars aplenty would have echoed around Mourne in millennia past as men strove to erect the many mighty megaliths. Prosperity was the consequence of fertility coming on crops and animals and if this was ensured by the erection of phallic or vagina stones to the sun-god with all the attendant shouts, commands and roars of exertion necessary during construction, then there certainly were many 'screams of prosperity' heard across Ulster and the hills of Mourne in particular. The boundary of the territory of the *Ulaidh*, incidentally, was delineated by a series of ditches and earthworks, known variously as the 'Dorsey', the 'Black Pig's Dyke' or the 'Dane's Cast'. Folklore has excelled itself in the explanation of a Black Pig running rampant and ploughing up the earth into the defensive ditches with its tusks as it charged along. The real explanation of the derivation of the name is a little more prosaic. The Black Pig's Dyke comes from the Irish *Bleacht Pigín Diach*, meaning an 'Unfortunate milk vessel', ie. something that was easily and frequently broken, a reference to a useless defensive system that was all too easily penetrated. The alternative name the 'Dorsey' had a similar scornful vein. The Dorsey is from the Irish *Doras Sídhe* meaning 'Magic or Fairy Door'; ramparts that could be breezed though as if by magic. The final name, Dane's Cast, has nothing to do with the much later Vikings or Danish raiders but is likely a contraction of the Irish *Daoidheanna Casta*, 'intricate embankments'.

Later in the early medieval period, the people who occupied parts of present day county Down and Antrim, the previous stronghold of the *Fir Bolg* and *Ulaidh* would be referred to as *Cruithne*. It would seem from the Irish that, like the *Fir Bolg* before them, the *Cruithne* were given to the cult of fertility. The name of the

The low mound in the middle distance is now called Percy Bysshe. Its original name in Irish was *Pearsa bPise*, 'form of a vulva'. The quarry that the granite men opened at this fertility site can be seen at the front of the hill.

Overlooking the Annalong valley, the great phallic megalith on the slopes of Percy Bysshe hill was used during the war as a target by American forces on manoeuvres. Note the sleeping eye that gives animation to the stone.

people is derived from *Cruit-ne*, meaning 'very many mounds' which, given the predilections of the *Fir Bolg*, could be understood as 'vulvas'. The word *Cruit* means 'a hump on the back, a little eminence'; it would be used for instance if a scared cat arched its back in facing a dog, *chuir an cat cruit uirthe féin* – 'the cat hunched itself up'. Whether we speak of a 'hump, hunch, mound, bulge, swelling (*Boirrche*), bump or little eminence', the real significance behind the name for the ancients was probably sexual, particularly as a way of referring to breasts and vulvas.[7] Adding the suffix *–ne* to *Cruit* gave it the great collective sense of 'very many mounds'.

We should remember that it was not unusual then for mounds and swellings in the landscape to be given sexual connotations. Mention has already been made of Slievenamaddy coming from the Irish *Sliabh na mBáidhe*, meaning 'the mountain of love' on account of its resemblance to female genitalia but other hills in Mourne have been similarly regarded. A case in point is the hill in the middle of the Mournes with the incongruous name of Percy Bysshe (OS J3324). The hill would seem to have had a name substitution brought about by Victorian excursionists into the hills. The present name is a reference to Percy Bysshe

Shelley, 1792 – 8 July 1822, one of the major English Romantic poets who drowned in Italy. It was known that during his life Shelley had travelled to Dublin where he published his 'Address to the Irish People' and some wondered as a result if he had ever travelled to Mourne around that time. The name of the Mourne hill has nothing to do with the poet but is yet another mnemonic. The name is a derivative of the Irish *Pearsa bPise* which means 'form of a vulva'. The ancients looked on this low hill swelling up, as it were, between Slieve Lamagan and Slieve Bignian and thought of genitalia. The quarry-men, ever happy to extract granite from sites renowned for fertility, duly opened a quarry at the side of the hill. The location was used during the war for training and firing anti-tank artillery and even yet the occasional unexploded shell is found. Visitors passing by the start of Percy Bysshe bluff on their way to the head of the valley and Bignian's north tor, will see a great phallic megalith, with what is probably an ancient granite rubble trail leading up to it, on their right hand side. The upright monument served as a target for American forces on manoeuvres in the mountains during the war and the face of the stone that looks out over the Annalong valley is peppered with bullet holes.

Perhaps the most obvious formation for vagina stones is the close placement of two rocks that still leaves a gap between them. To make the fertility intention quite clear, a rock to symbolise the penis is frequently inserted in the gap. This practise is not unique to Mourne. Up at the Causeway coast a very famous example of the insertion of a phallic rock is the Grey Man's Path at Fair Head where the ancients wedged an unmistakable penile stone across a deep 'vaginal' gully.[8] Some in the past maintained that this rock has fallen into place, this despite the fact that the bridge is a composite of four stones with further stones in a support role as wedges on the left-hand side. The stone column that bridged the gap was not 'fallen' but deliberately placed in situ by the ancients. That this was long regarded as a phallic fertility stone is clear in Irish. The name 'Grey man's path' is only a mnemonic for *'Gríos mian puite'* meaning, 'the red-hot desire of the vulva'. On the next page, look carefully at the big truss stone on the left-hand side to see how the ancients cleverly employed it as a face stone with a large open mouth at the top, crying out, as it were, in the ecstasy of sexual climax.

Here in Mourne, apart from the stones already illustrated at Eagle Rock cliff, cliff gully stone insertions are found inter alia at Spellack, Upper Cove, Slieve Bearnagh south tor, and in the south side of Slieve Bignian's north tor. A particularly important rock insertion is to be found at Buzzard's Roost. This is the name of a great crag high on the north-eastern shoulder of Slieve Bignian's north tor, though the name originally derived from the large chasm that bisects the crag. Facing east as it does, the fissure just catches the light of winter solstice dawn. The chasm was regarded as a great vagina by the ancients who wedged a particularly large stone in it symbolic of the fissure being penetrated and fertilised by the 'phallic' insertion. Buzzard's Roost actually has a number of stones wedged

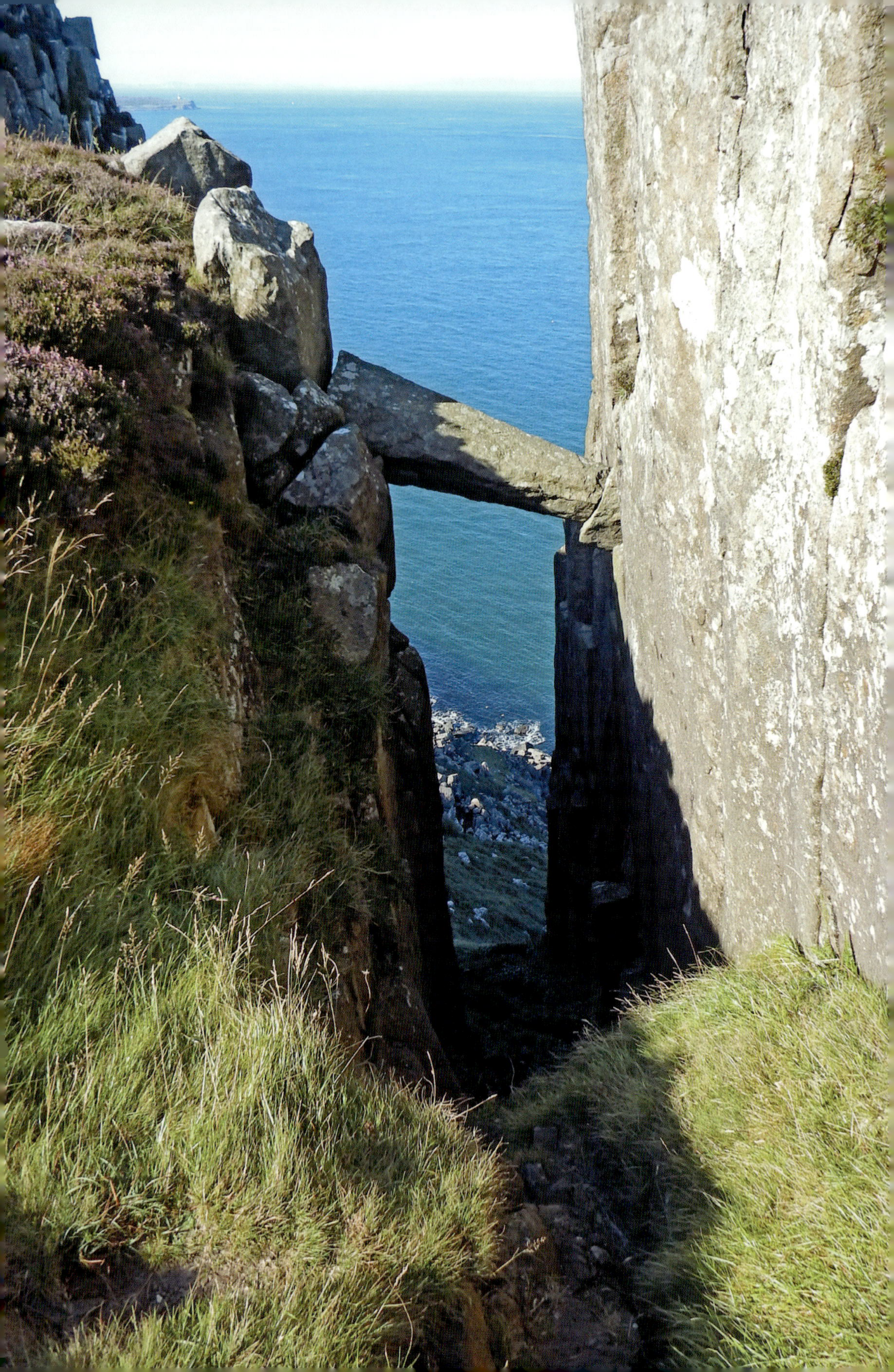

Above: This natural fissure at Fair Head was regarded as a symbolic vagina and has had a boulder dropped into it as a notional penis.

in it. I often imagine this fissure as an ancient equivalent of Rome's Trevi fountain where people of millennia past would toss boulders into the crevice wishing for fertility for the coming year. Usually the boulder would fall to the bottom of the fissure but if they were lucky the stone might jam between the rock sides. The solstice sun would then project the shadows of the lucky inserted stones even deeper into the gap. Standing at the entrance of the fissure you can count at least a dozen jammed stones high up and the floor is strewn with a multitude of rounded boulders that missed their chance of glory when they failed to wedge in the gap when thrown from the top.

The first climbing guide to Mourne described the recess as 'a speleological oddity'. It was first climbed on 18th September 1954 by W.B. Gibson and M. McMurray who had to enter into the deep chasm 45 metres through continuous

Left: The placement of this phallic stone across the deep gully at Fair Head was a monumental achievement for the ancients. The name of the defile, 'Grey Man's Path', is a mnemonic of the Irish '*Gríos mian puite*' meaning, 'the red-hot desire of the vulva'. Note the open-mouth ecstasy of sexual climax on the face stone on the left of the defile.

*The great fissure of Buzzard's Roost under Slieve Bignian's north tor, shows some of the fertility boulders deliberately wedged in the gap by the ancients. Buzzard's Roost is from the Irish bPis Ard Roiste, meaning 'high ripped vulva'.*

water drips before the very difficult 73 metre climb could begin. The present climbing guide sets the tone:

> 'Despite almost permanent dampness, the main central chimney on the crag gives an outing of great atmosphere which is just on the humorous side of character building and best savoured with a large party in high spirits or preferably full of spirits! Start in the very bowels of the cleft.'[9]

The large tilted phallic stone inserted by the ancients is now part of the climb. It is no surprise that climbers refer to it as a chock-stone. At the top edge of the cliff, the ancients also pushed out a great spear stone into the void and this is popularly regarded as the buzzard's beak. The name of the chasm and spear stone has nothing to do however with actual buzzards. Buzzard's Roost is yet another mnemonic of the Irish (*Creag na*) *bPis Ard Roiste*, meaning '(Crag of the) high ripped vulva'.

There is one more probable rock insertion worth a thought, namely the underwater stone at the entrance to Donard Cove. The Cove is a tremendous sea

# VAGINA STONES

A close-up of the great spear stone on top of Buzzard's Roost crag. The huge stone spear projecting out over the edge of the cliff is often thought of as the 'buzzard's beak'. The cliff has been undercut to accentuate the megalith which points over to Slieve Lamagan.

cave that was much loved by smugglers and the story of this being St Donard's particular residence until the day of Judgment would likely have been encouraged by them to discourage casual inspection.[10] This cave going, as it does, deep into the hillside, would have had obvious vaginal associations for the ancients. Until an underwater examination of the submerged rock at the entrance to the cave takes place, it can only remain an unconfirmed suspicion that the ancients deliberately manoeuvred a large phallic stone into the rocky entrance and dropped it on the sea-bed as a permanent mark to fertility.

The following selection of photographs will hopefully create awareness of the work of the ancient *Fir Bolg*, the womb men. As one becomes familiar with the sheer extent of worked and manipulated stones across the hills of Mourne, the enormity of effort would seem to require a time space of surely many thousands of years. As we cannot know how early the work began or how long remnants of pagan practice endured after the coming of Christianity, we have, by and large, preferred not to identify the monuments of Mourne with particular peoples or epochs but have chosen rather to refer to these early stonemen as 'the ancients'.[11]

Above: A classic example of vagina stones. These stones with their phallic insertion are to be found under Slieve Bearnagh slabs, above the 'Lecarry Loanin' path and not too far from the stile at the head of Pollaphuca valley. Look sideways at the right-hand stone to see the closed eye and the slightly open 'mouth' at the top, cleverly suggestive of disposition at intercourse.

Top right: This little pair of vagina stones on the eastern slope of Slieve Bearnagh await the summer solstice sun to appear over the distant shoulder of Slievenaglogh and the shadow of the penile stone to penetrate through the gap.

Bottom right: The natural shale stones in the foreground are a reminder that these two large granite boulders placed together to form a vaginal notch complete with a symbolic phallic stone between them, have been dragged quite a distance to this site on Luke's mountain where they receive the rays of the declining winter solstice sun.

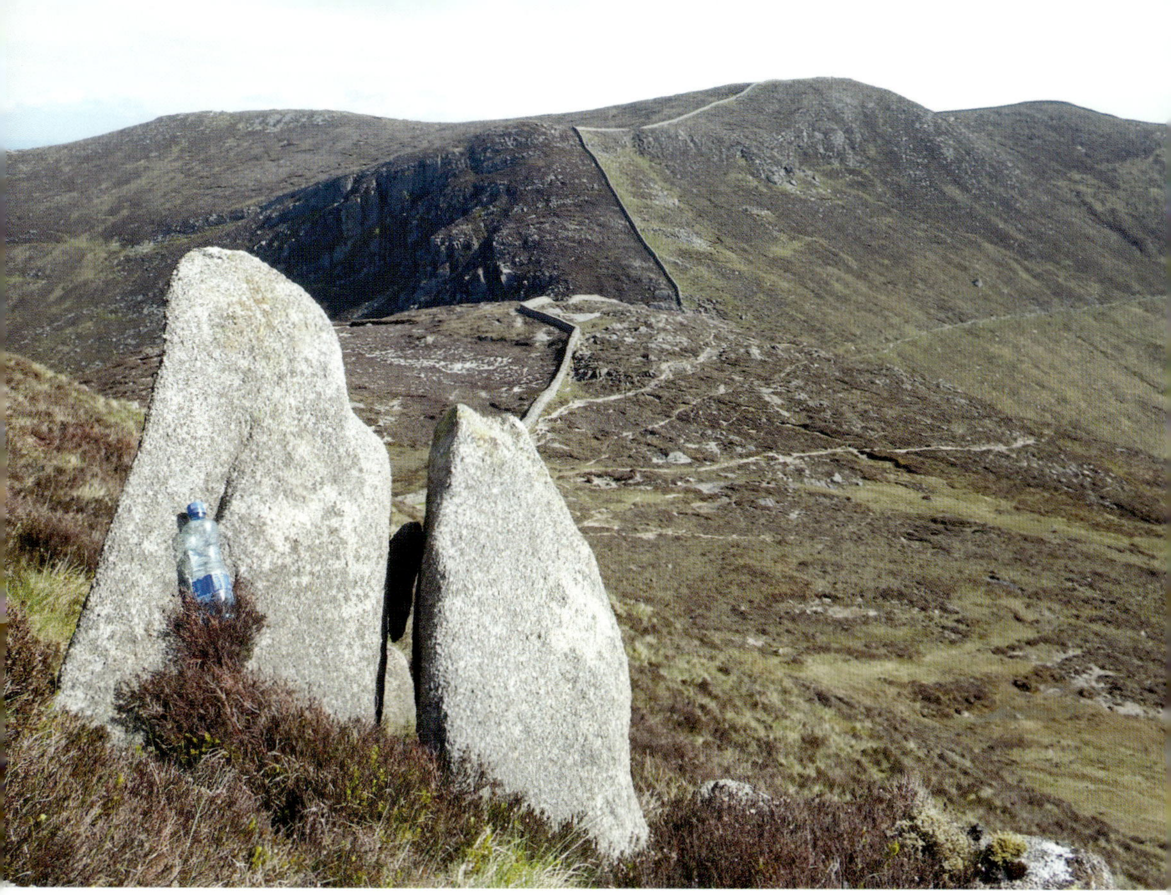

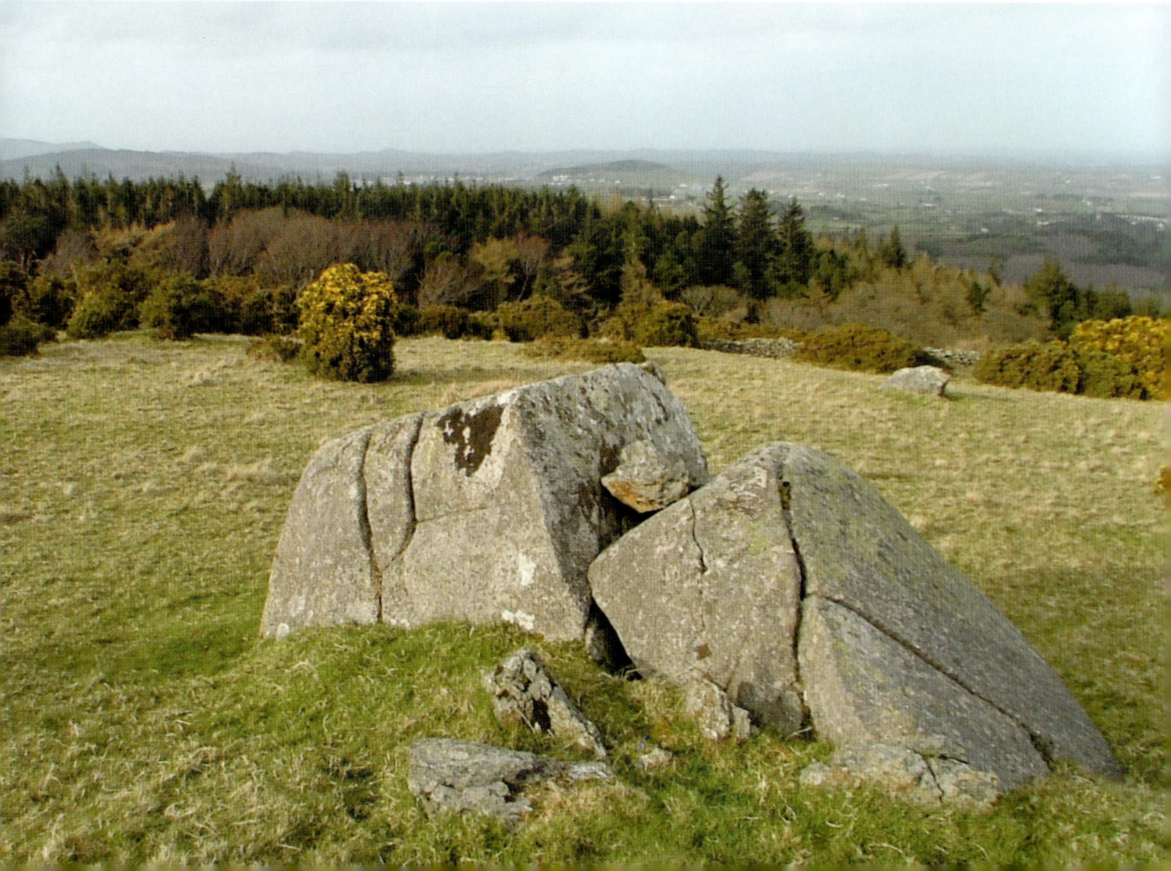

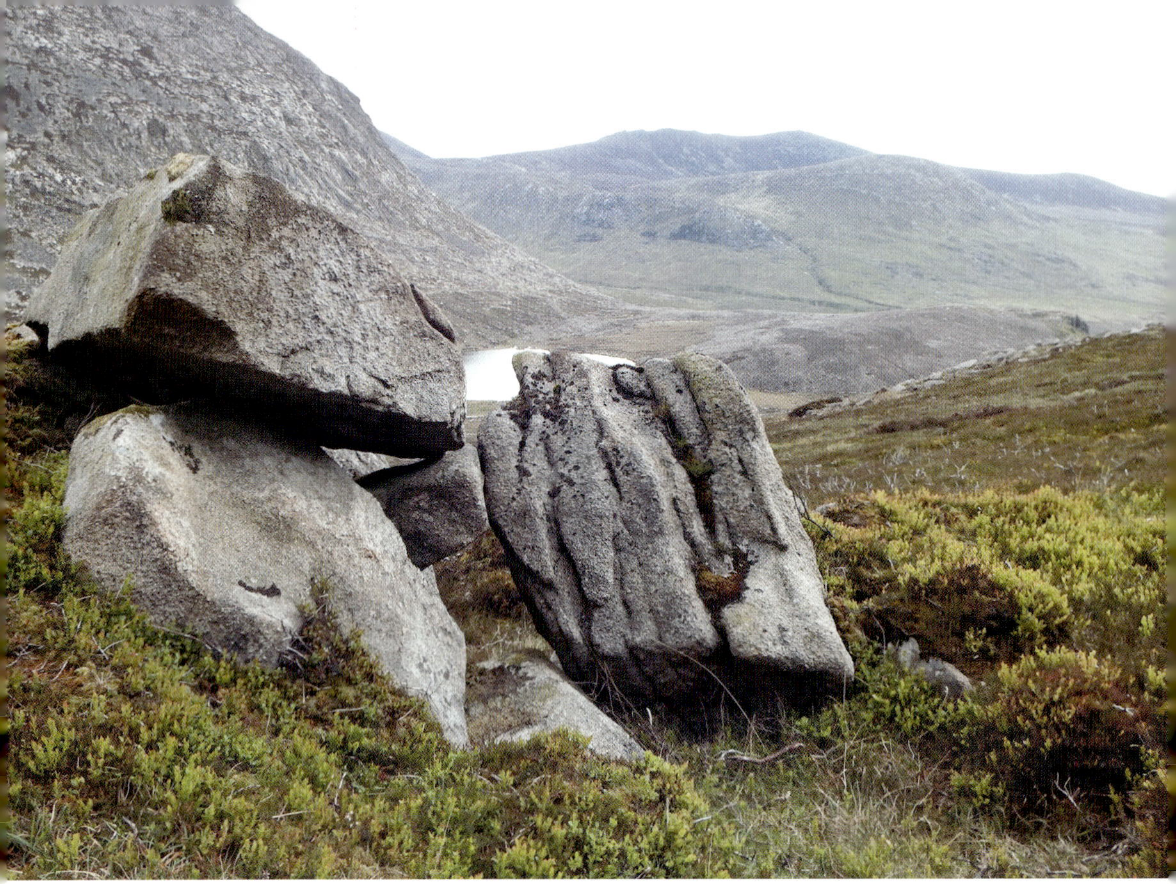

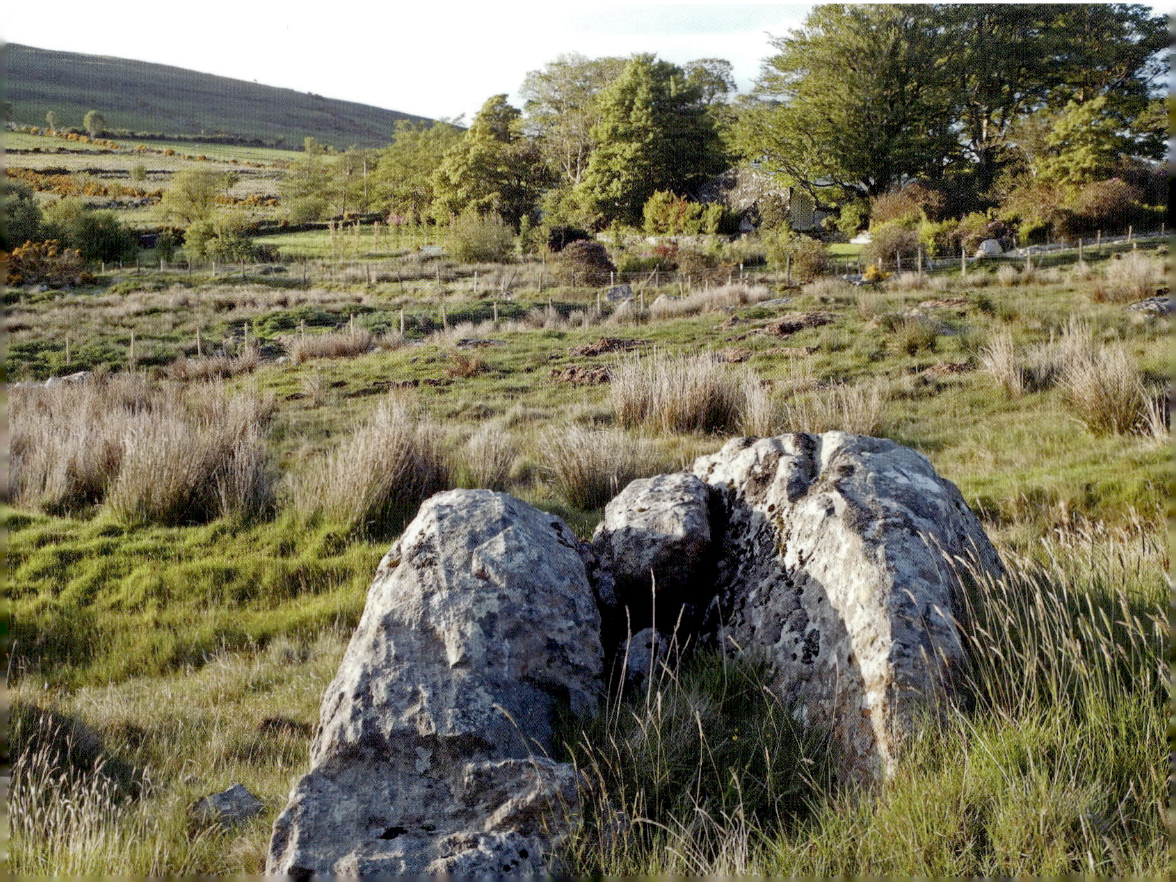

Top left: This arrangement of vagina stones under Bignian's North Tor looks to where the summer solstice sun will emerge from the womb-like side of Slieve Lamagan. The skyward looking face on the right stone is quite distinctive.

Bottom left: These compact vagina stones are on the western flank of Spelga mountain near the Kinnahalla Road.

Above: The ancients envisaged this gap on one of the Back Castle tors on Slieve Bignian's crest to be a vagina and inserted the boulder to represent a penis. There is also a small seat stone at the bottom of the gap below the boulder insertion. Speculation about the reason for the placing of the seat stone swings, inter alia, between it being as good a sheltering place for a watchman as might be found on an otherwise very exposed mountain-side, to it being a place bestowing special fertility to all those 'entering the womb' and sitting there for a while.

# Prehistoric Mourne: Inspiration for Newgrange

Above: Two stones have been inserted into this notional vaginal crack on Upper Cove cliff. A sourpuss face is on the projecting rock above them on the right; it would also cast a phallic shadow into the recess.

Right: These large vaginal stones are found on the front of Millstone mountain above the old quarry opened by John Lynn in 1824. The penile insertion points out over Dundrum Bay to St John's Point.

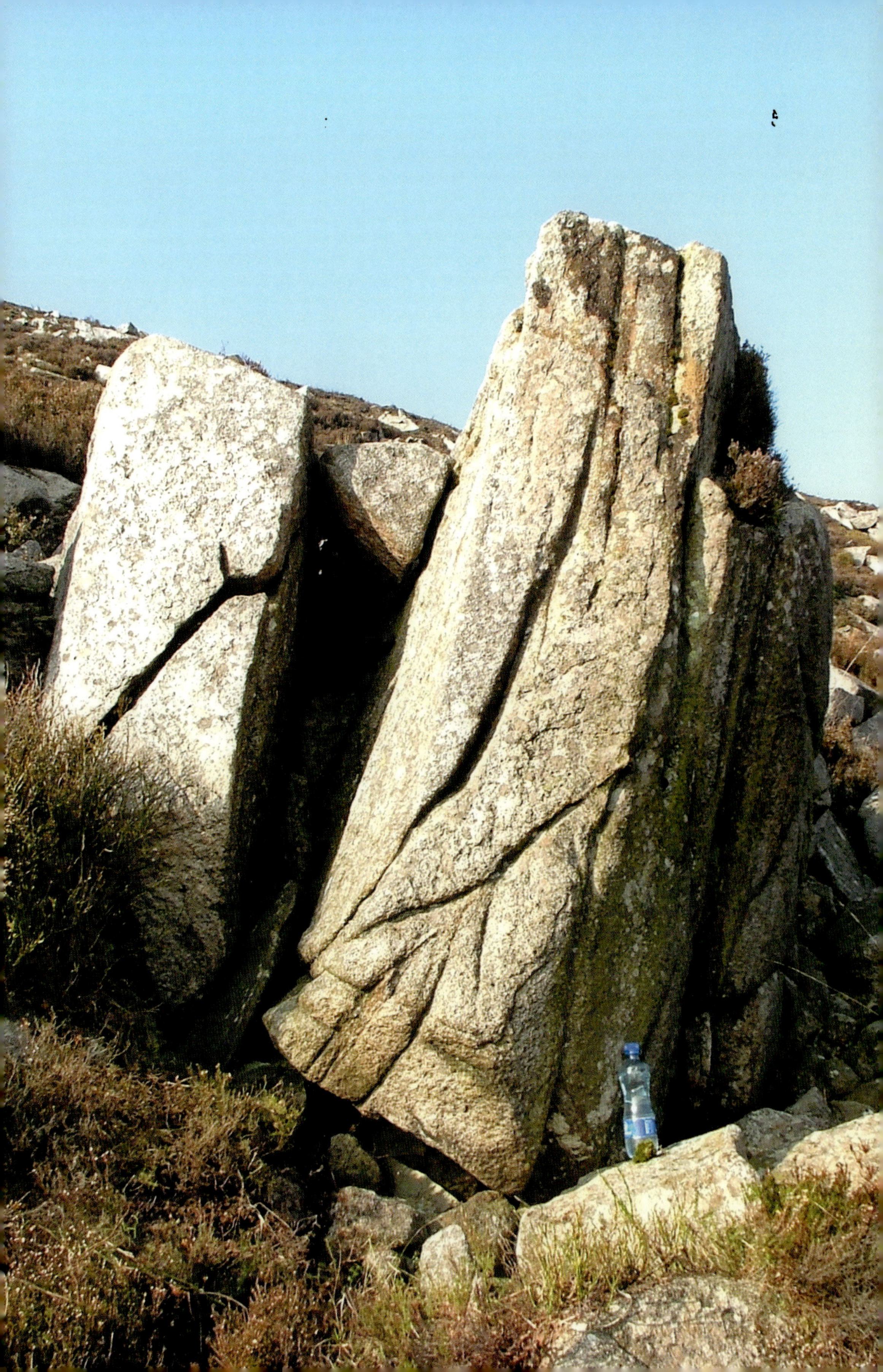

These are probably the most important pair of vagina stones in Mourne because Chimney Rock mountain gets its name from them. The name of the mountain is a mnemonic of the Irish *Shimleadh Roc*, meaning 'pretended gap' and refers to the arranged five foot gap between the summit tor on the right and the placed boulder on the left. The importance of this arranged gap becomes clear shortly after dawn on the winter solstice when the sun is seen to rise from the tip of the phallic shaped hilltop (seen here in the middle of the small photograph) to give the vaginal opening, that the gap symbolises, a fertility insemination of solar semen. So important was this auspicious conjunction of landscape and sun at the solstice that it made this mountain top a 'sanctuary' for the ancients as apparently verified by the multitude of arranged stones (burial sites?) across the summit.

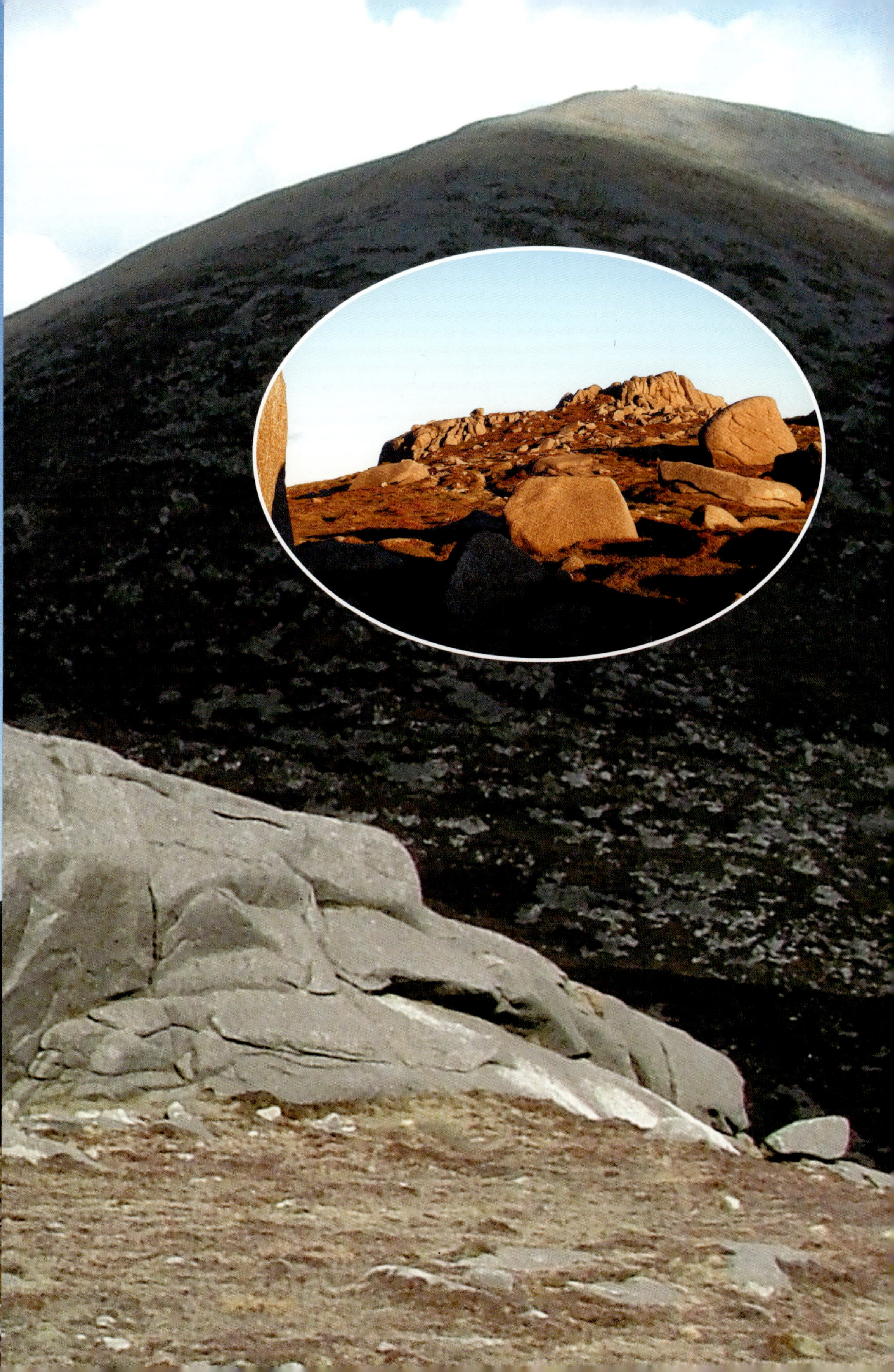

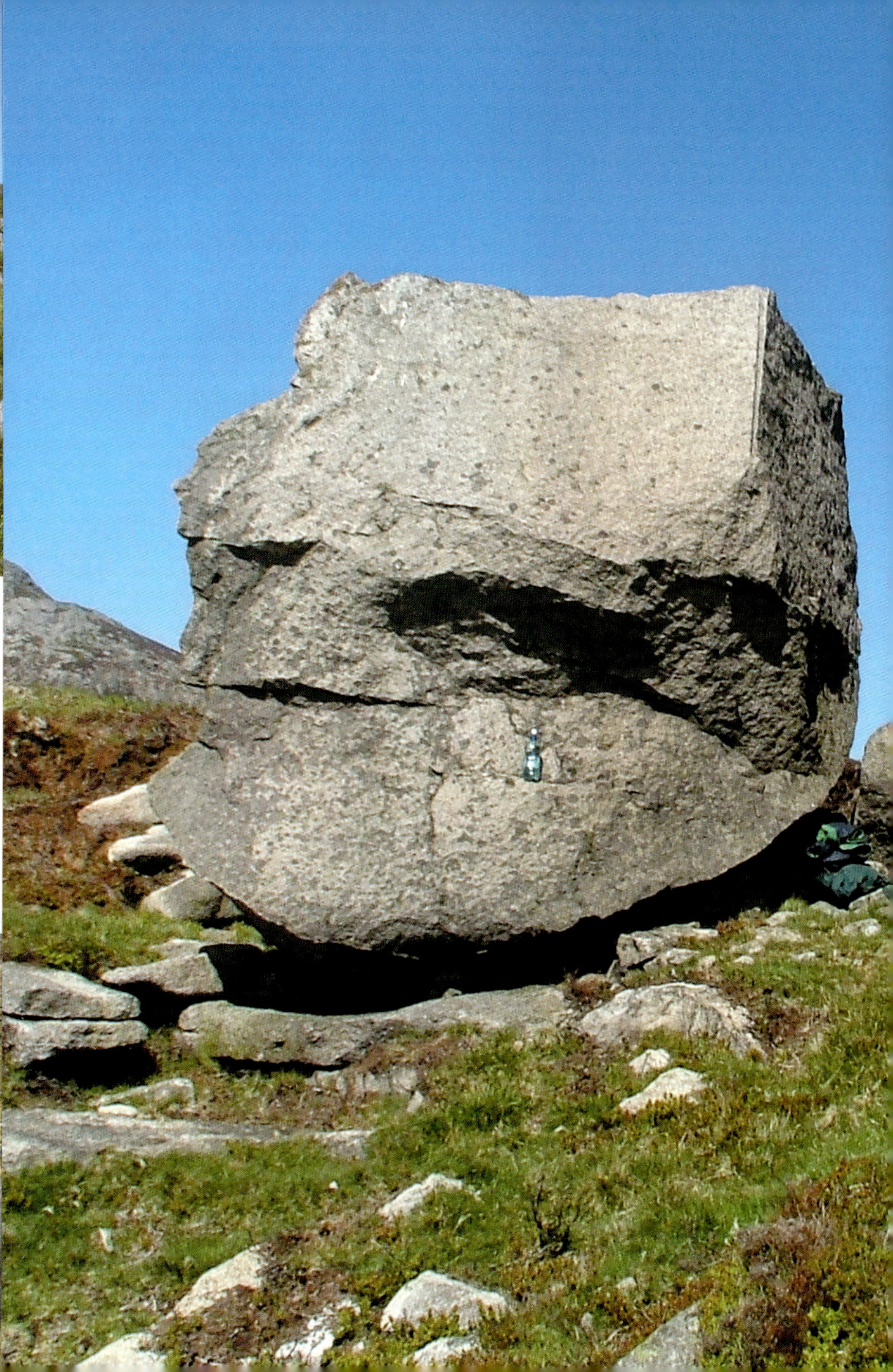

A frontal view of the vaginal stones on Douglas Crag. The size of these stones, their upright disposition, their solstice orientation and their commanding location atop the Douglas Crag cliff, mark these stones as immensely important. Also significant for chronological purposes is the visible line on the top inner corners of the stones where a long iron jumper bar was used to split them. The creation of these megaliths was not therefore in prehistoric times but anywhere from the early iron age to the hey-day of the granite men one hundred and fifty years ago. The implication is that the old religion endured in Mourne perhaps much longer after the arrival of Christianity than has been imagined.

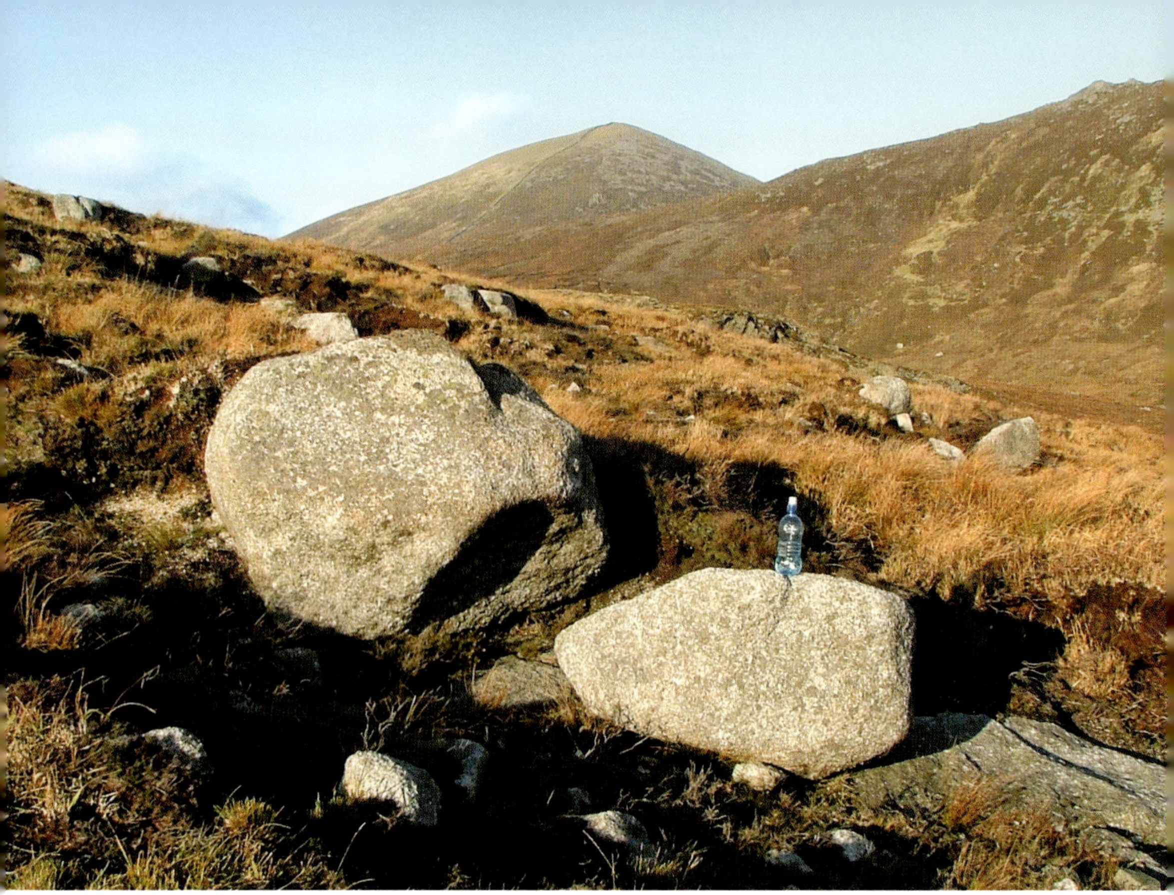

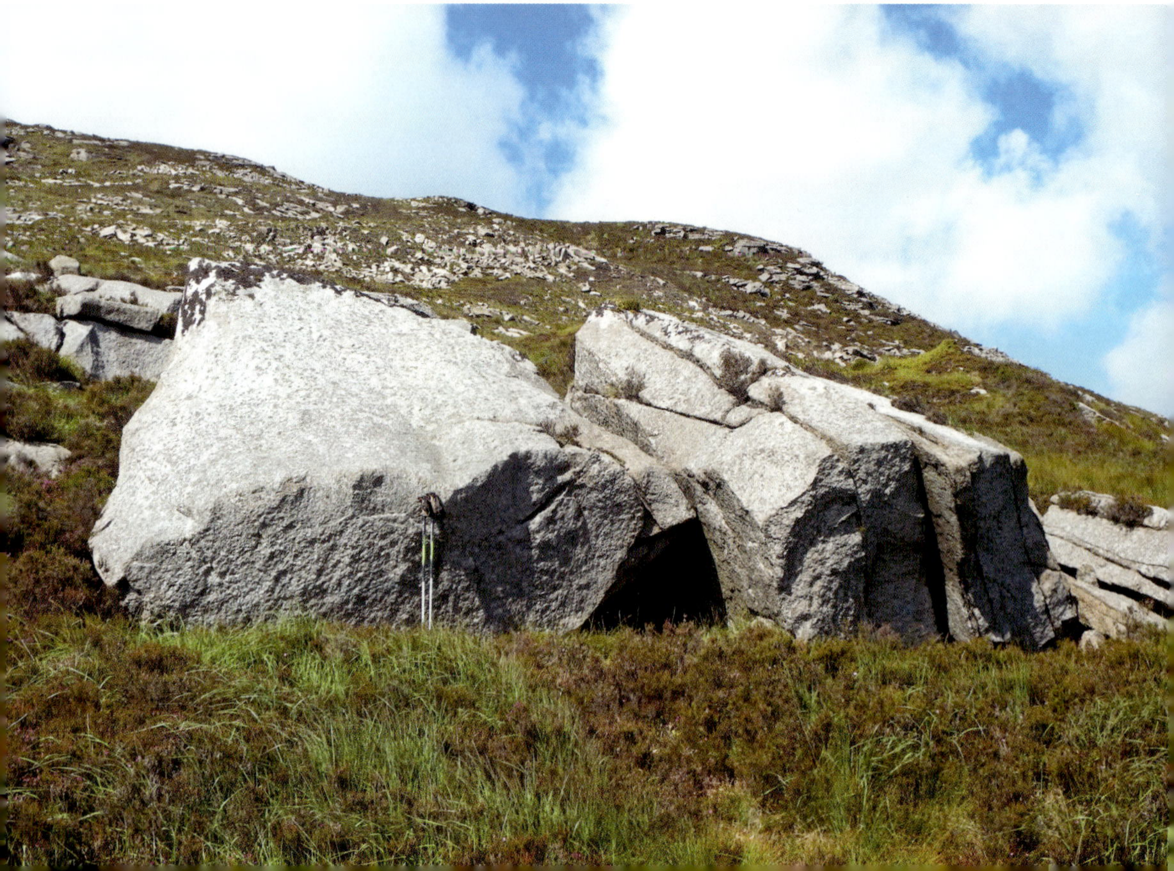

Top left: These pair of stones are found on the walk up to Rocky mountain. They are included here because one kind interpretation has it that the phallic stone on the right is addressing a vagina. The unkind interpretation is that the stones depict immanent fellatio.

Bottom left: These huge vagina stones are at the end of the Bloody Bridge valley on the left under the steep shoulder of Chimney Rock, before you come to the quarry. The opening between them awaits the penetrating fertility light of summer solstice dawn. The great size of the stones mark this as an important site, probably where the sun is to be seen rising from the top of Crossone mountain. Note the emphatic eye gash on the left-hand stone that turns it into a 'face' with a rather sharp nose.

Above: I found two granite axe-heads, left perhaps as offerings, in this vaginal split found at the back of Slievenagarragh summit under the shoulder of Chimney Rock. The opening has been carefully arranged to receive the dawn light of the winter solstice. There may be a further degree of sophistication with the angled spear stone in front of the opening; it likely has been positioned so that its tip casts a phallic shadow into the vaginal opening at the equinox, the time of planting the crops. The opening extends back for about a metre. In the foreground notice the face on the left-hand stone. Look at the cracks on the two right-hand stones to imagine eyes and mouths and look then at their positioning; what have the ancients tried to convey? (Answer on next page).

Above: This vista shot from one of Slieve Bignian's Back Castles later revealed a surprising depiction of cunnilingus on the rock face on the right. The summit of this tor, which can be seen by a great swathe of the Mourne lowlands, is covered with hammered out rock bowls meant for vigil fires lit while awaiting the solstice dawn.

Top right: The gap in this rock off the Banns Road awaits the fertility phenomenon of the summer solstice sun appearing from the top of distant Slieve Lamagan.

Bottom right: Between two of the tors on Slieve Bignian these huge vagina stones await the penetration of the early summer solstice sun cresting the gap of the tors.

Answer from page 241: The two stones have been carefully positioned to suggest they are either having a kiss or a nibble at each other. It is always worthwhile having a second look at stones to see if there could be any other purpose intended in their shapes, alignment, position or shadows. There is so much more waiting to be discovered. This book can, as it were, only open the door a fraction to the rich heritage in simple sculpted stone up in high Mourne. The ancients worked on these hills for thousands of years. There will certainly be many more treasures to be found.

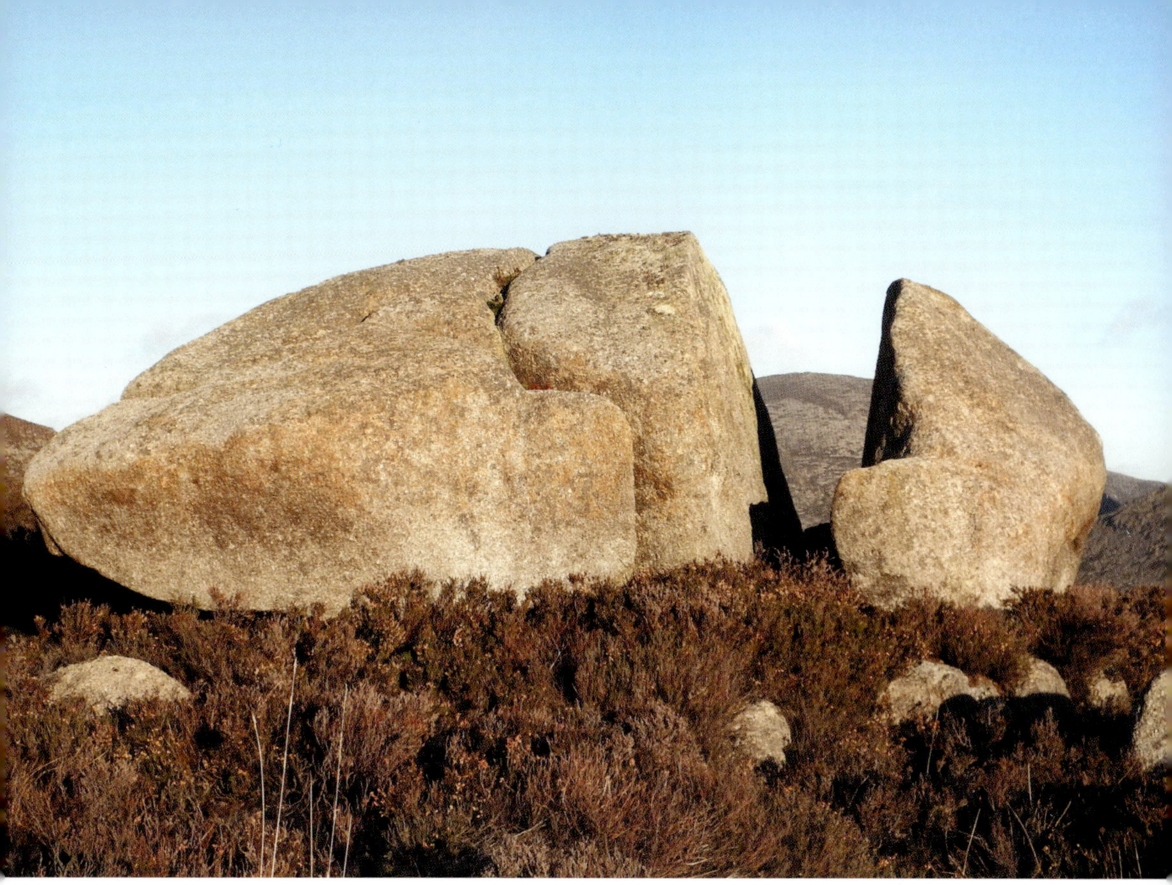

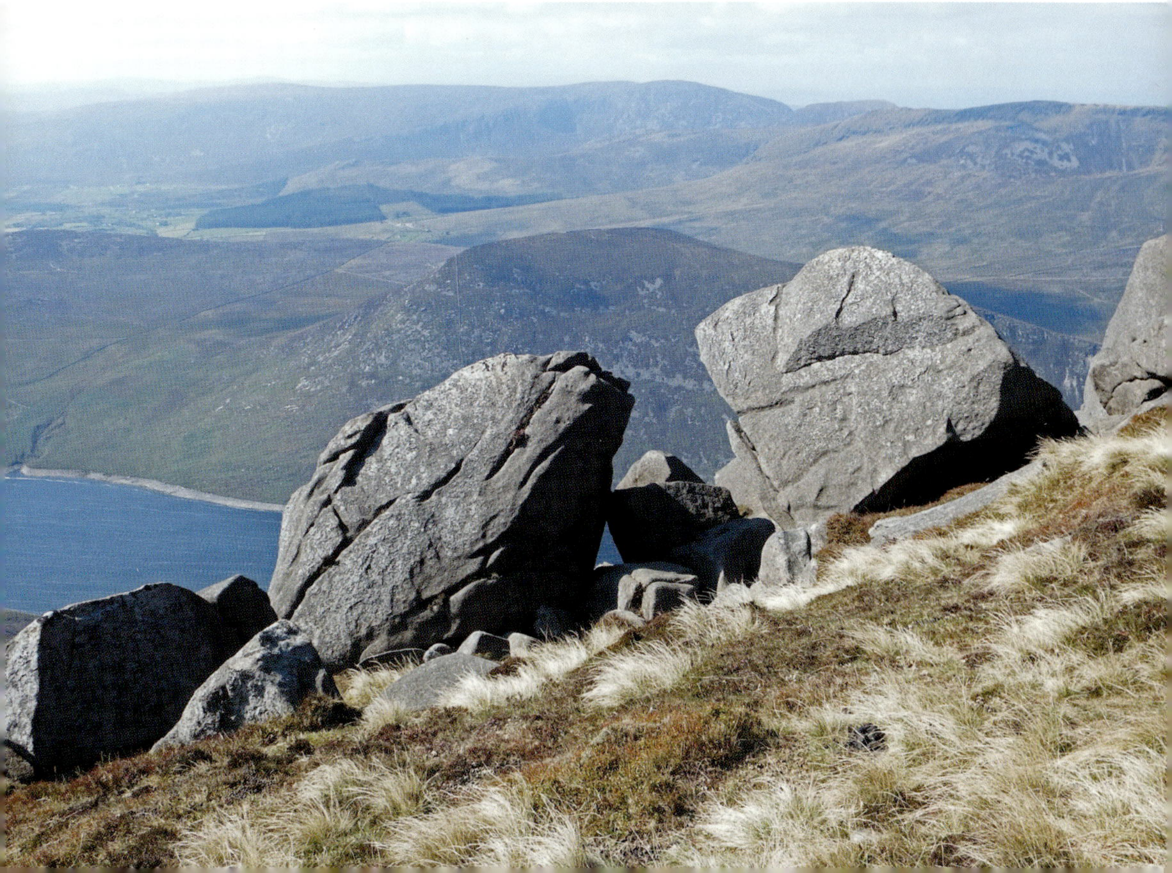

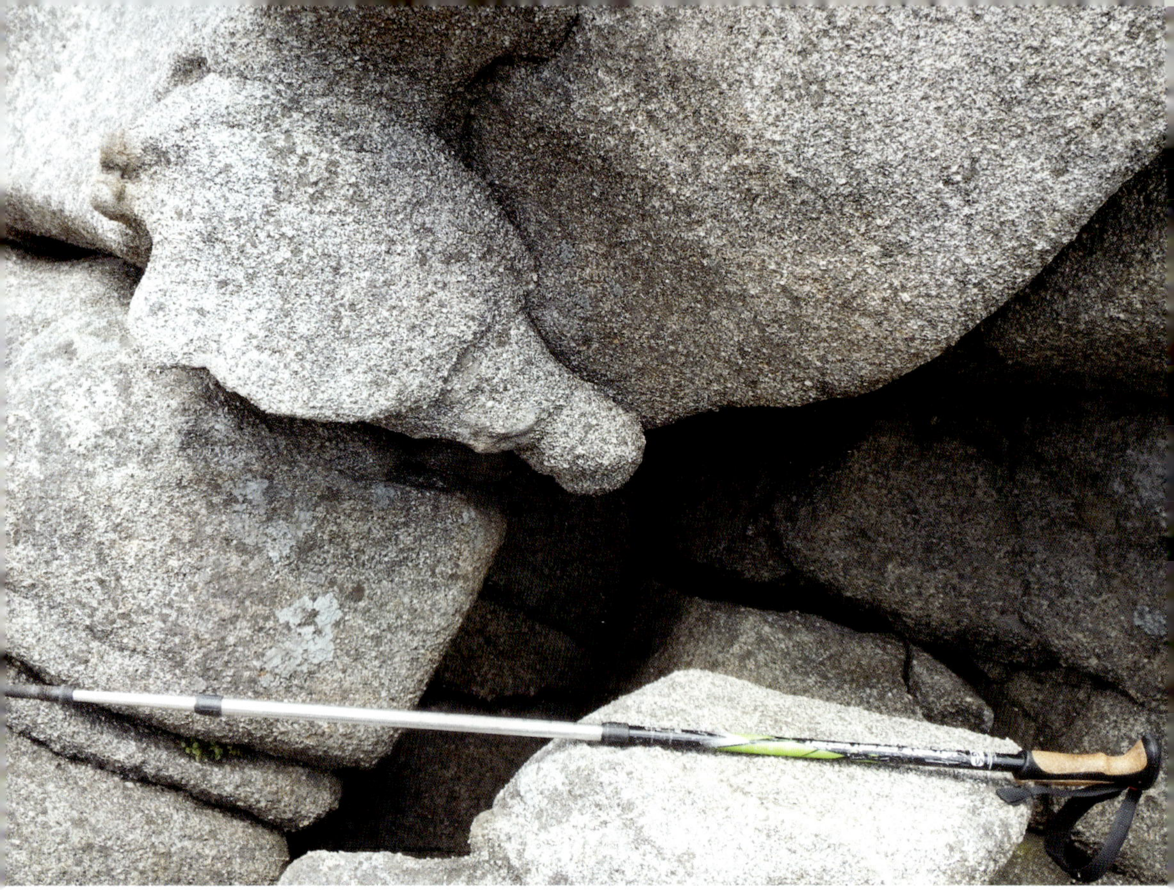
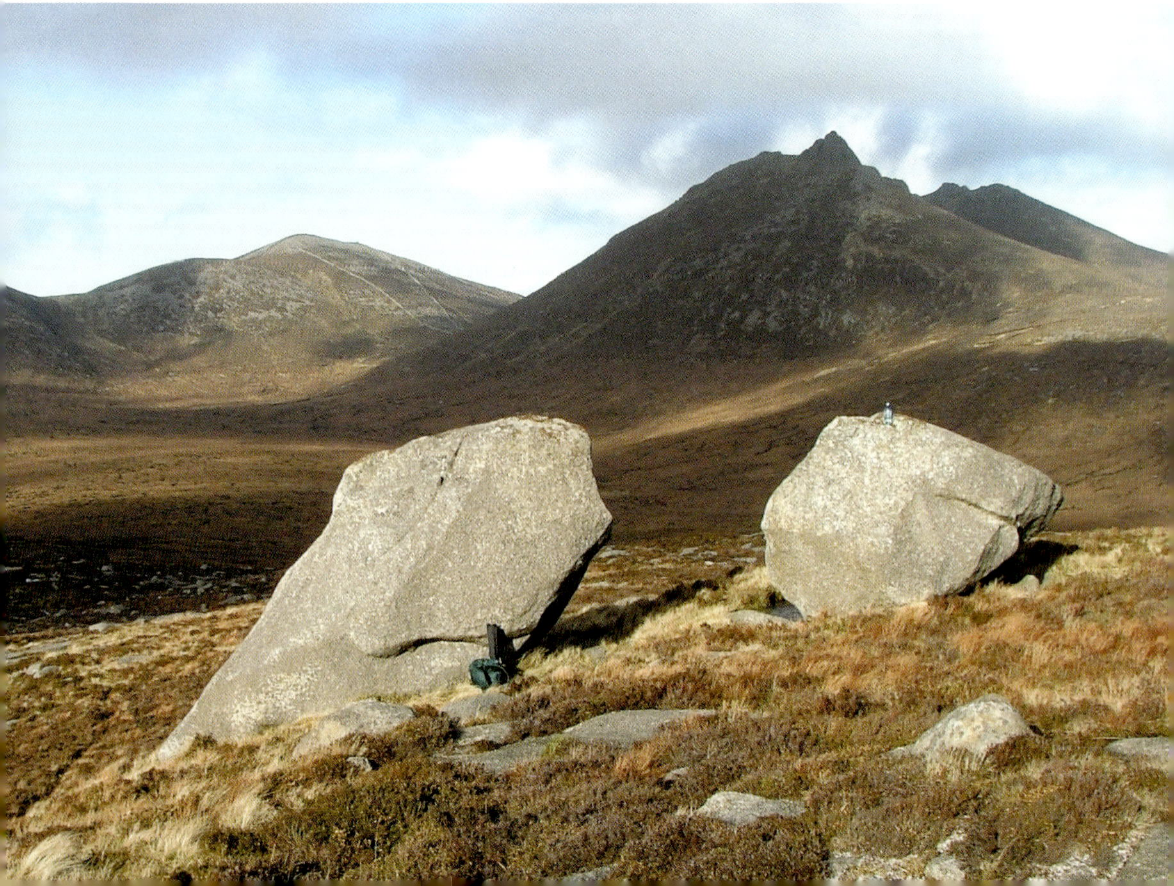

Top left: A phallic stone has been carved addressing a 'vaginal cavity' in the rock face on an outcrop on Slieve Meelbeg.

Bottom Left: Amid scenic splendour these two vaginal stones on the summit of Ben Crom, await the winter solstice sun. The solstice sun will emerge, as if from a womb, from the large gap between Slieve Bignian's north tors and penetrate the gap between these stones.

Above: In the centre, the small sunlit stone with a phallic head has been directed towards this hole near Ben Crom summit showing that the ancients interpreted this gap as a vagina. Doan mountain is in the background.

Above: This part of the river high up between Rocky mountain and Hares Castle has been treated as a vagina. The phallic spear stone in the foreground has been arranged to point at the 'menstrual flow'. A pointy nose face stone is on the right.

Top right: This split granite boulder has been deliberately placed here resting on top of shale bedrock. The reason for its placement may lie in the fact that, in the other direction, the gap between the stones is orientated on the summit of Spellack.

Bottom right: Note the shadow eyes and faces on both parts of this split boulder under Spellack. The placement of the two halves is quite suggestive of intercourse taking place and the orientation of the gap between the stones is aligned towards summer solstice sunrise.

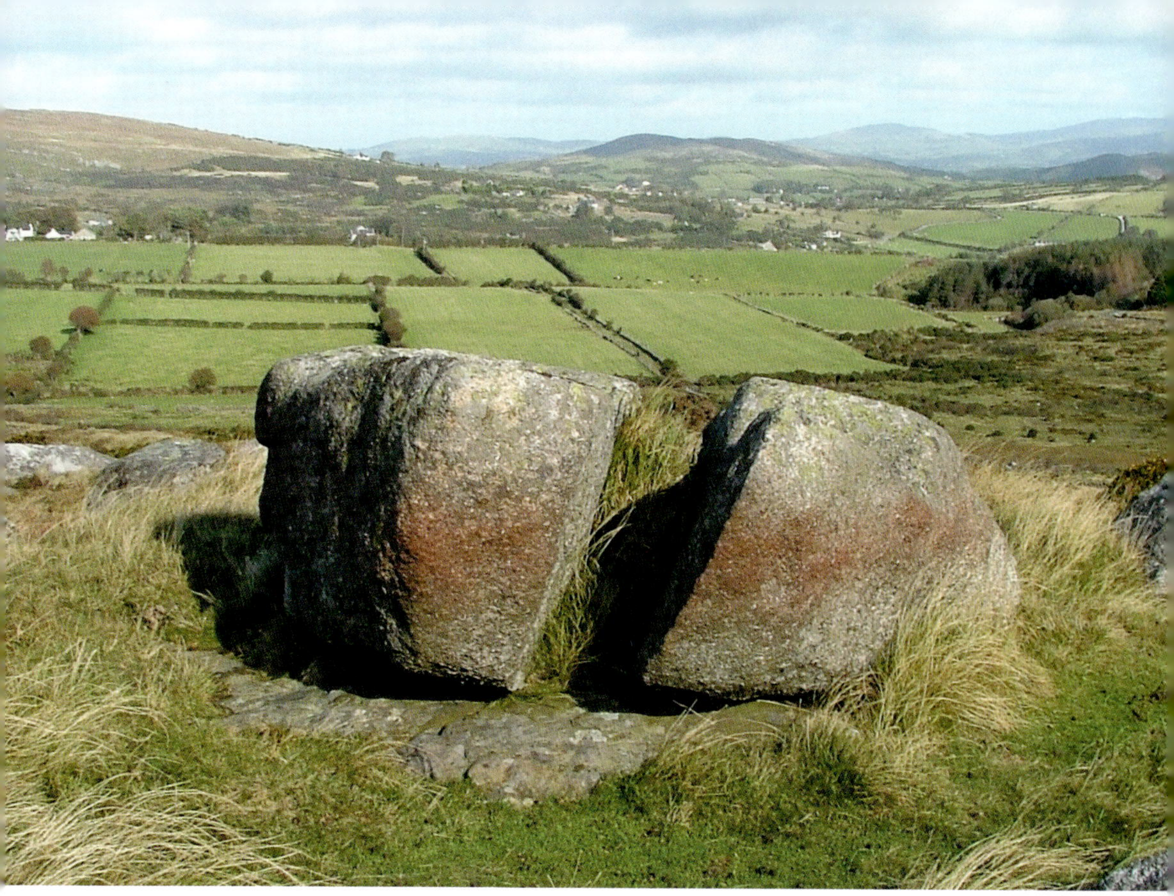

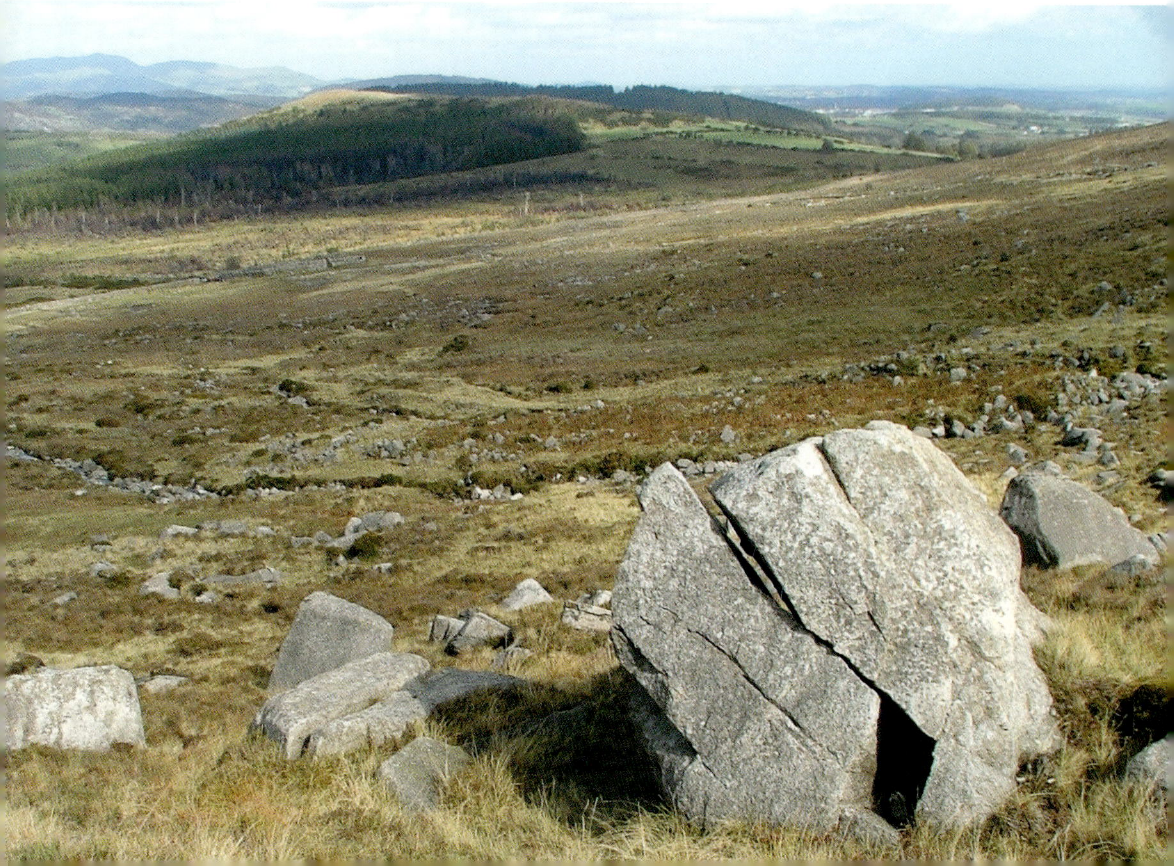

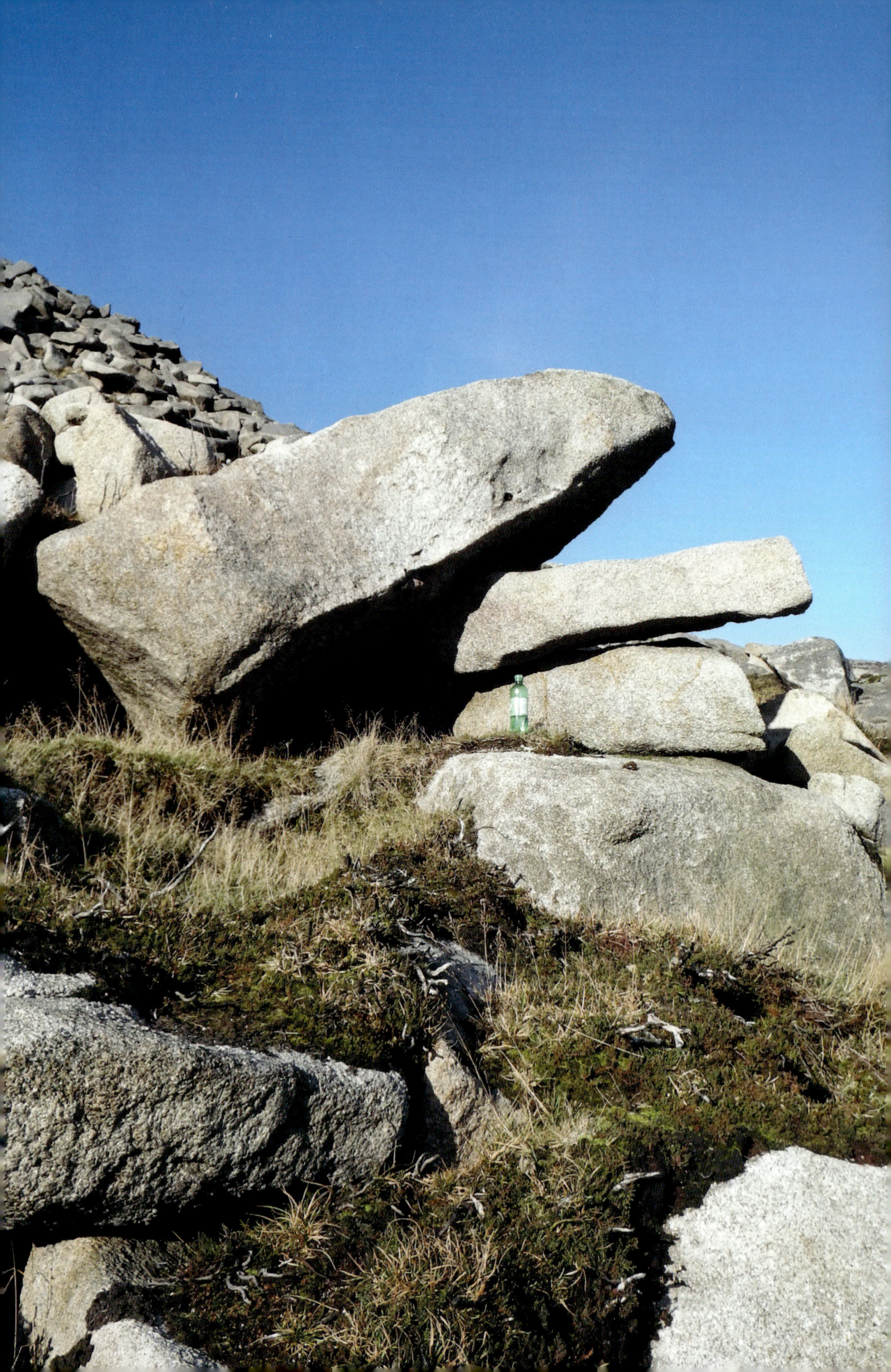

# BEGETTING STONES

After looking at phallic spear stones and vagina stones, we look now at some of the fertility stones marking procreation. *Gein* is the word in Irish for 'the act of begetting, being born.' The plural in Irish is *geinte,* and this has frequently been rendered in English as 'giant'. Thus we have the Giant's Causeway, Giant's tables, Giant's graves and a plethora of Giant's stones of which the best known one locally would be the Giant's Stone high on the slopes of Altnadua (OS J313353) a couple of miles outside Castlewellan. The name of the hill, Altnadua, gets its name from the megalith, in particular from the hollow on the bottom front of the stone which was similar to notches on stone axes where the wooden handle would be hafted to it. Altnadua hill is from the Irish *Alt na dTuagha*, 'the height of the axe'.[1] The act of begetting that bestowed the Irish *geinte* on the stone, which in turn became 'giant' in English, occurs at winter solstice dawn. It is from the Giant's Stone on Altnadua hill that the sun could be seen rising from the rounded 'pregnant' summit of Burrenreagh Hill. This was the sun being born from the earth to begin anew its life-giving cycle. A similar explanation connected with surrounding topography probably lies behind the Giant's Grave at Tollymore. It is also referred to as 'The King's Grave' and this is very likely a mnemonic from the Irish *Cian Greah*, meaning 'the distant ejaculation'.[2] The existing forest, however, presently precludes further explanation.

Like many of the place-names of Mourne the name of the Giant's Causeway has eluded understanding because the importance of the early religion of fertility which gave great prominence to the sun was not appreciated. We mention the Causeway coast here as an indication that the ancient fertility culture was not confined to Mourne but extended along the east and north coasts of Ulster. Forget all the fanciful blather of Finn Mac Cool building a causeway across the north channel so that he could fight his Scottish counterpart, Benandonner. There is certainly a geological connection between the coasts but such stories point up a certain desperation to try and explain how the name came about. There are a couple of Irish names in existence for the Giants Causeway, namely *Clochán an Aifir* and *Clochán na bhFómharach*, meaning respectively 'The pavement or stones of reproach' and 'The pavement of the Fomorians'. However, the real Irish name is to be found as a mnemonic of the present English. There are no written sources to verify it but the name of the Giant's Causeway is a phonetic simulation of the Irish (*Tí na*) *Geinte Cuais buidhe,* meaning '(The place of) the act of begetting of the

The small green water bottle scarcely conveys the huge size of the top phallic stone simulating the act of procreation. This megalithic creation is on the eastern shoulder of Slieve Lamagan, above the path leading from Lower Cove to Upper Cove.

PREHISTORIC MOURNE: INSPIRATION FOR NEWGRANGE

The hollow at the bottom of the Giant's Stone was reminiscent of a notch to haft a handle onto a stone axe and thus was the origin of the name Altnadua, from the Irish *Alt na dTuagha*, 'the height of the axe'.

The early summer solstice shadow cast by this decidedly phallic pillar gave the Causeway its name in Irish, namely (*Tí na*) *Geinte Cuais buidhe*, '(The Place of) the act of begetting of the sunny hollow'.

sunny hollow'. The action that verifies the name takes place at dawn of the summer solstice when the rising sun catches the high pillar headland at this part of the coast and casts its phallic shadow into the side of the bay between the cliffs as if penetrating the recess in the act of procreation. The phallic shadow didn't sit well with early Christianity who distained the phallic projection as a source of shame, hence the later name *Clochán an Aifir*, 'the pavement of reproach'.

Also at the Giant's Causeway is a large boulder on the rocky shore known as 'the Giant's Boot'. It is a great favourite with the tourists and the surface has acquired a shiny patina from the many who queue up to sit on it and have their photograph taken. I dare say they would be rather surprised to know they are sitting on an ancient fertility stone selected by the ancients for its upright phallic shape. It should be noted that the background cliff swells out greatly like a great pregnancy and we may imagine the ancients regarded the appearance of the summer solstice sun at the top of the swollen cliff as an auspicious birth from this earthly womb. The fertility nature of the Giant's Boot stone was clear in the original Irish for the name is only a mnemonic for (*Clogh na*) *Geinte Bod*, meaning '(The stone of) the begetting (ie. erect) penis'.

The popular Giant's Boot at the Giant's Causeway is a fertility stone. The name comes from the Irish *Geinte Bod*, 'the erect penis'. In the background the cliff swells out like a great pregnant womb and the megalith marks where the 'birth' of the sun from this womb can be seen at dawn of summer solstice.

Above: A panoramic view of the Mournes from the Giant's Stone on Altnadua hill. The site of the stone marks where the winter solstice sun is 'born' from the summit swelling that is Burrenreagh hill (out of sight to left of photograph).

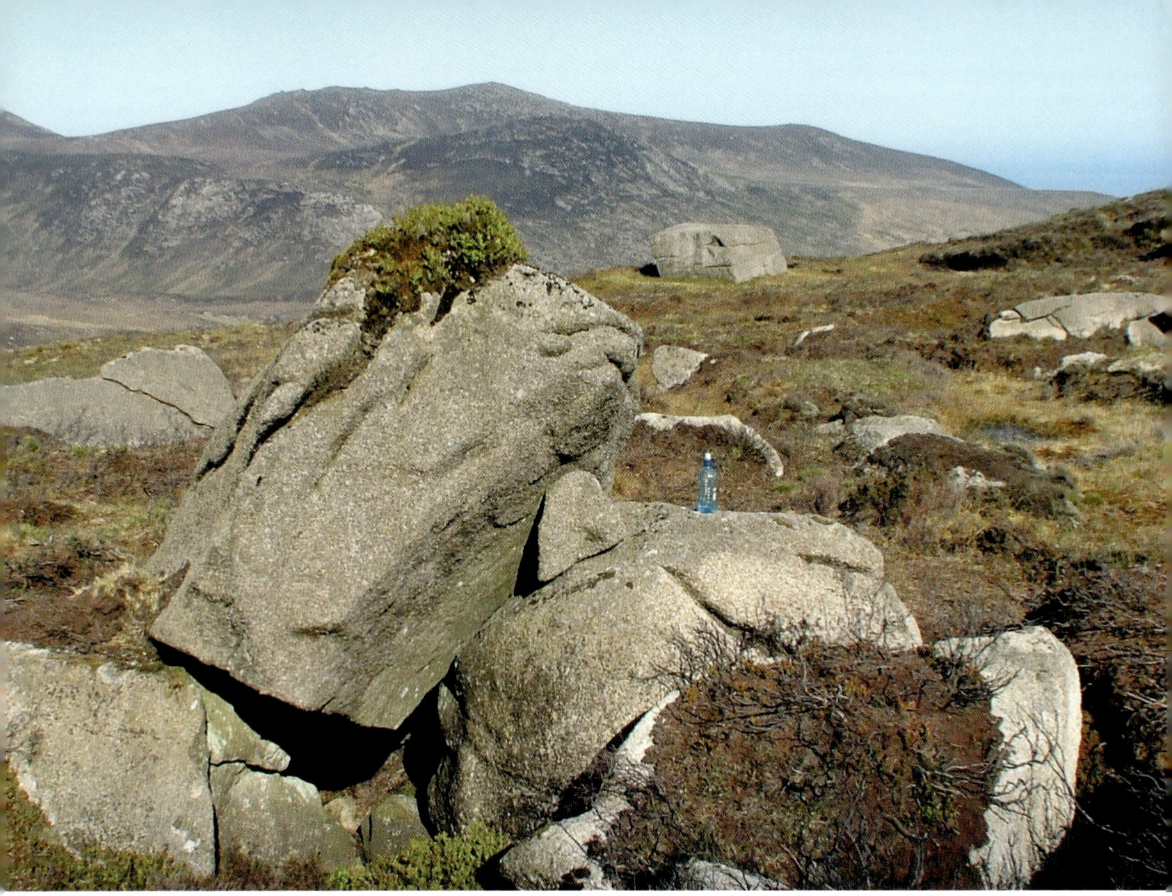
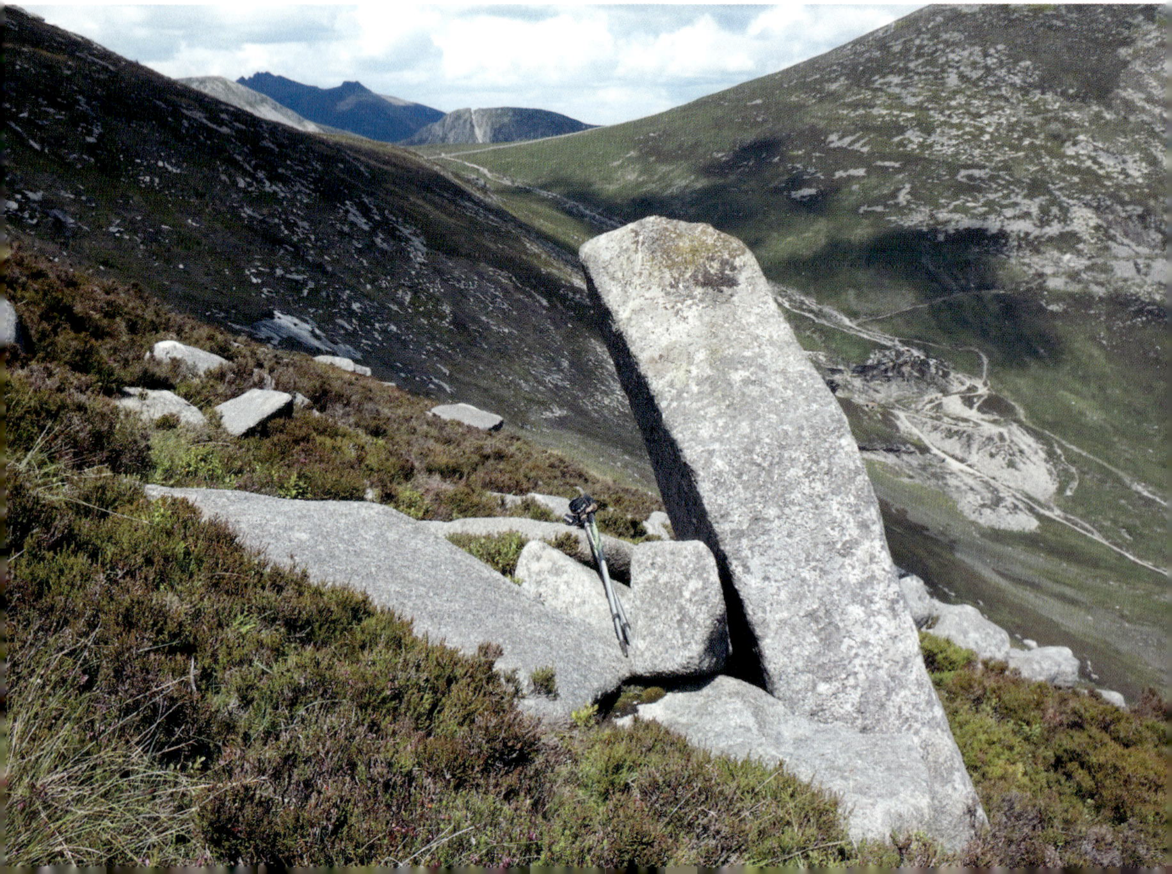

Top left: These large copulating stones are found on the path from Bignian Lough to the col between Bignian and Lamagan, under Buzzard's Roost cliff. Also noteworthy is the formidably large diamond shaped megalith in the middle background, one of the points of which looks to where the summer solstice sun sets between Slieve Bearnagh and Slieve Lamagan.

Bottom left: On the slope of Chimney Rock mountain this spear megalith points to where the winter solstice sun disappears behind the hillside above.

Above: This monument of 'The Lovers' is on the slopes of Chimney Rock mountain. It is a wonderful work of conceptual art. The stones are also arranged to ensure fertility as the gap between the 'bodies' is only fully penetrated at the time of the summer solstice dawn. This photo was taken at 9.30am on 12th April, but already the sun has moved well round.

Simulated copulation under Upper Cove cliff.

A phallic stone under Spellack looks towards Slievenaglogh. In the background is Clanawhillan Hill.

Like the arrangement of The Lovers this pair of stones is found on Chimney Rock and also carefully placed to receive the early summer solstice sun in the gap between.

The same pair of stones five hours later; the sun now highlights the phallic appendage that confirms the begetting nature of the megalith.

This trio of stones in the act of begetting is found above the path from Cove to Upper Cove; note how the smallest megalith is crying out.

More stones arranged in the act of begetting, this time on the south facing slope of Chimney Rock.

These stones, preparing for intercourse, are found in the megalith rich area under Spellack in the Trassey valley.

On the slopes of Slieve Bearnagh's north tor, this act of copulation depicts the smaller stone crying out.

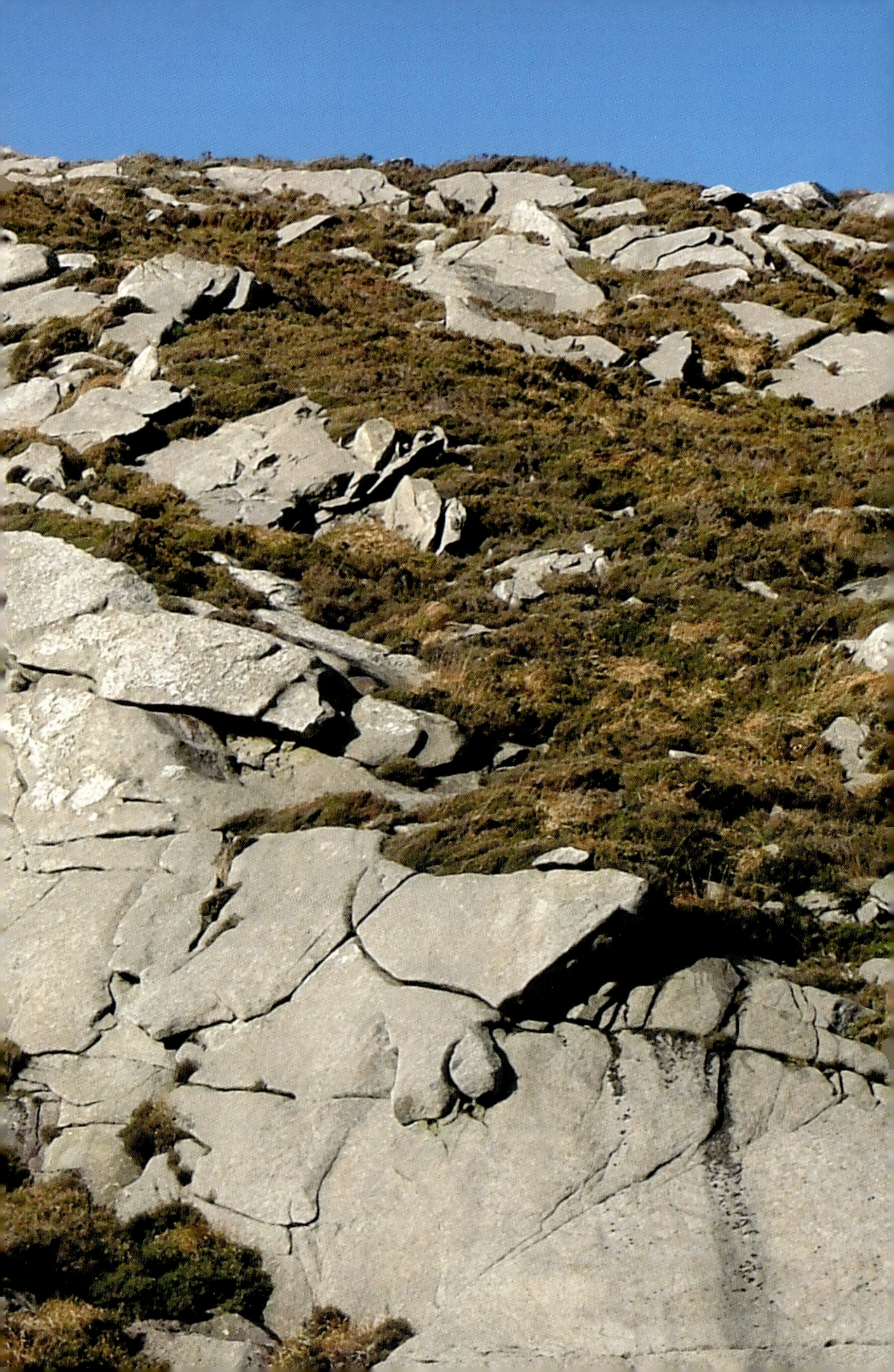

Opposite: First note the natural drainage tracks on the bottom right. The ancients exploited this feature to suggest abundant fertility through perpetual ejaculation when they reshaped the rock face as spear shaped male genitalia complete with two distinctive testicles. This rock sculpture is on the slope of Slieve Meelmore in Pollaphuca valley.

This page: A marvellous begetting creation on the shoulder of Slieve Lamagan nearest Percy Bysshe hill. I refer to these stones as 'The Tease' because, despite the obvious large size and tilt of the begetting stone, it has most precisely and delicately been left a mere 4cm from the stone to be serviced.

Above: An act of begetting stone on the heights of Thomas mountain overlooking Newcastle. Note the circular eye hammered in the face stone behind it.

Top right: This substantial stone, of phallic import, projects prominently on the slope of Chimney Rock mountain.

Bottom right: The reverse side of the same megalith reveals it to be an impressive *Gein* stone depicting a remarkable resemblance of a pair of mating seals with the mouth of the top male agape in sexual rictus. This side of the stone faces north-east directly towards summer solstice sunrise which occurs at 4.45am. Already at 9.58am on 24th July when this photograph was taken, this side of the stone is about to pass into the shade.

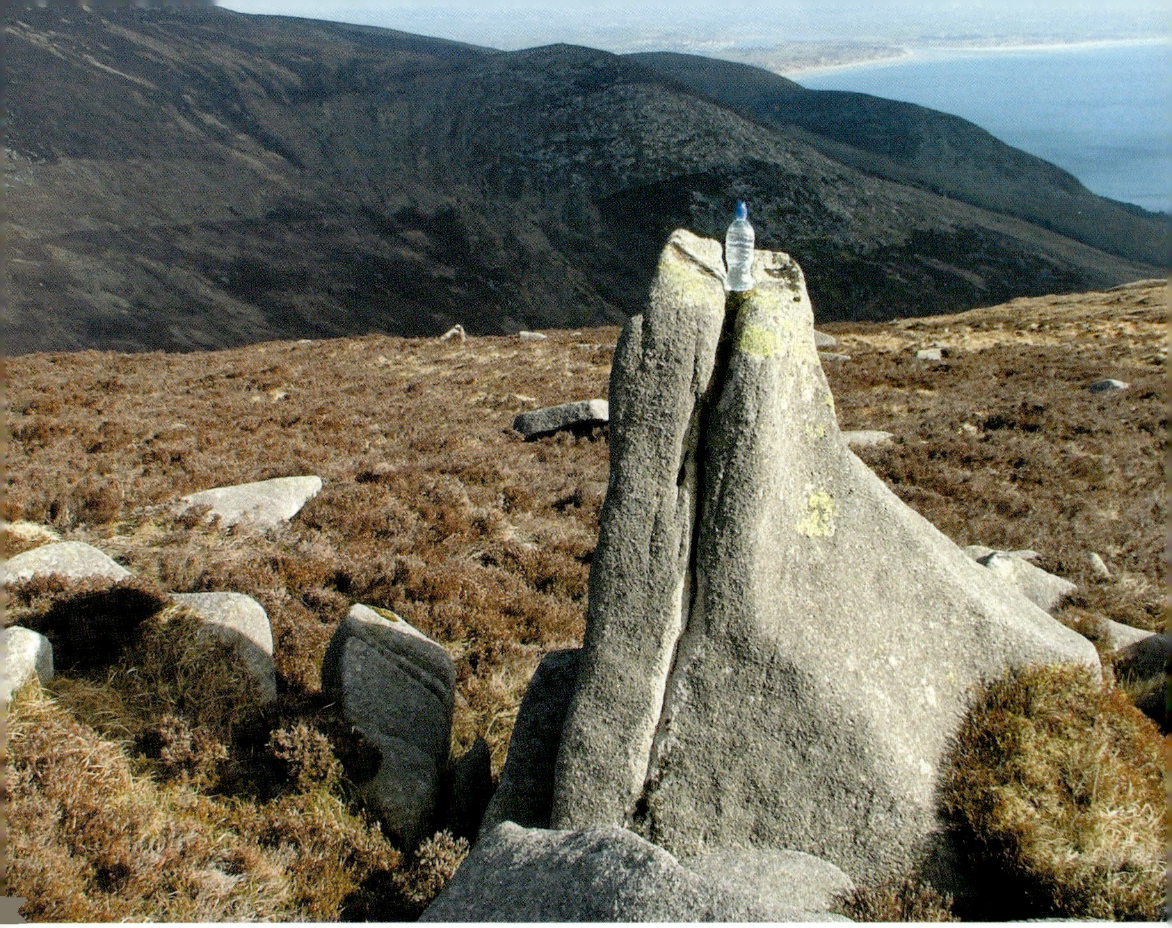

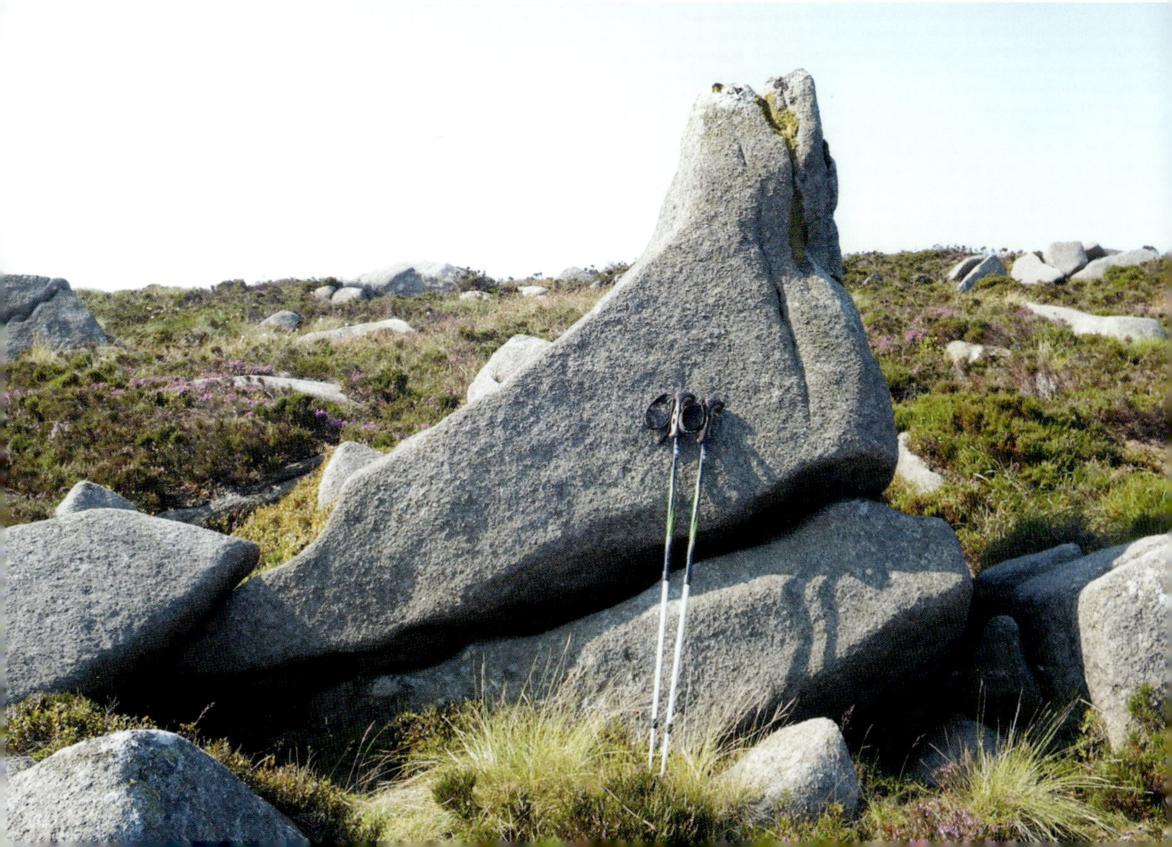

*The lower stone cries out in this close-up of the great Meelmore megalith first shown on page 114/115.*

*Rock infusions have been cleverly employed on the slopes of Slieve Bearnagh's north tor to create erect penises with emphatic corona.*

We earlier referred to the Causeway coast to show that the ancient fertility culture was not confined to Mourne but extended along the east and north coasts of Ulster. The names of quite a few places along Ireland's north east coast bear evidence of being derived from a fertility interpretation of the landscape. Annagassan in County Louth is a small sea-side village looking out onto Dundalk Bay. The name of the village is from the Irish *An-all Gasán*[3], meaning literally 'very great stalk'. The 'stalk' in this case was the projecting headland of the Cooley peninsula on the far side of Dundalk Bay which was envisaged as a monstrous penis. About a mile or so north of

262

Like a bull servicing a cow, these begetting stones on the lower slopes of Rocky mountain (OS J3525) are a classic example of the genre. They will be found when approaching Rocky mountain from the Quarter Road and past Long Seefin.

Annagassan is Jenkinstown where early man built a fort. Here in Mourne we have a similar name at Jenkin's Point, Glasdrumman, (OS J3822). Both are derived from the Irish *Gein Cian*, meaning 'the long distance act of begetting'. In County Louth the name comes from the dawn sun at summer solstice arising from the end of the Cooley 'penis' in a notional moment of ejaculation, as seen from distant Jenkinstown across Dundalk Bay. Similarly in Mourne, the distance act of begetting is the dawn sun of summer solstice arising from the end of St. John's Point headland as seen from Jenkin's Point on the far side of Dundrum Bay. A bit further south from Jenkin's Point we have Janet's Rock near Ballymartin (OS J353169); this name is derived from the Irish *Geineadh Roc*, 'the act of begetting hollow' although the interpretation of how the name came about is not so simple. The name might possibly come from the winter solstice sun being seen to set at the end of Lee Stone Point (OS J3314), but more likely from the shadow of nearby Black Rock casting a penile fertility shadow into the tiny bay at winter solstice dawn something akin to the headland at the Giant's Causeway casting its fertility shadow into the 'sunny hollow', the *Cuais buidhe*, only there it happens at summer solstice dawn.

263

Place-names in the vicinity of Belfast Lough also saw the landscape being interpreted in a sexual manner.[4] Holywood, on the south shore of Belfast Lough, had an early monastery founded by saint Laisrén son of Nasca before 640. The present ruins of the medieval Old Priory at the junction of High Street and the old Bangor Road were believed to be built on the site of Laisrén's previous foundation. Laisrén probably chose the site for his monastery to claim the place from the pagans for Christianity. The ancients had looked across Belfast Lough from Holywood and regarded the long substantial north side of the Lough as a huge penis. What made St Laisrén's site special to the pagans was that it was from here that the sun could be seen rising at the end of the 'penile' north shore at dawn of summer solstice at what is now Whitehead.[5] Mention of the name Holywood is found around the year 1275 in accounts on the great rolls of the pipe of the Irish exchequer. It is a mnemonic of the Irish (*Tí na*) *h-Olla Buid*, meaning '(Place of the) great penis'.

On the other side of the Lough, Carrickfergus received its name from a sexual understanding of the landscape. Place-names of Northern Ireland attribute the name to *Carraig Fhearghasa*, 'Fergus's Rock' after Fergus son of Eirc, founder of the kingdom of Dalriada. Other authorities maintained that the name of the town came from *Carraig na fairrge*, 'Rock of the sea'.[6] Certainly the Anglo-Norman knight John de Courcy built his castle on the 'rock of Fergus' in 1177. Carrickfergus is from the Irish *Carraig Fir Guis* where a sexual construct was originally put on the volcanic dyke sticking out into the waters of Belfast Lough; the rock on which the castle would be built. *Carraig Fir Guis* means 'the rock of the man of vigour', a reference to a manhood aroused. It was this phallic rock sticking out into the sea, on which the castle would be built, that gave the town its name.

Like English, Irish has numerous words for the male sexual organ a number of which, because they appear in the names of Mourne, are noted here. There is *Biach*, which Dinneen's dictionary, out of an abundance of sensitivity, delicately explained in Latin as, '*membrum virile*'. *Biach* is often rendered in English as the mnemonic 'back' and so we have the 'Back Castles' and also the slang name for the Mourne Wall given to it by its builders, namely 'the Back Ditch' from the Irish *Biach Dúithir*.[7] The Irish *Slat*, meaning normally 'a rod, switch or wand' is used in an obscene sense and this, as mentioned in chapter two, is behind the real meaning of Slievenaslat at Castlewellan, and 'The Slates' (OS J2423) under Eagle Mountain. Similar in meaning was the Irish word *Fé*, meaning 'a measuring rod'. The rod became a euphemism for the phallus and the word is found in the present

Interpreting the landscape sexually happened also in North Antrim. This natural rock spike of dolerite at Fair Head is at the entrance to the famous 'vaginal gully' known as the Grey Man's Path (illustrated in previous chapter). Fair Head is a mnemonic from the Irish *Fir Ead*, meaning 'being jealous of the man'. The main contender for the name must be a large upward thrusting block at the base of the cliff as seen from Ballycastle but this well endowed pillar is also a worthy example of the name.

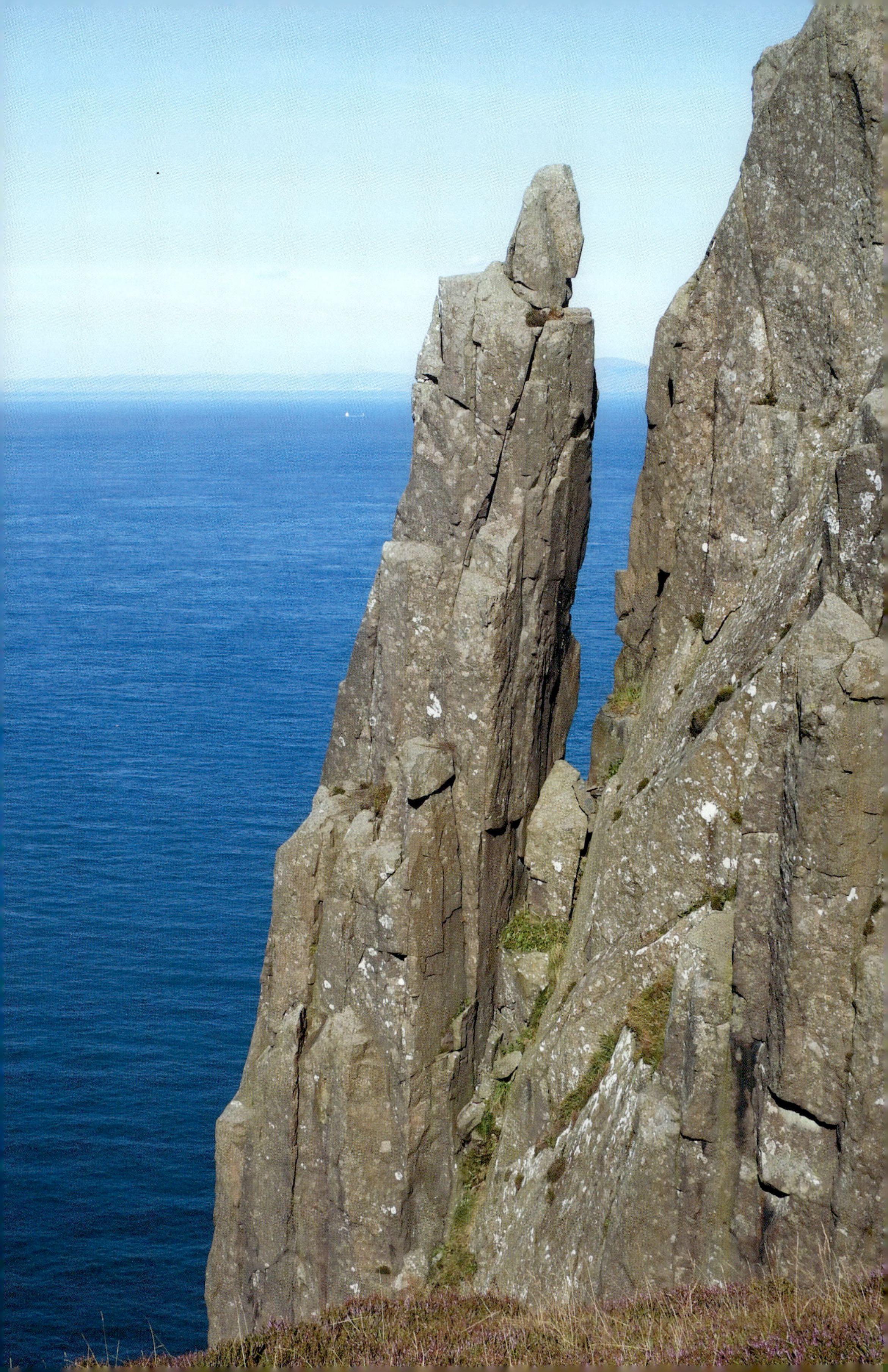

*These important begetting stones are on a little isolated mound in the old Drinneevar quarry, seen here in the background. They were known as* Braighde a eibhear óg a geinte, *literally 'prisoners of the new granite of the act of begetting'. On this side the profile of the bottom stone is not dissimilar to that of the fertility symbol, the pig.*

name of Glenaveagh, from *Gleann na bhFé*, 'glen of the (phallic) rod', between Kinnahalla and Spelga. Likewise the Irish *Gasán*, meaning 'stem, stalk' is sometimes found as a euphemism for the penis as in the name of the County Louth town, Annagassan, discussed earlier. We have *Moth* found in the name of Slievedermot which looms over Kilbroney valley; the Irish word *Dear, Déar or Diar*, being an intensive prefix conveying the meaning of 'huge'. Then we have the Irish word *Bod* mentioned above as part of the name of Holywood. Also of interest is the Irish *Dúd*, meaning a 'stump' and its close affinity *Dúid*, meaning 'the neck, a cad; the penis'. Although not found as part of Mourne names, the Ulster emigrants to America introduced the word to the lexicon of that country and, while now apparently dated and obsolete, it became for a while the disparaging American slang reference for a man; 'Dude'.

One of the most important begetting stones is also fortunately reasonably close to Newcastle at Drinneevar mountain. When granite was needed for the construction of Newcastle's quay at the start of the nineteenth century, the granite men opened a quarry at the back of Drinneevar at a favoured site. The quarry was located just where the shale overbearing gave way to granite and at a place regarded by the ancients as one of luck and fertility. Access was possible by a special road made diagonally up the flank of Drinneevar, starting from Delarey Terrace at the end of King Street. The importance of the site came also from it being mentioned, perhaps unknowingly, by the Irish scholar John O'Donovan who was gathering local place-names for the ordnance survey in 1834. The following note was made by Place-names of Northern Ireland when considering the derivation of the name of Drinneevar.

> 'Although the anglicized spellings of this place-name strongly suggest that it derives from Irish *Droinn Iomhair*, O'Donovan recorded a form *Dún Iomhair*, 'Ivor's Fort' in the ordnance survey name-books. Furthermore, there is a note in pencil on the ordnance survey letter map of the Mournes which reads 'Bridge of Ever oge a Giant'. It is clear that O'Donovan had heard some folklore concerning a giant called *Iomhar Og*, 'young Ivor' in the locality, and it is reasonable to assume that this is the character from whom Drinneevar derives its name.'[8]

The quarry site was special to the ancients who had erected begetting stones that pointed to where the winter solstice sun declined into a little swelling on the mountain-side to the south. Here the sun was penetrating the vulva of the earth which made the site one of great fertility and luck. As to the copulating stones

The lower of these fertility stones at Drinneevar quarry has been given the head of a turtle. Its head and body are of shale and its carapace is of granite. It is a simple yet very effective ancient sculpture.

*Like the fertility megalith at Drinneevar quarry, this stone high on the southern slope of Slieve Donard has been shaped like a turtle.*

themselves, the seaward side of the bottom stone could be regarded as having a snub nose and, as such, is not unlike that great fertility symbol, the head of a pig. The other side of the lower stone is of a higher order of importance. Look closely to see that the ancients selected a stone with a fusion of granite and shale, a sort of marriage of opposites and thus an auspicious symbol of fertility. The lower shale has been given the body and head of a turtle while the granite top is its carapace. The working of this stone is a beautiful little creation of ancient sculpture. I have found other turtle stones on Leganabruchan, Bignian tors and high on Slieve Donard's southern slopes.

The men quarried away at the granite and after the quay was built in 1807 production turned to square-setts and cribben (kerbs for footpaths). Over the years the quarry got bigger and moved deeper into the hillside yet in all that time the begetting stones were left undisturbed for it was believed that to move them in any way would incur severe misfortune. Eventually the begetting stones formed a little island in the quarry as the quarrymen worked around them. Left high and dry, the quarrymen eventually jokingly referred to the stones as 'prisoners' and they were called in Irish *Braighde a eibhear óg a geinte*, literally 'prisoners of the new granite of the act of begetting'. This was the source of the later mnemonic 'Bridge of Ever oge a Giant' and along with 'the nab' on Leganabruchan (from *Lagán an Bhruacháin*, 'little hollow of the little shelf') and the Slievenagarragh megalith skylined at the end of the Bloody Bridge valley, are among the few megaliths whose names still survive from the Irish. The pencil note recorded by O'Donovan refers therefore to the granite quarry at the back of Drinneevar mountain where the begetting stones still stand.

This pair of begetting stones is on the eastern extremity of Chimney Rock mountain with Slievenagarragh below.

This great spear pointed boulder on the lower slopes of Slievenagarragh has been oriented towards the summer solstice sunrise and then skilfully split to impart the suggestion of multiple copulation. Breaking a notch out of the front of the stone above the spear-point creates a good impression of a mouth for the middle stone and perhaps a nose for the bottom one.

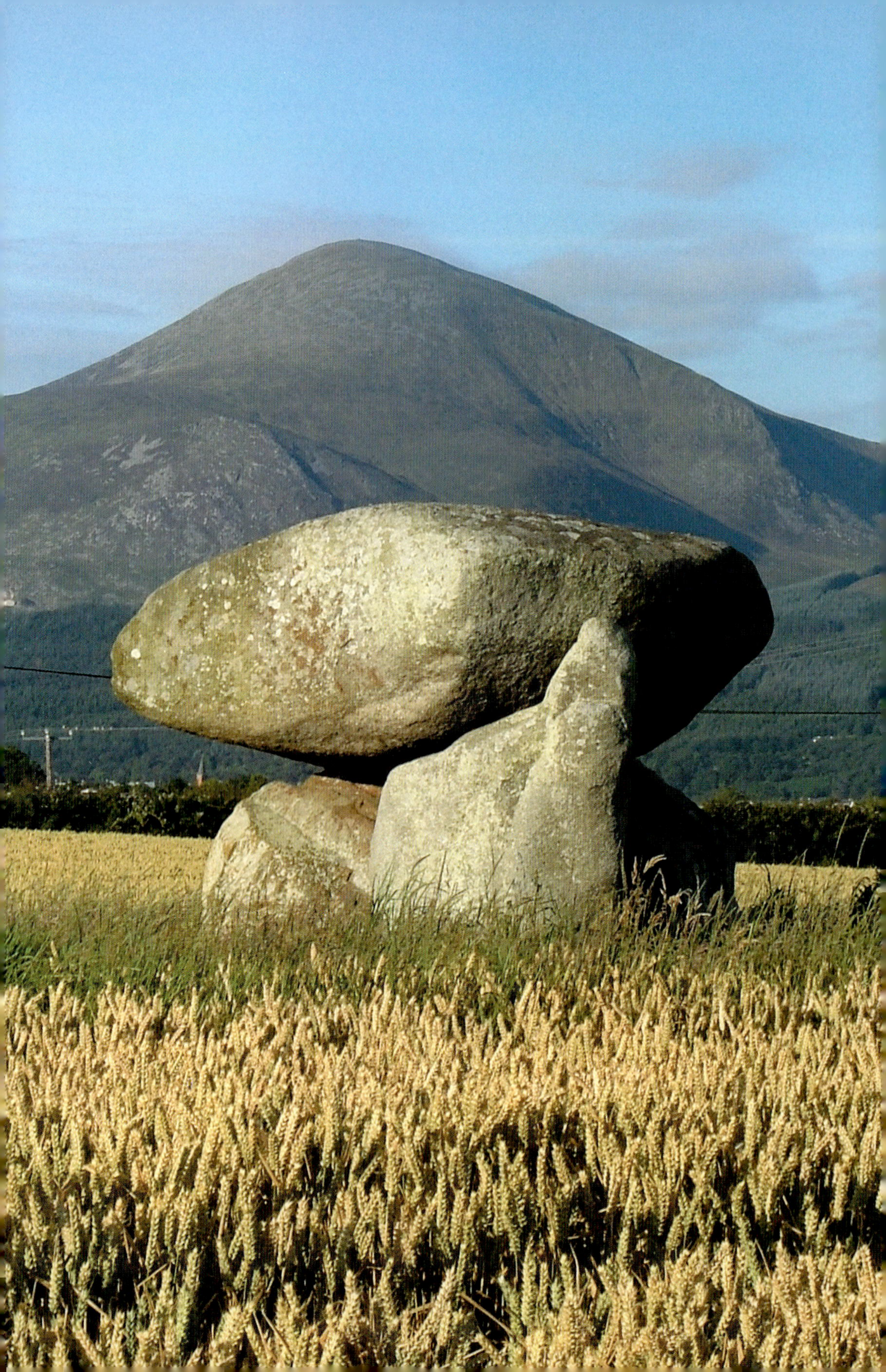

# SLIDDERYFORD DOLMEN

*'I went there early on with my father who had cousins living about half a mile away, men as native the ground as the Mesolithic inhabitants millennia before, moving as unobtrusively and purposefully as those hunter-gatherers with their fish-spears. Even then, I had some intuited sense of the prehistoric in the parochial ground, a feeling I retain and indulge when I return to the spot, as I often do, 'for tranquil restoration'.*

(FROM 'DIGGING TOWARDS THE LIGHT' BY SEAMUS HEANEY)

Although the Slidderyford dolmen lost the circle of stones that once surrounded it in the middle of the nineteenth century, it still remains a sun marker of great sophistication.[1] The word dolmen is reputed to have been introduced by a Frenchman. In the Cornish language, the term was *tolmen*, meaning 'hole of stone'. Ireland has about 190 dolmens, fourteen of which are in county Down, and Irish would always have had a name for these sites from very earliest times. Given the common root of Celtic language, the similarity of terms between Breton, Cornish and Irish should be no surprise. Indeed the Cornish term *tolmen*, meaning 'hole of stone'[2] starts to come close to the ancient fertility meaning. Dolmen is probably a contracted and eclipsed remnant of the Irish (*Clocha na*) *dTuill méin*, meaning '(Stones of the) hole of desire'. Spelling out the import of this, the desire was sexual and the gap or portal between the two front orthostats was the much yearned for vulva awaiting the impregnating solstice sun. Even the obsolete term Cromlech had a fertility derivation in Irish as *Crom-leacht*, 'the bent/stooped monument'. We mentioned earlier that Ben Crom mountain in the Mournes probably had its genesis in the Irish *Bean Crom*, 'the bent woman' where the mountain was imagined as bending down to expose the hill-side gully or notional vulva to the fertilising dawn light of winter solstice. In a similar fashion, the capstone of a typical tripod dolmen could be construed as bending over to enable the twin front orthostats to present themselves for copulation from the sun like 'friendly thighs'.[3] Slidderyford, Legananny and the two undocumented dolmens on Chimney Rock mountain that will be referred to later, all present their front portals to the setting sun, two at winter solstice and two at summer solstice. If other dolmens are reviewed in the wider context of their surrounding landscape, they should be found likewise to be connected with the sun and likely marking where the sun is seen to set into a 'vaginal' declivity or onto the top of a 'phallic' mountain. Kilfeaghan dolmen in Kilbroney parish, for instance, probably sees the winter solstice sun set in a notch or hollow on the distant

The dolmen at Slidderyford is a sophisticated sun marker with points on the capstone directed towards where the sun rises both at summer and winter solstice.

PREHISTORIC MOURNE: INSPIRATION FOR NEWGRANGE

Cooley peninsula. In Irish *Feagán* (genitive: *Feagáin*) refers to a groove in a spinning wheel. Kilfeaghan would have its name from *Caol Feagáin*, 'the narrow or precise point of the groove', ie. the dolmen marked the exact place where the setting sun could be seen declining into a distant notch on Cooley.[4]

Before coming to the dolmen itself, we take a quick look at the adjacent river Ore and the nearby standing stone in the Flush Loney. The river Ore is not named on the map and I have never heard it referred to in conversation. It is a tiny tributary of the Carrigs river and follows the edge between the former flat marshy area and the higher ground of the Flush Loney until it joins the Carrigs at the Twelve Arches. The name of the river comes from the Irish *Óir*, meaning 'fringe, border; limit, edge' and owed its origin to social rather than topographical reasons. The river is so named because it marks the boundary between the Annesley and the Downshire Estates. This is the reason for the round boundary pillar built at the confluence of the Carrigs and Ore rivers, seen from the Twelve Arches bridge.

The lost name of the river was only discovered because of an incident reported in the *Down Recorder*, on 22nd April 1911. 'About midnight on Easter Monday,

This little tributary of the Carrigs river is the Ore. It is from the Irish *Óir*, meaning 'border' and marked the division between the Annesley and Downshire Estates. The fancy pillar, inset on its circumference with rounded stones, is a boundary marker on the Annesley side of the river.

# Slidderyford Dolmen

*The old road to Belfast from Newcastle crossed the Carrigs river at the Twelve Arches bridge. An arch at either end is obscured in this photograph. Entrance to the field of the Slidderyford dolmen is under the tree seen at the end of the bridge on the left. The dolmen is a monument in state care but is sited on private land which should be respected.*

Robert Smith, 64, mill-worker, of Mill-hill, near Castlewellan, fell into the River Ore, at the twelve arches, on the Newcastle road. Mr Joseph McDowell, of Ardrossan, and a boy, Joseph Clark, also a visitor, were returning from a friend's house at the time, and heard cries of distress. Fortunately they carried a lamp, which enabled them to discover Smith clinging to a wire that stretches across the river at this place. With no little difficulty he was pulled to the bank. By this time he was utterly exhausted. The nearest household, Mrs Taylor's, was aroused. With the help of Sergeant Murphy, of the mounted police, Belfast, who happened to be at the house on holidays, and a man named Johnston, Smith, in an inanimate condition, was conveyed indoors, and only for Sergeant Murphy applying first aid for a long spell he would probably have succumbed. When the police arrived at Mrs Taylor's about 2.a.m., they found to their great satisfaction that the man was well on the road to recovery, and did what they could to complete it. Presently, well wrapped up in rugs and dry clothes, he was put on a side-car, the police accompanying him, and driven home to his wife.'

In referring to the standing stone in the Flush Loney the monument actually comprises two stones. The second large stone close to the upright pillar is largely hidden. It has a flat top and has been incorporated as part of the field boundary. Although much of the lower stone is obscured, it is likely that this was a pair of

*The phallic standing stone on the Flush Loney has a large companion stone incorporated into the field boundary. They probably were a pair of vagina stones, placed to allow the solstice sunlight between them. The name of the Flush Loney is sexual and comes from the Irish* Flosc Loinneach, *meaning 'joyful discharge'.*

vagina stones, so placed together that the winter solstice dawn and summer solstice sunset would shine between them. The standing stone was mentioned in earlier works but it was not realised then that the stone was a sun pointer[5]. There is a distinct edge on the stone which points across the road towards winter solstice sunrise. A careful look on the mountain side of the stone will reveal that the rock has been cut to impart a sleeping eye so it is also a face stone.

The Flush Loney itself is probably part of a very ancient pathway which skirted the great flat marshy area once known as Old Town drained by the Carrigs river.[6] On account of the nearby marshy area, now of course well drained, the name of the Flush Loney could easily be imagined as having come from the Irish *Fliuch*, meaning 'moist, wet, damp', but it was the standing stone rather than the marsh that had pre-eminence in determining the name. The name of the Flush Loney has a clear sexual and fertility connotation and is a close phonetic rendering of the Irish *Flosc Loinneach*, meaning 'joyful discharge'.[7]

Slidderyford dolmen is an iconic fertility and sun marker. As a sun marker the dolmen records winter and summer solstice sunrise together with winter and

*A little mouth has been created under this nose on the capstone. This is the point that looks to where the sun rises on the longest day, the summer solstice.*

summer solstice sunset. For good measure attention has also been paid to the equinox. We may only imagine what other information, garnered over millennia, was lost when the twelve stones that once encircled the monument were removed. It is the capstone that marks the sunrises. The back of the capstone, that part away from the mountains, has a pronounced natural point which is carefully directed to summer solstice sunrise. The front of the stone didn't have a convenient point so part of the capstone was broken off to create a shallow spear point directed to winter solstice sunrise. A small knob of granite was still retained on the capstone to the left of this shallow spear point to act as an eye which is more noticeable when the evening sun casts a shadow.

The orthostats of the dolmen have a story of their own to tell. Previously, and following on the description given by the great Irish naturalist Robert Lloyd Praeger, it was believed that the three orthostats were formed of one granite and two shale stones.[8] A closer examination reveals however that underneath the grey lichen covering, the eastern stone at the front is actually of sandstone, a rock not found in these parts. This stone in its original warm red colour would have been favoured by the ancients on account of its affinity with winter solstice dawn; so

275

*This photograph taken at 7.30am on the equinox highlights the artificial point on the capstone that is directed to where the winter solstice sun will rise.*

when they constructed the dolmen they placed it closest to the rising sun. The rock was probably shipped from the abundant outcrop of sandstone at Scrabo, Newtownards, brought down Strangford Lough, around St John's Point, over Dundrum Bay and into the inner bay to near Slidderyford. Indeed, some big flakes of sandstone have been found in the dolmen field after ploughing, suggesting that at least some of the missing stones of the now lost stone circle were also of sandstone too.

If you are fortunate to be at the dolmen towards sunset at the summer solstice it will be found that this is the one time that the back end of the sandstone block is illuminated and it is then possible to see that the stone has been given a sleeping eye, the suggestion of a nose and from the vertical chop marks on the upper half of the stone, what would seem to be a representation of long hair.[9] The place of the setting sun at summer solstice can also be precisely determined. It is necessary to lie down and look through the narrow slit between the two orthostats on the seaward side. A large notch has been cut out of the bottom of the granite orthostat and by sighting through the narrow gap and along the point of the notch you can see exactly where the sun sets over by distant Bunkers Hill.

SLIDDERYFORD DOLMEN

The underneath side of the sandstone orthostat really only sees the full sun as the sun sets at summer solstice. This photo was taken at 8.55pm on 28th June and reveals what seems to be a sleeping eye, a nose and the suggestion of hair in the vertical chop marks on the left. Sandstone is not found locally and it would have been necessary to ship this stone in from Scrabo over twenty miles away.

*When looking through the narrow slit between the seaward orthostats and sighting along the notch at the bottom of the granite orthostat, as marked here with the red stick, the precise point of summer solstice sunset can be found over by Bunkers Hill.*

    Another name that was collected by the ordnance survey in 1834 was *Ath na gcloch beó*, 'the ford of the living stones', for which we can give three completely different but plausible explanations. The first possibility relates to the practice of animating stones, making simple faces on them, by adding an eye and a mouth and thus making them 'alive'. The remnant stone of the missing circle that has been rolled in under the dolmen is a face stone with a distinctive eye and mouth. We can only wonder if the other missing stones had also been so animated with faces and thus regarded as 'living stones'? A second explanation of the Irish would look on the monument as stones to live by, seeing them as a vital guide for the early farmers. Vertical lines have been scored on the underneath of the shale orthostat, marking shadows cast at the dawn of equinox, the all important time for planting and getting crops into the ground. The lines have been gouged into the shale rock just where the dawn shadow of the granite orthostat falls on the shale stone at that crucial time in the farming year making the stones a form of calendar and thus stones to live by. The name of Slidderyford is not from some former algae covered, slippery stones that might have constituted a crossing point on the nearby Carrigs river long before the Twelve Arches bridge was built. Apparently it was the gouged lines on the underneath of the shale orthostat that were important enough to give the monument its present name. The appellation of Slidderyford is likely a mnemonic from the Irish *Sliocht a buidhe fordail*, meaning 'the mark of the yellow wandering'. It is possible that the missing stone circle may have also played a part in the name but we will now never know. A third explanation is relevant here but truly comes into its own at the Legananny dolmen. This saw the upright orthostats as 'living' in the sense that they were seeking nourishment from the capstone. They were suckling. A careful look at the front orthostats of Legananny especially when the sun is shining across the side of the stones revealing small details, shows us the indentations of small hammered eyes. The top of the eastward orthostat has been indented to create a mouth open to suckle from the capstone both on the outside and underneath. The dolmen's name is from the Irish *Liag an nainge*, meaning 'Stone of the foster-mother'.[10] On the western, stepped orthostat, the downward line of a mouth has been hammered into the rock making the step feature into an open hungry mouth. We cannot know who was buried in this beautiful monument, but were it a king or a noble person from the ancient society, we might surmise from the little graphics that the structure was erected as a loving tribute by many foster-sons.

This stone, likely a remnant of the original stone circle, has been rolled underneath the dolmen. The shadow eye and the mouth hammered into it would allow it to be called a 'living stone'.

The shale orthostat at Slidderyford is in the act of suckling from the 'mother' capstone.

279

*This equinox photograph, taken at 7.24am, shows the shadow cast on the shale orthostat where grooved lines have been scored to denote the time for planting. These grooves probably gave us the name Slidderyford from the Irish* Sliocht a buidhe fordail, *meaning 'the mark of the yellow wandering'.*

Mention was made earlier that Slidderyford dolmen records winter and summer solstice sunrise together with winter and summer solstice sunset. It is at winter solstice sunset that the whole raison d'être for the siting of the dolmen is revealed. The location of Slidderyford dolmen is a fertility site par excellence. The ancients deliberately chose this location because it marked where the sun, at winter solstice, set into the mountain swelling, or vulva, on the shoulder of Commedagh. The swelling (*Boirrche*) at the side of Commedagh was regarded therefore as a gynaecomorphic feature and the front two orthostats were positioned and 'opened', like a bent over woman, to receive the fertility rays of the sun as it penetrated into the earth at this special time of the solar year. Slidderyford dolmen is certainly special.

*The winter sunlight highlights the shadows on the Legananny orthostats where eyes and the line of a mouth have been hammered into the rocks. The near stone has a dimple of a mouth at the top and whether the page is turned to the left or the right, the stone can still be construed as suckling. This explains how Legananny dolmen got its name; it is from the Irish* Liag an Nainge, *'Stone of the Foster-mother. Picture was taken at 1.40pm on 22nd November.*

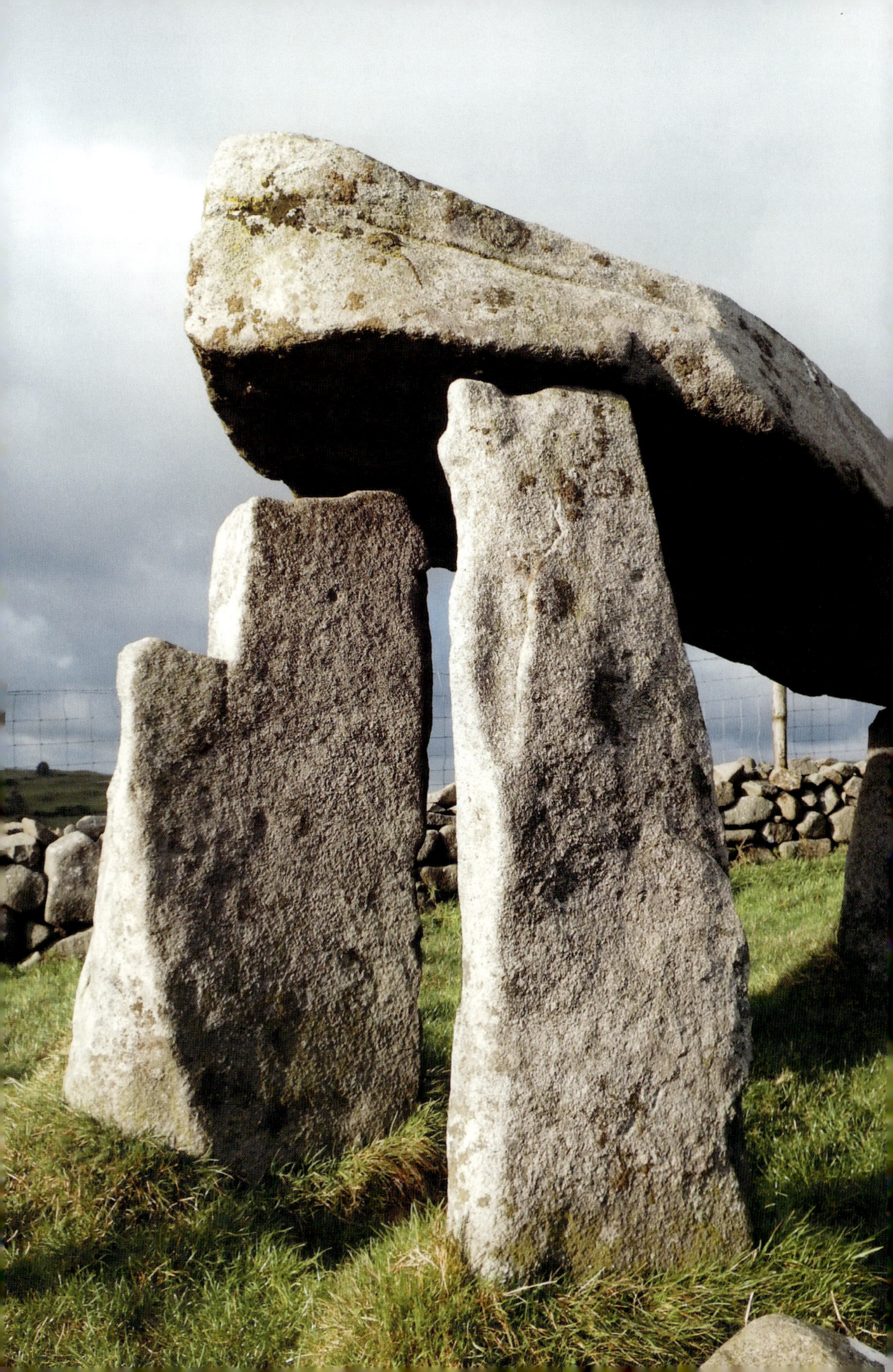

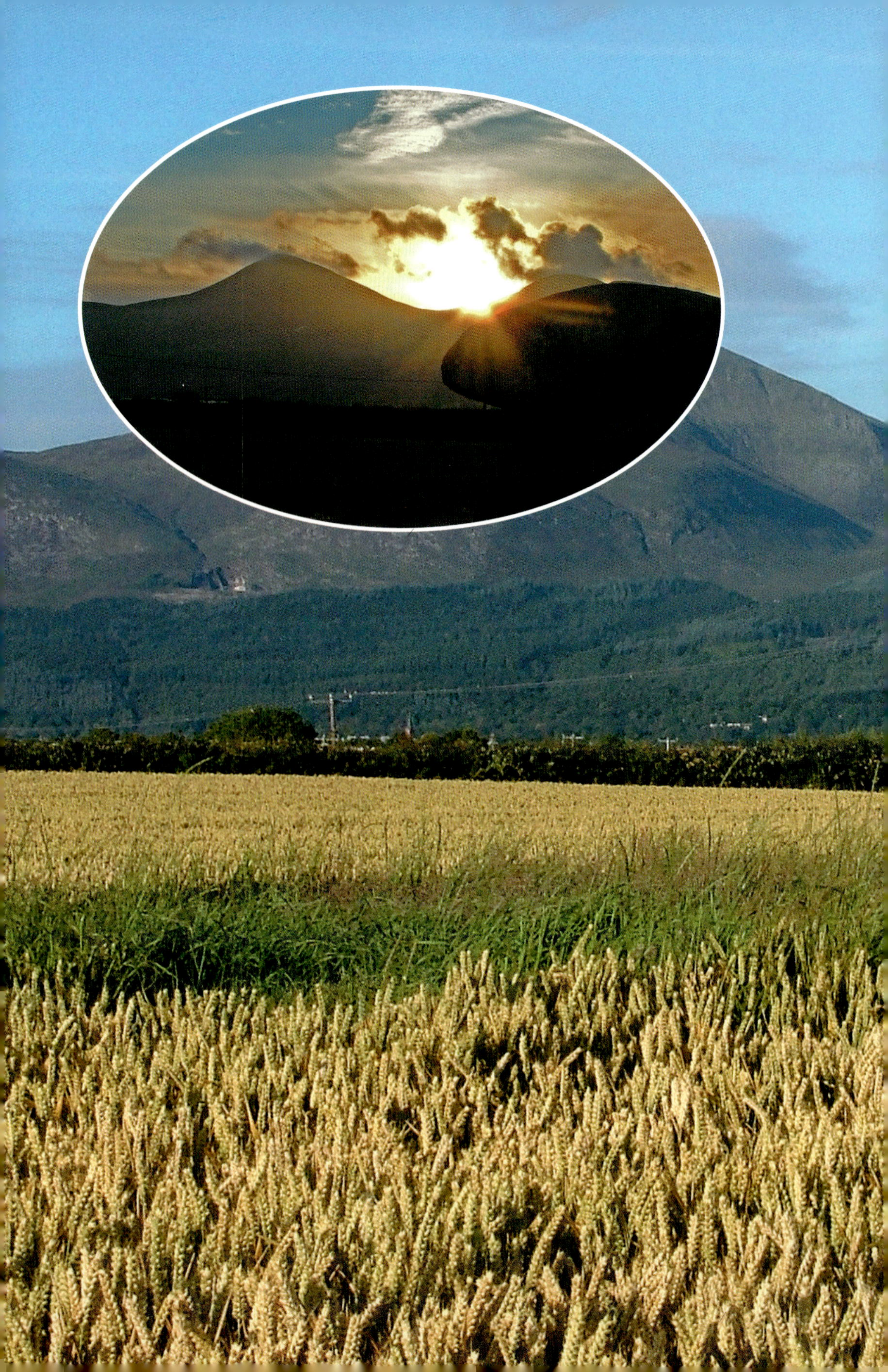

In a classic gynaecomorphic interpretation of the front of the Mournes, Slidderyford dolmen has been precisely located where the declining winter solstice sun can be seen entering the vulva of the earth, the *Boirrche* or swelling on the shoulder of Slieve Commedagh. The smaller inset photograph shows the setting sun at 3.07pm just shy of the solstice on 19th December.

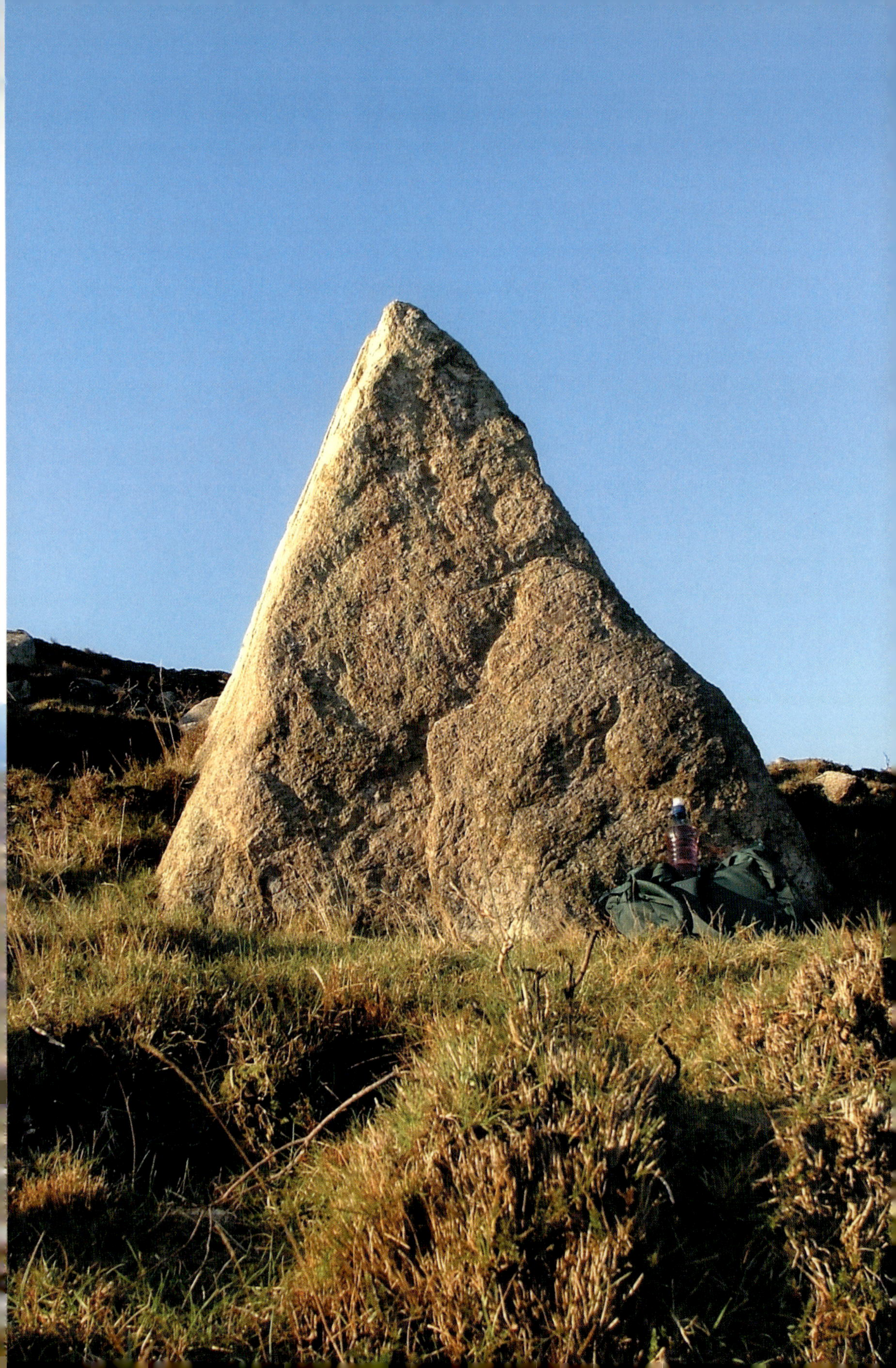

# THE BLOODY BRIDGE VALLEY & THE SPEAR OF ABUNDANCE

*'Lurid stories are told of the dark deeds which are supposed to have taken place here about the year 1641. The stories, however, are too contradictory to have any historical value and they only serve as so many of Ireland's stories do, to perpetuate the intolerance and religious bigotry which have disgraced our past and to which our present generation is not immune.'*

A CAUTIONARY WORD FROM REV. W. ARMSTRONG JONES, RECTOR OF ST. JOHN'S PARISH CHURCH, IN KILMEGAN RURAL DEANERY YEAR BOOK, 1949.

When John O'Donovan made his map of Mourne in 1834, he recorded the name *Carr na Bláthaighe* behind Slieve Donard at what is the location of the Bloody Bridge valley. No explanation for the name was offered and because the meaning and great significance of the name was apparently not understood, it did not subsequently appear on ordnance survey maps. Yet it is *Carr na Bláthaighe*, 'The Spear of Abundance', that made the Bloody Bridge valley one of the most important areas of Ireland thousands of years ago, important enough for the Neolithic builders of the great passage tomb of Newgrange to want to emulate it in their building.

In coming to understand this famous spear we must first remember again that the ancients endowed the landscape with human attributes. The countryside was interpreted sexually. Long strips of land like St John's Point, the sides of Belfast Lough, promontories or long straight shafts of sunlight were regarded as phallic and were symbolically imagined to have the same power and ability to infuse life as the male penis. Rounded hills, bulges or swellings (*Boirrche*) in the landscape were regarded as wombs or vulvas, for instance Slieve Builg on Bignian, Percy Bysshe hill, or Slievenamaddy the 'mountain of love'. As to the life-giving birth channel, the all important vagina, it would seem that the imagination of the ancients knew no limits. A gorge, a gully, a fissure, a cave, a cleft between rocks, flowing water, springs, the simplest crack small or wide, holes of any nature and even two boulders deliberately placed together with a gap between them as featured in the earlier chapter on vagina stones, all qualified to symbolise the female sacred source of life and fertility. Accordingly, the upper reaches of the

A young animal is shown suckling on the right hand side of this spear stone at the start of the upper Bloody Bridge valley. The stone was a reminder that one was entering the domain of the most famous ancient phallic spear in Ireland.

Bryansford is from the Irish *Braine Fuardha*, 'beginning of the cold zone'. The building on the left was formerly the six bedroomed Roden Arms Hotel which closed in September 1906 when its lease expired. Jocelyn, Lord Roden, then used it as his private residence.

**Some Local Place-names derived from Solstice Sunlight**

**Ballyginny:** The townland area around Maghera. It is from the Irish *Baile Geine*, 'townland of the act of begetting so called because, depending where one was within the townland, the winter solstice sun could be seen setting onto the top of Slieve Meelmore, into the [V] shaped notch or notional vagina at the side of Slieve Bearnagh, or onto the phallic tors of the same mountain. It was in this townland that the late James Spiers found a souterrain when ploughing his field in 1939.[1] The souterrains are often the only survivor of early raths and these, it would seem, were frequently built on sites thought to bring good fortune because they marked places of fertility interaction between sun and earth at solstice.

**Bryansford:** Despite earlier thoughts that the name derived from a ford over a stream[2] the name comes from the Irish *Braine Fuardha*, 'beginning of the cold zone'. The old Bryansford really began at the present back gate exit from Tollymore Park; from this point on, a traveller going towards Moneyscalp at solstice would now be in the shadow of the Drinns and so this marked the beginning of the gloomy frigid area.

**Bunkers Hill:** Bunkers Hill at Castlewellan is from the Irish *Bun Cíor* meaning 'jet (or dark) bottom' hill, from the bottom of the hill being in darkness at the winter solstice although the top is bright.

**Carnacaville:** There are three elements behind this name, the shape of Slieve Bearnagh's tor from Carnacaville, the way some potatoes used to be sown and the winter solstice sunset. The name of the townland in Irish would be *Carr na Caibeála*, the 'spear of kibbing'. Next time you leave Maghera village and drive past St Joseph's Primary School at 22, Carnacaville Road, look at the tiny rugged tip of Slieve Bearnagh sticking up at the back of the mountains. From here the tip of Bearnagh's tor is almost lost but enough protrudes to show itself. With apologies to the fairy tale of Goldilocks and the three bears, we could more precisely describe the appearance of Bearnagh's tor from this angle as 'daddy spear, mammy spear and baby spear'. In Irish the word for 'spear' is *Carr*. Normally from this location Slieve Bearnagh would hardly receive the slightest attention as so little of it can be seen. All this changes, however, at winter solstice sunset when the sun sets and highlights the mountain's pointed tip. Before 4.00pm, the time of sunset, the sun is down behind the mountain tip and giving it prominence by backlighting it. The third element of the name is the long obsolete practice of 'kibbing', or in Irish *Caibeail* (genitive *Caibeála*). Kibbing was the custom, practised by some, of sowing potatoes by burying the sets a few inches in the soil. With the demise of hand sowing of potatoes, the metaphor has lost much of its significance but at winter solstice at Carnacaville it still certainly seems that the sun is buried 'just a few inches' behind the tip of Slieve Bearnagh.

**Crock Horn Stream:** This leads down to Ballagh Bridge from the eastern slopes of Chimney Rock mountain and is from the Irish *Cróch-Oirean,* meaning 'Saffron yellow shore'; a reference to the colour of the solstice sunrise on the coast.

**Dolly's Brae:** Nowadays the name seems to be more associated with the road over Magheramayo hill and the events of 12th July 1849 when there was a clash between Orangemen and Ribbonmen that brought about a government inquiry. Many interesting explanations have been given for the derivation of this name including one fanciful legend that Dolly was the matronly owner of a shebeen in the area. The name however comes from the Irish *Doilbh Brí* and means 'gloomy hill'. The name belonged to the steep hill overlooking the road between Ballyward and Castlewellan and was so named because on winter solstice the hill left much of the area in darkness and shade.

This photograph of the Mournes was taken from Cathedral Hill, Downpatrick at 3.52pm on 29th December. The sun is setting in the middle of the Mourne mountain range and gave Downpatrick one of its early names, *Dun dá leithe glaise*, 'fort of the two bluish-grey halves.'

**Downpatrick:** One of the early historical names for Downpatrick was *Dun-da-lethghlas*, tentatively translated by Place-names project as 'fort of the side of the stream'.[3] This was likely proffered because an alternative translation didn't seem to make sense. But *Dun-da-lethghlas*, and variants, can be understood as 'fort of the two bluish-grey halves' (*Dun dá leithe glaise*); the key to understanding this is the setting of the winter solstice sun on the Mournes as seen from Cathedral Hill, once the site of a pre-historic ring fort. The winter solstice was so important for the ancients that the fort was named in relation to the setting sun. A grand panorama of the distant Mournes can be seen from the front of the cathedral. The sun sets exactly in the middle of this visible range, hence the reference to the two halves and their descriptive colour. The sunset location is on the shoulder of Shan Slieve and Slieve Corragh. Although Ben Crom cannot be seen, if the same line of sight was projected further into the Mournes it would come to this great fertility mountain. The name of the great Celtic god, Crom Dhu, was associated throughout Ireland with fertility rites, evil and sacrifice. The location of the setting winter solstice sun thus explains the second historical name for Downpatrick, Rath Celtchair. Celtchair was hitherto presumed to be a reference to *Cealtchair mac Uitheachair,* a mythical warrior of the ancient Ulster Cycle of Tales. The present proposal is that this name for Cathedral Hill refers to the sacrificial slaughter taking place out of sight at Ben Crom at solstice. Rath Celtchair is from the Irish *Ceilt Áir,* 'concealment of slaughter'.

**Glenfoffany:** When this local name was collected by the ordnance survey in 1834 it was rendered as *Gleann na bhFofanaidhe*. The place-names project recorded uncertainty and wondered about the name being a hybrid form but nevertheless suggested that it 'probably derives from *Gleann Fofannaí* in Irish where *Fofannach* refers to 'a place abounding in thistles'. However, with their deep roots and prolific seeding habits, thistles are very tenacious. These prickly plants, which cannot be grazed by herbivores, had they ever existed at Glenfoffany, are certainly not to be found there now. The vegetation that prevails is the usual heather with poor grass that is found all across high Mourne. The derivation of the name lies not with the spiny plant but with the appearance of the valley at winter solstice dawn. The valley then earned the name *Glan Fo-Fána*, 'bright below the slope'. The upper reaches of Leganabruchan that lies on the seaward side of this valley would be in shade at dawn but light would still fill the valley below. Thistles didn't come into it.

**Slievemoughanmore** (Slievemouganmore in pronunciation) in the Place-names of NI is 'of uncertain origin'. This is a significant mountain yet placed as it is on the more western side of the Mournes and overshadowed at the winter solstice to a large extent by adjacent Pigeon Mountain, the proposal is that the name derives from *Sliabh moiche gan mór* meaning 'mountain without a great dawn'.

**Wee Slievemoughan** is from the Irish *Uí sliabh moiche gan* and being completely overshadowed by its bigger neighbour at dawn thus gets the name of 'grandson or descendant mountain without dawn'.

A frosty Newcastle as seen from Millstone Mountain at 8.50am on 20th January. The light of sun on the landscape at the winter solstice was so important to the ancients that many names in the locality record whether they received sunlight or not.

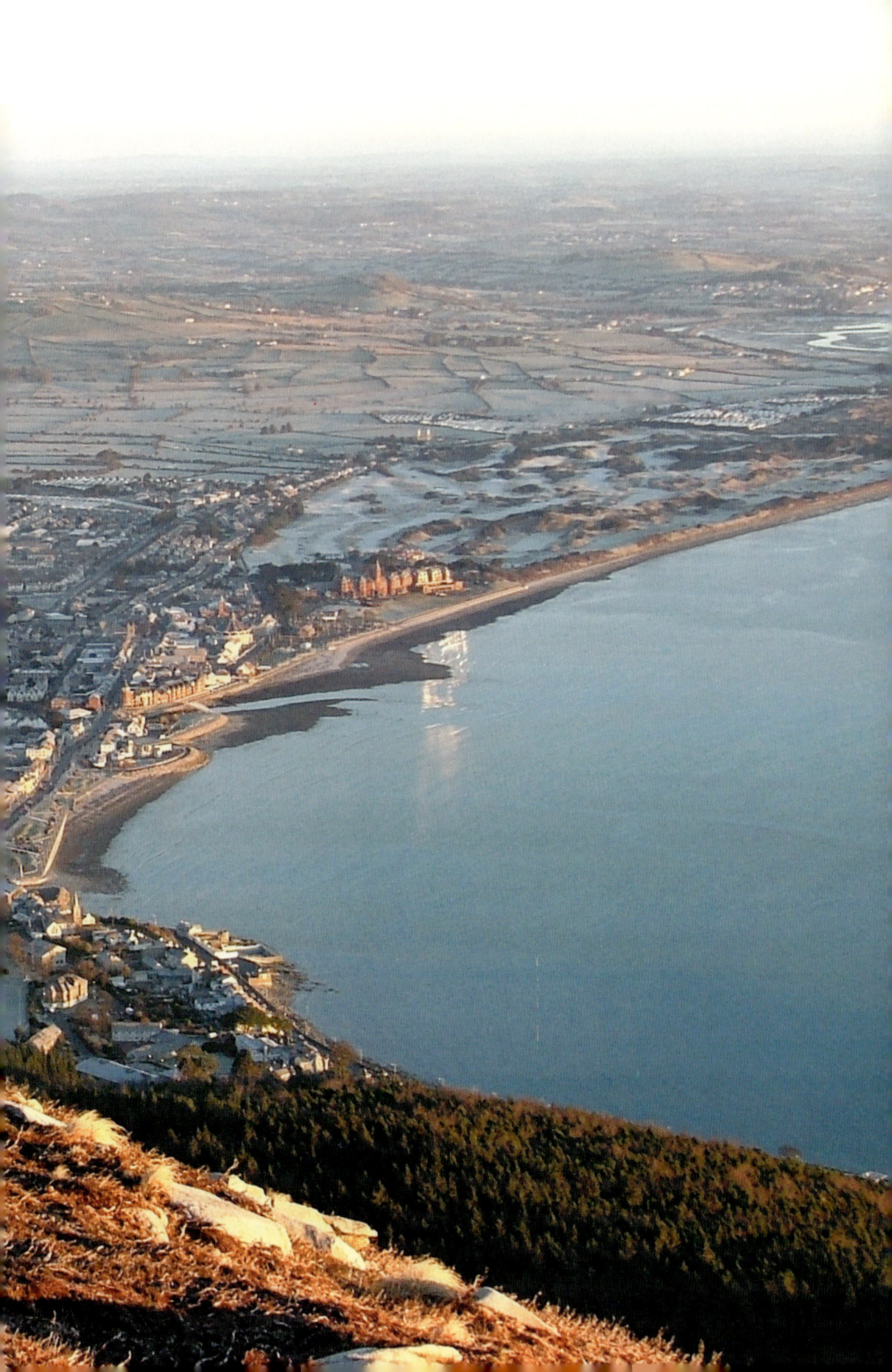

*The name of Hares Castle is from the Irish* h-Éirí Caise Tál, *'pouring forth of love of the rising'. The granite men chose to open their quarry at the 'fertility tip' of the phallic outcrop.*

anterior to 1834 but most probably the original Irish, understanding the summit as phallic, had a rendering like *Áirseóra Pearsa Caise Tál,* meaning 'The pouring forth of love/semen of the devil's feature'. In turn this was anglicised as 'Art Pierce's Castle', then back into Irish for the ordnance survey as '*Caislen Airt mhic Piarais*' before returning to English as the present Pierce's Castle.

Descending cloud has frustrated a number of attempts near solstice to witness the 'pouring forth' that the original Irish would have referred to, which would be the sun appearing at the front of the phallic mountain summit as if at the moment of ejaculation. The spectacle would seem to take place close to 10.50am winter time and one of the places to view it is where the ancients put a huge megalith in the bed of the river coming down from Altataggart mountain.[6] This huge stone is in the river-bed at J231251, just after the track crosses the bridge over the river. From low down beside the megalith and likely near the level of the river itself, the sun should come to touch the front of Pierce's Castle at solstice. At the other end of the year, the summer solstice, the spectacle is repeated in reverse. The setting sun at 21st June cast the shadow of Pierce's Castle onto Eagle mountain. The ancients marked with a huge boulder the spot where the sun again seemed to ejaculate from the rounded tip of Pierce's Castle. This monumental

## The Bloody Bridge Valley & The Spear of Abundance

megalith on Eagle's slopes had the name in Irish of *Buinne ceap*, 'the ejaculation stone', literally 'discharge block'. The stone is still there in all its prominence but the name moved round the corner to the col between Eagle mountain and Slievemoughanmore and *Buinne ceap* became the 'windy gap'.

There is a great similarity behind the names of Clanawhillan, Castlewellan, Greencastle and its former nearby neighbour, the old pre-reformation church of Kilnagreinan. All enjoy uninhibited sun at solstice. Clanawhillan, as mentioned on page 107, is from the Irish *Clochán an buidhe lán,* meaning 'clachan of the full sun'. Similarly the name of Castlewellan, for which I have heard numerous interpretations, gets its name from being able to enjoy full sun on winter solstice day without the light being interrupted by the mountains. Castlewellan is from the Irish *Caise Tál buidhe lán,* meaning 'pouring forth of love of the full sun'. One part on the outskirts of the town that gets little sun at the winter solstice is Corrie Wood as it is in the shade of Bunkers Hill. The present nursing home of that name was formerly the residence of Lord Annesley's estate agent, James Hugh Moore-Garrett, the man who collected the dreaded rent. He was quite an efficient agent

This large block near the quarry on Hares Castle has been detached yet deliberately left in a provocatively suggestive pose. The block faces over towards Bignian's phallic north tor. The stone may have been given fertility intentions but whether it also gave the name *h-Éirí Caise Tál* to this tor below Rocky is doubtful.

which is also another way of saying he was not afraid to evict people to protect the interests of the landlord. Indeed, on 28th March 1892 he wrote to 5th Earl Annesley, 'I had to evict two very poor old women....The name of the women is Hassard and the 'farm' is a bit of mountain in Moyad'.[7] I have no doubt that at that time, old Irish speaking residents of Castlewellan would have particularly enjoyed the irony of knowing the real significance behind the name of the agent's grounds. Corrie Wood is a mnemonic of the Irish *Coirigh Bod,* meaning 'sinner's penis', a reference, not unfortunately to the land agent, but to the phallic shadow of Bunkers Hill which stretched out over the area as winter solstice sunset approached. The sight of the sun setting on the summit of Bunkers Hill also likely gave the name to Diamond Hill further to the north-east at J3538, near Ballylough Lake. Diamond Hill is not really a hill in the sense of a high mass of land; this should be a clue that something else was intended by the name. We earlier mentioned on page 46 that Diamond Rocks in the Mournes was from Irish and meant 'Place of Origin Hollow'. The name of Diamond Hill would be derived from *Tí an Bhunaidh Áil,* 'Place of the origin of pleasure' as from this location the sun would be seen to set on the summit of Bunkers Hill and the hill summit was imagined as ejaculating.

In 1938 Fr Patrick Farry, a curate at Kilkeel, related a conversation he had with the late Canon Marmion, PP, VF, Dundrum (1870-1950) at the opening of Grange Church in 1926. The Canon had been born and reared in the area and was a member of the family who gave the ground for Grange church and contributed generously to the building. Canon Marmion provided the name and location of the lost church of Kilnagreinan which Fr Farry recorded as follows:

'There is also, in the same locality (as Grange Church), a tradition of an old pre-Reformation Church, Kilnagreinan – 'the Church of the sunny-spot'. Canon Marmion remembers the ruins of the old church on the ridge of ground overlooking the present Cranfield Golf Course, between the public road and the sea. He also states that there was supposed to be an old graveyard around the ruins, and that many people (when he was a boy) resented the action of the then owner when he ploughed up the field for the first time, because it had remained fallow in the knowledge of the oldest inhabitants.'[8]

Further west, Greencastle, the site of the Norman fort controlling the entrance to Carlingford Lough, has its name, not from the castle as we might reasonably expect but from the Irish (*Tí na*) *Gréine Caise Tál,* (Place of the) 'pouring forth of sun love'; like Kilnagreinan, Greencastle received the sun throughout the solstice day. So, just as Bryansford received its name because the Drinns cast shade at winter solstice on the road from that point on towards Moneyscalp, likewise across the Lough from Greencastle, Carlingford, being shaded by the mountains behind it, received its name, not from the Scandinavians as hitherto widely believed, but from the Irish *Cár Linn Fuardha,* 'Mouth of the cold pool'.

The name of Castlewellan is from the Irish *Caise Tál buidhe lán,* meaning 'pouring forth of love of the full sun'.

## The Bloody Bridge Valley, the Pass of Fire

The widespread understanding of how this valley got its name relates to the sad fact that during the war of 1641-42 somewhere in the Ballaghanery woods that once existed in the vicinity of the Bloody Bridge, English prisoners en route from Newry were killed by their Irish captors when a prisoner exchange deal fell through. In an unfortunate embellishment, which suited the ends of propaganda, it was later further proclaimed that the bodies of the prisoners were then thrown off the bridge so that the river ran red with blood. This was supposedly the reason the river and the old bridge were known as the Bloody Bridge.[9] There is a problem here however in that at least two different tragic stories were conflated. An important detail in verifying where the truth lies begins by checking the stonework underneath the old Bloody Bridge, now by-passed by the main Newcastle/Kilkeel road a few hundred metres away. Even a cursory look underneath the structure reveals that the bridge was originally only wide enough for a single horse and was later widened twice in its history. Centuries ago when the bridge was only 4/5 feet wide, two men riding home from Greencastle fair and knowing that only one horse at a time could cross the bridge, started a race

*The entrance to the Bloody Bridge valley at 7.40am on 28th February. It is two months after the solstice but the remnant of shadow cast by Carr's Face, where the quarry is, can still give a hint of the greater shadow cast ten weeks earlier. In the middle of the picture is the phallic tor on the western summit of Chimney Rock. It disappears from view as one climbs higher but is replaced with a heroic megalith on the skyline overlooking the upper valley.*

to get to the bridge first and cross it before the other. The first horse reached the start of the bridge but in its haste made the awful mistake of galloping out on the wrong side of the low parapet and thus careered into the void and fell onto the rocks below. The second horse racing close behind followed the same path in error before its rider could rein it in and both horses and riders were dashed on the rocks below.[x] This awful tragedy earned the river the Irish name *Mí-ádh Páis* meaning 'unfortunate or unlucky death'. This Irish name was subsequently sadly corrupted by Walter Harris to Midpace River when he named the local rivers in 1744[11]. The river did indeed once run red with the blood of horses and riders at some early historical stage. Now that the evidence of the events of 1641–42 have been painstakingly laid before us by scholars at TCD, it is long past time to set aside the toxic propaganda of prisoners bodies being desecrated by being thrown over the parapet into the river.

Despite the aforegoing, the name of Bloody Bridge valley now has a new and much earlier evolution thousands of years before the events of 1641 or the tragic horse race. Searches on top of the great western summit tor show its upper surface to be absolutely covered in deep rock bowls hammered into the granite. At least twenty bowls mostly filled nowadays with rain water have been counted on top of this landmark. Rather than being of geological origin, these bowls are man made. These are the bowls that would have burned with fire in the vigil for the dawn of winter solstice. In the dark hours waiting for the special sun to rise, the ancients would have lit fires probably using pig fat or oil from fish, seals or whales. Up on this height, with any wind blowing, the fires would have burned fiercely and made quite a spectacle in the darkness. It would have been a real conflagration and this impressive display is the likely early source of the valley's name. The name of the valley would have been from the Irish *Bladhm Bríghe*, 'Flame of power'. The subsequent tragedy of the horses galloping to their deaths was probably the occasion for the transition of the Irish name to the present English mnemonic. There are no written sources to offer verification but the multitude of granite bowls on the phallic summit tor stand in mute testimony.

A pleasing view along the top of Chimney Rock from the top of the great western tor of Chimney Rock. The tor is covered with bowls hammered into the granite in which fires of fat would have been burned in the vigil before the winter solstice dawn. The conflagration thus caused would have been magnificently impressive and easily seen down at road level and far out to sea. The spectacle gave us the name *Bladhm Bríghe*, 'Flame of power' which, under the influence of later tragedies, morphed into the English mnemonic Bloody Bridge.

The entrance to the Bloody Bridge valley as seen from the main road. Look for the landmark phallic tor on the skyline of Chimney Rock mountain. This is the tor pitted with fire bowls that would have blazed at the vigil for winter solstice dawn.

The origin of the name of Ballaghanery and its many variations lies with a literally outstanding topographical feature at the top part of the valley; a massive Neolithic megalith that boldly and dramatically dominates the faux valley skyline. The ordnance survey scholar, John O'Donovan, could only work at that time with what he was given by the survey officers or what he could glean himself from locals. Without the insight of the importance of the ancient religion of sun worship, it is no wonder that he wrote to headquarters from Newry on 12th May 1834, 'The names of the Mourne Mountains are very curious'. O'Donovan was aware of the importance of personally seeing features and at the end of the day on which he climbed Slieve Donard he concluded his report to Dublin with the remark:

> 'Those who have surveyed the land, who have lived in the neighbourhood, and who have, with their own eyes, seen those features, should furnish a list of their names spelled as well as they could catch the sound.'[17]

This huge stone was probably just casually dismissed as an accident of nature, just one of Mourne's many thousands of stones about which there was apparently nothing special. The early Irish however, knew of the deeper importance of this rock and had named the valley after it. The names recorded by Walter Harris

308

writing in 1744, ninety years before the ordnance survey, come closest to representing the truth of the Irish. Thus in his work *The Antient and Present State of the County of Down* he makes mention of the pass and includes a footnote.

'About three miles south of *New-Castle*, near the edge of this Barony, and that of the half Barony of *Mourne*, is the Pass of *Bealach-a-neir,* or *Ballyonery.*' To which is added the note:

(*Bealach* in *Irish* signifies a Path or Gap; so that *Bealach-a-neir* is the Path Way or Gap to the Mountain of Neir, which hangs over it, now corrupted into *Ballionery.*)

The mountain of Neir has caused much confusion as to its whereabouts as it was not marked on any maps. It has spawned many variations such as Ballogh Enary, Baloghe Neyrye, Ballaghnerye, Balloth-enevry, Ballotheneirry, Bealachaneir and today's present spelling of Ballaghanery. They all refer to the upper part of the Bloody Bridge valley. The mountain of Neir is from the Irish *Bealach an irille*, meaning 'the pass of the spike'; the spike being the massive megalithic phallic monument. The Irish word for point or spike, namely *ireall* (genitive *irille*) has been contracted by time and usage from *an irille* to *a-neir* and so we have Harris referring to the pass as *Bealach-a-neir.* When you walk up the old granite trail to the upper reaches of the Bloody Bridge valley and see high above the left side of the path the huge megalith so emphatically prominent, no clearer example could be given of how a dominant topographical feature was often the determining factor in naming an area.

Dominating the skyline of the upper Bloody Bridge valley, this great megalith gave the valley the name *Bealach an irille*, meaning 'the pass of the spike' and which has now become the name of the townland, Ballaghanery.

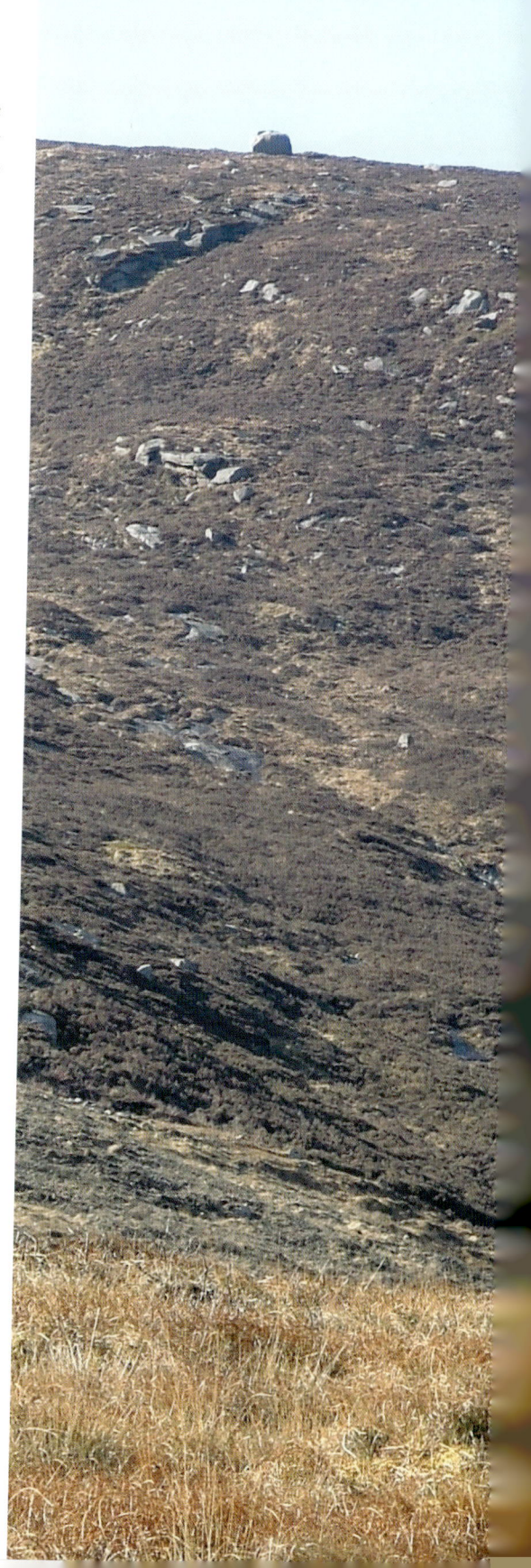

to highlight some particular feature or event that was so well known to the whole local community that just the mention of the name identified the area immediately to everyone. *Glas* meaning 'green', while correct in Irish, was just too common in usage to ensure a necessary unambiguous communal recognition. The very fact that the word was common would have permitted confusion with other 'green' localities and the possibility of the word being either corrupted or misinterpreted had to be considered. The answer is found in a new appreciation of the old name for the area that was collected by John O'Donovan in 1834, namely *Carr na Bláthaighe*, 'the Spear of Abundance'.

A javelin is a light throwing weapon about 2.6 metres, thrown overhand after the momentum of a short run. A spear was also a thrown weapon but it could be much stouter than a javelin and also used instead for thrusting as need depended. The usual preparatory poise for a spear or javelin was to grip the weapon in the centre of gravity and hold it far back behind the stretched throwing arm, before running and throwing it overhand as hard as possible at the target. Keeping this in mind, the alternative interpretation to *An Ghlasdromainn*, 'the green ridge', means setting aside the common adjective *glas* and substituting the very similar sounding Irish word *Gléas*. The change from the Irish *Gléas* to *Glas* was probably not a deliberate expunging of the old pagan name but a gradual elision through lack of understanding. Had O'Donovan been able to find an explanation for *Carr na Bláthaighe* he almost certainly would have included it on the ordnance survey maps; but he didn't. The verbal *gléas* has a wide range of meanings such as 'I harness, dress, prepare, trim, set in order, put in tune, and **poise (as a javelin)**'. Poise, as for a javelin, conveyed the idea of preparation for a flying projectile and accorded with the idea of waiting, anticipating and expecting the rays of the solstice sun shining straight and true like a spear up the Bloody Bridge valley. The original meaning of Glasdrumman would have derived from *An Gléasdromainn* meaning 'the poised ridge'; it was the starting place for the Spear of Abundance to be launched. From the Mourne plain to the ridge, the ancients imagined the sun figuratively poising itself for the preparatory run to throw its shaft of life-giving light. The starting place for the run was the coast and ended at the first hill of the Bloody Bridge valley which the ordnance survey unfortunately misnamed as Slievenagarragh; it really should have been *Gléasdromainn*, 'the poised ridge', for, as we shall see, the name of Slievenagarragh is a complimentary or alternative name for the very end of the Bloody Bridge valley, the part overhanging it and also known as Slieve Neir, 'the mountain of the Spike'.

At the other side of Dundrum Bay a similar elision took place with the name of Rossglass. 'The poised headland', which would be the real meaning of *Ros Gléas*, would seem to make much less sense than *Ros Glas*, 'the green headland', until it is connected with where the sun sets at winter solstice; that happens to be in the middle of the Mourne lowland, the place where the sun had 'poised' before throwing its dawn spear of light. There are no longer any remains of the original

This is the great megalith that dominates the skyline of the Bloody Bridge valley and gave it the name *Bealach an irille*, 'the pass of the spike' which subsequently gave us the names Mountain of Neir and the townland of Ballaghanery. The time is 10.04am on 18th March and the sun, shining across the bottom end of the stone reveals the hammered indentations where the ancients shaped the stone into the backend of a cow, complete with bony haunches and a curly tail. This is Slievenagarragh, from the Irish *Sliabh na Gair-Aigh*, 'mountain of the primeval (literally the 'great grand-daddy') cow'. This great fertility monument would be serviced by the dawn light of winter solstice.

The quarry on Carr's Face as seen on 18th March at 7.30am. The edge of this shoulder of Chimney Rock mountain generated the great phallic shadow of *Carr na Bláthaighe*, the Spear of Abundance. Carr's Face, or *Cairre Fás* as it is in Irish, was 'the beginning of the Spear'.

**Carr's Face, the beginning of the spear**

Carr's Face is marked on the ordnance survey map of Mourne as the high northeastern flank of Chimney Rock mountain. It is virtually identified with the former granite quarry that was worked at the top of that slope. The map also shows the line of the disused mineral railway that led up to the large bare slab of the quarry face. The line of the railway and the quarry spoil are easily seen by those walking up the old granite trail to the Mourne Wall and many must have asked themselves why the quarry-men went so high to obtain granite when there was plenty of the good stuff much lower down?[21]

Because we all deeply cherish the place of our birth and rearing, the derivation of place-names is taken very seriously. The depth of research of the Queen's Place-names project into their explanation for Carr's Face is obvious. They describe it as an English form. So before delving into variance it is fair to record exactly what they have said:

'Carr's Face, in the townland of Ballaghanery, derives its name from the surname Carr which in Ulster may be of Irish or Scottish origin (MacLysaght 1982, 50-1; Bell 1988, 31-1). Arthur Carr of Ballaghanery, together with his father Nicholas Carr and other members of that family, are recorded in a will dating to 1782 (*Reg Deeds abstracts ii §670*) and it is quite likely that Carr's Face derives its name from some member of this branch of the family.'[22]

Despite the proven past presence of a family named Carr in the local area the origin of the name of Carr's Face is much older; probably thousands of years older. Carr's Face in its present construct is indeed an English form but the name is a mnemonic, a sound-a-like, of the Irish *Cairre Fás* meaning 'the beginning of the spear'.[23] It is that part of the shoulder of Chimney Rock mountain known as Carr's Face that cuts off the winter solstice sunrise from the entire southern side of the upper valley yet allows the other side to be bathed in light. As the Irish *Cairre Fás* shows, Carr's Face was where the sunlight, the tip of the spear, started its flight. The Spear of Abundance was the huge phallic shadow spear generated by the low solstice sun and the shoulder of Carr's Face mountain. This annual ephemeral spear stretched out up the valley and penetrated the source of the female waters at the head of the valley to endow both it and all the area beyond towards Slieve

This quarry at the head of the Bloody Bridge valley was opened at the great fertility site touched by the point of *Carr na Bláthaighe*, the famous solstice shadow Spear of Abundance. Out of respect for the fecundity of the Spear, or more likely, out of fear for their own well-being if they jeopardised the place touched by the fertility tip, the quarry men left a phallic plug of rock, seen on the left, jutting out into the quarry and worked away on either side of it.

The quarry-men went to exceptional lengths to open a quarry high on the heights of Carr's Face because this famous fertility location would have brought good luck to their efforts. Note again how the north tor of Slieve Bearnagh projects, phallic-like, from the very middle of the vaginal notch between Chimney Rock and Slieve Donard.

Bearnagh, with fertility for the coming year.[24] When next passing through the large quarry at the head of the valley, note how the quarry-men, respecting where the point of the sun's fertility spear landed, left a priapic granite plug in the middle of the quarry where the river flows, yet quarried extensively to left and right of it. The quarry-men of generations past who were still heirs to *seanchas*, the ancient knowledge, chose to go to exceptional lengths to quarry at Carr's Face. They did so, not because the granite itself was somehow extraordinary, but because they knew this was a 'lucky' site. It would be good to them and their efforts as the sun had been good to generations before them. Mourne was an inherently conservative place. When life was hard it was wise to stay with what had been tried, tested and proved. It was wise to be respectful and heed the ways of the ancestors; to cherish and cling to what they had done.

This then was the great Spear of Abundance, *Carr na Bláthaighe*. On winter solstice morning, Lugh, the great Celtic god of light, he who was known as *Lámh-Fhada*, 'the Long-handed' and able to throw his spear vast distances, lifted his red

# The Bloody Bridge Valley & The Spear of Abundance

spear with the dawn, poised himself on the plain and hill of *Gléasdromainn* and launched his famous spear of light and fertility from *Cairre Fás* into the vulva of the earth at the head of the valley and onwards over to the north tor of Slieve Bearnagh. This legendary line would be recognised for its importance by the builders of Newgrange who, in emulation, ensured that the same phenomenon of penetrating fertility light would be annually enacted at their great tomb and carved the celebrated line onto the middle of kerbstone one at the tomb's entrance and saw it through to its conclusion on the other side on kerbstone fifty-two.

Two walkers approach the tailings of the great quarry at the head of the Bloody Bridge valley.

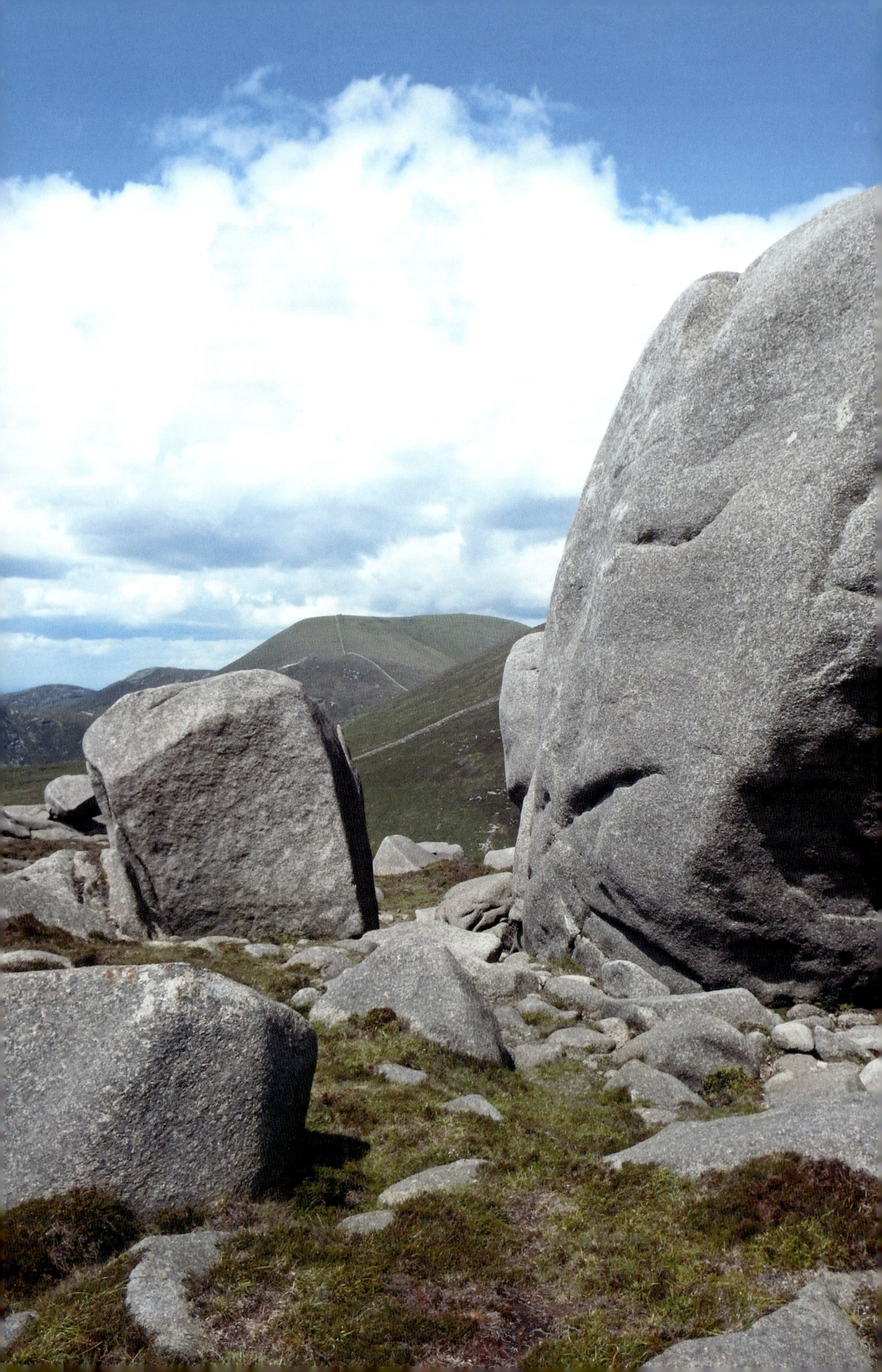

# CHIMNEY ROCK

*'In the time of Ptolemy the geographer (born A.D. 70) the Mourne district had acquired the name of Hieron, or 'the Sacred Promontory'.*
Canon Henry Lett, M.R.I.A., in Maps of the Mountains of Mourne in the County of Down, Ulster Journal of Archaeology, Vol 8, No 2, April 1902.

If ever there was a sacred landscape set aside for the ancestors, this is it. To understand the importance of this mountain to the ancients, obsessed as they were with procreation, life and fertility, it is best to look at the profile of Chimney Rock mountain from across Dundrum Bay. From Newcastle to Dundrum the outline of the mountain is masked by Millstone mountain, but from Ballykinlar onwards to St John's Point the gently rising plateau of the mountain stands out as a monstrous tumescent phallic shaft complete with a bulbous head at the end. It was this gigantic representation of male power and fertility that in part made this mountain irresistible for the ancients. Another compelling reason was the summit orientation of the mountain which pointed neatly towards the rising winter solstice sun. Many of the monuments of this mountain have already been illustrated in previous chapters. There are, however, so many other rocks, boulders and collections of boulders indicative of the hand of man, some more of which we will feature at the end of this chapter, that this whole mountain top was obviously seriously important. As one becomes aware of the multitude of arranged stones, it is obvious that incredible effort has been expended here.

The belief systems of the Neolithic are beyond certainty; we can only surmise and make reasonable assumptions. Did the ancients carry out so many impressive endeavours on Chimney Rock summit in order to honour their ancestors? Would each special arrangement of stones likely represent a burial? Were that the case the astonishing number of specially placed rocks and stones would make this summit plateau of Chimney Rock a truly large Neolithic cemetery and explain the designation of 'Sacred Promontory' made by Ptolemy nearly two thousand years ago. It is the orientation of the mountain plateau towards the winter solstice that may explain the preponderance of 'graves'. The unspoken thought behind so many burial sites and the remarkable moving of so many stones may lie in the idea of the deceased going to live in the sun at death and that they could return bringing help, prosperity and fertility at the solstice.

This is the famous artificial gap that gave the mountain its name. The opening simulated a vulva which was penetrated by the rising sun at winter solstice dawn. Chimney Rock is a mnemonic of the Irish *Shimleadh Roc* meaning 'pretended gap'. See the illustration on page 234/5. Note the close eye and the mouth hammered onto the front of the tor.

## The 'Horsemen' Tor

When professor Estyn Evans wrote about the fishermen of Mourne he left us a list of landmarks that were important to them.

> 'Nothing illustrates more clearly the intimate knowledge of Mourne and its mountains possessed by fishermen who were also farmers, the close association of land and water in this country where the mountains go down to the sea, than the landmarks which were used to guide the boats to and locate their fishing grounds. The names read like a poem. There are, for example, the Two Hills, the Blue Hills, the Three Tallies, and the North Mountain Foot; the Small Pike, the Long Land, and Marleys-on-the-Ditch; the Horsemen, the Bleachyards, McVeigh's-in-the-Glen, Rook's Chimney, Henry's Lumps, Nicky's Easens and the Old Mill Stump... Some of these numerous landmarks can readily be identified by the landsman for they are the hill-marks on Binnian and the other mountain tops. The Horsemen, for example, are the tors on Chimney Rock, with the General leading the others, his horse's back proudly curved against the clouds.'[3]

Many of these old place-names used by the fishermen would have had their genesis in Irish. In Dundrum Bay we have the two rocks 'Cow and Calf' that have claimed the lives of the unwary. Six men died here on the night of 4th December 1859, when the brig *Tikey*, sailing from Odessa with a cargo of 400 tons of barley, struck on the Cow and Calf Rocks. Before that a smuggler used his intimate knowledge of the Bay to lure a chasing revenue cutter onto the rocks. Lieutenant S. Mottley, commander of the cutter *Hardwicke*, with twelve guns, was chasing a smuggler that had landed contraband at Glasdrumman when she crashed into the rocks and was lost in October 1820.[4] The Cow and Calf got its name from the sea crashing into the gap between them; the name is likely a mnemonic of the Irish *Coireán Caib*, meaning 'the small cauldron of the mouth'.

In 1899, a former Newcastle coastguard told of going out in the lifeboat during a terrific storm. To the man's surprise there was little surf as the hurricane was so bad it had the effect of beating down the waves near the shore. The ship in danger was a schooner from Wales and it was being driven ashore at a fatal part of the coast, north of Newcastle, known as the Cut Throat. Four times an attempt was made to launch the lifeboat and the fifth attempt was successful when 'several hundred people caught the ropes and tried to launch it; The people pulled the boat out until they were up to their breasts in the water.'[5] The coastguard would have heard the coastal name 'Cut Throat' from the local Newcastle fishermen. Gory as the name sounds it really came from the Irish *An Cuithe Troch*, 'the pit of one fated to die'. In the days of sail, if an Atlantic depression changed the wind to an easterly or south-easterly direction, vessels coming up the Irish Sea often found themselves unable to tack against a gale and with no room to manoeuvre around St John's Point, found themselves inexorably being driven onto the rocks and shore of Dundrum and Tyrella. Indeed Schollogstown Hill, where my paternal ancestors used to farm, overlooked this dangerous coast around Tyrella, Minerstown and Rossglass. The name of Schollogstown evokes the many horrors of shipwrecks witnessed from this vantage point with the screams of dying men. It is likely a contraction of the Irish *Scol Áigh Tean*, 'Valiant shout of the shipwreck'. The rocks of Minerstown earned the grim name *Mian-Áir Tean*, 'Lust of slaughter of the shipwreck'.

An important boundary for fishing in Dundrum Bay was Hellyhunter Rock off Cranfield Point. This name was from the Irish *h-Eile Huintéir*, 'another aimless vagrant'. The rock was an 'aimless vagrant' as it didn't know where it was going; sometimes out of the sea, sometimes under the sea. It was a reef. This rock was a boundary marker and no trawling was allowed inside a line between it and St John's Point; or at least that was the idea.[6]

Once you have left the car park at the Bloody Bridge and, having crossed the road, are about to enter through the stile to walk up the valley alongside the river, pause a moment. Look to the western summit of Chimney Rock above the end of the Bloody Bridge valley to see the attenuated phallic shaped tor known to the fishermen of old as 'Horsemen'. This is the tor that has its granite top pitted with bowls in which the ancients would have burnt oil or fat in their pre dawn vigil at winter solstice. These fires gave us the Irish *Bladhm Brighe*, 'Flame of power', which ultimately morphed into the present name of Bloody Bridge. To arrive at the summit of Chimney Rock, the easiest route by far is to take the trail up to the Mourne wall and, when nearly there, bear off round to the left following the trail to the tor. Don't be tempted to leave the trail to the wall too early thinking to take a shortcut as you would end up in a real obstacle course up and down mucky peat banks. Savour the summit and its surroundings for there is so much to see. The ancients worked here for thousands of years and left behind such a multitude of works, many simple and small, but so much more than this book could embrace.

The western summit tor, the one seen from the main road, is the 'Horsemen' mentioned by Estyn Evans. Think not of galloping horses for the name is a mnemonic from the Irish *h-Oiris Méin*, and means 'landmark of pleasure', a reference to its phallic shape. The tor can be seen on the skyline from almost all of Dundrum Bay. There is something about the level part of the mountain in front of this tor that gives the suspicion the ancients may have quarried and removed surrounding rock projections so as to deliberately enhance the tor and to remove anything distracting from its phallic outline. The huge boulder that forms part of the gap in front of the tor had to be sourced from somewhere and likewise the huge nearby boulders that form part of The Lamagan Line on the western slope, the largest of which has already featured at the start of the first chapter. We cannot know the extent of their efforts to clear the vicinity around 'Horsemen' but great labours have been undertaken with the tor itself.

This tor on Chimney Rock was called by the fishermen 'Horsemen'. The Irish, *h-Oiris Méin*, recognised the tor's phallic shape for the name means 'Landmark of pleasure'. The strange name 'The top of ye mountain fote' in Mercator's map of Ulster 1595 belongs to Chimney Rock and not Slieve Donard. All becomes clear when we realize that 'fote' is really the Irish *Foithe* meaning 'wasp' and that the ancients had deliberately shaped this tor to replicate it. In the background on the slopes of Slieve Donard, the green patch of grass marks the great solstice ritual platform with its phallic rocking stone. To the right of this again is the second rock outcrop already illustrated on page 172.

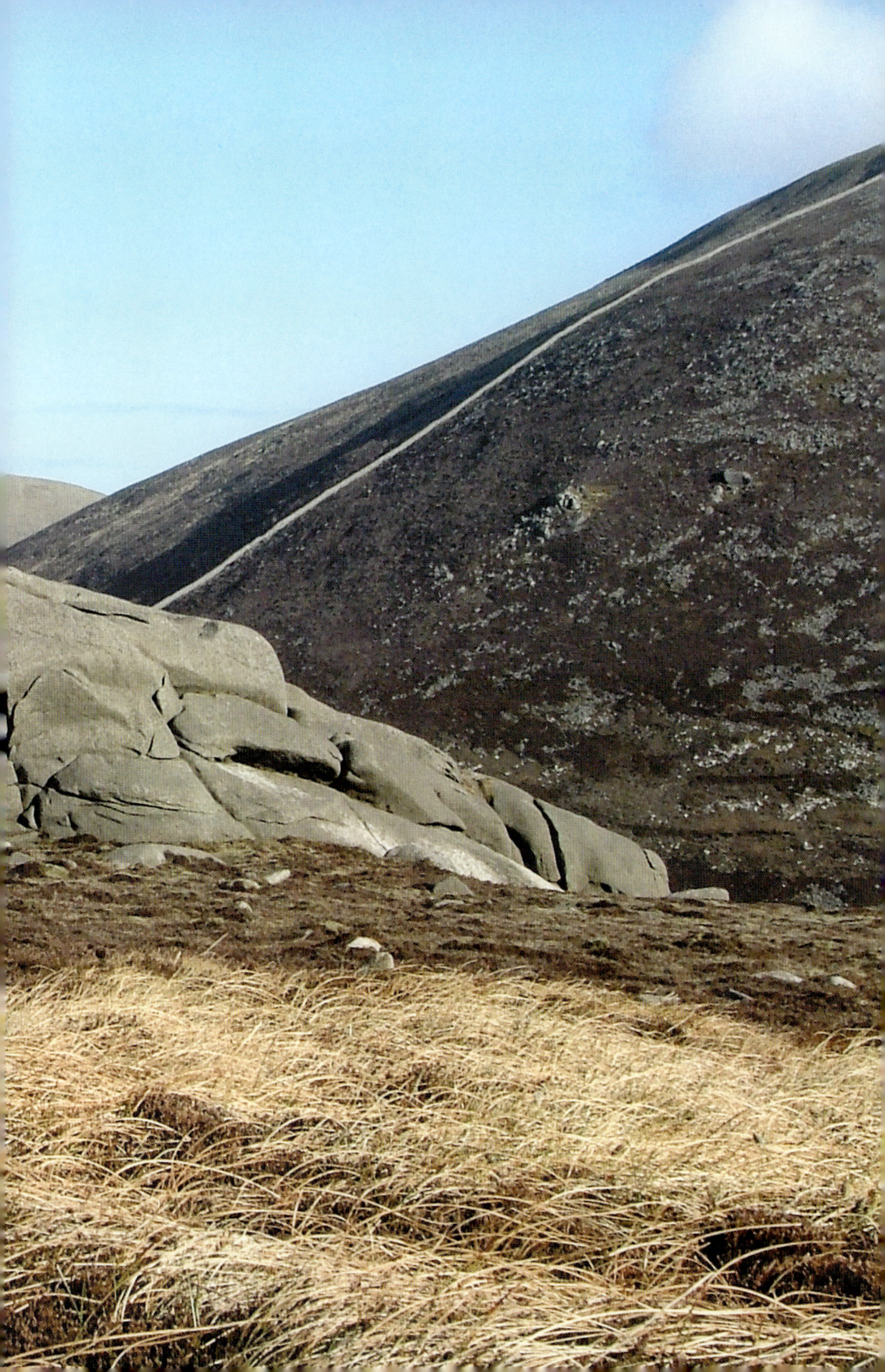

Prehistoric Mourne: Inspiration for Newgrange

Look carefully at the tor from the seaward side to appreciate how the ancients deliberately shaped this rock, not only into something phallic, but also into the outline of an insect which we imagine to be a bee. With its yellow and black body, the colours strongly associated with dawn, the bee may have held a place of special regard with the ancients on account of its colours as much as for its welcome honey. The tor has been apportioned into three segments typical of a bee's body with the head being particularly distinctive. The large front rounded dome has been given a sleeping eye suggestive of the compound eye of the bee and two large depression bowls have also been hammered out on top of the 'head' where the antenna would be. Low at the front of the bee's head the rock has been gouged to replicate the outline of the mandibles. Round the side of the bee's head the rock has been gouged to give the outline of a boar, repeating the idea mentioned previously on page 144, that the Lord of the Feast in the Otherworld tale of *Togail Bruidne Da Derga* was represented as a man carrying a pig on his shoulder. That other boulder which has a similar boar outlined on the side of it is near at hand. At the side of the tor the long low bench of rock represents the

This landmark tor on Chimney Rock has been shaped as a bee. This face features a closed sleeping eye, gouge marks to represent the mandibles and fire bowls hollowed out on the head where the antenna would be. On the side is the outline of the head of a boar which leaders of the clan were expected to provide for feasting.

The rock contours at the back of 'Horsemen' tor have been adapted into the shape of a boar's head with its mouth agape and above it a strategically placed eye. To the left again, the gouge in the rock can be seen as representing both a phallic meatus groove placed to face the rising summer solstice sun and the place of the bee's sting.

legs which in flight a bee stretches out straight behind it. The wings have almost been left to the imagination but the suggestion of something ephemeral and hazy is conveyed by a lightly chopped patch of rock where one would expect the wings to join the body. There are a number of suggestive shapes along the side of the tor which we leave to the eye of the beholder but it is hard to miss the outline of a nesting sea-bird with prominent head and beak. The ancients didn't tie themselves down in the creation of rock creatures and so it is no surprise to find not only the outline of a seagull at the side but, at the back end of the tor, the part facing towards the light of summer solstice dawn, another image suggestive of a boar with an open mouth. At the back there is also a gouge to represent a phallic meatus groove as well as the site of the bee's sting.

**The General**

This is the highest point of Chimney Rock mountain; it is the most eastern part, the bulbous part, the penile head of the full swelling or according to professor Estyn Evans's description, 'The Horsemen are the tors on Chimney Rock, with stone on the right side of the western or left recess of Newgrange chamber. Governor Thomas Pownall, one of the first to describe Newgrange, had surmised in the late eighteenth century that the characters were Phoenician and Vallancey then went one better and constructed an alphabet from them and read into it the name 'Angus'. He had also viewed his characters as not unlike a boat and the name stuck. Even George Coffey would later write, 'There is no doubt that the marking at Newgrange is a rude representation of a ship or galley similar to those of the Scandinavian rock-tracings.'[10] We will look at Newgrange in more detail later but suffice for the moment to record the belief that the passage of Newgrange is an emulation of Mourne's great *Carr na Bláthaighe*, the Spear of Abundance, and that the markings of the chamber's left recess depict Chimney Rock and the right recess roof Slieve Donard and its environs at winter solstice. Our photograph of the tor closest to Chimney Rock summit is believed to be the origin of the Newgrange markings sometimes known as 'Vallancey's Boat' although nature has tumbled the stones from their original setting.

From the summit cairn of Chimney Rock this line of boulders, like a grave barrow without the earth, stretches out towards the summer solstice sunrise.

This collection of boulders towards the end of Chimney Rock plateau, possibly the grave of an important leader of the ancients, is surmised to be the source of the image depicted on C4 at Newgrange. In comparing with the characters of 'Vallancey's Boat', shown below, the stones on this tor should be considered as having tumbled from their original positions and are now askew. The distinctive stone on the left, which in its primary position was probably intended to represent an erect phallus, is now tumbled from its original location and may now be showing us its reverse side. The dislodgment and tumbling might well have happened during the night of the Great Wind, *Oíche na Gaoithe Móire*, on 6th January 1839.

Compare these marks which became known as Vallancey's boat, with the photograph above. They are found inverted on C4 in Newgrange chamber and from the beginning have excited a lot of fanciful speculation. The contention is that all the markings on C4 depict Chimney Rock plateau from the 'view point of the risen solstice sun' which would be the centre of Newgrange chamber.

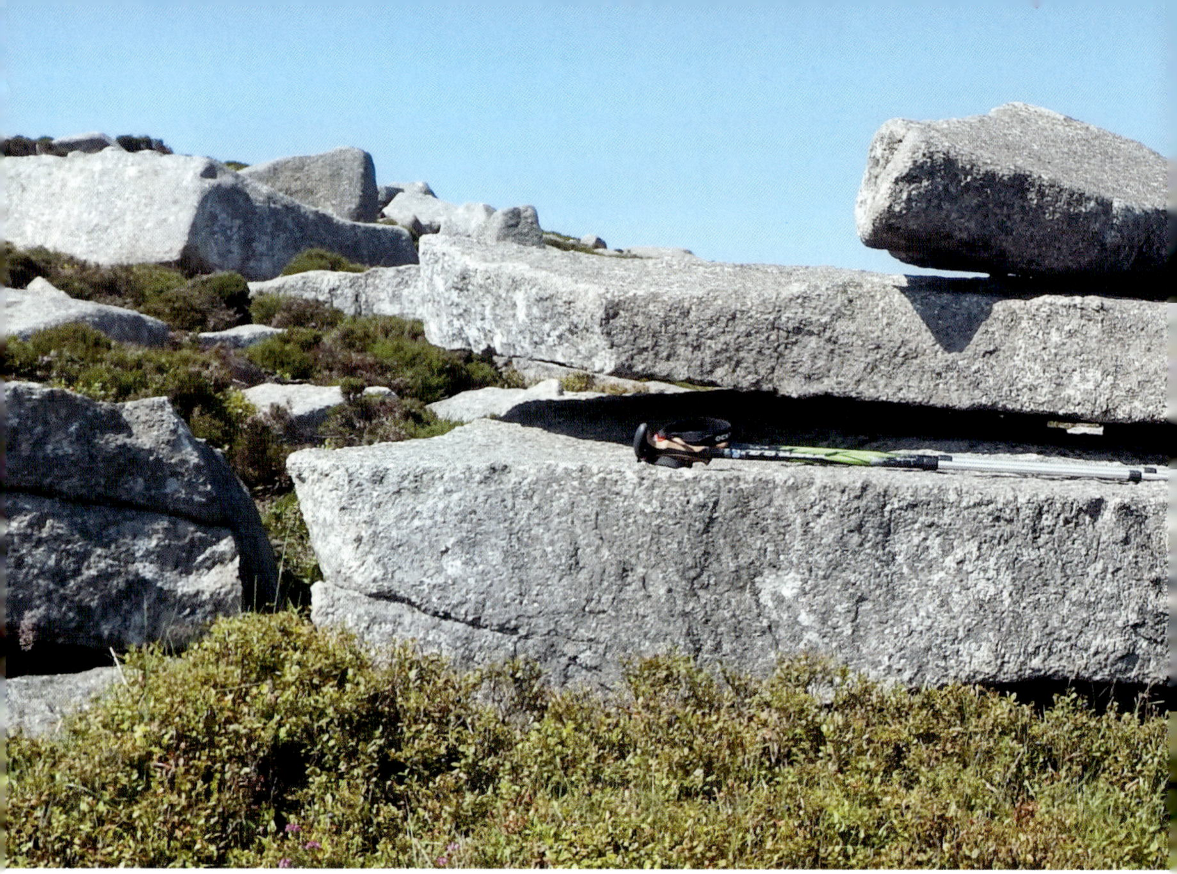

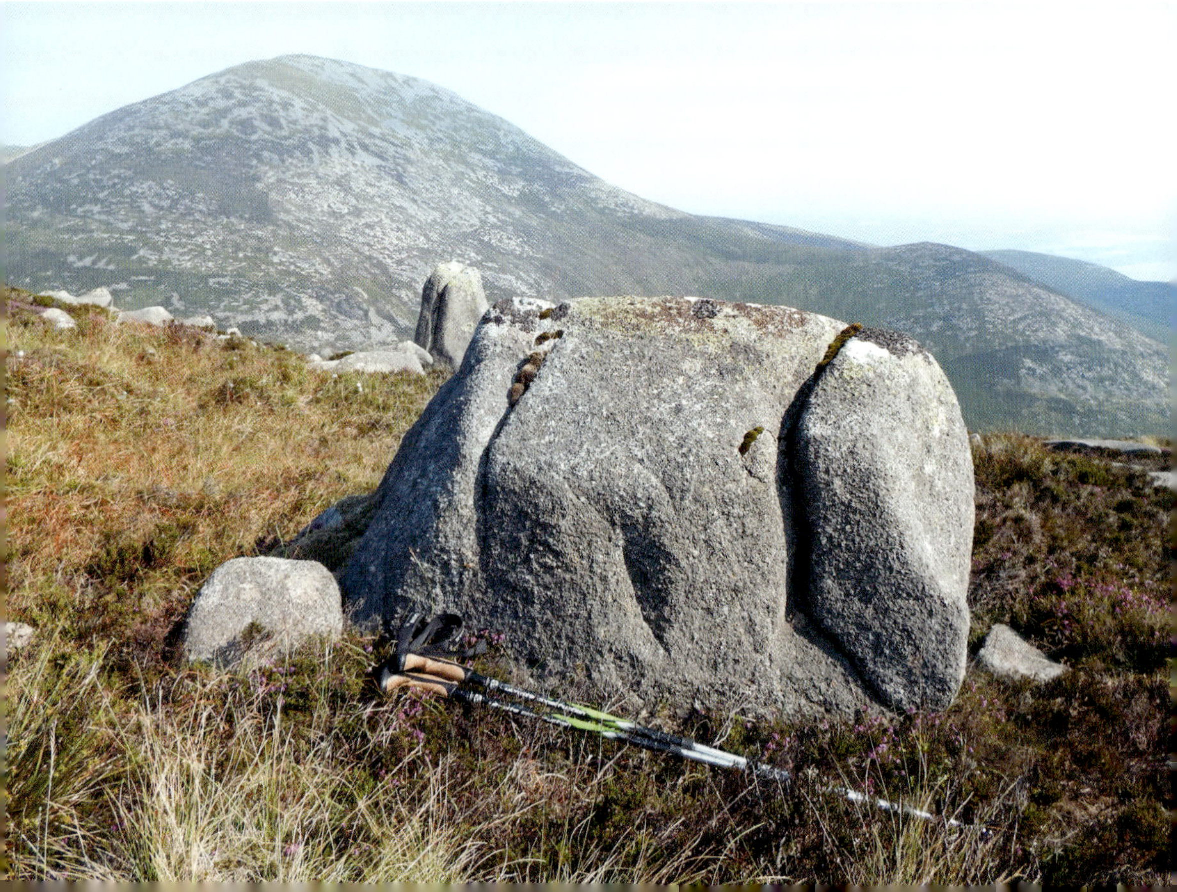

Above: It is only by walking round this beautiful attenuated triple decker monument on the seaward slope of Chimney Rock that its size and sophistication can be appreciated. It has a fertility opening between the bottom stones awaiting the penetrating light of summer solstice dawn; other points on the stones look to Slieve Donard, dawn of winter solstice and the summit of Chimney Rock.

Left: Chop a groove in the front and enhance the cracks on either side and suddenly a boulder is transformed into vaginal walls with a penis inserted between them. The very simplicity of the art work makes it all the more attractive and powerful. In the background is the phallic stone already featured on page 261.

Right: A stone is changed into a dormouse having a feed.

Above: An intriguing row of stones with their points uppermost, although the big middle stone may have toppled. Have fun interpreting. Might that be a squat version of a dolphin's head on the left and then near beside it the spatulate bill of a shoveler duck? The formation of this line is closely linked to chevaux de frise where closely packed upward pointing stones formed defences around forts such as at *Dún Aonghasa* (Dun Aengus) on Inishmore, Arran Islands.

Top right: This great spear stone is probably capping a grave. Note the sideward face underneath. To the left a cheeky little representation of nuzzling fellatio. Then again is the face underneath about to do the same?

Bottom right: Originally the rucksack and water bottle were placed against this stone to give scale to the shadow eye. Only later was it realised that in the background a large closed eye had been gouged on the rock face to make a great skyward looking face. Many times the work of the ancients has been missed in the field only to have been fortuitously recognised later when photographs have been reviewed on the screen.

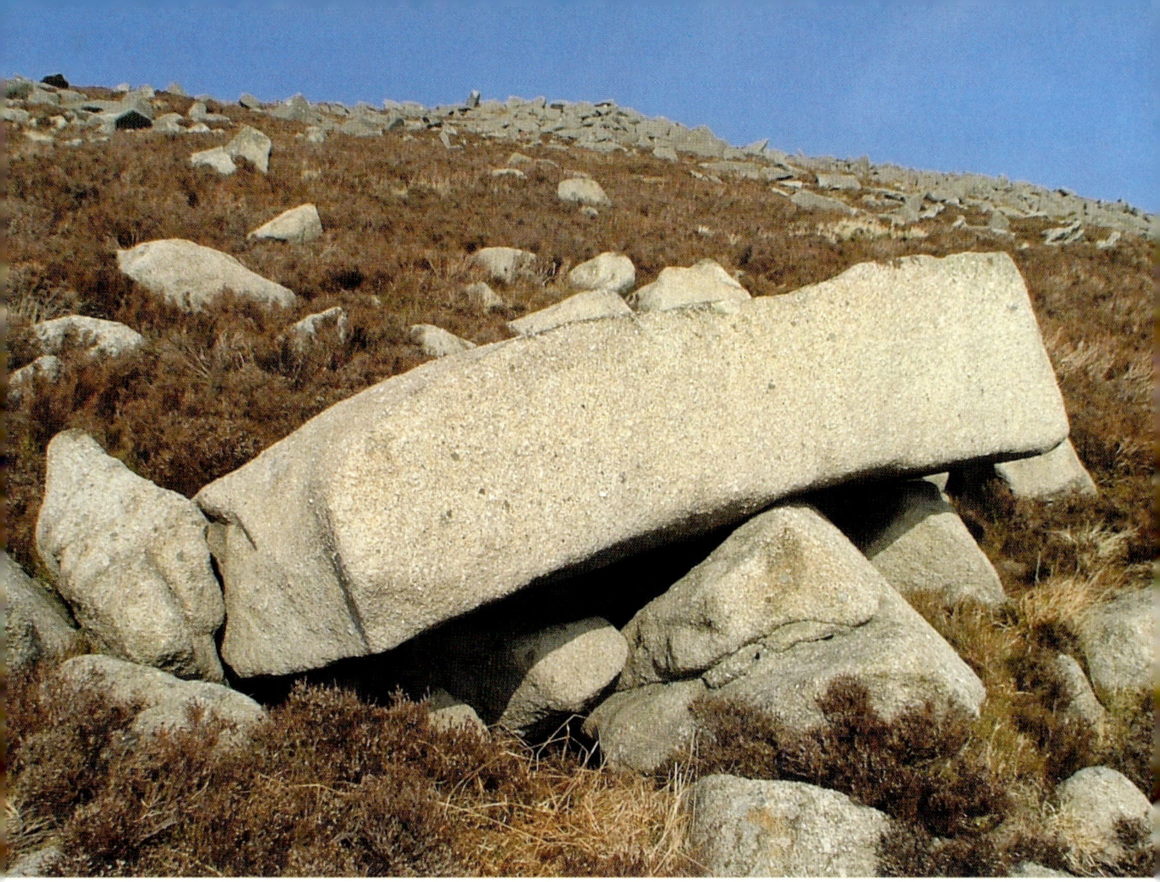

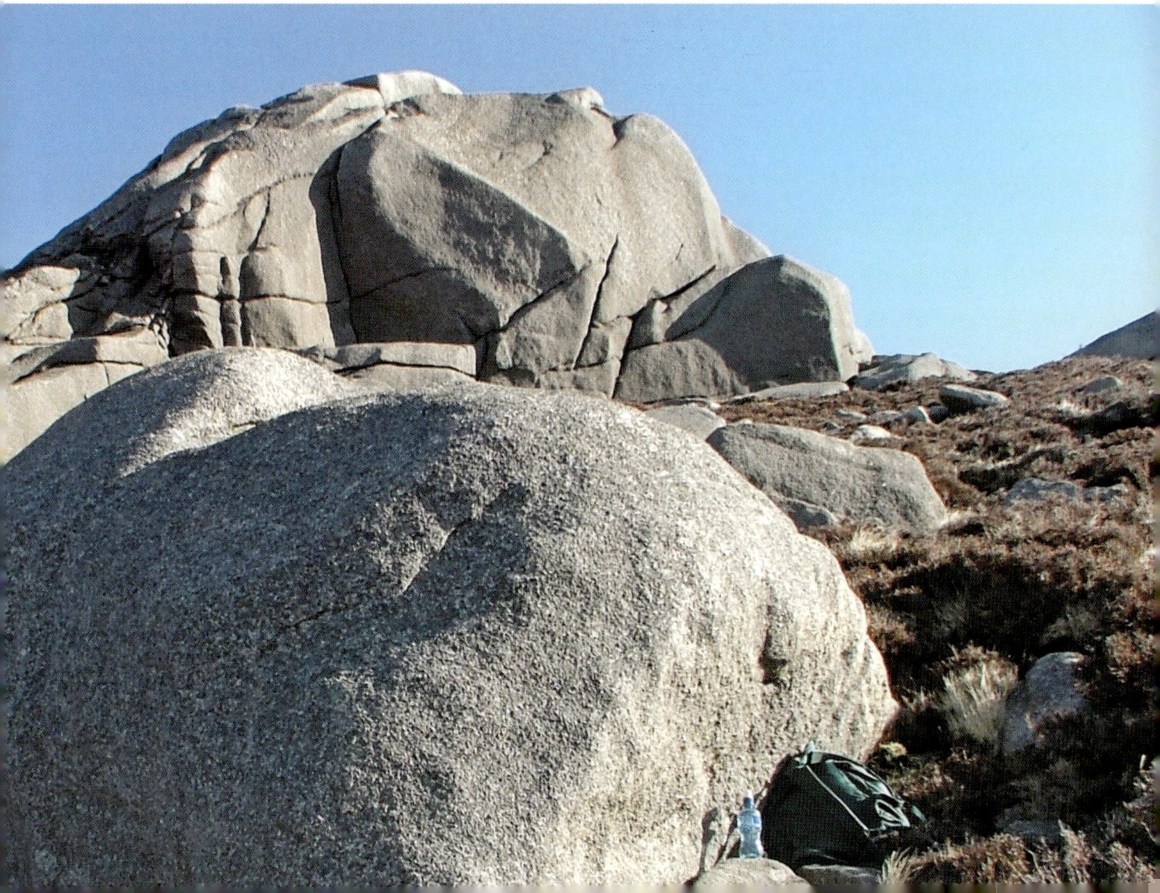

Above: If you find this grave flaunting its phallic tip that points towards summer solstice sunrise, have a seat along the side. This is a welcoming grave designed so that friends could comfortably sit around it and socialise while the 'spirit' presumably sat on the centre stone being admired for his priapic endowment. Perhaps in life the deceased was a *Seanchaidhe*, or storyteller of note accustomed to having people around him. I find this a very comical grave, certainly unusual but nonetheless very pleasant to sit beside.

Top right: This is more like what would be expected for a covered grave. There are many variations; it is all part of the joy of discovery on your journey through this ancient sacred landscape.

Bottom right: This is a *Gein* or 'begetting' stone on the eastern slope of Chimney Rock; it simulates copulation. The beauty of this creation is how the ancients used a formation of rock crystals to create an eye. Walk round the rock until you are facing Donard and a different creature emerges.

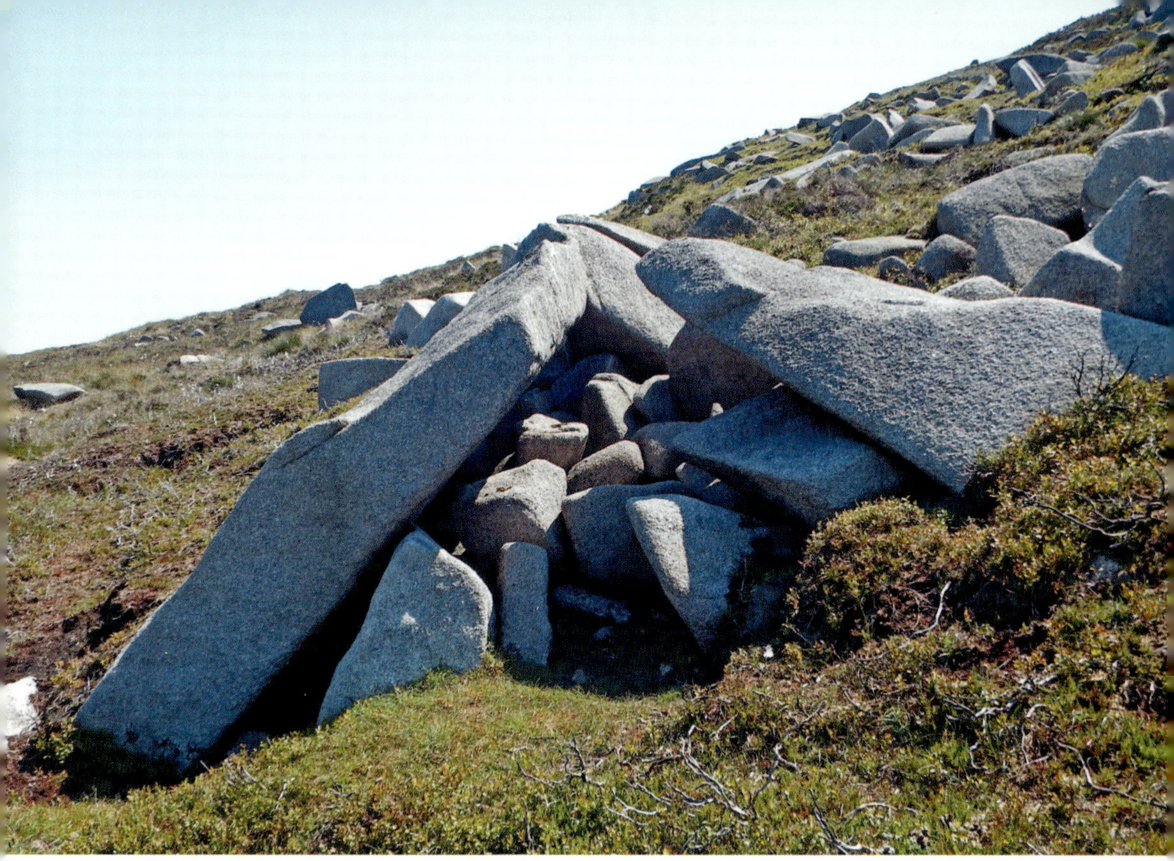

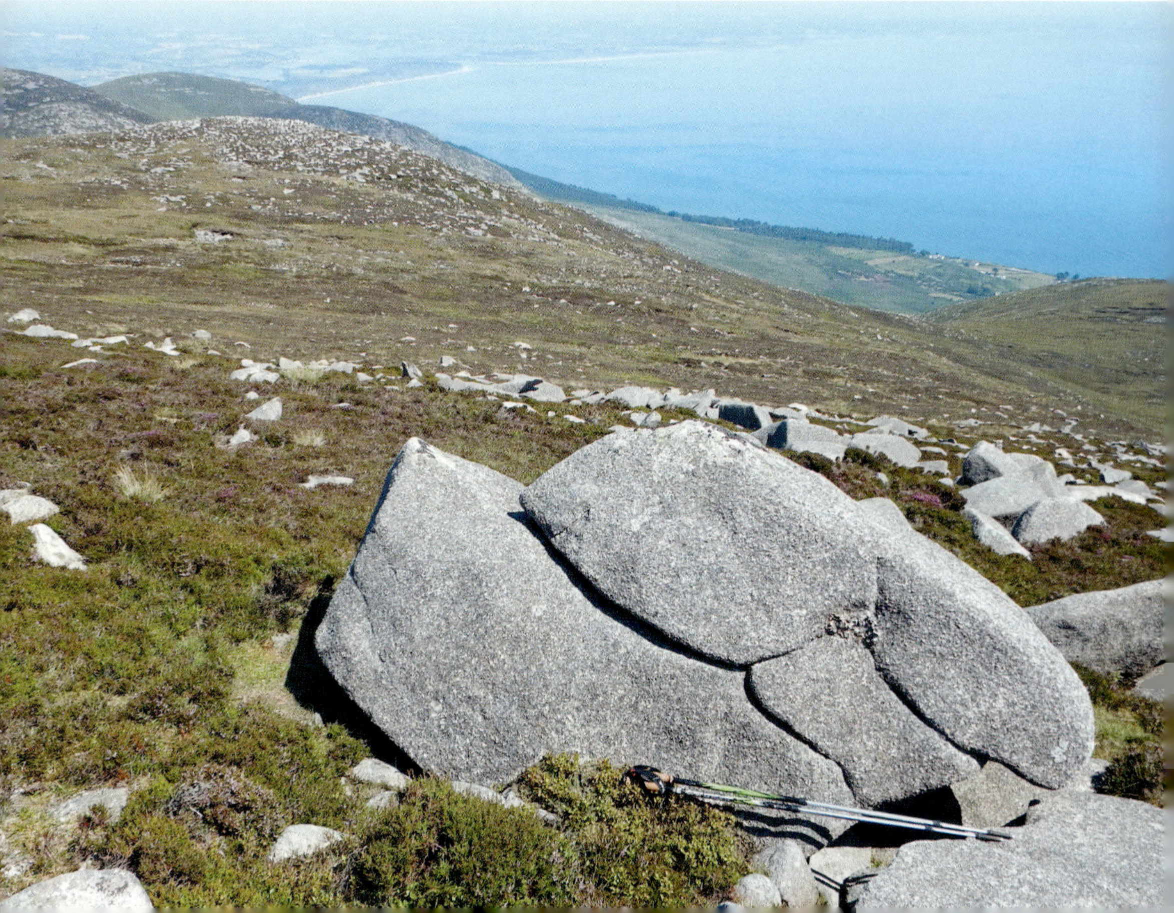

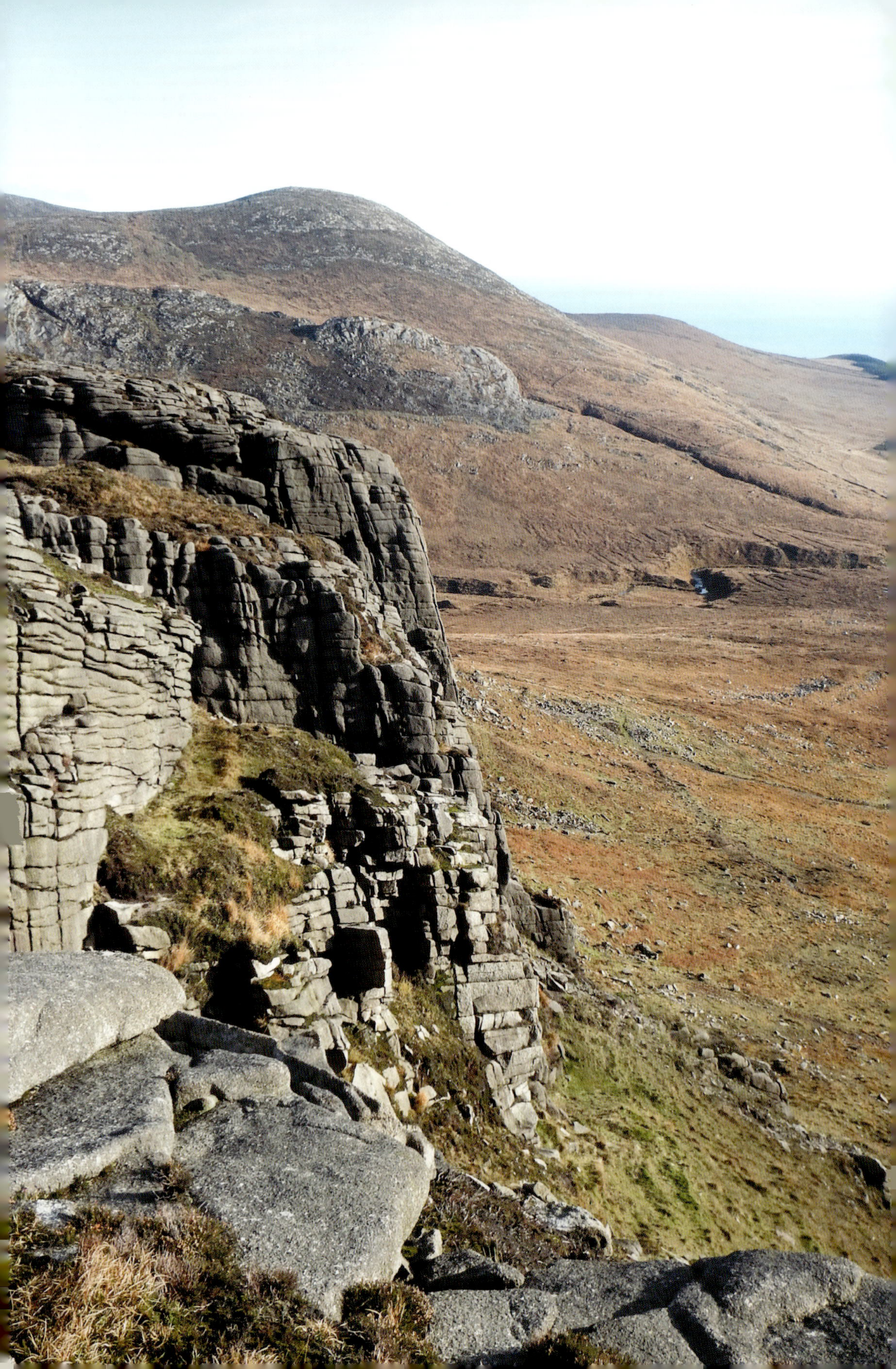

# UPPER AND LOWER COVE

*A banner must needs be the highest symbol of a family's or of a nation's traditions, of its glories, its heroism, its noblest aspirations, and as such it was and always has been venerated.*

THE O'NEILL OF LISBON SPEAKS OF HIS FAMILY'S CREST, THE RED HAND OF ULSTER, IN THE ULSTER JOURNAL OF ARCHAEOLOGY, NOVEMBER 1908.

A number of phallic and spear stones in this area of Mourne have already been featured but there are at least four further aspects of Upper and Lower Cove to be considered; These are the cliff face phallus, the solstice shadow of Rocky mountain, the great cave and the famous emblem of Ulster. In all of these the winter solstice sun has a major influence.

**The Phallus on the Cliff**

Lower Cove is an impressive wall of granite. It is beloved by climbers because of the challenge it provides, because it faces south and that it gets plenty of shelter from Slieve Lamagan; it is a pleasant location to spend a day on the rock face. The granite wall is divided by buttresses and present convention numbers these as one to four, starting from the left. Except where the points of the buttresses cast shadows, most of Lower Cove receives the first light of winter solstice dawn. Our interest is with the second buttress for this is where the cliff phallus is to be found.

In eons past the ancients noticed how a little spring of water issued half way up the cliff face and decided to enhance it as a symbol of fecundity. The brighter face of exposed granite shows where men, probably dangling from ropes from the top of the cliff, cut away at the granite to shape a suggestive phallus with its point terminating where the water issued from the cliff. The result of their skilful and undoubtedly strenuous efforts is a taut spear-like penis in permanent ejaculation; a truly impressive symbol of perpetual fertility. This remarkable example of ancient sculpture works on a number of levels; it welcomes the first light of winter solstice and, as such, is renewed in its fertility and potency. The early artist felt comfortable enough with the general suggestion of a spear point conveying or giving the impression of a penis that he felt free to develop the sculpture as a head. Readers are invited to examine the close up photograph. Making out a closed eye might be easy enough but after that the 'creature' is determined by the faults in the rock and whatever mythical idea was in the artist's

Looking over towards Rocky mountain and the Hares Castle from atop the cliffs of Lower Cove.

*The whiter granite shows the cliff face phallus with its weeping tip half way up this second buttress of Lower Cove.*

mind. Personally I have wondered at an open beaked bird and one that has a crest such as the waxwing, a berry eating winter visitor to these shores. The image of a penis in continuous ejaculation then becomes one of a bird drinking from an ever flowing spring. It is not necessary to connect with anything real for the artist has already achieved his purpose with something dynamic. That said and without wanting to read too much into it, this ancient carving, with what could be construed as a crest, would pass the expectations for a Phoenix. The early origins of this long-lived, regenerating creature are supposed to lie with ancient Egypt. Who knows however what stories may have been carried far from Mourne thousands of years ago about an indestructible bird associated with the sun, who drank from a spring of life and who was reborn every year at the winter solstice?

**Names and the Solstice Shadow of Rocky Mountain**

The sun rises on Mourne about 8.45am on the winter solstice. If it is one of those rare cloud free mornings, the sun will cast the shadow of Rocky mountain across the Annalong valley and into the incipient corrie between Slieve Lamagan and Cove mountain. On the map this equates to the plateau between the presently marked Lower and Upper Cove where Cove Lough is to be found. Rocky mountain

UPPER AND LOWER COVE

got its name from the Irish *Roicheadh*, meaning 'reaching, coming to, or, arriving at' and it refers to the mountain's phallic solstice shadow reaching across the Annalong valley and 'inserting itself' into the declivity between Lamagan and Cove. Many of the large face stones and megaliths that grace this little plateau of Mourne will be found, inter alia, to delineate the fleeting boundaries of this shadow phenomenon; some of the megaliths likely also mark further fertility connections between sun and landscape at the closing of the day. The perceived intercourse of sun and earth on this auspicious dawn is a relatively quick affair. The rising sun must grow in strength and brightness so as to be able to cast a shadow but by about 9.20am the whole liaison is nearly finished as the shadow withdraws from the declivity and, with the rotation of the earth, turns into the Annalong valley. All is over inside about forty minutes.

To understand the origin of Cove mountain we disregard ideas of a small sheltered inlet, for Cove is a mnemonic.[1] The name is from the Irish *Caob* which means 'a clod, a lump, a shovelful of clay'. As a 'lump', *Caob* is a euphemism for the penis and would refer firstly to the large phallic shadow projected by Rocky mountain into the Cove Lough basin on winter solstice morning. Secondly and at the

Could this sculpture, that would be lit by the favoured mid-winter first light, be the source of the ancient phoenix legend? The name 'phoenix' answers to the Irish *Fionn Áigh* meaning 'white thing of good luck'.

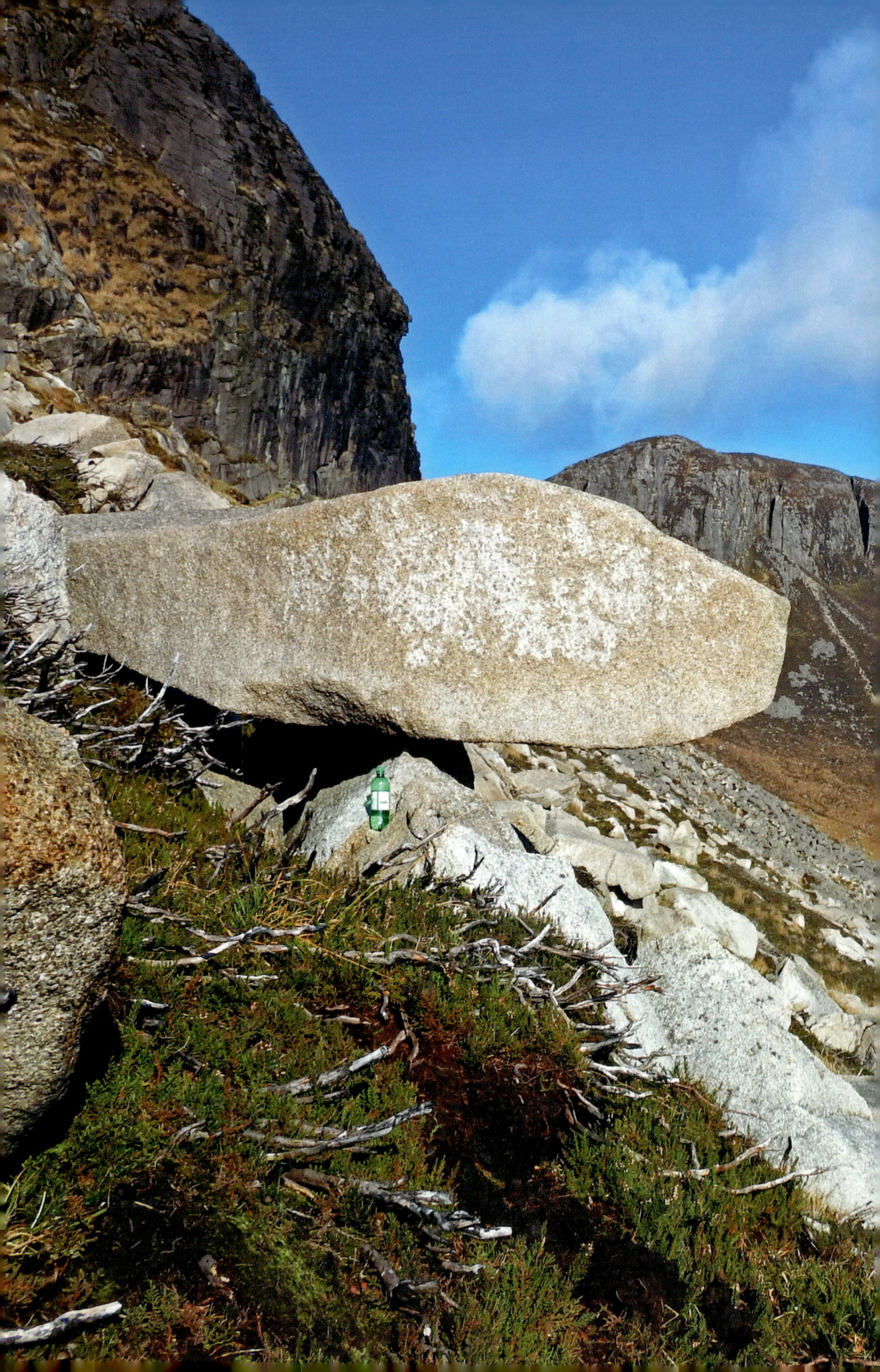

This large phallic stone, shaped to resemble a dog's head, points across the Annalong valley from the slopes under Cove mountain.

Prehistoric Mourne: Inspiration for Newgrange

The four buttresses of Lower Cove as seen from Percy Bysshe hill.

A large phallic stone on the slopes overlooking Lower Cove.

other end of the day, the name would refer to the great head of Cove mountain casting its phallic shadow into the vaginal declivity of the Annalong valley at sunset. The names of Upper and Lower Cove would also appear to be mnemonics. They both fit so conveniently onto the two scarp faces where the ordnance survey thought they belonged that it is hard to believe they could have an entirely different meaning in their original Irish. In the case of Upper Cove the name is likely derived from the Irish *Upatha*, meaning 'charms, sorcery, enchantment'. The place for the pagan prayers was the corner of the cliff overlooking the Annalong valley as it received the first light of winter solstice dawn. The flat area here is regarded as the former ritual platform and still has its stone chair together with runnels hammered into the floor of the rock surface as illustrated on page 491. Here also on the rock face below is the great ancient symbol of Ulster of which more in a moment. The name of Lower Cove brings us back to the Phallus on the second buttress. Rather than allude to the perpetually ejaculating penis on the rock face, scornful Christians described it as *Lobhar* meaning 'sick'. Instead of it being a weeping penis or drinking bird, the sculpture was now looked on as vomiting.

The time is 3.56pm on 2nd December and as the solstice approaches so the phallic shadow of Cove, seen here on the left, extends into the 'vaginal' Annalong valley. It is this phallic 'lump' of a shadow, *Caob* in Irish, that gave us the mnemonic Cove.

'You climb up through a very narrow passage to the top of the rock and land on one of the most beautiful, most magnificent and romantic spots that can well be conceived.' (Harris, 1744). Here a snowy Slieve Donard is seen from the top of Lower Cove.

Bignian, known to the fishermen of old as 'Buckie'[3], with the winter solstice sun sinking onto the top of it, stretched out its bold shadow in an apparent colossal climactic ejaculation. The cave that the ancients created to receive this potent fertility light was therefore regarded as a gigantic vagina. Burying someone at the back of the cave would probably have been in the hope of their regeneration or some form of new life for the deceased's spirit. Whatever their beliefs about life after death, the ancients were certainly prepared to go to a lot of effort to attain it.

**Ulster's Ancient Emblem came from Mourne**

Behind the surviving gable of Clonduff old church in the townland of Ballyaughian, is the burial place of Arthur Magennis who lived at Cabra and died in 1737. Look at the coat of arms on the grave to see that it is surmounted by a boar, the great ancient symbol of fertility, and that the right red hand can also be clearly seen. From the twelfth century the Magennises were the principal territorial lords of Iveagh in south Down. The great Irish genealogist, Edward MacLysaght, noted:

## Upper and Lower Cove

'…by 1598 the Magennis chief of the time, whose father was officially regarded as 'the civillest of all the Irish in these parts', had joined Tyrone (who was his brother-in-law) and thus 'returned to the rudeness of the country'. A generation later their loyalty to Ireland and the ancient faith was undoubted.'[4] Sandstone is not a local material and its use here as a headstone is rather unusual; the colour red was associated with the rising sun and the old fertility religion. The stone therefore could be construed as passing on the subtle message of respect for the sun worshipping beliefs of the forefathers as well as enhancing the right red hand which was an integral part of the crests of the Magennis and O'Neill clans. Back at the start of the 1900's there was much doubt about whether Irish heraldry had ever attained a shape sufficiently definite to justify its comparison with other nations or even possessed in former times an allegorical design that could be considered a national emblem. It was into this debate that The O'Neill of Lisbon stepped in 1908. Before the flight of the Earls, the O'Neills had been the dominant family in Ulster for more than a thousand years and during this long period down to the 16th and 17th centuries, the 'right red hand' was their main

The time is 2.52pm on 2nd December and solstice is still a few weeks away. The shadow of Lamagan is stretching out over Upper Cove but in the foreground the shadow of the principal Back Castle of Bignian is reaching out towards the cave of Lower Cove. The final touch of this priapic point at solstice sunset would have made this a place of spectacular renewal.

# Prehistoric Mourne: Inspiration for Newgrange

The often heard legend of the cutting off of the left hand and casting it ashore to win a race and a kingdom was given short shift a century ago by one of the greatest authorities on heraldry in Ulster, John Vinycomb, M.R.I.A. who dismissed the story as 'not of any account'.

The origin of the red hand belongs with the ancient sun worshippers of Mourne. Can we imagine that moment of solstice dawn. After the long vigil of the night, arms were spread wide with hands raised and opened in greeting to the rising sun. The outstretched hands joined the incantations of light and the beseeching words to the great sun for fertility and good fortune during the coming year. Here in Mourne the ancients noted that as the solstice sun rose on the Annalong valley, the very end of the cliff-face overlooking the valley was the one part that received the first light. To strengthen their welcome for their god and thus their chances of their prayers being successful, they undertook the astounding task of stripping back the great vertical weathered cliff face, exposing fresh granite that flushed an orangey red in the first light of the day. The granite was not just arbitrarily removed but was deliberately stripped back to give the form of an enormous right hand. At dawn, sunlight has to pass through more of the earth's atmosphere and meets more air molecules that scatter away the blue light; what is left is mostly the red component and this makes the rising sun seem red. This phenomenon intensified the rock's natural warm colour. For the first half hour then of dawn light, the huge hand on the cliff-face of Cove would glow a ruddy orange. Before too long the sun would rise higher and the light would become brighter and colours changed. In the normal light of day the fresh granite appeared so much cleaner, vivid and intensely white by comparison with the nearby grey weathered granite. This daylight change of colour brought about the new name of *Snab Bán*, 'the white fragment' for the cliff face; later this part of the mountain would be known as Slieve Snavan. For this important part of Mourne it is no surprise that the cliff had yet another name, Gedic. This alternative was from the Irish *Geadach* (genitive: *Geadaighe*) meaning 'having a white star on the forehead (as a horse)'. It is a surprise that such a famous symbol did not leave its own name on this part of the landscape, *Lámbh dearg*, 'the right red hand'. God knows what events took place on the cliff top of Lower Cove at solstice dawn; perhaps such awe and dread

*A copy of the seal of Hugh O'Neill who died in 1364. The Irish Aodh (Hugh) is latinised by 'Odo'. The legend on the seal (Sigillum) is S. ODONIS ONEILL REGIS HYBERNICORUM ULTONIE+. This extremely ancient seal was brought out of Ireland and sold at auction to Mr Otway Cave for £73 in 1784.*

had been generated over the millennia that even the mention of the name would have been circumscribed with great anxiety and alarm lest it bring down 'bad luck'. Superstitious fear was very powerful in the country and had been for centuries; it may well have been deemed prudent to use a euphemism for *Lámbh dearg* such as the alternatives already mentioned, *Snab Bán* or *Geadach*, rather than awaken the ire of the old gods. To appreciate the enormous deference and reverence given to this great cliff-face hand, even a thousand years after the coming of Christianity, we should reflect again on the significance of what the O'Neill stated:

> 'It was ever venerated by the people, followed by the armies, and gave origin to the celebrated war-cry of *Lámbh dearg Eirinn Abú!* 'the red hand of Ireland for ever'; and I don't know of any country where an emblem of heraldry has more warmly and enthusiastically been allied to popular and patriotic feeling than this one.'

Sometimes grains of truth remain jumbled up in old legends. We can never know what took place on the top of Cove as the solstice sun appeared, but it is not impossible that instead of the legendary hand being thrown from a boat, that a person or animal was thrown in sacrifice from the cliff top to win, not a kingdom, but success and prosperity for crops and animals for the coming year. The conducting of sacrifices on the top of Lower Cove could provide an explanation for the existence of runnels hammered into the rock near the cliff edge; they could have served to remove blood which would otherwise make the edge of the cliff slippy and dangerous. The right red hand on the rock of Cove will only retain the deep warm colour for twenty to thirty minutes after sunrise. Anyone who wants to see the event must be blessed with a cloud-free morning and be prepared to walk up into the Mournes initially in dark and then through the grey twilight to be in place to see the end of Cove. It certainly gives a very healthy respect for the ancestors of millennia past who would have been out on the mountains all night in anticipation.

Ritual platform with phallic spear point chair atop Lower Cove; please avoid cliff edges.

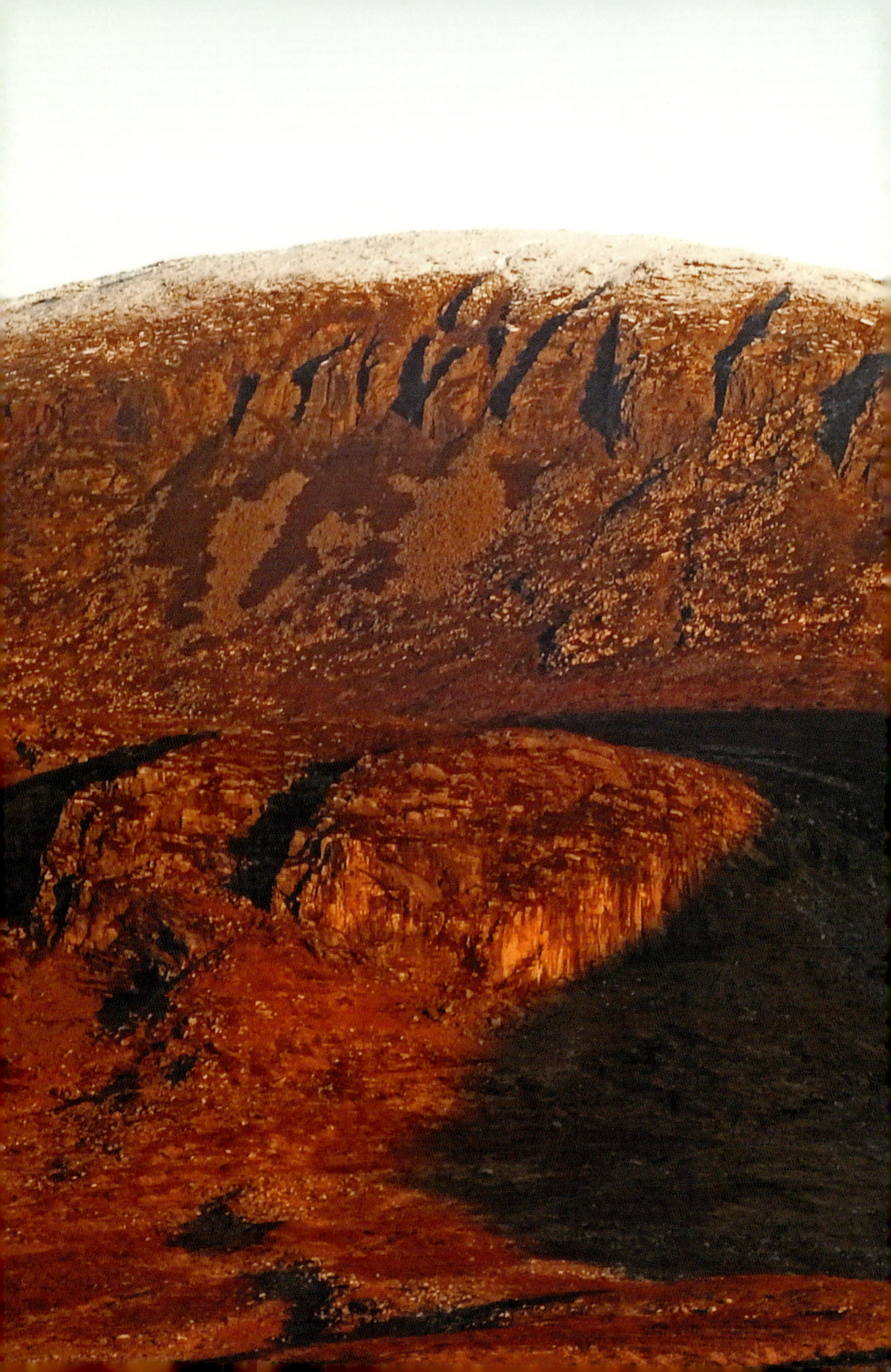

The time is 9.13am on 29th December. The great phallic shadow of Rocky mountain is withdrawing from the declivity of Cove Lough. On the corner of the cliff towards the lower left, and overlooking the Annalong valley, the warm sunlight of dawn highlights the ancient right Red Hand welcoming the first light of the new sun. The Magennis clan, Lords of Mourne, took this ancient symbol as their insignia and in turn it was adopted by the Earl of Tyrone and subsequently became the great emblem of Ulster. Have a look at the cliff face in normal light as shown earlier on pages 194-196.

Courtesy of Photographic Unit, National Monuments Service

# NEWGRANGE AND MOURNE

*'Newgrange is unhesitatingly regarded by the prehistorian as the great national monument of Ireland; in the words of the late Seán Ó Ríordáin, 'one of the most important ancient places in Europe'.*

THE BEGINNING OF COLIN RENFREW'S INTRODUCTION TO PROFESSOR MICHAEL J. O'KELLY'S WORK, *NEWGRANGE; ARCHAEOLOGY, ART AND LEGEND*, THAMES AND HUDSON, LONDON, 1982

Life was much quieter around Newgrange when I paid my first visit there now nearly fifty-five years ago. Professor O'Kelly and his team had not yet started the excavations that would make this great tomb world famous and result in it being inscribed as a world heritage site in December 1993. It was a peaceful sunny summer's day back then and there was no-one around. While my father went looking for the key-holder to come and obligingly unlock the little entrance gate, my brother and I spent time climbing the overgrown hill and wondering to ourselves what was so special about a big dark hole in the ground. Little did we know. Reflecting now on visitor numbers that hover around a quarter of a million a year and on the remarks above of the famous Cork archaeologist Seán Ó Ríordáin, one cannot help wondering what the implications are for Mourne with its wealth of megaliths and its treasure house of Neolithic sculpture, for Mourne is the inspiration behind Newgrange. Before looking at the Mourne connection which is best exemplified in the Newgrange art work, first a review of this great passage grave to offer some explanation of yet unanswered questions.

### Name:
After the mystical speculation of Charles Vallancey on Newgrange, it was hardly surprising that Sir William Wilde poured scorn on Vallancey's thought that the name Newgrange might be a reference to *Grian*, the sun, saying instead that the name was 'evidently of English introduction'.[1] Seán Ó Ríordáin suggested that the name might be a corruption of *An Uamh Greinè*, 'the cave of Grainnè', a mythological Irish figure who made a tour of Ireland in a year and a day and carried large stones in her apron that were sometimes thrown down to make her bed; in the end Ó Ríordáin preferred the explanation that 'it seems more likely it is a straightforward Anglo-Irish estate name'.[2] Since then the understanding of Newgrange has been interpreted as of Norman derivation, being a satellite farm

The entrance to the great passage tomb of *Brú na Bóinne* showing the highly decorated kerbstone, K1, which is a stylised map of Mourne.

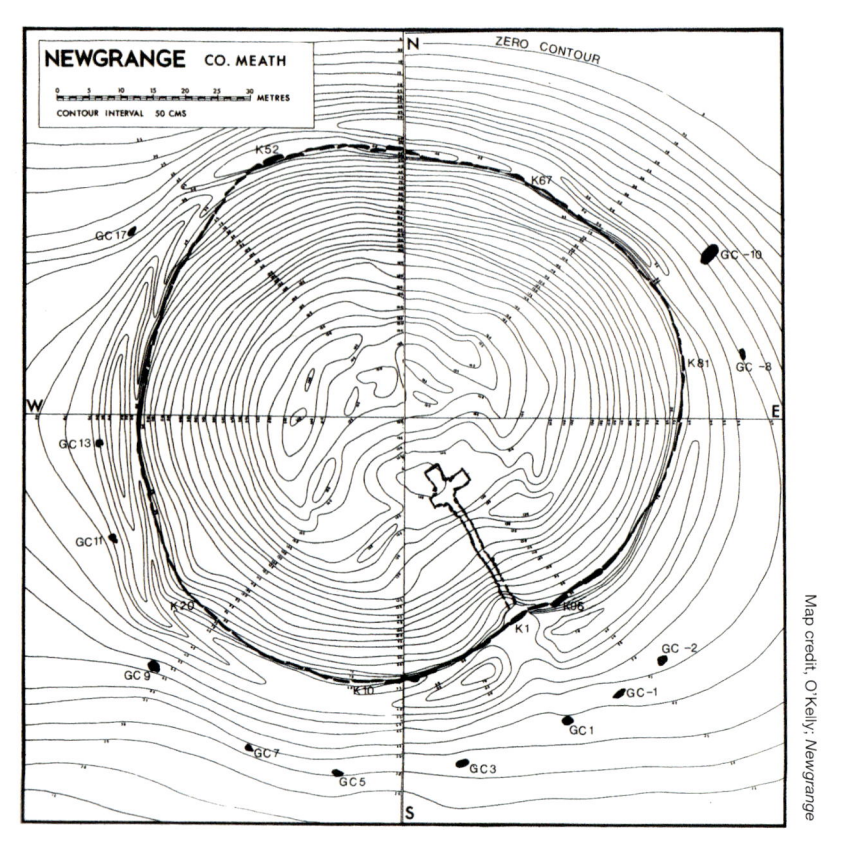

The surveyed outline of Newgrange before Professor O'Kelly started his excavations showing the flattened end of the monument.

> 'When the slip had been removed from in front of the kerbstones it was found that, while most of them were set in boulder-packed sockets, others had been set up on boulders. This arrangement seems to have been adopted so that the finished kerb should have as even a top line as possible having regard to the varying sizes and shapes of the slabs and it was later found that the arrangement was a consistent one.'[6]

During the restoration, for instance, the longest kerbstone K12 was one of the kerbs 'readjusted back onto their built-up stone supports'. May we suggest that the kerbstones are another symbolic part of the New Sun. At Newgrange the winter solstice sun rises from the distant hills but at Mourne the new sun emerges from a grey sea. The kerbstones, besides initially fulfilling the function of retaining the turves and water rolled stones from which the mound is constructed, acted as a symbolic level horizon from which the upper part of the mound, the new sun, could be seen at the moment of rising.[7] Not all the kerbs have yet been revealed. Just as kerbstone K67, on the northeast side of the mound, received special

A close-up of the sun rising over Ballykinlar. The ancients based the shape of Newgrange on the shape of the early morning sun deformed by the refraction of light through the atmosphere. This distortion flattened or squashed the sun's normally circular shape.

decoration on account of it facing towards summer solstice sunrise, so perhaps later archaeologists may have the joy of discovering another decorated kerbstone on the yet unexcavated part of the mound that faces towards winter solstice sunset and that this also would have a Mourne motif.

**Use of Quartz**
Before he died, professor Michael O'Kelly was acutely aware of the criticism around his restoration of the great quartz façade of Newgrange.[8] It is significant that on the dedication page of his book about Newgrange he quoted from the 1900 presidential address of Dr E. Wright given to the Royal Society of Antiquaries, who said: 'To be a restorer of ancient monuments one should be sheltered by a triple coat of brass, but even a repairer of such required a coat of mail.' I note with sadness some of the criticisms subsequently printed about O'Kelly's work, that the quartz wall constituted 'a monumental mistake', that it

*The name Newgrange is from the Irish Nua-Grian meaning 'New Sun' which is epitomised by the beautiful restored façade of white quartz. This New Sun emerges as if from the grey horizon of the sea at Mourne, symbolised here by the levelled ring of grey kerbstones*

'inflicted a 1960's standard of office-block design upon a structure that had stood for five thousand years…' and that 'it has been included in an international list of the world's worst archaeological reconstructions'. Such criticism can be like a boomerang. Who remembers now how horribly wrong the eminent archaeologists Ó Ríordáin and Daniel were when they scorned Newgrange folklore that said 'The rays of the rising sun at certain times of the year penetrate the opening and rest on a remarkable triple spiral carving in the central chamber'. Such an account they said was 'an example of the jumble of nonsense and wishful thinking indulged in by those who prefer the pleasures of the irrational and the joys of unreason to the hard thinking that archaeology demands.'[9] A decade later professor O'Kelly made the discovery of the winter solstice sun light penetrating Newgrange chamber, proving that the reviled folklore was substantially correct after all. As one who remembers the mound as it was before restoration I can only record my personal appreciation for the efforts that professor O'Kelly made that we might enjoy what we see today. It is only right that he and his wife Claire have been commemorated on the downstairs wall in the *Brú na Bóinne* visitors' centre. We all owe them a great debt of gratitude. It may be correctly discerned that the present writer does not belong to the school of minimal restoration; sympathetic and careful restoration by all means but it would have been disrespectful to the work of the ancients to have left their monument 'a ruin'.[10]

But what of the quartz? The Irish word for quartz is *Grianchloch*, literally 'sun stone'. The ancients had a very deliberate purpose for going to the trouble of bringing the quartz to Newgrange all the way from County Wicklow; they were building a New Sun. It was more than a tomb, a womb, a mansion or an abode for the spirit dead that they were building; it was their very god, the sun, that was being honoured by this construction and no effort would be too much or take too long in such a cause. The quartz was never intended to be a fancy path of cobbles or a terrace as some have suggested, it was deliberately sourced for its white reflective properties to create as perfect a replica of the sun as possible.[11] The only other question might be whether some ancient had such sharp eyesight and been able to safely look at the dawn sun so as to perceive the minute presence of sun-spots that might subsequently have been represented on the façade by the darker round stones of granite from Mourne?

**The Composition of the Mound**
It is one of the details that the tour guides narrate to present-day visitors, that Newgrange mound is built up of loose water rolled stones estimated to weigh two hundred thousand tonnes. Along with the stones the excavators found layers of turves that had been stripped from a substantial area around the mound. The removal of the fertile top soil with the turves would have been a large sacrifice to a people who depended on this resource for the grazing of their cattle. Besides the huge investment in labour involved, the accuracy of the solstice sunlight annually penetrating the central chamber shows that the undertaking was also thought out and meticulously planned. There was nothing haphazard about it; as professor O'Kelly said:

> 'We came to realize that we were not dealing with questions of brute force and mere strength of numbers so much as with intelligent and well-organized

method, more on the lines of the organization and division of labour practised today in any comparable undertaking. ...We have no doubt whatever that the whole undertaking was carefully thought out and planned from first to last and carried out with something like military precision.'[12]
Accordingly, we have always thought that the selection of the building material for the composition of the mound was also carefully planned and may have had hitherto unrecognised immense symbolic purpose and value.

The economy of the Neolithic was based on their crops and cattle, with cattle being an especially valued form of mobile wealth. The good soils and rich grazing of the Boyne valley made this part of Ireland prime farming land and it doubtlessly supported many livestock for the Neolithic people. To appreciate the symbolism of the material that makes up Newgrange I would like to suggest a new understanding of the name of the river Boyne. The proposition looks to the Irish *Bóin*, which means 'a little cow'. When the Irish collective suffix *–ne* is added to the end of *Bóin* we then have *Bóin-ne* 'very many little cows'. Such I believe was the early understanding of *Bóin-ne*, the name of the river which flowed through this rich dairy country. The symbolism comes from collecting a stone from the river, a stone that has been born from this source, rolled and shaped and finally deposited on the flood-plain. The stones, we may speculate, coming as they did from this sacred source, were themselves symbolical 'little cows'. Constructing the great mound with two hundred thousand tonnes of this water rolled material was the equivalent of making a treasure house of bovine wealth of unbelievable proportions. The 'very many little cows' of course had to be 'fed' so the people stripped the grass turves of a vast surrounding area to lay the sods alongside the stones on the mound, securing the stones in place and providing a perpetual symbolic food source. With the mound made up of millions of well fed 'little cows', the ancients had, in their eyes, constructed their new sun with the most valuable of all material, herds of cows. And as for the larger water rolled granite boulders now interspersed throughout the quartz façade; if they were not possible sun-spots, might they have been regarded as prime bulls from Mourne, themselves annually renewed by the touch of the solstice sun like the megalith of the primeval cow called Slievenagarragh, and now set to service the little cows in perpetuity? This new sun mound that the ancients had painstakingly created would henceforth be a treasure store of incalculable symbolic wealth. Dead ancestors buried in such a tomb would be surrounded with riches beyond imagining in their new life.

**The Great Entrance Kerbstone of Newgrange**

After years helping her husband at Newgrange, studying all aspects of the mound's art and reflecting on what she had discovered, Claire O'Kelly was absolutely correct and quite prescient when she declared about K1, 'there is therefore nothing accidental about the siting or the ornamentation of this fine slab'. She further declared 'that the symbolical meaning was the original inspiration for Irish passage-grave art'.[13] The problem for all those who have looked upon this most enigmatic of stones was to discern just what was this symbolic content and the meaning that lay behind the decoration. Many, like Ó Ríordáin, had thought the spirals and artwork to be just decoration or ornamentation, others prehistoric graffiti and it was Claire O'Kelly who cautiously summed up the present consensus that Newgrange art was 'geometrical and non-representational, at least in an overt sense'.

In more recent times it has become obvious that offering an explanation for the art of Newgrange would be fraught with great scepticism and ridicule. The learned work of Geraldine and Matthew Stout stated, 'The meaning of megalithic art is generally dismissed as the puerile pursuit of the pseudo-scientist. Explanations include astronomical and geographical interpretations'. To this they added:

'Interpretations come in cycles, which often reflect the cultural background of the period: feminism, Freudianism, materialism, etc. Current interpretations, therefore, have more to do with the time we live in than with the Neolithic. It is also impossible to escape the legacy of the drug culture and its attendant interest in mysticism and shamanism. The inconvenient truth is, that in the absence of the original artists, we can never hope to have more than the very vaguest concept of what they were trying to convey.'[14]

Be that as it may, one is now free to set forth the geographic and symbolic meaning of this hitherto magnificent and inscrutable work of art with the conviction that the artist's concept is not a mystery but is indeed understandable. The real problem has been that until now we just have been looking in the wrong place. To find the answer one must look to Mourne rather than the Boyne valley.

To adapt the slogan of the Ronseal advert of 1994, the famous entrance kerbstone at Newgrange, referred to from now on as K1, *does exactly what it says on the tin*. The geographic explanation for K1 and indeed for the other highly decorated stones K52 and K67 is simple, they are all stylised maps depicting major winter and summer solstice events of the Mournes over forty miles away. Make no mistake; Newgrange is copying the sacred promontory of Mourne which thousands of years ago must have had fame, perhaps even then of international import, far beyond what we can imagine today. K1 identifies with Mourne. It is as if K1 was saying for Newgrange, 'just as the rising winter solstice sun exactly penetrates the vulva of the earth at the Bloody Bridge valley in the Mournes, so likewise the sun precisely penetrates me at winter solstice as well'. The vertical groove down half the centre of K1 has a name in Irish; this is *Carr na Bláthaighe*, 'The Spear of Abundance', the name collected at Mourne in 1834 by John O'Donovan during the ordnance survey. The spirals are no less than the mountains surrounding the Bloody Bridge valley. The decorated stone K52 will be considered when we look at Slieve Bearnagh and K67 when we look at Slieve Bignian.

  The ancient master-sculptor who made out the map of Mourne across the entrance stone also imparted the sense of dynamic movement to symbolise the shaft of light flying through the dawn. When the Stouts were giving their description of the entrance stone they introduced the idea of water, making an analogy of the spirals with 'waves'. 'The curving, loose ends of the spirals', they said, 'carry around the foot of the stone in tubular waves…'. Looking at the many sculptures in stone of whales and sea creatures around the hills of Mourne, one can be in no doubt that the ancients were very familiar with the sea and the denizens of the deep. They would have been skilled sailors. If you have ever sculled a boat you will be familiar with the eddies left in the water after the oar has finished its stroke. The same image of swirls of water, with clockwise spirals on the left of *Carr na Bláthaighe* and anti-clockwise spirals to the right of the line, conveys the idea of the spear of light splitting the air and swirling the darkness

The four mountains along one side of the Annalong valley are the spirals along the bottom of K1. Here, from left to right as seen from the Carrick Little track are, Lamagan, Cove, Beg and Slieve Commedagh.

**Number Code to interpret K1 Entrance Stone at Newgrange.**

1. The centre groove is *Carr na Bláthaighe,* 'the Spear of Abundance' and refers to the winter solstice sun casting a penetrating shadow into the 'vulva' of the upper Bloody Bridge valley.
2. Carr's Face, a shoulder of Chimney Rock mountain; it is from the Irish *Cairre Fás,* 'the beginning of the spear'.
3. Chimney Rock mountain; this spiral has many nicks and notches marking major megaliths.
4. Rocky, the 'reaching' mountain; its phallic shadow reaches over the Annalong valley at dawn of winter solstice.
5. Long mountain; an extended shoulder of Chimney Rock. The name is a mnemonic of *Luan,* meaning 'Light' as its long flank receives the uninterrupted light of solstice dawn.
6. The summit tor end of Slieve Bignian.
7. The junction between the Annalong valley and the valley between Slieve Lamagan and Slieve Bignian. This may well therefore be Percy Bysshe hill, the name being a mnemonic of the Irish *Pearsa bPise,* 'form of a vulva'.
8. Slieve Bignian, or more likely that part known as Douglas Crag with its monstrous megalith marking the summer solstice sunrise from between Donard and Chimney Rock, ie. kerbstone 67.
9. Slieve Lamagan.
10. Cove mountain: including Lower Cove, Upper Cove and Cove mountain; the numerous later nicks on this part of K1 witness to the importance of Cove at winter solstice. Cove is also the lower of the spirals on the famous Triple Spiral motif on chamber stone ten.
11. The Slash. Professor O'Kelly always thought this line was trying to impart a message as the gouge in the stone went below the grass-line! It represents the line of sight from the important ritual platform on the south side of Slieve Donard, through the top of the Devil's Coachroad on Slieve Beg, over to the flank of Slieve Bearnagh's north tor (which last is not featured on the kerbstone; Bearnagh is the innermost of the triple spirals on C10).
12. Slieve Beg: probably a contraction of the Irish *Beaghán* meaning 'a sting', a reference to the phallic ridge of rock in the Devil's Coachroad gully. Beg is the upper of the triple spirals on chamber stone ten and it likewise has a faint line across it equivalent to the aforementioned slash.
13. The three sun/earth fertility connections, depicted as three double diamonds, visible from parts of Curragh Ard marsh. See pages 89-91.
    a) The winter solstice sun seen rising from the top of Drinnahilly
    b) The sun rising out of the notch between Drinnahilly and Shan Slieve
    c) The sun seen at the tip of Slieve Thomas
14. Slieve Commedagh.
15. Slieve Donard: Note where the slash line starts half-way up the south facing slope at the ritual platform.

Kerbstone One at the entrance to Ireland's premier prehistoric monument of Newgrange has, for a long time, been the most photographed yet the most enigmatic stone in Ireland. This superb example of ancient art is a stylised map of the Mourne Mountains about forty miles north of the Boyne (See key code on adjacent page). At Mourne the early inhabitants, the *Fir Bolg* (men of the womb), celebrated the first light of winter solstice sun casting a large phallic shadow up the Bloody Bridge valley in a great symbolic act of sexual congress between sun and earth. It is as if K1 was saying for Newgrange, 'just as the rising winter solstice sun exactly penetrates the vulva of the earth at the Bloody Bridge valley in the Mournes, so likewise the sun precisely penetrates me at winter solstice as well'. This shaft of fertility light at Mourne

372

was called in Irish *Carr na Bláthaighe*, 'The Spear of Abundance', and is replicated by the central groove on the stone. This kerbstone would have been carefully chosen by the ancients and it is no accident that the megalith is of a pronounced penile shape. The sexual symbolism has been further emphasised by quite suggestive depictions of fellatio by both adjacent kerbstones. Many of the little nicks and notches on the spirals coincide with important megaliths at Mourne. The slash down two-thirds of the entrance stone just left of the central bar is not an accident but was a later addition to mark the important line of sight from the ritual platform on Slieve Donard, through the top of the Devil's Coachroad, over to the flank of Slieve Bearnagh.

373

aside as it flies on its way to penetrate the earth bringing it fertility. It is no accident either that the great stone used to display this act of annual procreation between sun and mother earth should itself be decidedly priapic in shape. K1 was probably deliberately chosen for its evocative appearance and phallic form.

In understanding K1 there is another factor to consider. The tomb itself is the new sun, so the blaze of light that flies through the air notionally creating the swirls, like a boatman rowing as fast as he can, is coming **out of** the tomb, out of the new sun, rather than going into it. Hence on K1 the Mournes are entered via the Bloody Bridge valley from the top of the stone. I will always remember the eureka moment when the understanding of K1 came; it was on 6th March 2011 after a walk in the mountains following the death of a relative. There had always been an awareness of approximate similarity between the spirals on the stone and the use of contours on a modern map. The subliminal idea existed that the spirals could possibly represent mountains. But the moment of comprehension came when a connection was made with the four lower spirals and the four mountains along the Annalong valley, Commedagh, Beg, Cove and Lamagan as seen from the Carrick Little track. The other mountains came as a matter of course. We who are spoiled nowadays with GPS, precision maps and photographic reality, should make allowances for scale and exactness. K1 is after all a work of approximation rather than an exact map, it is stylised, representative, and suggestive and as such it actually works quite well.

The four mountains along the west side of the Annalong valley may answer a different mystery that puzzled many from the time of Colgan, the seventeenth century hagiographer. In the Book of Leinster, which lists the mothers of the saints of Ireland, Derinilla, the mother of St Donard was given the epithet *Derinilla Ceathair Cícín*, 'Derinilla of the four paps'. Anxious to ensure that this strange description of Derinilla did not brand her as some kind of monster with four breasts, Colgan attempted to explain it by saying she had given the milk of her breasts to sons born of four different husbands.[15] It is more likely however that her husband, Echu, the last pagan king of Mourne and son of Muiredach, gave his wife the valuable grazing rights to the Annalong valley and that the description of 'four paps' relates to the four mountains, Commedagh, Beg, Cove and Lamagan, rather than Derinilla herself.

**K1 and the Slash Sightline through the Devil's Coachroad**

There is further internal evidence on K1 that this entrance stone of Newgrange is an appreciation of Mourne. To the left of the central groove there is a thin line like a slash in the rock that stretches down about three-quarters the height of the stone. In most artistic representations of K1, including the monumental work of Claire O'Kelly, this line is air-brushed out, being thought of as an unfortunate accident to the stone and just an irrelevant distress line. Professor Michael O'Kelly

The great phallic chair on the ritual platform of Slieve Donard and in the background the dark gully of the Devil's Coachroad on Slieve Beg with the north tor of Slieve Bearnagh beyond it. This is the sightline 'slash' down the left front of Newgrange entrance stone that extends below the area of spiral carving.

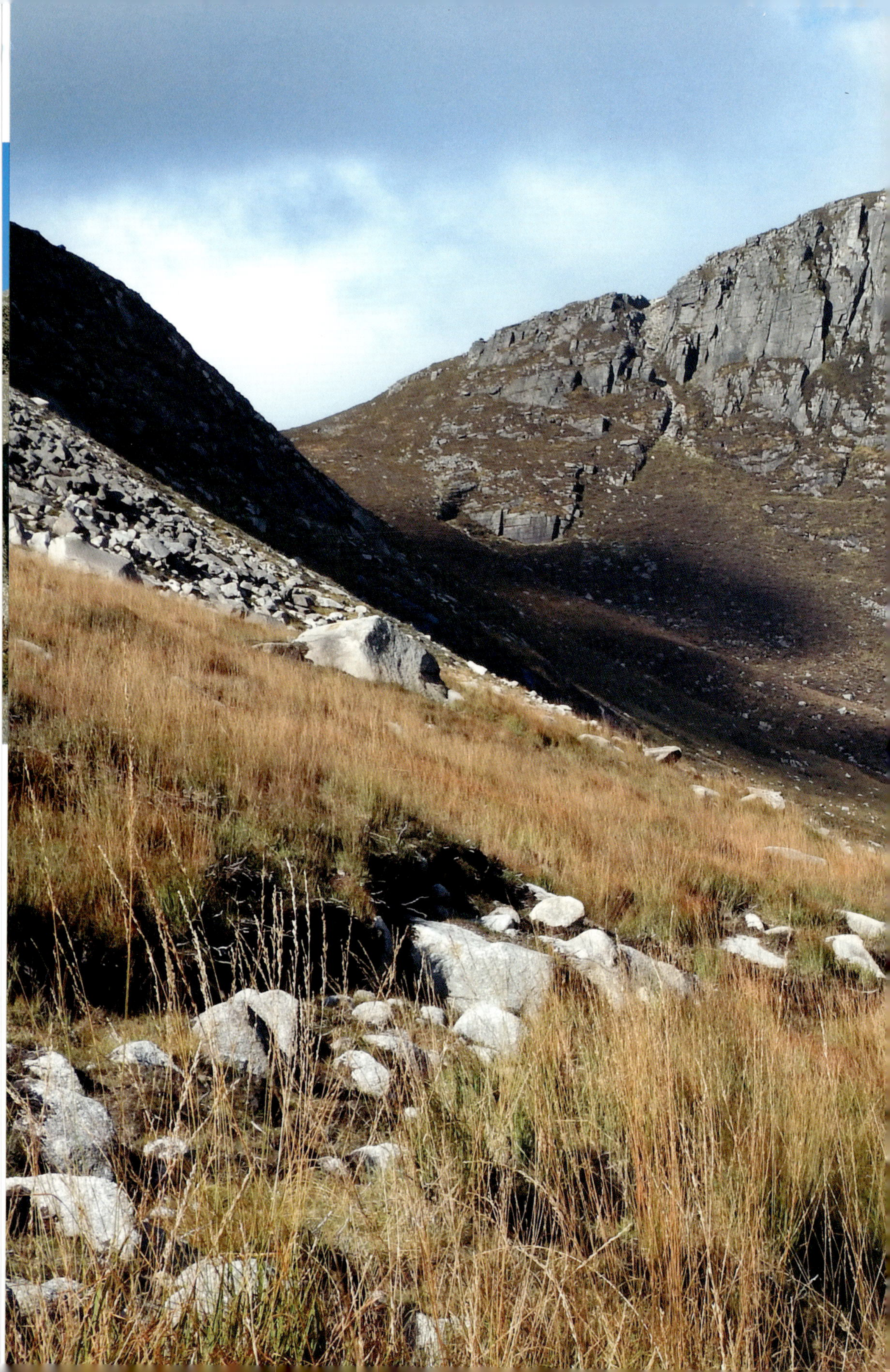

Slieve Beg at the head of the Annalong valley. The name of the mountain may be a contracted remnant of the Irish *Beag-Náire* meaning 'shamelessness'.

*The rock at the top of the Devil's Coachroad has been made whiter by mauling, doubtlessly to symbolise a seminal discharge.*

possibility that the name of Slieve Beg may have been a contracted remnant of the Irish *Beag-Náire* meaning 'shamelessness', or from *Beaghán* meaning 'a sting', a euphemistic reference to the phallic ridge. The old name of Annahole may not be a mistranscription after all but a further allusion to the Coachroad as *Ana h-Uilc*, 'plenty of an evil thing'. The name of Annalong is not far distant either as it is from the Irish *An-All Loime*, meaning 'very great nakedness'; a clear hint to the massive erect stone penis in the gully of the Devil's Coachroad. With a name like that it would be no surprise that good Christian people would have quickly elided it to *Áth na Long*.

**From the Entrance Passage of Newgrange to the Triple Spiral**

Such is the narrowness of the entrance passage into Newgrange mound that guides ask visitors to remove back-packs so as not to get caught or jammed. Only one person at a time can go along the passage and it reminded me acutely of the middle narrower fissure on Slieve Lamagan above Lower Cove that can only be squeezed into sideward. Such strictures only reinforce the idea of walking in the very footsteps of the ancients.[19] The planning of the passage-way was as methodical and deliberate as the rest of the tomb and like the K1 entrance stone it mimics Mourne and in particular the upper reaches of the Bloody Bridge valley that is pierced at solstice by *Carr na Bláthaighe*, 'The Spear of Abundance'. Visitors going along the passage at Newgrange do not usually realise that they are going uphill until the guide tells them that there is a two metre rise in ground level between entrance and the final chamber. This is a deliberate imitation of the rising trail of the upper Bloody Bridge valley. Further, the ancients went to much trouble to build a sinuous passage-way rather than a straight one which would have been much easier. It would not have been necessary to slightly twist the passage-way to constrict the path of solstice light as this could have been done much more simply by reducing the width of the roof-box. We surmise that the reason for the gently winding passage-way was to copy the turns of the upper reaches of the Bloody Bridge river. Such twists and turns were probably intended to give the reassurance of familiar surroundings to ancestral spirits buried on the sacred promontory of Chimney Rock; the features of the passageway would have been recognizable to the spirits in their imagined comings and goings and make them still feel included and belonging even though this clan had moved to the lush pastures of the Boyne. It was always important to be respectful towards the ancestors so as not to incur their displeasure and have bad luck. Likewise we may be sure that the ancients who took such care in the planning and execution of this great monument would have been aware of the spring welling up from the socket of R8 and that this too was made to replicate the Crossone river or the other tiny tributary from Donard's flank into the Bloody Bridge river in its upper reaches.

Others before now have remarked how analogous the central chamber of Newgrange is to a womb. Standing in the central chamber with one's back to the passage, a visitor has just followed the equivalent of the processional route at Mourne up the Bloody Bridge valley to the place where the great Spear of Abundance impregnated the earth at solstice dawn. At Mourne, the area between Chimney Rock and Slieve Donard is known as the Bog of Donard. Six months later at the summer solstice from the plateau of Douglas Crag under Slieve Bignian, the sun can be seen rising, or as the ancients would have preferred it, being born from the [V] shaped notch or womb between Slieve Donard and Chimney Rock. The bog of Donard got its name from this summer solstice event and not from the presence of the peaty and marshy ground in this area. The bog of Donard is a mnemonic of the Irish *Bolg an Donn Árd*, 'the womb of Donard'. This solstice 'birth' is the meaning behind the spirals and diamonds on kerbstone 67 which itself has been deliberately placed on the north-east side of Newgrange mound facing where the summer solstice sun rises. So important was this birth of the sun from the earth that the place where it can be witnessed was marked on Douglas Crag by the biggest megalith in Mourne.

*The fern would have been an ideal image of fecundity for the ancients; each pointed leaf was like a mini phallic spear but the real importance was the fertility symbolism of the plant unfolding in spring as if it were a penis straightening out and becoming tumescent.*

and which we referred to earlier. This is the same line also found on the front entrance kerbstone as the slash that goes down below the end of the carving on the stone. (See key code for K1, number eleven on page 371).

Newgrange is rightly acclaimed as the great national monument of Ireland. Mourne, which was its genesis and inspiration, now likewise deserves due status as one of the most important and influential areas of Megalithic Ireland. Looking again at the vast corpus of the endeavours of the ancients, the animal stones, the face stones, together with the vaginal, priapic and begetting stones, the right Red Hand of Ulster and the great ancient sanctuary that is Chimney Rock mountain,

# NEWGRANGE ABD MOURNE

we are most certainly privileged to have such a vast heritage of riches on our doorstep. The farmers and landowners who have hitherto preserved and protected Mourne need all possible safeguarding themselves as the future development of this ancient legacy is brought to the wider appreciation of mankind. It would be most unfortunate to reveal these treasures only to have defacement such as the graffiti chiselled in stone at Cloghmore, despoliation through rampant erosion from thousands of extra feet, the mortification of a rise of rubbish discarded throughout the beautiful mountains or the strictures of strangulating regulation from officialdom. Such are some of the challenges ahead but the future is bright indeed. Mourne has much to offer and Mourne deserves to be fully recognised as a world heritage site.

This world famous icon of Newgrange is a depiction of the end of the Spear of Abundance. Clockwise from the top the spirals represent Slieve Beg, Cove mountain and Slieve Bearnagh. Note the line through the Slieve Beg spirals; this is the line of sight from Donard, through the Devil's Coachroad, over to Slieve Bearnagh.

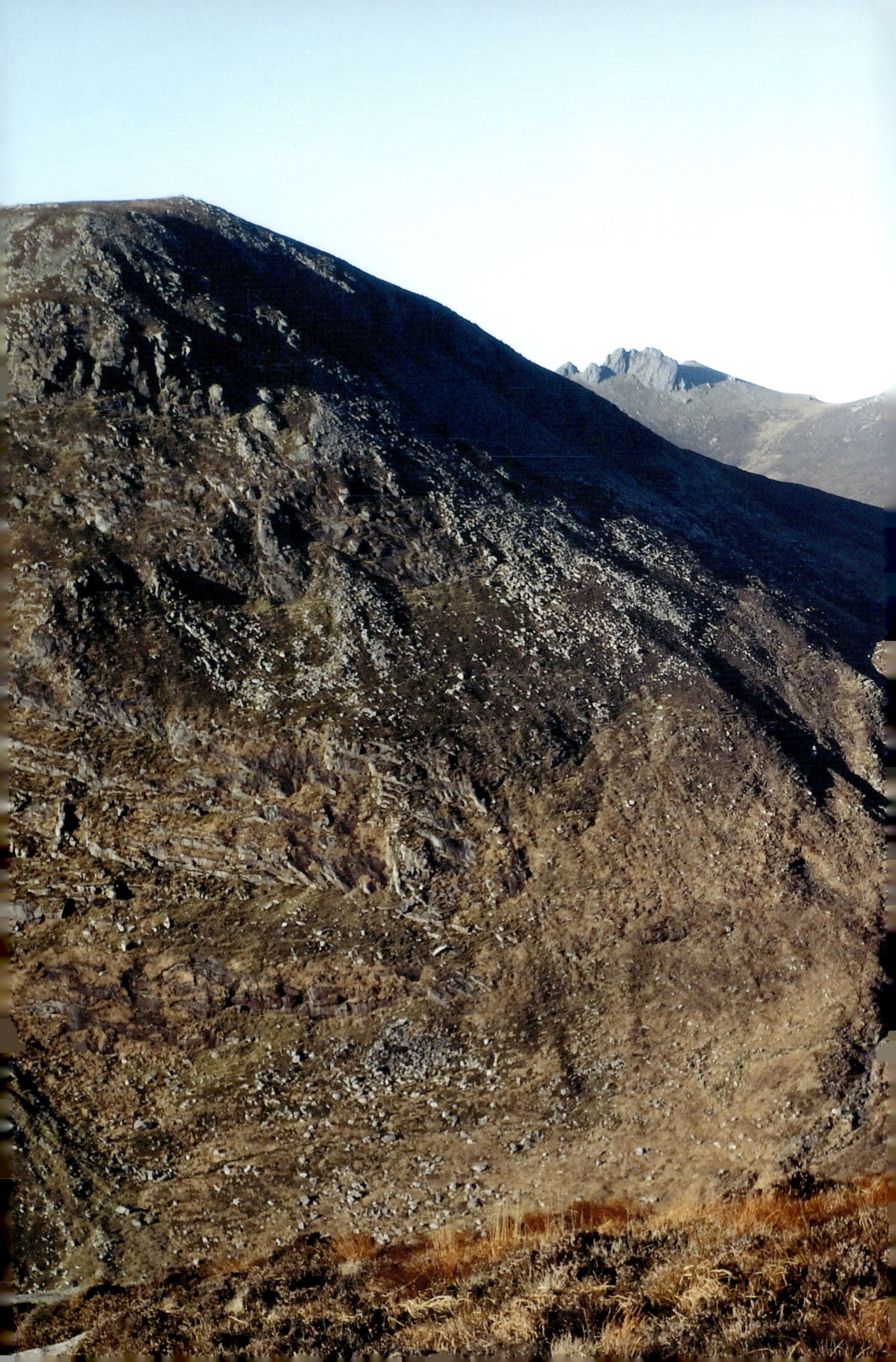

This is the view represented by the famous Newgrange triple spiral; Cove mountain on the left (the bottom spiral), Slieve Beg on the right (the top spiral) and in the middle beyond Slieve Bearnagh (spiral closest to the back wall) where the great solstice Spear of Abundance ended on the north tor.

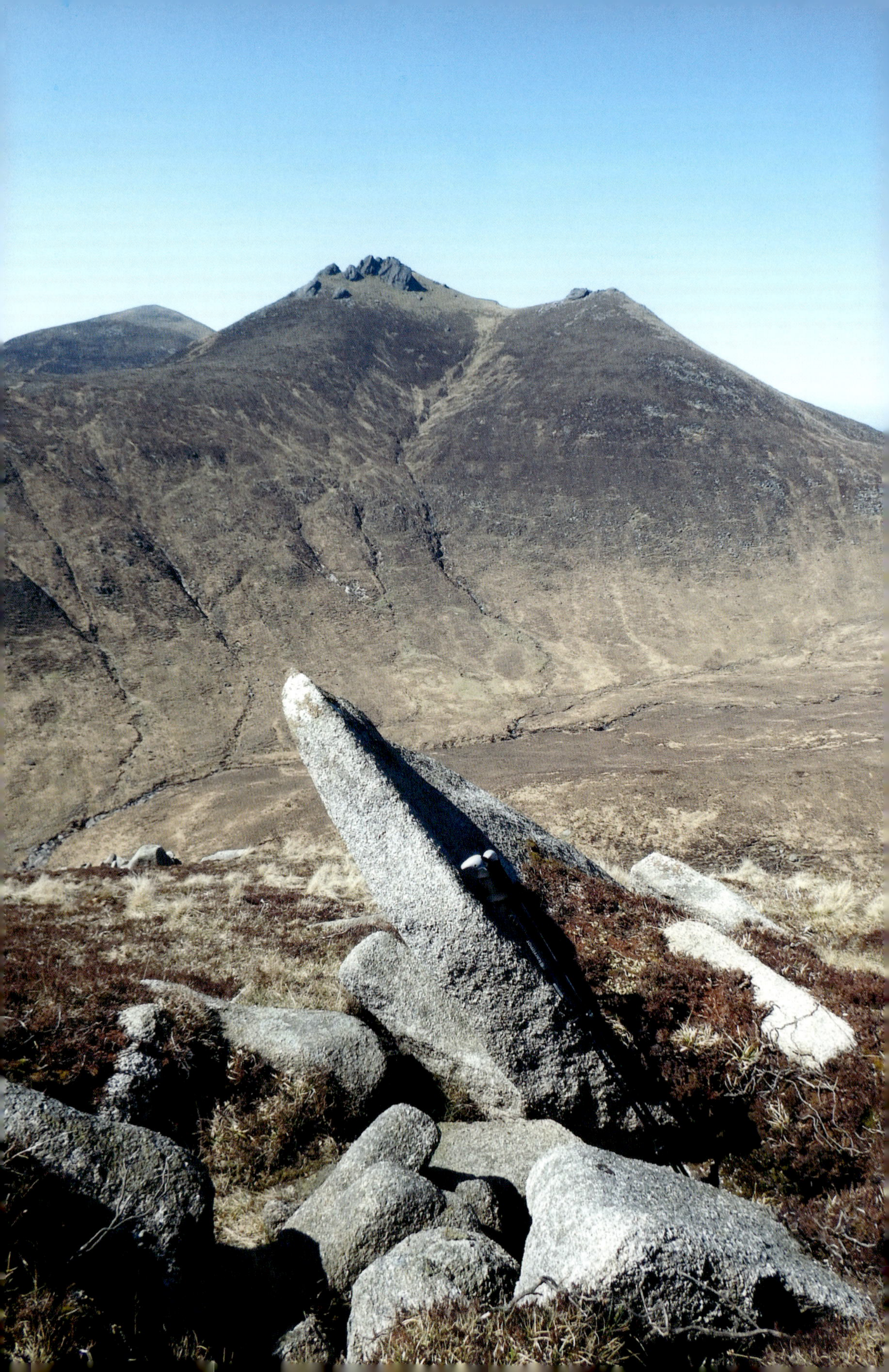

# SLIEVE BEARNAGH

*'These mountains bear noble names given by ancient peoples, names that resonate with the folk memories of many millennia….'*

(p.16, THE MOUNTAINS OF MOURNE; A CELEBRATION OF A PLACE APART, BY DAVID KIRK, PUBLISHED BY APPLETREE PRESS, BELFAST, 2002.)

Professor Estyn Evans was in lyric mode when he referred to the tors of Bignian and Bearnagh.

'The typical Mourne summit is a clean symmetrical dome, aesthetically satisfying but rather monotonous and dull to the climber, for whom the way ahead is always hidden on a convex slope. In this setting of smooth profiles the broken craggy tops of Binnian and Bearnagh strike a dramatic note. To anyone who reads the map with intelligence and feeling, the contours of the Mournes will sing together sweetly, but the hachured scars of the tors rise above the harmony like a thrilling descant.'[1]

The present name of Slieve Bearnagh is in Irish *Sliabh Bearnach*, meaning 'gapped mountain'. The name presumes an analogy with a row of teeth where one is missing in the middle, leaving the 'gap'. Mention has already been made of a not dissimilar analogy for the pass of the Bloody Bridge and the pass beside Slieve Loughshannagh where the operative Irish looked at was *Séanasach* meaning 'a pretty gap between the two front teeth'.

In all, four possible names can be considered for Slieve Bearnagh with the present version being very likely a corruption of the earliest which was one of phallic approbation. These four names are Bearnagh, Gapped Mountain, Broken Mountain and the Irish (*Ár*) *bhFear-na*. No doubt other names have been lost but those that remain testify to this being a mountain of importance for the ancients. As for lost names, were it not for a singular mention in a tale by Richard Rowley we would likely have lost the name of Lecarry Loanin' which runs along the flank of Slieve Bearnagh in Pollaphuca valley[2].

## (*Ár*) *bhFear-na* - '(Our) Man!'

Although it is not attested by written sources, the most likely origin for the name of Bearnagh is the similar sounding Irish (*Ár*) *bhFear-na* meaning '(our) man!' This is the eclipsed version of *Fear*, 'man' in Irish, to which has been affixed the emphatic Irish *–na*. The name works on two levels. Firstly and as already mentioned when examining Carr's Face quarry, Bearnagh's north tor was the place

A phallic megalith on the western slope of Cove mountain
with the tors of Slieve Bearnagh in the background.

of special significance as the termination point at winter solstice dawn of *Carr na Bláthaighe*, the 'Spear of Abundance'. This north tor was visible at the very centre of the vaginal notch formed between Chimney Rock and Slieve Donard as seen from Carr's Face quarry. Being in the centre of the vaginal notch gave it the inevitable interpretation of representing the male penis; the name *bhFear-na* is an Irish synecdoche, substituting the less discomforting whole of 'our man' for the sexual part. Secondly, the ancients fashioned the semblance of a face on the front of the tor by the judicious removal of rock to make two shadow eyes and a mouth; 'our man'. A close look at the mouth of this face reveals a sculpture within a sculpture for it has been crafted to give the head of a boar. When the shadows are right, another face can be discerned to the right of it. Likewise, the very summit of the tor has been subtly worked to give a huge boar's head, the outline of which is perhaps more clearly obvious from Slieve Meelmore. The huge summit boar has a great brooding shadow eye and been given a typical snub snout by removing a chunk of rock from the tor. It is a masterful work of symbolic art but it is only one of many works for, not content with moving so many boulders on this hill-side, the ancients have utilised the shapes and forms of the rock and by making a line here and a gouge there, have, as it were, filled a mountain side canvas with rock art of face stones. *BhFear-na* can be seen as more than a term of approbation for the tor's sexual interpretation but also an appreciative recognition of the multitude of suggestive art forms and especially the great face at the end of *Carr na Bláthaighe*. Professor Evan's description of the tors as a 'thrilling descant' is even more sublime than imagined. The decline of the ancient religion would have seen the morphing of *bhFear-na* to the more innocuous present *Bearnach*. If the old name has all but disappeared, the rock art however, fortunately endures. You must let the imagination wander slowly over the boulders and rock faces and see it afresh through the eyes of the ancients. The ancients spent a long time working on this mountain; even if you have already looked carefully you will still find new insights and discoveries with each further visit.

Incidentally, creating a boar's head out of a mountain top is not unique to Bearnagh. The same can be said for Slieve Lamagan when viewed imaginatively from Bignian in the morning. Have you ever closely looked at Slieve Thomas on an early spring or summer morning? One can only wonder if the little gully on the face of Thomas was deliberately deepened to create a shadow eye making the whole rounded head of Slieve Thomas into quite a plausible boar's head with the Black Stairs being the snout. The concept of a whole mountain being made into a boar's head is certainly quite impressive but the work required to achieve it would be modest; indeed, compared with making the Mourne Wall in the last century,

In the foreground is the former winch for lifting heavy granite blocks at Carr's Face quarry. In the background and exactly in the [V] shaped notch between Chimney Rock and Slieve Donard is the north tor of Slieve Bearnagh; the distant tor was thus viewed lasciviously and earned it the approbation in Irish of (*Ár*) *bhFear-na*, '(our) man!'

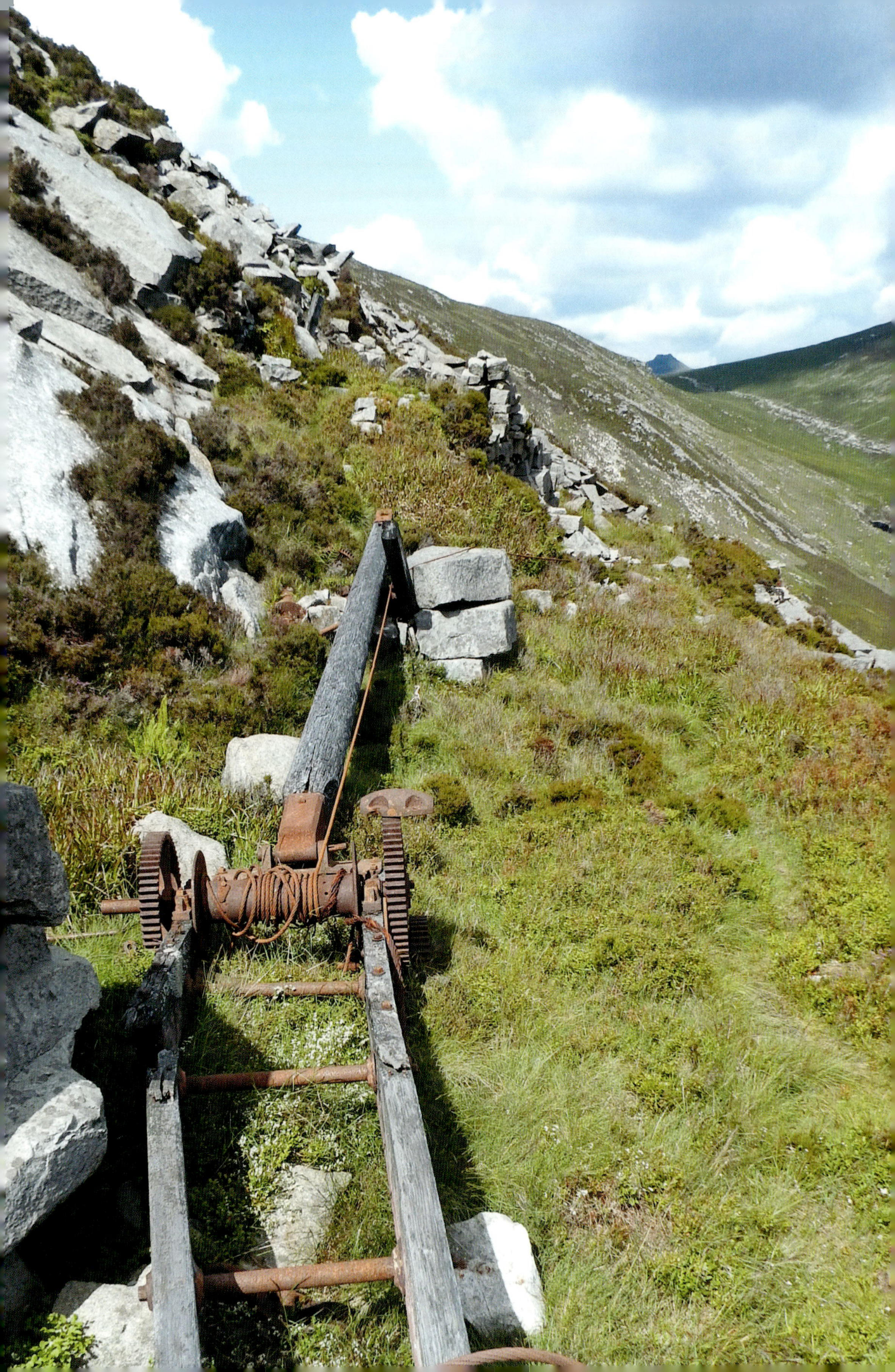

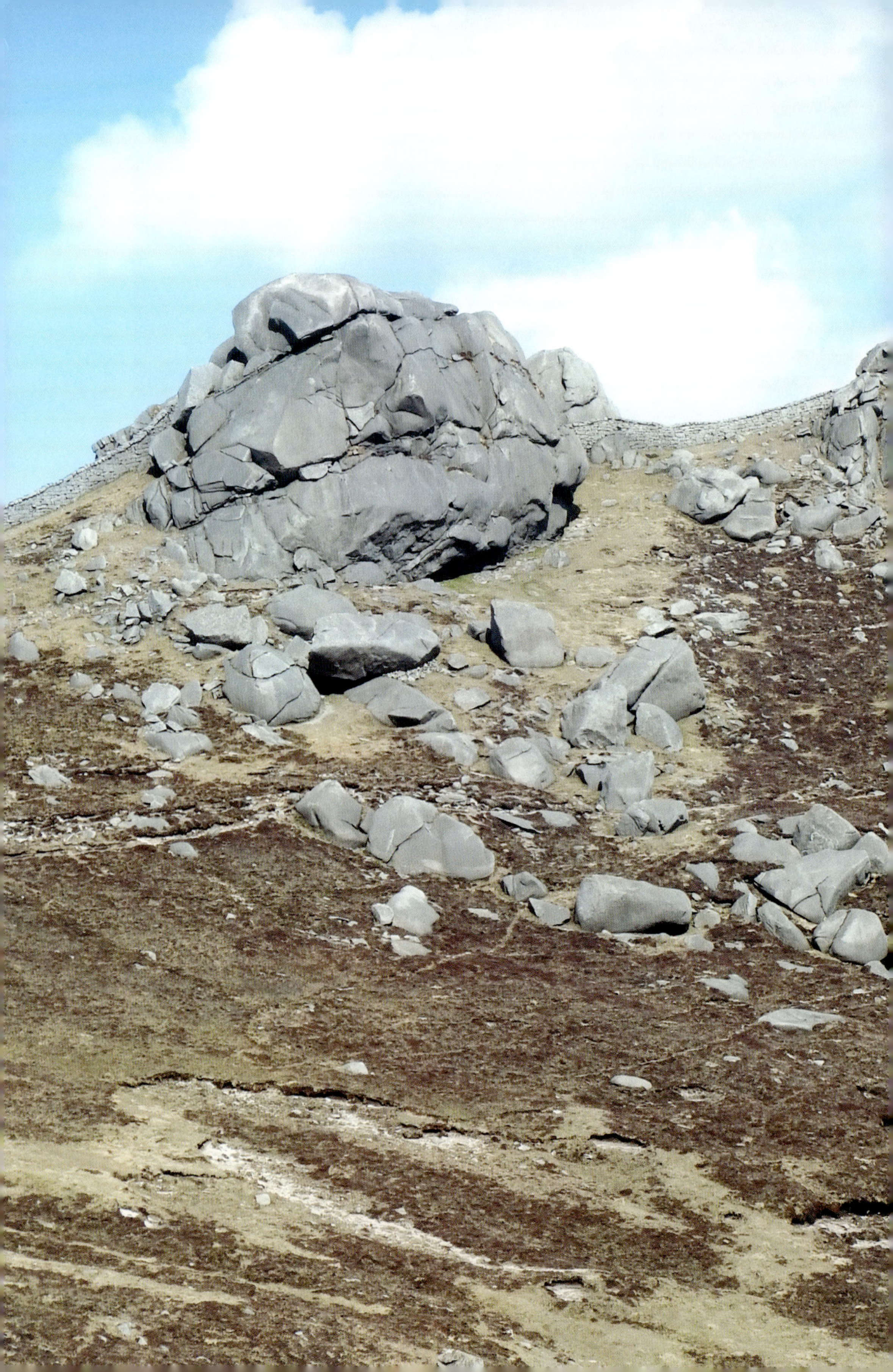

*This view of the tors of Slieve Bearnagh from the far side of Lough Island Reavy makes it easy to understand why the mountain was referred to in English as 'gapped' mountain.*

sunrise and sunset of both solstices. A number of stones have been built up around the base of the megalith providing a wind break and shelter for some seeking protection from the elements. The men of Mourne who built the Mourne wall may have rested underneath but the shelter is probably much older. The entrance to the shelter faces towards appearance of first light at summer solstice. Note how the pointed stone near the entrance has been so placed that the rising sun would cast its shadow into the opening. This opening has been treated as a vagina. Sunset on the summer solstice sees the sun touching the side of the north tor. Look again at the large rounded neighbouring megalith to the south of the shelter megalith to see that a phallus has been outlined on top of it which points to the side of the north tor. Because this priapic outline is on the top of the huge boulder it is not obvious as you walk past; it illustrates how new insights and discoveries can always continue to be made.

*The cluster of megaliths below the north tor of Slieve Bearnagh, the end of the Spear of Abundance, marks this as a very special fertility location and greatly desired as a burial place. Three important megaliths are near the top of the tor; to the left the large bulbous stone with a penis gouged into the top, beside it in the middle, under the centre of the tor, the largest block, and then its 'slice of pie' companion to the right. Note also the meatus groove line on the bulbous summit that emphasises this tor's phallic credentials.*

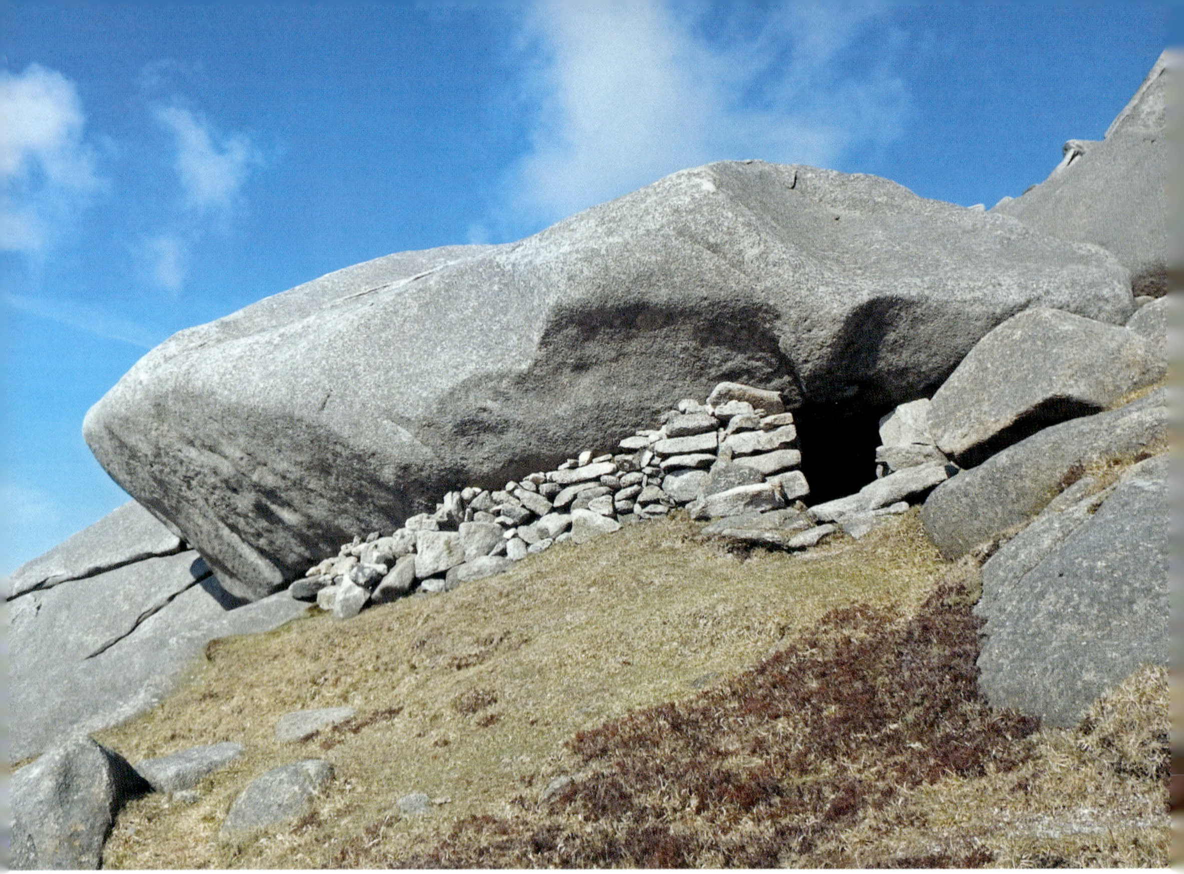

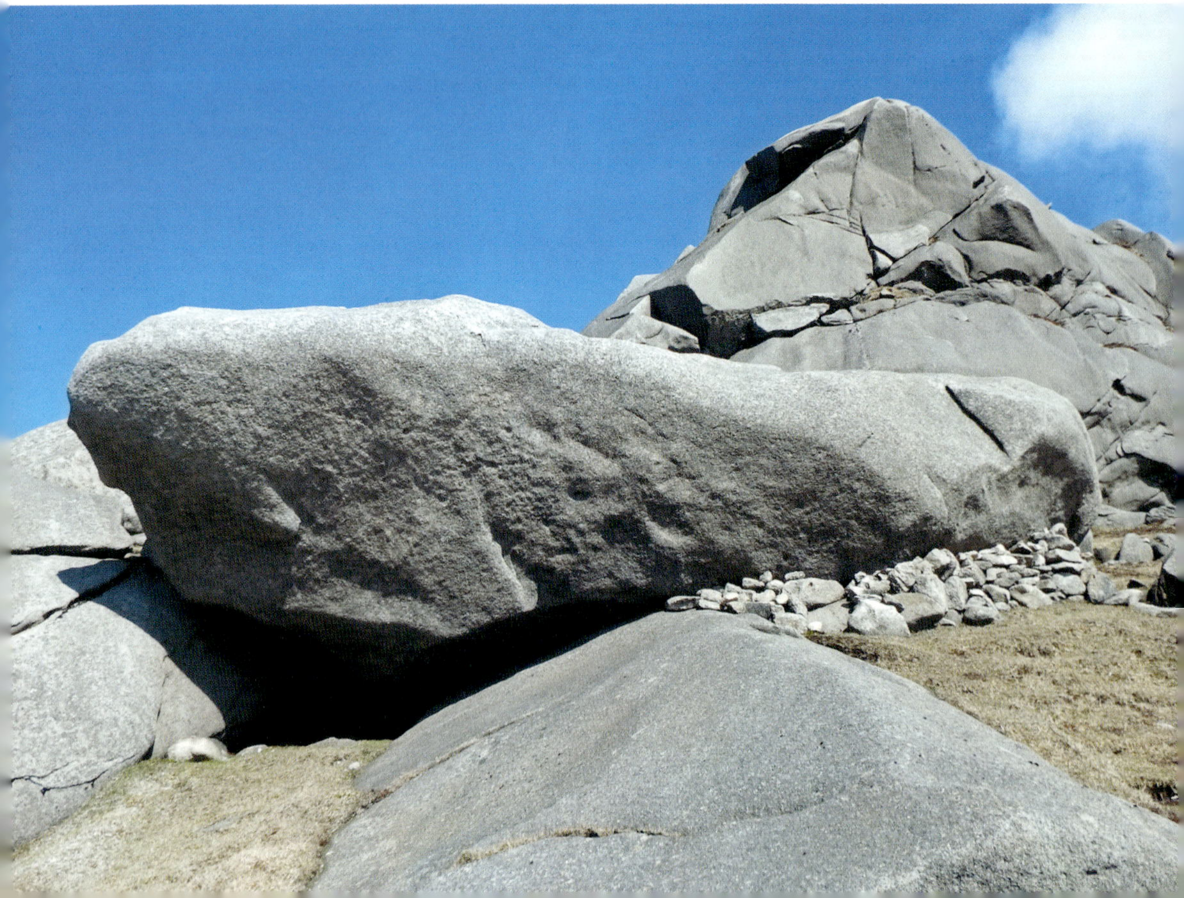

Top left: The entrance to the shelter under the great megalith opens to first light at summer solstice dawn. The stone to the right of the entrance has been so placed that its phallic shadow may penetrate into the vaginal opening underneath at this time of fertility.

Bottom left: The right hand side of this monstrous block has been given a gouged line to simulate a penile corona but the real beauty is the faint outline of two boars revealed by the shadows on the rock. The easiest to see here is a young animal, head high, on the centre of the stone and to its left, another animal with its snout down. They compliment the huge background boar, with dark brooding shadow eye and well defined flat snout that is on the summit of the tor.

Above: The back end of the same stone in the evening light of 3rd June; by hammering out a shadow eye the ancients have transformed this part of the megalith into the semblance of a conger eel's head.

Right: This little sculpture of a conger eating its prey is to be found at the corner of Slieve Bearnagh's north tor. The round eye in relief is a detail of beauty.

A large boulder of quite substantial weight has been deployed on Slieve Bearnagh's summit tor by the ancients to simulate fellatio.

megaliths and face stones on Slieve Bearnagh's slopes we certainly have riches aplenty. Many other treasures on Slieve Bearnagh have already been illustrated, as for instance on pages 8, 158-161 and 213 but so many more await appreciation.

### Broken Mountain

On the face of it the fourth name 'broken mountain' would seem to be an awkwardly translated variation of 'gapped mountain'. Both names, gapped and broken mountain, were collected by the ordnance survey in 1834. It is most fortunate for us that the name Broken mountain was preserved and not discarded as an apparently clumsy rendering for 'gapped'. The name is a vital link with Slieve Bearnagh's pagan past, revealing its importance during that vigil period before winter solstice dawn. Broken mountain is a mnemonic from the Irish *Breo Cian* meaning 'long distance fire'. This is the reason for the hitherto mysterious circular bowls deep in the granite on the very summit of Bearnagh's north tor[3]. The great granite bowls acted as receptacles for a monstrous vigil fire that would have been witnessed on solstice night over a vast area of south Down. Being a fire associated with the gods, the Bearnagh fertility fire would have been held in great awe. It had probably been lit on this mountain top for many thousands of years.

On the south side of Bearnagh's summit tor is this suckling stone. In the left background another part of the tor is also suckling and to its right is the profile of the only smiling face stone I recollect finding in Mourne. In the middle background a little animal is shown sleeping.

Detail of the small sleeping animal with its four little legs and a tiny penis; this is a beautifully sensitive work of ancient sculpture.

405

These large man-made bowls on top of Slieve Bearnagh's north tor would have been used for dramatic vigil fires at solstice. The pyrotechnics gave the mountain the former name of 'Broken' from the Irish *Breo Cian*, 'long distance fire'. The lower lip of the bowl on the left beside the rucksack would have allowed burning overflow to pour down the meatus groove on the front of the tor.

There are many granite bowls on the tops of the mountains of Mourne, particularly on Chimney Rock and at various parts of Slieve Bignian but the double bowl on top of Slieve Bearnagh's north tor must surely be one of the largest in Mourne. The double bowls on Bearnagh are quite deep although one is much bigger and deeper than the other and both together measure at least one and a half metres in length; they would have held very many litres of flammable material and produced a very substantial fire. The use of the Irish *Breo* to refer to the flame is also quite instructive as this is a word usually used for a fire that proceeds from burning putrid matter such as fish, etc. The likelihood is that the ancients had saved up dripping from roasting pigs, rendered blubber from seals and oil from fish and whales. The highly flammable oil would have been carried to the mountain tops in bulbous animal skins. The pot-holes had been prepared as round making it easy to place bulging spherical skin bags into them. During the vigil, extra bags could be dropped into the smaller hole to keep the larger bowl topped up and sparing the attendant from being splashed with burning oil. The positioning and overlapping of the two bowls was carefully thought out to

Two of the man-made bowls in the granite tor of Chimney Rock that would have held solstice vigil fires. The tors of Slieve Bearnagh are in the middle distance.

facilitate a huge pyrotechnic event. Even nowadays people constantly need to be warned that in the event of a chip-pan going on fire it should never be extinguished by throwing water on it as it only causes an explosion and a much bigger fire. The placement of the two granite bowls slightly overlapping was probably deliberately planned to facilitate such a great fiery explosion for dramatic effect. With the fire of oil burning nicely, a sealed skin of water could be dropped into the smaller bowl giving the attendant time to scramble clear before the skin ruptured and the water and burning oil mixed with a thunderous explosion that would have hurled a fire-ball high into the night sky. Such a sudden, huge and powerful conflagration would have lived up to the description of *Breo Cian*, 'long distance fire', as the display would have been visible in the dark across all of south Down and even to the Belfast and Craigantlet hills. It would have been an event of power, awe, excitement and dramatic impact; making a spectacular dénouement, commanding respect and preparing watchers to salute the dawn. The great explosion would have had another purpose. The furious contents of the bowls would have undoubtedly boiled over and the burning overflow would have followed the lower rock slope, venting itself down through the meatus channel on the eastward side of the phallic summit. The great initial explosion, jetting fire high into the night sky would have been a deliberate simulation of ejaculation; it was always intended for the fiery 'semen' to dribble down over the front of the tor as the fullest expression of fertility. Even though these sensational pyrotechnics would have been practiced for thousands of years and even discontinued perhaps for another one and a half thousand years after the coming of Christianity it is sad to realise that this ancient name of *Breo Cian*, albeit in the modified form of 'Broken Mountain', has apparently only finally dropped from usage in the last eighty years.

**Slieve Bearnagh and K52 of Newgrange**

When considering the axis of symmetry at Newgrange, professor O'Kelly found that a good line ran from the centre of the entrance stone, K1, to the centre of Kerbstone 52, the decorated stone at the back, or north north-west side, of the monument. An excavation was made here so that the kerbstone could be re-erected from its fallen position and also to check out the then widely held possibility that the decorated stone K52 heralded the entrance to another tomb. No secondary tomb was found but now the crisp decoration that covered the whole front of the stone could be appreciated. If there was no second tomb the question remained unanswered as to why the ancients had gone to such trouble to create this work of art and then to place it at the back, in direct line with the entrance stone? Because Newgrange had been deliberately orientated to the winter solstice sunrise, the professor was wary to dismiss this alignment as a mere coincidence. That both stones were decorated with a central line was a further

The beautifully decorated kerbstone 52 at Newgrange represents Slieve Bearnagh at Mourne and in particular how the winter solstice sunrise is viewed from the southerly summit tor. The water-rolled stones in the background were collected from the Boyne flood-plain and used to build up the mound; these were the symbolic 'very many little cows', or *Boin-ne*, for the use of the dead ancestors.

This is the view eastwards from the platform on Slieve Bearnagh's summit tor. Compare and match with the left side of decorated kerbstone K52 above.

The ancient platform, perhaps used for ritual, on Slieve Bearnagh's summit tor. The view eastwards from this platform is mirrored in the spirals of K52. The platform itself is redolent with sexual symbolism, from the obvious fissure on the left that the sun penetrated on winter solstice morning, the phallic spear stone below the rucksack, to the tiny *geinte* stones on the far right. If you find the thin shadow eye (up at the top, straight above the rucksack) then the rock behind the platform can be imagined as a great 'face'.

unifying factor but as to why the second decorated stone had been placed at the back the professor left the question open.

Time moves on and now thirty-three years after professor O'Kelly felt obliged to park the question it can be stated that the beautifully decorated stone of K52 is the Mourne equivalent of Slieve Bearnagh. As the photographs demonstrate, the left side of K52 with its circles and swirls is a magnificent rendering of the view eastwards from a small platform built onto a granite outcrop on the southerly summit tor of Bearnagh. The Mourne wall butts into the outcrop and it is most fortunate that the builders of the wall did not plunder this platform for building material. It seems that along the length of the wall the builders left severely alone those stones they perceived to have been placed in situ by the ancients. From the slang name of 'the back ditch' that they gave to their wall, many of these builders it would seem, were Irish speakers and, like the quarry-men, custodians of the ancient knowledge or *sanas*; thus a mixture of respect for the work of the ancients, tradition, and a good dose of fear about bringing bad luck on themselves if they disturbed the stones of the ancients, saw all such stones being left untouched.[4]

There is a noticeable symmetry in the overall shape of K52. With its raised corners at either end the megalith could be said to have a good resemblance to the rear end of a cow, with the corners being the bony haunches and the wide central groove the tail. Given the importance of the cow in the ancient economy, this resemblance is probably no accident. Likewise the profile of the top of the stone would appear to be no accident either for when it is compared to the panorama of Mourne as seen from the summit tor of Slieve Bearnagh, that part from Slieve Donard to Slieve Bignian's north tor, then the outline of the landscape and the top of K52 have a remarkable affinity. Care has even been taken to gouge the top of the stone above L5 cup-mark to symbolise the Bloody Bridge valley and on the other side of the central groove the zigzag pattern on top right of centre would equate to the western flank of Chimney Rock mountain. Everything about Newgrange was carefully thought out in advance and this would apply even more so to a megalith on which so much time and effort would be expended in depicting its message.

Adjacent pages give numerical key codes proffering explanations for the spirals and details on the stone. The photograph taken from the ritual platform on Slieve Bearnagh is certainly worth more than the proverbial thousand words in demonstrating that K52 left side relates to this mountain. This discovery was made in June 2011 but it would be four more years, all but a few weeks, before the right side of K52 yielded up some of its secrets. Because advancing years have made it impossible to climb up and check the very top of Bearnagh's summit tor, one must leave it to others to eliminate the possibility of any further viewpoint

Slieve Bearnagh from the Tullyree Road.

Pot of Legawherry — Commedagh — Slieve Beg — Donard — Ritual Platform — Bloody Bridge Valley

Slieve Corragh — L14, Tributary from Slieve Bearnagh — Notch of Devil's Coachroad — Hatched area on K52

This is the view eastwards from the southerly end of Slieve Bearnagh's summit tor. Although Slieve Bignian's north tor could not be included at the right end, nevertheless the profile of the distant mountains can be seen to match the profile of the top of K52.

412

R8, Winter Solstice Sunrise
The exact position will depend on one's viewpoint from Bearnagh's summit tor.

Chimney Rock · Spence's Mountain · Rocky Mountain · Slieve Lamagan · Ardmally · Douglas Crag · Forks Mountain

Bignian North Tor out of picture

Cove · L13, Tributary · Tip of Megalith illustrated on bottom of page 213 · Ben Crom Reservoir

The location of the rising solstice sun on the shoulder of Chimney Rock mountain depends on one's viewpoint from the summit tor; preference should be given to the ritual platform.

413

### Prehistoric Mourne: Inspiration for Newgrange

**Tentative Number Code to interpret the Left-side of K52 at Newgrange**
**Spirals:**

L1  Slieve Commedagh. The gouge to the right hand side spirals could represent the great megaliths on the side of the mountain illustrated on pages 77 & 80/81 but in comparison with the view from Bearnagh's ritual platform a determination for The Castles on the south flank of Commedagh is equally tenable.

L2  Slieve Donard.

L3  Chimney Rock Mountain. The notch towards the bottom left would likely equate with the phallic tor called 'Horsemen' illustrated on page 326/327.

L4  Cove Mountain.

**Cupmarks:**

L5  Apex of the 'Spear of Abundance' shadow, *Carr na Bláthaighe*. It could also represent *Bolg an Donn Árd*, 'the womb of Donard'. See page 385.

L6  Inconclusive. There are many megaliths on the south side of Chimney Rock however this probably represents the end of the shadow cast by the summit tor of Slieve Bignian at winter solstice sunset. A large quarry on the mountain's flank marks the spot.

L7  Inconclusive. It may represent something that is now under the waters of the Ben Crom reservoir or the megalith on the south-west slope of Cove mountain opening this chapter.

L8  This cupmark marks the Shelter Stones. These megaliths are illustrated on page 39.

L9  This could possibly be the great Diamond Rock megalith illustrated on page 48/49 but also the fertility megalith on Slieve Corragh illustrated on pages 100/101.

L10  Not as pronounced a hollow as the others and possibly a later addition. Inconclusive, but could answer to the megalith on the col above the Pot of Legawherry illustrated on page 99.

L11  Positional information with this cupmark is too imprecise to make a determination. The mark could refer to a megalithic creation on the slopes of the Pot of Legawherry and even extend to the Spinkwee megalith illustrated on page 153.

**Rivers:**

L12  The master carver has skilfully utilised this crack on the face of the kerbstone to represent the tributary source of the Kilkeel river.

L13  The zigzag lines between the carved diamond patterns and the triangles at the bottom neatly represent the second tributary to the Kilkeel river.

L14  The very short vertical chop line joining into the zigzags of thirteen, apparently a later addition, would represent the rivulet flowing down between Bearnagh's tors. Companion tributaries are marked on the other half at R21.

**Other:**

L15  The symbolical 'cow's tail' on K52; this central groove represents the sight line of the winter solstice sunrise from Slieve Bearnagh's summit tor to the southern end of Chimney Rock known as Long mountain from the Irish *Luan*, meaning 'light' or 'radiance'.

L16  Apparent later addition of a trapezoid; it bears a great resemblance to the profile of the 'slice of pie' megalith that was the spear-tip ending the 'Spear of Abundance', *Carr na Bláthaighe*; this would represent a 'difference of opinion' from the main theme depicted on K52. The central groove is not *Carr na Bláthaighe*, as on K1 but a different winter solstice spectacle from Slieve Bearnagh's summit tor.

# Prehistoric Mourne: Inspiration for Newgrange

**Tentative Number Code to interpret the Right-side of K52 at Newgrange; offered, as at auction, 'with all faults'.**

R1  The cup-marks inside the cartouche are the three mountains of Slieve Donard, Chimney Rock and Cove mountain.

R2  Cartouche Two: Spences mountain, Rocky mountain and Lamagan. The suggestion of a tiny depression to the right of the third cup-mark would be Percy Bysshe hill.

R3  North tor of Slieve Bignian.

R4  Cartouche: Ben Crom then the spear head of winter solstice dawn that penetrates the 'vaginal' gully; the 'half' a cup mark denoting the smaller part of Ben Crom beyond the gully then Doan mountain.

R5  You are here; the viewpoint believed to be the ancient platform on Slieve Bearnagh's summit tor.

R6  Slieve Bearnagh's north tor.

R7  Inconclusive; but the great megalith of Diamond Rock could answer for this.

R8  The winter solstice sunrise from the shoulder of Chimney Rock mountain through the Cove/Lamagan col; exact position of sunrise depends on one's viewpoint on Slieve Bearnagh.

R9  At the other end of the year and pointing in the opposite direction is summer solstice sunset. The two tiny spear points, in the middle between R8 and R9, would then represent sun direction at summer solstice sunrise and winter solstice sunset.

R10  Being in a declivity on the surface of K52, it is suggested that this enclosed spear point is the winter solstice dawn shining up the lower Annalong river valley.

R11  The winter solstice dawn shadow of Slieve Bignian's summit tor being cast towards the north tor.

R12  Inconclusive. Likely the solstice sunset shadow of Slievenaglogh over onto Slieve Bignian.

R13  This unenclosed cup-mark suggests a megalith rather than a mountain and the great pair of vagina stones on Slievenaglogh cliff top are the prime contender.

R14  A partial cup-mark; perhaps a later addition? There are many good megaliths on Slieve Meelbeg that could answer but preference goes to the great compound megalith at the head of Happy Valley.

R15  Summer solstice sunset between the 'breasts' of Cove and Lamagan.

R16  Summer solstice sunset between the north and summit tors of Slieve Bearnagh.

R17  Inconclusive. Shadow from Bearnagh's north tor at summer solstice sunset?

R18  Inconclusive. Winter solstice sunset through the Hare's Gap?

R19  Inconclusive. Winter solstice sunset through the col between Donard and Commedagh?

R20  Inconclusive. Summer solstice sunset through Donard and Chimney Rock col into the Bloody Bridge valley?

R21  At the bottom of the stone, three faint vertical lines, are most likely a later addition; these are companion tributaries to the Kilkeel river, similar to that referred to on the other half of the stone at L14. Look again at the opening photograph in the chapter to see the background streams.

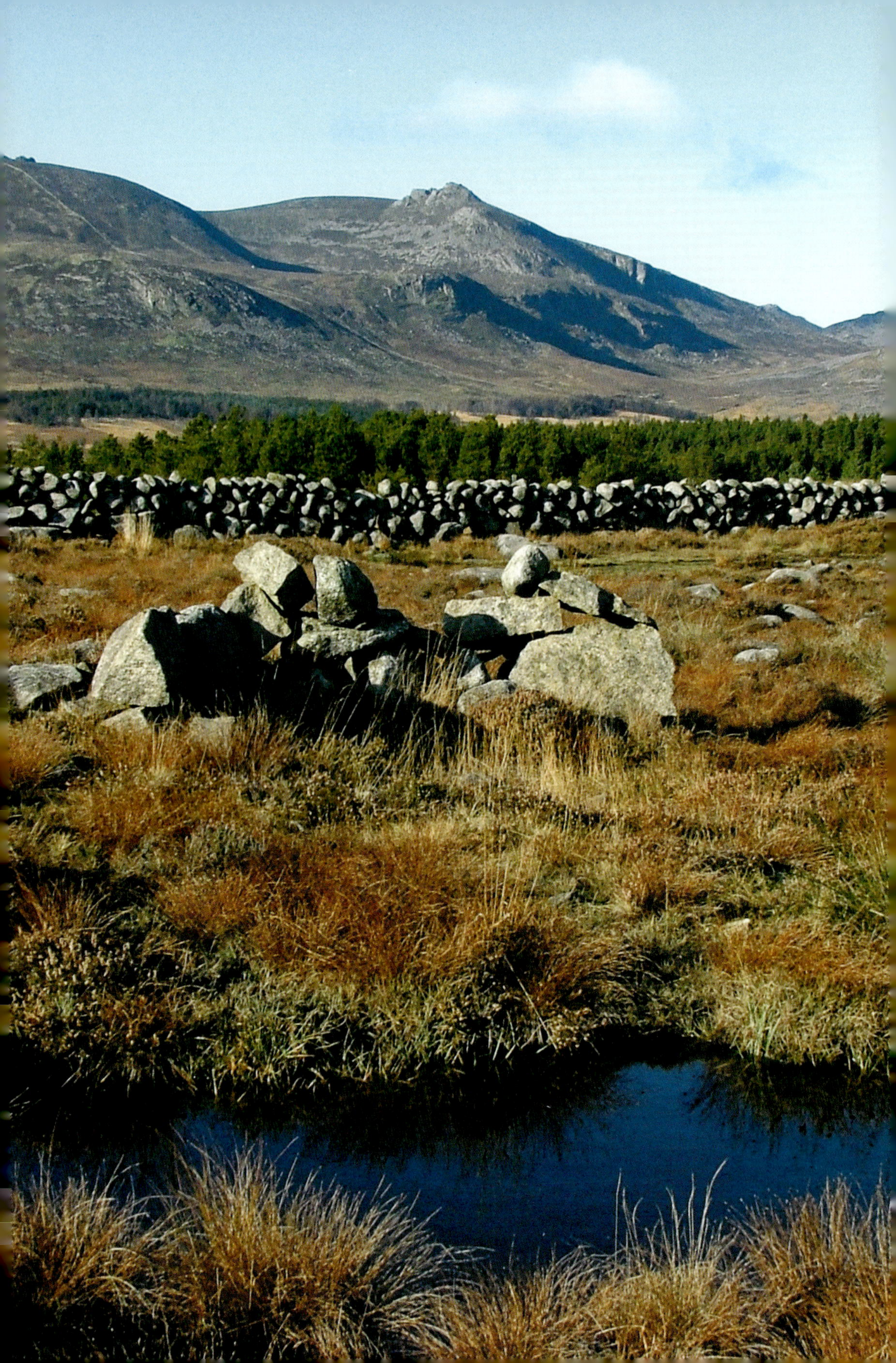

# SLIEVE BIGNIAN AND VICINITY

Slieve Bignian is to lower Mourne what Slieve Donard is to the Newcastle area. Both mountains dominate the landscape below them and give us scenery of extraordinary majesty. The side profile of Bignian has been likened to an eagle with outstretched wings. It certainly is a jumbo mountain, which is just a handy way of remembering that the height of the summit tor is 747 metres; that's 2448 feet in old money.[1] Like the other peaks of the high Mournes, Bignian received great attention from the ancients. Whether they looked at the priapic tors along the spine of the mountain, the great phallic up-thrusting north tor or the swollen womb-like bulge at the western end, this long mountain, judging by its many megaliths and face stones, was special to the fertility loving *Fir Bolg* of millennia past. On its slopes is the biggest megalith of Mourne, if not in all Ireland; a place of such apparent sacred importance that it featured on the highly decorated kerbstone sixty-seven at Newgrange (referred to henceforth as K67). But before examining this great mountain we first take a look at its southern vicinity.

**From Happy to Silent Valley**

The Silent Valley is one of two valleys in Mourne that were known as Happy Valley. Although unfortunately not so named on the OS map, the second Happy Valley is that between Slieve Meelmore and Slieve Meelbeg at J297287. Various explanations have been proposed for this name including that it was due to joyful picnic parties that were a feature during the late nineteenth century. The name of Happy Valley however has nothing to do with picnics and cheerful visitors or for that matter, miners; it is a mnemonic of the Irish *hAilpa Balla,* the 'protuberances of the ramparts', a reference either to the tors along the top of Bignian above or the spear stone megaliths on the other side of the valley both on top of rock outcrops and pushed out over the imposing cliffs of Slievenaglogh. Certainly in the case of the second Happy Valley accessed from the Trassey Road car park at J293296, a huge compound construction with a very large and ostentatiously phallic point can be found high on the northern flank of Slieve Meelbeg. When you see the size of this creation, the number of large rock slabs involved and the awkwardness of the steep slope, it can only produce the greatest respect and admiration for the skill and determination of the ancients. If the phallic point of

The distinctive peak of Bignian's North Tor as seen from the far side of the Annalong Valley. In the foreground is the rough remnant of a booley shelter.

the megalith is anything to go by, this site of ancient labours marks where the summer solstice sun can be seen rising from the bulging shoulder below the summit of Slieve Meelmore. It is also possible that at the other end of the year the same location marks where the winter solstice sun can be seen at the top of Slieve Meelbeg.

The transition from Happy Valley to the present name of Silent Valley was already accomplished by June 1895 and would seem to have happened fairly quickly[2]. The story that the name came about because no birds sang there was an attempt to put an explanation on the English and was first recorded in 1940 by Jack Loudan in his telling of the history of the Belfast water supply[3]. The clock had started ticking on the name change during the summer of 1887 and spring of 1888 when the driest season for many years was experienced in Belfast as an acute water shortage. The demand for water in Belfast had risen from four and a half million gallons to ten million gallons a day and consumption was rising rapidly. The risk of trade dislocation to the manufacturing mills was becoming an alarming prospect. Accordingly, in July 1891 the Belfast Water Commissioners commissioned their civil engineer, Luke Macassey, to advise them where to obtain water of quantity and quality. Lough Neagh was too low and not clean enough. McAuley's lake near Ballynahinch was looked at as were possibilities at Upper Bann, at Clady, Glenravel and Glenarm. Macassey's recommendation came inside a few months and he elected for Mourne. The location was certainly high enough, it could provide a practically inexhaustible supply of water and this itself was beautifully pure, indeed exceptionally so and, importantly, there would be little opposition from the interests of river landowners. Inside two years a Bill was introduced in Parliament to obtain a supply of water to Belfast from the Mourne mountains.[4] The effect in Mourne was electric. The area had been spared the worst depredations of emigration but there was little work besides fishing, cutting granite and the small farms. The prospect of a dam being built and the jobs that would come with it was the talk of the Kingdom. There was great excitement. The news brought great hope that, with jobs, sons and daughters might be able to stay at home[5]. This was the milieu for the name change from Happy Valley to Silent Valley. That the name changed so quickly over the four years between the time the search for water was commissioned in July 1891, the passing of the Water Supply Act in 1893, to the great party in the valley to mark the cutting of the first sod in 1895, is an indication both of the enthusiastic anticipation that the news had generated and that Irish was still in widespread usage at that time. The name of 'Silent Valley' is a mnemonic of the Irish *Súile an Balla*, meaning simply 'expecting the rampart'.

Not far from the entrance to the Silent Valley the Head Road crosses Colligan Bridge (J308204). As this was the location where one could notionally 'look up the legs' of the Silent Valley – the steep sides of Slievenaglogh on one side and Slieve

The great compound megalith high on the slopes of Slieve Meelbeg; this was the source of the name Happy Valley. It is from the Irish *hAilpa Balla*, 'protuberance of the rampart/high slope'.

Bignian on the other, being the 'legs' – the origin of Colligan was the Irish *Col na geine*, 'lust of the act of begetting'. The [n] of the article *na* has been elided from everyday speech. This name is not the only instance of the gynaecomorphic interpretation of the landscape in the locality. Moolieve mountain, one of the foothills of Bignian that overlooks the dam, received its name from a sexual construct being put upon its rounded shape. Some had reasonably thought the name came from *Maolshliabh* 'bare/round mountain' but like Slievenamaddy above Newcastle, the mountain's shape was interpreted as female genitalia and the tantalising outline earned it the Irish name *Muilleadh*, 'inciting or urging'. The present form is likely a syncopation of *Muilleadh Sliabh*, 'inciting mountain'. Following on from the mountain's sexual interpretation, the adjacent southern extremity of Moolieve, Scardan Hill, was probably so named to reflect the female urethral opening as the name *Scárdán* in Irish means 'a spout, a jet, a squirt'. Perhaps this 'discharge' from the landscape influenced the name of Sally Lough below the dam as Sally is only a mnemonic of the Irish adjective *Salach* 'dirty, soiled, impure, unclean'.

*The impounded water of the Silent Valley dam as seen from the heights of Slievenaglogh. Moolieve mountain lies beyond on the left and, with its shape being construed as female genitalia, the name is probably a contraction of the Irish Muilleadh Sliabh, 'inciting mountain'.*

**Banns Road and Slievenaglogh**

Only three trees now exist at the end of a field on the right side as you enter on the Banns Road marking the site of what once was the McEvoy household, the only cottage that graced the lovely but lonely rocky road into the Mournes and Lough Shannagh. Until the Belfast Water Commissioners started to clamp down in 1904 on the digging of turf on the 9,000 acres they had acquired by act of parliament, this road was one of the main access routes used by the people to obtain their fuel from the mountain bogs. From his doorway during the course of the year Stephen McEvoy would have witnessed hundreds of neighbours making the long walk to the bogs with their *sleaghán* (pronounced 'shlawn'), the special spade with a wing at one or both sides to cut the turf sods. Cutting the turf was hard work as was the stacking or 'footing' of the turves afterwards. The term 'footing' came from the Irish *fothain* meaning 'sheltering or protecting'; the long cut turves were erected like little teepees or shelters to let the air flow around them and dry them out. When the turves were dry the families brought the turf alongside the road and built them up into stacks until the cart or donkey and creel could bring them to the family home for the winter. The rows of turf banks, from the Irish *Bannc*, gave us the present name Banns Road.

    The Banns Road is the best way to get to Slievenagore and Slievenaglogh that lie to the west of the Silent Valley. The summit and eastern flank of Slievenagore is peppered with small quarry openings. The quarry men favoured fertility sites and Slievenagore, rather than deriving from 'mountain of the goats' as presently proposed, could be from the other form collected by the ordnance survey *Sliabh na gCor* meaning the 'mountain of the cast'.[6] At summer solstice, the shadow of Bignian and its tors would be cast onto various points along Slievenagore as the sun rises. These projecting tors were regarded as erect phallic members throwing a potent phallic shadow and a stronger likelihood is that the name of Slievenagore is instead from the Irish *Sliabh na gCoire*, 'mountain of sin'. After a steep climb up the side of Slievenaglogh, you have a commanding view down into the Silent Valley with its deep blue waters. On the other side of the valley the Ardley river tumbles down between Wee Bignian and the heights above. In its contracted form there can be no certainty about its original meaning but a couple of possibilities might be *Árd lic* or *Árd Léige*. The first possibility would have viewed Wee Bignian

The ridge of Slieve Muck as seen from the Banns Road. This road was the access route to the bogs for turf and gets its name from the turf stacks or *Bannc* that were built along it awaiting collection.

*The white speck on the cliff edge just above the centre of the picture is the megalith nominated for the name of Slievenaglogh.*

in erect phallic mode for *Árd lic* means 'wanton or lascivious height'. The second, and most likely possibility, was that the name referred to the megalith on the heights above marking where a phallic shadow would be cast across the Silent Valley by the summit of Slievenaglogh at sunset on the winter solstice. That spot would have been deemed a place of special renewal, an important fertility location. *Árd Léige* means 'Height of the boulder/headstone'. We mention Ardley and the possible meanings of its name as this part of Bignian has apparently been confused with Ardmally. We will return to the name of Ardmally when looking at the other side of Slieve Bignian for Ardmally is the neighbouring foothill to Douglas Crag.

On a good day the walk along the path atop the cliffs of Slievenaglogh is a treat. Here, apart from the heart-lifting scenery, one may have the pleasure of seeing the common lizard among heather that has not been burnt in recent times and in the skies above the peregrine falcon patrolling its territory. The cliffs are a favoured nesting place for these protected raptors so if you happen to be walking here in spring and find the bird screeching and circling you overhead, then know that you are being warned off because there is a nest in the vicinity and that it is

*Slievenaglogh as seen from the Silent Valley. The white speck on the very right of the picture is a great megalith incorporated into a wall. This stone probably lies along the sightline that sees the sun rising either from the top of Wee Bignian or Moolieve.*

The megalith of Slievenaglogh is positioned where the rising winter solstice sun appears, with great fertility symbolism, at the top of Wee Bignian mountain.

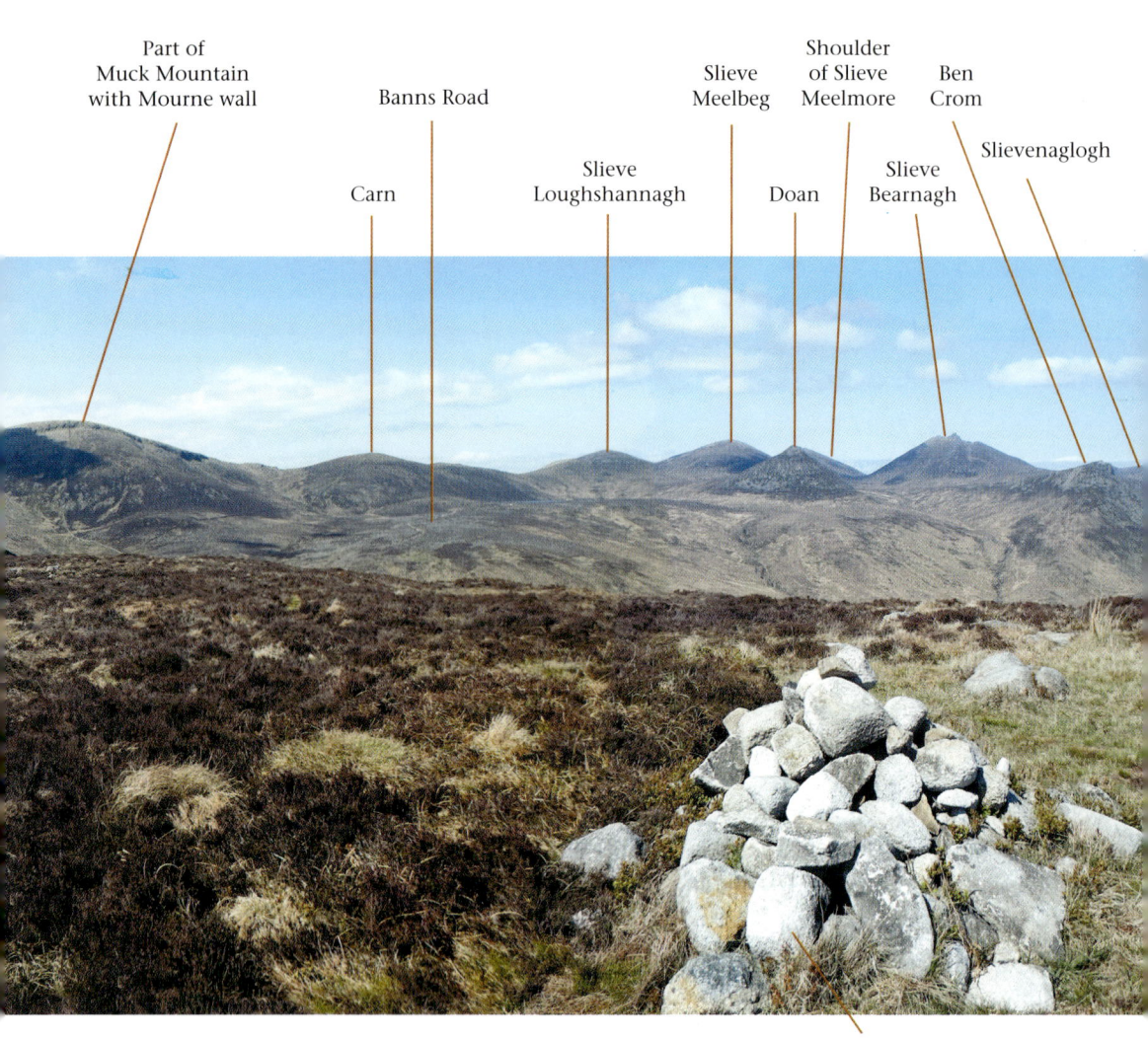

Part of Muck Mountain with Mourne wall — Banns Road — Slieve Meelbeg — Shoulder of Slieve Meelmore — Ben Crom — Slievenaglogh — Carn — Slieve Loughshannagh — Doan — Slieve Bearnagh

Cairn on Slievenaglogh

best to move on sharpish. Slievenaglogh is a name borne by two mountains in Mourne, the other being above the seaward side of the Trassey valley. The name is from the Irish *Sliabh na gCloch* and unfortunately receives the insipid translation of 'mountain of the stones/rocks'. The translation is not incorrect but gives the impression that the mountain is just a particularly stony place whereas in fact the names of both mountains are derived from significant stones, or what should be acknowledged as important megaliths erected by the ancients. In the case of the Trassey valley Slievenaglogh, the megaliths have been pushed out over the edge of the cliff to point towards winter solstice sunset and have been featured on the cover and title page of this book. There are a number of megaliths towards the end of Slievenaglogh above the Silent Valley and also a very prominent one built into a wall along the bottom side of the mountain. One of the great stones that gave its name to the mountain is on the cliff edge and well along the Silent Valley.

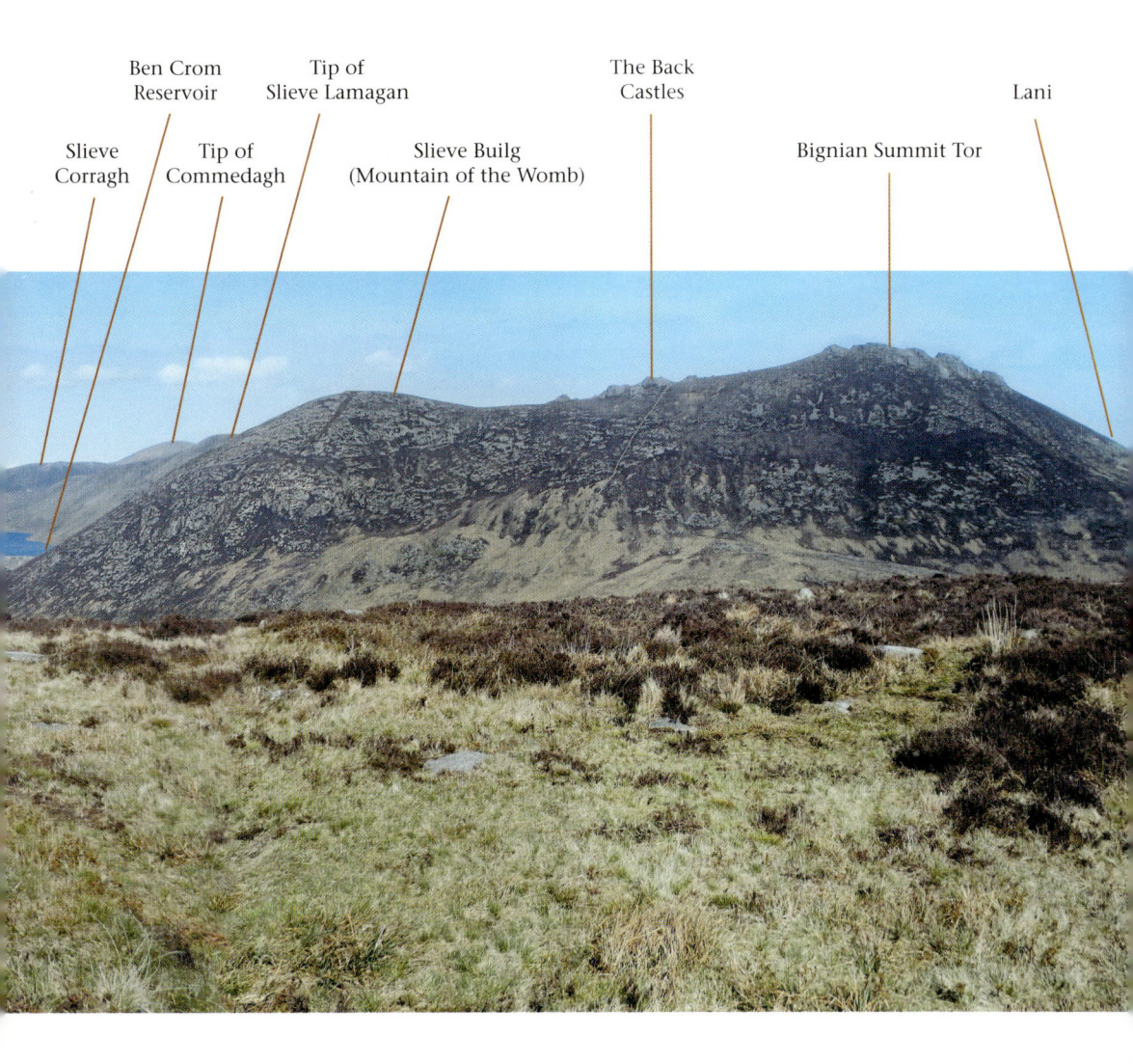

Labels on photograph (left to right):
- Slieve Corragh
- Ben Crom Reservoir
- Tip of Commedagh
- Tip of Slieve Lamagan
- Slieve Builg (Mountain of the Womb)
- The Back Castles
- Bignian Summit Tor
- Lani

It apparently marks both where the rising winter solstice sun, with profound fertility symbolism, could be seen emerging from the top of Wee Bignian; and at the other end of the year, at summer solstice sunrise, it would seem that the same location enjoyed the spectacle of the sun rising from the bulging womb like swelling of Bignian known as *Sliabh Builg*. Near this megalith the ancients placed two further great stones with a gap between in simulation of a vagina to mark the birthing of summer solstice sun from this womb of Bignian. At the bottom of Slievenaglogh slope, the great stone incorporated into the wall is easily seen from the road running along the reservoir. The megalith likely lies on the sightline that sees the sun rising either from the top of Wee Bignian or Moolieve. The translation of Slievenaglogh might therefore be better understood as mountain of the fertility megaliths or 'mountain of THE stones'.

## Prehistoric Mourne: Inspiration for Newgrange

### Miners Hole

Having walked along to the end of Slievenaglogh you come to the area marked on the map as Miners Hole. Nearby is Miners Hole river. The origin of the name has been attributed to 'the activities of prospecting Cornish miners, some of whom were brought over by Lord Kilmorey to search for ores in places such as Leitrim townland in Clonduff'.[7] However, Miners Hole is yet another name in the same category as Hare's Gap, Annalong Buttress, Devil's Coachroad, Cow and Calf, Happy Valley, Cut Throat, Raven Rocks, Buzzard's Roost, Lindsay's Leap, Windy Gap, Chimney Rock, Silent Valley, or Percy Bysshe. They all seem to make sense in English but are really the sound of Irish in an English skin, otherwise mnemonics. Miners Hole is from the Irish *Mian Áir Olc* meaning 'evil desire of slaughter'. The origin of the name lies, not with rock prospectors or diggers of holes, but with the attenuated phallic spear head shadow cast by the cliff end of Slievenaglogh on winter solstice morning. The shadow received this name because it stretched out and pointed over in the direction of Ben Crom where the whispered tradition remembered the dreaded sacrifices that were made to the fertility god Crom Dhu on that particular morning. Likewise the nearby river was

The spear point on this very substantial megalith points to the notch between Slieve Lamagan and Bignian where the summer solstice sun would emerge. Appearances are deceptive from this angle; the face stone is quite long and on the far side it is easily higher than most men. Phenomenal effort would have been required to bring such a stone to this location; and this is just one of many in the surrounding area.

The Ardley River.

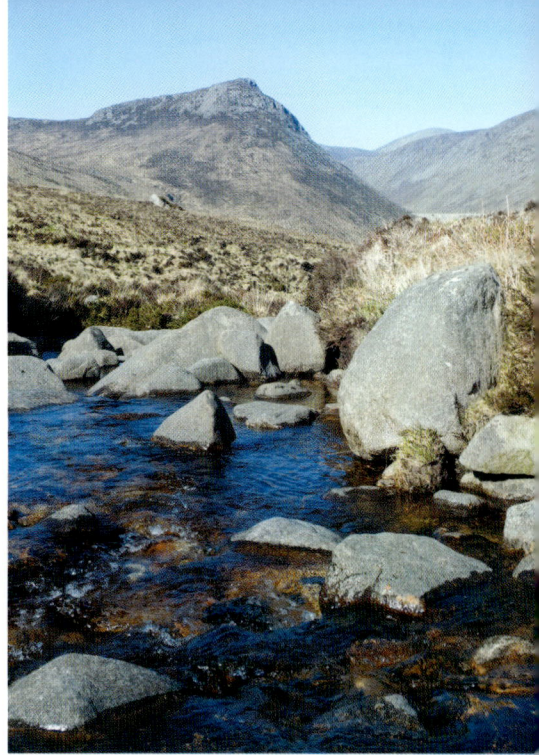

Miners Hole River flowing towards Ben Crom, the mountain of sacrifice.

similarly named because of its proximity as it flowed towards the same mountain before cutting across the shadow and cascading downhill into the valley below.

Two large boulders on Slievenaglogh slope not too many metres south of the Miners Hole river waterfall near the river's entry-point into the reservoir, are probably megaliths awaiting an explanation for their raison d'être. Indeed the slopes east of the Banns Road near this part of the Miners Hole river are an interesting hunting ground for the endeavours of the ancients. The larger the stone, the more likely it is to be a marker of the sun's solstice appearance on top of or from between some surrounding mountains. If there is a defined point on the boulder it will usually be found to indicate towards where the sun appears or disappears and thus supplying the explanation for the megalith's existence. Some of these boulders are of very significant sizes, as for instance the one apparently marking where the summer solstice sun appears at the pointed tip of Ben Crom.

A little phallic sculpture on Slievenaglogh cliff top.

431

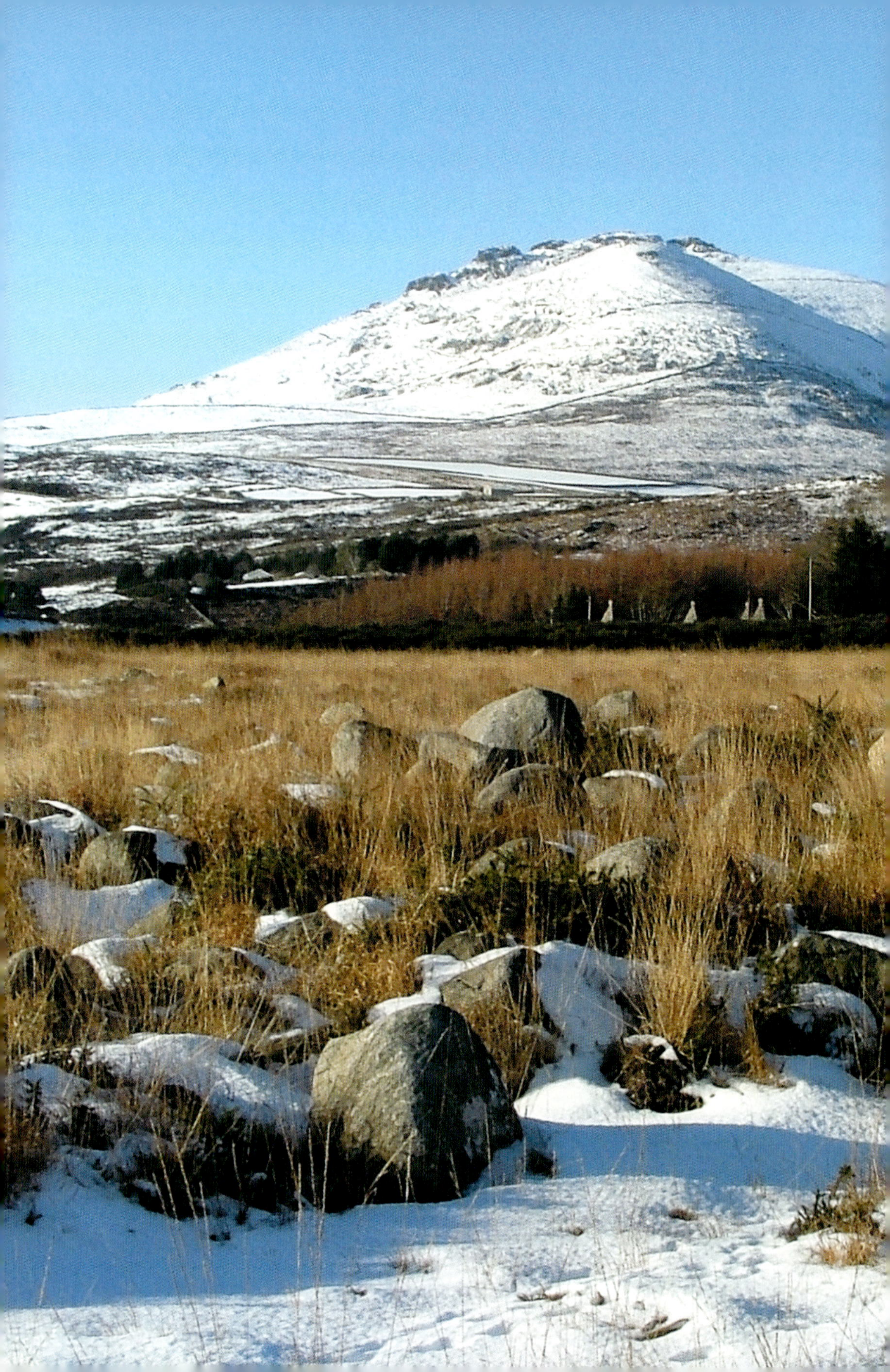

Slieve Bignian as seen from the Quarter Road on 5th December.

## Forks Mountain and The Maid of the Sweet Brown Knowe

Forks River is to be found on the map of Mourne but for some strange reason Forks mountain itself is not listed or named. It is an adjunct at the very end of Bignian overlooking the townland of Ballyveagh and is located at J326233. The name comes from the Irish *Foirceann* meaning 'end or extremity' although others might argue for *Forc* on account of the mountain's rather priapic top. *Forc* means 'a table fork or a prong', a description which retains the sexual nuance and is plausible when the mountain is viewed from the seaward end of Bignian's summit tors. A sexual construct was certainly put on the mountain in the past. In Irish the adjective *Forc* means 'firmness or stiffness'. The sexual aspect is obvious in the name of Ballyveagh townland. Viewed from the Head Road below, the twin peaks of Bignian and Forks were interpreted as a pair of firm breasts and the townland had the Irish name *Baile Bé*, 'townland of the maid or woman'. In 1834 the ordnance survey also recorded a name 'Birch Town'; this again was a reference to a couple of firm stiff breasts for the name was only a mnemonic of the Irish *Beirt Teann* meaning 'a tight pair'.[8]

A walk along the front or seaward side of Forks mountain is a humbling experience. One cannot help be awed at the multitude of quarries and the endeavours that had to be made in recent centuries by the men of Mourne to eke a living from the land. The piles of quarry scree, the tippings, the profusion of plug and feather marks on rock and yet more quarries at each turn of the track speak profoundly of a hard existence. One is humbled when confronted with the magnitude of effort, the exertions for survival, the sweat and struggles inevitably bound up in these silent piles of stone. In centuries to come these quiet quarries will tell a tale comparable to the efforts of the ancients in their erection of so many megaliths. This is the area of Mourne that has given rise to 'The Maid of the Sweet Brown Knowe'. If the name is familiar to you it probably is because you have heard versions of the eponymous song by the Dubliners or the Clancy Brothers, the start of which is as follows:-

> *Oh, come all you lads and lassies, and listen to me a while*
> *And I'll sing for you a verse or two that will cause you all to smile;*
> *It's all about a fair young man I'm going to tell you now*
> *How he lately came acourtin' of the maid of the sweet brown knowe...*

Twenty years ago Charles Cunningham told how this song belonged to Mourne. 'This song has always been claimed as one of Mourne's own. I heard my grandfather and a man called Rodgers singing it together over fifty years ago. They were sitting on a big stone ditch in a field called Park-na-gore up along the Mill River in Moneydarraghmore. They pointed out to me where the place the song referred to was, up on the face of the mountain. The Brown Knowe is at the foot of the Forks Mountain, which is to the front of Slieve Binnian when looking up from Annalong. It is in the townland of Ballyveaghmore at

Bignian is on the left and Forks mountain is on the right. When viewed from this angle the mountains resembled a pair of breasts and earned the Ballyveagh townland the name of *Baile Bé*, 'townland of the maid or woman'. Note the extensive quarries across the face of both mountains; this is the source of the 'Maid of the Sweet Brown Knowe'.

about the 1,000 foot line. To the east is the Laney and the Carrick; to the south-west, a bit further away, is Crockanroe. It is approached by a lane in from the Head Road about 200 yards south-west from Ballyveagh Road end.'[9] When next you hear the song, think of the men of Mourne sweating away in the quarries on Forks mountain. 'Maid of the Sweet Brown Knowe' is at the same time a mnemonic and a humorous, sexual description by the quarrymen of their work. It is from the Irish (*Tí na*) *mBiadh Súighteán Broinne Nó*, meaning '(The Place of) Sucking the food of the Famous Breast', namely extracting the granite from the mountain.

Access roads were needed for the men to get to the quarries and for the granite to be hawled back down the mountain-side. The front of Forks and Bignian were criss-crossed with the quarries and little tracks; this is the area referred to by Charles Cunningham as 'Laney', a name not marked on any map. The name is Irish and refers to the multitude of tiny trails from quarry to quarry; it comes from *Lání*, the plural of *Lána*, 'a lane or a narrow road'. The other name mentioned, the

*This sliver megalith enjoys the most beautiful of views from the slope of Forks mountain. The top of the stone is aligned to Slieve Donard.*

small curved hill of Crockanroe, is from the Irish *Cnoc an Ró,* 'the hill of the cast' and probably had its name from being the place to see the spectacle of the fertility shadow of Wee Bignian cast across this hill as the sun set on top of the mountain at winter solstice. On the heights above the granite would have been put onto slipes to be taken down the mountain by horse or donkeys pulling these special wheel-less sledges.[10] From the quarries the stone was brought to the many little farms for dressing into cribben, sills, building stone or square setts. This work gave us the name for the townlands of Brackenagh – east, west and two uppers. Brackenagh is an amalgam of two words of Irish, *Breacadh,* 'carving, chipping, bespattering...' and *Niacha,* 'a small particle, a little bit (as of a chip of granite)'. The sound of this industry was captured by a young Church of Ireland clergyman in what must surely be among the most beautiful reminiscing lines of local alliteration.

> 'Of the Mournes I remember most the mist,
> The grey granite goosefleshed, the minute
> And blazing parachutes of fuchsia, and us
> Listening to the tiny clustered clinks

Not far above the sliver megalith is this priapic pointed stone which bears a remarkable likeness to a mute swan with the bulbous knob atop its beak.

> Of little chisels tinkling tirelessly
> On stone, like a drip of bird's beaks picking
> Rapidly at scattered grain....'[11]

Forks mountain received plenty of attention from the ancients for the slopes and summit are rich in face stones, spear stones and animal sculpture.

### The Name of 'Bignian'

Given its length and great size it is no surprise that there are quite a number of names associated with Bignian. Some of these are the North Tor, South Tor, Summit Tor, Ardley, Laney, Forks mountain, Maid of the Sweet Brown Knowe, Ardmally, Douglas Crag, Buzzard's Roost, Blue Lough Buttress, the Back Castles, Bucky and Slieve Builg, referred to by Canon Lett as Slieve Bug. Undoubtedly many further names have been lost.[12] It has been a happiness in this work to have drawn attention to three old names around Bignian presently missing from maps of Mourne but hopefully worthy of inclusion in the future, namely Forks mountain, Ardmally and Slieve Builg or Womb mountain. As to the spelling of

At the top of Forks mountain this sizeable spear stone points to where the winter solstice sun will appear above the adjacent summit rocks.

Bignian itself, readers will have noticed that this is the form used throughout this work instead of Slieve Binnian on the present ordnance survey activity map of the Mournes. Bignian was the name form recorded by the scholar John O'Donovan in his notebooks in 1834 and, when properly understood, has seemed eminently the most appropriate name to continue with. Indeed, I deem it a great pity that the old form of Bignian that was in widespread use until the war was subsequently replaced on maps.

Over twenty years ago the Place-names project of Queen's University did us all a great service by collating the varieties and usages of names throughout Mourne as found on a multitude of maps and manuscripts. They must have had an invidious job when making their choice of name for the mountain for, unsurprisingly, it has three if not four names among the name versions collected. First to the form 'Bignian' used in this work by deliberate preference; this is the form found on Williams Map of 1810 and used again by John O'Donovan a couple of decades later. Part of the problem has been the existence of two very similar sounding names, namely *bPinginn* and *Binneán*. It was the first form that was most prevalent in the early part of the twentieth century and which was the name in common usage on postcards of Mourne, albeit in a variety of spellings. The form *bPinginn*, which we explain in a moment, seems to have presently lost pre-eminence simply because the eclipsed Irish obscured its origins whereas the form *Binneán* was straightforward to understand. Place-names project made a telling comment when speaking about this mountain: 'It seems that the element *sliabh*, (mountain), was prefixed relatively late and that originally the feature was referred to only as *Binneán*.' As rightly pointed out 'the mountain is often referred to simply as Binnian'. The present proposition is that, rather than having the element 'Slieve' attached relatively late that it was elided at a very early stage and is only now being re-introduced onto a modified name. The understanding behind the version 'Bignian' depends on eclipse in Irish and on the way the rock stacks at the summit tors and along the top of the mountain are weathered. The tors have been described by some as 'moneystacks' because the horizontal weathering of the granite made them appear like piles of money; a most apt description indeed and one that had appealed to the people of Mourne long ago. We should remember that pre decimal pennies were large coins and counting out two hundred and forty to make a pound, with twelve pennies to the shilling,

A strategically placed eye and a little mouth change this rock to a very passable turtle. The top of Forks mountain is rich in face stones. They don't have to be recognisable creatures but it is fascinating to see how the mind of the ancient sculptor worked in giving interpretations to the surrounding rock surfaces.

*The weathered tors with their strong horizontal lines were reminiscent of stacks of money and gave the mountain its name in Irish, (Sliabh na) bPinginn '(mountain of the) money' of which only the eclipsed remnant of 'Bignian' and variants is left.*

made an impressive row of bollards of bronze. The name Bignian is an eclipsed remnant of the Irish (*Sliabh na*) *bPinginn*, 'Mountain of the Money', where the operative Irish word originally was *Pinginn*, 'penny, money, wage'. The first part of the name '*Sliabh na*' was elided and the Irish [*na*] which caused the eclipse, in this case [*b*] in front of [*P*], was lost sight of. All that was left was the sound 'Binginn' and this would be found in a variety of spellings, Bignian, Bignean, Bingian and Bingion to mention a few.

**Megaliths of the South and Summit Tors**

The megaliths under the south tor of Bignian are worthy of very special note on account of their size, the steepness of the slope and the consummate skill that would have been necessary to manage the massive stones in such a challenging location. In circle one, two massive stones are at the centre of a cluster that still has much to reveal. One of the prime reasons why this location was of immense importance to the ancients is easy to discern from the alignment of the stones.

A pair of hares enjoy the sun on Forks mountain.

They point to the top of Forks mountain where the summer solstice sun will be seen to rise. The whole shape of Forks mountain has the appearance of a firm breast but the small rocky tip of Forks could be perceived as a tumescent phallus making the location of the megaliths under the south tor one of powerful fertility.

A gap has also been left between the large megaliths making them a pair of vagina stones so that the locality and the theme of fertility was only further enhanced at the other end of the year when the dawn light of winter solstice penetrated the 'vaginal gap' in a great moment of renewal. The light between the gap is further channelled upslope into a notch of two more face stones. There is fertility symbolism everywhere. One can only wonder at the 'open mouth' stone slightly down slope that was probably carefully positioned to direct the early winter solstice sun through its 'mouth' to the underneath of the great spear stone that looks over to Forks. Again one can only ponder the judicious removal of rock from the tor above to create the semblance of an eye turning the snub nosed part of the tor into the suggestion of a boar's head. Indeed there is evidence all around of an imagination fertile with sculptural possibilities. The ancients made shadow eyes and mouths on so many rock surfaces, transforming them into 'faces'. Many a time I had walked past these creations without realising their existence or because I was too close to perceive the artist's grand intention; afterwards, when photographs were examined, richness upon richness became apparent. For the sake of example, attention has been drawn to two interpretations, namely 'the boar's eye' on the second tor and 'the raven's head' on the fourth tor. Enjoy the discovery of many more.

The summit tors of Slieve Bignian as seen from Forks Mountain. South Tor on the left is the lowest of the tors and may well have received its name from the monumental megaliths below it. Many megaliths mark sites where the winter solstice sun appears in the notches between the tors as if being born from a vaginal opening.

A case can be made that the awe of the great megaliths marking summer solstice sunrise from Forks mountain gave the South Tor its name. The great size of the stones may be gauged against the trekking poles which, by comparison, are really insignificant in the photographs. The sheer size of these stones and how they would have been manhandled still generates astonishment, amazement and admiration. Although it cannot be verified, I strongly believe that the name of '**South**' tor is only a shortened mnemonic of the Irish **Suaith**nidheacht, meaning

This mountain-side has been the scene of stupendous labours and alone would have been sufficient to warrant the origin of the name of Mourne from the Irish (*Sléibhte na*) *mBúir-na*, 'The mountains of very many roars'

'a marvel, a prodigy'; a well deserved allusion to the stunning achievement of placing these great stones. Behind and upslope from the megaliths is another cluster of rocks which do not seem to be accidental falls. Follow the points of the spear stones and imagine the winter solstice sun disappearing into the notch between the first two tors, where this notch is again perceived as vaginal. The gynaecomorphic interpretation of the landscape has certainly been lavishly observed on these environs of Bignian.

Above: A close-up view of the first two tors of Bignian. A select three groups of megaliths have been circled but there are many more. <u>South</u> Tor, on the left, probably derived its name from the extraordinary megaliths below it. The name would be a shortened mnemonic of the Irish *Suaithnidheacht*, meaning 'a marvel'. Note how a shadow eye on the rock face of second tor has transformed that part of the tor into a boar's head.

Top right: Circle One: These great megaliths mark where the summer solstice sun can be seen rising from the summit of distant Forks Mountain. The 'open mouth' megalith, down slope to the right, comes into play at winter solstice dawn. The trekking poles straddling the two stones in the foreground are virtually lost, such is the size of this megalith.

Bottom right: Circle One: The megaliths are a pair of vagina stones, so arranged as to receive the fertility light of winter solstice dawn into the gap between them. The larger megalith on the left has a multitude of subtle 'faces'; one looking to the sky, another open mouth version to Forks and an interesting nose facing left to the tor. The various possible artistic interpretations are a tribute to the skill of the ancients. On the lower stone on the right, the ridge along the side has a close resemblance to the distinctive flipper of a humpback whale; for scale note the size of the trekking poles at the tip of the stone.

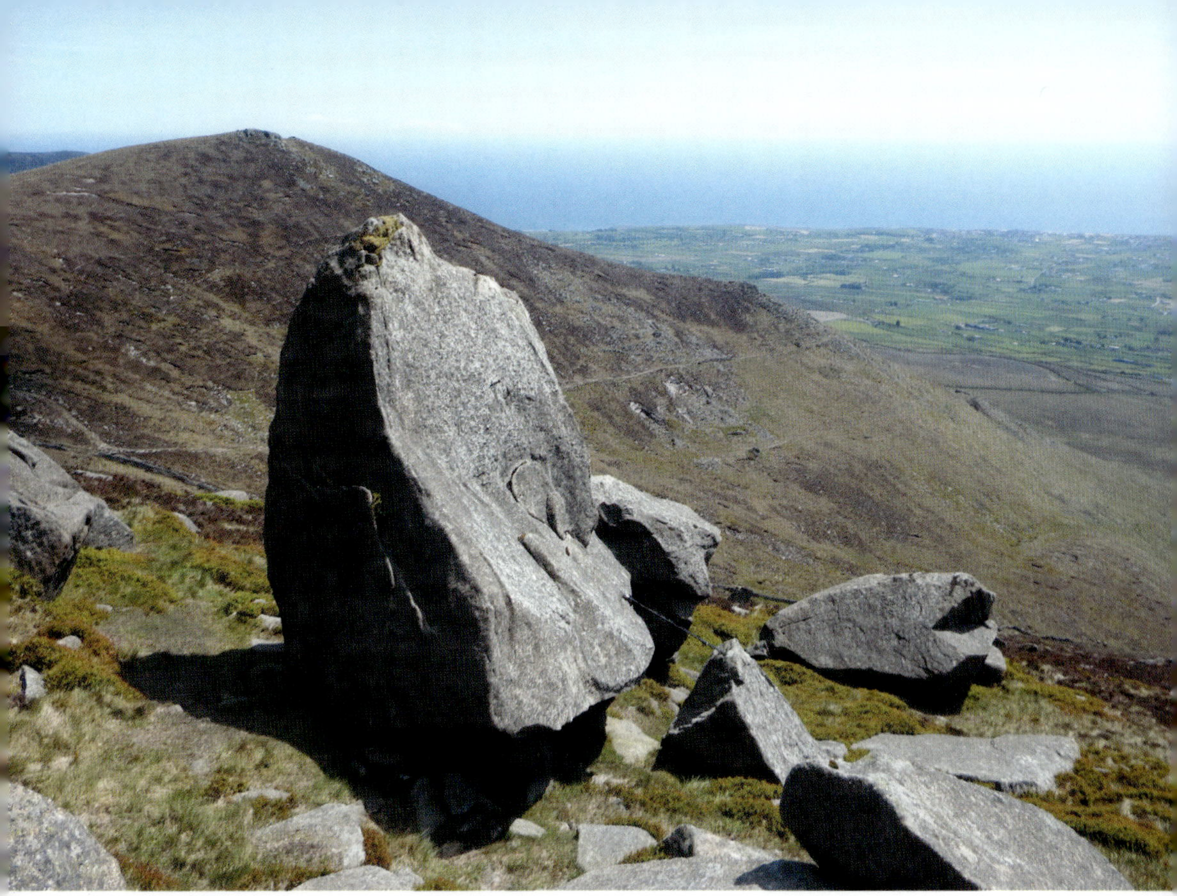

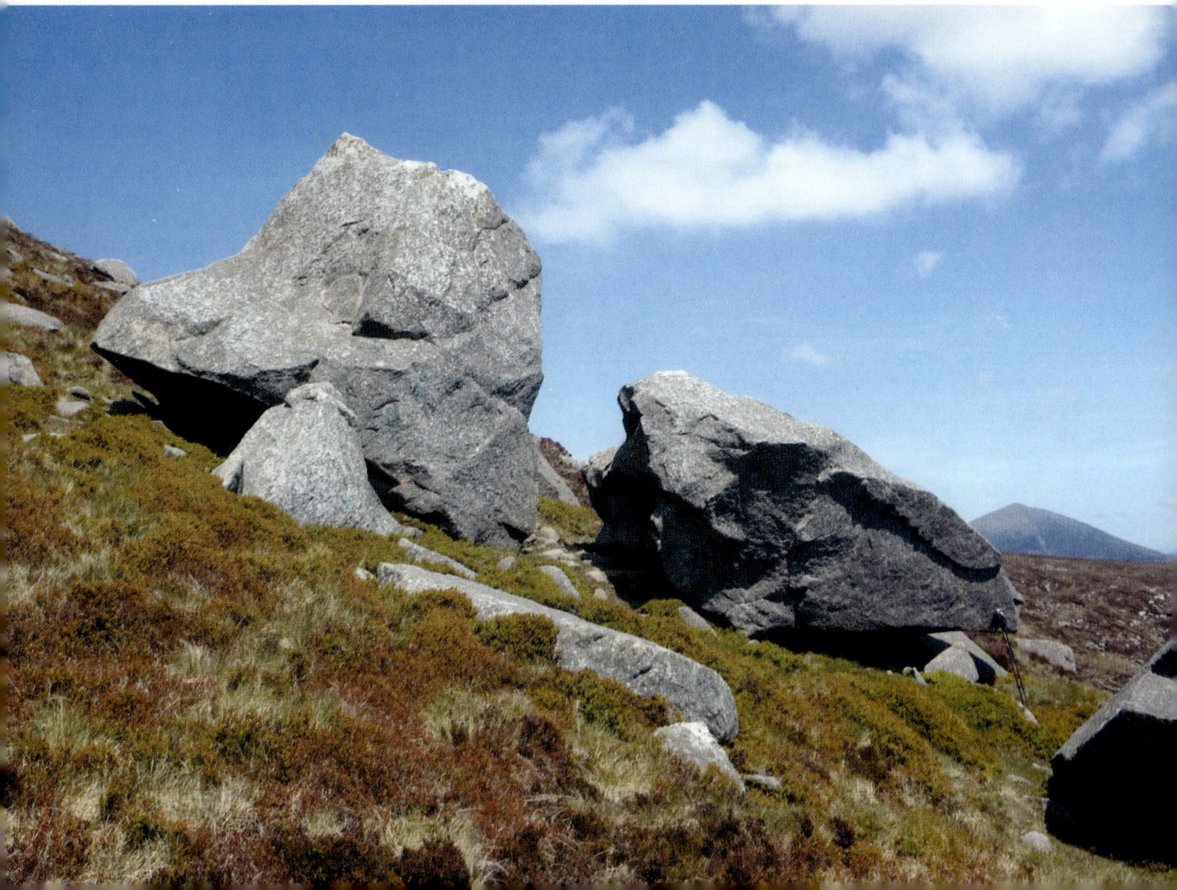

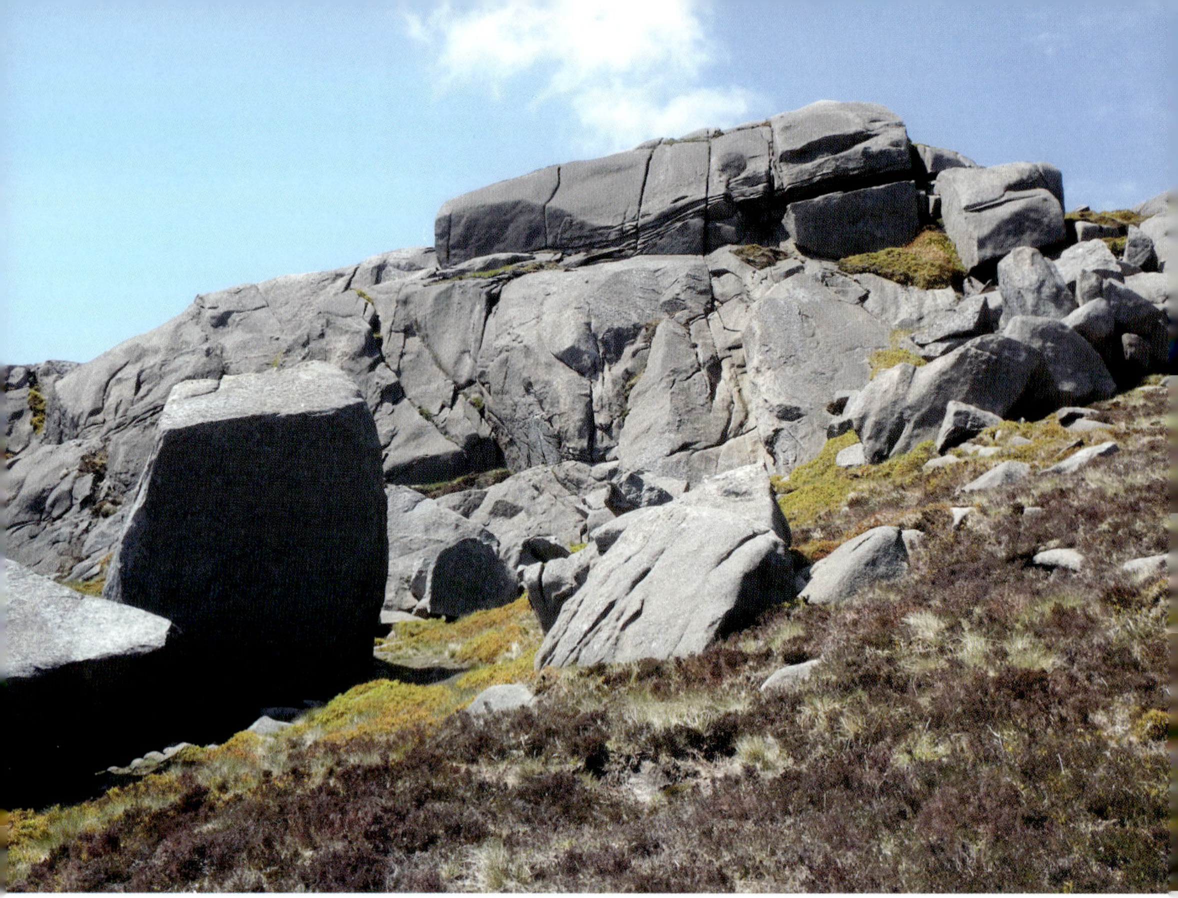
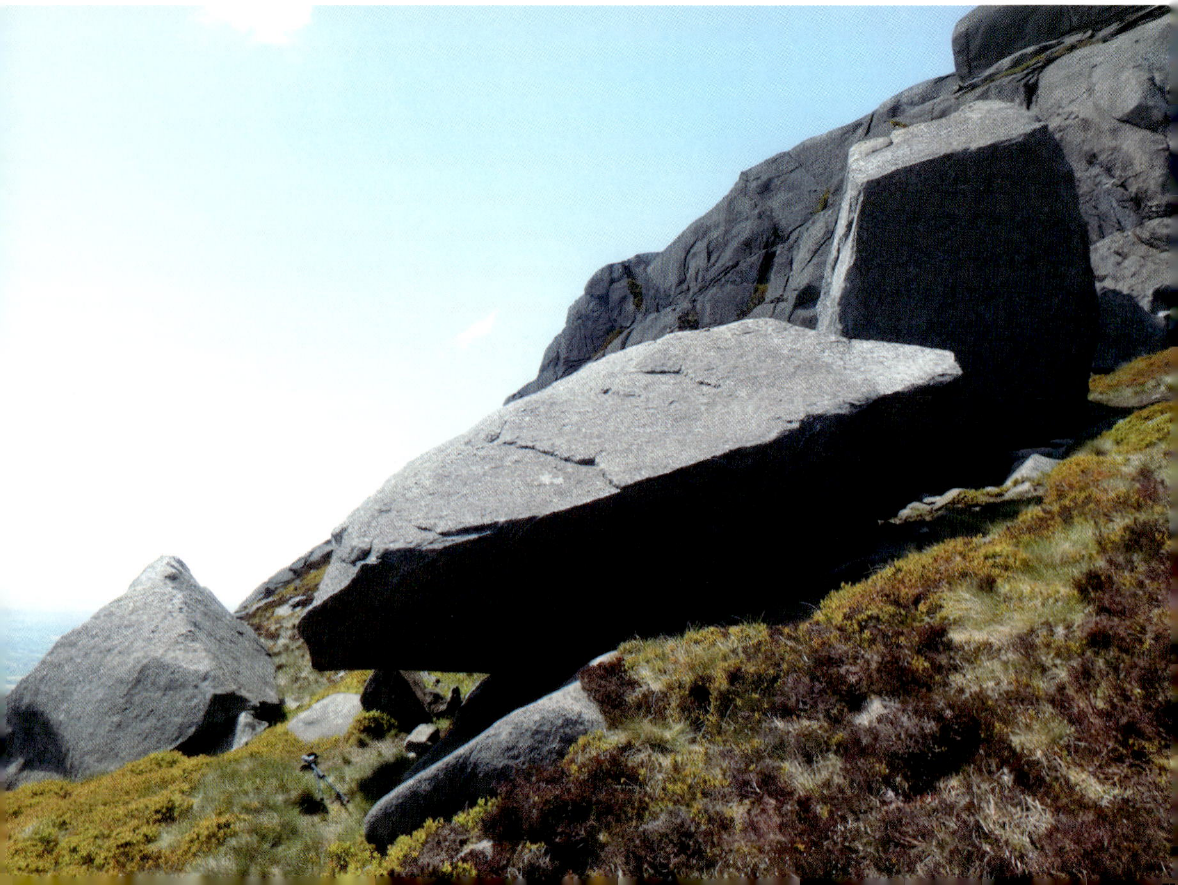

Top left: Circle One: The spear point directed over to Forks mountain top is more obvious in this picture taken down slope. The higher end of the upper stone points towards the snub nose part of the tor above; this projection above is ambiguous enough to be interpreted as either a phallus or as an approximation to a boar's head complete with great shadow eye….or both. On the left, the tor sports another snub nose and a well placed shadow eye to make a further boar.

Bottom left: Circle One: The great lower spear stone points emphatically over towards the summit of Forks mountain. The trekking poles on the ground below the spear tip are almost lost in size; and then, besides the megaliths, we must remember the anchoring base stone below.

Above: Circle Two: In the gap between south and second tor is a special favourite, a megalith of a viviparous lizard; this remarkable sculpture is a counter-balance for the great spear stone on which it rests.

Circle three: This pair of vagina stones would seem so much part of the hillside that its subtle alignment could be easily overlooked. The gap between the rocks is pierced at winter solstice as the sun clears the gap between South and Second tor. When looking through the gap it can be appreciated that the flat back of the great stone is neatly aligned with Slieve Donard.

The many megaliths under the third tor of Bignian, including the two circled here, seem to mark where the summer solstice rises at the end of the great phallic mountain of Chimney Rock giving a simulation of ejaculation.

Circle Four: The nose of this intimidating face may point over to winter solstice sunrise but the placement of this huge megalith also marks where the summer solstice rises at the end of distant phallic Chimney Rock mountain. The bottom picture is the same stone viewed a little lower down slope and illustrates the skill of the ancient sculptor who has provided us with yet another face. The anchor stone on which the megalith rests is a very substantial slab in its own right and should not be overlooked in assessing the enormous labours involved.

Above: The fourth tor of Bignian. The ancients made many 'faces' on the shoulders, boulders and rock surfaces of Bignian; the raven's beak, to the left of the wall, is quite distinctive. In mythology the raven was the harbinger of darkness and death, especially death in battle.

Top right: Circle Seven: This megalith is one of a number of megaliths perched along the top edges of the tors. Slieve Commedagh is in the background.

Bottom right: Some of the more important megaliths under Bignian's summit tor. This tor is also rich in 'faces'. The large spear pointed rock to the left of circle eleven has already been illustrated on page 155. This photograph was taken at 11.30am on 10th June; as the sun moves to the other side of Bignian later in the day the shadow eyes chopped into the rocks disappear and with it the opportunity to find faces.

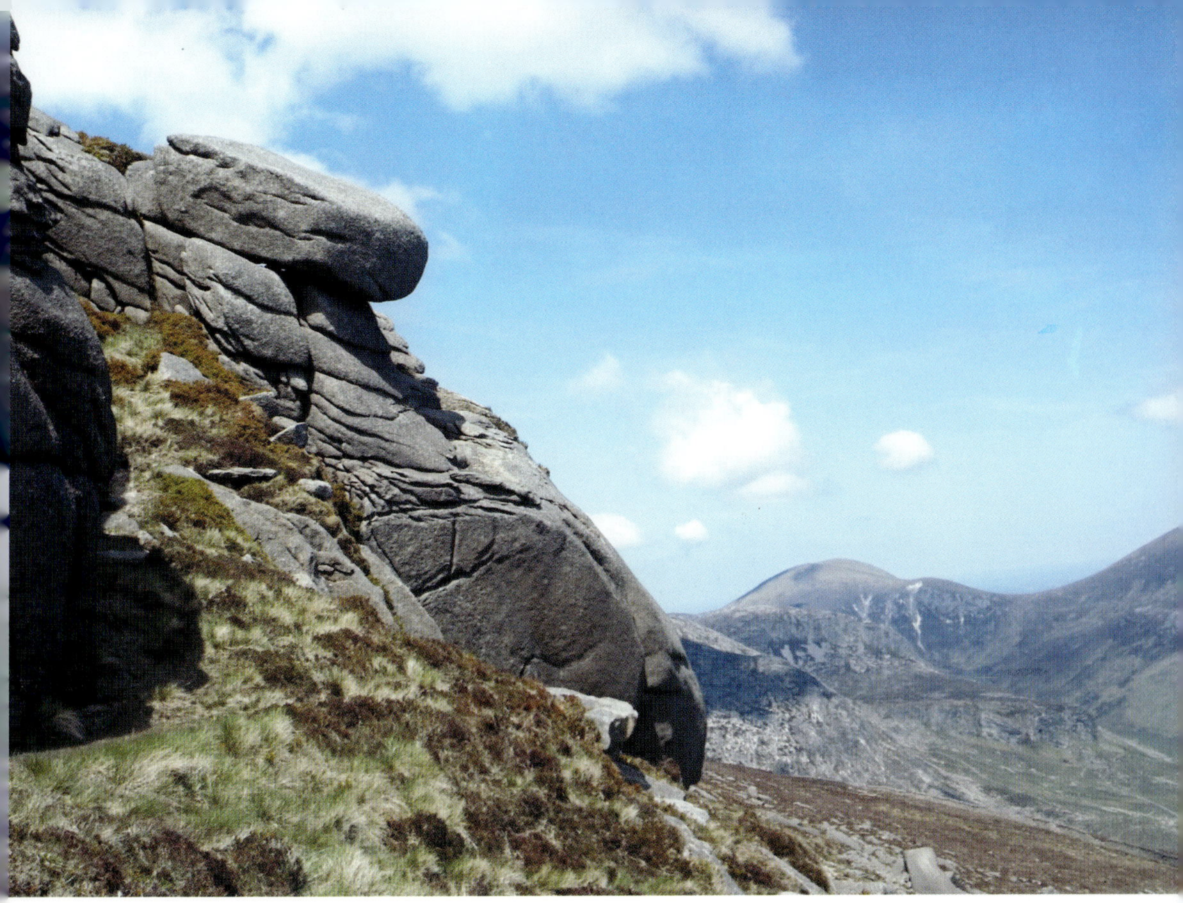

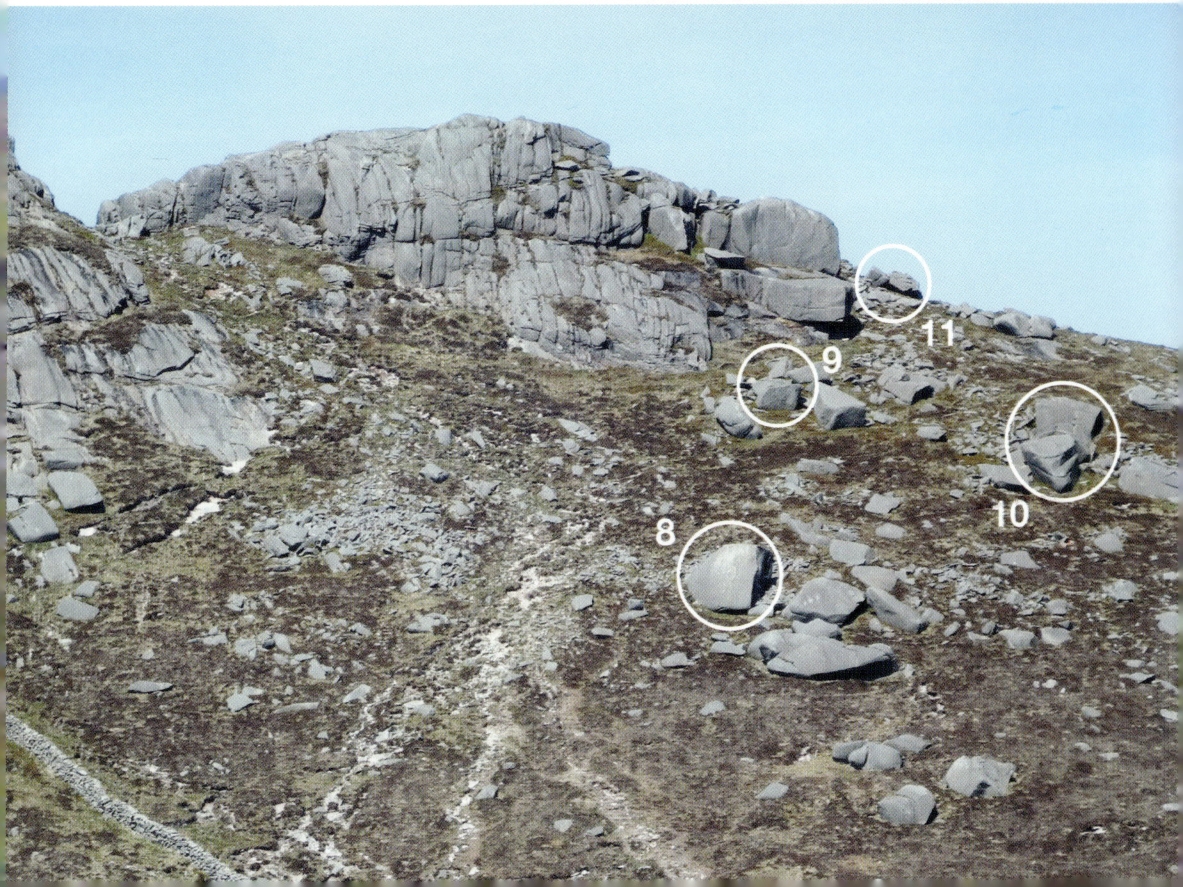
11
9
10
8

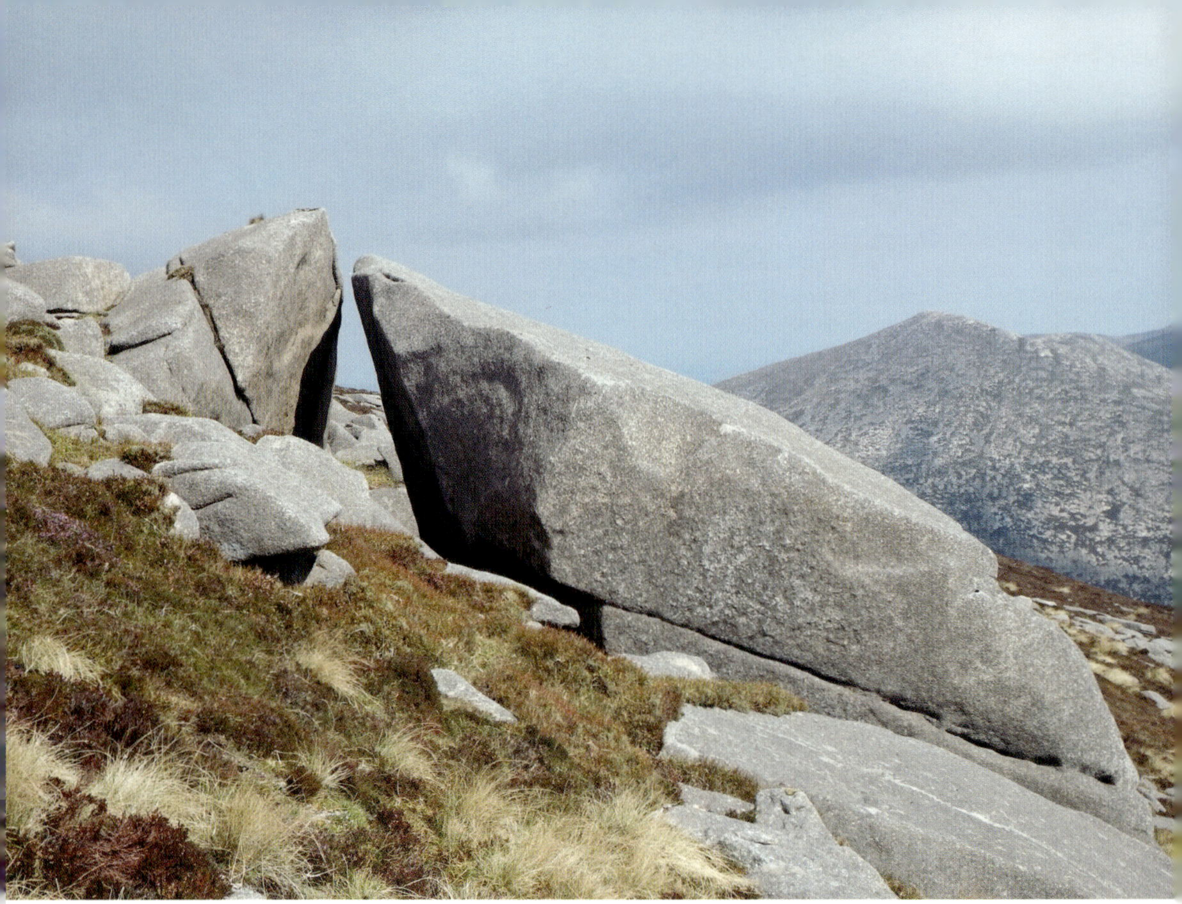

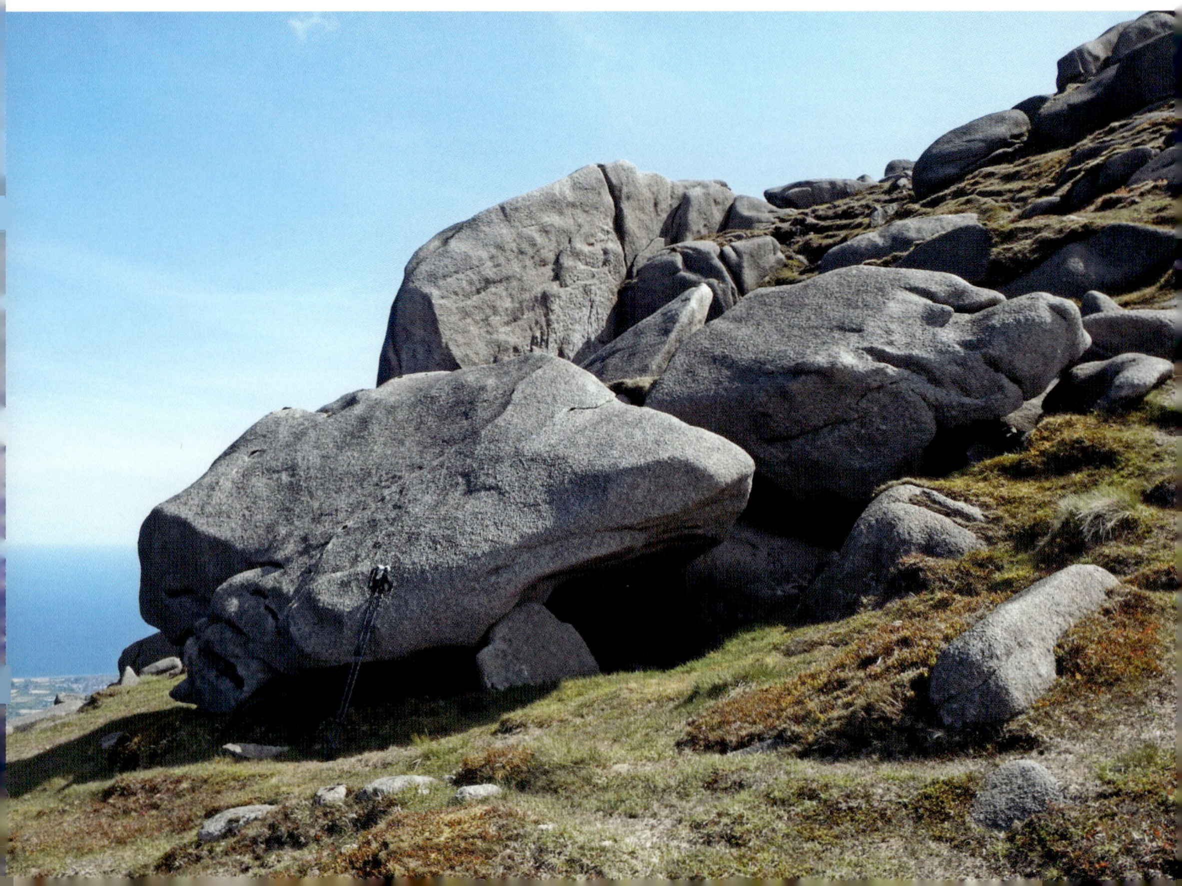

Top left: Circle Ten: The gap between the stones awaits the fertilising light at the end of the winter solstice day. There is a delightful interplay at the top of the gap where the tips of the two stones would appear to be about to give each other a kiss.

Bottom left: Circle Eleven: These megaliths are noteworthy for their shapes. The bottom chocked stone bears the resemblance to the front of a dolphin's head while the stone above it is a turtle. One must consider the possibility that the fertility loving Fir Bolg deliberately selected them on account of the remarkable and proportionally large size of their reproductive organs.

Above: A view of the Back Castles on Bignian's spine.

A panoramic view of the fields of Mourne from Bignian.

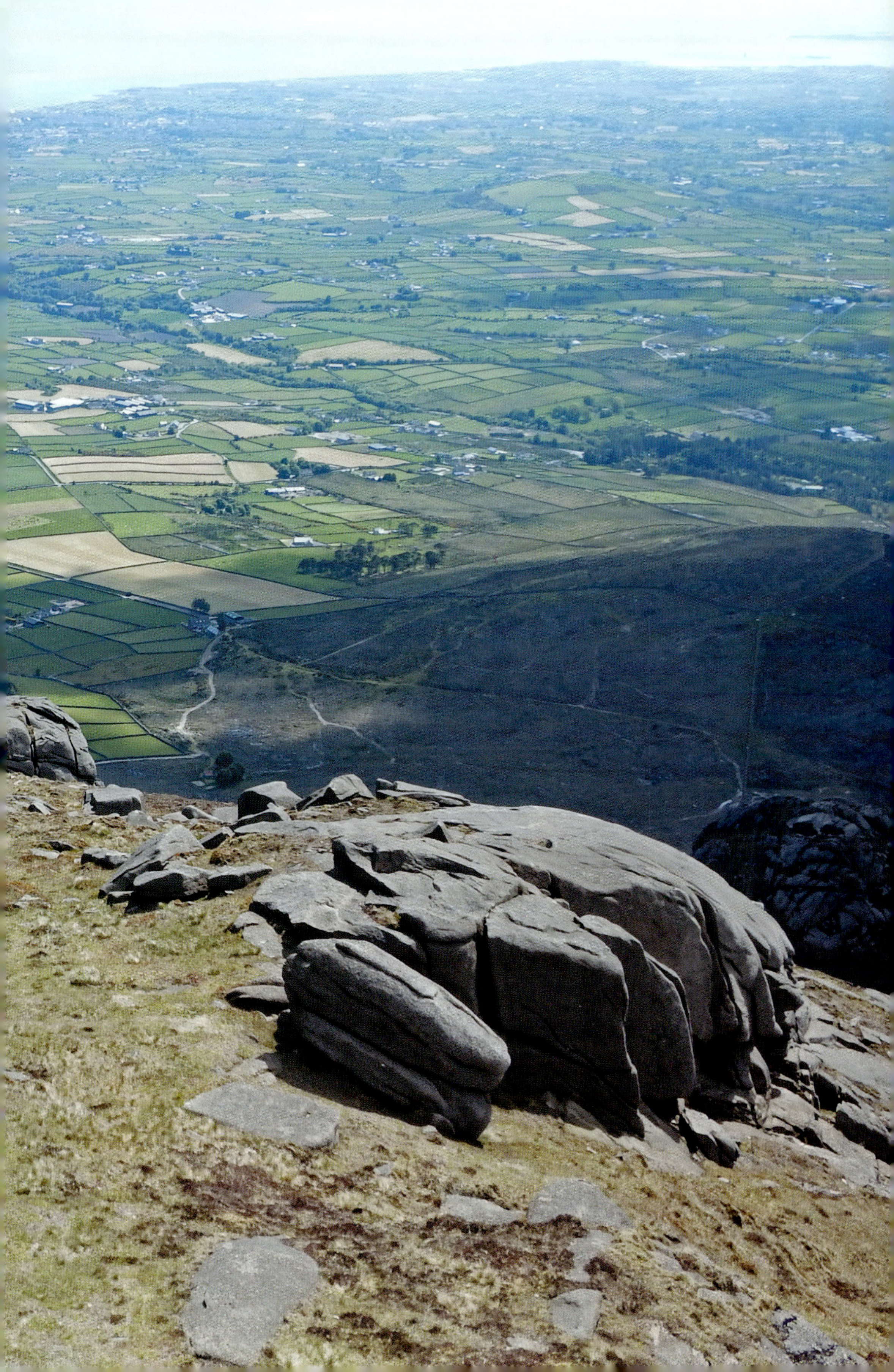

Maid of the
Sweet Brown Knowe
(Quarries)

Forks Mountain

Bignian Summit Tor

Ardmally

Annalong River Valley

Slieve Bignian as seen from Rocky at midday on 5th November.

Back Castles

Slieve Builg

Blue Lough Buttress

The Great Boar's Head Megalith
Viewpoint for Newgrange K67

Bignian North Tor

Buzzard's Roost

Douglas Crag

Percy Bysshe Hill

Spear Stone pointing to Bignian Summit

This megalith on Douglas Crag has been carefully wedged in place with chock stones.

The snub nose and eye gives this megalith the profile of a boar's head.

Chop marks for an eye and a mouth have made this megalith into a face stone.

The little eye, pointy nose and mouth give this megalith a close resemblance to a shrew.

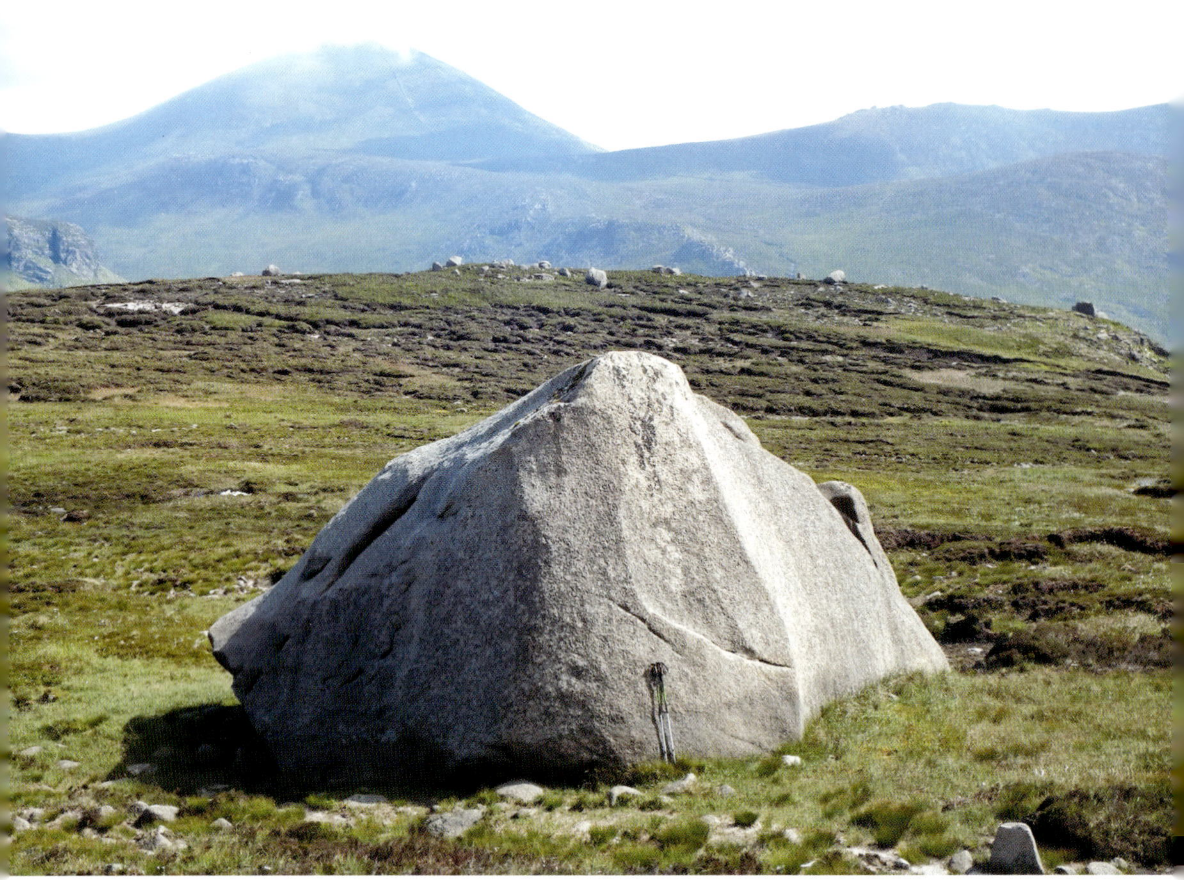

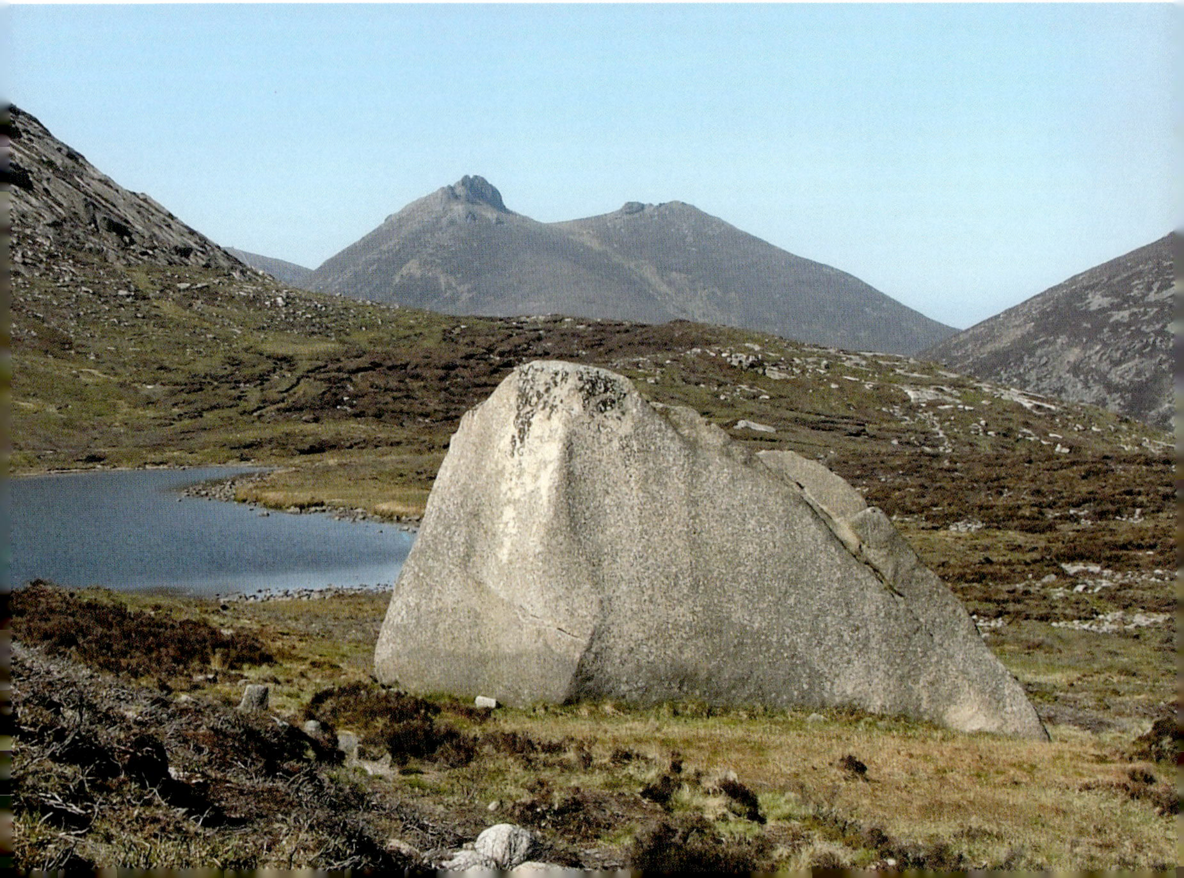

## SLIEVE BIGNIAN AND VICINITY

summit of Chimney Rock mountain and marked, we believe, by the great megalith of circle eight. Three double diamond motifs were already encountered on the left side of K1 and, as explained on page 371, are likewise viewpoints for important sun/earth fertility conjunctions. We might tentatively suggest that on the left side of K67 the linked lozenges and triangles followed by yet more lozenges below the triangles are duration markers indicating the number of days the sun is partially visible on its journey towards the notch, then completely visible at the notch and then retreating back to partial before disappearing for another year.

Top left: This huge boar head megalith marks where the summer solstice sun is born from the vaginal notch between distant Slieve Donard on the left and Chimney Rock on the right. Note the profusion of other megaliths marking the same event on Douglas Crag in the middle distance.

Bottom left: As a further reason for the vast labours in locating this monumental boar megalith, the nose also points to the notch on the right, between Slieve Bearnagh and Slieve Lamagan, where the declining summer solstice sun was deemed to enter and impregnate the earth.

Bottom: The Newgrange decorated kerbstone, K67, which faces east towards the summer solstice sunrise, is a depiction of the same solstice at Mourne where the sun rises from the vaginal notch between Slieve Donard (left spiral) and Chimney Rock (right spiral). The top 'diamond' is the rising sun and the 'double diamond' on the bottom is the viewpoint for the spectacle from Douglas Crag on Slieve Bignian.

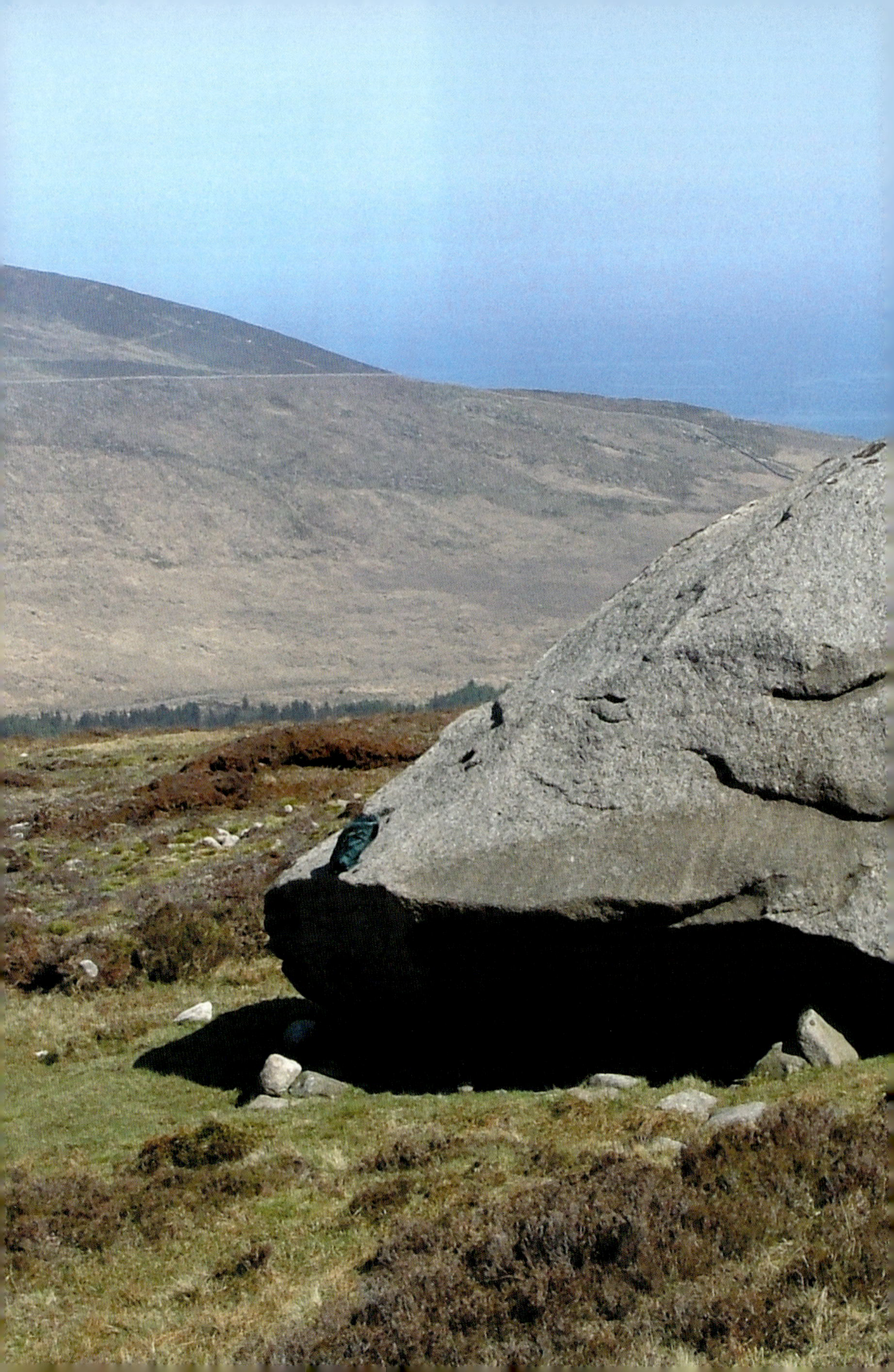

This great boar head megalith is probably the largest in Mourne competing only with the huge vagina stones under Bignian's North Tor. This monstrous megalith marks the birth of the summer solstice sun from the earth's vagina, the notch between Slieve Donard and Chimney rock. At the end of the same day it also marks the impregnation of the earth by the sun setting into another notch between Slieve Bearnagh and Slieve Lamagan. Such is the size of the megalith that the rucksack on the nose of the stone is quite insignificant.

## The North Tor and the name 'Binnian'

Having mentioned the origin of Bignian as coming from the Irish (*Sliabh na*) *bPinginn*, 'Mountain of the Money', it is timely to look at the present name found on maps, namely Slieve Binnian. Both forms were collected by the ordnance survey in 1834. As Place-names project inform us, Binnian is from the Irish *Sliabh Binneáin* 'mountain of the little peak'.[15] Those who know the Mournes and Slieve Bignian in particular will recognise that the name Binnian, 'the little peak', properly belongs to the North Tor with its pointed phallic summit so beloved by the ancients. It would be a pity if the tail was to wag the dog and that the name *Binneán*, that refers exactly to the north end of the mountain, should dispossess the name for the more widespread weathered topographical features along the rest of the mountain. In the past the name *Binneán* did not apply to the tors along the centre of the mountain as these had their own distinctive name, the Back Castles. These upright Back Castles were regarded as phallic, bestowing great fertility when the winter solstice sun set behind them; their name was a mnemonic for *Biach Caise Tál,* meaning 'yielding of penis love'. The Back Castles however are good examples of the weathering of the granite that resembled moneystacks or *bPinginn*.

There is another possible name variation for the mountain namely 'Great Bennyng' mentioned on Lythe's Map of 1568. After Bignian and Binnian this would represent a third name. These early English place-names were frequently adaptations of the sound of the Irish; in the case of Great Bennyng this is now beyond verification. Great Bennyng may likely be a telescoped mnemonic of the Irish (*Tí na*) *gCreathair Binneáin,* (Place of the) Sanctuary of the Little Peak'. We may gauge the likelihood of this part of Bignian being regarded by the ancients as a sanctuary from the gynaecomorphic interpretation still possible on the topography, from the presence and orientation of huge megaliths, the existence of what may reasonably be interpreted as a ritual stone chair half way up a cliff face, the shaping of a great slab of rock into a plausible boar's head, the interpretation from Irish that can be put on the name of North Tor besides that already mentioned of Great Bennyng, the presence on the tor of numerous large fire bowls hammered out of the granite, but above all the interaction of the sun on the landscape at the beginning and end of the winter and summer solstice day.

The North Tor is not one convenient projection but rather two large tors separated by a small col. The climbing fraternity distinguish them as north tor east and north tor west.[16] We begin our circuit of the tor on the lower reaches of north

> The North Tor of Slieve Bignian has a very distinctive summit. From the Blue Lough and under Slieve Lamagan it appeared as phallic. This was the source of the Irish name *Sliabh Binneáin* 'mountain of the little peak' which has now been applied to the whole length of the mountain.

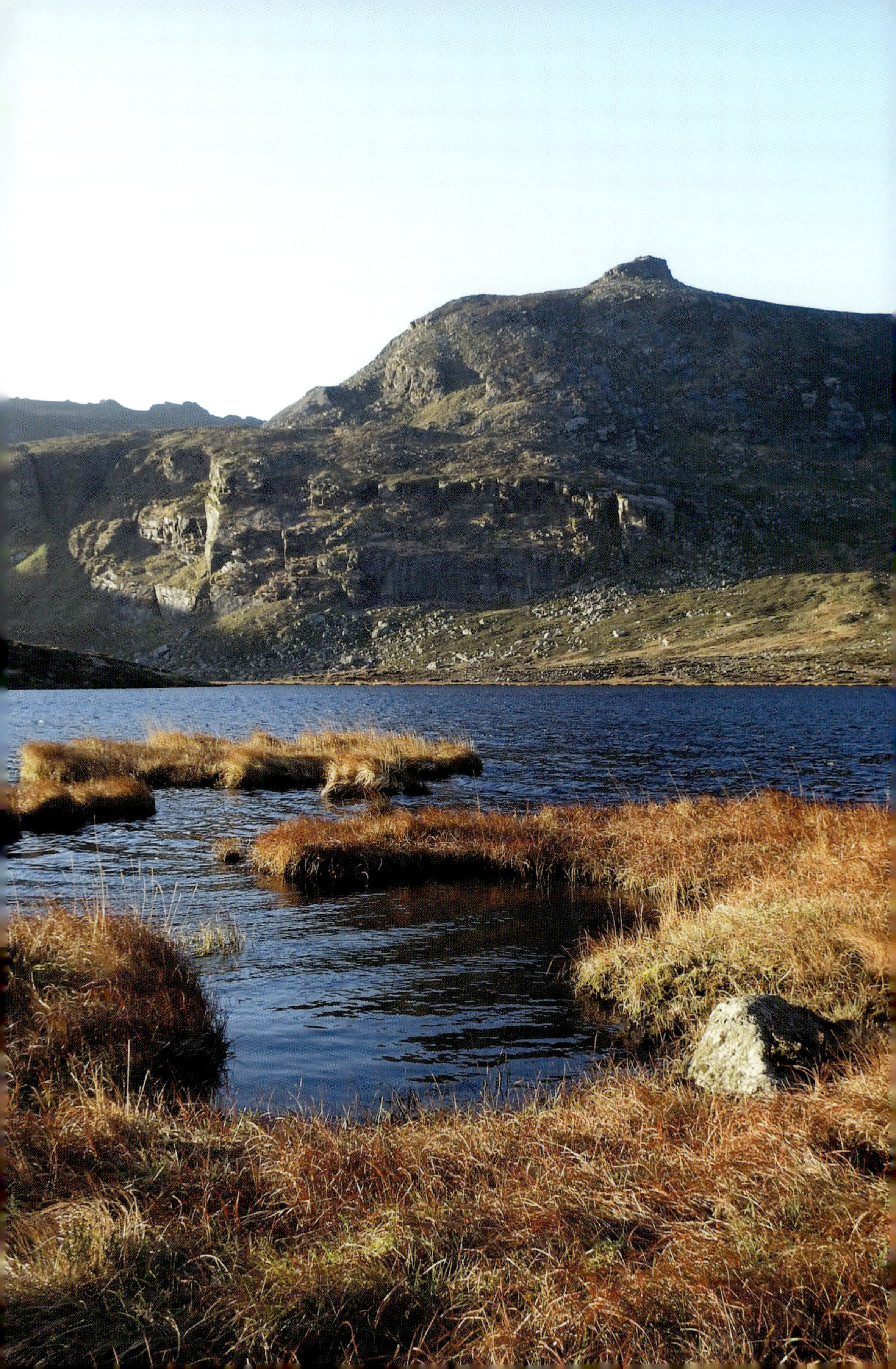

## Prehistoric Mourne: Inspiration for Newgrange

tor east, the part of the tor closest to Slieve Lamagan and overlooking the Blue Lough valley. It is from the valley below that the 'little peak' is best seen and its similarity to an erect penis understood. When the high slope under the peak is examined, it would appear that the ancients further enhanced that interpretation by supplying a pair of stone testicles on the slope below. A great slab of rock was indented to give the rough impression of two massive testicles to compliment the erection above. Both slabs are extensively undercut at the front and despite their sagging similarity from below, a close examination shows that both 'testicles' have points directed over to Slieve Donard. One wonders if the great labours at this location were on account of it being the place to see the dawn summer solstice sun emerging from the top of Slieve Donard, a display that would certainly have been interpreted as sun and earth coming together at a moment of ejaculation.

Below: Bignian Lough with the North Tor in the background. Note the megalith on the slope in the middle of the picture.

Top right: Half way up the slope behind this capstone is the huge divided slab simulating a pair of testicles complimenting the apparent erection of the tor above.

Bottom right: Part of the great slab that has been undercut and in the left background Slieve Donard.

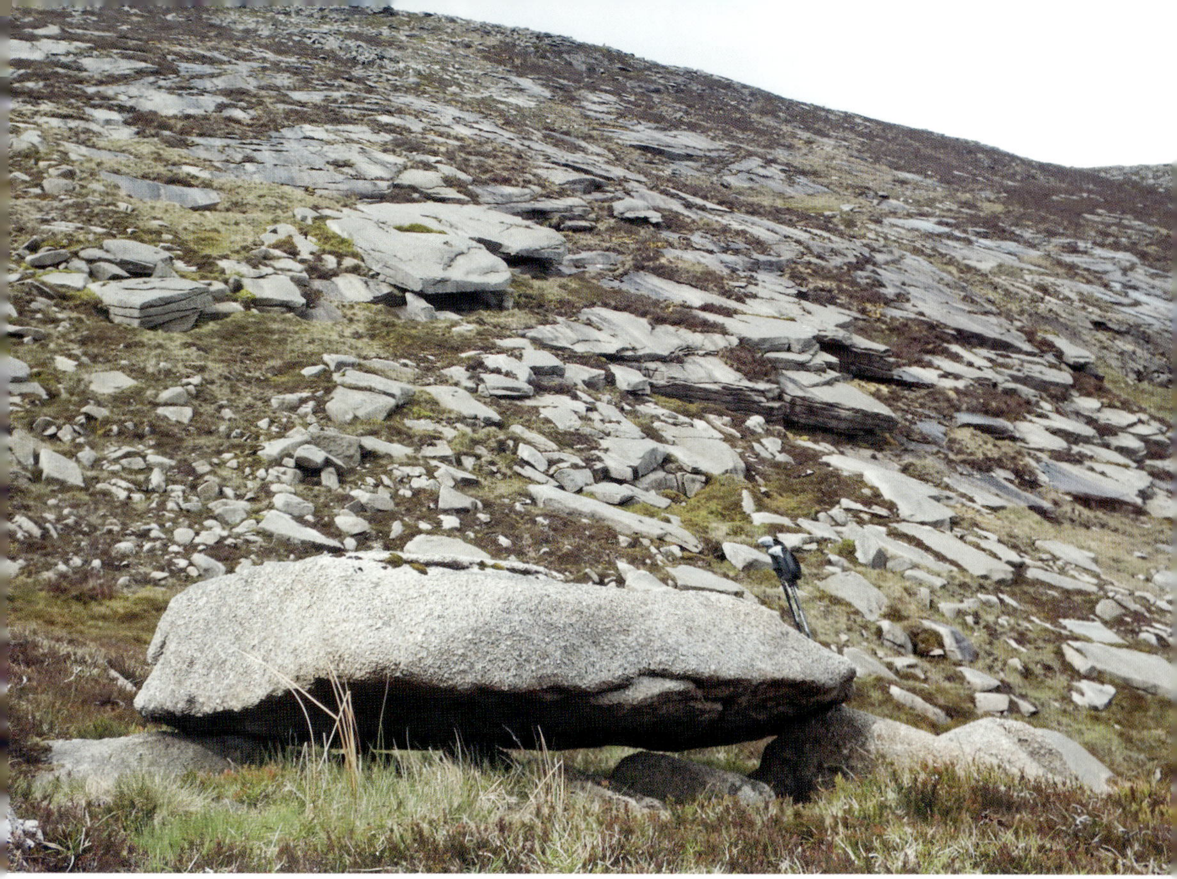

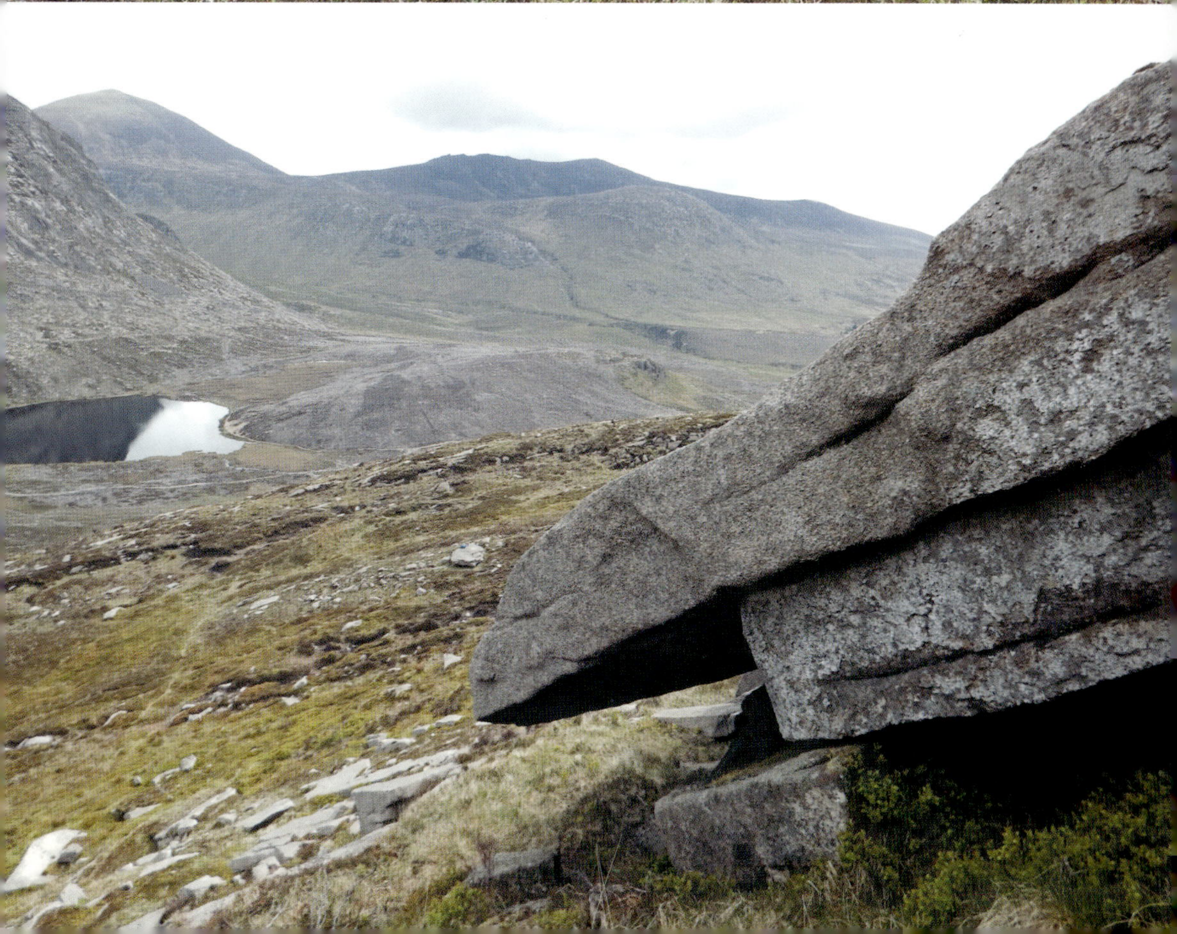

A stark Lamagan seared of all vegetation by fire. The mountain bears many megaliths on the slope facing Bignian's north tor. Lamagan was viewed as a huge vulva and had its name from the Irish *Lab an Geine*, 'considerable lump of a woman'. During the first world war the mountain was used for target practice by the Home Fleet anchored in Dundrum Bay and many rusting metal shards can still be found all across the top of Percy Bysshe hill, the small hill left of centre.

One only has to look at the west slope of Slieve Lamagan to realise how important the phallic north tor was to the ancients. The slope of Lamagan is absolutely covered with megaliths, most of them spear stones which point towards the top of the north tor. As illustrated already on page sixty, the declining winter solstice sun casts the phallic shadow horn of Bignian's north tor onto Lamagan's side. This perceived sexual interest gave Lamagan its name in Irish, *Lab an Geine*, 'considerable lump of a woman', the 'lump' of course being the vulva[17]; the shadow horn (*Sleabhac* in Irish) at solstice gave us the mnemonic 'Lamagan Slabs'.[18] Climbing from rock to rock across the slope of Lamagan and moving from one megalith to another, made one marvel at how the ancients could have moved so many large stones when footing was so dangerous; but they did, even up to the higher reaches.

The presence of great fire bowls hammered out of the granite support the idea of the north tor once being a very important ritual place for the ancients. The great double bowl on the summit of Slieve Bearnagh, once known as Broken Mountain, otherwise *Breo Cian* 'long distance fire', had been imagined to be the largest of bowls and was certainly much larger than any of those previously found atop Chimney Rock, until that is, one came across the monstrous bowl under Bignian's north tor east. You would pass close to it while on the easy way to the top of the tor.[19] The bowl is more than two metres across. The flame from this great bowl lit during the night of winter solstice would have been witnessed by those keeping vigil around the Annalong valley and been visible also on the plains below in a rather restricted part of Mourne, namely Moneydarragh, Annalong and Mullartown. Large bowls had also been found on top of one of the Back Castle tors and these would have given a striking pyrotechnic display to a far wider landscape below. These bowls at the Back Castles were clustered right across the top of the rock. It would have seemed as if that whole part of the mountain was on fire. Both parts of the north tor would have been well illuminated. One large boulder in the very middle of the north tor col has a couple of bowls and there are two large examples on top of north tor west. Among the boulders under southerly north tor west is a little bowl high on the rock. Climbers will recognise it as 'Triggers', described in the climbing guide book as 'a one move problem that has become somewhat of a classic. The original starts on the two obvious hand holds and jumps for the bowl'. From further back along the spine of Bignian it becomes more obvious that this particular large boulder has been worked on to make it a face stone. The bowl could be viewed as part of the mouth.

One of many of the large fire bowls on this larger Back Castle Tor. This eminence has a commanding view over much of Lower Mourne so the solstice fire would have been seen over a wide area. In the background is the split North Tor.

This fire bowl is in the middle of the col of the North Tor. In the background is the summit of Bignian and to the right of it some of the Back Castles.

The more the surfaces and shadows of the north tor, east and west, are examined as the sun passes throughout the day, it becomes apparent that a great multitude of faces have been created on all parts of the tor. Not all are obvious close up, indeed scarcely so, but it would seem that many of these beastly faces were intended to be observed on approach along the spine of the mountain from the southerly summit. When the sun is right the inside cliff of north tor east above the col becomes a massive boar's head. It is not the only such representation of the animal for it appears again on the rock face under the great fire bowl. Again on the northern side of the col, overlooking Ben Crom reservoir, the rock face under the ritual platform is another boar's head. This animal head, approaching twenty feet in height, has been rendered so smoothly on the rock face as to appear natural and effortless. It has taken great skill to create such a graceful sleeping eye on the granite without leaving any sharp edges on the rock surface and all while probably hanging from a rope as well. It is the work of someone with impressive talent and rare ability, a master craftsman indeed. Such workmanship only further distinguishes the small platform that graces this stone boar's head. This small ledge, which seems eminently worthy to be referred to as a ritual platform, is

Towards the lower right is surely the largest of fire bowls of Mourne as seen from the top of North Tor East. The bowl is easily over two metres in length and is an indication of the importance of this tor to the ancients. Also visible below near Bignian Lough is the huge boar megalith marking solstice sunrise from the notch between Slieve Donard and Chimney Rock.

distinguished by a stone seat for the ancient master of ceremonies. The location allowed good observation of winter solstice sunrise over at the Back Castles as well as sunset at summer solstice.[20] Just getting the fairly substantial stone seat onto this high ledge was no mean feat in itself. One must insert a necessary word of caution here. Even the ancients who used this location would have needed nimble agility to access it. This is not a location that can be lightly scrambled up to; rather it should be treated with serious respect and only be attempted with due discretion, proper preparation and good protection.[21]

With the north tor having the appearance of a tumescent phallus from the Annalong valley below and the deep col cleaving the tor in the middle evoking resemblance to a vaginal notch, it is no surprise that such fertility associations supported the idea of the north tor being a sanctuary in ancient times. One can imagine the vigil wait for solstice dawn being spent in chanting, prayers, petitions for fertility, recitation of charms, making of spells for good luck and calls upon the dead ancestors for protection. It reminded me of Richard Rowley's poem *Thinkin' Long* the first verse of which sees an old man reflecting beside his fire.

> 'It's time the lamp was lit,
> A sit my lone,
> Watchin' the firelight play
> On the cracked hearth-stone.
> Oul' dreams go through my head,
> Like words o' a song.
> A'm sittin' here my lone,
> An A'm thinkin' long.'[22]

Rowley had obviously heard this local expression and was quite taken with it to the extent of making a poem around it. The expression 'thinking long' seems to be quite local to Mourne; an aunt of mine who had taught in Kilcoo was well familiar with it but her husband from another county had never heard of it. It has the meaning of taking one's time over something, being slow and deliberate or giving something careful consideration. This is still fairly close to the ancient meaning in Irish. The local expression 'Thinking long' is a mnemonic that has

The boar's sleeping eye has been so smoothly rendered on the rock face as to appear completely natural. The portrayal of such a deceptively simple image belies the magnificent skill behind its execution; a skill made all the more amazing for having been achieved with primitive tools. On top of this boar rock, as seen on the opposite page, is a small platform and seat probably used for ritual.

The ritual seat at Bignian's North Tor col. From this vantage point the ancient master of ceremonies had a clear view of the winter solstice sunrise penetrating the fertility notch of the col. The blocks behind the sheep would appear to have been deliberately placed across the gap so that over on Ben Crom the first sight of the winter fertility sun 'being born' from the notch would be raised making it possible to witness the spectacle from that mountain's summit rather than somewhere lower down the cliff face.

Bignian's north tor as seen from back along the spine of the mountain. The penetration by the sun of the great gynaecomorphic notch between west and east tors at winter solstice dawn brought assurance of annual fertility to the earth. The ancients added their own monstrous megaliths, the greatest of which are the two very large boulders below the centre of the picture. The positioning of these two vagina stones, which are also carefully aligned on the summit of north tor east, was an achievement of literally monumental proportions. Given how steep is the slope, the sourcing and delicate placing of these stones, bigger than any at Stonehenge, must command profound awe, amazement and absolute admiration for this astonishing achievement by the early men of Mourne. This megalithic creation alone, would have justified the origin of the name of Mourne from the *Irish Sléibhte na* mBúir-na, 'the mountains of very many roars'. Also of importance is how the ancients spalled rock from the top of the right side of the central col to create a great shadow eye and turning that part of North Tor East into a giant boar's head when seen from back along Bignian's spine. The effect is lost close-up which makes the grand scheme even all the more remarkable. Turning the mountain top into the great fertility symbol of a boar gave the North Tor even greater eminence as a place of ritual.

preserved for us the Irish *Tincheadal Luain* meaning, 'Incantation of light' and harks back to the ancient chants and mantras that went on interminably in pagan times during the vigil for the rising of the solstice sun. Such chants, it would seem, likely echoed around the north tor from the ritual platform and as a result gave the tor its name. Just as the south tor seems to be a shortened mnemonic of the Irish *Suaithnidheacht*, 'a marvel', so the North Tor is thought to be a mnemonic of the Irish (*Sliabh na*) **n-Ortha**, meaning '(mountain of) prayers/incantations'.[23]

The glory of the north tor and its confirmation as a place of immense importance to the ancients must surely be the gigantic pair of vagina stones below the col. If one could go back in time, five or six thousand years, there are so many questions one would look answers for. Examine the photographs and ask yourself first how much you think these great boulders weigh. Where exactly on the heights above were the stones sourced, how were they quarried, how were such immense weights prevented from crashing and tumbling down the mountain slope, how many men were involved in moving the stones and even the basic question itself…how do you go about moving them with precision? There is also the question of why they undertook such massive labours and why here? An answer may be postulated by a careful look at the topography and making surmises on where the solstice sun rises and sets. From above the vagina stones it is apparent that the gap between the vagina stones is aligned on the distant Back Castles and further that from this angle these tors have a very obvious penile outline. The great vaginal stones under the north tor have been positioned to catch the light of the winter solstice sun as it rises from the Back Castles and the earth and sun combine to create an imaginary moment of ejaculation; the immense efforts of the ancients in placing these huge vaginal megaliths was with the purpose of insuring solstice impregnation of the earth by 'solar semen'. The location of the vagina stones under the north tor was doubly important for it would seem that at the other end of the year, at sunset of the summer solstice, the vagina of stone was again impregnated by sun in ejaculating mode as it touched the top of the phallic north tor east as it set. There are probably many more secrets that the stones and tors will reveal in the future. It would seem, for instance, that the lower point of the larger of the vaginal stones also has an alignment over to the horizon where the sun would rise at equinox between the peaks of Snaefell and South Barrule on the distant Isle of Man.

Such indeed are some of the treasures left us by the ancients on the length of Slieve Bignian. There is much more of ancient times to be discovered and understood throughout the Mournes. The reason for the positioning of many megaliths still awaits the presence of the sun at the time of the solstice and should it come then suddenly there are so many places that one would like to be at the same time. I have been walking the hills, looking at the rock faces and works of the ancients for many years yet every time I go out it seems there are always more discoveries, new insights and better understandings. The work of discovery is a most satisfying task even if it seems never-ending. So as to be able to make a conclusion of this book so much has had to be left 'for another day'. Faced with so many more corners to explore and looking at a multitude of photographs that cannot be included here, one can only take comfort from the words of a wise person who said: 'Leave a little bit for the angels.' Enjoy your own discoveries for there are certainly many more treasures out there. The ancients have left us many more happy surprises.

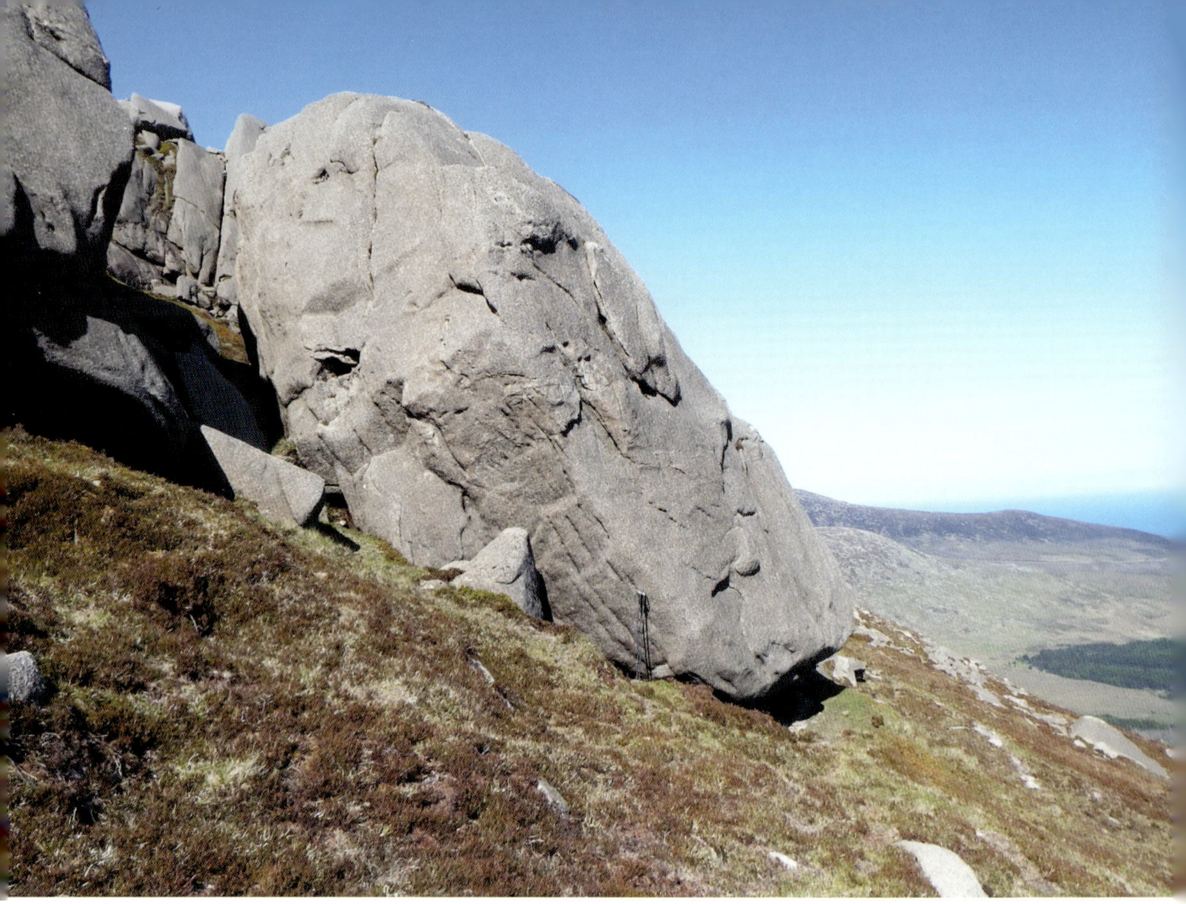

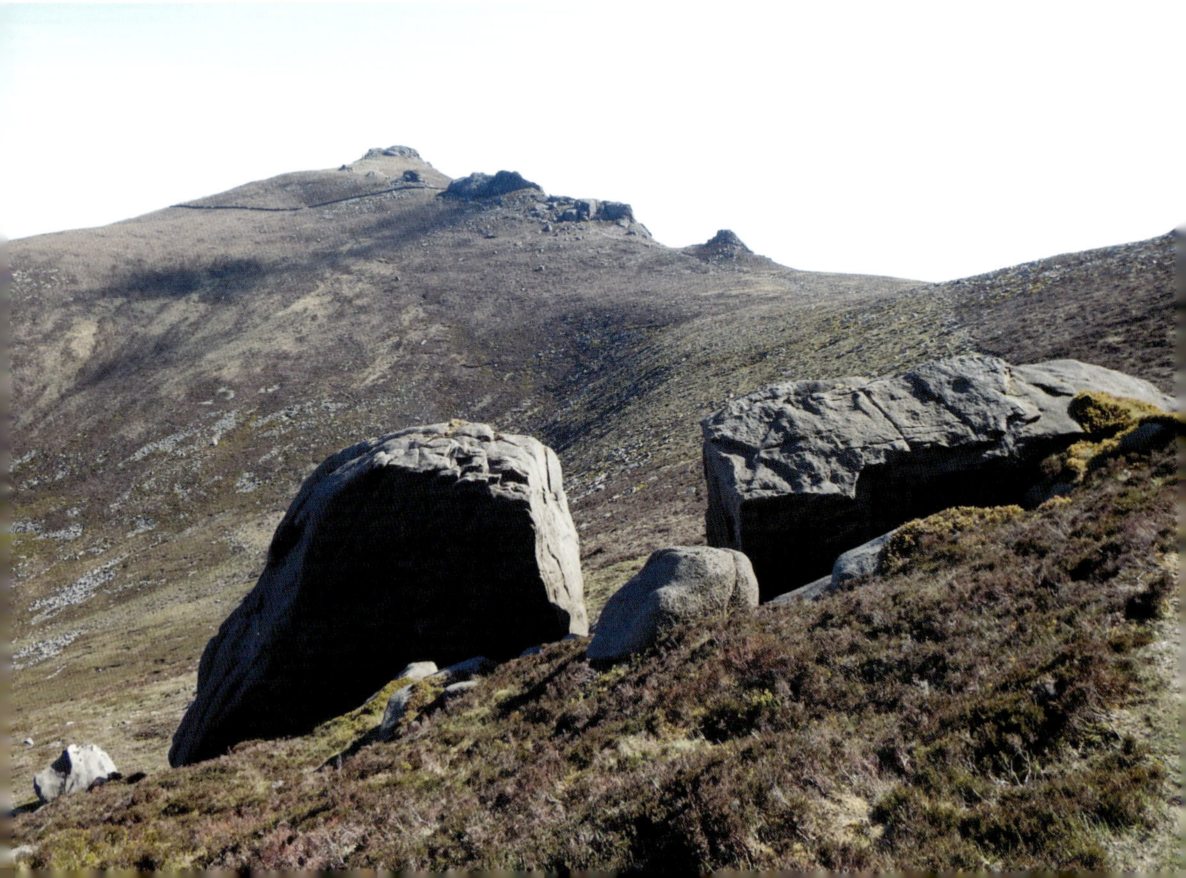

Top left: The trekking poles propped against the bottom of this megalith, the larger of the pair of vagina stones under Bignian's north tor, help to give an impression of the size of this monster stone that the ancients somehow manoeuvred with precision on the steep slope.

Bottom left: On the slope above the great vagina stones you can see the alignment of the opening faces over to the Back Castles and from this angle the middle Castles have a distinctly penile shape. Solstice sunrise appearing at the end of this phallic mountain top made this a fertility location of enormous importance.

Above: From this location at summer solstice the declining sun touches the top of North Tor East, seen here in the background through the vaginal notch of the stones, sending its impregnating solar semen into the gap.

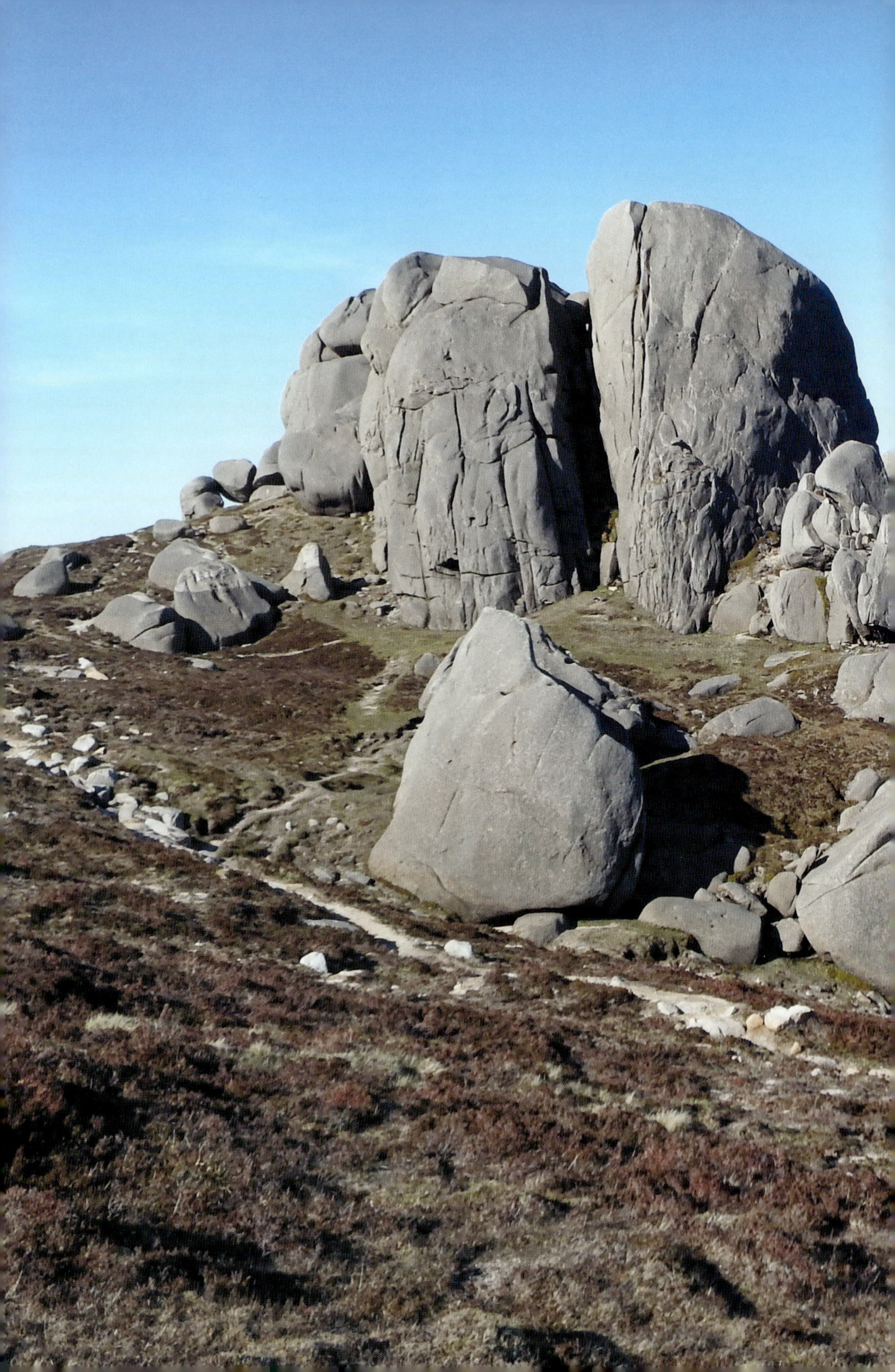

The cleft splitting Bignian's north tor west was regarded as a great vagina by the ancients. At the top of the split the ancients wedged a large stone, (just the tip visible here emerging from the shade), so that its penile shadow would insert itself into the crack to bring fertility as the sun set at winter solstice.

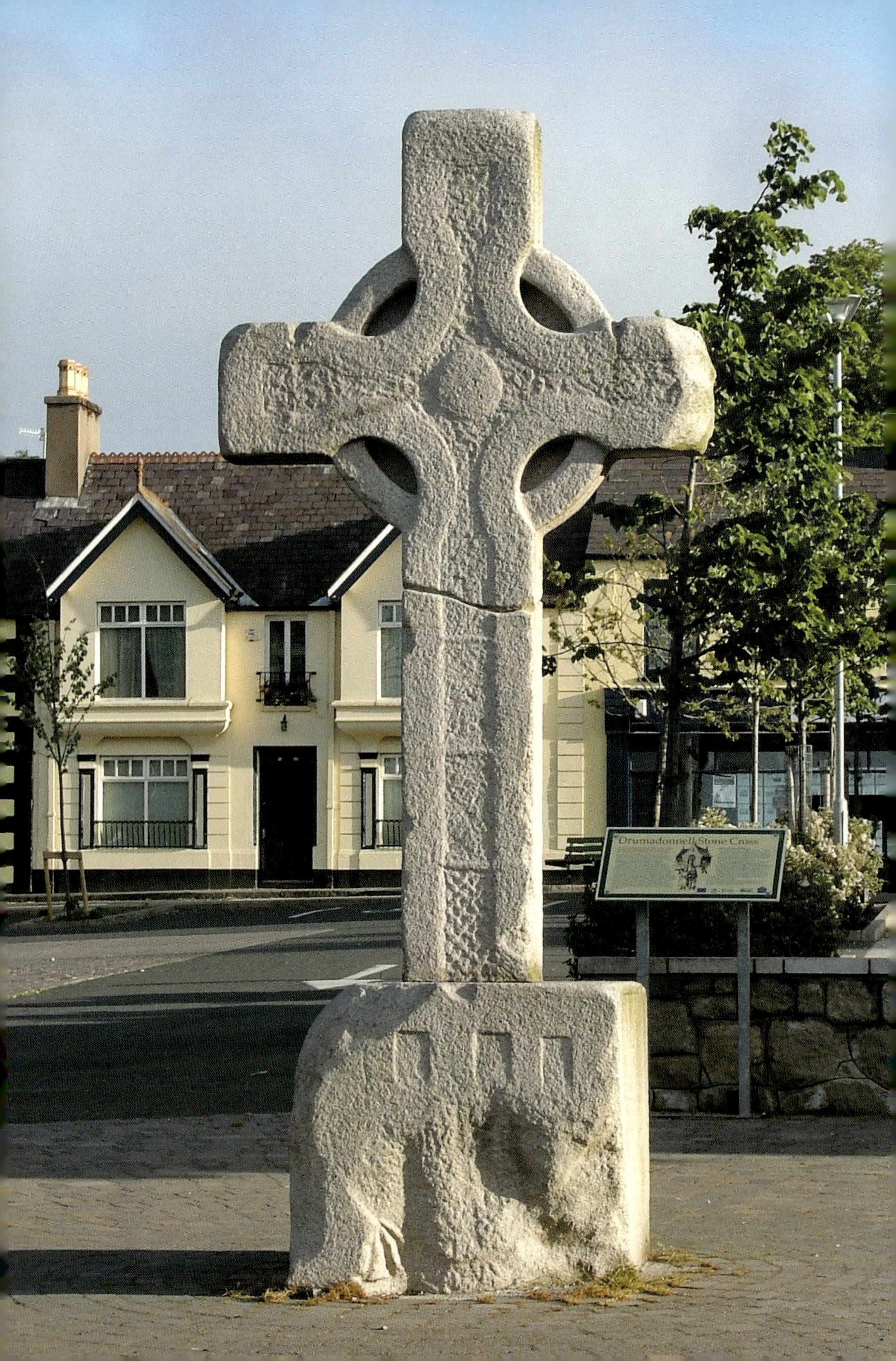
Drumadonnell Stone Cross

# THE COMING OF CHRISTIANITY

*Judging by this extract from a laughingly partisan ballad about Dolly's Brae, we may well wonder how deeply St Patrick's message was absorbed into warlike Irish hearts.*

> *'If you'd a-heard them cursed infidels whenever they got by,*
> *They began to shout and roar like brutes but soon we let them fly.*
> *They robbed our Catholic houses too when we were in the fray,*
> *Contending with the soldiers, that night on Dolly's Brae.*
>
> *Unless you turn and go to Mass, your souls they are undone*
> *And yield your heart in earnest to the blessed Virgin's son;*
> *Yes, and be obedient to the Pope, whom you do curse I know*
> *Or you will be rewarded in the regions down below.*
>
> *For you must know our Holy Church from erring still is free,*
> *No sinful man with Satan's spawn can ever injure she*
> *And you will be rewarded all upon your dying day,*
> *So let no man induce you for to walk near Dolly's Brae.'*[1]

The great struggle between paganism and Christianity supposedly had a watershed in the person of St Donard's father, Echu, son of Muiredach. Echu was the last pagan king of Mourne. He clashed with St Patrick earning his anger and a curse. The story is told in *Bethu Phátraic* (Echu being spelt 'Echaid').

'Patrick said to Echaid son of Muiredach, that no king would ever descend from him, and that of his race, there would never be a troop [large enough] for a folkmote or an army in Ulster, and that his race would be in scattering and in dispersion, that his own life would be short, and that he would come to a violent end. For this reason was Patrick [hostile] to Echaid, as the most skilled say. Two maidens had offered their maidenhood to the Lord. Echaid bound them on the seastrand under waves, for they refused to worship idols and to marry. When Patrick heard that, he entreated the king concerning them, and got them not. 'Thy brother Cairell, whom thou smotest with a rod,

*In the Upper Square of Castlewellan stands this faithful replica of the Drumadonnell Cross which may date from the 9th century. Christianity finally took root in Mourne after millennia of adherence to the ancient pagan religion. Great skill was shown by the craftsmen who made this granite cross especially in the panels of interlaced and spiral decoration. The original is safely in store at Castlewellan Forest Park.*

*This large boulder in the corner of Bangor Cemetery formerly rested on Glasdrumman shore where it was known as the 'Lighthouse' Stone. This name was a mnemonic of the Irish Lia h-Íosa, 'The Jesus Stone' for it was believed that the martyrs of Mourne were tied to this rock to be drowned by the incoming tide.*

he', said Patrick, 'since he granted me a goodly boon, will himself be a king, and from him there will be kings and princes over thy children and over the whole of Ulster'….

However, Echaid's wife knelt at Patrick's feet. Patrick blessed her, and blessed the child that lay in her womb, namely, the wonderful, renowned son Domangort [Donard] son of Echaid. He it is whom Patrick left in his body, and he will live therein for ever.'[2]

While there is always the possibility that this story reflects the memory of some myth, it likewise could well have happened at it has been told.

Fast forward to 1908 and on 12th December of that year George Herbert Brown, J.P., died. He was a man well known in Newcastle as he was a patron of the popular summer horticultural show and just the previous year had acted as a judge at the Newcastle regatta and sports. Our point of interest lies with the headstone for his grave. This was secured by another J.P., a relative called Mr John Thompson. To mark George Herbert's grave at Bangor cemetery, arrangements were made to remove a massive ten ton boulder from the shore at Glasdrumman,

488

near the hut where the deceased gentleman had spent so many pleasant days. The locals knew this stone as the 'lighthouse' rock. It was reported that it took seventy-seven men to move the boulder from its bed. Certainly it was a headstone with a difference. The grave is to be found in the far corner of Bangor cemetery, taking the avenue to the left upon entering the gate. We cannot know now whether this mammoth boulder was selected on account of any associated folklore prevalent at the time or whether it was randomly chosen for its size, availability and proximity to George Brown's holiday residence. There is more to the name of this stone than meets the eye and in a sense John Thompson did us all a favour for, had he not picked this named stone, the knowledge of its importance would surely have been lost. The boulder is indeed large but, despite its significant size, it could not reasonably be construed to have a passing resemblance to a lighthouse. Its importance lies in its name, for 'lighthouse' is a mnemonic from the Irish *Lia h-Íosa*, 'The Jesus Stone'. It is believed that this is the boulder to which the martyrs of Mourne were tied when they refused to worship the pagan gods and indulge in the fertility rites. The stone looks quite peaceful now in the corner of the cemetery. It is a face stone, for part of the boulder has been chipped to give the impression of a closed sleeping eye. I cannot think that the gentleman justice could have been aware of the history of the stone he selected. For the maidens who refused Echu it would have been a torturous demise made all the worse by the inevitability of their deaths; waiting for the inexorable tide coming in to drown them as they lay tied to the rock.

**St Patrick, Sacrifice and Armour's Hole**

In any consideration of human sacrifice in prehistoric Mourne, Armour's Hole must have a prominent place. Mention has already been made of the possibility of sacrifice at Spellack mountain with people being thrown from the summit to mark the summer solstice. It has already been mentioned that the present name might have been elided from the Irish *Spealadh* meaning the 'act of shedding, flinging to waste, scattering abroad'. At the Bloody Bridge the ritual platforms on either side of the upper valley are contenders for places of sacrifice. On the Chimney Rock side, runnels are found hammered into the rock on the platform that faces towards summer solstice sunrise. If this was a site for a dawn vigil fire on which, for instance, a pig would be roasted in anticipation of feasting then the runnels would serve the function of removing whatever dripping and fat was not consumed in the flames. Such an anodyne explanation however, is made more in hope for the likelihood is that the runnel was made to gather blood that otherwise would have made the surface of the cliff platform dangerously slippy. The cliff-top platform at the corner of Lower Cove also has runnels which would have served the dual purpose of collecting blood at a time of sacrifice but also of channelling water out over the cliff face in simulation of ejaculation. It would seem that over

This elevated platform at Chimney Rock in the upper reaches of the Bloody Bridge valley looks out over towards Crossone mountain and summer solstice sunrise. Below are the trails above the quarry leading to the Mourne Wall. If the rock slab on the left was used as a sacrificial altar, the substantial runnel hammered out of the rock below it would have served to drain away slippery blood.

the last few hundred years the growth of heather and turf deposits have clogged up a good part of the water catchment on the top of Cove for the waterfall that formerly jetted out over the top of the cliff as recorded by Walter Harris in 1744 no longer seems to function. He had noted that

'after rain a stream rushes from the west side of the said Rock, which shooting from the top falls in a large cascade.'[3]

When looking at the derivation of the old names for Downpatrick we mentioned how Rath Celtchair is from the Irish *Ceilt Áir*, 'concealment of slaughter', a reference to Ben Crom, the great mountain of sacrifice, which lay hidden beyond where the sun set. Any gory details of what may have happened here are mercifully lost in the mists of the mountains. If people were ever thrown from the top of the cliff as part of sacrifices for fertility, then this is where it likely happened. We can only wonder at the thoughts and fears of victims being lead up the mountain to their fate. Irish has an interesting expression which is probably very old, it is *Lá na Sléibhe*; the literal meaning is 'Day of the Mountains' but the actual meaning is 'the Day of Doom'. Another site with an ominous name in Irish is Miners Hole at J3024, mentioned in the previous chapter. Rather than owing its name to fancied activities of Cornish miners as was proposed, it is derived from the winter solstice phallic shadow of Slievenaglogh stretching out yearningly over towards Ben Crom and thus the shadow was called *Mian-Áir Olc,* 'Evil desire of slaughter'.

The earliest mention of Armour's Hole is a short reference by Walter Harris in 1744.

> 'On this coast near Bealachaneir Pass is a deep narrow Cave, wrought by the violence of the surges into a rock of flint; and on the brow of the hill not far from it by the sea-side is a large hole, like the shaft of a mine, into which the sea rolls underneath, called Armar's hole, from which one James Armar, murdered here by his son James about the year 1701, who deservedly suffered for the fact at the ensuing assize.'[4]

The ordnance survey notes about the cave are brief but give us the added detail that 'Armour's Hole is a long cavity, extremely narrow, not being more than 3 or 4 feet broad and about 40 feet deep. The waves beat in with fury at the bottom'. The story of Armour's Hole, horrible though it may be, is probably a very ancient tale embodying the folk memory of multiple obscene killings that took place here

Here on the edge of Lower Cove cliff, the grooves hammered in the rock may have served to remove blood from sacrifices and also funnel rain-water out over the cliff in simulation of ejaculation.

*A party of people stand on top of Ben Crom mountain. This mountain, Bean Crom as it was in Irish or 'stooped woman' was seen as presenting herself towards the winter solstice sun for fertilisation. In Ireland the name of the god Crom Dhu was notorious for sacrifice and many undoubtedly took place on this summit.*

in pagan times when human sacrifices were made for fertility. The very name Armour is a clue; in Irish *Ár Mór* means 'great slaughter'. The story told by the *Dublin Penny Journal* is as follows:

> 'Edward Armor was a wealthy widower whose wild and reckless son had little regard for anyone other than a lady called Mary O'Hagan. He was also an excessive gambler who squandered his father's wealth. Having got himself into considerable debt, Edward junior sought the help of his father who refused to support him any longer. The son was enraged and decided to take his father's life that he might do as he liked with his wealth. He devised a plan whereby he informed his father of his wish to marry Mary and, with that purpose in mind, requested his father to accompany him to her house to seek her parents' consent. As he did not want anyone to know of his intentions he suggested that his father set out on his own and he would follow him later. Having given his father a head start, the younger Armor pursued him, dragged him off his horse, and threw him into the pit now known as Armor's Hole. However, a group of smugglers, on hearing both the father's shriek and the sound of galloping horses, decided to investigate and matter and discovered

the body. Edward junior was subsequently traced to a distant public house where he was allegedly found in the process of selling his father's horse. He was brought to Down jail and, having appeared for trial, was sentenced to be executed. It is said that Mary O'Hagan went mad on hearing of Edward's crime and died within a few months of his execution.

When Tom Porter retold the story in *12 Miles of Mourne* in 2000, the name of the victim was Thomas Armer, now giving us three different Christian names of James, Edward and Thomas. If anything, these variations are an indication of the antiquity of the story. Originally the tale would have been handed down in Irish and interesting possibilities are revealed when the phonetics of the names are looked at a little more closely. The Thomas Armer of Tom Porter's version could be rendered as *Tuama Áir Mór,* giving us a name for the defile of death; it means 'tomb of great slaughter'. There is a rising sense of the possible enormity of horror perpetrated here with the name 'James'. The name James has a passing closeness to the Irish *Iomad*, meaning 'too much, plenty or a great number'; the same might be said of the Irish *Iomáin* where the idea would be driving people towards the chasm. *Iomáin* means 'act of driving, tossing, flinging...'. Making such interpretations is highly speculative but the accretion of similar possibilities brings a tenuous credibility. Might the name Edward have been derived from the Irish for 'sacrificing', namely *Íodhbairt*? The last name in the story is Mary O'Hagan possibly from *Marbhadh a h-Aigéine,* with the meaning 'slaughtering of the abyss'.

Close by Armour's Hole is the little stream of Srupatrick. Most visitors will only realise they are crossing Srupatrick when they see the 'Welcome to Mourne' sign at the side of the road. The tiny stream marks the boundary between Mourne and Iveagh and until 1972 marked the administrative boundary for the town of Newcastle after it separated from the union of Kilkeel at the start of the twentieth century.[5] Srupatrick, or Patrick's stream, was alleged to be as far as St Patrick came in his mission of converting this part of Ireland. The legend has been recorded for us by professor Evans in his seminal work, *Mourne Country,* and it is worth quoting the relevant part.

> 'The conversion of Mourne to Christianity was, it must be supposed, a slow process, for this isolated region, steeped in old custom, would have offered strong resistance to new ideas. There is a tradition that St Patrick founded a church somewhere in the Kingdom which has long since disappeared, but this runs counter to a stronger tradition that the Saint did not set foot beyond St Patrick's Stream, which was so named because it was the limit of his travels. The story goes that when he reached the little river that marks the northern boundary of Mourne he took off his sandal and threw it... As he threw it he uttered a prophecy: "The length of that there will never be blood spilled"... One cannot help feeling that St Patrick was not well received when he entered the mountain pass.'[6]

The two main reasons lying behind most ritual sacrifice would have been to please the gods and to assert the power of the rulers to decide who lived and who died. St Patrick and his disciples played an important role in the ending of the barbaric practice of human sacrifice in Mourne by bringing the gentle message of the gospel and defeating the curses of the sun-worshipping priests. The strange behaviour of St Patrick throwing his sandal in the vicinity of Srupatrick, taken in conjunction with the prophecy of ending bloodshed, can be reasonably interpreted as Christianity putting an end to killings at Armour's Hole. Some have thought to wonder how far St Patrick's sandal flew or its significance for wherever it landed but there really is no need to look further than Armour's Hole for when 'sandal' is transposed into Irish it gives us *An Scáine Dall* 'The Black Fissure'.

Returning to the remark by professor Evans that he felt 'St Patrick was not well received when he entered the mountain pass', this has a serious implication for the term 'Kingdom of Mourne' beloved by the local tourist industry. It is pleasing to think of tourists being welcomed here in kindly Kingdom of Mourne. They most certainly are; but unfortunately it is the legend of the poor reception given to St Patrick that endures in the kingdom title. The word 'kingdom' does not bespeak a region that was once a monarchical state; rather it is from the Irish *Cean Doim*, 'miserable welcome'. The Irish *cean* normally means 'affection, passion' but can be used about the reception given to a guest as in the phrase *Ní cean gus a dtig*, 'he was not welcome'.[7]

Even the slogan favoured by the tourist board 'kindly' Mourne, which was mentioned by Estyn Evans in his classic *Mourne Country*, is from the pagan past and refers rather to *Cian Lia*, 'distance standing stone', where a stone marked a significant far off connection between sun and earth as seen from that location. When the Yorkshire Ramblers' Club visited Mourne at the start of the twentieth century they recorded two names for Commedagh, namely 'kindly Commedagh' and also 'Meadow mountain'. For all the levelness of its summit, it really would be stretching the imagination to describe the top of Commedagh as a 'meadow'. Like Deers Meadow at Spelga, Meadow mountain should be understood rather as 'dagger' mountain, from the Irish *Meadóg*. Commedagh casts its own awesome shadow on winter solstice morning. The megaliths on Commedagh's flank, illustrated on pages 77, 78 and 80-81, are a possible source of the adjectival mnemonic heard by the Yorkshire Ramblers, 'Kindly Commedagh'; it is from *Cian Liaga* 'distance stones'. In understanding the Irish etymology of 'kindly' we would not dismiss the English meaning and would look to the remarks of Estyn Evans.

> 'The phrase 'kindly Mourne' sums up the gentleness of a well-loved countryside. John O'Donovan, in his letters for the Ordnance Survey, wrote in 1834 of the people of Hilltown that they were 'a kind warm-hearted and tractable people'. Of Mourne folk he said that 'the more Irish they are, the more civil, obliging and intelligent you will find them – and the more Scotch, the more reserved, cautious, cold and unobliging'. Evidently his stay was too

short to penetrate this reserve, but time has softened the differences between the two stocks, and it is my experience that they all deserve the epithet 'kindly'.[8]

It is to be desired that visitors will continue to take away the very best of memories. As to helpfulness received and the lasting impression it can make, what better than the words of John O'Donovan on his reception in 1834.

'In the Irish district from Slieve Donard to Slieve Croob, I found farmers to leave their work and go with me for the distance of 4 miles to introduce (me) to others.'[9]

## St Patrick and Driving Out the 'Snakes'

Back in the twelfth century the Welshman Giraldus Cambrensis, after a visit to Ireland in 1185 as secretary to prince John, passed dismissive comment on the absence of snakes in Ireland.

'Of all sorts of reptiles, Ireland possesses those only which are harmless, and does not produce any that are venomous... Some indeed conjecture, with what seems a flattering fiction, that St. Patrick and the other saints of that country cleared the island of all pestiferous animals; but history asserts, with more probability, that from the earliest ages, and long before it was favoured with the light of revealed truth, this was one of the things which never existed here, from some natural deficiency in the produce of the island.'[10]

Indeed it is accepted by naturalists that snakes were unable to inhabit Ireland as the country had been early isolated after the ice age by rising sea-levels. The legend still endures throughout the world that St Patrick rid Ireland from snakes as the people were converted from paganism to Christianity during the fifth century. If there never were snakes to be banished in the first place how could the legend be so widespread and enduring; what happened?

The answer lies in a combination of the Irish language, in Irish farming, particularly with an analogy involving the milking of animals and in understanding the greatness of the accomplishment of Patrick in ending the pagan fertility practises associated with sun worship. We should also remember that at a purely human level it would have been exceedingly embarrassing, awkward, and distressingly uncomfortable for Christian converts to acknowledge that any of their ancestors engaged in pagan debauchery; a euphemism was called for to alleviate explicit mention of something that was humiliating to talk about. The nature of the ceremonies that took place at winter solstice dawn cannot be known; we may only guess. May we imagine that processions took place bringing up candidates to be initiated or victims to be sacrificed. The vigil fires would have been lit on the mountain tops and preparations for feasting attended to. Incantations, prayers and petitions would be offered up, perhaps involving long repetitious and trance inducing chanting, drumming, singing or dancing. The

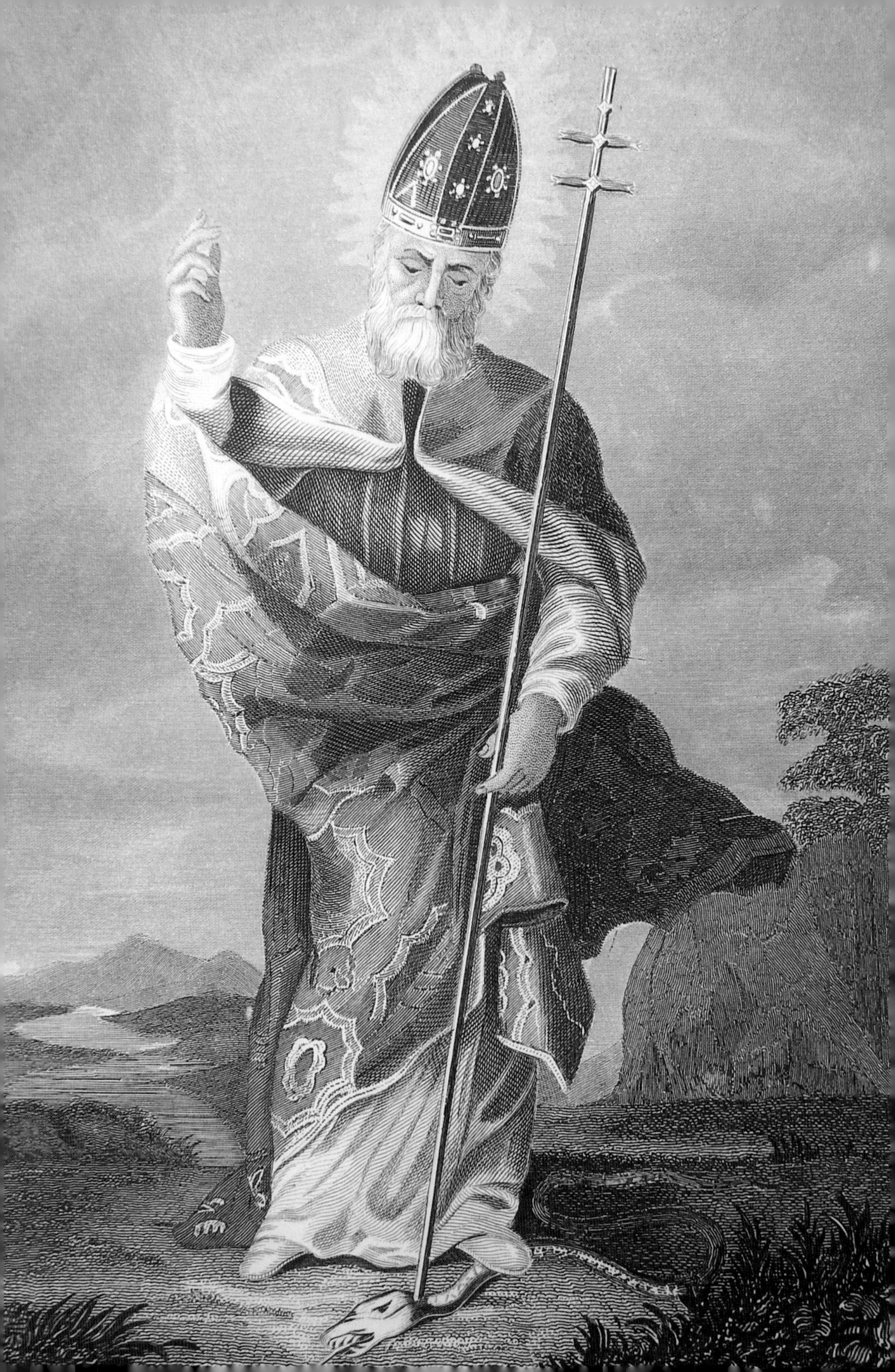

coming of the fertility light of the new sun was probably a signal for complete indulgence in sexual licentiousness, the beginning of a sexual orgy. Rather than give graphic details of what went on at these ceremonies redress was had centuries ago to a farming analogy of milking the animals. The operative Irish word that conveyed the import of what went on without spelling out the dissipation was *Sniogaigh*, 'milking the very last drop, milking after the teat-flow ceases, draining completely'. The parallels with unrestrained hedonism that went beyond the ending of semen flow were obvious. It was this utterly dissolute behaviour that St Patrick ended by his preaching. By bringing the message of the gospel, of love, mercy, restraint, purity and no bloodshed, Patrick terminated the pagan fertility rituals. The sexual excesses represented by *Sniogaigh* were banished. 'Snakes' is both a metaphor and an English mnemonic for the Irish *Sniogaigh*. So indeed St Patrick did banish the 'snakes' from Ireland. Patrick ended the wanton sexual practices that had been followed for millennia but while the English speaking world from Giraldus Cambrensis to the present day have heard about the 'snakes', none seem to have known about the deeper meaning of *Sniogaigh*. Perhaps, for all we know, the stream that bears St Patrick's name at the Ballagh, namely Srupatrick, may have been used to baptise converts. Returning again to Patrick's action mentioned above, that St Patrick threw his sandal and prophesied no more blood, there may yet possibly be another residual message. There is a closeness of sound between the English 'Patrick threw...' and the Irish *Aithrighe Truagh* but significantly *Aithrighe Truagh* means 'deep repentance'.

**St Patrick and the Shamrock**

Customs must be changing. Sixty years ago I remember that wearing shamrock on St Patrick's Day would have been *de rigueur*. I also remember that the best place to find it at Newcastle was among the rock ballast between the railway lines out past the station. Nowadays the custom of wearing a sprig seems to be declining but the shamrock is still one of the most identifiable emblems of Ireland.

There is no written evidence of St Patrick ever having used the shamrock as a teaching aid. The long standing legend tells of St Patrick taking up a leaf of shamrock and pointing to three separate leaves on one stem to explain the mystery of the Blessed Trinity when early converts had difficulty grasping the concept that in One God there were three Divine Beings, really distinct and equal in all things. The emphasis in Ireland has always been with the three leaves of the shamrock; surprising there is no reference to the lovely little yellow flowers. Aer Lingus has the trefoil on its wings, bowls of shamrock are presented annually to

This engraving from *Lives of Irish Saints and Martyrs* is the work of Archibald L. Dick (c.1793-1856) of Brooklyn, New York. It is a classic rendering of St Patrick driving out the snakes from Ireland. The mountains of Mourne are featured on the bottom left. Might an Irish emigrant have informed the engraver of the enormity of Mourne's pagan past?

An etching in glass of St Patrick on the back door of St Patrick's church, Bryansford, showing the symbols of snakes and shamrocks.

the American president at the White House on St Patrick's Day and there will be advertisements galore featuring the leaves but no-where will the flowers be found. The adoption of the shamrock by Christianity is a case of an erstwhile pagan symbol being taken over and 're-invented'. The attraction of the plant to the pagans was its little yellow petal flower that was a great symbol of the sun. On the shamrock it is the yellow flowers that turn into the seeds so the flower represented not only the sun but also the promise of fruitfulness. The sun was the great god of fertility and as such was often synonymous with the human source of fertility, the female vagina. It was the yellow flower of the shamrock, suggestive of the

498

sun, that gave the plant its name. The present word in Irish for shamrock is *seamróg* (a Munster variation would be *Simearóg*) but the earliest derivation I believe comes from a compound of *Sámhais Roc*. The aspirated version of *Sámhas* would have a sound similar to the beginning of our local river the Shimna, where the Irish for bulrushes, *Simhean*, has the [sh] sound, as in 'shawl, sheaf or ship'. It is easy to understand why the little flower of the shamrock needed to be overlaid with a Christian interpretation for in pagan times the original *Sámhais Roc* [*Shámhais*] had an explicit sexual meaning that would have been incompatible with the Christian message. *Sámhais Roc* means 'hole of bodily pleasure'.

## 'Trí Fiacla Óir' – Three Gold Teeth?

There is one little mystery of Mourne recorded in the Annals of the Kingdom of Ireland under the year 739. The annals tell us:

> 'The sea cast ashore a whale in Boirche, in the province of Ulster. Every one in the neighbourhood went to see it for its wondrousness. When it was slaughtered, three golden teeth were found in its head, each of which teeth contained fifty ounces. Fiachna, son of Aedh Roin, King of Ulidia, and Eochaidh, son of Breasal, chief of Ui-Eathach [Iveagh], sent a tooth of them to Beannchair, where it remained for a long time on the altar, to be seen by all in general.'[11]

Giraldus Cambrensis, the welsh historian with the Norman invasion, also recorded the story but was rightly sceptical; 'I should suppose', he said, 'that these teeth had rather the outward appearance of gold than that they were really such; and that the colour they assumed was a presage of the golden times of the future conquest immediately impending'. There may be a message nonetheless in this story of the whale, though at this distance in time any deliberations are tenuous. Where does the kernel of truth lie? The story relates to Mourne, the place of *Beanna Boirche,* 'the peaks of swellings', it is probably very early and we look at it here with an eye to the sacrifices at Armour's Hole. The origin of this tale has yo-yoed from Irish into English before the annalists set the 'new version' down again in Irish; there is a distinct possibility that the story is connected with the sacrifices to the sea god of the early Forhóire and ultimately to the triumph of Christianity over these sacrifices symbolised by the 'gold' tooth being placed on the altar at Bangor for a long time.

We consider that the annalists have given us a translation of the English mnemonic sound of the original Irish. A couple of parts are worth looking at namely 'three gold teeth' and 'whale'. There were never meant to be literally 'three gold teeth'. What we may have however is the English sound of the Irish *treabh gola Teathra* that has the meaning 'tribe of the pit or chasm of Teathra'. Significantly here *Teathra* was the Formorian god of death and of the sea. On account of this story relating to Mourne one cannot but help think of the sacrifices at Armour's Hole and that these sacrifices were likely in appeal or propitiation to this sea god *Teathra*. Regarding the aspect of sacrifice there is an ominous similarity between the god *Teathra* and the word *téatair*; the Irish *téatair* means 'a rope, a binding, a tether'. The inference that the story originally dealt with the struggle between paganism and Christianity is suggested by the sound of 'whale', possibly *Buailim* (*Bualadh*) meaning 'I strike, defeat'. The various possibilities from the phrase 'fifty ounces' were really too wide-ranging to be helpful but the notion of tension or struggle between the two ideologies could still be suggested by 'ounces', this possibly being the sound of *Ionnsaighe*, 'attacking, assaulting'. Such musings could never really hope for anything conclusive. However the successful progress of Christianity in South Down is best exemplified by the adaptation and replacing of former pagan sites around the circumference of Dundrum Bay by many catholic churches.

**Local Church Sites: From Paganism to Christianity**

Some old maps of Ireland give the name of Holie Bay to Dundrum Bay. The reason was to be found in the number of Christian churches around its periphery. Within less than a mile of the shores of this bay were formerly situated eleven churches in ancient days. Starting from the south, the first church on the margin of the bay was Ballaghanery, then Maghera, Drumcaw, Rathcath (Clough), Lismohan, Killyglinnie, Ballykinlar, Tyrella, Rathmullan, Rossglass, and St John's.[12] Contrary to the map makers expectations the proliferation of churches was not an indication of sanctity but perhaps closer to the opposite. The locations for these churches had been sites of pagan significance. Some other church sites we would also look at are Ballymoney, Kilmegan, Dugganstown, Kilmeloge, and Massforth. Dundrum Bay was not the only place in the diocese where pagan sites had been adopted. In 1878 monsignor O'Laverty had written:

> 'It is worthy of remark that many of the ancient churches of Down and Connor stand in the immediate vicinity of sepulchral mounds, testifying that their founders were too wise unnecessarily to outrage the feelings of their disciples, who had that traditional regard for what was hallowed by their ancestors, which is so characteristic of the Celtic race. The ancient churches of Dundonald, Holywood, the Knock, Ballymahon, and Donaghadee, and many others erected close by mounds for sepulchral or religious purposes, seem to have been ecclesiastical structures intended to replace their Pagan predecessors.'[13]

**St Mary's, Ballaghanery**

It was long a source of mystery as to why a church should have been built in what is, even now, a place remote from population settlement. With the Bloody Bridge

With its deep frowning eye, this 'face' on the floor of the Slieve Donard ritual platform, oozes a profound sense of menacing evil. On the right is the phallic rocking stone; this platform may well have been the scene of debauched rituals.

valley being a nerve centre for pagan practices in ancient times and having ritual platforms on the sides of both Slieve Donard and Chimney Rock, it would have been essential for Christianity to declare its presence in this vicinity. St Mary's was a site of particular pagan importance as it was from here about 8.10pm that the sun could be seen setting on the top of Slieve Donard at summer solstice. Also after millennia of human sacrifice in the locality, we can be sure that enormous superstition would have prevailed. Travellers would have had to deal with fear and a very real dread of evil spirits when they had to pass the entrance to the Bloody Bridge valley and the nearby chasm of Armour's Hole. We should not underestimate the comfort and courage conferred to them by the presence of the chapel.

The menace and fears of the powers from the abyss was captured by local poet Richard Rowley in his work entitled *At the Ballagh*. A dying shepherd spoke of the

The precarious ruins of St Mary's chapel, Ballaghanery in 2004 before the timely restoration of the arch. Apart from its proximity to the very nerve centre of paganism at the Bloody Bridge valley, St Mary's was built at this location to comfort passing travellers and more importantly to claim the site from paganism because it was from here that the sun could be observed setting on the summit of Slieve Donard at 8.10pm on the summer solstice; the moment of sunset is seen here in the smaller picture.

day he saw the very face of evil when he harboured angry thoughts in his mind against someone who was going to take a field he had long rented away from him.

'This was the story that oul' Davy told

Lying upon his death-bed....

He couldn't work or rest and the anger burned fierce in his heart until he gripped his ash-plant and left the mountain eager to meet his enemy, 'murder in my heart an' blasphemy on my lips.' While on his way something far out at sea caught his eye. It was the shape of swirling fog but black and dark, rushing across the water straight for the land until it hung all trembling in the air above him.

I looked an' saw
Its misty curtains open. From its heart
Black as if hewed from ebony a face
Glowered upon me, leanin' out to peer
Into my face. Twin branching horns o' jet
Sprang from its head, an' in its taloned hand
Was clutched a spear o' steel hideously pronged
Wi' triple white-hot points. But oh ! its eyes,
Its eyes were terrible. They glowed an' blazed
Red-hot like fire or white like molten lead,
Through me they looked into my very soul,
And saw the evil thoughts deep in my heart,
And when they saw, the sharp-fanged lips outstretched
Into a grin o' malice an' wicked glee.
A wind sprang up, the cloud was whirled away
And as it passed I heard a fiend-like screech
Of horrible laughter. When I dared look up
O'er Donard's peak I saw a huge dark cloud
Suddenly burst in flame an' disappear.[14]

Davy would safely lose his anger when a ray of sun shone out yet he never forgot the evil he encountered. It is significant that this tale was located at the Ballagh. The poem is didactic, telling of the dangers of giving way to anger. We cannot know whether such a death-bed story was ever really told but given Rowley's propensity for writing and basing his stories on what he had heard from local characters, there is quite likely a grain of truth behind this tale. Allowing even for a generous dose of poetic licence, there is a stronger likelihood that even so recent as ninety years ago, when these lines were penned, Rowley was encountering widespread and firm beliefs in fairies, banshees and evil spirits of the night. The deep seated and latent fears of the ancient gods lingered long; such fears elicited words of wisdom that Rowley put into the mouth of a *Seanchaidhe* or one versed in folk-lore, stories and the wisdom of the ages about the dangers of dabbling with the ways of the spirits or wee folk.

*Crouched over the ashes,*
*The Shanachie spoke,*
*'Tis ill to take gifts*
*From the Hidden Folk;*
*Drink not their drink,*
*Eat not their bread,*
*Share not their shelter,*
*The Shanachie said.*[15]

## Ballymoney, Kilcoo, with a look at Carnmoney and Moneyscalp

The eclipsed Irish word *Buinne* lies behind the meaning of the townland of Ballymoney, Kilcoo parish, where the ruins of old Ballymoney church are situated. I have stood in the holy ground of Ballymoney where my maternal ancestors were buried, awaiting the winter solstice sun to check where it would rise. Writing about the ruined church of Ballymoney, Mgr James O'Laverty said:

> 'Near the site of the altar are interred the remains of Friar Burns, who died in the 74th or 75th year of his age, about the year 1817. The friar was born in Ballymagreehan; he generally resided in Burren-reagh, and was the last of the Dominicans in this locality.'[16]

The sun finally rises just after 9.20am from behind the broad summit of Slievenaman. The roughly circular nature of the cemetery would suggest that the site was originally an early rath, located here for fertility reasons on account of this sunrise bestowing fertility. Christianity adopted the former pagan site by building a church here. Ballymoney would be from the Irish *Baile na mBuinne*, 'Place of the (sexual) discharge'. There doesn't appear to be anything distinctly phallic about where the sun emerges from the top of Slievenaman. One can only imagine that the *Fir Bolg* culture was so suffused with thoughts of fertility and procreation that just the appearance of the sun from the top of a hill was enough to conjure thoughts of ejaculation.

The name of Kilcoo likely comes from winter solstice sunrise at the old Ballymoney chapel. It is a contraction of the Irish *Cill an Cúibe*, 'church of the bend'. There was always a possibility of the name coming from the entrance to the chapel site for, after walking down the fairly straight loney, church-goers had to go round a bend in the path to the entrance gate on the west side. More likely however, the name of the chapel came from the shape of Slievenaman hill as it gently rises and curves before stretching out at an even level. From the site of the chapel this was where the winter solstice sun appeared at the top of the curved bend of the hill, hence the 'church of the bend'. The calendar of patent rolls of James 1 of 1614 gives an alternative rendering of Ballynerened for Ballymoney. Thinking again of where the solstice sun rises, perhaps Ballynerened may be derived from *Baile na Reang*, 'townland of the hill-ridge'?

The place-name of Ballymoney townland is not unique for a similar derivation lies behind Carnmoney, County Antrim. Carnmoney gets its name from a perceived ejaculation from sun and earth connecting at winter solstice. The name of Carnmoney comes from the Irish *Carr na mBuinne*, meaning 'the spear of squirting forth'. The vicinity below the Church of Ireland at Church Brae, Carnmoney, sees the winter sun connect with the angular spear point head of Belfast's Cave hill. From this location, the sharp angled cliff head was viewed as a 'corner' and thus gave us the Parish of Coole, from the Irish *Cuile*, 'of a corner'.

The cemetery and back gable of old Ballymoney chapel, Kilcoo, destroyed in 1641.

Christianity had adopted this pagan location long ago for this is an ancient church site.

More locally one might also mention Moneyscalp. Located at J3232, overlooking the Bryansford Road and the back end of Tollymore Forest Park, the name of this hill would likely be from the Irish (*Tí na*) *mBuinne Scailpe*, meaning (Place of the) 'issuing forth of the cleft'. There is no need to look for an actual cave, fissure or distinctive cleft on the Moneyscalp hillside, easier and all as it presently would be after the logging of a large part of the plantation. Rather the name derives from where the winter solstice sun can be seen rising from the distant hollow between the Drinns, the name of two hills in Tollymore Park. This probably accounts for the siting of the cashel at J327329; these stone forts or early farm enclosures often favoured auspicious sites of fertility. It would have given status and brought 'good luck' to live at a place where the sun could be seen being born from the notch of the earth at the solstice. This solstice event accounts for the other name for Moneyscalp found in the Down Rent Roll of 1692, namely 'Money-flulare'.[17] The image here is of the great moist vulva of a brood mare or she-ass giving birth for the name comes from the Irish for such an animal,

505

*The present chapel of St Malachy, Kilcoo, was dedicated in June 1901 to replace an earlier chapel. This church is about a mile from the old Ballymoney chapel.*

namely *Láir* (genitive *Lára*); the full derivation being (*Árd na*) *mBuinne Fliuch-Lára*, (Height of the) 'discharge of the moist mare'. [18]

### Kilmegan

From the Irish *Cill Mí-Geine*, 'Church of evil conception'. During repairs at the church some decades ago, a banana shaped souterrain was found in the car park going underneath the edifice. This is an instance of Christianity having claimed a former pagan site, probably an early rath or farmstead. The early farmers chose this site as a favoured place to build as it marked where the winter solstice sun could be seen setting onto Slieve Meelmore and into what they imagined as a great swollen vulva. For the ancients this was an important fertility site. Christianity not only claimed the site but branded the distant solar spectacle as 'evil'. To be quite clear then, the 'evil conception' referred to the distant setting sun and not to the church. The nearby cross-roads see the start of the Hollybush road. Hollybush is only a rendering of the Irish *h-Olla Buas,* 'very great paunch', a further description of Slieve Meelmore at solstice.

Kilmegan church is in the townland of Moneylane. This townland name is from Irish and also alludes to the fertility event of the winter solstice sun setting on Slieve Meelmore; the Irish is (*Baile na*) *mBuinne lán*. Dinneen translates *Buinne* as 'a discharge, a spouting, a squirting forth'. The moment of the sun settling on and touching Slieve Meelmore was regarded as a moment of a full, complete and monumental ejaculation into the swollen mountain vulva. The Irish behind Moneylane, (*Baile na*) *mBuinne lán*, means '(townland of the) full squirting forth'.

### Dugganstown

This name is not recorded on the OS maps but is a local name in Tollymore Park for the ruins of the old church built by Lord Roden for his retainers. The ruins can still be found amid the trees down off the road that heads west from Horn Bridge;

a tentative reference would be J342324. These ruins have a decorative entrance arch studded with eleven large water rolled stones, perhaps one for each of the apostles but excluding Judas. Previously these ruins were thought to be the remnant of a barn or other farm outhouse. The isolated location for this church may be explained on similar grounds to that of St. John's Point or St Mary's at Ballaghanery; it was a redeeming for Christianity of a site formerly of pagan significance. In autumn when the leaves have fallen, it is easier to see the track where the old path formerly came up the hill to the church. This local name was given to me by Sarsfield Flynn, a former member of Newcastle Urban District Council, who had worked in the Park for many years as a forester. The name is possibly derived from the Irish *Dubh Gein tonn*, 'dark lower act of begetting'. The surrounding

The Church of Ireland at Kilmegan has claimed for Christianity a former pagan site where the winter solstice sun could be seen setting on Slieve Meelmore.

trees obscure observation of how the solstice sun plays out the 'act of begetting' but the assumption is that the former church marked where the winter solstice sun appeared from between the two hills of the Drinns. A 'higher' act of begetting would have prevailed had the sun emerged from the summit of the Drinns rather than between them and certainly the darkness of the valley below and that of the back-side of the Drinns, hidden from the sun, would have warranted the description 'dark'. With the sun shining through the gap between the two Drinns hills, the site of Dugganstown would be the winter equivalent of Spinkwee stone which, on the other side of the Drinns, marks the appearance of the summer solstice between the same gap.

## Kilmeloge

Kilmeloge enclosure is found at J344184 in the townland of Ballyveaghmore and is included here because the place was thought to be ecclesiastical in origin on account of the start of the name; *Cill* in Irish means 'a church, a church-yard, a burial place'. Mgr O'Laverty recorded that 'the people have lost every tradition

Deep among the trees of Tollymore Park are the ruins of the old chapel of Dugganstown, believed to mark a former pagan site possibly in Irish *Dubh Gein tonn*, the 'dark lower act of begetting'.

regarding it, yet the place is considered *gentle* (his italics and emphasis), and it is therefore wonderfully well preserved'[19]. The word 'gentle' is the clue that the site was important for fertility reasons, such as the sun setting on top of one of the mountains at solstice. 'Gentle' is really a mnemonic from the Irish (*Tí na*) *Geinte Táil*, '(Place of) Pouring forth of begetting'. The start of the name may come instead from the Irish *Caol* rather than *Cill* with the meaning of 'a narrow part, a slender thing' and would be a reference to Kilmeloge being the precise spot to witness the 'pouring forth of begetting'. This 'pouring forth' presumably comes from the sun being in such contact with the landscape at solstice that allowed a sexual construct to be put on it but there are presently no observations to advance our understanding.

**Massforth**

This is the name of the principal church of Upper Mourne, the parish of Kilkeel. The name unfortunately is not found on the present ordnance survey map but it

'Massforth gets its name from the shape of Knockchree hill, seen here on the left, where the summer solstice sun sets. It would be from the Irish *Más Fuartha*, 'Hips of cooling'.

deserves to be as it is an ancient name. The present church was opened in 1879, a year after Mgr O'Laverty penned the following lines in his diocesan history.

'During the time of persecution, Mass was celebrated in the open air at a place called the Mass Forth, in the townland of Ballymacgeough. It was only in the year 1811 that the parish priest, the Rev John MacMullan, commenced the erection of a chapel on the spot hallowed by so many traditions. It was however, the year 1818 before the chapel was completed by his successor, the Rev Richard Curoe. A few years ago, the Rev George Maguire replaced this chapel with a magnificent church, which is now nearly completed...It is built of squared granite and presents a very superior specimen of masonry.'[20]

Despite the long association of the area with religious worship, the name of Massforth does not come from the sacrifice of the Mass which in Irish would be *Aifreann*. Instead the name is of fertility origin and derives from a sexual eye being put on the dip between the nearby hill of Knockchree between which the sun would decline at summer solstice. Massforth is more likely from the Irish *Más Fuartha*, 'Hips of cooling'.

It is 9.22pm on 28th June and the photographer's shadow is stretching out towards Maghera church of Ireland. Only a stump of the round tower now exists (out of sight on the left) but formerly its shadow would have protectively extended over to the old chapel to 'shield' it from the pagan fertility spectacle of the summer solstice sun setting on top of Bunkers Hill.

## Maghera

This ecclesiastical site was built on an earlier rath itself located at a place of fertility significance. From the rath the winter solstice sun can be seen rolling down the flank of Slieve Commedagh as it sets. For some years I had believed that the round tower had been deliberately placed away from the chapel lest there should be the slightest hint of a phallic shadow from the tower being cast over the chapel and 'tainting' it; there could be no suggestion that paganism still had dominance over Christianity. The round tower has indeed been deliberately placed. Had its purpose been as a watch tower or a look-out post for danger then it would have made more sense to place it on the higher ground a little more to the south and closer to the present glebe. But the round tower, which served as a bell-tower, was intentionally placed to act as a shield. There is one time during the year that the tower did cast its shadow over the old chapel and that was at sunset of the summer solstice. It would seem that the tower was deliberately sited to block any view from the chapel of the sun setting on the summit of Bunker's Hill, an event

THE COMING OF CHRISTIANITY

that carried obvious connotations of sexual ejaculation for the ancients. The tower was so sited to 'protect' the chapel and its community from the former pagan spectacle.

**Drumcaw, Clough and Lismohan**

Drumcaw is certainly a secluded little ruin. You have to travel up a farm track off the Manse Road from the back of Seaforde and the ruin will be found down in a field between two ridges. As far back as 1878 when Mgr O'Laverty wrote his history of Down & Connor diocese, the graveyard was long under tillage. Fortunately the small church was retained in the middle of the field although it is now completely covered in ivy and the interior filled with stones. Why the church was built in such a remote location remains unknown but the answer will probably be found at winter solstice on the ridge above which has a most commanding aspect of the Mourne range.[21]

Near to Drumcaw is the village of Clough. The church that once stood here and went by the name of Rathcath is long gone. Given the veneration with which such sites were held, even if in ruins, the suspicion is that it was removed by

The ancient church of Drumcaw was one of eleven ecclesiastical sites that formerly existed around Dundrum Bay.

someone who would have been untrammelled with such respect and the main suspect is the landlord Sir Francis Annesley. Clough was originally the possession of the McCartans, but in 1612 it was granted by James 1st with the surrounding lands to Thomas Fitzmaurice and in 1615 it came by purchase into the hands of Sir Francis Annesley, Baron of Mountnorris. Three years later his estates in county Down were elevated into a manor which was called after the village then known as Cloghmaghericatt.[22] By 1622, the church of Rathcath, like Drumcaw, was declared in be in ruins by the Protestant bishop. The church was supposed to have stood near the Norman rath and it is possible that Annesley used the stone of the church to build a home. More than twenty years later Walter Harris would write that Clough 'is a well laid out village wherein is a good mansion house of Francis Annesley, Esquire, near which is a Danish rath...'[23] The ruinous site of the Annesley mansion in Clough faces the [T] junction with the Castlewellan Road.

While in the vicinity of Clough, a quick look to the south to Mountpanther, the hill famous for the ruins of the great Georgian mansion. There are no wild cats involved in this name. It is yet another mnemonic from Irish, in this case *Mannt Pianta* and gets its name from where the distant winter solstice sun was seen to set into what appeared to be a tiny declivity on the Mournes. The thinking behind the name is the same as for Tievedockaragh, *Taobh Dochrach* 'painful slope', where the large phallic shadow of Rocky mountain was imagined to hurt the vaginal valley between Crotlieve and Tievedockaragh as it squeezed in tightly at dawn of summer solstice. In the case of Mountpanther, *Mannt Pianta* means 'gap of pains'.

Like the church of Rathcath the two churches of Lismoghan and Killyglinnie are also gone. Regarding Lismoghan, O'Laverty tells us that 'about 100 yards south-west of the 'Lis' or fort, formerly stood a little chapel, called by the people, Killywoolpa'. As this site is very near the tidal inner Dundrum Bay, the name Killywoolpa was probably from the Irish *Cill a Buaile Pactha,* 'Church of the filling up of water'. The church and graveyard were apparently destroyed in the early part of the nineteenth century. Significantly, the Lis or fort that does survive at J429388 is on the exact same sunset line as the dolmen at Slidderyford and witnesses the winter solstice sun setting onto the swelling on the side of Slieve Commedagh as previously illustrated on page 282.[24] In 1518 the name of this fort was recorded as Lesmalstyke alias Ballykinlor; this is likely a rough spelling of *Lis Mala Stiúgtha,* 'fort of the dying (sun) hill-brow'. Interestingly, if the same line of the setting sun was extended further north-east is would bisect with the former site of Ballydugan chapel which the historian, bishop William Reeves, recorded was 'part of the garden of Ballydugan House'.[25] The name, like Dugganstown in Tollymore earlier mentioned, could be from the Irish *Dubh Gein,* 'dark act of begetting' only in this case the begetting is the setting sun (hence 'dark') penetrating the 'vulva' on the side of Commedagh.

The church of Killyglinnie may be gone but its disused graveyard is located at J424374 near the inner bay of Dundrum. This church marked the pagan fertility

## THE COMING OF CHRISTIANITY

site where the winter solstice sun copulated with the earth as it descended into the great vaginal hollow between Slieve Donard and Commedagh. The name of the church would be from the Irish *Cill an Gleanna*, 'church of the glen'. Formerly, and before the chapel of Ballykinlar was completed about 1784, Mass was celebrated every other Sunday at the nearby four roads of Carrickinab. A lovely tradition was preserved that when the priest would be celebrating Mass, a Protestant farmer in the neighbourhood, called Mr Craig, used to keep watch on a hill in his farm in order to give timely notice of the approach of the priest-hunters. The people remarked that good fortune ever afterwards attended Mr Craig and his family.[26]

### Ballykinlar

Regarding Ballykinlar, it was Walter Harris who ascribed the derivation of the name to Bailecaindlera, 'the town of the candlestick' because it was 'appropriated to Christ Church, Dublin, for wax-lights'. This interpretation arose because John De Courcy had granted Lower Ballykinlar by charter to the Dublin church about the year 1200.[27] Whatever the reason for De Courcy's patronage there is no mention of candles or lights in the charter. Harris looked to the Irish *Coinnleóir*,

The old graveyard is the original site of Ballykinlar chapel. In the background, on the hill, is the present church of St Patrick and St Joseph.

*The time is 3.34pm on the 28th December and the sun can still be seen setting on the summit of Slieve Donard from the front steps of Ballykinlar church.*

'a candlestick' as the explanation for the name of Ballykinlar. This is not, however, the reason for the origin of the name though in a sense it comes close. Perhaps the first thing to say about the present Ballykinlar chapel is that it is not on the exact same site as the ancient establishment. The old chapel was on an island the name of which was preserved in De Courcy's charter as 'Inislochaculin'. The lake on which the island was situated was drained in 1814. It was in 1782 that the recently appointed Rev John Macartan, a native of Ballymaginaghy near Castlewellan, renewed the chapel on the island.[28] Seventy years later it was necessary to replace the chapel by a new one and they even got as far as laying the foundation stone on 17th July 1885 before it was discovered that the original site would not bear the weight of the intended church. Fortunately the Marquis of Downshire granted a new site on a nearby hill a few hundred yards to the east on which the present church of St Patrick and St Joseph is built. One unfortunate aspect of the church's construction was that a stone circle that had stood from ancient times in the townland of Tubbercorran, on the road from Corbally to Ballykinlar was blasted with powder and the stone removed for the building of the church. The significance of the ancient chapel site, marked by the present graveyard, becomes apparent at winter solstice sunset. It was from this site that the sun could be seen setting on the summit of Slieve Donard. This is the event that gave Ballykinlar its name; looking to the sun setting on Donard, the Irish named the place *Baile cinn láir*, 'town of the middle of the head', from *ceann* (genitive *cinn*) meaning 'head', but also 'top, peak, topmost part' and *Lár* (genitive *láir*) with the meaning 'middle, midst, centre'. The ancients would have regarded the sunset spectacle as a powerful acting out of ejaculation. It would have been a special place for them and probably accounts for the existence of two artificial islands or crannogs on which, after the lake was drained, were found bronze spears, axes and other antiquities. Having a cemetery at this location for the faithful who looked to the resurrection and eternal life was entirely appropriate and a suitable adoption of an erstwhile pagan site.

Interestingly, by marking a line on the map between old Ballykinlar cemetery and the top of Slieve Donard, the line cuts through that part of Murlough Sandhills where Dr Oliver Davies and Miss Masie Gaffikin noted a number of ancient burial sites before the war. Further discoveries by professor E. Evans and Masie Gaffikin in 1948 led to extensive excavations during 1950-51 by A.E.P. Collins and these plotted burial sites would have approximately followed the line along which the sun would be seen setting on Donard showing that the burial sites of the ancients were not random but deliberate in their choice of location. Site eight at Murlough is an exception but it is on the same line as Killyglinnie where the solstice sun would set into the 'vaginal notch' between Slieve Donard and Slieve Commedagh.[29]

## Tyrella

The present Church of St John of the Church of Ireland closely occupies the site of the former chapel that had fallen into ruin after the suppression of the monasteries. Again, like the other chapels around the circumference of Dundrum Bay, this location had originally been a place of pagan significance on account of where the sun set on the distant Mournes at winter solstice. The history of the present church was traced by the Downpatrick historian J.W. Hanna in the Downpatrick Recorder, March 1862.

> 'About 1800 the greater part of the walls of the old building were removed by the Rev. Mr Hamilton as materials for effecting additions to Tyrella house and erecting a garden wall. At that time he purposed having a new church erected on the old site but the board of First Fruits refused making any grant owing to the small number of members of the Established Church resident in the parish. Nothing towards that object was done until the year 1839.
> The work was commenced in 1839 by the removal of the debris of the old building, including portions of the western and north walls, the latter lying quite close to the road. These fragmentary portions were about three feet thick, built of undressed stone, cemented with lime mortar, and showed that

Place of winter solstice sunset

St John's Church of Ireland at Tyrella marks where the winter solstice sun sets on the summit of Chimney Rock mountain, partially visible to the right of centre. The name Tyrella is from the Irish *Tí Ralach* meaning 'place of the huge person', a discrete way of referring to distant Chimney Rock which was his huge penis.

this had been a transition church, perhaps of the 11th or 12th centuries. At the west end were found, lying among the accumulated stones and mortar, two holy water stoups of freestone and in the adjoining grounds great quantities of human and horse bones, remains of coffins and uninscribed headstones, which were subsequently removed and buried in a large grave to the east of the old cemetery near the river side. The cemetery must have been at one period very extensive, as it stretched from south of where the present church stands across the road into the townland of Clanmaghery, in an adjoining field of which great quantities of human bones have been repeatedly found. As a place of interment, it began to be disused about ninety years past (ie. circa 1770).'

The old medieval catholic church had been built at this site to claim it for Christianity. As mentioned earlier in our chapter on Chimney Rock mountain, the original medieval church marked where the winter solstice sun sets on top of the bulbous seaward summit of Chimney Rock; the whole mountain being regarded by the ancients as a great tumescent phallus. This is how Tyrella got its name; it

*It is 3.49pm on the 28th of December and the setting winter sun casts its colourful glow over Rathmullan church.*

is from the Irish *Tí Ralach* meaning 'place of the huge person', which was really a roundabout but more discreet way of referring to his huge penis.[30] The knob summit of Chimney Rock was referred to by the local fishermen as the 'General'. This name is a mnemonic of the Irish '*Gein Rálach*', 'Gigantic act of begetting'; another reference to the whole mountain being regarded as a swollen penis and, as mentioned, a strong contender for the origin of the Atlantis story; Atlantis only being a composite of the Irish *At Lan Thíos*, 'Full swelling in the north'.

**Rathmullan**

The old church of Rathmullan certainly had an exotic history, belonging to the Knights Hospitallers or the Order of St John of Jerusalem, and enjoying exemption from the ecclesiastical tax imposed by the first Franciscan pope, Nicholas 1V in 1292 on account of their services and losses in Palestine. The church suffered during the dissolution of the monasteries and the Protestant bishop reported in 1622 that the church was in ruins. These ruins were removed about 1703 when the present Protestant church which occupies the site was erected. The name of Rathmullan is presumed to have come from the mound about three hundred

It is a week after the solstice and at 4.09pm on the 28th December the sun is setting at the end of the Mourne plain. The ancients regarded the sun setting at the end of the protruding land as a sexual union culminating in ejaculation. St John's chapel was built to claim this pagan site for Christianity.

about why early Christians had gone to the trouble of erecting a church here. It would be years before the answer emerged that the solution lay with the setting sun on the winter solstice. From the promontory of St John the plain of Mourne stretched out from the mountains to the sea. This attenuated plain was regarded as phallic and when the winter solstice sun set at the very end it could only be regarded as a moment of exceptional fertility with land and sun joining to bring about ejaculation. This would account for one of the old names for St Johns. When bishop Malachi of Down was making a grant to the abbey of St Patrick in 1183, the chapel of St John was referred to as Stechian. It is possible that this was a corrupted version of the Irish *Stéig Áine*. *Stéig* has the meaning of 'a slice, a strip, a portion of land', a reference to the attenuated plain of Mourne across Dundrum Bay where the highly symbolic sexual union of sun and distant coast took place annually at winter solstice sunset. The full meaning of Stechian or *Stéig Áine* would be the 'strip (of land) of pleasure'.[34] It is possible that the very designation of St John for the chapel may have been influenced by the Irish *Gein*, meaning 'the act of begetting'. Might there have been an old, unrecorded name of *Gein Poinnte*, 'begetting point', that was Christianised to John's Point? It would also have helped that the feast of St John, the beloved disciple, apostle and evangelist, has long been celebrated in the Christian calendar on 27th December, very close to the solstice.

These churches around Dundrum Bay, namely St Mary's Ballaghanery, Maghera, Drumcaw, Rathcath (Clough), Lismohan, Killyglinnie, Ballykinlar, Tyrella, Rathmullan, Rossglass, and St John's, together with the others mentioned, all bear witness to the enduring faith of our ancestors. The sun worshipping days of Mourne's pagan past have gone so we need not be diffident about claiming the works of the ancients as part of our heritage. As we look on and indeed admire the many works of the ancients throughout prehistoric Mourne, their achievements stand testimony to the dignity of man. The more we look on their accomplishments, the more we can remind ourselves of how far we have come and how very fortunate we are for the faith brought to us by St Patrick. To him we leave the last word:

> 'For the sun which we see rises every day for our benefit at his behest, but it will never reign nor will its radiance endure, but all who worship it will come to a bad end in wretched punishment as well. But we who believe in and adore the true sun, Christ, who will never die, nor will anyone die who has done his will, but he will last for ever just as Christ lasts for ever, Christ who reigns with God the Father almighty and with the Holy Spirit before ages and now and for all ages of ages. Amen.'[35]

# NOTES

CHAPTER 1
## A good place to live

1. *Eat your Greens: An Examination of the Potential Diet Available in Ireland During the Mesolithic,* Rachel Maclean, UJA, Vol 56, 1993
2. Nutritious hazelnuts: page 3 of *A History of Ulster,* by Jonathan Bardon, Blackstaff Press, Belfast, 1992
3. Mount Sandel, Co. Derry. This was an early Mesolithic site with hearths, pits and post-holes, on the estuary of the River Bann near Coleraine; an area of about 1,000 sq. metres was excavated by P.C. Woodman during the years 1973-1977, revealing four hearths occupied in succession. The hearths and rubbish-pits contained burnt remains, amongst them animal bones (including those of wild pig), hazelnut shells and flint tools; these pits yielded bones of salmon, sea-bass, eel and flouder, and seeds of apple and water-lily. Bird remains included duck, pigeon, grouse, goshawk and capercaillie (wood-grouse).
4. *Excavations in the Sandhills at Dundrum, Co Down, 1950-51* by A.E.P. Collins, UJA, Vol 15, 1952
5. *Notes on Irish Sandhills* by Rev L.M. Hewson, JRSAI, Vol 68, part 1, June 1938
6. Collecting blackberries noted in *Down Recorder* 8th October 1910. Nowadays the hundredweight means 100lbs but in 1910 the imperial long hundredweight would have prevailed, namely 112lbs or 8 stone which is equal to 50.80 kg.
7. Spence's Mountain (J3624): page 171, *Place-Names of Northern Ireland,* Vol 3, The Mournes, 1993.
8. The lore surrounding Domhnach na bhFraochóg or Blaeberry Sunday is comprehensively treated in *The Festival of Lughnasa, a study of the survival of the Celtic festival of the Beginning of harvest,* by the late Máire MacNeill (1904-1987); it was first published by Oxford University Press in 1962. The chief custom of the festival was the resorting by the rural communities to certain heights, or water-sides to spend the day in festivity, sports and bilberry-picking. This masterful work of scholarship is noteworthy for the thoroughness with which Máire MacNeill gathered all details of the life of St Donard. See also, *Picking Bilberries, Fraochans and Whorts in Ireland; the Human Story* by Michael J. Conry.
9. Page 80-81, *The Antient and Present State of the County of Down,* Dublin 1744. The season of scarcity was June and July when the previous year's crop was exhausted and the present year's crop of potatoes was not yet ready.
10. The inquiry into trawling in Dundrum Bay was conducted by the Fisheries Branch of the Department of Agriculture in the Annesley memorial hall and was reported in the *Down Recorder* 25th July 1908.
11. Letter by Observer to the *Down Recorder* 27th June 1908.
12. Details of the prosperous herring season from the *Down Recorder* 7th November 1908.
13. Page 106 of *Exploring Prehistoric Europe,* by Chris Scarre, Oxford University Press, 1998.
14. Salmon in the Shimna; *Down Recorder* 27th June 1903. For more on salmon in Dundrum Bay and on the salmon pools in the Shimna, see *Where Donard Guards* pages 224-226. The 'twenty-footer' pool on the east side of the Shimna bridge had an earlier name of Collins Pool. This place where the salmon gathered likely derived from the Irish *col linn* meaning the forbidden pool, ie. not to be fished in; not that it stopped the poachers visiting it.
15. For more on Maggie's Leap, both the human tragedies and the origin of the local name, see pages 164-169 of *Where Donard Guards* and *Slieve Donard's Domain* pages 49-52.
16. Letter of Rev J.R. Moore to Lord Elliott concerning the Bill for the regulation of Fisheries in Ireland. Rev Moore was seeking an extension of time for fishing on the 'small river called the

Newcastle or Tullymore river'. "As owing to its peculiar position the fish do not come up until the end of June, or beginning of July and the period by law prohibits fishing after the 12th August consequently the period being so short it is scarcely worth the expense of furnishing the necessary tackle nets, etc." Letter of 4th May 1842, page 244 of PRONI D. 1854/6/2.

17  When I asked local farmer, Hugh Rodgers, about the whereabouts of Kilnahattin, he pointed over to the foot of Leganabruchan. 'Over there somewhere', he said. Kilnahattin has sometimes been confused with St Mary's chapel, Ballaghanery as the start of the name was understood as *cill,* the Irish for 'church'. This part of the name however is probably derived from *caol* meaning 'a narrow, or precise point'. Bad weather during recent winters has precluded observations to verify that the 'precise point' as marked by the Sperm whale megalith or another megalith in the vicinity, derives from a location where an observer would see the sun connect with the landscape in symbolic fertility perhaps at either Drinneevar or at Slievenagarragh. Kilnahattin is from the Irish *Caol na h-Athainne* meaning 'the place of the firebrand'. The head of a Sperm whale contains a liquid wax called spermaceti from which the whale derives its name. Spermaceti was used in oil lamps, and candles and it would be particularly apt for this whale to represent a firebrand. I have noticed another long megalith (not photographed) at the foot of Leganabruchan so only further observations, most likely of where the sun sets at the winter solstice, may determine why these stones have been placed where they are or indeed, whether 'the place of the firebrand', like the very name of Leganabruchan itself, is a remnant from the days of smuggling.

18  Tollymore Park, a Northern Ireland Forest Park Guide, (1959), page 37, has the following: "*Parnell's Bridge:* This bridge crosses the Shimna about half a mile upstream of the point where the Spinkwee flows into it, and is said to have been named, like the point called Parnell's View, after Sir John Parnell, who was at one time Chancellor of the Exchequer in Ireland, and a relative of both the Roden family and Charles Stewart Parnell of Avondale." Sir John Parnell (1744-1801), was best known for opposing the Act of Union between Great Britain and Ireland in 1801 and for this he was dismissed from office. Before this, Sir John was a Commander of Irish Volunteers and had been instrumental in winning the right to vote for Irish Catholics and for them to enter Parliament, sentiments which would hardly have endeared him to Robert Jocelyn, 3rd Earl of Roden who was a Grand Master of the Orange Lodge and who was himself dismissed from his post as a Commissioner for Peace after a public inquiry into his part in the 1849 fracas of Dolly's Brae.

19  Mammals available in Mesolithic Ireland listed by Rachel Maclean in *Eat Your Greens,* UJA, Vol 56, 1993. The natural history of pigs in Ireland is complex. There are no skeletal remains of wild boar that predate the arrival of humans in Ireland and some argue that boars are not native to Ireland in the sense that they had established themselves on the Irish land mass without human intervention. Some scholars also maintain that the red deer was introduced to Ireland during the Neolithic period and was not present during the Mesolithic.

20  On 24th June 2009 the Mourne Observer posed the question, 'Driver take me to Carrowmurwaghnemucklagh' and suggested it lay around the Pot of Pulgarve or around Spinkwee. The author's reply to the Mourne Observer is given in full for the information it contains about pigs and the boundaries of Tollymore.

'Would it be a surprise if, in your quest to reach Carrowmurwaghnemucklagh, the taxi-driver took you to the vicinity of Sunnyholme caravan park on the Castlewellan Road rather than the exalted reaches of Pulgarve or Legawherry in the Mournes? Carrowmurwaghnemucklagh is an anglicised version of an old Irish name for part of the townland of Tollymore.

Reference to it is found in a land grant made by King James 1st, in the 10th year of his reign (ie. circa 1613) to Sir Arthur Magennis, knight of Rathfriland. The king confirmed to Sir Arthur Magennis "the lands of Dromange, Newcastle, Ballybegg, Morolock half townland, Tullymore half townland, containing the two quarters of Carrowlissenefrin and Carrowmurwaghnemucklagh, Ballybegg to be free of compositions and risings out." (original spellings retained)

But the taxi is going to Carrowmurwaghnemucklagh. In the Irish this is *'Ceathrú muirbheach na muclach'* meaning 'the quarter of the level stretch of the droves of pigs' and centuries ago the flat land along the floodplain of the Burren suffered from such poor drainage that it was more likely to suit pigs than any other form of livestock or agriculture. The boundary of Tollymore extends approximately from the swings in the islands park, across Bryansford Avenue to the Burren and follows that river to a pronounced bend in its course not far from Tesco's supermarket before taking in a rough triangular portion on the river's east bank. The Tollymore townland boundary can still be discerned behind the houses on the Castlewellan road by old hedges and tree lines. The apex of the triangle at this part of Tollymore would be Sunnyholme caravan park. The area in this part of the floodplain of the Burren river is the most likely location for the area once known as *'Ceathrú muirbheach na muclach'.'*

21 Article in *The Times* Monday 15th April 2013 by Simon de Bruxelles, *Wild boar in rangers' sights as forest population soars.*

22 Regarding another name for Slieve Muck: on page 17 of *Mourne Country*, Professor Evans notes: 'On the east a stony scree or 'dry quarry' to use the local name, occupies the hillside below the shale escarpment. Lighter coloured patches among the stones of the scree are disposed so as to resemble, when seen from a distance, the letters POV; and a little imagination has completed the word Poverty. I have often heard Slieve Muck referred to as Poverty Mountain.'

Poverty Mountain is derived, not from differing coloured patches on the scree but from the Irish for the phallic megalithic stones at the southern end of the mountain which catch the winter solstice sun and in doing so cast their potent and symbolically fertilising shadow into the notional vagina of the White Water valley the route of B 27, the Moyad Road. The name is a mnemonic for the Irish *Poibar Tí*. The word *Piobar* (gen. *piobair*) is the Irish for 'pepper', figuratively meaning 'poison', and also' fussiness' and 'excitement'. *Poibar Tí* translates as 'place of (sexual) excitement'.

23 Egg collecting on page 51 of *Slieve Donard's Domain*, Ballaghbeg Books, 2011.

Chapter 2

# Mourne: The Mountains of Sex

1 Page 53, *Ordnance Survey Letters Down*, ed. Michael Herity, Fours Masters Press, Dublin 2001
2 Ibid.
3 Letter of 12th May 1834, page 68 of *Ordnance Survey Letters Down*, Four Masters Press, Dublin 2001
4 Letter of 16th May, ibid.
5 Canon Lett's paper, *Names of Places in the Mountains of Mourne*, was reproduced in volume twelve of the Ulster Journal of Archaeology in 1906. Also of local importance is O'Donovan's manuscript map of the Mourne Mountains, which was produced in the same journal, volume eight, page 137, in 1902.
6 The examination of Mourne place-names as possible mnemonics began with a scrutiny of *Lindsay's Leap*, on the front of Thomas mountain. See the final chapter 'A Neolithic monument above the quarry' in *Slieve Donard's Domain*, Ballaghbeg Books, 2011.
7 *Déar* in Irish (also found as *Dear*, or *Diar*) is an intensive prefix meaning 'huge'. *Meadóg*, (genitive *meadóige*), is translated in Dinneen as 'a dagger, dirk or poniard, a short knife; a knife of unusual size or shape'. The prefix *Déar* also features in another Mourne name, Slievedermot (OS. 1928), which is not a personal name but a mnemonic for the Irish *Déar-Moth* meaning 'huge penis'.
8 'King's Meadow', page 125 of Walter Harris's, *The Antient and Present State of the County of Down*, 1744.
9 I have noticed that very many of the quarries of Mourne have been opened at sites formerly rich in pagan significance. The stone for Newcastle harbour was sourced away behind Drinneevar at a place already marked with *gein* (act of begetting) stones. The quarrymen seem to have been the last custodians of the old knowledge. They must have regarded granite sourced from these special sites as lucky. The quarrymen went to incredible lengths to access

these pagan sites; witness the steep mineral railway constructed up to Carr's Face on the upper edge of Chimney Rock mountain.
10. The Irish dictionary of Pádraig Dinneen is used throughout for the translation of Irish. In his *Official Tourist Guide to County Down and Mourne Mountains,* page 173, Robert Lloyd Praeger gives the following: '...the range was named *Beanna Boirche* (Banna Borka), the peaks (literally **horns**) of Boirche.' The 'horns of swellings' also conveys the sexual import of the old name.
11. *MacCana's Itinerary 48-9,* and quoted on page 124 of *Place-Names of Northern Ireland, Vol 3, The Mournes.* The proposal that Mourne was really a tribal name imported from county Monaghan was again raised by Francis Byrne in 1973 on page 128 of his scholarly work *Irish kings and high-kings,* London.
'In 1165 Ua Cerbaill once again acted as peace-maker between Muirchertach (now high-king of Ireland) and Cú Ulad's son and successor Eochaid. In return he was granted the territory of Benna Bairrche – the Mourne Mountains, which derive their present name from the migration thither of the Mugdorna from Ua Cerbaill's lands in Monaghan.'
12. See 'When Newcastle was called Shyleke', pages 52-54 of *Where Donard Guards,* Ballaghbeg Books, 2007.
13. See Newry and Mourne Council website.
14. Doan as *Do an mí-áil caib*: *Do* is the Irish for 'two; *an* is an intensive prefix meaning 'very'; *mí* in Irish is a negative separable prefix that conveys the sense of 'bad'; *áil,* as earlier mentioned, means 'pleasure, desire'; *cab,* (genitive *caib*), plural idem, means 'a head, a mouth, a gap' and so we can understand Doan as 'two very evil heads of pleasure'.
15. Sally Lake in the Silent Valley: Sally Lake in the gardens under the present dam would seem to have been imagined as a lake of seminal discharge for in Irish *Salach* (genitive *Salaighe*) has the meaning, 'dirty, soiled, impure, unclean, despicable, polluted, defiled'. See Dinneen page 935. Rather than being connected with Doan mountain, the 'pollution' was more likely perceived to have come from Scardan Hill (OS J3121) under Moolieve. *Scárdán* in Irish means 'a spout, a squirt'; and would have had a sexual meaning.
16. See *Place-names of Northern Ireland,* page 181 of *The Mournes; An Úrach* has been translated as 'the clayey/verdant river' probably because of thoughts about the sediment it would carry. The alternative translation given of 'newness' or 'freshness' does not relate to water quality but to the genesis of the river by the fertilising sun at the moment of solstice sunset.
17. 'Drusy cavities'; page 46 of *Mourne Country* by Professor E. Estyn Evans, Dundalk, 1951. The name Richey is mentioned. This was Dr James Ernest Richey, an eminent geologist, who read a paper to the Geological Society on 15th June 1927 on 'The Structural Relations of the Mourne Granites'. He would later treat of 'The Tertiary ring complex of Slieve Gullion' in 1932.
18. I have found rocks pierced by the hand of man on Leganabruchan, the Trassey valley, Douglas Crag, the rock face of Chimney Rock, the slopes of Slievenagarragh, the south tor of Slieve Bearnagh and south of Lower Cove. There is a very good example on the ridge line of Drinneevar where a boulder has been pierced on the top and has an exit hole on the side. The round shaped megalith that probably gave Slieve Corragh its name has a nearby rock surface pierced with a large hole. If memory serves me, this hole is some metres away on the Donard side.
19. On the western side of the north tor of Slieve Bignian, for instance, you can see two holes in the rock. The top shows the existence of crystals and the bottom hole is a shattered mess where explosives were used to access the interior hollow.
20. Letter of 19th April 1834 to Thomas Larcom, Mountjoy Barracks.
21. Page 190; chapter on 'The Elder Faiths' from *Mourne Country,* Dundalgan Press, Dundalk, 1951.
22. An example of whitewashed brass finials can still presently be found at the first house on the left past the entrance to Tollymore Park on the Bryansford Road.
23. Bearnagh Slabs: Richard Rowley has preserved for us an old Mourne name in his story, 'The Choosers of the Slain' (*Tales of Mourne,* London, 1937). The opening sentence on page 217 is: 'I had come up the Lecarry loanin' behind Bearnagh, had climbed the flanking slope and crossed the col to the Hare's Gap.' From the context, Lecarry loanin' would be the path under Bearnagh along the side of Pollaphuca Hollow. It is from the Irish *Leacrach,* (genitive *leacraighe*), meaning appropriately 'abounding in flags'.

24 If you happen to have access to *Rock Climbs in the Mourne Mountains*, produced by Mountaineering Ireland in 2010, have a good look at the photograph of Buzzards Roost at the top of page 75 and note the remarkable phallic shadow cast by Blue Lough Buttress on the left of the picture. Likewise on top of page 79, the right hand side of the photograph shows how the topography generates the shadow.

25 Crocknafeola: *Place-names of Northern Ireland,* Vol 3, The Mournes, page 134.

26 Ben Crom: page 126, *Place-names of Northern Ireland,* Vol 3, The Mournes.

27 For the building of the old quay and the specifications for the thousands of perch of dressed stone required see pages 83-89 of *Where Donard Guards,* Nicholas Russell, 2007. The Ballagh quarry and the access road are illustrated in the section, 'Early Trails on the Mountain', pages 139-142, of *Slieve Donard's Domain*. Regarding the ridge of rock along the access road which is illustrated on page 141, look down at the lower part of the outcrop to see a formidable eye carved in the rock to make a 'face stone'. Other face stones are featured in chapter three though why the ancients went to so much effort to create them we can only guess.

28 See final chapter of Slieve Donard's Domain, 'A Neolith monument above the quarry'. The realisation that many of the names of Mourne had been changed into mnemonics brought about a complete examination of local names and was the stimulus for this present book.

29 John Fagan's memories of the great Clannabarcaigh hurling team were recorded in a *Souvenir of Newcastle's First GAA week, 1954*. This was held in St Patrick's Park from Sunday 25th July to Sunday 1st August. The author's grandfather, Dan Curran, the first town clerk to Newcastle Urban Council, was one of those who played against Newry and beat them in the final of the Co. Down league. But Newry protested maintaining that the winning point scored was wide of the posts. The team captain Peter Murray and Dan Curran rode bicycles to Armagh to fight against the protest. They won by one vote, and they brought the medals home.'

30 I record my appreciation to Eddie O'Hagan of Castlewellan Road for these reminiscences of Irish being spoken in Glasdrumman. Further information on the subject can also be found in *Irish in County Down Since 1750,* by Ciarán Ó Duibhín, published by Cumann Gaelach Leath Chathail, in 1991.

31 For further illustrated information on Amy's River see pages 187-188 of *Slieve Donard's Domain,* Nicholas Russell, Ballaghbeg Books, 2011.

32 Page 55 of *Ordnance Survey Letters Down* by Michael Herity, Four Masters Press, Dublin 2001.

33 Peter Wilson conducted a basic survey of this structure and recorded his discoveries in *Archaeology Ireland,* Vol 26, No 14, Issue No 102, Winter 2012, as *'An unusual Stone Structure on Slieve Donard'*. He felt it was probably not a prehistoric monument because, inter alia, 'the north-south alignment of the stone structure is not one that is commonly encountered with megalith tombs'. I feel more will eventually be revealed about these stones and that it will be discovered that the ancients chose this location and alignment because of significant interaction of the sun with the distant landscape, most likely at winter solstice sunset and that present hidden fertility implications will be made known. I am more sympathetic to these rows of stones originating from the hand of man rather than being the product of strong frost action (periglacial processes) as mentioned in the article. Perhaps Mr Wilson's article may persuade other archaeologists to conduct a more extensive survey.

34 Millstone Mountain an 'open air museum'; see the chapter 'Millstones' and page 189 in particular in *Slieve Donard's Domain,* by Nicholas Russell, Ballaghbeg Books, 2011.

35 The interpretation of the origin of Attical largely stems from the Irish *Col,* 'lust'. The original meaning of Annalong, which will be looked at later on, is probably more provocative. Place-names of Northern Ireland, Vol 3, The Mournes, page 17, gives the Irish *Áit Tí Chathail,* meaning 'Cathal's dwelling place' for the origin of Attical. The Irish *Col* is again used with the meaning of lust, in the origin of Colligan Bridge (J308204), where one could notionally 'look up the legs' of the Silent Valley; the original would have been *Col na geine,* 'lust of the act of begetting' but the [n] of the article na has been elided in everyday speech).

36 BCDR, *Official Tourist Guide to County Down and Mourne Mountains,* by Robert Lloyd Praeger, page 171, printed by McCaw, Stevenson & Orr, Belfast, (2nd Ed) 1900.

37 Regarding the mirror stone at the head of the Glen River Valley, speculation is reserved to these footnotes. While the flat area of the stone faces the summer sunrise, the higher other

end of the stone points towards the top of the col and one presumes it looks to where the winter solstice sun would rise out of the col. At the end of the summer solstice day it is also possible that from the mirror stone's location the sun may be seen setting on top of Slieve Commedagh. This mirror stone, lying as it does along the path to Donard, is worthy of further observations to reveal its significance.

38  Craignagore: 'Rock of the Projection' is from the Irish word *Corr*, (genitive *Cuirre*), meaning 'a projection, snout, peak, bill,'. Thoughts of pagan ritual fertility practices initially suggested a possible derivation from the Irish *Craig na gCoriach*, meaning 'rock of the sinners'. Ancient ritual practices cannot be proved but the rock spear point most certainly can so I have stayed with *Craig na gCuirre*. Remember that because of the eclipse the [C] of *Cuirre* is not sounded. If I may also tentatively give directions, on the map take the dotted forest road east of Drinnahilly and after the steep part the road becomes more level. Although a nice straight stretch of road beckons ahead, leave the road at the dog leg turn and continue eastwards through the grass a few dozen metres and then turn slightly downhill into the thick of the forest looking for a rocky outcrop. You are coming to the outcrop from the rear and need to continue round through the trees to the front. The spear point platform is not particularly large but is reasonably distinctive. When in the future the forest is felled one can only hope that the powers that be would consider leaving the area in front of the rock unplanted and open that the beauty of the site as well as the orientation of the rock to the solstice can be appreciated. With the forest road already nearby, Craignagore has the potential for easy development as part of Mourne's ancient pagan past.

39  The Barony of Clanbrassil became extinct with the death of John Strange, 5th Earl Roden, who held the title from 1880 until his death on 3rd July 1897. It is no surprise that 5th Earl Roden often features in the correspondence of 5th Earl Annesley. Like Earl Annesley, 5th Earl Roden served in the Scots Fusilier Guards where he was a Lieutenant Colonel. He served in the Crimea War and was at the battle of the Alma, Balaclava and Inkerman. Hugh 5th Earl Annesley was shot in the face at the battle of the Alma. The Clanbrassil title expired with Earl Roden because he died *sine prole mascula,* ie, without sons.

40  The meanings of Drinnahilly are outlined on page 137 of *Place-names of Northern Ireland; Mournes*. The associated name, The Drinns, is treated on page 138.

41  Slievenaslat: The application of sexual interpretations to place-names based on the sun at solstice extends northwards beyond Slievenaslat but it is a matter of regret not to have either the time or space here to expand on them or to satisfy the many possibilities presented by these names. The name of Wood Road, for instance, that runs from Clonvaraghan village over to Backaderry may be much older than any timber plantation. It probably comes from the Irish *Bod* (genitive *Buid*), meaning 'penis' as it is from this road that the winter solstice sun is seen setting on top of Curlets Hill. Then we wonder, might the first part of Backaderry be from the Irish *Biach*, meaning 'erect penis'; possibly *Biach an deoraidh* meaning 'the erect penis of the wanderer', a reference to a phallic shadow moving with the setting winter sun? Many further insights connecting place-names with solstice await to be recorded.

42  Ibid, pages 114-115.

43  The source of the Tullybrannigan river is often erroneously believed to be the stream on the eastern flank of Slievenabrock, probably because it is easily seen from Newcastle town. This river was certainly the boundary between the Roden and Annesley estates and the source of the river is marked at the crest by upright stones built into the top of the wall. This wall that follows the stream uphill was built in 1841 by Lord Roden to enclose his sheep walk and to deter trespass westwards along Curragh Ard from Newcastle. The cost of the wall was £44 and half of it was paid by Lord Annesley in order to protect his interests, namely Lady Annesley's plantations. The correspondence relating to the building of the wall is found in PRONI. D.1854/6/2 in two letters between Rev John R. Moore, trustee for Lord Annesley, then a minor, and Captain Hill, land agent for Lord Roden. The letters are dated 22nd September 1840 (page 46) and 23rd September 1841 (page 157). The stream mearing the two estates is referred in the correspondence as 'the rivulet'. The Tullybrannigan river proper, however, has its source in the marsh, Curragh Ard, between Slievenabrock and The Drinns, as per the ordnance survey activity map. The marsh is overlooked by the face feature that gave the Tullybrannigan area its name.

44  On account of the spelling of the Irish *Brannda*, 'a reef' in the derivation of the name, I strongly support the spelling of Tullybrannigan, with the double [n], as featured on the old road name sign and not the spelling Tullybranigan as recently found on the Mournes activity map.
45  *Place-names of Northern Ireland; Mournes*, page 166.
46  Slieve Corragh: Pierced fertility holes have long been associated with betrothal. The tradition was that couples would make their promises while holding hands through the hole. In Northern Ireland we have the famous example of the Doagh Holestone. See also the illustration of the pierced rock at the Hares Gap on page 45.
47  *Spinnc Buidhe* the 'sunny pointed stone': *Buidhe*, or in modern Irish *Buí*, is usually understood as 'yellow' or 'golden'. The older Irish of Dinneen offers also the further understanding of 'sunburnt, sunny, summerlike'. The stone can certainly be called golden when lit with the first dawn light.
48  Page 257, *Slieve Donard's Domain*, by Nicholas Russell, 2011, Ballaghbeg Books.
49  Sunset for the local area at the winter solstice is given as 15.57 hours. This presumes the sun setting on a flat horizon. Anyone hoping to witness the sun setting into the 'fertility notch' from Luke's mountain needs to be present long before the time above. Because the sun sets quite quickly it is not possible to follow the sun descending into the notch by racing diagonally up the hill. Place-names of Northern Ireland have recorded (on page 107) the 1629 form of 'Clonculllyne aut Lurgorue al. Balledryneny'; these variations for Clonachullion, otherwise 'Lurgorue' and 'Balledryneny', would seem to also be descriptions of tracking the declining sun up the slope of Luke's mountain. Lurgorue stems from the Irish *Loirgim Ruadh*, 'I trace or follow the red one', while 'Balledryneny' looks to the idea of ascending, as in the Irish *dréim*, 'the act of climbing'.
Some of the large boulders or 'face stones' on the slopes of Luke's mountain may perhaps later be demonstrated to be dual purpose, marking not only the fertility phenomenon of the winter solstice but a similar event at summer solstice sunset horizon.
50  Newell's Cross is treated in *Place-names of Northern Ireland, Mournes*, on page 63.
51  Spellack: See *Place-names of Mourne*, page 171
52  The use of the term 'fairies' was examined in a light-hearted article by Manchán Magan entitled *Away with the faeries'*, in *The Irish Times Magazine*, 15th March 2014. This brought to mind the remarks of Sean O'Faolain in *The Irish*, 1947: 'This medley of myth and realism must have forged a strangely dual mind in the race that found itself oscillating so gently between both. Possibly the greatest degree of objectivity that the native mind can have reached when listening to these half-credible, half-incredible wonders – which, as with the folk of today or yesterday, was not just something adverted to occasionally and briefly but something impinging on them at every hour of their lives – was that of the old West Cork woman who was recently asked, 'Do you really believe in the fairies?' and who replied, 'I do not, but they're there!'
53  The big unanswered question is why the ancients picked this forbidding location requiring such demanding exertions. No observations at solstice have been possible. Maybe the sun appeared at the top of one of Slieve Bearnagh's tors; I think it more likely to mark the setting of the winter solstice sun into the [V] shaped notch or vagina at the end of Pollaphuca Valley.
54  See 'Earlier names of Slieve Donard' on page 117 of *Slieve Donard's Domain*, Ballaghbeg Books, 2011.
55  The Hare's Gap: *h-Éirí Cheap*: *Éirí* is from the Irish word *Éirghe* and means 'act of rising, arising, getting up, ascending; becoming'. It is used here in a sexual sense. Some might be more familiar with its usage in the phrase *Éirí Amach na Cascá* meaning 'The Easter rebellion or insurrection'.
56  Further details of the smuggling trade, including signalling posts and caves for hiding contraband, are in the chapter 'Smugglers on the Mountains'. The Brandy Pad is dealt with on pages 65 to 71 in *Slieve Donard's Domain*, Ballaghbeg Books, 2011.
57  I am happy to amend this error about Spelga which is found on page 125 of *Slieve Donard's Domain*.
58  For Butter mountain the ordnance survey recorded the Irish name *Sliabh an Ime* 'mountain of the butter', but this would be a classic case of the original Irish *bothach* having been

changed into the English mnemonic 'butter' and in turn being translated back into Irish. Butter indeed may have been buried in the locality but it was the collection of summer booley huts on the south east flank of this hill that gave the place its name. It is worth noting the extensive former turf banks across the valley on the side of Slieve Loughshannagh where the occupants of the booley huts cut their winter turf while minding the cattle during the summer. See also page 121 of *Slieve Donard's Domain* for illustrated mounds of booley sites at Spelga valley reservoir.

59 The Irish word *Páis* can be translated as 'suffering' or 'affliction' but here it has the meaning 'death'. The word was used with the same meaning in an early name for the Bloody Bridge river which was named by Harris as the Midpace River. This name was a corruption of the Irish *Mí-ádh Páis* meaning 'unfortunate or unlucky death' and was an allusion to the accidental deaths of riders racing to Newcastle from Greencastle fair. In the haste the horses misjudged the proper edge of the bridge parapet and galloped instead over the edge of the void to the rocks below before they could be reined in. See *Slieve Donard's Domain*, page 165.

60 Examination of Slievenamiskan; *Place-names of Northern Ireland; The Mournes*, pages 168-169.

61 Deers' Meadow: In his *Names of Places in the Mountains of Mourne*, UJA, 1906, Canon W.H. Lett recorded the existence of a name 'Dead Man's Cairn'. He described this as 'a heap of stones in the Deer's Meadow half a mile south of fork of roads, on right hand going towards Kilkeel. One of the customary heaps raised by each traveller as he passes by, placing a stone on it, to mark the spot where the dead body of a man had been found.' There may have been more to the name than the reverend gentleman imagined. The name probably has no connection with the finding of dead bodies but is instead a mnemonic of the Irish *Déad mí-áin*, meaning 'tooth of evil pleasure'. The cairn would have been a marker to the length of the phallic shadow that gave Deers' Meadow its name. I do seem to remember a story however, of a carter who died here while bringing goods from Kilkeel to Hilltown but the name on the map would have been established long before his unfortunate demise.

62 Early alternative names for Hen Mountain: *Place-names of Northern Ireland; The Mournes*, pages 141-142.

63 Folklore based on fact: quote from page 93, *The Sunbird*, by Wilbur Smith, Pan Books, London, 1997.

64 Page 28 of *Place-names of Rostrevor* by Rev Bernard J. Mooney, Newry Reporter, 1950. Place-names project of Northern Ireland declare the name to be 'of uncertain origin'.

65 St Bronagh's chapel: While standing by the wall of the old chapel, I have watched the sun emerge from the rounded slope of Slievebane (J1918) at about 10.30am on 19th December. Slievemeel (J2120) performs in a similar manner to Slievedermot early on winter solstice and its name is likely a corruption of the Irish *Sliabh Mí-Áil*, 'mountain of evil pleasure'.

Perhaps someone will later follow up the suggestion that the great megalith on the upper crest of Leckan Beg marks the winter solstice sun appearing at the top of Slievemartin, making it the winter equivalent of the summer solstice dawn spectacle of the sun appearing at the top of Slievemartin as seen from Cloghmore? Likewise, if the winter solstice sun is seen from Slieve Roosley to rise from the notch between phallic mountains Crenville and Slievedermot, a reconciliation of Roosley's name of 'Boduck' given on the Map of Down in 1755, might then be possible. 'Boduck' may well be a corruption of the Irish *Bod Oiche*, 'Penis hole'.

One of the meanings of the Irish word *Rúisc* is 'a shot or discharge'. Through a sexual interpretation of the landscape, Slieve Roosley may have been given its name from being the perceived recipient at solstice of a 'solar seminal ejaculation' from the phallic mountains further down the valley. Perhaps a megalith, *Rúisc Lia*, 'ejaculation stone' may be later identified?

66 Pages 191-192 of *Official Tourist Guide to County Down and Mourne Mountains*, by Robert Lloyd Praeger, 2nd Edition (revised), McCaw, Stevenson & Orr, Ltd., Belfast, 1900.

67 Ibid; page 187: 'the humpy profile of Ballynagelty, (*baile-na-ngealtaigh*, 'the town of the madmen') – 1,297 feet – rising far above the sickle-shaped gravel-spit and whitewashed hamlet of Killowen built on a raised beach.' May the good residents of Killowen be relieved their hamlet was not formerly a place of madmen.

Chapter 3

# The Face Stones of Mourne

1 Harold Carson expanded on the idea of Mourne Faces in an article *'Faces in the Mournes'*, in Volume 5, 1992, of Twelve Miles of Mourne, The Journal of the Mourne Local Studies Group. From his prompting the Mourne Observer ran a five week feature on the topic. Likewise Neil Johnston, writing in the 'Ulster Log' in the Belfast Telegraph, used the interesting word *'phizzogs'* to characterize the big illustrated effigies. *Piseog* in Irish means 'witchcraft, sorcery; a charm, a spell'. *Piseoga* were chiefly directed to obtaining cures of man and beast and to conserving and increasing farm products such as butter, milk, young stock, etc. But probably due to the impression that these stone images were accidents of nature, public interest drained away.

Also an exhibition entitled 'Sculptures of Mourne' was shown at Newcastle Library from 1st to 11th July 2014. It was comprised of twenty photographs taken by Wesley Rollins and many showed excellent examples of face stones and some photographs of the Mourne Wall.

2 Page 49 of *Ireland in Pre-Celtic Times* by R.A.S. Macalister, Maunsel and Roberts, Dublin, 1921.

3 Balor: The mythological tales can be interpreted in many ways. T.F. O'Rahilly saw Balor, quite fittingly, as another manifestation of the Irish supreme deity, namely the sun-god.

4 An illustration of the 'Balor' megalith together with the routes of the three climbs, 'Chimney Slab', Chimney Arête' and 'Power up the Mac', is found on page 156 of *Rock Climbs in the Mournes*, published by Mountaineering Ireland, 2010. This is the same stone featured at the start of chapter one with a boar's head on another side of the boulder.

5 Without fear of either exaggeration or contradiction, there are thousands of stones across the hills of Mourne that the ancients have simply decorated with eyes and mouths. One of the hardest jobs was the editing or whittling down of the many hundreds of such face stones to the representative sample presented here. Undoubtedly many other and even better faces are out there to be found. The finding and interpreting of these ubiquitous stones adds greatly to the pleasures of a day's walk in the hills.

Chapter 4

# Spear and Phallic Stones of Mourne

1 Cribben: The term 'cribben' is the Mourne name for long lengths of granite that were used as kerbs for footpaths and that marked the edge of the road. The name is from the Irish *Craoibín* which described an old practice when taking home the turf in creels from the bog. Creels were usually taken home in pairs astride a donkey's back but occasionally they were carried home by either a man or woman on their backs and it was not very pleasant to have bits of turf going down the back of your neck. The practice of *Craoibín* was to put a row of turf-sods standing upright around and over the mouth of a creel to keep in the smaller pieces of peat. The analogy of upright turfs marking and protecting the edge of the creel saw the term easily transferred to marking the edges of roads and the lengths of granite that were used for that purpose.

2 *The Grave of St Patrick*, Vol V1, No 2, April 1900, Ulster Journal of Archaeology, by F.J. Bigger. The name Slievenalargy, from where the slab was sourced, is from the Irish *Sliabh na Leirgí*, meaning 'mountain of the declivities'. The original location of the slab on the mountain is now lost but when in situ it would have pointed to the appropriate notch or vaginal declivity on the distant Mournes where the winter solstice sun set, hence the name, and probably also to another notch involved at summer solstice. Francis Bigger makes it clear that the selection was of a large **natural** slab. The stone did not have to be quarried as is presently suggested on information plaques near the saint's grave. The Irish word *Learg* (genitive *Leirge*, plural, *Leirgí*) has a number of meanings, 'a path, way, footstep; a plain, a piece of good level land;

# NOTES

    slope, declivity, a track; a battle-field, a battle, a rout.' Place-names project elected for the version *Sliabh na Leargadh*, 'mountain of the sloping expanse'.
3. Damage at St Patrick's Grave: *Downpatrick Recorder,* 25th October 1902.
4. Page 123 of *The Antient and Present State of the County of Down,* Walter Harris and Charles Smith, Dublin 1744.
5. Idem, page 82.
6. In light of Harris's comments it was not unreasonable, for instance, for David Kirk to mention in *The Mountains of Mourne: A Celebration of a Place Apart.*, page 18, 'The Vale is the Annalong valley and Snavan is Lamagan and Cove mountains, then regarded as one.' The Vale is indeed the upper reaches of the Annalong valley but Snavan is only a tiny part of Cove.
7. We are examining Slieve Snavan but the other mentioned location, *Slieve-neir*, is that part of Chimney Rock mountain at the head of the Bloody Bridge valley. It is a reference to the mighty megalith that dominates the skyline of the valley in the upper reaches. When all else is in darkness in the valley at winter solstice morning, this megalith in on the line that receives the first sunlight. Slieve Neir is derived from *Sliabh nIrille,* 'mountain of the spike'. More on this when dealing with Chimney Rock.
8. The purpose of the runnels near the top of the cliff could be to funnel rain water over the edge in imitation of fertility ejaculation, or to drain away blood from sacrifices and direct it to the 'red hand'.
9. *Maps of the Mountains of Mourne in the County of Down,* by Rev Canon H.W. Lett, MRIA, in Ulster Journal of Archaeology, Vol 8, July 1902.

CHAPTER 5

# Vagina Stones

1. Pages 112/114 of *Slieve Donard's Domain* by Nicholas Russell, Ballaghbeg Books, 2011.
2. Partholan: Earlier commentators such as Thomas F. O'Rahilly in *Early Irish History and Mythology*, page 75, have stated: 'The name Partholan is non-Irish, being a borrowing of Latin, Bartholomaeus'. My own persuasion is that the name, like Slángha, is indeed Irish and a very symbolical one at that. The name is a contracted amalgam of the Irish *an Parthas Oileán,* 'the garden or paradise island' from the attractiveness of the country to the first settlers.
3. We append the footnote of John O'Donovan whose publication in 1851 of the edition of the Annals of the Four Masters, with translation and notes, was a major step forward in the study of Irish history. Commenting on the year 2533 he said: 'Sliabh Slángha was the ancient name of Sliabh Domhanghairt, or Slieve Donard, in the south-east of the county of Down. The cairn of Slángha is still to be seen on the summit of Slieve Donard, and forms a very conspicuous object. The hero Slángha is now forgotten by tradition, but the memory of St. Donard is still held in great veneration throughout the barony of Iveagh and the Mourne mountains.'
4. Page 150 of *Complete Guide to Celtic Mythology* by Bob Curran, Appletree Press, Belfast, 2000.
5. P.W. Joyce's explanation of *Fir-Bolg*: Chapter Two: *'Fir Bolg. Bolg. Bulga.'*, page 43-44, of *Early Irish History and Mythology* by T.F. O'Rahilly.
6. *Rath Murbholg*: See page 23 of *Where Donard Guards* by Nicholas Russell, Ballaghbeg Books, 2007.
7. The Cruithne people: The very many humps could refer to people continually hunched, pulling ropes, in the business of erecting many megaliths. Alternatively, if one was to make a topographical interpretation, one might think of Cruithne as people from drumlin country although this restricts their area of influence to mid and south Down.
8. The Grey Man's Path: Illustrated, for instance, on page 195 (Plate 164) of *Ireland's Eye, The Photographs of Robert John Welch,* by E. Estyn Evans and Brian S. Turner, Blackstaff Press, 1977.

PREHISTORIC MOURNE: INSPIRATION FOR NEWGRANGE

The caption records: 'In 1892, Welch, perching himself casually but somewhat perilously on a fallen column which bridges 'The Grey Man's Path', 'used a village boy 14 years old to make the exposure, cap off and on, say one second' (The cap belonged to the camera). The note on the back of the original print states that 'the right angle cliff top will cut twine' and goes on to explain that the path leads from the top of the cliff (636ft) down a fissure formed by denudation along a fault plane in the cliff. The drop from the column on to the path about 60ft. but my carcass would not have stopped till it reached the talus top 400 feet below had I slipped off.' As we have already mentioned in the main text, this megalith has not 'fallen' into place but is a deliberate placement.

9   The Sheugh: *Rock Climbs in the Mourne Mountains,* published by Mountaineering Ireland, 2010. The first Mourne climbing guide was produced in 1959 by Dr Phil Gribbon and the Sheugh is described on p.19. The photo showing the Buzzard's Roost fissure also shows a climbing rope down the right-hand rock face where Ricky Bell was preparing for a strenuous ascent.
10  Donard Cove with illustrations: pages 52-54, *Slieve Donard's Domain,* Ballaghbeg Books, 2011
11  A common interpretation is that the advent of farming brought greater stocks of food and thus allowed great undertakings in society. Generally, therefore, great works in stone are attributed to the Neolithic period beginning about 4,000BC. The thrust of chapter one, 'A good place to live', leaves open the possibility however of the great works in Mourne beginning much earlier and even possibly back to the early Mesolithic.

CHAPTER 6

# Begetting Stones

1   The local road name has unfortunately been misspelt and is presently given as 'Altnadue Road' and this despite the presence of Altnadua House.
2   Strictly speaking the Irish word *Greabh* means 'a nappy excrescence on wool' but given a sexual interpretation it could be understood as semen; it is liberally translated here as 'ejaculation'.
3   Annagassan: Derived from three Irish words; *An-,* an intensive prefix meaning 'very', when prefixed to adjectives (which next see); *All,* an adjective meaning 'great' – it is also found as *Oll* in compound words and has the similar meaning of 'great, huge, monstrous…'; *Gasán,* meaning 'stem, stalk' but here as a euphemism for the penis.
4   It must be left to others to check the likelihood that the name of the Giant's Ring at Ballynahatty, near Shaw's Bridge, has been derived from the Irish *Geinte,* 'of the act of begetting', and that the site owed its early importance to significant solstice fertility interaction between the landscape and the sun on the surrounding horizon.
    Similarly, the derivation of the name of Bangor is interesting if presently inconclusive. An explanation for the name is given in the old Irish text *Táin Bó Fraích,* as follows: 'The Connaught warrior *Fróech* and the Ulster warrior *Conall Cernach* were returning to Ireland from the Alps with Fróech's cattle when Conall's servant, Bicne mac Láegaire, died at the place which then came to be known as Inber mBicne, today Bangor Bay. When they came to shore, the cattle shed their horns, thus giving rise to the name *Trácht mBennchoir,* 'the strand of the horn-casting'. (*Place-names of Northern Ireland, Vol 2, The Ards,* see, Parish of Bangor, pages 141-150, by A.J. Hughes and R.J. Hannan, Institute of Irish Studies, 1992.) Folklore often contains kernels of truth. Could St Comgall have chosen the site for his monastery, as would St Laisrén at Holywood, to claim for Christianity a previous pagan site? The tale of the cattle shedding their horns would be interpreted as an allegory for pagan fertility phallic shadows (the horns) giving way to Christianity. Bangor is now so built up that direct sight-lines to possible places of contact between sun and landscape at the solstices from Bangor Abbey are impossible. We might speculate however that the summer solstice sun setting on distant Knockagh hill, the site of the great war memorial, the hill having a height of 390 metres, might be one possibility. *Bennchor* is taken to derive from the Irish

# Notes

*Beann* (genitive *Beinne, Beanna*) meaning 'horn' and *Cor*, 'act of wearying, growing tired'. With the coming of Christianity, the pagans 'grew tired' of the sexual interpretation of the landscape and the symbolic phallic shadows of the old fertility religion.

5   Whitehead is located at the base of Muldersleigh Hill at the entrance of Belfast Lough. Place-names of Northern Ireland have recorded that Muldersleigh Hill appeared in 1605 in the inquisition taken at Antrim, as Mullaslee, although no suggestions were made for the origin of the name. I would tentatively suggest that, because it was from Hollywood across the Lough that the summer solstice sun could be seen rising from Muldersleigh Hill (earlier Mullaslee), that the name is a somewhat corrupted version of the eclipsed remnant of the Irish (*Tí na*) *mBuilg-léas*, meaning '(Place of the) bright spot'.

The fertility theme also extends to Belfast Lough which was anciently known as *Loch Laoigh*, in the Annals of Tigernach (See Placenamesni.org). This is 'the Lough of the suckling calf' and the name probably derives from the shape of Belfast Lough which has a close resemblance to a large teat, beloved by very young calves.

6   Carrickfergus: See page 12 of *Carrickfergus and its Contacts*, by Rev John F. MacNeice, Rector of Carrickfergus and Archdeacon of Connor, printed by Matthews Bros, Carrickfergus, 1928.

7   The slang term for the Mourne Wall is discussed in the chapter of that name on page 236 of *Slieve Donard's Domain*, by Nicholas Russell, Ballaghbeg Books, 2011. *Dúithir* means 'dawn, morning'.

8   Derivation of Drinneevar: *Place-names of Northern Ireland, Vol 3, The Mournes*, page 138. See also speculation about the possible location of a 'bridge' before it was appreciated that the 'bridge' was a mnemonic; page 248, *Slieve Donard's Domain*, Ballaghbeg Books, 2011.


Chapter 7
# Slidderyford Dolmen

1   Slidderyford Dolmen and the stone circle that once surrounded it were treated earlier on pages 2-7 of *Where Donard Guards*, 2007, Ballaghbeg Books.

2   Beyond mentioning that dolmens were early tombs or burial chambers, there is no mention in Wikipedia of any association of dolmens with fertility.

3   Were it not for pressure of space it would have been a delight to follow up the urging of one of the proof readers who wrote to me saying: 'Do you think you might consider giving a foreword or a separate chapter to educating your readers on the central role of sexuality in paganism? He reminded me of the words of Queen Medb of Connacht in the *Táin Bó Cuailnge* to her messenger when she was looking the loan of the magnificent bull of Cooley. 'If Dáire himself comes with the bull I'll give him a portion of the fine Plain of Ai equal to his own lands, and a chariot worth thrice seven bondmaids, and my own friendly thighs on top of that'.

And all without a blush. (Thank you for that Eddie). [Quote taken from Thomas Kinsella's translation of the *Táin*.]

4   Kilfeaghan: *Caol Feagáin*, 'the narrow or precise point of the groove'. Awaiting confirmation of where exactly the solstice sun sets on Cooley as seen from this location. *Feagán* could also refer to the rim of a spinning wheel so it is also possible for the sun to set on top of a distant hill. *Cill* is the Irish for 'church', but when 'Kil-' is encountered in a place-name, more etymological consideration should be given to possible derivation from the Irish *Caol*, with the sense of 'narrow, slender, fine of point', or as rendered here, an exact location, a precise point. The name Kilnahattin, for instance, in the locality of the Bloody Bridge, specifically the slopes of Leganabruchan, definitely does not refer to St Mary's chapel, Ballaghanery [This confirmed to me by local farmer, Mr Rodgers, who emphatically pointed away from the ancient chapel and over to the mountain-side.]

5   Flush Loney Standing Stone: See *Where Donard Guards*, p.7-9. There is an illustration of the second block buried in the hedge. Also, *Slieve Donard's Domain*, p.62-64, where the carving

on the stone of Jeremiah Atkinson's name, he who was the greatest local smuggler, was seen as a rude victory sign to Earl Annesley who was in charge of the Customs Service.

6 Old Town: This does not imply an ancient settlement but rather is from the Irish *Oll-Tonn*, meaning 'great level marsh'. A century ago, there was a boreen from about the entrance to the site of Tesco's supermarket on the Castlewellan Road stretching across the fields behind the Burrendale Hotel. It was known at the guttery lonen because of the poor drainage that blighted the area. Newspaper reports of that time frequently speak of flooding afflicting Castlewellan and Dundrum Roads.

7 *Flosc Loinneach*, meaning 'joyful discharge': The *raison d'être* for the siting of Slidderyford Dolmen is the winter solstice sunset. Hopefully others may someday determine that the Flush Loney standing stone marks where the declining winter solstice sun can be seen touching Slieve Commedagh in such a manner as to suggest a notional solar seminal discharge. By putting a sexual interpretation on where the solstice sun sets, the 'joyful discharge' is to be seen coming, not from the stone, phallic and all as it is, but from that part of the distant Mourne landscape.

French Nook (OS 3833): This name just off the nearby Dundrum road, while still on the map, is now obsolete. Like the explanation above, the name refers to where the winter solstice sun sets onto the mountains (most likely the top of Donard) and is a telescoped mnemonic of the Irish *Frionnsa na n-Uaigha*, 'fringe of the graves'.

8 Praeger's description of Slidderyford mentioning two shale orthostats and one granite is from page 161 of the *Official Guide to County Down and the Mourne Mountains*, McCaw, Stevenson & Orr, Belfast, 1900 (2nd edition); in the 1924 edition it would be page 140. Of particular interest also is his mention of a substantial but sadly closed souterrain which would have great potential as a tourist attraction like Binders Cove at Finnis. 'It lies 90 yards south of the cromleac, and is about 60 feet long, 4 feet wide, and 6 feet high, enlarging towards the west end, and having a square recess near that extremity.'

9 One man who was present at Slidderyford dolmen on the summer solstice of 1912 was a W. Murphy; he carved his name on the inside of the shale orthostat. Hopefully the days of such selfish and insensitive defacement are long gone. However it would seem that the idea of the dolmen and sun at solstice being connected was exercising minds over a century ago.

10 Legananny: Fosterage was one of the leading features of Irish social life, which prevailed from the remotest period and survived, though in a modified form, even so late as the seventeenth or eighteenth century. It was practised by persons of all classes, but more especially by those in the higher ranks. The most usual type of fosterage was this:- A man sent his child to be reared and educated in the home and with the family of another member of the tribe, who then became foster-father, and his children the foster-brothers and foster-sisters of the child. While young persons were generally fostered in this manner, in families, some were put in care of distinguished ecclesiastics; many of the Irish saints were fostered in this way, whose early training in a great measure determined their future life. St Columcille was fostered and educated in childhood by a holy priest named Cruithnecan. (See *A Social History of Ancient Ireland*, Vol 2, page 14, by P.W. Joyce, Longmans, Green & Co, London, 1903.)

Other explanations for the name of Legananny are that it is derived from *Liagán Áine*, 'Áine's standing stone', Áine being an Irish goddess (Place-names of Northern Ireland). Some have favoured the proposal made by John O'Donovan that the name came from *Lag an Eanaigh*, 'Hollow of the bog'. (See the centenary book *Leitrim Fontenoys, 1888-1988*, page 4, 'A rugged land', Printed by W.& S. Magowan, Newry, 1988).

11 Visit www.ni-environment.gov.uk to check the monuments of Northern Ireland on the website of NIEA, Sites and Monument Record. The database has information on approximately 15,000 sites.

12 Not ever wishing to stay so late on the mountains as to be caught in the dark, no sightings of sunset from the dolmen locations have been attempted. I record the thought (guess, shrewd assessment, flight of fancy, suspicion, whatever....), that the locations of these monuments are linked with the sun. Both dolmens would seem to be directed towards summer solstice sunset. May others enjoy the discovery that the stones look beyond themselves to a fertility event on the horizon.

CHAPTER 8
# The Bloody Bridge Valley and the Spear of Abundance

1. The story of the discovery of the souterrain in James Spiers field is told and illustrated on p.40, *Where Donard Guards,* Nicholas Russell, Ballaghbeg Books, 2007. When pointing out the location to the author, James still recalled the large stones that formed the sides of the narrow passage. 'We left the cave open for about a fortnight so that the neighbours could see it', he said, 'then I put the stone back over the hole. I had to sow the barley.' He also remembered two other souterrains in the townland and a third, with a wave of his hand, 'on over a bit'. There was no realisation then of a possible linkage with winter solstice setting on Slieve Meelmore.
2. Bryansford was described and illustrated on p.63-64, *Where Donard Guards,* Nicholas Russell, 2007. It is realised now that the name had its source in Irish and not from an English understanding of a ford over a stream or river, ostensibly created by one Brian McHugh McAholly Magennis.
3. *Dun dá leithe glaise*: Jocelin, the Cistercian monk of Furnes had his own version of how the name came about. Writing in the twelfth century in his 'Life and Acts of Saint Patrick' Jocelin fancifully attributed the name to the freeing of the hostages of Dichu by an angel.
'...the angel again appeared and freed them from their prison-house, and from the power of their enemies. And from the place wherein they were confined he bore them through the air, as was formerly the Prophet Isaiah; and he left one of them in a place in Down, where is now erected the church of Saint Patrick, and the other on a neighbouring hill, surrounded by a marsh of the sea; and he broke asunder the chains wherewith they were bound: and each place is even to this day, from the broken chains, called *Dun-daleathglas*.'
This version, connecting the 'two halves' mentioned in the Irish with the two ancient forts, Cathedral Hill and the Mound of Down, in the absence of any other explanation, had widespread acceptance for a long time. See page 53 of *Life and Acts of Saint Patrick*, edited by Edmund Swift, Hibernia Press, Dublin, 1809.
4. Hares Castle: Prof Estyn Evans featured an engraving that imagined the Hares Castle as a crouched hare; see figure 25 on page 52 of chapter Drumlins and Eskers in *Mourne Country*, Dundalgan Press, Dundalk, 1951. The image is pleasing but nonetheless incorrect for the names of Mourne derive from Irish rather than English.
5. Pierce's Castle: See page 147 of *Place-Names of Northern Ireland, Vol 3, The Mournes.*
6. Solstice at Pierce's Castle & under Tornamrock: The tiniest glimpse of sun seen through the clouds while waiting beside the megalith in the river bed, has made me wonder if the slight wobble in the earth's axis now shows the sun sliding across the top of Pierce's Castle? Such observations I must leave to others. Long before the approximate 10.50am transit at Pierce's Castle, the sun appears over Eagle mountain. It seems the ancients quarried the top of Tornamrock to bring down numerous large stones to mark where the sun appears from Eagle's summit at winter solstice. Chief among these boulders is a very large 'mirror' stone, the sloped flat surface of which faces towards Eagle. Further down the valley and just where the track takes its first rising dog-leg turn, look for the large boulder on the lower slope of Rocky mountain. It is believed to mark where the winter solstice sun will finally set into a notch on the distant Carlingford mountains as seen down along the Kilbroney river valley.
7. Annesley Copy-Letter Book: The letter extract is from an old copy-letter book for the Annesley estate for the years 1890-1894, which was rescued from a rubbish heap in the Annesley Memorial Hall (the former rent office) by Eamon McMullan when the property was bought by the Glee Singers. These letters were later digitally transcribed and are in the author's possession. They provide many very interesting tales of the growth of Newcastle at the end of the 19th century, including how the present golf course of Royal County Down was very nearly sold to the War Department as a firing range and how the deal to build the Slieve Donard Hotel was almost cancelled because Annesley wouldn't guarantee a water supply.
8. Kilnagreinan: See *Penal-Day Traditions in Mourne,* in the 1938 edition of the *Journal of the Down & Connor Historical Society.* The site of the old church is believed to be that marked at J273105 with an asterisk as 'mound'. Cranfield Golf Course is long gone but the remains of

the graveyard can still be detected as a slightly raised area in a field to the left and almost at the end of the Cranfield Road, past the entrance to the Cranfield House Hotel, and just before the entrance to the present caravan site. If using Google maps, note the shadow of a raised rectangular area in the field opposite the caravan site. How long the church building continued to function it is now impossible to say. The Abbey of Newry was dissolved shortly after the Reformation and its lands were granted to Nicholas Bagenal, ancestor of the Kilmorey family. The graveyard, however, would appear to have remained in use long after the church as it is listed in a report dated 1881 as one of a number of Mourne graveyards vested in the Commissioners of Church Temporalities in Ireland (HC 1881 vol XXVlll).

Tom Cunningham of Belfast drew attention to Fr Farry's article in a letter to the Mourne Observer on 31st March 2004. Fortunately for us all, Tom Cunningham later expanded on his letter and fullest details can now be found in an excellent illustrated article entitled *Kilnagreinan: A Forgotten Mourne Church*, which appeared in the Journal of the Mourne Studies Group *12 Miles of Mourne*, pages 14-22, of vol 9, 2010. The link to the Cistercian Abbey of Newry was also comprehensively examined. In the future it may perhaps be verified that Kilnagreinan was built where it was to claim the site from paganism, as would be the case, if for instance, the winter solstice sun was seen to set on top of one of the Carlingford Hills.

9   The events of 1641/42 at the Bloody Bridge were extensively examined by Thomas Fitzpatrick in his book, *The Bloody Bridge and other papers relating to the Insurrection of 1641 (Sir Phelim O'Neill's Rebellion)*, printed by Sealy, Bryers and Walker, London, 1903. The details of the killings of the prisoners and a different explanation of how the Bloody Bridge earned its name were mentioned in *Where Donard Guards*, pages 64-70, Ballaghbeg Books, 2007. The question was further looked at in *Slieve Donard's Domain*, page 165, Ballaghbeg Books, 2011. See following note.

10  The facts of the tragic horserace can be found in an article *Round Rostrevor* in the Down Recorder, 22nd August 1874. After years of work by Trinity College Dublin it is now fortunately possible to view free on-line at 1641.tcd.ie the digitised depositions of the five thousand who gave evidence before the commissioners of enquiry. Have a look, for instance, at the deposition of Thomas Trevor, Co Down, taken on 12th May 1653, reference MS 837 folio 086r-087v.

11  Walter Harris in *The Antient and Present State of the County of Down*, Dublin, 1774, mistakenly refers on page 143 in his work to the Bloody Bridge River as the 'Midpace River - which falls almost perpendicular from the mountains'. Harris's account of how the English prisoners were 'most barbarously cut, slashed, hacked and at length hanged' at a wood at Ballaghanery is to be found on page 93 of the same work.

12  Ancient Stories: Especially 'Carlingford Volcano' in Michael George Crawford's *Legendary Stories of the Carlingford Lough District*, printed by the Frontier Sentinel, Newry, 1913.

13  *Aodh*: The word means 'fire' in Irish. It is frequently used as a man's name. Hugh is often its English equivalent.

14  Muntereddy: No interpretation for this has been found but given that the Roden estate included a fair part of the northern foothills of Mourne, from Tullybrannigan to Clanawhillan and also embraced the commonage of mountain pasture, may I suggest *Muin Tír Éidigh*, the 'accursed upper back region'. *Éidigh* in Irish is an adjective meaning 'ugly, detestable, hateful, horrible, accursed'. The land would have been deemed 'accursed', not because it was poor mountain land but because, being under the shadow of the higher mountains, it did not receive the early winter solstice light. *Muin* has a number of different meanings but because of the high topography we have preferred *Muin* with the sense of 'the neck and shoulders, the upper back, the neck, the back of the neck', meaning of course the upper region of foothills.

The grant to Brian Magennis, itemising the seven and a half townlands he received, is found in the calendar of the Patent Rolls of the Chancery of Ireland, Pat 8 James 1, page 193. Also in February 1611, Ever MacPhelimy Magennis was granted eleven townlands of Owtertirry (*Uachtar Tíre* – 'the upper part of land') called Ballycastlewellan.

15  Raven Rocks: Lying between the Bloody Bridge and Glen Fofanny rivers, this is marked on the OS map below Crossone at J3727. The anomaly of the name is obvious to anyone who

# NOTES

knows the terrain or cares to look again at the area between the two rivers. There are no large rocks suitable for nesting, no trees, no eminences and certainly no cliffs. The name is a mnemonic from the Irish *Ruibhne Ruic* meaning 'lance of the hollow'. Stay on the north side of the bloody Bridge and, instead of crossing the river, follow the old granite trail that used to serve Crossone. The hollow is a large saucer shaped depression on the hillside below Crossone and as such offered a slight bit of shelter. If the spear stone was ever upright, as the shaped bottom of the stone suggests it would have been, it has now unfortunately been tossed down and damaged. At some stage granite men decided to split the stone spear, but did it so as to separate the stone neatly into two almost equal halves that are now a few feet apart; they now appear as two spears, their sharp points facing towards the rounded, breast like summit, of Crossone. A low pile of stones placed at the top end between the halves would also suggest that the intervening 150cm space had been used as a simple shelter. If you ever find this particular lance you will discover that it was originally a particularly fine megalith on which someone probably worked for hundreds of hours, rubbing and grinding the granite down to achieve a sharp point. It is a special tactile experience to feel the outside tip of the original stone as it was before it was split. Run your fingers over the top 30cm or so of the former granite lance. Your hand will feel that the surface, while not completely smooth, is still amazingly good. A fine silky, perfectly polished finish was probably never intended as much as a symbolic sharpness. To appreciate the effort of someone grinding the side tips of the lance, just move your hand further down the side of the stone to feel the rough and surprising difference. The breaking of this stone was indeed a tragedy but at least the parts are still there.

16   Ballaghanery townland information is from *Topographical Index; Census of population of Northern Ireland, 1926.* HMSO, reprint of 1947.
The very comprehensive listing of early names for Ballaghanery is to be found on page 20-21 of *Place-Names of Northern Ireland, vol 3, The Mournes,* Queen's university, 1993. When writing in 2007 about Ballaghanery, on page 22 of *Where Donard Guards,* an explanation was assumed based on the 1549 letter of Nicholas Bagnal of Newry who urged the Lord Deputy Bellingham 'to induce Magenis to cut the great pass called Ballagh Enary'. The mistaken inference was to suggest that the pass 'Enary' might possibly have been so called after King Henry Vlll. The significance of the Irish *Bealach an irille,* meaning 'the pass of the spike' was not then understood.

17   Letter of John O'Donovan from Castlewellan on 23rd April 1834 the day he climbed Slieve Donard. 'Up this steep and rocky passage I skipped from stone to stone with the agility of a goat, but was obliged to wait for my guide whom age had rendered less vigorous.' O'Donovan was then aged 28 years and had the energy of youth but I have a very special admiration for a man who after such a strenuous day and after he had returned to his quarters at Castlewellan then sat down to write for five hours about his experiences. [He recorded the time he started and finished his letter] Such dedication to his mission still deserves our respect and we have all been immensely enriched because of his commitment.

18   The Irish word *Maidhm* (pronounced like 'mime') is both male and female. The various meanings given in Dinneen's dictionary (page 697) are; act of bursting, etc.; a burst, rupture, eruptions or breach, a cataclysm, a breaking surge, a retreating wave, a swell; an explosion or crash; a deep hole caused by a burst, or made by a stream, a mountain pass; a battle, a rout or defeat; a defeated army; severe injury; a large amount. The list is surprising extensive but because of the topography we elected to use the translation of 'a mountain pass'.
There is yet another meaning not explicitly mentioned by Fr Dinneen, who was a Jesuit, but a meaning that can be most clearly inferred from his range of options, namely the breach, rupture or deep hole that is the female vagina. The unique geography of the valley sees the winter solstice sunrise 'pierce' the very middle of it. The sun at dawn 'penetrates' the valley where the water flows out from the bog at the top thus most symbolically fertilising mother earth on the very day of the sun's new birth.

19   The full deliberations about the meaning of Shannagh-More, map reference J3827, are given on page 151 of *Place-Names of Northern Ireland, vol 3,* The Mournes. Lough Shannagh, map reference J2926, however, based on a local interpretation, is translated on page 182 of the

537

PREHISTORIC MOURNE: INSPIRATION FOR NEWGRANGE

same work as 'lake of the foxes'. Slieve Loughshannagh, map reference J2927, has received the translation given to the adjacent lake to become 'mountain of the lake of the foxes'. This is as given on page 157 of the same work.

20   Alternative to Slieve Loughshannagh: Place-names project have done us a great service by collecting and thus preserving another name for Slieve Loughshannagh, namely Slievahilly. It is well removed from Cock mountain to which it has been referred; the Irish collected for Cock mountain in 1834 being *Sliabh a choilligh*. It is tentatively proposed here that not only is Slievahilly independent of Cock mountain in its own right, but that it is a slightly corrupted version of *Sliabh a h-Áil*, 'mountain of pleasure'. The 'pleasure' is related to the phallic shadow of Doan mountain being cast onto it at dawn of winter solstice.

21   Words will always be insufficient to acknowledge the labours of the granite men climbing up to Carr's face quarry every day to toil at back breaking work. The effort of the people of Annalong, like councillor David McCauley, to preserve the memory of the granite men throughout Mourne is far-sighted and deserves our fullest recognition. It was a delight to record the following remarks in *Slieve Donard's Domain* on page 159:

'David passionately believes that we should give deeper appreciation to the skills our forefathers achieved extracting, cutting, moving, dressing and building with this stone. I note with pleasure that a project is presently underway to record and photograph all the granite workings in the Mournes. It is a precious heritage and a legacy that holds a rich potential for tourism. The skills and memories are still there even if the quarries are closing. Granite is a beautiful stone and the memory of those who worked it and their monumental efforts deserve to be cherished for future generations.'

22   Explanation for Carr's Face found on p128 of *Place-Names of Northern Ireland, Vol 3, The Mournes*, published by the Institute of Irish Studies in 1993.

23   Carr's Face: The word *Cairre* is the genitive of *Carr* the Irish for 'spear'; *Fás* in Irish means 'the act of growing, or becoming' and is perhaps better known as the name of Ireland's former National Training and Employment Authority.

24   We cannot be sure to what extent, if any, the quarrying on Carr's Face may have resulted in possible alterations to the original path of the Spear of Abundance. Despite the removal of a vast amount of granite, the effect on the mountain's shadow is surely most minimal.

CHAPTER 9

# Chimney Rock

1   Choosing a burial site: In March 1858 when workmen, employed by the Marquis of Downshire, were making an embankment from Keel Point, near Dundrum to Murlough, they found a stone coffin and nine urns all filled with charred human bones. All but one of the urns was destroyed by the workmen. I have wondered if there was anything special about selecting this place as a burial site? May others later verify that it is from Keel Point that the winter solstice sun can be seen setting on top of Slieve Commedagh, making this indeed an excellent fertility location and in the eyes of the ancients a very worthy place to bury their dead. For notification of the discovery of the urns see the *Down Recorder*, 13th March 1858; also p. 11-12, *The Early Settlers,* in the 2007 publication *Where Donard Guards*, Ballaghbeg Books, printed by Bairds.

2   Atlantis: The first appearance in literature of the story of Atlantis is in Plato's writing of *Timaeus and Critias*. Much of the writing might be seen as the result of Plato's fertile imagination and as the first example of science fiction. The destruction of Atlantis may be a reference to the widespread devastation of northern Europe wrought by the three Storegga underwater landslides off the Norwegian coast that involved the collapse of an estimated 290 kilometres of coastal shelf around 6225–6170 BC.

The Irish of *At Lán Thíos* is as follows: *At,* means '**a swelling**'; *Lán,* an adjective, means '**full**, complete, satisfied, perfect'; *Thíos,* means 'down, beneath, beyond, **in the north** (ie. from a Mediterranean perspective)'.

NOTES

The story of Atlantis has inspired a vast library of works, but our focus is Prehistoric Mourne. We are content to let the phallic profile of Chimney Rock, the multitude of enormous megaliths of Mourne which necessitated a highly organised society, the sheer number of arranged stones/burials on the summit of Chimney Rock, the explanation of the name of Atlantis from the Irish, the reality of the Storegga slides and the propensity for human nature to tell a good story about gigantic sex, to collectively offer a reasonable explanation for one of mankind's longest standing mysteries.

3   Landmarks: page 152, in the chapter *Luggers and Long Lines,* of *Mourne Country,* by Professor E. Estyn Evans, Dundalgan Press, Dundalk, 1951. Also, the professor has put an English plural interpretation on what is essentially a singular Irish word. As *h-Oiris Méin* means 'landmark of pleasure' is could feasibly be applied to the whole mountain as Professor Evans has done but for the sake of a precise point helpful to fishermen out on Dundrum Bay I have interpreted 'Horsemen' as applicable to one tor, the most westerly one. Applying the name 'Horsemen' to all five mini summits of Chimney Rock would seem to defeat the navigational necessity of obtaining precise bearings while out at sea. But then I'm not a seaman. The interpretation of 'landmark' can remain open.

4   Shipwrecks: For the sinking of the *Tikey* and *Hardwicke* see p.198 of *Where Donard Guards*. The chapter on Dundrum Bay gives an extensive list of the shipping lost in what was described as 'one of the most dangerous bays for shipping in Ireland'.

5   Down Coastguard's Reminiscence: See *Down Recorder,* 6th May 1899. Eight men were rescued from the stricken vessel. The coastguard never forgot that rescue. It wasn't that the storm was so bad, for it really was; he remembered because one of those he rescued was his own brother.

6   Hellyhunter Rock: See *Trawling from Steam Vessels off Parts of the East Coast of Ireland,* forbidding beam trawling within three miles of Hellyhunter Rock; *Down Recorder,* 25th August 1900. Nearby is another reef marked with a buoy and called *New England*. This reef was also a great danger and inconvenience to fishermen. The name comes from the Irish *Neac Ainleanamhna* meaning 'Nail of Persecution'.

7   Derivation of Tyrella: The Irish *Rail* (genitive *Ralach*), (f.), normally means an oak tree but it also has a figurative sense of 'a huge person'. It is quite similar to the adjective used earlier in the translation of 'General', *'Gein Rálach'* meaning 'gigantic act of begetting'. The adjective *Rálach* (genitive *Rálaighe*) carries an accent and means 'gigantic, monstrous', or sometimes 'anything large'.

8   Commemorative Plaque to B-26 Marauder: Details of the crash were first given in Twelve Miles of Mourne by Ernie Cromie, a member of the Ulster Aviation Society, and with his permission, repeated with an illustration on pages 226-7 of *Slieve Donard's Domain*.

9   Charles Vallancey: See Webb's *Compendium of Irish Biography* comprising sketches of Distinguished Irishmen and of Eminent Persons connected with Ireland by Office or by their Writings. Dublin, 1878.

10  Art at Newgrange: page 43 of George Coffey's *Newgrange and other incised tumuli in Ireland*.

CHAPTER 10
# Upper and Lower Cove

1   Cove: Place-names project sums up the received understanding. 'Evans believes that the first element of this name (Cove Mountain) is a corruption of the word 'cave' and the form from Williamson's map (of 1810), if accurate, would certainly support this'.
There are a number of words in Irish that could be used for the word 'cave' depending on the circumstances, namely, *Uaimh, Cuas, Uain, Scailp, Fochla, Prochlais or Pluais*. None of these, however, sound like 'cove'.

2   The Cave of Lower Cove: page 123 of Walter Harris's *The Ancient and Present State of the County of Down,* Dublin, 1744; reprinted by Arthur Davidson, Spa, in 1977. It is on the same page that Harris makes the sorry slip of saying 'Snavan, in Irish, signifies to creep'. Slieve

Snavan is from the Irish *Snab Bán* 'the white fragment'. The Irish for 'creeping, or crawling' is *Snáigheach*.
3   Buckie: See page 148 of Professor Evan's *Mourne Country*. Buckie was the name given to one of the middle tors of Slieve Bignian because of its resemblance to a type of lugger which carried a tall standing lug with staysail and jib. The name of the boat may have been derived from a sexual interpretation put on the tall standing lug, namely *Biach Āil*, 'Penis of pleasure'. As such the name would have also been considered suitable for one of Slieve Bignian's priapic tors. Another lugger name, Dandy Smack, may have come from the Irish appreciation of its handling capability namely *Dáin Déithe Smacht*, 'Control of a gift of wind'.
4   Magennis: pages 157-158 of Edward MacLysaght's *Irish Families, their Names, Arms and Origins*, Hodges Figgis & Co., Dublin, 1957.
5   O'Neill on the Red Hand: The O'Neill of Lisbon was rebutting an article by Rev Canon Ffrench, M.R.I.A., which had been written under the heading of 'The arms of Ireland and Celtic tribal heraldry'. O'Neill's reply was *The Heraldic Emblem of Ireland* and it appeared in the November 1908 edition (Vol 14, No 4) of The Ulster Journal of Archaeology. It was appropriate that O'Neill's reply should feature in this journal as, ever since the first volume of the first series began in 1853, it had featured the Red Hand on the cover with the words *Laimh Dhearg Eirinn*. The second series which began in 1895 had from the outset continued the use of the Red Hand and, better still, had employed the signet of the O'Neill family on the covers.

CHAPTER 11
# Newgrange and Mourne

1   Page 199 of *The Boyne and the Blackwater* by Sir William Wilde, published in 1849.
2   Pages 16-18 of *Newgrange*, Thames and Hudson, London, 1964. Professor Ó Ríordáin died in 1957 before the book was published. Fortunately had co-written two thirds of this important work with his friend Dr Glyn Daniel before his untimely death.
3   *Brugh* or *Brú*: See page 45, *Newgrange in early Irish Literature*, in Prof M.J. O'Kelly's *Newgrange*, Thames and Hudson, 1982.
4   Lecale a womb? In referring to *Brú na Bóinne* as a womb, I have felt that the 'womb men', the *Fir Bolg*, could likewise have considered the location of the stone circle at Ballynoe townland, to have been the appropriate womb centre of Lecale, then virtually an island and mostly surrounded by water or swampy marsh. Others, making observations of where the sun sets on the Mournes at winter solstice, may probably later confirm that this location was selected for its fertility associations.
5   *Ibid*: page 46.
6   Levelling of Kerbstones: See page 70, chapter 5 on *'The Cairn Slip'*, and page 109 *The Kerb*, of M.J. O'Kelly's *Newgrange*. Also, page 8 of *Newgrange* by Geraldine and Matthew Stout, CUP, 2008, where 'the kerbstones at Newgrange were raised above or lowered below the old ground surface to keep a horizontal alignment'.
7   Kerbstones: It may be worth recording the idea, which unfortunately cannot be expanded here, that besides representing a notional horizon for the rising solstice sun, the placement of the kerbstones and possibly their decoration, hidden or otherwise, may be sympathetically related to a notional great ring around the inner Mournes that has the Bloody Bridge valley as its centre. K1 equates with *Carr na Bláthaighe* at the Bloody Bridge and extends through the tomb to match with Slieve Bearnagh on K52. I have often imagined for instance, K12 the longest kerbstone around the mound, as being notionally equivalent to Slieve Bignian. The creation of a boar's head in the middle of K12 also happens to strategically match the location of the largest megalith in Mourne which also has a boar's head on it. This is illustrated in conjunction with K67 in the chapter on Slieve Bignian.

NOTES

8   Criticism of O'Kelly's reconstruction: It seems O'Kelly made only the gentlest of replies to critics although their words must have hurt him deeply. On page 115 of *Newgrange*, he wrote: 'Visitors have said to us that it is now 'too modern looking' and that they preferred it when it was 'so romantic'. This is to forget that Newgrange must have been 'modern looking' also to the Boyne valley people of about 2500bc when it was first built.'
9   Ó Ríordáin's mistake about Newgrange: See page 19 of Ó Ríordáin & Glyn Daniel's *Newgrange*.
10  Leaving Newgrange a ruin? See page 5 of *Newgrange* by Geraldine and Matthew Stout, CUP, 2008. Although the author is a long standing member of the Ulster Archaeological Society, the views expressed about restoration are personal.
11  Facing with quartz: If the ancients originally placed the quartz on the front of the mound in a great semi-circle suggestive of a half risen sun, it would account for the quartz being thickest at the entrance where the sun would be 'biggest' and why the quartz tapers away on either side.
12  A planned construction: pages 118-121 of *Newgrange*, by M.J. O'Kelly, 1982.
13  K1 ornamentation: See Claire O'Kelly's chapter *Corpus of Newgrange Art*, pages 146-149, of *Newgrange, archaeology, art and legend*, 1982, Thames & Hudson, London.
14  Page 18, Chapter 2 *The Entrance*; *Newgrange* by Geraldine Stout & Matthew Stout, Cork University Press, 2008
15  Derinilla of the Four Paps: page 90, *The Festival of Lughnasa*, by Máire MacNeill, Oxford University Press, 1962.
16  Reaching Donard's Platform: Do not be tempted to take a 'direct route' from the Bloody Bridge quarry up to the platform as it would be much more strenuous climbing through the heather. Following a sheep trail over from the Mourne wall is definitely much easier.
17  Two Devil's Coachroads: See under Devil's Coachroad on page 216, Appendix 3, *Mourne Country*,1951.
18  Annalong: Page 54 of *Place-Names of Northern Ireland, Vol 3, The Mournes*, QUB., 1993.
19  Slieve Lamagan fissures: There is no doubt that the middle fissure received attention from the ancients who would have regarded it as a vaginal opening. You don't have to squeeze in too far before you come to a phallic spear stone about waist height jammed across the opening and pointing outwards. This is probably as far as the winter solstice sun could enter this particular crack. Manoeuvring such a heavy bit of granite and the stone that supports it in such a very confined space certainly called for skill and great strength.

CHAPTER 12
# Slieve Bearnagh

1   Bearnagh tors: page 15 of *Mourne Country*, chapter on 'The Mountains'.
2   Lecarry Loanin': The name is found in the opening sentence of Rowley's tale, *The Choosers of the Slain*, on page 217 of his 1937 work *Tales of Mourne*. The name is directly from the Irish *Leacraighe*, 'abounding in flags'.
3   'Pot-holes': Until now only natural causes have been considered for the existence of 'pot-holes' on the summits of various mountains. Their presence was referred to by professor Evans but in the context of whether the tors had been covered with ice or not. The comments of professor Evans are found on pages 49/52, *Drumlins and Eskers, Mourne Country*, 1951, Dundalk.
   'The great crags on top of Bearnagh have every appearance of having been shaped by ice, however much frost action has shattered them. In several instances the tors have large circular pot-holes such as are usually associated with the work of running water, but this cannot be used to prove that ice must have risen above them since similar pot-holes are a feature of granite tors in areas such as Cornwall which were unglaciated.'

PREHISTORIC MOURNE: INSPIRATION FOR NEWGRANGE

4   'The Back Ditch': See page 236 of *Slieve Donard's Domain,* Nicholas Russell, Ballaghbeg Books, 2011. The name 'Back Ditch' is a mnemonic of the Irish *Biach Duithir* and would have been a sexual curse on the hard, backbreaking work of building the wall. It would translate as the 'morning f***'.
5   Perhaps it will be later shown that the Spear Tip megalith doubles as an indicator of where the summer solstice sun disappears behind the north tor?

CHAPTER 13
## Slieve Bignian and vicinity

1   Height of Bignian at 747 metres. To continue the analogy with jumbo jets, one might also mention Slieve Commedagh which is 767 metres.
2   The name of 'Silent Valley' was used in paper reports on the excursion from Belfast to the valley in June 1895 when the chairman of the Water Commissioners brought down a large party including the Lord Mayor of Belfast.
3   Explaining 'Silent Valley': page 86, *In Search of Water being a History of the Belfast Water Supply,* by Jack Loudan, published on the occasion of the centenary of the Belfast City and District Water Commissioners, 1840-1940, Wm Mullan & Son, Belfast. This explanation was picked up and repeated by W.H. Carson on p.14, 'The Silent Valley before the Dam', in *The Dam Builders, the Story of the men who built the Silent Valley Reservoir,* Mourne Observer Press, 1981.
4   In March 1893 the Grand Jury at Downpatrick were cautioned by the County Surveyor, P.C. Cowan about the Belfast Water Supply Bill; '…and as the works include a tramway for use during construction, that may seriously affect the county interests, I would suggest that this Bill should receive your careful consideration.' Later, in 1905, P.C. Cowan would carry out the inquiry into the Castlewellan gravitational water scheme.
5   Irish Emigration Statistics: An appreciation of the importance of the proposed dam to the local economy might be better understood by reflecting on emigration statistics. In 1896 the number of emigrants who left Irish ports was 39,226; of these 7,434 were from Ulster. Records about emigration from Ireland only started after the famine from May 1851. From that date to December 31st 1896, the total who left was 3,690,123; this broke down to 1,934,826 males and 1,755,297 females. See the report of the Registrar-General in the *Down Recorder,* 20th March 1897.
   The great hope for jobs would later be tempered when the Belfast Water Commissioners started to enforce their ownership of the 9,000 acres of Mourne. The quarries at Hares Castle and Percy Bysshe bluff had to stop working and the land was no longer let for sheep rearing. Many tenants were also inconvenienced at the loss of their tubary rights; all this in spite of strenuous objections in parliament by Jeremiah MacVeagh, MP for South Down.
6   Slievenagore: this is treated on page 167 of *Place-Names of Northern Ireland, Vol 3, The Mournes,* by Mícheál B. Ó Mainnín, Institute of Irish Studies, QUB, printed by Bairds, 1993.
7   Miners Hole: page 146, *Place-Names of Northern Ireland, Vol 3, The Mournes.*
8   Townland of Ballyveagh: page 28, *Place-Names of Northern Ireland, Vol 3, The Mournes.* The form of 'Baile Riach' was also recorded. This name may have derived from the overt sexual appearance of the mountains and the notion that the 'breasts' were being flaunted. The name *Baile Reabhrach* means 'wanton townland'.
9   Maid of the Sweet Brown Knowe: Location identified by Charles Cunningham on p.45 of Vol 7, *Twelve Miles of Mourne,* 1996 Journal of the Mourne Local Studies Group.
   Head Road: Mentioned in the location description for the Brown Knowe; this high road loops round the bottom of the mountains from the Quarter Road to the Moyad Road. It gets its name from the aspirated Irish *h-Íodh,* where the word *Íodh* means 'a bracelet, a ring, a collar'.
10  Slipes: Some Mourne slipes were illustrated by professor Evans on p.118 of *Mourne Country.*
11  Little chisels tinkling tirelessly: Lines from the poem *Ireland,* by W.R. Rodgers in his collection *Awake! And other poems.* Rev Rodgers gathered his poems and sent them to press

# NOTES

in London in 1940. The first printing was entirely destroyed by enemy action but fortunately for us he persevered, the work was reset and first published in July 1941 by Martin Secker & Warburg, Essex Street, London.

12 Lost names: Hopefully some of the old fishermen's' names for landscape features as mentioned on page 324 will be later identified. They are likely mnemonics of the Irish and this is the medium by which they should first be considered for interpretation.

13 Ardmally: The name is treated under the Ardley River, p.174/5, *Place-Names of Northern Ireland, Vol 3, The Mournes*.

14 Douglas Crag summer solstice: When camped on Douglas Crag to witness the early morning sunrise, it was with the expectation that the sun would be seen rising between Slieve Donard and Slieve Commedagh. Computer graphics that purported to show where the sun would rise had marked the Commedagh/Donard col as the rising place. The disappointment at not being able to photograph the sunrise was more than compensated by the brief but vital corrective glimpse of where the sun really rose from Douglas Crag; it was a salutary lesson on the importance of personal observation.

15 Slieve Binnian, the name presently favoured by the ordnance survey and Place-Names project, is considered on p. 153 *Place-Names of Northern Ireland, Vol 3, The Mournes*.

16 Climbing at Bignian: See Bignian on pages 23-60 in *Rock Climbs in the Mourne Mountains* by Simon Moore, Craig Hiller and Ricky Bell, published by Mountaineering Ireland, Dublin 2010. They point out that the exposed tors have big crystals and the friction for climbing is 'unique'. I have always enjoyed the many stories that lie behind the naming of Mourne climbs and the name of the thirty metre climb 'The Penguin on Newcastle Beach' put up in 1981 on North Tor West is a little gem. This excellent route, as a guide book tells us, was 'named in dedication to a proprietor (T.S.) of the local climbing shop who mistook a damaged guillemot for a penguin and telephoned the RSPB with news of his discovery'. He received much banter from his clientele over his honest mistake.

17 The name of Lamagan: Although the name of the mountain is now spelt with an [m], the local pronunciation which is true to the Irish is 'Lavigan'. The great naturalist Robert Lloyd Praegar also drew attention to the pronunciation of Lavigan on page 227 of the 1900 edition of *Official Tourist Guide to County Down and Mourne Mountains* (unfortunately edited out of the 1924 edition). For the various names of Slievelamagan see pages 162/163 of *Place-Names of Northern Ireland, Vol 3, The Mournes*. I don't know why the ordnance survey decided to spell the name all one word, Slievelamagan.

18 Lamagan Slabs: Lamagan Slabs on the ordnance survey map is the slope facing Bignian's north tor and above the Blue Lough and gets its name from the Irish for the shadow horn. It is not to be confused with the large expanses of sloped rock a couple of hundred metres further right on the corner of the mountain overlooking Percy Bysshe hill. These later sloped rocks beloved by climbers are called 'slabs' in the English sense of the word and provide the longest routes in the Mournes, including the classic climbs of FM, Arcadia, Cherchez-La and Upper FM.

19 Easy Route to top of Bignian's North Tor East: I very nearly gave up trying to access the top of the North Tor. I followed the path until it required a rock climb. There is no need to undertake any climbing as a convenient and infinity easier route is available a bit lower down from the steep impasse by venturing to the right/seawards and up round the back of the difficult part. As for North Tor West summit, approach it on its western side and not from the steep gully in the col.

20 Summer solstice sunset: One of the 'holy grail's' for the ancients would have been the sight of summer solstice sun setting on the phallic tors of Slieve Bearnagh. The viewpoint that could witness such a fertility spectacle would have been very important. Could the north tor platform claim this further distinction?

21 Caution on the hills: The most important of footnotes but really only a reiteration of common sense. Although having no connection with Mountaineering Ireland, I can only completely concur with the caveat given in their 2010 guide book that 'hill walking, climbing and rambling are activities that can be dangerous and may result in personal injury or death. Participants should be aware of and accept these risks and be responsible for their own actions and involvement.'

Incidentally, I never made it up to the stone seat and have been curious to know whether the seat might be a logan stone, a 'rocker'. Perhaps sometime, someone will tell me.
22  *Thinkin' Long*: Page 68 of Richard Rowley's collection of poems, *City Songs and Others*, published by Maunsel & Co, Dublin & London, 1918.
23  *Ortha*: This Irish word for 'charm, curse, prayer or incantation' had so many uses in past times. Then, you had the like of *Ortha an leonta*, 'the sprain-cure', *Ortha na fiacaile*, 'the toothache charm', or *Ortha an dídin*, the protection-prayer, said while going three times round the house.

CHAPTER 14
# The coming of Christianity

1  Dolly's Brae: The shadow cast from the Annesley demesne by the Moorish Tower hill left Dolly's Brae in the shade on winter solstice morning. It earned this part of Magheramayo the Irish name *Doilbh Brí* meaning 'gloomy hill'.
2  Human sacrifice at Mourne: page 225 of *Bethu Phátraic*, from *The Tripartite Life of Patrick, with other documents relating to that Saint*. Edited by Whitley Stokes, Eyre & Spottiswoode, London, 1887. See also page 89 on The Mountain Pilgrimages in Máire MacNeill's marvellous work of scholarship, *The Festival of Lughnasa*, Dundalgan Press, Dundalk, 1962. Every snippet of information about St Donard is recorded here.
3  The waterfall of Cove: Phenomenon recorded on page 123 of Walter Harris's *The Antient and Present State of the County of Down*, Dublin, 1744. Reprinted by Arthur Davidson, Spa, 1977.
4  Near Bealachaneir Pass is a deep narrow Cave: This comment from Harris refers to Smugglers' Hole which was illustrated on page 57 in the chapter 'Smugglers on the Mountains' in *Slieve Donard's Domain*, Ballaghbeg Books, 2011.
Armour's Hole: Earliest reference, page 81 of Walter Harris's *The Antient and Present State of the County of Down*, Dublin, 1744. Reprinted by Arthur Davidson, Spa, 1977.
See also page 55 of *Place-names of Northern Ireland, Co Down, Vol 3, The Mournes* which reprints the fullest version from *Dublin Penny Journal*, 20th September, 1834. This is more comprehensive than the ordnance survey notes published by the Institute of Irish Studies; see page 47 in *Ordnance Survey Memoirs of Ireland, Vol 3, Parishes of County Down 1, 1834-6, South Down*.
A very readable version including the ballad of Edward Armer is to be found in *The Murder of Thomas Armer*, penned by Tom Porter; see pages 12-14, in *12 Miles of Mourne, Vol 8, 2000*, Journal of the Mourne Local Studies Group.
5  Council Boundary: One of the granite boundary markers for Newcastle council can still be seen at the side of the road at Srupatrick. This is one of three out of the original five markers to still survive. The present markers are at Srupatrick, on the upper Tullybrannigan Road where it crosses the river and the third one is presently buried but safe in a hedge on the Bryansford Road facing the junction with the end of the Tullybrannigan Road where it leads down to Priest's Bridge.
6  Srupatrick: *Mourne Country*, pages 99-100 in chapter 11, Raths and Saints, published by Dundalgan Press, Dundalk, 1951. The same idea of St Patrick stopping at the stream reappeared in *St. Colman's Church, Massforth, Upper Mourne; Centenary Souvenir, 1879-1979*.
7  The Ordnance Survey Letters Down, edited by Michael Herity in 2001, bears out the fraught welcome encountered by St Patrick in this part of South Down. In the letter of John O'Donovan to his superior in the ordnance survey [letter dated 24th April 1834 from Downpatrick] O'Donovan recorded the tradition of how Donnart 'at this time a fierce and warlike chief', on missing his bull, 'swore by the wind, sun and the moon, that he would banish Patrick and his clergy out of his territory. With that...he assembles his chosen troops and coming to where Patrick, his family and adherents were, accuses the saint of having sent his servant to steal his bull....' The perilous episode that could have resulted in

bloodshed ended with Donard being converted after the miraculous restoration of the bull. The tradition was further recorded that 'the warlike Donnart became a meek and humble disciple and after having become acquainted with the mild spirit of the Gospel, and seen the strict morality and self-refusal recommended in the book of life, he was induced to resign his chieftainship, abandon his fortified residence, give up the savage amusements of hunting the elk and other timid animals of the plain, and betake himself to fasting and praying on the highest apex of that wild and desolate range of mountains which formed the Southern boundary of his territory.' After lighting the first Easter fire at Slane and facing the wrath of the high king we know that St Patrick certainly did not lack for courage. Perhaps, however, after this dangerous encounter with the warlike Donnart and having the safety of his adherents in mind, the saint may have prudently elected not to proceed any further south beyond Donard's territory. The story of the conversion of St Donard is covered in more depth in the chapter 'Earlier names of Slieve Donard' on pages 116-117 of *Slieve Donard's Domain*, Ballaghbeg Books, 2011.

8   Kindly Commedagh and also Meadow Mountain: See Lewis Moore's article *The Ancient Kingdom of Mourne* in Yorkshire Ramblers' Club Journal, Volume 1, No 3, pp 155-172, Leeds, 1901.
Kindly Mourne: E.Estyn Evans, page 4 of *Hills and the Sea* in *Mourne Country*, Dundalgan Press, Dundalk, 1951.

9   Helpful farmers: O'Donovan's letter of 24th April 1834 from Downpatrick to Thomas A. Larcom, Mountjoy Barracks, Dublin.

10  Of reptiles and those which are not found in the island: Chapter 23 of *The Historical Works of Giraldus Cambrensis*, edited by Thomas Wright, published by H.G. Bohn, London, 1863.

11  Three Gold Teeth: *Annals of the Kingdom of Ireland* by the Four Masters: translation and publication by John O'Donovan in 1851; reproduced by Edmund Burke, Dublin 1990. The same story is referred to by Giraldus Cambrensis in his work *The Topography of Ireland*, distinction 2, chapter 10, 'Of a fish which had three golden teeth'; referring to this wonderful fish, he said that it was cast ashore at Carlenfordia, now Carlingford, which is opposite the Mourne mountains; but Giraldus, who only knew the whereabouts, marks the place by the nearest English castle. The notice of the casting of this whale with the three golden teeth is given in Irish in the Annals of Ulster at the year 752, in nearly the same words as used by the Four Masters; and in the Annals of Clonmacnoise at 740.
The normal spelling for tooth in Irish is *Fiacal* (genitive *Fiacaile*) (f.) with the meaning 'a tooth, tooth of a comb or other denticulate object; edge or verge; a tooth-like crag.' The spelling of *Fiacla* is retained as found.

12  Eleven Churches around Dundrum Bay: the original list included the church of Kilbride (Bright). It was raised in 1830 and nothing remains of it. Although Kilbride has been omitted, I included instead the site of Killyglinnie.

13  Church Sites: pp. 10-11, 'Kilkeel or Upper Mourne', *Diocese of Down & Connor, Vol 1*, by Rev James O'Laverty, Duffy & Son, Dublin, 1878.
In the absence of any observations one can only speculate about old Kilkeel chapel being on a former site of pagan interest. Perhaps later another may verify whether the name of Kilkeel might come from the Irish *Cill Caoile* with the meaning 'church of the loins'. Could it be a possible reference to the winter solstice sun setting into a narrow gap or perhaps the pointed top of an eminence on the Cooley mountains? The Irish *Caoil* (genitive *Caoile*) (f.), has the meaning of 'loins; the waist'.

14  *At the Ballagh:* Richard Rowley's poem of the shepherd's death bed tale is found on pages 51-59, in *The Old Gods and other poems*, printed by Gerald Duckworth, London, 1925.

15  From 'The Shanachie', in Richard Rowley's *The Piper of Mourne*, McCord, Belfast, 1944.

16  Friar Burns: page 40, *Parish of Kilcoo*, in O'Laverty's *Diocese of Down & Connor, Vol 1*, Dublin, 1878.

17  Moneyscalp & Money-Flulare: the names have been collated on pages 111-112 of *Place-names of Northern Ireland, Co Down, Vol 3, The Mournes*.
In place-names, see also Moneydarragh on pages 50-51. I record my suspicion that the 'money' part of the name also comes from the eclipsed Irish *mBuinne*, although at the time of writing there are no observations to allow an explanation.

545

18. Moist Mare fertility: Mention should also be made of Lord Limerick's Follies sited on the edge of the demesne. See page 44 of *Tollymore Park, The Gothick Revival of Thomas Wright and Lord Limerick*, by Peter Rankin of The Follies Trust, 2010. Perhaps rather than 'spirited heralds of the structures of utility' inside the demesne, these rather phallic endowed follies may have earned their placement from the sun at solstice.

19. Kilmeloge: This is spelt as 'Killmologe' by Mgr O'Laverty who treated with it in the Parish of St Mary's or Lower Mourne, pages 25-27, Vol 1, *An Historical Account of the Diocese of Down and Connor*, Dublin, 1878. A tentative suggestion for the origin of the name might be *Caol Mí-Log*, with the rough gist of 'precise spot (to see the) evil hollow'. The hollow presumably would be some part of the horizon, such as a notch or a valley on which a sexual interpretation had been conferred by the setting sun.

20. Massforth: Upper Mourne, page 22, Vol 1, *An Historical Account of the Diocese of Down and Connor*, Dublin, 1878. The sight of the sun setting into a vulva of Knockchree at summer solstice was probably one of the reasons for the location of the chambered grave behind the church. The orientation of the stones of the grave however would suggest an alignment with a different sun event, presently not visible, but likely to have been winter solstice sunset.

21. Drumcaw: Present understanding gives *Droim Cath*, 'ridge of battles'. However the Irish *Cath* can have another explanation besides 'a battle or a war'; it could also be translated as 'a temptation' and this would allow a sexual interpretation on the landscape at solstice; until more observations are made the nature of any likely gynaecomorphic 'temptation' must remain speculative. The church is placed low enough in the valley under the ridge with the result that the mountains cannot be seen so it cannot witness or be tainted by the spectacle that impressed the ancients. I had wondered at the possibility of the sun setting on the summit of Slieve Croob at summer solstice as seen from the church's location but after a visit at midsummer this can be discounted.

22. Clough: Mgr O'Laverty's history, pages 36-58, the Parish of Ballykinlar, Vol 1, *An Historical Account of the Diocese of Down and Connor*, Dublin, 1878.

23. Clough: See p.496 of *A History of the County of Down* by Alexander Knox, Dublin, 1875. We would also mention here that the chapel of Clough seems to be on the same line of the setting winter solstice sun as the church at Kilmegan. The local name Cumran, best known perhaps from the Primary school, is surmised to be from the Irish *Comair Rann*, 'exact division' and may refer to the mid-winter sun dividing the Mourne mountain range as seen from Cumran hill neatly in two.

24. Lismahon Rath (this is the present spelling on OS map): I have a preference for the old spelling 'Lismoghan' though rather than looking to O'Laverty's explanation that the name comes from *Lis Mogán*, 'fort of the footless stocking', I imagine instead *Lis na mBoghanna* 'fort of the curves', the curves being the swelling on the side of Slieve Commedagh where winter solstice sun sets and the curve of Commedagh itself.

25. Ballydugan chapel: page 30, *Ecclesiastical Antiquities of Down, Connor and Dromore*, by Rev William Reeves, Hodges & Smith, Dublin, 1847.

26. Good Neighbour: The story of Mr Craig keeping watch during Mass at Carrickinab is on page 58, Vol 1 *Diocese of Down and Connor*, Parish of Ballykinlar. The name of the present road leading from Ballykinlar to the site of the former chapel of Killyglinnie, Carrickinab Road, is from the Irish *Carraig a n-Abadh*, 'Rock of the Abbot'.

27. Ballykinlar: The charter of John De Courcy (in Latin) is found in Rev Reeves *Ecclesiastical Antiquities*, page 211 and in O'Laverty (in English), Vol 1 *Diocese of Down and Connor*, Parish of Ballykinlar, pages 38-41.

    Also of interest to researchers would be the series of articles in the *Downpatrick Recorder* from January to May 1862 by J.W. Hanna entitled *Gossipings about the parishes of Tyrella and Ballykinlar*.

28. Fr. John Macartan: He received his education in the College de Lombardes, Paris and was ordained by Rt. Rev Dr. Macartan of Down and Connor on 14th March, 1773. He died 21st February 1814 and was buried in Maghera.

29. Murlough Burial Sites: The location of burial sites on the Murlough peninsula are mapped on page 3 of UJA Vol 15, parts 1 & 2, 1952, in *Excavations in the Sandhills at Dundrum, Co Down, 1950-51* by A.E.P. Collins. This article also contains many B&W photographs of the diggings. We may also surmise that the location of the urns found at Keel Point in March

1858 was determined by the spot being regarded as auspicious and fertile on account of where the winter solstice sun set on the Mournes. For more on this see pages 11-12 of *Where Donard Guards,* Nicholas Russell, Bairds, 2007.

30   Derivation of Tyrella: The Irish *Rail* (genitive *Ralach*), (f.), normally means an oak tree but it also has a figurative sense of 'a huge person'. It is quite similar to the adjective used earlier in the translation of 'General', *'Gein Rálach'* meaning 'gigantic act of begetting'. The adjective *Rálach* (genitive *Rálaighe*) carries an accent and means 'gigantic, monstrous', or sometimes 'anything large'.

The church of St John's at Tyrella was consecrated and opened for public celebration of Friday 16th September 1842. The church needed to be rebuilt within three decades and even now, with a congregation of about only twenty families, the problems of on-going maintenance remain.

Ballynoe: *Baile Nó*, 'the famous townland' is famous for its stone circle. Rough reckoning suggests that Ballynoe is on the same alignment with Tyrella church and the all important phallic summit of Chimney Rock. If others can later verify this alignment it would certainly be a great *raison d'être* for the ancients having built the circle where they did. Virtually surrounded by water as the ancient territory of Lecale was, the ancients may also have imagined their stone circle as being in the very centre or womb of Lecale, imparting to this site even greater status as a place of fertility and new life. The great mound of Newgrange was similarly thought of as a womb because it was located in a 'belly' or great loop on the river Boyne. While on this idea of the stone circle being in the centre of a topographical womb, the same might be said of the Giant's Circle, the Ballyanhatty complex. The townland of Ballynahatty is situated in a loop of the River Lagan and in a great bulge between the Lagan and Minnowburn stream. This would also explain the old name for the same place of Ballylary of 1605 found in the Irish Patent rolls of James 1; Ballylary would be from the Irish *Baile Láir*, 'town of the middle or centre'. The circle would appear to be on alignment with Holywood, (*Tí na*) *h-Olla Buid*, meaning '(Place of the) great penis', and the rising summer solstice sun at the end of the 'phallic' northern side of Belfast Lough (see again page 266). An orientation towards the rising sun might explain Ballynahatty as from *Baile na h-Áithe*, 'townland of fire'.

31   Schollogstown: This hill, overlooking the northern sweep of Dundrum Bay, witnessed many a ship and crew being blown onto the rocks and lost during storms. The name is thought to come from the Irish *Scol Áigh Teinn*, 'Valiant shouts of distress'.

32   Rathmullan: page 51, Vol 1, *Diocese of Down and Connor*

33   Rossglass: page 72, Vol 1, *Diocese of Down and Connor*

34   St John's: See pages 22-25, *Notice of the Ancient Chapel on St John's Point, in the County of Down,* by the Archdeacon of Down; Ulster Journal of Archaeology, vol 2, 1854.

Lecale: We have noted the many churches along the coastline of Lecale that have been grafted onto sites formerly important to pagans on account of the phallic interpretations put on the distant Mournes at winter solstice sunset. Accordingly, the very name of Lecale must now be considered to derive, not from *Leath Chathail* 'Cathal's district', but from the Irish *Leath Caoile*, 'The district of the loins'.

35   From the Confession of St Patrick, section 60. Translation from *The Life and Writings of the Historical Saint Patrick*, by Bishop R.P.C. Hanson, Seabury Press, New York, 1983.

Blue Lough from under Bignian.

The trail home down the Annalong Valley.

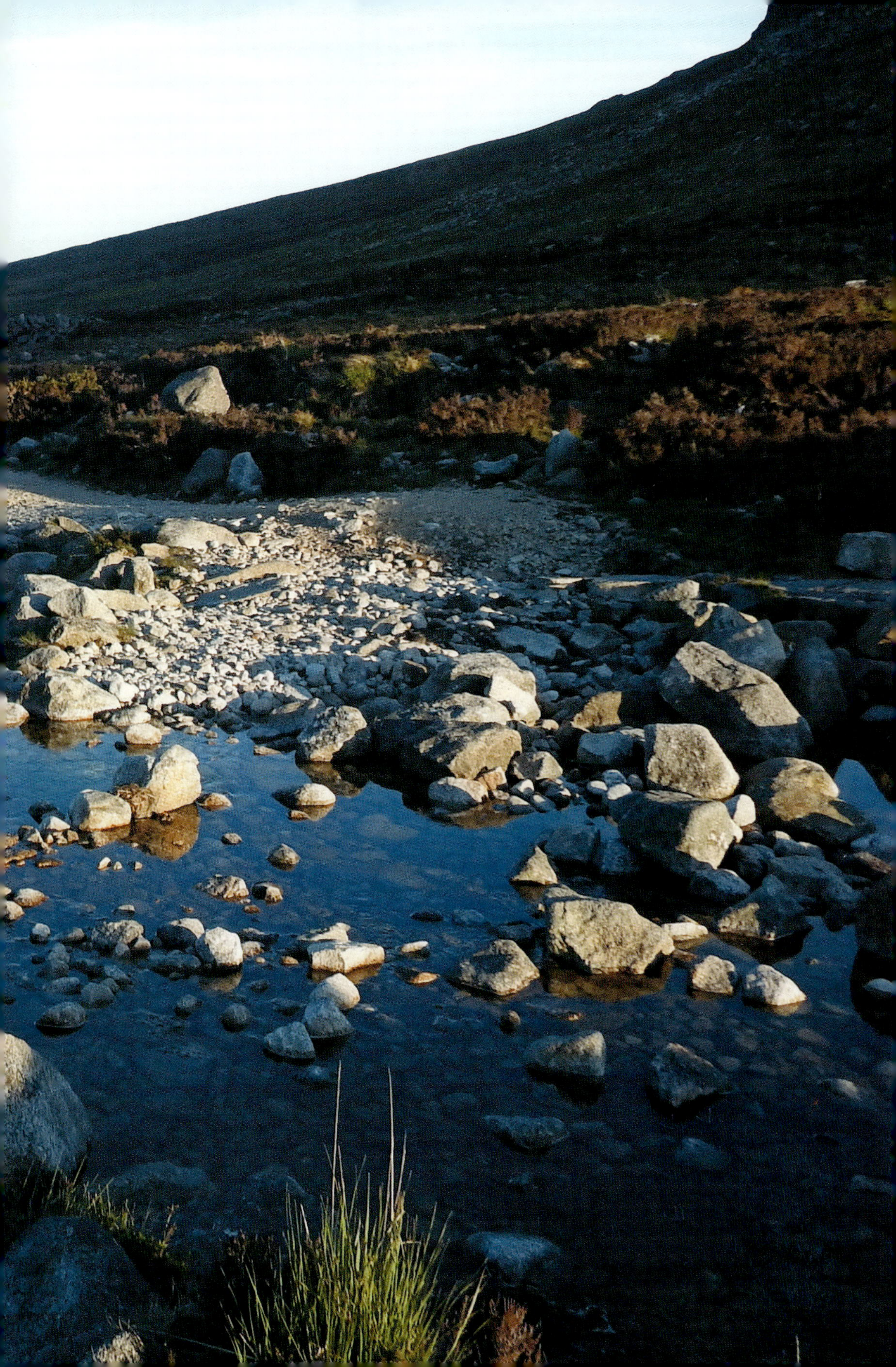

# BIBLIOGRAPHY

Andrews, J.H.*'More suitable to the English tongue': The cartography of Celtic Placenames*, Vol 14, No 2, Winter 1992, *Ulster Local Studies*

Antpöhler Werner *Newgrange, Dowth & Knowth; a visit to Ireland's Valley of the Kings*, Mercier Press, Cork, 2000

Archaeology, Ireland *Brú na Bóinne, Newgrange, Knowth, Dowth and the River Boyne*, various authors, originally published as a supplement to Archaeology Ireland, volume 11, no 3. Later special edition published in 2003 (ISBN 0953442632)

Atkinson, Archdeacon E.D. *Dromore, An Ulster Diocese*, Dundalgan Press, 1925

Bardon, Jonathan *A history of Ulster*, Blackstaff Press, Belfast, 1992

Battersby, William *The Age of Newgrange; Astronomy and Mythography*, Costello Print, Navan, 1997

Beatty, William *Beatty's Guide to Newcastle and Vicinity*, 3 editions, 3rd by R. Carswell & Son, Queen Street, Belfast, 1904

Bermingham, Nóra *The Bog Body from Tumbeagh*, Wordwell, Bray, 2006

Bhreathnach, Edel *Tara*, Government Publications, Dublin, 1995

Bigger, Francis Joseph *Inscribed Stone, Clonduff, Co Down*, UJA (2nd series), Vol 4, No 3, April 1898

Bonwick, James *Irish Druids and Old Irish Religions*, published 1894

Bordaz, Jacques *Tools of the Old and New Stone Age*, David & Charles,

Borlase, William C. *The Dolmens of Ireland*, Chapman and Hall, 1897

Bowen, E.G. *Britain and the Western Seaways*, Thames and Hudson, 1972

Boylan, Henry *A Dictionary of Irish Biography*, Gill & Macmillan, Dublin, 3rd edition, 1998

Bradley, Richard *The Prehistory of Britain and Ireland*, Cambridge University Press, 2007

Bradley, Richard *Image and Audience; Rethinking Prehistoric Art*, Oxford University Press, 2009

Brannon, N.F. *A trial excavation at St John's Point Church, County Down*, UJA, Vol 43, 1980

Brannon, N.F. *Standing Stone near Downpatrick, County Down*, being part of Five Excavations in Ulster, 1978-1984, pages 90-91, including an illustration, in UJA, Vol 49, 1986

Brennan, Martin *The Boyne Valley Vision*, Dolmen Press, Portlaoise, 1980

Brewer, Paul *Ireland – History, Culture, People*, London, 2001

Briggs, C. Stephen *Stone resources and implements in Prehistoric Ireland: a review*, UJA, Vol 51, 1988

Brooke, Rt Hon William *St Patrick and the Old Religion of Ireland*, Dublin 1874

Brothwell, Don *Variation in early Irish populations: a brief survey of the evidence*, UJA, Vol 48, 1985

Buckley, Anthony D. *Beliefs in County Down Folklore*, Chapter 20, Down, History and Society, Geography Publications, Dublin 1997

Buckley, Victor M. *Archaeological Inventory of County Louth*, Stationery Office Dublin, 1986

Burl, Aubrey *The Sun, The Moon, and Megaliths; Archaeo-Astronomy and the Standing Stones of Northern Ireland*, (The Oliver Davies lecture for 1985-1986), UJA, Vol 50, 1987

Burl, Aubrey *Rings of Stone; the prehistoric stone circles of Britain and Ireland*, Hampshire, 1979

Burl, Aubrey *Great Stone Circles*, Yale University, 1999

Cambrensis, Giraldus *The Topography of Ireland, its miracles and wonders*, edited by Thomas Wright, published by H.G. Bohn, London, 1863

Capper, Wilfrid *Caring for the Countryside; a History of 50 years of the Ulster Society for the Preservation of the Countryside*, Bangor, 1988

Carr, Peter *An Early Mesolithic site near Comber, Co Down*, UJA, Vol 50, 1987

Carson, W. Harold *Faces in the Mournes*, Vol 5, 1992, in *12 Miles of Mourne*

Case, H. & ApSimon, A. *The Neolithic and Earlier Bronze Ages in the North of Ireland,* IIS, Queen's, Belfast, 1970

Case, Humphrey *Settlement-patterns in the North Irish Neolithic,* UJA, vol 32, 1969

Castleden, Rodney *The Stonehenge People; An exploration of life in Neolithic Britain 4700-2000BC,* Routledge & Kegan Paul, London, 1987

Chambers, S.W. *Places of Interest in Northern Ireland: South Armagh, Newry and the Mourne Mountains,* being a wartime brochure for HM Forces, issued under the auspices of Command Welfare, 1941

Chart, DA (ed) *A Preliminary Survey of the Ancient Monuments of Northern Ireland,* 1940

Chessell, Henry *National Parks for Britain,* Cornish Brothers Ltd., Birmingham, no date but early post WWll

Coffey, George *Newgrange and Other Incised Tumuli in Ireland,* 1912, republished by Blandford Press, 1977.

Collins, A.E.P *Excavations in the Sandhills at Dundrum, 1950-1951,* Ulster Journal of Archaeology, vol 15, p 2-25, 1952

Collins, A.E.P *Excavations at Two Standing Stones in Co Down,* (being Drumnahare and Carrownacaw) UJA, Vol 20, 1957

Collins, A.E.P *Further investigations in the Dundrum Sandhills,* Ulster Journal of Archaeology, vol 22, p 5-20, 1959

Collins, A.E.P *Kilfeaghan Dolmen, Kilkeel, Co Down,* UJA, Vol 22, 1959

Collins, A.E.P & Wilson, B. *The Slieve Gullion Cairns,* Ulster Journal of Archaeology, vol 26, p 19-40, 1963

Collins, A.E.P & Waterman, D.M. *Millin Bay, a late Neolithic cairn in Co Down,* Archaeological Research Publications N.I., Belfast, 1955

Collins, A.E.P. *Excavations at Mount Sandel, lower site, Coleraine,* UJA, Vol 46, 1983

Colum Padraic (ed) *A Treasury of Irish Folklore; The stories, traditions, legends, humour, wisdom, ballads and songs of the Irish People,* Wings Books, New York, 1992

Conradh na Gaeilge *Placenames and Townlands of Lower Mourne,* May 2007

Conry, Michael J. *Picking Bilberries, Fraochans and Whorts in Ireland; the Human Story,* Carlow, Ireland, 2011

Conwell, E.A. *Examination of the ancient Sepulchral Cairns on the Loughcrew Hills, County of Meath,* PRIA, lX, 1866

Conwell, E.A. *On the Identification of the Ancient Cemetery at Loughcrew, Co. Meath,* PRIA, 1872

Cooney, Gabriel & Mandal, Stephen *The Irish Stone Axe Project, Monograph 1,* Wordwell, Bray, 1998 [See also a review of this work by Sinéad McCartan in UJA Vol 59, 2000]

Cooney, G. & Grogan, E. *Irish Prehistory: a Social Perspective,* Wordwell, Bray, 1999 [See also a review of this by J.P. Mallory in UJA Vol 59, 2000]

Crawford, Michael George *Legendary Stories of the Carlingford Lough District,* The Frontier Sentinel, Newry, 1913

Crawford, O.G.S. *The Technique of the Boyne Carvings,* Proceedings of the Prehistoric Society, 21, 1955

Cummings, Vicki (ed.) *The Neolithic of the Irish Sea; Materiality and traditions of practice,* Oxbow Books, Oxford, 2004

Cunningham, Noreen & McGinn, Pat *The Gap of the North; The Archaeology & Folklore of Armagh, Down, Louth and Monaghan,* O'Brien Press, Dublin, 2001

Cunningham, Tom *Kilnagreinan: A Forgotten Mourne Church,* pages 14-22 in the Journal of the Mourne Local Studies Group, *12 Miles of Mourne, volume 9, 2010*

Curran, Bob *Complete Guide to Celtic Mythology,* Appletree Press, 2000

Curtin, Jeremiah *Tales of the Fairies and of the Ghost World collected from oral tradition in South-West Munster,* David Nutt, London, 1895

Dames, Michael *Mythic Ireland,* Thames and Hudson, London, 1992

Daniel, Glyn *The Megalith Builders of Western Europe,* Hutchinson & Co., London, 1958

Daniel, Glyn *Megalithic studies in Ireland, 1929-79,* (The Estyn Evans lecture for 1979), UJA, Vol 43, 1980

Davidson, R.C. *Rock Scribings in Co Down,* UJA, Vol 13 1950

Davies, Oliver *Stone Circles in Northern Ireland,* UJA, Vol 2, part 1, 1939

Davies, Oliver *Large Prehistoric Enclosures in Ireland,* UJA, Vol 9, 1946

De Bhaldraithe, Tomás *English – Irish Dictionary,* Dublin, 1959

De Breffny, Brian *Heritage of Ireland,* Weidenfeld and Nicholson, London, 1980

De Breffny, Brian *Ireland – A Cultural Encyclopaedia,* Thames & Hudson, 1983

De Paor, Máire and Liam *Early Christian Ireland,* Thames and Hudson, London, 1958

De Paor, Liam *Portrait of Ireland – Past and Present,* Rainbow Publications, 1985

De Valéra, Ruaidhri & Ó Nualláin, Sean *Survey of the Megalithic Tombs of Ireland,* Vols 1-6, Dublin Stationery Office,

De Vismes Kane, W.F. *The Black Pig's Dyke: The Ancient Boundary Fortification of Uladh,* Proceedings of the RIA, Vol 27, Section C, No 14. Hodges, Figgis & Co. Dublin, 1909

Dickson, John M. *Observations on our Ancient Cills,* UJA (2nd series), Vol 6, No 3, July 1900

Dillon, Paddy *The Mournes; Walks,* O'Brien Press, 2000

Dinneen, Rev Patrick *Foclóir Gaedhilge agus Béarla, an Irish-English Dictionary,* Dublin, 1927

D.O.E. *Rostrevor, Conservation Area,* February 1979

D.O.E. *Mourne, Area of Outstanding Natural Beauty,* 1986

Doherty, Gillian *Anglicization and the Ordnance Survey,* being chapter nine in *The Irish Ordnance Survey, History, Culture and Memory,* Four Courts Press, Dublin, 2004

Donegan, Maureen *Fables and Legends of Ireland,* Mercier Press, Dublin, 1976

Doran, J.S. *My Mourne,* Mourne Observer

Doran, J.S. *Hill Walks in the Mournes,* Mourne Observer

Doran, J.S. *Turn up the Lamp, Tales of a Mourne Childhood,* Appletree Press, 1980

Doran, J.S. *Wayfarer in the Mournes,* Outlook Press, 1980

Dubourdieu, Rev John *Statistical Survey of the County of Down with observations on the means of improvement,* Dublin, 1802

Dweeryhouse, A. R. *The Glaciation of North-Eastern Ireland,* Quarterly Journal of the Geological Society, Vol 79, 1923

Ellison, Cyril *The Waters of the Boyne & Blackwater,* Dublin 1983

Eogan, George *A Decade of Excavations at Knowth, Co Meath,* Irish University Review, Spring 1973

Eogan, George *Report on the excavations of some passage graves, unprotected inhumation burials and a settlement site at Knowth, Co. Meath,* RIA, Vol 74, Section C, No 2, 1974

Eogan, George *Knowth and the passage-tombs of Ireland,* Thames and Hudson, London, 1986

Eogan, George *Prehistoric and Early Historic Culture Change at Brugh Na Bóinne,* Proceedings of the Royal Irish Academy, Vol 91, C, number 5, Dublin, 1991

Erskine, Thomas *Mourne, a photographic portrait,* Clonlum Publications, 2006

Evans, E. Estyn *Irish Heritage; the Landscape, the People and their Work,* Dundalk, 1942

Evans, E. Estyn *A Lost Mourne Megalith – and a Newly-Discovered Site,* UJA, Vol 11, Parts 1 & 2, 1948

Evans, E. Estyn *Mourne County: Landscape and life in South Down,* Dundalgan Press, Dundalk, 1951

Evans, E. Estyn *Irish Folk Ways,* Routledge & Kegan Paul, London, 1957

Evans, E. Estyn *Prehistoric and Early Christian Ireland,* London, 1966

Evans, E. Estyn *Ireland and the Atlantic Heritage,* Lilliput Press, Dublin, 1996

Evans, John G. *The Environment of Early Man in the British Isles,* London, 1975

Farry, Fr Patrick *Penal-Day Traditions in Mourne,* from vol 9 of *Down and Connor History Society Journal*

Flanagan, Deirdre *Place-names as Historical Source Material,* Part 1 appeared in the first edition Vol 1, No 1, October 1975 of *Ulster Local Studies,* the sequel Part 2, in Vol l, No 2, May 1976

Flanagan, Deirdre *Exemplary Guide to the Study of a Placename,* from Vol 3, *Journal of the Federation of Ulster Local Studies,* circa 1977

Flanagan, L.N.W. *A Neolithic Site at Drumadonnell, Co Down,* UJA, Vol 29, 1966

Forbes, Diane *Slieve Donard: A new challenge for the National Trust,* article in journal of Mourne Local Studies Group, *12 Miles of Mourne,* Volume 5, 1992

Forde-Johnston, J. *Prehistoric Britain and Ireland,* Dent & Sons, 1976

Forsythe, Wes & Gregory Niall *A Neolithic logboat from Greyabbey Bay, County Down,*

Four Masters *Annala Rioghachta Eireann; Annals of the Kingdom of Ireland from the earliest period to the year 1616,* with translation and notes by John O'Donovan, Hodges, Smith & Co., Dublin, 1856 (reprinted by De Búrca Rare Books, Dublin 1990)

Fourwinds, Tom *Monu-mental about Prehistoric Antrim,* Dublin, 2008

Frazer W. *Notes on Incised Sculpturings on Stones in the cairns of Sliabh-na-Calliaghe, near Loughcrew, Co Meath,* PRSA, 1893

Freitag, Barbara *Sheela-na-Gigs, Unravelling an Enigma,* Routledge, Abingdon, 2004

Fry, Malcolm F. *Paddle your own; The Logboat in the North of Ireland,* Historic Monuments and Buildings Branch, DOE, 1988

*Preserving ancient and historic monuments and sites in State Care in Northern Ireland, c 1921 to c 1955*
- *Part one: establishing a system of care,* UJA, Vol 62, 2003
- *Part two: establishing a system of care,* UJA, Vol 64, 2005
- *Part three: reorganizing the system of care,* UJA, Vol 65, 2006
- *Part four: fresh departures in the system of care,* Vol 66, 2007

Gardner, Arthur *Britain's Mountain Heritage and its preservation as National Parks,* Batsford, London, 1942

Garnett, Jacqueline Ingalls *Newgrange speaks for itself; Forty carved Motifs and related Site Features,* Trafford Publishing, 2005

Gibson, Alex & Simpson Derek *Prehistoric Ritual and Religion,* Stroud, 1998

Goddard, Ian C. *Fire in Prehistoric Land Management,* UJA, Vol 46, 1983

Gregory, Lady *Complete Irish Mythology,* Slaney Press, 1994

Groenenman-van Waateringe, W. *The Ballynoe Stone Circle Excavations by A.E. Van Giffen, 1937-1938*

Hall, Valerie *The Making of Ireland's Landscape since the Ice Age,* The Collins Press, Cork, 2011

Hamilton, M. *Local History and the Irish Language,* Vol 13, No 2, Winter 1991, *Ulster Local Studies*

Hamlin, Ann & Lynn, Chris *Pieces of the Past,* HMSO, 1988

Harbison, Peter *The Archaeology of Ireland,* London, 1976

Harbison, Peter *Pre-Christian Ireland, from the first settlers to the early Celts,* Thames and Hudson, London, 1988

Harbison, Peter *Pilgrimage in Ireland: the monuments and the people,* London, 1991

Harbison, Peter *Treasures of the Boyne Valley,* Gill & Macmillan, Dublin, 2003

Harding, Dennis *Prehistoric Europe; The Making of the Past,* Oxford, 1978

Harris, Walter & Charles Smith *The Antient and Present State of the County of Down,* Dublin 1744, reproduced by Davidson Books, Ballynahinch, 1977

Hartnett, P.J. *Newgrange Passage Grave, Co Meath,* JRSAI, 1954

Hartnett, P.J. *The excavation of two tumuli at Fourknocks (Sites 11 and 111), Co Meath,* RIA, Vol 71, Section C, No 3, 1971

Hayes, Tom *Using Astronomy in Archaeology: A Look at the Beaghmore Alignments,* UJA, Vol 58, 1999

Hayes, Tom *Megalithic Technology,* UJA, Vol 64, 2005

Hensey, Robert *First Light; The Origins of Newgrange,* Oxbow Books, Oxford, 2015

Herity, Michael *Irish Passage Graves; Neolithic Tomb-Builders in Ireland and Britain 2500 B.C.,* Irish University Press, Dublin 1974

Herity, Michael & Eogan, George *Ireland in Prehistory,* Routledge & Kegan Paul, 1977

Herity, Michael *Ordnance Survey Letters Down,* Four Masters Press, Dublin, 2001

Hewson, Rev. L.M. *Notes on Irish Sandhills,* JRSAI, Vol 66, p 154-172, 1936

Hewson, Rev L.M. *Notes on Irish Sandhills,* JRSAI, Vol 68, p 69-90, 1938

Hickey, Helen *Images of Stone; Figure Sculpture of the Lough Erne Basin,* published by Fermanagh District Council, 1976

Hirons, Kenneth R. *The Changing Vegetation of the Mournes,* Vol 2, 1988, in *12 Miles of Mourne*

HMSO *Topographical Index* (Townlands), *Census of Population of Northern Ireland,* 1926

HMSO *Ancient Monuments of Northern Ireland,* various from 1926

HMSO *The Ulster Countryside; Planning Advisory Board,* 1947

Hoare, Sir R.C. *Journal of a Tour in Ireland,* London, 1807

Hull, Edward *Explanatory Memoir of the Geological Survey of Ireland, including the country around Newry, Rathfryland and Rostrevor in the county of Down; and the Mourne Mountains* Alex Thom, Dublin, 1881

Hull, Eleanor *Pagan Ireland,* M.H. Gill & Son, Dublin, 1923

Jones, Carleton *Temples of Stone; Exploring the Megalithic Tombs of Ireland,* Collins Press, Cork, 2007

Jope, E.M. *Porcellanite Axes from factories in North-East Ireland: Tievebulliagh and Rathlin,* UJA, Vol 15, P 31-55, 1952

Jope, Edward Martyn (Ed) *The Archaeological Survey of Northern Ireland, County Down,* HMSO, Belfast 1966

Joyce, P.W. *The Origin and History of Irish Names of Places,* Vol 1-2, M.H. Gill & Son, Dublin, 1891, Vol 3, produced in 1913

Joyce, P.W. *A Social History of Ancient Ireland,* Vol 1-2, Longmans, Green & Co., London, 1903.

Joyce, P.W. *The story of Ancient Irish Civilisation,* London, 1907

Joyce, P.W. *The Wonders of Ireland and other papers on Irish Subjects,* Longman, Green, and Co. Dublin, 1911

Joyce, P.W. *Old Celtic Romances, translated from the gaelic,* Dublin, 1920

JRSAI *Slidderyford Cromlech, Newcastle, Co Down,* page 299 with illustrations on page 300

 *Ballynoe Stone Circe, Co Down,* page 300-302, *Slieve Donard, in the County of Down,* pages 230-233

 *Kilfeaghan Cromlech, Co Down,* pages 264-266

 *Souterrain at Slidderyford, near Dundrum, Co Down,* p 266-268

 All five articles above from *The Journal of the Royal Society of Antiquaries of Ireland,* Part 3, Vol 35, 30th September 1905, printed by Hodges, Figgis & Co. Dublin

J.S. (a private publication) *Eire Ard, Inis Na Righ: Fragments of Ancient Irish History,* Darien Press, Edinburgh, 1894

Keatings, Margaret *The Mourne Mountains; a Guide Map for Walkers,* NITB

Kennedy, Gerald Conan *Irish Mythology; a Guide & Sourcebook,* Killala, 1991

Kennedy, Patrick *The Bardic Stories of Ireland,* M.H. Gill & Son, Dublin, 1886

Kinsella, Thomas *The Tain, from the Irish epic Táin Bó Cuailnge,* Oxford University Press, 1969

Kirk, David *The Mountains of Mourne; a Celebration of a Place Apart,* Appletree Press, Belfast, 2002

Knowles, William J *Sepulchral Pottery,* UJA (2nd series), Vol 1, No 2, January 1895

Knowles, William J. *Report on the Prehistoric Remains from the Sandhills of the Coast of Ireland,* Royal Irish Academy, Vol 1, No 2, 1889

Knox, Alexander *A History of the County of Down,* Hodges, Dublin, 1875

Lalor, Brian (ed) *The Encyclopaedia of Ireland,* Gill & McMillan, Dublin, 2003

Lawson, Leonard *25 Walks in Down District,* The Stationery Office, 1998

Lett, Canon Henry W., *Mosses, Hepatics and Lichens of the Mourne Mountains,*

 Proceedings of the Royal Irish Academy, series 3, Vol I, 1889

Lett, Canon Henry W., *Ancient Canoe found near Loughbrickland, Co. Down,* UJA (2nd series), Vol 1, No 2, January 1895

Lett, Canon Henry W. *Maps of the Mountains of Mourne in the County of Down,* UJA (2nd series) Vol 8, No 1, January 1902

Lett, Canon Henry W., *Slieve Donard in the County of Down,* a paper read before the Royal Society of Antiquaries of Ireland, 3rd July 1905

Lett, Canon Henry W., *Names of Places in the Mountains of Mourne,* U.J.A. 1906

Lewis, Samuel *A Topographical Dictionary of Ireland,* London, 1837

Lewis-Williams & Pearce *Inside the Neolithic Mind; consciousness, cosmos and the realm of the Gods,* Thames & Hudson, London, 2005

Lucas, A. T. *Cattle in Ancient Ireland,* Boethius Press, 1989

Lynn, Chris *Navan Fort, Archaeology and Myth,* Wordwell, Bray, 2003

Lyle, Paul *Between Rocks and Hard Places; discovering Ireland's Northern Landscapes,* The Stationery Office, 2010

Macaulay, Anne *Megalithic Measures and Rhythms; Sacred Knowledge of the Ancient Britons,* Floris Books, 2006

MacDonald, Philip *Archaeological investigations at Kilhorne, Moneydarragh Mor, Co Down,* UJA, Vol 66, 2007

Mac Cana, Proinsias *Celtic Mythology,* Hamlyn, London, 1970

MacKie, Euan *The Megalith Builders,* London, 1977

Maclean, Rachel *Eat your Greens: An Examination of the Potential Diet Available in Ireland During the Mesolithic,* UJA, Vol 56, 1993

Mac Manus, D.A. *The Middle Kingdom; The Faerie World of Ireland,* London, 1959

MacMillan, Rev Archibald & Brydall, Robert *Iona; Its History and Antiquities; Its Carved Stones,* Houlston & Sons, London, 1898

MacNeill, Máire *The Festival of Lughnasa: A study of the survival of the Celtic festival of the beginning of harvest.* Oxford University Press, 1962. (*inter alia,* Slieve Donard: pages 84-96)

MacSween, Ann & Sharp, Mick *Prehistoric Scotland,* Batsford, London, 1989

Mac Uistin, Liam *Exploring Newgrange,* O'Brien Press, Dublin, 1999

McCaughan, Michael *The Irish Sea; Aspects of Maritime History,* IIS, 1989

McCionnaith, L. *Foclóir Béarla agus Gaedhilge,* (English-Irish Dictionary), Dublin 1935

McComb, A.M.G. & Simpson, D. *The Wild Bunch: Exploitation of the Hazel in Prehistoric Ireland,* UJA Vol 58, 1999

McComb, Anne *Random finds of flint objects in the area of the Shimna River near Bryansford, County Down,* UJA Vol 64, 2005

# Bibliography

McComb, William *McComb's Guide to Belfast, the Giant's Causeway and adjoining districts of the Counties of Antrim and Down*, Belfast, 1861

McCoy, Jack *An Index to the Mourne Observer, 1949-1980*, SEELB, 1984

McMahon & O'Donoghue *Brewer's Dictionary of Irish Phrase & Fable*, Weidenfeld & Nicolson, London, 2004

McNally, Kenneth *Standing Stones and other monuments of early Ireland*, Appletree Press, 1984

McNally, Kenneth *Ireland's Ancient Stones, A Megalithic Heritage*, Appletree Press, 2006

Malley, A.J. *The Recording and Study of Field Names*, issue 5, being Vol 3, No 1, November 1977 of *Ulster Local Studies*

Mallory, Jim & Hartwell, B. *Down in Prehistory*, Chapter One, *Down, History and Society*, Geography Publications, Dublin 1997

Mallory, J.P *Trials excavations at Tievebulliagh, Co Antrim*, UJA, Vol 53, 1990

Mallory, J.P. & McNeill, T.E. *The Archaeology of Ulster*, IIS, Queen's, Belfast, 1991

Malone, Caroline *Neolithic Britain and Ireland*, Tempus Publishing, Stroud, 2001

Maringer, Johannes *The Gods of Prehistoric Man*, Weidenfeld and Nicolson, 1960

May, J.M. *Javelin and Arrow-Heads from the Lower Bann Valley*, UJA, Vol 2, part 1, January 1939

Midlands-East Tourism *Newgrange, Co Meath...a step back in time*, no date

Milton, Kay *Our Countryside our Concern; The policy and practice of conservation in Northern Ireland*, Bairds, 1990

Ministry of Development *Mourne*, HMSO, 1970

Mitchell, Frank *The Irish Landscape*, Collins, Glasgow, 1976

Mitchell, Frank *The Way that I followed*, Country House, Dublin, 1990

Mitchell, W.I. (ed.) *The Geology of Northern Ireland*, 2nd, Baird, 2004

Moffat Alistair *The Sea Kingdoms; The story of Celtic Britain & Ireland*, HarperCollins, London, 2001

Mooney, Fr Bernard *Place-Names of Rostrevor*, E. Hodgett printers, Newry, 1950

Moore, Donald (ed.) *The Irish Sea Province in Archaeology and History*, Cambrian Archaeological Association, Cardiff, 1970

Moore, Michael J. *Archaeological Inventory of County Meath*, Stationery Office Dublin, 1987

Moore, Sam *The Archaeology of Slieve Donard; A Cultural Biography of Ulster's Highest Mountain*, Down County Museum, 2012

Morris, Ronald W.B. *The Prehistoric Rock Art of Argyll*, Dolphin Press, Dorset, 1977

Morris, Ronald W.B. *The Prehistoric Rock Art of Galloway & The Isle of Man*, Blandford Press, Dorset, 1979

Morton, Grenfell *Victorian and Edwardian Newcastle*, Friar's Bush Press, 1988

Morton, Dr WRM *Unurned Cremations from Site 1, Dundrum Sandhills*, Ulster J. of Archaeology, Vol 22

Mould, Daphne Pochin *The Mountains of Ireland*, Gill and Macmillan, Dublin, 1955

Mould, Daphne Pochin *Irish Pilgrimage*, M. H. Gill & Son, Dublin, 1955

Murphy, Anthony & Moore, Richard *Island of the Setting Sun; In Search of Ireland's Ancient Astronomers*, The Liffey Press, Dublin, 2006

Murphy, Michael J. *History from the Mournes and Ravensdale, County Louth*, issue 14, Vol 7, No 2, Summer 1982, *Ulster Local Studies*

Murray Emily & Logue, Paul *Battles, Boats & Bones; Archaeological Discoveries in Northern Ireland 1987-2008*, NIEA, 2010

Nelms, H. *The structure of Newgrange*, pages 54-55, in *Antiquity* No 55, 1981

Nelson, E. Charles *Shamrock; Botany and History of an Irish Myth*, Boethius Press, Aberystwyth, 1991

North, John *Stonehenge; Neolithic man and the Cosmos*, Harper Collins, London, 1996

O'Brien, Tim *Light Years Ago; a study of the Cairns of Newgrange and Cairn T Loughcrew, Co Meath, Ireland*, Black Cat Press, Monkstown, Co Dublin, 1992

O'Connell, Catherine *The Irish Peatland Conservation Council – Guide to Irish Peatlands*, Dublin, 1987

O'Curry, Eugene *Lectures on the manuscript materials of Ancient Irish History*, Dublin 1861, reprinted by Four Courts Press, 1995.

Ó Dónaill, Niall *Foclóir Gaeilge-Béarla*, Rialtas na hÉireann, 1977

O'Donovan, John *Glossary in which the disguised form of Irish words in their English dress are unmasked and their general and local meanings pointed out with observations upon the fluctuating state of the orthography and general and particular rules laid down to fix it drawn from analogy and approved custom*, 1830

O'Donovan, John *Annals of the kingdom of Ireland by the Four Masters*, Dublin, 1856, reprinted by De Búrca, seven volumes, 1990

O'Donovan, John *Sanas Chormaic; Cormac's Glossary* [O'Donovan was the translator and annotator in conjunction with Whitely Stokes] Irish Archaeological and Celtic Society, Calcutta, 1868

Ó Duibhín, Ciarán *Irish in County Down since 1750*, Cumann Gaelach Leath Chathail, 1991

O Duinn, Sean *In Search of the Awesome Mystery: Lore of Megalithic, Celtic and Christian Ireland*, Columba Press, 2011

O'Grady, Standish Hayes *The Pursuit after Diarmuid and Gráinne the Daughter of Cormac Mac Airt; Transactions of the Ossianic Society*, Dublin, 1857

Ó hÓgáin, Dáithí *The Sacred Isle, Belief and Religion in Pre-Christian Ireland*, Boydell Press, 1999

Ó hÓgáin, Dáithí *Historic Ireland; 5,000 years of Ireland's Heritage*, Gill & McMillan, Dublin, 2001

Ó hÓgáin, Dáithí *The Lore of Ireland; An Encyclopaedia of Myth, Legend and Romance*, Boydell Press, Woodbridge, 2006

O'Kelly, J. *Excavations and experiments in Ancient Irish Cooking Places*, Journal of the Royal Society of Antiquaries of Ireland, 1954

O'Kelly, Claire *Illustrated Guide to Newgrange and the other Boyne Monuments*, Cork, 1967

O'Kelly, Claire *Passage-grave Art in the Boyne Valley*, Proceedings of the Prehistoric Society, Vol 39, 1973, London

O'Kelly, Claire *Concise guide to Newgrange*, John English, Wexford, 1976

O'Kelly, Michael J. *The megalithic tombs of Ireland* in Antiquity and Man: Essays in Honour of Glyn Daniel, Thames and Hudson, London, 1982

O'Kelly, Michael J. *Newgrange; Archaeology, Art and Legend*, Thames and Hudson, London, 1982

O'Kelly, Michael J. *Early Ireland; An introduction to Irish Prehistory*, Cambridge University Press, 1989

Ó Mainnín, Mícheál B. *Place-Names of Northern Ireland, Vol 3, The Mournes*, Institute of Irish Studies, Queen's, 1993

Ó Maolfabhail, Art *Keep Townland Names Alive*, issue 6, being Vol 3, No 2, May 1978, Ulster Local Studies

Ó Mórdha, Pilip *The medieval kingdom of Mugdorna, p 432-447*, Clogher Record, Monaghan, 1972

O'Rahilly, Thomas F. *Early Irish History and Mythology*, The Dublin Institute for Advanced Studies, 1946

Ó Ríordáin, Sean P *Lough Gur Excavations; Carraig Aille and the 'Spectacles'*, RIA, vol LII, Section C, No 3, Hodges & Figgis, Dublin, 1949

Ó Ríordáin, Sean P. & Daniel, Glyn *Newgrange and the Bend of the Boyne*, Thames & Hudson, 1964

Ordnance Survey N.I. *Activity Map: The Mournes including Slieve Croob*, Land & Property Services, Belfast, 2009 [This is the latest of the Maps on the Mournes – 'Designed with outdoor enthusiasts in mind'. A good map is indispensable to follow the names of the many places mentioned in this book.]

O'Sullivan, Muiris *Megalithic Art in Ireland*, Dublin, 1993

O'Sullivan, Sean *The Folklore of Ireland*, Batsford, London, 1974

Oram, Hugh *Old Newcastle*, Stenlake Publishing, 2008

Patrick, J. *Midwinter Sunrise at Newgrange*, in Nature, 249, 1974

Pearsall, Ronald *Myths and Legends of Ireland; Tales of a Magical and Mysterious Past*, Todtri, New York, 1996

Petrie, George *The Round Towers of Ireland*, Royal Irish Academy, Dublin, 1845

Piggott, Stuart *Neolithic Cultures of the British Isles; A study of the Stone-using Agricultural Communities of Britain in the Second Millennium B.C.*, Cambridge University Press, 1954

Piggott, Stuart *The Prehistoric Peoples of Scotland*, Routledge & Kegan Paul, 1962

Pointing, Gerald & Margaret *The Standing Stones of Callanish*, Stornoway, 1977

Pooler, Rev Charles *St Patrick in Co. Down; An address delivered in St Patrick's Cathedral, Dublin on St Patrick's Day, 1904*, Dublin, 1904

Power, Patrick C. *Sex and Marriage in Ancient Ireland*, Mercier Press, 1976

Praeger, Robert Lloyd *The "Preservation" of Ancient Monuments* [a Mourne farmer tells Praeger how he dynamited a dolmen and a neighbour cut up another because 'there's a power o' money in it'.] UJA, (2nd Series) Vol 4, No 2, January 1898. This article must have been very influential as three months later powers were devolved to County Councils to prosecute where any

ancient monuments or remains 'are being dilapidated, injured, or endangered'.
Praeger, Robert Lloyd *Official Guide to County Down and the Mourne Mountains,* Marcus Ward, 1898, & second edition 1900
Price, Victor *Apollo in Mourne,* Blackstaff Press, 1978
Private Owner *Newcastle Area in the Downpatrick Recorder, 1836-1950*
Proudfoot, Lindsay (ed.) *Down, History & Society,* Geography Publications, 1997.
Public Record Office *Calendar of State Papers relating to Ireland, 1509-1670*
Quinlan, John *The cooking places of Stone Age Ireland,* JRSAI, 1887
Raftery, Barry *Pagan Celtic Ireland; the enigma of the Irish Stone Age,* Thames and Hudson, 1994
Raftery, Joseph *Prehistoric Ireland,* Batsford, 1951
Rees, Alwyn & Brinley *Celtic heritage; Ancient Tradition in Ireland and Wales,* Thames and Hudson, London, 1961
Reeves, Rev William *Ecclesiastical Antiquities of Down, Connor and Dromore,* Hodges and Smith, Dublin, 1847
Reeves, Rev. William *The Seal of Hugh O'Neill,* page 255, Vol 1, first series, Ulster Journal of Archaeology, Belfast, 1852
Roberts, Anthony *Sowers of Thunder; Giants in myth and history,* London, 1978
Rowley, Richard *The Old Gods and other poems,* Duckworth, London, 1925
Rowley, Richard *The Big Grey Man, A legend of Mourne,* Mourne Press, no date
Rudgley, Richard *Secrets of the Stone Age,* London, 2000
Ruggles, Clive *Astronomy in Prehistoric Britain and Ireland,* Yale University, 1999
Russell, Nicholas *Where Donard Guards,* Ballaghbeg Books, Newcastle, 2007
Russell, Nicholas *Slieve Donard's Domain,* Ballaghbeg Books, Newcastle, 2011
Ryan, Michael (ed) *The Illustrated Archaeology of Ireland,* Country House, Dublin, 1991
Salmon, John *Druidical Sacrifices in Ireland: Were there human victims?* UJA (2nd series) Vol 1, No 3, April 1895, continued in Vol 1, No 4, July 1895 and concluded in Vol 2, No 1, October 1895
Scarre, Chris *Exploring Prehistoric Europe,* Oxford University Press, 1998
Sharkey, John *Celtic Mysteries; The Ancient Religion,* Thames & Hudson, 1975
Sheane, Michael *Ulster and Saint Patrick,* Stockport, 1984

Shee, E. *The techniques of Irish passage-grave art; Megalithic Graves and Ritual,* Jutland Archaeological Society, Xl, 1973
Sheridan, Alison *Early Settlers of Mourne,* Vol 3, 1989, in *12 Miles of Mourne*
Sheridan, J.A. *Porcellanite artifacts; a new survey,* UJA. 49, 1986
Sherry, Brian (ed) *Along the Black Pig's Dyke; Folklore from Monaghan and South Armagh,* published by Castleblayney Community, 1993
Simpson, D.D.A. *Irish Axe Hammers,* UJA, Vol 53, 1990
Stanley-Jones, E. *A Guide to walking in the Mournes,* Mourne Observer, 1962
Stewart, A.T.Q. *The Shape of Irish History,* Blackstaff Press, 2001
Stout, Geraldine *Newgrange and the Bend of the Boyne,* Cork University Press, 2002
Stout, Geraldine & Stout Matthew *Newgrange,* Cork University Press, 2008
Streit Jakob *Sun and Cross; The development from megalithic culture to early Christianity in Ireland,* Stuttgart, 1977
Swift, Edmund L. *The Life and Acts of Saint Patrick the Archbishop, Primate and Apostle of Ireland – now first translated from the original Latin of Jocelin, the Cistercian Monk of Furnes,* Dublin, 1809
Thomas, Julian *Understanding the Neolithic* (being a revised 2nd edition of *Rethinking the Neolithic*), Routledge, London, 1999
Thomas, N.L. *Irish Symbols of 3500 BC,* Mercier Press, Dublin, 1988
Turner, Colin *The Mournes,* Cottage Publications, 1997
Twohig, Elizabeth Shee *The Megalithic Art of Western Europe,* Clarendon Press, Oxford, 1981
Twohig, Elizabeth Shee *Irish Megalithic Tombs,* Shire Publications, Princes Risborough, 2004
Uí Chonboirne, Máire *Place Names of Lecale and Kinelarty; Logainmneacha Leath Chathail agus Chineál Fhathartaigh,* Lecale Gaelic Society, Downpatrick, 2015
Vallancey, C. *Collectanea de rebus Hibernicis,* Dublin, 1824
Van Hoek, M. *The Prehistoric Rock Art of County Donegal,* Ulster Journal of Archaeology, in two parts, Journal 50 and 51
Viney, Michael *A living Island; Ireland's Responsibility to Nature,* Comhar, 2003
Viney, Michael *Ireland; a Smithsonian Natural History,* Blackstaff Press, 2003

Waddell, John *The Prehistoric Archaeology of Ireland,* Galway University Press, 1998

Waddell, John *Rathcroghan: archaeological and geophysical survey in a ritual landscape,* Wordwell, 2009

Wakeman, W.F. *Archaeologia Hibernica,* Dublin 1848

Wakeman, W. J. *Canoe found at Portadown,* UJA (2nd series) Vol 5, No 1, October 1898

Wall, C.W. *Mountaineering in Ireland,* F.M.C.I. guide, Dublin, 1976

Wallace, Patrick & Ó Floinn (eds) *Treasures of the National Museum of Ireland; Irish Antiquities,* Gill and McMillan, Dublin, 2002

Waring, John B. *Stone Monuments, Tumuli, and Ornament of Remote Ages with remarks on the early Architecture of Ireland and Scotland,* The Strand, London, 1870

Warner, Richard *A cooking place at Fofannybane, Co Down,* Vol 4, 1991, in *12 Miles of Mourne*

Water Service *The Silent Valley,* D.O.E. publication, May 1986

Watson, E. *The Megalithic and Bronze Ages in County Antrim,* UJA, Vol 8, p 80-118, 1945

Webb, Alfred *A Compendium of Irish Biography,* Gill & Son, Dublin 1878

Welsh, Harry *Tomb Travel; A guide to Northern Ireland's megalithic monuments,* N.I. Environment Agency, 2011

Welsh, Henry *Field Surveys undertaken by the Ulster Archaeological Society in 2006,* UJA, Vol 67, 2008

Wilde, Sir William R.W. *Beauties of the Boyne and the Blackwater,* Dublin 1848, reprinted by K.Duffy, Galway, 2003

Cambridge Archaeological Journal, pages 243-59, 10:2, 2000

Wilson, BCS *The First Inhabitants,* chapter one in *Lecale, a study of Local History,* Queens University, 1970

Wilson, W. *The Post-Chaise Companion or Travellers Directory through Ireland,* Dame Street, Dublin, 1786

Wood, John Edwin *Sun, Moon and Standing Stones,* Oxford University Press, 1978

Wood-Martin, W.G. *Pagan Ireland: An Archaeological Sketch* being a handbook of Irish pre-Christian Antiquities, Longmans, London, 1895

Wood-Martin, W.G. *Traces of the Elder Faiths: Fairy and Marriage Lore,* series started in UJA (2nd series), Vol 3, No 3, April 1897, continued in Vol 3, No 4, July 1897, again in Vol 4, No 1, October 1897 concluding in Vol 4, No 2, January 1898. The articles were subsequently published under the title *Traces of the Elder Faiths in Ireland: a handbook of Pre-Christian Traditions* by Longmans Green & Co, London, 1902.

Woodman, Peter *Settlement patterns of the Irish Mesolithic,* UJA, Vol 36 & 37, 1973-1974

Woodman, Peter *The Mesolithic In Ireland; Hunter Gatherers in an Insular Environment,* Oxford, B.A.R. series, 1978

Woodman, Peter *Stone and Flint Implements: A Key to Prehistoric Settlement,* issue 9, Vol 5, No 1, Winter 1979, *Ulster Local Studies*

Woodman, Peter *Excavations at Mount Sandel, 1973-1977,* HMSO, 1985

Woodman, Peter *Problems in the colonisation of Ireland,* UJA, Vol 49, 1986

Woodman, Peter, et al *The Archaeology of a Collection; The Keiller-Knowles Collection of the National Museum of Ireland (Monograph series 2),* Wordwell, Bray, 2006. [William James Knowles amassed a huge collection of some 15,000 prehistoric artefacts. The Dundrum sandhills were one of his favourite hunting grounds.]

Wright, Thomas *The History of Ireland from the earliest period of the Irish Annals to the Present Time,* London, no date.

Yates, Paul *Mourne,* Nicholson & Bass, 2005

Young, Robert M. *Vestiges of Primitive Man in the County Down,* UJA (2nd series), Vol 4, No 1, October 1897

# INDEX

Altataggart mountain 300
Altnadua 249, **250-251**
American Army & USAF 222, 331
Amy's River 67, 69
Annagassan 262-263, 266
Annalong 46, 216-217, **383-384**, 434, 475
Annalong Buttress 58, 59
Annalong Valley 58, 59, 60, 154, 194-195, 198-199, 200-201, 222, 237, 290, 311, 334, 344, 349, 356, 358-359, 370, 374, 376, 379, 421, 460, 475, 477
Annals (see Four Masters)
Annals of Ulster 116
Annesley 17, 85, 93-94, 272, 301, 302, 512
Ardley River 425-431
Ardmally 43, 426, 437, 460-462
Armour's Hole 489-494, 499-501
Armstrong, Rev W. 289
Atlantic 9, 517, 538/f2
Atlantis 322-323
Attical 82-84
Aughnahoory 44

Backaderry 527/f41
Back Castles 43, 231, 242, 264, 298-299, 353, 457, 470, 475, 476, 477, 481, 482-483
Back Ditch, The 264
Badger 21
Ballagh 123, 501-503
Ballaghanery 303, 307-309
Ballydugan 512
Ballyginny 292
Ballykinlar 9, 321, 500, 513-515, 521
Ballylough 2
Ballymagreehan 93, 504
Ballymahon 500
Ballymartin 263
Ballynagelty **137-138**
Ballymoney (Kilcoo) 106, 500, 504-505
Ballynahatty circle 547/f30
Ballynoe stone circle 547/f30
Ballyveagh 434-435
Ballyveaghmore 434, 507

Ballyward 293
Balor 142
Bangor (also Beannchair and Beannchor) 488-489, 499, 532/f4
Bann River 128, 242
Banns Road 83, 424-425
Bartlett (map maker) 314
Basking Shark 9, 10, 11
Beanna Boirche **35-37**, 38, 40, 64, 75, 282-283, 289, 307, 310, 499
Bear 21
Bearnagh Slabs 58
Beech nuts 1, 2
Begetting Stones 37, 114-115, **248-269**, 340-341, 450
Belfast 46
Belfast Lough 264, 289, 533/f5
BCD Railway 170
Benandonner 249
Ben Crom 31, 38, 39, 40, 43, 44, 59, 61, **62-64**, 100-102, 167, 192-193, 205, 214-215, 244-245, 271, 291, **294**, 311, 376-377, 430-431, 476, 479, 490, 492
Bilberries (see under Blaeberries)
Bigger, Francis Joseph 169
Binnian (see Slieve Bignian) 45
Binnian Lough 252-253, 472, 477
Bishop's Seat, The 198, 290, 307
Blackberries 2
Black Pig's Dyke 221
Blackstaff River 322
Black Stairs, The 71, **72**, 73, 396
Blaeberries 2, 522/f8
Blaeberry Mountain 2
Bloody Bridge Valley 21, 30, 42, 145, 173, 182-183, 198, 240-241, 268, 285, **288-319**, 325, 369, 374, 376, 385, 411, 489, 490, 500-502
Blue Lough 205, 470-471
Blue Lough Buttress 58, 59, 61
Boar (including Pigs) 19, 21,
22, 26, 141, 142, 145, 164, 266, 268, 328-330, 352, 354, 394-396, 400-401, 403, **414-415**, 441, 444, 447, 463, 464, **466-469**, 470, 476-480, 489
Boazio (map maker) 95
Bog of Donard 385-386
Bowls (see Rock Bowls)
Boyne River 362-363, 372, 385, 409
Brackenagh 436-437
Brandy Pad 44, 47, 49, 107, **120-122**, 141, 163, 178-179
Broughnamaddy 51
Brown, George Herbert 488
Bryansford 292-293, 298, 302, 307, 498
Bryansford Avenue 2
Bryansford Road 12, 42, 95, 107, 126, 134, 505
Bunkers Hill 276, 278, 293, 301, 510
Burns, Friar 504
Burrenreagh 249, 251, 504
Burren River 12
Butter Mountain 128
Buzzard's Roost 43, 223-227, 252-253, 430

Cambrensis, Giraldus 495-499
Carlingford Lough 51, 302, 306
Carn Mountain 40, **47-50**, 311
Carrickfergus 264
Carrick Little 154, 370, 374
Carrigs River 272-273, 274, 278
Carrickinab 513
Carnacaville 293
Carnmoney 504
Carrowmurwaghnemucklagh 21
Carrownaforling 93-94
Carr's Face 290, 291, 303, **316-319**, 371, 376, 393, 415
Carson, William H. 141
Cascade River 96, 102
Cassy Water 51
Castles of Commedagh 40, 178-179, 298-299

559

Castlewellan  33, 93, 170, 249, 293, 298, 301, 306
Cat  21, 26, 30, 222
Cattle  28, 367-368, 411
Causeway Coast  223, 225, 262
Chimney Rock Mnt  1, 2, 21, 23, 27, 28, 36, 68, 142, 145, 146, 154, 158-159, 166, 184-191, 197, 199, **234-235**, 240-241, 252-253, 255, 256, 261, 271, 284-287, 290, 293, 299, 303, 305, 308, 311, 314, **320-341**, 371, 385, 388, 394, 407, 411, 415, 430, 448-451, 467, 475, 489, 490, 516
Christianity  169
Cillan Fort  42
Cistercians  362
Clanawhillan (also as Clonachullion)  104, 106-**108**, 119, 154, 254, 301
Clanbrassil  90
Clanmaghery  516
Clark, Joseph  273
Climbing  225, 343, 351, 475
Cloghmore  135-139, 389
Clonachullion (see Clanawhillan)
Clonduff  35, 52, 53, 56, 352, 354, 430
Clonmacnoise  170
Clough (also Rathcath)  500, 511-512, 521
Coastguard  6, 324-325
Cock & Hen Mountain  54, 126, 128, 131, **134-135**
Cock Mountain  54, 56, 128, **131-134**
Cockles  5, 26
Cod  5
Coffey, George  332
Coiscéim na Caillí  (see Maggie's Leap)
Colgan (hagiographer)  374
Colligan Bridge  422-423
Collins, A.E.P.  1, 515
Cooley Mountains  57, 262, 272
Corrie Wood  301-302
Council  (Newry & Mourne)  39
Cove Mountain (including Upper & Lower Cove)  58, 120, 165, 167, 197, 198-199, 202-203, 223, 232, 248-249, 254, 256, 290, 334, **342-359**, 370, 371, 374, 387, 389-391, 392-393, 415, 489, 491
Cow & Calf  324, 430
Crab  5, 6, 26
Craig, Mr  513
Craignagore  88-89
Cranfield  302, 325
Crawford, Michael G.  306
Crenville Mountain  135-136, 220
Crockanroe  435-436
Crock Horn Stream  293
Crocknafeola Hill  61
Crom Dhu  430, 492
Cromwell, Hugh  66
Crossone Mountain  29, 46, 146, 286, 290, 307, 315, 385, 490
Crotlieve  52, 57, 512
Cruithne  221-222
Cunningham, Charles  307, 434, 435
Cunningham, Stephen  71
Curoe, Rev Richard  509
Curragh Ard  90-92, 95, 315, 371
Curran, Dan  526/f29
Cut Throat, The  324, 430

Dalriada  264
Daniel, Glyn  366
Da Vinci, Leonardo  35
Dane's Cast  220-221
Davies, Dr Oliver  515
De Courcy, John  264, 513-514
Deer  20, 21, 195
Deers Meadow  34, 35, 50, 82, 131, 1134, 494
Delarey Terrace  267
Derinilla  374, 488
Devil's Coach Road  178-179, 371, 373, **374-384**, 387, 389, 430
Diamond Hill  302
Diamond Rocks  **42-47**, 44, 49, 112
Dick, Archibald L. (engraver, New York)  497
Dinneen, Rev Patrick  36, 37, 47, 83, 93, 95, 112, 127, 128, 220, 264, 506
Doan Mountain  40, **42-44**, 46, 49, 118, 211, 245, 311

Dog  21, 166, 189, 222, 285-287
Dolly's Brae  293, 487
Dolmen  (see also Slidderyford, Legananny)  284-287, 323, 330
Dolphin  338, 456-447
Donaghadee  33, 500
Donard  (see Slieve Donard)
Donard Bridge  17
Donard Cove  226-227
Donard Lodge  16
Doran, Arthur  65
Douglas Crag  8, 31, 206-207, **237-239**, 371, 385-386, 426, **462-469**
Downpatrick  33, 169-171, **294-295**, 490
Downpatrick Recorder  170, 272, 515
Downshire  272, 514
Drinnahilly  40, 67, **89-93**, 169
Drinneevar  **64-65**, 123, 181, 266-268
Drinns, The  10, 12, 13, 89-92, 103, 153, 293, 302, 505, 507
Dromena  298
Drumcaw  500, 511, 512, 521
Duck  23, 338
Dugganstown  (in Tollymore Park)  500, 506-508, 512
Dundonald  500
Dundrum  299, 321
Dundrum Bay  5, 10, 16, 26, 169, 219, 220, 232, 312, 321, 324, 325, 474, 500, 511, 512, 520

Eagle Rock  71-78, 82, 84, 175, 223
Eagle Mountain (near Attical)  82-83, 97, 264, 300-301, 397
Earls, The Flight of  355
Echu (king of Mourne, also as 'Echaid')  374, 487
Eels/Elvers  7, 12, 26, 401-402
Eggs  22, 23, 26
Emigration  35, 422
Evans, Professor E. Estyn  34, 45, 52, 119, 182-183, 323, 324, 325, 329, 382, 393-394, 493-494, 515

Face Stones  8, 9, 47, 49, 93, 95, 111-113, 118, 128, 136,

# INDEX

138, **140-167**, 216-217, 236, 247, 260, 274, 338-339, 377, 388, 394, 405, 410, 430, 441, 449, 451, 454-455, 465
Fagan, John 65
Fair Head 223, 225, 264-265
Fairies 53, 110-111, 221
Fairy thorn 53, 54
Famine 35
Farry, Rev Patrick 302
Feeney, Eddy 66
Fennell, W. J. 170
Fern 386-388
Fertility Gates 54-57
Fiddlers Green 138
Finlieve Beg 51
Finn Mac Cool 249
Fir Bolg 142, 219, 220, 227, 372, 421, 499, 504
Fire Bowls (see Rock Bowls)
Fishermen 3, 5, 7, 10, 12, **324**, 325
Fitzmaurice, Thomas 512
Flax 43
Flinn, Charles 2
Flush Loney **272-274**
Flynn, Sarsfield 507
Foffany Dam 153
Forest of Dean 21
Forks Mountain 43, **434-439**, 441, 442, 444-445, 447
Four Masters, Annals of 35, 219, 499
Fox 21, 310-311
Fraochóga (see under Blaeberries)
French Nook 534/f7
Frogs 16, 17, 26, 147, 455

GAA 65, 356
Gaffikin, Masie 515
Giants Causeway **249-251**, 263
Gannet 23
Gedic 198
Geese 12, 23
Gein Stones (see Begetting)
General, The 43
Genome 14
Gibson, W.B. 225
Glasdrumman 65, 66, 263, **311-315**, 324, 488
Glasdrumman Hill (*Gléasdromainn*) 190-191, 210-211, 290, 518-519

Glenaveagh 126-127, 266
Glenfoffany 17, 171, 295
Glen River & valley 16, 17, 71, 79, 82, **84-87**, 147, 148-149, 175, 179, 310, 455
Grange church 302
Great Gap, The 310
Great Gully 82, 97
Greencastle 298, 301-302, 303
Grey Man's Path 223-225, 264
Grouper fish 4, 5
Grouse 26
Guard Dog Dolmen 285-287, 330
Guga Hunt 23

Haddock 5
Hamilton, Rev Mr 515
Hanna, J.W. 515
Hanolock 12
Happy Valley 421-423, 430
Harbour, The 64, 65, 176-177, 266, 268
Hare 441
Hares Castle 184, 246, 298-301
Hares Gap 23, 26, 45, 87, 116, 118-122, 162, 382, 397, 430
Hardy, Paddy 1
Harris, Walter 5, 35, 194-196, 206, 290, 303, 308, 351, 352, 490-491, 512, 513
Haws 2
Hazelnuts 1, 2, 21, 26
Head Road 434
Heaney, Seamus 271
Hen Mountain (see Cock and Hen)
Hermit's Glen 84-86
Herring 5
Hewson, Rev Lindsay 1
Hilltown 494
Hindu Kush 97
Hollybush Road 506
Holywood 264, 266, 500
Horn Bridge 506
Humpback Whale 13
Hurling (Clann na Bárcaighe) 65

Ice House 13, 84
Institute of Irish Studies 34

Irish Language 35, 65, 66
Isle of Man 481
Iveagh 353, 493

James, Mr 33
Janet's Rock 263
Jansson, Joann 198
Jenkin's Point 263
Jenkinstown 263
Jocelyn, Col. 6
Joyce, P.W. 219

Kelly, Professor Michael 69
Kilcoo 106, 298, 478, 504-505
Kilbroney Parish 51, 135-137, 220, 266, 271
Kilfeaghan dolmen 271-272
Kilkeel 5, 302, 493
Kilkeel River 44, 46, 49
Killyglinnie 500, 512-513, 515, 521
Killywoolpa 512
Kilmegan 500, 506-507
Kilmeloge 500, 507-508
Kilmorey, Lord 430
Kilnagreinan 301-302
King's Meadow 35
King Street 267
Kinnahalla 124-128, 130, 230-231, 266
Knock 500
Knockchree 509
Knockgoran 195-201, 315

Lamagan Slabs 58, 59, **60**
Laney 435
Leabhar Gabhála 219
Lecale 33
Lecarry Loanin 228, 393
Leestone 3, 4, 5, 6, 263
Leganabruchan 10, 12, 146, 181, 182-183, 268, 295, 315
Legananny 271, **279-281**
Legawherry, The Pot of 95-102
Leinster, The Book of 374
Leitrim Lodge 299
Lett, Canon Henry William 34, 40, 43, 195, 198, 321, 437
Library 7
Limerick, Lord 195
Limpet 5
Lindsay's Leap 105, 430

561

Linenhall Library  356
Lismohan  500, 512, 521
Lizard, Viviparous  184-185, 186-187, 426, 447
Long Mountain  371
Long Seefin  58, 263
Longstone  216-217
Loudan, Jack
Lough Island Reavy  399
Lough Neagh  422
Lough Ree  170
Lough Shannagh  43, 424
Luke's Mountain  75, **104-106**, 108, 151, 228-229, 236
Lynn, John  146, 232-233
Lynx  21
Lythe & Mercator (map)  47, 470

McAuley's Lake  422
McCauley, David  538/f21
McClean, Master Joseph  106
McDowell, Joseph  273
McEvoy, Stephen  424
McLindon, John  35, 47, 57
McMurray, M.  225
Mac Aodha (map maker)  383
Macartan, Rev John  514
Macassey, Luke  422
Mac Domhnaill, Aodh  307
Maclean, Rachel  21
MacLysaght, Edward
MacMullan, Rev John  509
Magennis  306, 353, 356
Magennis, Arthur  352, **354**
Magennis, Brian MacHugh  307
Magennis, Catherine  353
Maghera  220, 292, 293, 500, 510-511
Magheramayo  293
Maguire, Rev George  509
Maid of the Sweet Brown Knowe  43, **434-435**, 460-461
Maggie's Leap  7, 23
Main Street (Newcastle)  12
Marmion, Canon  302
Massforth  500, 508-509
Mercator, Gerald (map maker)  195, 198
Mice  26, 28, 29
Middle Tollymore Road  1, 298
Midpace River  303

Millstone Mountain  64, 67, 68, 70, 146, 169, 174, 232-233, 296-297, 321
Miners Hole  430-431, 490-491
Minerstown  325
Mirror Stone  23, 26, 86-88, 121
Monaghan, County  37
Moneydarragh  475
Moneydarraghmore  434
Moneylane townland  506
Moneyscalp  96, 292, 302, 504-506
Moolieve Mountain  423-424, 426, 429
Mooney, Fr Bernard  34, 135
Moore-Garrett, James Hugh  301-302
Mottley, Lieutenant S.  324
Mountpanther  512
Mount Sandel  1, 23, 219, 522/f3
*Mourne Country*  34, 45, 182-183, 382, 493-494
Mourne (meaning of)  37-39, 40
Mourne Mountains  33, 34, 43, 52, 64, **176-177**, 195, 220, 242, 266, 284, 294, 308, 310, 321, 322, 369, 370, **372-373**, 374, 406, 422, 437, 443, 480, 497, 511, 520
Mourne Wall  54, 55, 118, 120, 158-159, 264, 316, 325, 377, 394, 399, 410
Mourne Way  92, 153
Moyad Road  57, 61, 302
Mullartown  311, 475
Murlough  1, 5, 176-177, 515
Murphy, James  5
Murphy, Sergeant  273
Murray, Peter  526/f29

Neolithic burial site  284
Newcastle  37, 66, 296-297, 299, 306, 307, 309, 321, 488, 493, 497
Newell's Cross  107
Newgrange  69, 71, 89, 284, 289, 291, 319, 322, 331-333, **360-391**, 397, **408-419**, 421, 462, 463, 466-469
Newtown Road  57

Newry  33, 39, 135, 136, 303, 308
North Tor (Bignian)  60, 61

Octopus  7
O'Donovan, John  33, 34, 35, 37, 43, 47, 52, 57, 67, 75, 116, 131, 267, 268, 289, 299, 307, 308, 311, 312, 314, 315, 369, 438, 462, 494, 495
O'Hagan, Eddie  526/f30
O'Hagan, Mary  492-493
O'Kelly, Claire  366-367, 463
O'Kelly, Professor Michael J.  361, 363-367, 374, 408-410
O'Laverty, Mgr. James  500, 504, 507, 509, 511, 512, 518
Old Town  274
O'Neill, Hugh the Great  353
O'Neill, The (Lisbon)  343, 355-357
Ordnance Survey  33, 34, 43, 50, 91, 96, 105, 116, 125, 131, 134, 135, 194, 198, 267, 278, 295, 300, 307, 312, 369, 397, 404, 421, 425, 470, 491, 494, 508
Ore River  272
Ó Ríordáin, Seán  361, 366, 369
Otter  21
Oxford  219
Oysters  5

Parnell's View  10, 12, 13
Patton's Bridge  17
Percy Bysshe  **221-223**, 259, 289, 348, 371, 430, 474
Periwinkles (see under Winkles)
Phallic Stones  **168-217**
Phoenix  344
Pierces Castle  57, 298-300, 334
Pig (see Boar)
Pigeon Mountain  58, 59, 61, 295
Pine Marten  21
Pish-Metter  307
Place-names project, Queens  3, 35, 47, 52, 61, 64, 74, 88, 91, 96, 105, 108, 119, 124, 125, 126, 127, 137, 295, 299, 307, 314, 316, 349, 383, 438, 462, 518

# INDEX

Plaice 5
Pollaphuca Hollow 3, 6, 7, 9, 10, 20, 108-118, 121, 141, 164, 210-211, **212-213**, 228, 258, 393
Porter, Tom 307, 493
Pownall, Governor Thomas 332
Praeger, Robert Lloyd 85-86, 136, 137, 275
Ptolemy 220, 321, 322
Pulgarve 79

Quarter Road 58, 263, 432-433
Quarry 66, 92-93, 109, 118, 121-123, 125, 154, 221, 233, 241, 266, 316-319, 376, 425, 434-437, 451

Ram 23, 27
Rathcath (see Clough)
Rathfriland 33, 52, 306
Rathmullan 500, 517-518, 521
Raven 441, 452
Raven Rocks 307, 430
Razor-shells 5, 26, **205**
Red Hand, The 343, **352-357**, 388
Rede Joints 46
Reeves, Bishop William 512
Renfrew, Colin 361
Rhys, Sir John 219
Richey, Dr James Ernest 46
Ritual Platform 21, 88-89, 357, 371, 375, **376-379**, **409-414**, 474, 476-479, 489-491, 501
Rock Bowls, 242, 308, 330, 404, 406-407, 470, 474-477
Rocky Mountain (three of) 50-58, 128, 184, 198, 199, 240-241, 246, 263, 299, 323, 343-345, 358-359, 371, 512
Roden, Lord 6, 292, 307, 506
Rodgers, Hugh 523/f17
Rose-hips 2
Rossglass 312, 325, 500, 518-519, 521
Rostrevor 34, 57, 136, 220
Round Seefin 58
Rowley, Richard 393, 477-478, 501-503
Royal Irish Academy 43

Sally Lough 423
Salmon 7, 26
Sandbank Road 134
Sand eels 5
Scardan Hill 50, 423
Scarva 306
Schollogstown 325, 518
Scotland 23, 64
Scrabo 276-277
Seaforde 511
Seagulls 22, 24-25, 210-211, 214-215, 329
Seals 3, 5, 8, 9, 26, 261
Shamrock 497-499
Shannagh More 310-311
Shan Slieve 97-98, 103-104, 294
Shark (see also Basking Shark) 9, 402
Sheep 27, 153
Shelter Stones 38, 39, 63
Shimna River 6, 7, 12, 16, 22, 499
Shrew 19, 21, 32, 33, 198, 465
Silent Valley 25, 42, 50, 141, 180, 204-205, 215, **421-424**, 430
Skara Brae 5
Slates, The 82-84, 264
Slidderyford dolmen 9, 11, 75, **270-283**, 512
Slieveanowen 51
Slieve Bearnagh 8, 9, 20, 40, 44, 68, 105, 106, 109, 110, 118, 120-122, 125, 141, 151, 158-159, 160-161, 164, 166, 178-179, 210-211, 212-213, 223, 228-229, 257, 262, 286, 291, 292, 293, 318-319, 370, 373, 375, 376, 387, 389-391, **392-419**, 466-469, 474
Slieve Beg 162, 290, 370, 371, 374, 375, 376, **379-384**, 387-391
Slieve Bignian 36, 42, 43, 59, 64, 118, 141, 145, 154, 180, 184, 198, 202, 204-205, 223, 226, 231, 242, 242-243, 245, 268, 284, 301, 352, 370, 371, 393, **420-485**
Slieve Bolg (also Builge, Bug) 42, 43, 289, 429, 437
Slieve Commedagh 75, 77-82, 85, 97, 148-149, 175, 178-179, 198, 280-283, 370, 371, 374, 452-453, 463, 494, 510, 512, 515
Slieve Corragh 45, 46, 96, 97, 98-99, 100-102, 294
Slieve Croob 93-95, 123, 495,
Slievedermot 40, 135-137, 266,
Slieve Donard 13, 21, 26, 29, 33, 42, 46, 67, 70, 71, 74, 78-79, 81-82, 84, 85, 87, 110, 113, 147, 148-150, 165, 172-174, 178-179, 189, 194, 198-199, 219, 220, 268, 289, 290, 308, 311, 322, 332, 352, 371, 373, **376-379**, 389, 394, 403, 421, 436, 448, 463, 467, 472-473, 495, 501, **514**
Slieve Donard race 71
Slieve Lamagan 31, 38, 39, 40, 58, **60**, 63, 64, 141, 204-205, **206**, 218-219, 223, 227, 242-243, 248-249, 259, 323, 325, 334-335, 343, 344, 353, 370, 371, 374, 384, 394, 430, 466-469, 470, 472, **474**
Slieve Loughshannagh 311, 393
Slievemageogh 82-83
Slievemartin 40, 135, **136-139**
Slieve Meelbeg 244-245, 421-423
Slieve Meelmore 20, 23, 24-25, 75, 106, 108, **111-118**, 141, 154, 178-179, 210-211, 212-213, 258, 262, 292, 394, 396, 421, 506-507
Slievemiskan 51
Slievemoughanmore 295, 301
Slieve Muck 19, 22, 47, 50, 59, 61, 62, 128, 129, 207, 323
Slievenabrock 89-90, 92, 95-98
Slievenagarragh 191, 210-211, 241, 268-269, 312, **313-315**
Slievenaglogh (at Trassey) 47, 75, 105, 106, 118, 120, 124, 151, 152, 156-157, 228-229, 236, 254, **382**, **428-430**

563

Slievenaglogh (at Silent Valley) 50, 206-207, 421, 422, 424-431, 428, 491
Slievenagore 62, 425
Slievenalargy 170
Slievenamaddy **39-42**, 51, 79, 84, 88, 222, 289, 423
Slievenaman 154-155, 311, 504
Slievenamiskan 34, 35, 51, 124, 128, 130-132
Slievenamuck 311
Slievenaslat 83, 93-94, 264
Slieve Neir 195, 307-309, 314-315
Slievenisky 123
Slieveroe 51
Slieve Slángha 219
Slieve Snavan 194-198
Slieve Thomas 9, 13, 14-15, 64, 66, 67, 68, 71, 75, 79, 84, 87, 105, 214-215, 260, 394
Smacks, fishing 5
Smith, Robert 273
Smuggling 88, 324, 492
Snaefell 481
Snakes 495-498
Sole 5
South Barrule 481
Spaltha 124, 126-127
Spear of Abundance 284, **288-319**, 332, 369, 370, 371, 373, 385-386, 394, 397, 414-415, 519
Spear Stones 22, 73, 76, 88, 90, 118, 123, **168-217**, 338, 343, 351, 357, 438, 447
Spelga 34, 124, 126-132, 230-231, 266, 494
Spelga Dam 35, 51, 164
Spellack 9, 106, **107-109**, 112, 151, 156-157, 223, 246-247, 257, 489
Spence's Mountain 2, 403
Sperm Whale 10, 12
Spiers, James 292
Spinkwee valley 9, 89, 95, **102-104**, 153, 315, 507
Srupatrick 493-494, 497

St Bronagh's chapel 136-137
St Donard 42, 116, 227, 374, **377-379**, 487
St John's, Church of Ireland (Tyrella) 330, 515-516, 521
St John's Parish 289
St John's Point 169, 232, 263, 289, 321, 324, 325, 500, 507, 519-521
St Laisrén 264
St Mary's, Ballaghanery 198, 290, 500-502, 507, 521
St Patrick 169-171, 487-489, **493-498**, 521
Stoat 21
Stokes, Whitley 219
Stonehenge 480
Stout, Geraldine & Matthew 369, 370
Strangford Lough 276
Squirrel 21
Swan (Whooper & Mute) 12, 23, 26, 87, 121, 125-126, 437

Taylor, Mrs 273
Thierafurth 298
Thompson, John 488-489
Tievedockaragh 52, 57, 512
Tollymore 21, 298
Tollymore Forest Park 10, 92, 195, 249, 292, 505-508, 512
Tom & Jerry 26, 28, 29, 30
Top of the Hill 67-69, 174
Trassey River & Valley 9, 107, 111, 118-121, 124, 151, 152, 154, 157, 236, 257, 310, 421, 428
Triple Spiral, The 384-391
Tuama (see Slieve Thomas)
Tuatha Dé Danann 110
Tubbercorran stone circle 514
Tullybrannigan 90, 92, **95-97**
Tullybrannigan River 12
Tullynasoo 93
Tullyree Road 56, 411
Turbot 5

Turtle 31, 181, 206, 267, 268, 439, 456-447
Twelve Arches, The 272-273
Tyrella 325, 330, 500, 515-517, 521

Ulster 116, 198, **220-221**, 249, 262, 321, 355-359, 487, 499
Ulster Journal of Archaeology 43, 170, 343, 355

Vagina Stones 218-247
Vallancey, Charles 323, 331-333, 361-362
Venus 41
Vikings 220, 221
Vinycomb, John 356

Wales 31
Wasp 326-330
Water Commissioners, Belfast 422
Water Supply Act 422
Wee Bignian 43, 425-431, 436
Wee Slievemoughan 295
Whale 9, 10, 12, 13, 14-15, 26, 66, 86, 444-445, 499-500
Wheat 26
Whitehead 264, 533/f5
Whiteside's Garage 7
White Water 61, 83
Whiting 5
Whortleberries (see under Blaeberries)
Wild Forest Lane 298
Wilde, Sir William 361
Williams (map) 64, 438
Williamson (map maker) 34
Windy Gap 82-83, 301-302, 397, 430
Winkles 5, 6
Wolf 18, 21
Wolfhound 189
Wright, Dr E. 365

Yellow Water 83

564

*Children playing in front of Hamersley Iron housing in Tom Price, Western Australia, 1974 [Wolfgang Sievers, courtesy National Library of Australia Wa.pic-vn 3308495-v].*

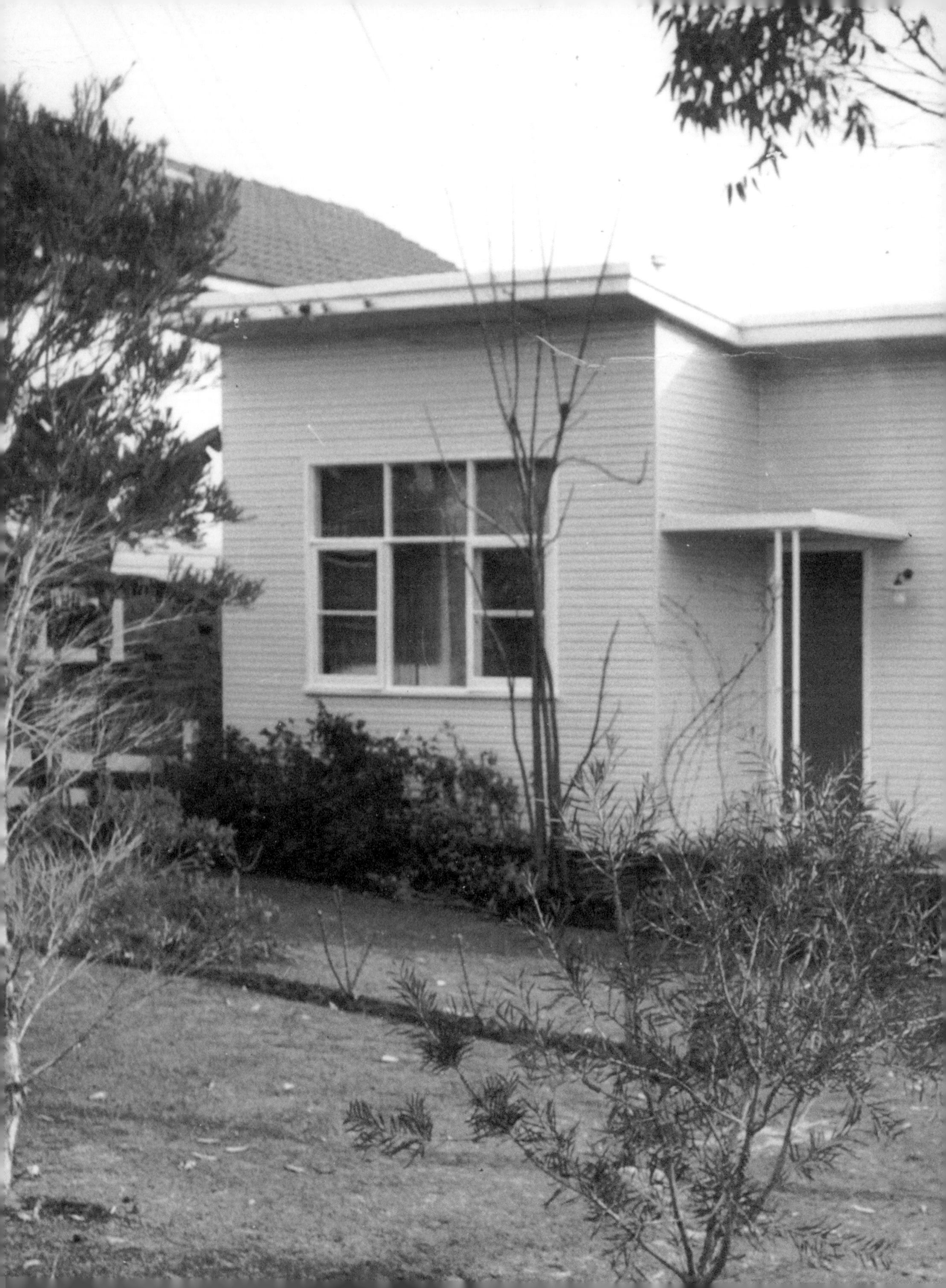

This book is dedicated to my parents Gerhard and Robin Weller who bought their first home in the western suburbs of Sydney in 1962 and raised happy kids.

JOHN GLENN: *Just to my right I can see a big pattern of lights, apparently right on the coast.*
NASA: *Roger...that is Perth and Rockingham that you are seeing.*
JOHN GLENN: *The lights show up very well and thank everyone for turning them on.*

*Face of the Earth.*™
*[ArcScience Simulations. c. 2008.]*

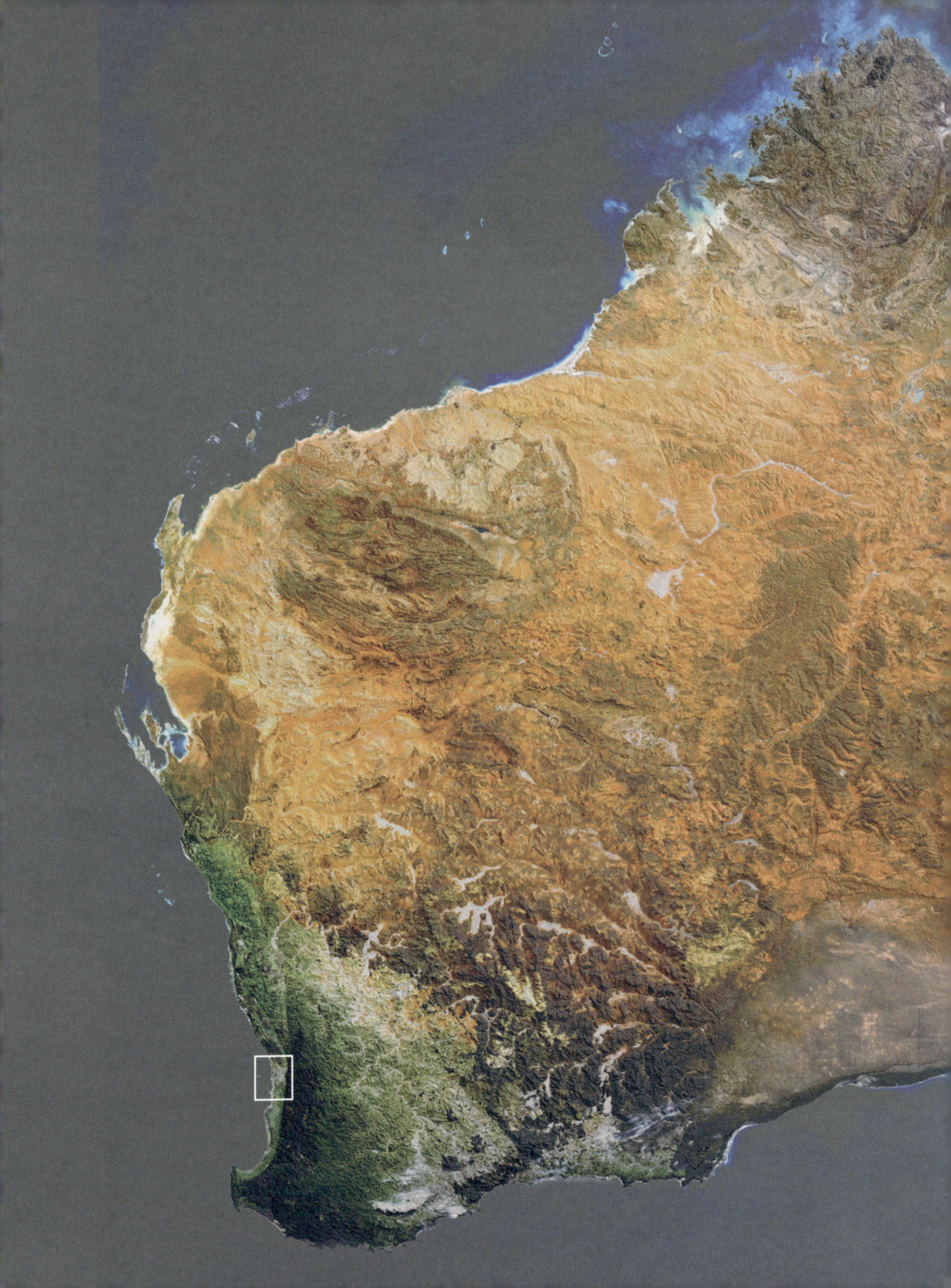

# Unlike the light-footed nomad who ranged across the landscape attuned to its flux and flow, cities, because they are fixed in one place, must bring everything unto themselves.

Ever since the first villages clustered around rudimentary farmland in Mesopotamian floodplains, settled people have struggled to draw sustenance from their surrounding landscape. With some food in storage, the ancient city temporarily freed itself from nature's cycles and incubated larger numbers of people than the surrounding ecosystem would otherwise (nomadically) have sustained. Because the city then invariably exhausts its surrounding land it must, if it is to survive, spread further afield. The ever-expanding city must trade what it has in surplus for what it doesn't. Collectively, cities thus form a network of interdependence and antagonism, a web that now covers the whole planet. In order to survive, the city has literally had to go to the ends of the earth. The city has become the world. This sketch of the problem of settlement is borne out to this day as Perth exhausts its hinterland to produce crops, some of which are exported back to sustain populations in the Middle East, the very landscapes where the first cities began. Now that there is no more new territory from which to replenish its stocks, the world-city must, for the first time in its history, try to creatively adapt to its environmental limits.

The city of Perth in its regional landscape context.
Landsat imagery provided by the ACRS at Geoscience Australia, and digitally enhanced by Landgate (Western Australian land information authority).

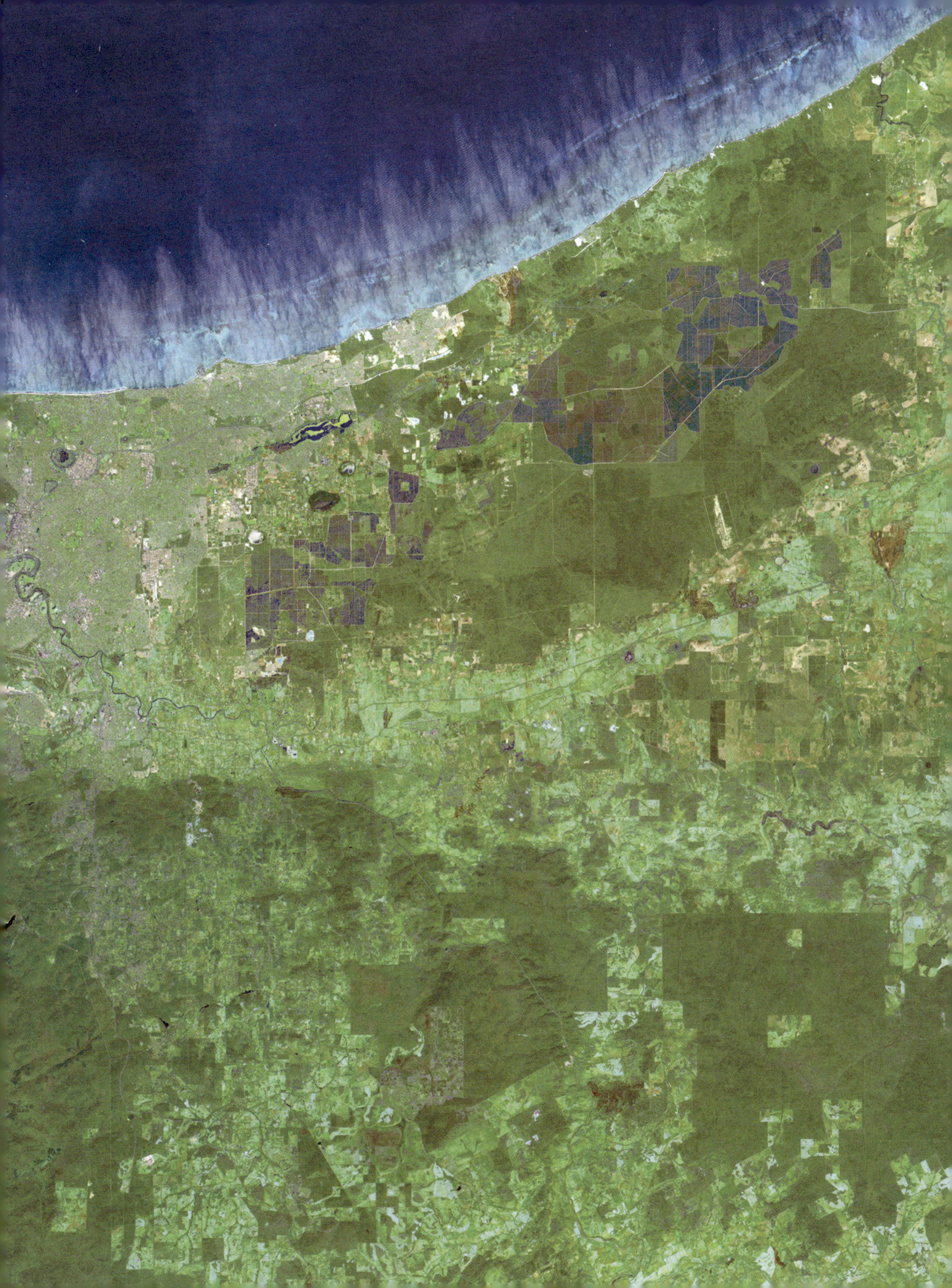

Perth's current population of circa 1.5 million is predicted to more than double by 2050. To accommodate this influx we need to build at least 700,000 homes. More than housing, the city's entire infrastructure will have to double. What was built in 179 years will need to be reproduced in 40.

## A Note on Structure and Content

This book documents two years of work by a team of researchers based at The University of Western Australia Landscape Architecture program, funded by the Australian Research Council. The project concerns the creation of different scenarios for the future of Perth's urban form. Although the city of Perth is the central subject, the methods and ideas you will find in this book could be applied and adjusted to suit any city experiencing rapid growth.

While based on empirical data, the work documented here is also speculative. It's what is called research by design: when creative processes are used in tandem with more conventional research practices. The product is a form of 'landscape urbanism', an emerging international school of thought that argues for shaping cities with greater regard for their landscape conditions. Landscape urbanism suggests a form of urbanity that respects the constraints of the landscape's ecology but also seeks out opportunities for development, which draws inspiration from that landscape.

The book's structure and content follows the process of the research. We begin by situating Perth in its historical context then survey its physical and cultural conditions. We then map Perth's landscape systems so as to find any constraints and opportunities for growth. These constraints and opportunities in turn help define and generate a range of scenarios for the large-scale development of the city into the future. These scenarios embody Australian Bureau of Statistics' projections that Perth's population will at least double in the next four decades. The scenarios objectively manifest this projection in horizontal and vertical forms of urban growth. The scenarios are all set against the benchmark of the status quo: what is referred to in the book as Business as Usual. The practice of Business as Usual is documented by a visual essay, The Cutting Edge. When discussing Business as Usual we reflect on the difficulties of innovation at the level of conventional development by visiting two exemplary projects: one in far-flung suburbia, Wungong Urban Water; and the second in the city centre, the New Perth Waterfront. As a complement to the otherwise very large-scale scenarios, toward the end of the book we also zoom in to look at housing and offer some examples of innovative work being done by Perth's best architects.

While this research process can be traced linearly through the book, it is not the only route one can take. The book is intended as a resource, something that can be dipped into at different points and at different times by anyone interested or directly involved in making the city.

Preface, by Charles Waldheim — XIII

# 1 INTRODUCTION — Richard Weller and David Hedgcock — 015
# 2 DATABASE — 047
# 3 LOCAL CULTURE — 131
# 4 MAPPING — 147
# 5 METHOD — 165
# 6 BAU CITY — 179
# 7 THE CUTTING EDGE — 201
# 8 BAU+ — 237

*Wungong Urban Water: An innovative model, by Brett Wood Gush* — 239
*A suburb 'as if the landscape really mattered?', by Richard Weller* — 250

# 9 NEW SCENARIOS — 257
# 10 HORIZONTAL SCENARIOS — 261

*POD City* — 265
*Food City* — 275
*Car Free City* — 291
*Seachange City* — 297
*Treechange City* — 305

# 11 VERTICAL SCENARIOS — 309

*Sky City* — 341
*Perth's New Waterfront* — 355
*River City* — 361
*The Path of Density, by Anthony Duckworth-Smith* — 371
*Surf City* — 375

# 12 DIVERCITY — 389
# 13 DREAM HOMES — 397

*Dream Homes, by Dale Alcock* — 399
*Hyper Housing, by Simon Anderson* — 403
*Think Brick, by iredale pedersen hook* — 419
*Prix d'Amour, by Jon Tarry and Darryn Ansted* — 429

*Acknowledgements* — 443
*Media & Publications* — 445
*Contributors* — 447
*Index* — 449

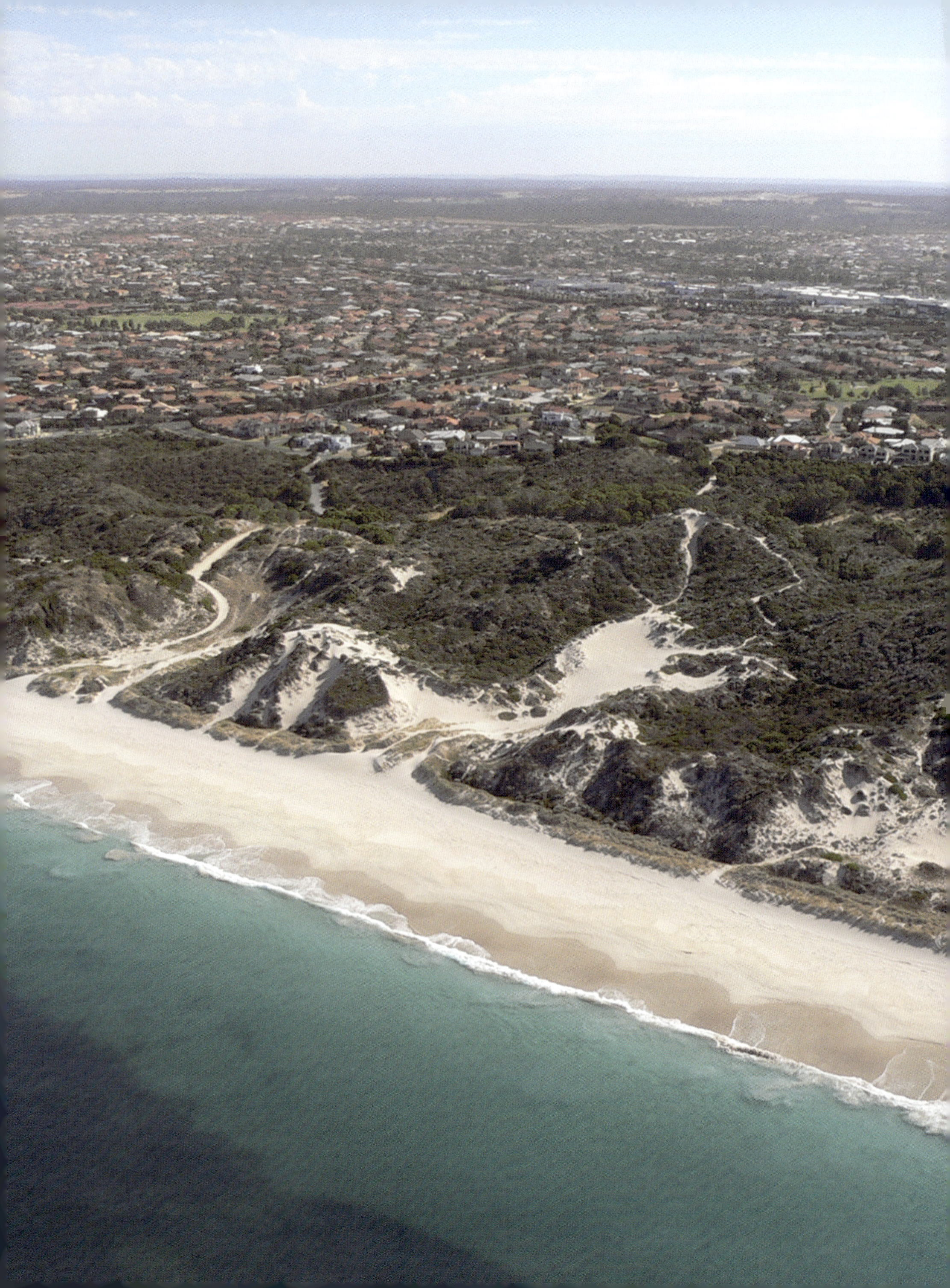

## News from Nowhere

Perth first registered in international media in 1962 by turning on its lights to illuminate the South-Western coast of Australia for astronaut John Glenn orbiting the earth in Friendship 7. As chronicled in Tom Wolfe's *The Right Stuff*, the luminous outline of Perth's growing urban bounds afforded the astronaut a moment of terrestrial orientation during an otherwise disorienting series of short days and nights in orbit. With the publication of *Boomtown 2050*, the outline of Perth's urban agglomeration once again affords international audiences a momentary sense of self-recognition amid the disorientation and dross of contemporary urbanisation. Regardless of its distance from the conditions for urbanisation in other parts of the globe, Perth, as described here, is both legible to local readers while illuminating the conditions for urban form internationally.

Perth's singularity and remoteness make it an unlikely indicator of tendencies and trends evident elsewhere. Perth is closer to the urban populations of Indonesia and Malaysia than to the eastern Australian metropolises of Sydney or Melbourne. Even the city's own website describes Perth, with no small pride, as the most remote urban centre in the world. Notwithstanding the contradictions of such a depiction, Perth has consciously constructed an image of itself as a city at the edge of the urbanised world, at once remote from and insulated from the natural and cultural references representing ersatz urban form in the western world. Self-consciously constructed distance aside, the Perth carefully described in this publication by Richard Weller and his colleagues at the University of Western Australia emerges as an uncannily reliable reflection of urban conditions internationally.

In spite of the historical and cultural conditions specific to Perth's history and future delineated in *Boomtown 2050*, contemporary Perth demonstrates an accelerated aggregation of the ecological eclipse and territorial tendencies of cities across the globe. The city is growing at a pace that merits comparison with its Asian contemporaries and easily outpaces the American equivalents of Las Vegas and the like. Perth's growth predictably outpaces the sustainability of its considerable natural resources, and long ago outstripped the regional supply of fresh water. Despite this lack of sustainability, even the most cautious projections suggest the city will continue to explode with immigrant population over the coming decades.

In the context of the city's ongoing unsustainable growth the publication of *Boomtown 2050*, and the research it assembles, offers a timely and authoritative account of the numerous questions facing Perth's residents at the intersection of environmental affordance, urban form and public policy. Beyond those local concerns, the publication offers international audiences a compelling image of the use of design as a form of urban research. Weller's text, photographs, drawings, diagrams and design proposals construct an impressive array of empirical research into the conditions of the contemporary city and the disciplines that aspire to describe it. In doing so, the publication promises to once again use the illuminated outline of Perth's urban extremities to shed light on the decidedly global conditions for remote urban populations. It should be required reading for students of the city worldwide.

*Charles Waldheim*

# 1

# INTRODUCTION

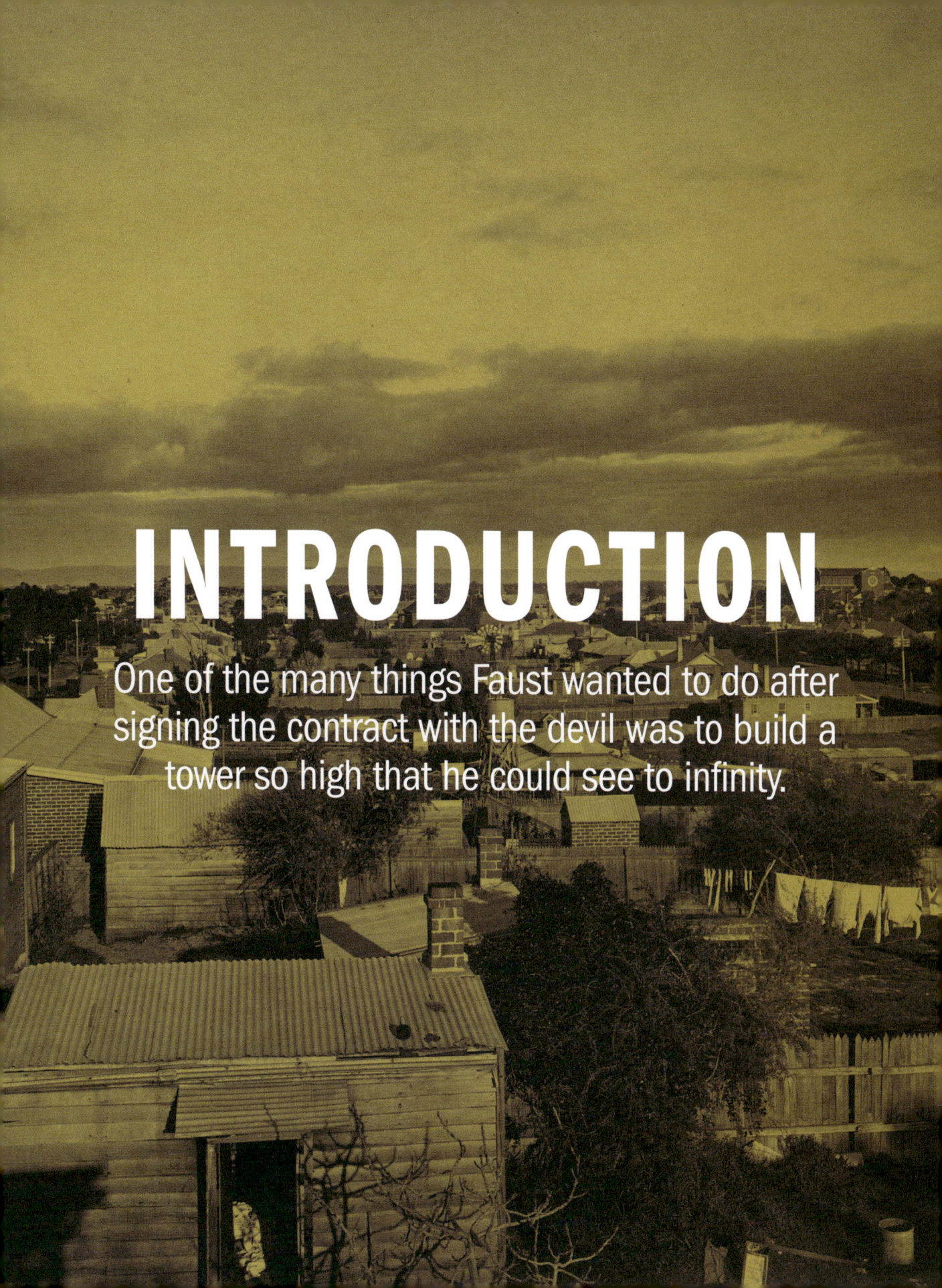

One of the many things Faust wanted to do after signing the contract with the devil was to build a tower so high that he could see to infinity.

Swan R.
Ellen R.
Guildford
Road from Guildford to York
Halfway Ho.
Perth
PERTH
Mt Eliza
Perth Wr
Pt Belches
Pt Pelican
Pt Heathcote
Melville Wr
Pt of Perth
Pt Walter
Helena R.
Canning R.
Kelmscott
Rocky
Rous Hd
Swan R.
Fremantle
T. Harrison
G. Robb
Woodman Pt
Clarence
G. Dunnage
Cockburn
Sound
T. Watson
Brown Hill
T. Peel
English Miles
Halfway Ho.
to York
Helena R.
Continuation of the Helena R.

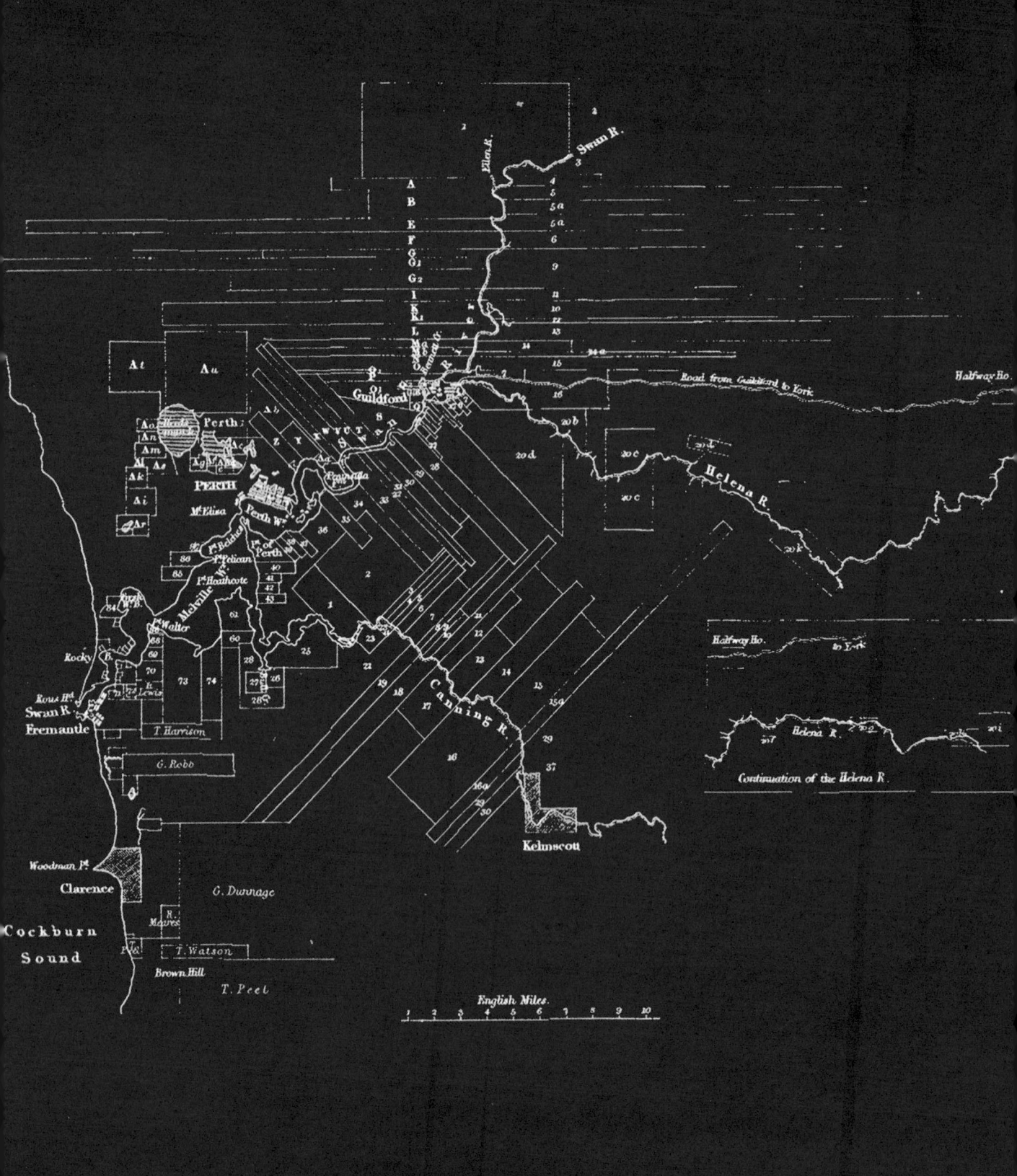

# BOOMTOWN 2050

To build this tower a village had to be removed – an allegory for tradition that always stands in the way of what we optimistically still refer to as 'progress'. Upon realising that his creative powers were also destructive, Faust experienced anxiety then guilt and regret. Regardless, Mephistopheles spurs Faust onward, exhorting him not to look back. Exhorting him to be modern! And so it goes: the infinitely creative force of modernity is coupled with, and seems impossible without, its counterpart – destruction. Since Goethe penned the tale of Faust in 1806 there have been just over 200 years of such progress and the destruction of the world has burgeoned; so much so that the very atmosphere into which Faust's tower would soar, the clear air through which he would see to infinity is itself now polluted by our actions. As a consequence 'our' world now heats up, the icecaps melt and the oceans rise. The waters of life now lap corrosively at the base of the Faustian tower. Many of the images in this book are views from somewhere within that allegorical tower. But they are not about the infinite, rather, they suggest that the city cannot just violently progress, it must now creatively adapt to its limits.

History has shown that cities are very adaptable. Some cities have a record of settlement for over 2000 years as generations of settlers have moved in, rebuilt and expanded the urban fabric to meet the emerging demands of such factors as defence, production and cultural expression. Cities have demonstrated a tremendous responsiveness to social, economic and environmental imperatives. For all its contemporary ills, the city still engages the senses, motivates the individual and generates new lives and lifestyles at an ever-increasing rate. Cities are living monuments to a long history.

Perth has only a short history – less than 200 years – but in that time it has grown from a pioneer outpost to a modern metropolis. It has adapted to revolutions in production, employment, transport and technology. The comfortable suburban environment that Perth has become now faces the prospect of radical change. In a booming economy, predicted to last for decades, populations are now queuing up to call Perth home. We could just go on producing more of the same form of suburbia that we currently enjoy but questions of the availability of cheap oil, food and water, and changing lifestyles, suggest that alternative forms of urbanism need to be explored.

This book is about recognising, documenting and addressing future urban change in Perth and challenging us all to think about the future impact of this growth on the character of the city. The various development scenarios we present in this book are intended as

*Perth's original sub-division, 1839 [Courtesy State Library of Western Australia, Battye Library: rare map 24 1. 12].*

*Canning Road, Bicton [courtesy State Library of Western Australia, Battye Library, 10539P].*

realistic development options but more than anything they are intended to incite more creative debate about what Perth might become by 2050. The time is right for Perth to discuss and plan its future. Indeed it has the luxury to do so: unlike many others in the world this city is not yet out of control. Perth has a strong planning tradition and a well-organised planning administration, but in order to fulsomely debate its future the community requires clear and compelling visions of alternatives to conventional suburban sprawl.

The early European agricultural settlement of the Swan Coastal Plain was not a success; however, important lessons were learnt through the bitter experience of failure. Early exploration sought out the less-sandy soils of the Pinjarra Plain, Swan Valley and ultimately the ancient clays of the escarpment and beyond. The agricultural settlers quickly left the sand plain to the artisans, administrators and entrepreneurs, who would form the kernel of urban settlement that in later years was to grow into the Perth Metropolitan Region.

The scattered, dispersed and predominantly rural settlement of the Swan Coastal Plain finally gave way to more distinctively urban characteristics with the discovery of gold in the distant regional areas of the colony in the 1890s. The early centres of Fremantle, Perth and Guildford were vital as a conduit to the Goldfields for the thousands of prospectors and miners that descended on the fledgling colony.[1] In the 10 years between 1891 and 1901, the population in Perth grew from 16,000 to 61,000.[2] The increasing population quickly led to the overcrowding of existing residential accommodation. When development reached capacity, squatter colonies (mainly tent cities) sprung up on the outskirts of existing settlements in areas like East Fremantle and Subiaco.[3] In these overcrowded and transient environments disease spread rapidly. Water-borne diseases such as typhoid and cholera were an ever-present threat given the lack of fresh water and the inadequate provision for sewerage disposal.[4] In such an environment the landscape was less of an inspiration as it was a constant reminder of the harsh and alien conditions of a newly settled continent.

The lure of gold brought more than adventure-seekers to the colony. It also brought genuine wealth. The state treasury that had struggled for so long to meet its debts to the United Kingdom was rewarded with the royalties that flowed from the discovery and exploitation of the colony's resources. Public works could now be planned and implemented. From 1890 to 1900 ports, roads, bridges and water-supply provision were all built in a huge expansion of public infrastructure that was to have a major impact on lives and lifestyles in the region.[5]

1. Stannage, C.T., *The People of Perth: A Social History of Western Australia's Capital City*, Perth City Council, Perth, 1979.

2. McCarty, J.W., 'Australian Capital Cities in the Nineteenth Century', Schedvin, C.B. and McCarty, J.W. (eds), *Urbanization in Australia: The Nineteenth Century*, Sydney University Press, Sydney, 1970.

3. Webb, M., 'Urban Expansion, Town Improvement and the Beginning of Town Planning in Metropolitan Perth', Gentilli, J. (ed), *Western Landscapes*, University of Western Australia Press, Perth, 1979.

4. Webb, M., 'Urban Expansion, Town Improvement and the Beginning of Town Planning in Metropolitan Perth', Gentilli, J. (ed), *Western Landscapes*, University of Western Australia Press, Perth, 1979.

5. Le Page, J.S.H., *Building a State: The Story of the Public Works Department of Western Australia 1829-1985*, Water Authority of Western Australia, Perth, 1986.

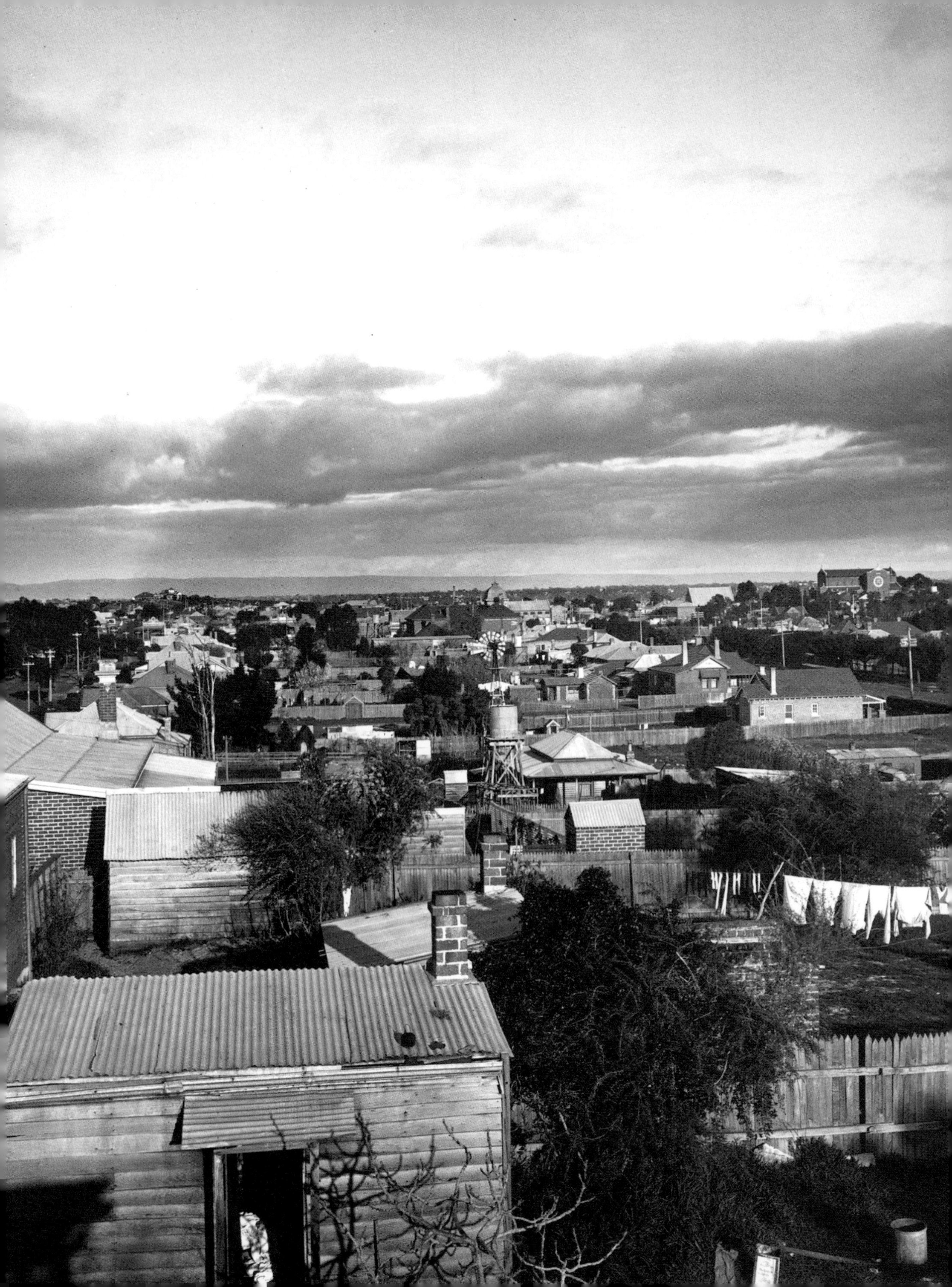

While so much of the early settlement took on the bush as a natural frontier to be conquered, the emergent city parks at least paid due homage to the role of nature as an antidote to the overcrowded slum housing that had begun to dominate the city. The obvious enjoyment of the parks as centres of recreation kept the seeds of a landscape tradition alive among Perth's populace. It was this tradition that was ultimately to infuse the suburbs with a sense of landscape, if not a sense of place.

The landscape setting of early suburbia is a classic tale of pioneering. The bush was the background to this setting and it was never far away. But in the houses and gardens the quest for order, permanence, regularity and uniformity prevailed. Beginning with the front garden the residents imposed their Anglo-Saxon will and values on the landscape transforming it totally into an image of their making. While the back garden took longer to succumb to such ministrations, the potential and possibilities had been revealed and as the century unfolded so too did the landscape of suburbia.

Suburban growth away from the increasingly congested centres of Fremantle and Perth became a viable option with the introduction of suburban railways, beginning in 1881 and followed shortly after by the introduction of trams.[6] This public transport infrastructure allowed families to live away from the crowded and increasingly unhealthy city centres, yet maintain a link to their employment and service opportunities. With none of the constraints of walkability, suburban life spread the urban region beyond its narrow confines and created the next generation of pioneers. These pioneers faced the same challenges as the early settlers that went before them: the heat, the sand, the isolation and the omnipresent bush.

Early suburban development was largely uncontrolled, and houses and even suburbs developed around Perth and Fremantle in an almost random distribution. Many lots put up for sale were slow to be developed. Others were never sold and many more were left in the hands of speculative purchasers who had no development intentions.[7] The subdividers of this early suburban land had few responsibilities to their future residents. There was no requirement to build roads or provide any services. The acquisition of a suburban lot invariably gave the purchaser a pegged area of largely undisturbed bushland fronting an unmade road reserve that could be some distance from the nearest suburban service centres. However, the lack of services did secure two important characteristics of these early suburbs: the land was both cheap and plentiful. In addition, some of the much derided natural conditions of the land began to be turned to the advantage of the suburban pioneers.

6 Selwood, J., 'Public Transport and Urban Growth', Gentilli J. (ed), *Western Landscapes*, University of Western Australia Press, Perth, 1979

7 Selwood, J., 'Public Transport and Urban Growth', Gentilli, J. (ed), *Western Landscapes*, University of Western Australia Press, Perth, 1979.

*Maylands backyards, 1920s [courtesy State Library of Western Australia, Battye Library, 001738D].*

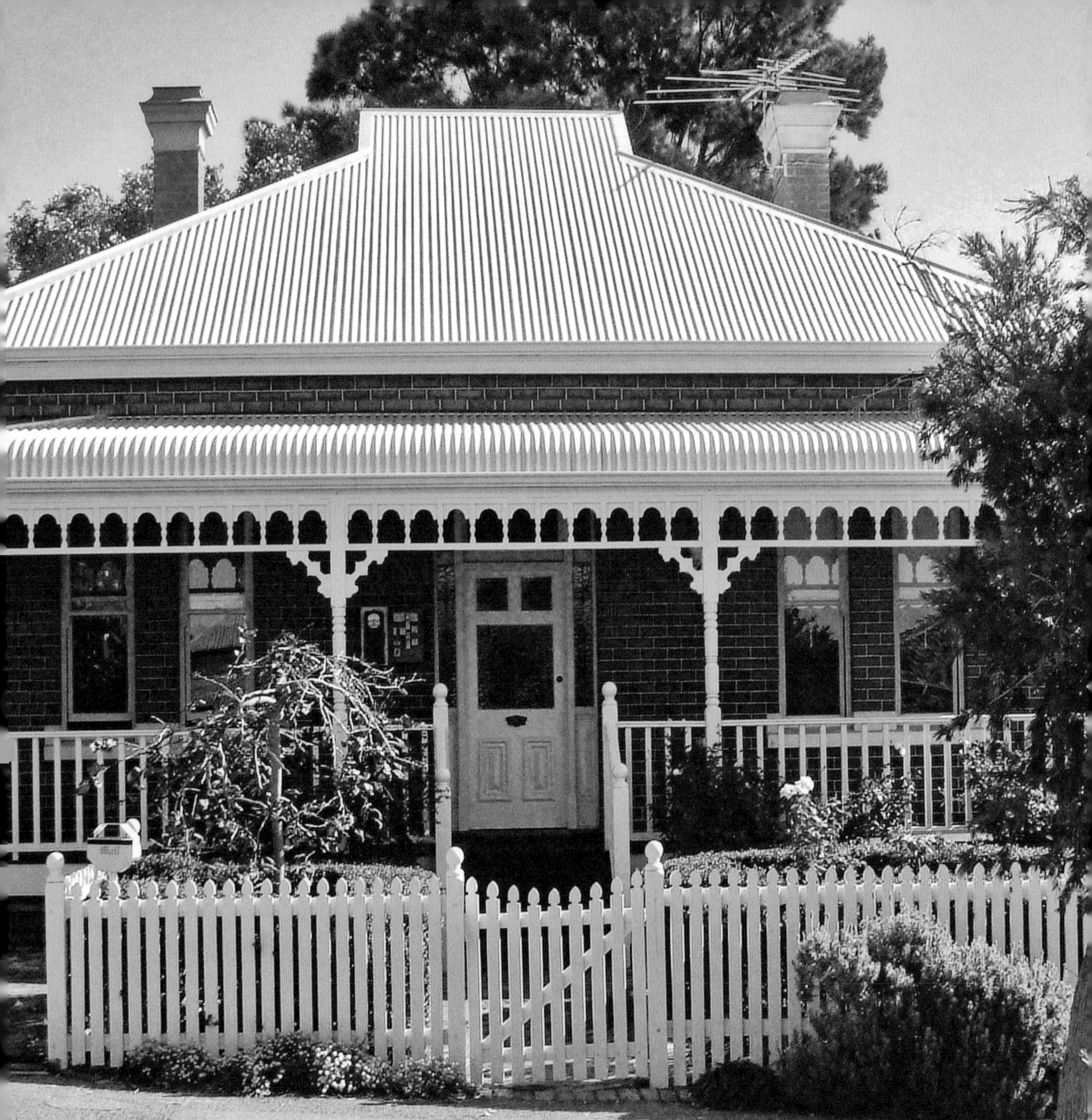

With no reticulated water available, residents were vulnerable to summer drought but over most of the Perth region the groundwater system provided ready access to a reliable, if not exactly palatable, supply of water. Wells were dug and windmills were constructed to draw the water to the surface. The lack of sewerage was also overcome by making use of that much maligned natural characteristic of the coastal plain: sand. Sand proved to be an excellent filter for the septic tanks that were developed to treat domestic waste. While this form of self-sufficient infrastructure provided significant independence for the new suburban resident it also carried a significant health threat: the potential pollution of a resident's water source from their own sewage. By the turn of the century it was known that such pollution was the cause of a number of debilitating and often deadly diseases such as dysentery and typhoid.[8] The solution required water extraction to be isolated from sewerage disposal and authorities began insisting on minimum lot sizes to ensure that adequate separation could be achieved. The recommended standard of the day was a quarter of an acre (1,012 m$^2$).[9]

It was the combination of the natural bush setting, the absence of developed roads, reticulated water, sewerage and electricity services, and the large quarter-acre blocks that gave the early suburbs their enduring qualities of space, nature and independence. Certainly the lot sizes were considerably larger than the mainly modest houses required by the early suburban settlers. Large backyards were typical and their functional qualities suited the developing character of suburban pioneers. The remaining trees on the lots were used for fuel to heat the home, to cook and to boil the water for the weekly wash. There was plenty of space for waste to be burnt and buried and a range of livestock such as horses, goats and even cows could be suitably accommodated to serve a range of important functions for the residents.[10] As John Freeland explains 'the often extensive backyards were more likely to be utilitarian with vegetable plots, poultry runs, workshops, wood sheds, fruit trees and the essential clothes lines'.[11] With the backyards of suburban lots devoted to the functional necessities of suburban life the frontage of the lots could be developed for more aesthetic purposes.

While there was such a strong spirit of independence in these early suburbs, communal life was not slow to evolve. Early settlers banded together to lobby the state government for the provision of services and when this was resisted they applied, via petition, to establish Road Boards (the earliest form of local government) with the authority to levy rates on householders to provide for the basic services that the subdividers had neglected to

8  Webb, M., 'Urban Expansion, Town Improvement and the Beginning of Town Planning in Metropolitan Perth', Gentilli, J. (ed), *Western Landscapes*, University of Western Australia Press, Perth, 1979.

9  Hedgcock, D. and Hibbs, T., 'Perth's Suburban Traditions: From Orthodoxy to Innovation', Hedgcock, D. and Yiftachel, O. (eds), *Urban and Regional Planning in Western Australia. Historical and Critical Perspectives*, Paradigm Press, Perth, 1992.

10  Stannage, C.T., *The People of Perth: A Social History of Western Australia's Capital City*, Perth City Council, Perth, 1979.

11  Cuffley, P., quoted in Mullins, P. and Kynaston, C., 'The Household Production of Subsistence Goods: The Urban Peasant Thesis Reassessed', Troy, P. (ed), *A History of European Housing in Australia*, Cambridge University Press, Cambridge, 2000, p. 148.

provide.[12] The road became an important symbol for the suburbs. Local rates paid for their construction, local labour was used to clear and grade the reserves but most importantly they became the environment in which people traversed, met their neighbours and ultimately they became the shared public space of local community. Roads provided the window onto other people's lifestyles and the residents were aware that judgements were being formed on the public face that their houses and gardens presented to the street.

While the rear of houses were characterised by the location of 'lean-to' kitchens, laundries and toilets opening on to a yard that supported so many of their functions, the frontages of houses provided a very direct contrast. The design of early 20th Century houses (and indeed many other buildings) had long understood the importance of façade.[13] It was on the front elevation of housing that poorly laid brickwork was disguised by tuck-pointing. It was the front verandah that displayed the intricate carpentry required for laddering and spindling. Front windows and doors used leadlights as a form of decoration and entrances were corbelled and coined to embellish their significance. These treatments are all indicative of the importance of 'appearances' for the early suburban dwellers and their front gardens evolved to complement the values they espoused in their buildings. As Robert Freestone puts it 'The front yard was both a zone of display and a social contract, a semi public space of neatness encoding a statement about individual personality in the context of community'.[14]

If the front garden was to reveal something of the values of the occupants, the reading of its development sees two distinct but related themes emerge. Firstly, there was a clear reaction against the palette of the surrounding natural bushland with order, uniformity and colour being espoused in garden plans; and secondly, there was the enduring nostalgia for the plants of the 'mother country'. By the end of the 19th Century the hose and the lawnmower had been invented and Australian suburbia seized on their possibilities.[15] The most obvious outcome was the flat, square-trimmed lawn. These lawns dominated front gardens forming a tradition that is as dominant today as it was 100 years ago. It covered the hot, dry and dusty sand on which the suburbs were built and provided a clear contrast to the surrounding bushland.[16] While lawns also provided a very functional surface for a range of recreation activities this did not fit with the evolving role of the front garden. These gardens were to be seen and admired. They were rarely 'used'.

There was great pride in presentation and despite the summer heat, shade trees were rarely planted in front gardens. Such planting would have hidden the house from the street

*Municipal Gardens, Subiaco [courtesy John Viska].*

and that was the antithesis of what the façade treatments were all about. Although front fences were rare, where they did exist they were low and permeable with open pickets and wire mesh being the favoured materials.

Town planning legislation was introduced into Western Australia in 1928 and one of the first powers to be used was the control over the subdivision of land. The newly established Town Planning Board quickly set about imposing controls over the development industry. Over a relatively short period, control over the construction of streets, the provision of services and the staging of development were introduced.[17] New suburbs were now required to connect to the developing mains water and sewerage systems. Gas and electricity were also being provided and the road system was beginning to respond to the emerging needs of public and private transport. Suburbs began to be designed rather than just subdivided and parks and other amenities became enmeshed into the tapestry of these new communities.

With suitable infrastructure service provision the size of lots could be reduced and the quarter-acre block that had so typified development in the first half of the century began to be reduced. No longer was there the need for septic tanks, wells, firewood and rubbish pits. Lot sizes reduced steadily in the post-war period, initially to 800 m² and down to 600 m² by the 1960s. Serviced land was more valuable and as the cost of land increased so too did the pressure to reduce lot sizes.

The planning of suburbs also introduced more rigid controls over the siting of houses on lots. Front, rear and side setbacks were standard local government controls and with these setbacks so the distribution of space between front and rear gardens became more codified and uniform. The large imposing front gardens were institutionalised in the application of planning standards and 7.6 m (25 feet) front setbacks were common right up until the 1970s.[18] The staging of subdivision approval to improve the balance between lots being created and homes being built upon them saw the emergence of a clearer development front and the pattern of isolated houses in bush settings rapidly disappeared.

But probably of most significance to the relationship between suburban development and its natural landscape setting was the introduction of land clearing and re-contouring as a prelude to development. Suburbs developed in the first half of the 20th Century are distinguished by the retention of their natural contours and characteristics. The often erratic undulations of the coastal plain sand dunes dominate the suburban landscape particularly in the younger dune areas closer to the coast. In this environment, house lots

12  Berry, C., 'The Evolution of Local Planning', Hedgcock, D. and Yiftachel, O. (eds), *Urban and Regional Planning in Western Australia. Historical and Critical Perspectives*, Paradigm Press, Perth, 1992.

13  Freeland, J.M., *Architecture in Australia: A History*, Penguin, Victoria, 1968.

14  Freestone, R., 'Planning, Housing, Gardening: Home as a Garden Suburb', Troy, P. (ed), *A History of European Housing in Australia*, Cambridge University Press, Cambridge, 2000, p. 128.

15  Baskin, J. and Dixon, T., *Australia's Timeless Gardens*, National Library of Australia, Canberra, 1996.

16  Baskin, p. 96.

17  Hedgcock, D. and Hibbs T., 'Perth's Suburban Traditions: From Orthodoxy to Innovation', Hedgcock, D. and Yiftachel, O. (eds), *Urban and Regional Planning in Western Australia. Historical and Critical Perspectives*, Paradigm Press, Perth, 1992.

18  Halkett, I., *The Quarter Acre Block*, Australian Institute of Urban Studies, Canberra, 1976.

1835  1900  1925  1941  1950

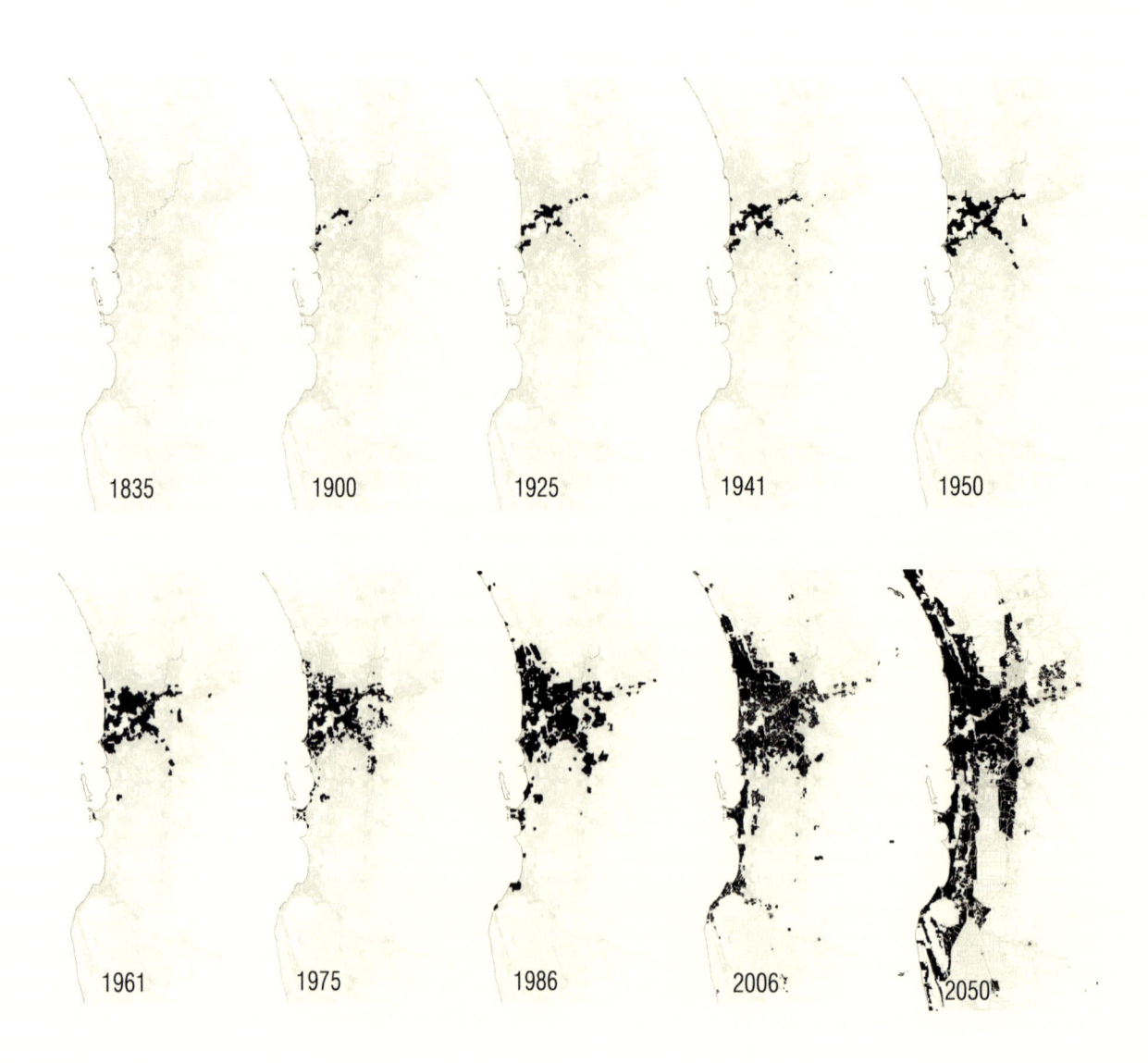

1961  1975  1986  2006  2050

were often sloped with marked falls between the front and rear of lots and, in seeking a flat building surface, limestone foundations were built to accommodate the contours.[19] This elevation of the house above the ground level clearly differentiated residences from their natural surrounds but so too, as the setting evolved, did it physically separate the house from its emergent yard and garden.

While the elevated sandy soils of the coastal plain have never been a major impediment to development, their lower-lying swampy swales did constrain the consistent spread of suburbia. Some swamps and wetlands were filled and drained but this was an expensive exercise in a period where there was limited mechanisation in the development industry. With the advent of heavy earth-moving machinery in the post–World War II period the natural contours were no match for the grader's blade. The more dramatic dunes and swales were quickly transformed into lower-lying undulating contours and the prerequisite for such re-contouring was the clear-felling of the remaining bushland. The natural landscape was re-engineered into a new environmental reality. What greeted the post-war suburban pioneer was not the omnipresent bushland but the flat, featureless sandpit of the suburban frontier. Any semblance of the natural palette had disappeared and an empty canvas awaited the suburban dreams that were forming (and being formed) in the minds of future residents.

Robin Boyd famously described such development as the Australian ugliness 'condemning the small mindedness that he perceived as leading not only to the destruction of the landscape but also to the creation of inappropriate gardens. In his view little of significance could come from such a suburban wasteland'.[20] But such a view reflects some of the elitism and arrogance of the Modern movement that was to succumb to the power of the vernacular in the seed change years of the 1960s. Herbert Gans referred to this distinction as the difference between 'creator orientation' and 'user orientation'. John Fiske also noted that the different perspectives involved in viewing culture were either 'mass produced' or 'popularly fashioned'.[21]

The 1960s was a period of growing economic prosperity. New waves of migrants arrived in Western Australia chasing the dreams of family lifestyles and home ownership in spacious suburbs that were in clear contrast to the economic, social and physical conditions they left behind in the congested cities and regions of Europe. At the same time established post-war Perth families began to raise their expectations regarding their lifestyles in the suburbs.

*The growth of Perth from 1835–2006 including a 2050 projection if the city continues to sprawl.*

19 Farrelly, F., 'A Snapshot of Plants in new Subdivisions in Perth in 2003', MA thesis, The University of Western Australia, Perth, 2003.

20 Holmes, K., 'In her Master's House and Garden', Troy, P. (ed), *A History of European Housing in Australia*, Cambridge University Press, Cambridge, 2000, p. 164.

21 Greig, A., 'Project Homes or Homes as Projects: Fashion and Utility in Twentieth Century Australia', Troy, P. (ed), *A History of European Housing in Australia*, Cambridge University Press, Cambridge, 2000, p. 221

THE PERTH METROPOLITAN REGION SCHEME

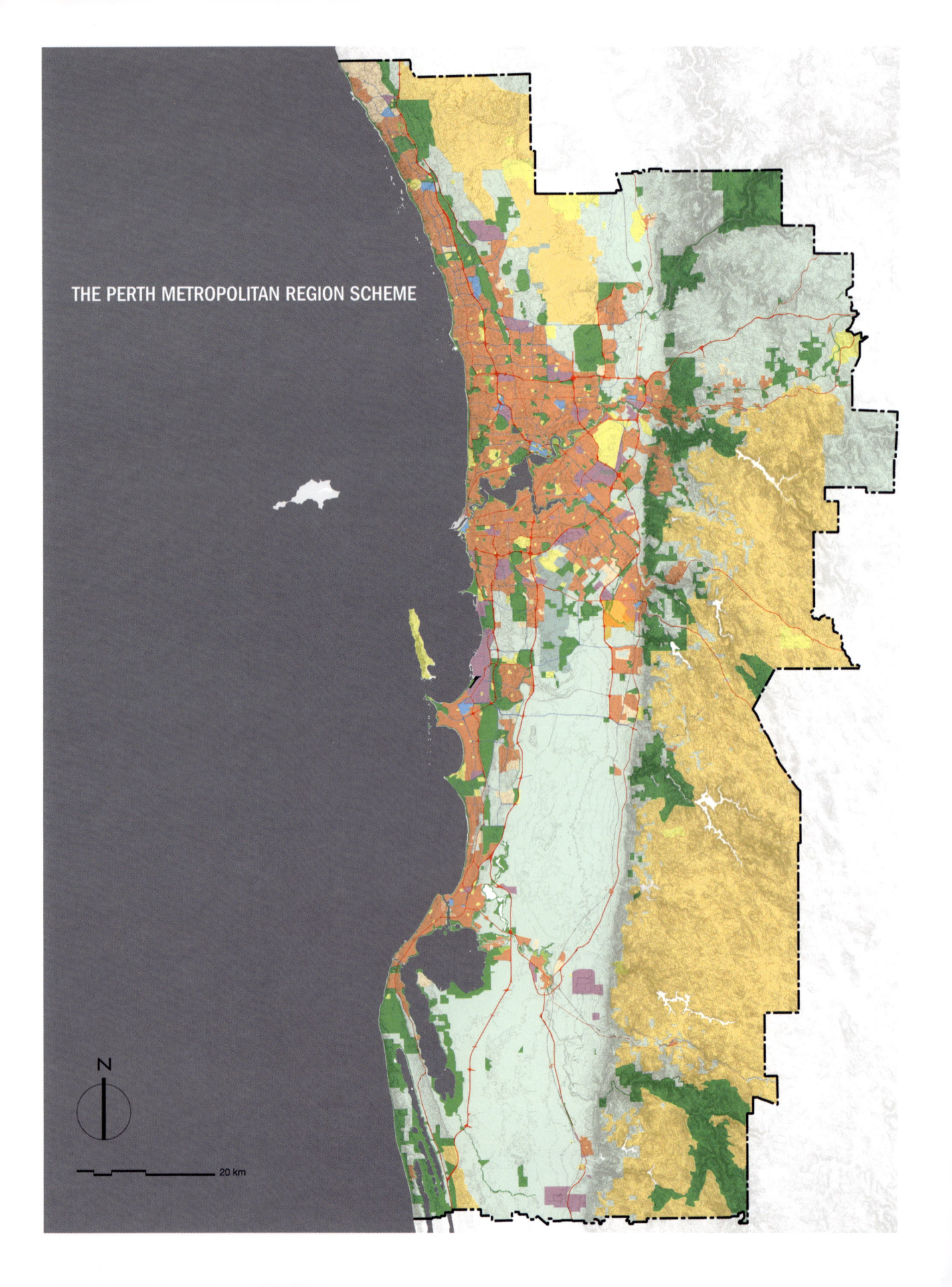

20 km

In the public domain the development of parks and open spaces was equally destructive on the natural environment. The planning system had ensured adequate land was being set aside for recreation outside of individual homes and by the end of the 1950s all developers were having to cede to the Crown 10% of their development area for the purposes of public recreation.[22] This provided extensive areas of undeveloped land but as this land transferred to local government control the great majority of the space was cleared, graded and turfed to accommodate the perceived need for organised sporting activities. Although the surveys of the day identified less than 5% of the population being involved in such activity, it consumed over 80% of the public land set aside for recreation.[23] There was no relief to the prevailing anthropomorphic character of suburbia in its local open spaces. However, the concept of regional open space, developed in the work of Stephenson and Hepburn in 1955, provided a precursor to the changing attitudes towards bush protection that was to dominate the latter part of the century.

The Stephenson and Hepburn plan for the metropolitan region proposed that larger areas of regional open space be set aside for conservation and recreation purposes. These tracts of land – such as the escarpment, wetlands, and river and ocean foreshores – were identified as an important public resource that required government resumption and management to secure their natural qualities. They proposed a system of regional taxation on landowners in the Perth Metropolitan Region to fund the acquisition of these spaces.[24] By the 1960s Perth had a statutory region plan – the Metropolitan Region Scheme – that identified the location of these 'parks and recreation reserves, and the Metropolitan Improvement Tax, which, although scaled back from its original conception, provided a consistent revenue flow to fund the acquisition of regional open space. Singleton noted that the major contribution of these planning initiatives was 'the beginning of a system of regional parklands in which many of the best natural attributes of the region are now represented'.[25] Over the years the protection and enhancement of these spaces not only ensured that the natural setting of the coastal plan was preserved, albeit in a rather modified and scattered form, but it also elevated the status of bushland as areas to be enjoyed and embraced rather than feared and reviled, a sentiment that had been so pervasive for much of the century. This appreciation of the city's natural setting bodes well for a city that, in the 21$^{st}$ Century, will have to preserve and also reconstruct its local ecology.

Like most North American and Australian cities, Perth is now predominantly a flatland of free-standing suburban homes and their related infrastructure. In a word, *sprawl*. At an average density of six homes per hectare Perth is now one of the most sprawled (or should

22 Town Planning Department of Western Australia, 'A Report on Public Open Space', Town Planning Board, Perth, 1981.

23 Stephenson, G. and Hepburn, A., 'Plan for the Metropolitan Region Perth and Fremantle', Government Printers, Perth, 1955.

24 Stephenson, G. and Hepburn, A., 'Plan for the Metropolitan Region Perth and Fremantle', Government Printers, Perth, 1955.

25 Singleton, J., 'Environmental Planning on the Swan Coastal Plain', in Hedgcock, D. and Yiftachel, O. (eds), *Urban and Regional Planning in Western Australia: Historical and Critical perspectives*, Paradigm Press, Perth, 1992, p. 236.

we say spacious) cities on earth. From top to bottom the city is now over 120 kilometres long and it covers 100,000 hectares. Roads are the warp and weft that hold this thin carpet of urbanism together. Naturally then, Perth has the fourth highest car ownership ratio in the world. In its current form, Perth can function only so long as we have cars or some kind of individual people movers that run on cheap, abundant energy. In the future, however, there is no guarantee that this will be the case.

Because our city is designed to suit cars, when viewed from the street the dominant element in most homes is now the double garage and a much reduced front lawn. Small versions of 18th Century English aristocratic estates from which the dream of suburbia stems, those front lawns and their attendant ornamental plants depend on water and fertiliser to sustain their image. But the Swan River, if it is to survive as an ecosystem, can't take more of the phosphate we liberally apply to our lawns or the agricultural landscapes of the hinterland which in part stock our supermarkets with the paradisiacal illusion that we can eat whatever we want, whenever we want. Despite severe water shortages, Western Australians use 12 times more water than the global average. Any new forms of urbanism will need to harvest and recycle water.

Since 1950 front and back yards in suburbia have become smaller and houses have become bigger. Although 24% of Perth's homes are occupied by individuals, they are generally designed and built to house families. The average price of such a house is $446,000, and to sustain an individual (ecological footprint) in such housing now takes 14.5 hectares of land, seven times the world average. Western Australians, Saudi Arabians and Singaporeans share the increasingly dishonorable status of being the most unsustainable people on the planet.

Perth's weighty ecological footprint is exacerbated by the city's isolation. Perth's economy is based on the extraction and exportation of minerals and natural gas in exchange for which it imports most of the things its citizens need and desire. Very little of what constitutes the average Perth lifestyle is made locally. Whilst information now transcends distance and is relatively cheap to move, the stuff of the material world is not. So long as commodity prices are high and global networks of exchange are well oiled, Perth transcends its local environmental and economic limitations and remains a highly affluent (and conservative) society. Whilst its isolation might help defend against microbes and missiles, because Perth is so dependent upon networks of exchange over vast distances it is, like a spider in a web, highly vulnerable to any perturbations in the

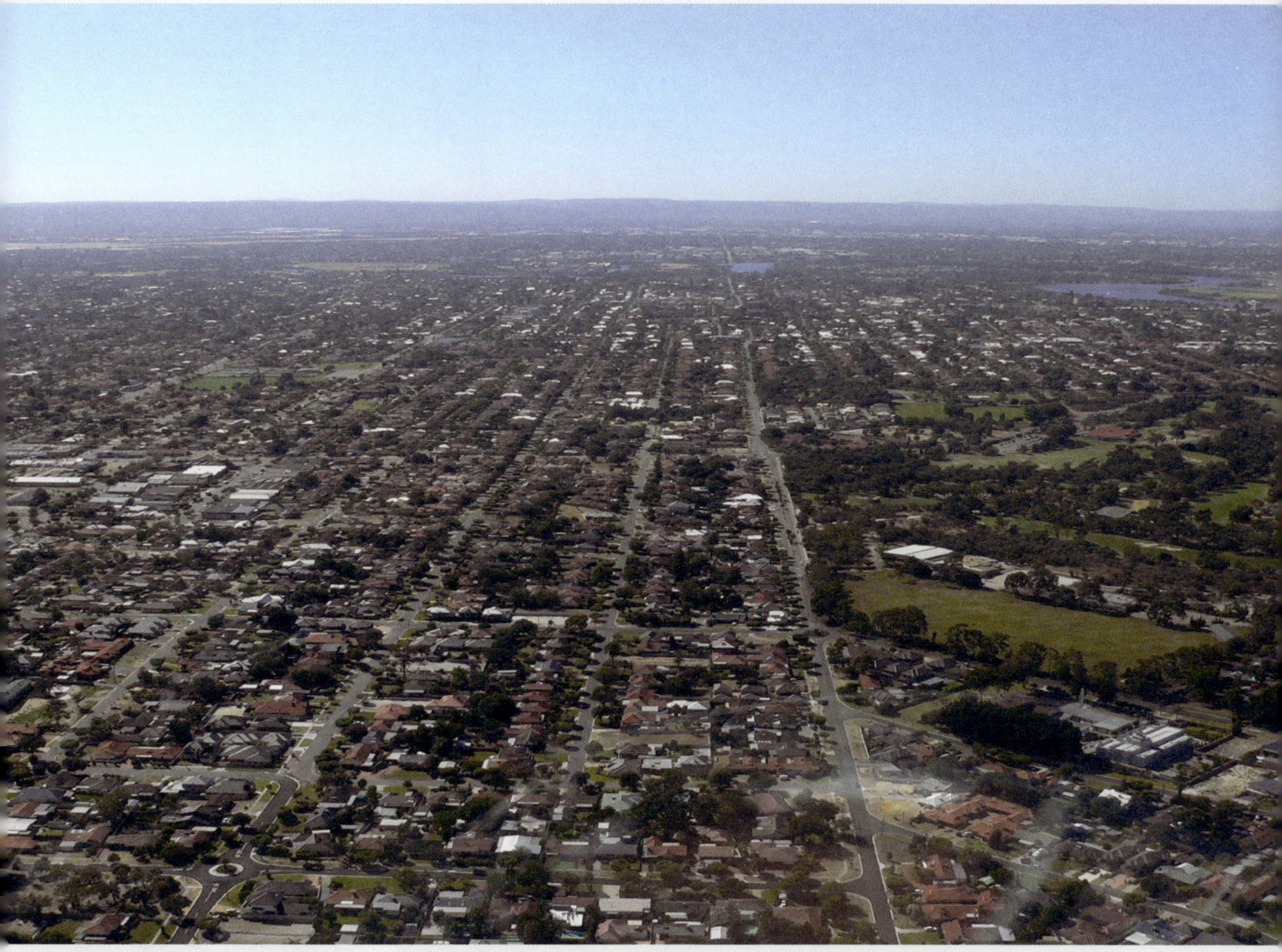

Contemporary Western Australian suburban housing. 'The Ultimo',
Dale Alcock Homes [Joel Barbitta, D'Max].

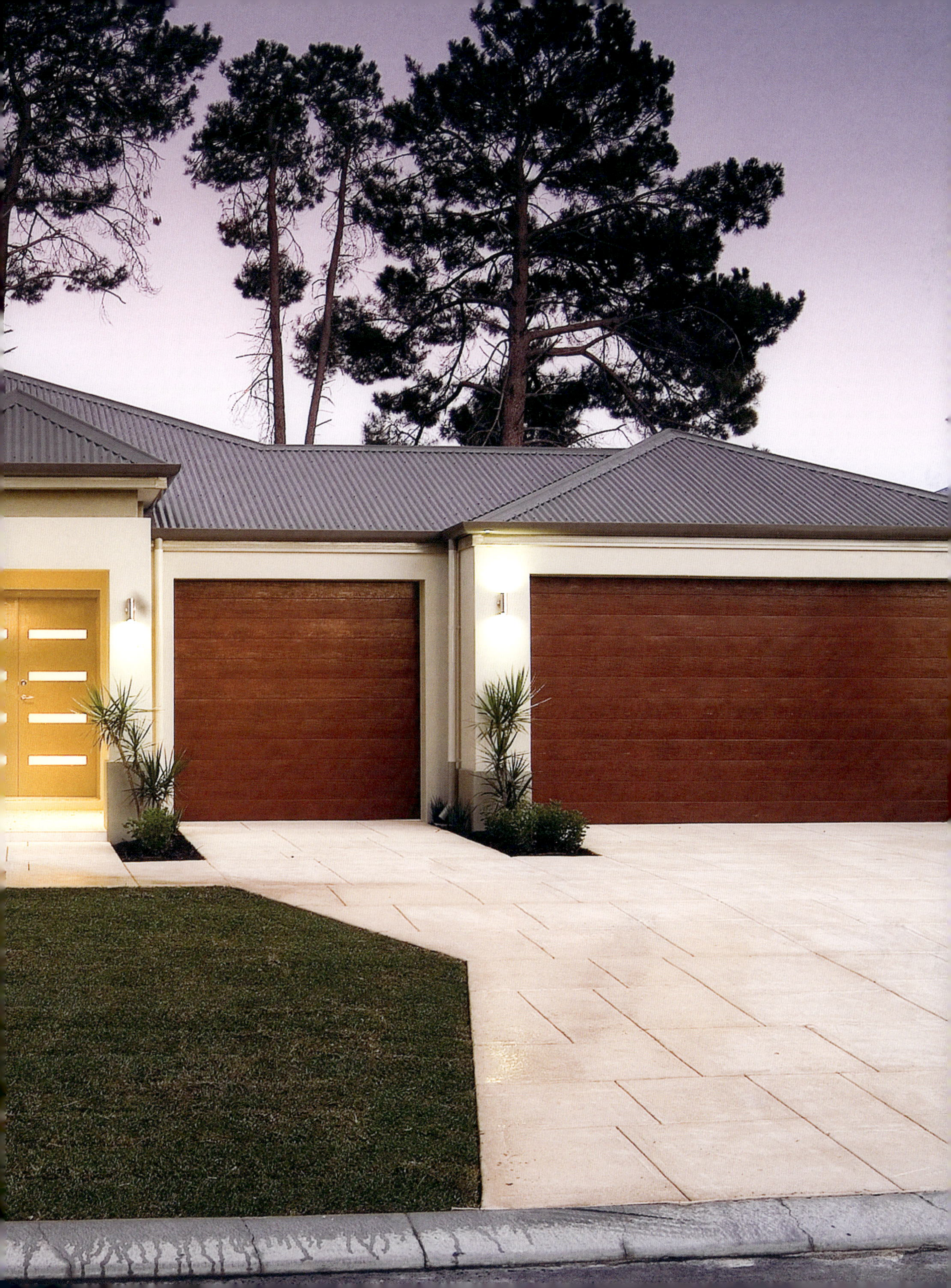

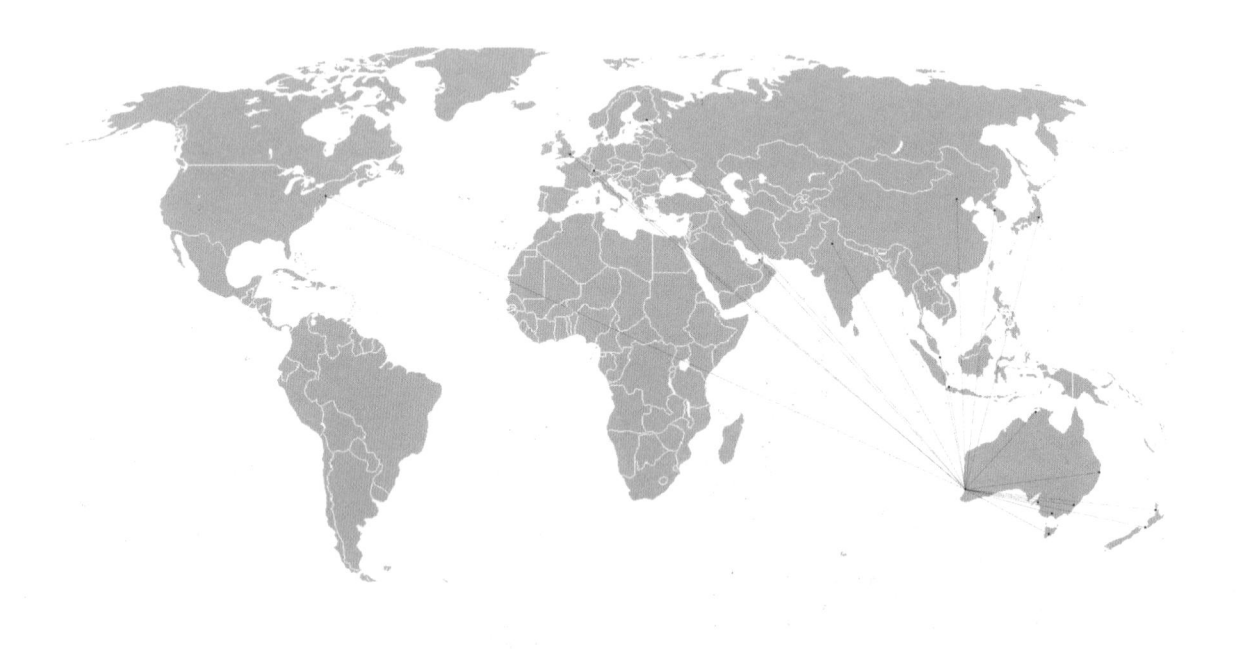

*Perth's major trade links.*

global system. Isolation in this sense is not so much a geographic form of security as a potential 21st Century liability. Accordingly, Perth will need to shock-proof itself against global perturbations by not only developing economies of greater diversity and depth but by creatively adapting the city to its landscape and creating more sophisticated and self-sufficient infrastructure.

Perth is also increasingly self-conscious about creating a vibrant urbane culture so as to attract and retain the sorts of people Richard Florida refers to as 'creatives'.[26] Perth, a 'get rich quick' mining town and the world's most isolated city, is not noted for its creativity. Because of looming ecological limitations on the one hand and a rapidly growing economy and population on the other, that will have to change.

In synchronisation with its environmental and technological limitations, Perth's population might one day reach a plateau, but since its founding in 1829, fuelled by periodic mineral booms, it has grown more or less continuously. When we began this research the Australian Bureau of Statistics (ABS) predicted that Perth's population of circa 1.5 million would double to reach three million by the year 2050.[27] To accommodate the projected 2050 population increase, 651,078 new free-standing homes (based on 2.3 people per dwelling) or 788,147 apartments (based on 1.9 people per dwelling) will need to be built. Pending land availability, the housing industry in Perth says it can build 20,000 homes per annum so in terms of sheer numbers it is *do-able*. But housing is one thing: the infrastructure needed to sustain such vast residential landscapes is quite another. It stands to reason that if the population of the city doubles then the entire infrastructure of the city will also have to double. *Everything* that was built in 179 years will need to be reproduced in the next 40.

This book is not about whether the predicted increase in population is right or wrong, rather, this book is about how that increased population should be housed in new urban form. Even if, for some reason, Perth never becomes a city of three million people surely it is still worthwhile to consider ways the city could develop – if only to reflect back on its current suburban homogeneity, a form of urbanism many believe to be already unsustainable. The last time the population doubled (1970–2000) it gave rise to Perth's vast northern suburbs. Should we simply recreate that form of urbanism in the next 40 years, only this time southwards where land is readily available?

When we began modelling the urban design scenarios described in this book around the highest ABS figure of a 2050 population of three million people, some thought we were being dramatic. Now, at the time of this book going to press, the ABS has issued

26 Florida, R., *The Rise of the Creative Class – And How it's Transforming Leisure, Community and Everyday Life*, Basic Books, New York, 2002.

27 Australian Bureau of Statistics (ABS) offers three figures for population growth, a high, medium and low. We concluded that our study should be predicated on the highest figure as this will in all likelihood be achieved some time in the 21st Century if not by 2050.

As in so many cities experiencing growth, the fundamental question for Perth now is — grow up or go sprawl?

new figures suggesting that Perth's population could far exceed three million people by 2050. The doubling of the population with which we began this research is now the most conservative of the ABS projections for Perth. The highest projection is a total population of 4.2 million by the year 2056. While this figure far exceeds the number around which we began our modelling, the outcomes of our research meet this new figure in two ways. Firstly, through a process of mapping Perth's regional landscape we have identified 118,000 hectares of land suitable for suburban development. This is more than enough land to accommodate an additional 2.7 million people living in conventional low-density suburbia should Perth decide to continue sprawling. Secondly, assuming that such a Business as Usual model of development is inappropriate for the 21st Century, then it is equally possible to accommodate the latest predicted population increase with a combination of the other scenarios we offer. If one were to literally construct all the scenarios that we present in this book, then Perth would be a city of even more than the ABS's highest prediction of 4.2 million people. However, simply accommodating such numbers is not the only issue. The urban form of that accommodation and the quality of life it generates is what ultimately matters.

As in so many cities experiencing growth, the fundamental question for Perth now is: to sprawl or not to sprawl? The international sprawl debates are intense and often split sharply down the middle. Those debates go something like this. The case *against* sprawl is that it is flab to what should otherwise be a taut body. Sprawl is wasteful because it is destructive of agricultural land and precious habitat. Its non-porous surfaces increase run-off that damages waterways, and its free-standing homes are inefficient with regard to energy and infrastructural costs. Sprawl is car-dependent with increasingly long commutes that, in turn, add to the problem of global warming. Sprawl leads to social problems because it isolates people in a landscape of homogeneity. Sprawl is thought to lack culture and community because it lacks density and a sense of place. And finally, sprawl is ugly and people only buy into it because they have no other choice.

The case *for* sprawl is politically supported by economic liberalism and a suspicion of any regulatory planning that inhibits individual rights vested in land. Additionally, if one accepts conventional economic modelling, sprawl is cheap to build and thus enables people to enter the real estate market. Sprawl-scape is an economic powerhouse and to oppose this on either environmental or aesthetic grounds is elitist. Further, it is argued that new suburbs are safe. Replete with generous open spaces and new schools, suburbia is

**SPRAWL HAS NEARLY WRECKED THE HUMAN HABITAT OF NORTH AMERICA AND MOST OF IT IS DEPRESSINGLY BRUTAL, UNHEALTHY AND SPIRITUALLY DEGRADING.** James Howard Kunstler

IN ITS IMMENSE COMPLEXITY AND CONSTANT CHANGE THE CITY IS THE GRANDEST AND MOST MARVELLOUS WORK OF MANKIND.

Robert Bruegmann

thought to be a better place than dense urban neighbourhoods for raising children. The suburbs lack congestion and despite their increasing distance from the CBD, people like driving. And in any case, are not both cars and homes becoming more energy efficient and isn't the government creating new basins of local employment and amenity in the new suburbs? Finally, a free-standing home and a garden is the quintessence of the Australian way of life – it's what people want and *they* don't think it's ugly.

These stark arguments for and against sprawl are reinforced by the language used. For example, Adam Rome, Professor of History at Pennsylvania State University, speaks of land that is 'lost' to development[28] and Frederick Steiner, Professor of Landscape Architecture at the University of Texas, refers to 365 acres of land being 'consumed' by sprawl in North America every hour.[29] On the other hand Robert Bruegmann, Professor of Urban Planning at the University of Illinois, complains that even to say sprawl 'consumes' land is prejudicial.[30] The author and ardent sprawl critic James Kunstler says that sprawl 'has nearly wrecked the human habitat of North America', and most of it is 'depressingly brutal, unhealthy and spiritually degrading'.[31] Yet, as he flies out of Los Angeles, Bruegmann extols the contemporary city as 'the grandest and most marvellous work of mankind'.[32]

Perth's current planning policy, known as 'Network City', purports to be an alternative to piecemeal suburban sprawl. Fundamentally, Network City is not a masterplan but a set of principles which, through an emphasis on Peter Calthorpe's celebrated notion of Transit Oriented Developments (TODs), aim to limit sprawl.[33] Network City's authors, the Western Australian Planning Commission (WAPC), envisage Perth becoming a polycentric city whereby infill development will create higher-density enclaves clustered around approximately 120 nodes (sites such as shopping centres, train stations, campuses and medical facilities) within the existing suburban fabric of the city.[34]

Although Network City is widely recognised as a good set of principles, it has some problems. Firstly, predicated on the city reaching a population of 2.2 million (an extra 375,000 free-standing dwellings) in the year 2031, Network City is a relatively short-sighted document. Secondly, of the 375,000 homes that will need to built to house the predicted 2031 population, Network City recommends that 60% be built within the existing city limits, and 40% (150,000 homes) be assigned to peri-urban (greenfield) land. And yet, according to our calculations there is in the Perth Metropolitan Region currently 23,000 ha of land *already* committed for suburbanisation and this land alone could accommodate 276,000 free-standing homes at orthodox low density.[35] Thirdly,

---

28 Rome, A., *The Bulldozer in the Countryside: Suburban Sprawl and the Rise of American Environmentalism*, Cambridge University Press, New York, 2001, p. 264.

29 Steiner, F.R. (ed), *The Essential Ian McHarg: Writings on Design and Nature*, Island Press, Washington, 2006, p. xvi.

30 Bruegmann, R., *Sprawl: A Compact History*, The University of Chicago Press, London, 2005.

31 Kunstler, J.H., *The Geography of Nowhere: The Rise and Decline of America's Man-made Landscape*, Simon and Schuster, New York, 1993, p. 10.

32 Bruegmann, R., *Sprawl: A Compact History*, The University of Chicago Press, London, 2005, p. 225.

33 Calthorpe, P. and W. Fulton., *The Regional City: Planning for the End of Sprawl*, Island Press, Washington, 2001.

34 Department for Planning and Infrastructure, <http://www.dpi.wa.gov.au/networkcity/1214.asp>, viewed 2008.

35 Although often zoned for 20 homes per hectare the 2006 *State of the Environment Report* concludes that the average built suburban density is 12.5 homes per net hectare. It is upon this average that our density calculations are based. *State of the Environment Report* (Draft), Environmental Protection Authority, 2006, p. 229.

## CURRENT ZONING

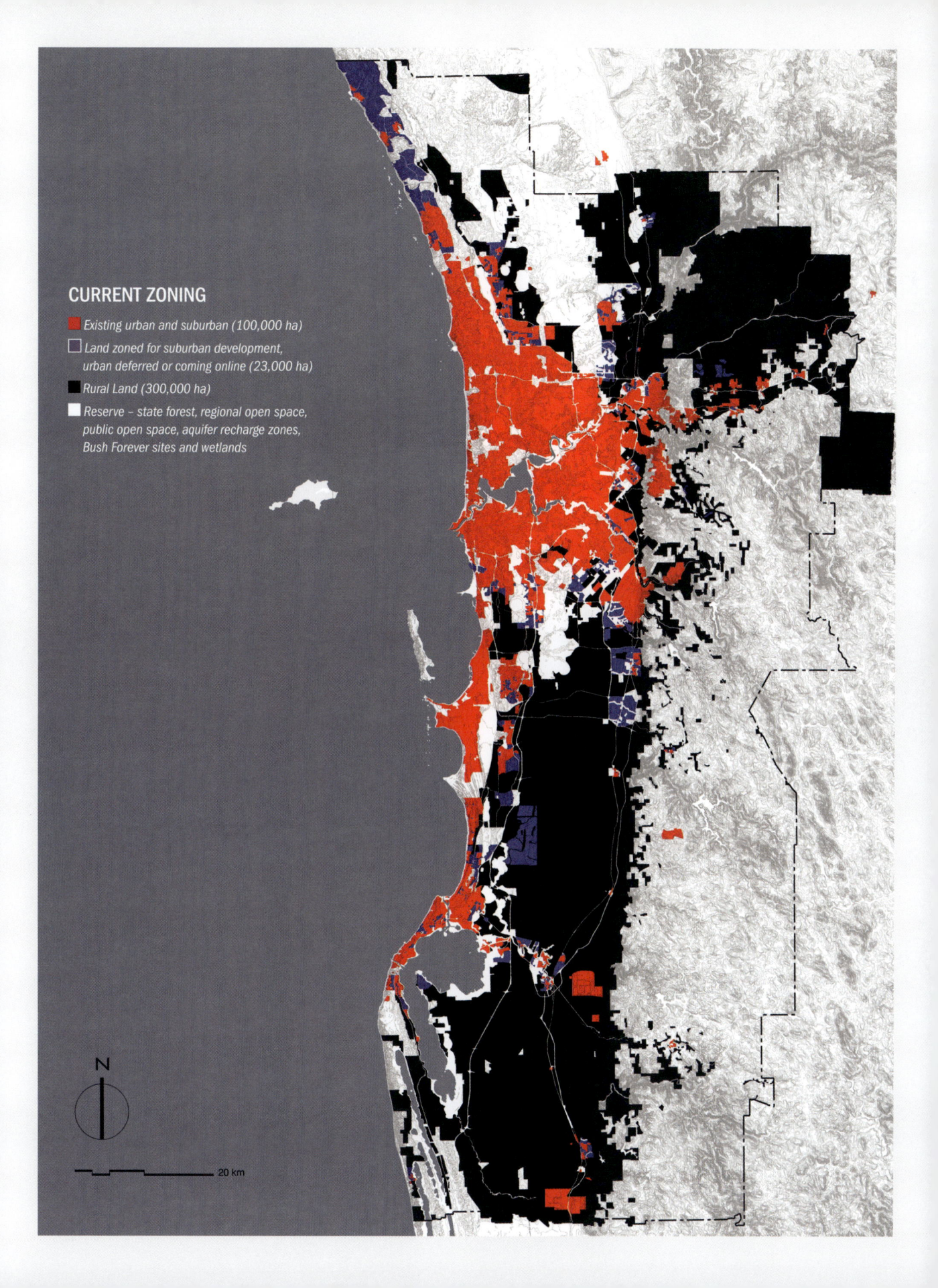

- Existing urban and suburban (100,000 ha)
- Land zoned for suburban development, urban deferred or coming online (23,000 ha)
- Rural Land (300,000 ha)
- Reserve – state forest, regional open space, public open space, aquifer recharge zones, Bush Forever sites and wetlands

N

20 km

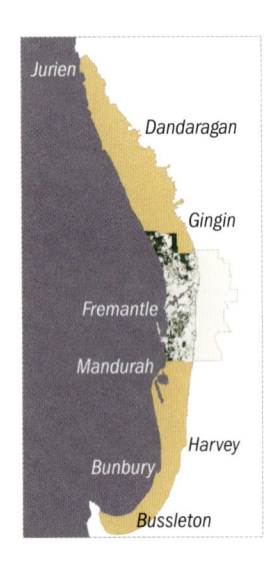

*Perth within the larger context of the Swan Coastal Plain bioregion. The Swan Coastal Plain falls within the South-West Australian Hotspot, one of 34 such places in the world. A Hotspot is a place with unique and threatened biodiversity.*

Network City's emphasis on polycentricism is problematic because many of the 120 nodes or 'activity centres' it has identified for increased density are currently unattractive to consumers. This is because they are typically places within the existing suburban fabric of the city that have been built primarily as service nodes for cars, not people. Such activity centres, if they are to become the epicentres of thriving and relatively dense residential development, will require substantial reconstruction to make them attractive civic spaces. Such reconstruction in turn drives up costs for infill development making it potentially unaffordable relative to greenfield suburban development with which it must directly compete.

The final concern we have with the government's Network City document is that it is just words. Network City offers the public no plans or images of the urbanism it recommends. Because it has no clear imagery, Network City has failed to gain traction in the public imagination and there seems to be considerable confusion amongst both professionals and the public as to how any of its words will be translated into form.[36]

Our research, as documented in this book, is to be understood as a supplement, not an alternative to Network City. Network City is one good scenario for the future of the city and we offer others. To do this our approach tries to overcome the limitations we have identified with Network City in three ways. Firstly, our development scenarios are based on 2050, not 2031, population projections. This provides greater long-term depth to large-scale planning strategies, which in turn can better inform current decisions. Secondly, all the urban forms that emerge from our scenarios are depicted accurately in panoramic images that can be easily understood by both professionals and the public. And finally, instead of creating one masterplan, or in the case of Network City one policy, we offer multiple scenarios. The reason for this is to aid debate about the future form of the city but it also suggests that the city needs to pursue several options simultaneously.

Without taking sides in the sprawl versus anti-sprawl debate we present alternative development scenarios which work both horizontally and vertically with regard to the existing landscape conditions of the city. In short, we are offering five alternative scenarios for spreading development – POD City, Food City, Car Free City, Seachange City and Treechange City; and three scenarios for vertical development – Sky City, River City and Surf City. All the scenarios can be compared with what we refer to as BAU (Business as Usual) City, the scenario that Perth just continues doing what it has done so effectively for the last 178 years: building suburbia on greenfield sites.

What distinguishes the scenarios from many urban planning studies is that we have approached the city holistically from a regional landscape perspective. Consequently the scenarios we have developed all explicitly relate to and are directed by landscape conditions. This regional landscape perspective is not an innovation, rather it is part of a tradition that can be traced back to the 1920s when the pre-eminent urban historian Lewis Mumford, on the shoulders of his mentor Patrick Geddes, advocated that planning proceed with a holistic sense of a bioregion so that 'all its sites and resources, from forest to city, from highland to water level, may be soundly developed, and so that the population will be distributed so as to utilize, rather than nullify or destroy, its natural advantages. [Regional Planning] sees people, industry and the land as a single unit.' [37]

This holistic interpretation of the city and its environment has, however, been largely ignored by late 20th Century suburban development in Australia. Perth has fewer excuses for such ignorance than other Australian cities for it was about Perth's landscape that Professor George Seddon in 1972 wrote *A Sense of Place*, an internationally acclaimed book that foregrounded the landscape as an ecological structure for, and a cultural influence upon, the city.[38] But apart from one sentence in the conclusion of his book where he warned against the (rumoured) possibility of 10 million people settling on the Swan Coastal Plain (i.e. Dunsborough to Geraldton) by 2072, Seddon only described the landscape as it was, not what it might become. Our research focuses almost exclusively on the future.[39]

Because of water shortages the noted palaeontologist Dr Tim Flannery recently declared that Perth could become 'the 21st Century's first ghost metropolis'.[40] In the very long term Flannery may be right: this old and arid landscape is not suited to large numbers of stationary people. But what we think Flannery really means to say is that the way we live now is unsustainable and that the future no longer just happens – it must be designed.

That ultimately is what this book is about. It is about Perth designing its future. It is about Perth becoming a more diverse city. It is about Perth becoming a more exhilarating city. Most importantly it is about Perth becoming a more resilient city. To be resilient to environmental pressures is, in an evolutionary sense, to be able to adapt. To adapt means taking risks with new forms.

*Richard Weller and David Hedgcock*

---

36 For Network City to become real and gain momentum, a demonstration project – the creation of an alluring activity centre with associated high-density residential development – must be creatively designed and well constructed as soon as possible. In fairness to the government such projects are on the drawing board.

37 Hall, P., *Cities of Tomorrow: An Intellectual History of Urban Planning and Design in the Twentieth Century,* 3rd edn, Blackwell Publishing, Oxford, 2002, p. 161.

38 Seddon, G., *Sense of Place: A Response to an Environment. The Swan Coastal Plain, Western Australia,* University of Western Australia Press, Perth, 1972.

39 Seddon, p. 258.

40 Davies, A., 'Sydney's Future Eaten: The Flannery Prophecy', *Sydney Morning Herald,* 19 May 2004. Flannery also ignores the construction of new desalination plants, changing consumption patterns and the possibility of us better capturing the 100 gigalitres of wastewater that is annually discharged into the ocean from our sewerage systems. He also misses the point that any new development (and a retrofitting of existing development) could harvest and store a massive quantity of stormwater which washes uselessly into the ocean each year. The Perth region is also undergird by large aquifers that some believe could be further exploited.

Because of water shortages the noted palaeontologist Dr Tim Flannery recently declared that Perth could become 'the 21$^{st}$ Century's first ghost metropolis'. In the very long term Flannery may be right: this old and arid landscape is not suited to large numbers of stationary people. But what we think Flannery really means to say is that the way we live now is unsustainable and that the future no longer just happens – it must be designed.

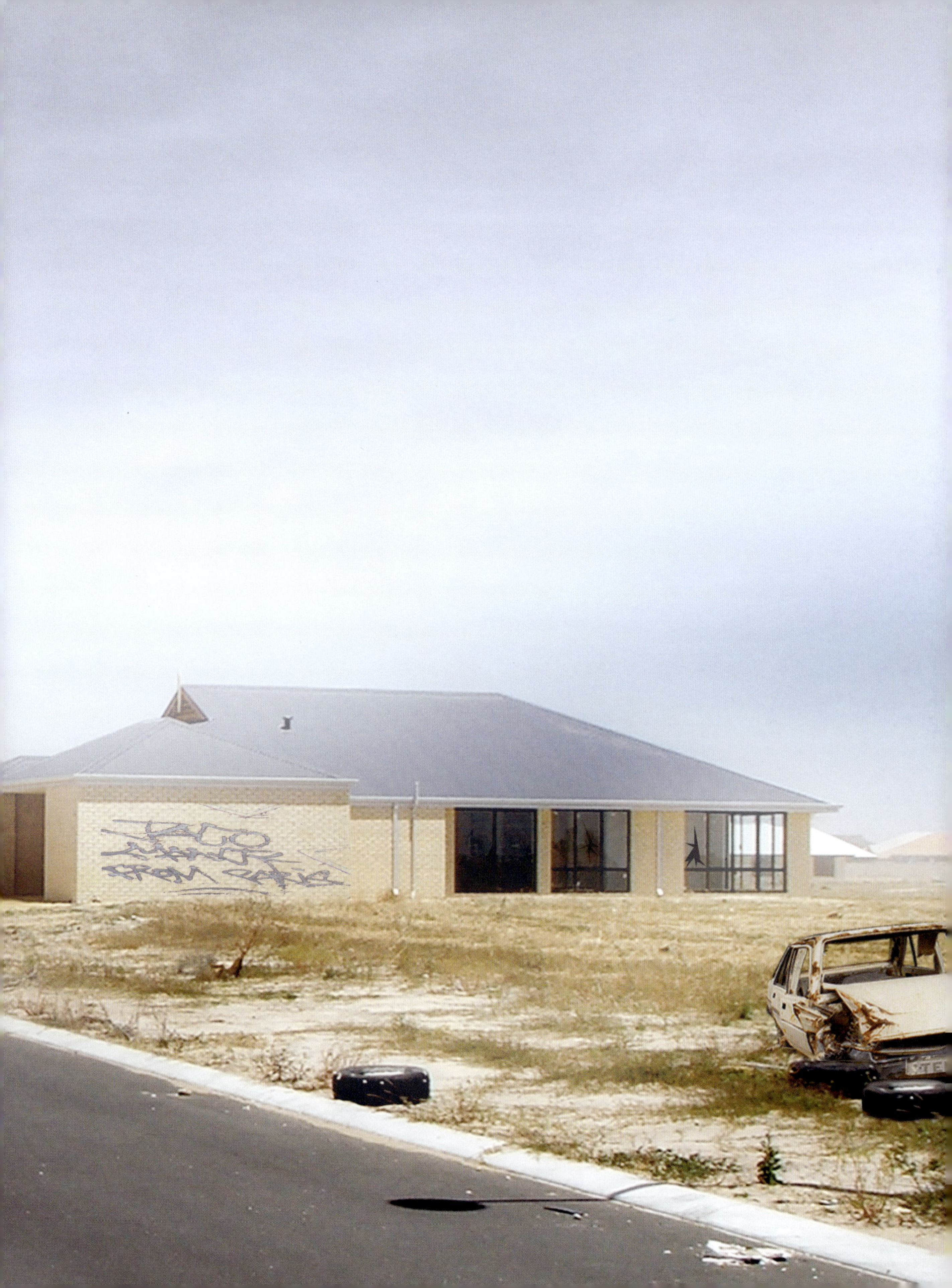

2

# DATABASE

By bringing together data from a wide array of sources this statistical essay provides an holistic account of the city. It is intended as a useful resource, but the information contained herein can also be used in evaluating the various urban design scenarios presented later.

Disclaimer: Information in this statistical essay is provided in good faith. However accuracy and appropriateness of the information is not guaranteed, and the authors and the UWA Press disclaim all liability in respect of any omission occurring in reliance on the facts contained within.

Perth is one of the most isolated capital cities in the world. Adelaide, the nearest capital city, is 2,692 km by road.

**7.72 million sq km[1]**

**2.53 million sq km[2]**

Perth

The South-West Australia Hotspot is one of the world's 34 Biodiversity Hotspots (most biodiverse areas in the world). The Perth Metropolitan Region falls within this zone.[3] There are 8,000 taxa of vascular plants in the Hotspot[4] of which 1,500 (19%) occur in the Perth metro area.[5]

- Rural 36%
- State forests 30%
- Urban 12%
- Parks and recreation 12%
- Waterways 3%
- Public purposes 2%
- Road reserves 2%
- Industrial 1%
- Urban deferred 1%
- Rural - water protection 1%

*Western Australia: 33% of Australia – the largest land area of any Australian state. Coastline length: 12,500 km – a third of the Australian coastline. Population: 1.96 million[6] – 10% of Australia's population. Distance north-south: 2,391 km.[7] Distance east-west: 1,621 km.[8]*

*The relative proportions of Perth's Metropolitan & Peel Region zone categories (2003). Metropolitan development zones include: urban, urban deferred, central city area, industrial & special industry, rural, rural-water protection, and private recreation. Land reserved for public purposes includes: parks & recreation, railway & port Installation, state forest, civic & cultural, waterways, primary and other regional roads, and public purposes. Note that port installations and civic and cultural zones are not represented (0.02% and 0.01% respectively).[9]*

# SITE

*New Perth Waterfront development (see page 355)*

*Wungong Urban Water (see page 239)*

Perth and Peel urban and urban deferred zoned area: 99.4 thousand hectares.

1. Geoscience Australia, <http://www.ga.gov.au/education/facts/dimensions/areadime.htm>, viewed September 2008.

2. Geoscience Australia, <http://www.ga.gov.au/education/facts/dimensions/areadime.htm>, viewed September 2008.

3. del Marco, A. et al, Local Government Biodiversity Planning Guidelines for the Perth Metropolitan Region', Western Australian 'Local Government Association, West Perth, 2004, p. 35.

4. del Marco, p. 35.

5. Powell, R. and Emberson, J., 'Growing Locals: Gardening with Local Plants in Perth', Western Australian Naturalists Club Inc., Nedlands, 1996, p. 73.

6. Western Australia's population at the 2006 Census was 1,959,088. Australian Bureau of Statistics (ABS), 2006 Census QuickStats:<http://www.censusdata.abs.gov.au/>, viewed September 2008.

7. ABS, Catalogue No. 1300.5, *Western Australian Yearbook No. 34 – 1998*, Canberra, 1998.

8. ABS, Catalogue No. 1300.5, *Western Australian Yearbook No. 34 – 1998*, Canberra, 1998.

9. Department for Planning and Infrastructure (DPI), internal databases quoted in <http://www.planning.wa.gov.au/publications/mdp/mdp2003/10_Chapter%205.pdf>, viewed April 2007.

**DATABASE**

# Perth is set to experience the fastest rate of growth of any Australian city in history.[1]

1   Birrell, B., Presentation at the Committee for Economic Development of Australia (CEDA) Population Forum, Perth, 27 June 2008.

2   ABS, Catalogue No. 3222.0, *Population Projections, Australia, 2004–2101*, Canberra, 2005.

3   ABS, Catalogue No. 3222.0, *Population Projections, Australia, 2006–2101*, Canberra, Last updated 4 September 2008.

## 2005

| CAPITAL CITY/BALANCE OF STATE | 2004/ACTUAL | 2051/A | 2051/B | 2051/C |
|---|---|---|---|---|
| Sydney | 4,225.1 | 6,311.6 | 5,608.8 | 5,292.1 |
| Balance of New South Wales | 2,495.7 | 3,796.3 | 3,133.9 | 2,668.2 |
| New South Wales | 6,720.8 | 10,107.9 | 8,742.7 | 7,960.4 |
| Melbourne | 3,593.0 | 5,894.6 | 5,041.1 | 4,566.8 |
| Balance of Victoria | 1,370.0 | 1,534.2 | 1,533.0 | 1,624.4 |
| Victoria | 4,963.0 | 7,428.7 | 6,574.1 | 6,191.2 |
| Brisbane | 1,777.7 | 4,202.0 | 3,354.7 | 2,778.1 |
| Balance of Queensland | 2,110.4 | 4,382.8 | 3,544.3 | 2,966.0 |
| Queensland | 3,888.1 | 8,584.8 | 6,899.0 | 5,744.1 |
| Adelaide | 1,123.2 | 1,326.8 | 1,203.9 | 1,138.5 |
| Balance of South Australia | 409.5 | 409.3 | 376.8 | 399.0 |
| South Australia | 1,532.7 | 1,736.1 | 1,580.7 | 1,537.5 |
| **Perth** | **1,454.6** | **2,999.2** | **2,453.6** | **2,017.6** |
| Balance of Western Australia | 523.5 | 891.0 | 710.9 | 560.9 |
| Western Australia | 1,978.1 | 3,890.2 | 3,164.5 | 2,578.6 |
| Hobart | 202.2 | 286.9 | 219.6 | 178.2 |
| Balance of Tasmania | 280.1 | 333.2 | 233.5 | 157.2 |
| Tasmania | 482.2 | 620.1 | 453.0 | 335.4 |
| Darwin | 109.4 | 295.5 | 232.3 | 153.0 |
| Balance of Northern Territory | 90.4 | 175.0 | 117.7 | 71.3 |
| Northern Territory | 199.8 | 470.5 | 350.0 | 224.3 |
| Australian Capital Territory | 324.1 | 547.1 | 401.6 | 289.5 |
| Total capital cities | 12,809.3 | 21,863.7 | 18,515.7 | 16,413.8 |
| Total balance of states & territories | 7 279.6 | 11 521.7 | 9 650.1 | 8 447.0 |
| Australia | 20,091.5 | 33,389.8 | 28,169.7 | 24,864.5 |

*Australian capital cities: actual and projected population ('000).*

*Above are the ABS population projections with which we began the research. The very latest figures as shown on the opposite page forecast even larger populations for all Australian cities.[2] The ABS provides population data in three series, A, B and C to show a range of projections for analysis.*

**50**
**DATABASE**

# GROWTH

## 2008

| CAPITAL CITY/BALANCE OF STATE | 2006/OBSERVED | 2007/OBSERVED | 2026/A | 2026/B | 2026/C | 2056/A | 2056/B | 2056/C |
|---|---|---|---|---|---|---|---|---|
| Sydney | 4,282.0 | 4,334.0 | 5,487.2 | 5,426.3 | 5,358.2 | 7,649.0 | 6,976.8 | 6,565.2 |
| Balance of New South Wales | 2,534.1 | 2,554.0 | 3,189.9 | 2,968.8 | 2,780.2 | 4,140.1 | 3,233.4 | 2,646.1 |
| New South Wales | 6,816.1 | 6,888.0 | 8,677.0 | 8,395.1 | 8,138.5 | 11,789.1 | 10,210.2 | 9,211.3 |
| Melbourne | 3,743.0 | 3,805.8 | 5,272.3 | 5,038.1 | 4,861.7 | 7,970.7 | 6,789.2 | 6,100.9 |
| Balance of Victoria | 1,383.5 | 1,399.1 | 1,626.1 | 1,624.1 | 1,636.3 | 1,879.6 | 1,749.1 | 1,742.9 |
| Victoria | 5,126.5 | 5,204.8 | 6,898.3 | 6,662.2 | 6,498.0 | 9,850.3 | 8,538.3 | 7,843.8 |
| Brisbane | 1,819.8 | 1,857.0 | 2,908.0 | 2,681.1 | 2,465.6 | 4,955.1 | 3,979.3 | 3,237.0 |
| Balance of Queensland | 2,271.1 | 2,324.5 | 3,645.4 | 3,356.9 | 3,129.7 | 5,966.3 | 4,759.6 | 3,998.2 |
| Queensland | 4,090.9 | 4,181.4 | 6,553.3 | 6,038.0 | 5,595.2 | 10,921.3 | 8,738.9 | 7 235.2 |
| Adelaide | 1,145.8 | 1,158.0 | 1,410.8 | 1,384.5 | 1,391.8 | 1,848.5 | 1,651.8 | 1,623.7 |
| Balance of South Australia | 422.1 | 426.2 | 531.5 | 499.8 | 451.0 | 691.4 | 552.7 | 406.7 |
| South Australia | 1,567.9 | 1,584.2 | 1,942.3 | 1,884.4 | 1,842.9 | 2,539.9 | 2,204.5 | 2,030.4 |
| **Perth** | **1,518.7** | **1,554.1** | **2,455.2** | **2,267.6** | **2,112.1** | 4,164.4 | **3,358.4** | **2,815.5** |
| Balance of Western Australia | 540.6 | 552.0 | 796.8 | 732.9 | 660.5 | 1 207.6 | 935.0 | 702.3 |
| Western Australia | 2,059.4 | 2,106.1 | 3,252.0 | 3,000.5 | 2,772.7 | 5,372.0 | 4,293.4 | 3,517.7 |
| Hobart | 205.5 | 207.4 | 266.8 | 245.3 | 228.2 | 367.2 | 279.7 | 224.0 |
| Balance of Tasmania | 284.5 | 286.0 | 338.5 | 307.0 | 277.5 | 411.1 | 291.2 | 202.6 |
| Tasmania | 490.0 | 493.4 | 605.3 | 552.3 | 505.7 | 778.3 | 571.0 | 426.6 |
| Darwin | 114.4 | 117.4 | 189.3 | 165.2 | 142.4 | 334.9 | 243.0 | 169.2 |
| Balance of Northern Territory | 96.3 | 97.5 | 140.1 | 119.8 | 100.8 | 238.1 | 158.6 | 94.9 |
| Northern Territory | 210.6 | 214.9 | 329.4 | 285.0 | 243.3 | 573.0 | 401.6 | 264.2 |
| Australian Capital Territory | 334.1 | 339.8 | 462.5 | 416.5 | 373.0 | 683.2 | 509.3 | 374.2 |
| Total capital cities | 13,163.3 | 13,373.4 | 18,452.0 | 17,624.7 | 16,933.0 | 27,973.0 | 23,787.5 | 21,109.6 |
| Total balance of states & territories | 7,532.2 | 7,639.3 | 10,268.2 | 9,609.2 | 9,036.1 | 14,534.2 | 11,679.6 | 9,793.7 |
| Australia | 20,697.9 | 21,015.0 | 28,723.0 | 27,236.7 | 25,971.9 | 42,510.4 | 35,470.0 | 30,906.1 |

*The population projection with which we began the research as shown on previous page has now become the most conservative ABS projection for Perth's population growth by 2056, as shown in table above.[3]*

'The huge predicted urban growth demands new approaches to housing, the water supply infrastructure and waste management practices if Perth is to progress towards sustainability.'[4]

4 Grace, W., 'Sustainable Urban Living – a Perth Perspective', Paper presented to the National Housing Conference, Perth, October 2005.

5 Wikipedia Contributors, 'Perth, Western Australia', <http://en.wikipedia.org/wiki/Perth,_Western_Australia>, viewed August 2008.

6 Western Australian Planning Commission (WAPC), Greater Perth Population and Housing 'Discussion Paper No. 2', WAPC, Perth, 2003, p. 9.

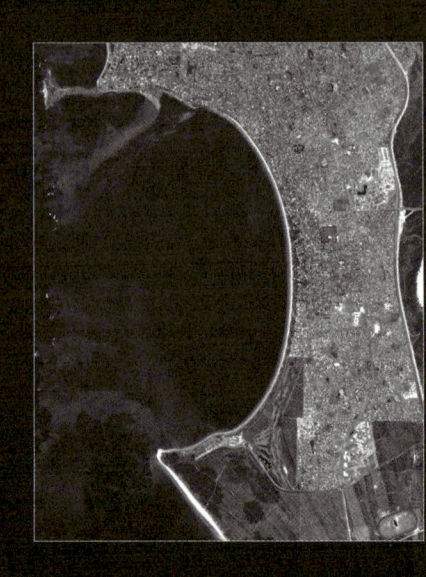

| YEAR | POPULATION |
|---|---|
| 1901 | 36,274 |
| 1911 | 106,792 |
| 1947 | 272,528 |
| 1961 | 420,133 |
| 1971 | 641,800 |
| 1981 | 809,036 |
| 1991 | 1,142,646 |
| 2001 | 1,325,392 |
| 2006 | 1,519,500 |

| YEAR | URBAN DEVELOPMENT |
|---|---|
| 1925 | 66 sq km |
| 1962 | 257 sq km |
| 1974 | 378 sq km |
| 1983 | 495 sq km |
| 1995 | 559 sq km |
| 2002 | 631 sq km |

*top left: Warnbro Sound ca. 1970, right: Warnbro Sound 2008*
*bottom left: Perth metropolitan area population table,[4] right: Approximate extent of urban development.[5]*

# GROWTH

Perth was founded in 1829. By 1830 Western Australia's European population had reached 1,500 on 36 immigrant ships.[7] The first settlers were predominantly young, most were males, and 70% came from major urban centres in the south-east of England.[8] Aboriginal people are estimated to have numbered around 15,000 in the South-West at the time.[9]

Perth grew slowly from its inception due to poor conditions for agriculture, and the city remained relatively small in size until the gold rushes of the 1890s stimulated growth.[10] Perth's population doubled in the 30 years from 1971 to 2001 and Australian Bureau of Statistics' projections indicate a doubling again by 2051 to a population of around three million.[11] Currently around 950 people are moving to Western Australia every week.[12] If the current rate of growth continues (and current predictions are that it will), Perth could reach a population of well over three million by 2050,[13] exceeding current forecasts.[14] National demographer Bob Birrell believes that Perth could be the fastest growing city in Australian history and may 'face traffic, health and housing chaos in coming years' if it doesn't 'heed the early warning and plan ahead'.[15] By world city standards, Perth's annual growth rate of 2.4% seems moderate when compared with cities such Beihai as in China, which is growing at an annual rate of 10.58%.[16] Considering that it has taken Perth 179 years to develop current city infrastructure for 1.5 million people it would, however, seem a considerable task to repeat this in the next 40 years.

7   Appleyard, R.T. and Manford, T., *The Beginning*, University of Western Australia Press, Perth, 1979, p. 150.

8   Appleyard and Manford, p. 147.

9   Wikipedia Contributors, 'Swan River Colony', <http://en.wikipedia.org/wiki/Swan_River_Colony>, viewed April 2008.

10  National Museum of Australia, 'Perth Town, the Capital of the Swan River Colony Founded by Captain James Stirling in 1829', Canberra, <http://www.nma.gov.au/advancedSearchResultsItemDetail.jsp?irn=383>, viewed April 2008.

11  ABS high-level population projection for Perth, 2051. ABS, Catalogue No. 3222.0, *Population Projections, Australia, 2004–2101*, Canberra, 2005.

12  Birrell, B., CEDA Population Forum, Perth, 27 June 2008.

13  Perth accommodates approximately 73% of Western Australia's population. Calculations based on ABS data.

14  As at the time of writing, April 2008.

15  Birrell, B., CEDA Population Forum, Perth, 27 June 2008.

16  Beihai in southern China is a city of 1.4 million people and is predicted to reach 5.8 million by 2020. Vom Hove, T., 'The World's Largest Cities and Urban Areas in 2006 and 2020' in City Mayors Statistics, <http://www.citymayors.com/statistics/urban_intro.html>, viewed April 2008.

In the years 1950–2006 Perth's population grew at an average of 22,500 people per year. The population is currently growing by approximately 27,000 people per year.[1]

**1,518,700** Perth's population 2008.

**4,200,000** Perth's projected population, high level, 2051.[2]

**61.5%** Percentage of Perth residents born in Australia. The Australian-born population for Perth and Peel was 923,044.

**31.3%** Approximately one third of Perth's residents were born overseas. 142,424 were born in England.

**730,634** Perth's total labour force population.

**627,421** Number of dwellings in Perth (includes unoccupied).[3]

**67.2%** Percentage of family households in Perth.

**23.6%** Percentage of single person households in Perth.

**2.5** Average number people/Perth household 2006.

**2.3** Projected average number people/Australian households 2050.[4]

**91.1%** Percentage of Western Australians living within 50 kilometres of the coast. Australian average is 85%.

**1,090** People/km$^2$ – Perth's urban area average density.

**79.1** Western Australia's life expectancy for males. National average is 78.7 years.

**83.8** Western Australia's life expectancy for females. National average is 83.5 years.

*Demographics: Core data.[5]*

# DEMOGRAPHICS

By 2050, 50% of the Australian population will be over 45, and more than a quarter will be over 65.[6]

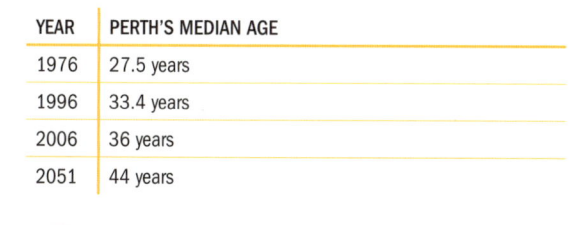

| YEAR | PERTH'S MEDIAN AGE |
|---|---|
| 1976 | 27.5 years |
| 1996 | 33.4 years |
| 2006 | 36 years |
| 2051 | 44 years |

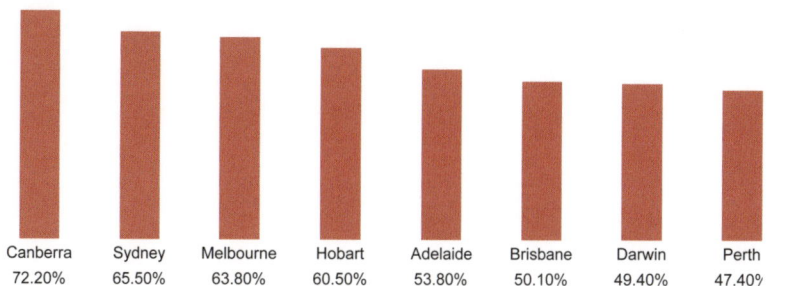

| | Canberra | Sydney | Melbourne | Hobart | Adelaide | Brisbane | Darwin | Perth |
|---|---|---|---|---|---|---|---|---|
| | 72.20% | 65.50% | 63.80% | 60.50% | 53.80% | 50.10% | 49.40% | 47.40% |

| | Sydney | Melbourne | Brisbane | Adelaide | Perth | Hobart | Darwin | ACT |
|---|---|---|---|---|---|---|---|---|
| 2006 | 4,282.00 | 3,743.00 | 1,819.80 | 1,145.80 | 1,518.70 | 205.5 | 114.4 | 334.1 |
| 2056 | 7,649.00 | 7,970.70 | 4,955.10 | 1,848.50 | 4,164.40 | 367.2 | 334.9 | 683.2 |

top: Change in median age in Perth Metropolitan Region.[7]

middle: Australian cities: Percentage of overseas migrants with a bachelor degree or higher by destination, 2001–2006. Perth attracts fewer people with university qualifications than all other Australian capital cities.[8]

bottom: Australian capital cities and regions: Population size (x 1000), observed and projected, 2006–2056 (ABS High-level projections, 2008). The Australian Bureau of Statistics revised its population projections following the 2006 Census. High-level projections for Perth were revised upwards to 4.2 million people. Mid-level projections indicate a population increase of 116%, the highest for all Australian cities 2006–56.[9]

1. Water Corporation, *Water Forever: Options for our Water Future*, Perth, 2008, p. 16.
2. The ABS released in September 2008 a revised high-level population projection for Perth to 4.2 million people. This is an additional 1,038 people per week. Mid-level projections indicate an additional 650 people per week.
3. This includes dwellings in the Peel statistical region.
4. Foran, B. and Poldi, F., *Future Dilemmas: Options to 2050 for Australia's population, technology, resources and environment*, CSIRO, Canberra, 2002.
5. ABS, Catalogue No. 1338.1, *New South Wales in Focus, 2008*, Canberra, 2008; ABS, Catalogue No. 2030.5, *Perth: A Social Atlas, 2006, Census of Population and Housing*, Canberra, 2006; ABS, 2006 Quickstats, *Perth*, Canberra, 2007; ABS, Catalogue No. 3222.0, *Population Projections, Australia, 2004–2101*, Canberra, 2005.
6. ABS, Catalogue No. 3222.0, *Population Projections, Australia, 2004–2101*, Canberra, 2005.
7. Western Australian Planning Commission (WAPC), *Greater Perth: Population and Housing Discussion Paper Two*, WAPC, Perth, 2003. ABS, Catalogue No. 3222.0, *Population Projections, Australia, 2004–2101*, Table 15: Projected population, Components of change and summary statistics, Perth, ABS, Canberra, 2006.
8. Comparative Capitals, FORM, Perth, 2008. Based on ABS data.
9. ABS, Catalogue No. 3222.0, *Population Projections, Australia, 2006–2101*, Canberra, 2008.

55
DATABASE

# Western Australia will need up to 400,000 additional workers over the next decade to sustain its resources boom.[10]

**20,910** — Indigenous Australians (1.5%) in Perth and Peel regions.

**452,888** — Perth residents born overseas. Perth has the highest proportion of people born overseas of any Australian capital city, except Sydney.

**157,567** — Number of people (22.6% of Perth's labour force) with a bachelor degree or higher qualification.

**111,068** — Number of people (16.1% of Perth's labour force) employed as technicians and tradespeople: the highest of all Australian capitals.

**306,033** — Number of people (or half of Perth's labour force) with no qualifications.

**26,941** — Number of unemployed in Perth.

**445,910** — Number of full-time employees in Perth (61%).

**26,000** — Estimated number of fly-in fly-out workers in Western Australia.[11]

Perth population, top 10 countries of origin (bar chart):
- Ireland
- Vietnam
- Singapore
- India
- Italy
- South Africa
- Malaysia
- Scotland
- New Zealand
- England

(x-axis: 0 to 160,000)

top: Demographics data.[12]

bottom: Perth population, top 10 countries of origin. Perth's migrant population is highly Anglo-Celtic in origin.[13]

# DEMOGRAPHICS

'Perth's population is forecast to grow at 45% between 2005 and 2021. "This is absolutely massive, completely unprecedented…It's a massive task for building infrastructure."'[14]

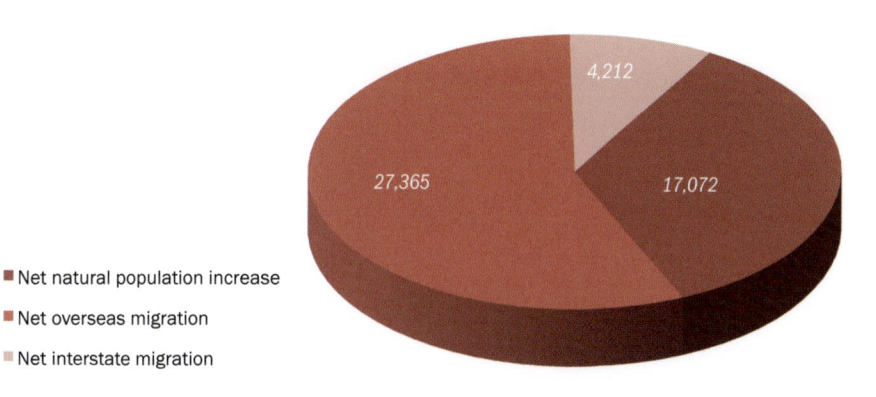

- Net natural population increase: 27,365
- Net overseas migration: 17,072
- Net interstate migration: 4,212

### Western Australia: net population increase 2006–07

Western Australia's net population increase was 48,649 in the 12 months to September 2007. Economist Shane Wright has estimated that 33,300 interstate and overseas migrants moved into Perth in 2005–06,[15] or 641 people a week. In 2008 this increased to an estimated additional population into Perth of 712 per week (and an estimated 950 people per week for the state). Western Australia has been described as 'the nation's economic powerhouse' with 10% of the national population producing 13% of national GDP[16] and is dependent on overseas immigration to power the current resources boom. The Western Australian Chamber of Commerce and Industry estimates that Western Australia needs 400,000 additional workers over the next decade in order to sustain the recent rates of economic growth.[17] This would mean an additional 769 people a week into Western Australia, or an additional 577 people coming to Perth weekly just to meet employment demands of the next decade: a housing demand of approximately 230 dwellings weekly[18] or 11,960 houses annually.[19]

---

10  Chamber of Commerce and Industry Western Australia report quoted by The Hon. Gary Gray, Parliamentary Secretary for Regional Development and Northern Australia, CEDA Forum, 27 June 2008.

11  Western Australian Minister for State Development, *Submission to the Productivity Commission: Research Study into the Economic Impacts of Migration and Population Growth*, <http://www.pc.gov.au/__data/assets/pdf_file/0011/9758/sub027.pdf>, viewed March 2008.

12  ABS, Catalogue No. 2030.5, *Perth: A Social Atlas*, 2006 Census of Population and Housing, Canberra, 2006.

13  ABS, *2006 Census QuickStats: Western Australia*, Canberra, 2006.

14  Bob Birrell quoted in Maley, P., 'Population explosion makes Perth the prime mover', *The Australian*, 27 June 2008.

15  Wright, S., 'Boom times draw thousands to WA', *The West Australian*, 22 March 2008, p. 54.

16  Pearson, J., CEDA Population Forum, Perth, 27 June 2008. A summary of the report can be accessed online, <http://www.news.com.au/perthnow/story/0,21598,22719155-2761,00.html.>

17  Pearson, J., CEDA Population Forum, Perth, 27 June 2008.

18  Assuming a household size of 2.5 people per dwelling.

19  Graph drawn from ABS data quoted in Wright, S., 'Boom times draw thousands to WA', *The West Australian*, 22 March 2008, p.54.

**57**
**DATABASE**

X2

# INFRASTRUCTURE

**36** Hospitals

**453** Primary and secondary schools

**5** Universities

**11** Colleges (TAFE)

**43** Police stations and offices

**23** Fire stations

**12,751** Kilometres of road

**69** Train stations

**14** State Emergency Service (SES) units

**3** Airports

**2** Ports

**24** Museums

**10,502** Kilometres of sewers in Perth region

**9** Sewerage treatment plants

**11** Dams

**1** Desalination plant (+1 in process for 2011 production)

**7** Artesian groundwater extraction stations: Mirabooka, Gwelup, Wanneroo, Jandakot, Neerabup, Lexia, Yanchep/Two Rocks)

**103** Water pumping stations

**12,537** Kilometres of water mains

*Infrastructure, Perth metro area 2007.*

'For every population increase of 10,000 people, new services and infrastructure will be required such as: 4,000 new homes, a shopping precinct half the size of a Westfield shopping centre and an additional 20 MW of power to keep it running.'

Western Power online advertisement, <http://www.westernpower.com.au>.

2.5 net d/ha

10 net d/ha

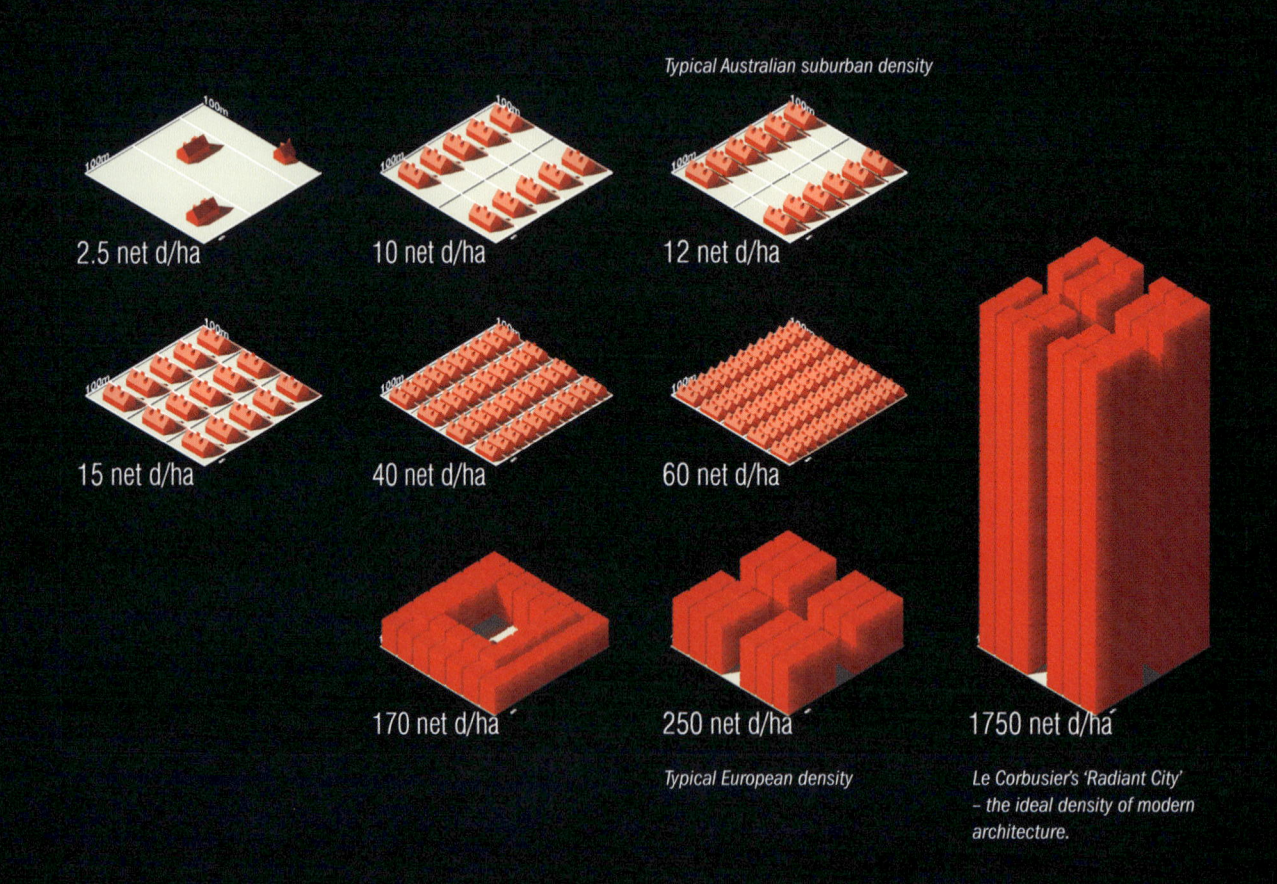

*Typical Australian suburban density*
12 net d/ha

15 net d/ha

40 net d/ha

60 net d/ha

170 net d/ha

250 net d/ha

*Typical European density*

1750 net d/ha

*Le Corbusier's 'Radiant City' – the ideal density of modern architecture.*

*Standard urban densities (dwellings per hectare).*

# SUBURBANITY

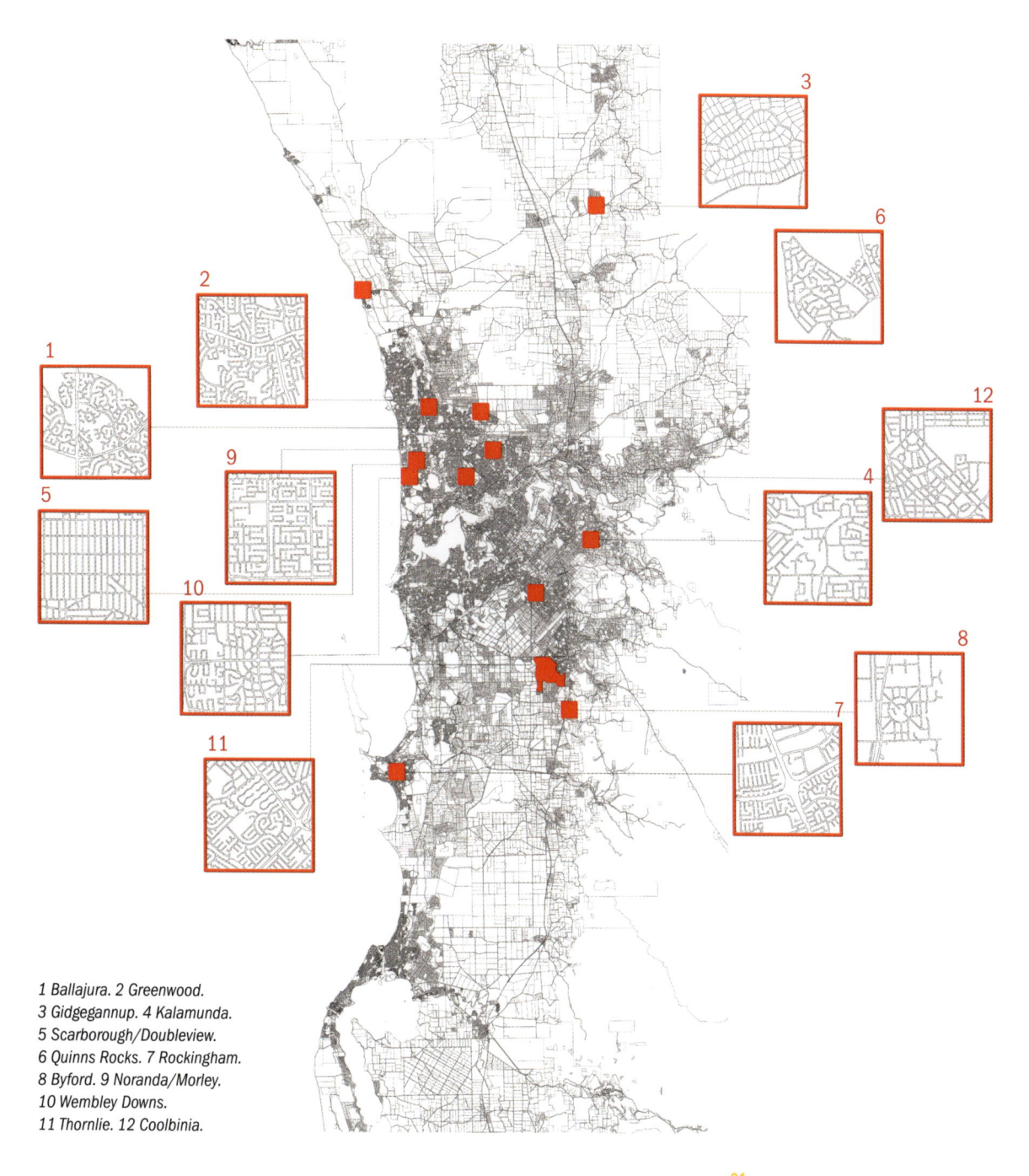

1 Ballajura. 2 Greenwood.
3 Gidgegannup. 4 Kalamunda.
5 Scarborough/Doubleview.
6 Quinns Rocks. 7 Rockingham.
8 Byford. 9 Noranda/Morley.
10 Wembley Downs.
11 Thornlie. 12 Coolbinia.

61
DATABASE

'Australians spend about $5.3 billion per year on wasted food...This represents more than 13 times the $386 million donated by Australian households to overseas aid agencies in 2003.'[1]

**309** Licensed or registered landfills in Western Australia.

**3.2** Million tonnes of total metropolitan waste disposed to landfill. This includes household, industrial and building waste.

**1.4** Million tonnes of household waste generated in Western Australia in 2006-07.

**1,015,210** Tonnes of total household waste generated in Western Australia in 2006-07 went into landfill (75%).

**338,204** Tonnes of total household waste generated in Western Australia in 2006-07 was diverted for re-use or recycling (25%).

**692** Kilograms/capita of total household waste generated in Western Australia in 2006-07 went into landfill.

**1.2** Million tonnes of organic waste (garden and green waste, food, sludges and manures) was disposed to landfill (2006-07).

**4** Million tonnes of organic carbon could be made available for soil improvement in agriculture annually from Australian recycled organic landfill material.

**25%** Water savings can be achieved by applying recycled organic material to soil, where fertility and viability has become degraded through intensive farming.

**3%** Reduction in emissions by removing organic waste from Australia's waste stream.

**650,000** Tyres sent to Western Australia's landfill annually. Only one company is recycling tyres in Western Australia. Another two companies are baling and mono-filling tyres for possible future recovery. The tyres will be exhumed or mined when rubber becomes more valuable.[2]

**60%** (Approximate percentage) of waste tyres are sent to landfill.

*Data source[3]*

# WASTE

## Australia ranked seventh in a survey of 30 OECD countries in total municipal waste generation per capita.[4]

kg/capita

Bar chart values (approximate):
- USA: ~760
- Australia: ~690
- Spain: ~650
- UK: ~580
- France: ~540
- Italy: ~540
- Sweden: ~480
- Canada: ~420
- Japan: ~400
- Mexico: ~340
- China: ~115
- India: ~100

Pie chart:
- Municipal and household: 26%
- Commercial and industrial: 19%
- Building and demolition: 55%

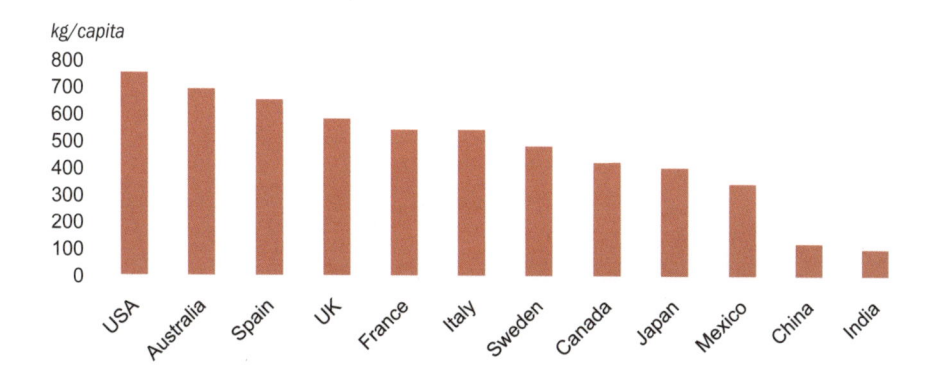

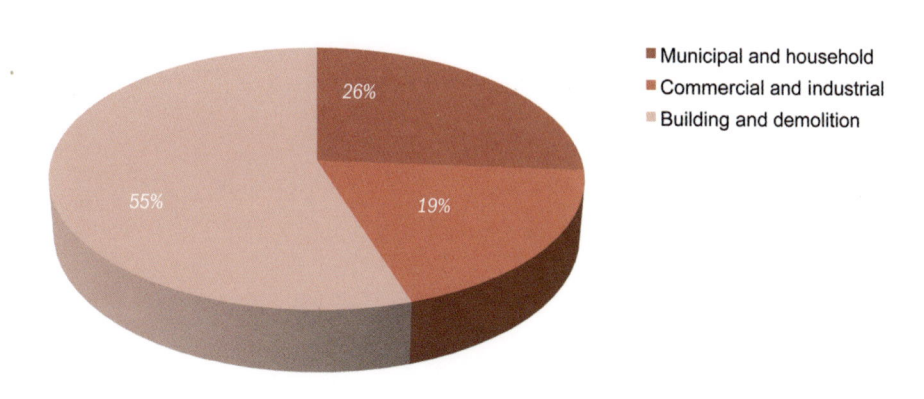

top: OECD: Total kilograms of municipal and household waste generated per capita 2005. Australia ranked seventh in a survey of 30 OECD countries in total municipal waste generation per capita.[4]

bottom: Waste deposited in Perth metropolitan landfills 2004.[5] Since 2001 there has been a steady increase in the amount of building waste disposed to landfill correlating with an increase in boom-related building activity.[6]

---

1. Hamilton, C. et al., 'Wasteful Consumption in Australia: Discussion Paper Number 77', The Australia Institute, Canberra, 2005.

2. Department of Environment and Conservation, 'Review of Total Recycling Activity in Western Australia 2006/07', Department of Environment and Conservation, Subiaco, 2008.

3. Data in this table is sourced primarily from ABS, Catalogue No. 4613.0, Canberra, 2007, and Zero Waste, <http://www.zerowastewa.com.au/documents/zwpds_phase1_0607.pdf>, viewed April 2008.

4. OECD Factbook 2008: Economic, Environmental and Social Statistics, <http://puck.sourceoecd.org/vl=14590885/cl=13/nw=1/rpsv/factbook/index.htm>, viewed April 2008.

5. Zero Waste, <http://www.zerowastewa.com.au/data/dis6/>, viewed 2007.

6. Data in this table is sourced from The Environmental Protection Authority (EPA), State of the Environment Report Western Australia 2007, Department of Environment and Conservation, Perth, 2007, Australian Bureau of Statistics, Catalogue No. 4648.0.55.001, Detailed Energy Statistics, Australia, 2001–02, Canberra, 2004; Econnect; Sustainable Energy Development Office (SEDO), <http://energy.wa.gov.au/pages/emissions.asp>; <http://www.abs.gov.au/AUSSTATS/abs@.nsf/productsbyCatalogue/0C2AA58A90E887B3CA256E60007BAB57?OpenDocument>, viewed June 2008.

‘Western Australia has the highest per capita rate of solid waste generation in Australia. Strong links exist between waste generation and economic growth.’[7]

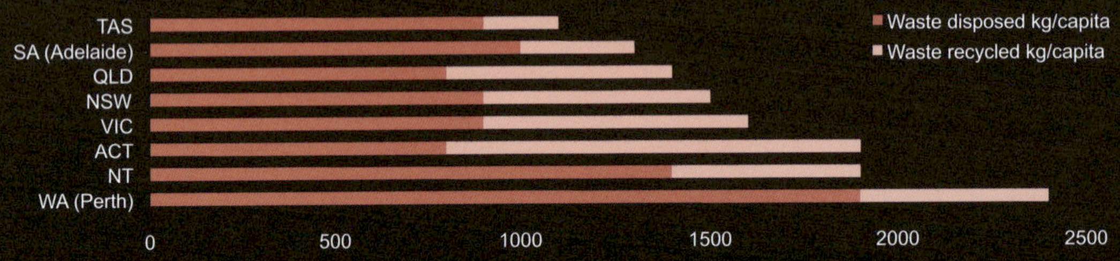

TAS
SA (Adelaide)
QLD
NSW
VIC
ACT
NT
WA (Perth)
0
500
1000
1500
2000
2500
Waste disposed kg/capita
Waste recycled kg/capita


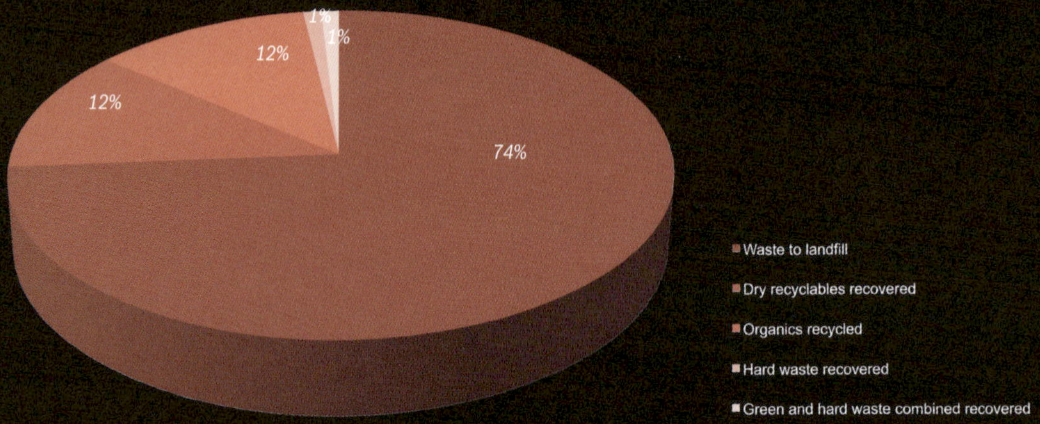

1%
1%
12%
12%
74%
Waste to landfill
Dry recyclables recovered
Organics recycled
Hard waste recovered
Green and hard waste combined recovered


*top: Total solid waste flows 1999/2000. Perth's total waste is high due to high levels of building and construction activity and high consumption levels.*[8]

*bottom: Western Australia's municipal waste destination, 2006-07. Three-quarters of waste goes to landfill in Western Australia.*[9]

# WASTE

# Total waste disposed to landfill in the Perth metropolitan area averaged at 1.9 tonnes per capita in 2004,[10] or more than two VW Beetles per person per year.

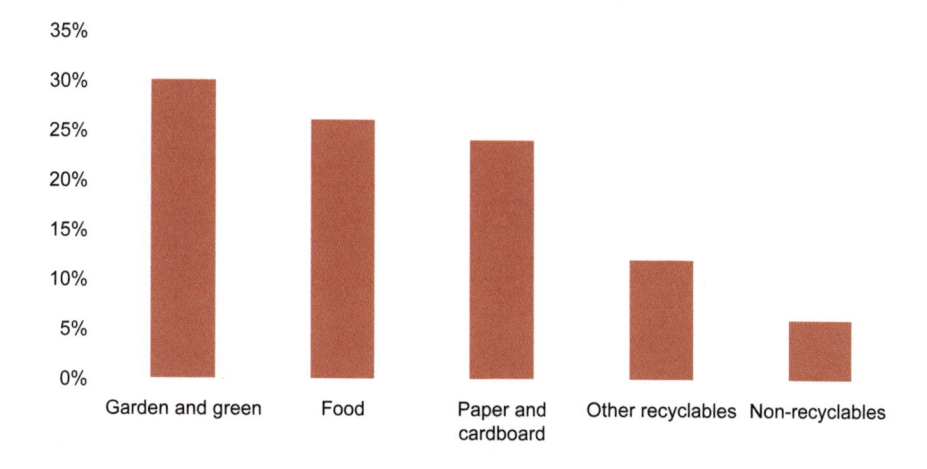

7. The Environmental Protection Authority (EPA), *State of the Environment Report Western Australia 2007*, Department of Environment and Conservation, Perth, 2007; Australian Bureau of Statistics, Catalogue No. 4648.0.55.001, *Detailed Energy Statistics, Australia, 2001-02*, Canberra, 2004; Sustainable Energy Development Office (SEDO), <http://energy.wa.gov.au/pages/emissions.asp>; <http://www.abs.gov.au/AUSSTATS/abs@.nsf/productsbyCatalogue/0C2AA58A90E887B3CA256E60007BAB57?OpenDocument>, viewed June 2008.

8. 2006 Australian State of the Environment Committee, Australia State of the Environment 2006, <http://www.environment.gov.au/soe/2006/publications/drs/indicator/346/index.html>.

9. Zero Waste Plan Development Scheme (ZWPDS) Phase 1 Report 2006-07, <http://www.zerowastewa.com.au/documents/zwpds_phase1_0607.pdf>, viewed 2007.

10. Towards Zero Waste, <http://www.zerowaste.com.au/data/>, viewed July 2008.

11. Zero Waste Plan Development Scheme (ZWPDS) Phase 1 Report 2006-07, <http://www.zerowastewa.com.au/documents/zwpds_phase1_0607.pdf>, viewed 2007.

12. Paulin, B., 'Submission to the Productivity Commission: Inquiry into Waste Generation and Resource Efficiency', <http://www.pc.gov.au/__data/assets/file/0012/22521/sub081.rtf>, viewed August 2008.

13. Wastenet, <http://www.wastenet.com.au>, viewed 2008.

| Category | Percentage |
|---|---|
| Garden and green | 30% |
| Food | 26% |
| Paper and cardboard | 24% |
| Other recyclables | 12% |
| Non-recyclables | 6% |

above: Municipal and household waste composition 2005. Metropolitan Perth generates about 1.2 million tonnes of organic waste annually[11] and much of this goes to landfill. Over half is food and garden waste and another 24% is paper and cardboard, which is also biodegradable. Organic waste is a valuable resource that can be used to help improve soil quality. Bob Paulin, agronomist at the Western Australian Department of Agriculture, believes that of the 'potential agricultural markets, horticulture and particularly intensive vegetable, vine and fruit growing offer the most potential because of their intensive use of inputs (fertiliser, irrigation and pesticides) and their usual proximity to urban waste generation'.[12] Organic wastes disposed to landfill decompose and produce methane, a significant greenhouse gas.[13]

65
DATABASE

Australia's rainfall is the lowest of all continents in the world (excluding Antarctica). Despite this, Australia has one of the highest per capita water consumption rates in the world.[1]

| | |
|---:|:---|
| **1** | Inland waters outfall. |
| **5** | Treated sewerage ocean outfalls. |
| **9** | Sewerage treatment plants. |
| **54** | Properties served per kilometre of water main. |
| **57** | Properties served per kilometre of sewerage main. |
| **101** | Water distribution storage facilities. |
| **103** | Water pumping stations. |
| **624** | Sewerage pumping stations. |
| **10,502** | Kilometres of sewerage mains and channels. |
| **12,537** | Kilometres of water mains. |

| | | |
|---|---|---|
| KL | 1 Kilolitre | 1000 Litres |
| ML | 1 Megalitre | 1000 Kilolitres |
| GL | 1 Gigalitre | 1000 Megalitres |

| WATER SOURCE | VOLUME |
|---|---|
| surface water | 85,233 ML |
| groundwater | 145,533 ML |
| desalinated water | 18,120 ML |
| recycling | 4,951 ML |
| Total | 244,100 ML |

top: Perth Metropolitan Region: water supply infrastructure.
bottom: Perth Metropolitan Region: water sources 2006–07.[2]

# WATER

'South-West Western Australia is one of the most water challenged parts of the country, experiencing Australia's highest rates of climate change and dryland salinity amid rapid population growth and associated development.'[3]

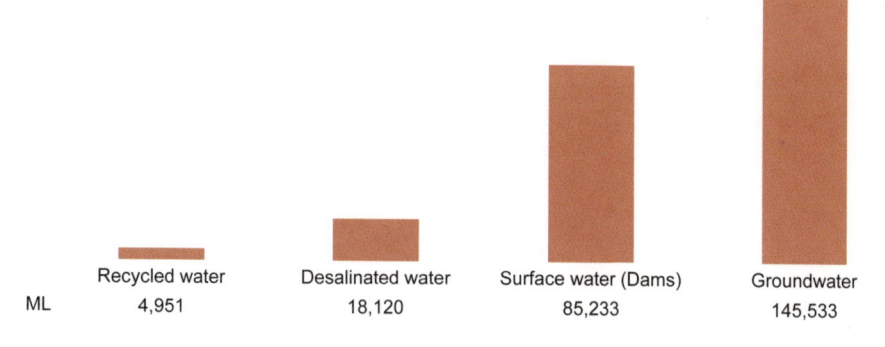

| | Recycled water | Desalinated water | Surface water (Dams) | Groundwater |
|---|---|---|---|---|
| ML | 4,951 | 18,120 | 85,233 | 145,533 |

Perth: Metropolitan water sources 2006–07 (megalitres).[4]

The dominant source of water for domestic and commercial use in Perth is groundwater from aquifers beneath the Swan Coastal Plain.[5] This makes Perth unique among Australian capital cities, which mostly rely on surface water. Perth's surface water is collected in 11 dams; and the Kwinana Desalination Plant has recently come online supplying 45 GL annually (17% of drinking water supplies). Perth's water sourcing has changed markedly since the 1970s when dams supplied the majority of Perth's water. With a 70% reduction in rainfall runoff since the mid-1970s, the Water Corporation predicts that surface water supply could become completely obsolete in 50 years.[6]

## Perth groundwater

Approximately 60% of Perth's drinking water is supplied from the Gnangara Mound aquifer.[7] 22,000 km$^2$ in area, Gnangara Mound stretches from Guilderton to Fremantle and out to Bullsbrook. Rottnest Island would fit into the mound more than 115 times. The mound is ecologically important and supports Perth's system of wetlands. The water table of the aquifer has reduced, and recharge has decreased by about 25% over the last 25 years.[8]

1. GetGreen, <http://www.getgreen.com.au/2007/04/09/australian-water-crisis-facts/>, viewed 2008.
2. National Water Commission, *National Performance Report 2006-2007: Urban Water Utilities*, Water Services Association, Melbourne, 2008.
3. CSIRO, <http://www.csiro.au/science/psfk.html.>, viewed July 2008.
4. National Water Commission, *National Performance Report 2006-2007: Urban Water Utilities*, Water Services Association, Melbourne, 2008.
5. Australian Academy of Technological Sciences and Engineering, *Western Australia: Water Policy Issues in Climate Uncertainty*, 2005. <http://www.atse.org.au/index.php?sectionid=129>.
6. Water Corporation, *Planning For New Sources of Water*, <http://www.watercorporation.com.au/W/water_sources_new.cfm>, viewed 2007.
7. Water Corporation, *Planning For New Sources of Water*, <http://www.watercorporation.com.au/W/water_sources_new.cfm>, viewed 2007.
8. Banks, A., 'Gnangara users break water rules', *The West Australian*, 11 January 2007, p. 6.

# 'Per capita water consumption in Perth is higher than in all other state capitals and Perth ranks amongst those cities most likely to endure water stress in the coming decade.'[9]

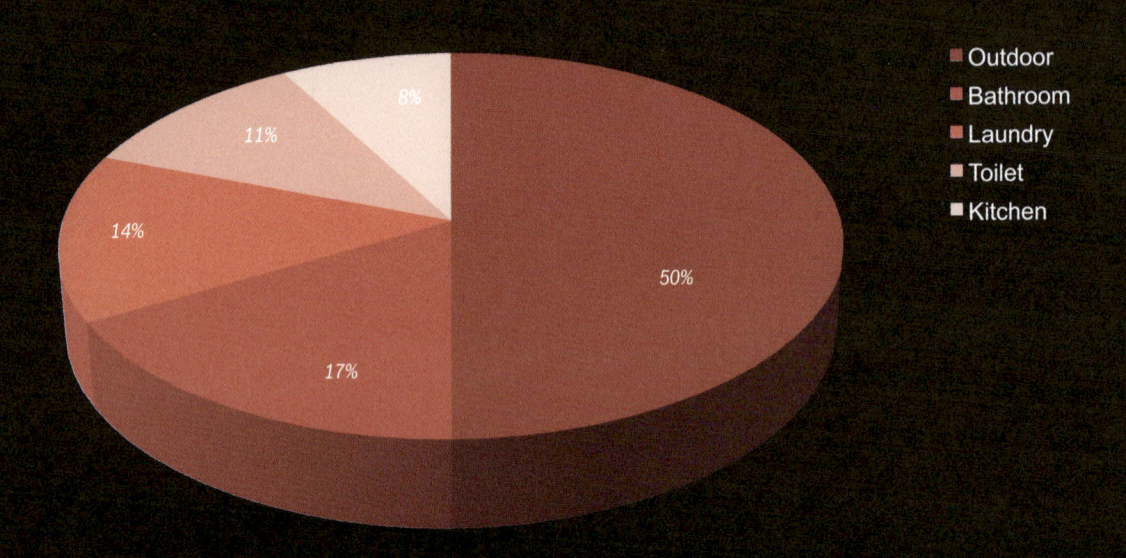

- Outdoor: 50%
- Bathroom: 17%
- Laundry: 14%
- Toilet: 11%
- Kitchen: 8%

| DOMESTIC WATER USAGE | VOLUME |
| --- | --- |
| Average Perth household use 2006–07 | 282 kL |
| Perth average domestic water use per person 2002–07 | 107 kL |
| Perth average total water use per person 2002–07 | 153 kL |
| Average potential annual rainwater tank water supply | 50 kL |

| WATER SUPPLY/USE | VOLUME |
| --- | --- |
| Average annual per residential property | 281 kL |
| Total residential | 168,969 ML |
| Total commercial, industrial and municipal | 46,419 ML |
| Total urban | 235,153 ML |

| WASTEWATER | VOLUME |
| --- | --- |
| Residential and non-trade waste sewerage collected | 109,537 ML |
| Trade waste sewerage collected | 6,300 ML |
| Sewerage collected per total property | 198 kL |
| Total sewerage collected | 115,837 ML |

top: Western Australia: Domestic potable water use 2005–06.[10] Half of all household water used by Western Australians is for outdoor and garden purposes. In Perth the average household used 282 kilolitres of water for domestic purposes in 2006–07.[11] Water used outdoors, and in toilets and laundries, does not have to be of drinking standard[7] so conceivably around 141 kL could be supplied to households annually through third pipe schemes for non-potable household purposes.

middle: Domestic water usage: Perth (per annum).[12]

bottom left: Perth Metropolitan Region: Water usage 2006–07.[13]

bottom right: Perth Metropolitan Region: Sewerage/wastewater 2006–07.[13]

'Key issues regarding water usage in Perth are: a low re-use of water; few domestic rainwater tanks; a selection of plants and grasses not necessarily chosen for dry conditions; and a general lack of appreciation of water as a valuable and relatively scarce resource.'[14]

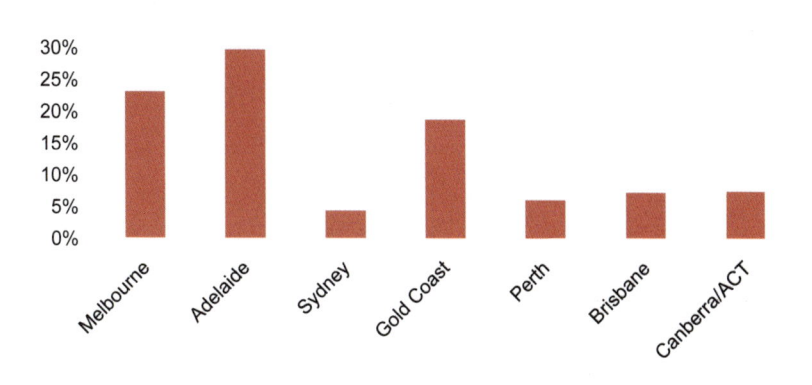

9. Horwitz, P. et al., 'South-West jewel must not be a water mine for Perth', *The West Australian*, 26 March 2007, p. 12.
10. National Water Commission, *National Performance Report 2005–06: Major Urban Water Utilities*, Water Services Association of Australia and National Water Commission, Melbourne, 2007.
11. Water Corporation, Water Forever website, <http://www.thinking50.com.au/go/conserve/energy-efficiency/household-energy-use-and.>, viewed 2008.
12. Water Corporation, *Water Forever: Options for our water future*, Perth, April 2008.
13. National Water Commission, *National Performance Report 2006–07: Urban Water Utilities*, Water Services Association, Melbourne, 2008.
14. Australian Academy of Technological Sciences and Engineering, *Water Resources for Perth and the Goldfields: Report of a West Australian Division Study, Executive summary*, 2002. Online at <http://www.atse.org.au/index.php?sectionid=129.>
15. National Water Commission, *National Performance Report 2006–07: Urban Water Utilities*, Water Services Association, Melbourne, 2008.
16. Water Corporation, *Water Forever: Options for our Water Future*, Perth, April 2008, p. 20.
17. Water Corporation, 'Water Futures', <http://www.thinking50.com.au/go/water-futures.>, viewed May 2008.
18. Water Corporation presentation, <http://www.watercorporation.com.au/_files/Presentations/20061110.pdf.>, viewed August 2008.

Australian capital cities: Percentage of effluent recycled 2006–07.[15] Perth's recycling of wastewater remains relatively low at 6% in comparison with other Australian capital cities. The state's water authority plans to increase this to 12% by 2012 in progression towards a target of 20%. Water Corporation's long-term target is to recycle 30% of treated wastewater in Perth.[16] Under consideration is groundwater replenishment using recycled water, similar to the Groundwater Replenishment System in California, and The NEWater scheme in Singapore.[17] In 2007, around 100 GL of wastewater is potentially available for re-use each year,[14] currrently, the majority is treated and pumped out to sea. Water Corporation anticipates that, long term, recycled water could provide 70 GL/year drinking water, or half of the projected required source capacity by 2050.[18]

# Perth's water footprint is about 4% above the national and state average.[19]

| | |
|---:|---|
| **99.97%** | Percentage of water in wastewater discharged into the ocean (0.03% is particulate). |
| **320** | ML/day treated wastewater discharged off the Perth metropolitan coastline. |
| **116,800** | ML/annum (117 GL) treated domestic wastewater discharged off the Perth metropolitan coastline. |
| **90** | Average household recyclable greywater from bathroom and laundry in 2007 in kL. |
| **148.7** | ML/day (or 54,785 ML/annum) of greywater could be produced by Perth's 437,300 detached residential houses.[20] |
| **35** | GL/annum greywater could be used for water supply in Perth by 2060. Water Corporation anticipates that 15 GL could be supplied by greywater systems in Perth and another 20 GL by community greywater systems and treated for water supply.[21] |
| **32.75** | GL/annum total water used on Perth's irrigated agricultural areas (6,000 hectares) in 2005-06.[22] |
| **21%** | Percentage of all public water supply in Perth is used by business and industry.[23] |
| **50%** | Percentage of Perth's total annual residential water usage (84,485 ML) could potentially be supplied by recycled water (for use on gardens). Total Perth residential usage is 168,969 ML.[24] |
| **6%** | Percentage of Perth's effluent is recycled. |

above: Perth wastewater figures.

# Average Perth household water consumption increased 5% to 282 kL in the 2006–07 year. This required 370 kWh of electricity for treatment and about the same again to transport the water.[25]

| RECYCLED WATER USAGE | VOLUME |
| --- | --- |
| Industrial and commercial | 4,833 ML |
| Irrigation | 118 ML |
| Total recycled water supplied | 6,958 ML |

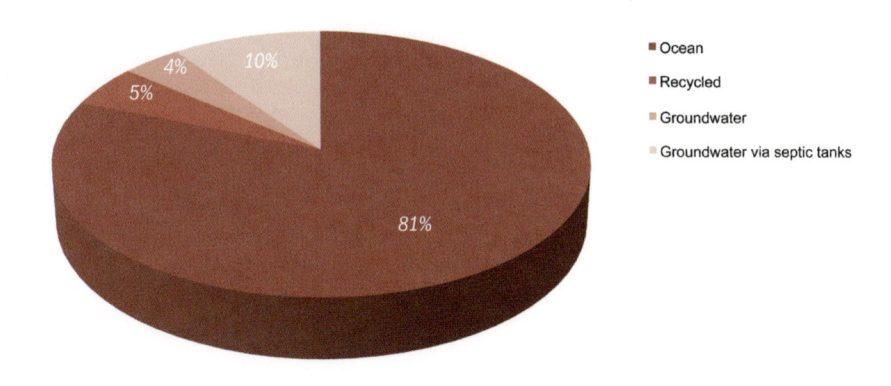

Pie chart — Percentage of treated wastewater by destination:
- Ocean: 81%
- Recycled: 5%
- Groundwater: 4%
- Groundwater via septic tanks: 10%

top: Perth Metropolitan Region: Recycled water usage.

bottom: Perth Metropolitan Region: Percentage of treated wastewater by destination.[26]

81% of Perth's treated wastewater is discharged into the ocean from outlets at Ocean Reef, Swanbourne and Cape Peron. Treated waste outlets are more than a kilometre from the shore. Perth's recycled wastewater is mainly used on irrigated public open space and for industry.[27]

19 Australian Conservation Foundation, Consumption Atlas, <http://www.acfonline.org.au/consumptionatlas/>, viewed June 2008.

20 Calculated using ABS 2006 Census data for housing.

21 Water Corporation, *Water Forever: Options for our Water Future*, Perth, April 2008, p. 51.

22 ABS, *2006 Census QuickStats, Western Australia*, Canberra, 2006.

23 Water Corporation, *Water Forever: Options for our Water Future*, Perth, April 2008, p. 14.

24 Calculated from National Water Accounts data.

25 Water Corporation, <http://www.thinking50.com.au>, viewed June 2008.

26 Water Corporation, *Water Forever: Options for our Water Future*, Perth, April 2008, p. 41.

27 Water Corporation, *Water Forever: Options for our Water Future*, Perth, April 2008, p. 40.

'Western Australia's potential intermittent generation resource is substantial and diverse, from onshore and offshore wind energy, solar energy and wave energy generation.'[1]

**98%** Percentage of Western Australia's primary energy needs supplied from fossil fuels.

**50%** Percentage of Western Australia's total electricity supply generated by gas-fire.

**136,408** Terajoules of natural gas consumed by Western Australia in 2001–02.

**17,329** Gigawatt hours of electricty consumed by Western Australia in 2001–02.

**426** ML of petrol consumed by Western Australia in 2001–02.

**1,608** ML of diesel consumed by Western Australia in 2001–02.

**2/3** Western Australia's greenhouse gas emissions are produced from fossil fuel combustion.

**2.7%** Forecast growth rate of Western Australia's annual electricity consumption. Most of the increased demand will come from the mining and commercial sectors.

**18%** Transport comprises 18% of Western Australia's total primary energy use.

**46%** Increase in peak electricity consumption over the past six years from 2,446 MW in 2000 to 3,575 MW in 2006–07 summer.[2]

**22,000** New homes were connected to Western Power's electricity grid in 2001.[2]

**30,000** New homes were connected to Western Power's electricity grid in 2006.[2]

**6%** The Western Australian Government's renewable energy target for the South West Interconnected System for 2009–2010.[3]

| PJ | petajoule | $10^{15}$ J |
| TJ | terajoule | $10^{12}$ J |
| GJ | gigajoule | $10^{9}$ J |
| MJ | megajoule | $10^{6}$ J |
| kJ | kilojoule | $10^{3}$ J |
| hJ | hectojoule | $10^{2}$ J |

left: 'The SI (International System of Units) unit of energy is the joule (J), equal to one watt per second; one kilowatt hour is exactly 3.6 megajoules, which is the amount of energy transferred if work is done at a rate of one thousand watts for one hour.'[4]

# ENERGY

'There is enough room in the WA wheatbelt to power the SWIS by mallees...perhaps the only energy system that is a net [carbon] sink.'[5]

The South West Interconnected System (SWIS) is the major electricity network in Western Australia. Power generation in the SWIS is predominantly from natural gas and coal, both non-renewable energy sources. The SWIS operates in isolation from power systems in the other Australian states due to a distance of 1,500 kilometres between system extremities.[6]

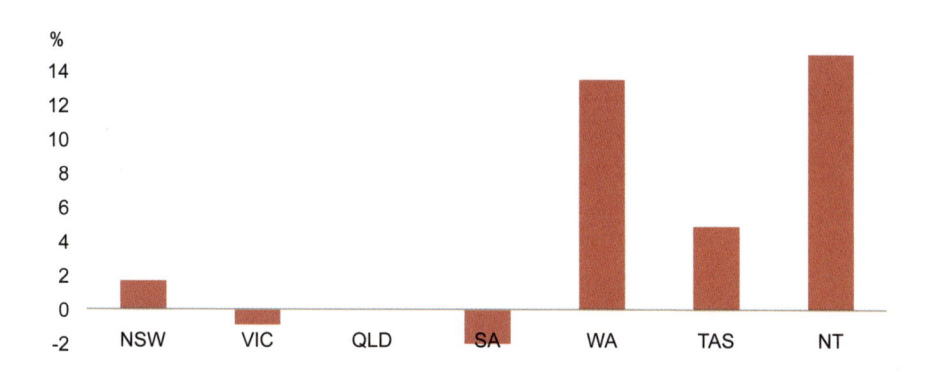

*Australian states: percentage of growth in energy consumption, 2006-07.*[7]

Western Australia's energy consumption grew by 13% in 2006–2007 reflecting the boom conditions of strong economic and population growth. Western Australia contributed the most overall to Australia's growth in energy consumption in 2006–2007.

1. Econnect, Draft Independent Report, 'Maximising the Penetration of Intermittent Generation in the SWIS', Econnect Project No. 1465. Report commissioned by the Office of Energy, Government of Western Australia, 2005. Online at <http://www.eriu.energy.wa.gov.au/cproot/655/4246/1465%20SWIS%20Report%20Consultation%20Rev%20000.pdf>, viewed September 2008.

2. Western Power, <http://www.westernpower.com.au>, viewed 2008.

3. Riwoe, D., et al., *A Review of Energy and Greenhouse Gas Emission Projections for Western Australia*, ABARE Report Prepared for Western Australian Greenhouse and Energy Taskforce, Canberra, 2006.

4. Wikipedia online, <http://en.wikipedia.org/wiki/Watt>, viewed 2008.

5. Harrison, D., 'Bioenergy and Integrated Wood Processing', Powerpoint presentation for the National Oil Mallee Conference, Perth, 14 March 2008, <http://www.oilmallee.com.au/pdf/conference/DonHarrison.pdf>, viewed September 2008.

6. The Environmental Protection Authority (EPA), *State of the Environment Report Western Australia 2007*, Department of Environment and Conservation, Perth, 2007; ABS, Catalogue No. 4648.0.55.001, *Detailed Energy Statistics, Australia, 2001-02*, Canberra, 2004; Econnect; Sustainable Energy Development Office (SEDO), <http://energy.wa.gov.au/pages/emissions.asp>.

7. ABARE, Australian Energy Statistics: Australian Energy Update 2008, <http://www.abareconomics.com/interactive/energyUPDATE08/>, viewed September 2008.

DATABASE

# Western Australia has the lowest national participation rate in state green power programs, at only 0.5% of Western Australian households.[8]

| | |
|---|---|
| **0.5%** | Western Australia's green power program participation rate, the lowest rate in Australia. |
| **15.5** | GJ/capita: Western Australia's 1990 residential energy use. |
| **17.2** | GJ/capita: Western Australia's 2005 residential energy use. |
| **15** | kWh/day: average electricity consumption of households connected to the SWIS in 2004. Total of 5,500 kWh. |
| **4,000** | MW: installed capacity of the SWIS. The power system is small by international standards. |
| **14,000** | MW: total installed capacity of the world's biggest wind energy generator in Germany. Germany has poorer wind conditions than Western Australia. |
| **2,600** | MW: peak demand in summer (mainly due to air conditioning). |
| **1** | kWh of electricity consumed from Western Power's electricity grid emits approximately 0.992 kg of carbon dioxide. |
| **1** | kWh of natural gas consumed emits approximately 0.219 kg of greenhouse gases. |
| **1** | kWh of wood consumed emits approximately 0.328 kg of greenhouse gases. |
| **2** | MW is the power rating of a typical wind turbine (2007). Offshore generators will rate up to 5 MW. |
| **10** | MW–500 MW is the typical maximum output of a wind farm in 2007. |
| **50%** | Percentage of Denmark's installed electricity capacity produced by intermittent generators (mainly wind). |

| | |
|---|---|
| MW | megawatt |
| KWh | kilowatt hour |

'Power and energy are frequently confused.'[9]

'Energy efficiency improvements in Australia have occurred more slowly than in other nations. From 1973–74 to 2000–01, technical energy efficiency in Australia improved by 3%. The International Energy Agency has found that Australia's energy efficiency has improved at less than half the rate of other countries.'[10]

8   The Environmental Protection Authority (EPA), *State of the Environment Report Western Australia 2007*, Department of Environment and Conservation, Perth, 2007.

9   Wikipedia, <http://en.wikipedia.org/wiki/Watt>, viewed 2008.

10  Your Building, An introduction to energy efficiency in commercial buildings, <http://www.yourbuilding.org/display/yb/An+introduction+to+energy+efficiency+in+commercial+buildings>, viewed 2008.

11  Western Power, <http://www.westernpower.com.au>, viewed 2008.

12  Western Power, Advertisement at <http://www.westernpower.com.au>, viewed April 2008.

13  Grace, W., 'Sustainable Urban Living – A Perth Perspective', National Housing Conference, Perth, October 2005.

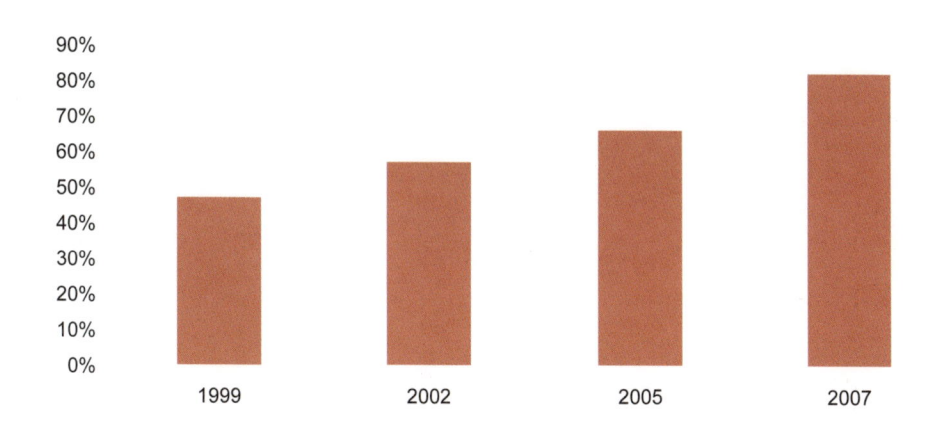

above: Western Australia: Percentage of homes with air conditioners.[11]

Western Australia now has the highest percentage of homes with air conditioners in Australia.[12] As a result, peak electricity demand has grown at a significantly higher rate than average demand, and is forecast to grow 25% faster than average demand in the next 10 years. Passive solar dwellings perform well without air conditioning but conventional, mass-market project houses generally perform poorly and require air conditioning to maintain adequate levels of thermal comfort. According to William Grace, 'Although the housing industry has made a start…a much more rapid take up is necessary to ensure that energy-efficient design is the basis of all new housing.'[13]

# 'Over the past 15 years, residential energy use per capita has increased by 15% in Western Australia.'[14]

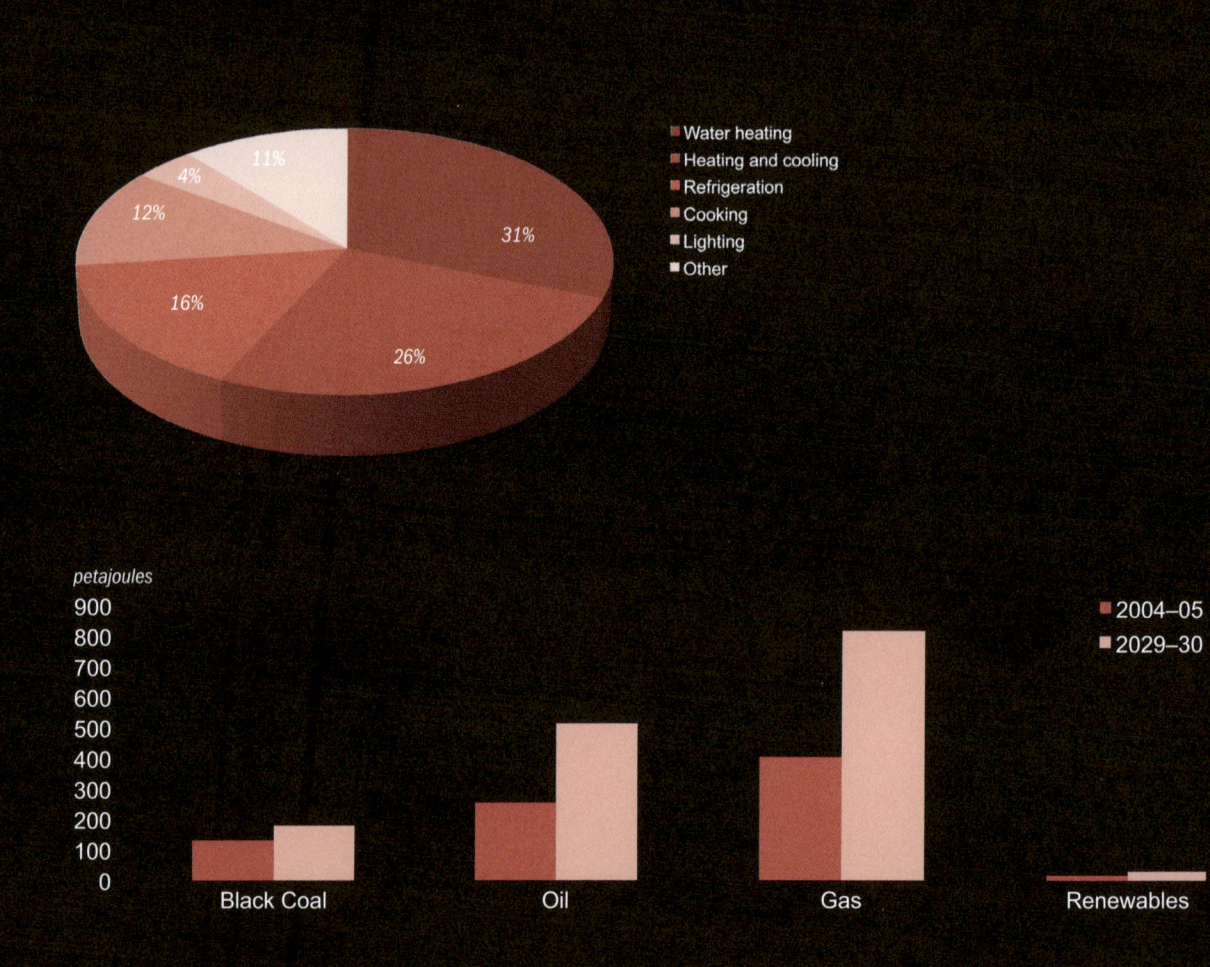

- Water heating — 31%
- Heating and cooling — 26%
- Refrigeration — 16%
- Cooking — 12%
- Lighting — 4%
- Other — 11%

Bar chart (petajoules) — 2004–05 vs 2029–30:
- Black Coal: ~130 / ~180
- Oil: ~260 / ~520
- Gas: ~420 / ~830
- Renewables: ~10 / ~30

*top: Western Australia: Energy use in a typical Western Australian home.[15] In 2004, average electricity consumption of households connected to the SWIS was approximately 5,500 kW hours.*

*bottom: Western Australia: total energy consumption by fuel type.[16] 50% of Western Australia's electricity is gas generated.*

# ENERGY

'The state is reliant on fossil fuels. 98% of Western Australia's primary energy needs are supplied from fossil fuels.'[17]

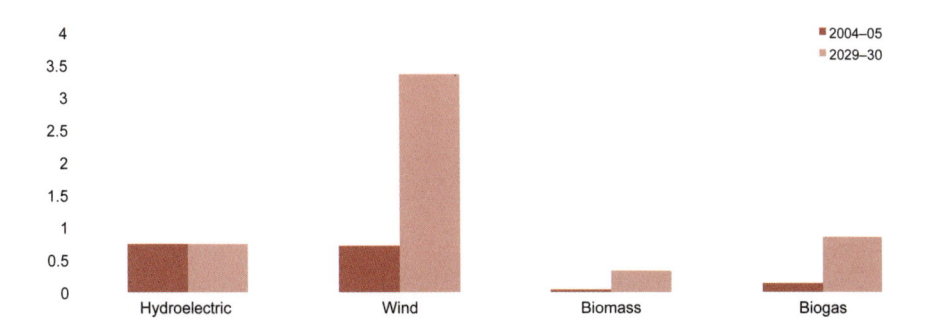

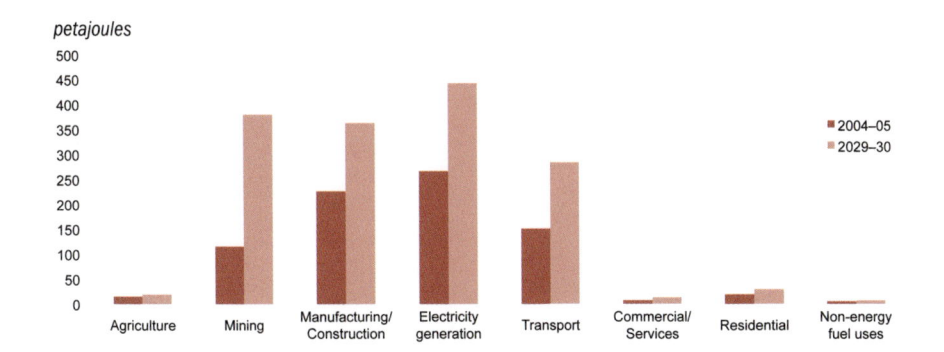

14. The Environmental Protection Authority (EPA), *State of the Environment Report Western Australia 2007*, Department of Environment and Conservation, Perth, 2007.

15. Sustainable Energy Development Office, <http://www.sedo.energy.wa.gov.au/pages/energy_smart_homes.asp>, viewed 2008.

16. Riwoe, D., Cuevas-Cubria, C. and Akmal, A., A *Review of Energy and Greenhouse Gas Emission Projections for Western Australia*, ABARE Report Prepared for Western Australian Greenhouse and Energy Taskforce, Canberra, 2006.

17. The Environmental Protection Authority (EPA), *State of the Environment Report Western Australia 2007*, Department of Environment and Conservation, Perth, 2007.

18. Riwoe, D., Cuevas-Cubria, C. and Akmal, A., A *Review of Energy and Greenhouse Gas Emission Projections for Western Australia*, ABARE Report Prepared for Western Australian Greenhouse and Energy Taskforce, Canberra, 2006.

19. Riwoe, D., Cuevas-Cubria, C. and Akmal, A., A *Review of Energy and Greenhouse Gas Emission Projections for Western Australia*, ABARE Report Prepared for Western Australian Greenhouse and Energy Taskforce, Canberra, 2006.

top: Western Australia: Projected renewable energy generation (petajoules).[18]

bottom: Western Australia: Total energy consumption (petajoules) by sector, current and projected.[19] Western Australians are energy hungry and have high levels of consumption in all major sectors: in the home, fuel use for travel and indirectly through production and freight of the goods and services consumed.

77
DATABASE

'Transport's current dependence on cheap oil supplies is not a sustainable activity. Estimates of the life of cheap oil supplies range from 3 to 50 years.'[1]

**37** Million vehicle kilometers were travelled in Perth in 2004. This is an increase of around 50% since 1991. On average, Perth drivers travel the equivalent of 500 times around the world (more than 20 million km) daily in cars.[2]

**14,200** The total length of road in Perth and Mandurah (in km). This is 9.4% of all roads in the state (not including forestry roads).

**3.1** Car trips per Perth person per weekday.

**10.7** Perth road per capita (metres).

**8.3** Australian road per capita (metres).

**6.9** USA road per capita (metres).

**2.4** European road per capita (metres).

**631** Perth CBD parking spots per 1,000 persons.

**489** Australian CBD parking spots per 1,000 persons.

**468** USA CBD parking spots per 1,000 persons.

**238** European CBD parking spots per 1,000 persons.

**$0.9** Billion AU$: estimated social and environmental cost of road congestion, Perth 2005.

**$2.1** Billion AU$: estimated social and environmental cost of road congestion, Perth 2020.

**10x** Total travel in Australia's urban areas has increased tenfold over the past 60 years.

**100%** Percentage increase in train use at Subiaco station (1998–2002) following completion of the Subi Centro housing development.

**60** Million passengers per annum: rail patronage is expected to double from the current figure of around 30 million following completion of southern suburbs rail link. This will result in a substantial greenhouse gas reduction.

# TRANSPORT

In Western Australia the proportion of people cycling or walking to work has almost halved in the last decade.[3] In contrast, cycling in Copenhagen has increased 65% in 30 years from 1962.[4]

**Perth is one of the most car-dependent cities in the world.**

Of 84 world cities, Perth ranked (1995):
- Third highest in road infrastructure length per capita.[5]
- Fourth highest in car ownership.[6]
- Sixth highest in CBD parking spaces per job.[7]
- 81.5% of all trips are made by car in Perth. This rises to 90% in newer suburbs on the urban fringe.[8]
- 84% of Western Australians use private vehicles to get to work or study compared to 72% in Sydney.[9]
- 10% use public transport to get to work.[10]

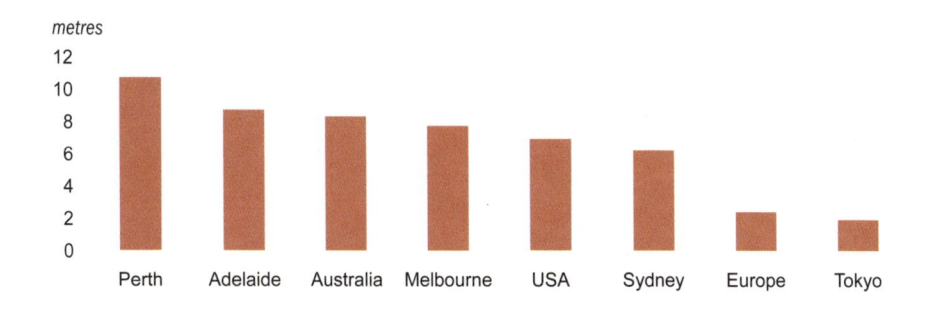

*metres*

| Perth | Adelaide | Australia | Melbourne | USA | Sydney | Europe | Tokyo |
|---|---|---|---|---|---|---|---|
| ~11 | ~9 | ~8.5 | ~7.5 | ~7 | ~6.5 | ~2.5 | ~2 |

above: Australian capital cities compared with Europe, Tokyo and USA: Length of road per capita (metres).[11]

left (and continued over page): Perth transport data.[12]

---

1. RAC WA quoted in *Hope for the Future: The Western Australian State Sustainability Strategy*, Department of Premier and Cabinet, Western Australian Government, Perth, 2003.

2. Based on world circumference of 40,076 km at the equator.

3. Shilton, T., 'Commuters in WA the laziest in the nation', *The West Australian*, 22 November 2007, p. 13.

4. Rogers, R. and Power, A. *Cities for a Small Country*, Faber and Faber, London, 2000.

5. Public Transport Authority, Western Australian Government, Powerpoint presentation, <http://www.pta.wa.gov.au>, viewed 2008.

6. Public Transport Authority, Western Australian Government, Powerpoint presentation, <http://www.pta.wa.gov.au>, viewed 2008.

7. Public Transport Authority, Western Australian Government, Powerpoint presentation, <http://www.pta.wa.gov.au>, viewed 2008.

8. Department for Planning and Infrastructure, <http://www.dpi.wa.gov.au/travelsmart/14954.asp>, viewed April 2008.

9. Ministry of Transport, *Transfigure: 2006 Employment and Commuting*, <http://www.transport.nsw.gov.au/tdc/documents/tf2008-01-transfigures.pdf>, viewed June 2008.

10. ABS, *Perth Social Atlas 2006*, Canberra, 2006.

11. Public Transport Authority, *Options for Sustainable Transport*, UDIA Sustainability Forum, Perth, 2007.

12. Data in this table is sourced from *State of the Environment Report WA*, 2007; Main Roads Western Australia, *Annual Report 2007*; Main Roads Western Australia, internal databases 2008; Public Transport Authority, 2007, *Options for Sustainable Transport*, UDIA Sustainability Forum, Perth, 2007; Department of Environment and Conservation, Western Australian Greenhouse Strategy, 2006.

**79**
**DATABASE**

| | |
|---|---|
| **250,000** | Daily car trips in Perth are less than one km – the equivalent of a 10- to 15-minute walk or a five-minute bike ride. |
| **4,400,000** | Personal vehicle trips are made in Perth daily. |
| **5–7** | Kilometres: car use substituted per kilometer of efficient public transport used. |
| **6.3%** | Percentage of all Perth trips that are walking and cycling. In Europe figures range from 35% to 45%.[13] |
| **60,369** | Western Australians who travelled to work by public transport on census day, 2006. Commuters were mostly living near city centres or within easy access to public transport.[14] |
| **1** | Litre: For every litre of petrol used in cars, 2 kg of $CO_2$ is released.[15] |
| **4** | $CO_2$-e released annually by an average car.[16] |
| **68%** | More greenhouse emissions released in transporting an equivalent number of passengers by car than by electric rail. |
| **67,000** | The greenhouse gas saving for the Perth to Mandurah railway's first year full operation (tonnes of $CO_2$-e). |
| **1,000,000,000** | AU$: Per annum cost of Western Australian road crashes – a major cause of deaths of Australians aged between 6 and 28.[17] |
| **3** | Perth: urban transport related emissions (tonne/capita $CO_2$). |
| **1** | Singapore and Amsterdam: transport related emissions annually (tonne/capita $CO_2$). |
| **13%** | Percentage of Western Australia's emissions are from transport. |
| **60** | Average daily travelling time in Western Australia (minutes). |
| **650,000** | Tyres sent to landfill annually in Western Australia. |

*$CO_2$-e is the abbreviation of carbon dioxide equivalent and is the standard measure for greenhouse emissions.*

# TRANSPORT

'Approximately 70% of Perth's new residential development still occurs at or beyond the boundaries of currently developed areas. Expansion in these locations, with limited services and little or no local employment, exacerbates vehicle dependence.'[18]

13. Landry, C., 'Innovation builds a healthier city', *The West Australian*, 7 July 2007, p. 57.
14. ABS, *Perth Social Atlas 2006*, Canberra, 2006.
15. Carbon Neutral, <http://www.carbonneutral.com.au/climatechange.htm>, viewed June 2008.
16. Carbon Neutral, <http://www.carbonneutral.com.au/climatechange.htm>, viewed June 2008.
17. *Perth Walking: The Metropolitan Region Pedestrian Strategy*, Department for Planning and Infrastructure, Perth, 2000.
18. *State of the Environment Report WA*, 2006.
19. ABS, Catalogue Number 4102.0, *Australian Social Trends 2008: Public Transport Use for Work or Study*, Canberra, 2008.
20. ABS, Catalogue Number 4102.0, *Australian Social Trends 2008: Public Transport Use for Work or Study*, Canberra, 2008.
21. ABS, *Perth Social Atlas 2006*, Canberra, 2008.

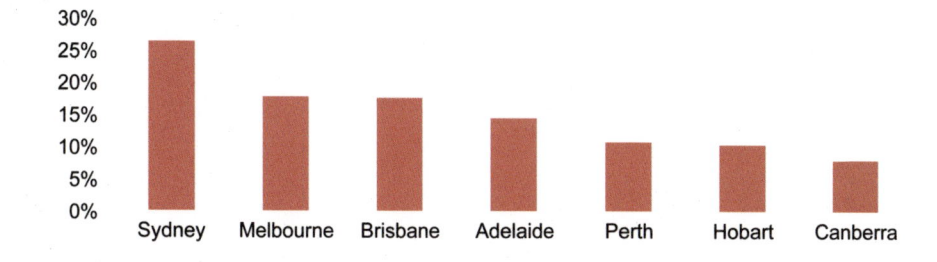

Australian capital cities: Percentage of adults using public transport to get to work or study, 2006.[19]

Public transport usage declined substantially in Australia in the 30 years following World War II. This correlates with a large increase in the registration and use of private vehicles in Australian cities.[20] In Perth, it has been found that public transport usage is highest in a 5 km radius of Perth's CBD, along train lines and main arterial roads.[21]

**81**
**DATABASE**

# TOD (Transit Oriented Development) aims to maximise access to public transport. Curitiba, Bogota, Toronto, Calgary, Portland, Japan, Singapore, Hong Kong and cities in Denmark, Sweden, France, and the Netherlands have implemented TOD principles into their city planning.[22] Dallas, in Texas, is currently doubling its light rail network, planning 400 km of rail.

The Network City planning strategy for Perth[23] aims to reduce car dependence by encouraging non-car modes of travel and supporting higher residential densities around neighbourhood centres and public transport hubs.[24]

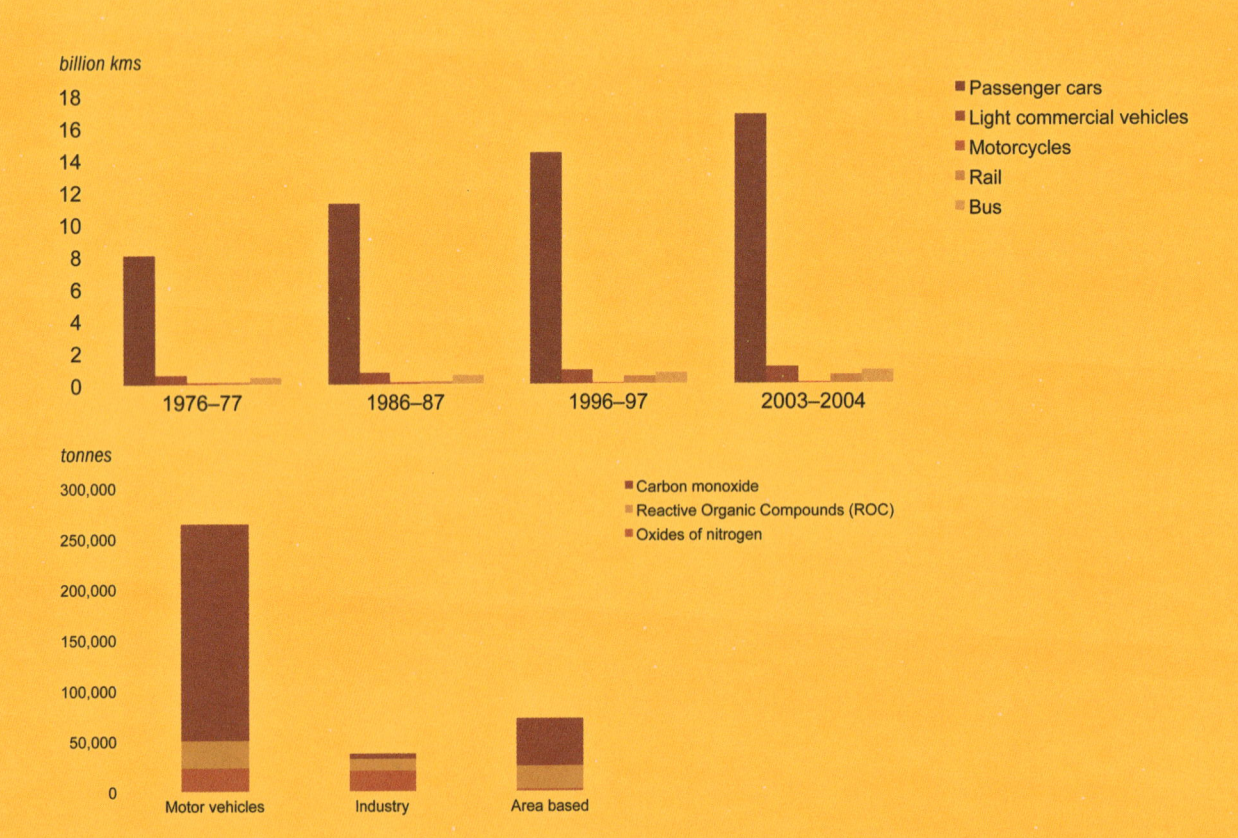

top: Total passenger kilometres travelled in Perth annually (billion kms).[25] Total car travel in Australian urban centres has grown tenfold in the last 60 years. Average growth in car traffic for Australian capital cities is projected to be in the range of 23% between 2005 and 2020. 'This implies a substantial increase in the level of car traffic on our current city networks.'[26]

bottom: Perth: Annual emissions due to human activity, 1992 (tonnes).[27] Motor vehicles are the major source of all emissions in the Perth metropolitan area. Vehicles contribute 80% of carbon monoxide and 42% of nitrous oxides emissions to the Perth airshed. Overall, transport contributes 13% to Western Australia's greenhouse gas emissions.

# TRANSPORT

# Western Australia has an average of 2.1 cars per household, the equal highest rate in the country.[28]

'It is widely recognised today that the most effective way of building a "transit metropolis" is to tightly integrate dense, mixed-use development around stops on a fixed-route transit network, thus maximising walk-up patronage and multiple trip making. This is the approach from Curitiba and Ottawa with their bus ways, through the urban rail systems in European cities, and in the modern Asian cities such as in Japan, Hong Kong and Singapore (Cervero, 1998). Bus or light rail feeders to the main rail system are also widely exploited.'[29]

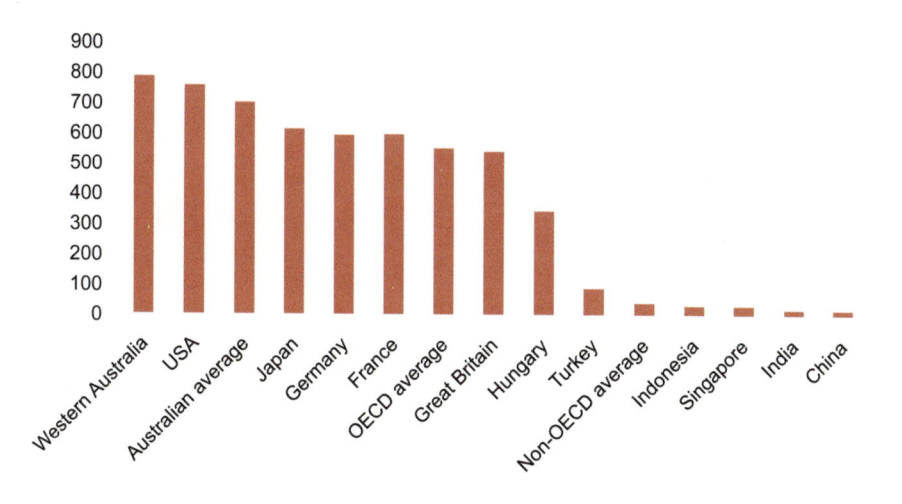

World comparisons: Vehicles per 1000 population, 2006.[30]

22 'Transit Oriented Development', Wikipedia online, <http://en.wikipedia.org/wiki/Transit-Oriented_Development>, viewed June 2008.

23 Western Australian Planning Commission, *Network City*, 2005, <http://www.wapc.wa.gov.au>, viewed June 2007.

24 Western Australian Planning Commission, *Development Control Policy 1.6: Planning to support Transit use and Transit Oriented Development*, Perth, 2006.

25 Bureau of Infrastructure, Transport and Regional Economics (BITRE), *Australian Transport Statistics Yearbook 2007*, Canberra, 2008.

26 Bureau of Infrastructure, Transport and Regional Economics (BITRE), *Estimating Urban Traffic and Congestion Cost Trends for Australian Cities*, Working Paper 71, Canberra, 2007.

27 Environmental Protection Authority/Western Power, *The Perth Photochemical Smog Study*, EPA, Perth, 1996.

28 ABS, *Perth Social Atlas 2006*, Canberra, 2008.

29 Kenworthy, J. R., *Transport Energy Use and Greenhouse Gases in Urban Passenger Transport Systems: A Study of 84 Global Cities*, Murdoch University, Perth, 2003.

30 Organisation for Economic Cooperation and Development (OECD), *OECD Factbook 2008: Economic, Environmental and Social Statistics*, 2008; ABS Catalogue No. 9309.0, *Motor Vehicle Census, Australia, 31 March 2006*, <http://www.abs.gov.au/AUSSTATS/abs@.nsf/ProductsbyReleaseDate/06010F4E7D145276CA257394000EC89A?OpenDocument>.

'Emissions are first and foremost a problem created by the affluent industrialized nations. The USA and Australia have greenhouse gas emissions averaging 22 and 28 tonnes per head respectively, compared to less than 1 tonne for many developing nations, including China. The sustainable level of emissions has been estimated to be about 3.5 tonnes for every person on planet Earth.'[1]

# EMISSIONS

On a per capita basis, Western Australia's emissions are higher than Australia's and other developed countries including the USA and UK.[6]

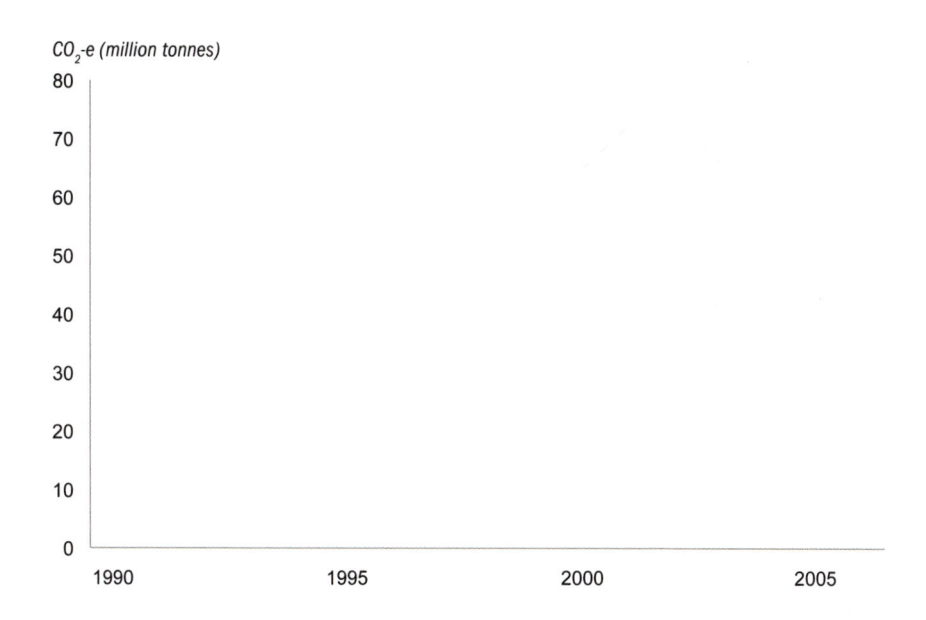

$CO_2$-e (million tonnes)

1990　　1995　　2000　　2005

Western Australia: Growth in total $CO_2$ emissions (million tonnes) 1990–2006.[7]

Western Australia's total $CO_2$-e emissions in 2006 were 70.41 million tonnes, an increase of 12% since 1990. The Greenhouse and Energy Taskforce recommended that Western Australia should 'slash its greenhouse gas emissions by two-thirds by 2050 [on 2000 levels], endorse a national carbon trading emissions scheme and aim to derive 20% of all electricity used in Perth and the South-West from renewable sources by 2020.'[8]

1. Lenzen, M., 'Individual responsibility and climate change', Environmental Justice Conference, The University of Melbourne, October 1997.
2. Calculation based on 36.6 tonnes per capita per annum x 1.5 million people = 54.9 million tonnes. The state's total emissions were 70.49 million tonnes in 2002.
3. Carbon Neutral, <http://www.carbonneutral.com.au/comp_calc_backg._info_proposal_format.pdf>, viewded 2008.
4. Grace, W., 'Sustainable Urban Living – a Perth Perspective', National Housing Conference, Perth, October 2005.
5. Environmental Protection Authority (EPA), State of the Environment Report Draft: Western Australia 2006, Department of Environment and Conservation, Perth, 2006.
6. The Environmental Protection Authority (EPA), State of the Environment Report Western Australia 2007, Department of Environment and Conservation, Perth, 2007.
7. Australian Government Emissions Information System, <http://www.ageis.greenhouse.gov.au/GGIDMUserFunc/QueryModel/QueryModelElectricity.asp#resultStartMarker>, viewed August 2008.
8. Banks, A. and Taylor, R., 'Tough greenhouse gas targets a risk for WA', The West Australian, 6 February 2007, p. 4. The Greenhouse and Energy Taskforce report is available online: Western Australian Department of Environment and Conservation website, portal.<http://environment.wa.gov.au/portal/page?_pageid=54,5690266&_dad=portal&_schema=PORTAL>.

**85**
DATABASE

'The residential sector is responsible for producing 63 million tonnes $CO_2$-e of greenhouse gases per annum – around 20% of Australia's total emissions. The sector shows a 23% increase over the period 1990–95, the largest absolute increase in sectoral emissions over that period. These emissions represent some 9 tonnes $CO_2$-e per dwelling per annum. In addition to these emissions that arise from everyday energy use, the energy embodied in the 120,000 new houses added to the stock each year adds another 6 million tonnes $CO_2$–e.'[9]

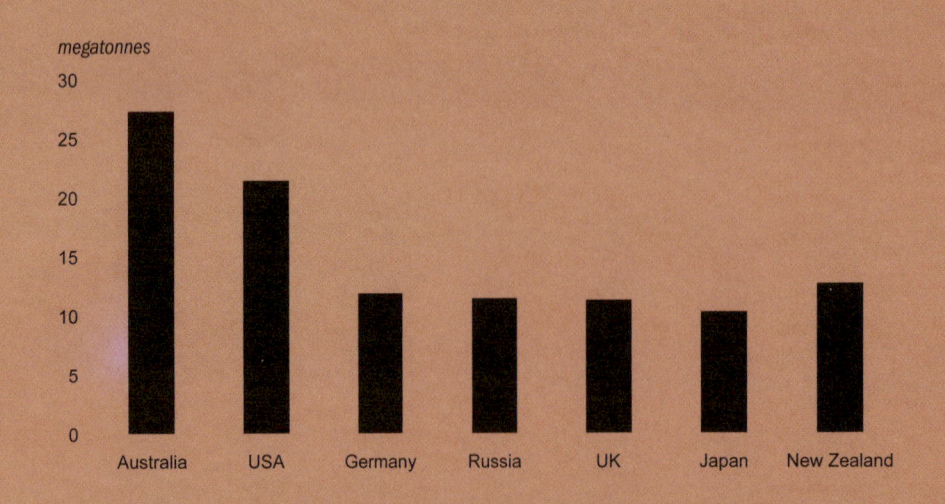

Per capita greenhouse gas emissions in megatonnes (Mt) 2001.[10]

Australians generate the highest level of emissions per capita in the industrialised world. Hal Turton argues that although 'Australia accounts for [only] 3.4% of total Annex I emissions, Australia's total emissions exceed those of major European economies such as France and Italy (each with around three times Australia's population) and are only 20% lower than those of the UK.'[11]

# EMISSIONS

'Australia's overall greenhouse emissions are relatively small – about one percent of global emissions. However...we have one of the highest per capita greenhouse emissions in the world.'[12]

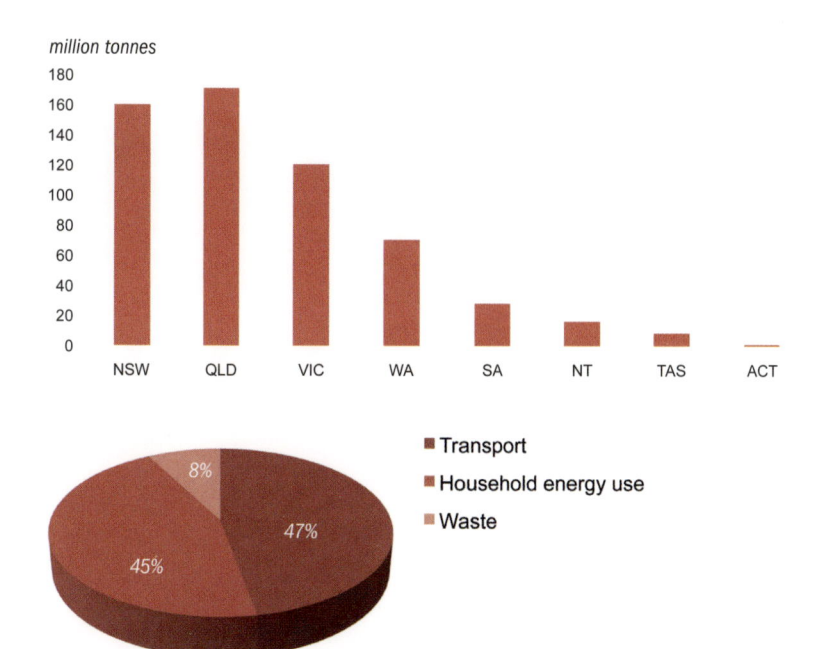

*million tonnes*

| State | Emissions |
|---|---|
| NSW | ~160 |
| QLD | ~170 |
| VIC | ~120 |
| WA | ~70 |
| SA | ~28 |
| NT | ~15 |
| TAS | ~8 |
| ACT | ~0 |

- Transport — 47%
- Household energy use — 45%
- Waste — 8%

*top:* Australian states: Total greenhouse gas emissions 2006 (million tonnes).[13] Australia's total greenhouse gas emissions in 2006 amounted to 576 million tonnes of carbon dioxide equivalent.

*bottom:* Western Australia: Domestic sources of greenhouse gas emissions, 2006.[14] The main sources of Western Australian domestic emissions are transport, domestic energy use and waste. Home heating and cooling (26%), water heating (31%) and refrigeration (16%) contribute most to domestic energy consumption. Therefore, improving the energy efficiency of homes is an effective way of reducing greenhouse gas emissions.

9   Grace, W., 'Sustainable Urban Living – a Perth Perspective', National Housing Conference, Perth, October 2005.

10  Turton, H., 'Greenhouse gas emissions in industrialised countries. Where does Australia stand?', Discussion Paper No 66, The Australia Institute, 2004.

11  Turton, H., 'Greenhouse gas emissions in industrialised countries. Where does Australia stand?', Discussion Paper No 66, The Australia Institute, 2004.

12  Department of Environment and Conservation, *Western Australian Greenhouse Strategy*, 2006. Online at <http://portal.environment.wa.gov.au/portal/page?¬_pageid=54,5691452&_dad=portal&_schema=PORTAL>, viewed June 2008.

13  Department of Climate Change, *State & Territory Greenhouse Gas Inventories 2006*, Australian Government, 2008. Online at <http://www.climatechange.gov.au/inventory/stateinv/index.html>, viewed September 2008.

14  Department of Environment and Conservation, *Western Australian Greenhouse Strategy*, 2006. Online at portal.<http://environment.wa.gov.au/portal/page?¬_pageid=54,5691452&_dad=portal&_schema=PORTAL>, viewed September 2008.

**DATABASE**

**952.72** Billion AU$: Australia's GDP (2006-07).

**5.7** Billion AU$: Gross value of agricultural production Western Australia (2005-06).

**127.8** Billion AU$: Gross State Product Western Australia (real, 2006-07).

**61.5** Billion AU$: Gross State Product per capita Western Australia (real, 2006-07).

**22.13** Billion AU$: Western Australia's total imports (2006-07).

**60.51** Billion AU$: Western Australia's total exports (2006-07).

**4.3** Billion AU$: Value of Western Australia's agricultural exports (2005-06).

**9%** Western Australia's total export value was from agriculture.

**13.7** Billion AU$: value of Western Australian exports to China (2006-07).

**12** Billion AU$: value of Western Australian exports to Japan (2006-07).

**5.7** Billion AU$: value of Western Australian exports to India (2006-07).

**5** Billion AU$: value of Western Australian exports to Republic of Korea (2006-07).

**2.8** Billion AU$: value of Western Australian exports to United Kingdom (2006-07).

**2.4** Billion AU$: value of Western Australian imports from Singapore (2006-07).

**2.6** Billion AU$: value of Western Australian imports from Western Japan (2006-07).

*above: Western Australian import and export data[1].*

# ECONOMICS

Mineral resources are Western Australia's top commodity exports, constituting approximately 86% of the state's merchandise exports.[2] Over half (54.8%) of Western Australia's agriculture production is exported overseas.[3]

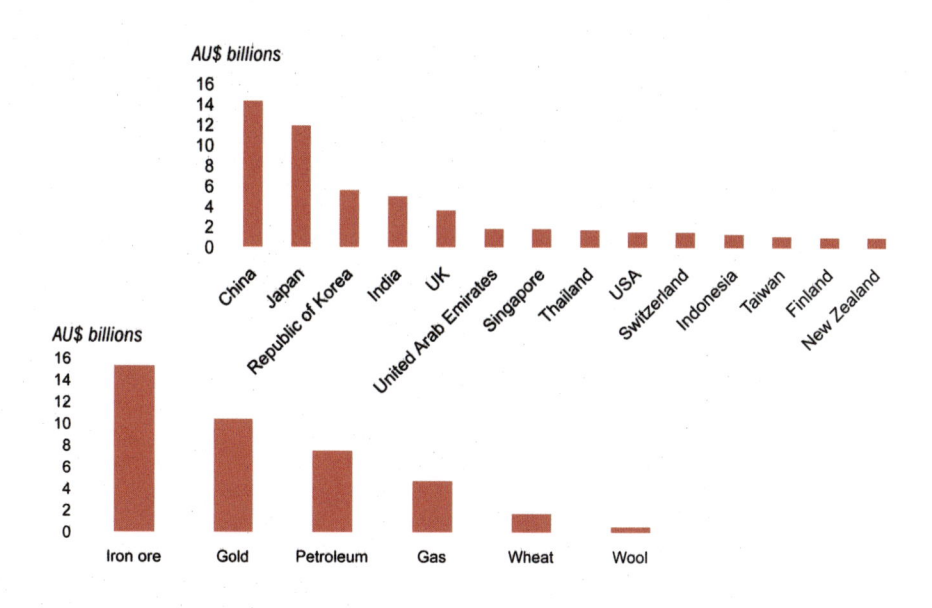

*AU$ billions*

|  |  |
|---|---|
| China | ~15 |
| Japan | ~12 |
| Republic of Korea | ~6 |
| India | ~5 |
| UK | ~3 |
| United Arab Emirates | ~2 |
| Singapore | ~2 |
| Thailand | ~1.5 |
| USA | ~1.5 |
| Switzerland | ~1 |
| Indonesia | ~1 |
| Taiwan | ~1 |
| Finland | ~1 |
| New Zealand | ~1 |

*AU$ billions*

|  |  |
|---|---|
| Iron ore | ~15 |
| Gold | ~10 |
| Petroleum | ~7 |
| Gas | ~5 |
| Wheat | ~1.5 |
| Wool | ~0.5 |

top: Western Australia's major export markets by value 2007 (AU$ billions).[4]
bottom: Western Australia's major export commodities 2006–07 (AU$ billions).[5]

[1] ABS, Catalogue No. 1306.0: *Western Australia at a glance*, Canberra, 2008; ABS, Catalogue No. 5206.0: *Australian National Accounts: National Income, Expenditure and Product*, Canberra, 2008; ABS, Catalogue No. 7121.0: *Agricultural Commodities 2005/2006*, Canberra, 2006; EPA, *State of the Environment Report WA*, 2007; Department of Industry and Resources, Powerpoint presentation 2007, <http://www.ecc.online.wa.gov.au/documents/000090V02.Mike.WILSON.ppt.>, viewed 2008; Australian Bureau of Agricultural and Resource Economics, 2007; AusLink, <http://www.auslink.gov.au/publications/reports/pdf/Perth_Adelaide_Corridor_Strategy.pdf>, viewed June 2008.

[2] Department of Industry and Resources, Powerpoint presentation quoting ABS data for 2007, <http://www.ecc.online.wa.gov.au/documents/000090V02.Mike.WILSON.ppt.>, viewed 2008.

[3] ABS, 'Feature article 2: The Agriculture Industry in Western Australia', *Catalogue No. 1367.5: Western Australian Statistical Indicators, March 2007*, Canberra, 2007.

[4] Department of Industry and Resources, Powerpoint presentation quoting ABS data for 2007, <http://www.ecc.online.wa.gov.au/documents/000090V02.Mike.WILSON.ppt.>, viewed 2008.

[5] ABS, Catalogue No. 1306.5: *Western Australia at a glance*, Canberra, 2008.

**53.1** Billion AU$: Estimated value of Western Australia's mineral and petroleum industry exports 2007.

**16.7** Billion AU$: Western Australia's petroleum export value 2007.

**16.1** Billion AU$: Western Australia's iron ore export value 2007.

**7** Billion AU$: Western Australia's nickel export value 2007.

**4.7** Billion AU$: Western Australia's alumina export value 2007.

**4.1** Billion AU$: Western Australia's gold export value 2007.

**1.8** Billion AU$: Western Australia's lead, copper and zinc export value 2007.

**756** Million AU$: Western Australia's mineral sands export value 2007.

**306** Million AU$: Western Australia's salt export value 2007.

**264** Million AU$: Western Australia's coal export value 2007.

**13.6** Western Australia's salt export volume in million tonnes 2007.

**152,085** Western Australia's gold export volume in kilograms 2007.

**264** Western Australia's iron ore export volume in million tonnes 2007.

**160,457** Western Australia's nickel export volume in tonnes 2007.

**50%** Percentage of Australia's total value of mineral and petroleum sales from Western Australia.

**71%** Percentage of Australia's total oil and condensate production from Western Australia.

**2.2** Billion AU$: Western Australia's import value from United States of America (2006-07).

**1.9** Billion AU$: Western Australia's import value from United Kingdom (2006-07).

**1.5** Billion AU$: Western Australia's import value from China (2006-07).

# ECONOMICS

## Western Australia's Gross State Product per capita increased by 2.8% per year from 1993 to 2004, exceeding the national annual growth rate of 2.6%.[7]

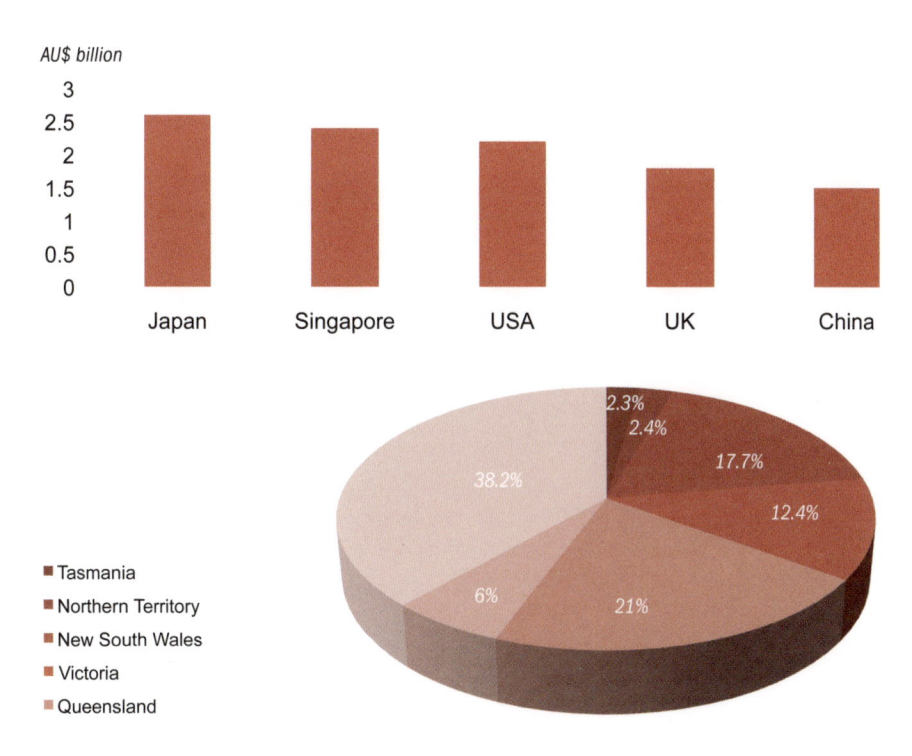

*AU$ billion*

| Japan | Singapore | USA | UK | China |
|---|---|---|---|---|
| ~2.6 | ~2.4 | ~2.2 | ~1.8 | ~1.5 |

Pie chart:
- Tasmania: 2.3%
- Northern Territory: 2.4%
- New South Wales: 17.7%
- Victoria: 12.4%
- Queensland: 21%
- (6%)
- (38.2%)

*top:* Western Australia's imports: Top five import markets by value 2006–07 (AU$ billion).[8]
Western Australia's imports are primarily from Asian markets.

*bottom:* Australia: Merchandise exports by state 2007, not including services.[9]
Western Australia accounts for almost 40% of Australian exports.

*left:* Western Australia's resources sector export and import data 2007.[10]

---

6  ABS, *Perth Social Atlas 2006*.

7  ABS, Catalogue No. 1306.5, *Western Australia at a glance*, Canberra, 2008.

8  Department of Industry and Resources, 'Statistics and Economics', Powerpoint presentation quoting ABS figures for 2007.

9  ABS, Catalogue No. 1306.0: *Western Australia at a glance*, Canberra, 2008; ABS, Catalogue No. 5206.0: *Australian National Accounts: National Income, Expenditure and Product*, Canberra, 2008; ABS, Catalogue No. 7121.0: *Agricultural Commodities 2005/2006*, Canberra, 2006; EPA *State of the Environment Report WA*, 2007; Department of Industry and Resources, Powerpoint presentation, 2007; Australian Bureau of Agricultural and Resource Economics, 2007; AusLink, <http://www.auslink.gov.au/publications/reports/pdf/Perth_Adelaide_Corridor_Strategy.pdf>, viewed June 2008.

DATABASE

**9.1** Million tonnes wheat (2005-06).

**131,000** Tonnes cattle and calves (2005-06).

**107,800** Tonnes wool (2005-06).

**22.13** Million sheep and lambs (2006-07).

**2.32** Million meat cattle (2006-07).

**9.09** Million tonnes of barley for grain (2006-07).

**15.3** Billion AU$: iron ore (2006-07).

**10.4** Billion AU$: gold bullion (2006-07).

**7.5** Billion AU$: petroleum and petroleum products (2006-07).

**4.7** Billion AU$: natural gas and gas products (2006-07).

**1.7** Billion AU$: wheat (2006-07). As a percentage: 50% of the national export total.

**517** Million AU$: wool (2006-07).

**4.5** Million tonnes of non-bulk freight was moved between Perth and the eastern states in 2005 (not including mining and grain). This is forecast to double in the next 20 to 25 years.

**1,800** Metre long trains. The current economic length of a train on the east-west corridor is 1.8 km, stacked double.

# ECONOMICS

Perth is one of the world's most isolated capital cities. International and interstate transport is vital in supporting the state's economic and social viability.

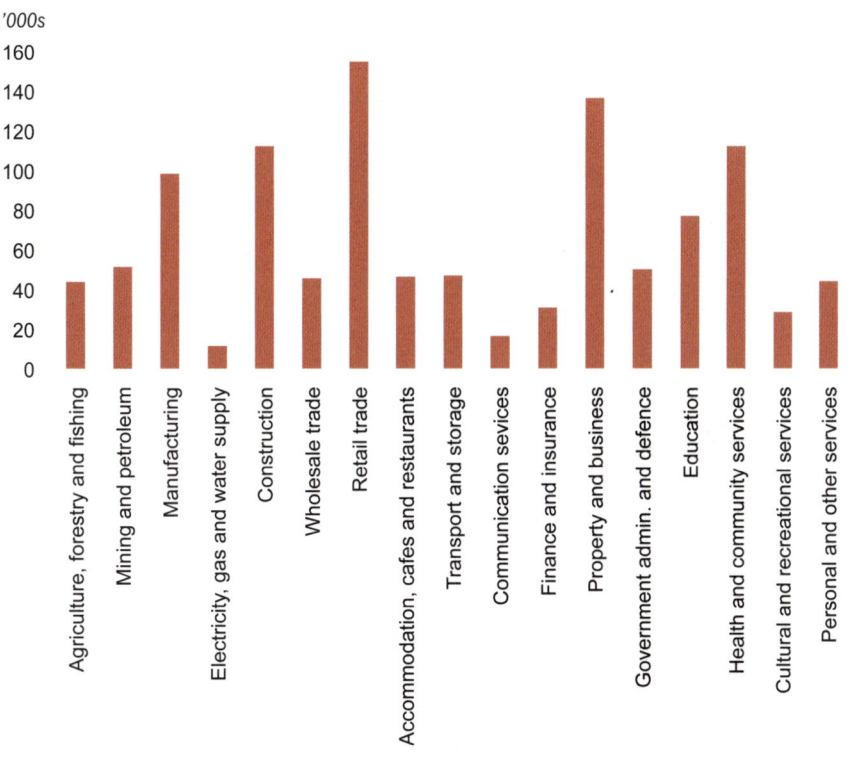

10  Department of Industry and Resources, unpublished data quoting ABS figures for 2007.

11  Department of Industry and Resources, Powerpoint presentation quoting ABS, Department of Industry and Resources and OECD Economic Surveys, Department of Consumer and Employment Protection.

12  ABS, Catalogue No. 1306.0: *Western Australia at a glance*, Canberra, 2008; ABS, Catalogue No. 5206.0: *Australian National Accounts: National Income, Expenditure and Product*, Canberra, 2008; ABS, Catalogue No. 7121.0: *Agricultural Commodities 2005/2006*, Canberra, 2006; EPA, *State of the Environment Report WA*, 2007; Department of Industry and Resources, Powerpoint presentation, 2007; Australian Bureau of Agricultural and Resource Economics, 2007; AusLink, <http://www.auslink.gov.au/publications/reports/pdf/Perth_Adelaide_Corridor_Strategy.pdf>, viewed June 2008.

above: Western Australia: Employment by industry sector, 2007 ('000).[11]

Western Australia's economy supports high numbers of employees in the retail, construction and property sectors in 2007. Total direct and indirect employment in the mining sector amounted to approximately 20% of state employment. 55% of all jobs created in Western Australia in the 1990s resulted from growth in the resources sector.[12]

left: Western Australia: Major commodities produced and exported.[13]

93
DATABASE

Europe
Western Australia
Perth ecological footprint for three million at 14.5 hectares per person (2050)
Perth ecological footprint for 1.5 million at 14.5 hectares per person (2007)
Perth metropolitan area

# FOOTPRINT

## Western Australia 'now has one of the highest per capita rates of consumption in the world'.[1]

Western Australia's large ecological footprint (14.5 hectares per person) is due to the state's resource based economy, high standards of living and high personal consumption rates. Food, housing and transport are the major impacts on Western Australia's environment. Land use associated with food alone makes up 46% of the state's ecological footprint. This figure is large because of the agricultural (crop and livestock) components of food production. Western Australia runs livestock over large areas of land at low densities.[1]

[1] EPA, *State of the Environment Report*, WA, Department of Environment and Conservation, 2007.

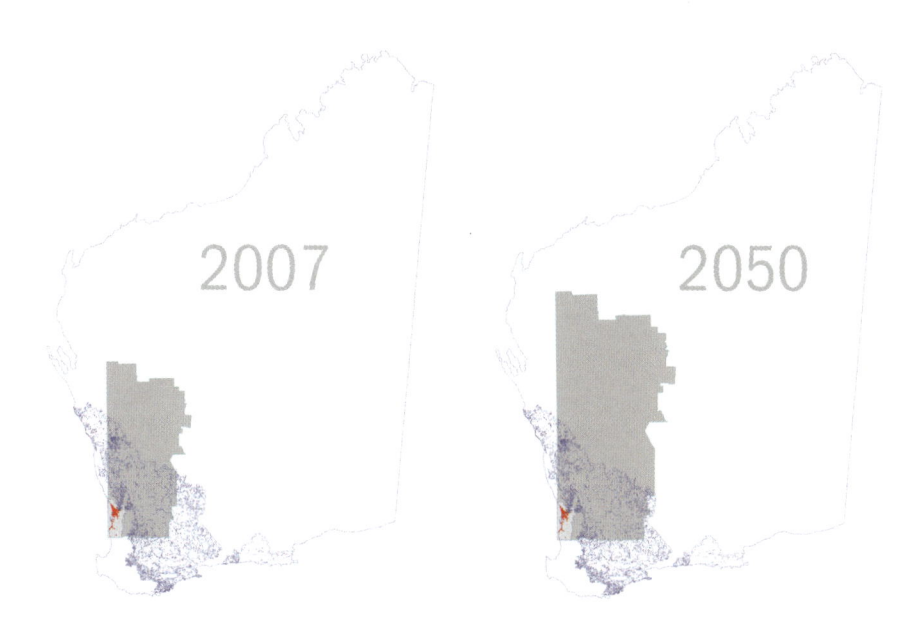

above left: 2007: 21.7 million hectares = footprint for 1.5 million Western Australians.
above right: 2050: 43.4 million hectares = footprint for three million Western Australians.
left: Perth's ecological footprint size scaled to Europe and Western Australia.

**95**
DATABASE

'In the 50 years since the end of the Second World War, Australian cities have been transformed from fairly tightly knit core-and-spoke configurations, to sprawling suburban low-density configurations. This transformation of urban land use has been accompanied and made possible by a rapid improvement and spread of the road system, and an even more rapid expansion in per person car ownership'.[2]

Sydney
4,119,190 inh.

Los Angeles
17,263,000 inh.

Tokyo -Yokohama
33,190,000 inh.

Calcutta
13,940,000 inh.

Mexico City
19,620,000 inh.

Singapore
4,163,000 inh.

London
13,945,000 inh.

Berlin
4,101,000 inh.

Tehran
10,740,000 inh.

Rome
3,900,000 inh.

Shanghai
13,580,000 inh.

Perth
1,496,227 inh.

Phoenix
2,907,000 inh.

Paris
10,600,000 inh.

Melbourne
3,592,591 inh.

Taipei
7,260,000 inh.

*City footprint maps show metropolitan built-up areas.*[3]

# FOOTPRINT

'There are about 10 billion hectares of bioproductive land in the world. There are about six billion people on this earth. Therefore, everyone is entitled to about 1.7 hectares of this bioproductive land to support them. If you need much more, you are using someone else's resources.'[4]

2 Bureau of Infratructure, Transport and Regional Economics, *Information Sheet 014, Urban Transport: Looking ahead*, 1999, <http://www.btre.gov.au/info.aspx?NodeId=61&ResourceId=30>, viewed September 2008.

3 van Susteren, A., *Metropolitan World Atlas*, 101 Publishers, Rotterdam, 2007.

4 Eamus, D., 'Sydney's Ecological Footprint – A Size 11 Problem?', <http://www.onlineopinion.com.au/view.asp?article=1189>, viewed September 2008.

5 WWF Living Planet Report and Conservation Foundation of Australia's Consumption Atlas data.

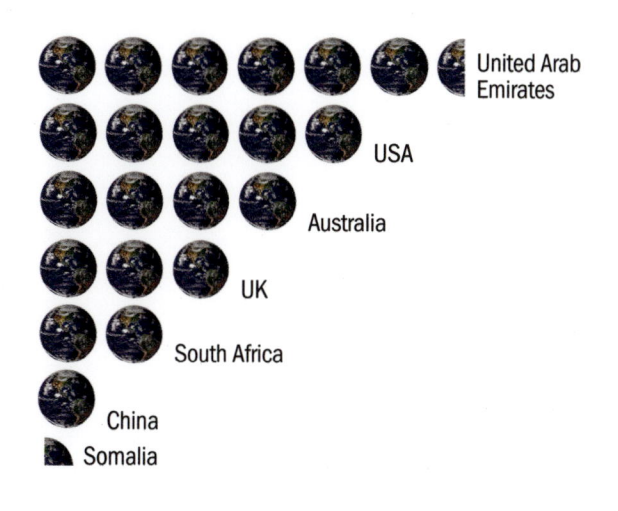

United Arab Emirates
USA
Australia
UK
South Africa
China
Somalia

above: *If the world lived as Australians do, we would need four planets to support us.*[5]

**134,596** People living alone aged over 15 years: 11.6% of the population.

**45%** Percentage of sole person households living in inner city suburbs.

**40,087** Single parent families with dependent children: 10.5% of all families.

**173,735** Couples with no dependent children: 45.6% of all families.

**60%** 60% of families with no dependent children were found in inner city suburbs, and in the Mandurah region; Bouvard, South Yunderup.

**207,658** Dwellings under mortgage or under a rent/buy scheme. At 40.2% of all occupied homes, Perth has the highest proportion of homes being purchased of all capital cities.

**230,956** Homes with broadband access: 44.4% of homes.

**306,033** Employed people with no qualifications above school level: 42.2% of the labour force.

**211,840** People 15-64 years who were not in the labour force: 23% of the labour force. Two-thirds of these were women.

**26,941** Unemployed people: 3.7% of the population.

**202,494** Students, five years and over.

**125,484** Students attending government schools: 62% of students.

**157,567** People in the labour force with a bachelor degree or higher: 22.6%.

**26,629** People not fluent in English: 2.1% of the population five years and over.

**449,628** Overseas-born people: 33.6% of population. The second highest proportion of all capital cities, following Sydney.

**20,910** Indigenous Australians.

**245,600** People 60 years and over: 17% of the population. High numbers of these were living in coastal areas of Rockingham and Mandurah and within a 10km radius of Perth city centre.

**89,020** People aged 0-4 years: 6.2% of the population.

**111,000** Increase in resident population in the five years to 2006: 8.4% increase. Population increases were largely in outlying suburbs but also East Perth due to densification of housing.

# SOCIAL

'We need urban environments that are easy to navigate and that provide lots of opportunities for random encounters between people in the community. In the terms used by urban planners, we need environments that are high in connectivity, permeability and accessibility.'[1]

'Research reveals that 60% of WA's primary school students live less than a 20-minute walk from school but most are still driven every day.'[2]

One in six Australians are obese or 3.71 million people – 17.5% of the population. The annual cost of obesity in Western Australia comes to $6 billion. 'Long term planning on issues such as urban design…is urgently needed.'[3]

left: Perth/Mandurah region social data.[4]

[1] Moore, T., *Towards Improved Support for Families of Young Children: The Role of Communities*, Centre for Community Child Health, Royal Children's Hospital, Melbourne, 2005.

[2] 'Close to Home', *Uniview*, Summer 2008.

[3] Deed, G., *The West Australian*, 22 August 2008, p. 3.

[4] ABS, Catalogue No. 2030.5, *Perth: A Social Atlas, 2006 Census of Population and Housing*, Canberra, 2006.

'There is a particular danger for Perth, with the boom well in place and 12–14 hour working days beginning to bite'.[5] West Australians average 41 hours a week at work, an hour more than the national average and three hours more than workers in Canberra.
An additional two hours a day in the car getting to and from work 'is now a fact of life for many people living in Perth's outlying suburbs'.[6]

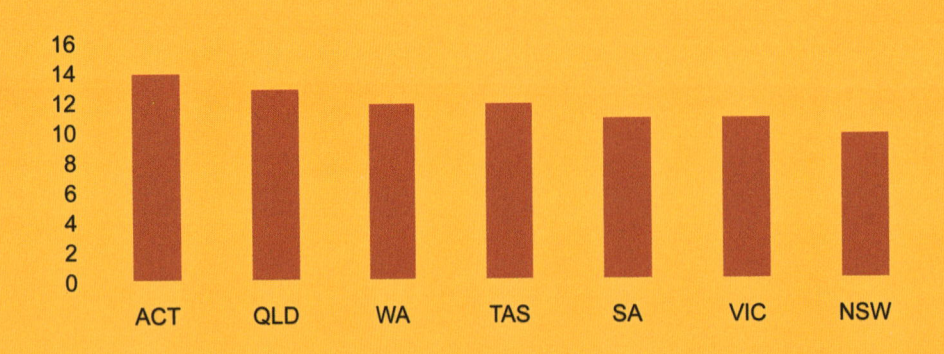

Australian states: Incidence of long-term mental health conditions per 1,000 total population.[7]
Western Australia has the third highest percentage of population with long-term mental health conditions.

There were 13,391 homeless people in Western Australia in 2006, compared with 11,697 in 2001. The homelessness rates in Western Australia and Queensland are significantly higher than in other Australian states at 68 homeless people per 10,000 population compared to 40–50 homeless per 10,000 population in other Australian states.[8]

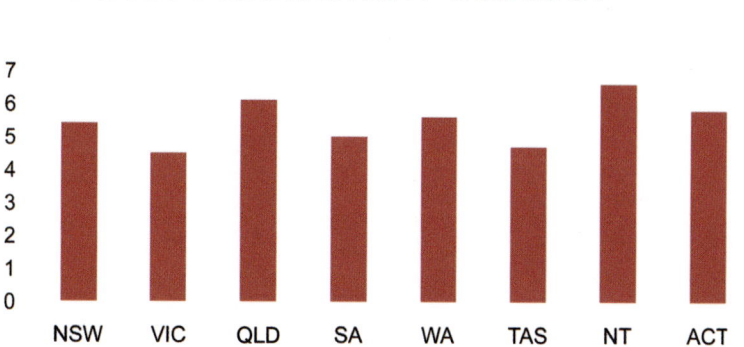

5 Landry, C., 'Innovation builds a healthier city', *The West Australian*, 7 July 2007, p. 57.

6 Riley, S., 'Freeway run for City workers turns to a crawl of up to an hour', *The West Australian*, 2 July 2007, p. 5.

7 FORM, *Comparative Capitals: A Creative Capital Research Project*, FORM, Perth, August 2008.

8 ABS, Catalogue No. 2050.0, *Counting the homeless 2006*, Canberra, 2006.

9 ABS, Catalogue No. 1338.1, *New South Wales in Focus 2008*, Canberra, 2008.

Australian states: Victims of personal crime, 2005 (percentage of population).[9]
As a percentage of population, Western Australia ranks fourth of all Australian states.

'The measures…for housing include reducing the size of new housing; the adoption of passive solar design as a principle for all new housing and housing retro-fits; reducing the embodied energy per unit floor area; and adopting solar hot water as a standard. The potential for dramatic reductions in scheme water use arising from water efficient fixtures, rainwater tanks and recycling are identified as appropriate responses to the critical water supply issues facing Perth.'[1]

**66%** Dwellings in Western Australia with insulation in 2005, compared to the national average of 61%. The proportion of insulated dwellings in WA increased from 52% in 1994.

**57%** Households in Western Australia using fluorescent lights, 32% used other energy-saving lights.

**55%** Western Australian households who applied at least one measure to regulate heat through windows, compared to the Australian average of 48%.

**17%** Houholds in Western Australia using solar energy in their homes, the second highest level in Australia after the Northern Territory and three times the national average of 5%.

**70%** Between 1994 and 2005, there was an increased use of whitegoods in Western Australian dwellings, notably air conditioners (36% to 70%), dishwashers (17% to 34%), clothes dryers (41% to 48%) and washing machines (95% to 97%). Computer uptake also increased from 47% in 1999 to 70% in 2005.[2]

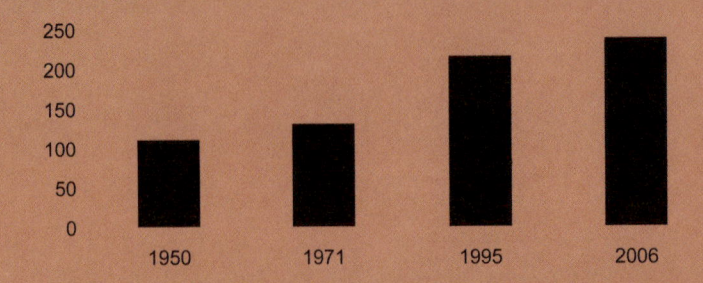

Western Australia: Typical house size, 1950 to 2006 ($m^2$).[3] Western Australia's typical house size has more than doubled since the 1950's from 110 $m^2$ to 237.5 $m^2$ in 2006-07[4] while the average number of occupants per household has decreased by approximately 40% over the same period.

# HOUSING

'A house is not just a house, it is far more. A house involves land, water, electricity, and a whole range of issues that have to come together. Each one is a separate department in the city and unless you can bring them all together as a single team you will never provide a fully serviced urban environment.'[5]

|  | Peri-urban | Low-density | High-density |
|---|---|---|---|
| Allotments per ha | 5 | 15 | 40 |
| Lot size, m² | 1,500 | 467 | 175 |
| Roof area, m² per lot | 250 | 230 | 105 |
| Paved area, m² per lot | 100 | 50 | 35 |
| Pervious area, m² per lot | 1,150 | 187 | 35 |
| % of area impervious | 20 | 42 | 70 |
| % of area allotments | 75 | 70 | 70 |
| % of area road corridor | 15 | 20 | 20 |
| % of area open space | 10 | 10 | 10 |

Typical urban development patterns for residential land use, Melbourne and Brisbane.[6]

1 Grace, W., 'Sustainable Urban Living – a Perth Perspective', National Housing Conference, Perth, October 2005.

2 ABS, Catalogue No. 4602.0, *Environmental Issues: People's Views and Practices*, March 2005, accessed online, September 2008.

3 The Environmental Protection Authority (EPA), *State of the Environment Report Western Australia 2007*, Department of Environment and Conservation, Perth, 2007; ABS, 'Average floor area of new residential buildings', Catalogue No. 8731.0, *Building Approvals, Australia*, Canberra, 2008.

4 ABS, Catalogue No. 4102.0, *Australian Social Trends 2007*, Canberra, 2007.

5 Baskin, J. in Burdett, R. and Sudjic, D. (eds.), *The Endless City*, Phaidon, London, 2007, p. 487.

6 Table from: Institute for Sustainable Resources, 'Integrated Stormwater and Treatment and Harvesting: Technical Guidance Report', Monash University, Melbourne, 2006. Online at <http://iswr.eng.monash.edu.au/research/projects/stormwater/final_report.pdf>, viewed October 2008.

7 Real Estate Institute of Western Australia (REIWA), 2008.

103
DATABASE

# HOUSING

$443,000

June quarter 2008 median Perth residential house (above) and land (opposite) prices (AU$).[7]

104
DATABASE

$250,000

LOT 858
PH: 9322 6734
BURNS BEACH

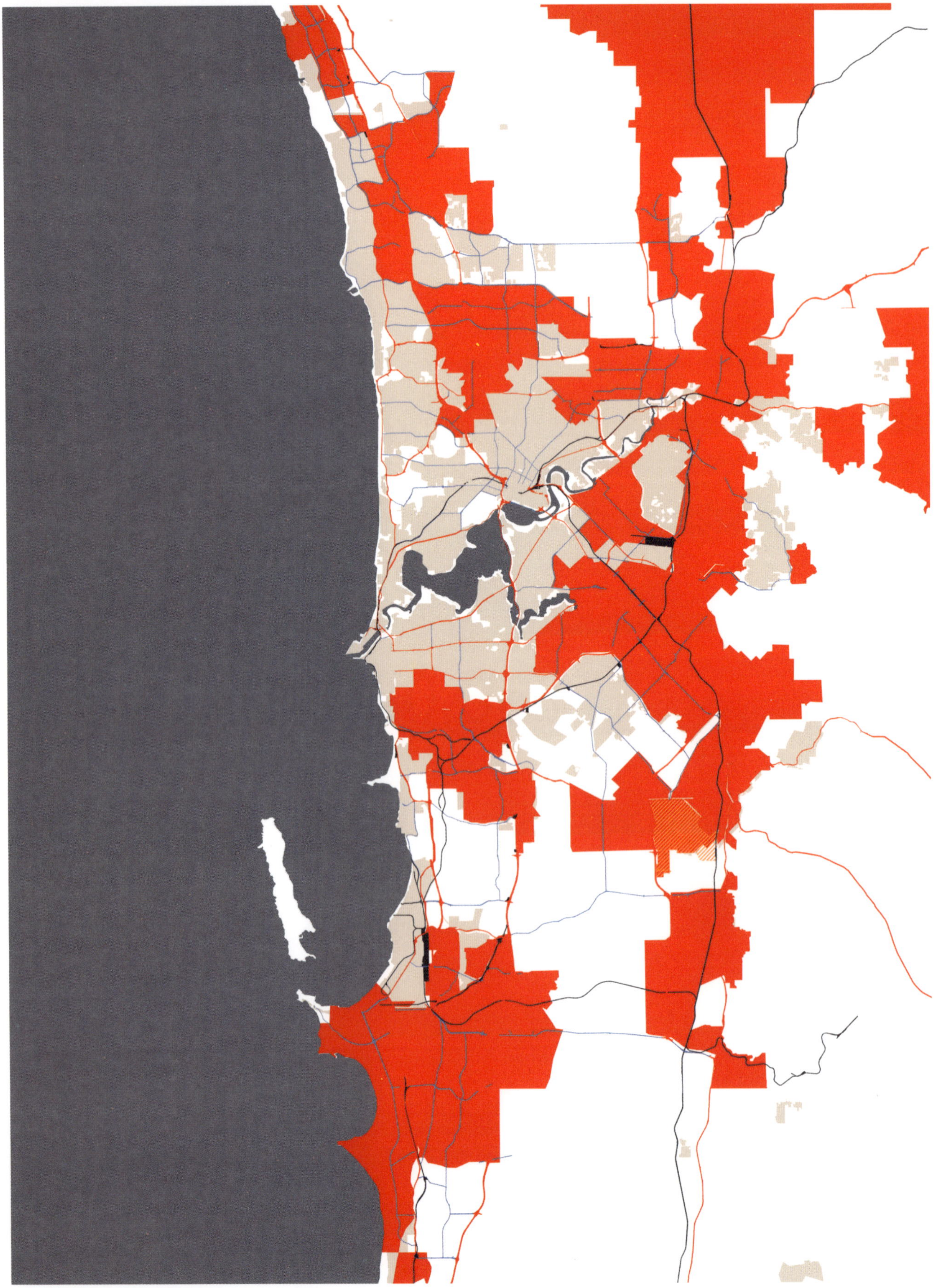

# HOUSING

A Perth household required an annual income of $133,000 to purchase a median priced house ($446,000). A growing number of households will struggle to attain home ownership.[8]

8 Shelter WA, <http://www.shelterwa.org.au/publications/news/Presentation_State_of_Affordable_Housing_2007.pdf>, viewed April 2008.

9 Real Estate Institute of Western Australia (REIWA), Median residential house prices, March 2008.

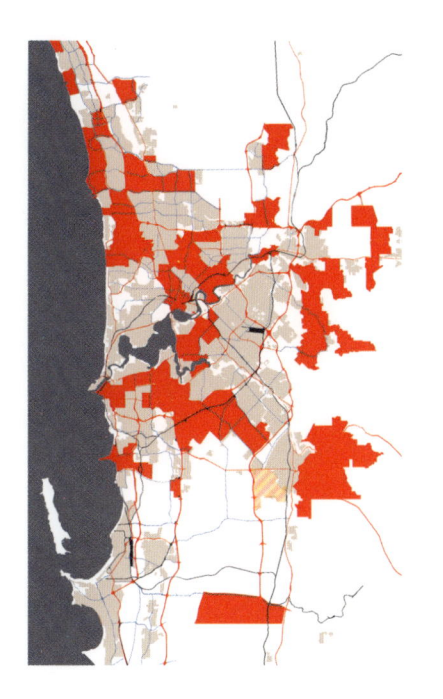

left: Perth median house price under AU$500K
above left: Perth median house price AU$500–800K
above right: Perth median house price AU$800K+[9]

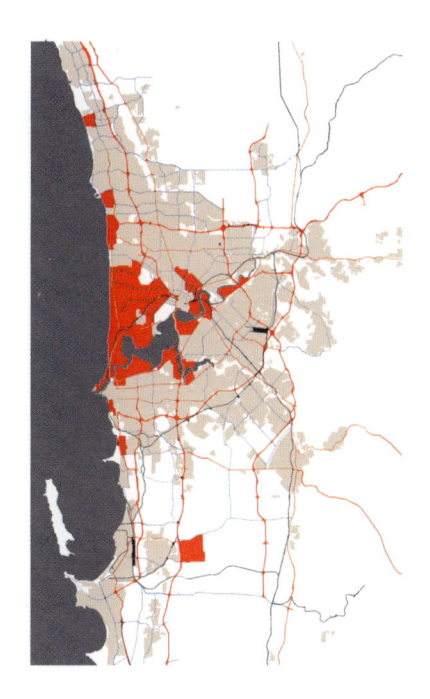

In June 2007 none of Perth's 291 metropolitan suburbs were affordable to purchase for households in the bottom 40% of the income range or households in receipt of the median income.[10] Typical bank home loans in Perth are five times annual income.[11]

| | |
|---|---|
| **24,621** | New residential buildings completed. |
| **203,115** | AU$: average value of new residential building. |
| **2.16** | AU$ billion: total value of non-residential building completed. |
| **698** | Perth median lot size 698 sq metres, 1991–92. |
| **559** | Perth median lot size 559 sq metres, 2004–05. |
| **78.1%** | Separate houses. |
| **11.9%** | Semi-detached, row or terrace houses. |
| **9.4%** | Flats, units and apartments. |
| **67.2%** | Family household. |
| **23.6%** | Lone person household. |
| **3.6%** | Group household. |

Western Australia: building activity 2006–07[12]

Mission Australia recommends a range of strategies [to address homelessness and housing affordability issues in Perth] including creating more affordable housing in the heart of our capital cities, combating the trend of low-income people living on the suburban fringe and travelling hours to work.[13]

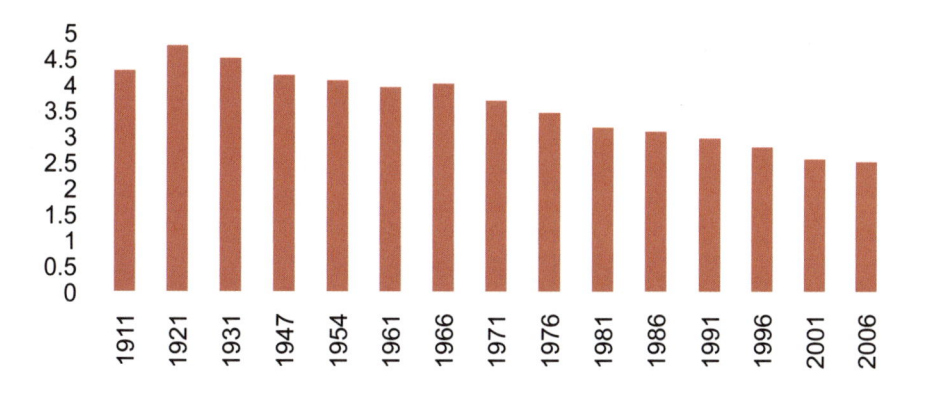

10   Shelter WA, <http:www.shelterwa.org.au/publications/news/Presentation_State_of_Affordable_Housing_2007.pdf>, viewed April 2008.

11   Shelter WA, <http:www.shelterwa.org.au/publications/news/Presentation_State_of_Affordable_Housing_2007.pdf>, viewed April 2008.

12   Data in this table is sourced from ABS, Catalogue No. 1306.5, *Western Australia at a Glance 2008 Revised*, Canberra, 2008; Western Australian Planning Commission; ABS, *2006 Census Quickstats: Perth*, Canberra, 2007.

13   Mission Australia, 'UN Report on Australian housing crisis rings true', 12 June 2007, <http://www.missionaustralia.com.au/news/media-releases/42-media-releases/182-un-report-on-australian-housing>, viewed September 2008.

14   'Greater Perth Population and Housing Discussion Paper 2', Western Australian Planning Commission, Perth, 2003; ABS, *2006 Census Quickstats: Perth*, Canberra, 2007.

15   2050 projection from Foran, B. and Poldy, F., 'Future Dilemmas: Options to 2050 for Australia's Population, Technology, Resources and Environment', CSIRO Sustainable Ecosystems, Canberra, 2002.

*Western Australia: Number of people per household 1911–2006.*[14]

Western Australia's average household size has dropped from a high of 4.7 people per household in 1921 to 2.5 people in 2006. Projections indicate that the Australian average household occupancy rate will continue to decline to around 2.3–2.4 people per household by 2050.[15]

Perth is facing a housing affordability crisis unprecedented in recent times with an unaffordability ranking very close to that of London. Perth is still marginally more affordable than Sydney with house prices eight times the median household income compared to Sydney at almost nine.[16]

| RANK | CITY | NATION | RATIO |
|---|---|---|---|
| 1 | Los Angeles, CA | US | 11.5 |
| 2 | Salinas, CA | US | 10.9 |
| 3 | San Francisco, CA | US | 10.8 |
| 4 | Honolulu, HI | US | 10.3 |
| 5 | San Diego, CA | US | 10.0 |
| 6 | Mandurah (Perth region) | Aus | 9.5 |
| 7 | San Jose, CA | US | 9.3 |
| 7 | Sunshine Coast | Aus | 9.3 |
| 9 | UK Bournemouth & Dorset | UK | 8.9 |
| 10 | Belfast | UK | 8.8 |
| 11 | Sydney | Aus | 8.6 |
| 11 | Gold Coast | Aus | 8.6 |
| 13 | Kelowna | Canada | 8.5 |
| 13 | Santa Rosa, CA | US | 8.5 |
| 15 | Vancouver | Canada | 8.4 |
| 16 | Exeter & Devon | UK | 8.2 |
| 16 | Ventura County, CA | US | 8.2 |
| 18 | London (GLA) | UK | 7.7 |
| 19 | Perth | Aus | 7.6 |
| 20 | Tauranga | NZ | 7.5 |
| 21 | London Exurbs | UK | 7.4 |
| 22 | Melbourne | Aus | 7.3 |
| 22 | Victoria | Canada | 7.3 |
| 24 | Rockingham (Perth region) | Aus | 7.2 |
| 25 | Miami-West Palm Beach, FL | US | 7.1 |

*Severely unaffordable world cities, 2007.[17]*
*Ratio = multiple of house prices to annual income.*

# HOUSING

'The standard block size that defines our sprawling cities was initially mandated to separate dwellings in order to halt the spread of bubonic plague and, later, to accommodate septic tanks. By continuing to embrace it, we have launched a litany of problems, one of which is a generation of parents and children who think the only safe way to get to school is to be driven.'[18]

16  4th Annual Demographia International Housing Affordability Survey: 2008 Ratings for Major Urban Markets, <http://www.demographia.com/dhi-ix2005q3.pdf>, viewed April 2008.

17  4th Annual Demographia International Housing Affordability Survey: 2008 Ratings for Major Urban Markets, <http://www.demographia.com/dhi-ix2005q3.pdf>, viewed April 2008.

18  Giles-Corti, B., Centre for the Built Environment and Health, The University of Western Australia, quoted in, 'Close to Home', *Uniview*, Summer 2008.

19  *Comparitive Capitals*, FORM, Perth, 2008, based on ABS 2006 Census data.

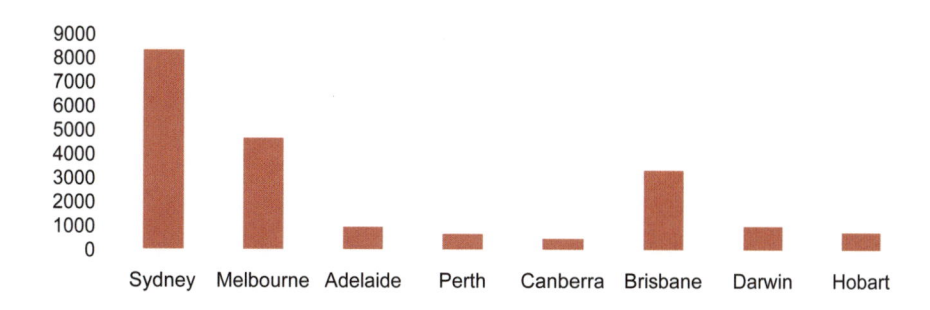

*Australian capital cities: Inner city population density, 2006 (persons per sq km).*[19]

Perth's inner city is the fastest growing municipality of any Australian capital city, but currently has a lower population density than most other Australian capital cities at 639 people per square kilometre. Perth's inner city population has grown from around 9,000 in 2001 to approximately 13,000 in 2008.

DATABASE

'The world will need one billion more hectares of arable land by 2050 – roughly the area of Brazil and far more land than will be available.'[1]

**34.9** kg beef
**17.5** kg mutton and lamb
**19** kg pork
**30.8** kg poultry
**10.8** kg seafood
**23.3** kg dairy
**135** kg fruit and fruit products
**162** kg vegetables
**137** eggs
**67.7** kg flour
**7.9** kg breakfast food
**7.1** kg rice
**53.4** kg bread
**7.1** kg nuts
**0.9** kg tea
**2.4** kg coffee

# FOOD

'The argument for developing green cities...rests on the fact that we harvest nutrients from across a nutrient poor continent and then concentrate them, and water, in our cities. Cities thus contain the two ingredients most vital to food production – large amounts of water and large amounts of nutrient, which are currently mostly wasted by pumping them into the ocean to get rid of a few bacteria. This is a truly illogical thing to do.'[2]

1  Vogel, G., 'Upending the Traditional Farm', *Science*, Vol. 319, 8 February 2008.
2  Cribb, J., Unpublished discussion, March 2008.
3  ABS, Catalogue No. 4306.0, *Apparent Consumption of Foodstuffs*, Canberra, 2000.

left: Australian annual food consumption per capita in kilograms 1997/98[3]

'Urban farming will be our biggest paradigm shift. Our likely food future will be focused on organic systems within urban and peri-urban boundaries. Organic hydroponics, organic aquaculture and aquaponics – high-tech food production teamed up with green roofs.'[4]

| | |
|---|---|
| **1,209,810** | Tonnes of Asian vegetables produced in Perth, of a total Western Australian crop of 1,798,493 tonnes (2006–07). |
| **179,148** | Kilograms of lettuce produced undercover in Perth, of a total Western Australian crop of 205,820 kg (2005–06). |
| **3,856** | Tonnes of lettuce produced outdoors in Perth, of a total Western Australian outdoor crop of 7,586 tonnes (2005–06). |
| **63,597** | Square metres of lettuce grown undercover in Perth (2005–06). |
| **2,194,180** | Kilograms of strawberries produced in Perth (1997). |
| **85** | Hectares of strawberries in Perth (1997). |
| **11** | Hectares of wheat grown for grain in Perth (1997). |
| **28** | Tonnes of wheat produced for grain in Perth (1997). |
| **771,552** | Kilograms of oranges produced in Perth (1997). |
| **24,034** | Orange production trees planted in Perth (1997). |
| **783** | Hectares of vineyards in Perth (1997). |
| **6,204** | Tonnes of grapes (fresh weight) produced in Perth (1997). |
| **6,749** | Tonnes of potatoes produced in Perth (1997). |
| **5,385** | Tonnes of potatoes produced in Perth (2005–06). |
| **124** | Hectares of potatoes in Perth (2005–06). |
| **112** | Hectares of tomatoes in Perth of a total of 350 ha in Western Australia (2005–06). |

'In Paris of a century ago, 100,000 tonnes of high-value out-of-season crops were grown on 1,400 hectares, around one-sixth of the surface area of the city, using about one million tonnes of horse manure. They used to heap up to 0.3 m of horse manure on top of their vegetable beds every year, and used many different methods to control soil and air temperature. They were able to grow between three and six crops of fruit and vegetables a year, making a good living on no more than 0.75 hectares.'[5]

left: Fruit and vegetable production in Perth.[6]

[4] Wilson, G., 'Urban Food will be our Biggest Paradigm Shift', *News Bulletin 2: Cities must Grow Fresh Food from Organic Waste*, Urban Agriculture online, <http://www.urbanag.org.au/urbagnews2.pdf>, viewed August 2008.

[5] Deelstra, T. and Girardet, H., 'Urban Agriculture and Sustainable Cities', Thematic Paper, Resource Center on Urban Agriculture and Forestry, Leusden, 2000.

[6] Data in this table is sourced from National Farmers Federation, <http://www.nff.org.au/farm-facts.html>, viewed May 2008; ABS, *Agricultural Commodities: Small Area Data, Australia, 2006-07*, Canberra, 2008; Vegetables WA, <http://www.vegetableswa.com.au/>, viewed May 2008; Australian Natural Resources Atlas, <http://www.anra.gov.au/topics/agriculture/statistics/wa/sd-perth.html#stats>, viewed August 2008; ABS, *Agricultural Commodities 2005/2006*, Canberra, 2006; ABS, *Western Australia at a Glance, 2008*, Canberra, 2008.

'In all production areas, difficulty in obtaining sufficient water and land for expansion as well as other factors...can lead to pressure to subdivide... This can significantly and irreversibly limit future options for agriculture in an area.'[7]

**12,872** Farms in Western Australia; or 9.3% of Australian farms engaged in agricultural production.

**81,269** Holdings in hectares with agricultural value, Perth 1997.

**64,913** Holdings in hectares with agricultural value, Perth 2006-07.

**9-11** Megalitres/hectare of irrigation is required to produce a 16 week summer carrot crop on sandy soil near Perth (9,000-11,000 kL/hectare) with conventional agricultural methods.

**2,123** The area of fruit and nut orchards in hectares in the Perth region 2006-07.

**1,315,689** Orchard fruit trees in the Perth region 2006-07.

**1,858** Hectares: vegetables grown for human consumption, Perth 2006-07 (1,930 hectare in 2005-06).

*top: Perth food production.[8]*

*bottom: Western Australia: Potential supply of nitrogen rich input materials by area, available for horticulture (tonnes N/yr available for horticulture).[9] Perth, Harvey and Gingin have the greatest potential supply of nitrogen rich material suitable for organic horticulture development. Perth has the potential for increased organic industry in the production of fruit and vegetables on the coastal plain; grapes, olives, citrus, avocados, vegetables and melons and has close proximity to organic nutrient sources.*

'The [Perth] region's restricted and limited rainfall necessitates the use of supplementary irrigation to produce most crops and to improve yield and market quality within the coastal plain. The soils of the Spearwood land system are generally suitable for horticulture and particularly vegetable production.'[10]

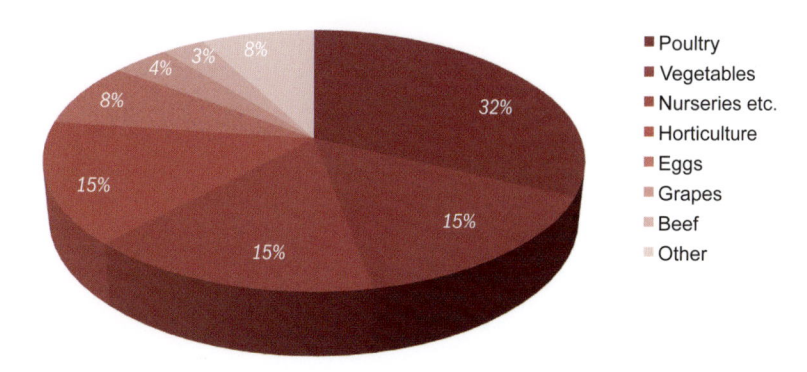

- Poultry 32%
- Vegetables 15%
- Nurseries etc. 15%
- Horticulture 15%
- Eggs 8%
- Grapes 4%
- Beef 3%
- Other 8%

Perth metropolitan region: Proportion of Gross Value Agricultural Production (GVAP) by agricultural commodity. Total value AU$277 million, 1996–97.[11] Poultry and vegetables were the major agricultural commodities (in terms of value) produced in the Perth metropolitan region in 1996/97.

7  Kininmonth, I., *Issues paper – Agriculture in the Perth Metropolitan Region: The Importance of Agriculture in the Perth Region*, Agriculture Western Australia, Perth, 2000.

8  Data in this table is sourced from National Farmers Federation, <http://www.nff.org.au/farm-facts.html>, viewed May 2008; ABS, *Agricultural Commodities: Small Area Data, Australia, 2006–07*, Canberra, 2008; Vegetables WA, <http://www.vegetableswa.com.au/>, viewed May 2008; Australian Natural Resources Atlas, <http://www.anra.gov.au/topics/agriculture/statistics/wa/sd-perth.html#stats>, viewed August 2008; ABS, *Agricultural Commodities 2005/2006*, Canberra, 2006; ABS, *Western Australia at a Glance, 2008*, Canberra, 2008.

9  McCoy, S., *Organic Horticulture: Strategic Opportunities for Western Australia*, Bulletin 4622, Department of Agriculture, Perth, 2004.

10 Kininmonth, I., *Issues paper – Agriculture in the Perth Metropolitan Region: The Importance of Agriculture in the Perth Region*, Agriculture Western Australia, Perth, 2000.

11 Cook, D., Anna, G., and Hatherly, C., *Agriculture Statistical Overview 96/97: Perth Metropolitan Region, Sustainable Rural Development Program*, Agriculture Western Australia, Perth, undated.

'Changing consumer tastes and demands are also increasingly influencing where and how agriculture is undertaken. International trends and local experience indicate an increasing demand for organic and fresh food grown near to where people live. In association with this trend farmers' markets are growing along with agri-tourism in the urban periphery. These trends are expected to continue as consumer awareness of diet and the importance of fresh food grows.'[12]

**1** Hectare will feed 50 people according to Dutch farming methods excluding wine, tobacco, meat.

**114** Hectares for poultry production.

**2,000** Hectares for fish production.

**7,950** Hectares of dairy pasture for milk production.

**1,278** Hectares for outdoor vegetable production.

**161** Hectares for indoor vegetable production.

**824** Hectares for rice production.

**5,550** Hectares for sugar beet production.

**1,600** Hectares for coffee production.

**304** Hectares for tea production.

**2,948** Hectares for fruit production.

**In a survey conducted for the United Nations, cities worldwide already produce about one-third of the food consumed by their residents on average. This percentage is 'likely to grow in coming decades, given that the need for urban agriculture could be greater now than ever before'.**[13]

12 Kininmonth, I., *Issues paper – Agriculture in the Perth Metropolitan Region: The Importance of Agriculture in the Perth Region*, Agriculture Western Australia, Perth, 2000.

13 Halweil, B. and Nierenberg, D., in their report published in the 'State of the World 2007' by the Washington-based Worldwatch Institute. Quoted by Tacio, H. D., 'Urban farming can help feed city millions', peopleandplanet.net: people and food and agriculture.

14 Fairlie, S., 'Can Britain feed itself?' *The Land*, Winter 2007-08.

15 The KM3 project by MVRDV was designed City for one million people in a 5x5x5km cube. MVRDV based their calculations on Dutch food consumption statistics and high-tech agricultural production (excluding beef, sheep and pork). MVRDV, *KM3: Excursions on capacities*, Actar, Rotterdam, 2005.

**Data used in the Boomtown 2050 research**[14] **(see Food City page 275)**
Chemical farming methods (excluding meat production) = feeds 14 people/ha
Traditional UK organic farming methods (excluding livestock) = feeds 7.5 people/ha

*left: The land areas needed to feed a population of 1 million people according to intensive Dutch farming practices.*[15]

'In Shanghai, only 20% of the land administered by the city authorities is actually built on; 80% of the land, mainly in the urban perimeter, is used for crop growing, making the city region self-sufficient in vegetables and producing much of the rice, pork, chicken, duck and carp. With their unique system of governance, Chinese cities administer vast adjacent areas of farmland and aim to be self-sufficient in food from this. Is this model of urban–rural linkages relevant to cities elsewhere in the world?'[16]

**306** Deer in Perth (1997).

**17,552** Pigs in Perth (1997).

**24,856** Meat cattle in Perth (1997).

**2.32** Number of meat cattle in millions produced in Western Australia (2006–07).

**2,926** Milk cows (in milk and dry) in Perth (1997).

**4,639,523** Meat chickens grown on contract in Perth (1997).

**12,147,237** Dozen eggs produced for consumption in Perth (1997).

**22.129** Numbers of sheep and lambs in millions produced in Western Australia.

**9.09** Number of million tonnes of barley for grain.

*Western Australia Agriculture/Farming activity 2006–07.*[17]

'Land use planning processes have not considered the strategic importance of agricultural land in the Perth region and have tended to follow the market rationalist view driven by urban property development processes...New integrated approaches to land use planning for these areas should be investigated that have regard to the possibility of multiple land use objectives.'[18]

### Vertical farm project, New York[19]

1 x 30-storey tower: designed to supply eggs, meat, vegetables and fruit for 50,000 people. Upper floors would grow hydroponic crops; lower floors would house chickens and fish to consume plant waste. Based on the concept that well designed greenhouses use as little as 10% of the water and 5% of the area required by farm fields. 150 vertical farms could produce food for the entire city of New York. New Yorkers eat 100 kg fresh vegetables per year.

16  Deelstra, T. and Girardet, H., 'Urban Agriculture and Sustainable Cities', Thematic Paper, Resource Center on Urban Agriculture and Forestry, Leusden, 2000.

17  Data in this table is sourced from National Farmers Federation, <http://www.nff.org.au/farm-facts.html>, viewed May 2008; ABS, 71250D0010_200607 Agricultural Commodities: Small Area Data, Australia, 2006-07, Canberra, 2008; Vegetables WA, <http://www.vegetableswa.com.au/>, viewed May 2008; Australian Natural Resources Atlas, <http://www.anra.gov.au/topics/agriculture/statistics/wa/sd-perth.html#stats>, viewed August 2008; ABS, Agricultural Commodities 2005/2006, Canberra, 2006; ABS, Western Australia at a Glance, 2008, Canberra, 2008.

18  Kininmonth, I., Issues paper – Agriculture in the Perth Metropolitan Region: The Importance of Agriculture in the Perth Region, Agriculture Western Australia, Perth, 2000.

19  Despommier, D., The Vertical Farm Project, Columbia University, New York, 2008. Despommier envisages blocks of vertical farms in the world's biggest cities, each tower providing enough food and water for 50,000 people per year with no waste. Plants would be grown hydroponically using NASA plant lists of suitable varieties. A prototype should be built within five to 10 years.

The UN Development Programme estimates that 800 million people are involved in urban farming worldwide. Most of these are in Asian cities.[20] Until the mid-1990s, when massive population growth and rising demand overwhelmed local food supplies, urban farmers in China's 18 largest cities were able to produce over 90% of locally consumed vegetables and half of all the meat and poultry. Hong Kong still produces two-thirds of the poultry, half the vegetables, and 40% of the fish it consumes. Singapore produces all of its meat and fish and one-quarter of its vegetables.[21]

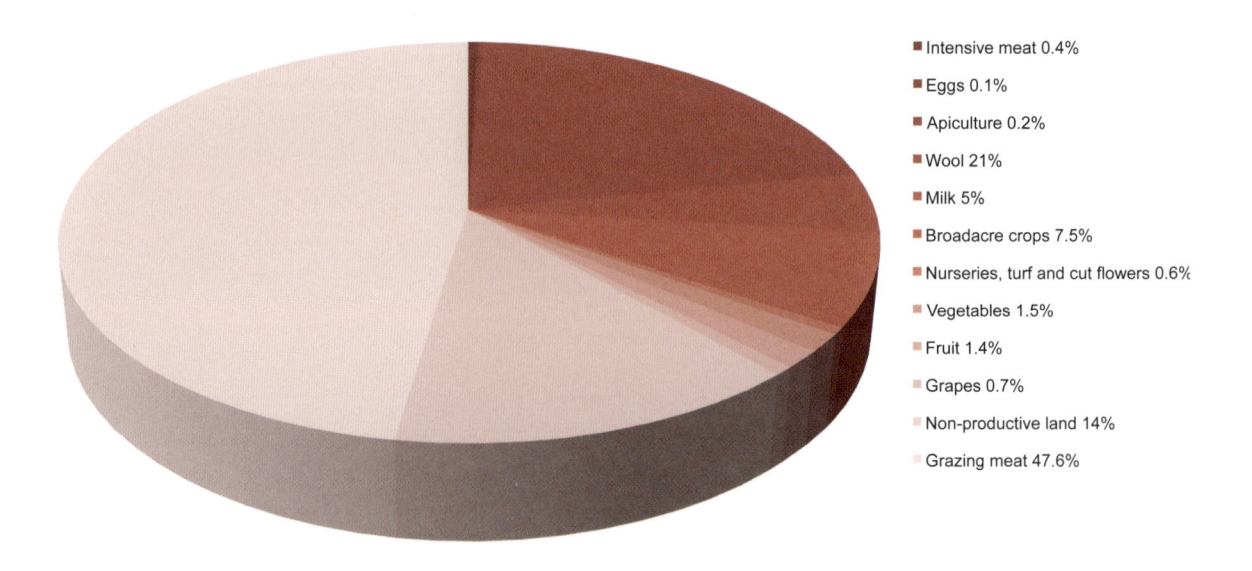

- Intensive meat 0.4%
- Eggs 0.1%
- Apiculture 0.2%
- Wool 21%
- Milk 5%
- Broadacre crops 7.5%
- Nurseries, turf and cut flowers 0.6%
- Vegetables 1.5%
- Fruit 1.4%
- Grapes 0.7%
- Non-productive land 14%
- Grazing meat 47.6%

*Perth Metropolitan Region: Area of farm production for major agricultural activities, 1996/97 (ha).[22]*
*The Perth Metropolitan Region has a diverse agricultural sector. Urbanisation is a major threat to the sustainability of these industries due to competition for land and water resources. Perth's agricultural sector accounts for 6% of all farmland in the South-West region.*

'Geographically the [Perth Metropolitan] region is well located to continue supplying high quality products to export markets in both the Asia region and the Northern hemisphere. It is able to grow a variety of products due to the suitability of its climatic zone and is strategically well positioned to take advantage of world consumer demand for clean and safe quality food. It has regular and efficient air and sea links which enable it to distribute perishable products worldwide.'[23]

20 Tacio, H. D., 'Urban farming can help feed city millions', peopleandplanet.net: people and food and agriculture, <http://www.peopleandplanet.net/doc.php?id=2940>, viewed September 2008.

21 'Towards sustainable cities', peopleandplanet.net: people and cities, <http://www.peopleandplanet.net/doc.php?id=1490>, viewed January 2008.

22 Cook, D., Anna, G., and Hatherly, C., *Agriculture Statistical Overview 96/97: Perth Metropolitan Region, Sustainable Rural Development Program*, Agriculture Western Australia, Perth, undated.

23 Kininmonth, I., *Issues paper – Agriculture in the Perth Metropolitan Region: The Importance of Agriculture in the Perth Region*, Agriculture Western Australia, Perth, 2000.

# One Perth eucalypt can support 600–1000 insect species, one exotic tree relatively few.[1]

**266,000**    Area of native vegetation in hectares mapped in the Perth Metropolitan Region in 2001. Of this: 191,000 hectares is protected and 75,000 hectares is unprotected (Local Natural Areas).

**58,000**    Area of native vegetation in hectares located on private land in the Perth Metropolitan Region and was unprotected. 12% (6,960 ha) of this was zoned for intensive urban development under the Metropolitan Region Scheme in 2001.

**80,000**    Approximate area in hectares of the Perth Metropolitan Region mapped as wetlands. Perth's wetlands are classified as conservation; resource enhancement; and multiple use, management categories based on condition and values. About 14,000 hectares of native vegetation is associated with these wetlands. An estimated 80% of the wetlands on the Swan Coastal Plain has been lost or degraded.

**10,000**    Approximate area in hectares of native vegetation in the Perth Metropolitan Region is located within 50 metres of waterways and provides important ecological linkages.

**500**    A system of Regional Ecological Linkages (green corridors) has been mapped and is currently being implemented by the Perth Biodiversity Project.
The corridors are 500 metres wide and aim to link significant natural areas as important 'stepping stones' within a comprehensive corridor linkage system. 'Perth Greenways' (Tingay and Associates 1998) were a precursor to the Ecological Linkage System and are incorporated where viable.

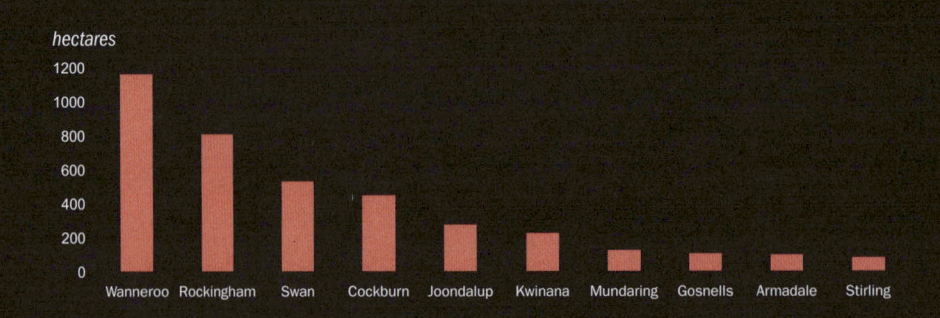

*top: Perth's native vegetation.[2]*
*bottom: Perth Metropolitan Region: Top 10 municipalities by area cleared, 2001–2004 (hectares).[3]*

The coastal cities of Wanneroo and Rockingham had the highest rates of native vegetation clearing between 2001 and 2004 (1,158 ha and 805 ha respectively). During this period Wanneroo averaged an annual clearing rate of 296.5 ha, and Rockingham averaged 289.5 ha.

# ENVIRONMENT

Nearly 900 hectares of native vegetation was cleared per year from the Perth metro area between 1998 and 2004 (more than one football oval per day). About 15,000 hectares was approved for clearing in 2005–06 (about 10 football ovals per day). Most of this was on the urban growth front and associated with housing and infrastructure development.

1 Powell, R. and Emberson, J., *Growing Locals: Gardening with Local Plants in Perth*, Western Australian Naturalists Club Inc., Nedlands, 1996, p. 48.

2 del Marco, A. et al., *Local Government Biodiversity Planning Guidelines for the Perth Metropolitan Region*, Western Australian Local Government Association, West Perth, 2004.

3 Environmental Protection Authority, *State of the Environment Report: Western Australia 2007*, Department of Environment and Conservation, Perth, 2007.

4 Powell, R. and Emberson, J., *Growing local: Gardening with Local Plants in Perth*, Western Australian Naturalists Club, Nedlands, 1996.

### Native animals[4]

Perth has over 70 known species of reptile – the highest number recorded for any city in the world. Most of these are lizards. The Perth region originally had around 30 species of native mammal. Kangaroos, wallabies, water rats, bats and possums are still common in some parts of Perth. The Perth subregion is recognised as one of the world's top biodiversity hotspots because of its huge diversity of endemic species and the significant threats posed by clearing and urban development.

**60** — Distance in kilometres from Fremantle to Ellen Brook in the upper Swan River Estuary. Six kilometres along the Canning River to Kent Street Weir.

**10–20** — Estuary water levels increase by 10-20 centimetres in winter due to the influx of water from the Leeuwin Current. Much of the urban development on low-lying land around the Swan–Canning Estuary is at or below mean sea level zero (Australian Height Datum).

**12** — The Swan River's main basin is a drowned river valley from the Pleistocene epoch and it is 12 kilometres in length, 2 kilometres wide and about 21 metres deep (in Mosman Bay).

**121,000** — The area in km$^2$ of the catchment area for the Swan, Avon and Canning rivers, however most of the water in the Swan–Canning Estuary originates in the higher rainfall areas of the Darling Escarpment and Swan Coastal Plain.

**10,000** — Estimated number of waterbirds residing in the Swan–Canning Estuary annually (1980s). The Swan Coastal Plain wetland system supports waterbird population and diversity.

**50%** — Percentage of the wetlands between Yanchep and Rockingham which had been drained by 1966. In 1991 it was thought that 70-80% of the wetlands on the Swan Coastal Plain had been lost or degraded.

**49** — The area in hectares of the Perth river foreshore that was filled for the Narrows Interchange and freeway development between 1955 and 1959. Dredging of river channels in the Swan–Canning Estuary was constant between 1892 and 1976. Much of the dredge spoil was used for infill programs. Twenty-eight hectares of the foreshore was filled in the Mounts Bay area alone.

**15,000** — Number of waterbirds in mid-spring to late autumn: the Swan–Canning Estuary is the final destination for large numbers of trans-equatorial migrant waterbirds from the Northern Hemisphere. The tiny (30 gram) birds fly about 25,000 km each way and a single bird may fly 400,000 km in a lifetime. Before the dredging and walling of the Swan River the numbers may have been much higher. Countries along the East Asian - Australasian flyway are signatory to treaties aimed at protecting bird feeding grounds.

**87** — Different species of waterbirds used the Swan–Canning Estuary in the 1980s.

**31** — Species of Swan–Canning Estuary waterbirds are listed in the Japan–Australia Migratory Bird Agreement which binds signatory countries to protect species.

**3** — Major habitats for wading birds remain on the Swan–Canning Estuary. These are at Como (40 hectares), Alfred Cove (130 hectares) and Pelican Point (20 hectares).

**40** — Approximate amount in kilograms of phosphorus applied to each hectare of urban gardens annually. Fertiliser applied to suburban gardens and agricultural land leaches into the catchment system of the Swan–Canning Estuary and contributes to a large nutrient store in soils and river sediments. These nutrients provide fuel for outbreaks of toxic algal blooms following summer floods.

**5,000** — Approximate amount in tonnes of phosphorus applied in total to Perth metropolitan gardens annually. This is double the application rate in agricultural areas.

**3,406** — Number of black swans in Swan Coastal Plain recorded in 1992. Colonial records site flocks of 500 but they are now found infrequently on the Swan River due to loss of habitat.

**500** — Area in hectares of the main species of seagrass in the Swan–Canning Estuary. Paddle weed sea grass, *Halophila ovalis*, covers about 20% of the estuarine basin in shallow sandy areas.

**284,100** — Number of people who fished recreationally at least once in 1987.

**544,300** — Number of people who fished recreationally at least once in 1999. Some species such as black bream are fully or over exploited in some areas.

ENVIRONMENT

'The most effective way to provide connectivity across the landscape for as many species as possible is to protect existing natural areas as stepping stones within broad bands (linkages) that connect the larger, more viable natural areas. 50 m is the minimum width required for viability of corridor linkage areas.'[5]

5   del Marco, A. et al., *Local Government Biodiversity Planning Guidelines for the Perth Metropolitan Region*, Western Australian Local Government Association, West Perth, 2004, p. 48.

6   ABS, Catalogue No. 4613.0, *Australia's Environment Issues and Trends 2006*, ABS, Canberra, 2006.

7   Brearley, A., *Ernest Hodgkin's Swanland: Estuaries and Coastal Lagoons of South Western Australia*, UWA Press, Perth, 2005.

above: Australian states: Total forest as percentage of land area.[6]

Western Australia has the least remaining forest of all Australian states (10%), when viewed as percentage of total land area. South Australia is close behind with only 11% remaining.

left: Swan-Canning Estuary data.[7]

127
DATABASE

'Western Australians have a preference for larger houses and fewer people per household compared to other parts of the world. This results in large land areas being needed to accommodate urban centres and consequent clearing of native vegetation and farmland for housing.'[8]

**23** Native tree species on the Swan Coastal Plain. Of these only eight are common including tuart, marri and jarrah, three banksia species, a casuarina and an acacia species.

**1,500** Species of plants (approximately) are native to the Perth Metropolitan Region.

**50** The area of a typical Perth garden (mainly grass) would have once grown around 50 species of native plants.

**100+** Species of terrestrial orchids occur in the Perth Metropolitan Region.

top: Perth vegetation data.[9]
bottom: Australian states: Native forest area 2003 ('000 ha).[10]
Western Australia's remaining forests are primarily native vegetation. Plantations comprise an additional 352,000 hectares, making up a total Western Australian forest area of 25,716,000 hectares.

# ENVIRONMENT

'In addition to the ecological impacts of reduced water availability, Perth's waterways are suffering from excessive nutrient inputs from leaching of fertilisers applied to the city's 500,000 residential gardens and municipal parks.'[11]

8  Environmental Protection Authority, *State of the Environment Report: Western Australia 2007*, Department of Environment and Conservation, Perth, 2007, p. 137.

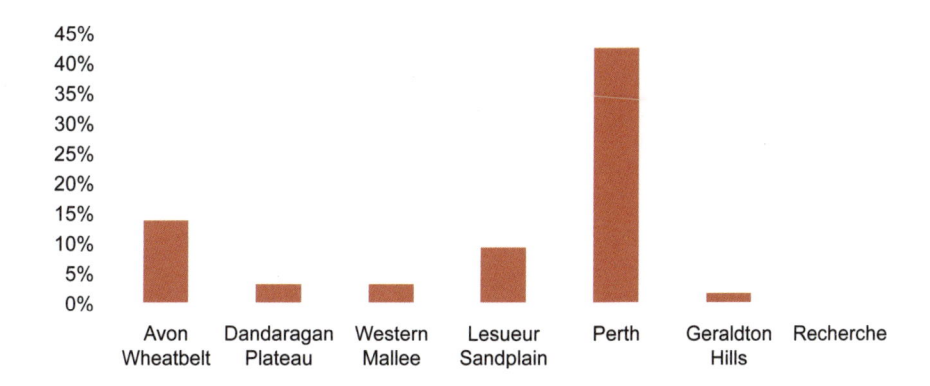

9  Seddon, G., *Sense of Place: Response to an Environment, the Swan Coastal Plain Western Australia*, Bloomings Books, Melbourne, 2004; Powell, R. and Emberson, J., *Growing Local: Gardening with Local Plants in Perth*, Western Australian Naturalists Club, Nedlands, 1996.

10  ABS, Catalogue No. 4613.0, *Australia's Environment Issues and Trends 2006*, ABS, Canberra, 2006.

11  Grace, W., 'Sustainable Urban Living – a Perth Perspective', National Housing Conference, Perth, October 2005.

12  Environmental Protection Authority, *State of the Environment Report: Western Australia 2007*, Department of Environment and Conservation, Perth, 2007.

above: Western Australia: Subregions with more than 50% of native vegetation cleared, showing percentage of total threatened ecological communities found in subregion.[12]

The Perth subregion (Swan Coastal Plain) contains 42% of the South-West's threatened ecological communities. The Swan Coastal Plain region stretches from Jurien Bay in the north to Dunsborough in the south and the Darling Scarp to the east.

# 3

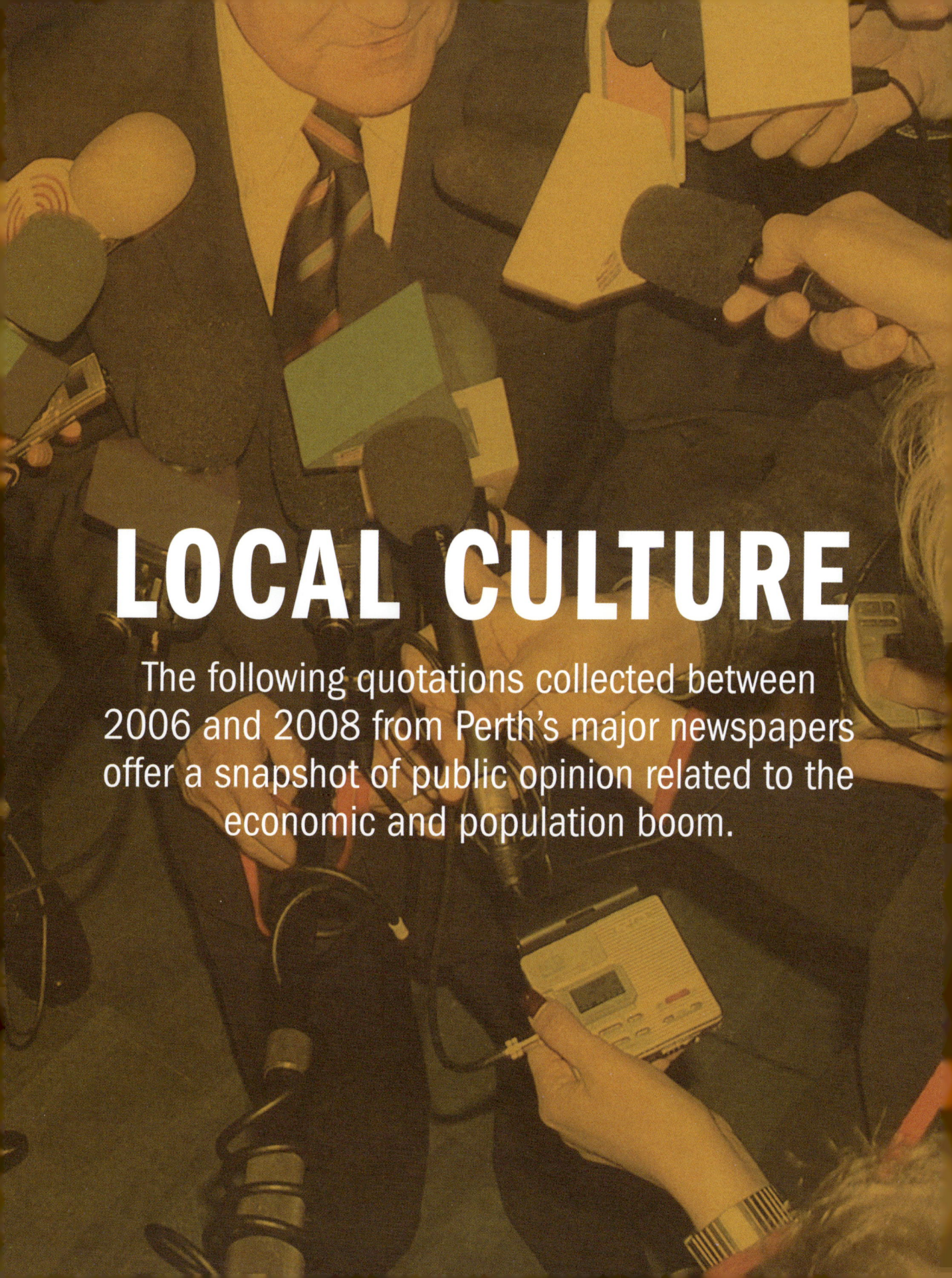

# LOCAL CULTURE

The following quotations collected between 2006 and 2008 from Perth's major newspapers offer a snapshot of public opinion related to the economic and population boom.

These quotations are organised thematically, not chronologically, and cover a range of topics. The quotes have been selected so as to represent the diversity of views and the level of debate that constitutes the local culture in relation to the future of the city.

# THE BOOM

## Money is poison for creativity. Jorg Imberger, *The West Australian*, April 25 2008.

The real future of Perth is not in Perth's hands but in Melbourne and London where Rio Tinto and BHP Billiton run their organisations. Peter Dowding, *The Weekend Australian Magazine*, September 6 2008. The benefit of the boom and the wealth is restricted to a few...The place is a joke. Perth more or less runs itself. It rolls along not through any intelligence, but through its natural strengths. Warren Anderson, *The Weekend Australian Magazine*, September 6 2008. In the midst of the State's biggest resources boom, West Australians are falling behind the rest of the nation when it comes to finishing school or completing tertiary study. Shane Wright, *The West Australian*, August 8 2007. It is estimated that about 20,000 West Australian children leave home hungry every day. The boom has been great for some, but a disaster for others. Let's hope that after the carnival is over there won't be too many tears. Jo Spagnolo, *The Sunday Times*, June 10 2007. Perth is the most expensive city in Australia for retirees thanks largely to WA's mining boom. Kate Campbell, *The West Australian*, August 29 2007. The upper end of the market is doing ridiculous things and that's purely a sign of the wash of money coming out of the mining industry. A year ago $9 million was a high price paid in Perth for a house. That has not only been eclipsed but left for dead as houses sell for up to $15 million...Luke Saraceni, *The West Australian*, January 3 2007. These days if you drive around at night you see homeless people in places you have never seen them before. Lisa Baker, *The West Australian*, May 18 2007. While mining and oil and gas sectors continue to drive our prosperity we are building our strengths like never before...we are becoming a centre of excellence for marine engineering and technology. The same applies to our flourishing creative industries. Our local music and fashion scenes are setting the pace. There is so much potential. Alan Carpenter, *The Sunday Times*, March 2 2008. Being known as the quarry for the rest of the world is not going to broaden the wellbeing of Western Australians. I feel you should make a difference in your home town and the window of opportunity we're seeing now with the resource boom will come only once in a lifetime. Lynda Dorrington, *The Australian*, July 17 2007. This is a time when we are being highly recognised for our key resources and achieving great wealth from them. It is time to proudly stand up and say we are a city of energy in all we think, say and do. Cities do not successfully grow unless people are fully included and engaged in the process: cities must look and feel good and with the encouragement of the cultures that exist here we can create a Perth culture that will be upheld as something truly special. Lisa Scaffidi, Speech to the WA Wine Press Club. Welcome to future Perth. Last year plans for 183,636 m² of office space and 2,993 residential apartments were approved by the City of Perth and construction is either underway or set to start on more than two dozen high rise projects that will redraw the city skyline...most of the new buildings are residential towers between 70 m and 115 m in height sold out before construction even begins. Daniel Hatch, *The West Australian*, April 7 2008. The State Government is targeting an ambitious 2011 deadline to launch one of Australia's biggest new satellite cities which could eventually provide affordable housing for 90,000 people just 10 km from fast growing Mandurah...The environmental challenges included assessing the risks of acid sulphate soils, providing drainage for waterlogged areas, dealing with odours from a piggery and addressing concerns about mosquitoes. Mark Drummond, *The West Australian*, June 9 2007. Coal Tycoon Ric Stowe has sold a $300 million 243 hectare parcel of land in Perth's rapidly growing northern corridor to a syndicate headed by listed developer Peet in WA's biggest residential property sale. The site will be divided up into 2,800 lots and is expected to bring in about 1.4 billion in land sales. Peet's shares firmed two cents to $3.91. Kate Emery, *The West Australian*, January 8 2008. It's time that our politicians and planners took the long term view of where this [growth] is leading us and what sort of city and countryside we are leaving for future generations. Exponential growth is the way a cancer behaves. Harry Cohen, *The West Australian*, February 26 2008. We need a government with vision for the future that can provide an appropriate development plan for Perth. Rob Druitt, Real Estate Institute of Western Australia, September 7 2008.

# POPULATION

## Population to hit 4.3m *Sunday Times,* September 7 2008.

The CCI (Chamber of Commerce and Industry) has calculated that WA needs an additional 400,000 workers over the next decade in order to sustain the recent rates of economic growth. Deirdre Willmott, *Subiaco Post,* April 5 2008. It's not just a skills shortage but a people shortage. The state is short of doctors, teachers, and electricians but it is also short of people to work in restaurants, nursing homes, and public transport. It is short of people to mow lawns, build homes, park cars and cut hair. This is not aberration but a state of permanent challenge. The state, indeed the world, has entered a new era of a chronic lack of people. Mike Nahan, *The West Australian,* February 23 2008. Conservatively, the world will need to accommodate about 150 million refugees from rising sea levels for a one meter sea level rise. Most will come from our nearest neighbours in Asia. Presumably Australia will wish to assist. With a current population of 20 million and our perceived vast space, we will come under a great deal of pressure to accommodate at least 60 million. Jorg Imberger, *The West Australian,* April 14 2008. Why we should allow more people to migrate to WA based solely on the needs of the mining boom is inexplicable. More workers deplete our natural resources even faster. Switzerland, Oregon and other places all have immigration barriers – why not WA? Given the pressure for us to take in climate change refugees surely that is where our priorities should lie. Jorg Imberger, *The West Australian,* April 25 2008. Federal opposition backbencher Wilson Tuckey says WA's north will be invaded by Asian nations unless the state and federal governments do more to develop and populate the region. Joe Spagnolo, *The Sunday Times,* May 17 2008. What's the bet that none of those charged with the responsibility for planning in WA have asked or attempted to answer the question: what level of population would suit Perth? Note that this is a different question to 'what level of population is sustainable'. Although Ms MacTiernan and a few of her party friends may want a Manhattan style 24/7 atmosphere for this paradise, many more like it just the way it is. We must say enough is enough and start discouraging people from coming here. Colin Delane, *The West Australian,* February 26 2008. Perth's outer suburbs are waking up to the sounds of crying babies as young families transform them into booming nappy valleys. Alison Batcheler, *The West Australian,* July 21 2007. New suburbs should have been opened up long ago but we have all these environmentalists shooting them down before even gestation and a thousand other bureaucratic impediments suffocating things from getting off the ground. David M Abott, *The West Australian,* March 22 2008.

# SUBURBIA

All the bush that is destroyed to make more and more houses for Perth is heartbreaking. I consider myself partially responsible because I live in Butler where it was bush until quite recently. I hope the State Government will find a solution before it's too late. Elena R. Themeliadou, *The West Australian*, February 11 2008

The State Government has unveiled plans for a new coastal satellite city between Joondalup and Yanchep that it claims will be the greenest in Australia. It was envisaged that Alkimos would be powered entirely by green energy and water would be recycled for possible use in neighbouring market gardens. Sam Riley, *The West Australian*, June 22 2007. Eco-friendly houses are now available for sale in Olive Waters Eco Village, a new estate being built in the rapidly developing suburb of Falcon, Mandurah. The site is between the estuary and ocean and is walking distance to the Miami shopping centre and Woolworths. *Sunday Times, ReadersMART*, June 3 2007. The Sustainable New Home, a national survey of more than 7000 households, was conducted by Connection Research and found less than a quarter of new home-buyers wanted to live in a new subdivision. And despite an increased awareness of sustainability, the report found most people were unfamiliar with the concept of 'green subdivisions'. Fewer than one in five regarded the status of a subdivision as 'green friendly' as an important factor in choosing where they would live. Laura Phillips, *The West Australian*, March 22 2008. Pressure from the building industry has forced the State Government to delay the introduction of controversial new building regulations which would potentially add thousands of dollars to the cost of a new home. The Building and Sustainability index, or BASIX, which aims to improve household water and energy efficiency was due to be in place early this year. Eloise Dortch, *The West Australian*, February 5 2007. Historically WA has been a place where a person on a modest income could buy a house of their own. This has been a major factor in attracting people from interstate and overseas and keeping the young here...housing affordability is now the biggest barrier to attracting and keeping people. The main criticism is that suburbia consumes too much land. We have plenty of land. Suburbia like its partner the car, has been one of the great liberating forces of history. We should foster it not strangle it. Mike Nahan, *The West Australian*, March 26 2008

# TRANSPORT

In my grandmother's lifetime she has seen milk delivered from a horse and cart, a man land on the moon, and watched her great grandchildren dance live on a computer screen. We must be prepared to embrace similar changes in magnitude when it comes to utilising alternative modes of transport and how our energy sources are generated. Phil Haberland, *The Sunday Times*, June 1 2008

Planning for mobility based purely on private motor cars will fail the community. Alannah MacTiernan, *The West Australian*, February 23 2008. In Perth every day 250,000 car trips are made of less than 1 km and 750,000 trips are made of less than 3 kms. Trevor Shilton, *The West Australian*, October 22 2006. Up to 30% of motorists will leave their car in the garage if petrol stays over $1.50, a survey has found. Shane Wright, *The West Australian*, May 24 2008. With 1.6 billion passenger trips on the London Tube last year, there were 1806 reported assaults. In Perth there were 161 assaults. That translated to one assault for every 222,360 trips on the Perth trains compared with one assault for every 885,935 trips on the Tube. Carmelle Sander, *The West Australian*, April 20 2008.

# CLIMATE CHANGE

# A study was done by the Swan River Trust's technical advisory panel, a group of 15 experts in climate change. According to the panel a large part of South Perth could be underwater in 100 years. Angie Raphael, *Community Southern Gazette*, January 2 2008.

About 94,000 WA coastal homes will be at risk if sea levels rise as predicted. Dr Ray Walls, *The Sunday Times*, April 29 2007. Animals and plants which are found exclusively in the South-West would be moved to wetter areas of WA under an emergency plan to save rare species from the ravages of climate change. Chris Johnson, *The West Australian*, June 23 2007. WA should slash its greenhouse gas emissions by two-thirds by 2050, endorse a national carbon trading emissions scheme and aim to derive 20 per cent of all electricity used in Perth and the South-West from renewable sources by 2020, a State Government task force has recommended. Amanda Roberts and Robert Taylor, *The West Australian*, February 6 2007. Australia's policy should be to be carbon neutral from 2010 by establishing a carbon charge on each element of carbon in the economy equivalent to the cost of sequestering this carbon…In Australia at the moment this would be around $13 per tonne of $CO^2$. Each Australian produces around 13 tonnes of greenhouse gas a year – 20 million would create a fund of around 3.5 billion. The carbon fund established for this charge would then be available for projects that can demonstrate zero or negative $CO^2$, including carbon sequestration in trees, geosequestration, biofuels, and renewable power. Peter Newman, *The West Australian*, April 28 2007. The head of the Future Farm Industries Co-operative Research Centre predicted yesterday that woody crops such as mallees could occupy up to 15 per cent of the farmland across vast areas of the Wheatbelt as biofuels and carbon offset programs sparked a major change in WA farming in the next 10 years. Kate Tarala and Jodie Thomson, *The West Australian*, May 22 2008. Perth Council wants to cut the city's carbon emissions by planting about 5000 trees in the CBD. It will also pay for another 81,000 trees to be planted elsewhere in the state. *The Sunday Times*, April 8 2007. Starting this month 105 trees will be planted for every house built by Plunkett Homes. *The Sunday Times*, 'Home', January 13 2008. Solar heat from the desert is the power of the future. Dr Gerry Wolff, *The West Australian*, January 14 2007. Uranium mining is the way of the future as the world goes nuclear to combat climate change. Mike Nahan, *The West Australian*, December 8 2007. Australia's mid-century 30 million will be twice as wealthy but heavily dependent on health services, continually searching for new water supplies and forced into using nuclear energy. Torrance Mendez, April 27 2007.

# Building medium density housing between three to five storeys high with choices of single bed units to penthouse suites would be a great start. Such densities would be more likely to deliver the lifestyle the Gen Y are seeking.
Trevor Smith, *The West Australian*, May 20 2007.

Unlike many years ago where people used to look at apartments and say – well that's a flat, I'd never live there because it's for people who can't afford a house – attitudes have totally changed. Luke Saraceni, *The Sunday Times*, August 28 2007. If you've considered apartment living, now's the time to buy, with Perth's median apartment price of $485,000 overtaking the median house of $470,000. Jessica Zoiti, *The Sunday Times*, August 28 2007. Changing social patterns often are revealed in demand for different kinds of housing. A city should be able to offer all options. Editorial, *The West Australian*, March 19 2008. The Real Estate Institute of WA wants the State Government to impose a minimum number of new flats, units and townhouses in each council area in a bid to ease the housing crisis. Kim Macdonald, *The West Australian*, August 13 2007. A $600 million plan to radically change the face of Leederville has taken a major step forward with the town of Vincent ready to call for expressions of interest from the private sector to build three high rise towers providing office space, retail and residential housing. Sam Riley, *The West Australian*, June 23 2007. It is really urgent that we limit the buildings' plot/size ratio. The current thinking of increasing the dwelling density and living space so that we are moving towards lots filled totally with buildings is very bad for the mental wellbeing of people. Jorg Imberger, *The West Australian*, April 25 2008. We've got ourselves into a situation of building a very low-density community which is the antithesis of what you really need for creating a walkable, pedestrian friendly environment. Billie Giles-Corti, *The West Australian*, January 30 2008. The propensity for dogs to sniff each other's bums means you end up meeting lots of nice dog owners. Paul Murray, *The West Australian*, December 23 2006. Dalkeith residents have rallied to put a stop to high density development in one of Perth's most exclusive suburbs. The People Against Density in Dalkeith (PADD) group was formed after the City of Nedlands released a concept plan which proposes to redevelop the Dalkeith Village area. Raquel de Brito, *The West Australian*, February 17 2008. Five to 10 storey buildings over most of the site are completely out of context with the streetscape character of Subiaco and the Subi-Centro area which is generally three storeys…There is no justifiable planning ground for buildings of this height and they should be no more than three to four storeys. Chester Burton, *The West Australian*, February 22 2008. Ms MacTiernan said she was 'very disappointed' with the council's response and 'thought the council understood Network City planning principles'. Daniel Hatch, *The West Australian*, February 22 2008.

# INFILL DEVELOPMENT

I always say we're not trying to mow down the existing residential fabric but where we do get some opportunity for infill we should be a little bit more creative than just R20 (20 homes per hectare). Alannah MacTiernan, *The West Australian*, February 22 2008. Ms MacTiernan has told local authorities that she will override them if they do not make the necessary high density zoning change. Kate Campbell, *The West Australian*, March 24 2008. What this current government has been all about is pursuing this myth of urban sprawl and trying to impose a style of dwelling on people that many people don't want. Simon O'Brien, *The West Australian*, March 24 2008. Fierce resistance to higher-density development in some Perth suburbs is largely due to ill-informed community debate and a 'not in my backyard mentality', WA's head planning bureaucrat claims. Many wrongly believed the push for greater density in Perth suburbs was about creating skyscrapers and much of the community debate overlooked the benefits of creating more compact neighbourhoods through a mix of two and three storey buildings that fitted in with surrounding single storey homes. Dawn Gibson, *The West Australian*, March 18 2008. Nineteen year old Curtin University planning students Sean Morrison and Michael Di Lazzaro lead FuturePerth, a group with a founding membership of almost 30 people in favour of high density and inner city development. It was created in response to what Mr Morrison called the 'not in my backyard' attitude of the older generation and particularly the response to the Perth Waterfront Project from long-established think tank CityVision. Daniel Hatch, *The West Australian*, June 25 2008. Our role is to inform the local community to stop them believing the hysteria from groups like Keep Cott Low and the Fremantle Society that development is dangerous... The State Government's Network City planning policy was a good document but its implementation had been poor. Sean Morrison, *The West Australian*, June 25 2008. The State Government has admitted it is unlikely to achieve its goal of confining 60 per cent of Perth's new homes to existing suburbs, a key plank of its long-term plan to reduce urban sprawl. Dawn Gibson, *The West Australian*, February 11 2008. In Cottesloe Acrophobia (fear of heights) is particularly acute. Sufferers have complained for years that buildings of height will ruin Australia's best beach, though they have never quite explained how. The local council, one of Perth's smallest has been emboldened by an influential local acrophobics' society and insists that buildings by the sea must not exceed 12 metres. Bad design is bad design and height limits do nothing but encourage it. Diversity is the key. Gareth Parker, *The West Australian*, December 29 2007. Anti-high-rise groups and residents in the City of Stirling had called a special electors meeting demanding the council withdraw a planning amendment which would allow development up to 12 storeys on one site. Two-thirds of the 400-strong crowd voted down the motion. Daniel Hatch, *The West Australian*, March 11 2008. By comparison with Barcelona and Dubai we seem fractured and timid. Not exactly frightened of our own shadow. Maybe just frightened to stand tall enough to throw one. Paul Murray, *The West Australian*, September 18 2007. As a city Perth has always been very immature in offering living opportunities in the central business district so we are catching up on where other cities around the world are. Peter Gianoli, *The West Australian*, April 7 2008.

# HOUSING AFFORDABILITY

House prices in Perth, though slowing now have climbed an astounding 161% since 2002. Food prices have climbed almost 25% over that same time period. But sitting between the two is the growth in wages which are now more than 40% higher than they were six years ago.

Shane Wright, *The West Australian*, April 28 2008

Despite similar population densities and household income levels, Perth has rapidly become one of the least affordable cities in the world while Houston remains one of the most affordable. Dawn Gibson, *The West Australian*, December 26 2006. Housing affordability in WA is much worse than first thought, with new figures showing there are 90,000 households suffering either mortgage or rental stress. Andrew Probyn, *The West Australian*, August 25 2007. Does it take a child to point out the obvious in the housing affordability debate? Too many people want to live in cities, demanding too many resources in terms of water, power, roads and transport. We need to cut Australia's immigration. C. Hughes, *The West Australian*, March 20 2008. It is difficult to believe that families struggling to meet payments on unnecessarily capacious homes are happier than were their parents or grandparents in much smaller dwellings. Tony Rutherford, *The West Australian*, July 1 2007. It is interesting to note Australian architects seem not to be much involved in the current debate – unlike the 60s and 70s when innovative low-cost housing was all the go among socially aware young architectural graduates. Tony Rutherford, *The West Australian*, July 1 2007. Developers are continuing to push up the price of land despite lot sales slumping to their lowest in almost 8 years, an Urban Development Institute of Australia survey of 40 big developers shows. It estimated that the average lot price in Perth rose 2% in the March Quarter to $293,055, almost $90,000 more than two years ago. Dawn Gibson, *The West Australian*, May 10 2008. The price of new homes in Perth would plummet by more than $180,000 if the State Government relaxed its planning policies to free up more land on the city's fringes, a national think tank has estimated. Perth developers were forced to pay $156,000 for a typical 550 m$^2$ block of housing land, which equated with $2.84 million a hectare, in a city where land should be the cheapest in the world. Dawn Gibson, *The West Australian*, December 26 2006. Having fallen embarrassingly short of its target to release 20,000 blocks of land this financial year, the State Government has revealed it will not set a target for 2008. Graham Mason, *The West Australian*, May 24 2007. The dream of home ownership will be lost for thousands of young families as Perth's residential land shortage worsens dramatically over the next 20 years, resulting in a huge shortfall of almost 60,000 lots, a new property report has warned. Dawn Gibson, *The West Australian*, January 13 2007.

# ARCHITECTURE

Many [buildings] are poorly oriented and lack adequate sun control, balconies are small and invariably accommodate the air-conditioning condenser unit rendering them virtually useless, unit layouts and finishes are basic and lack imagination and in many instances their relationship to the immediate environment is ignored.

Rod Mollet, *The West Australian*, September 12 2007.

Just pretend you have won the Olympics. Charles Landry, *The West Australian*, March 10 2007. The rush to cash in on WA's booming housing and construction market had given rise to bland, boring, box like buildings that would leave a legacy of concrete eyesores across Perth, top architects warned yesterday. Sam Riley, *The West Australian*, September 12 2007. And when I'm in Perth I don't feel stimulated by it, like I do when I'm in other cities. St Georges Terrace is a soulless windswept concrete canyon and the Hay Street Mall remains an aesthetic disaster. When was the last time you saw a marvellous piece of architecture go up? Paul Murray, *The West Australian*, December 23 2006. Beauty is in the eye of the beholder but I think the biggest problem is the lack of creativity in building design and built form. We need new and exciting architectural ideas that will stimulate debate. Troy Pickard, *The Sunday Times*, April 30 2008. You cannot make a great city through a simplistic bottom-line approach. The results are too mean spirited, courage is constrained, imagination curtailed and good experiments fall away to leave a city short of verve and style...I also do not want to talk about 'the great Perth lifestyle' or beaches, barbeques and beer. Charles Landry, *The West Australian*, February 10 2007. It didn't take Mr Landry long to form solid ideas about what is holding Perth back. The two issues which have resonated most strongly with me were his observations on Perth as 'the city that says no' and...the way we are swamped by suburbia. Interestingly one of them is psychological and the other physical, showing that town planning alone cannot correct a city's problems. Paul Murray, *The West Australian*, March 3 2007.

# URBANITY

The person who wants Perth to say 'yes' is Lord Mayor Lisa Scaffidi, voted in last year. She is the right person at the right time...her excitement about her job and her city is genuine. She talks of a new city waterfront development and of cross town linkages and an urban renaissance that involved not only big-wheelers but also families and artists' lofts. She wants the city, which more or less clears out after dark, to be lived in again.

Paul Toohey, *The Weekend Australian Magazine*, September 6 2008.

It's almost like there is too much wide open space. Donald Bates, *The West Australian*, August 21 2007. The Carpenter government has announced plans to develop the main city foreshore in a way that can only be described as a copy of Singapore or Hong Kong. This is simply crazy and ignores the whole context the river offers...We should make both the Swan River and King's Park nature reserves stopping any further development of the shoreline on the Swan. Jorg Imberger, *The West Australian*, April 25 2008. Alan Carpenter says the latest Perth city foreshore plan is a goer, and so it should be. It is bold and visionary and holds tremendous promise for the desperately needed invigoration of the city. Editorial, *The West Australian*, February 15 2008. If Alan Carpenter can find $300 million to make Perth beautiful, why can't he find $300 million ASAP to build another hospital? G. Cook, *The West Australian*, February 15 2008. It will signal a real coming of age for Perth, finally freeing itself from a suburban mindset to emerge as a cosmopolitan city, not just a collection of shops and offices. The day we start digging up that lawn will be the start of Perth's renewal. Paul Murray, *The West Australian*, February 16 2008. The Perth waterfront is ugly, crass and kitsch. Ben Juniper, *The West Australian*, March 14 2008. First, bringing the water and the city together is surely a positive move and long overdue. It will energise both the city and the water. Second, getting greater mixed uses into the heart of the city will bring Perth alive. Third, great public spaces and distinctive architecture are surely a good aim. Charles Landry, *The West Australian*, March 8 2008.

Perth City Council architect Craig Smith has given a scathing critique of the Perth Waterfront project, saying it is not a logical extension of the city, the proposed buildings do not interact with each other and the concept fails to engage with what is already there. Daniel Hatch, *The West Australian*, April 18 2008. One of the Councillors who recommended that Perth City Council reject key features of the State Government's foreshore plan works for an architectural firm developing several buildings that would have their views interrupted by the project's skyline. Cr Hardy rejected suggestions he had a conflict of interest. Daniel Hatch, *The West Australian*, April 17 2008. A low-key vision for the city foreshore in which low-rise waterfront development is coupled with an entertainment and marina precinct similar to Sydney's Darling Harbour will be revealed today by urban think tank, CityVision. CityVision's plan covers the same area as the government's but Mr Adam believed it better met the basic principles of successful waterfront development. Beatrice Thomas, *The West Australian*, June 19 2008. We are told tall buildings are bad, the view from Kings Park will be destroyed, we need to spend money on hospitals and that reclaimed grassland is somehow natural. How ridiculous. The youth and progressively minded people of Perth are utterly sick of the negativity surrounding the development debate. Sean Morrison, *The West Australian*, July 4 2008. Perth City Council should lose its planning powers if the central business district is to get a much-needed injection of life and culture, former Victorian premier Jeff Kennett said yesterday in another attack on Perth's lack of vision. Comparing WA's insular mentality to that of North Korea, Mr Kennett said it was clear the PCC had failed to make the most of the city's assets. Planning and Infrastructure Minister Alannah MacTiernan said Mr Kennett had an 'Idi Amin Complex' and 'loved telling people what to do.' 'I don't like the idea of people coming out and saying this is a crap city, it's not a crap city, it's a bloody good city," Ms MacTiernan said. Ben Spencer and Gareth Parker, *The West Australian*, March 15 2007. Curtin University Professor Greg Craven, a Victorian, says it beggars belief that a city blessed with 'the world's best river' instead turned its back to face a railyard...'Why are so many of our cleverest graduates as soon as they finish their degree leaving to go interstate?' Professor Craven muses. 'Overseas is one thing, but Melbourne, for God's sake?' Gareth Parker, *The West Australian*, July 29 2006. The Perth Waterfront Project and the State Government's Network City planning policy would be scrapped under a Liberal government, Colin Barnett said yesterday. The Liberal leader said people did not want skyscrapers on the city foreshore and the plan would create an exclusive enclave for corporations and rich apartment owners. Ms MacTiernan said it was 'complete nonsense' to suggest public access to the waterfront would be restricted. Mr Barnett did not understand the need for a 21st-Century precinct in Perth. FuturePerth chairman Sean Morrison said the belltower and convention centre showed what happened when bold and creative visions were watered down. He urged Mr Barnett not to sacrifice the 'quality and vision' of the waterfront project, saying Perth's population was set to double over the next 40 years and the environmental and infrastructure costs meant urban sprawl could not continue. Daniel Hatch, *The West Australian*, September 3 2008. I reckon the spiritual leader of Tibet would agree with me when I say 'Bugger the Swan River foreshore! Let's focus on the suburbs!' The Dalai Lama's promotion of compassion, human values, and religious harmony will come to fruition not from the lofty heights of golden temples and gambling Meccas, but rather in the humble, everyday interactions that take place within the streets of our suburbs. Phil from the Burbs, *Sunday Times*, 2007.

# WATER

## Total sprinkler bans will destroy Perth.
Peter Nattrass, *The Sunday Times*, April 8 2007.

When I said Perth could become the first ghost metropolis that was true, but the Government acted and got a de-salination plant going. Tim Flannery, *The Sunday Times*, February 18 2007. What next major water source is limitless? It's 'Desal #2. Government of Western Australia advertisement, *The Sunday Times*, May 20 2007. Water Corporation principal engineer Gary Crisp said WA's coastline boasted 'some of the best conditions in the world' for constructing successful desalination plants. Jodi Elston, *West Australian*, August 24 2007. Big front lawns are outdated and no longer sustainable in WA's increasingly parched climate. David Templeman, *The Sunday Times*, August 5 2007. The Water Corporation has called for the death of the traditional backyard garden, warning WA will not achieve its water usage targets if residents stick to thirsty species such as petunias, azaleas, roses and wide expanses of lawn. Gabrielle Knowles, *The West Australian*, April 22 2008. Dr Gill said the Water Corporation was planning to replace surface water and meet demand for potable supplies of 470 gigalitres annually by 2060 with four desalination plants, recharging underground aquifers with recycled wastewater, continued use of groundwater, industrial reuse and community-based schemes designed to cut consumption. Suellen Jerrard, *The West Australian*, April 11 2008. It's odourless and tasteless. There is no known risk to human health. We have been reassured by the experts that it contains no viruses, bacteria or hormones. It has passed through a multi-stage refinement process that can include ultraviolet disinfection, advanced oxidation, reverse osmosis and ultra filtration. It's probably more pure than water from your tap and some bottled water. But we don't want to drink it. David Kav, *The West Australian*, March 31 2007. When Colin Barnett suddenly dropped a proposal for a Kimberley water canal into the election debate two years ago he sought to stir the public imagination by revisiting a grand WA tradition. This has to do with big ideas for a big state. Editorial, *The West Australian*, January 13 2007. God says in the Bible: 'When I shut up the heavens so that there is no rain, or command locusts to devour the land or send a plague among my people, if my people…will humble themselves and pray and seek my face and turn from their wicked way, then I will hear from heaven and will forgive their sin and will heal their land,' 2 Chronicles 7:13-14. It's obvious from the verses above what we need to do to make it rain but I cannot see it happening…Lin Brown, *The West Australian*, April 24 2007. …a vast subterranean and surface system of drains was begun in and around Perth in 1912 and 1913…This drainage system now involves about 800 km of subterranean and more than 4000 km of surface drains. The water authority has no idea how much water these drains empty into our rivers and the ocean each year. Richard Titelius, *The West Australian*, July 30 2007. A group of eminent WA scientists has launched a scathing attack on the plan to tap the South West Yarragadee aquifer to boost Perth's drinking water supplies. Amanda Banks and Graham Mason, *The West Australian*, March 26 2007. The precautionary principle means you must look at all potential risks and if any seem to lead to irreversible problems, then you should not proceed. This project [tapping the Yarragadee] has no such problems. It is a wonderful resource, deep underground flowing substantially out to sea. Professor Peter Newman, *The West Australian*, April 3 2007. Perth's suburbs are sinking as much as 5 cm a year as a result of widespread pumping of water from aquifers under the city, satellite research reveals. Daniel Hatch, *The West Australian*, March 17 2008. Parts of the Swan River would be dead within 10 years unless farmers and gardeners stopped using fertilisers which caused choking algal blooms and massive fish deaths, WA's top environmental watchdog has warned. Kim Macdonald, *The West Australian*, February 28 2007.

# FOOD

**For decades they stood up to the relentless march of suburbia – tending their small patches of land as housing developments sprang up around them. But the combination of a booming population and skyrocketing land values is killing the humble suburban market garden which now only occasionally breaks up the sprawl of tiled rooftops...**
Jodie Thompson, *The West Australian*, May 10 2008.

Rising food prices have led to a dramatic increase in the number of people growing their own food. Giovanni Torre, *The West Australian*, April 28 2008. Agriculture Minister Kim Chance conceded WA was facing major food security issues as fruit as vegetable growers faced urban encroachment, water availability issues, competitions form cheap imports and tight margins. He said longer-term solutions lay in strategic planning particularly for land use rather than increased regulation. Giovanni Torre, *The West Australian*, April 28 2008. **Australia's biggest supermarket group yesterday added its voice to warnings that shoppers can expect to pay even more for food this year because of rising global prices for fuel and agricultural commodities.** Sean Smith and Shane Wright, *The West Australian*, January 31 2008. WA will struggle for food by 2020. Jodie Thomson, *The West Australian*, May 10 2008. The ambitious Ord River irrigation scheme could more than double if the Government's expansion plans are successful. After battling public perceptions that it's a white elephant, the scheme is set to come into its own by expanding from 13,000 hectares of irrigated agriculture to 29,000 hectares fed by Lake Argyle. The Ord irrigation area produces between 50 million and 70 million dollars worth of crops a year. Gareth Parker, *The West Australian*, January 13 2007. When you are talking about 2040 you are basically talking about generational change. By then we could be using farming systems we don't even know about yet. Slade Brockman, *The West Australian*, July 19 2007.

4

# MAPPING

In determining opportunities and constraints for the future growth of the city, it is important to accurately map the city's landscape conditions and factor these into any future development.

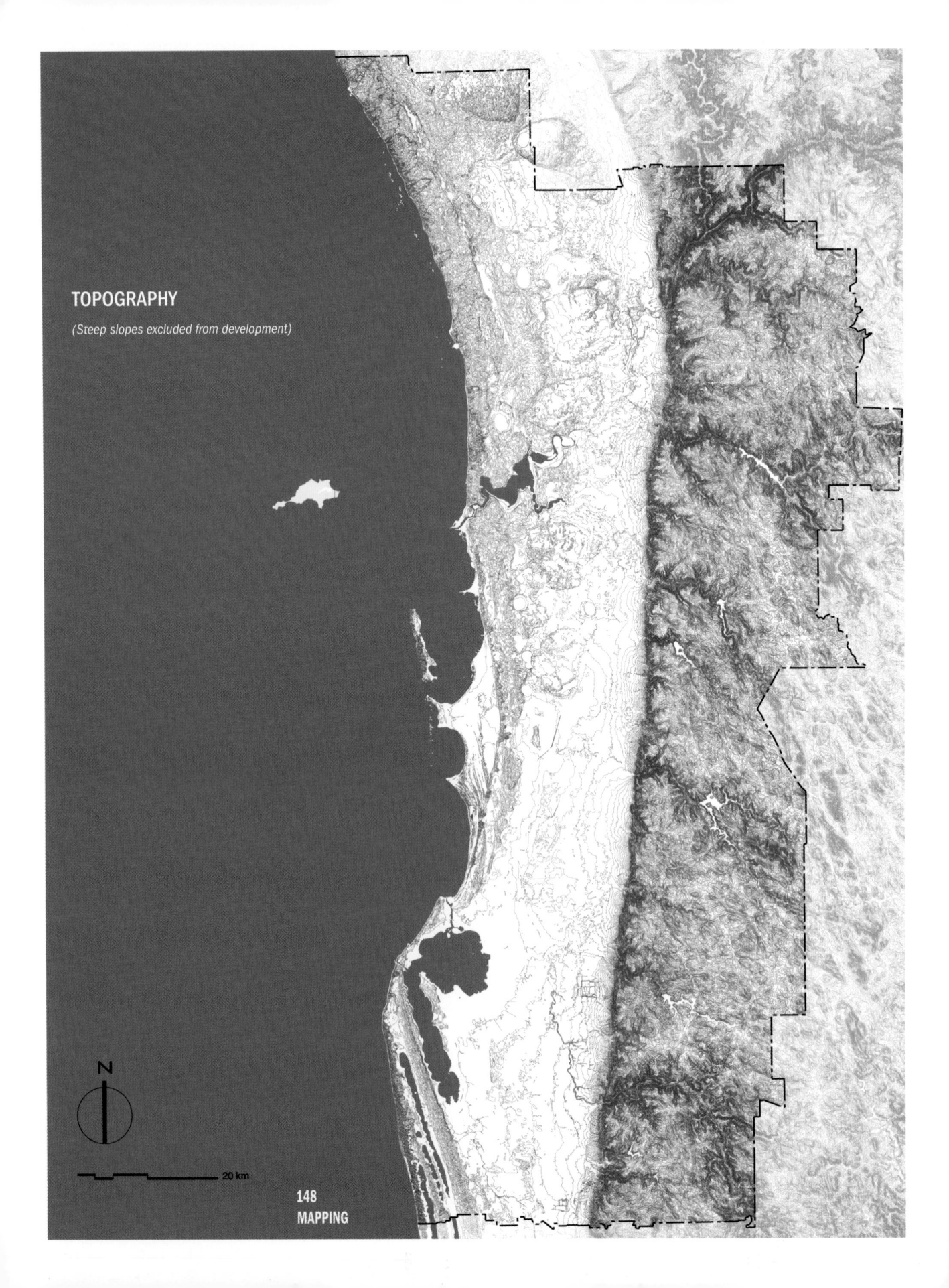

# TOPOGRAPHY
*(Steep slopes excluded from development)*

148
MAPPING

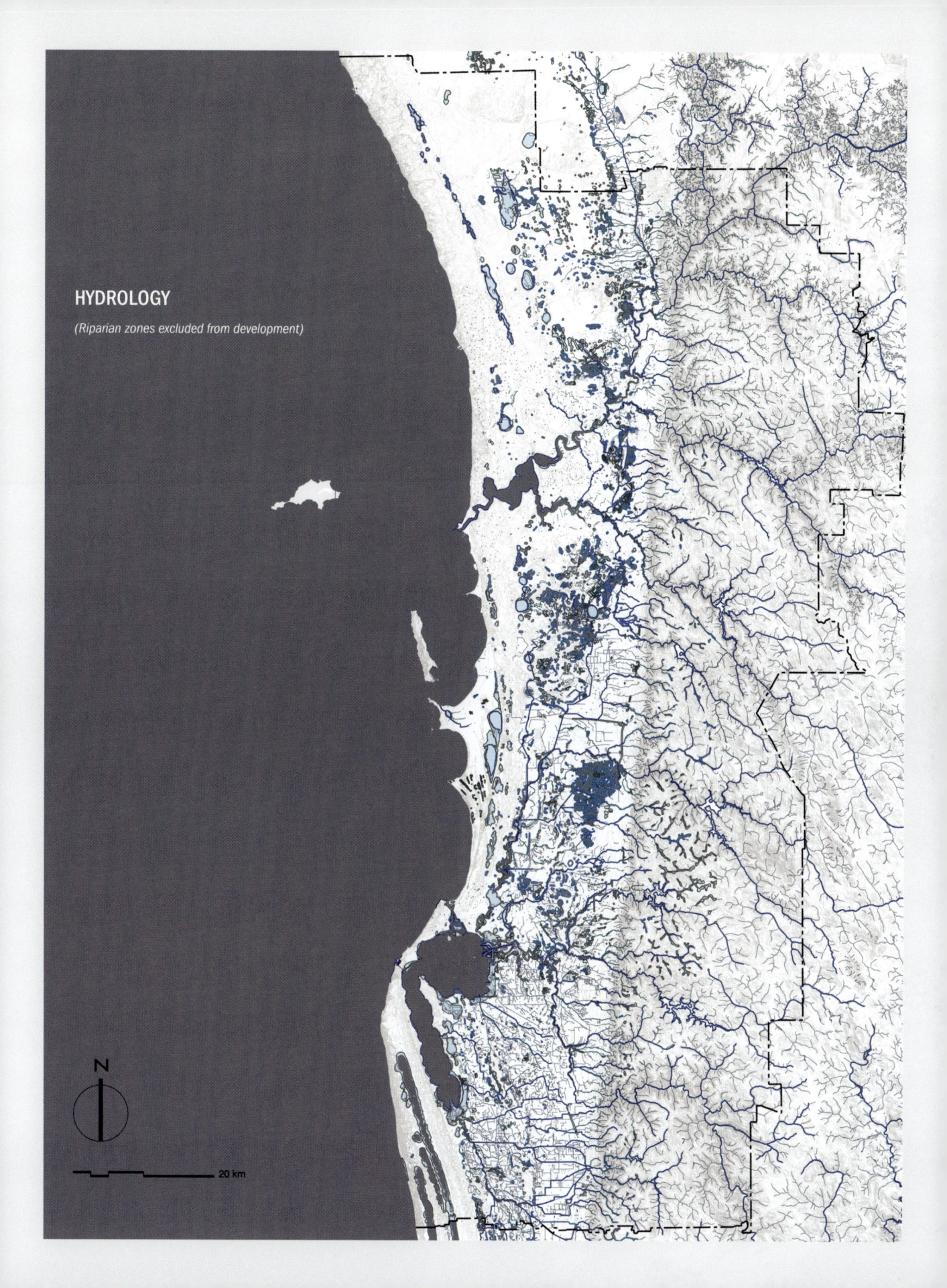

# HYDROLOGY
*(Riparian zones excluded from development)*

20 km

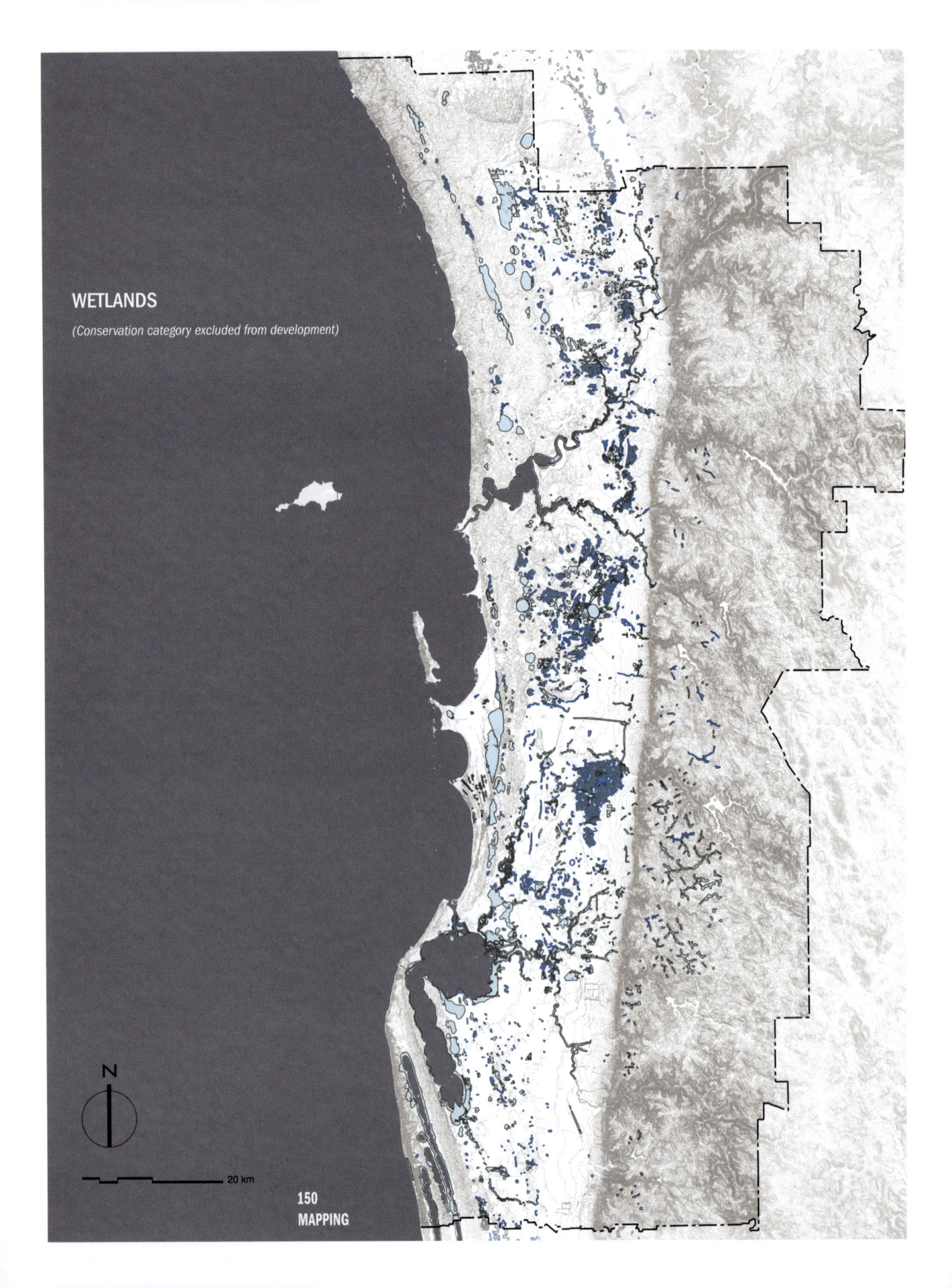

# WETLANDS
*(Conservation category excluded from development)*

20 km

150
MAPPING

## WETLANDS

*Resource enhancement – developable*

20 km

GROUNDWATER CONTOURS

20 km

152
MAPPING

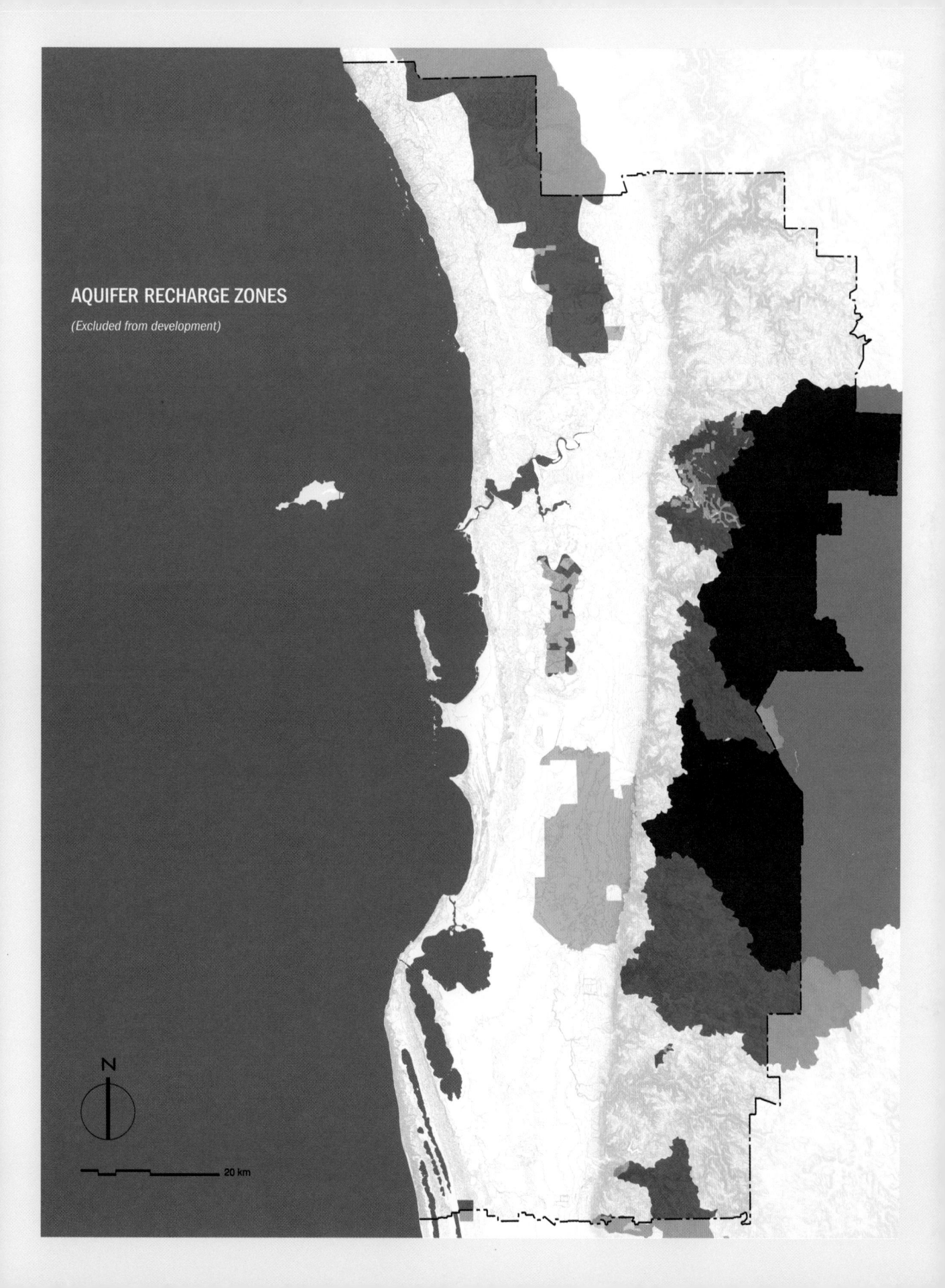

# AQUIFER RECHARGE ZONES
*(Excluded from development)*

20 km

# REMNANT VEGETATION
*(Including state forests excluded from development)*

20 km

154
MAPPING

**PUBLIC OPEN SPACE**
*(Excluded from development)*

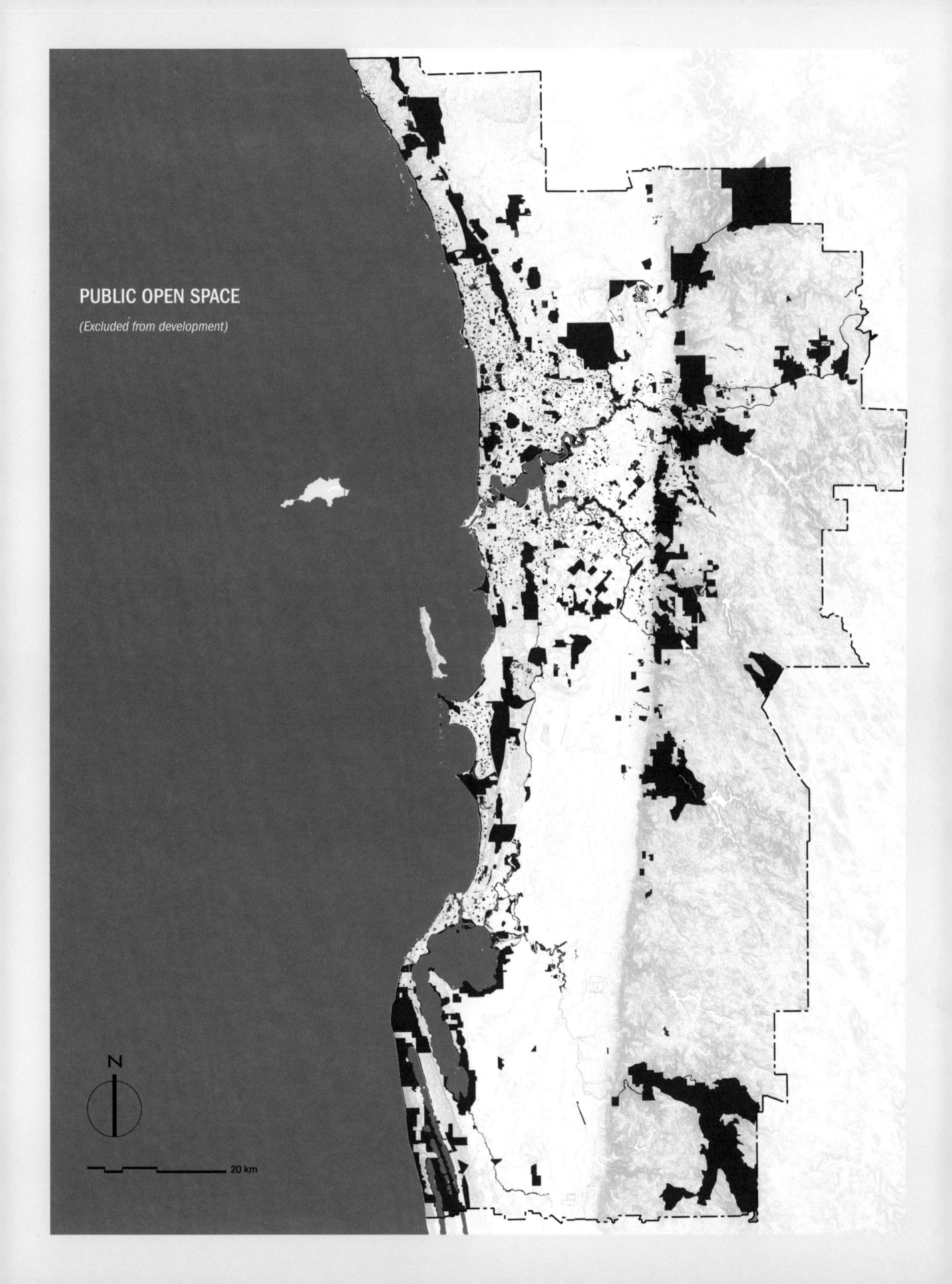

N

20 km

**BUSH FOREVER SITES**
*(Excluded from development)*

20 km

156
MAPPING

**INDIGENOUS CLAIMS**

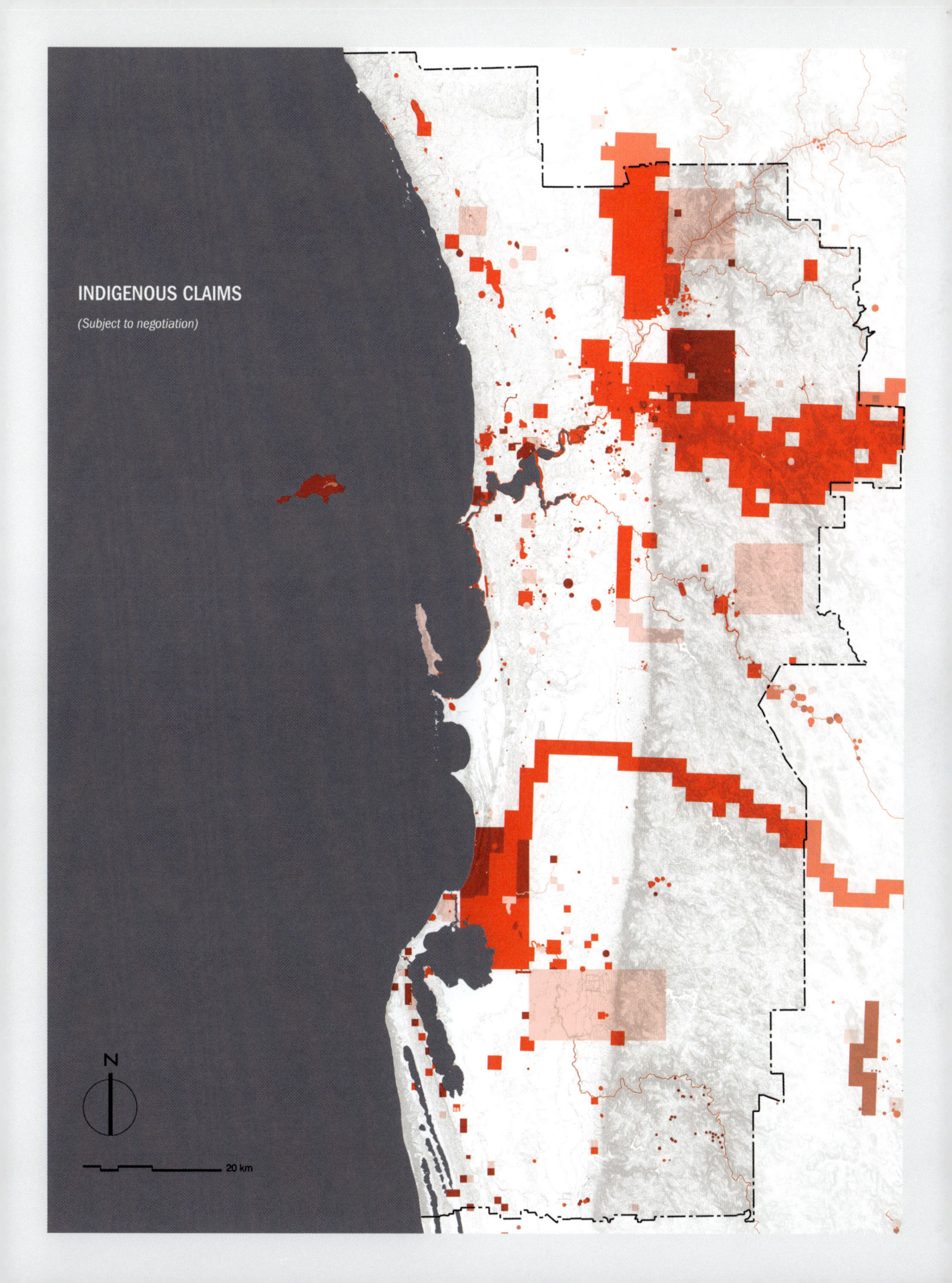

*(Subject to negotiation)*

20 km

POWER GRID

20 km

158
MAPPING

ROAD AND RAIL

20 km

WASTEWATER

N

20 km

160
MAPPING

SCHEME WATER

20 km

REGIONAL HABITAT MATRIX

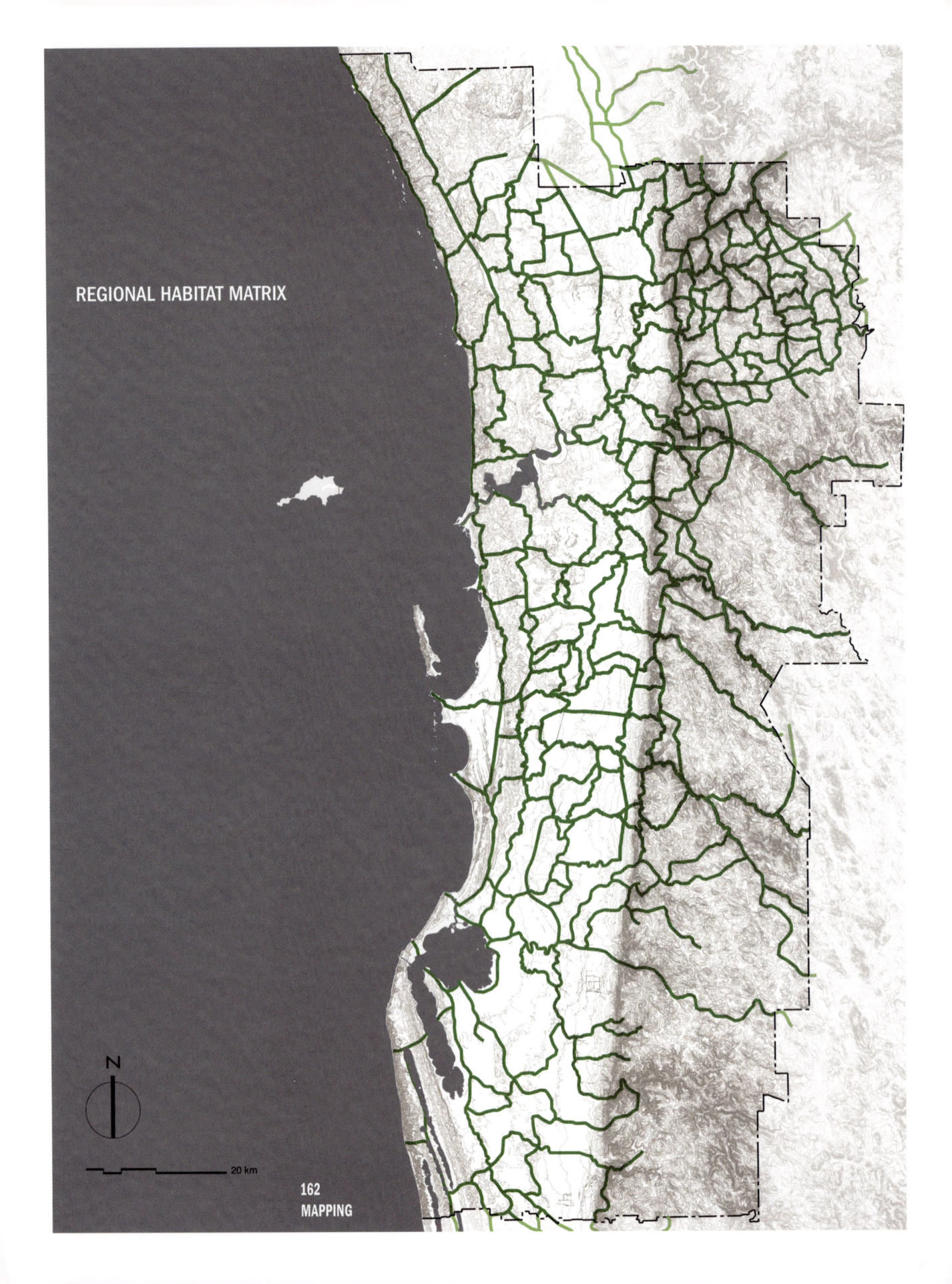

162
MAPPING

## CURRENT ZONING

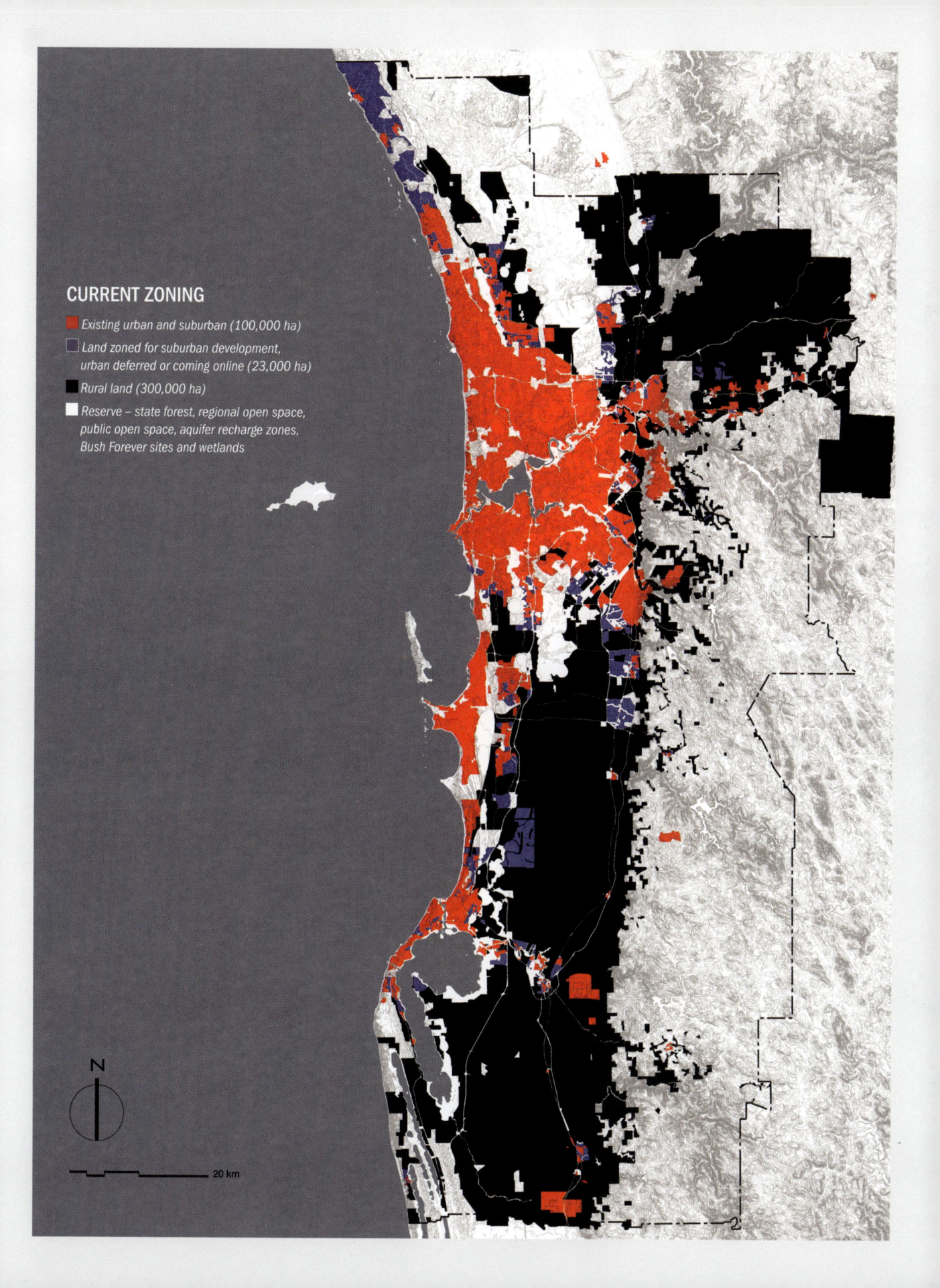

■ Existing urban and suburban (100,000 ha)
■ Land zoned for suburban development, urban deferred or coming online (23,000 ha)
■ Rural land (300,000 ha)
□ Reserve – state forest, regional open space, public open space, aquifer recharge zones, Bush Forever sites and wetlands

20 km

5

# METHOD

To begin the process of creating multiple urban-growth scenarios we have appraised Perth from a regional landscape perspective. The landscape thus forms the foundation from which the various urban-growth scenarios emerge.

METHODOLOGY

Urban Design     *Scenarios*     Landscape Planning

Landscape Urbanism

McHarg     MVRDV

Constraints     Opportunities
Greenfield     Infill

*Representation,
public communication,
political action*

# METHOD

To begin the process of creating multiple urban-growth scenarios we have appraised Perth from a regional landscape perspective. The landscape thus forms the foundation from which the various urban-growth scenarios emerge. When studied the landscape indicates limitations and opportunities for development that can render urban form more site-specific than is commonly the case in cities that have understood their landscape as a mere impediment to growth.

Such regionalism is part of a tradition in planning that can be traced back to the 1920s when the pre-eminent urban historian, Lewis Mumford, advocated that planning proceed with a holistic sense of a bioregion so that 'all its sites and resources, from forest to city, from highland to water level, may be soundly developed, and so that the population will be distributed so as to utilise, rather than nullify or destroy, its natural advantages. [Regional planning] sees people, industry and the land as a single unit.'[1]

Four decades later this is almost precisely the basis upon which Ian McHarg (1920–2001) developed his ecological planning method, known colloquially by the title of his famous book *Design with Nature*.[2] McHarg's life work was devoted to developing a planning methodology which could be universally applied to logically determine where development should and should not occurr. His philosophical and practical intention was to achieve a maximum 'fitness' between culture and nature. For McHarg, the pure logic of landscape systems, as described by scientists, provided the master narrative to which, what he perceived to be a civilisation built on hubris, should be corrected. For McHarg, the existing landscape provided guidelines by which cities should be shaped.

McHarg's method, known as 'sieve mapping' was to layer maps of all the various elements that collectively make up a landscape and then define the optimal conditions for certain types of development. For example, one might say that houses should only be built on north-facing slopes of a certain steepness, with a certain geology, in areas where there is no existing vegetation. By layering all the individual maps of the landscape and allowing the maps to cancel one another out wherever they do not meet these conditions, the resultant (or sieved) map has logically determined the places where these conditions are met and thus where housing should be sited.

Of course, what may or may not be the optimal conditions for certain types of development and the values upon which we develop places are more complicated than McHarg's method suggests. McHarg tried to refine the method to make it account for this complexity. With the benefit of over four decades of planners applying and innovating upon

1 Hall, P., *Cities of Tomorrow: An Intellectual History of Urban Planning and Design in the Twentieth Century* (3rd ed.), Blackwell Publishing, Oxford, 2002, p. 161.

2 McHarg, I., *Design with Nature*, Natural History Press, Philadelphia, 1969.

*Topography*

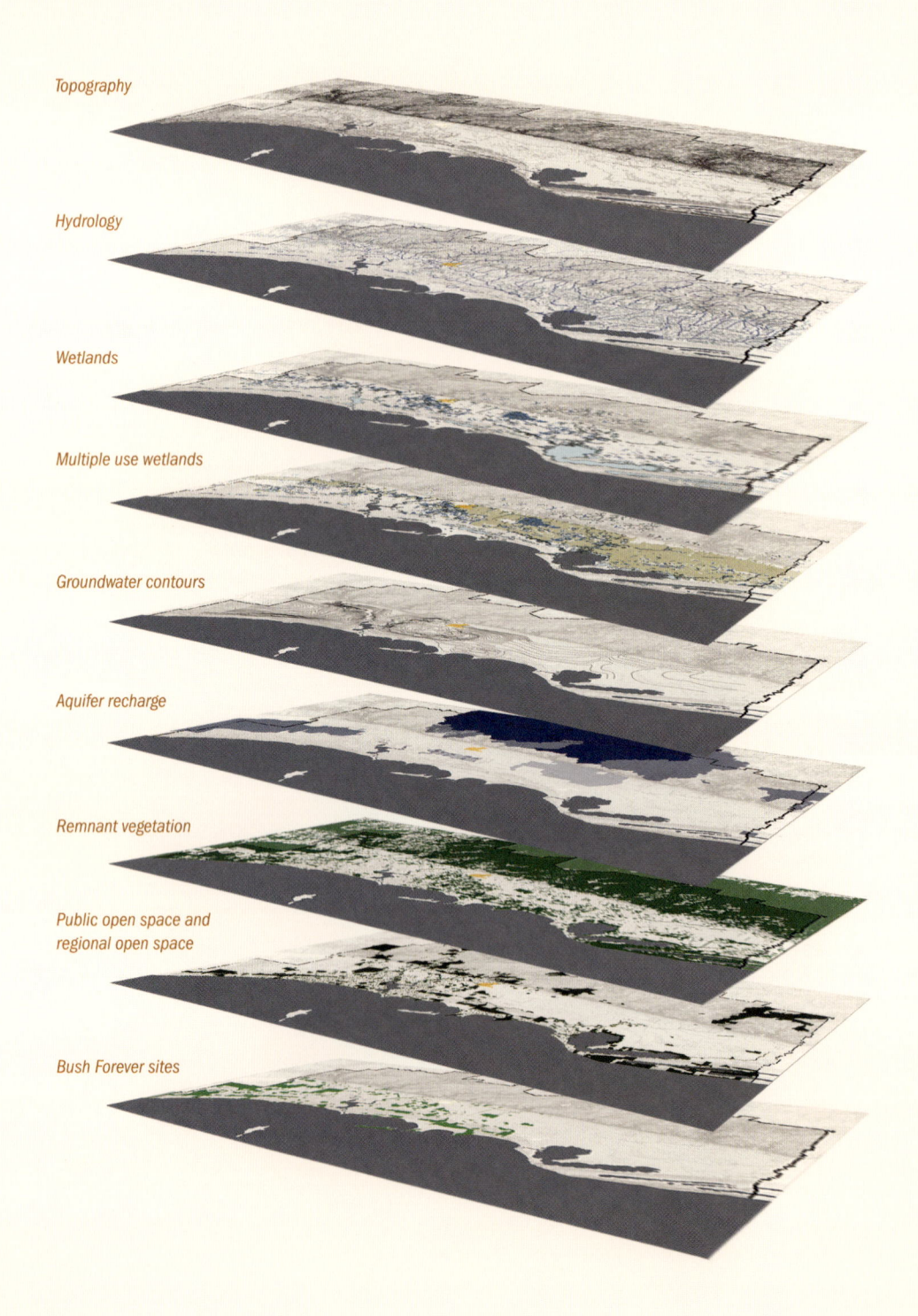

*Hydrology*

*Wetlands*

*Multiple use wetlands*

*Groundwater contours*

*Aquifer recharge*

*Remnant vegetation*

*Public open space and regional open space*

*Bush Forever sites*

**168
METHOD**

METHOD

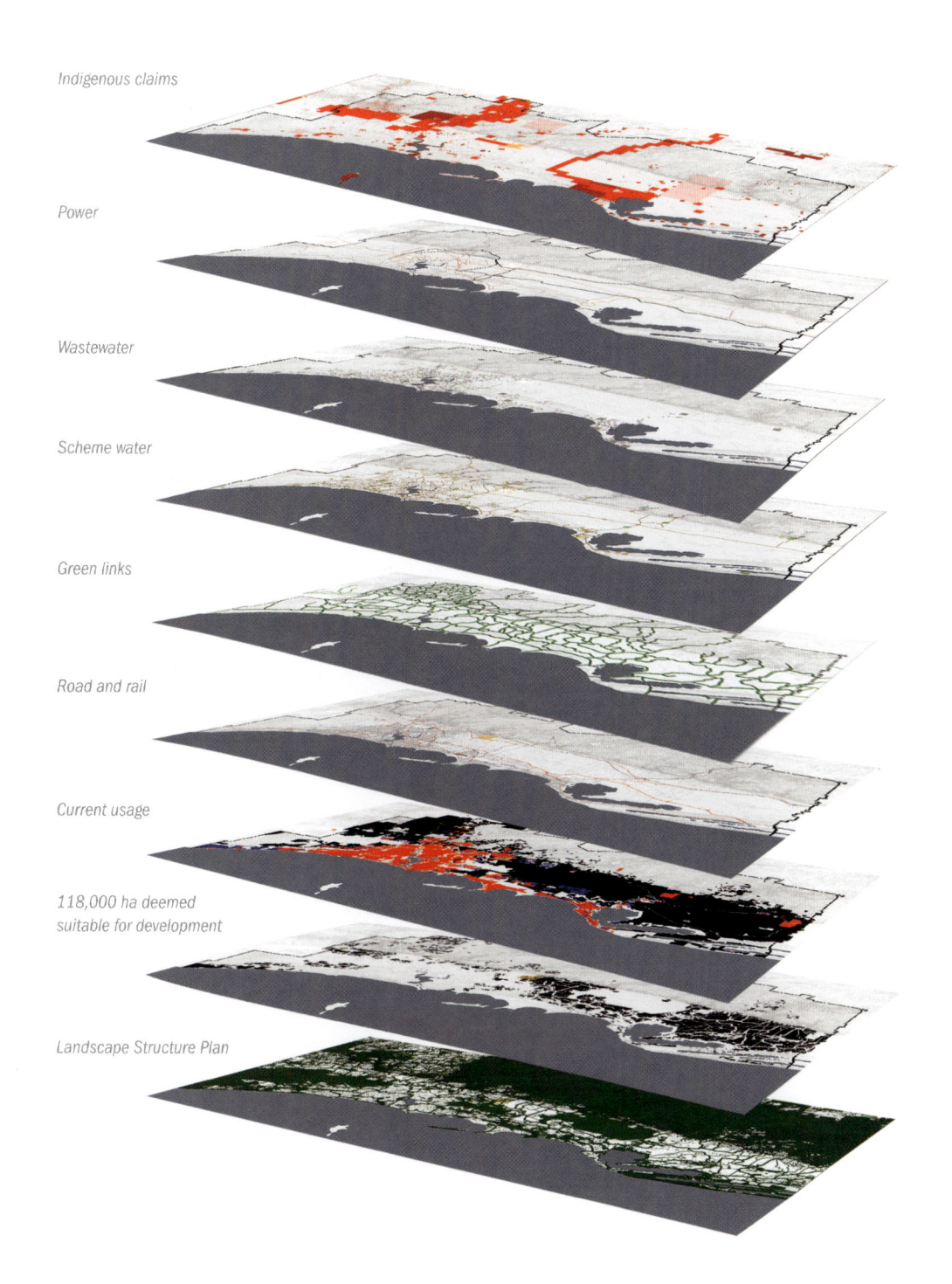

*Indigenous claims*

*Power*

*Wastewater*

*Scheme water*

*Green links*

*Road and rail*

*Current usage*

*118,000 ha deemed suitable for development*

*Landscape Structure Plan*

## COMPILATION MAP

The compilation of all the mapping layers and subsequent subtraction of all development extinguishing layers leads to both a Landscape Structure Plan for the whole city and a final map (see following pages), which identifies land that is (from a biophysical perspective) suitable for development.

20 km

McHarg's method, it seems, however, that we may never arrive at a perfectly logical (and computerised) mapping system that absorbs all the data of the city and the landscape and reconciles the two in harmony. The world just doesn't work that way.

Nonetheless, McHarg's method remains good at determining where, on a large scale, it would be sensible to build and not to build in regard to fundamental landscape conditions. Applying the basic method to the Perth Metropolitan Region we concluded that existing vegetation, wetlands, flood zones, riparian buffer zones, aquifer recharge zones and steep slopes greater than 25% should be exempt from development potential. In addition to subtracting (or sieving) these 'no-go' areas we have made allowance for a regional network of public open space and habitat corridors, which shouldn't be impinged upon by development. The result of this process of sieving is a final Landscape Structure Plan for the whole city.[3] (See map page 172.) What is indicated as green on this map cannot be developed and what is white can be.

When the habitat corridors and the other no-go areas are subtracted from the Perth Metropolitan Region there remains 118,000 hectares of currently undeveloped land suitable for suburban growth, enough land for 1,246,080 dwellings or an additional 2,865,984 people, should the city decide to continue sprawling. Almost all of this land is degraded rural land with little to no current agrarian productivity. Of this land 66,000 hectares is classified as 'multiple use wetlands': it can be developed but often requires fill in order to increase the land's surface level above the groundwater so as to legally support typical suburban housing.

While McHarg's method remains proficient at identifying where not to develop, it is not necessarily good at determining *how* or *what* to develop. In this regard we have been concerned to avoid what Professor James Corner of the University of Pennsylvania referred to as the 'tyranny of positivism' in regard to McHarg's methodology, by not expecting the method to do any more than identify large-scale setbacks from certain natural systems.[4]

In regard to conceiving of how and what to develop, it is the Dutch design group, MVRDV, who have inspired us.[5] Where McHarg was profoundly distrustful of modernity's dream of unlimited economic progress and a world re-engineered to meet all our desires, MVRDV, in the spirit and the tradition of the Dutch landscape and culture from which they emerge, approach the challenges of contemporary development and ecological limitations with profligate optimism. Where McHarg believed the organism had to fit into its environment with minimal impact, MVRDV's proposals tend to hybridise natural and

3 This matrix of green corridors is recommended by the Perth Biodiversity Project and has for the purposes of our study been included as land that cannot be developed in any of our scenarios. del Marco, A. & Taylor, R., et al. *Local Government Biodiversity Planning Guidelines for the Perth Metropolitan Region*, Western Australia Local Government Association, Perth, 2004.

4 Corner, J., 'Discourse on Theory II, Three Tyrannies of Contemporary Theory and the Alternative of Hermeneutics', *Landscape Journal*, vol. 10, 1991, p. 117.

Corner makes a second, more recent, reference to planning that became slavishly deterministic when he writes: 'Too many followers of McHarg simply adopted a methodology for practice, and while most shared his ecological ethics and viewpoint, they failed to grasp the larger conceptual, innovative and artistic dimensions of what still lies dormant in the potential of ecological concepts.' Corner, J., '"Creativity Permeates the Evolution of Matter and Life": The McHarg Event: An Unfinished Project', *Ian McHarg: Conversations with Students: Dwelling in Nature*, Margulis, L., et al. (eds), Princeton Architectural Press, New York, 2007, p. 99.

5 For MVRDV see: <http://www.mvrdv.nl/_v2/.> In addition, for critical discussion of the theory and practice of MVRDV see: *Reading MVRDV*, NAi Publishers, Rotterdam, 2003.

## LANDSCAPE STRUCTURE PLAN

One by-product of the mapping process is a Landscape Structure Plan (LSP) for Perth. The LSP asserts a landscape structure for the city of Perth at a regional scale. It interlinks existing reserves with new reserves to form a holististic open space system, guaranteeing the health of some of the landscape systems that are essential to the ecology of the city. In principle the green areas are set back from development and when development occurs in the white areas then that development is expected to make an investment in the LSP's reserved lands.

20 km

## DEVELOPABLE LAND

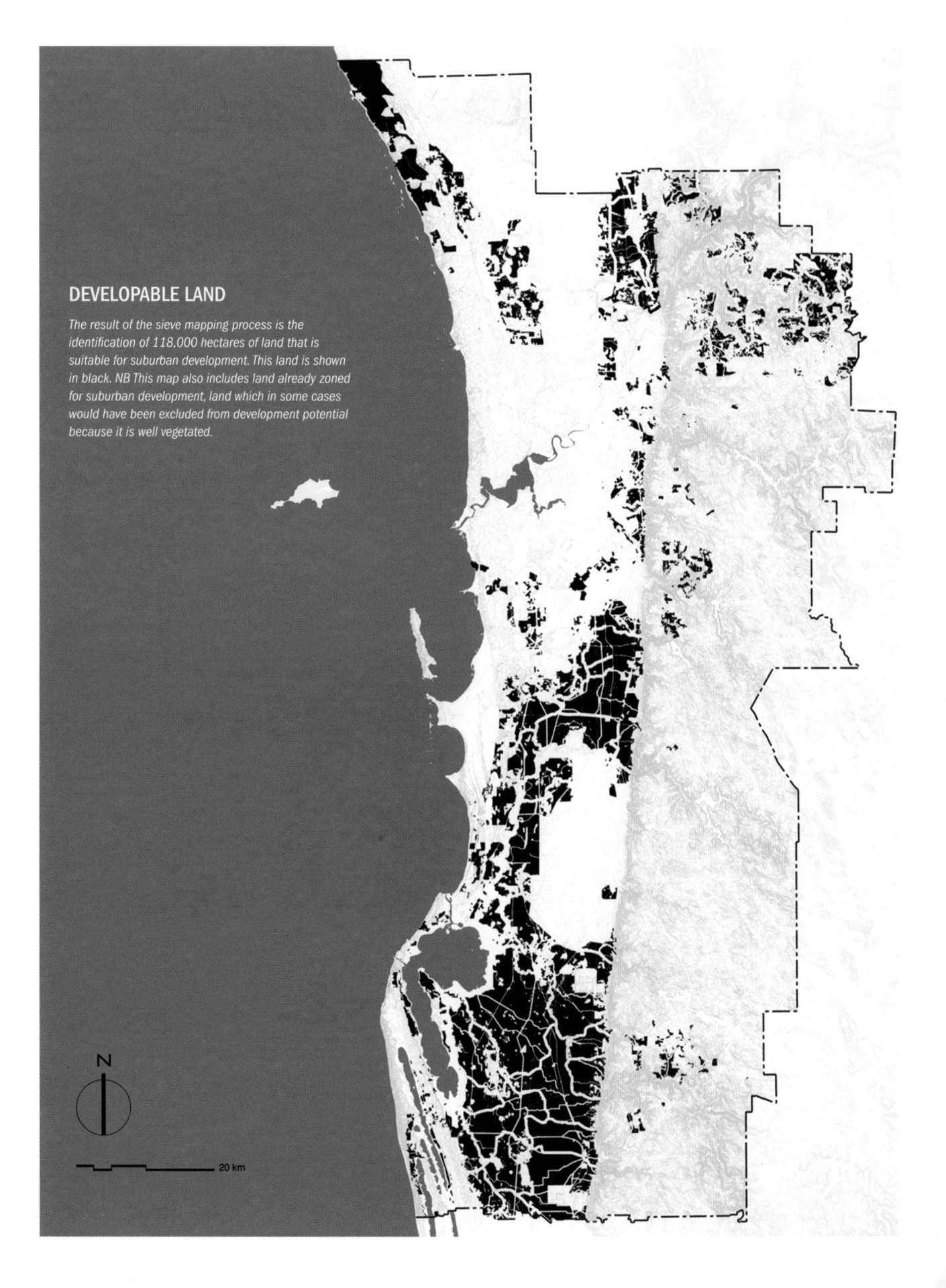

*The result of the sieve mapping process is the identification of 118,000 hectares of land that is suitable for suburban development. This land is shown in black. NB This map also includes land already zoned for suburban development, land which in some cases would have been excluded from development potential because it is well vegetated.*

20 km

With a 118,000 hectare land bank,

Perth could sprawl well beyond 2050.

175
**METHOD**

# METHOD

6   *KM3 Excursions on Capacities*, MVRDV Actar Publications, Barcelona, 2005.

7   A good example of MVRDV's scenario method is available in Eisinger, A. & Schneider, M. (eds), *Urban-Scape Switzerland: Topology and Regional Development in Switzerland Investigations and Case Studies*, Avenir Suisse, Berlin, 2003, pp. 212-235.

cultural systems into ingenious new growth trajectories. As polemic, MVRDV's work is brilliant, but as exemplified by their latest extrapolation, KM$^3$ – a 5 x 5 kilometre cube in which one million people could live a life utterly divorced from the land – it is also (perhaps intentionally) dystopian.[6] McHarg's philosophical antipathy toward the city, and his preoccupation with constraining it, is balanced by MVRDV's emphasis on leveraging ecological limits to generate creative opportunities. Inversely, MVRDV's proclivity for engineered excess is tempered by McHarg's genuine reverence for existing ecologies.

We have found that the combination of the differences between Ian McHarg's and MVRDV's approaches helps to cancel out their respective weaknesses. Although similar to McHarg insofar as they also believe in initially basing the design process on empirical data sets, MVRDV departs from McHarg's singular use of data to arrive at one resolutely correct masterplan by using the data (as we have done) to produce multiple development scenarios.[7]

In short, what we have found is that McHargian sieve mapping has been a good guide for determining where horizontal development should occur, whereas MVRDV's work has been inspirational in helping us conceive of bold vertical (infill) development scenarios. The scenarios documented in this book then demonstrate the results of combining the methods of both McHarg and MVRDV. This is what we call landscape urbanism.

*Whereas McHarg argued that cities should be shaped according to their landscape guidelines and within their landscape limits, the Dutch architects, MVRDV, have recently concluded that everything needed to sustain one million people can be contained in a 5 km cube. The image to the right shows this 5 km cube scaled accurately in relation to the CBD of Perth.*

177
**METHOD**

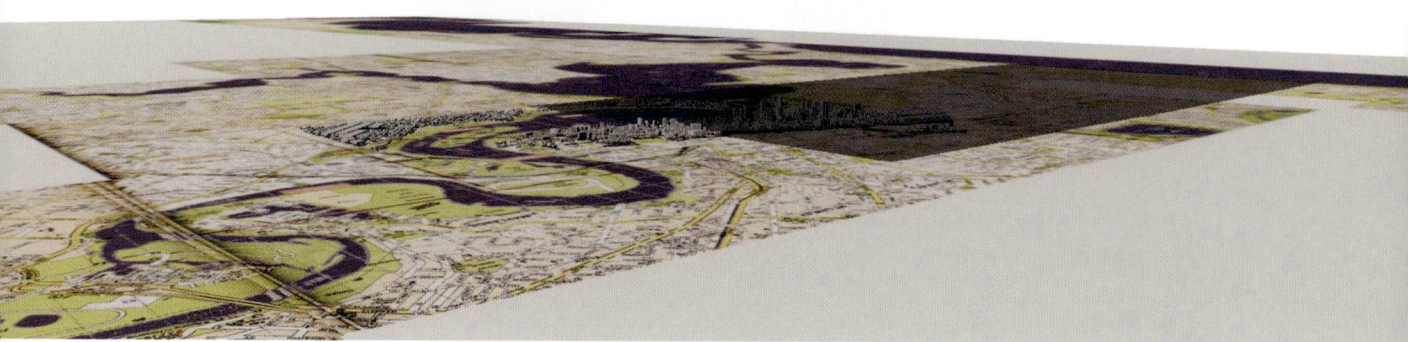

6

# BAU CITY

'Business as Usual'

Australian Dreamscape

*Photomontage by Andy Thomas*

# BAU CITY

In this scenario, to accommodate most of the predicted population increase, Perth would simply continue to build low-density suburbs the way it does now. With over 178 years' experience in a sandy landscape that can be easily remodelled, Perth is very good at constructing relatively high-standard suburbia. The standards for such suburban development are enshrined in the local development guideline 'Liveable Neighbourhoods.'[1] Covering everything from road layout to the design of public open spaces, 'Liveable Neighbourhoods' is a set of design guidelines conceived to ensure that our suburbs are well crafted at the human scale but it doesn't, and nor can it be expected to, substantively challenge suburban orthodoxy.

Supporting around 1.5 million people, the current urban footprint of Perth is 100,000 hectares. The average density is six dwellings per hectare (the average density in many European cities is 250 dwellings per hectare, often more). In addition to 100,000 hectares of built form, the Perth Metropolitan Region includes 300,000 hectares of rural land and 142,000 hectares of state forest. Based on sieve mapping (see Mapping) our analysis concludes that of this land, 118,000 is (including 23,000 hectares already zoned for development) appropriate for suburbanisation. Exempt from this 118,000 hectares are aquifer recharge zones, conservation category and resource enhancement wetlands,[2] state forest, floodplains, extant vegetation and steep slopes.

Industrial and other uses account for 12,000 of the 100,000 hectare urban footprint. Presumably this amount would need to be reproduced to sustain an extra 1.5 million people. Subtracting this area from the available 118,000 hectares leaves 103,840 hectares of land for potential residential development. If this land was developed at an average density of 12 homes per hectare (the typical density of contemporary suburban developments) then 1,246,080 new free-standing homes (2,865,984 people at 2.3 people per home) can be accommodated, significantly more than is needed by 2050.

Much of the 118,000 hectares of land remaining in Perth for possible suburbanisation has a high water table. That is, if you dig down a metre or so you will strike groundwater. Of the developable 118,000 hectares of land 66,000 hectares are classified as 'multiple use wetlands', a zoning that doesn't preclude development. In order to develop this land it must be built up above the water table so that the home's foundations are guaranteed to be at least 120 centimetres above the water table. If we accept that this practice of importing fill to elevate the profile of low-lying land is, as some argue, unsustainable, then we either need to design a new form of mass housing that can occupy this low-lying land, or preclude the land from residential development. If the latter became the case then we are left with only

[1] Western Australian Planning Commission, Liveable Neighbourhoods, 2007. Available at <http://www.planning.wa.gov.au/publications/liveable/LN_ed2.pdf>.

[2] Conservation category wetlands must be excluded and protected from development. Resource enhancement wetlands also need to be set aside from development but require rehabilitation.

CUT

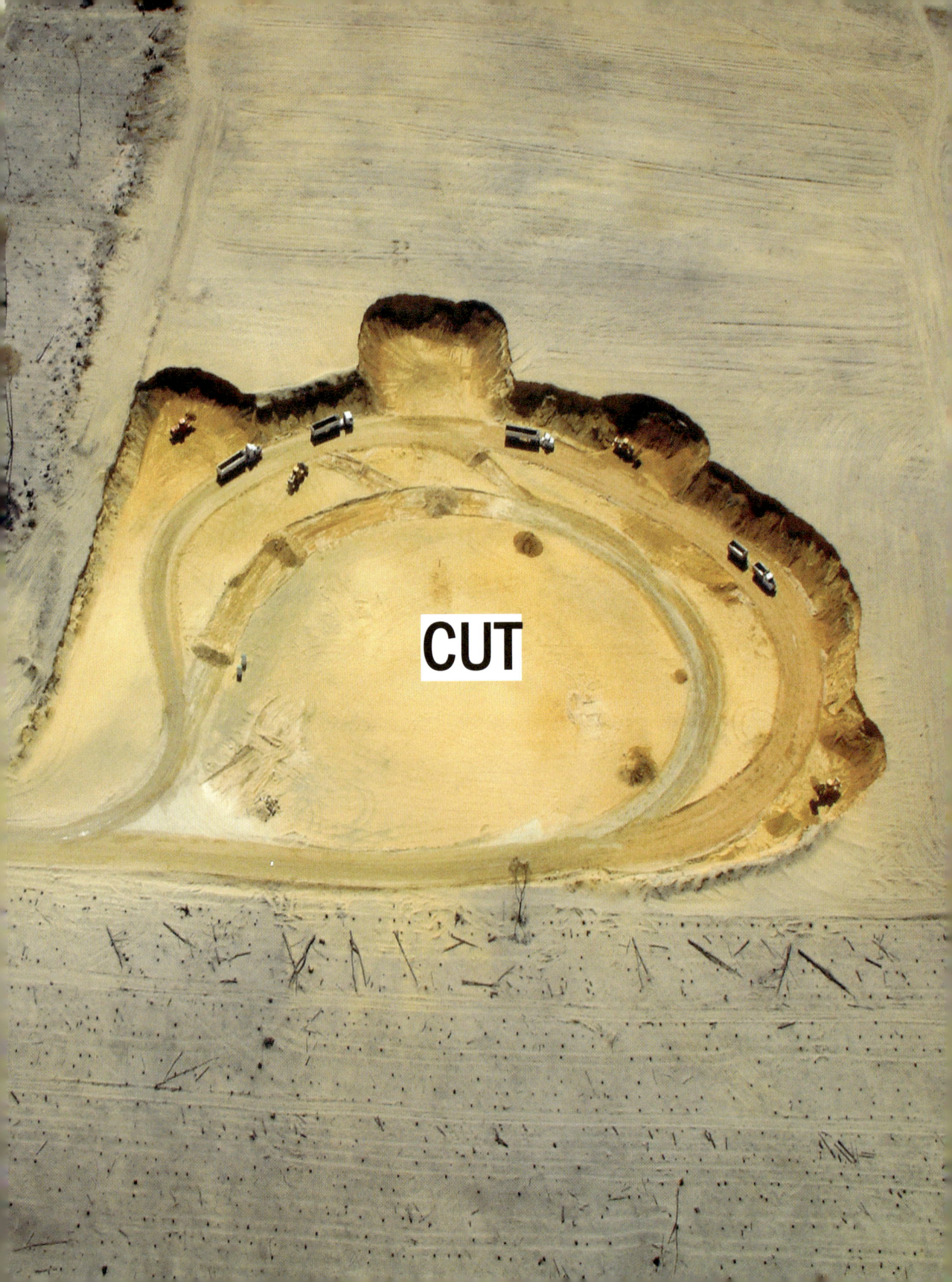

FILL

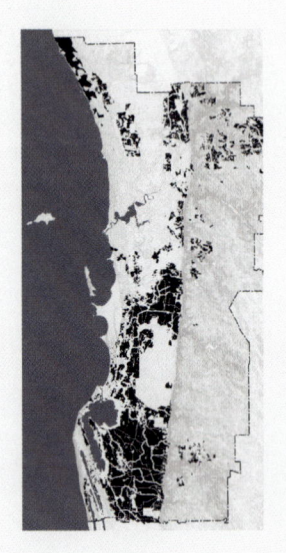

118,000 hectares of developable land

minus 66,000 hectares of multiple use wetlands

equals 52,000 hectares of developable land.

A rationalised BAU City developed to meet the 2050 population would then look something like this.

52,000 hectares of land from the original 118,000 that is technically suitable for Business as Usual suburban development. These 52,000 hectares could accommodate 624,000 homes for 1,435,200 people. If you look at the distribution of this land on the map on the page opposite, however, it is extremely fragmented and thus difficult to service and reconnect to the main organs of the existing city.

If, on the other hand, we continue to broach the problem of low-lying land with the use of fill then the conclusion is that Perth has a 118,000 hectare land bank and can continue to spread out, probably right through to the end of the 21st Century. To meet the predicted population increase of 1.5 million people upon which this research was originally based, 15,527 homes need to be built per annum. The local housing industry believes that if unhindered, it can deliver 20,000 homes per annum so on a strictly mathematical basis BAU City can facilitate Perth's predicted growth.[3] Currently, however, there is only 23,000 hectares of land zoned for suburbanisation. At an orthodox suburban density this land could accommodate approximately 634,800 people in 276,000 dwellings, significantly less than the predicted 2050 population increase.[4] In a Business as Usual scenario Perth will therefore have to rapidly release large tracts of peripheral land to meet demand.

As noted in the introduction, at the time of going to press the ABS had issued a new maximum projection for Perth's 2056 population. If the projection of a total 2056 population of 4.2 million people is borne out, then approximately 2.7 million additional people will require housing over the course of the next four decades. If these people are to be housed in free-standing homes then 1,173,913 homes are required. As we have seen, there is land available for 1,246,080 homes set out at an average density of 12 homes per hectare in the current Perth metropolitan area. To satisfy demand however the housing industry would need to increase production from 20,000 to more than 23,000 homes per annum.

If this BAU City scenario comes into being then from north to south, Perth would become a 170-kilometre-long city, a flatland of suburban sprawl covering over 200,000 hectares of land. From today's perspective it is dubious as to whether cars running on fossil fuels (or any other efficient form of individualised transport) will be available to service such a vast suburban landscape. This problem could be partially overcome by the creation of a comprehensive public transport matrix (see page 291), assuming this matrix can be retrofitted into the existing suburban fabric of the city so as to link the new suburbs of BAU City with the existing city.

BAU City not only runs into serious problems pertaining to mobility it also raises questions about access to employment and civic amenity. New localised basins of employment and

[3] In conversation with Dale Alcock.

[4] Although often zoned for 20 homes per hectare the *2006 State of the Environment Report* concludes that the average built suburban density is 12.5 homes per net hectare. Environmental Protection Authority (EPA), *State of the Environment Report Western Australia (Draft)*, Department of Environment and Conservation, Perth, 2006, p. 229.

## BAU CITY

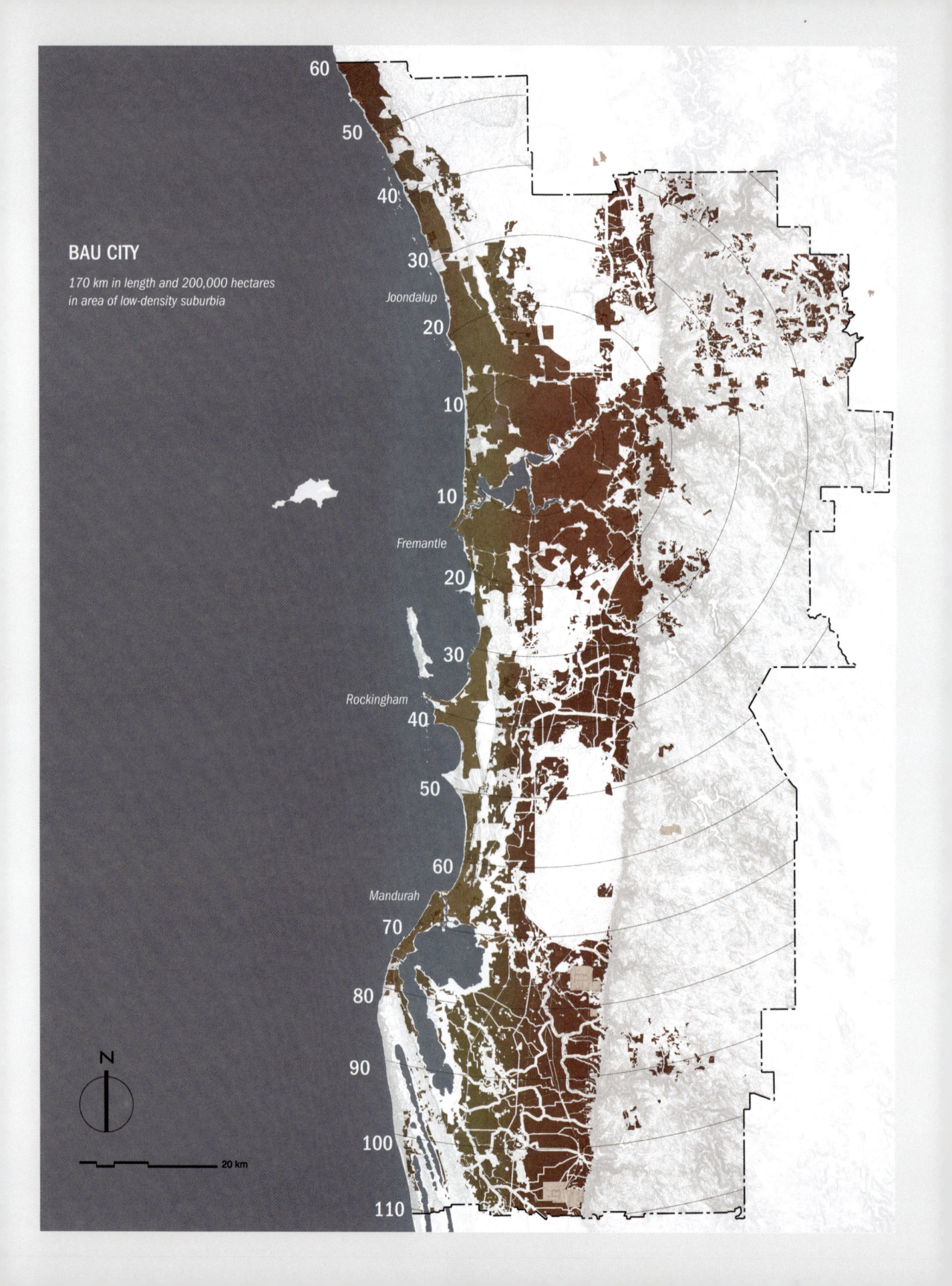

*170 km in length and 200,000 hectares in area of low-density suburbia*

Joondalup

Fremantle

Rockingham

Mandurah

20 km

civic amenity would need to be distributed across the vast suburban fabric of BAU City and the challenge will be to make these new centres attractive for future residents. The landscape upon which BAU City will be constructed is in itself relatively unattractive and can't be relied upon to provide relief from suburbia's notorious monotony.

## The problem of innovation

In accordance with current practice one could expect the new suburbs of BAU City to deploy increasingly innovative systems of transportation, energy creation, water use and housing construction. BAU City could be a landscape of gradual innovation but in the real world of contemporary suburbia, innovation is, at the best of times, hard won. Although the housing industry can probably meet demand if the land is released in time, the pace of BAU City's construction would surely outrun the pace of innovation necessary to make it a truly sustainable landscape in the face of the 21st Century's pressing environmental challenges. A fast-tracked BAU City will struggle just to maintain, let alone improve, design standards.

Even without extreme pressure the Fordist production system that underpins suburbia generally resists innovation. Suburbia is a package of so many interlocking parts that are delivered with such efficiency and within such narrow financial margins that each resists the other to radically change. Consequently, changes to suburbia tend to be aimed at the speed of delivery, not the quality of the product being delivered. Similarly, keeping abreast of fashion, changes to suburbia tend to be cosmetic, not structural. In short, it is far easier for our suburbs to look green, than be Green.

If suburbia is to become a more ecologically sophisticated form of urbanism then, among other things, it needs to adapt to the landscape systems it otherwise tends to erase. But it is hard to reconcile the land's ecological systems with suburban systems. The reason for this is fundamental: ecological systems are organic and boundless whereas suburban systems are mechanistic; ecological systems are radically site-specific whereas suburban systems are standardised and generic. If one is to design with ecological responsibility *and* creativity, then every site requires a highly nuanced and flexible response. Yet, due to the regulations that govern the layout of housing and its related infrastructure, suburban typologies are, in a word, inflexible.

Despite the majority of consultants and service providers wanting to genuinely improve their product, real innovation commensurate with the environmental challenges of the times is unlikely to come from within the system of daily production. With urgency, innovation needs to be mandated and facilitated. The alternatives to Business as Usual offered in this book aim to kick-start that process.

2008

2050

The last time the population of Perth doubled (1970–2000) the northern suburbs were created. Are we simply going to replicate that in the next few decades towards the south?

BAU CITY

191
BAU CITY

Changes to suburbia tend to be cosmetic, not structural. In short, it is far easier for our suburbs to look green than be Green.

1750
Stourhead, England

2008
Perth, Australia

BAU CITY

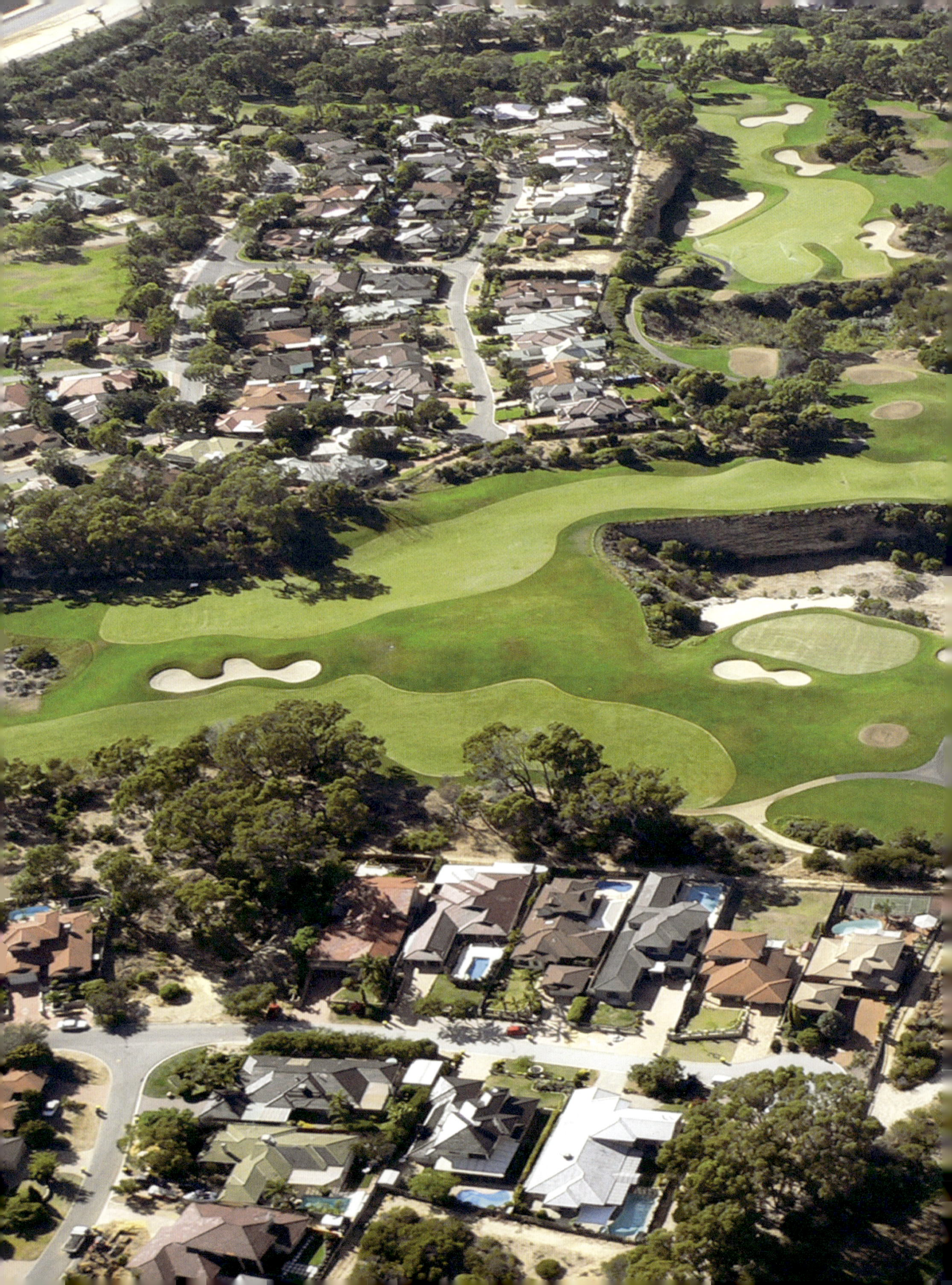

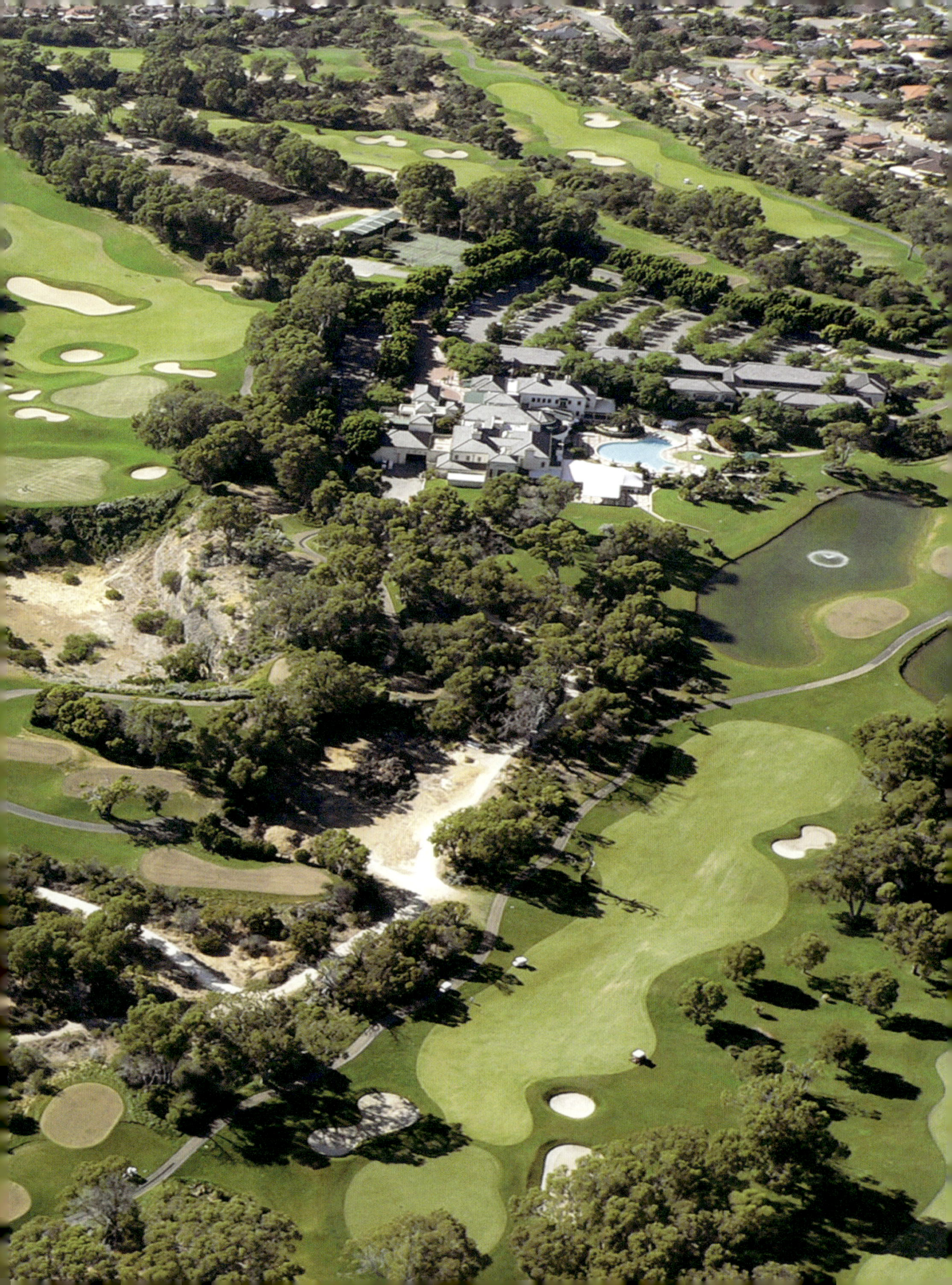

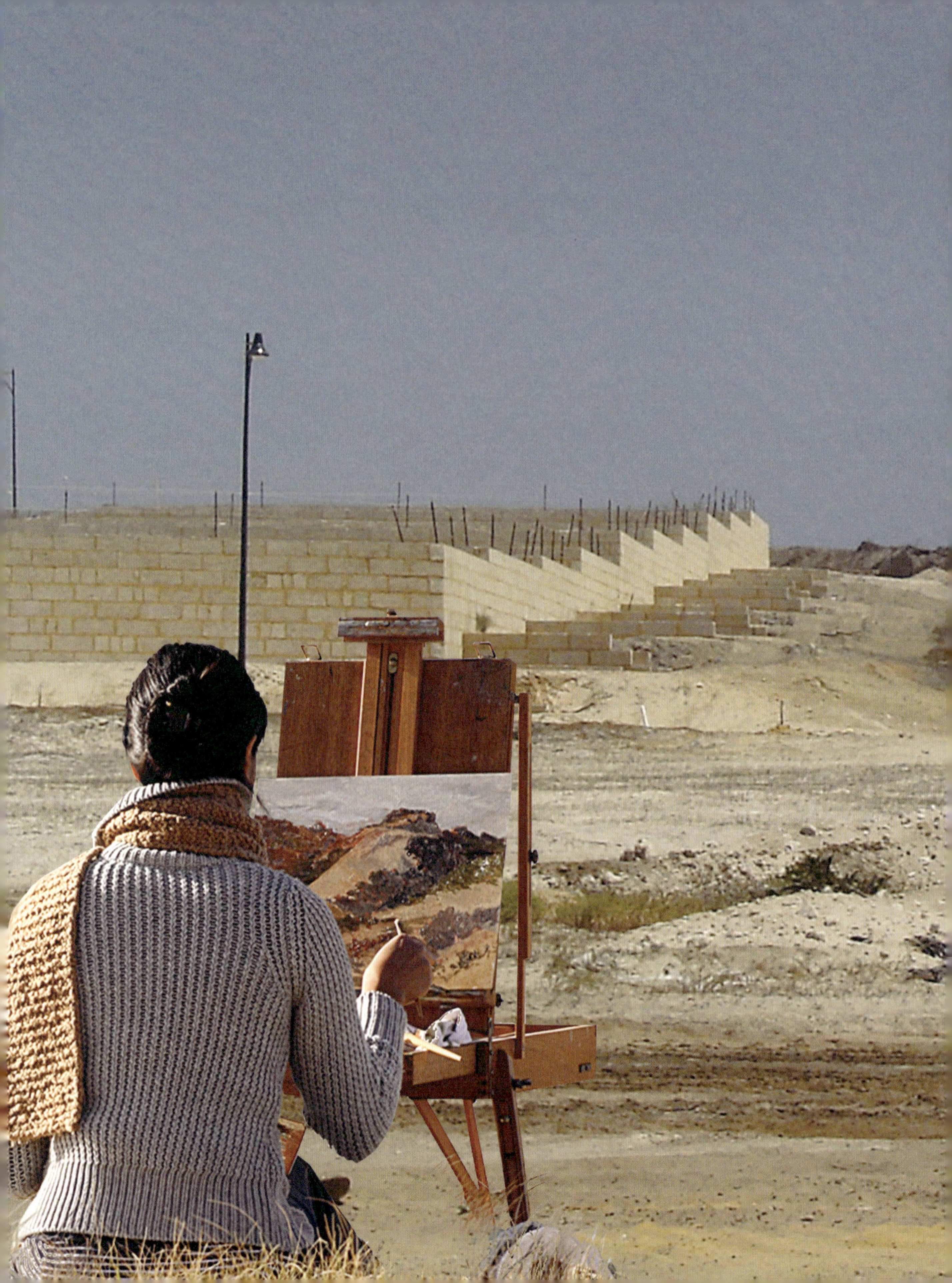

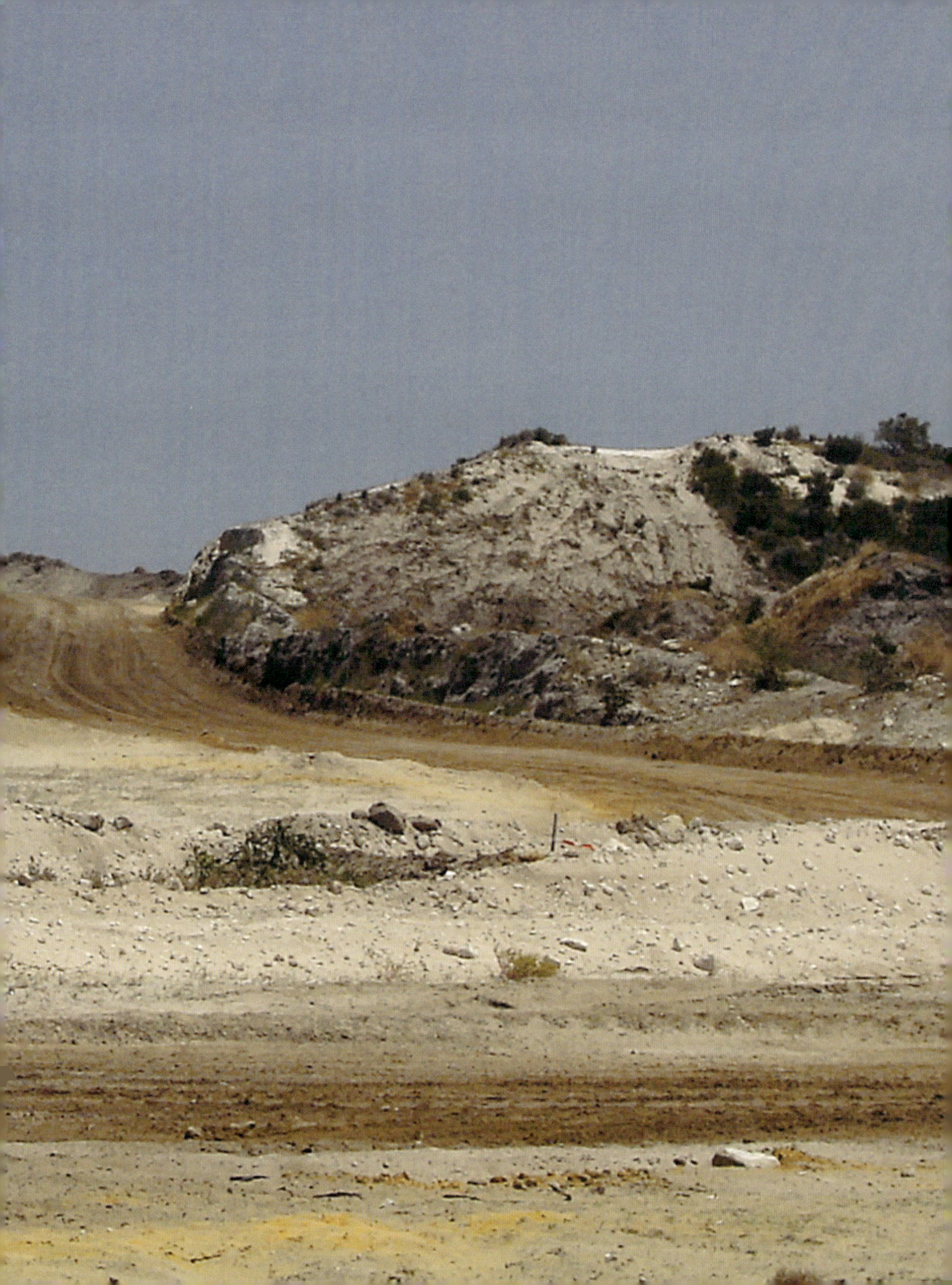

WWW.PEET.COM.AU

New Land
Pre-release.

# LakeLands
PRIVATE ESTATE
— A Community In Harmony With Nature —

Phone 9581 8835
www.lakelands-estate.com.au

PEET | Estates

7

# THE CUTTING EDGE

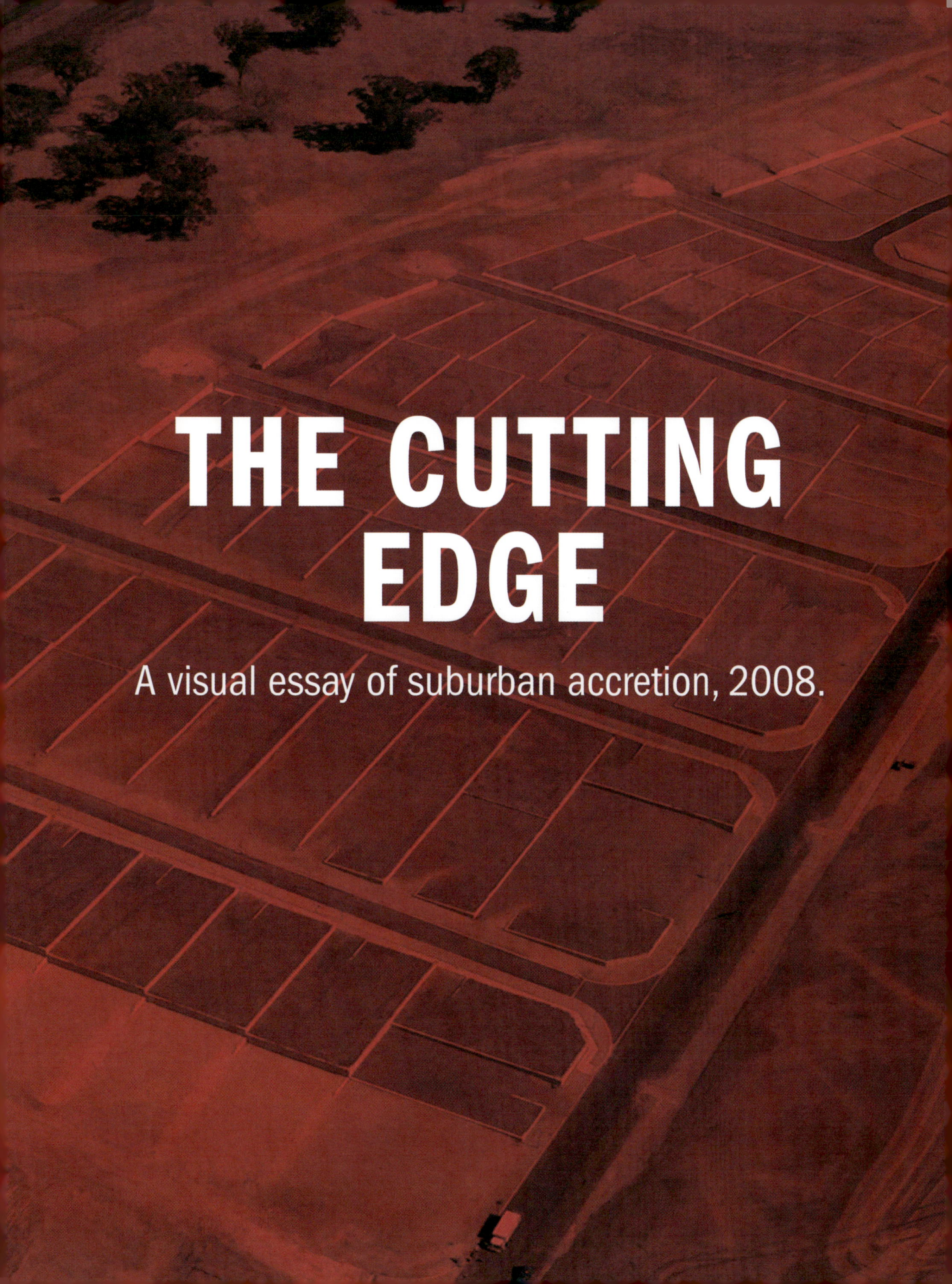

A visual essay of suburban accretion, 2008.

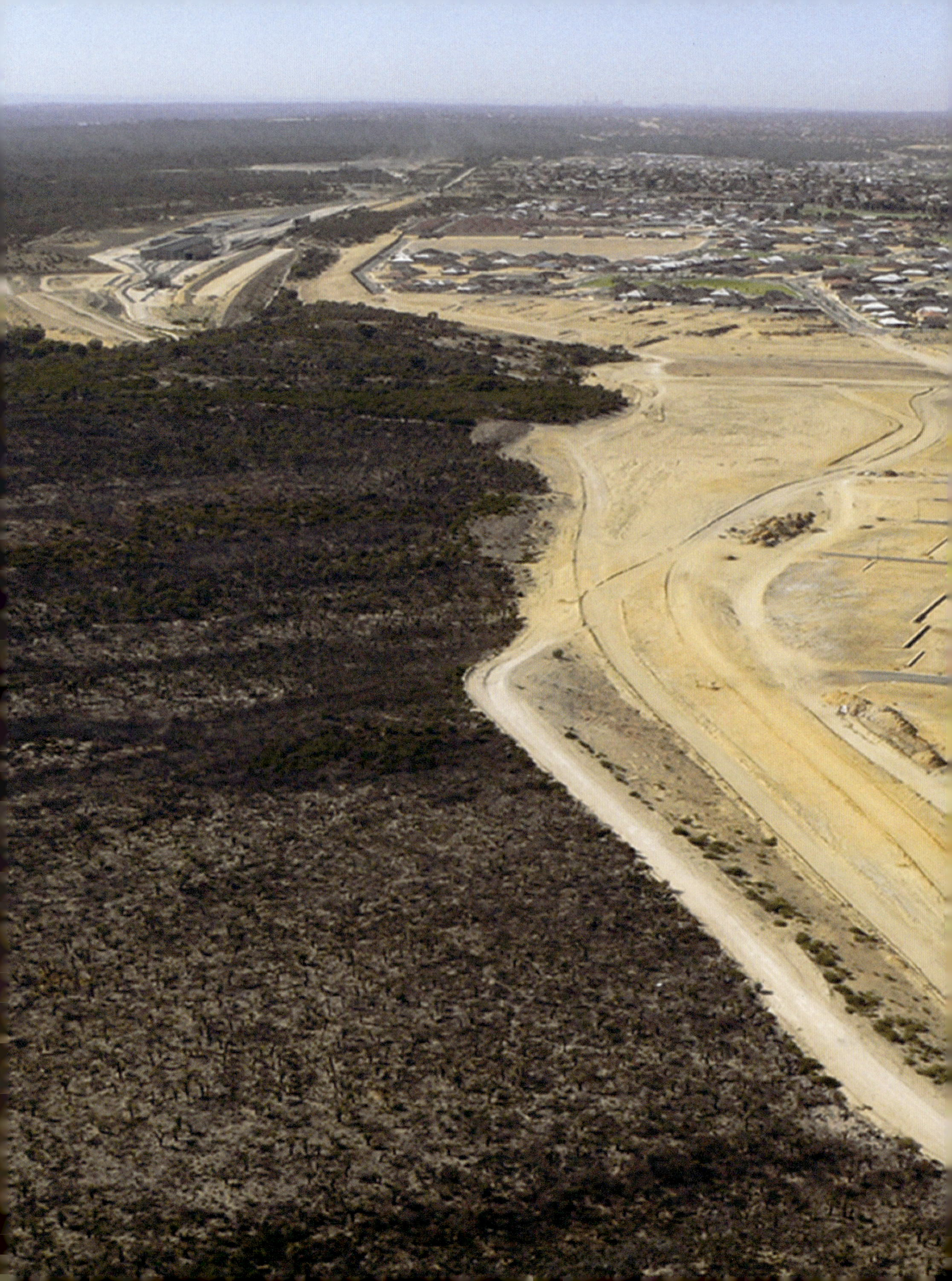

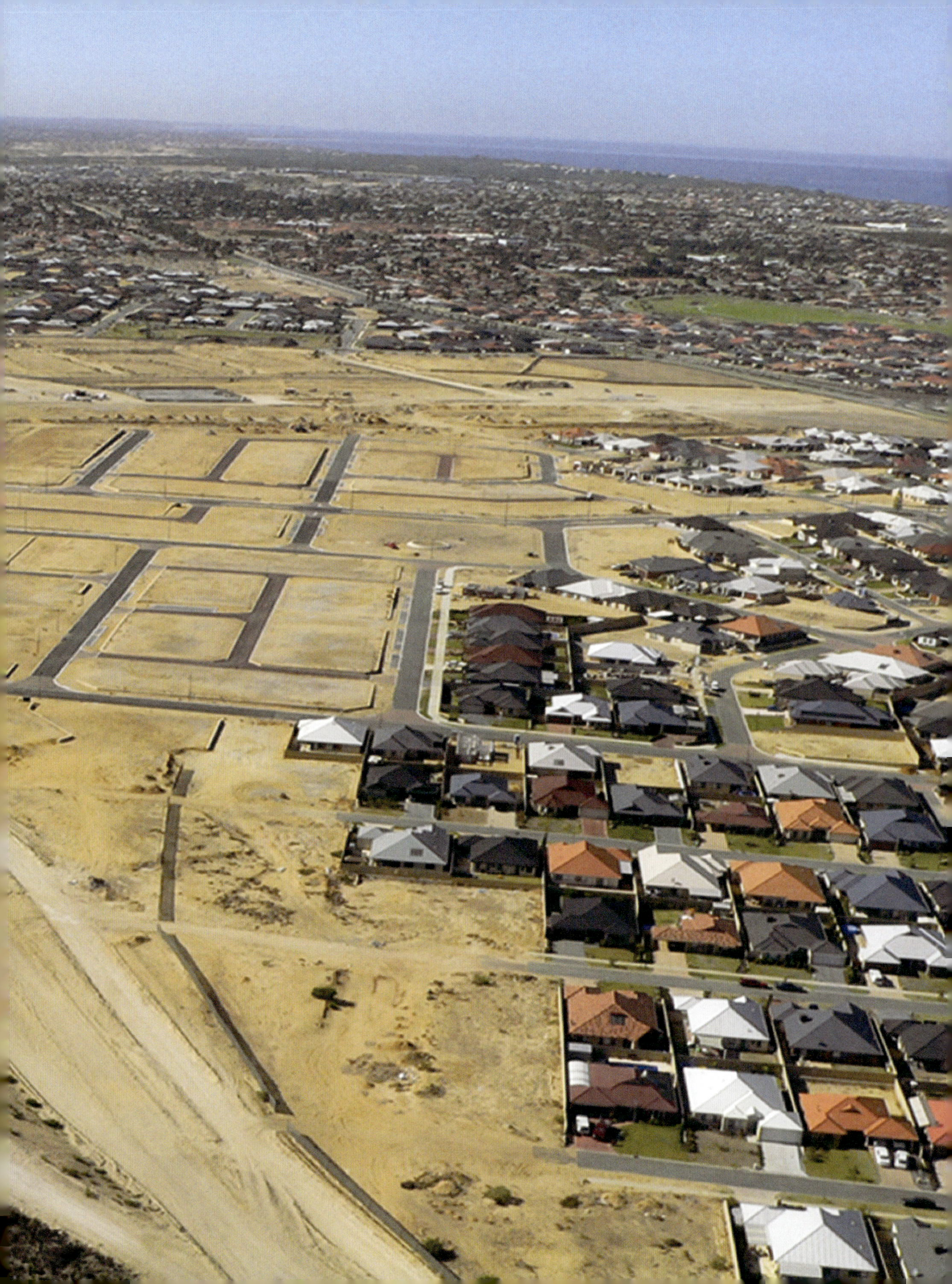

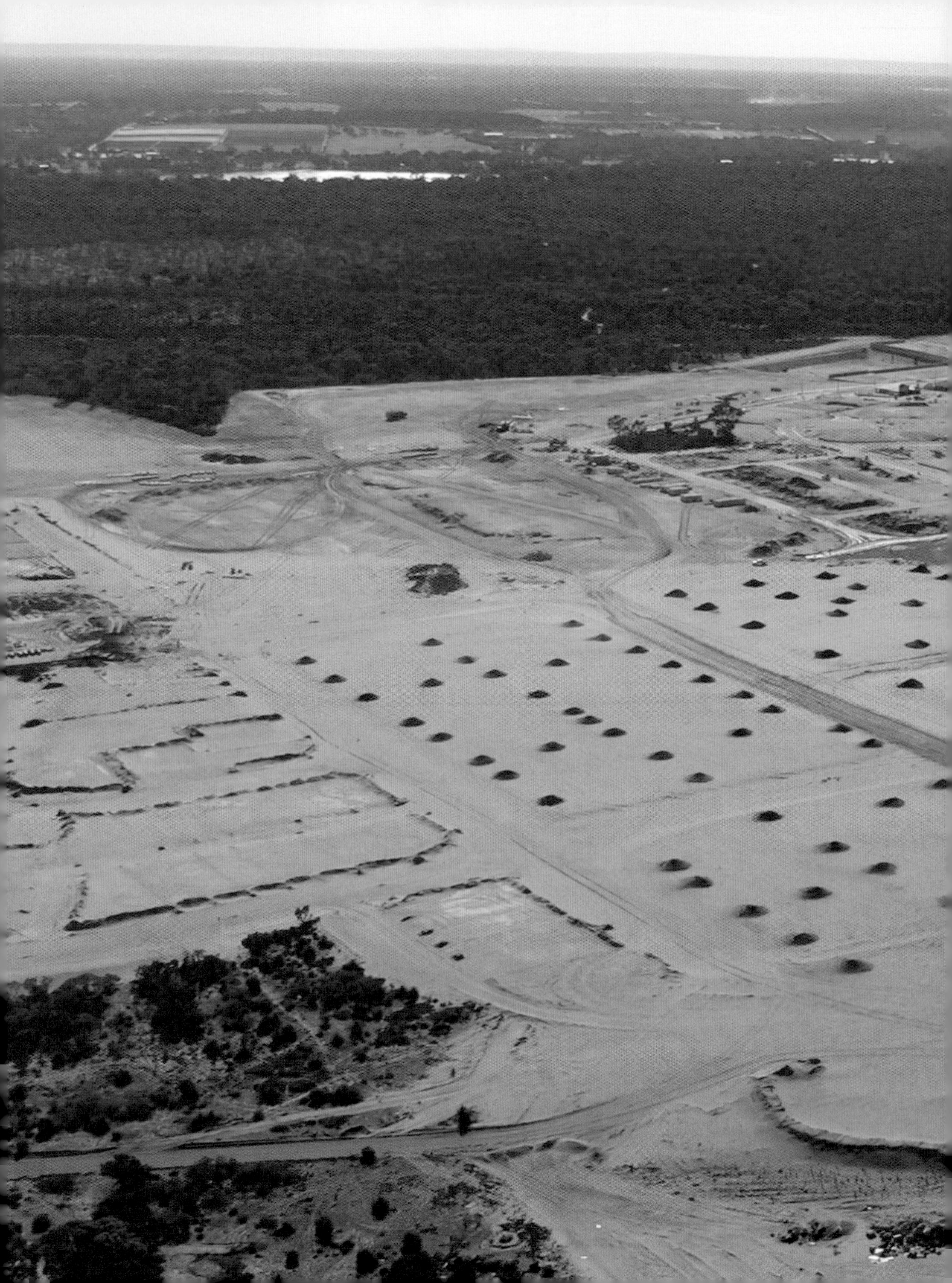

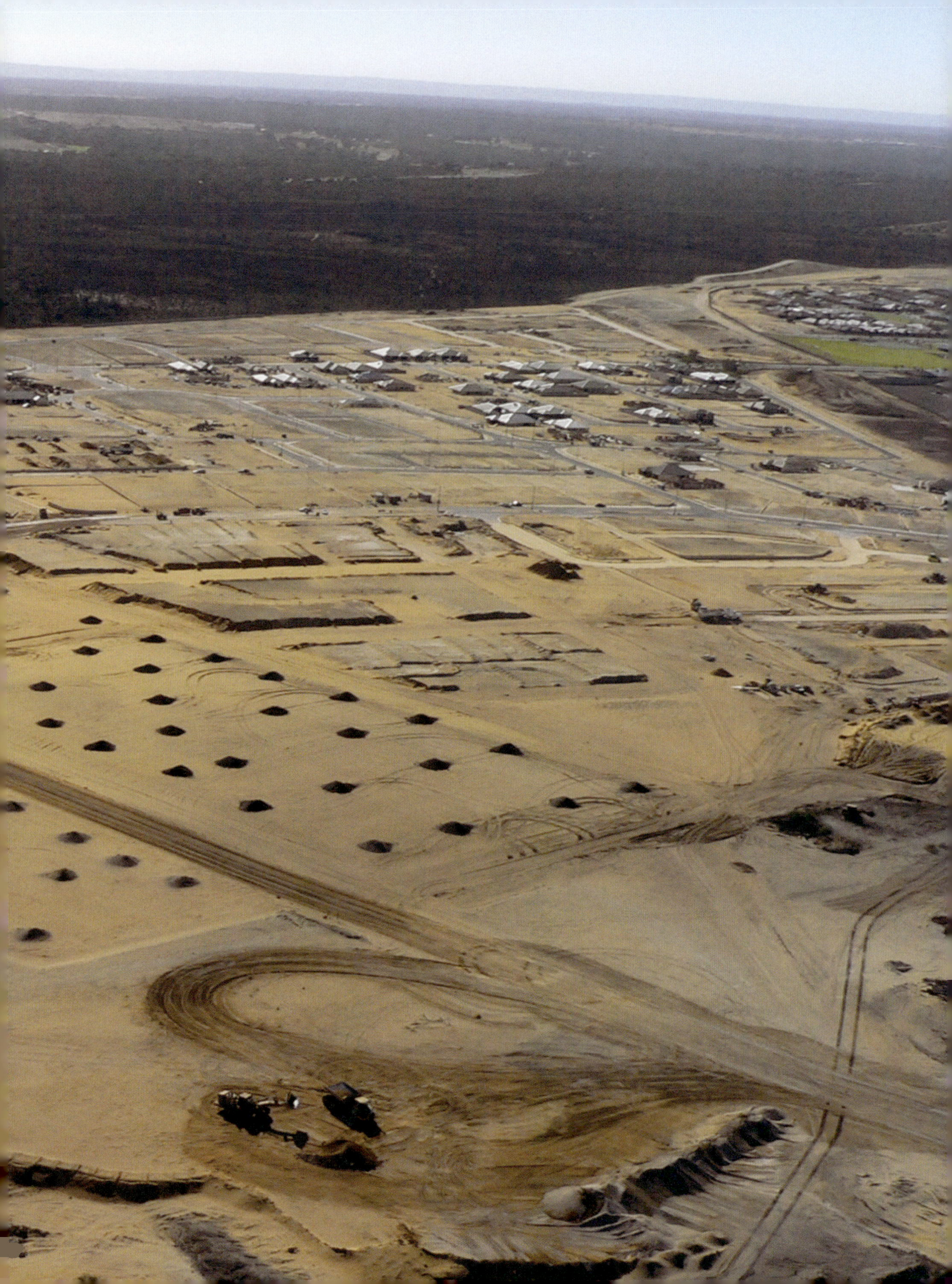

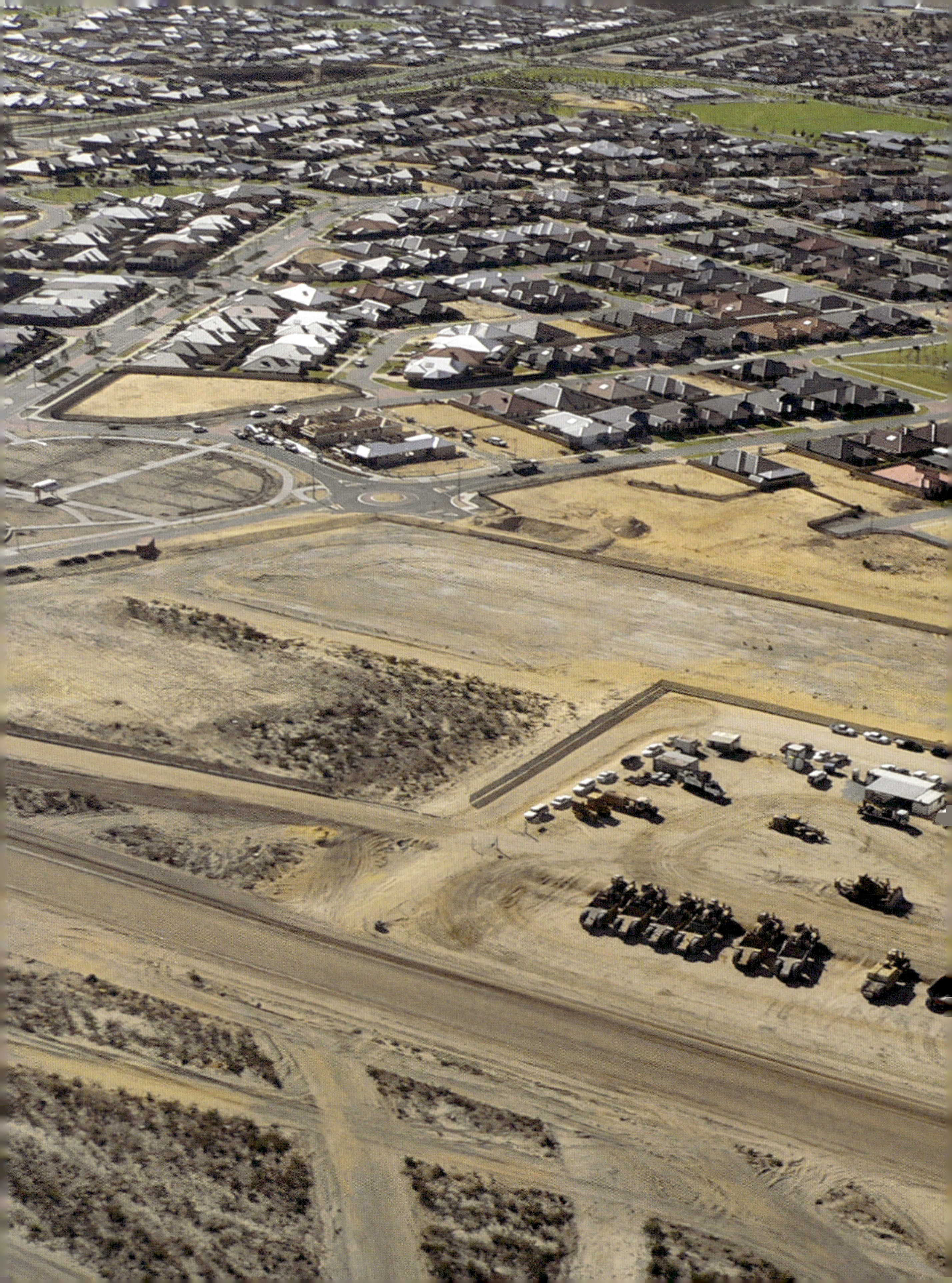

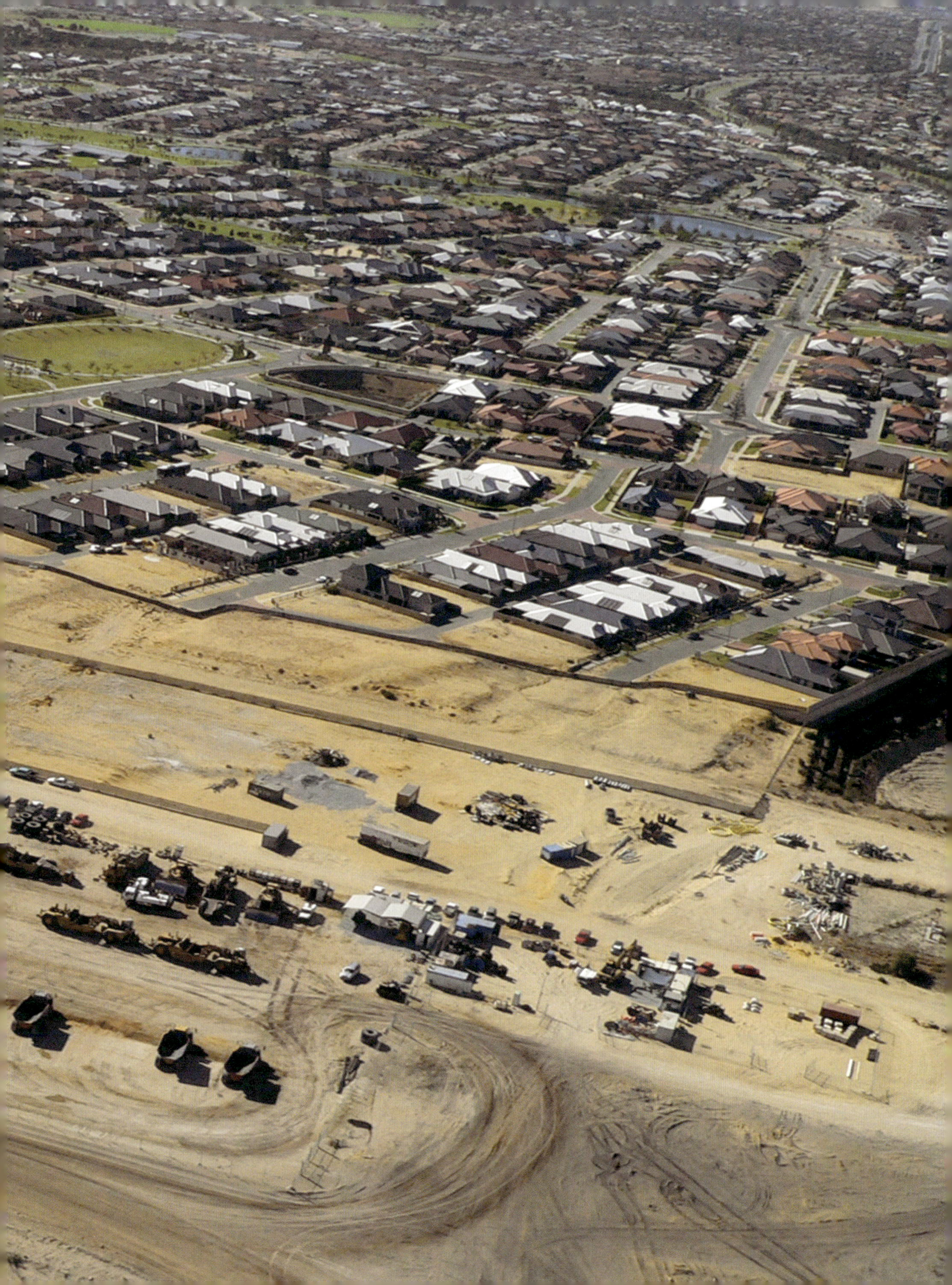

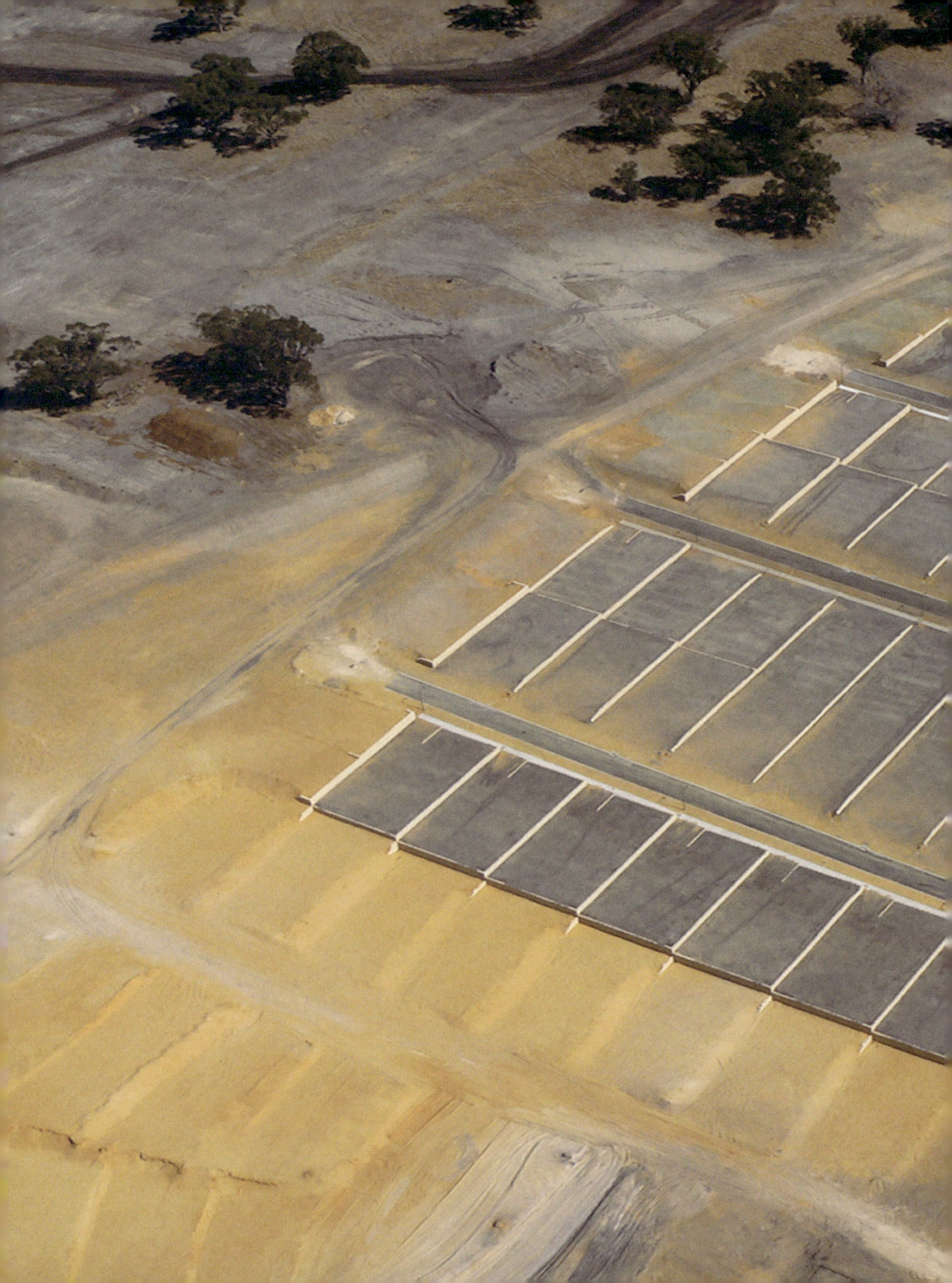

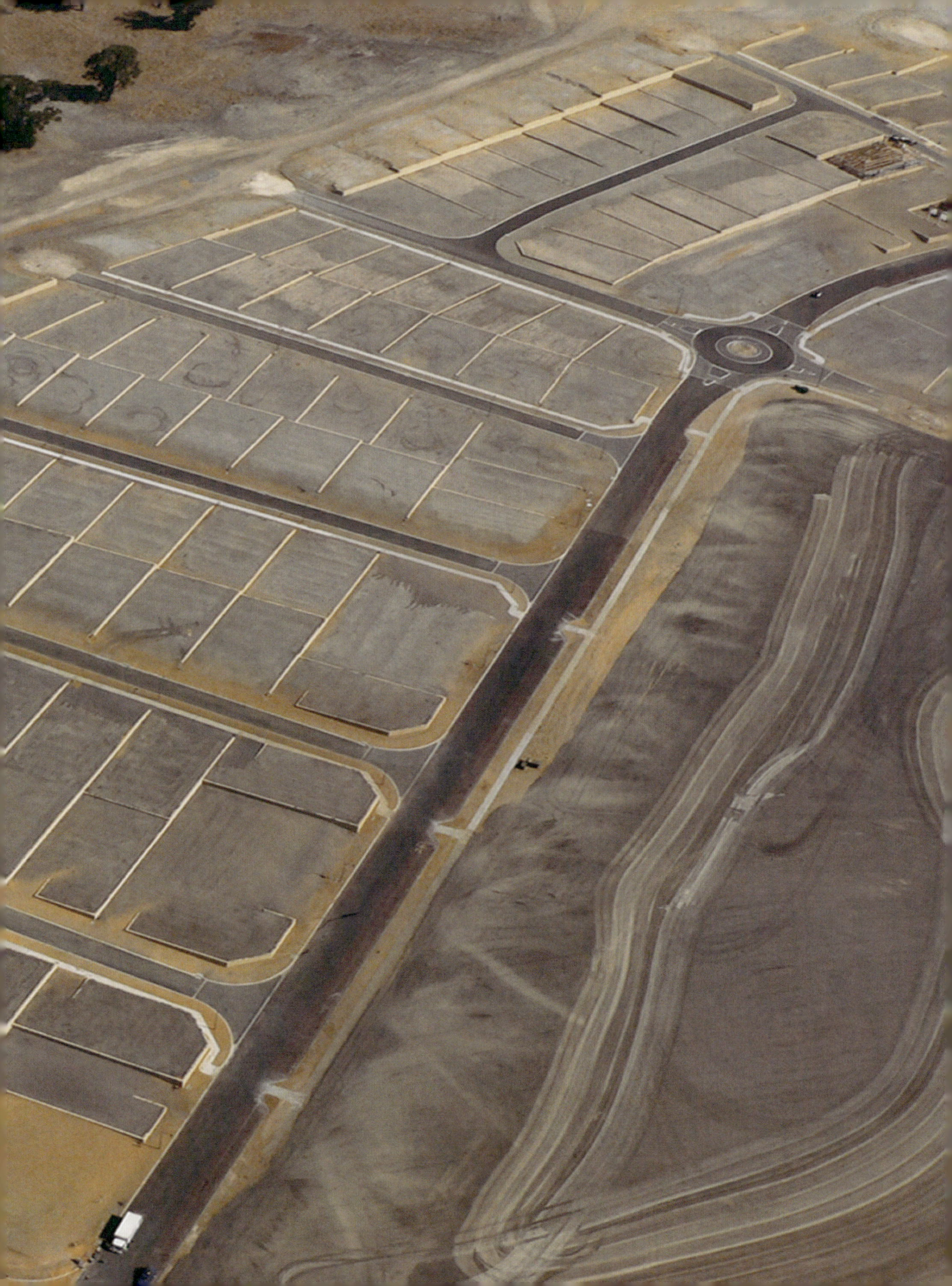

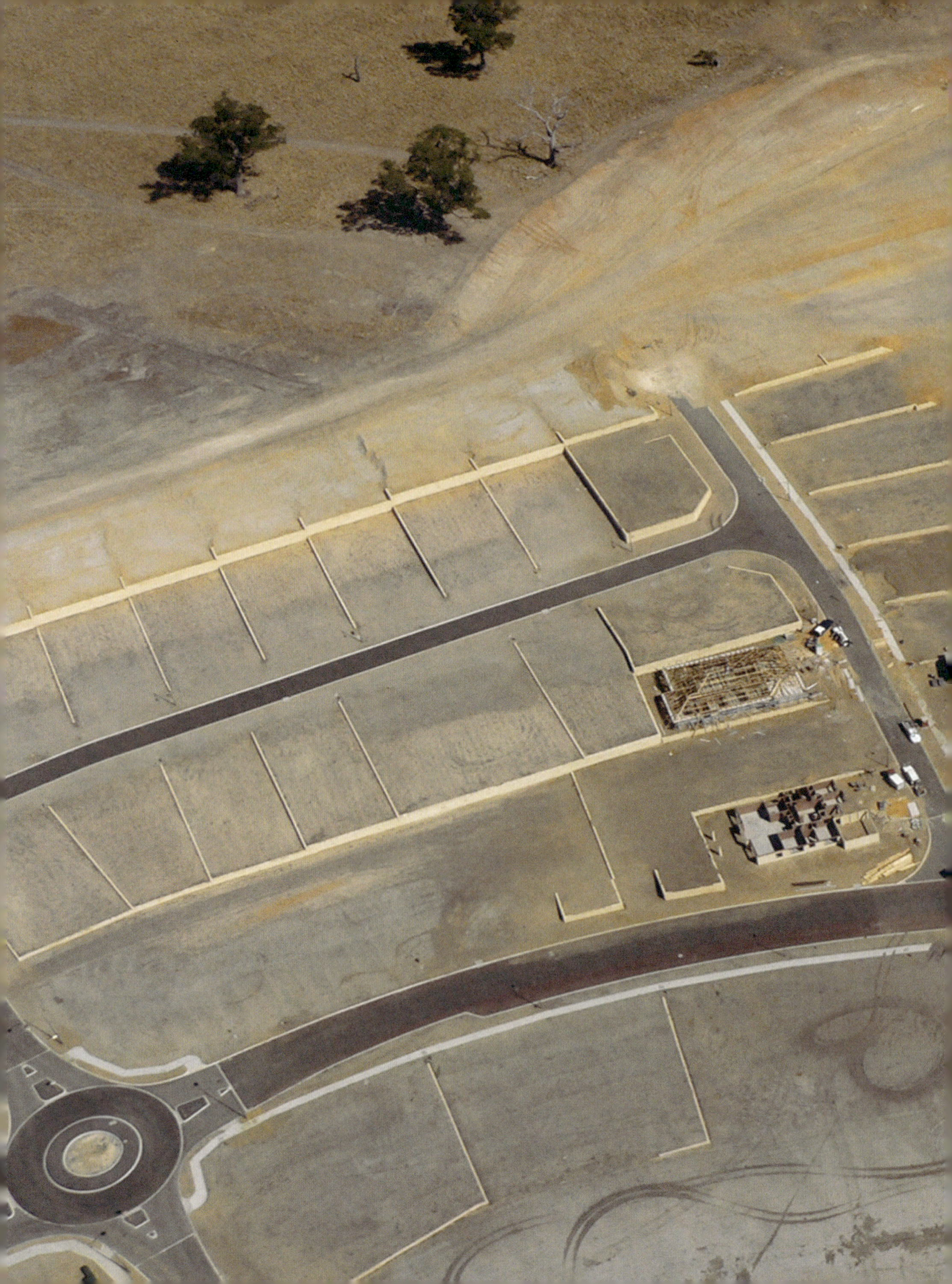

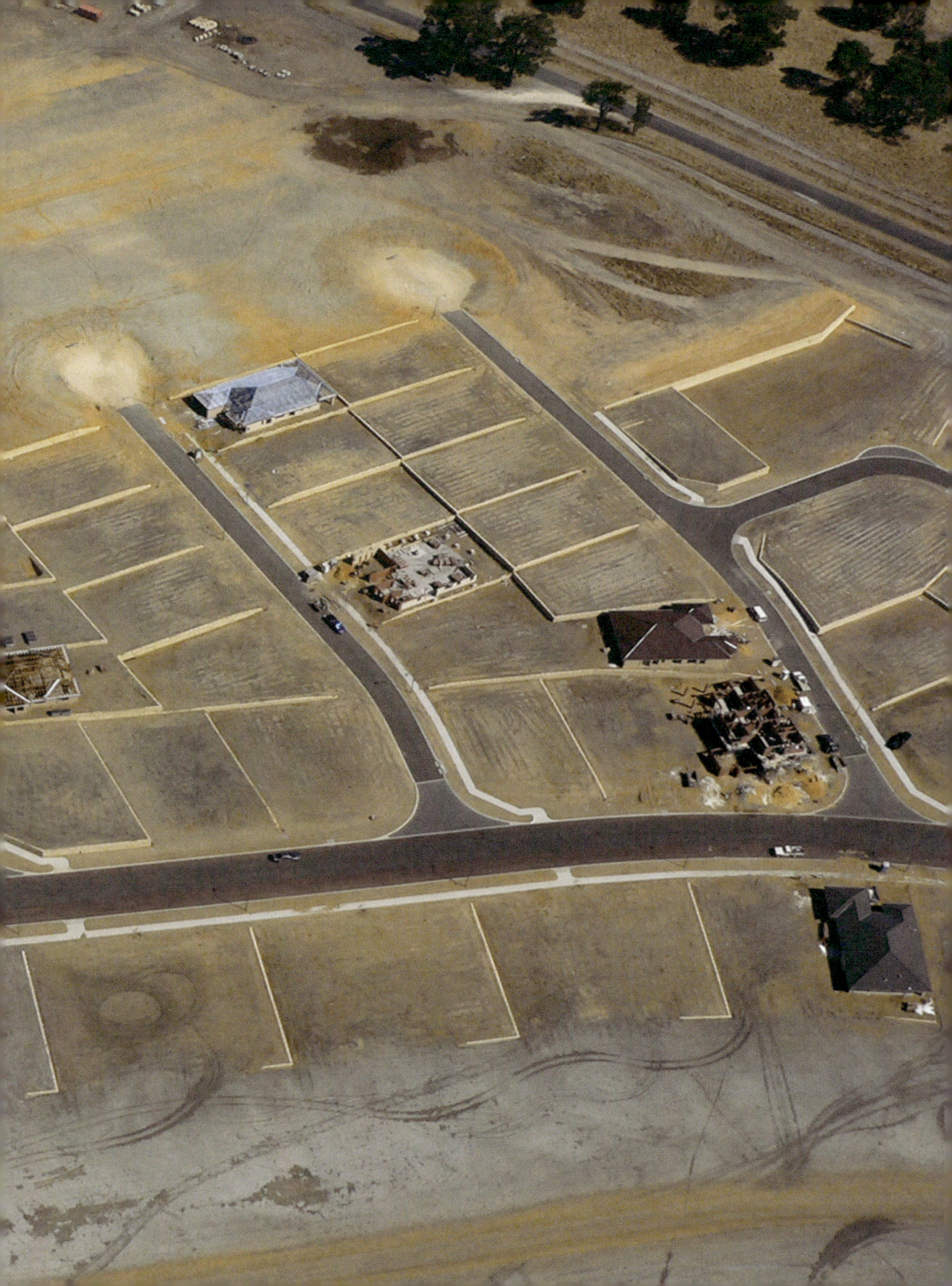

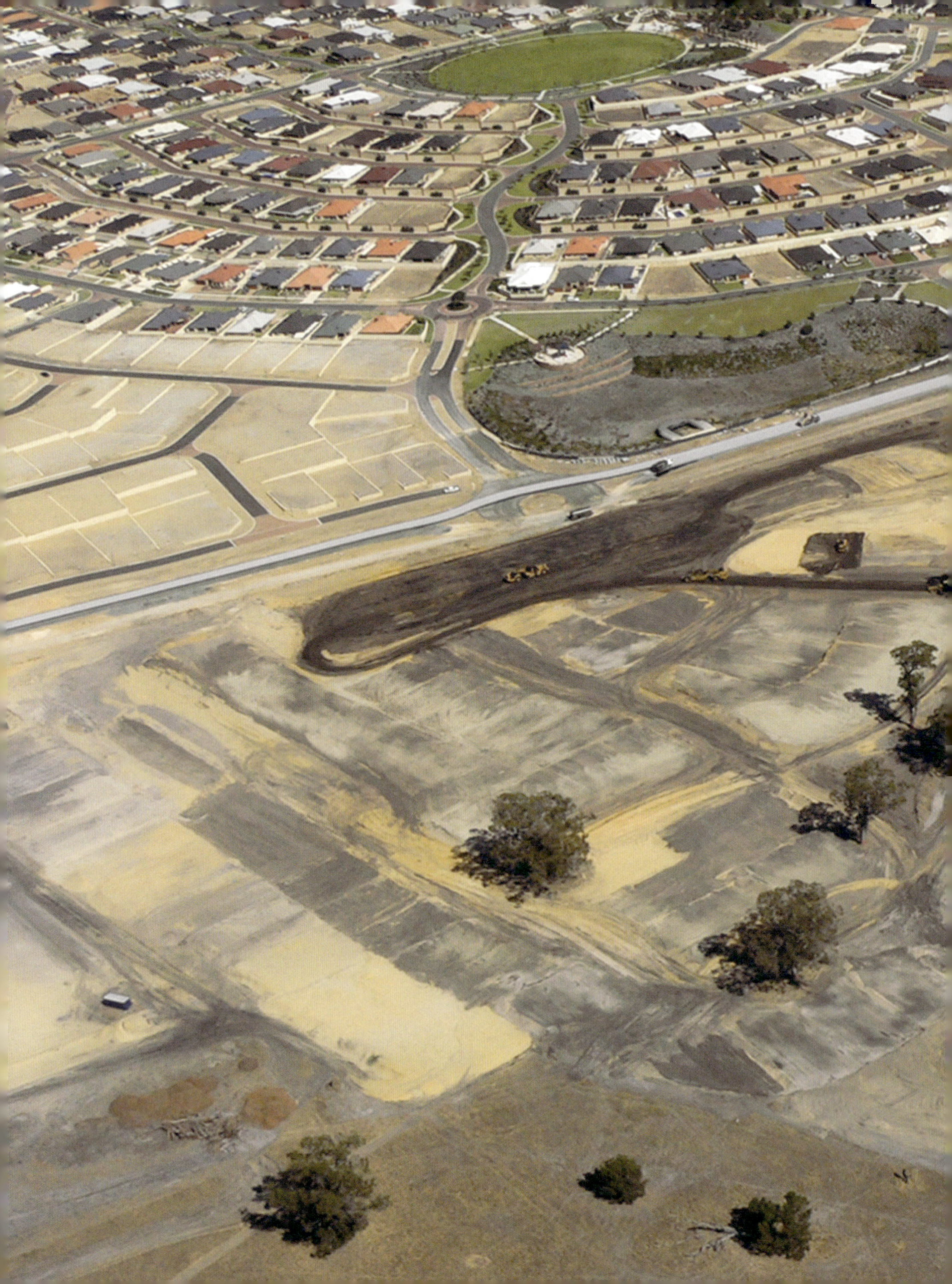

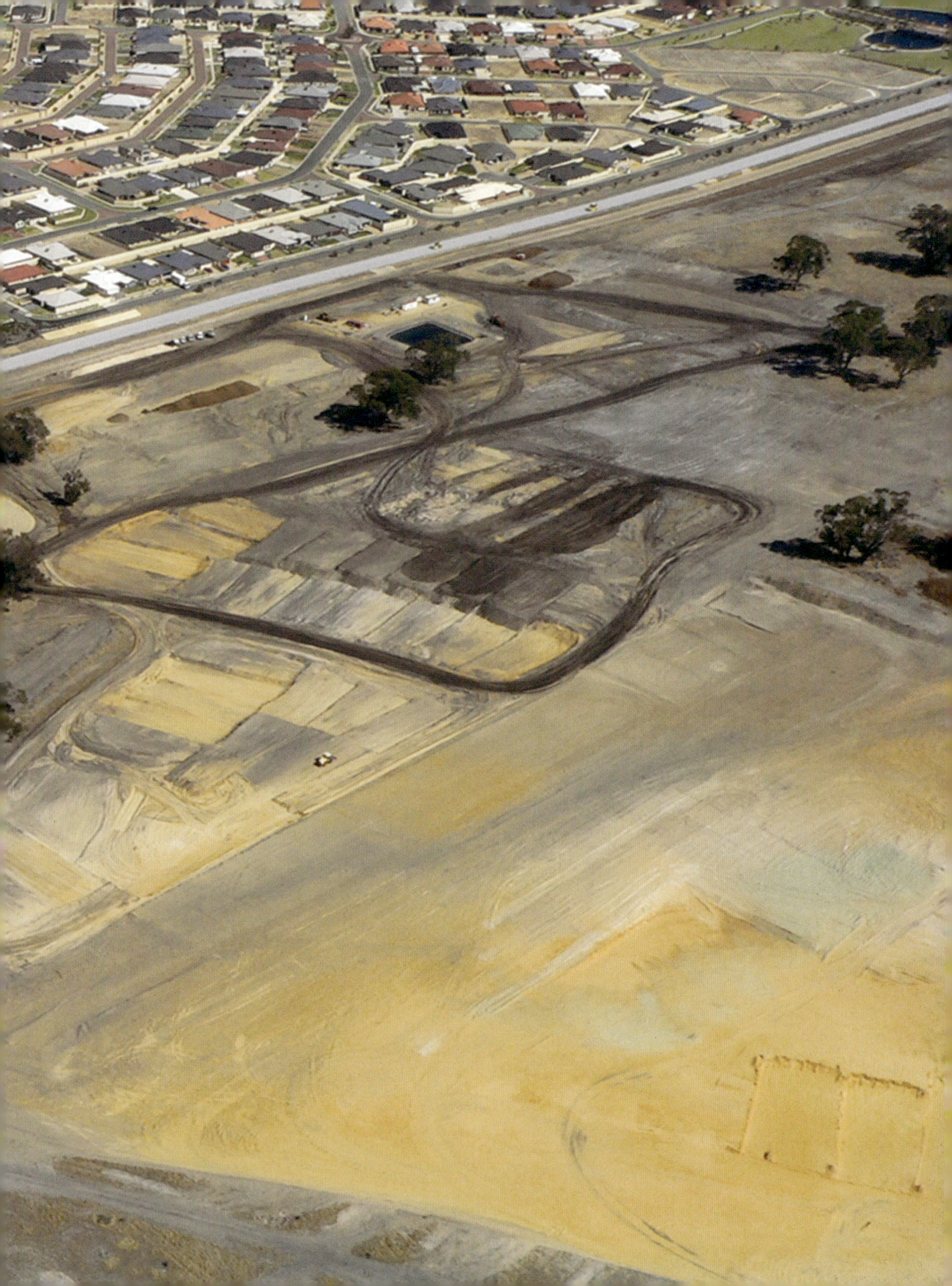

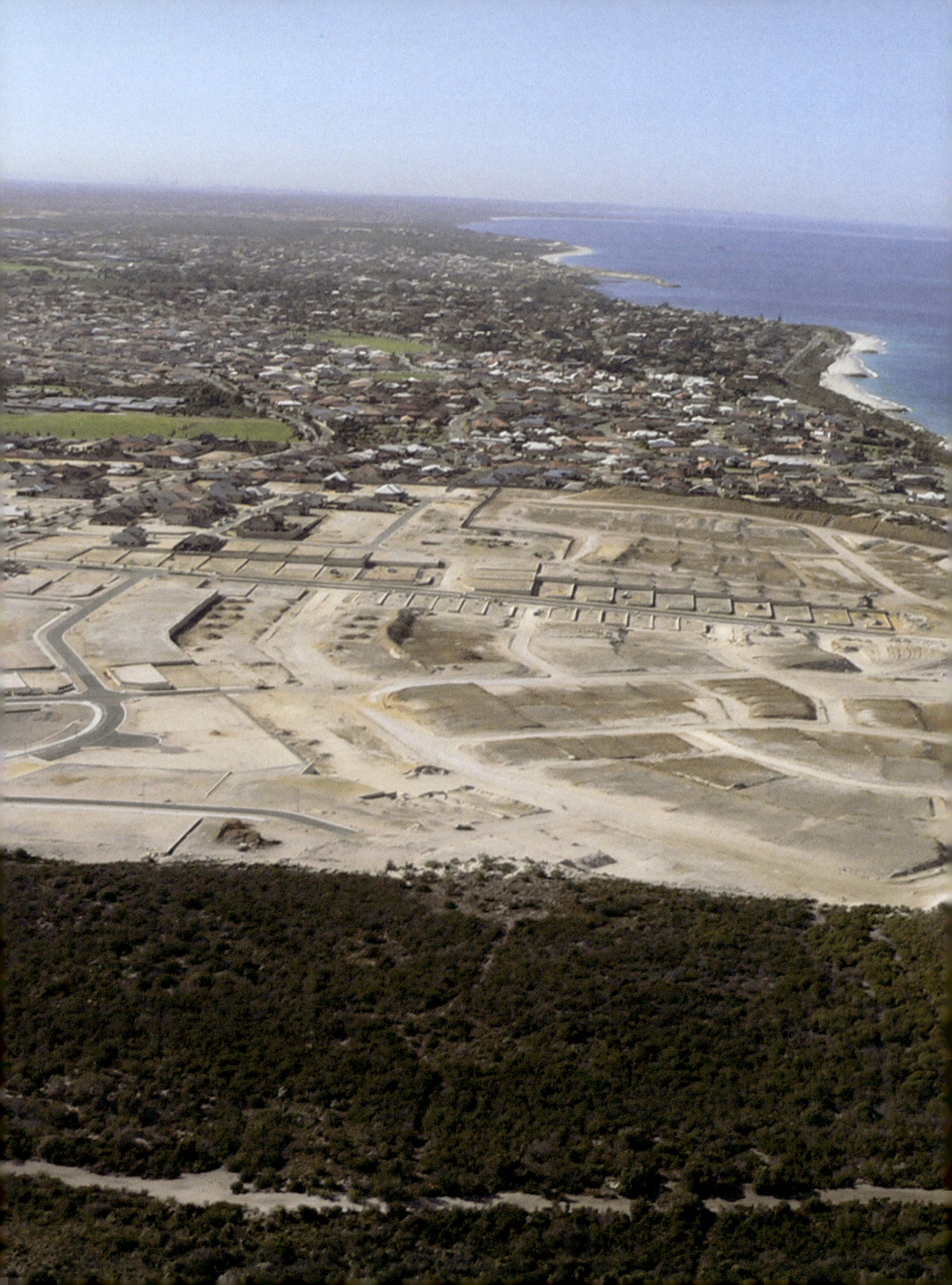

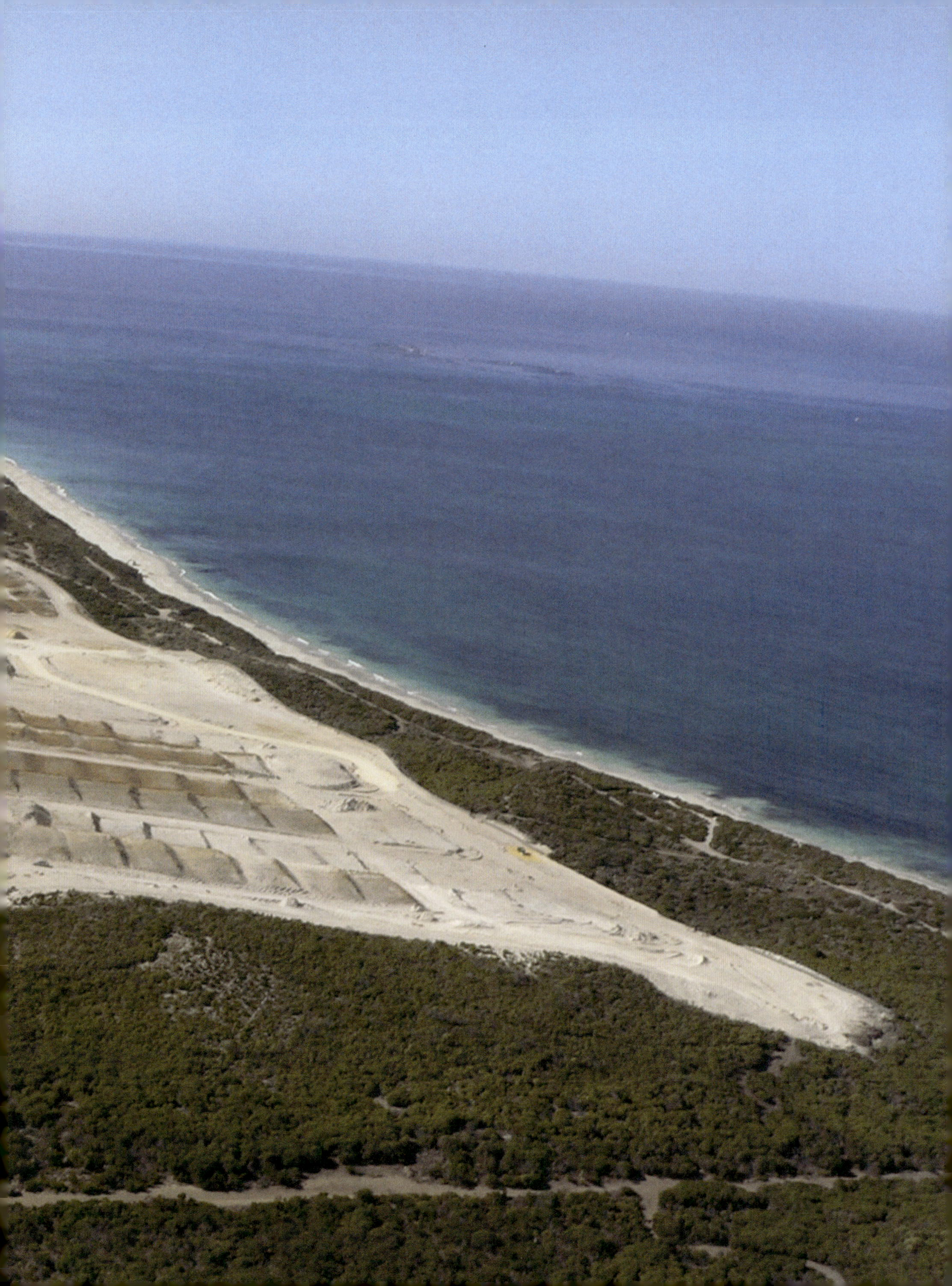

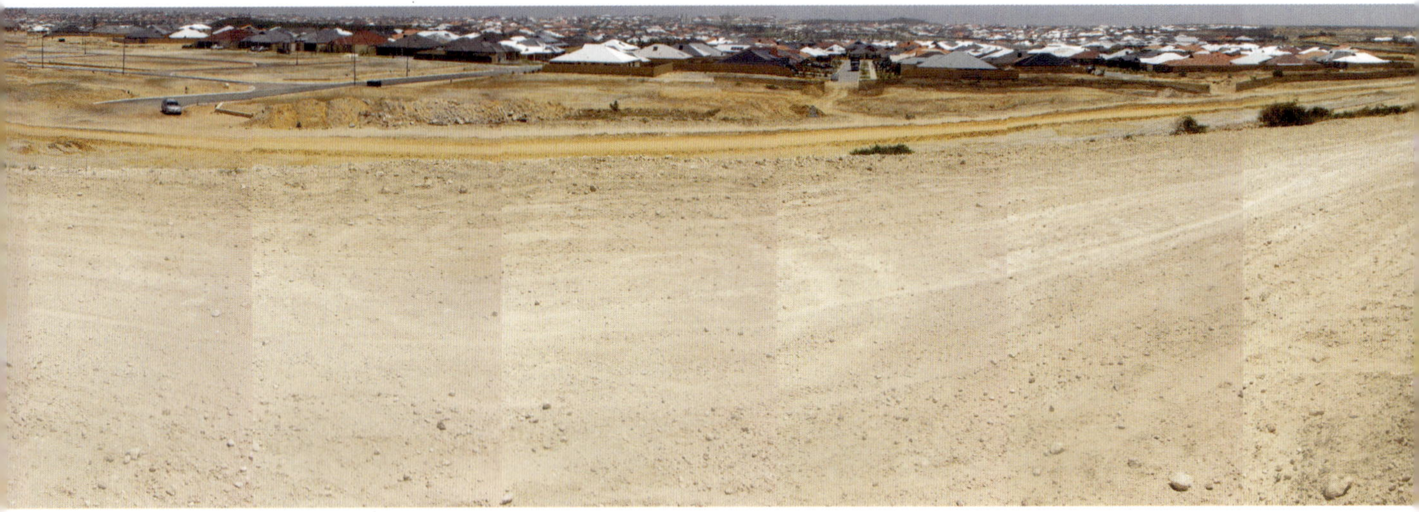

# THE CUTTING EDGE

**217**
**THE CUTTING EDGE**

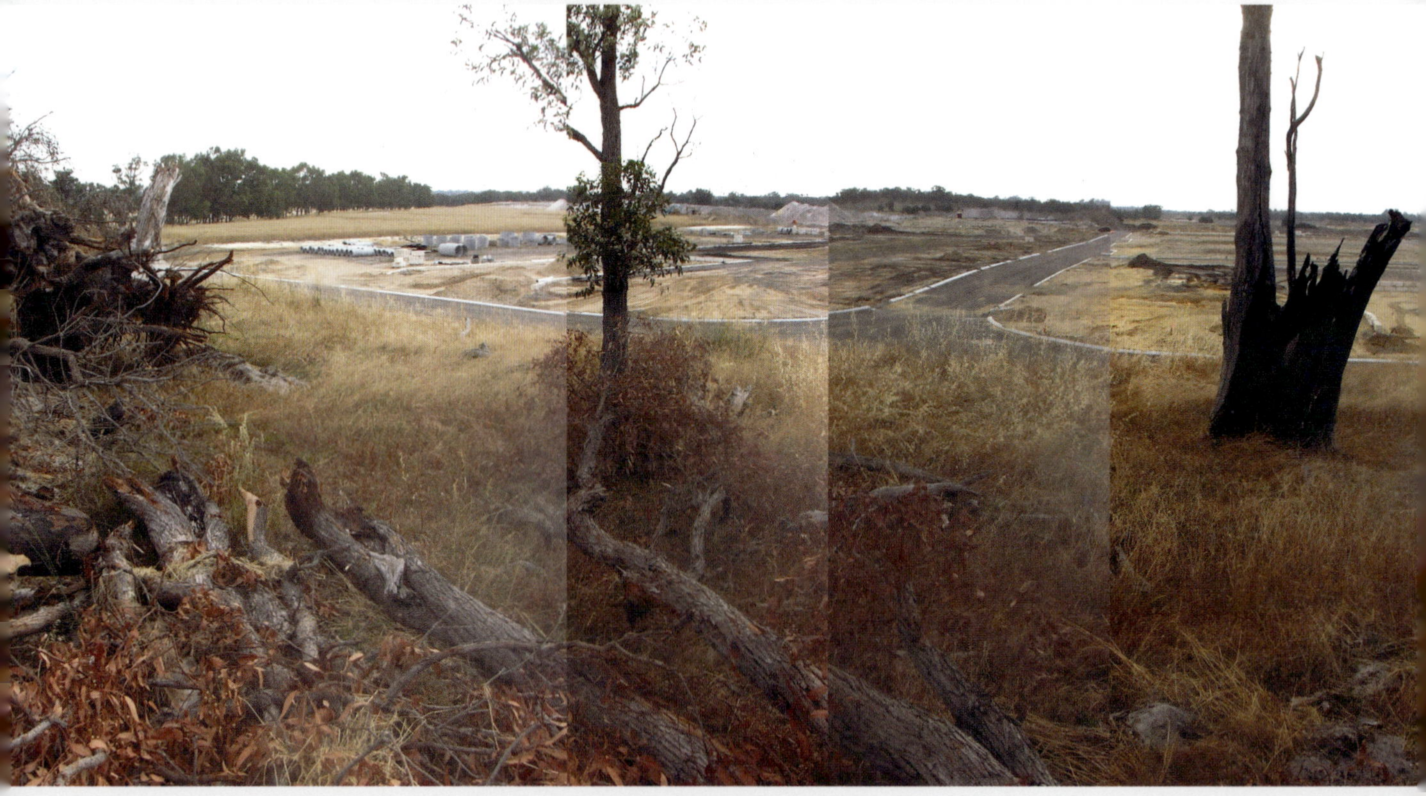

219
**THE CUTTING EDGE**

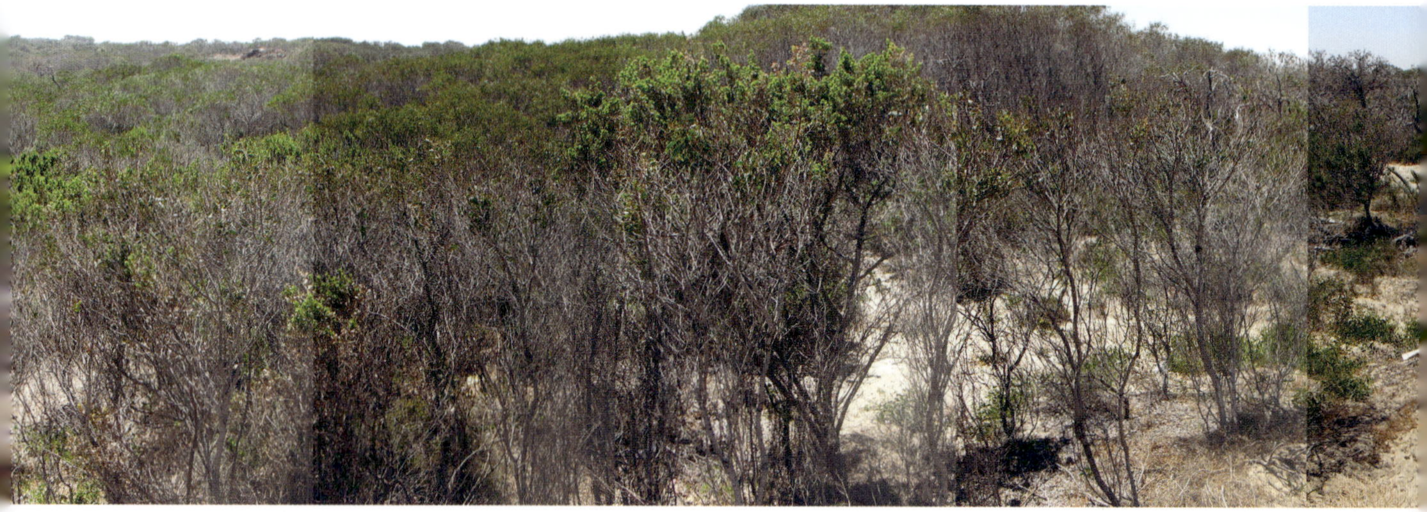

# THE CUTTING EDGE

**221**
**THE CUTTING EDGE**

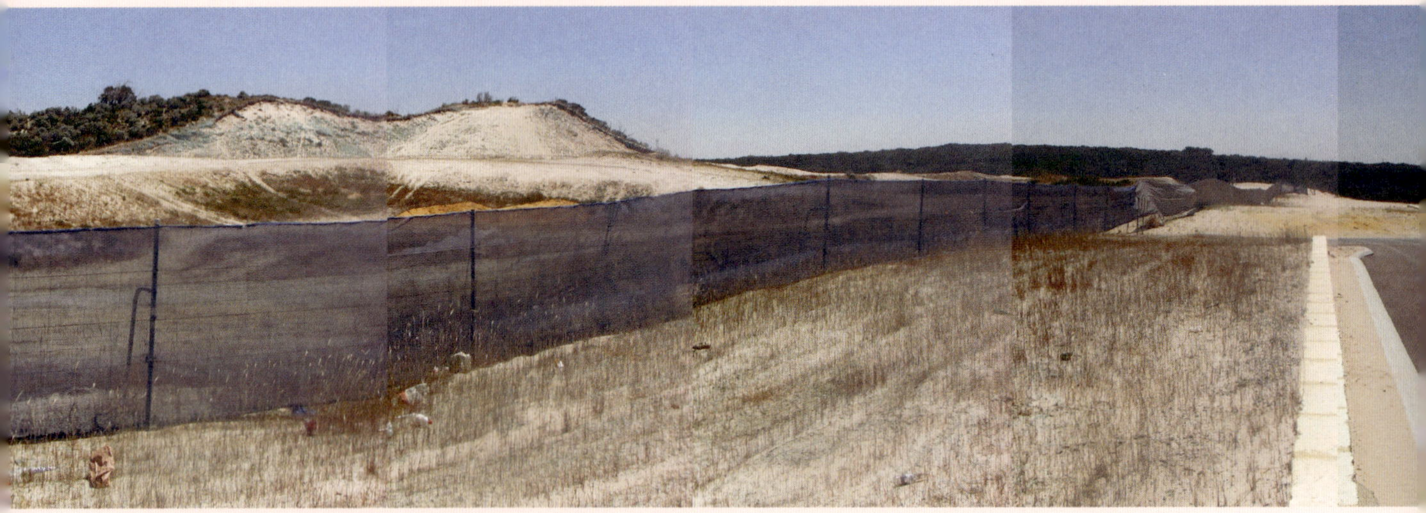

THE CUTTING EDGE

223
THE CUTTING EDGE

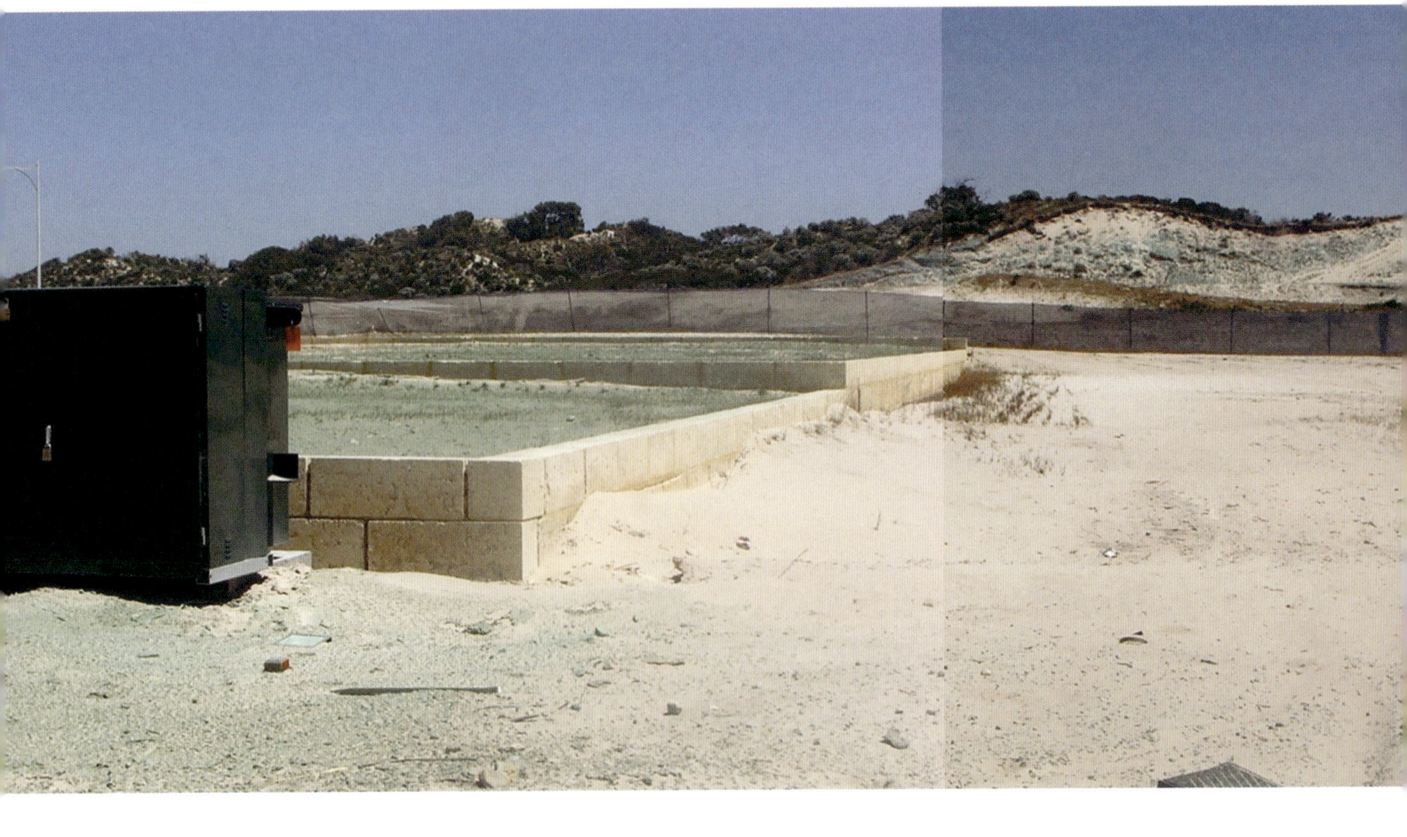

# THE CUTTING EDGE

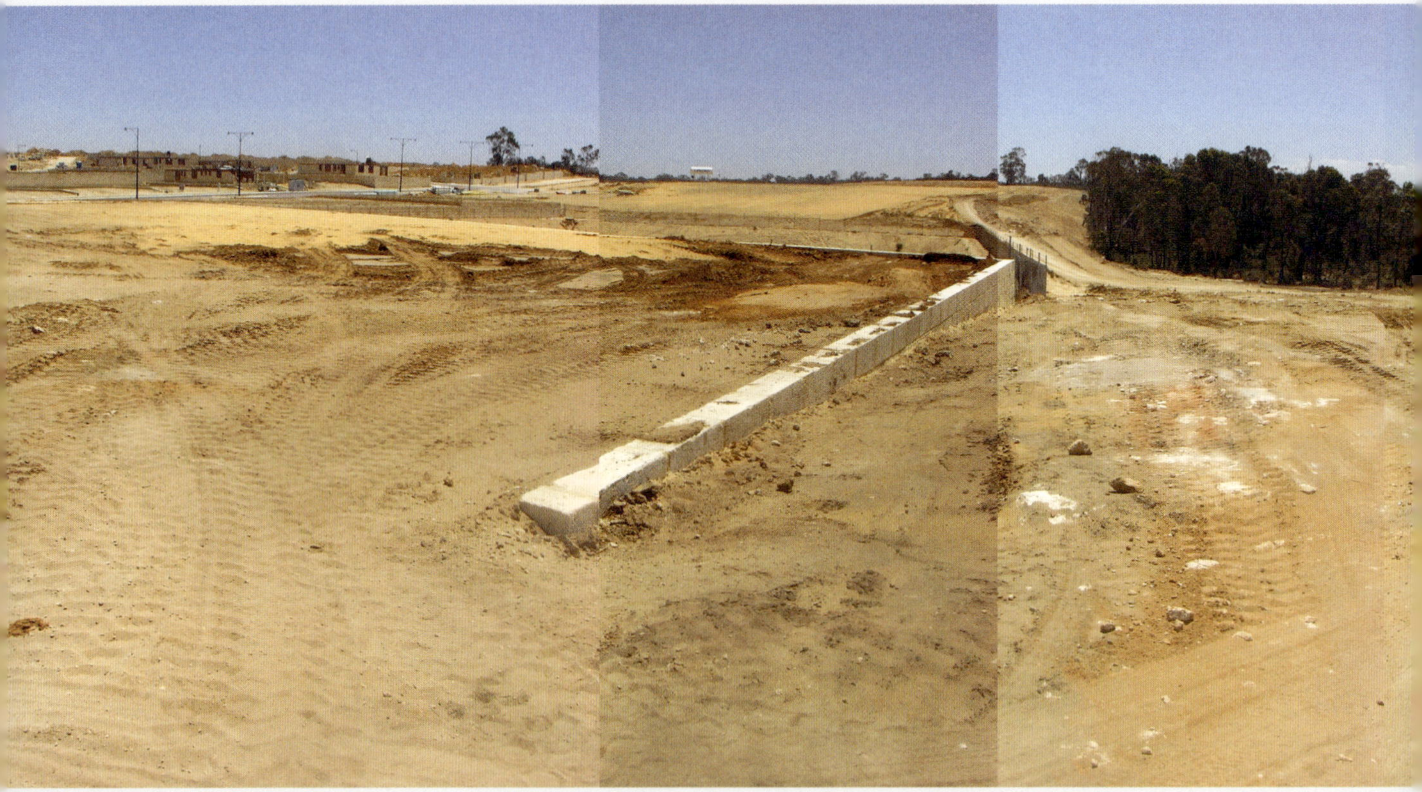

THE CUTTING EDGE

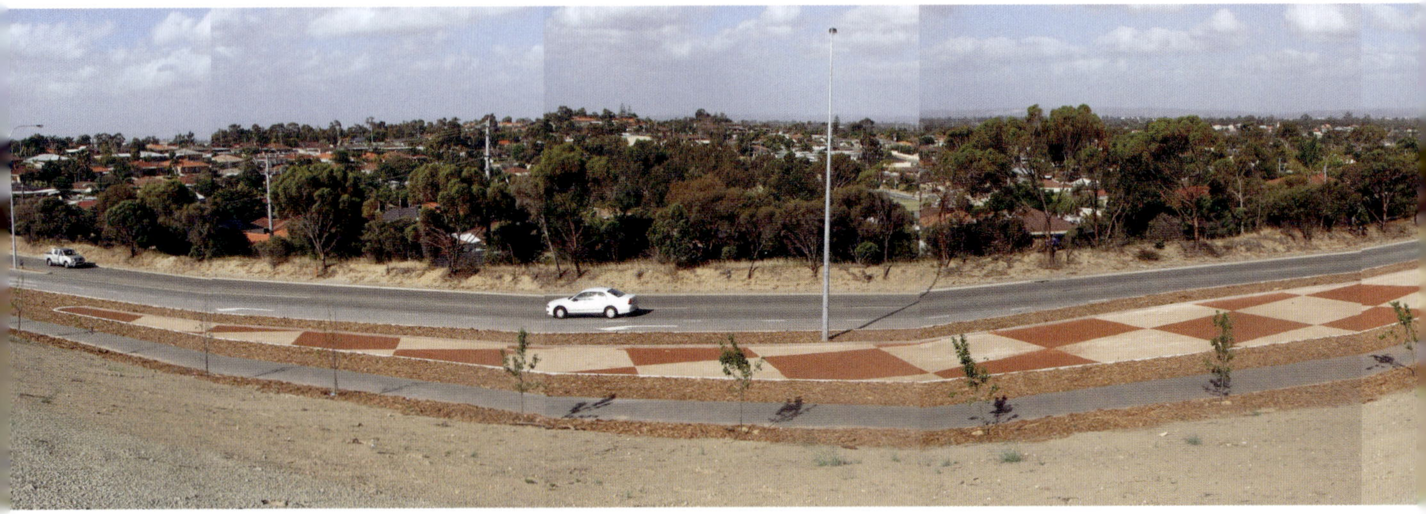

THE CUTTING EDGE

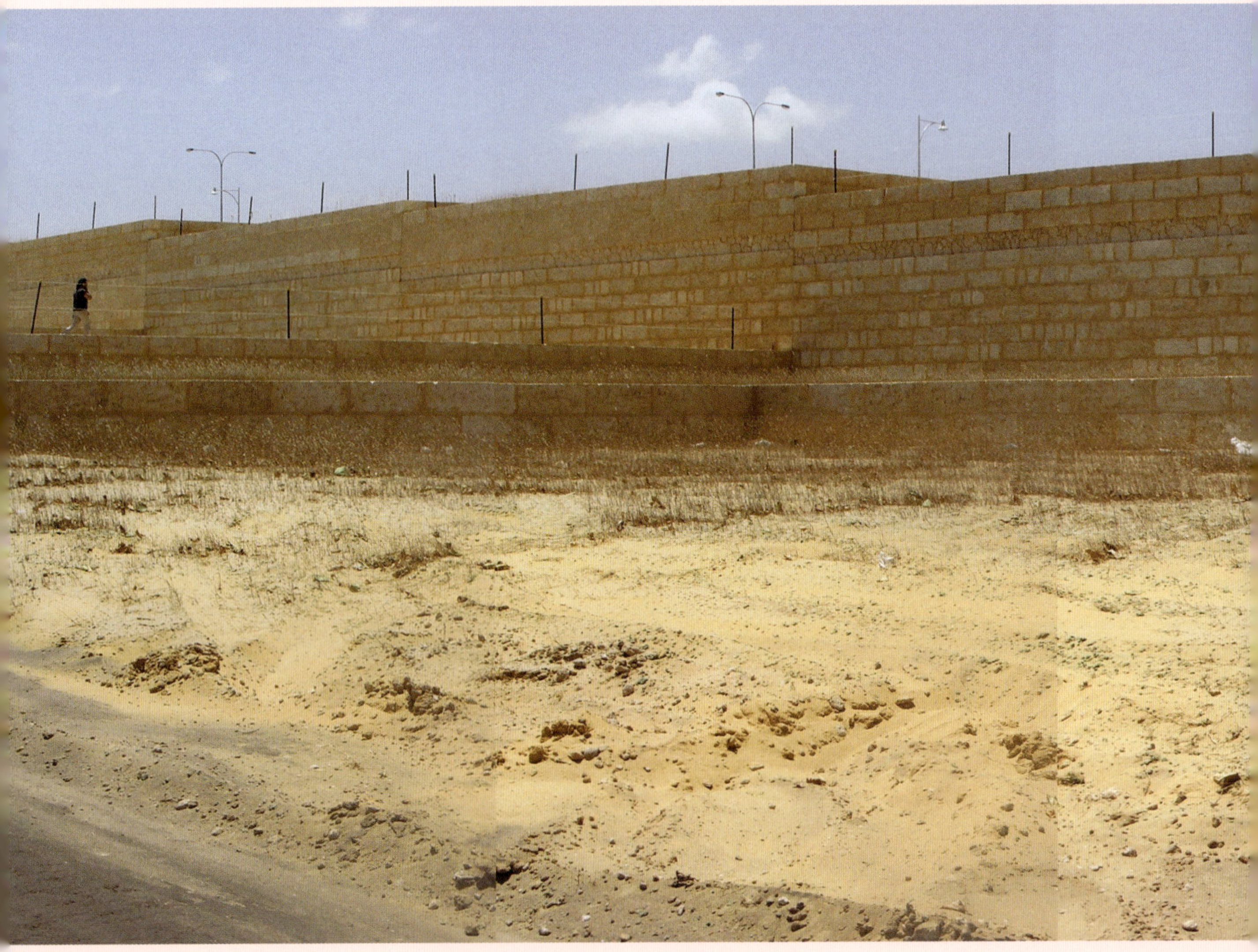

231
THE CUTTING EDGE

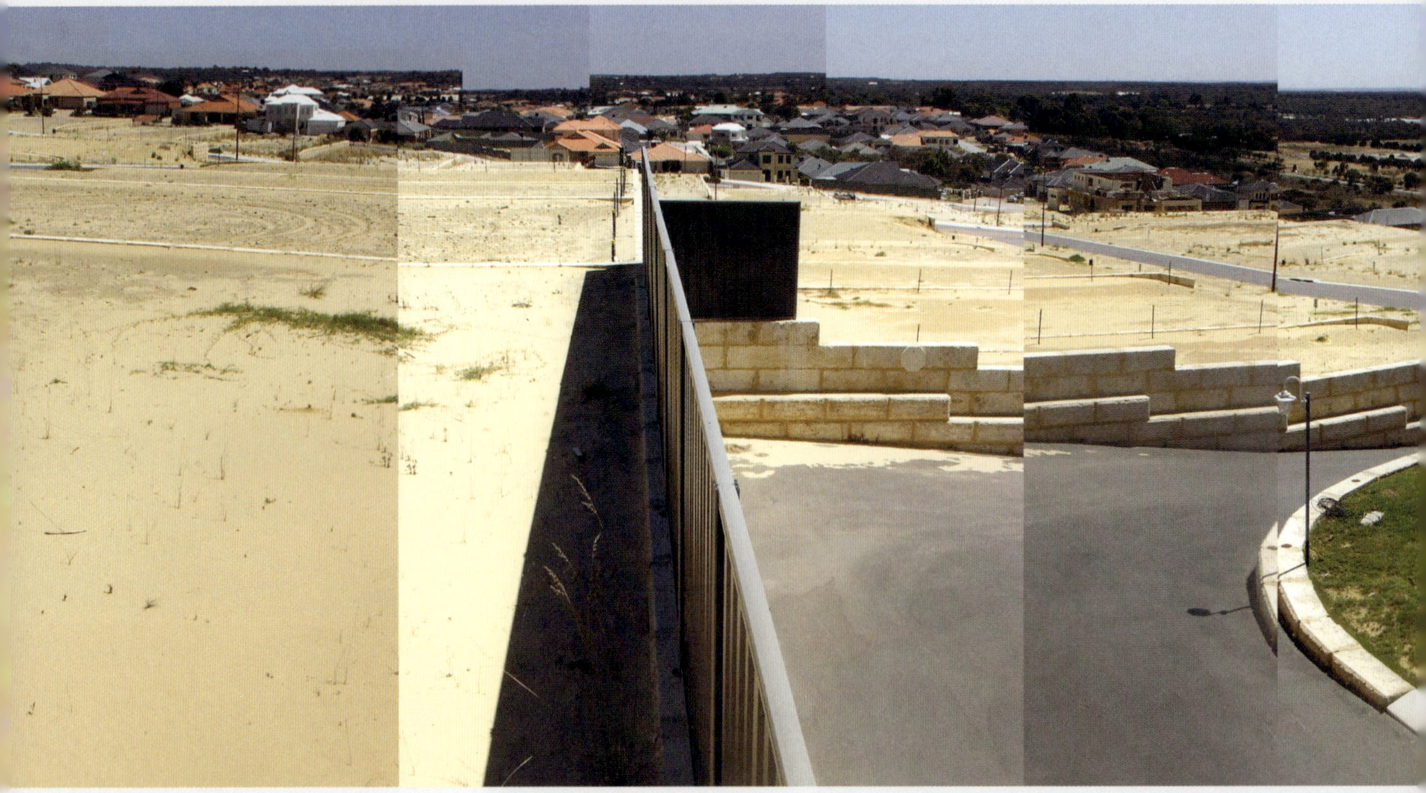

THE CUTTING EDGE

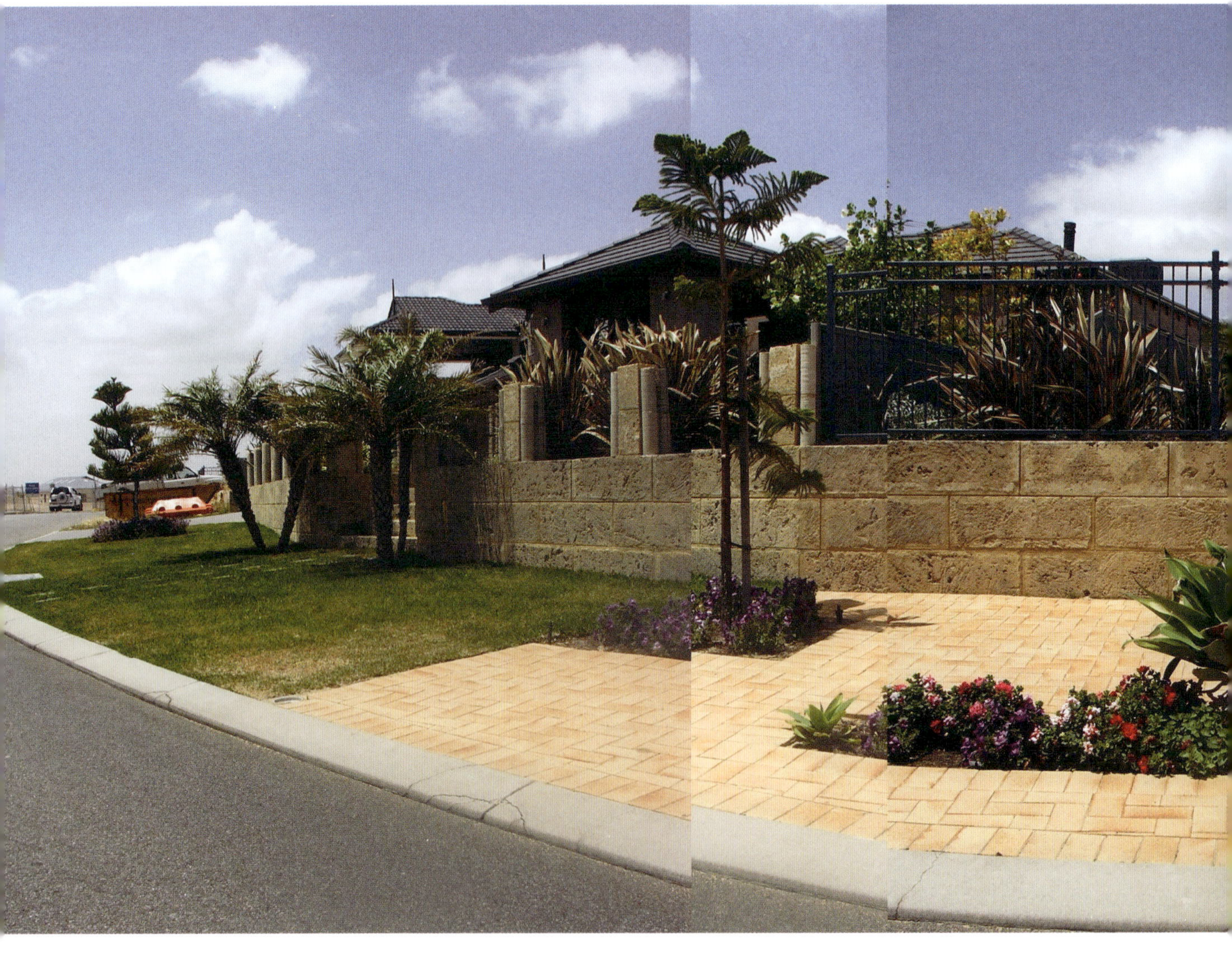

THE CUTTING EDGE

8

# BAU+

'Business as usual is no longer good enough.'

Hon. Alannah MacTiernan, Minister for Planning and Infrastructure, 2007.

Wungong Urban Water

20 km

# BAU+

## A suburban case study

The Wungong Urban Water project (WUW) encompasses an area of over 1,400 hectares and will yield 16,000 homes over a 15-year construction period accommodating an anticipated population of 40,000 people. The Armadale Redevelopment Authority (ARA), responsible for the development, initially approached The University of Western Australia landscape program and asked for a concept masterplan *as if the landscape really mattered*.

In addition, the ARA encouraged innovation across all aspects of the development. Soon after the UWA Landscape Structure Plan (LSP) was presented, The Planning Group joined the project as the lead planning consultants to refine the LSP's concepts and guide a full team of consultants through almost five years of masterplan development.[1]

A key aspect of the ARA's endeavour to deliver sustainable and viable development was the establishment of a partnership with the Commonwealth Science and Industry Research Organisation (CSIRO) and its Water For a Healthy Nation research project. The project was directed by Matt Taylor of CSIRO who, along with the ARA's business manager of planning, Jamie Douglas, facilitated a collaborative planning approach through which policy and established doctrine were constantly challenged in the search for the right outcome.

This is not usually how suburbia is produced and so the project can be reviewed as a case study regarding the degrees to which innovation can be built into the contemporary suburban planning and construction process.

## Wungong Urban Water: an innovative model

Armadale was identified as a major centre in the 1955 Stephenson Hepburn Plan[3] for Perth and the land around Armadale was identified for urban growth. The Metropolitan Regional Scheme[4] determined the land as urban and urban deferred in 1996 while Network City[5] and the Southern River/Wungong/Brookdale District Structure Plan[6] proposed a 'liveable neighbourhoods' structure over the area. In early 2004 the area was included in the ARA area to give the state government direct control of planning in Wungong and special powers to assist the urban development of the area.

The Wungong project area currently consists of relatively flat land with high clay content soils. The combination of soils, water entering the site from the escarpment, and poor drainage means the land experiences short periods of seasonal surface inundation. Due to the presence of water a significant area of the site has been unsuitable for farming and has remained as wetland. The site is also at the headwaters of one arm of Perth's river

---

Design team
 Richard Weller, Tinka Sack and The Planning Group

Design team advisors
 Shami Howe and Patric de Villiers

Design team support
 Andrew Nugent, Mike Rowlands, Jon Everett, Julia Robinson, Alexandra Farrington and Dr Margaret Grose

Core consultant team
 Matt Taylor (director), ATA Environmental Scientists, JDA Hydrologists, GHD Engineering, Worley Parsons Traffic Engineering, and Tempus Archeology

1. A complete documentation of the project is available at <http://www.landcorp.com.au/portal/page?_pageid=1033,1&_dad=portal&_schema=PORTAL&nav=wungong>.

2. The project is also the only urban area in Australia to receive acknowledgement and funding under the federal government's Water Smart Australia program.

3. Stephenson, G., *Plan for the Metropolitan Region, Perth and Fremantle: A Report Prepared for the Government of Western Australia*, Government Printing Office, Perth, 1955.

4. Western Australian Planning Commission, *Metropolitan Regional Scheme as amended from time to time*, 2008. Available at <http://www.wapc.wa.gov.au/Publications>.

5. Western Australian Planning Commission, *Network City: Community Planning Strategy for Perth and Peel*, 2004. Available at <http://www.wapc.wa.gov.au/Publications>.

6. Ministry for Planning, *Southern River/Wungong/Brookdale District Structure Plan*, 2001. Available at <http://www.wapc.wa.gov.au/>.

'It is possible to design better developments only if strategically situated, interdependent networks of open space, streets, utilities and land use can be planned and designed together from the outset.'

Girling, C. and Kellett, R., *Skinny Streets and Green Neighbourhoods: Design for Environment and Community,* Island Press, Washington, 2005. p. xiv.

*The Wungong Urban Water site, 1,500 hectares of low-lying degraded rural land adjacent to the existing township of Armadale.*

*The avenues (straight lines running north-south) define the main public open spaces of the masterplan and also function as drainage swales, retaining and cleansing stormwater before releasing it in to the site's natural drainage system and ultimately into the Wungong River, which leads into the Canning and Swan rivers further downstream.*

system. Consequently, water management and water quality were determining factors of the masterplan and will be crucial to the overall environmental credibility of the project when constructed.

The UWA LSP proposed an urban development with an integrated urban water-management system structured around a matrix of 'park avenues' and 'living streams' to maintain and enhance the area's natural and rural character. Integrated water-sensitive urban design, water-resource planning and environmental protection has resulted in an innovative total water cycle for the Wungong development and reduced dependence on imported scheme water. The development will also fund the restoration of the Wungong River, its wetlands and tributaries.

The primary element of the masterplan's water-management system is a system of linear swales framed by avenues of trees. The avenues will contain rows of eucalypt-lined green space with central swales leading to the Wungong River. The avenues create a meeting place for nearby residents and extensive pedestrian access throughout the development. The creation of these avenues challenges the Western Australian Planning Commission's 'Liveable Neighbourhoods' policy, which to a degree perpetuates the notion that open space must provide for field-oriented sports.[7] A unique system of accrediting open space has also been developed so that a wider variety of types of open space can be supported as part of the developer contribution to open space.

The Wungong Urban Water masterplan also investigated relationships between district solar orientation and constraints such as topography, ecology, heritage, road layout, ownership and lot orientation. The results demonstrated that the highly desirable east–west lot orientation is possible for up to 90% of the lots in some areas, significantly more than the Liveable Neighbourhood's target of 75%. This innovative solar orientation planning at a district level will make it easier for builders to achieve energy performance targets, for households to consume less energy and for people to enjoy the benefits of northern winter sun entering their main living areas.

Another innovation that sets a precedent for suburban development is the way in which the masterplan recognises the Aboriginal heritage of the landscape. Aboriginal heritage sites in the masterplan area have been identified as culturally and scientifically significant. An unprecedented number of Aboriginal sites have been incorporated into the public open space matrix, environmental buffers and other compatible land uses to enable preservation of these sites. This provides a unique framework for developing

[7] Western Australian Planning Commission, *Liveable Neighbourhoods*, 2007, Available at <http://www.wapc.wa.gov.au/Publications>.

Developable land

Schools

Roads

Community parks

Avenues (stormwater, public open space matrix)

Wungong River system

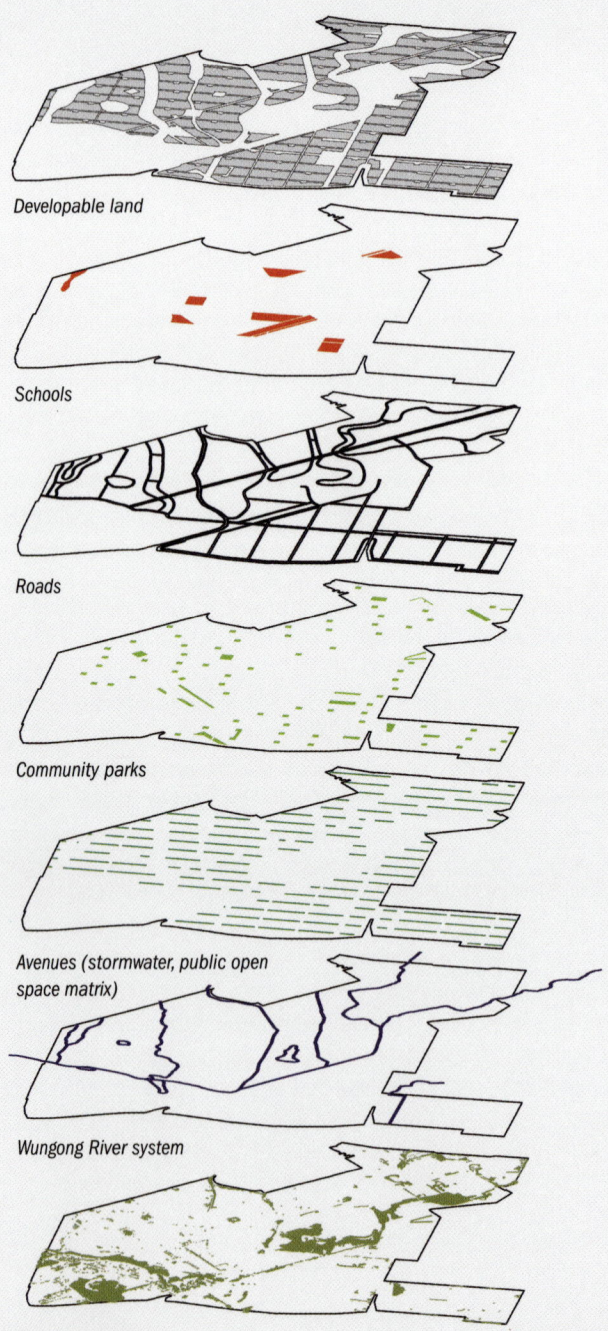

Existing vegetation

The original Landscape Structure Plan for Wungong Urban Water by The University of Western Australia.

- Existing vegetation
- Brook Parks, Wungong Bushland
- Wungong River Park
- Avenues
- Community parks
- Indigenous Cultural Centre & park
- Developable land
- Roads
- Community and commercial centres
- Regional commercial-industrial centres
- Schools
- Golf course & existing rural properties

245
BAU+

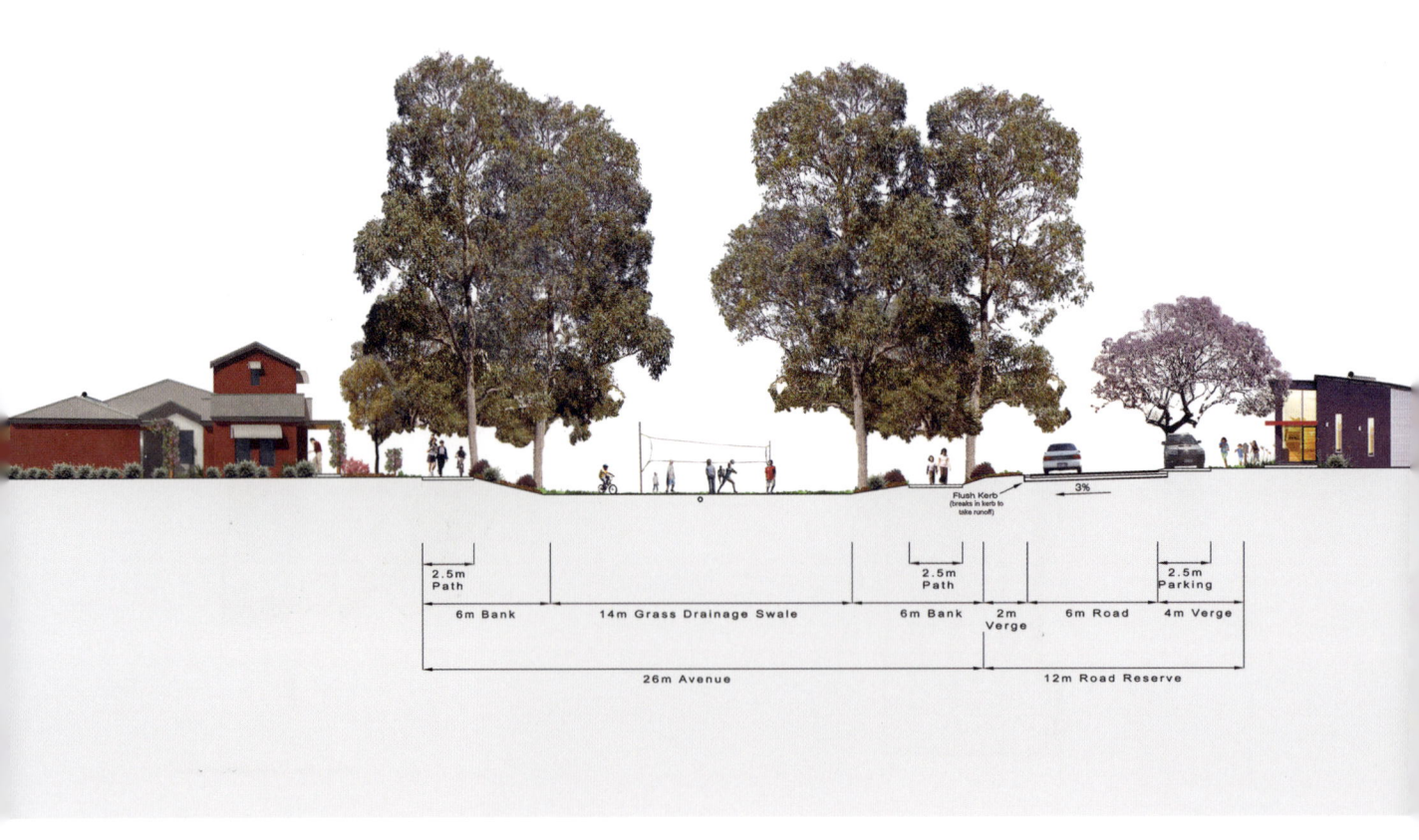

*Cross-section through a park avenue.*

on-country interpretation and promoting broader scientific and public understanding of Aboriginal culture.

Unlike traditional planning schemes the Wungong Urban Water project uses also 'place codes' to influence the quality of elements such as built form, streetscapes, and public open space. Placed-based planning is an innovative approach to town-planning, creating greater variety of development that responds better to individual sites and climatic conditions. Seven 'place codes' will guide development from the intensive district centre to conserved passive open space. These codes specify levels of quality and are tailored to the different parts of the site. 'Place codes' are site-specific; an improvement on the otherwise generic guidelines applied to vast tracts of suburban development.

*Brett Wood-Gush*

Well integrated, linear, public open space can play an effective part in reducing the $6 billion obesity epidemic afflicting our society.

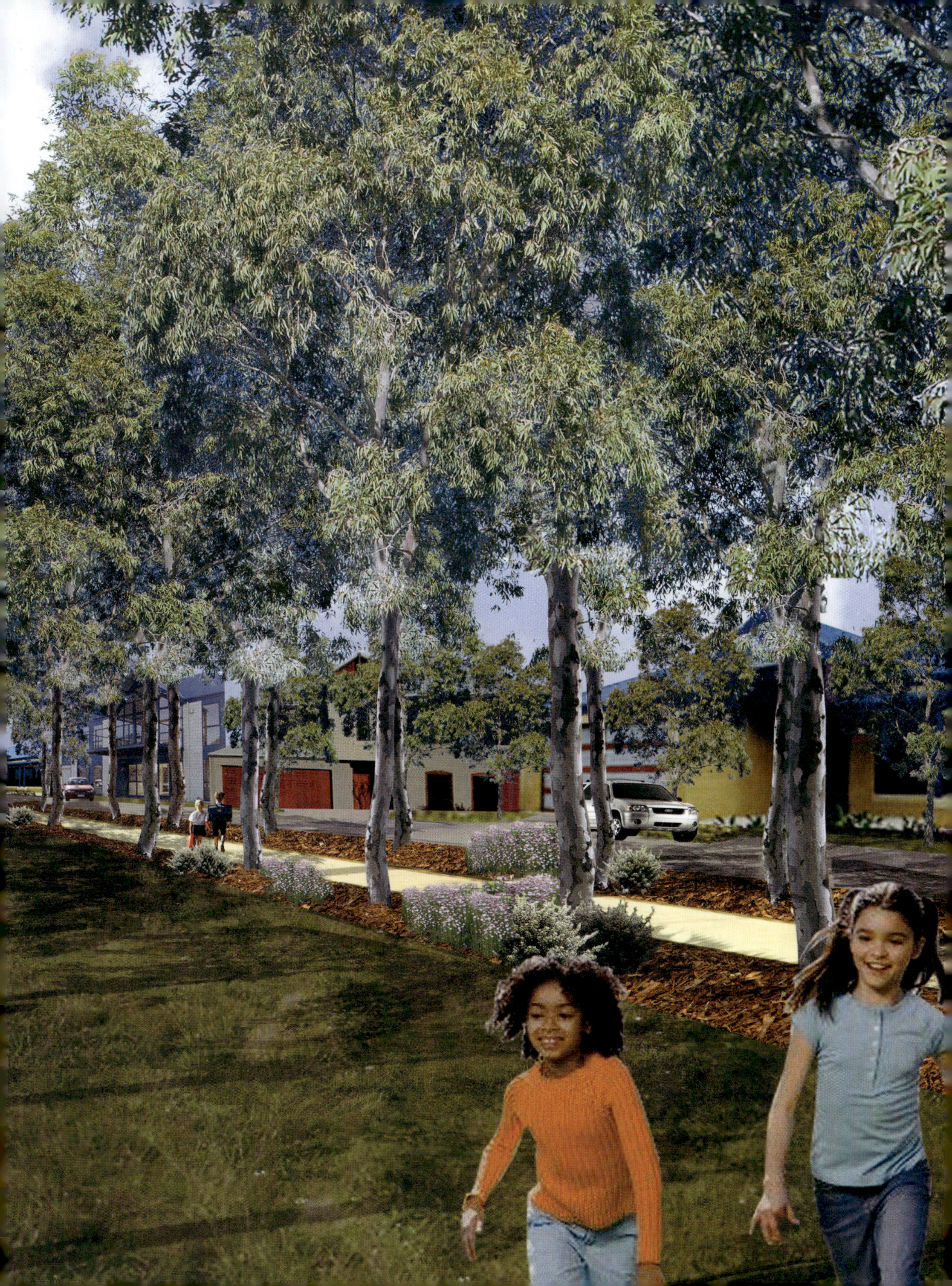

## A suburb 'as if the landscape really mattered'?

In response to the Armadale Redevelopment Authority's request for a masterplan to be created 'as if the landscape really mattered' we drafted the following design priciples to guide our work:

- Protect, interlink, and enhance existing vegetation deemed of cultural and ecological value.
- Create a holistic matrix of public open space (POS) that transcends individual property ownership and is robust, simple, and multi-functional.
- Integrate with the POS matrix a comprehensive stormwater management system as a legible infrastructural component of the project.
- Assert the POS matrix as the primary guidelines for subsequent development.
- Create a POS system that encourages streets and housing to be orthogonally (north–south and east–west) aligned to maximise passive solar access.
- Create an iconic site identity not through suburban pastiche but through the use of substantial plantings of endemic vegetation.

The following text describes how these design principles are enshrined in the final masterplan for the Wungong Urban Water development.

Without fill, the water table in this landscape is generally too high for houses built on concrete pads, the construction technique that dominates the local housing market. This, as well as the site's location at the headwaters of Perth's riparian system, its remnant wetlands, and regional water shortages, made water-sensitive design a dominant theme of the Wungong development.

Immediately we set aside and buffered all the existing wetlands, riparian zones (drainage lines surrounded by vegetation), and stands of significant vegetation. We then needed a simple system of drainage lines that would take all the water from the future suburban subdivisions and link into the site's natural drainage systems. This comprehensive drainage system, we concluded, would also function as a POS system. Ideally that system would form an interconnected matrix across the whole site, transcending the boundaries of the many smaller subdivisions that would form over the next 15 years in order to complete the project.

In Western Australia, in addition to land set aside for environmental protection, a development must also allocate 10% of its developable area to POS. To create a holistic, interconnected matrix of POS, we took the standard 10% POS allocation and stretched it into thin 'ribbons' across the entire site. The rule guiding the layout of these ribbons was that no future resident should ever be more than 100 metres from public open space.

A second rule was that the width to which an open space in a suburban context could be reduced before it was no longer visually and functionally viable was around 30 metres. Following these rules resulted in the superimposition of 40 kilometres of POS ribbons spaced 200 metres from one another across the whole site. These strips of POS became known as park avenues.

Each park avenue is defined by four rows of trees, which frame a central grassed open space. This open space functions as both a passive recreational area and a swale system. The swales within the avenue strip nutrients before discharging stormwater into the groundwater or into the revegetated zone of the Wungong River which bisects the site. In what is a hot site in a hot climate, the avenues also work to channel cool air through the development, in summer functioning as windbreaks filtering harsh easterly winds. Rear-loaded housing is prescribed to address the avenues, encouraging community ownership and passive surveillance of the public open space. Adjacent to one side of the avenue is a small road, ensuring general public access.

By virtue of their linearity, avenues encourage people to move along their length, an important consideration with regard to high obesity rates. People will also be enticed along the avenues because each one leads to the Wungong River and, as a rule, to a 3,600 $m^2$ community park situated at the heart of each neighbourhood. Similarly, each of the eight schools in the final masterplan is connected to a park avenue, making the POS matrix a safe and effective system for children. Some roads necessarily cross the avenues, but they are kept to a minimum. The avenues not only convey stormwater and people, but wildlife can also utilise this interconnected matrix. Finally, by virtue of their visual clarity and functionality, the avenues provide what would otherwise be raw suburban development with a distinctive and binding character on a scale commensurate with the development. The simple, low-maintenance typology of the avenue could thus achieve a lot with very little.

However, when an archaeological survey of the site revealed a plethora of important Aboriginal sites and these were (rightly) included in the overall POS calculation, the total POS figure was well over the mandatory 10% of the developable land. Consequently, every second avenue became a 'road avenue', meaning it retained its form as an avenue defined by four rows of trees, but a road replaced the internal open space. The continuity of the avenues as the structuring device for the whole development was thus maintained, but in the final scheme, residents now would find themselves potentially up to 200 metres from the nearest park avenue.

The avenues cut across the boundaries of the 35 different land holdings that comprise the site area and were understandably perceived by developers as complicating the orthodox development process. Striated by the avenues, the masterplan was criticised as over-designed

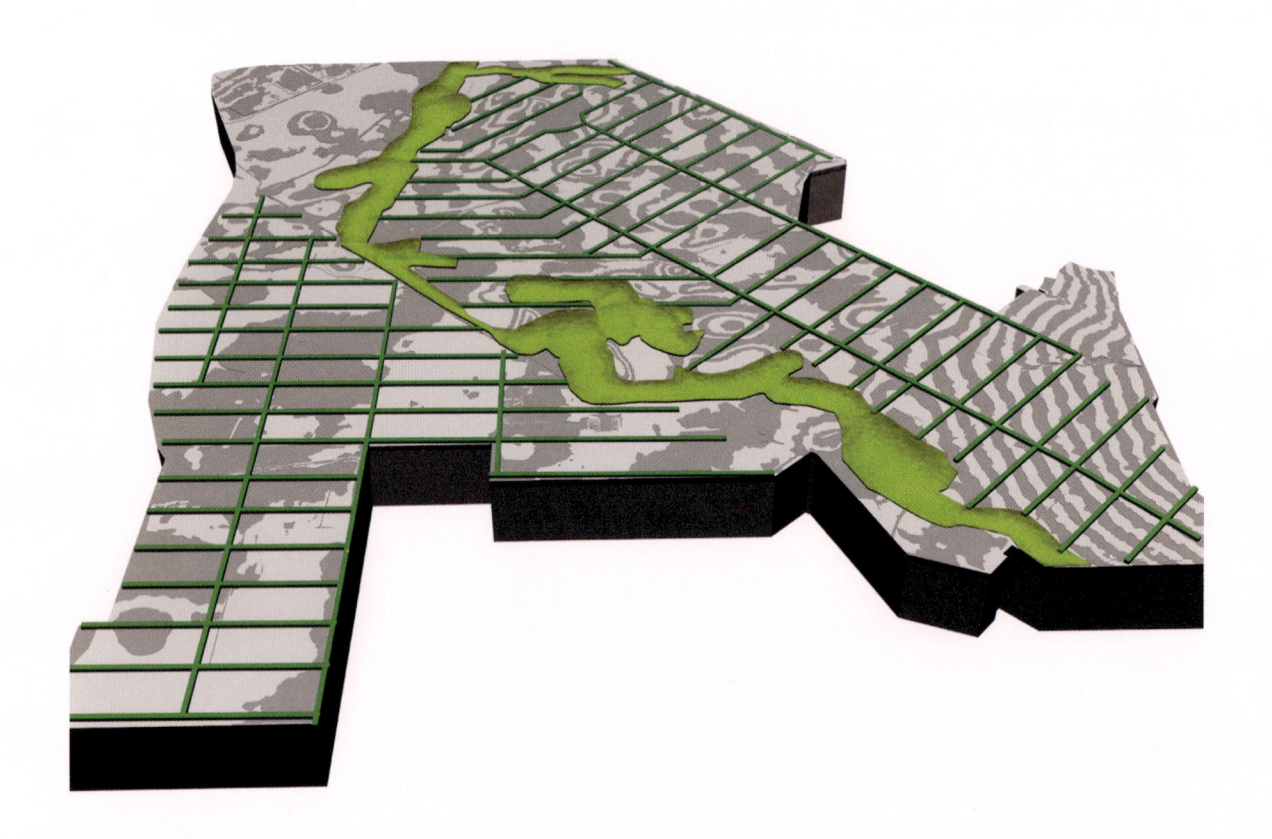

The public open space matrix of the Wungong Urban Water development forms an interconnected, ecologically and socially viable system whilst only using 10% of the site area.

and inflexible. As Andre Duany explains, 'Consultants thrive in a swamp of unpredictability. A masterplan that offers clarity is their mortal enemy as it immediately diminishes the value of their services. When such a plan is completed, they begin to stir, warning their developer clients. "Watch out – if that plan is passed you'll lose your flexibility!" Eventually the masterplan is rejected and the status quo prevails.' Indeed, to an extent the masterplan is inflexible, but not without reason. As already noted, the avenues guarantee an overall drainage system, a holistic matrix of interconnected POS, and help create a large-scale sense of place – all of which is unlikely to occur in their absence. To enable a degree of flexibility, we specified that an avenue could be adjusted to a distance of circa 40 metres to fit topographic nuances, but each development must ensure that the avenue enters and leaves any particular subdivision as demarcated on the masterplan.

What irked the various developers and their design teams most when they found they had to work with the overarching system of the avenues was that they were not free to shape the plans of their subdivisions as they normally would. They argued, somewhat ironically, that the avenues limited their ability to create a distinctive 'sense of place' for their particular project. We emphasised that the larger sense of place we were creating at masterplan scale with the avenues was more important than the branding of individual subdivisions.

The subdivision form that functions best within the structure of the avenues is simple grids. This too was intentional as grid layouts would maximise orthogonal housing orientation, in turn maximising passive solar energy opportunities. The masterplan aims to ensure that 90% of homes would be orthogonally orientated whereas many subdivisions achieve only 60%. Developers complained that this, again, was restrictive.

In the final masterplan the avenues on the northern side of the Wungong River are inter-cardinal, not orthogonal. The reason for this design change was partly that drainage was better served, but more so because the cadastral boundaries of the existing land ownership of the site are intercardinal.[8] It was considered difficult enough to ensure the avenues would link from one subdivision to another, but the complication of cutting across the existing grain of land ownership was expected to make construction absurdly complicated. Consequently, the consultant team explored and resolved ways of manipulating subdivision design within the intercardinal orientation of the avenues to maintain orthogonal orientation for the house lots without incurring a significant loss of yield for developers.

The many planning details of this masterplan conform to new urbanist principles. Residential areas are organised in accord with walkable distances to neighbourhood centres,

8 Many of Perth's cadastral boundaries are intercardinal. The origin of this can be seen in the first of Perth's sub-divisions as shown on page 16, wherein the geometry of the boundaries relates to the river not the compass.

9. Whilst acknowledging that 'precisely what green urbanism implies is evolving and unclear...' Timothy Beatley concludes that a greener city is one that would: reduce its ecological footprint; function in a way analogous to nature by developing a circular rather than linear metabolism; strive toward local and regional self sufficiency, and offer its citizens a healthier lifestyle and environment. Beatley, T., *Green Urbanism: Learning from European Cities*, Island Press, Washington, 2000.

10. Western Australian Planning Commission (WAPC), *Network City: Community Planning Strategy for Perth and Peel*, Western Australian Planning Commission, 2004. Available at <http://www.dpi.wa.gov.au/networkcity/1214.asp>.

streets form interconnected grids as opposed to cul-de-sacs, no buildings back onto POS, and generous streetscapes are prescribed. What 'sense of place' the housing stock will ultimately achieve remains to be seen, but the new urbanist strategy of developing relatively prescriptive aesthetic codes (place codes) has been adopted in a bid to regulate urban form.

The masterplan's avid protection and enhancement of existing wetlands, retention of remnant vegetation, and restriction of all plantings to species of provenance should form a coherent registration of local landscape character. Furthermore, retaining sites of Aboriginal significance adds to the project's registration of site-specificity. The masterplan's insistence on a comprehensive stormwater filtration system; orthogonal solar orientation and an interconnected matrix of public open space as dominant determinants of form shifts this project a few degrees from new-urbanism toward green-urbanism.[9]

While touted as innovative, the Wungong Urban Water masterplan's essential logic differs little from an established tradition of landscape architects bringing open-space networks to the fore in suburban planning. For example, Olmsted and Vaux's Riverside in Chicago (1869) integrated a generous public open space system; the Griffin's Castlecrag in Sydney (1920s) related roads and buildings to topography; McHarg's The Woodlands (1973) paid careful attention to hydrological systems; and Village Homes in Davis, California (1975) created a strong sense of community through the agency of its open spaces. Upon studying these precedents, it seems remarkable how advanced they were or, alternatively, how little landscape architecture in suburbia has progressed over the course of the 20th Century. Perhaps what is really needed in suburbia then is greater freedom at the level of individual expression with regard to built form and private property, but greater limitation with regard to broadscale ecological site conditions.

Smart growth advocates might well have argued against residential development in the Wungong project site in the first place. Indeed, the development cannot claim to be transit-oriented, nor does it include within its bounds any significant employment sources. In view of its approximately 30 minute drive from the central business district of Perth and average building density of 12 to 20 homes per hectare, each of which will in all likelihood have two cars, this development is extending sprawl, not resisting it.

A regional (smart growth) perspective can however be made to work both ways. For example, the addition of 40,000 new residents in this site will contribute significantly to the vitality of the adjacent township of Armadale, thus affirming Network City's ideal of a more polycentric city.[10] The change of land use from unregulated small-scale agriculture to a well designed and managed subdivision will also see considerable money spent on the site's degraded ecosystem. Consequently, the quality of the Wungong Urban Water site's waterways should improve, which in turn has beneficial downstream effects.

*Richard Weller*

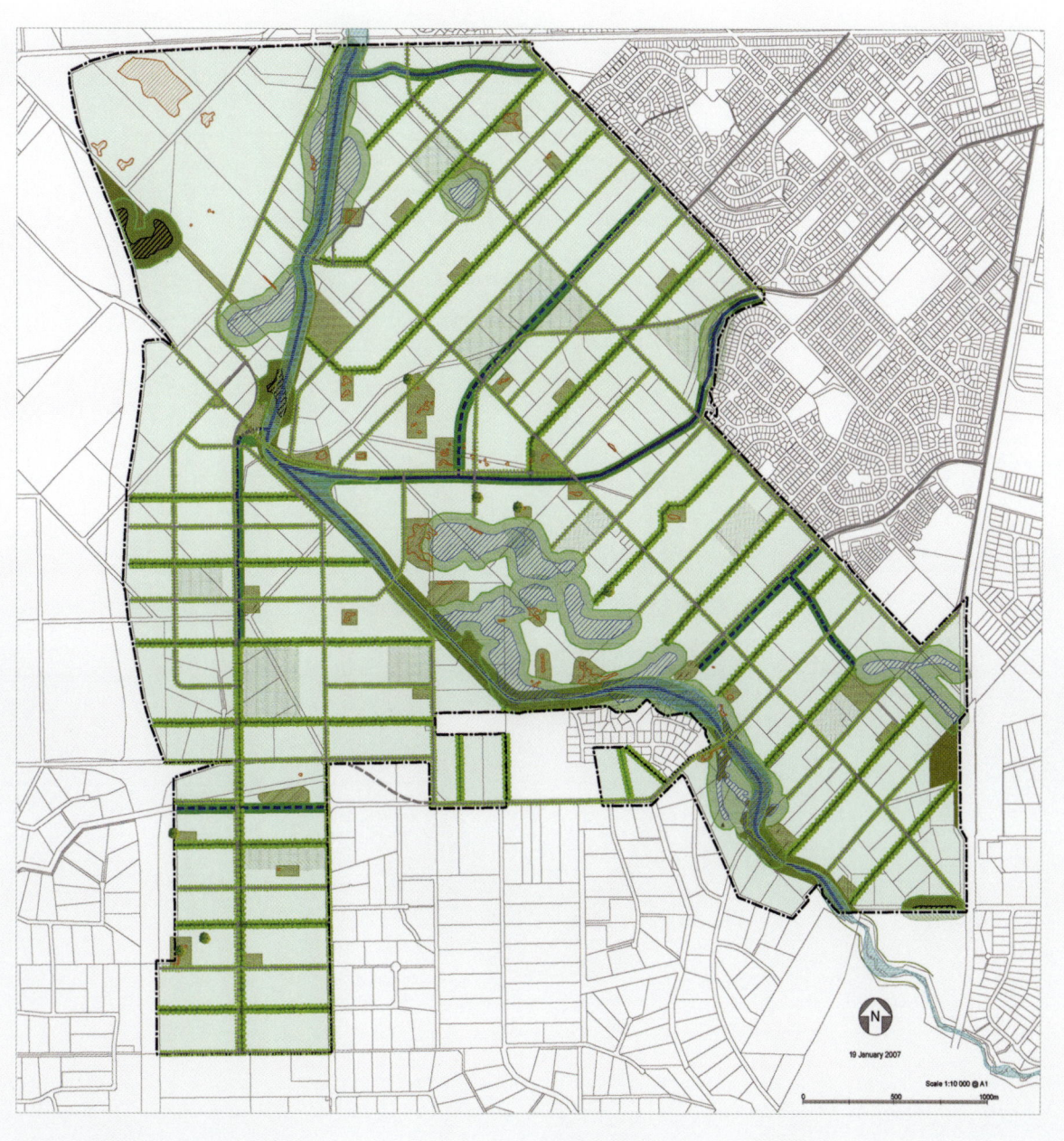

*The final Master Plan for Wungong Urban Water development by the University of Western Australia and The Planning Group in association with CSIRO and the consultant team (see page 239) directed by Matt Taylor (CSIRO) and Jamie Douglas (ARA).*

9

# NEW SCENARIOS

'Scenarios combine the rigour of theory and statistics with the essential flair and imagination necessary to the future of multifaceted issues embracing economy, society and the environment.'

Carrington, K., McIntosh, A. and Walmsley, J., *The social costs and benefits of migration into Australia*, Department of Immigration and Citizenship, <http://www.immi.gov.au/media/publications/research/social-costs-benefits/index.htm>, viewed 8 August 2007, p. 161.

Without taking sides in the sprawl versus anti-sprawl debate we are presenting alternative development scenarios, which can apply both horizontally and vertically with regard to the existing landscape of the city. In short, we are offering five alternative scenarios for spreading development across the Perth metropolitan and regional landscape: POD City, Food City, Car Free City, Seachange City and Treechange City, and three scenarios for vertical (infill) development; Sky City, River City and Surf City. The vertical scenarios are also prefaced by three examinations of conventional infill development at different densities across the current built-up area of the city area. All the scenarios can be compared with what we refer to as BAU (Business as Usual) City: the scenario that Perth continues doing what it has done so effectively since 1826 – building low-density suburbia on greenfield sites.

None of the scenarios have been intended as singularly correct answers to the problem of housing extra millions of people. Each scenario intentionally takes one big idea and 'runs with it'. They do this not for dramatic effect but to help clarify and attract debate about the potentials and the problems that all types of development have concealed within their airbrushed perspectives. Although we believe it is necessary to give planning ideas real form and represent development in a way people can understand, it is important that the images are not taken too literally. The images are not designs intending to be built as illustrated. They are far from it. They are what we call 'data-scapes'. That is, they accurately locate development and show its density but they do not pretend to show the human scale of development. The scenarios are simply large-scale planning concepts, which would, under normal circumstances, be subject to design resolution at a much finer grain. To illustrate this point, two 'designed' projects are included in the book: one zooms in on horizontal suburban development – Wungong Urban Water, and the other zooms in on vertical infill development, the New Perth Waterfront. These projects function in the book as test cases. Both are real projects, operating within the milieu of 'Business as Usual' but they offer certain innovations that are relevant to Perth's suburban and urban future.

Some no doubt will find the images of the scenarios somewhat brutal and mechanistic but we have intentionally elected to keep them so. We have not attempted to make the images of the scenarios sensual and enticing as one would normally find in images of development. We intentionally kept them as just empty shells of urbanism, so you, the reader, might descend from the panoramic heights to which we take you and then occupy these possible futures with your own imagination. It is our hope that by keeping the images of the scenarios bold and simple, as mere data-scapes, that readers might more easily bring to them their own opinions.

# INTRODUCTION

In producing the scenarios we gave ourselves a license to 'crash through' the normal contingencies that reduce so many developments to insipid, compromised creations. We felt this bold approach was necessary in Perth right now to prise open and incite debate. We have not wrung our hands over the aesthetic, political and social implications of each scenario. This is not to say that the urban scenarios in this book have been created in splendid isolation from the complex life of the city, on the contrary, it is precisely because we know how complex the city is that we wanted to keep things as simple as possible.

Equally intentional was that there be nothing purely conceptual, utopian or unbuildable in the scenarios. This book is not about fabulous cities of the imagination. Each scenario has been constructed with relatively simple and known building typologies in mind. Even though the primary aim of this research is to incite debate, each scenario has been prepared not just for argument's sake but with a view to being tested by more detailed design and partially built. Then we can properly assess which aspects of the scenarios can survive in the marketplace and how they perform ecologically and socially. Only then could we really assess whether they are better than the status quo.

We also hope that by showing development on such a large scale and placing that development in the context of the city's whole future, it might encourage communities to look beyond their own backyards when assessing the merits of the different scenarios. For example, a development project that proposes a few, or even one high-rise building on our coastline is likely to meet with fierce resistance. If, however, we approach the matter from the perspective of the whole coastline and in turn set this in the context of the whole city and the question of how to house extra millions of people, then perhaps the debates about development will be less myopic.

This is not to say that communities are not right to resist poorly designed development when they see it threatening their immediate sense of place. But if communities saw that development was being coordinated as a part of a larger holistic strategy, say, for the whole coastline and not just treated in terms of council jurisdiction, and if this was appreciated as an alternative to further sprawl, then perhaps development could be appreciated as an opportunity and not a disaster. Admirably, Perth's Network City planning policy attempted to situate development in a holistic framework and the scenarios that follow can best be appreciated as elaborations of, not contradictions to, that approach.

# 10

# HORIZONTAL SCENARIOS

With a population of only 1.5 million and an urban footprint of 100,000 hectares, Perth is already one of the most sprawling cities on earth.

## DEVELOPABLE LAND

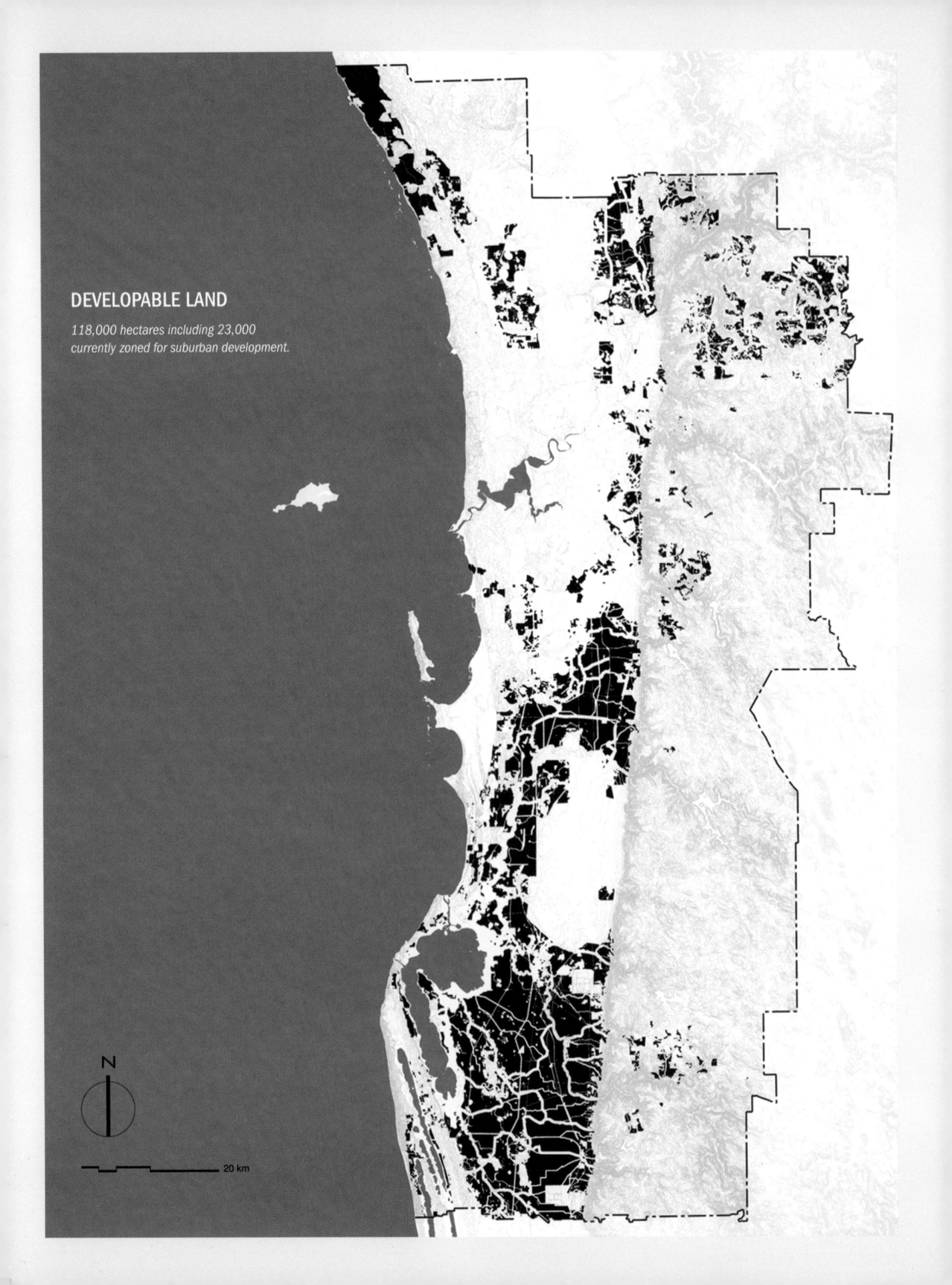

*118,000 hectares including 23,000 currently zoned for suburban development.*

20 km

# INTRODUCTION

As previously noted, there are currently 23,000 hectares of Perth's peripheral landscape zoned for suburban development. At an orthodox suburban density of 12.5 homes per hectare this land will accommodate 276,000 dwellings and 634,800 people.[1] It is likely that this development will be conventional, albeit with the modicum of innovation the Business as Usual model affords. The following alternative scenarios are based on accommodating 1.5 million people in the available landscape beyond the current edge of the city, but they can all accommodate more if necessary.

Our analysis of Perth's landscape concludes that there is 118,000 hectares of land (including the 23,000 already zoned for development) within the Perth Metropolitan Region suitable for suburbanisation. This land is not part of aquifer recharge zones or conservation category wetlands or resource enhancement wetlands,[2] is not flood prone, not vegetated and not steep. Of this land, 66,000 hectares is classified as Multiple Use Wetlands, meaning that it is low-lying but can be developed. Much of this land requires the addition of fill in order to increase its surface level above the water table sufficiently so that conventional homes can be legally constructed.

The first of our horizontal scenarios, POD City largely avoids this low-lying land by proposing that 1.5 million people be accommodated in 48 new towns, each with a density four times that of conventional suburbia. The second of our scenarios, Food City, also involves increased density and suggests that the remaining low-lying land be utilised for high-tech organic agricultural production. The Food City scenario leads to a third, Car Free City, a system of public transport which can be built into greenfield areas and retrofitted through our existing suburbs. The fourth and fifth scenarios, Seachange City and Treechange City, avoid this 118,000 hectares of land altogether by shifting focus to land beyond the current boundary of the Perth Metropolitan Region.

The 118,000 hectares of land we have identified as suitable for development is subdivided by the Perth Regional Habitat Matrix, (page 162), a system of habitat corridors originally planned by the Perth Biodiversity Project team.[3] These habitat corridors represent a city-wide network of reconstructed habitat primarily following riparian zones to connect existing fragments of bushland. One segment of this matrix can be seen at a larger scale cutting through the middle of the Wungong Urban Water masterplan as shown on page 255. When the whole habitat matrix is included and all the areas of land deemed not suitable for development excluded, the net result is a Landscape Structure Plan for the whole of Perth (see page 172). This Landscape Structure Plan requires much closer attention but in principle it says that what is green *cannot* be developed and what is white *can* be developed. It also implies that on a regional scale Perth should not only set aside the areas of green from development but that it should actively invest in this interconnected system as one of the vital organs of the city. The first two of the following scenarios, POD City and Food City operate within the guidelines of the Landscape Structure Plan.

---

[1] Although often zoned for 20 homes per hectare the 2006 *State of the Environment Report* concludes that the average built suburban density is 12.5 homes per net hectare. Environmental Protection Authority, *State of the Environment Report Western Australia (Draft)*, Department of Environment and Conservation, Perth, 2006, p. 229.

[2] Conservation category wetlands are considered wetlands in relatively pristine condition and must be protected from any development. Resource enhancement wetlands are those requiring ecological reconstruction and thereafter only limited human interaction.

[3] Del Marco, A. and Taylor, R., et al., *Local Government Biodiversity Planning Guidelines for the Perth Metropolitan Region*, Western Australia Local Government Association, Perth, 2004.

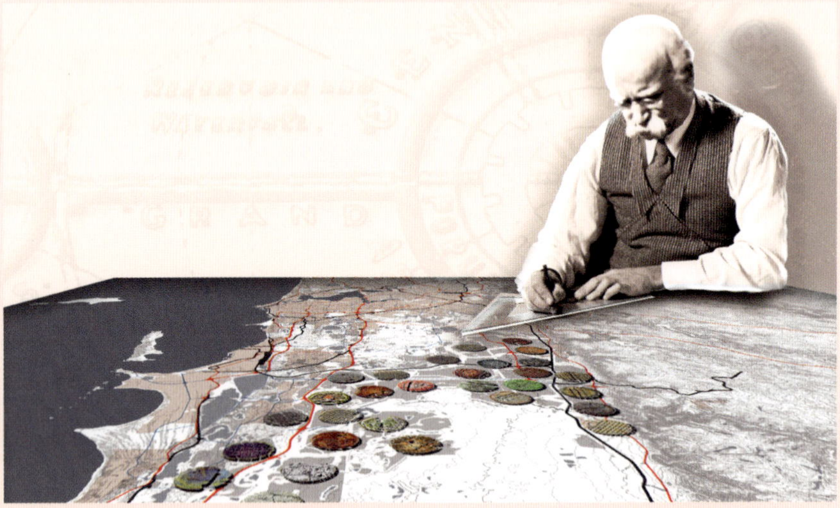
GRAND

# POD CITY

## Performance Oriented Developments (POD)

The English planner Ebenezer Howard's antidote to the unplanned 19th Century industrial city was a vision of relatively spacious new towns built in the countryside. Each 'Garden City' would accommodate 32,000 people at a density of about 40 homes per hectare surrounded by a rural estate/greenbelt of 2,020 hectares. These 'cities' were to be linked via rail to others in a decentralised mosaic around an extant central city. Land was to be held in common ownership and nourished by recycled human waste. Everyone in these new developments would be guaranteed sunshine, fresh air and above all, close proximity to 'the beauty of nature'.[4]

Published in 1898, Howard's original Garden City was conceived not only as a new form of urbanism but as a revolutionary social system: an embodiment of equity and a spiritual and material union of the country and the city.[5] This reconciliation between the city and the country would heal what he saw as the burgeoning pathologies of modern industrial life. Howard's appreciation of landscape was also profoundly ecological: for example, he described the landscape as the 'symbol of God's love and care for man…and all that we are and all that we have comes from it. Our bodies are formed of it; to it they return. We are fed by it, clothed by it and by it we are warmed and sheltered.'[6]

The Garden City's agrarian socialism failed to take root and the urban form Howard proposed has been routinely criticised for conflating arcadia with urbanity only to create a banal suburban hybrid of the two.[7] Additionally, in contemporary terms, Howard's Garden City isn't necessarily any more ecological than any other form of urbanism. The Garden City is, as Robert Freestone points out:

> *a spatial fiction as ecological footprints extend far beyond any neat notions of a discrete hinterland…Genuine green cities demand multifaceted processes of environmental management (eg; low energy usage, wastewater treatment, pollution controls, recycling, nature conservation, endangered species legislation, public transportation ridership etc).*[8]

These criticisms notwithstanding, we think that if tailored to the emerging environmental and social conditions of the 21st Century and freed from what appears to us now as the pastoral and social naiveté of the original, the essential idea and scale of the Garden City (approximately 32,000 people set in generous, productive open space) is compelling.

---

[4] Freestone, R., 'Greenbelts in City and Regional Planning', Parsons, K. and Schuyler, D. (eds), *From Garden City to Green City: The Legacy of Ebenezer Howard*, The Johns Hopkins University Press, Baltimore, 2002, p. 72.

[5] Howard, E., *To-morrow: A Peaceful Path to Real Reform*, Swan Sonnenschein, London, 1898.

[6] Young, R.F., 'Green Cities and the Urban Future', Parsons, K. and Schuyler, D. (eds), *From Garden City to Green City: The Legacy of Ebenezer Howard*, The Johns Hopkins University Press, Baltimore, 2002, p. 202.

[7] The Garden City ideal morphed in form and content as it travelled to Europe, America and Australia. It was never realised as a self-contained autarkic socio-political unit and its densities where it was realised rarely met the original prescription. A string of planners who worked in or visited Perth, most notably Sir John Forrest, Harold Boas, W. E. Bold, Sir Patrick Abercrombie, Gordon Stevenson and Alistair Hepburn, all to varying degrees advocated Garden City ideals. Suburbs such as Floreat and City Beach and some of Perth's extensive parklands remain as legacy.

[8] Freestone, R., 'Greenbelts in City and Regional Planning', Parsons, K. and Schuyler, D. (eds), *From Garden City to Green City: The Legacy of Ebenezer Howard*, The Johns Hopkins University Press, Baltimore, 2002, p. 98.

Ebenezer Howard's original Garden City diagram (in grey) scaled to, and superimposed over, the Wungong Urban Water masterplan (see page 255). The inner circles represent buildings and the surrounding hexagonal zone is greenbelt and agricultural land.

Both developments house roughly the same number of people but because the density of the Garden City was four times that of conventional suburbia it covers far less land.

We will need to build 48 of these in order to house 1.5 million people.

POD CITY

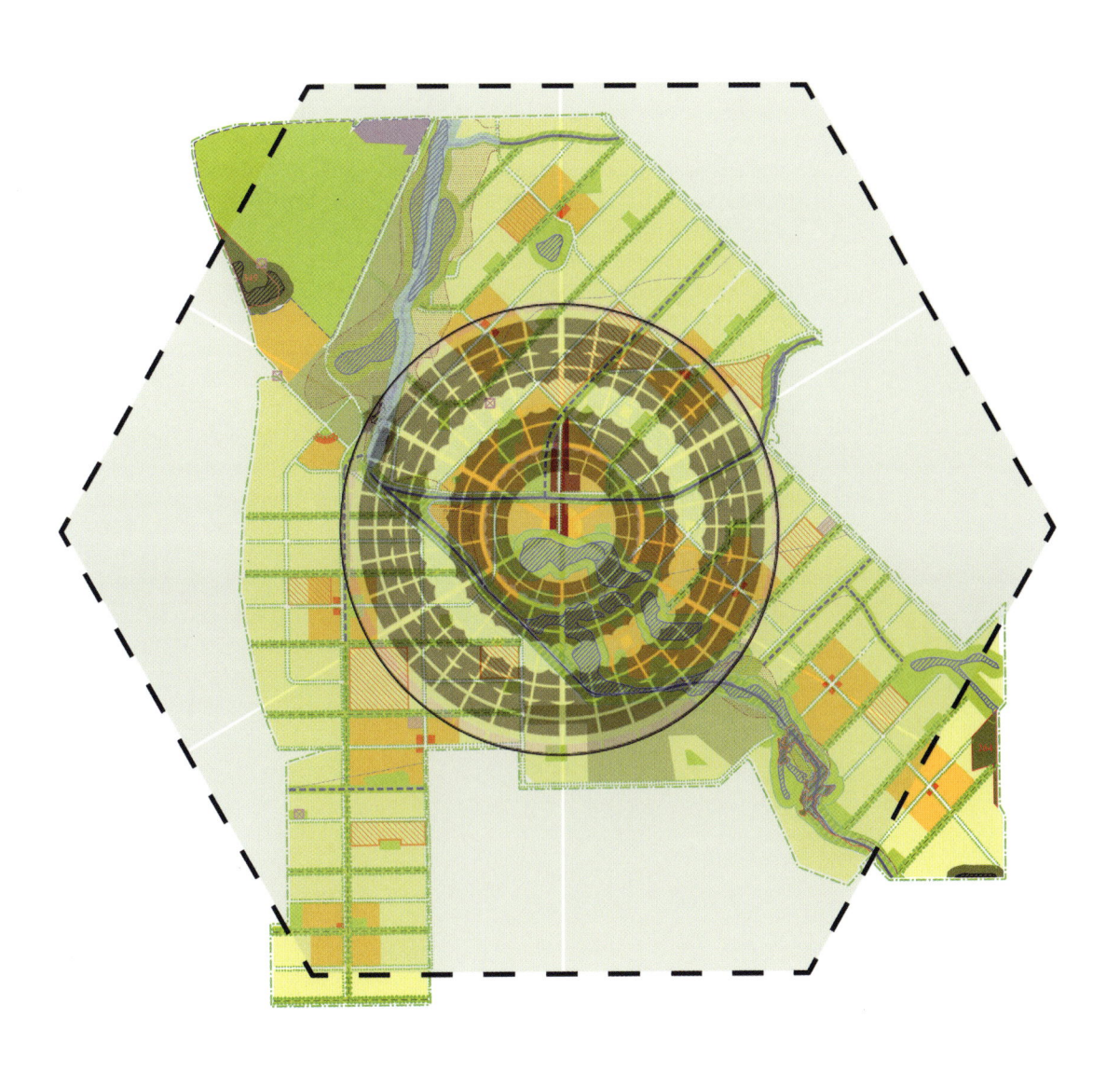

267
HORIZONTAL SCENARIOS

# POD CITY

We are thinking of the Garden City as a new kind of 21st Century village, a POD. The acronym stands for Performance Oriented Development; meaning that these new villages would be not only be Transit Oriented Developments (TOD – the somewhat reductive mantra of contemporary planning), but that their overall ecological performance would be the rationale behind their development codes. A POD would be a holistically designed metabolic system, one where, contrary to Howard's original, more attention is paid to the ecology of its infrastructure than the politics of its society.

To absorb Perth's projected 2050 population increase of 1.5 million people we would require 48 such PODs. To house an extra 2.7 million people (the highest and most recent ABS projection) we would require 84 PODs. Set at different advantageous points within the 118,000 hectares of available land (degraded cleared land close to public transport and not requiring fill) the PODs have an average density at least four times greater than conventional suburbia. The collective footprint of the 48 PODs is 19,392 hectares, leaving a land bank of 98,608 hectares which could become parkland, renewed agricultural land and reforestation zones. This land inbetween the various PODs would also contain civic institutions, industrial zones and recreation facilities that would serve to conjoin and be shared by the otherwise morphologically distinct PODs. At least two of the PODs would be university towns.

In what would be an unprecedented international design event, a cast of multi-disciplinary teams could be charged with sourcing the most innovative technologies for the development of the 48 new PODs of Perth. To appreciate the scale of this undertaking, bear in mind that it has taken over 60 consultants five years of work just to complete the plan for Wungong Urban Water (page 255) – the equivalent of one POD.

**HORIZONTAL SCENARIOS**

POD CITY

20 km

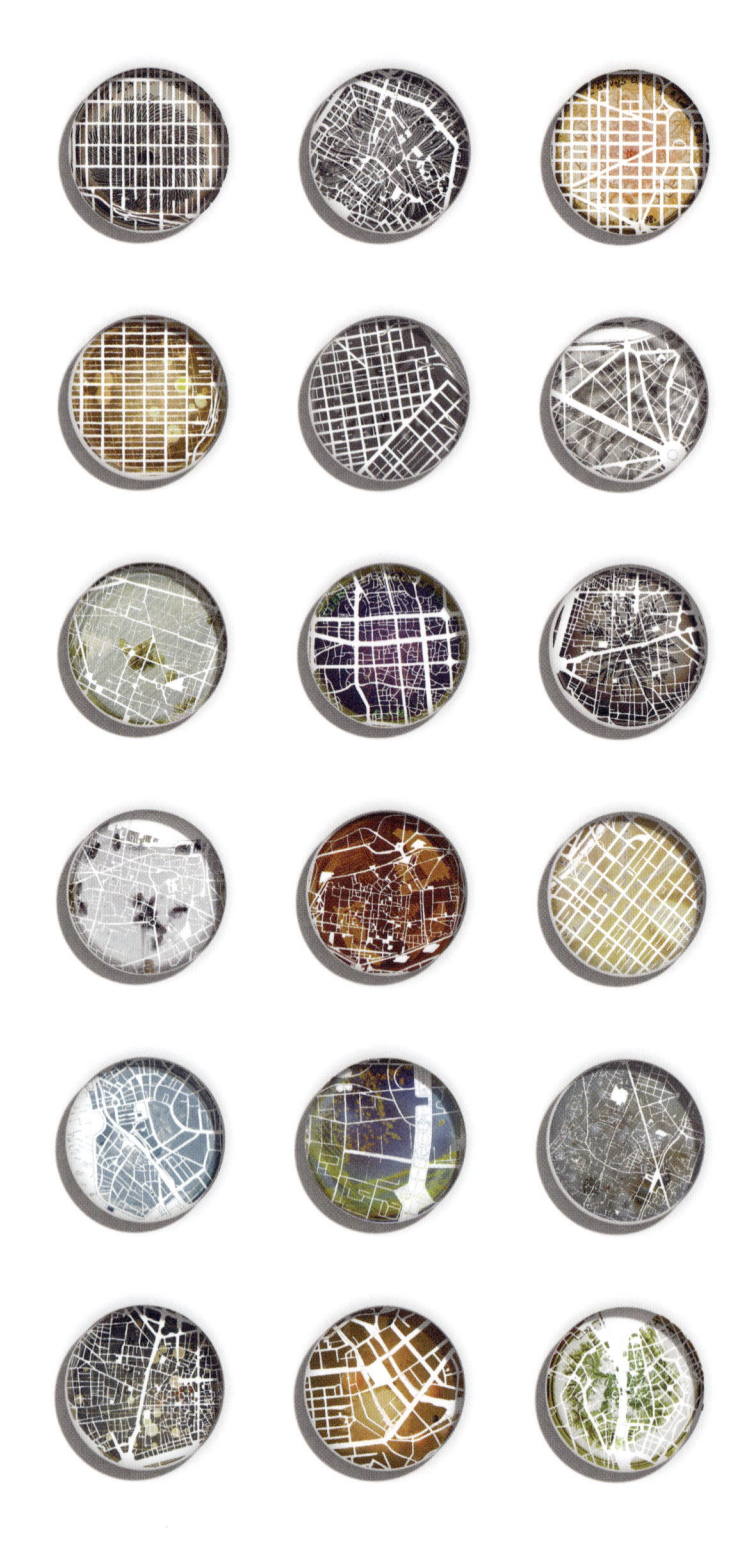

*The 48 PODs of Perth, each housing 32,000 people and designed as innovative 21st Century developments with densities four times that of conventional suburbia.*

POD CITY

271
HORIZONTAL SCENARIOS

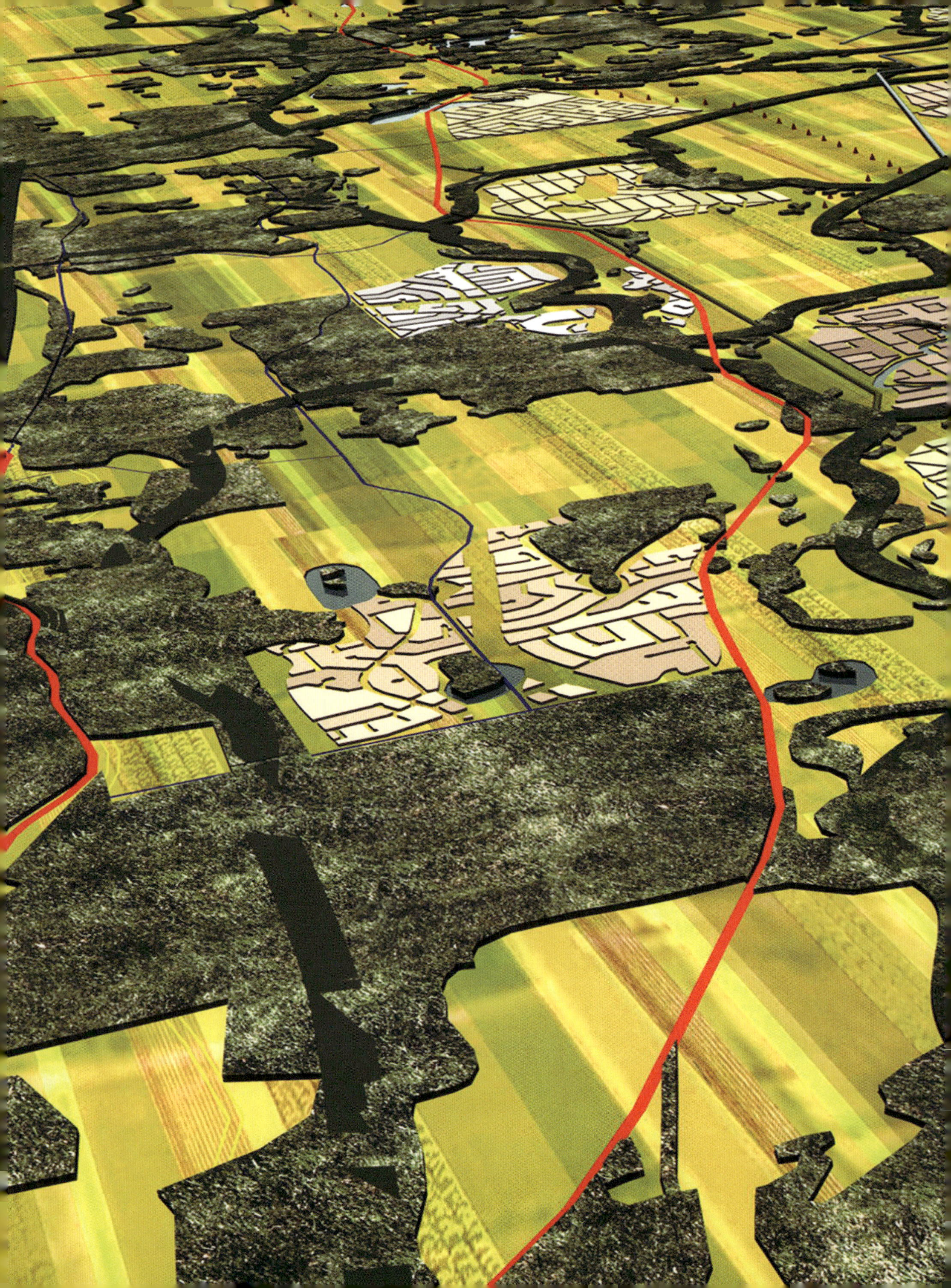

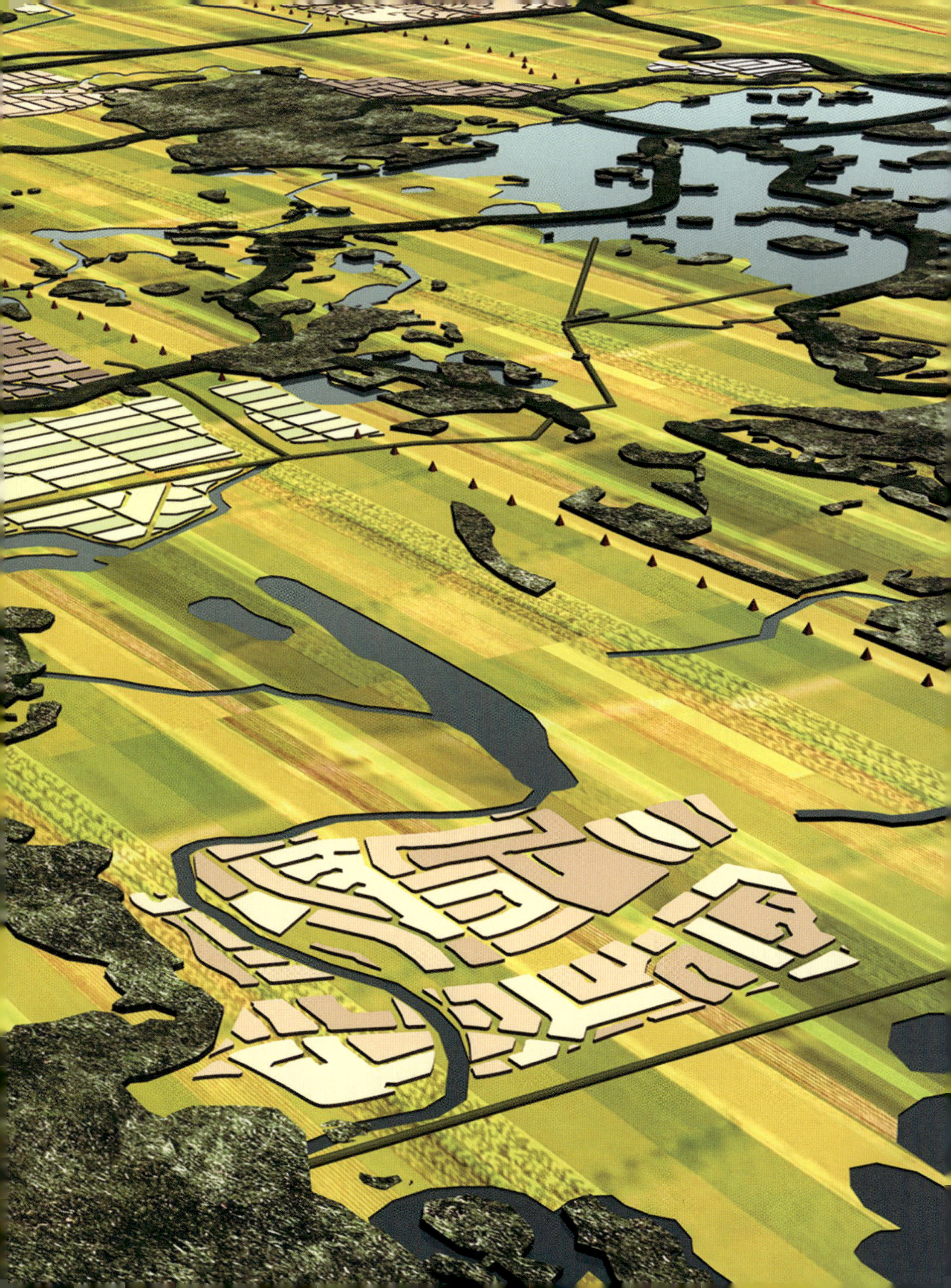

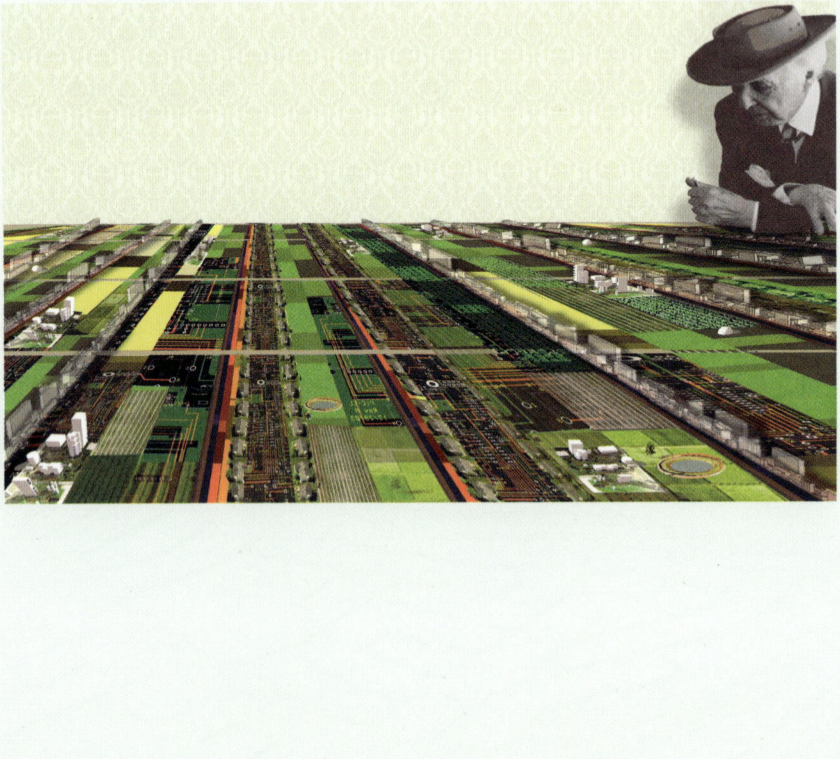

# FOOD CITY

As an urban-planning proposition for the future development of Perth our concept of Food City stems from architect Frank Lloyd Wright's 1930s concept of Broadacre City.[9] Wright believed that the modern city should not be a concentration of buildings in juxtaposition to an agrarian hinterland, rather, that the city and the landscape should be reconfigured as the warp and weft of a vast carpet spread across the entire continent of North America. The future Wright saw was one of agrarian virtue, one based on unlimited petrochemical horizons.

From our 21st Century perspective, Broadacre City's low densities (the original was to be 2.5 homes per hectare) and its car dependency are problematic. However, the notion that the urban and agricultural landscape be woven together into a new synthesis was prescient and can be productively reinterpreted to suit contemporary environmental challenges.

Certainly, in the past (and today where large backyards permit) many Australians' supplemented their diets with home-grown produce. Although such do-it-yourself alternatives to the global agribusiness necessary to sustain contemporary cities are probably futile, there is growing interest in what Andre Viljoen and Katrin Bohn refer to as Continuous Productive Urban Landscapes (CPULs) as a core component of more sustainable forms of urbanism.[10] Not only could our suburban landscapes become more interesting places if they were integrated with productive agricultural landscapes but Perth's ecological footprint of 43.7 million hectares (for the 2050 population assuming no change in current lifestyle) could be significantly reduced if food, in particular, was produced within the city limits.[11]

According to the Dutch planners MVRDV contemporary high-tech European farming methods can produce much of the food consumed by a population of three million on 60,000 hectares of land.[12] Of course, the yields of food that can be derived from the Australian landscape are generally far less than those derived from the European landscape but innovative mechanical and organic systems of farming can overcome this. Following MVRDV's allocations we can at least subtract 60,000 hectares (and an additional 14,160 for industrial and other purposes as per the existing city's amount of industrial estate) from the 118,000 hectares of degraded rural land, which we have identified as suited to suburban development. This leaves 43,840 hectares for the new residential urban footprint of the additional 1.5 million people predicted to live in Perth by 2050. If these additional 1.5 million people resided in this land area the resultant density would be 15 dwellings per hectare, six times the density Wright originally envisaged and almost three times the density of Perth's current average density. This density is, however, only slightly higher than the average density of contemporary suburbs. If an additional 2.7 million people were to live in Perth by 2056

[9] A good survey of Broadacre City and its implications is: Zygas, P. K. (ed), *Frank Lloyd Wright: The Phoenix Papers. Volume 1: Broadacre City*, Arizona State University: Herberger Center for Design Excellence, Phoenix, 1995.

[10] Viljoen, A., Bohn, K. and Howe, J., *Continuous Productive Urban Landscapes: Designing Urban Agriculture for Sustainable Cities*, Architectural Press, Oxford, 2005.

[11] Environmental Protection Authority, *State of the Environment Report Western Australia (Draft)*, Department of Environment and Conservation, Perth, 2006, p. 12. The ecological footprint of a Western Australian is 14.5 hectares (36.25 acres) per person. According to the EPA this figure is derived from the amount of land, both locally and globally, necessary to produce the food and other resources consumed by a single citizen. The figure also includes land necessary for landfill and carbon sequestration. For graphic depictions of Perth's ecological footprint see page 95.

[12] This figure does not include broadacre crops, wine or tobacco. MVRDV, *KM3 Excursions on Capacities*, Actar Publications, Barcelona, 2005, pp. 288–9.

## PERTH FOOD BOWLS

A  Food bowl for 1.5 million people: 30,000 hectares
   (minus wheat, wine tobacco and fodder – MVRDV)

B  Food bowl for three million people: 60,000 hectares
   (half the available land for development much of
   which is classified as Multiple Use Wetlands).

20 km

as the ABS has most recently predicted, then we would need to set aside 84,000 hectares of land for food production. This leaves 19,840 hectares of land to house 2.7 million people resulting in a residential density of 60 homes per hectare (or 71 apartments). This is 10 times Perth's average current density.

We can also approach the Food City scenario from the scale of an individual suburban project. Take the Wungong Urban Water development (page 255) for example. What would the form of such suburban development be if it had to feed itself from its land? The high-tech intensive Dutch methods of agriculture upon which we have based the Food City scenario at the macro scale can feed 50 people per hectare so for the 40,000 people who would be accommodated by conventional suburban development of the Wungong site to feed themselves they require 800 hectares of land. Of the total site area 184 hectares are automatically set aside for environmental purposes leaving 1,298 for development. Subtracting 800 hectares from this leaves 498 hectare of land for residential development amounting to a residential density of 124 people per hectare, i.e., 53 free standing homes per hectare or 65 apartments per hectare. More traditional chemical methods of agricultural production will feed approximately 14 people per hectare (excluding broadacre crops and livestock). At this level of productivity we require 2,857 hectares or approximately twice the site area. Traditional organic methods of agricultural production will feed 7.5 people per hectare (excluding broadacre crops and livestock) so to feed 40,000 people at this rate of productivity would require 5,333 hectares, approximately four times the site area.

It is, however, highly unlikely that a high-tech (feeding 50 people per hectare) level of food production could be achieved in Australia, let alone in the Swan Coastal Plain of Western Australia. That said, the Swan Coastal Plain has a rich history of food production and despite climate change, soil loss and declining rainfall, the Perth area remains conducive to production. Whilst Australian suburbia may never be able to feed itself off its own site area the food miles required to feed the population could nonetheless be significantly reduced if we were to produce more food within the city limits.

Whereas Wright, in 1930s America, envisaged a utopia of the car, the 21$^{st}$ Century is likely to see its demise. Whilst there will always be some form of individual people movers (for those who can afford it), public transport systems could become the dominant mode of movement through the future city. Consequently, Food City as depicted on page 280 is organised around an 800-metre grid of public transport. This transport grid is further explained on page 291.

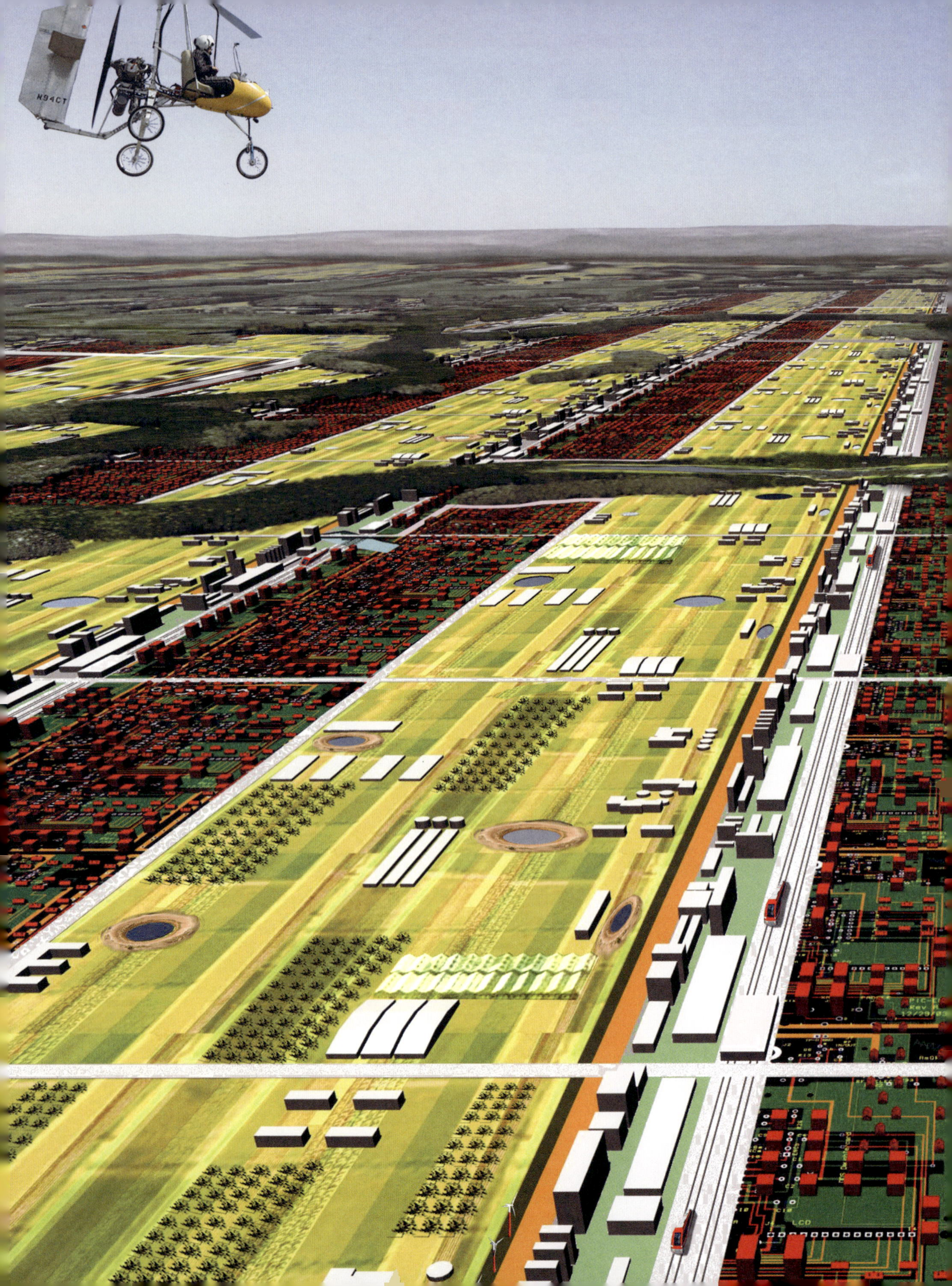

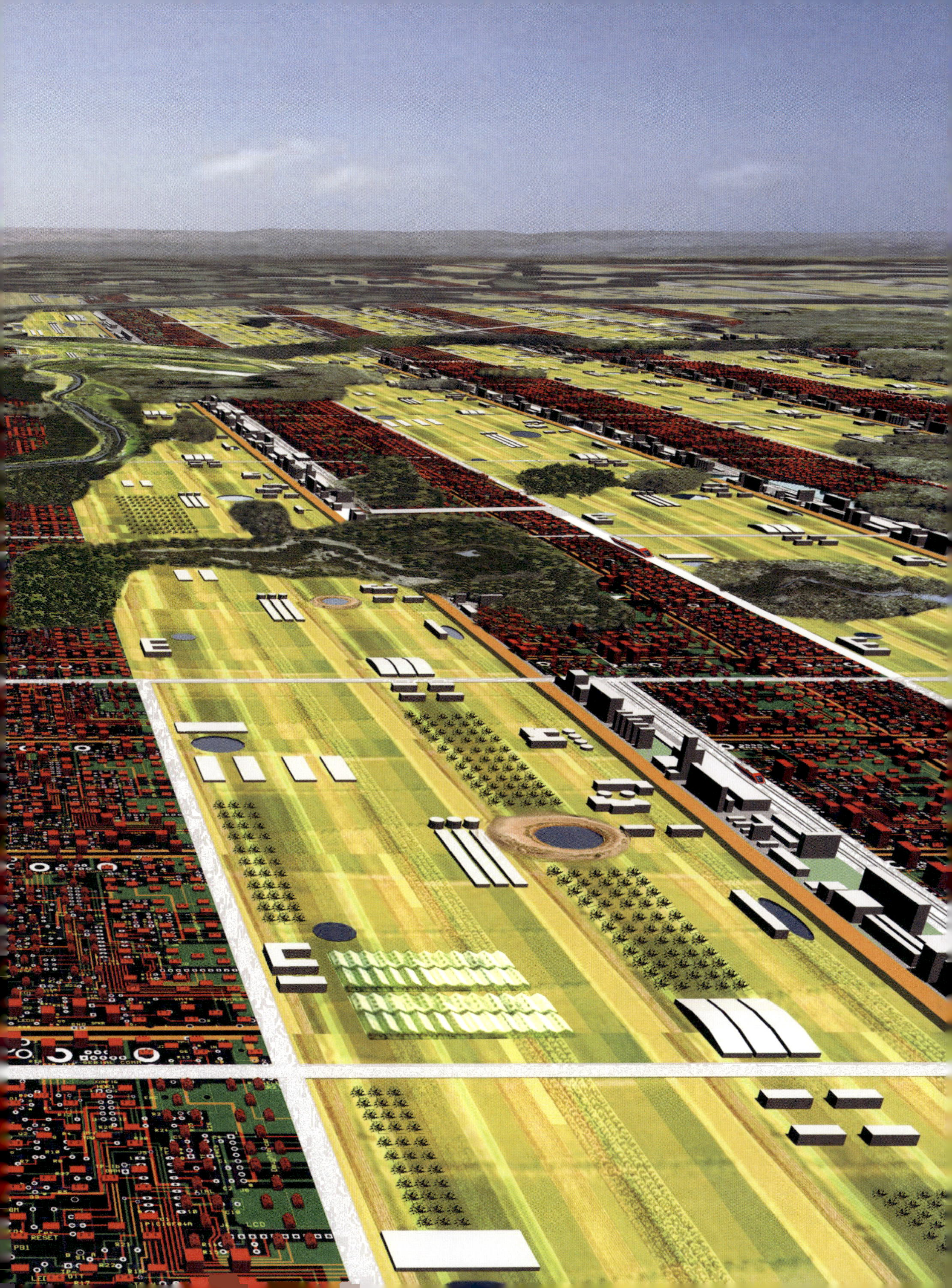

*Food City combined with an 800 x 800 metre grid of public transport. Each cell is 64 square hectares. Subtracting the land areas necessary for the transport system, streetscapes, and industrial and civic land uses, we are left with 44 hectares of land. In this formation Food City reaches a balance between a self-sufficient population and land area if the population of each cell is 1,091 living at a density of 20 dwellings per hectare. This amounts to a land-use distribution of 22 hectares for housing and 22 hectares for agricultural production in each 64-square hectare cell of Food City.*

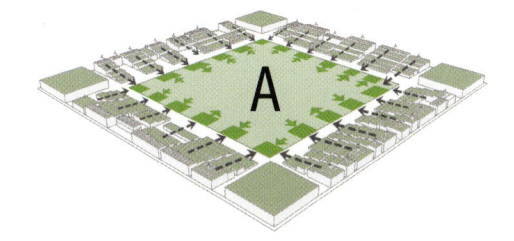

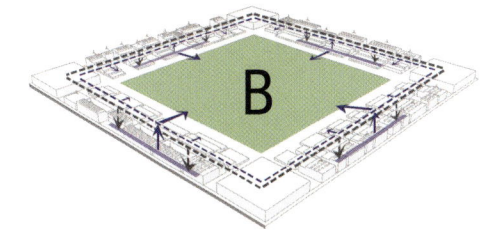

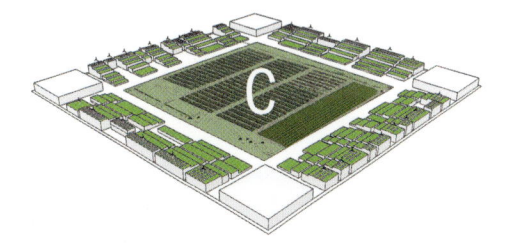

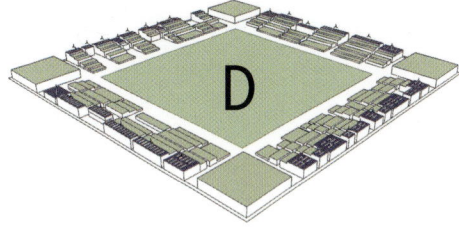

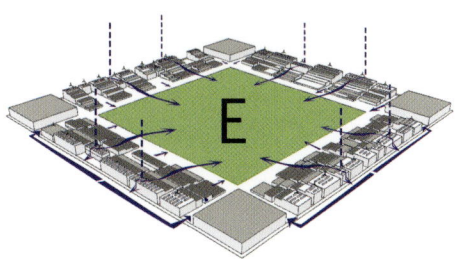

# FOOD CITY

A Compost
B Greywater
C Food
D Energy (solar and wind)
E Stormwater

This synthesis of public transport, built form and productive land suggests that the city be conceived and designed as one synergistic system. The buildings and the land could then directly exchange energy, materials, food and water. This would also be an urban environment in which citizens are more conscious of and involved in the very systems that sustain them.

**281**
**HORIZONTAL SCENARIOS**

# Applying the concept of Food City to a conventional suburban site.

*Conventional suburban development. The site is a total of 1,472 hectares of which 1,298 is residential. The proposed population is 40,000.*

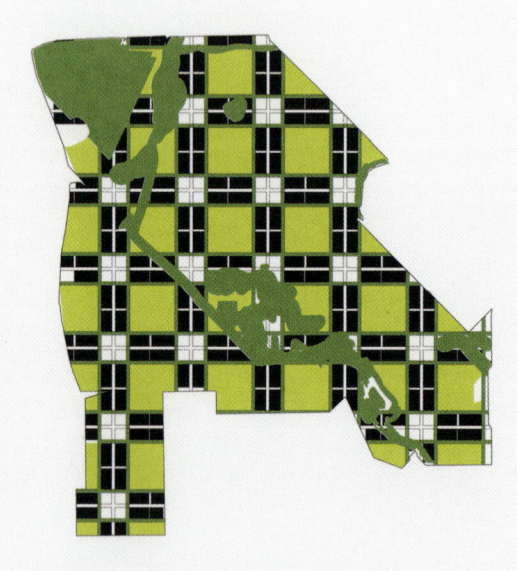

*Food City integrated with a grid of public transport.*

*Each block, 800 x 800 = 6,400 square metres, 64 hectares. Housing area: 21.57 hectares (34%), agricultural: 21.82 hectares (34%), tram boulevards: 5.5 hectares (8.6%), civic/industrial: 5.15 hectares (8.05%) and avenues/POS: 9.96 hectares (15.6%).*

*Using intensive Dutch farming methods, one hectare will feed 50 people excluding broadacre crops for livestock. Accordingly, the 21.82 hectares of agricultural land within each block will feed 1,091 people. These people would live in free-standing houses within the residential zone of each block at a density of around 20 dwellings per hectare. The total Wungong site will feed a total of 20,600 people on approximately 412 hectares of agricultural land.*

FOOD CITY

13 Data used in the *Boomtown 2050* research: Chemical farming methods (excluding meat production) feeds 14 people/ha; Traditional UK organic farming methods (excluding livestock) feeds 7.5 people/ha. From Fairlie, S., 'Can Britain feed itself?' *The Land*, Winter 2007–08.

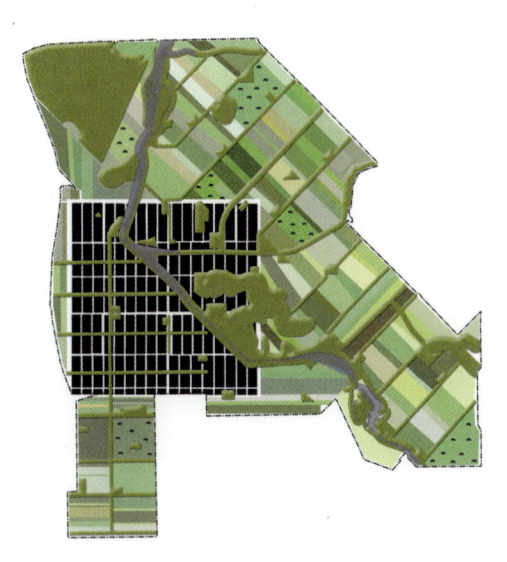

*An alternative form of the same concept, whereby 40,000 people live in a more compact townscape leaving much of the site available for food production.*[13]

283
HORIZONTAL SCENARIOS

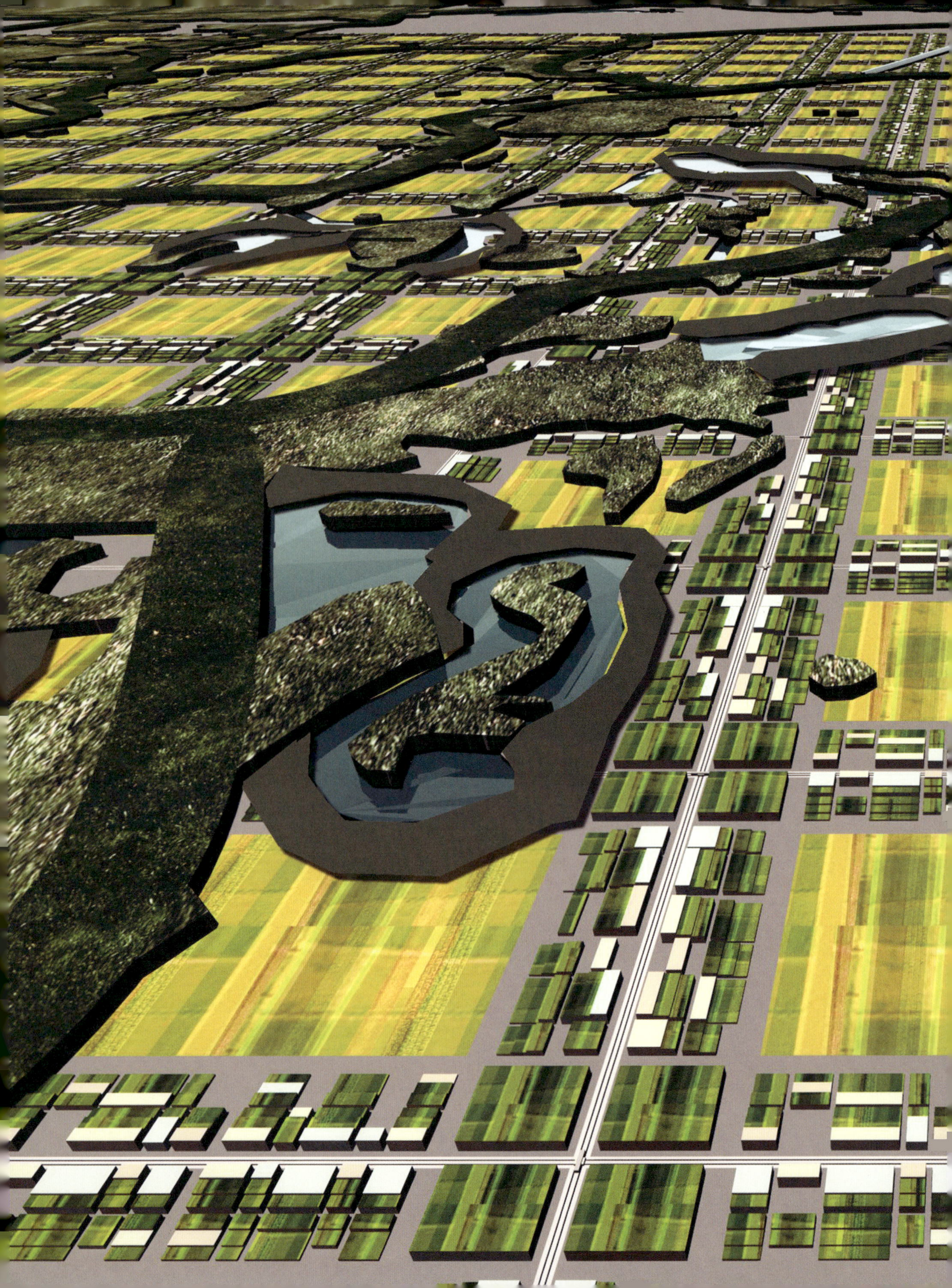

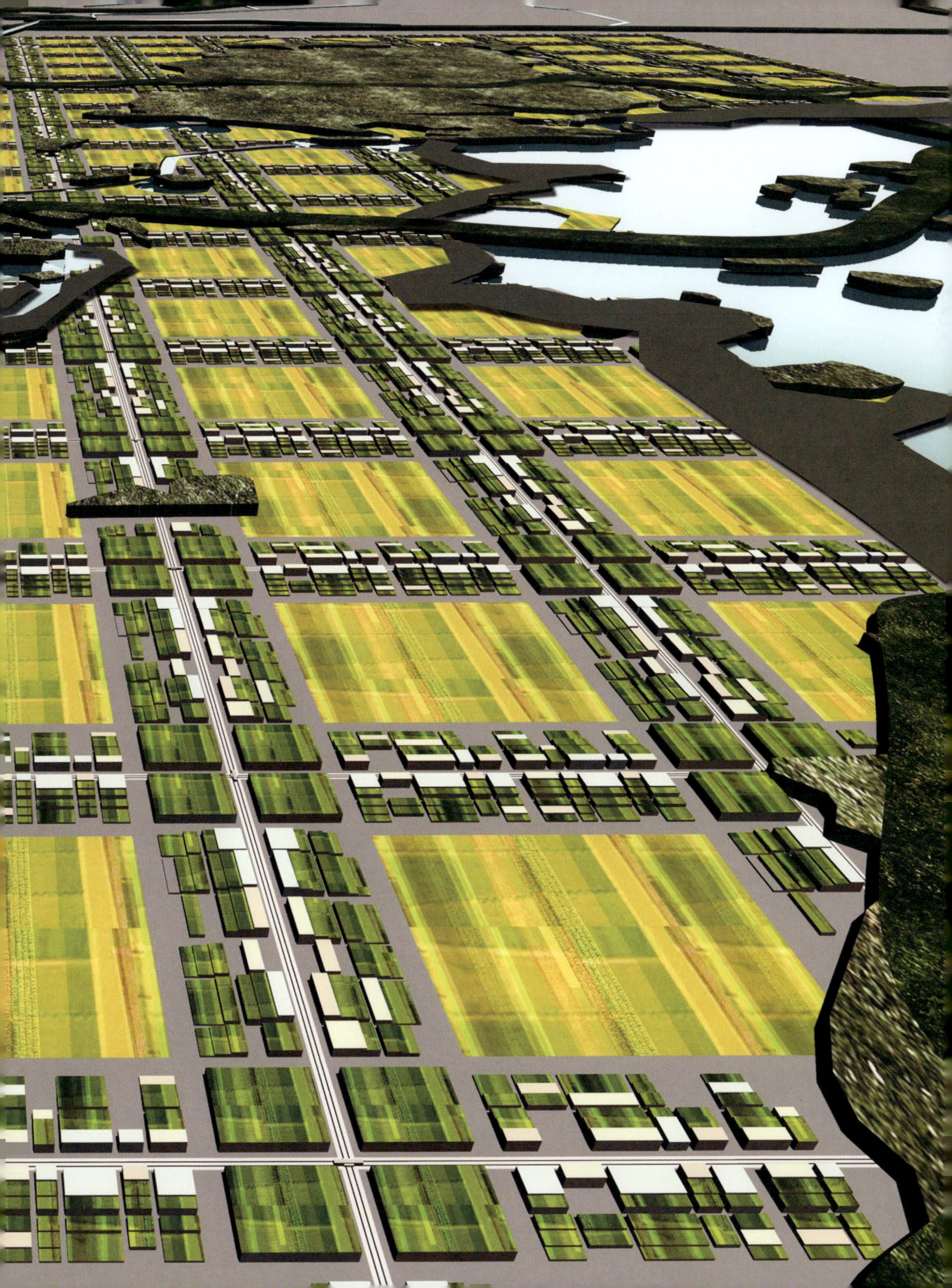

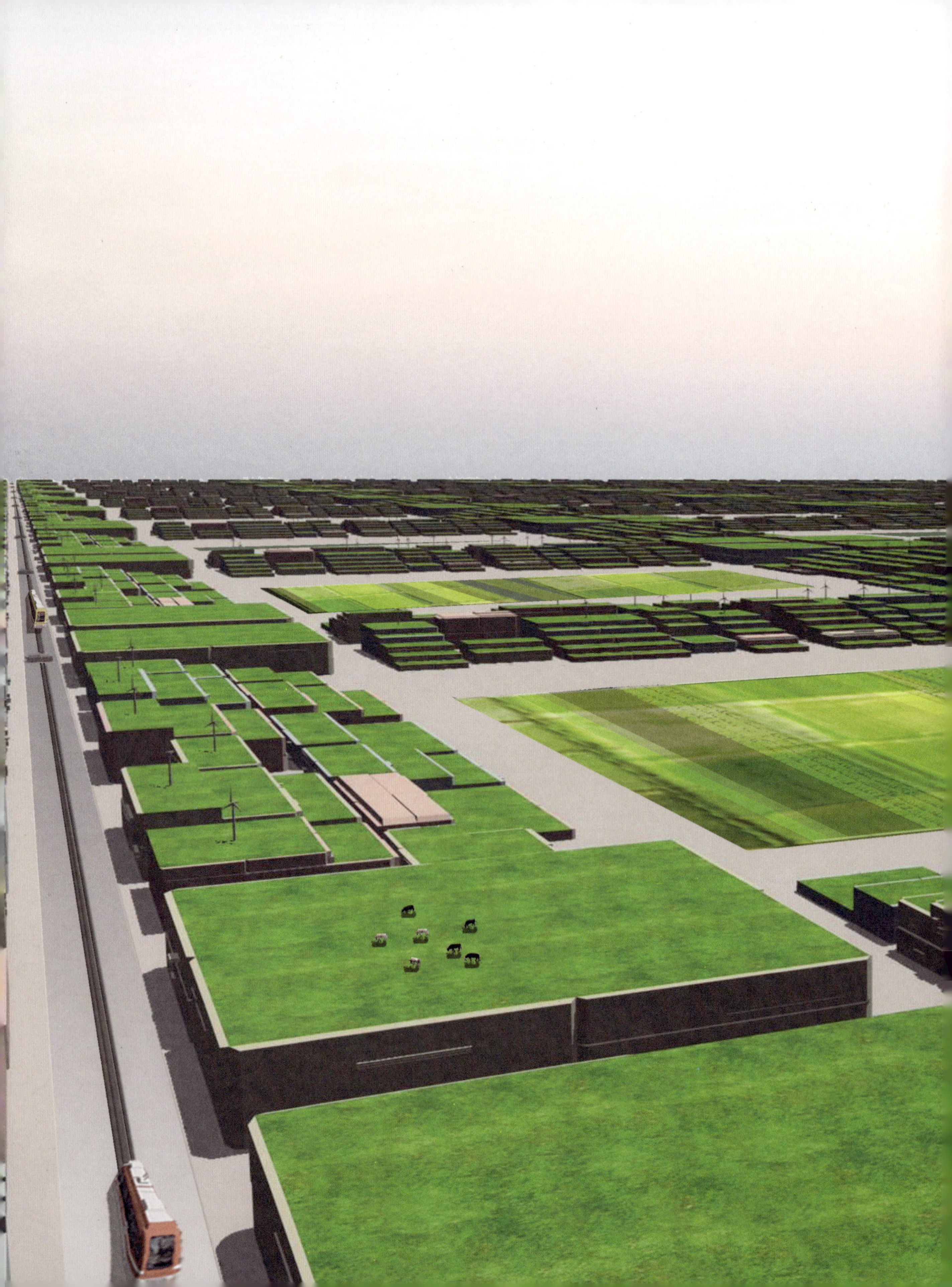

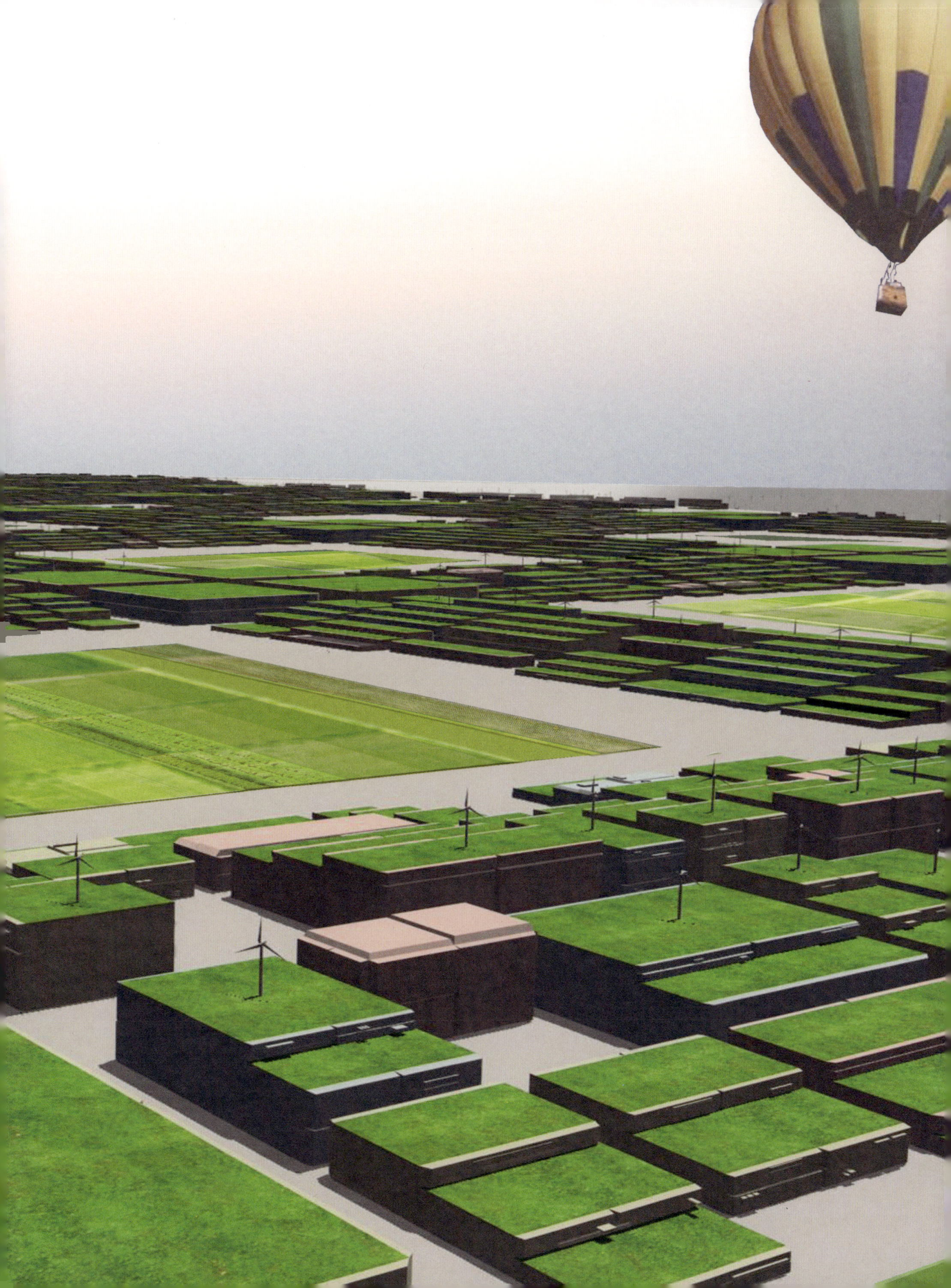

'In the next two generations the world must raise food production 110% – off a smaller and more degraded soils base, with two-thirds the water, costlier and scarcer nutrients, using less technology and under the hammer of climate change.'

Professor Julian Cribb, from 'The Coming Famine: Constraints to global food production in an overpopulated, affluent and resource-scarce world: the scientific challenge of the era', discussion paper on <http://www.sciencealert.com.au>, viewed January 2008.

## Speculating about ways to tackle this Professor Cribb says we must:

- Massively increase global public investment in agricultural research.
- Massively increase the rate at which new food production technologies are disseminated to farmers, especially in the poorer countries.
- Plan to peacefully limit the human population to two to three billion by the end of the century.
- Eliminate nutrient waste. Recycle all nutrients on farm, in industry, in restaurants, supermarkets, the home and in urban waste disposal systems back into the food chain.
- Develop 'green food' – alternative, low-input production systems, including urban horticulture, polycultures, algae culture and plant cell bioreactors – to feed urban populations on novel foods derived directly or indirectly from waste streams but with low environmental costs compared to agriculture.
- Develop 'Green Cities' in which crops are produced on roofs, walls and in waste areas, reducing urban energy use (heating and cooling) and using wastewater or stormwater. Recycle all urban water to limit demand on farm water.
- Develop systems that convert waste $CO_2$ and hydrocarbons into carbohydrates.
- Promote low-protein diets, vegetable consumption and low-input culinary traditions for affluent societies.
- Use advanced genetics, agronomics and other methods to enhance food production under recurrent drought and climatic instability.
- Integrate regional natural resource management so the needs of food production dovetail with those of the environment and other human activities, avoiding conflict and enhancing sustainability.
- Phase out commercial wild harvests, including fishing and forestry.
- Expand recording, conservation and banking of plant and animal genetics worldwide.

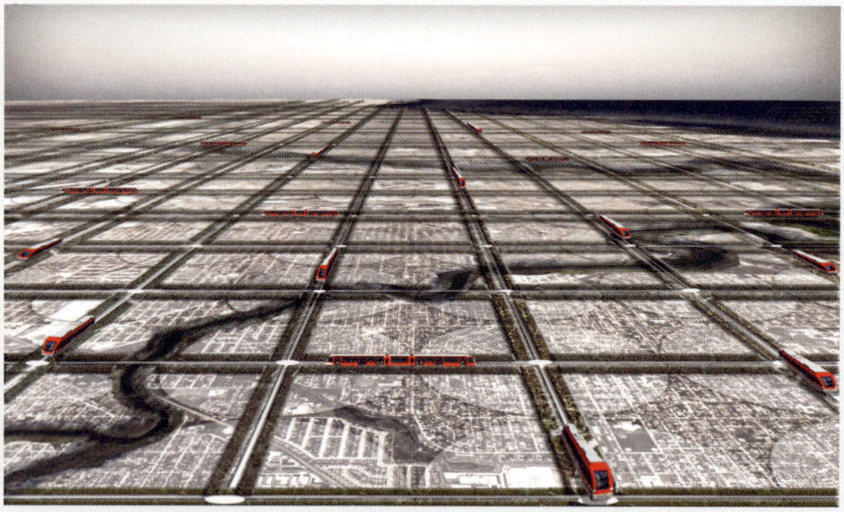

# CAR FREE CITY

Western Australians are producing 36.6 tonnes $CO_2$ emissions per capita per annum.[14] Western Australia's greenhouse gas emissions are significantly higher than for the rest of the world because of Western Australia's industry and export sector as well as high transport emissions resulting from an 'overwhelming reliance on motor vehicles for both people and freight movement'. The Greenhouse Energy Taskforce says Western Australia needs to 'slash emissions by two-thirds by 2050'.[15]

To varying degrees all the scenarios in this book assume that there will be complementary public transport innovations. This scenario of a Car Free City, however, exclusively expresses the possibility of a form of urbanism which is not determined by cars or other individual forms of mobility as the dominant modes of transport in the city. In anticipation of a time when petroleum is scarce and thus too expensive for most individuals, Car Free City takes Peter Calthorpe's concept of Transit Oriented Development (TOD)[16] to its logical conclusion and can be applied to both new greenfield development, the existing urban fabric and infill development.

Fundamental to the city with no cars is an 800-metre grid of roadways for some form of people movers (trams, light rail and/or buses). The people movers operate back and forth along the individual latitudinal and longitudinal lines of a grid. This grid would naturally adjust to suit topography and need to be retrofitted to the city in a way that endeavours to preserve the 800-metre graticule. Trucks and service vehicles would use the same grid system.

The 800-metre graticule ensures everyone is within a five-minute walk of a transit station, which would also function as a small commercial and civic centre. Such a grid would mean that any individual anywhere in the grid can get to any other point by a maximum of a short walk, two tram (or light rail or bus) rides and again, a short walk. For those who find the pedestrian component of this system either permanently or occasionally difficult or are returning home with goods and children, there could be a personalised electric buggy system operating from each transit station (one every 800 metres in all directions). A range of delivery services would become commercially available to augment the main public transport grid and emergency services would still require not only right of way but access to each home.

A single grid unit (neighbourhood) can contain anything from between 1,800 residents (conventional suburban density of 12 dwellings per hectare) up to 16,000 people at high density (250 dwellings per hectare). Each grid unit can also be variously devoted to industry, agriculture or residential and mixed-use development. The utilisation of this public transport grid in relation to the creation of agriculturally productive suburban landscapes can be seen on page 280.

Free from the domination of road layouts, the residential developments in Car Free City would have approximately 20% more land than our current car-oriented developments. Consequently, suburban densities can significantly increase and new housing typologies and public space arrangements could be explored without precluding emergency vehicle access to homes. Part of the 20% of land that is devoted to road surface in our current suburbs could then be retrofitted as riparian zones, stormwater filtration systems and linear public parks that encourage pedestrian movement.

[14] Environmental Protection Authority, *State of the Environment Report Western Australia (Draft) 2006*, Department of Environment and Conservation, Perth, 2006, p. 31.

[15] Greenhouse Energy Taskforce recommendation, Banks, A. and Taylor, R., 'Tough greenhouse gas targets a risk for WA', *The West Australian*, 6 February 2007, p. 4.

[16] Calthorpe, P. and Fulton, W., *The Regional City: Planning for the End of Sprawl*, Island Press, Washington, 2001.

20% of our suburbs are devoted to bituminous surfaces and the geometry of road design dictates suburban form. Freed from the dominance of cars our suburban environments could be significantly re-imagined.

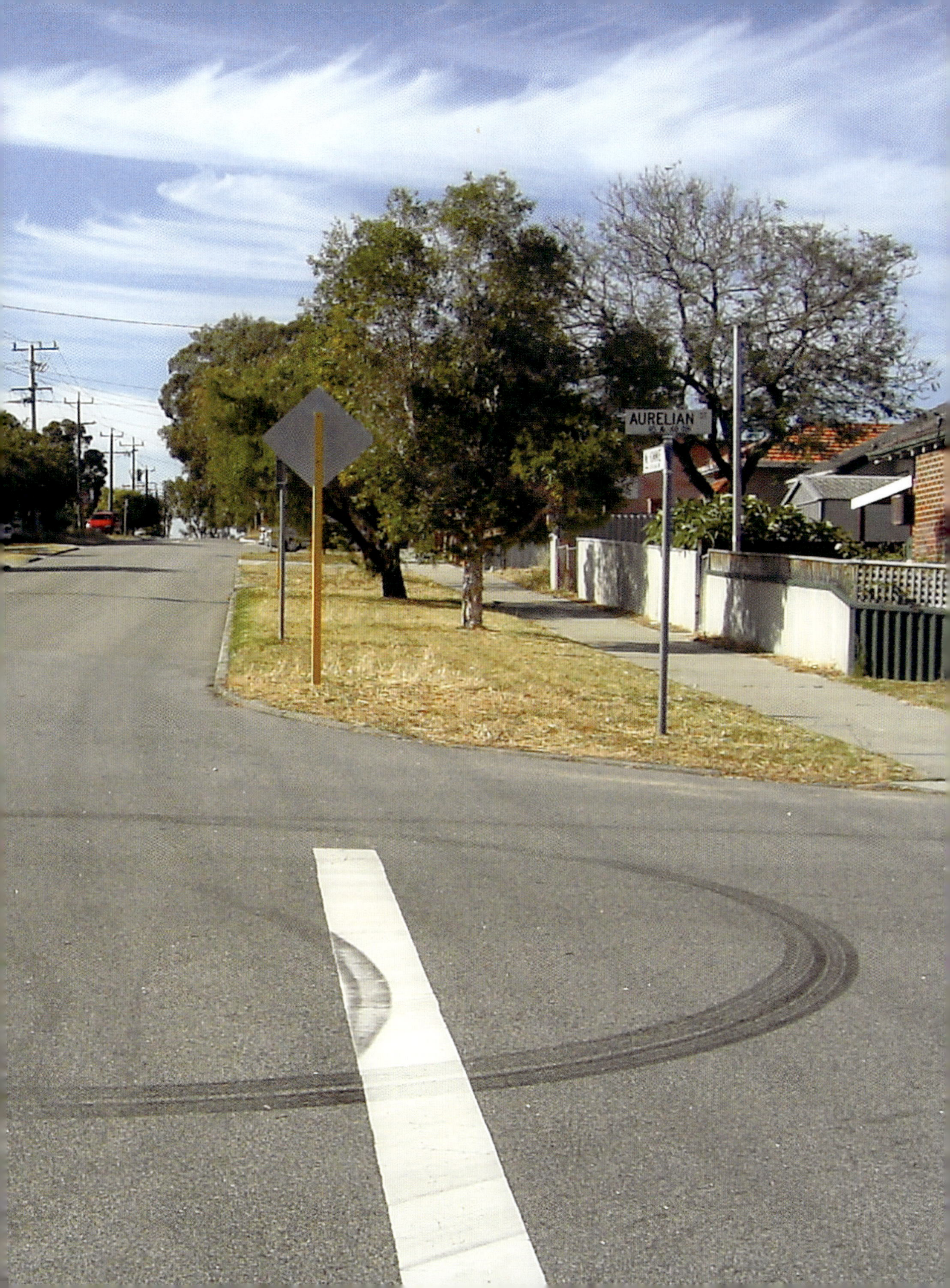
AURELIAN

*Car Free city is developed around an 800 metre grid of public transport (red lines). The system can be threaded through existing suburbs and allow new developments to be significantly denser than orthodox suburbia. Maps source: Jenkins, E.J., To Scale: One Hundred Urban Plans, Routledge, 2007.*

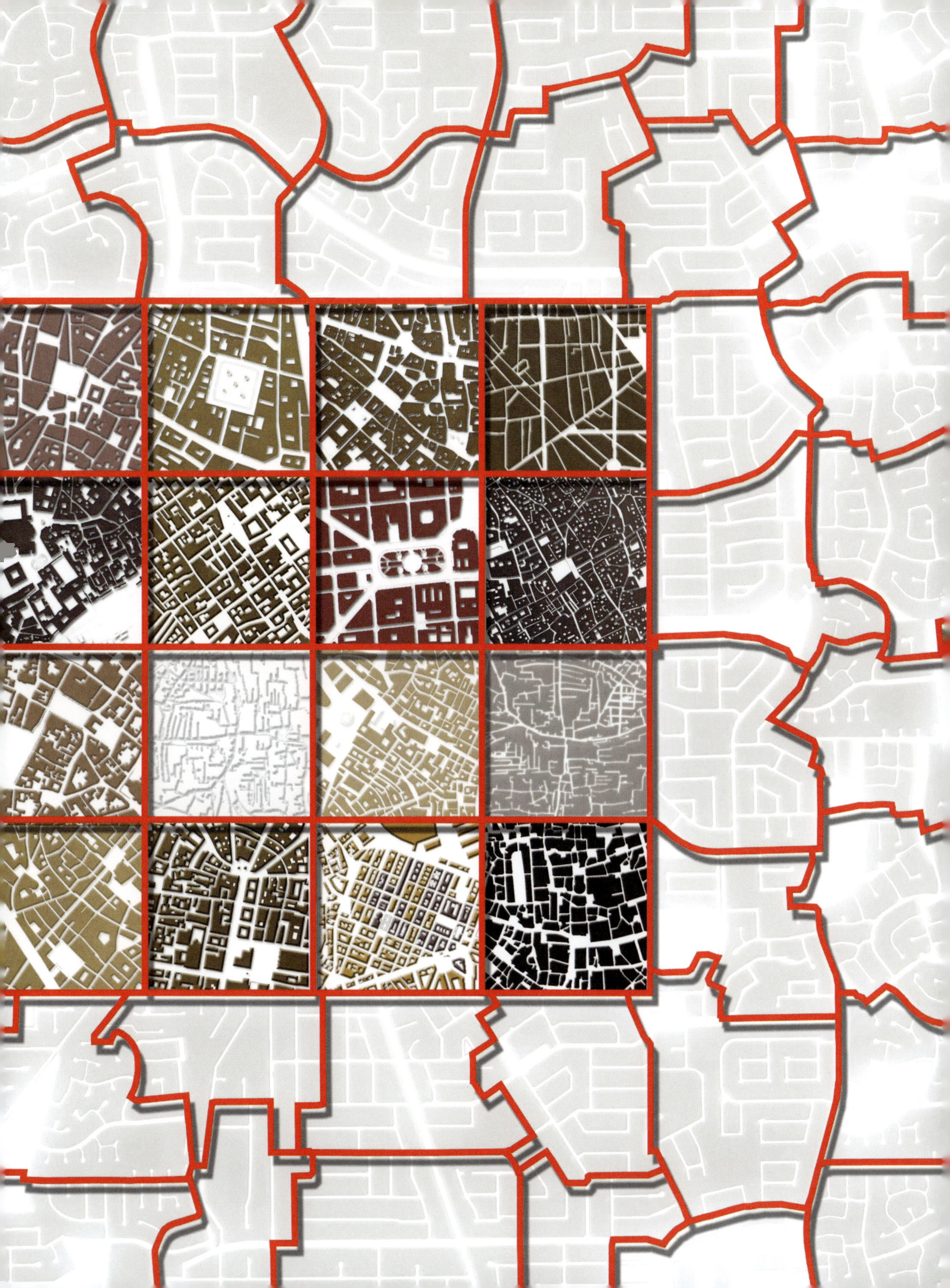

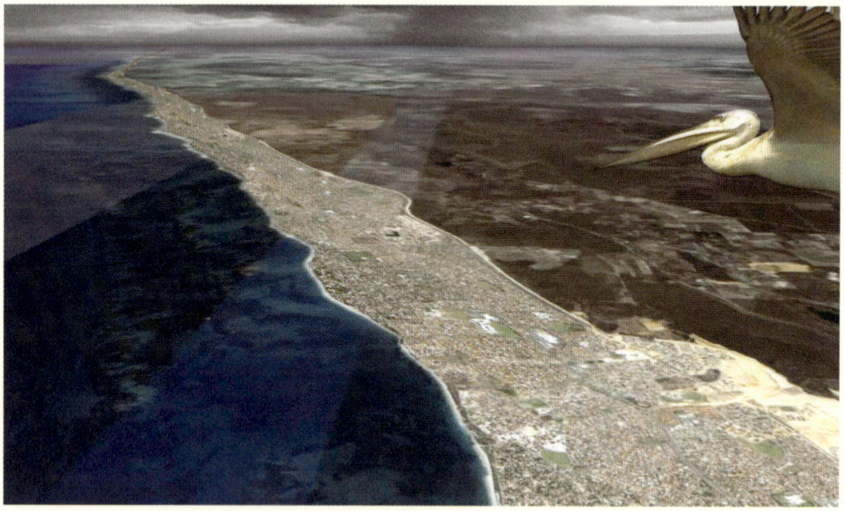

# SEACHANGE CITY

While Australian capital cities have all radically expanded in the last 35 years, during this time more than a million people have also left these cities for a beach lifestyle in coastal hamlets. This is known as the Seachange effect.[17] This scenario asks what if the future 1.5 million people coming to live in Perth opted for a seachange? It also relates to the common desire of an ageing population to retire near the coast and the Australian tradition of owning a small, cheap holiday home on the coast.

So that no citizen is further than a 25-minute walk from the beach – as a rule – this city would never reach more than two kilometres inland from the beachfront. Consequently, if spread out at the orthodox low density of 12 homes per hectare, Seachange City would be a linear city some 600 kilometres long. A northern and southern bullet train could deliver residents from Seachange City's extremities to the CBD of Perth in about 90 minutes (including a reasonable number of stops). This primary transport system would be supplemented by a light-rail system at a local level and hydrofoils could ply the coast.

This linear city would also be periodically punctuated by small town centres and curtailed by an urban-growth boundary and greenbelt to prevent it sprawling inland. Industrial areas could form pods of activity inland just beyond the main residential belt so that all residents are upwind of industry and waste recycling. Seachange City could offer a range of housing designed for coastal conditions, which would gradate in density; high at the beachfront to low at the inland border. Seachange City could satisfy Australia's ageing population with coastal retirement villages, it could offer city-dwellers coastal holiday homes and finally, it could provide idyllic lifestyle packages for the state's increasing number of 'fly in-fly out' workers, who work month-long shifts in remote mining towns.

Since this is one of the windiest coastlines on earth, Seachange City would be powered by wind turbines and water in part derived from small desalination plants. The city would also take advantage of characteristically fine weather and maximise the use of solar energy. Seachange City takes its final form by ensuring the protection of the dunes and only developing above a contour height of +2, a sort of urban Plimsoll line that anticipates rising sea levels associated with climate change.

[17] Burnley, I. and Murphy, P., *Sea Change: Movement from Metropolitan to Arcadian Australia*, University of New South Wales Press, Sydney, 2004.

# 1.5 million people living in low-density suburbia no further than 25 minutes' walk, from the beach creates a 600 kilometre-long city.

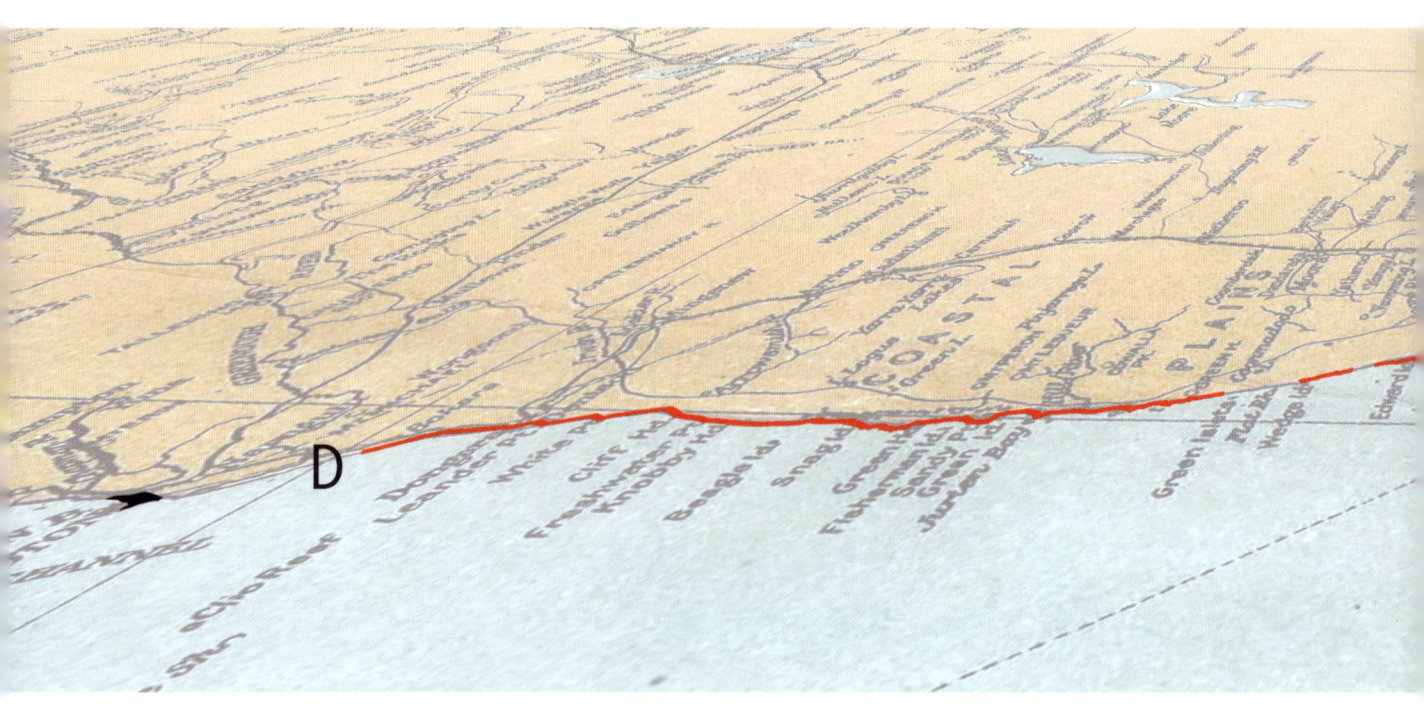

SEACHANGE CITY

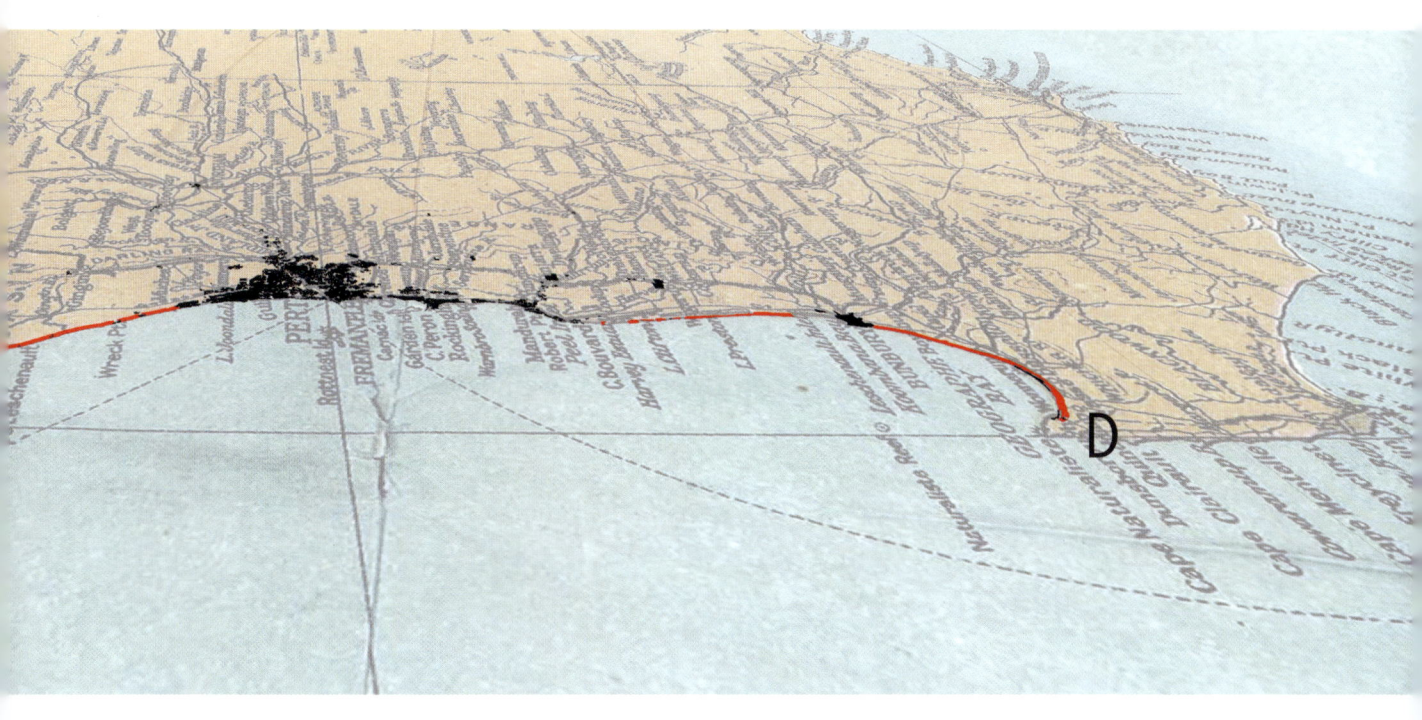

299
HORIZONTAL SCENARIOS

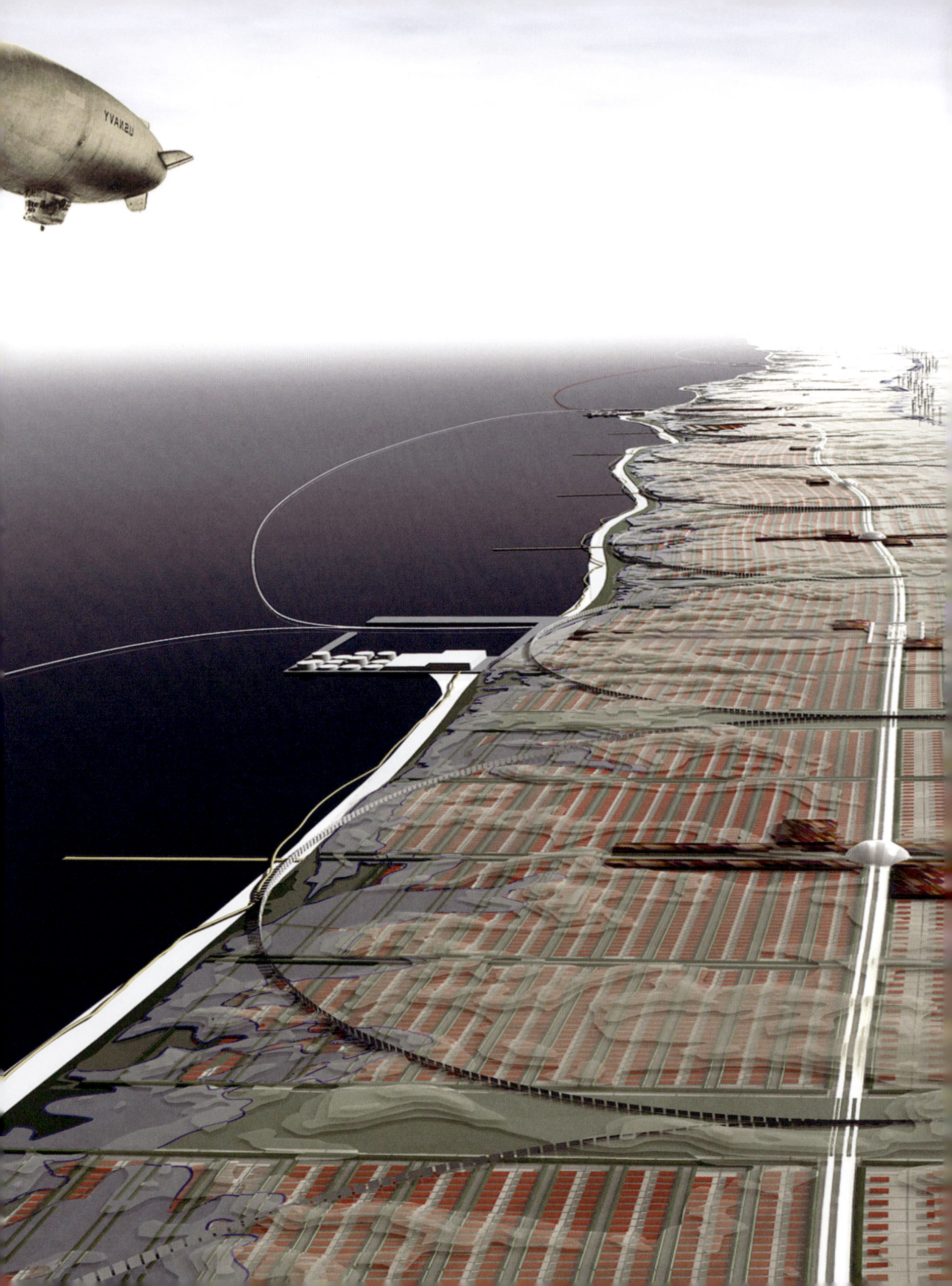
US NAVY

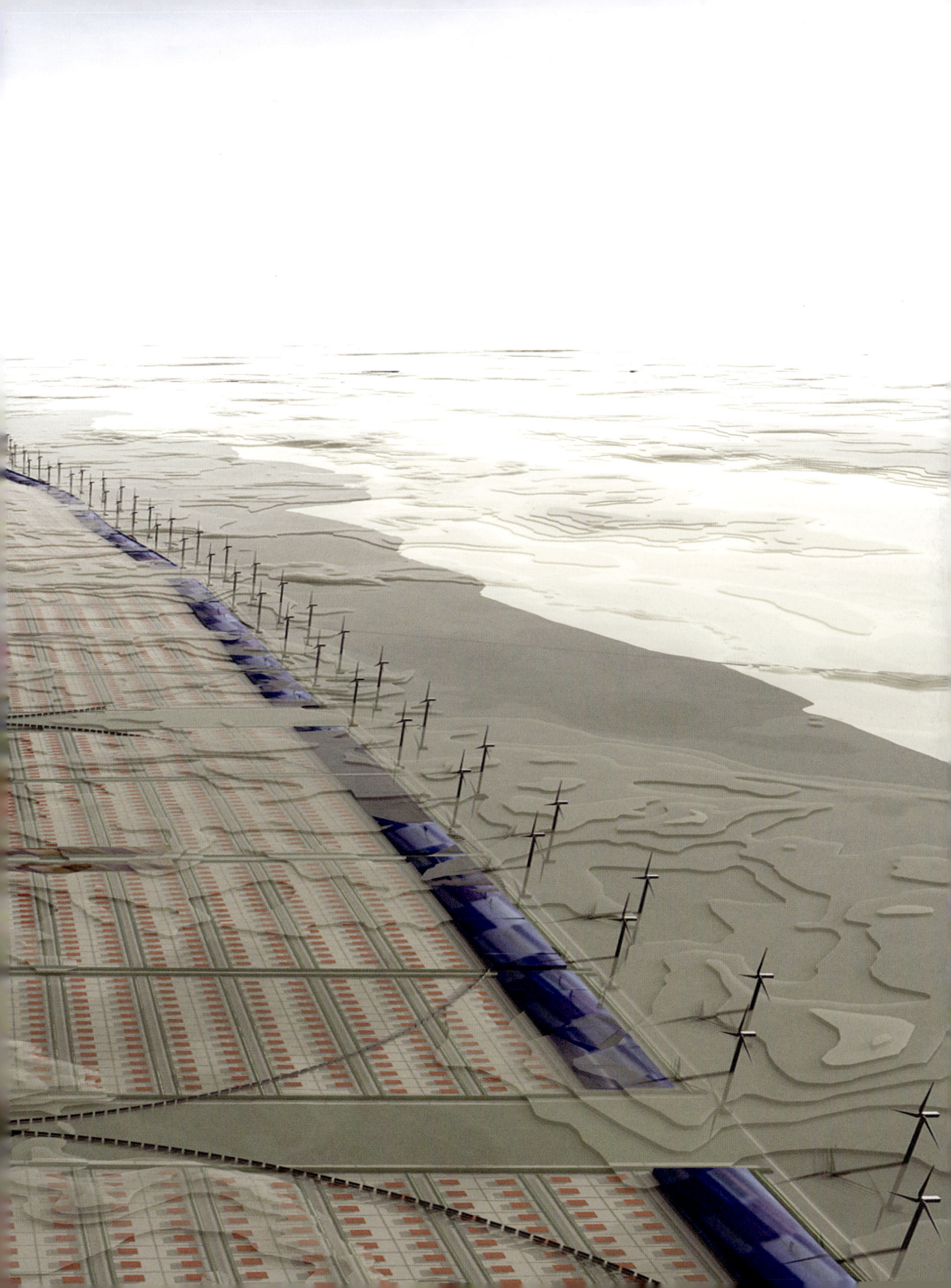

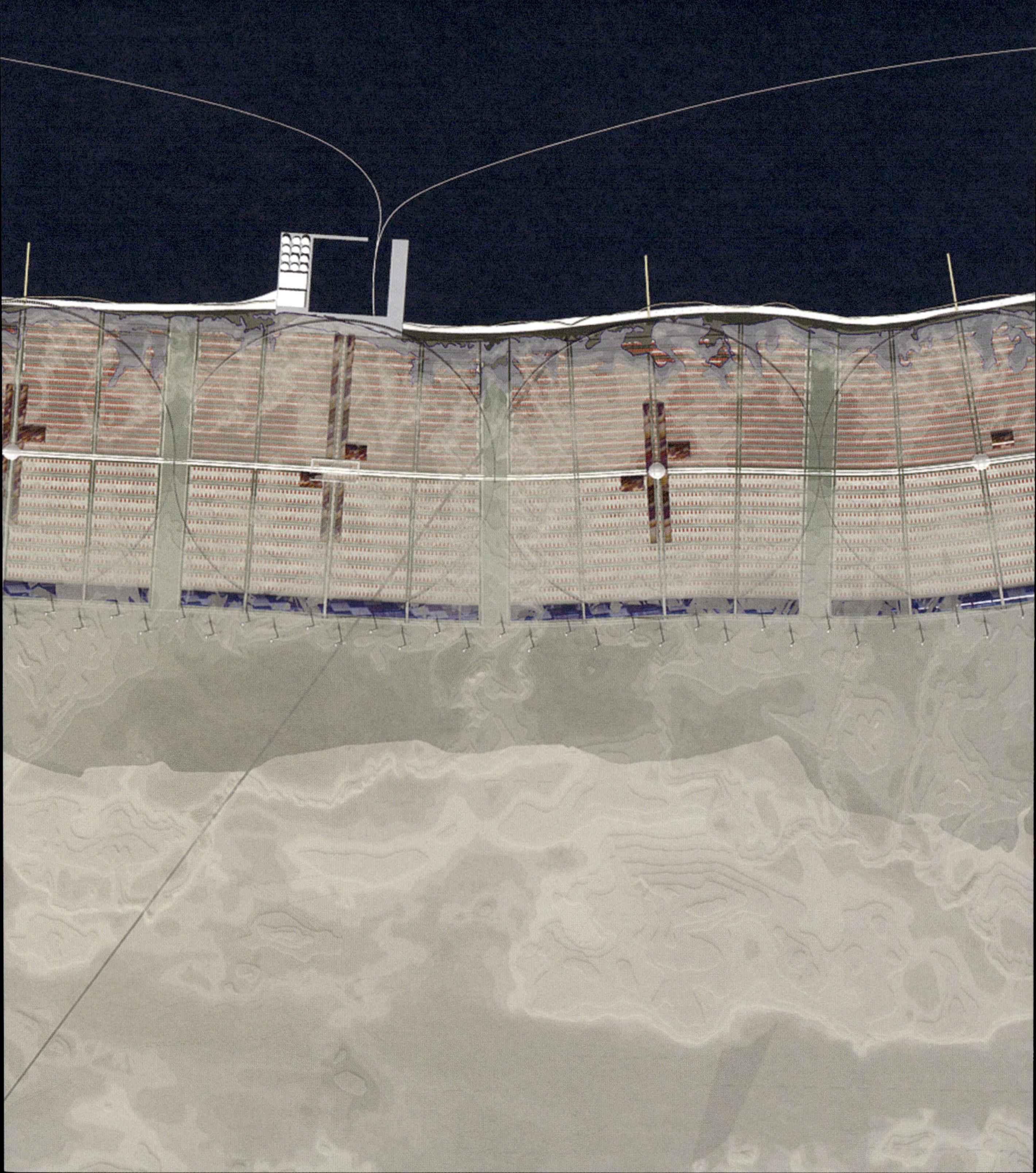

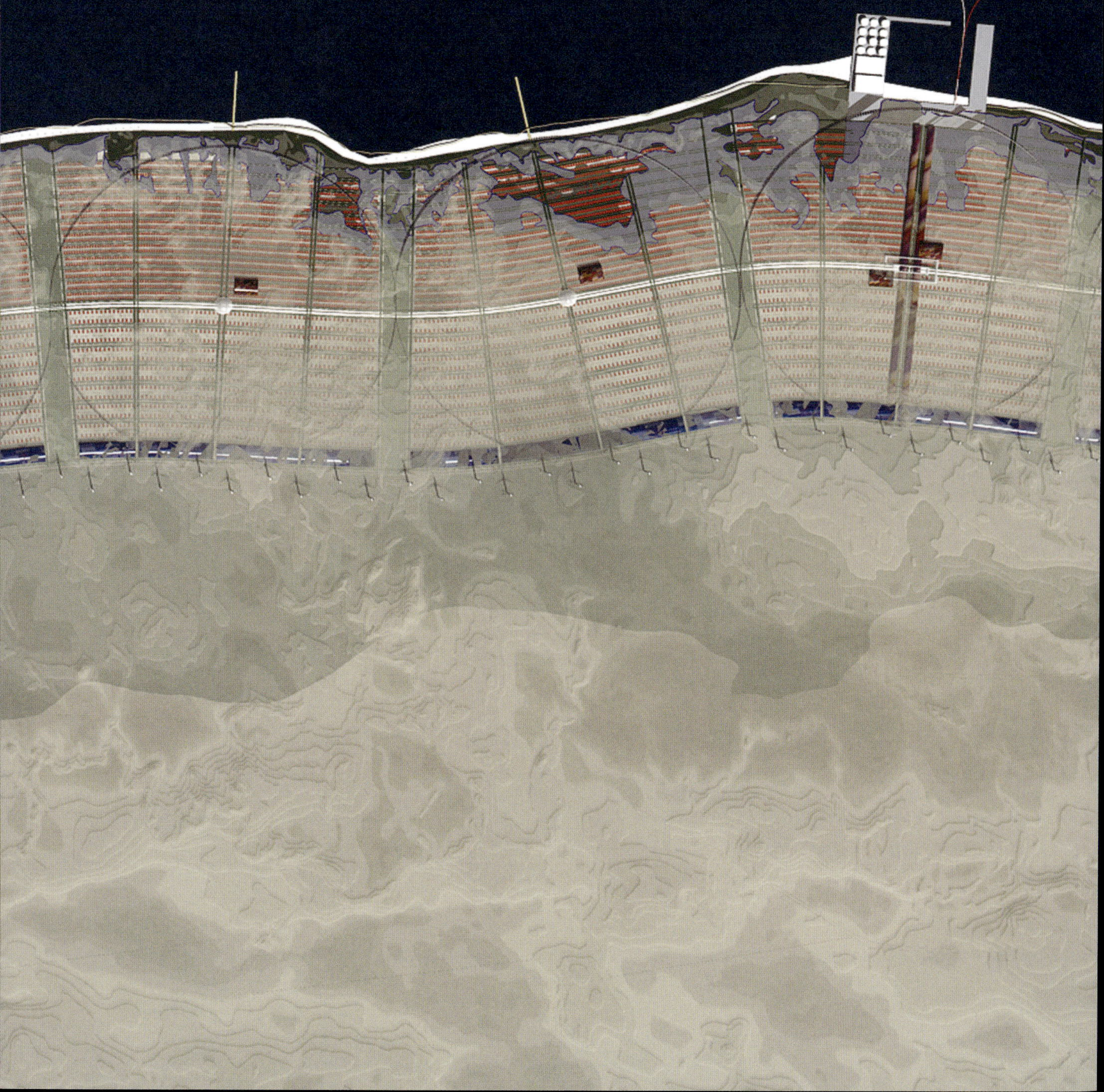

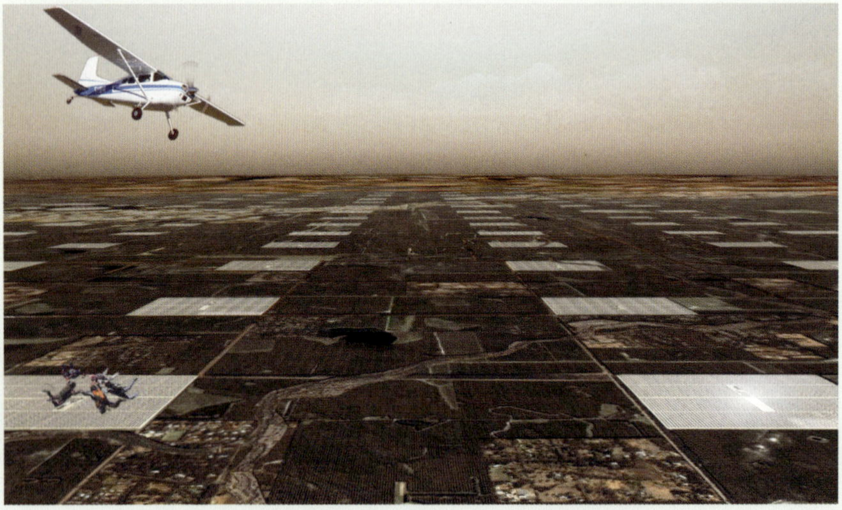

# TREECHANGE CITY

Just as many people have left major cities for a new life in coastal hamlets, some others, known as Treechangers, have relocated from coastal capital cities to inland rural landscapes. This scenario suggests that a bandwidth of land within approximately 1.5 hours' drive of the existing CBD be identified as a Treechange zone. The primary purpose of this zone, known as the Avon arc, is however to offset Perth's carbon emissions by 2050 by becoming a forest.

Western Australians are producing 36.6 tonnes $CO_2$ emissions per capita per annum.[18] A city of three million people with greenhouse gas emissions at current Western Australian rates would produce around 110 million tonnes of $CO_2$ emissions.[19] At least six trees are needed to offset one tonne of $CO_2$ in the Perth region.[20] Roughly 660 million trees taking up 6.6 million hectares would need to be planted to offset the emissions from a city of three million people.

The Avon Catchment around Perth is 11.8 million hectares of land of which 8.4 million is cleared. Current thinking is that at least 10% of the landscape needs to be replanted with woody perennials to balance regional groundwater tables.[21] If this reforestation was expanded, and continued to expand over time, large quantities of Perth's carbon emissions could be sequestered.[22]

As Perth grows and pressure builds in and around the existing city it is possible that more people will leave the Perth Metropolitan Region and move inland, particularly if more diverse economic and educational opportunities can be created there. The massive reforestation project of Treechange City could encourage other related industrial and agricultural activities. A new university devoted specifically to issues of agrarian landscapes and sustainable technologies would also be appropriate. Treechange City could also attract a significant number of people who are facing retirement in small, remote (and often dying) rural towns throughout the Western Australian wheatbelt by providing them with a rural way of life yet one with relative proximity to city services. People moving into Treechange City would live on small farms or cluster into rural hamlets dotted throughout this extensively reforested landscape.

In addition to the reafforestation of Treechange City would be the installation of an 8.7 x 8.7 km² solar array – the amount of solar surface necessary to power the city of Perth in 2050. It is also possible to apply some aspects of Food City and POD City to the Treechange City scenario so that Perth's hinterland becomes more productive and diverse.

---

18 Environmental Protection Authority, *State of the Environment Report Western Australia (Draft)*, Department of Environment and Conservation, Perth, 2006, p. 31.

19 Calculation based on 36.6 tonnes per capita per annum x 1.5 million people = 54.9 million tones.

20 Carbon Neutral, Carbon offset Calculator, <http://www.carbonneutral.com.au>, viewed November 2008.

21 Carbon Neutral, <http://www.carbonneutral.com.au>, viewed November 2008.

22 The science behind these calculations is rapidly evolving, making it very hard to arrive at conclusive data. What does become obvious is that reforestation alone cannot solve problems of carbon sequestration.

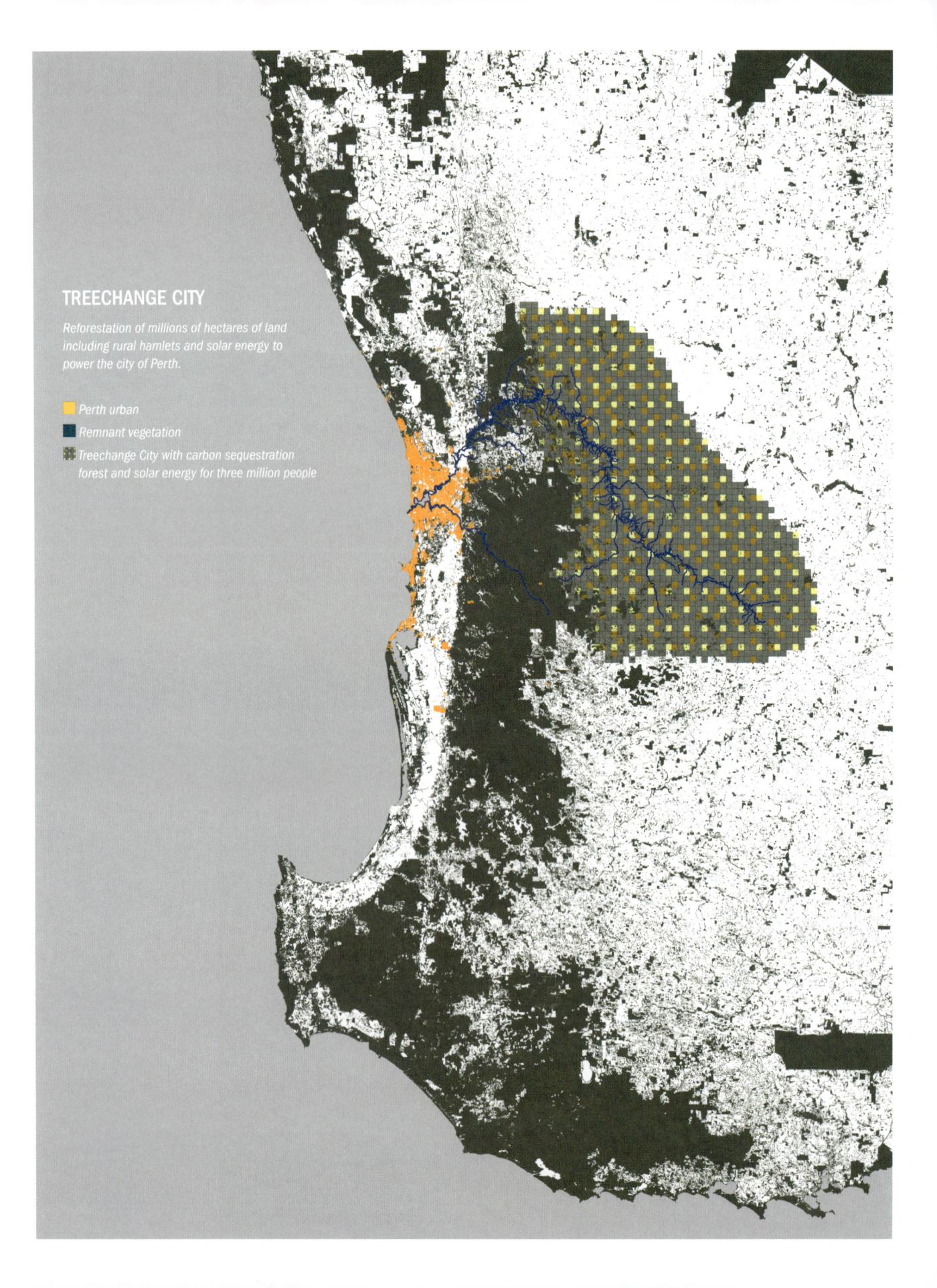

## TREECHANGE CITY

*Reforestation of millions of hectares of land including rural hamlets and solar energy to power the city of Perth.*

- Perth urban
- Remnant vegetation
- Treechange City with carbon sequestration forest and solar energy for three million people

TREECHANGE CITY

1 tree =

0.16 tonnes of
carbon absorbed

**307**
HORIZONTAL SCENARIOS

11

# VERTICAL SCENARIOS

If Perth is going to avoid extreme sprawl it will need to seriously engage with vertical development.

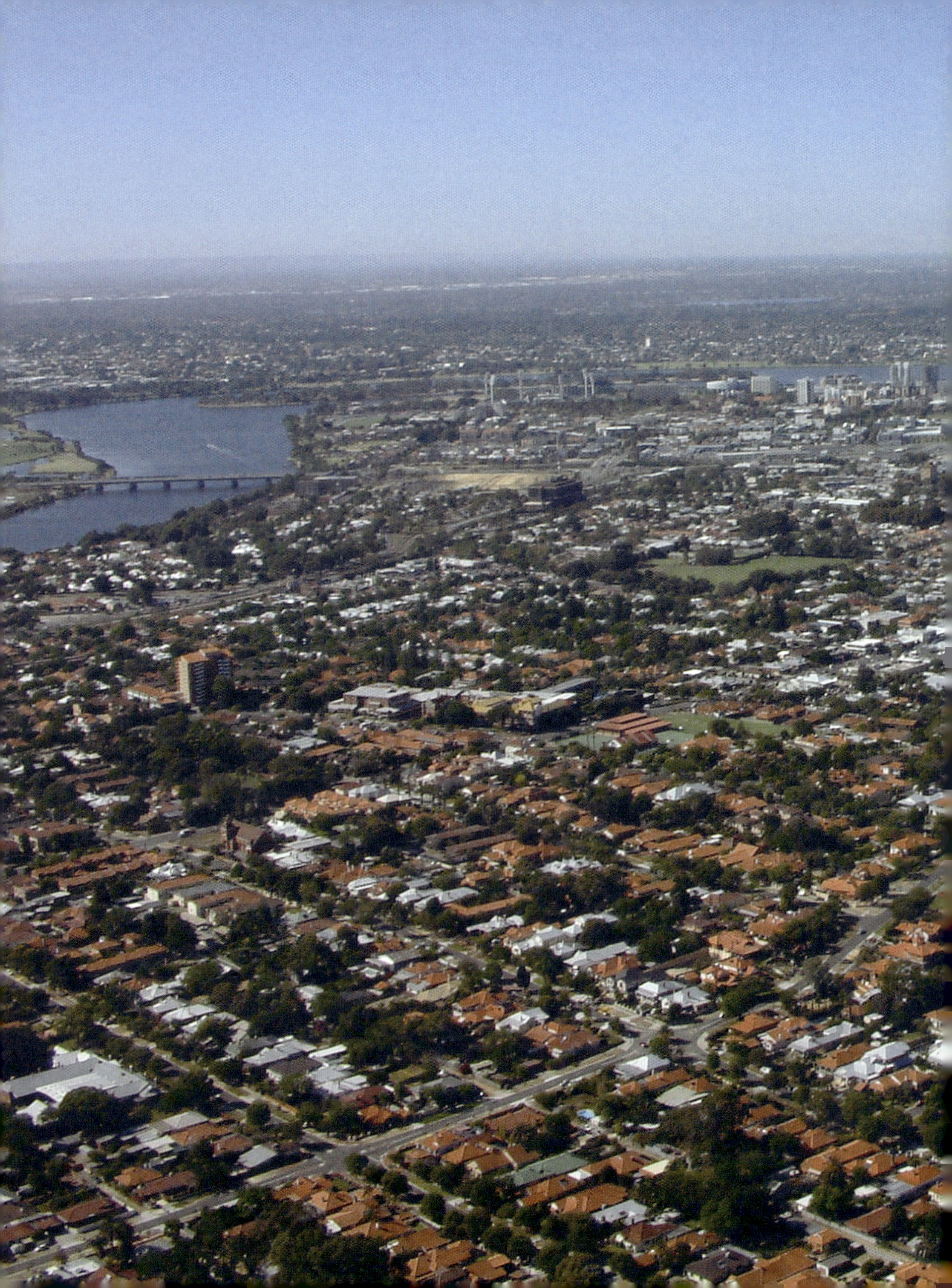

# N.I.M.B.Y!*

*Not In My Back Yard.

## CURRENT ZONING

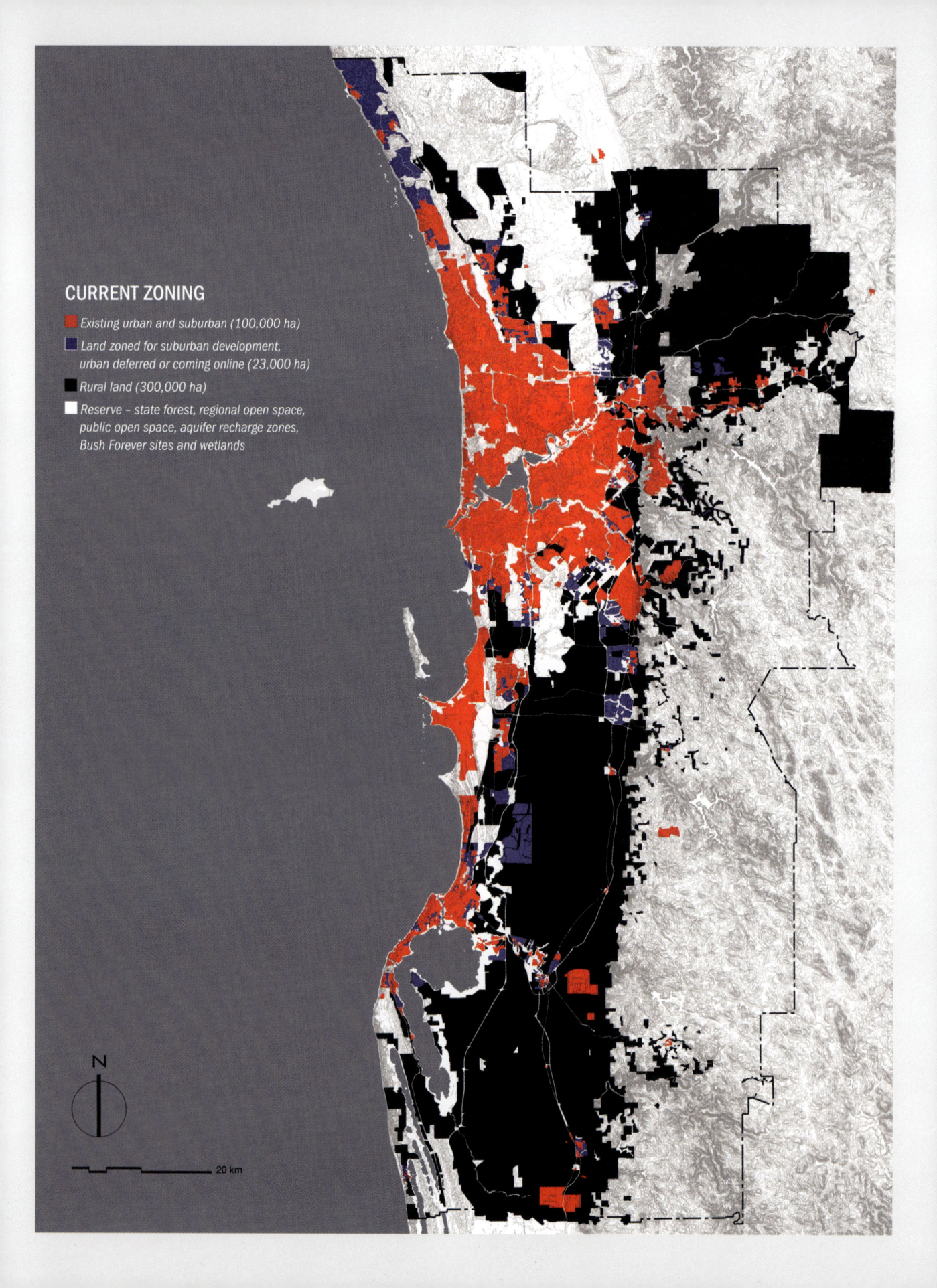

■ *Existing urban and suburban (100,000 ha)*
■ *Land zoned for suburban development, urban deferred or coming online (23,000 ha)*
■ *Rural land (300,000 ha)*
□ *Reserve – state forest, regional open space, public open space, aquifer recharge zones, Bush Forever sites and wetlands*

20 km

# INTRODUCTION

There is currently 23,000 hectares of land on the periphery of Perth zoned for or coming online for residential development. This land alone can accommodate 634,800 new residents at 12 homes per hectare. Subtracting these 634,800 people from the 2050 projection of an additional 1.5 million leaves 865,200 people (376,173 free-standing homes or 445,368 apartments) to be accommodated by infill development. For the purposes of conducting the vertical development scenarios we are setting a hypothetical urban-growth boundary around the city of Perth once these 23,000 hectares are developed. In this case Perth would have decided and found the political will to ensure that it not sprawl any further. Should the most recent ABS predictions of a further 2.7 million people living in Perth by 2056 occur and should the city maintain, even under that pressure, a restriction on sprawl then over one million apartments will need to be added to the existing urban fabric in the next four decades.

Often in local debate, the very people that as a matter of principle don't like new suburban developments (sprawl), also defend their own low-density residential neighbourhoods against infill development. Paradoxically, many of these people are also in principle for growth and development. Indeed, a city of three million people (or more) brings benefits that a city of 1.5 million cannot sustain. By couching development in terms of the city's collective future and its whole landscape, we hope that one of the effects of this research will be to inculcate a more broad-minded attitude to change. We hope to show that if large-scale infill development was organised in a concerted manner, then it could give more people access to areas of high amenity and add to the cultural vibrancy of the city. The fundamental principle guiding the distribution of increased density in the various vertical scenarios to follow is that it be concentrated near to high cultural or landscape amenity.

To demonstrate to the community the need for concentrations of vertical development, we conducted some basic and dispassionate infill development tests. For example, by distributing the required 376,173 new dwellings evenly across the entire area of existing city we find that an additional three dwellings have to be added per hectare of existing urban fabric. Or, if we add these 376,173 homes to only the inner ring of older suburbs where there is a strong desire for people to live, then we need to add 10 new dwellings per hectare of existing fabric. And finally, if the additional 865,200 people were to be accommodated within walking distance of the so called 'activity centres' identified in the government's Network City document then we need to add another 90 dwellings per hectare to those locations.

If we accept the latest ABS figures of an additional 2.7 million people living in Perth by 2056 and try to accommodate these people (minus the 634,800 people who will be housed in currently zoned suburban land) within the existing urban footprint then we need to add 897,913 free-standing homes or 1,086,947 apartments. This means we would need to try to fit an extra nine free-standing homes or 11 apartments per hectare of Perth's existing urban fabric. To appreciate exactly what this means, look outside your window and think about an area as big as a football oval and ask yourself where in that area of your neighbourhood could we add nine new homes or 11 apartments!

If you do not accept this level of development in your neighbourhood then we simply ask: where do you want people to live?

'Not in my backyard' is not an attitude suited to the challenges this city now faces. That said, we need our architects to show us how increased density in our suburbs can be a good thing. If we are to restrict sprawl, then they also need to do this in a way that keeps the costs of such development competitive with a free-standing home on the periphery of the city.

Mathematically these distributions do not seem problematic but when examining the addition of three, 10, or 90 dwellings per hectare to the existing suburban fabric one finds, in most situations, that there is a significant shortfall of opportunities for such additional development unless the existing fabric is demolished. The images on pages 324, 325, 330 and 331 show that in order to meet the required addition of three and 10 additional dwellings per hectare without the demolition of the existing urban fabric, high-rise development must be undertaken if Perth is to absorb the population increase within its existing urban boundary.

But even if density could be increased by a factor of three, 10 or 90, are these distributions in the best places for infill development? Adding three homes per hectare across the entire city is arguably just adding to an already sprawled form of urbanism. Adding 10 homes per hectare to the inner ring of older suburbs seems more reasonable as the backyards of existing suburban homes in these areas can be developed, and people living in these suburbs have easy access to relatively high amenity. Adding 90 homes per hectare around the government's activity centres is problematic because many of these areas are dominated by 'big box' shopping centres and transport hubs. Despite being close to shopping and transport these service centres are often unattractive places in which to live. The centres could be restructured to make them more appealing, but this increases development costs. Adding more people to such areas also risks compounding the social problems generally associated with high-density residential areas in areas of relatively low natural and cultural amenity. This is not to say these various distributions of infill development shouldn't be actively pursued where opportunities arise, but there is also need for more compelling forms of infill development if it is to become a genuine alternative to suburban sprawl.

One such compelling idea (being floated by Michael Kane, former advisor to Minister MacTeirnan) is for Perth to build a new orbital rail loop around the city's inner core and maximise density and jobs along it. The loop would give rise to a string of development hubs and would connect two major universities, several TAFE colleges, various medical hospital facilities, the airport, the CBD and several under-developed suburban community centres. These development hubs are where there is the highest potential for growth in the knowledge economy. The loop would intersect with all Perth's radial rail lines providing accessibility to all Perth's major high-density employment and activity centres. This string of development hubs along a new rail circuit would enshrine Network City ideals in one bold move and significantly boost the viability of Perth's overall public transport network. Many of the areas along this loop are, however, not exactly high in amenity but they could give rise to affordable higher density housing with excellent connectivity to jobs and the city centre.

Somewhat contrary to Network City's doctrinaire emphasis on Transit Oriented Development (TOD), Perth's most desirable areas to live are near its beaches, river and increasingly the CBD. We have therefore developed three vertical development scenarios attempting to capitalise on these major landscape attractors: Sky City, River City and Surf City.

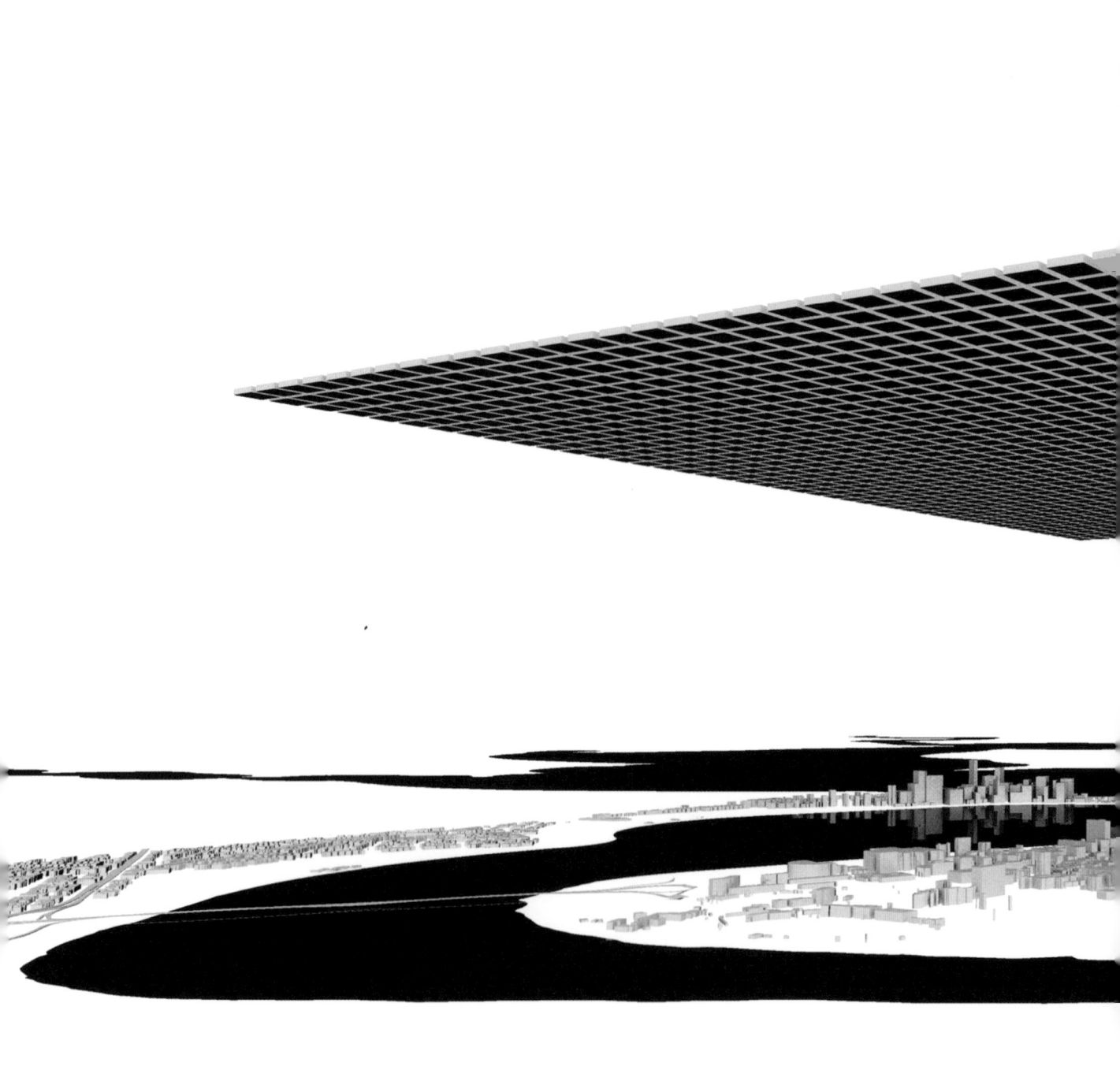

865,000 people in the form of a typical European city hovering over
the central city of Perth. Each block represents 1 hectare of five-storey
urbanism. All the following vertical scenarios concern ways in which
this mass can be brought to ground within the existing city.

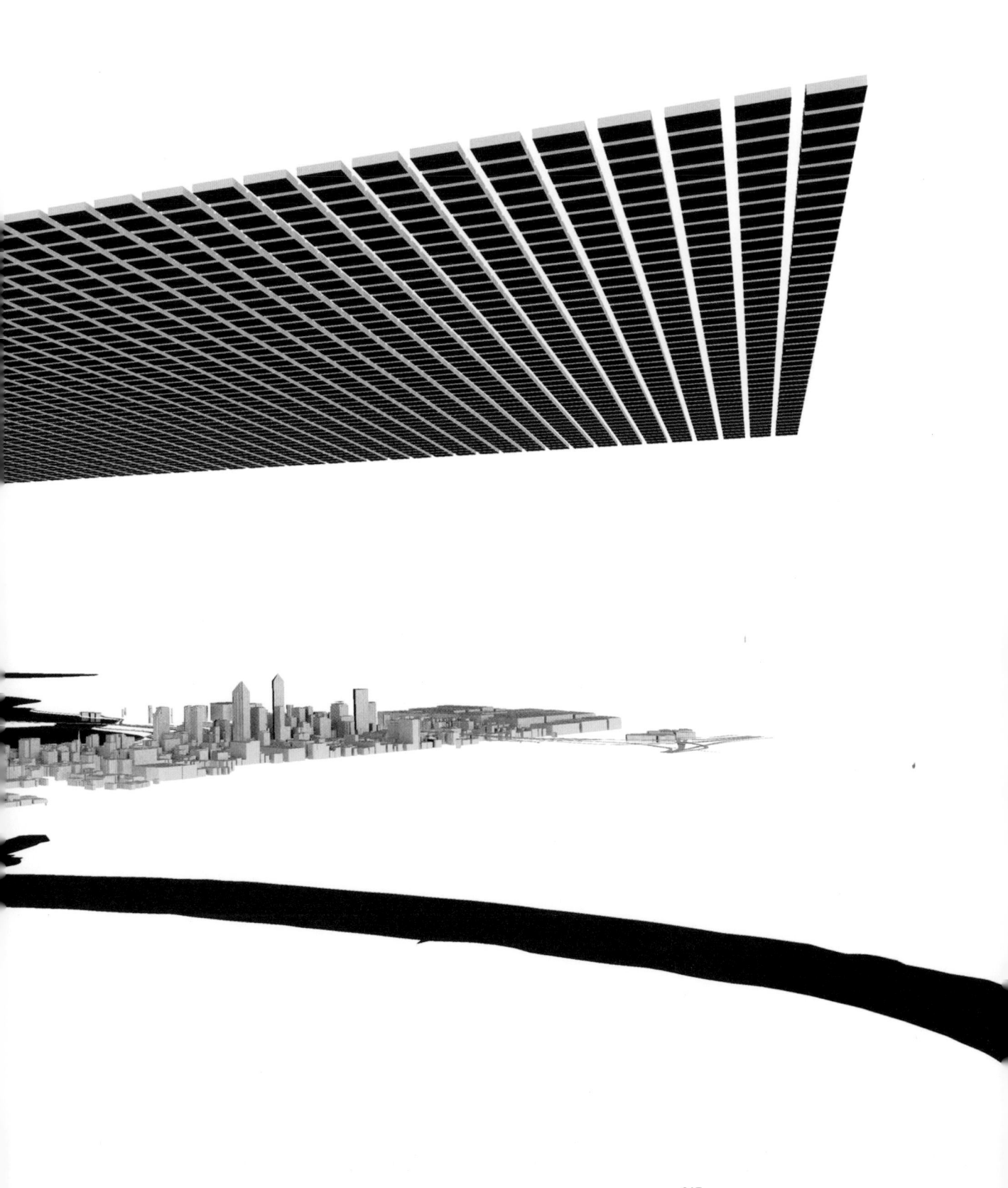

**VERTICAL SCENARIOS**

865,000

PARISIANS

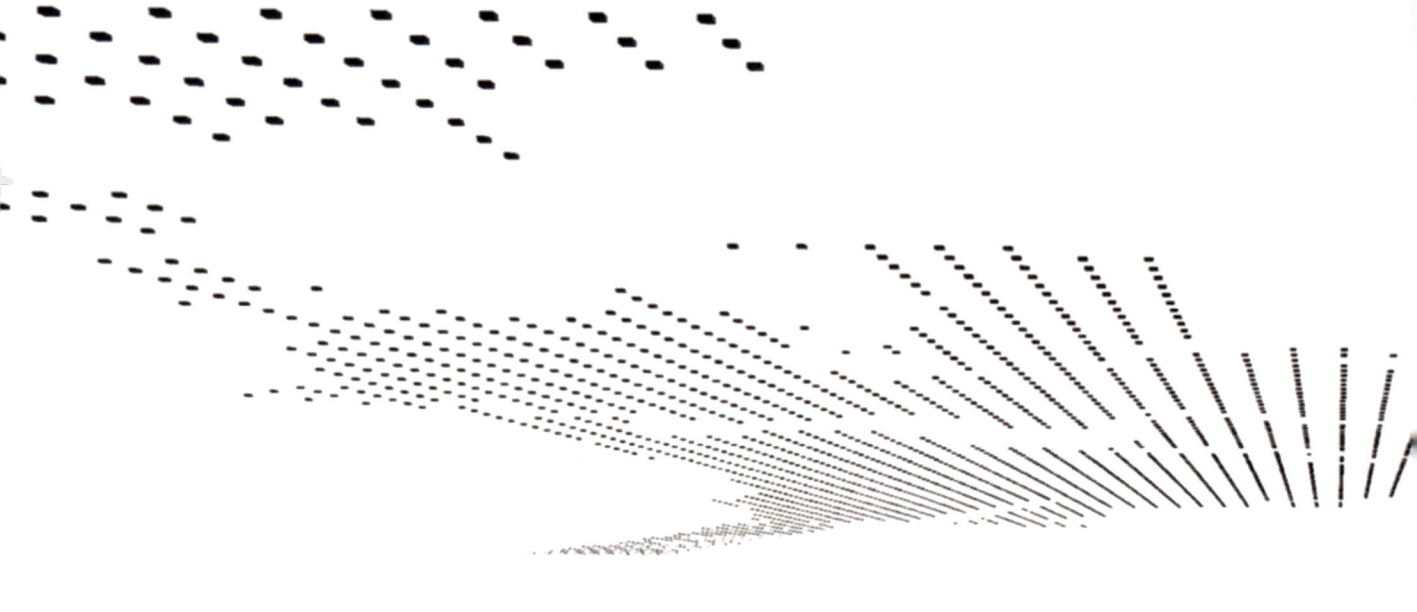

The density 'cloud' of 865,200 people
(376,174 homes) spread evenly over Perth's

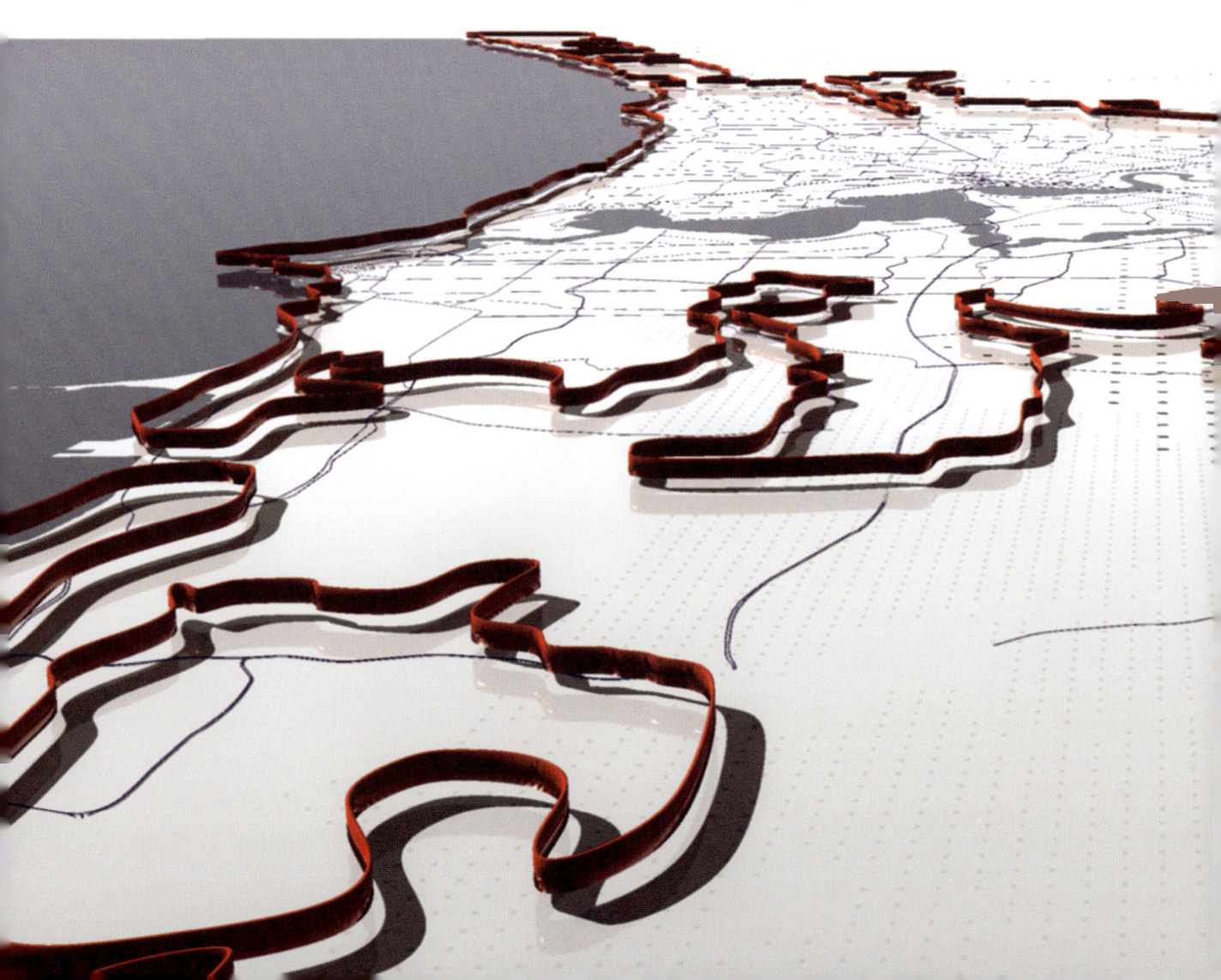

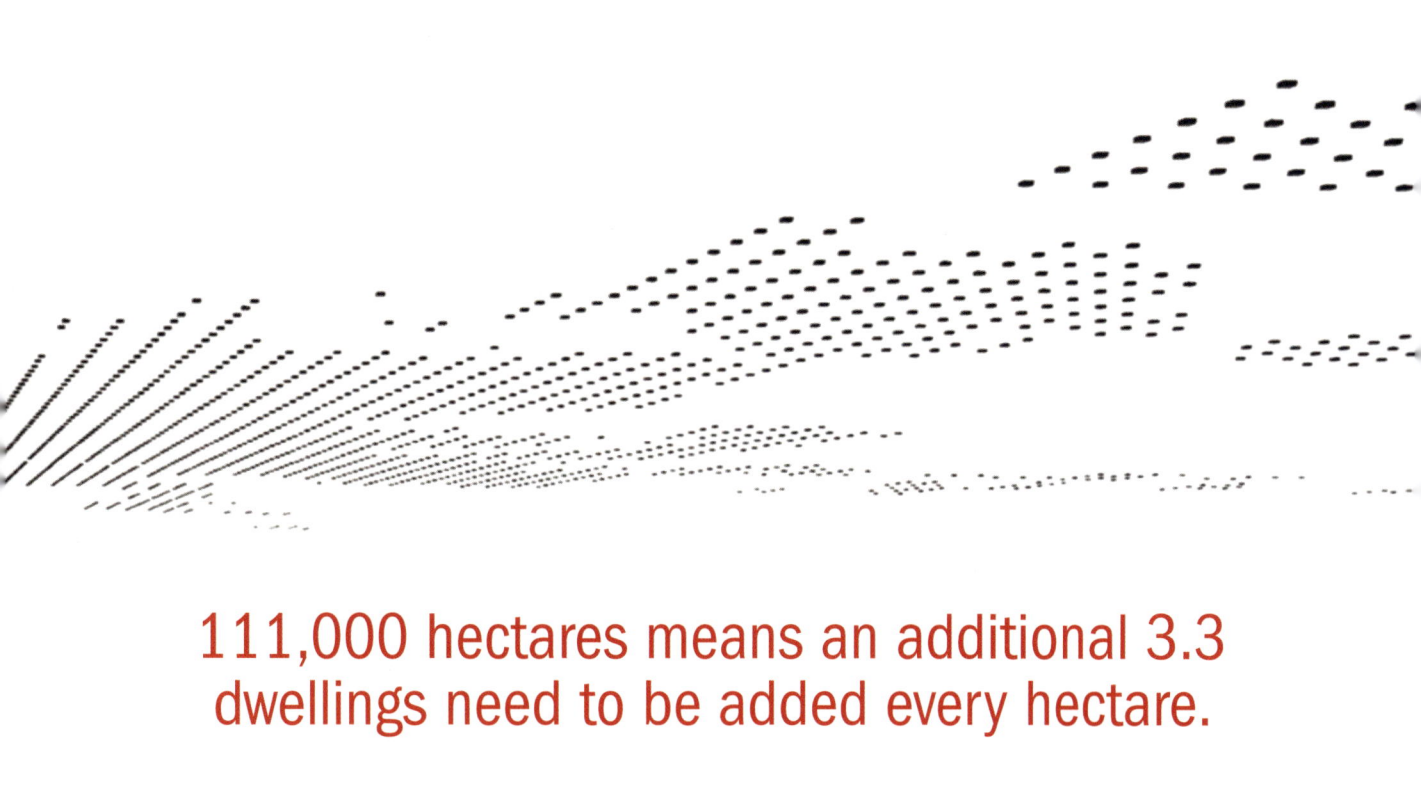

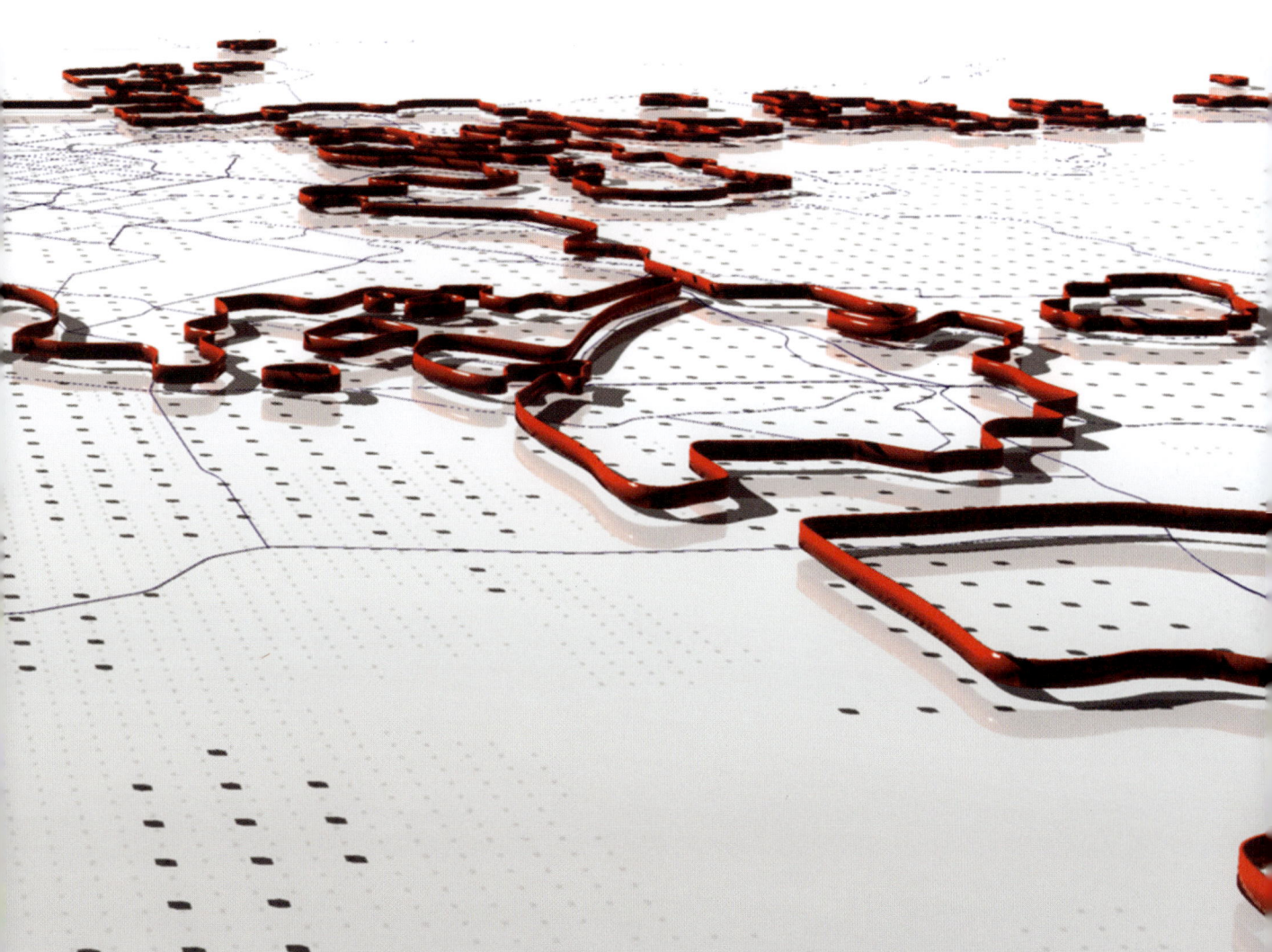

111,000 hectares means an additional 3.3 dwellings need to be added every hectare.

1 hectare

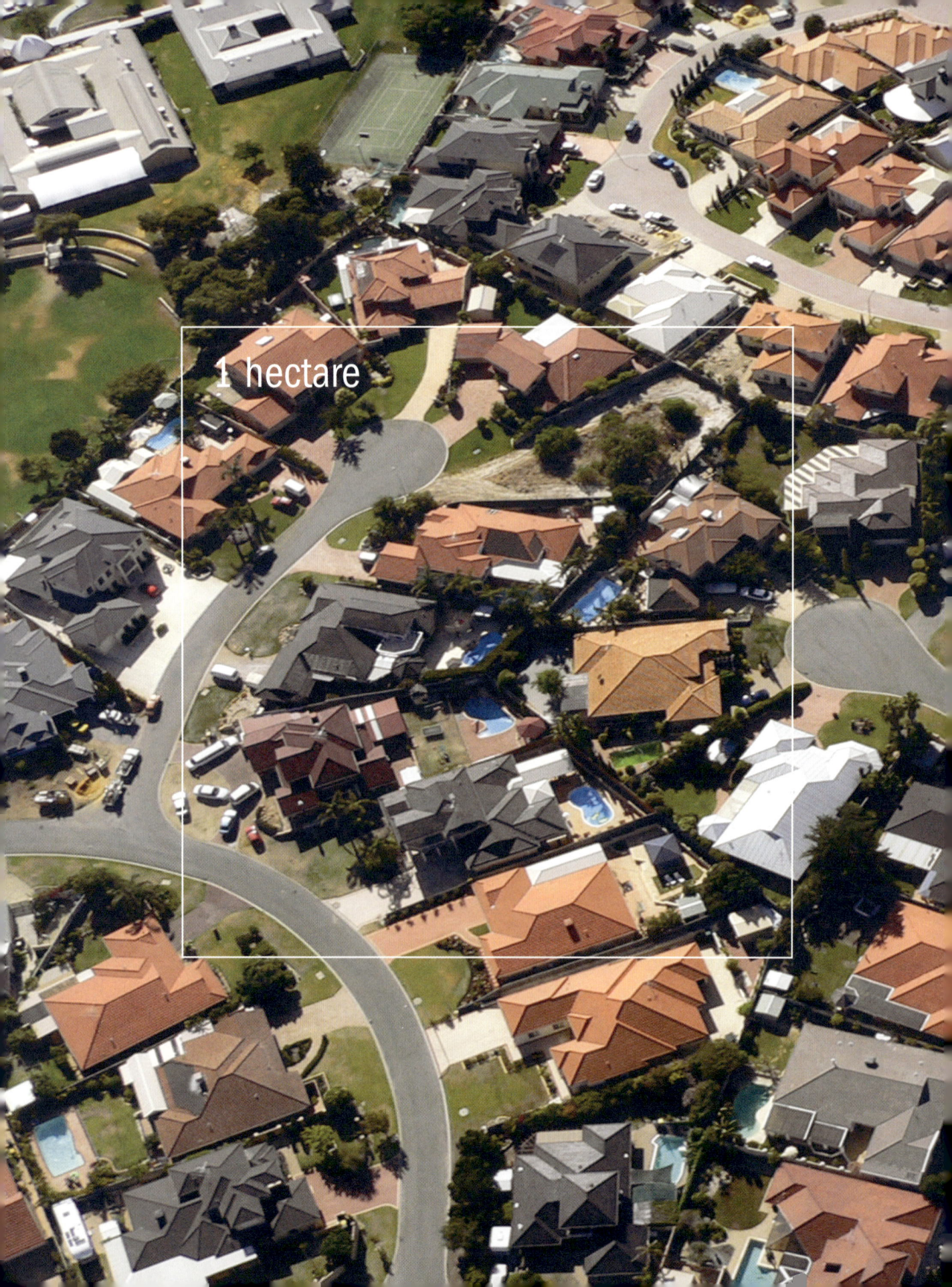

# BUT HOW CAN WE ADD THREE HOMES PER HECTARE HERE?

*above: Each grid represents 1 hectare.*

To test the requirement of adding 3.3 dwellings per hectare to the existing urban fabric we have taken 135 hectares of Ocean Reef, a typical Perth suburb. Without demolishing existing buildings we have only been able to add 120 new dwellings (276 people). Thus, there is a shortfall of 748 people from meeting the target of an additional 3.3 homes per hectare. Therefore if this community is to accept its share of the responsibility to house the increasing population and prevent the city from sprawling further then it needs to find a way of housing 748 people. One solution – as indicated over page – is to find sites for five 20-storey residential buildings.

# INTRODUCTION

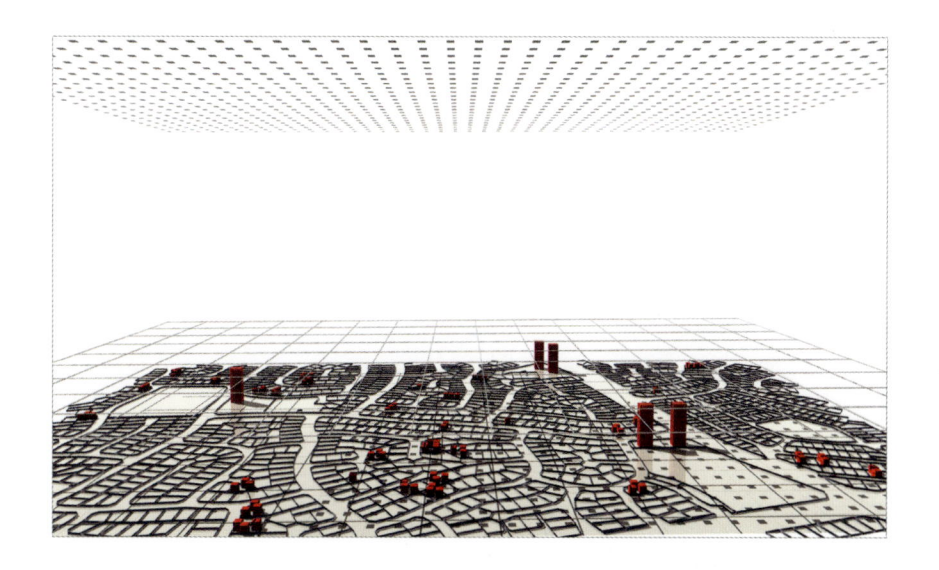

325
**VERTICAL SCENARIOS**

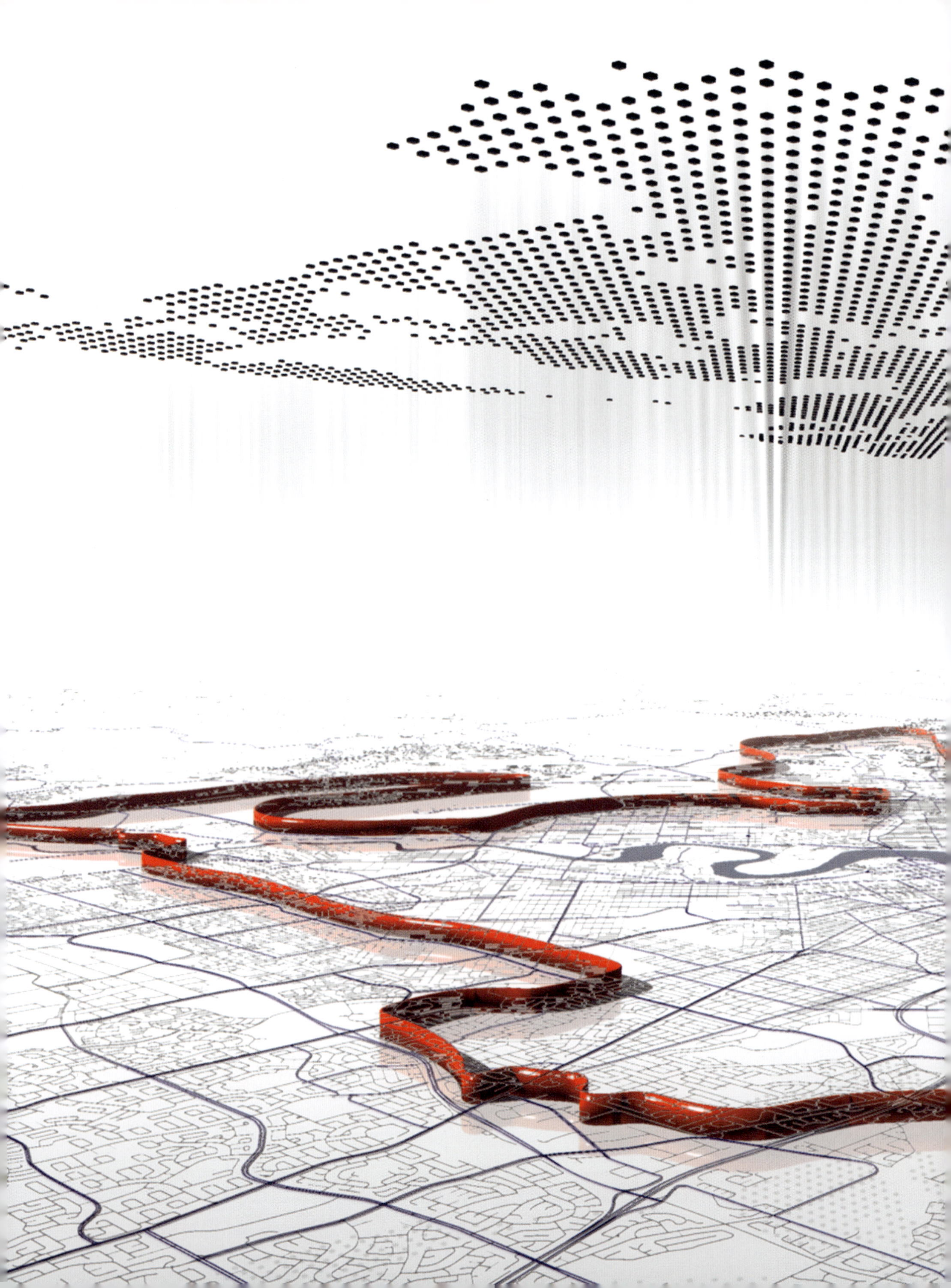

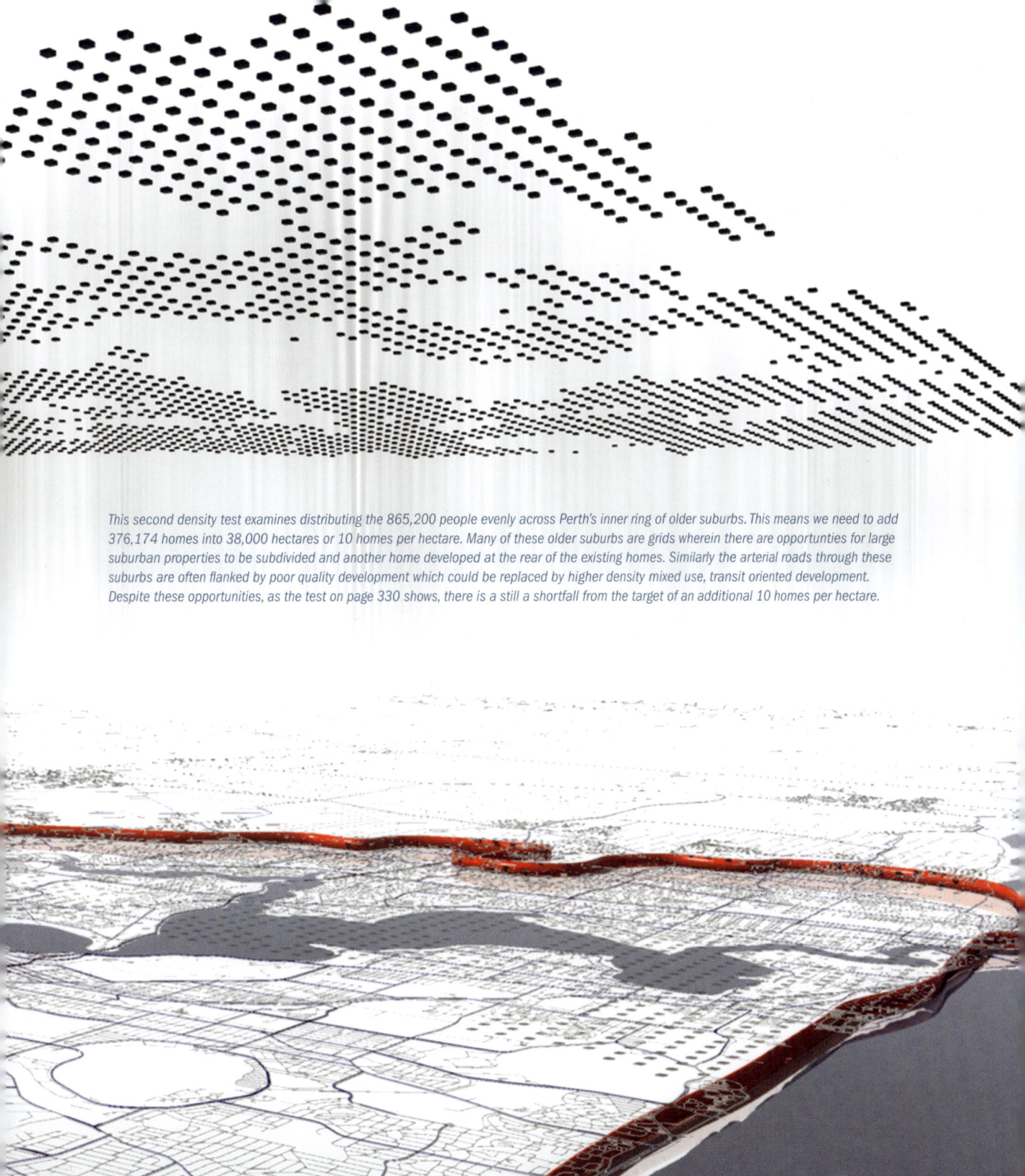

This second density test examines distributing the 865,200 people evenly across Perth's inner ring of older suburbs. This means we need to add 376,174 homes into 38,000 hectares or 10 homes per hectare. Many of these older suburbs are grids wherein there are opportunities for large suburban properties to be subdivided and another home developed at the rear of the existing homes. Similarly the arterial roads through these suburbs are often flanked by poor quality development which could be replaced by higher density mixed use, transit oriented development. Despite these opportunities, as the test on page 330 shows, there is a still a shortfall from the target of an additional 10 homes per hectare.

# HOW CAN WE ADD 10 HOMES PER HECTARE HERE?

1 hectare

# INTRODUCTION

Where we can rebuild areas of our suburbs then perhaps the best way to increase density and improve environmental performance is to invert the whole idea of freestanding homes surrounded by gardens.

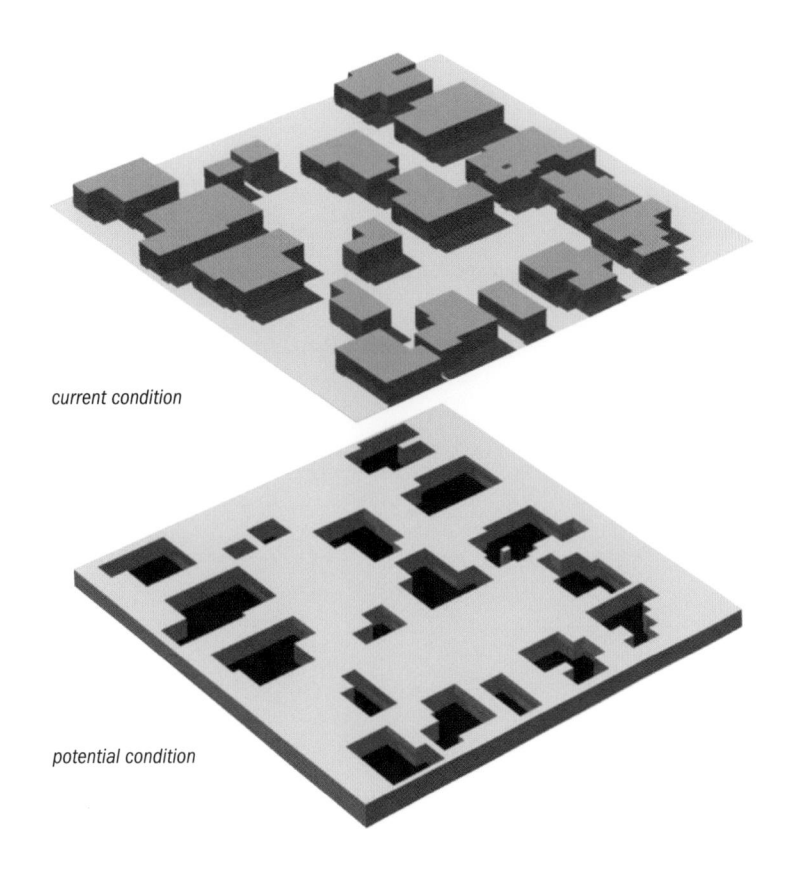

*current condition*

*potential condition*

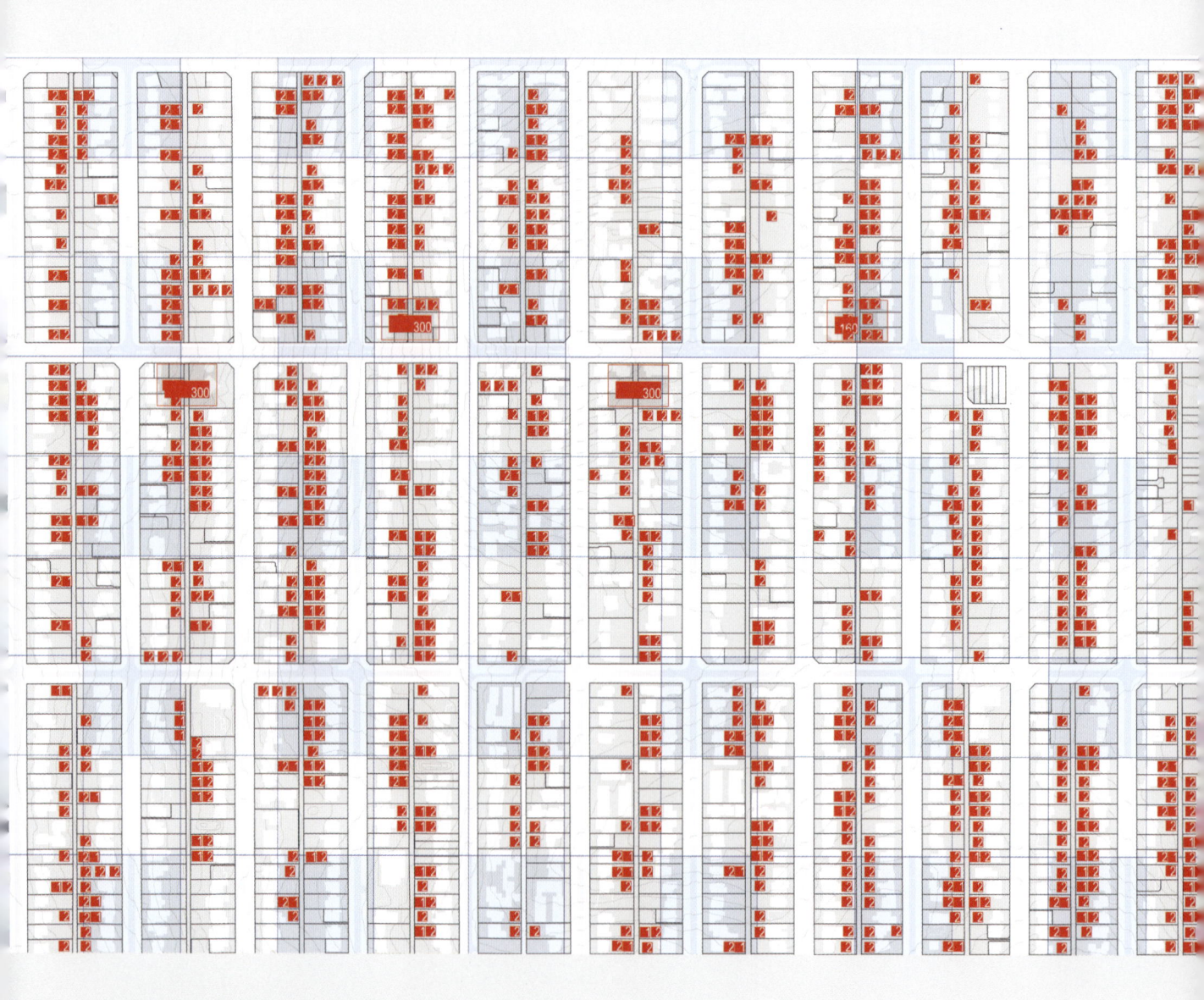

*above: Each grid represents one hectare.*

To test the possibility of adding an additional 10 homes per hectare we have taken 135 hectares of Doubleview and Scarborough. The target for this area is to add 1,350 homes (3,105 people) but we have only been able to find development opportunities to house 2,061 people. Therefore the shortfall of 1,044 people has to be accommodated in vertical development, for example four 25-storey towers.

INTRODUCTION

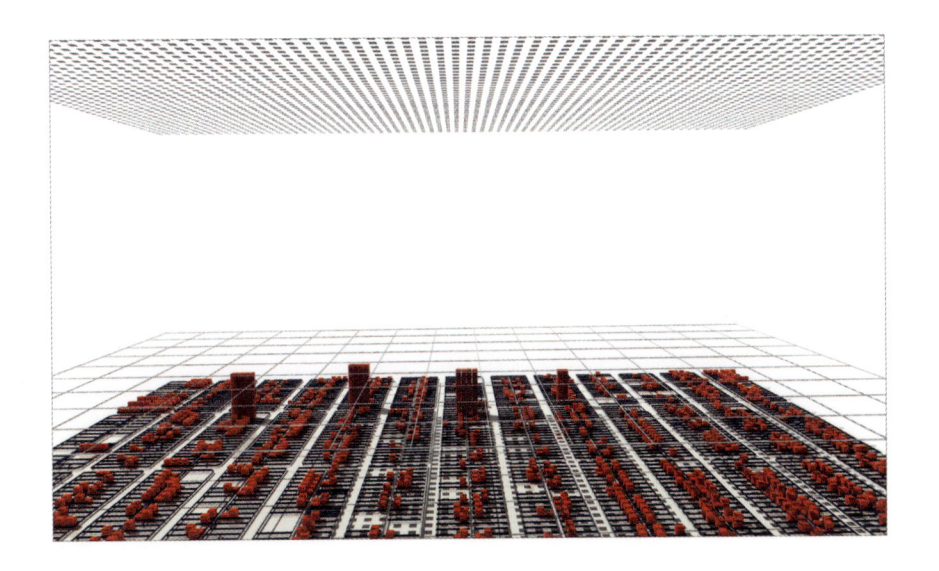

331
VERTICAL SCENARIOS

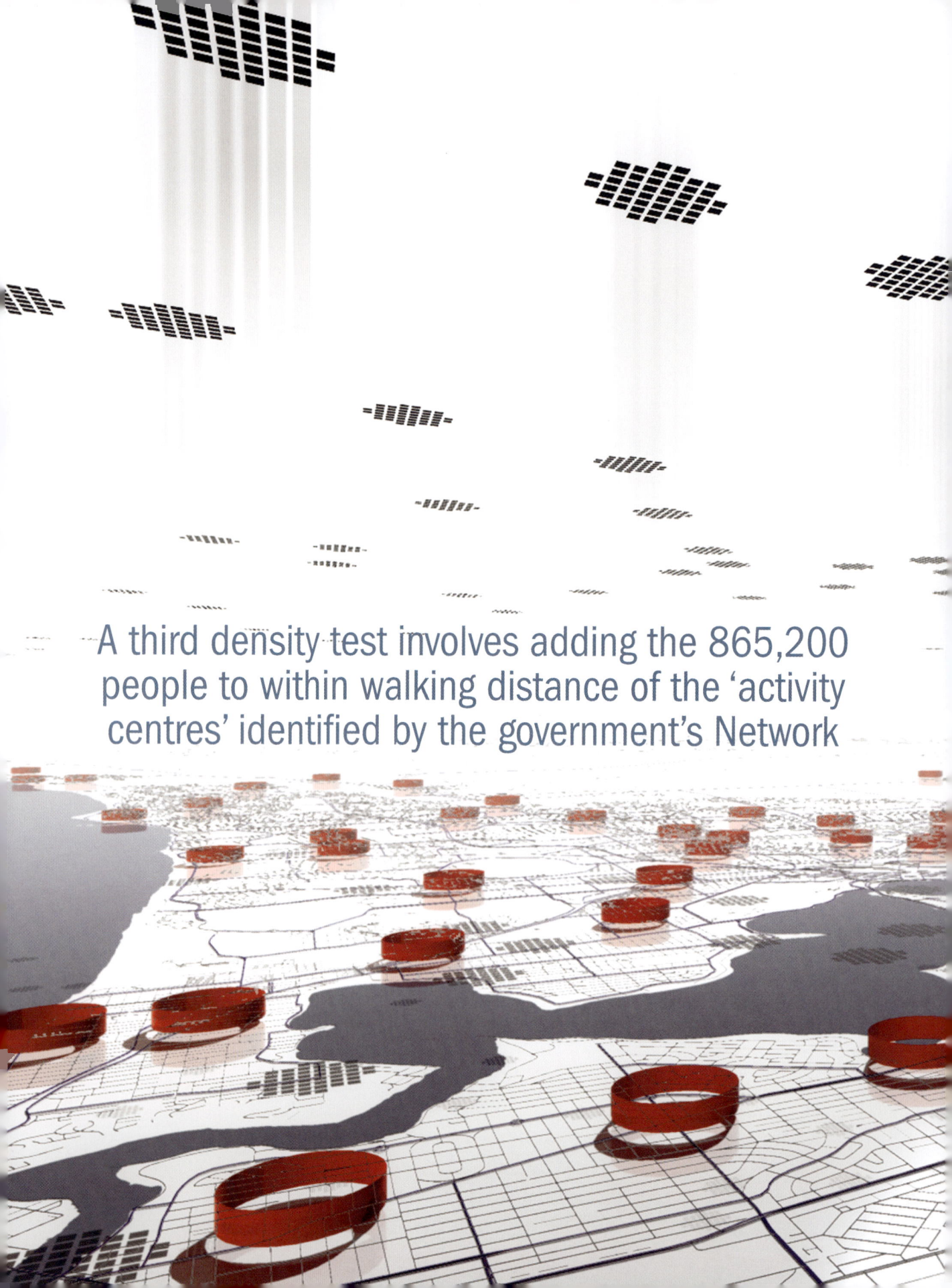

A third density test involves adding the 865,200 people to within walking distance of the 'activity centres' identified by the government's Network

City report. The result is that we need to add 90 apartments per hectare for all of the 50 hectares that comprise each activity centre.

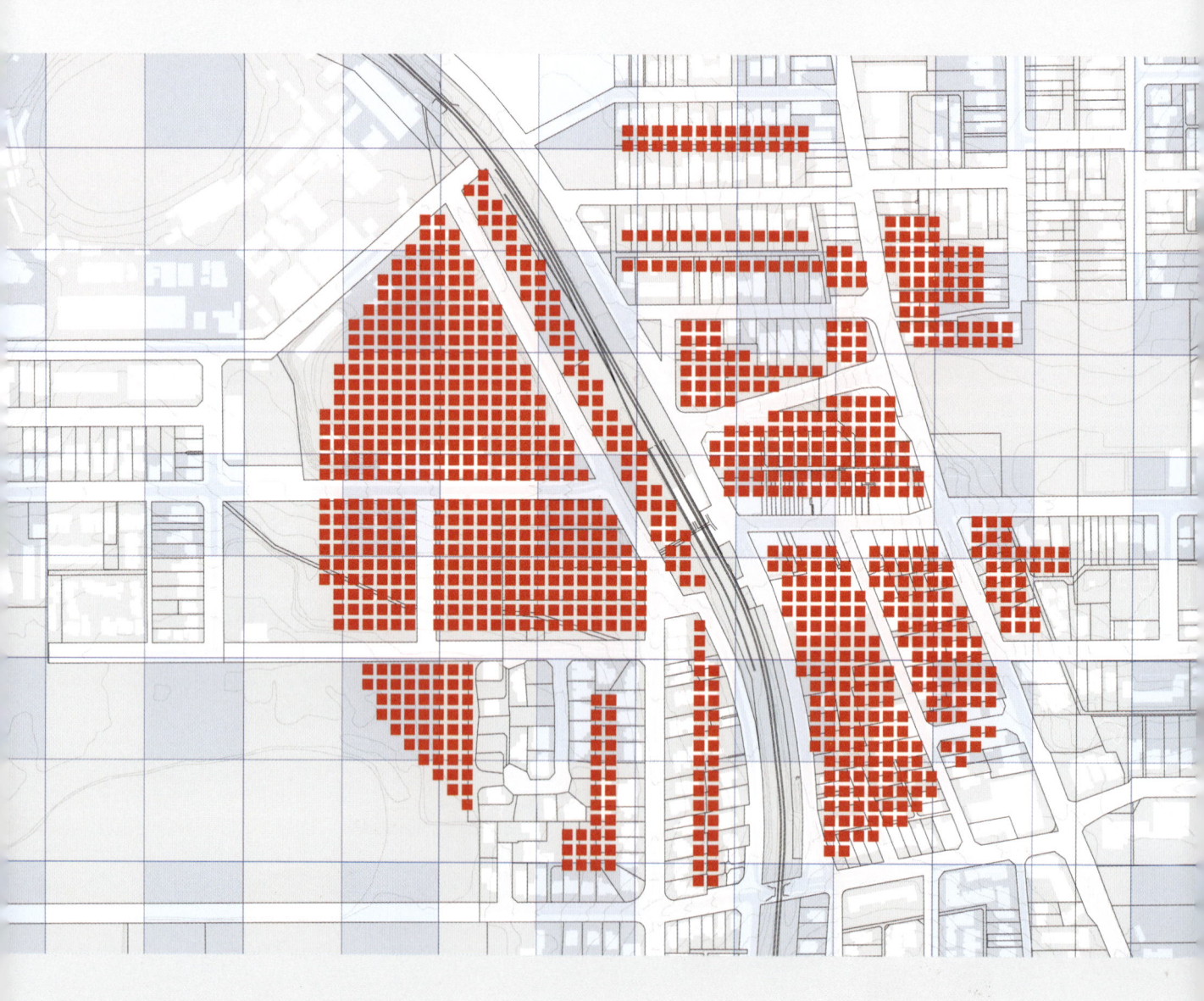

*above: Each grid represents one hectare.*

# INTRODUCTION

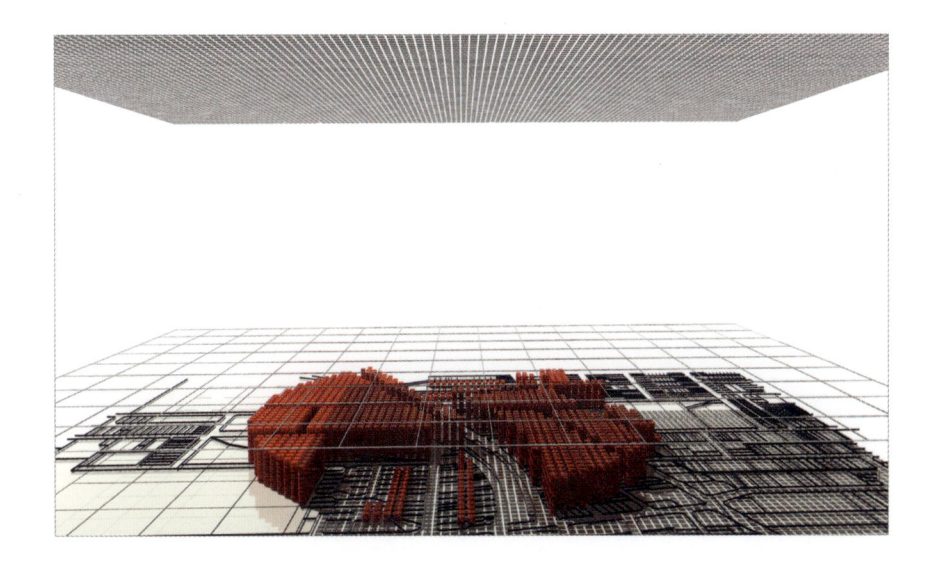

## 335
**VERTICAL SCENARIOS**

*A density increase of 90 dwellings per hectare within walking distance of the 120 activity centres identified in the government's Network City planning guidelines is neccessary if Perth is to accommodate an extra 865,000 people within its existing urban fabric.*

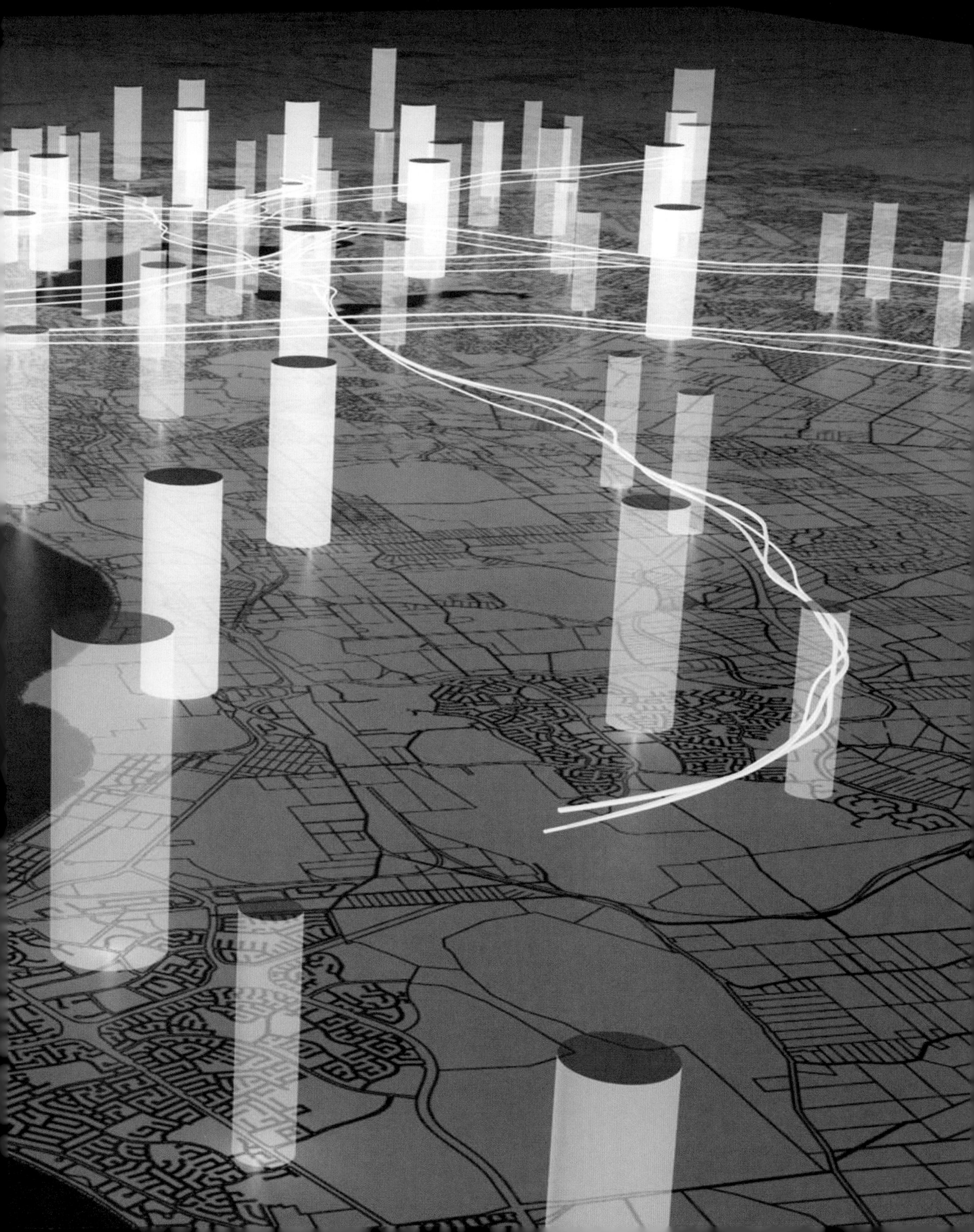

But why would you want to live in a higher density development close to transport and shopping centres when they look like this?

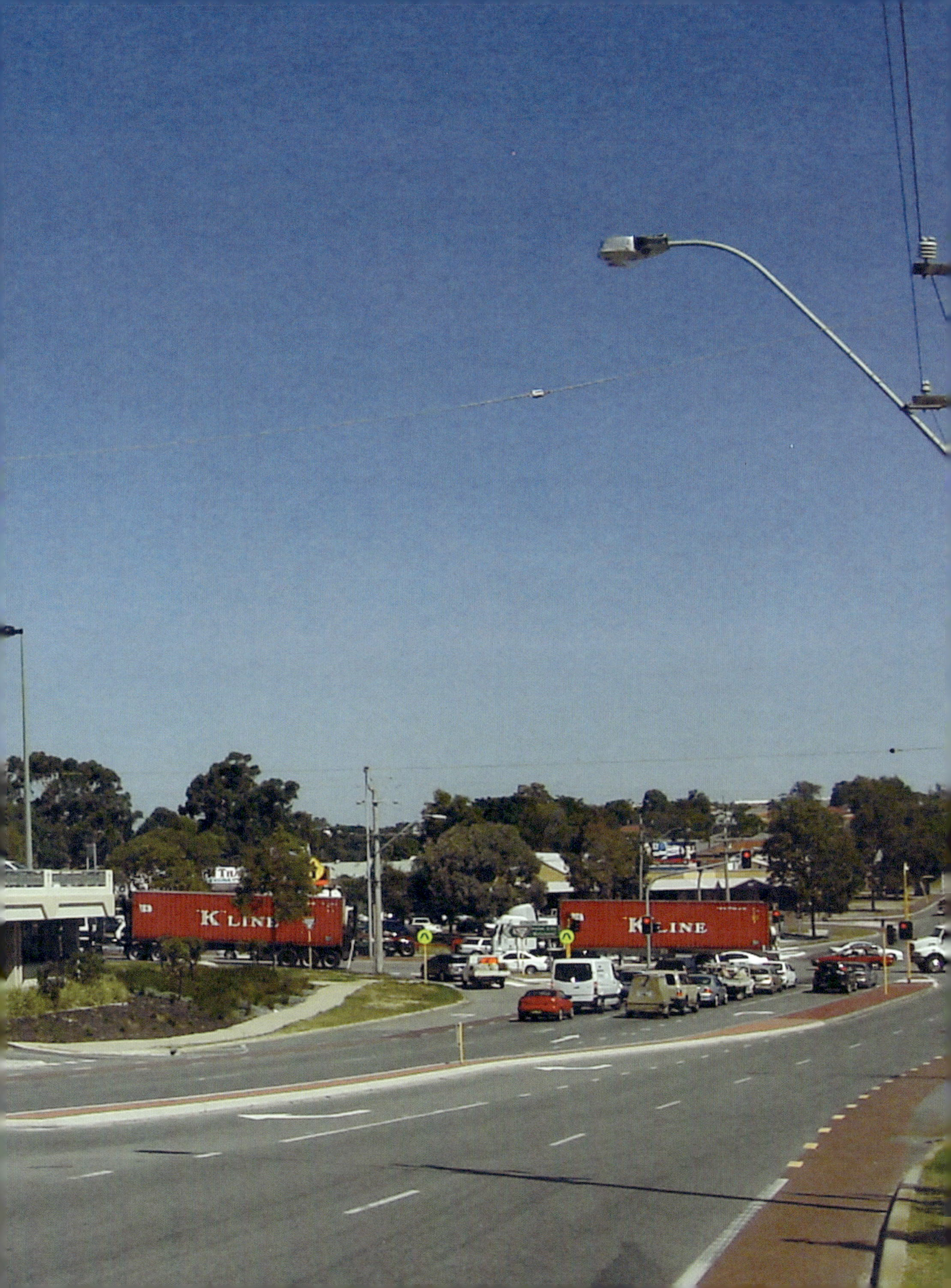
K LINE
K LINE

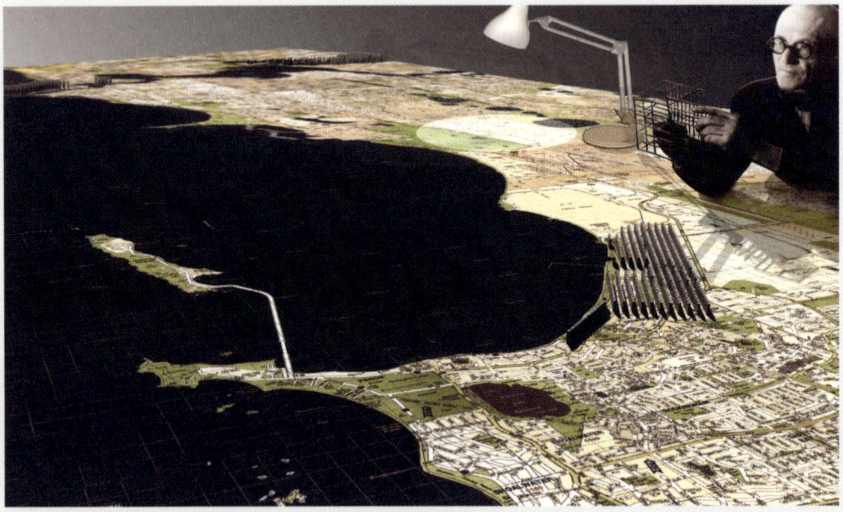

# SKY CITY

High-rise or high-density housing is uncommon in Perth and generally not the favoured form of housing in Australia. For most Australians it is inconceivable that someone should live under them or above them and that they should not have large homes and gardens. A free-standing home and garden is considered a birthright and tending one's lot is a national pastime. As Australian cities come under increasing population pressures and are thought to have already sprawled too far, this mindset is changing.

The ultimate proponent of high-density development was the modern Swiss architect Le Corbusier, whose original Radiant City model was conceived to house three million people (the predicted 2050 population of Perth) in an area of only a few kilometres. As shown over page this amounted to a density of 1,579 dwellings per hectare. The utopian model of Radiant City, along with modern architecture in general, was boldly conceived to alleviate the desperate need for mass housing in post-war Europe but when built quickly, cheaply and in areas of low amenity, Radiant City gave rise to some of the 20$^{th}$ Century's worst urbanism.

Stretching from London to Moscow and ultimately throughout the developing world, the essential formula of high-rise residential development in a car-dominated landscape is, with hindsight, widely recognised as a deleterious urban form.[1] However, if designed with attention to the users' real needs, and to public space, transportation links, microclimate and view-sheds, then high-rise development, which is close to good cultural or natural amenity, can be a successful method of housing large numbers of people.

One of the most perceptive critics of Radiant City was the American, Jane Jacobs. Based on her experience of living in Greenwich Village in Manhattan, Jacobs argued that the ideal density for a vibrant community was not 1,579 dwellings per hectare but 250 dwellings (475 people) per hectare, a density roughly 16 times that of conventional Australian suburbia and the sort of density found in many European cities.[2]

After the 23,000 hectares of land already zoned for suburbanisation on the periphery of Perth is built out, there still remain 865,200 people (and possibly many more) to be housed within the existing urban fabric of Perth by 2050. If these people were to be housed at a typical European density we would need to build a new city approximately 5 km$^2$. Florence, a city much loved by most who visit it, has a population of approximately 500,000 people (although it too is sprawling!). Perth could simply allocate some of its vast peripheral landscape to building a new Florence, albeit half as big again. But Florence is more than a form. It is a complicated layering of history in a particular landscape and culture, and to simply reproduce its form in a new location is no guarantee that the copy will be a success.

1 For a resounding critique of Le Corbusier's Radiant City see Hall, P., *Cities of Tomorrow: An Intellectual History of Urban Planning and Design in the Twentieth Century* (3$^{rd}$ ed.), Blackwell Publishing, Oxford, 2002, pp. 217-61.

2 Hall, P., *Cities of Tomorrow: An Intellectual History of Urban Planning and Design in the Twentieth Century*, (3$^{rd}$ ed.), Blackwell Publishing, Oxford, 2002, p. 72.

**VERTICAL SCENARIOS**

2.5 net d/ha

10 net d/ha

*Typical Australian suburban density*

12 net d/ha

15 net d/ha

40 net d/ha

60 net d/ha

170 net d/ha

250 net d/ha

*Typical European density*

1750 net d/ha

*Le Corbusier's 'Radiant City' – the ideal density of modern architecture.*

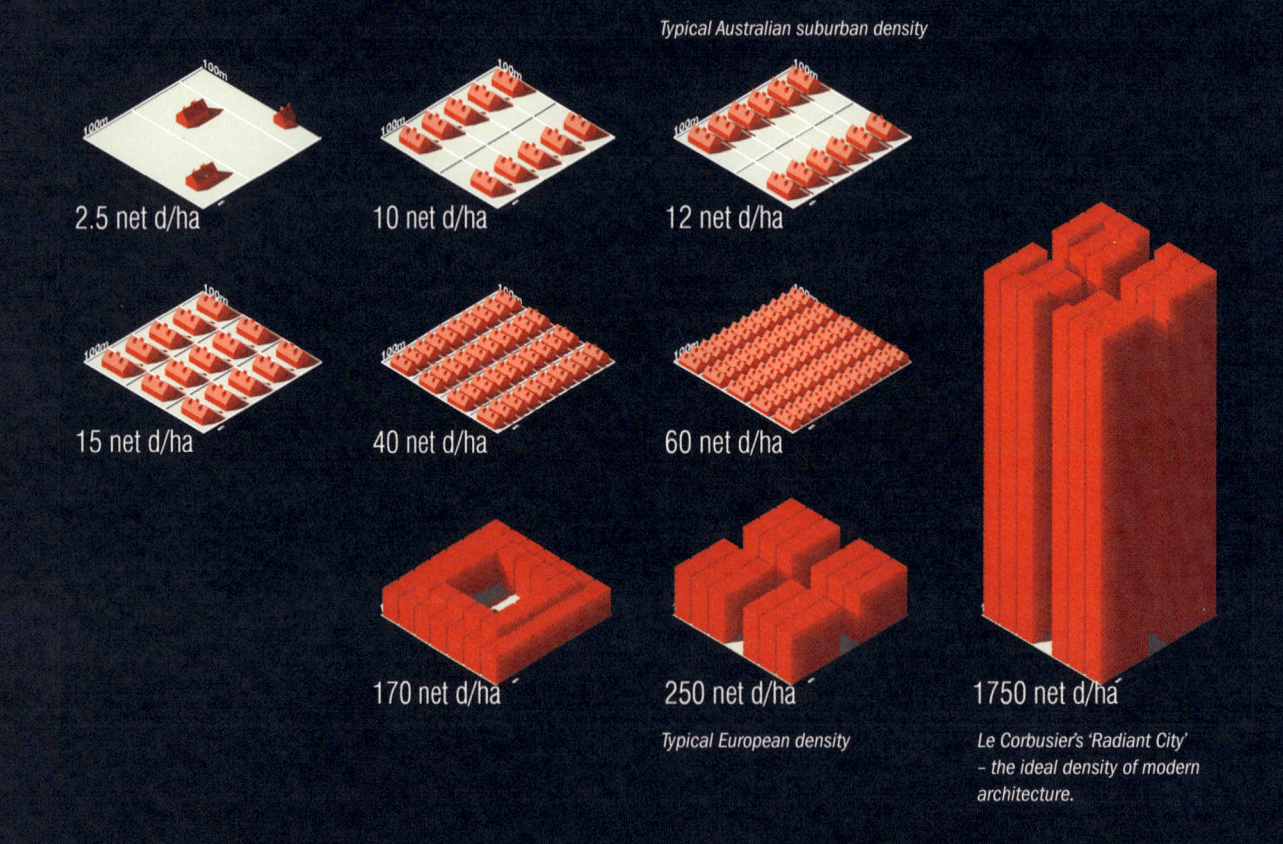

*Standard urban densities (dwellings per hectare).*

As Alex Marshall so nicely puts it, simply copying the form of great cities won't work because it 'resembles trying to grow a rose by starting with the patterns of its leaves and petals...You have to study the seed and the soil within which the seed is grown'.[3]

When we come to look for areas where we should develop high-density living in Perth it is, according to the lessons of the 20th Century, best to focus on areas that have high landscape and cultural amenity and which would, by becoming denser, augment and enhance that existing amenity. The Sky City scenario is based on finding places of high landscape and or cultural amenity within the existing city's boundary, in which 865,200 people could be housed at a density of 250 dwellings per hectare. We have identified three areas where this could reasonably occur: one around the existing CBD, a second at the mouth of the Swan River at Fremantle and a third on the coast, south of Perth in Rockingham. In the images that illustrate these sites we are not prescribing building heights as this is something best left for a design phase where the green attributes of buildings without lifts are typically played off against buildings that not only make economic sense but also provide maximum views.

Within close range of Perth's CBD we have identified 392.7 hectares of land on which, at a density of 250 dwellings per hectare, 98,175 dwellings could be built. This amounts to 186,532 people calculated at 1.9 persons per dwelling. Some of this undeveloped land is currently classified as public open space but for the purposes of this scenario we argue that since Perth has almost three times as much open space as it does built space (and almost no 'urbane' space) it can afford to relinquish some underused open space to urbanism. This approach is in part tested by the example of the New Perth Waterfront development documented on pages 355–59.

A second site for high-rise development is on the northern flank of the Swan River mouth at Fremantle. This site abuts the river to the south and the beach to the west and is adjacent to the much-loved town of Fremantle. It is also serviced by rail. These 185 hectares could accommodate 87,875 people living with beach on one flank, river on the other and the historical core of Fremantle across the river mouth. For this industrial land to become available, the working Port of Fremantle would have to be moved further south.

Whilst predominantly an industrial zone, the area surrounding the new port site further south also offers high landscape amenity and links with the existing coastal township of Rockingham. In the new port city of Rockingham we have concluded that an additional 170,793 people can be accommodated in high-density development.

The three components of Sky City can thus accommodate 356,843 of Perth's projected 2050 population. This represents a shortfall of 508,357 people and we need to look elsewhere within the existing city boundary for opportunities for vertical, high-density development. There are two following scenarios that do this: River City and Surf City.

[3] Marshall, A., *How Cities Work: Suburbs, Sprawl, and the Roads Not Taken*, University of Texas Press, Austin, 2000, p. 20.

# SKY CITY

*High-density development around the CBD of Perth.*

**344**
**VERTICAL SCENARIOS**

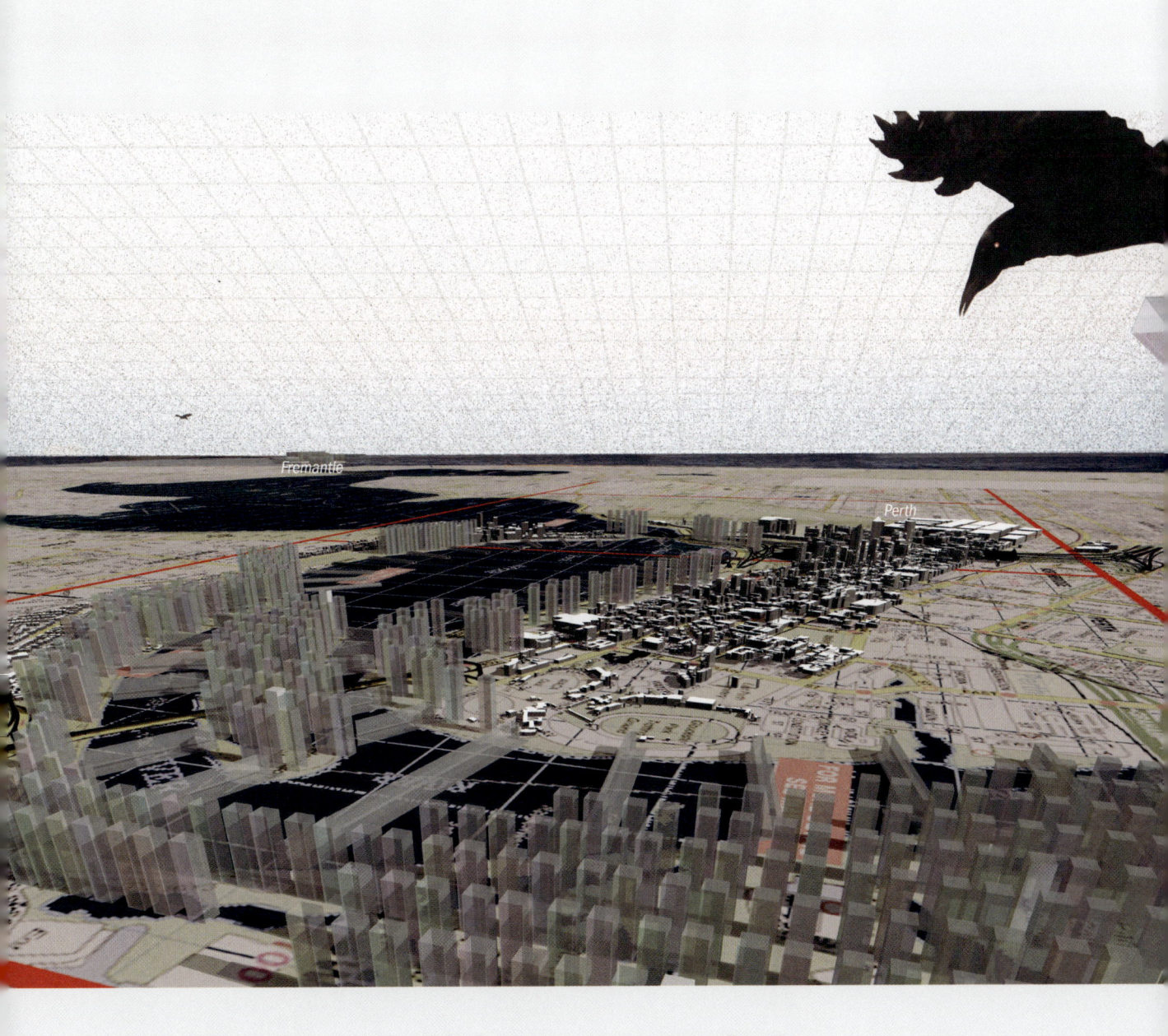

*View over high-density development around the CBD of Perth towards a second new mini-city at Fremantle.*

# HIGH QUALITY, HIGH DENSITY DEVELOPMENT IN AREAS OF HIGH AMENITY

Architecture by WOHA (Singapore)

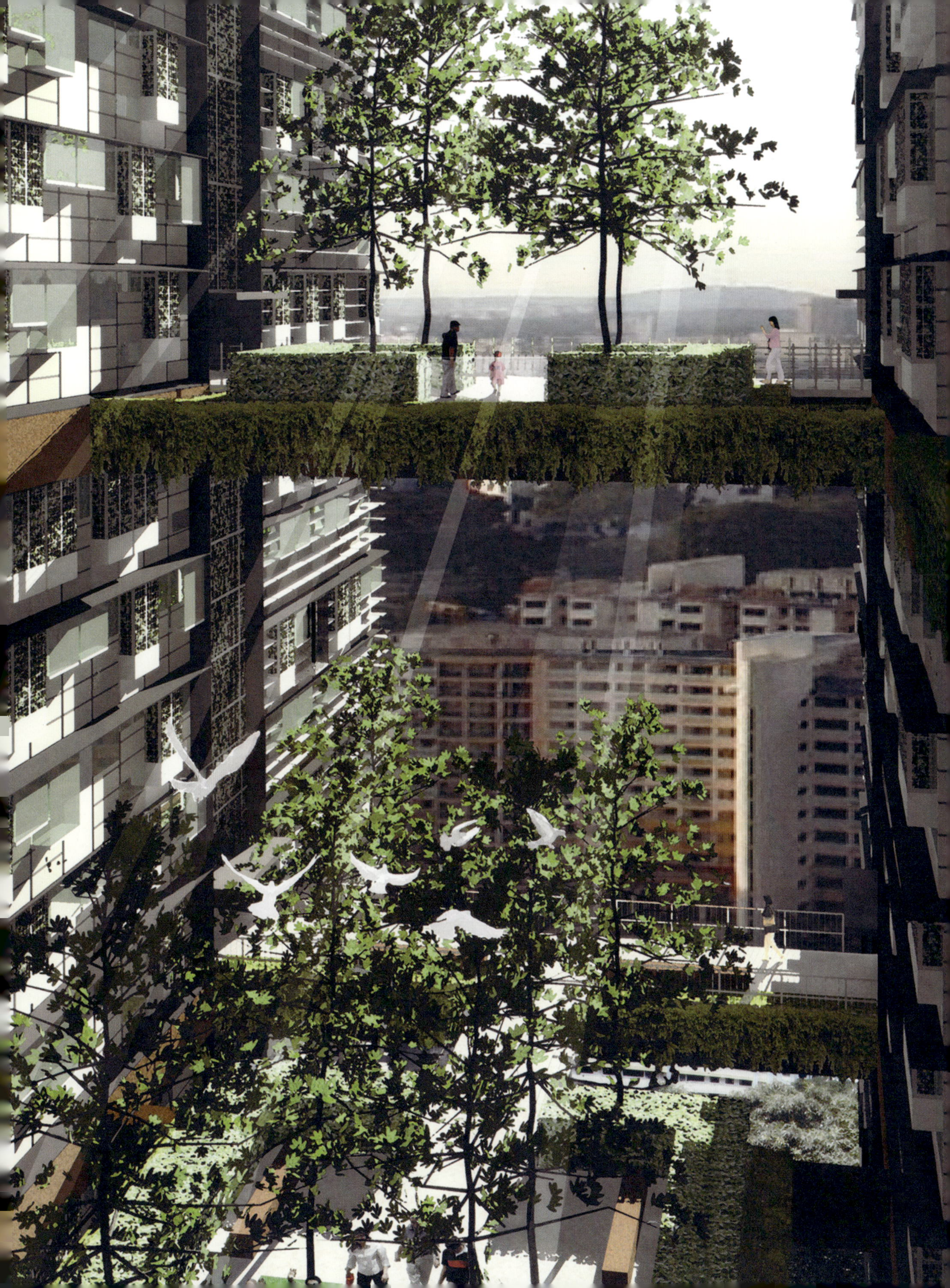

*Increased density can apply to public open space systems as well as housing. These images from Julian Bolleter's research into new public open space scenarios for Dubai could be transferred to any city endeavouring to restrict sprawl. These vertical landscapes could include a wide range of sporting and recreational activities, vertical farming, gardens and associated retail spaces.*

SKY CITY

349
VERTICAL SCENARIOS

... NOT vertical sprawl in areas of low amenity

BROWNLEE
TOWERS
A

*The port of Fremantle – an excellent site for high-density development.*

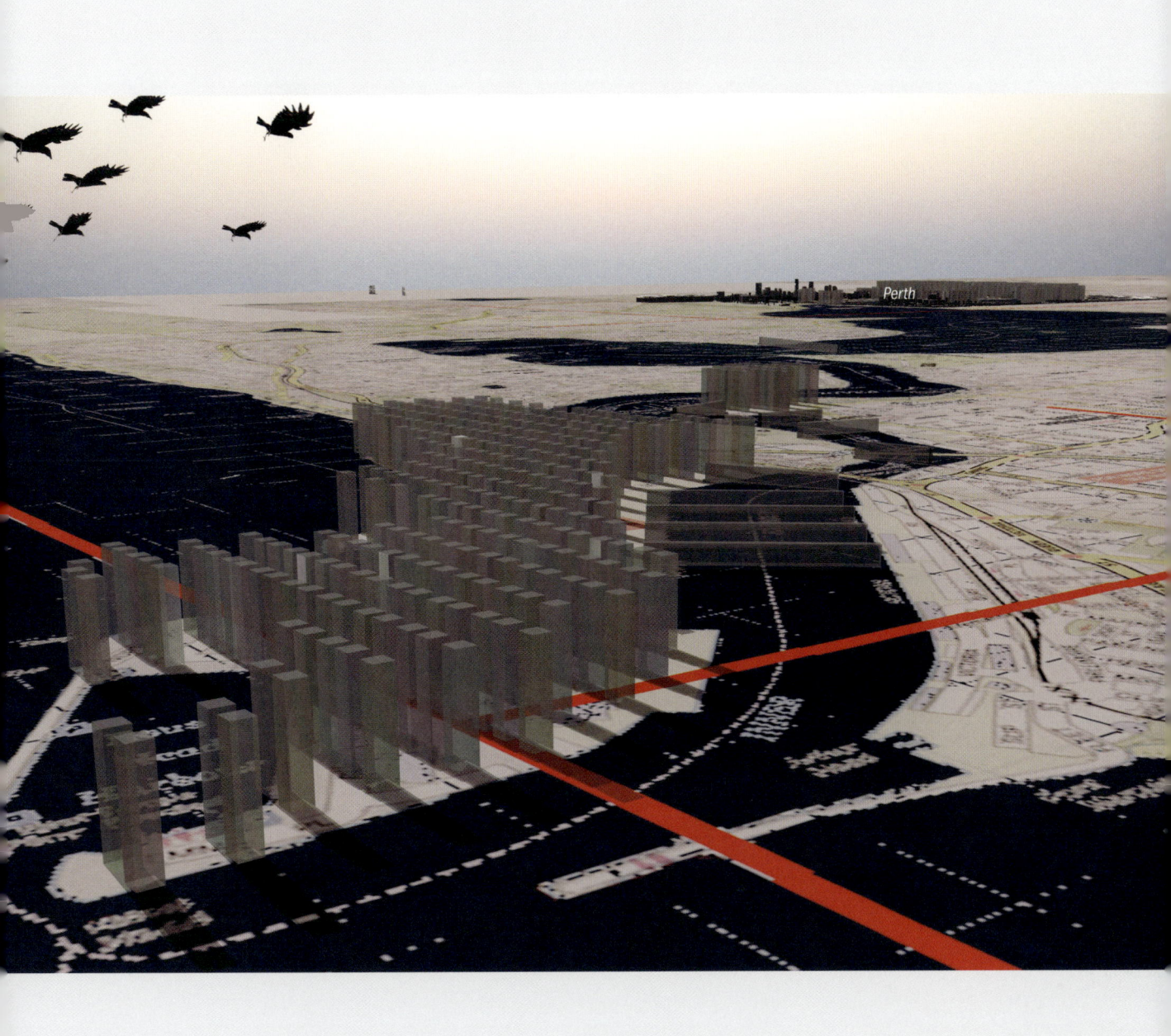

SKY CITY

Perth

**353**
**VERTICAL SCENARIOS**

*Image courtesy Ashton Raggatt McDougall.*

# PERTH'S NEW WATERFRONT

## A 'Sky City' test case

The New Perth Waterfront is a $3,360 million government initiative to enliven the CBD of Perth – a showcase of contemporary urban infill development. The project is an important test case as to whether Perth can build high-quality infill development that, unlike the current central business district, engages with the city's landscape setting and creates high-quality, public space. In the context of the larger planning scenarios documented in this book the New Perth Waterfront project operates as a zoomed in example of vertical development and shows that at the scale of urban design we can increase residential density and simultaneously create high-quality public spaces.

In 1829 when the Captain James Stirling sailed up the Swan River and landed in the area of what is now known as the Esplanade, he thought it was *the place* for a new city. He was wrong. It is windy and south-facing. Nonetheless, the city is now there and its modern grid is generally empty at the close of business.

At the turn of the 19th Century, despite already being partially filled in, the Swan River still lapped up against the edge of the fledgling city. The riverfront in the area of the Esplanade was a lively transport hub and entertainment area. In the 1960s the river edge was more extensively filled to make way for freeways and create a vast, flat public open space of grass that to this day no one really knows what to do with. Not many people promenade along the old Esplanade today. The city turned its back on the river and both the river and the city have suffered as a consequence.

The Perth Metropolitan Region has three times as much open space as it does built space and almost all that built space is suburban. Perth has over 140 kilometres of river edge and most of it is underused green-space. There is no urbanity on the Swan River, the central city's greatest amenity. Of the 140 kilometres of riverfront the New Perth Waterfront will develop only one, but it could be a significant breakthrough if it can demonstrate that development can enhance the city's livability and not negatively impact upon the river's ecology. Quality development should be encouraged on certain parts of the river and leveraged to help the Swan River Trust manage the larger issues that are impacting upon the river's health.

By 2050 many more people should live and work in the CBD and they will generally demand high-quality designed environments and services. In an area of 22.6 hectares this development will add 320,000 m² of office space, 55,000 m² of retail space, 12,000 m² of cultural space and 3,000 new apartments to the heart of the CBD. 5,700 people

*Project Management*
  LandCorp/DPI
*Urban Design*
  Ashton Raggatt McDougall
  Richard Weller and Oculus
*Planning*
  Roberts Day Group
*Heritage*
  Hocking Planning & Architecture
*Property*
  Colliers International
*Economics*
  Pracsys
*Civil Engineering*
  Wood & Grieve
*Marine/Coastal Engineer*
  MP Rogers & Associates
*Hydrology*
  Syrinx Environmental
*Survey*
  McMullen Nolan
*Geotechnical*
  Golder Associates
*Environmental*
  RPS Group
*Marine Environmental*
  WorleyParsons
*Transport Planning*
  WorleyParsons
*Structural Engineering*
  ARUP
*Quantity Surveyor*
  Ralph & Beattie Bosworth

*Image courtesy Ashton Raggatt McDougall.*

could live in this development and 23,000 could work there. This is a real city not a waterside theme park.

Countless designs have been done for this land between the city and the river in the past and all of them stymied by a profound scepticism toward vertical infill development in general and sentimentality toward the existing large open spaces in particular. This time the proposal to develop the area has real momentum but the project remains controversial and recent political and economic changes are a set back.

Despite its uncertain future we argue that this form of urbanism in this location is correct. Why? Firstly, it focuses energy around a new train station and builds the city out toward the river between William and Barrack streets, Perth's main north–south axes. Secondly, as a priority, the urban design uses built form to define potentially high-quality public space and enfolds the river into the city. There are two major public places framed by the urbanism: The Esplanade Square and The River Circle. The square could become the major civic forum for a working city, whereas The River Circle, a 500-metre round promenade, is more about framing the beauty of the river and offering leisure related activities protected from the wind. Both the circle and the square present Perth with grand civic spaces the likes of which it has never had. Finally, there is the right amount of development – neither too much nor too little as has bedevilled other schemes. And most importantly, the scale of the development is not suburban.

*Image courtesy Ashton Raggatt McDougall.*

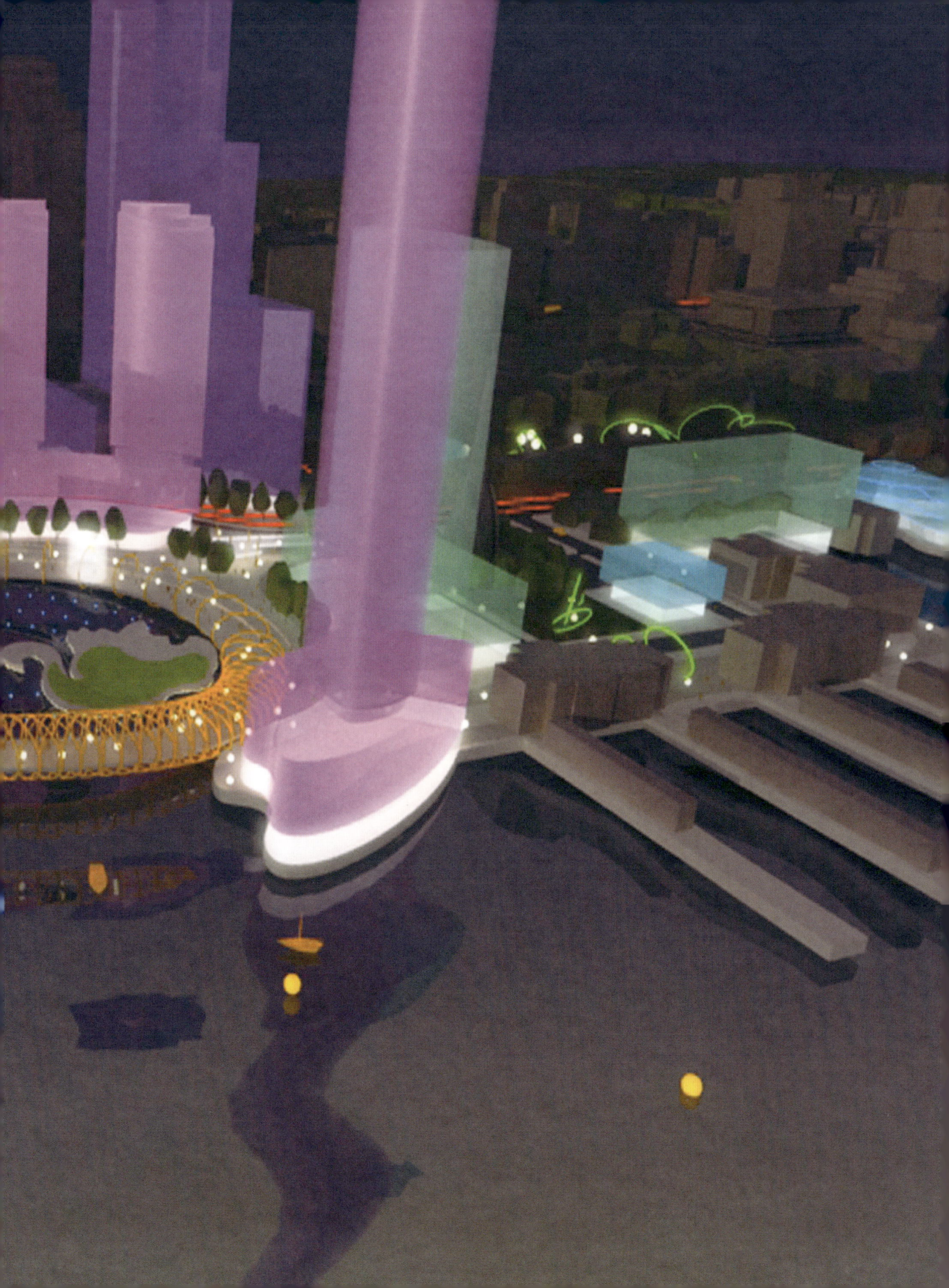

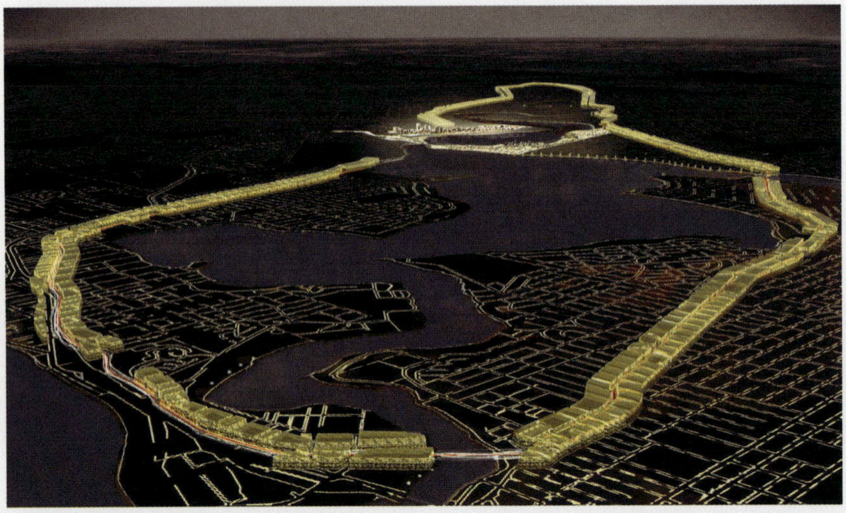

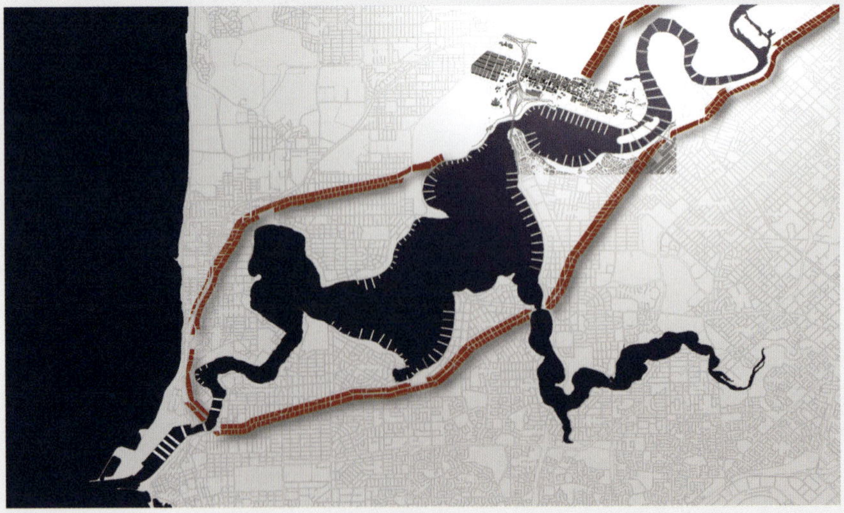

# RIVER CITY

The three mini-cities proposed in the Sky City scenario could accommodate 356,843 of Perth's projected 2050 population increase. This represents a shortfall of 508,357 people from the ABS projections around which our scenarios were originally modelled. If we take the most recent ABS projection of up to an extra 2.7 million people living in Perth by the year 2056 then (exempting the number of people accommodated in Sky City and in land already zoned for suburban development) Perth will need to accommodate 1,708,357 people within the existing urban fabric. Some of these people could be accommodated in variations of the tests shown earlier where an extra 3.3, 10, and 90 dwellings per hectare were added to the existing urban fabric.

The potential of the city to absorb more people in these ways notwithstanding, Perth's main residential attractors are its coastline and its river. The following two scenarios, River City and Surf City attempt to add significant numbers of people to these areas so that the reduced domestic space necessarily associated with high-density infill development is offset by proximity to the city's best natural amenities.

Significant residential development in the existing suburbs occupying the view-shed to Perth's river is extremely difficult. Not only is there a lack of sites that could be developed, but community resistance to development in these areas is fierce. Consequently, we have pulled back from the river edges and sought sites for development at the outer limits of the view-shed to the river. These sites generally correspond with two arterial roads: Stirling Highway running parallel to the river in the north and Canning Highway, parallel to the river in the south.

The land adjacent to these roads is feasible to develop: the existing buildings alongside these roads are generally low quality, and relative to sites directly adjacent to the river, the land is cheap. If developers could build high-rise apartments along these two roads, residents would be able to see the river and live within walking distance of the generous open spaces that flank it. High-density development along these two major arterial roads would also enliven these service corridors as commercial and residential zones. Public transport usage would increase, particularly if carriageways were expanded or an elevated light rail/monorail integrated into the restructuring of their sectional architectural profiles. Should the flanks of these arterial roads be developed at an average density of 250 dwellings per hectare, with allowances for situations where development is not achievable, we estimate that 250,000 people could be added to the city in this form.

Two additional components of River City are high-density residential finger-wharves and bridges. These elements do a lot to engage the river with urbanism but they are extremely expensive forms of development and collectively cannot accommodate more than about 50,000 people.

*left: The River City scenario: Increased density along the main roads framing the river, residential finger wharves and residential bridges into and across the river respectively.*

Why can't we increase development around the river and leverage that development to improve the river's ecology?

RIVER CITY

**VERTICAL SCENARIOS**

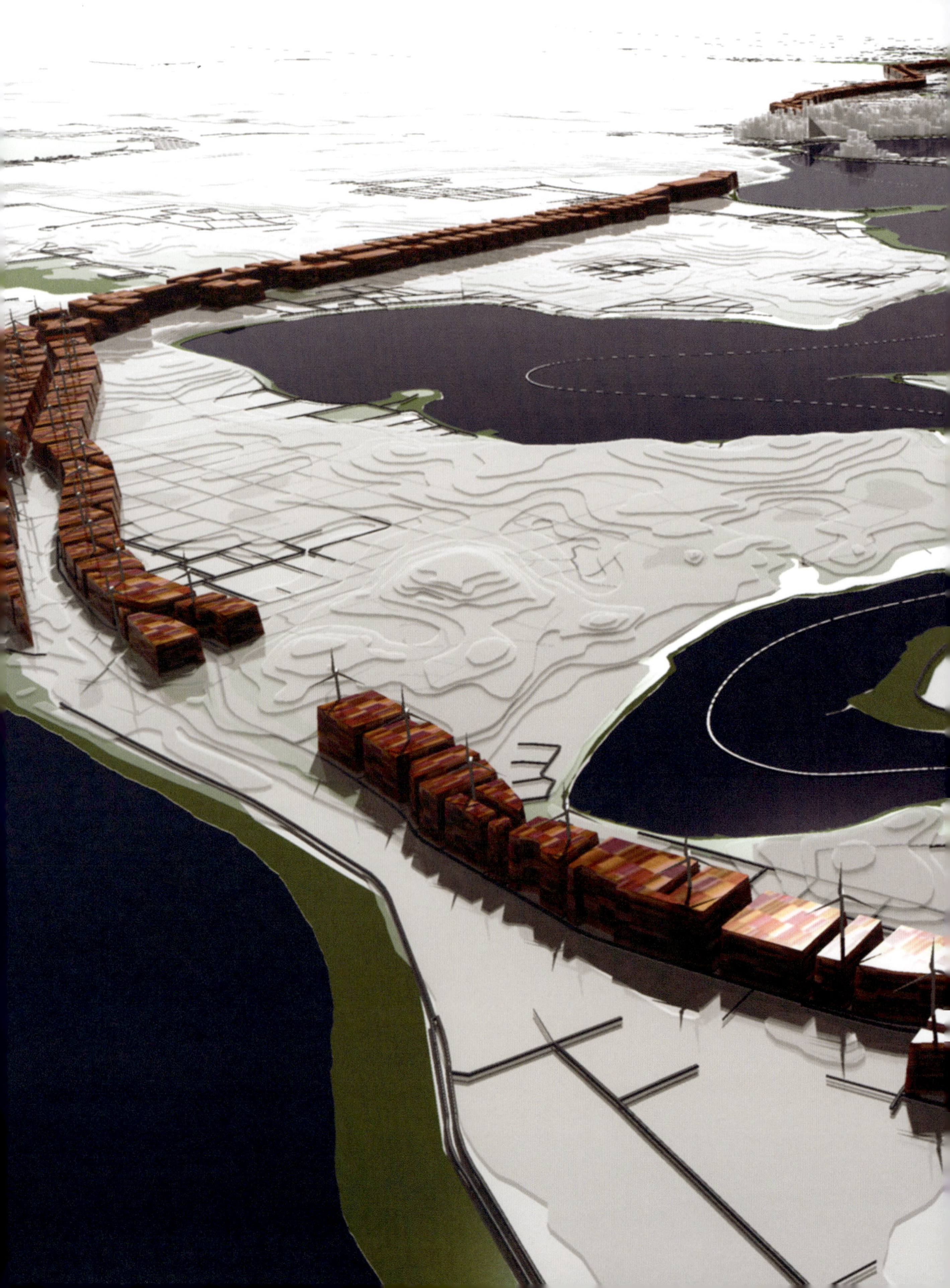

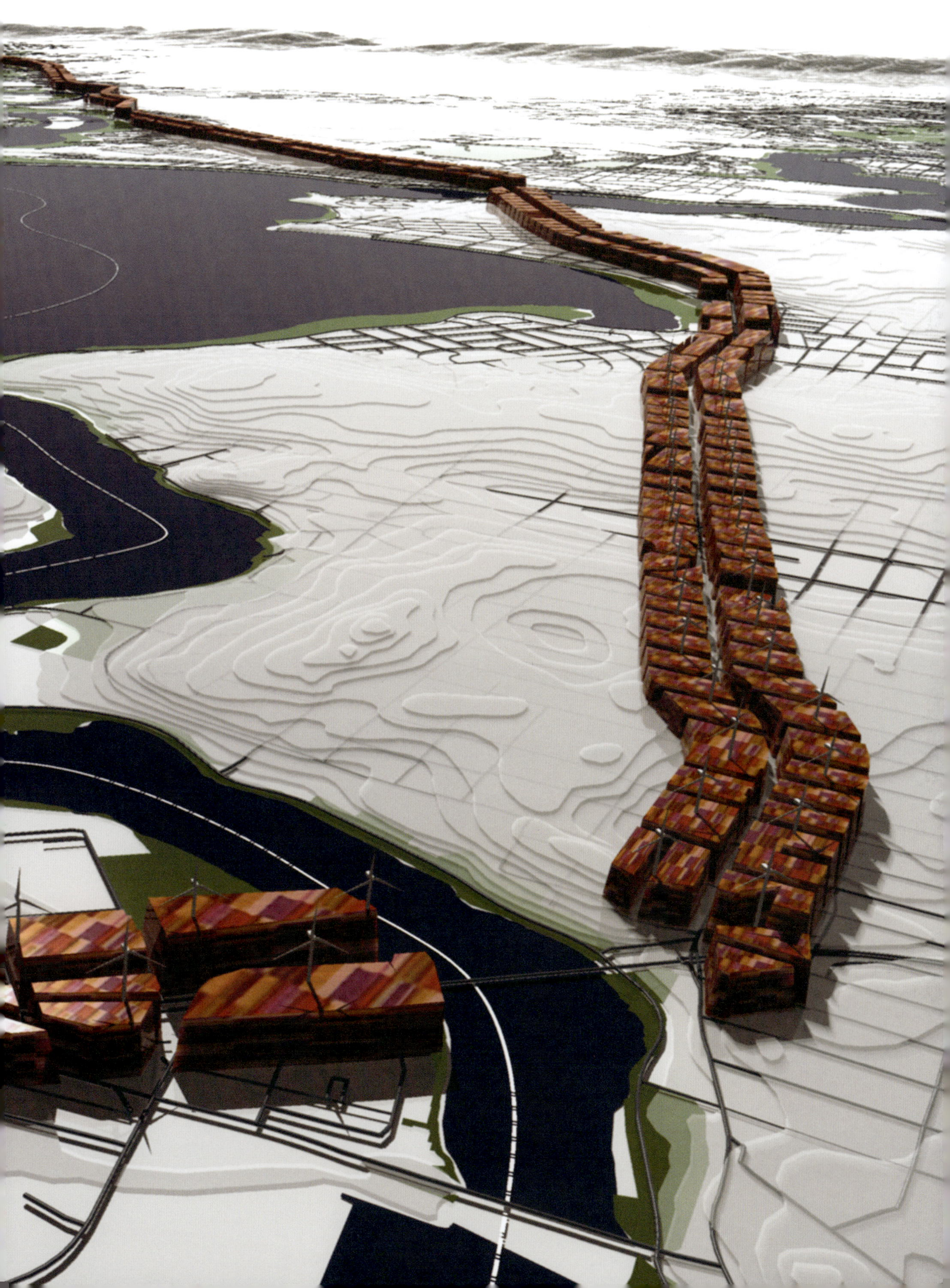

*Living bridges: six-storey residential structures across the river.*

RIVER CITY

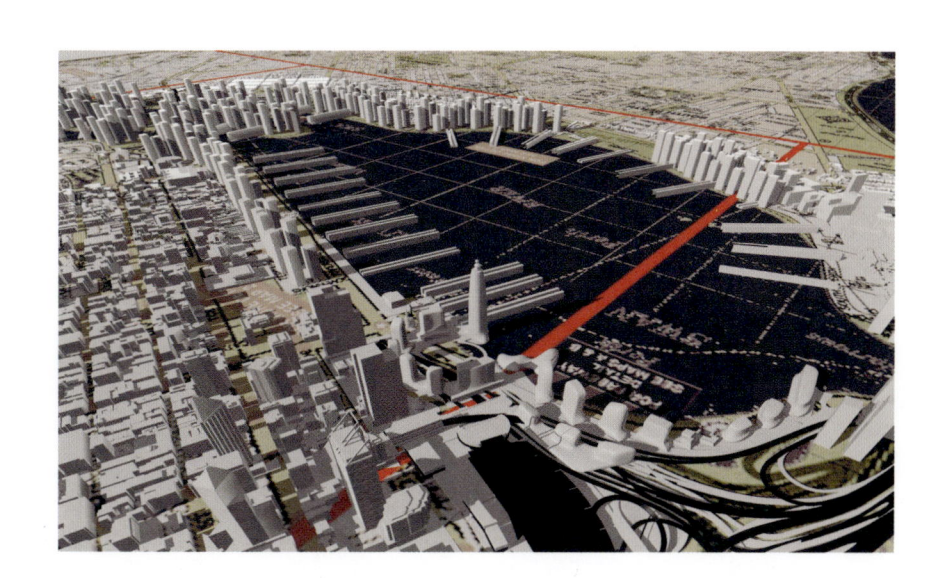

367
VERTICAL SCENARIOS

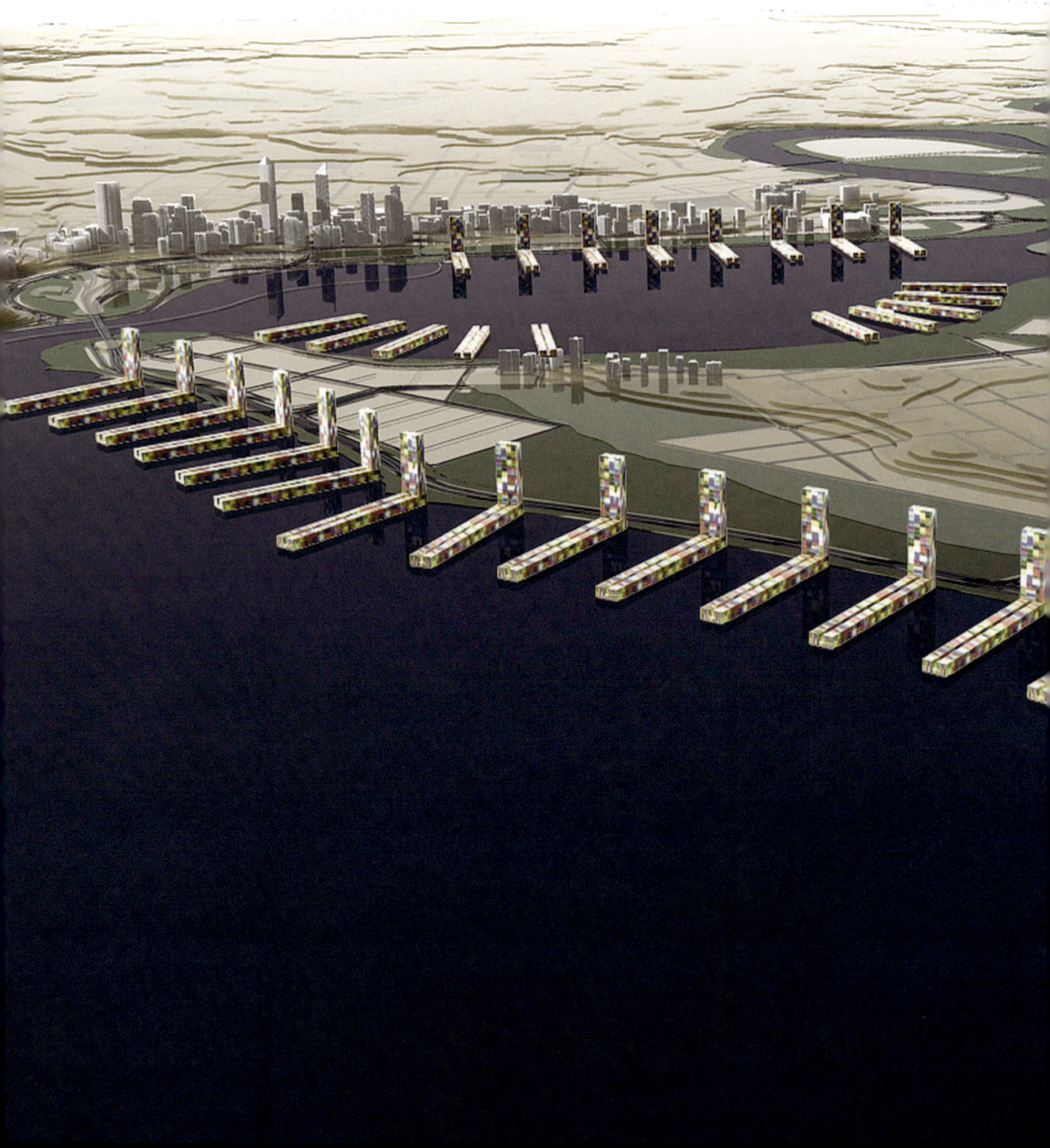

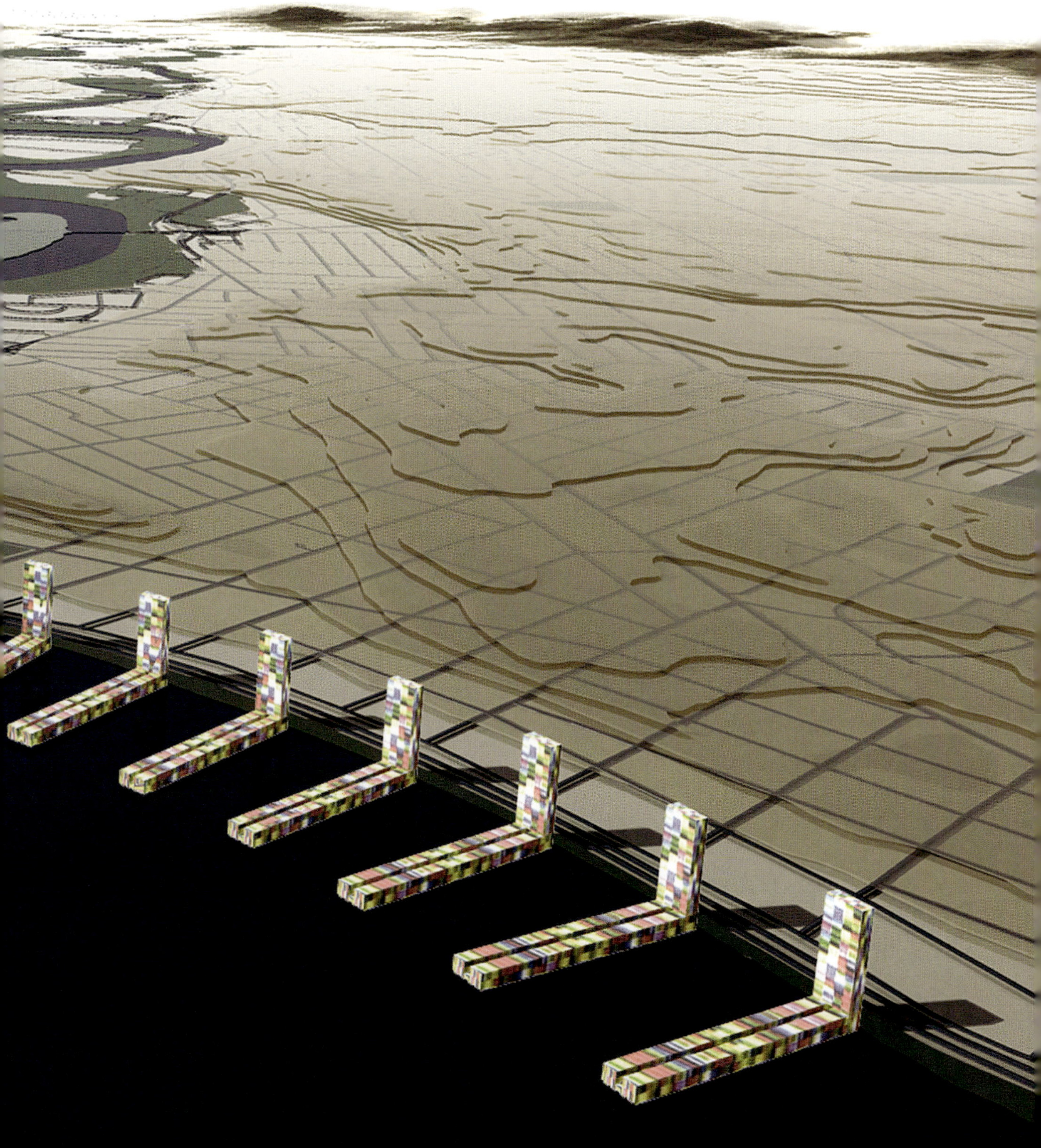

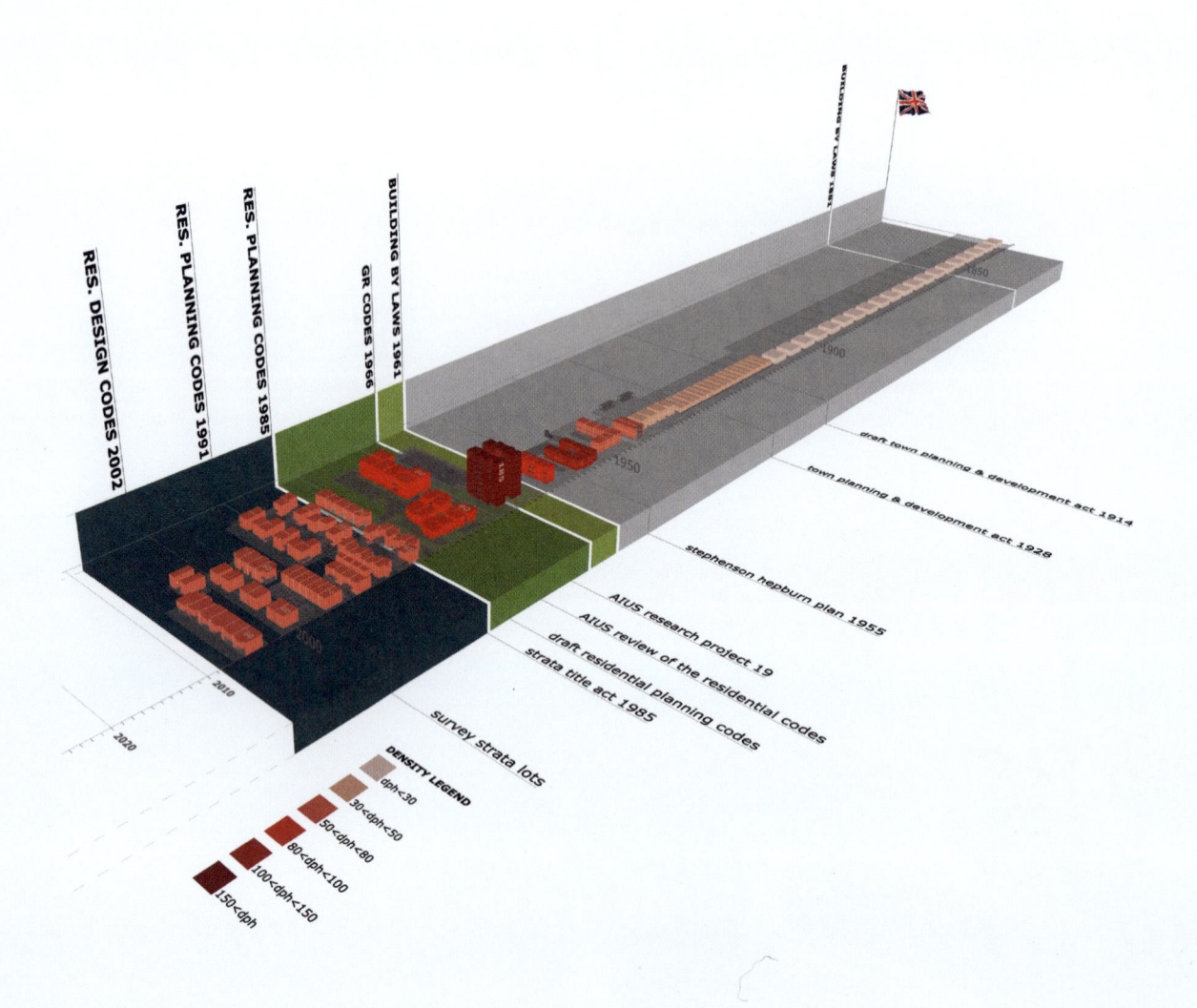

*An historical time line of Perth's urban density regulations.*

# THE PATH OF DENSITY

Arguments concerned with sustainability, housing demand, demographic change and affordability are currently contributing to a strategic push for increased dwelling densities in existing residential areas of Perth. During the 1960s, Perth's existing inner and middle suburbs experienced a brief but significant period of high-density urban consolidation. Prior to this Perth's only other notable exposure to high-density living arose from the building of flats in the 1920s and 1930s that were associated with the economic stress of the Great Depression.

The density boom of the 1960s coincided with local government's adoption of the General Residential Codes (GR Codes) which controlled the scale and form of multi-unit residential development. Importantly, through a plot ratio control mechanism, these codes allowed the building of large numbers of small dwelling units. Under these regulations housing developments in existing residential areas with densities in the range of 180 to 220 dwellings per hectare (dph) were not uncommon. In similar areas around Perth today it is difficult to find residential density zonings that are in excess of 60 dph.

Through development controls the architects of the GR Codes also deliberately pursued a particular type of building. The desired built form was one of tall apartment towers on large sites surrounded by communal gardens – referred to as garden apartments. There are many examples of such buildings from the 1960s dotted throughout the inner and middle suburbs of Perth. Ultimately this grand conception of garden apartment living rubbed up against the existing single homes next door and the vision faltered. It was the pursuit of this building typology that played a significant part in corrupting the understanding of the relationship between built form and high-density in Perth and in turn helped fuel a fear of urban consolidation.

The reaction to the apartment towers was relatively swift and severe. Height limits began to be imposed by local councils in an effort to moderate the scale of housing developments. This, however, meant that in many cases the development potential of a site could not be achieved. Subsequent reporting and regulation was to form the basis of the Residential Planning Codes which were adopted in 1985.

The Residential Planning Codes changed the way in which residential densities were defined – from plot ratio to dwellings per hectare. This allowed stricter control over the number and size of dwellings that could be built. Perhaps in response to the distress created by the apartment towers of the GR Codes local governments ascribed relatively meagre density provisions to much of the existing residential fabric.

In addition the new codes made further distinctions between group and multiple dwellings. This allowed local authorities to respond to the negative perceptions of units arranged one on top of the other and exclude them from most town planning schemes.

The new Residential Planning Codes and relatively sparse density provisions of local schemes resulted in the majority of multi-unit residential development being characterised by the lot-by-lot development of large floor-area group dwellings and a virtual extinction of the one bedroom units and two bedroom villas that had previously been built. This had the effect of severely restricting the diversity of new housing stock.

Changes to the Strata Titles Act in 1996 encouraged the subdivision of larger house lots in existing residential areas resulting in the propagation of vacant single home sites. These regulations encouraged battleaxe type development of individual dwellings.

It is this piecemeal development of large floor-area group houses and single dwelling battleaxes that characterises residential infill development in most of Perth today. Parking requirements, setback rules and overshadowing controls on relatively small blocks of land dictate large footprint buildings located centrally on the lot. These building forms leave little private or communal outdoor space other than that required for motor vehicle parking and manoeuvring. The resulting amenity of this type of development is questionable given the cramped arrangement of the building on the site.

In general, larger-scale multi-unit housing projects allow a more considered approach to the problems of efficiently using space, dwelling amenity and privacy that are so critical in this type of development. In addition, they hold much potential for implementing more effective sustainable design strategies such as creating opportunities for the provision of deep soil zones allowing rainwater infiltration into the local water table. (To their credit the GR Codes acknowledged some of these benefits and encouraged the amalgamation of land parcels by providing a density bonus for increasing site areas. The intent was to allow for efficiencies in the organisation of vehicles and greater amenity of the gardens.)

Under the current development paradigm for the majority of inner and middle suburban areas there is very little opportunity to provide smaller dwellings to help meet the substantial demands for increasing numbers of households, the provision of a more diverse range of dwelling types and more affordable housing options.

The reaction to Perth's high-density dallying of the 1960s is perhaps like many of Perth's topsy-turvy histories. The excess of the density boom has been followed by a period of arguably disproportionate restraint. There are signs that the density hangover may be

# THE PATH OF DENSITY

subsiding, at least at the tertiary levels of governance, as sustainability and affordability arguments support urban consolidation. Ultimately though, in the absence of state intervention, residential infill projects are played out on a local stage as municipalities control density on their patch through town planning schemes. The resistance to density in existing residential streets is still strong, as much local press will attest to, and it is this resistance which is telegraphed straight to the local officials and officers. Density is perceived as a caustic agent to the established character of quiet streets and is perhaps therefore thought to have similarly corrosive tendencies on the property values of traditional dwellings.

In order to achieve a more substantial density of infill residential development in the inner and middle suburbs, and avoid the local political quagmire, it seems prudent to seek out the land where there is less preciousness attached to established character. Arterial roadways and their adjacent strips of land are such areas. Many existing inner and middle suburbs are laced with these types of road which have evolved into busy motor vehicle transport routes. As an added incentive for higher-density development, these routes often also sustain a high frequency of public transport service as bus routes from the outer metropolitan areas converge.

Seeking to increase densities along arterial roadways combined with the sensitivity to density in bordering residential areas confines opportunities for development to a fairly narrow band close to the carriageway. Unfortunately these locations provide relatively inhospitable environs for dwelling – they are noisy and polluted and have well documented implications for human health. Traditional approaches to housing and its relationship to the street do very little to address these conditions.

Given this foreknowledge, the likelihood that motor vehicles will endure on these routes and the fact that the introduction of mass clean vehicle technology appears to be some way off, then what are the implications for architecture in these locations?

*Anthony Duckworth-Smith*

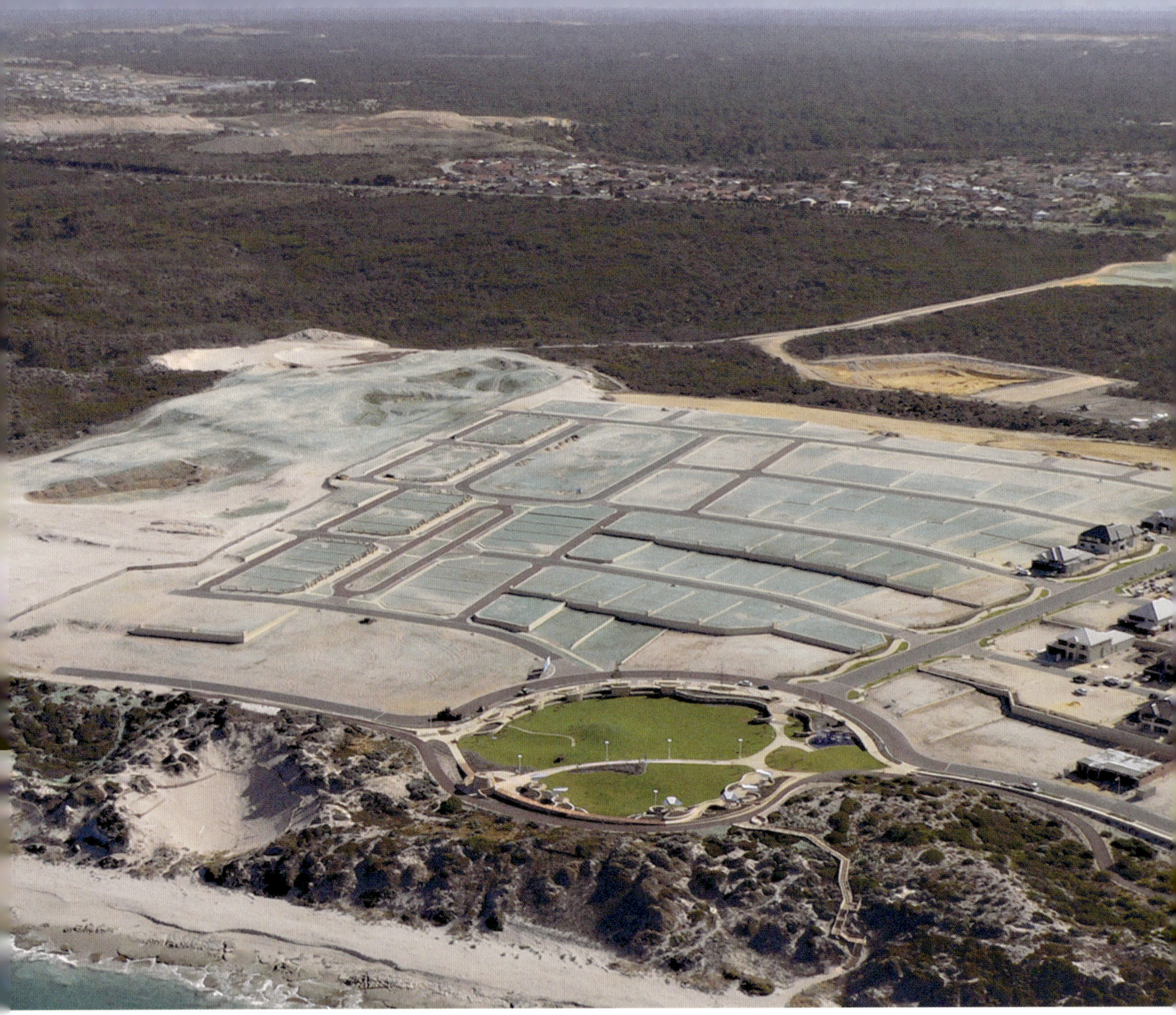

# SURF CITY

Perth has approximately 160 kilometres of beautiful coastline and nearly all of it is developed at a very low density. In principle, we believe it is desirable and possible to significantly increase the number of people living within the view-shed of, and walkable distance to, the coastline.

The standard practice of building low-density suburbia along the coastline, particularly north of the city, has resulted in the erasure of coastal topography and vegetation. It is virtually impossible to install conventional, car-based suburbs of brick and tile free-standing homes along the coast and retain anything but token remnants or reconstructed fragments of the coastal ecology. It is not common knowledge that the Swan Coastal Plain ecosystem (within the South-Western Botanical Region of Western Australia), is part of one of 34 global Hotspots of biodiversity.[4] Perth sits in the middle of the one of the earth's biologically richest and most endangered bioregions. Ignorance of this is compounded by the fact that the subtle vegetation of the Swan Coastal Plain also doesn't fit within the picturesque frames of verdant parks and gardens that typically sell suburbia. The existing vegetation is fire-prone, impenetrable and commonly home to snakes – in short, anathema to comfortable suburban living. In new suburban developments the existing vegetation and topography of the Swan Coastal Plain is routinely replaced with mixtures of green lawn and deciduous trees.

If we wish to conserve the unique biodiversity of the coastal landscape and still allow people to live close to the beach, the typology of free-standing low-density suburban development is simply inappropriate. To give more residents good views of the ocean and to preserve areas where the landscape is pristine, we need to reduce the footprint of buildings, increase their heights and set them well back from the coastal dunes. Any development has an impact but it can, in this manner, be minimised. In areas of the coast, which have already been extensively developed, buildings should also be high rise with a small footprint so as to minimise the destruction of the existing urban fabric, and add significant numbers of people to areas of high amenity.

An analysis of the opportunities for such development directed us toward adding a figure of 3,000 new residents for every kilometre of coastline – thus enabling an additional 450,000 people to live within the view-shed of the ocean and within walking distance to the beach. This averages out to a density increase of 40 dwellings per hectare, or one 25-storey residential tower every four hectares.

Development close to the beach in the midst of existing communities will, however, meet with extreme resistance. Indeed, Cottesloe, a coastal community, recently prohibited

[4] Mittermeier, R., Myers, N. and Goettsch Mittermeier, C. (eds), *Hotspots: Earth's Biologically Richest and Most Endangered Terrestrial Ecoregions*, CEMEX Conservation International, Mexico City, 1999.

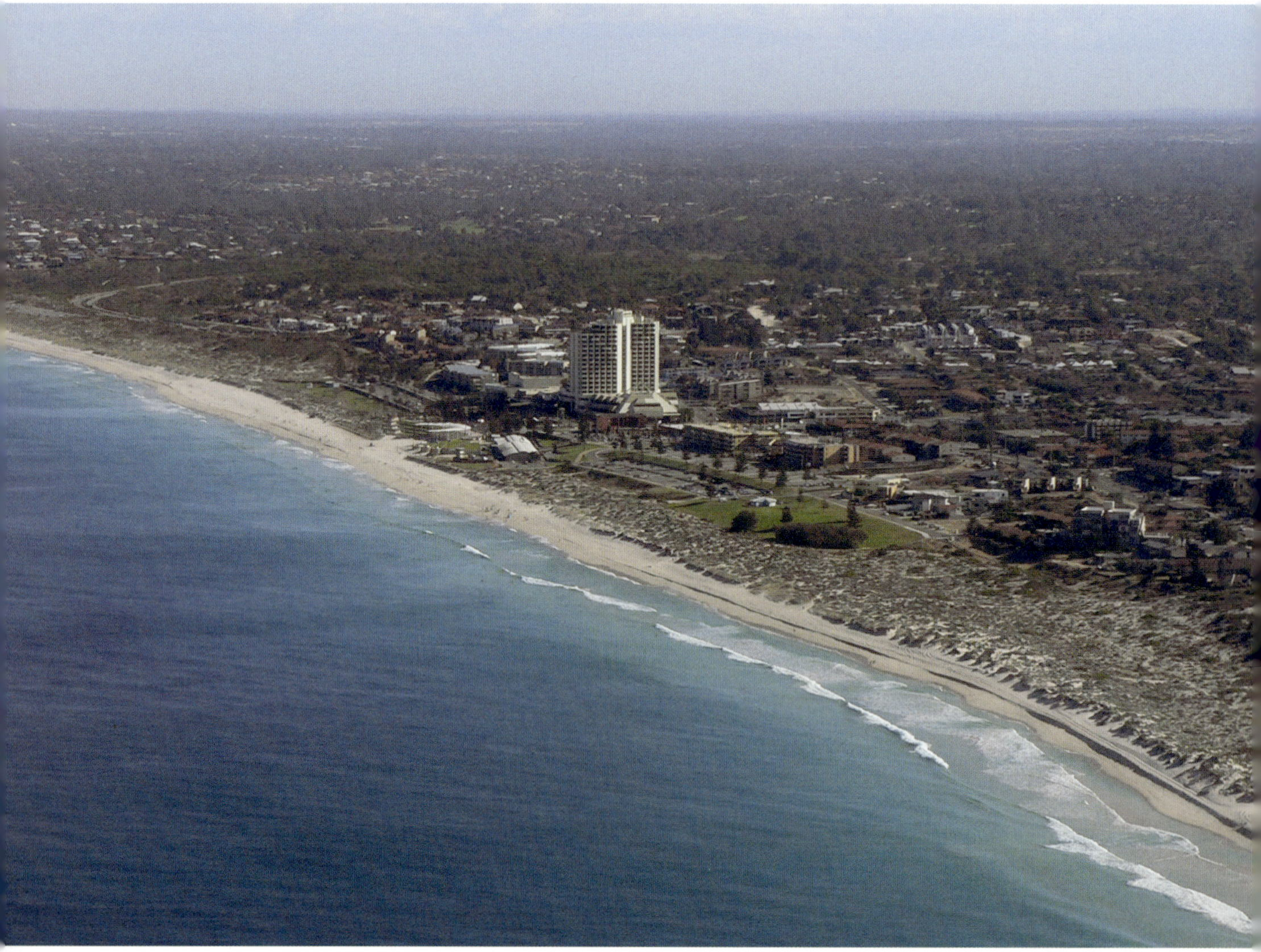

building above three storeys high. Consequently, as in the River City scenario we have pulled back from the coastal edge and shifted attention to the first ridgeline following the coast, the analogy being that if you arrive at the theatre late you don't stand at the front, but quietly take your place at the back. Here, along the coastal ridgeline, a band of land could be specifically rezoned for high-rise development to replace existing low-density suburbia. Alternatively, high-rise high-density development could be positioned alongside Perth's coastal highways which run parallel to the beaches but somewhat further inland than the coastal ridgeline.

An extra 450,000 people living along the coastline of Perth would not only make this otherwise exclusive zone more democratic, it would also create opportunities for enhancing the vibrancy of the coastal strip – a defining aspect of Perth worthy of mass celebration.

# SURF CITY

*above: 12-storey residential buildings every 500 m along the beachfront of the Perth Metropolitan Region.*

**378
VERTICAL SCENARIOS**

It is possible to increase the density along the coastal ridgeline – in this sense the landscape provides clear guidelines for development.

# SURF CITY

380
VERTICAL SCENARIOS

*above: 20-storey residential buildings following the coastal ridgeline of the Perth Metropolitan Region.*

*left: Viewed from offshore, Surf City creates a row of 'lighthouses' that reflect the gently undulating topography of the coastline.*

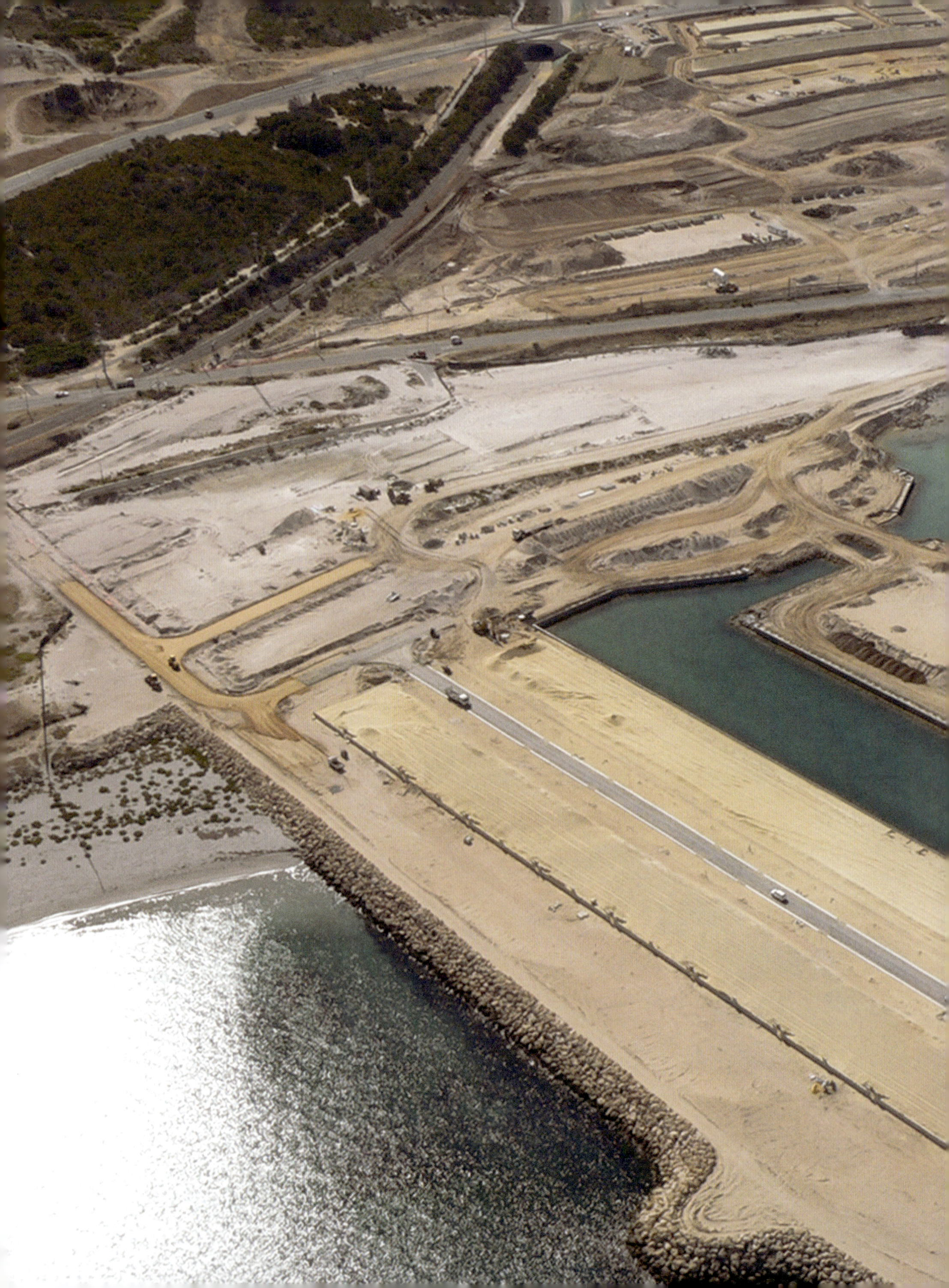

Is this the right way to treat our coastline?

*Coogee, Perth, 2008.*

4,500 people living in 30-storey towers takes up this much land.

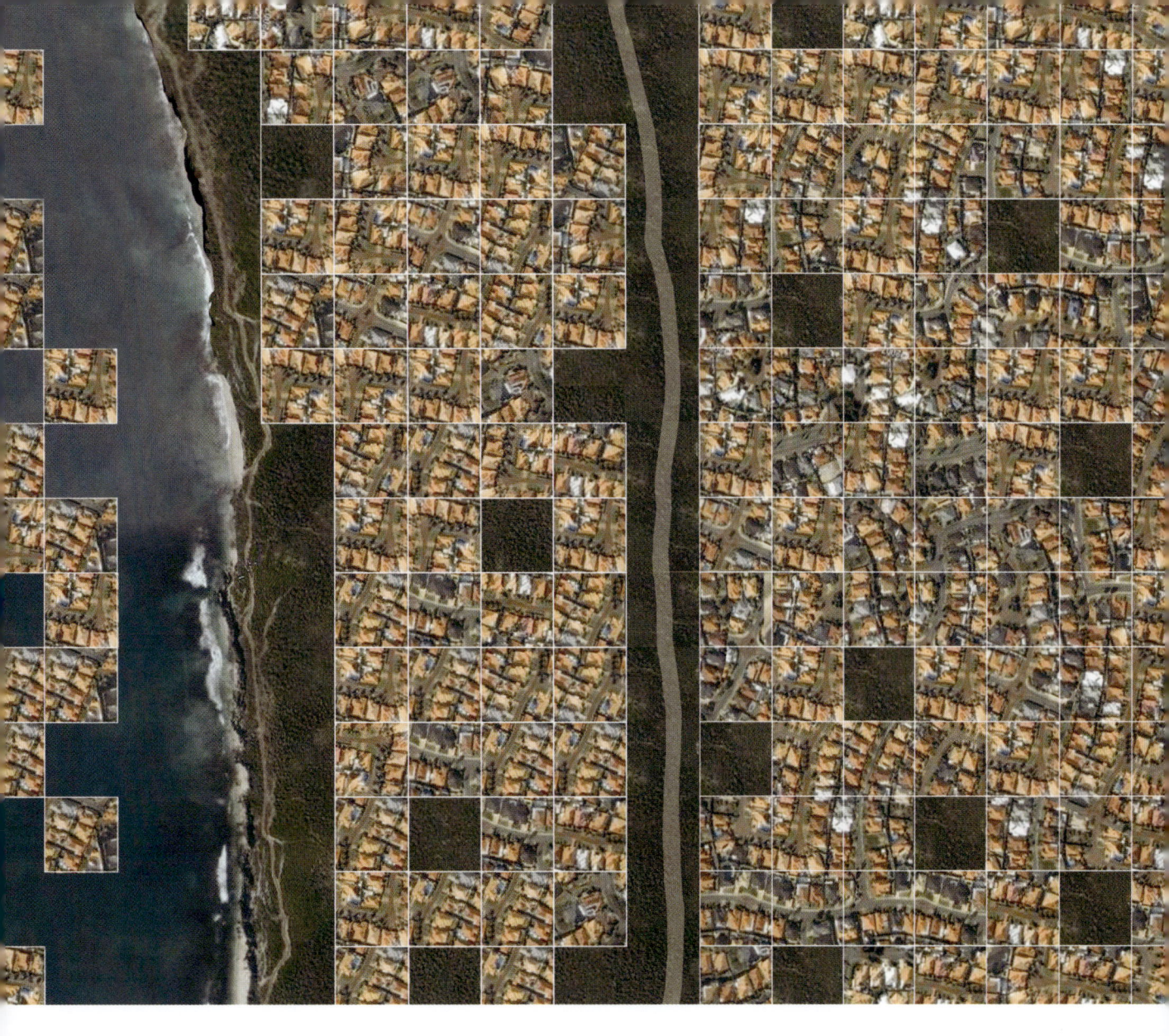

4,500 people living in conventional suburbia (12.5 dwellings per hectare) takes up this much land.

Before

After

SURF CITY

Landscape

Architecture

387
VERTICAL SCENARIOS

12

# DIVERCITY

Ultimately, this is what this book is about – Perth becoming a more diverse city, a more resilient city, a city that experiments with new forms.

Food City

River jetties

Sky City

POD City

Surf City

Sky City

*Living bridges*

River City

River City

Surf City

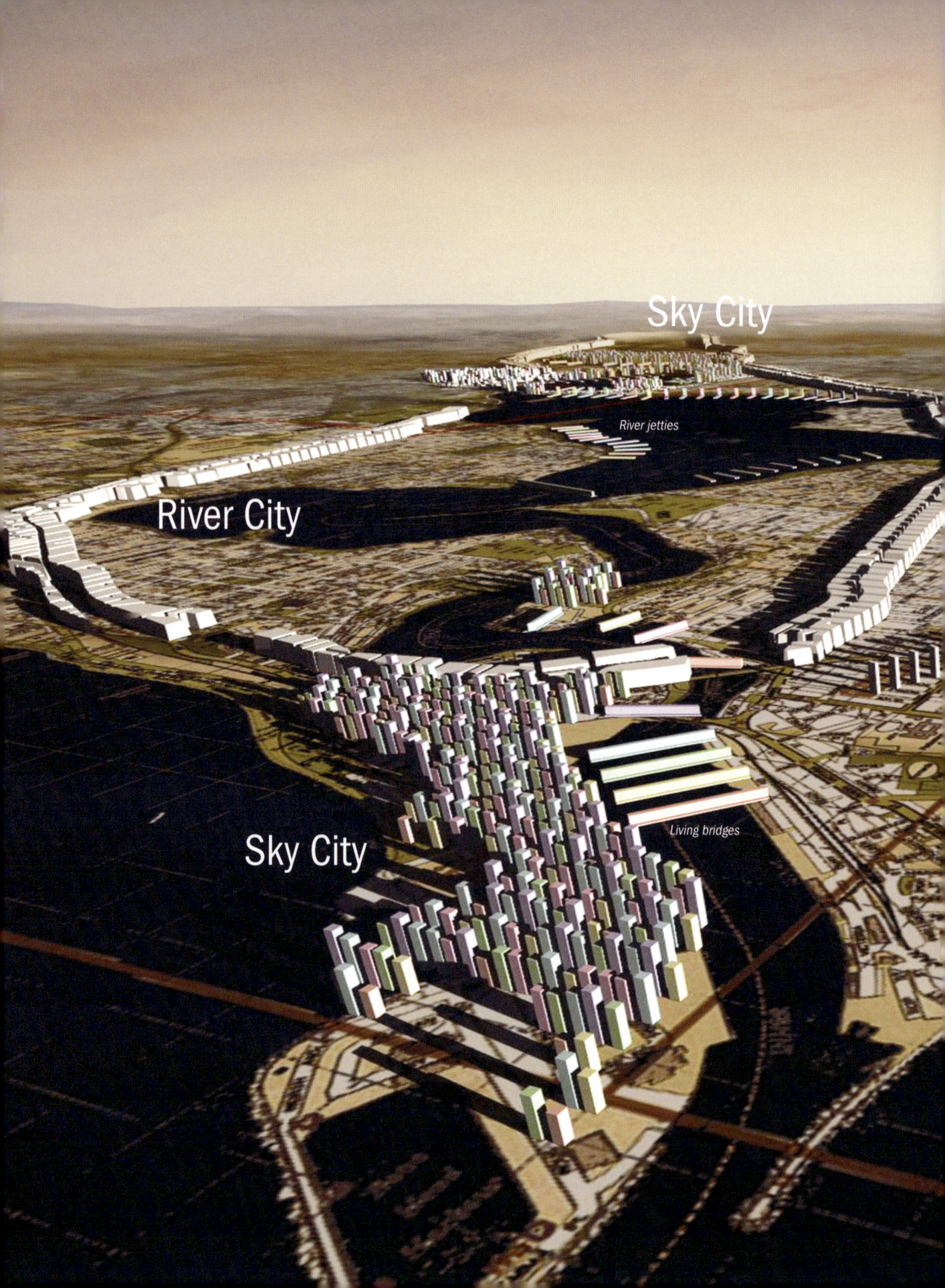

Sky City

River jetties

River City

Sky City

Living bridges

River City
Food City
POD City
Surf City

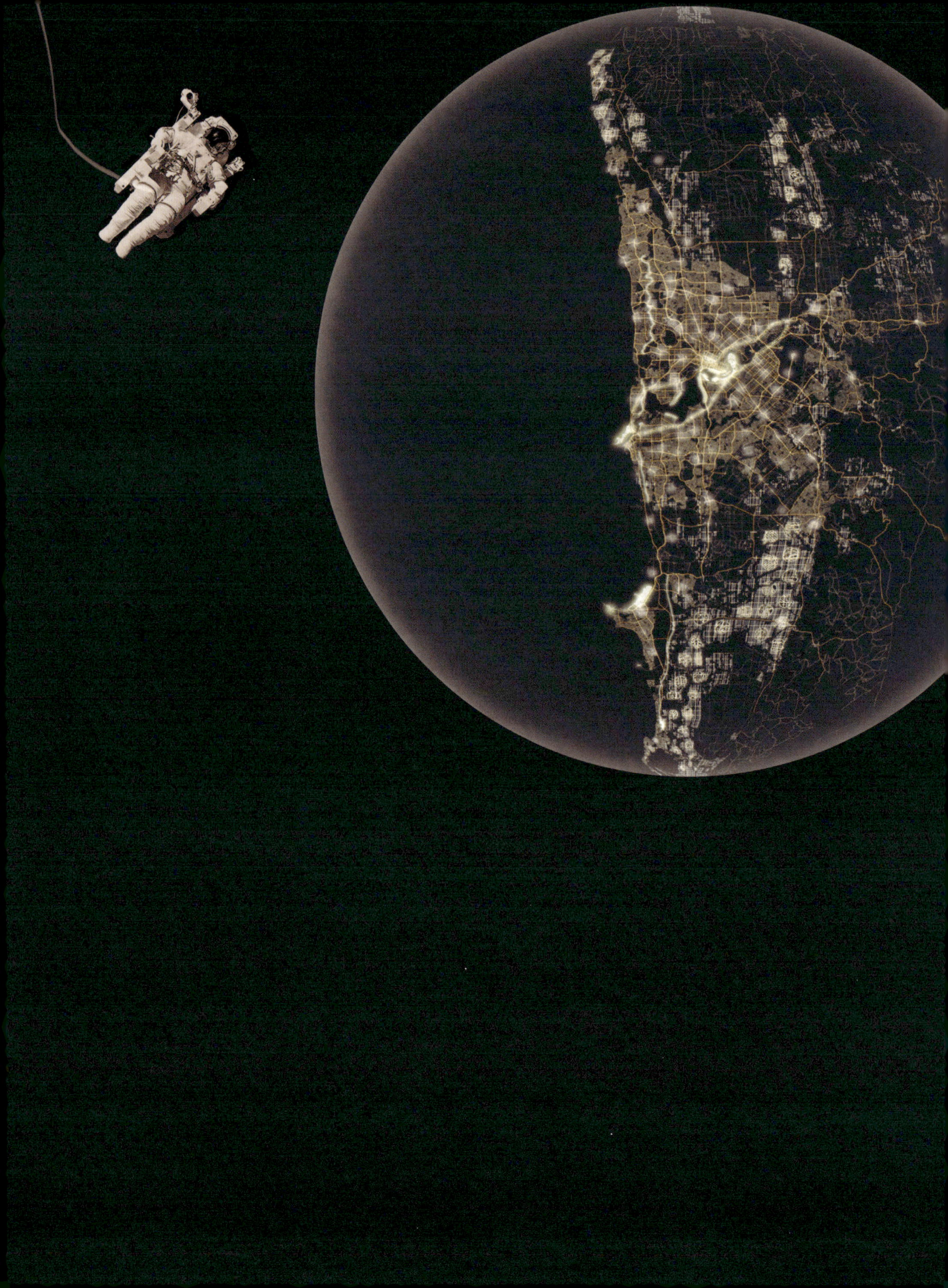

# DIVERCITY

To varying degrees all cities are trying to adapt their cumbersome urban forms to suit the socio-environmental challenges of the 21$^{st}$ Century. Unlike many other cities around the world though, Perth is not yet out of control: it can rationally and, as we hope to have shown in this book, it can creatively imagine, discuss and then design its future. Unless it responds rapidly as such, Perth will be overrun by a massive population increase and have no choice but to fast-track rampant suburban sprawl. With 118,000 hectares of land to move into, Perth could reproduce itself in the next 40 years to become the world's largest city inhabited by the lowest number of people. This could be the last great swathe of the Australian suburban dream. It could also be an ecological and social nightmare.

There is no one correct scenario for the future of the city. The alternative forms of urbanism presented in this book imply that Perth could both spread out further and go up higher. Each scenario in this book has advantages and disadvantages. All warrant closer examination by experts and the broader public. They are all points of departure requiring more detailed design and ultimately, partial construction. Only then can we really assess their economic, ecological and social feasibility. Only then could we really assess whether they are better than Business as Usual.

And as most Australians know, the suburban dream is very hard to beat. The latest Australian Bureau of Statistics figures suggest that Perth might have to accommodate an extra 2.7 million people by 2056. When we began this book we were working with a figure of 1.5 million additional people. A combination of the scenarios we have canvassed in this book could accommodate an extra 2.7 million people. Not everyone will agree with or even like the scenarios we have put forward but then we ask where and in what form will these future citizens live? Rather than building a brand new city somewhere else, it is our view that Perth should harness the energy of rapid population growth and through design create a more diverse city. In this sense the growth of the city is an exciting opportunity not a deleterious inevitability.

13

# DREAM HOMES

'Architects often criticise general or project housing. There is a lot to like about Australian project housing such as commodious standards of accommodation and its affordability, in particular its affordability compared to individually designed housing.'

Simon Anderson

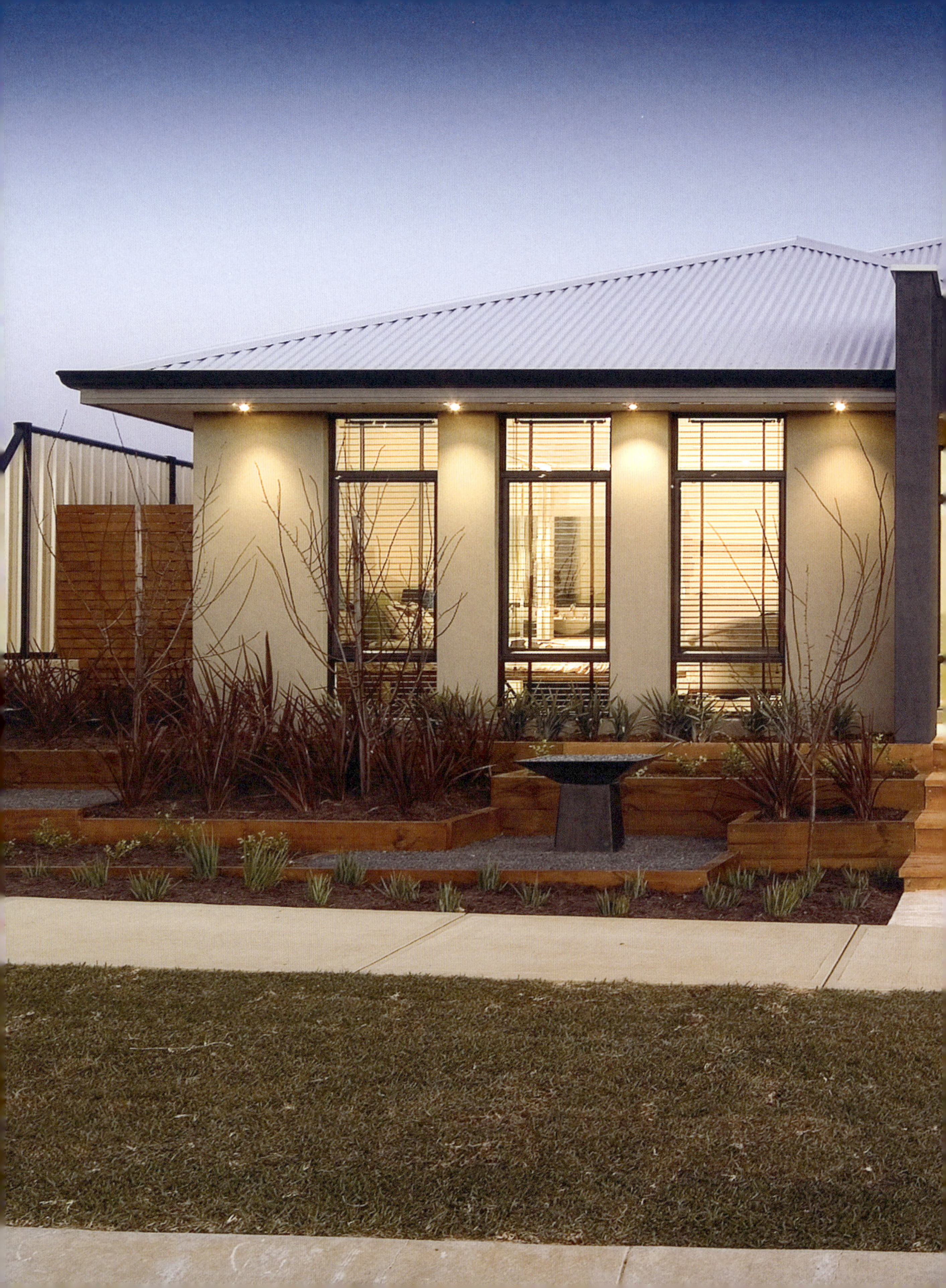

'Home builders cop a lot of flak and are accused of producing housing that is unimaginative, lacks innovation and is of poor design. The reality is that home builders are retailers and provide an affordable product to a consumer. The biggest challenge is to get consumers to be more daring and challenge the status quo. Consumers, who demand a well designed, adequate, energy efficient and responsive home will ultimately be served this. Our livelihood depends on meeting our clients' demands.'

Dale Alcock, 2008

# DREAM HOMES

*Dale Alcock Homes*

# Piazza

**DREAM HOMES**

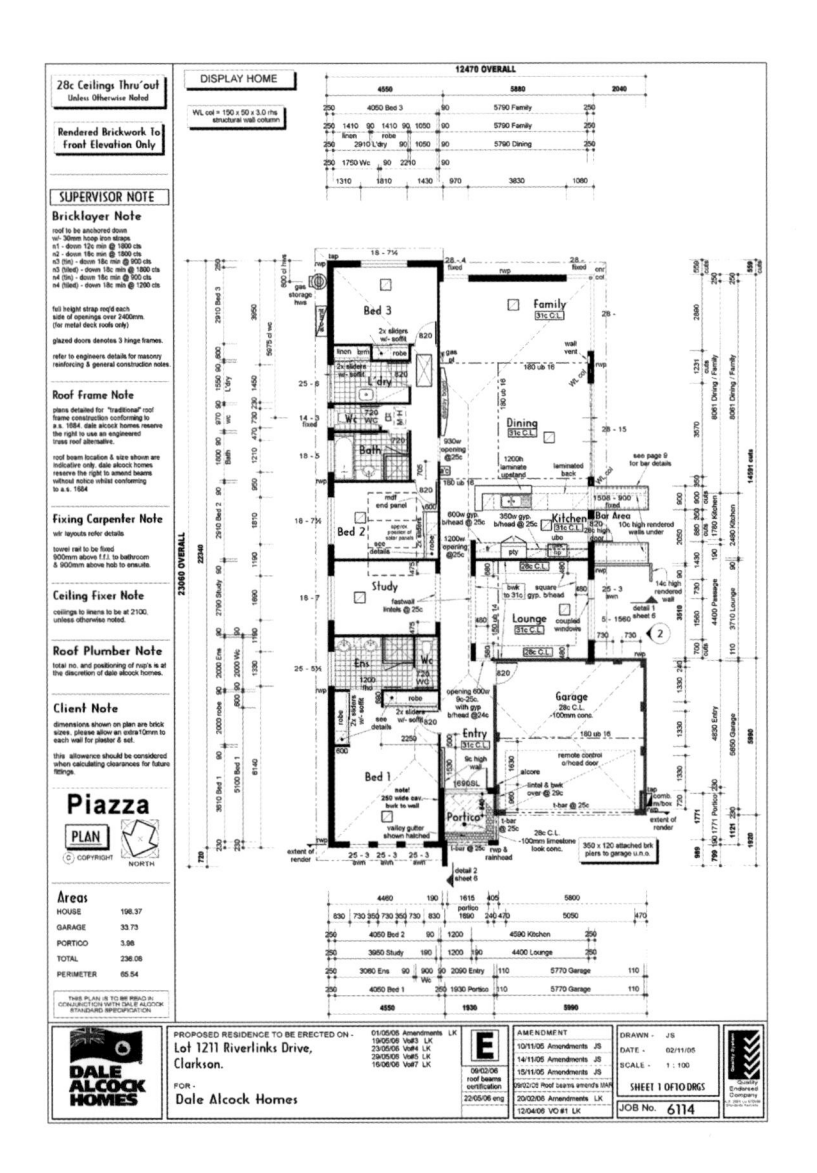

## New housing types for Perth

Architects often criticise general or project housing. There is a lot to like about Australian project housing such as commodious standards of accommodation and its affordability, in particular its affordability compared to individually designed housing. In fact much Australian and international residential heritage is nothing more than general housing produced by anonymous non-professionals, for example, Sydney's Paddington, Melbourne's Carlton and Perth's Fremantle.

Nevertheless, the acknowledged success of Australian general housing should not preclude critical analysis of built outcomes in an era of rapid demographic change, diminishing housing affordability and increasing environmental consciousness.

So what is there not to like about Australian general housing?

## What is wrong with Australian general housing?

Some critics argue that the houses are too large with average new project houses now commonly measuring nearly 300 m$^2$. These average houses could be smaller. Indeed they were smaller in earlier eras, but whether they are 150 or 300 m$^2$ is really more of a socioeconomic rather than an architectural question. An important characteristic of project housing has emerged in recent decades that is more open to architectural criticism, and this is the manner in which these 300 m$^2$ houses occupy their sites. Contemporary houses are built with very high site coverages compared to a generation ago, by virtue of housing sizes increasing, lot sizes decreasing and maximum site coverage rules being relaxed. The net outcome of these three inter-related practices has resulted in new suburban houses virtually covering their sites, removing the ability for the open space around the house, front and back yards to serve any other use than providing minimum standards of light, air and outdoor living areas. Important possibilities that suburban open space once provided are lost; the preservation and conservation of remnant vegetation, incorporation of significant tree planting, creation of biodiversity sanctuaries, maintenance of food production areas and the development of social sustainability facilities like sheds, workshops, studios and granny flats.

General housing is wasteful in several specific ways, though not in terms of structural efficiency or material usage. Many of the achievements of Australian general housing originate in the slow but steady development in masonry and masonry veneer building technology, a flourishing – but deregulated – specialised sub-contracting industry.

# HYPER HOUSING

Project housing is wasteful in the aesthetic pretences that pervade the general housing industry. Enormous quantities of applied finishes and decorative elements now contribute nothing more to the house than artifice. Builders offer similar floor plans with a choice of styles achieved through the addition of redundant labour and material to the relatively efficient skeleton of the house. Many aesthetic alternatives are historicist in nature. The production of the architectural features necessary to convey aesthetic choice requires the deployment of outmoded, costly skills and crafts and the replication of aesthetic features by cost-effective, imitative means also absorb significant resources.

In a related manner the planning of project housing is inefficient. While there is provision of useable space relative to circulation space, rooms are excessively programmed making them inflexible in use over initial and future occupation. Contemporary project housing is excessively functionally expressive. For example, home theatres of the 2000s will join 1980s games-rooms as relics of eras when fashions in leisure technology came to dominate house design. These rooms will have little for other purposes without significant building modifications. The flexibility of use for particular rooms is not good in project housing. Given that housing users are increasingly heterogeneous groups, any design that offers little flexibility of use is compromised.

The lack of compartmentalisation of project housing causes this inflexibility, does little to assist in the creation of privacy for different users and prevents the zoning of active and/or passive heating and cooling systems. As well as failing the flexibility test, project housing is not particularly adaptable or capable of being altered or extended, again in response to changing demographics and emerging needs for social sustainability. Large site coverages and single-storey houses permit very inefficient rooftop additions while traditional masonry construction makes internal alterations very labour-intensive and intrusive to occupants. Overall, contemporary project housing is neither flexible nor adaptable.

Finally, project housing offers limited passive environmental performance. Compact floor plans and relatively low ceiling heights are advantageous for active systems such as central heating and air conditioning systems, but environmental consciousness due to climate change now requires most to be made of passive systems. Contemporary project houses are not often suitable to sites of different orientations by virtue of their compact plans, frequently presenting only a small proportion of rooms to the sun. Likewise, compact-plan forms are difficult to effectively ventilate.

While project housing has undoubted strengths there are some significant weaknesses.

*Architect*
  Simon Anderson, UWA
*Project team*
  Simon Anderson
  Diana Goldswain
  Kate Sloss
*In-kind support*
  The Bundanon Trust
*Commercial building consultant*
  Highline Constructions
*Specialist concrete consultant*
  Concreto
*Specialist concrete building systems consultant*
  Reid Construction Systems

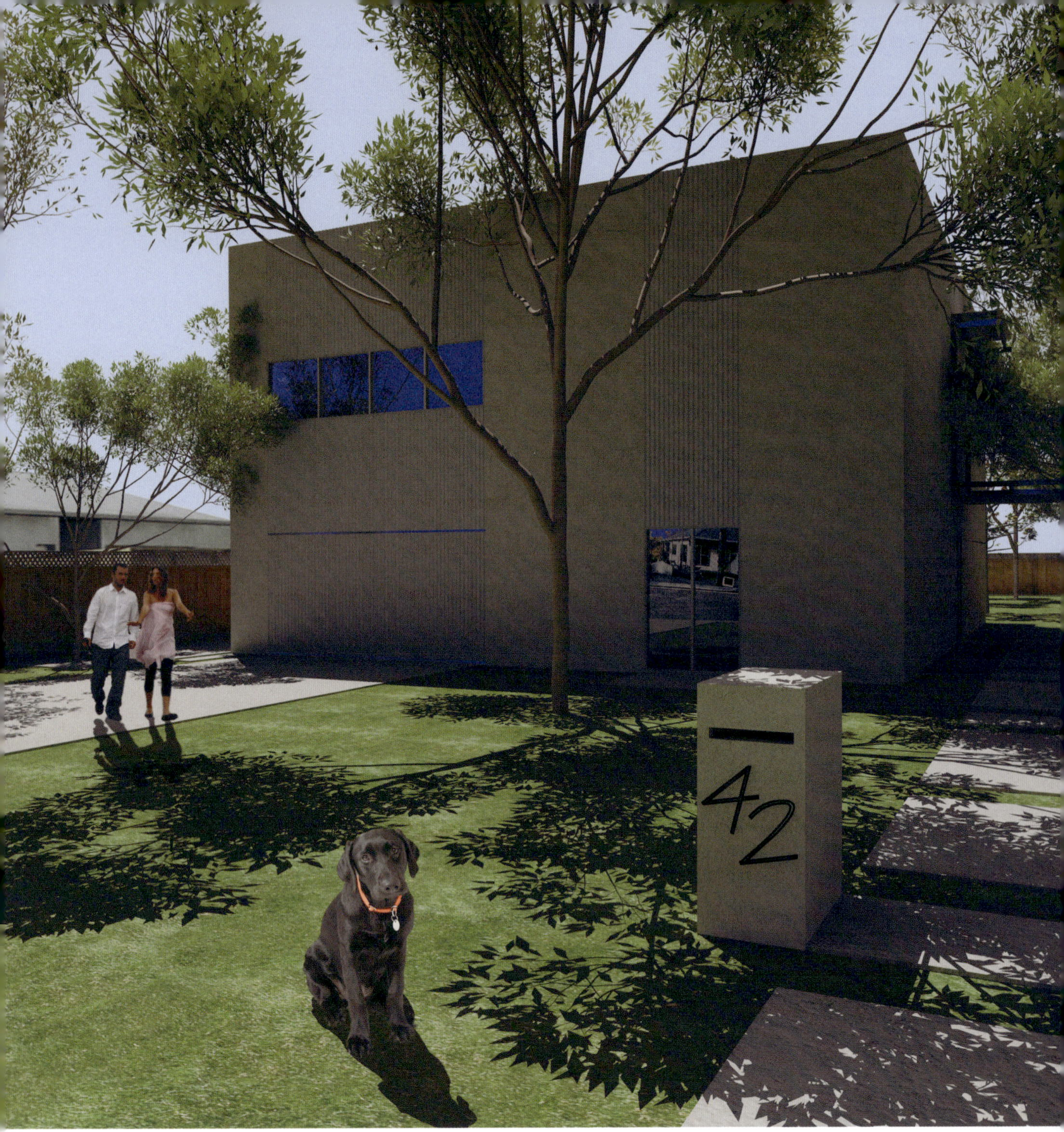
42

Project housing occupies too much of suburban sites; is not affordable enough; needs to be more flexible in use and easier to add and alter; and should do more to use the climate to facilitate human comfort, minimising energy consumption.

In response to the pressing issues of climate change, changing demographics and diminishing housing affordability, we need to keep the advantages of modern industrial building technology but reject the pretences of style and fashion. We should keep the good aspects of project housing that help meet new and emerging needs, but jettison the irrelevant and the wasteful.

## Hyper housing

We should build houses more like factories. General housing providers often talk about advances in industrial building techniques utilised in their industry while most low- to medium-density housing is produced using traditional materials and trades, and extensive sub-contracting. Yet one area of small-scale building provision, the commercial factory building, does show signs of advances in industrialised building techniques. The commercial imperative allows one to ignore history, style and aesthetics, and to concentrate on buildings as physical systems expected to have certain measurable outcomes. Many of the current topical issues in housing are measurable in some way. Issues such as affordability, sustainability and flexibility of use are essentially quantitative topics and warrant rational attention. This project does nothing more than attempt to develop alternative housing prototypes at low–medium density through systematically utilising the current techniques of the commercial factory building. After all, Rudolf Schindler and Charles Eames found it useful to do the same, while factory buildings from New York City to Fremantle are highly desirable houses after suitable conversion. Here we are designing factories with 'conversions' in place from the beginning although each of our prototypes could be built and sold as bare shells much in the way commercially-used factory buildings are.

Prototypical sketch designs are illustrated for a variety of low- to medium-density sites within the Perth Metropolitan Region. The designs would be suitable for similar climatic zones. Densities range from low to potentially high densities (R2 to R200+) with emphasis given to grouped dwellings over multiple dwellings. Hypothetical sites are used to explore alternative orientations and access patterns. Briefs are commensurate with available general housing in terms of total area, room sizes and functions. General housing clients

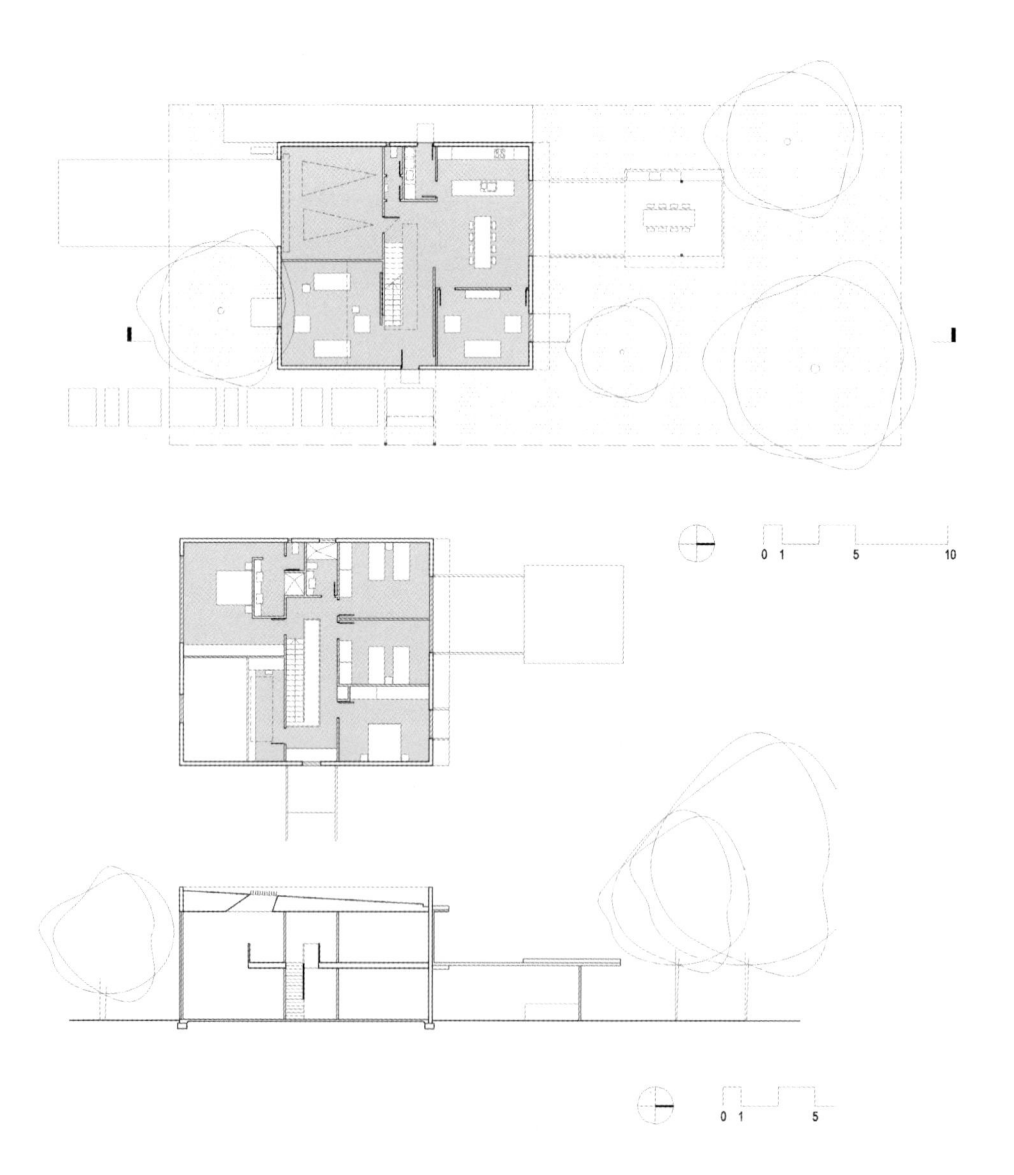

*The block house: the suburban prototype*

typically need affordable, low energy-use, contemporary houses for their own long-term occupation, yet want some flexibility to accommodate changing family structure, and desire some income/superannuation benefit from their house. Our designs are fully compliant with all authorities. All planning is prosaic, even generic, and intended to be more illustrative than definitive; circulation legible; wet areas compact and efficient. The prototypes are as big as project houses, cheaper to build and maintain, are more flexible and adaptable, use less energy to heat, cool and light, and have lower carbon footprints. Further, sustainability gadgets like greywater and photovoltaic systems could be easily added to the prototypes without compromising their architectural achievements.

### The block house: the suburban prototype

We started with the largest market – the single house on 500–1000 m$^2$ in a suburban area.

At this density (R10–20), local government authorities typically allow two-storey development with no streetscape policy given the heterogeneity of the suburbs, and require maximum 50% site coverage, large street setbacks, and smaller setbacks for all other neighbours for walls containing non-major openings, and space for two car parking behind the setbacks for each house.

On lots of this scale a free-standing rectangular volume can be positioned to achieve good solar access, street surveillance and nominal overshadowing. A block-like two-storey house was designed to optimise use of the selected building technology, allow for significant landscape retention and large tree planting, and to provide for possible future buildings to be added behind the new house. The upper storey also allows for distant views to break the insularity of single-storey suburbia, especially in very flat subdivisions. Alternative orientations can all be accommodated using a simple volume, albeit longer and more rectangular in aspect.

The planning maximises northern exposure and puts parents and children upstairs at opposite sides of the house separated by wet areas. Living rooms are downstairs with numerous doors, both internal and external, used to provide enormous flexibility of access and gradations of privacy control.

### The strip house: the urban prototype

Next we tried a more urban condition at medium to high density. We limited our design to terrace or row housing in the belief that it is an under-utilised typology worthy of re-investigation.

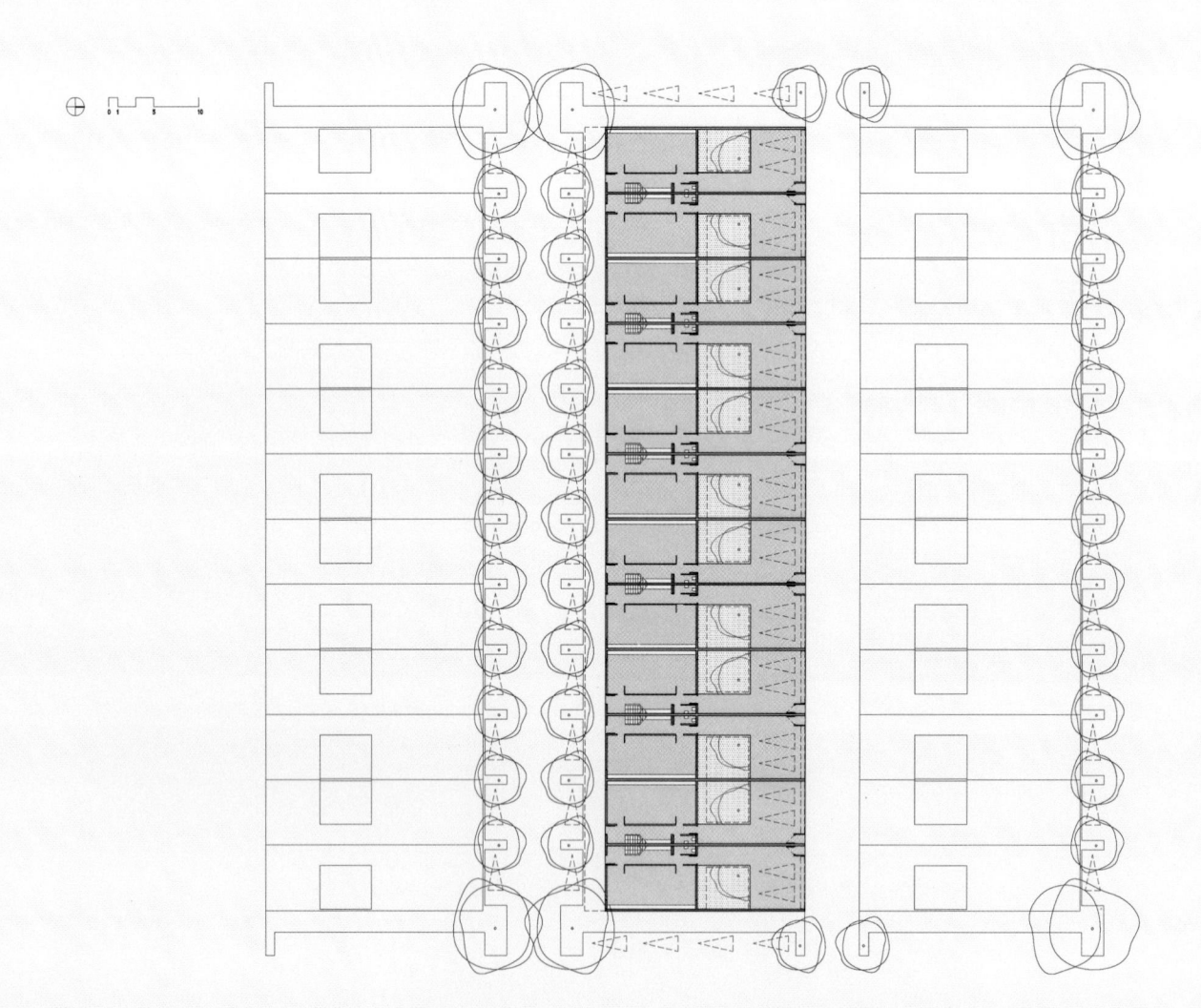

*The strip house: the urban prototype*

# HYPER HOUSING

Contemporary row housing in places like East Perth and Subi Centro, where up to five-storey houses have recently been built, is not really row housing: there is little sharing in any sense that terrace or row housing allows. In fact, East Perth and Subi Centro houses are really nothing more than large suburban houses compressed onto very small lots.

In medium- to high-density grouped housing the proportion of the individual lots is critical to achieving efficiency, in particular in relation to the provision of good car parking, service access, street planting and passive surveillance. A lot width of seven metres was chosen as it provides commodious accommodation and facilitates all of the above. It allows two cars to be parked on each lot with an additional bay on the street, which could be accessed using resident stickers. The seven-metre width then allows pedestrian access past the on-site cars, and planting of a significant street tree. Differential lot widths could also be added with some being smaller, say four metres with others larger, say nine metres. Further visitor/public parking is provided on the cross streets at a rate of six bays per number of houses on the block.

The strip of houses is designed as a terrace of four-storey houses using party walls for affordability and environmental efficiency. Four storeys was chosen as a conscious effort to lift density and to provide affordability in construction and in future rentals – it is hoped that the top storey could be cheap rent. A 12-metre high wall panel is used to form the houses. The full 280 m$^2$ of the houses can then be used in myriad ways by simply stratifying by floors. So the 'house' may be used as, for example, a 280 m$^2$ house for a large family, or the ground floor could be used as a 50 m$^2$ commercial space, on top of which is a 55 m$^2$ studio apartment and a 110 m$^2$ two-storey apartment. The full four-storey house would be attractive to a range of groups of people, and would by its ability to accommodate various usage patterns ensure a level of social sustainability and heterogeneity lacking – but needed – in new housing. It would be affordable and permit long-term occupation by extended families. It could be developed as shells for owners to finish as they need, would provide good investment and superannuation options for owners, and a great deal of potentially affordable rental accommodation.

A continuous street canopy is provided over the footpath to provide rain and sun protection for pedestrians, to improve the amenity of possible commercial uses on the ground floor, and to provide the separation needed to allow zero street setback to the upper floors. The street canopy could be transparent to solar radiation should it face north rather than south. Balconies could be added to the rear of the house at upper

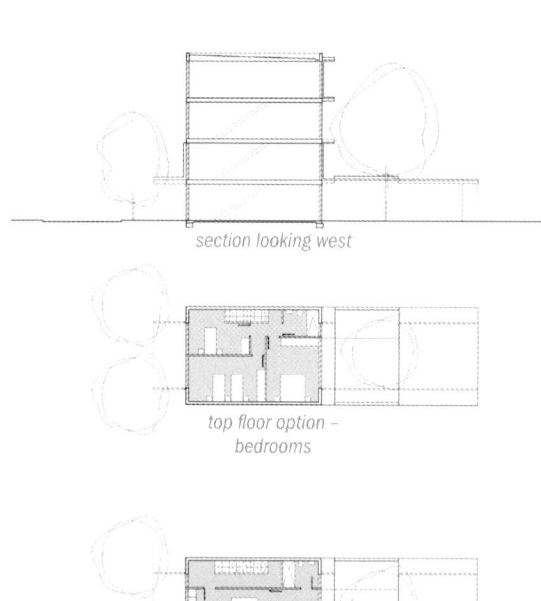

*section looking west*

*top floor option – bedrooms*

*middle floor option – studio apartment*

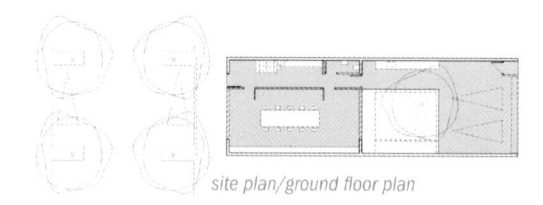

*site plan/ground floor plan*

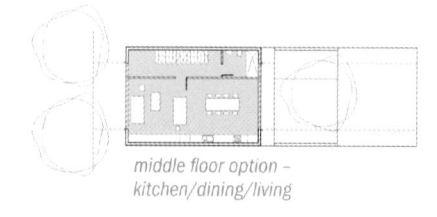

*middle floor option – kitchen/dining/living*

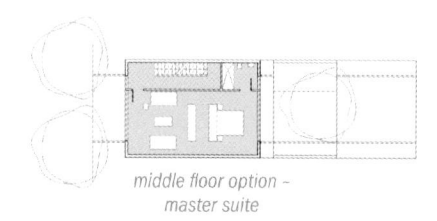

*middle floor option – master suite*

HYPER HOUSING

411
DREAM HOMES

section looking west

site plan/ground floor plan

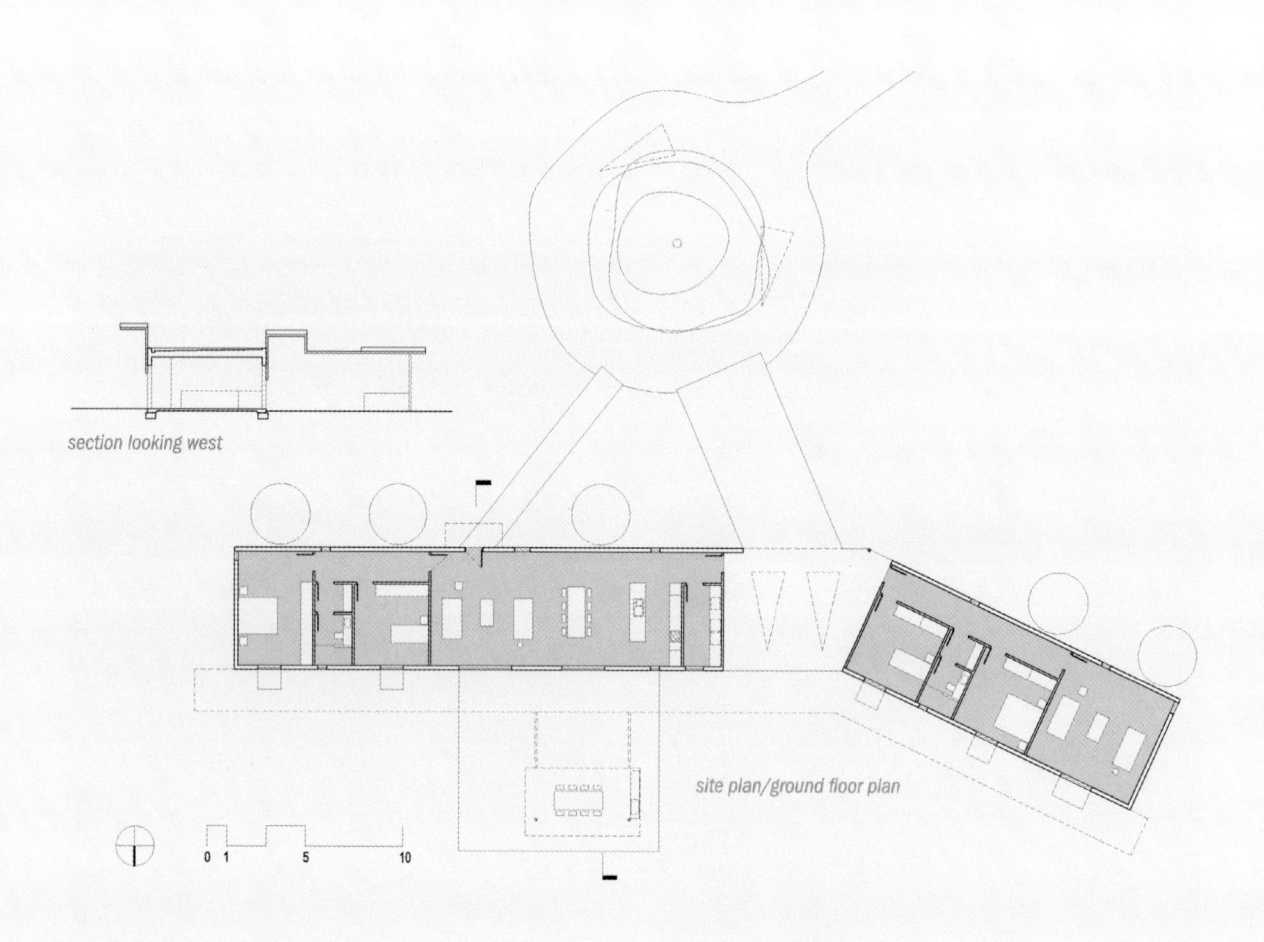

0 1 5 10

**The String House – the rural prototype**

levels, which could be offset so as to not overshadow the north-facing windows below. The courtyard is designed to be planted with a large deciduous tree, while the carport and covered walkway are designed to be covered in vines giving the entire rear of the house a verdant and overgrown appearance.

Front doors all open directly to the canopied street with back doors opening from the heavily planted car courtyard. All access is undercover, with the walk-up access system providing excellent privacy, cross-ventilation, security and the ability to accommodate changes in use at successive floors. The aggregation of the various rooms, apartments, commercial and service spaces is then suppressed in an over arching form designed to respond to the scale of the metropolis and the reality of the contemporary housing condition. Individuation in the expression of land uses and functions is limited to their natural variation within the overall design concept.

## The string house: the rural prototype

Finally we designed a semi-rural or rural prototype. At such densities (R2-5) and lower, local authorities typically have no requirements other than the Building Code of Australia. At these low densities, existing landform, contours, orientation and vegetation need to be accommodated. Hence an articulated, pavilioned and spreading single-storey house was strung across the site, reminiscent of Richard Leplastrier's Bayview House 1975.

The disconnected alfresco areas, also used on the suburban prototype, provide generous undercover areas but do not shade the interiors. Further, elevated sunhoods on the rural prototype provide sheltered verandahs of useable dimensions, again without overshadowing the interiors, and provide an amplification of horizontal scale in response to the location.

## The construction technique

All the houses are designed and built like commercial factory buildings. Off-form full-height insulated concrete panels standing on slab-on-ground form the structure and external walls. Panels will be poured on-site in various, limited numbers of sizes to allow for building efficiency and to provide the variety needed to accommodate residential design. A 'green cement' (one that does not use calcium carbonate chemistry) ensures carbon dioxide emissions from the concrete are negligible. A light steel roof structure ties the panels together and supports a low-pitched Zincalume roof lining. The panels

*The String House – the rural prototype*

HYPER HOUSING

415
DREAM HOMES

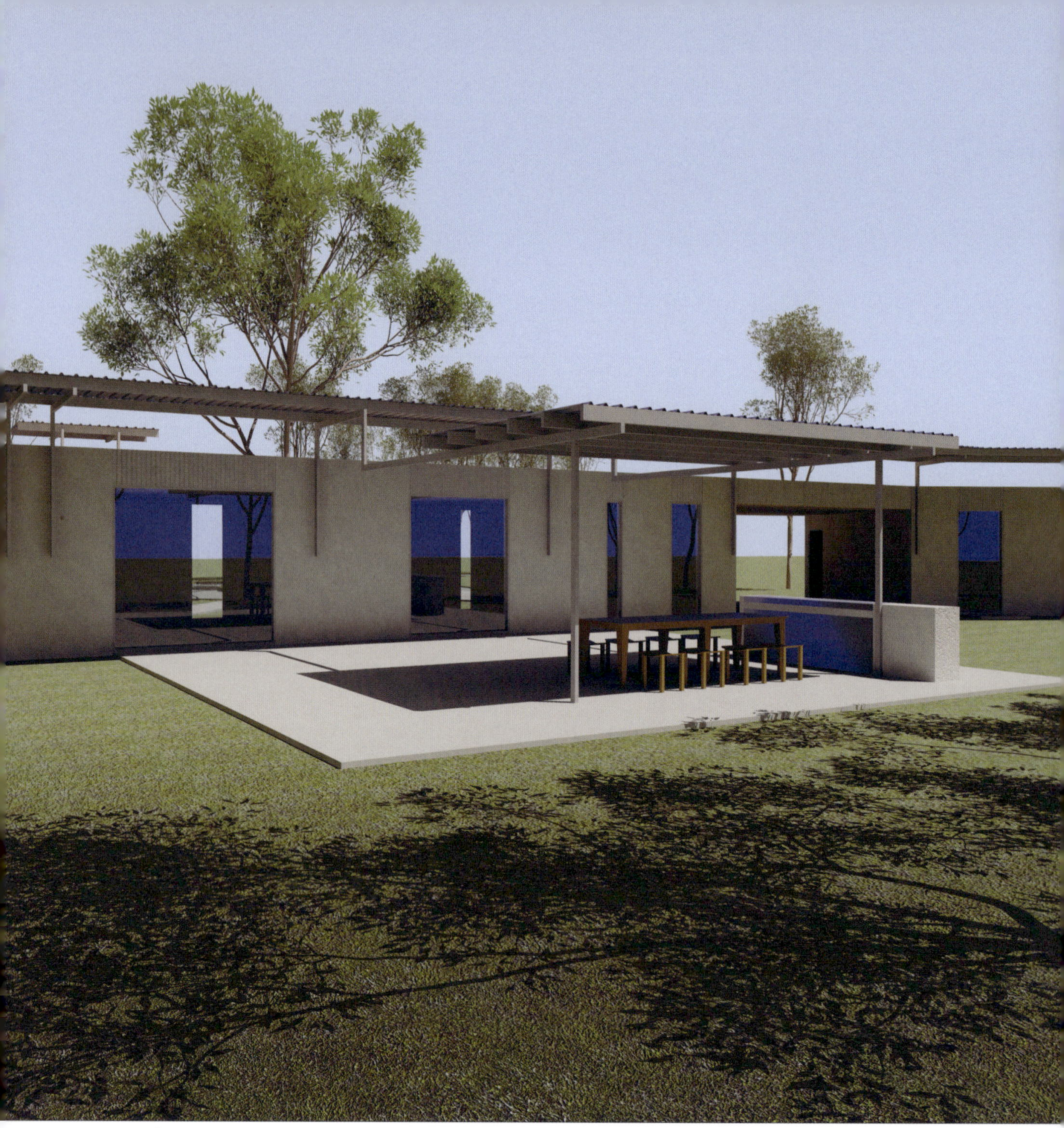

are all rectangular with no openings cast in. Panels could be manufactured off-site and engineered to accept further upper floors and can be recycled along with the steel roofing and internal walling.

The panels comprise 50 mm external non-structural skin, 25 mm rigid insulation and 125 mm internal structural skin. All walls can be erected in hours. The two skins are tied together with a proprietary tie while the external skin is reinforced with galvanised wire strips. Maintaining the panel width at 200 mm means that commercially available panel formwork could be used. External corners were mitred rather than butt-jointed to avoid thermal bridging, while protruding blade walls are avoided for the same reason.

A single industrial building sub-contractor will complete the earthworks, concrete footings, slab-on-ground, on-site panel manufacture and erection, steel roof framing and erection, roofing and insulation, paving and driveways.

All internal structure, framing, flooring, wall and ceiling linings are plantation timber and plywood, allowing a single carpentry sub-contractor to bring the houses to lock-up, apart from the aluminium external joinery and steel sun-shades which are manufactured and installed by a single sub-contractor. Wet areas use sheet materials, removing the need for a tiling contractor, while the cabinets are to be installed by the carpenter using flat-pack cupboards and benchtops. The last sub-contractor, apart from the obligatory plumber and electrician, is the painter who will spray-paint the entire interior with a low-sheen clear finish.

All fenestration occurs in the full height slots between panels with the remainder of the slots sheeted with Zincalume steel sheeting. The slots are parallel, ensuring structural efficiency for the wall panels and complete simplicity in their casting. The powdercoated aluminium joinery and cladding are pushed to the outside face of the panels to cover the exposed ends of the insulation at reveals, and to render the external face smooth rather than modelled. Sun-shading over openings in the concrete wall panels is provided by fixed galvanised steel sunhoods.

In the future the houses may be altered to produce independent houses of various possible configurations. And alterations would be easy for the occupier and allow the re-use of timber framing and linings.

*Simon Anderson*

**1** SUBURBAN DENSIFICATION: Occurs simultaneously from multiple points. The city centre is no longer the point of initial densification.

**2** GREENWOOD, PERTH: Typical 1970's low-density suburb, 20km from the city centre.

**3** BANKHURST ST, GREENWOOD: Typical 1970's project home at the end of its usable life. Median Cost $498,000.00.

**4** DEMOLITION: Decommissioned project home.

**5** BRICK RUBBLE: Debris from the existing house ready for reuse as screen walls and crushed brick paving.

**6** AFFORDABILITY AND DENSIFICATION: Subdivide into two properties.

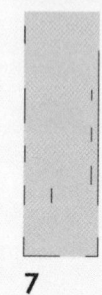

**7** RECYCLED BRICK: Material from previous house used as boundary walls and sun filtering walls.

**8** SOLAR COLLECTION: 2 Kw PV Cells + Roof windows for thermal mass heat gain.

**9** COURTYARDS: Flexible exterior space.

**10** INHABITABLE WALLS: Brick walls and recyclable cabinet work accommodating functional roles.

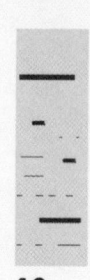

**11** WATER COLLECTION: Under floor storage of potable and grey water 40,000+ L.

**12** HEAT GAIN / THERMAL MASS: Contrasting dark floor and wall. Bricks mapping the movement of the sun for increased winter heat gain.

# THINK BRICK

### Boomtown and the forgotten suburb
Last year economic growth in Perth was greater than in China. Urban renewal and densification of the inner suburbs continues at a dramatic rate with brownfield sites, disused industrial precincts, old high schools and even out-of-date sport stadiums providing valuable land for the insatiable housing market. Single dwellings on large blocks of land are yielding to medium-density housing and chic apartment blocks dominate the market. At the other extreme, outer suburbs continue to expand with suburban Perth now over 100 kilometres of linear city hugging the Indian Ocean coast. Vast sums of government funding are poured into infrastructural projects to support new hubs of activity; community centres, education facilities, libraries and sporting complexes are rapidly constructed to match gleaming new shopping centres.

Somewhere in between these two dynamic environments is another Perth, the forgotten middle suburbs, such as Duncraig and Greenwood to the north, Riverton and Gosnells to the south and High Wycombe and Forrestdale toward the hills. So filled with optimism when they were built in the late 1970s and early 1980s these areas some 20 kilometres from Perth's CBD were cutting edge when this was the suburban edge. Now the brick and tile project homes that fill their cul-de-sacs look very tired and dated. These represent the median house price market of Perth currently at $498,000. Second highest in the country just behind Sydney, the middle suburbs are middle Australia in Perth. Poorly served by public transport and decayed underperforming schools, the car-dominated streets are empty like the shops in the local strip. These places unfortunately represent a pretty average situation for the 'average Australian'.

Poor affordability, rising inflation and soaring rents have combined to drive a decidedly divided market. Analysts tip continued volatility ahead as the tale of city versus country, blue-chip versus mortgage-belt, is played out.

### Affordable futures
It is in this context that we identify the primary issue of housing affordability but also the changing demographics of Australian families. The four bedroom, two bathroom suburban dream is no longer appropriate. A recent state government paper suggested that WA's population shall rise to 2.5 million by 2026. At this rate its population growth is almost double that of housing construction. Fundamentally, the population is getting older and number of children is declining rapidly, but ironically Western Australia is building larger

homes with more bedrooms and with fewer people living in them. *The Ageing of Aquarius*, a research document by Monash Professor Shane Murray, outlines that existing and new housing stock is primarily designed for the nuclear family: a detached house with three or more bedrooms, where rooms are program-specific. The spatial relationships between and within rooms and to outdoor spaces should be examined for alternative configurations that might better meet the needs of the contemporary household. Specifically, Western Australian housing stock is dominated by single detached housing (78%), limiting choice. Many singles and couples live in detached housing and must pay for excess capacity.

Fundamental to our proposal is that affordability must be addressed through appropriate land use and the development of suitable alternative housing typologies that respond to the changing demographic. Our proposal therefore seeks to establish a series of new dwelling configurations that address new and not so new family situations; single parent families, extended families, larger new immigrant families, empty-nesters and student cohabitation. But we must acknowledge the unique lifestyle of suburban Perth and understand that solutions that may be suitable in the Eastern States may not be embraced by the Western Australian public. The focus of our scheme develops a house type for an extended family where a granny flat could accommodate elderly relatives.

The project also seeks to establish more effective land-use principals. A typical 1000m$^2$ middle suburb lot size has been selected measuring 25 metres by 40 metres. We suggest two residences should replace the out-of-date project home that currently occupies the land. Our economic strategy suggests the typical property could be purchased for the median house price of $498,000, subdivided (effectively $250,000 each), then a pair of new houses built for $250,000 each. This would provide two new residences each for the median house price of an outdated project home at the end of its useable life. While our prescribed topic is the potential re-use of the brick, our concept is to minimise the need to re-use bricks by creating flexibility in the use of the dwelling, stretching its potential life toward future-proofing.

### Sustaining the brick

A 1999 Australian housing survey indicated that 76% of Western Australia's housing stock was double brick, a unique situation that should be exploited, but for the brick to remain dominant it must evolve into a more sustainable construction system. Our initial move is to re-use the brick and tile waste from the demolition of the existing residence as both

| COUPLE | COUPLE WITH CHILDREN | COUPLE WITH ADULT CHILDREN | COUPLE WITH ADULT CHILDREN AND ELDERLY PARENT | SECOND GENERATION |

**FUTURE PROOFING**
FLEXIBLE USE OF THE RESIDENCE AS THE FAMILY EVOLVES

**MINIMISE WASTE**
Minimise cutting of bricks

**MULTIPLE TYPES**
Single patron type

**DOUBLE STREET FRONTAGE**

**ALTERNATIVE ORIENTATIONS**

**THE EMERGING SUBURBIA**

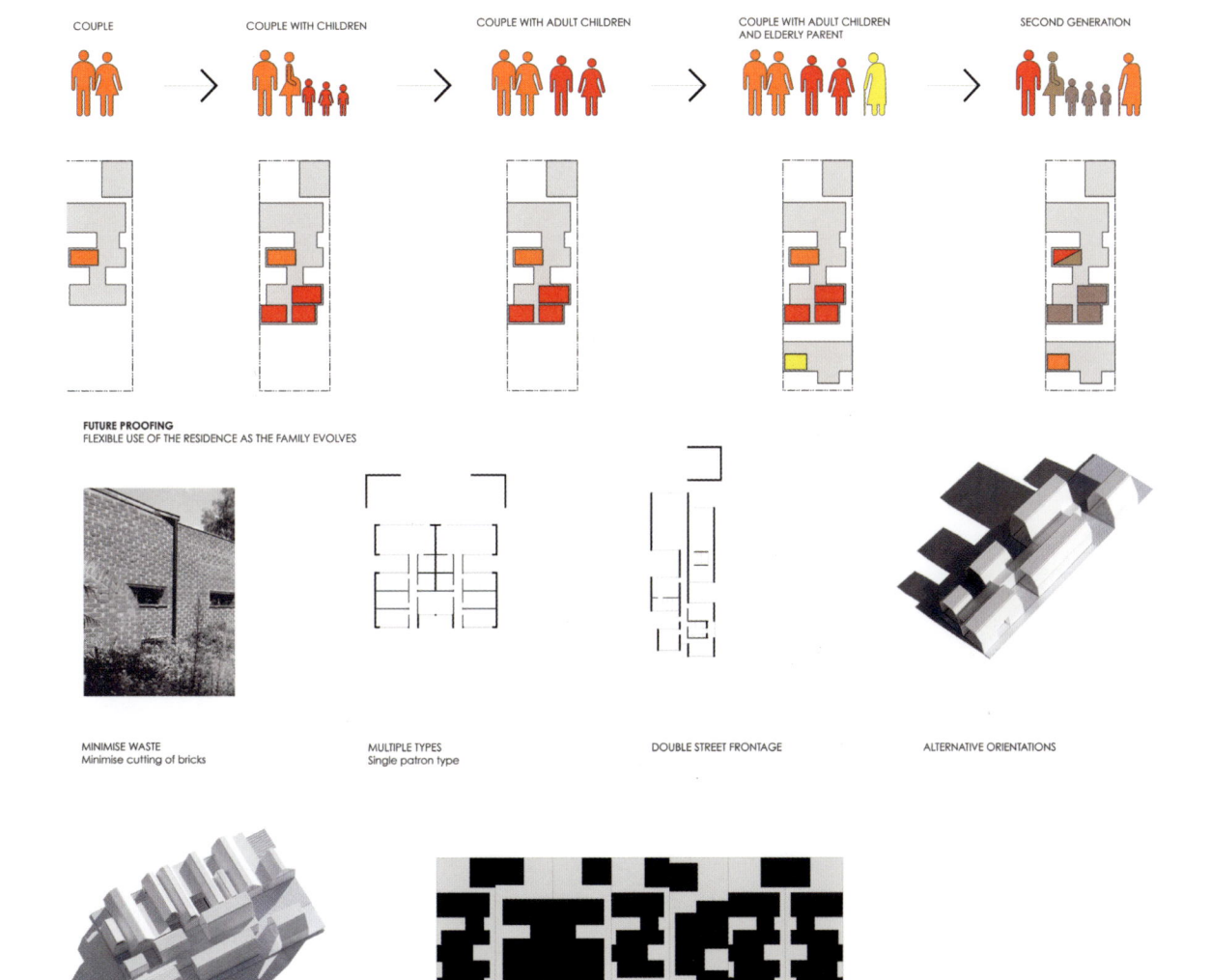

**EVOLVING STREET PATTERNS WITH INCREASED DENSITY**

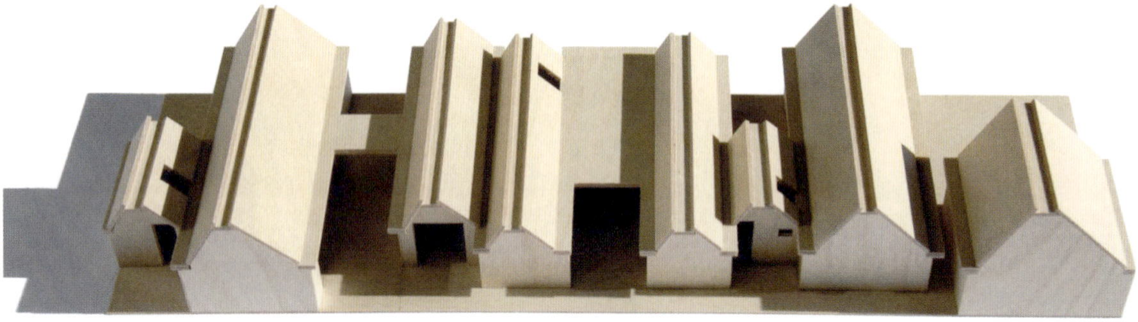

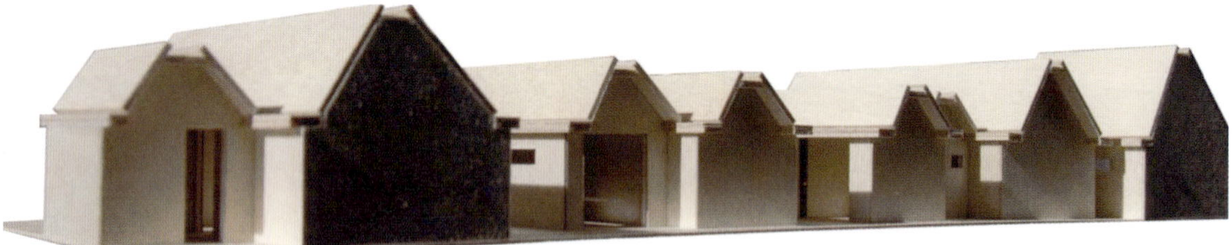

crushed-brick floor gravel and as infill for boundary walls with neighbouring property.

The primary concern for the new construction is its potential for re-use when the building is no longer required. A cavity wall interlocking brick system has been developed in association with Midland Brick where the hollow core of the brick is dropped over a series of recycled plastic reinforcement rods. As no mortar is used the masonry units shall be able to be re-used. A recycled plastic brick tie shall be developed to provide additional lateral stability. The top of each cavity wall shall be capped with a precast concrete ring beam that also forms a gutter to collect rainwater and serves as a pitching point for the recycled timber roof structure. The colour of the brick walls shall be determined by the manner in which they attract winter or summer heat. Strategically located dark-colour bricks shall collect additional heat-load from skylights that will capture winter sun in south-facing rooms. This idea is transferred onto the brick tile flooring system where darker coloured tiles shall be used to collect additional heat from the winter sun that is allowed to penetrate the space.

The roof is clad with fired clay tiles of a smooth surface to allow potable water collection. Beneath the tiles is R3.0 foil and batts to a painted screw-fixed plywood ceiling. A bank of photovoltaic solar cells shall be located on the north-facing roof on the main living spaces providing enough area to collect two kilowatts of power.

At ground level the traditional concrete slab in the main living areas has been replaced with a Rain Reviva in-ground water-tank system. Manufactured from high tensile recycled plastic the system is interlocking and trafficable. The footing for the walls shall provide perimeter stability for the water units and a sheet of structural ply shall be laid directly over the tanks, providing the base for the brick tiled floor. Each pod of the system holds 660 litres allowing 26,400 litres of storage under the main living space alone. The tanks under the service areas shall be independent and allow for collection and distribution of greywater only.

Door and window frames are identical in dimension to suit the module of the interlocking brick and manufactured from recycled jarrah. Cross-ventilation is vital in Perth and consistent small windows are inserted to ensure each room has the opportunity to capture and distribute afternoon breezes, shading is provided by the gutter overhang, and additional timber louvres as necessary. Recycled brick walls are constructed in a hit-and-miss manner to create a perforated brick brise-soleil in front of large panels of glass. All internal walls are cavity brick and act as perpendicular bracing to the lateral walls; the

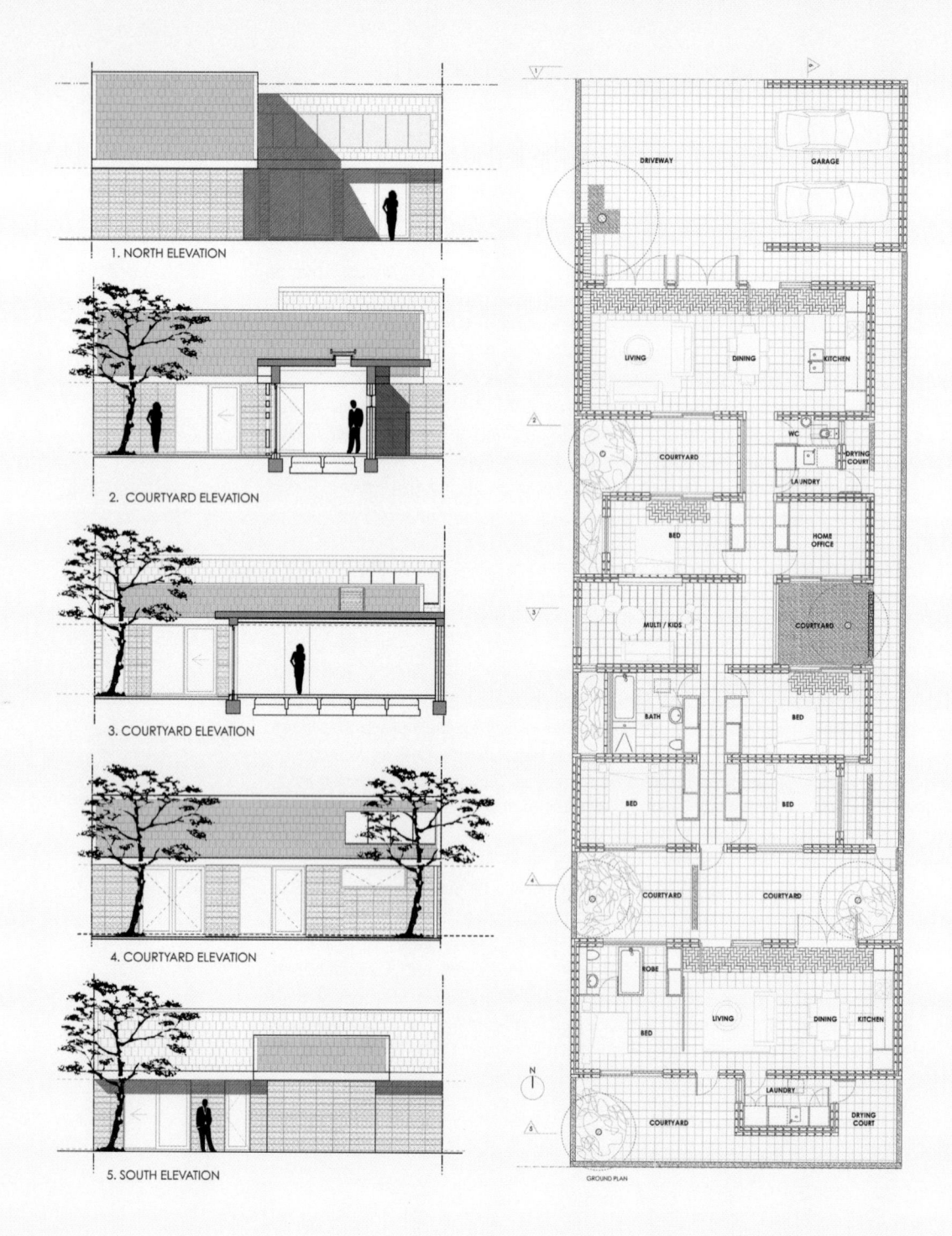

1. NORTH ELEVATION
2. COURTYARD ELEVATION
3. COURTYARD ELEVATION
4. COURTYARD ELEVATION
5. SOUTH ELEVATION

GROUND PLAN

additional cost is offset through careful planning and elimination of plasterboard from the project. Division of internal space is provided by pre-manufactured joinery units that form drop in elements that, in addition, hold the majority of internal doors.

Landscaping addresses the wasteful distribution of precious water onto greedy lawns. As an alternative we propose a 'drought proof' approach to the exterior spaces. This includes permeable gravel from crushed brick, brick paving, low water consuming local native plants, and deciduous trees in the courtyards that provide essential shading from east and west sun. All garden water shall be from the greywater tanks under the service areas.

*iredale pedersen hook architects*

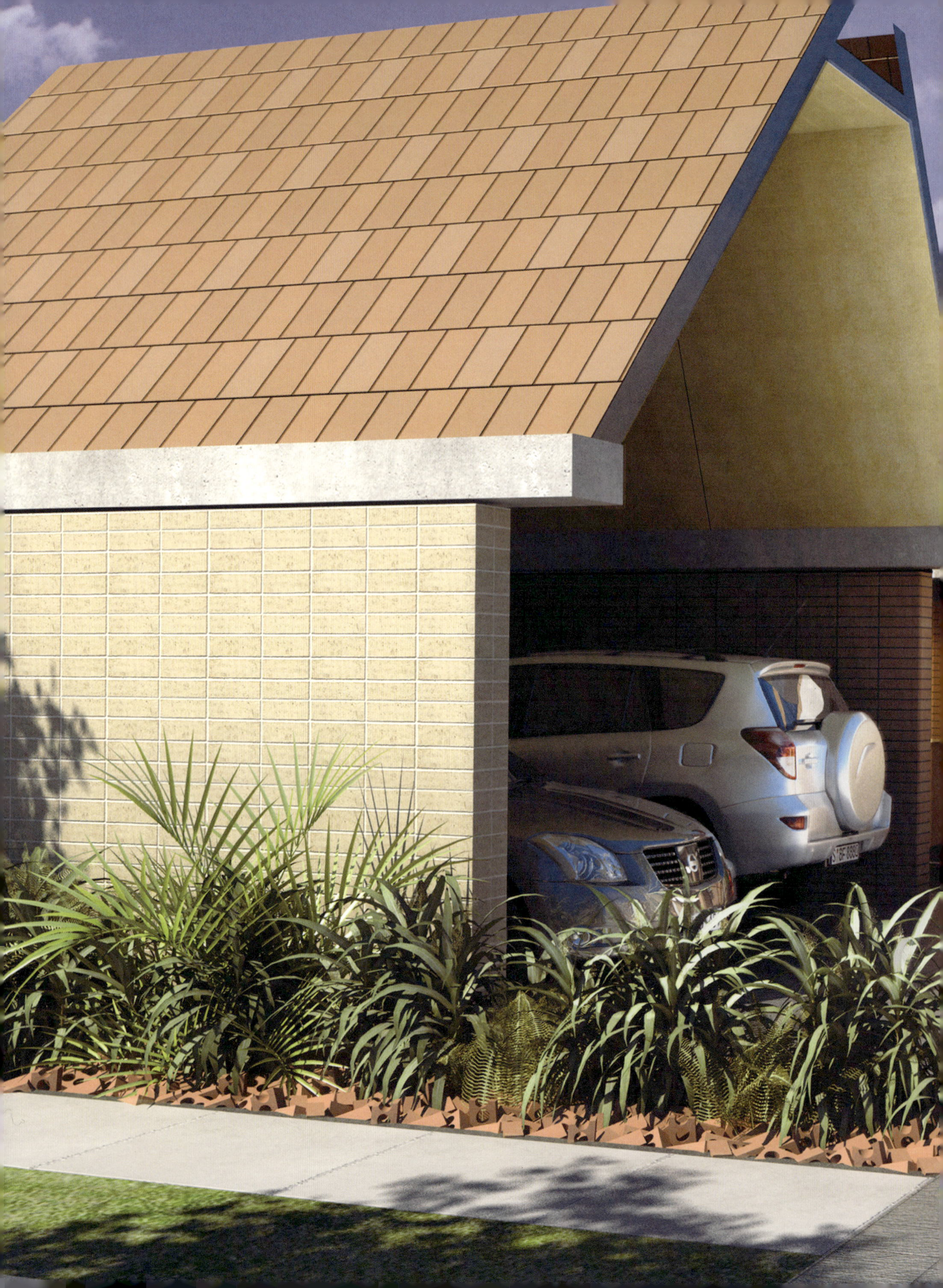

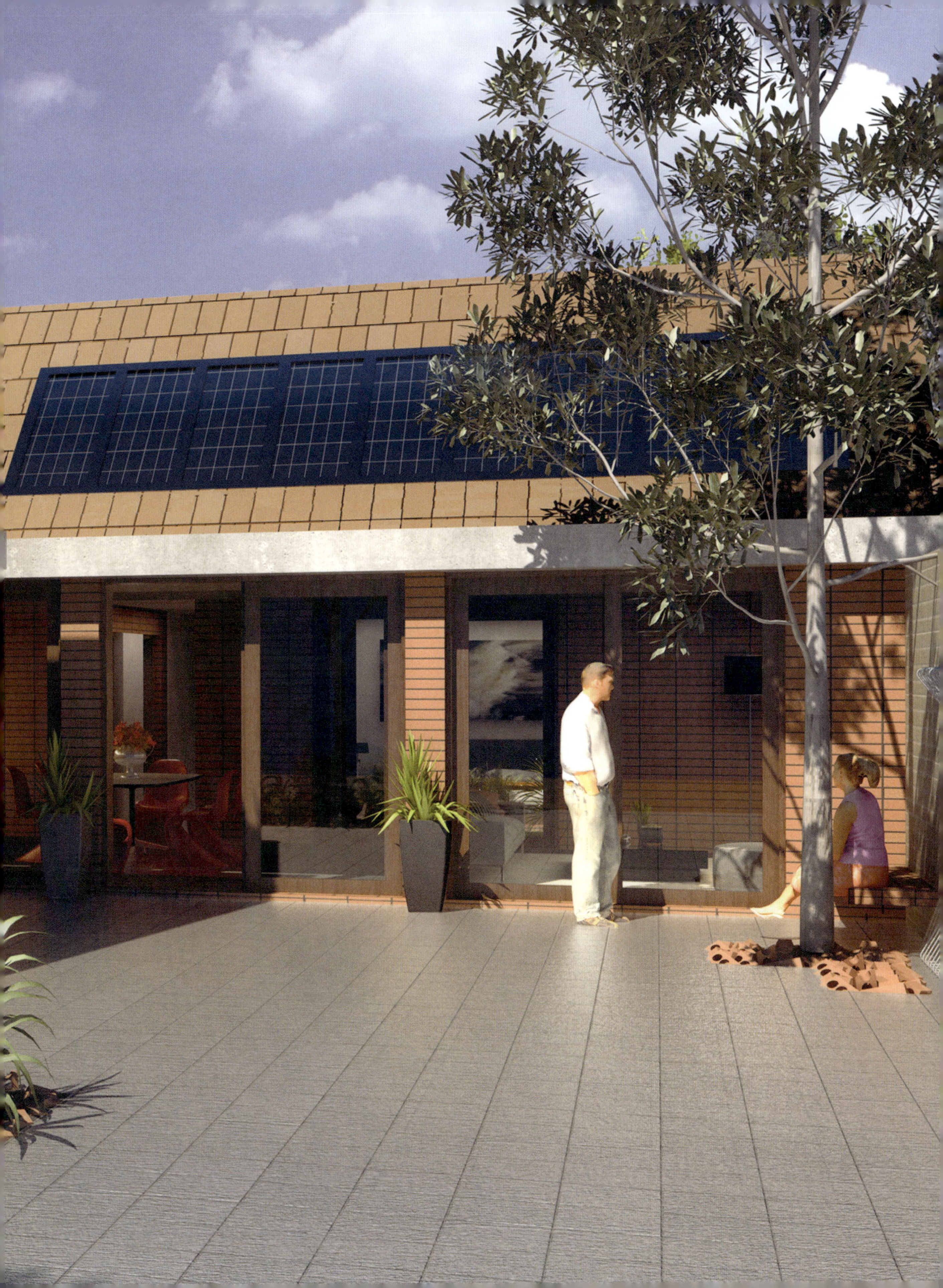

## Architecture as silver screen

On the following pages the photo essay 'Prix d'Amour' explores the significance of the 1990 house Prix d'Amour (Price of Love) through its demolition in 2006. Prix d'Amour was a Perth icon, arguably the apotheosis of Perth's primarily suburban culture. Prix d'Amour was based on the plantation house Tara from the 1939 film *Gone With the Wind*. The story was set in an aristocratic pocket of Georgia in the 1860s during the American Civil War. The film used the house as a set to locate the viewer in the same domestic sphere as the characters. Accordingly, as architecture it produced an intimate and stirring cinematic experience. When the set for Tara was used in the design of an actual dwelling in Perth 50 years later the spaces of reality and illusion collapsed. As a simulation – or a copy of a copy – it strived to replace reality with the illusion of the silver screen and succeeded in creating a local fiction.

Prix d'Amour resulted from Perth mining magnate Lang Hancock's rapid accumulation of wealth. A succession of lucrative mining ventures in the 1980s made Hancock one of the wealthiest individuals in Australia. Some of his ventures are more a source of national economic growth and pride than others. Besides iron ore mining, which is acknowledged as a driving force behind the Australian economy, the legacy of the Wittenoom asbestos mine is less celebrated.[1] Hancock's hyperbolic financial growth was at times converted into symbols in which his second wife Rose Porteous, née Lacson, shared.[2] Prix d'Amour was the eminent symbol which he built in 1990 for himself, Rose, their staff and poodles Snoopy, Linus, Dennis and Lulu. The whimsical aesthetic pastiche of decorative excess seen in the house characterised the couple, in particular Rose, who supposedly performed regularly at their Steinway piano in the ballroom of Prix d'Amour. As architecture the house came to represent another mine, although this time a mine of dreams and specifically sugar-coated ones. Its decorative appropriation and pastiche of baroque and neo-classical references – underpinned by clichés of the Hollywood dream factory and exhaustion with social responsibility – the house represents a postmodern moment. One is reminded of the image of the main character of Werner Herzog's film *Fitzcarraldo* (1982) listening to opera aboard a boat travelling down the Amazon after exorcising his megalomaniacal dream to take a ship over a mountain. Perhaps the 'price of love' to which the name of the house alludes is this cost of manufacturing dreams which here saw the silver screen draped over a Mosman Park block.

The house has been seen to symbolise Rose and Lang but it also reveals much about its detractors.[3] The house was designed by award-winning architects Wright and Palassis. The specific references made to Tara in the house include a lavish terraced garden setting, two-

# PRIX D'AMOUR

storey scale, a pristine white finish, a grand entrance, arched windows, balconies and an interior spiral staircase leading to a ballroom. Needless to say, the house interrupted the style of the other houses on the street, which were mostly built in the understated styles of the 1970s. This motivated much critique of the architectural direction pursued by Hancock. It became a screen for the projection of the broader society's architectural ethos and even morality.

The demise of the house was tragic and comic. The large arabesque wrought-iron gates remained closed as two years passed without occupancy. The opulent interior fittings were removed and a cyclone fence appeared around the deteriorating gardens. The interior was looted, the empty pool became a 'skate spot' and the entire building including the faux marble columns wore satirical graffiti. A security guard was employed and the demolition crew eventually arrived. Ironically, they tried to paint over the dollar signs that had been spray painted onto the building despite the demolition process already being underway.

The destruction of the house was a spectacle. Jon Tarry recorded the demolition for a 12-minute film, *A Rose No More,* at 7.45 am on Saturday 25 March 2006 from which this photo essay has been extracted. At the moment of the demolition a crowd gathered at the entrance and was given a 15-minute tour. Afterward, two workers swung sledge hammers in unison at the Juliet balcony until its railing crashed to the ground. Almost immediately, the mechanical arm of the excavator moved in to systematically smash each column of the grand entrance. When all eight had been punched to the ground the same mechanical arm pounded the canopy until it too crashed to the ground.

Historically, ruins have been invaluable in revealing their societies. They have also been a wellspring of romantic inspiration and continue to fascinate us. Recently the event of 11 September 2001 again revealed the sublime horror of grand forms being slowly consumed as destruction takes hold. They seem to remind us of our own mortality and the fragility of existence that we take for granted. The cycle of boom, construction and demolition has repeated in Western Australia. Prix d'Amour enacted this cycle on a small scale. It took appropriation to the superlative degree of simulation. By making a film set into reality, reality took on qualities of the screen that in this case saw the projection of dreams, romance, morality, fears, and desires that with its erasure ultimately came to signify nothing.

*Darryn Ansted with Jon Tarry*

[1] See the following for detail of Hancock's mining ventures: Duffield, R., *Rogue Bull: The Story of Lang Hancock, King of the Pilbara*, Collins, Sydney, 1979; Hancock, L., *Wake up Australia*, E. J. Dwyer, Sydney, 1979; Phillipson, N., *Man of Iron*, Wren, Melbourne, 1974; Wainwright, R., *Rose*, Allen & Unwin, Sydney, 2002.

[2] For a discussion of the obsession that the media had with the couple see Robinson, K., 'Of Mail-Order Brides And "Boys' Own" Tales: Representations of Asian-Australian Marriages,' *Feminist Review*, no. 52, 1996.

[3] Brian Wright won the 2005 Architects Board Award.

*Prix d'Amour.*
*[Newspix/Kerris Berrington]*

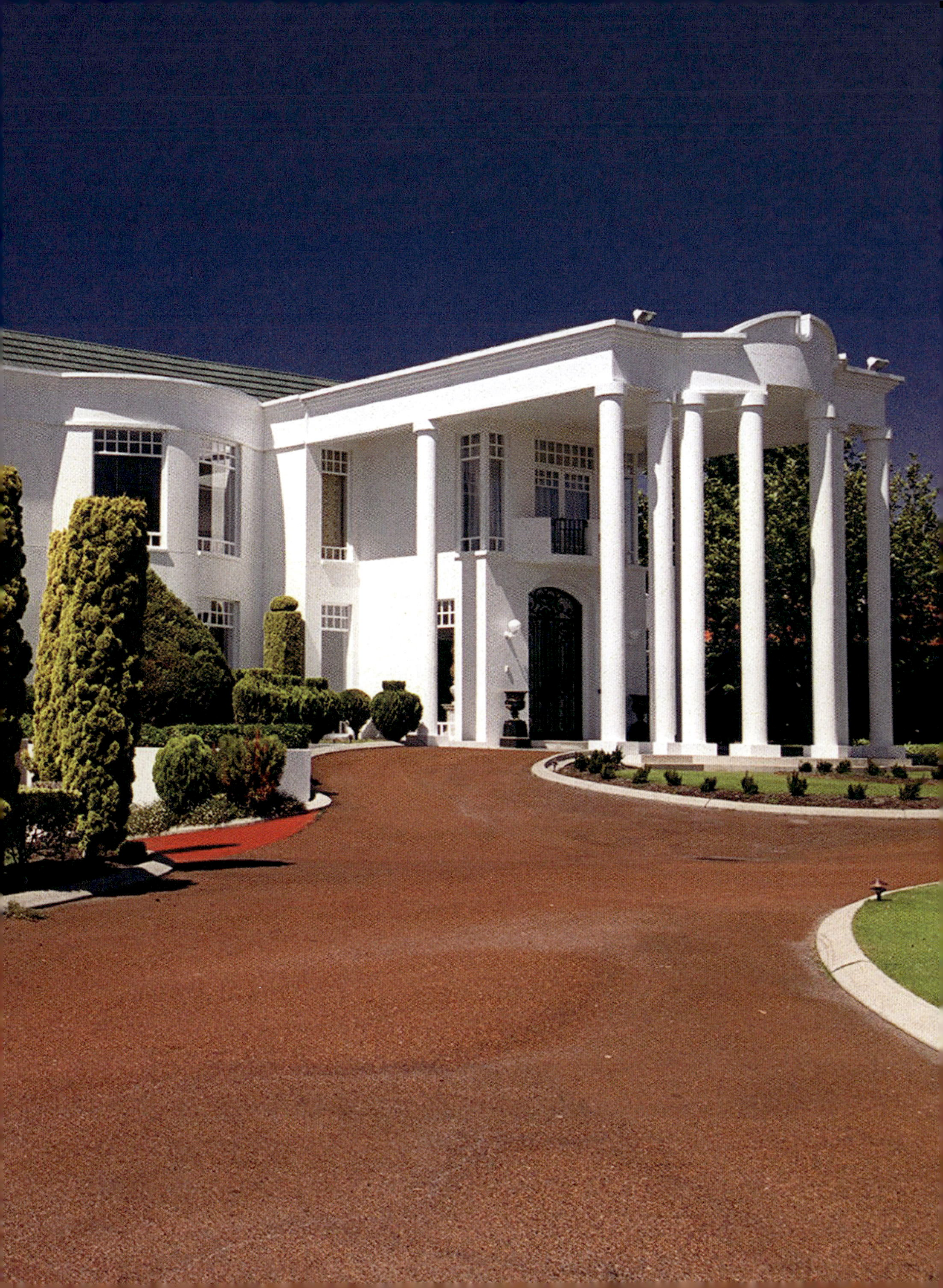

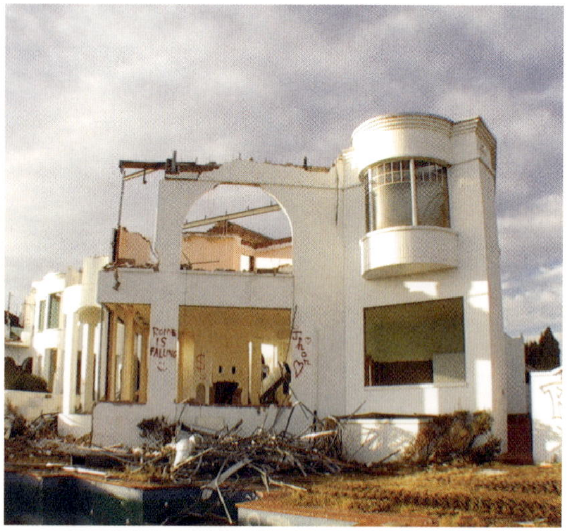

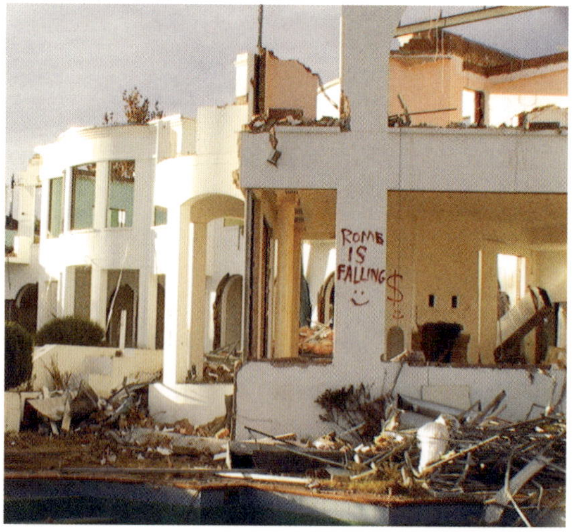
ROME IS FALLING

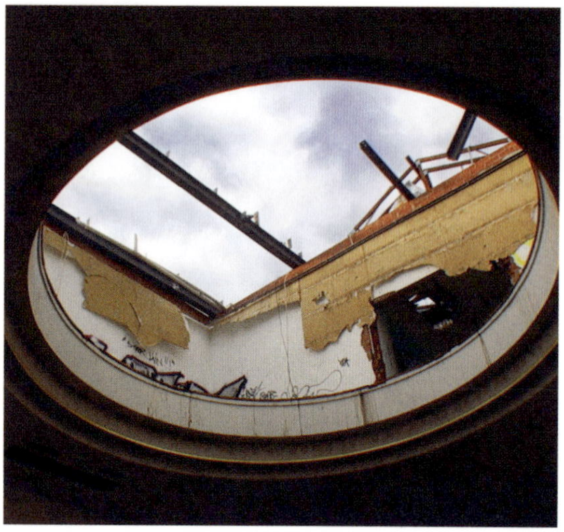

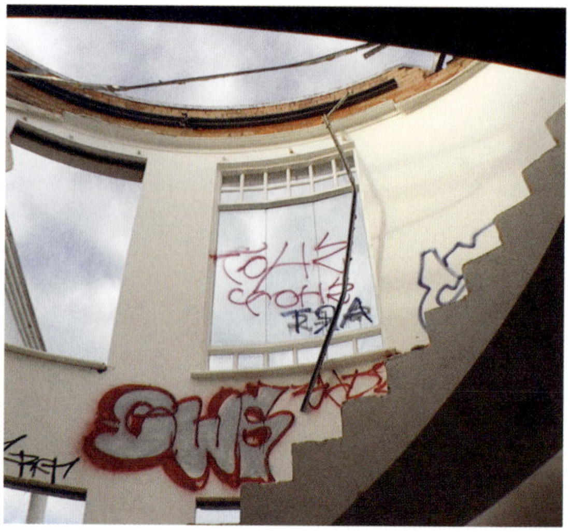

433
DREAM HOMES

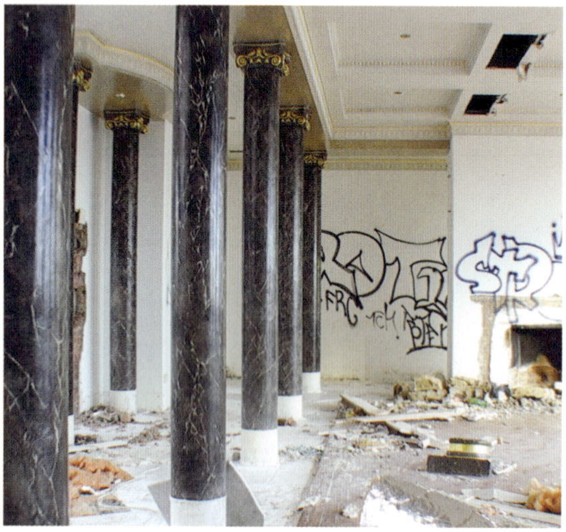
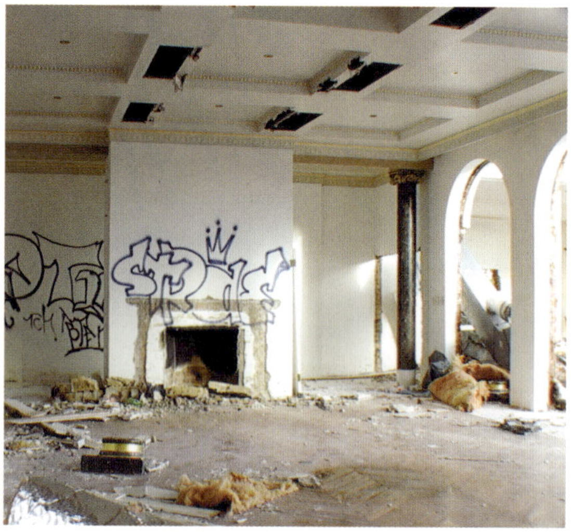
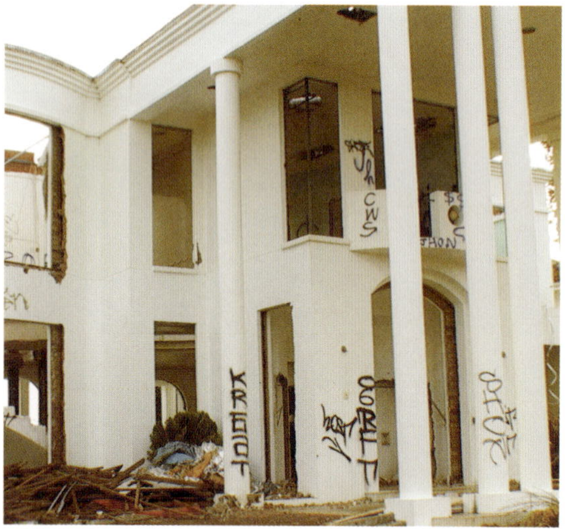
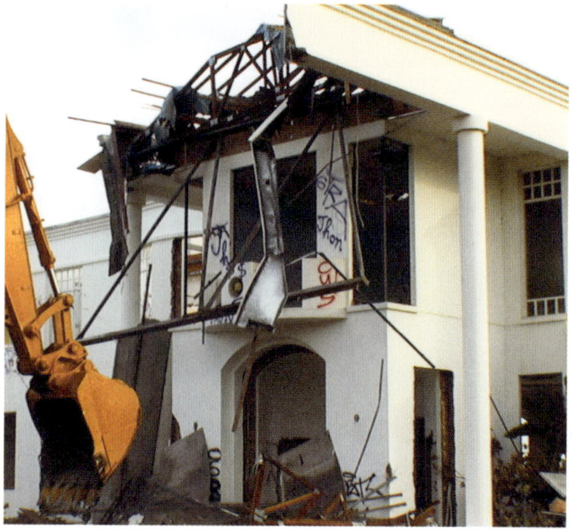

PRIX D'AMOUR

435
DREAM HOMES

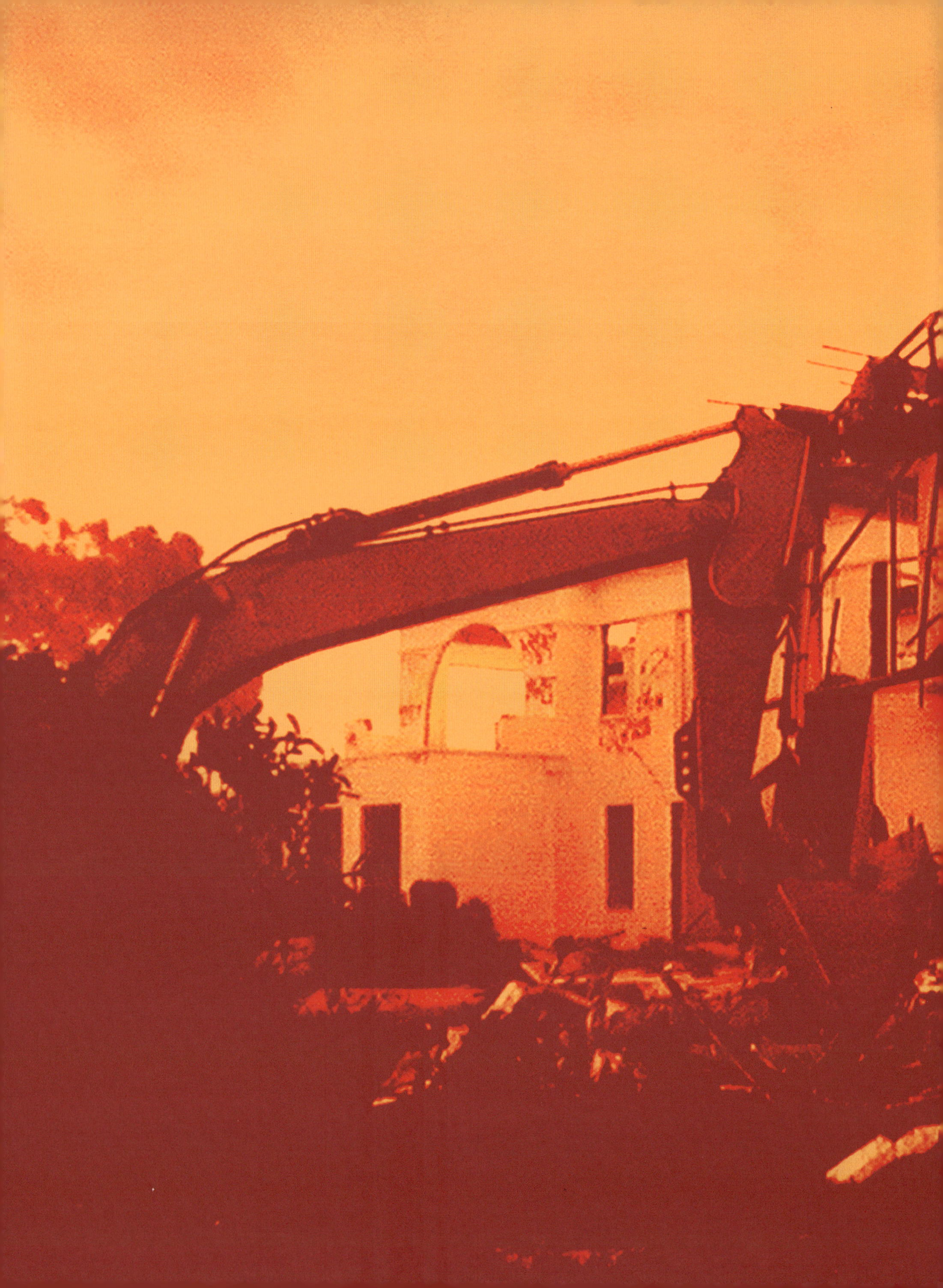

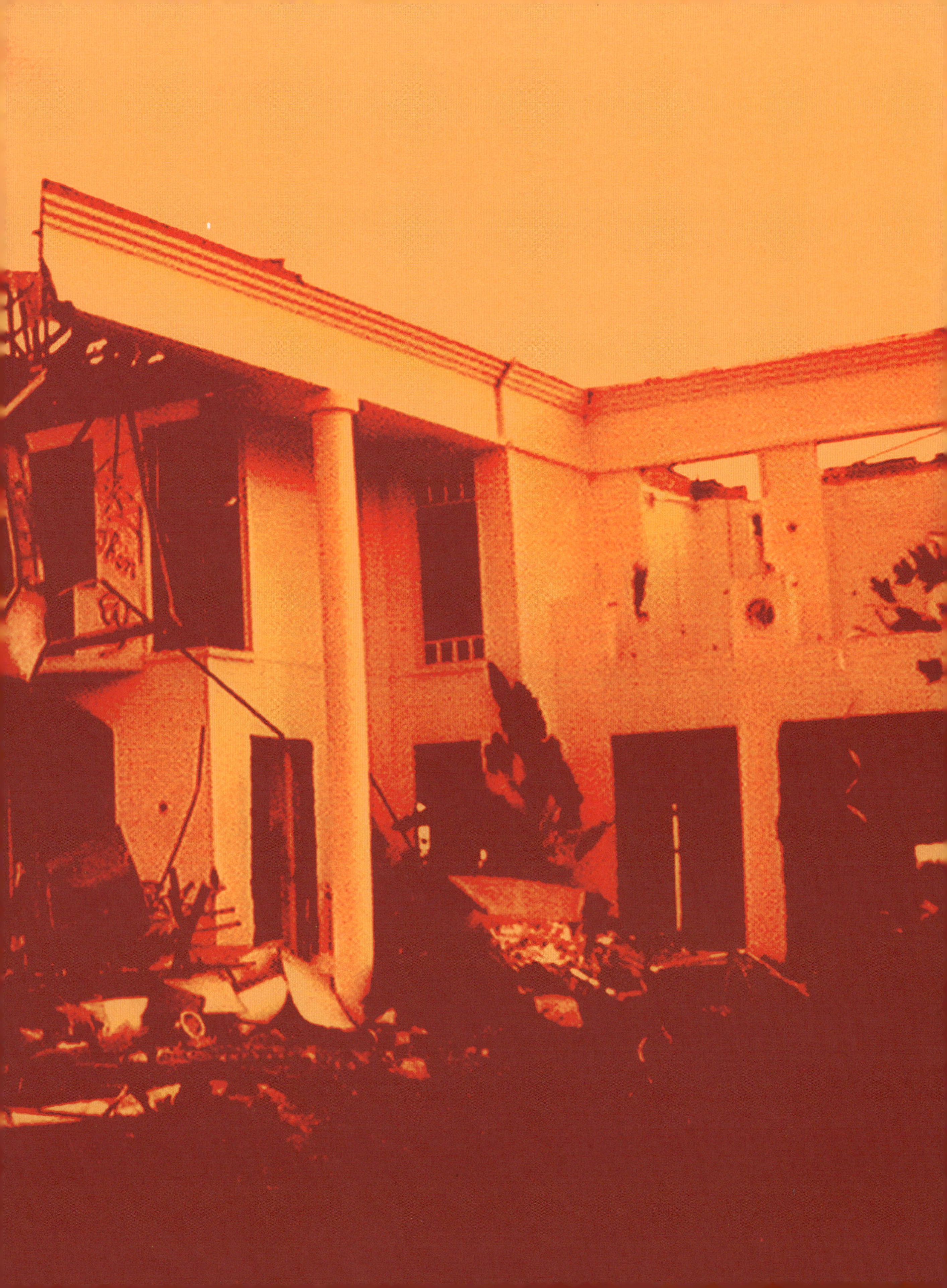

**IF THIS HOME COMES TO CONTAIN A FAMILY OF FOUR IT WILL TAKE 58 HECTARES OF LAND TO SUSTAIN THEM.**

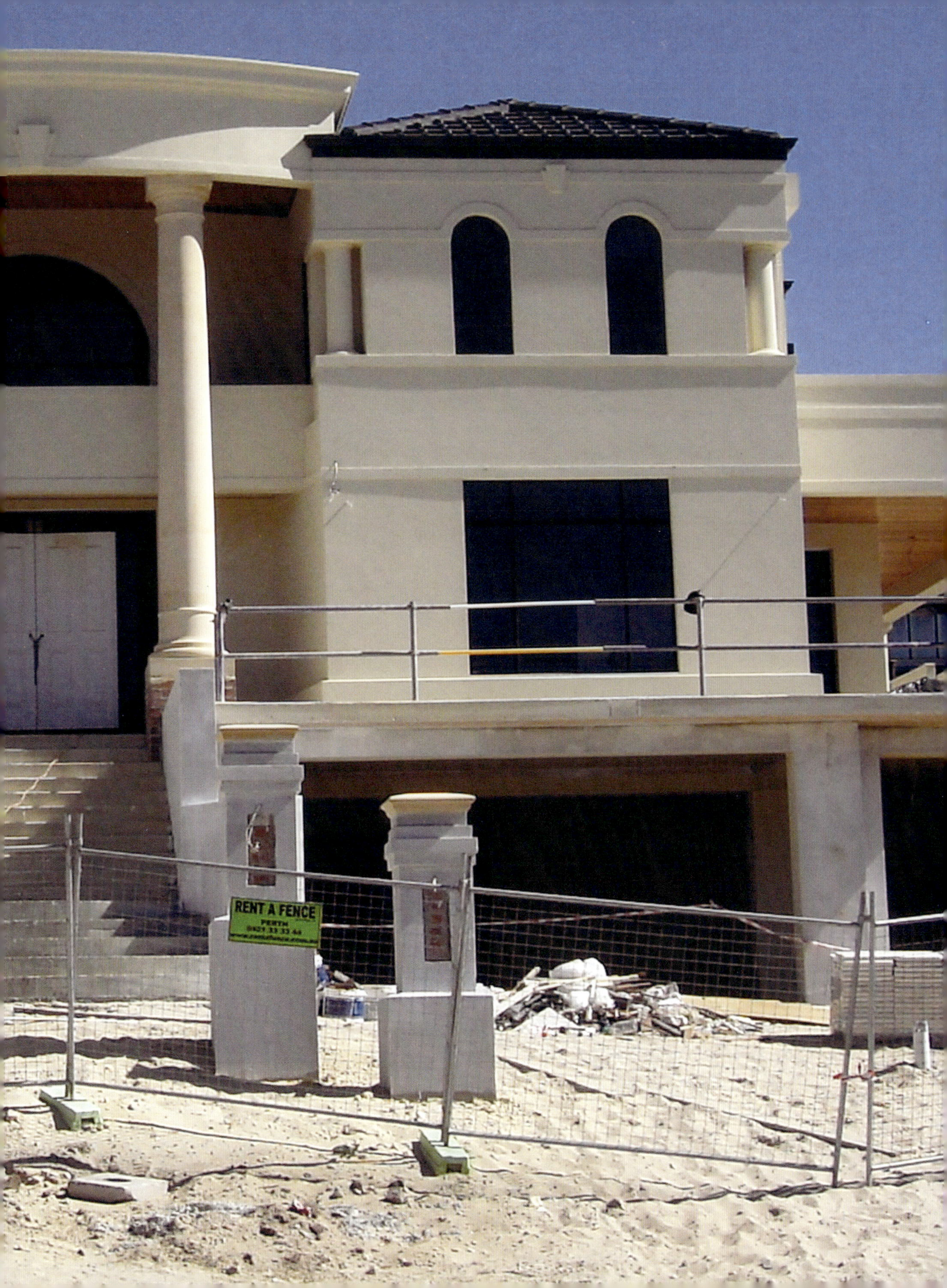
RENT A FENCE
PERTH

# This then is the true dimension of an average Western Australian suburban property. In this sense suburbia's aristocratic pretensions have now been fully realised.

| Goods/services | ha/person |
|---|---|
| Food and beverages | 6.69 |
| Clothing | 0.50 |
| Other products | 1.56 |
| Housing | 0.19 |
| Energy supply | 0.41 |
| Trade | 2.02 |
| Other services | 1.13 |
| Degraded land | 0.74 |
| Other | 1.25 |
| TOTAL | 14.50 |

Composition of the Western Australian ecological footprint.
*(Source data: Ecological Footprint accounting for Western Australia Report prepared on behalf of the Environment Protection Authority by Dr Peter Johnson from Prime Research in collaboration with the Environmental Protection Authority Services Unit. Environmental Protection Authority Perth, November 2006).*

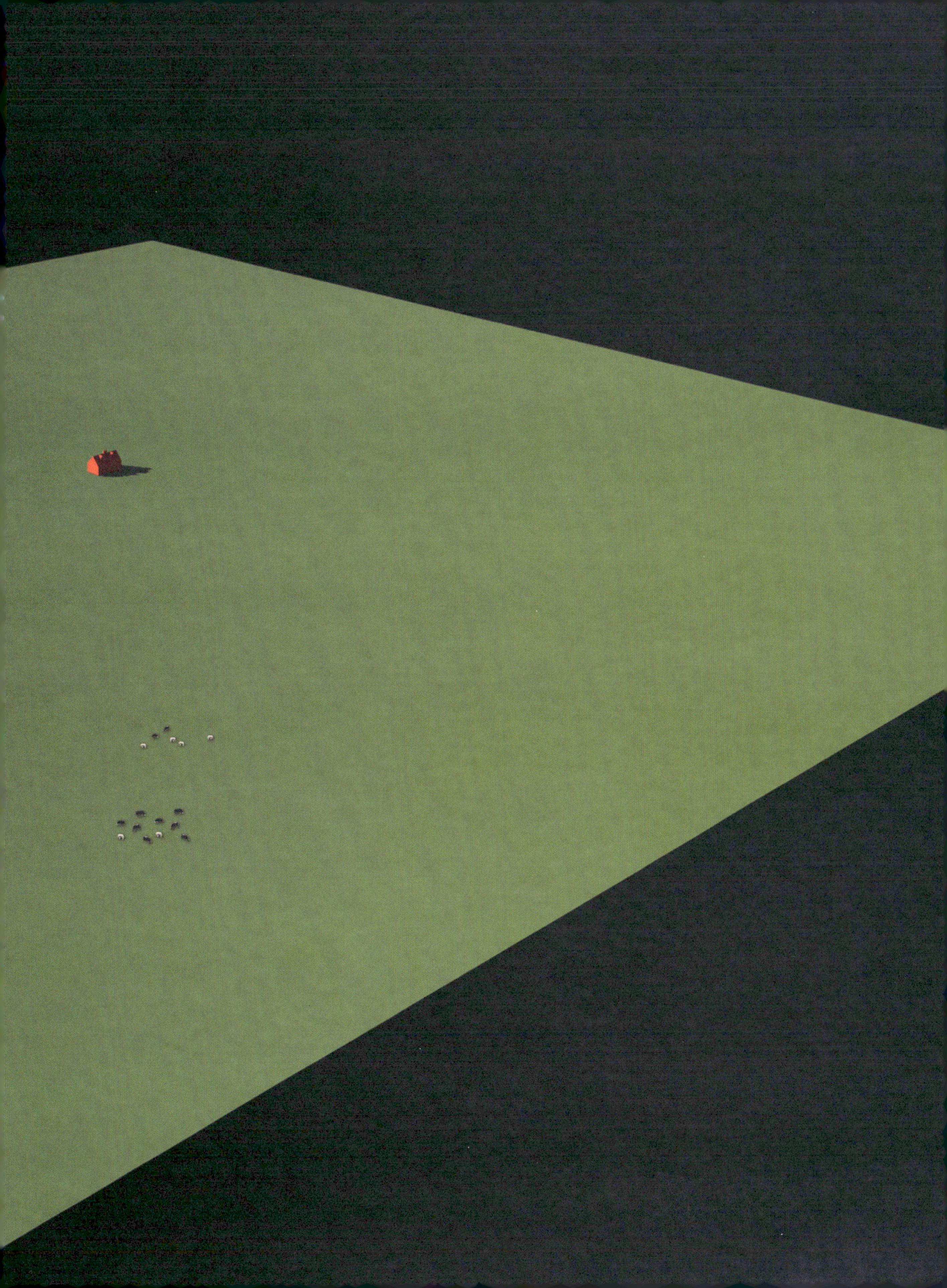

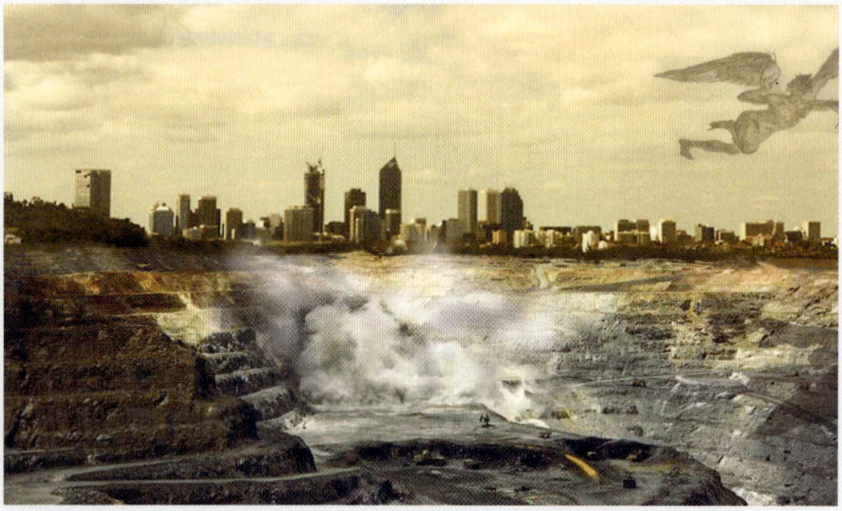

# ACKNOWLEDGEMENTS

The research documented in this book began in 2007 as a part of an Australian Research Council grant headquartered in the Faculty of Architecture, Landscape and Visual Arts at The University of Western Australia (UWA). The grant was directed by myself in association with Professor David Hedgcock, Dean, School of Built Environment, Art & Design at Curtin University of Technology. David has been knowledgeable, encouraging and a steadying influence. Karl Kullmann was (part-time) Research Associate to the project and Donna Broun, the (full-time) Research Assistant. Students Phivo Geogiou and Julia Robinson supported the research team. With a complicated brief and very little time, everyone rose to the occasion to quickly assemble the relevant data, conduct accurate mapping and produce compelling graphics.

Thank you also to all those who have contributed creative and written work to the book: Professor Charles Waldheim, Bernard Salt, Rob Adams, Professor Simon Anderson, Dale Alcock, Anthony Duckworth-Smith, Jon Tarry, Brett Wood Gush, Julian Bolleter, Ashton Raggatt McDougall, iredale pedersen hook and WOHA architects. We are also grateful to the following for their support, advice and/or assistance in gathering data: Dr Clarissa Ball – Dean Faculty of Architecture, Landscape and Visual Arts, Lord Mayor Lisa Scaffidi, Lynda Dorrington – FORM, Marion Fulker – Committee for Perth, Dr Alan Tingay – Environmental Scientist, Dr Martin Anda – Murdoch University, John Bartle – Department of Environment and Conservation, Andrea Beier – World Wildlife Fund, Melissa Dorant – Main Roads Western Australia, Professor Billie Giles-Corti – The University of Western Australia, Adjunct Professor Julian Cribb – University of Technology, Sydney, Dr Andrew Montgomery, Steven James and Matt Devlin – Department for Planning and Infrastructure, Dave Griffiths – Department of Environment and Conservation, Professor Steve Halls – Murdoch University, Damien Hassan – State Records Office, Howard Garner – Australian Bureau of Statistics, Shirene Hickman – Department of Environment and Conservation, Brad Jakowyna – Department of Environment and Conservation, Professor Helen Armstrong – Queensland University of Technology, Professor Kadambot Siddique – Institute of Agriculture, The University of Western Australia, Valerie K elly – Department of Agriculture and Food, Stephen Kovacs – City of Stirling, Peter Lampkin – Synergy, Peter Sanders – Western Australian Land Information Authority, Michael Toole – Australian Bureau of Statistics, Andrew Usher – Engineer, Dr Ray Wills – Western Australian Sustainable Energy Association, Dr Mathew Adams – Landgate, Martin Ford – Spacetime, Andy Thomas, Patric De Villiers – Urban Designer/Architect, Dr Ian Alexander – Geographer, Jamie Graham and Nathan Cantem – The University of Western Australia. Thanks also to the State Library of Western Australia and the Battye Library. If I have overlooked someone please forgive me.

With all the usual doubts about creative work (especially at this scale), I am also profoundly grateful to my wife, Dr Tatum Hands, who takes an active and critical interest in the work I do. I'd also like to acknowledge all the people, who in over 40 public and private presentations of this research have been both very encouraging and usefully critical. I am also appreciative of the enthusiastic team at UWA Press who have been great to work with.

Finally, a toast to my Research Assistant, Donna Broun. Without her boundless optimism, extraordinary work ethic and wide-ranging skills this book would simply not have been possible.

*Richard Weller*

## RELATED MEDIA

*Interview* Saturday Breakfast with James Lush, ABC Radio, Perth, 9 August 2008.
*News* Hatch, D. & Catanzaro, J., 'Population explosion looms large over state', *The West Australian*, 30 June 2008, p. 13.
*Documentary Feature* Harris, L., 'To Sprawl or Not to Sprawl', *Stateline*, ABC Television, 8 March 2008.
*Interview* The Morning Show, ABC Radio, Perth, 26 February 2008.
*Interview* Afternoons with Geraldine Mellet, ABC Radio, Perth, 3 March 2008.
*Voiceover* The New Perth Waterfront Website, www.perthwaterfront.com.au, viewed 22 February 2008.
*Feature* Fox, M., 'Brand New Day – Boomtown 2050', *The Sunday Times Magazine*, 21 October 2007, pp. 14-17.
*Feature* Williams, G., 'Designs On Us – Richard Weller', *The Sunday Times Magazine*, 11 September 2005.

## RELATED PUBLICATIONS

Weller, R.J., 'Planning by Design: Scenarios for a city of 3 million people', *JoLA: Journal of Landscape Architecture*, issue 6, 2008, pp. 6-13.
Weller, R.J., 'Boomtown 2050: "Spreading and Stacking: Part 1"', *Landscape Architecture Australia*, issue 118, 2008, pp. 21-24.
Weller, R.J., 'Spreading and Stacking: Part 2', *Landscape Architecture Australia*, issue 119, 2008, pp. 19-22.
Weller, R.J., 'The New Perth Waterfront: Designers Statements', *Architecture Australia*, vol. 97, no. 3, 2008, p. 42.
Weller, R.J., 'Landscape Sub-urbanism: Towards a Theory and Practice of Landscape Architecture in Contemporary Suburban Conditions', *Landscape Journal*, Wisconsin, issue 27, no. 2, 2007, pp. 255-270.
Weller, R.J., 'Boomtown 2050. Alternative Growth Scenarios for a Rapidly Growing City', *FORM: Shaping the Legacy*, 2007, pp. 48-53.
Weller, R.J., 'Sprawl-Scape', *Landscape Architecture Australia*, vol. 113, 2007, pp. 18-22.

## LECTURES AND BRIEFINGS

*The 2009 CY O'Connor Lecture* 'Boomscape', Perth Town Hall, Perth, 10 March 2009.
*Keynote Address* Professor David Hedgcock, 'Future Proof – Changing Development Paradigms', Urban Development Institute of Australia, WA State Conference, Bunker Bay, 24 October 2008.
*Guest Lecture* 'Development and Environment', Leadership WA, Perth, 13 August 2008.
*Guest Lecture* 'Boomtown 2050', Department of Agriculture and Food, Perth, 8 August 2008.
*Guest Lecture* 'Mapping Perth', Spatial Sciences Institute, Annual Conference, Curtin University, Perth, 25 July 2008.
*Keynote Address* 'Perth's Changing Face: Its Planning, its Population, its People', Committee for Economic Development Australia (CEDA), Perth, 27 June 2008.
*Public Lecture* 'The New Perth Waterfront', University of Western Australia, Perth, 19 June 2008.
*Guest Lecture* 'Boomtown 2050', WaterCorp Head Office, Perth, 16 June 2008.
*Guest Lecture* 'The Future of Landscape Architecture in Australia – The Boomtown 2050 Model', Hassell: Directors and Senior Associates (Australasia) Convention, Rottnest Island, 13 June 2008.
*Guest Lecture* 'Boomtown 2050 – Making Landscape Urbanism Work', Architecture Association, London, 14 April 2008.
*Guest Lecture* 'From Sign to Structure in Contemporary Landscape Architecture', Office of Martha Schwarz, London, April 2008.
*Guest Lecture* 'Urban Structures', ETH, Zurich, 23 April 2008.
*Guest Lecture* 'Recent Work', Ecole Nationale Superieure du Paysage de Versailles, France, 17 April 2008.
*Guest Lecture* 'Recent Design Work', University of Florence, 12 May 2008.
*Guest Lecture* 'Boomtown 2050', University of Florence, 14 May 2008.
*Guest Lecture* 'Design as Planning and Planning as Design', La Sapienze, University of Rome, 19 May 2008.

# MEDIA & PUBLICATIONS

*Guest Lecture* 'Boomtown 2050', Western Australian Department of Planning and Infrastructure, Perth, 28 March 2008.
*Guest Lecture* 'Boomtown 2050', Hassell, Perth, 3 April 2008.
*Public Lecture* 'The New Perth Waterfront', Government Architect's Lecture Series, Perth, 2 April 2008.
*Briefing* 'Boomtown 2050', Lend Lease, Perth, 25 March 2008.
*Briefing* 'Boomtown 2050', Office of the Minister for Planning and Infrastructure, Perth, 19 March 2008.
*Public Lecture* 'The New Perth Waterfront', AILA WA, University of Western Australia, Perth, 14 March 2008.
*Guest Lecture* 'Boomtown 2050', Honours Students in Urban History, Faculty of Architecture, Landscape and Visual Arts, University of Western Australia, Perth, 14 March 2008.
*Briefing* 'Boomtown 2050', Dale Alcock Homes Ltd, Perth, 13 March 2008.
*Public Lecture* 'Boomtown 2050', University of Western Australia Public Extension Series, Perth, 5 March 2008.
*Guest Lecture* 'Boomtown 2050', LWP Property Group, Perth, 27 February 2008.
*Guest Lecture* 'Boomtown 2050', ALCOA Industries Ltd, Perth, 25 February 2008.
*Guest Lecture* 'Boomtown 2050', Cameron, Chisolm, Nicol Architects, Perth, 22 February 2008.
*Launch Presentation* 'The New Perth Waterfront', Perth Convention Centre, Perth, 13 February 2008.
*Guest Lecture* 'Boomtown 2050', Australian Institute of Landscape Architects, Perth, 1 February 2008.
*Guest Lecture* 'Boomtown 2050', School of Population Health, University of Western Australia, Perth, 23 January 2008.
*Briefing* 'Boomtown 2050', Colliers International, Perth, 11 January 2008.
*Briefing* 'Boomtown 2050', Mirvac Fini Development Group, Perth, 7 January 2008.
*Guest Lecture* 'Boomtown 2050', Centre for Water Research, University of Western Australia, Perth, 16 November 2007.
*Guest Lecture* 'Boomtown 2050', Institute for Sustainability and Technology Policy, Murdoch University, Perth, 30 November 2007.
*Guest Lecture* 'Boomtown 2050', Western Australian Planning Commission and the Department of Planning and Infrastructure, Perth, 3 December 2007.
*Briefing* 'Boomtown 2050', Committee for Perth, Perth, 5 December 2007.
*Briefing* 'Boomtown 2050', Western Australian Chamber of Commerce, Perth, 29 November 2007.
*Briefing* 'Boomtown 2050', Invited Stakeholders, University of Western Australia Club, Perth, 8 November 2007.
*Guest Lecture* 'Boomtown 2050', 'Alkimos' Design Excellence Workshop, Perth, 2 November 2007.
*Public Lecture* 'Scenario Cities', Australian Institute of Landscape Architects, Sydney, 22 October 2007.
*Public Lecture* 'Suburban Disturbances', (EX)periment Design Forum, Adelaide, 20 October 2007.
*Guest Lecture* 'Scenario Cities', Urban Design Centre, Perth, 24 August 2007.
*Public Lecture* 'New Trends in Architecture', Form Gallery, Perth, 19 August 2007.
*Public Lecture* Boomtown 2050', Planning Institute of Australia, Perth, 5 July 2007.
*Public Lecture* 'The Dean's Lecture', Melbourne University, 13 March 2007.

### RICHARD WELLER

Richard Weller is Professor of Landscape Architecture at The University of Western Australia (UWA) where he has fostered a culture of landscape urbanism. In over 20 years of design practice Professor Weller has received a consistent stream of international competition prizes. His work has been widely exhibited including in a retrospective at the Museum of Contemporary Art in Sydney (1998). He has published over 50 papers on contemporary urban design and landscape architecture and has had a monograph of his work published by the University of Pennsylvania Press.

### DAVID HEDGCOCK

Professor David Hedgcock is Dean of the School of Built Environment Art and Design, a position he has held since the start of 2004. He began his academic career as a lecturer in urban and regional planning at the Western Australian Institute of Technology (the forerunner of Curtin University) in 1979. He was the Head of the Department of Urban and Regional Planning for over 10 years before taking up the role of Deputy Head of the School of Architecture, Construction and Planning in 2001.

### BRETT WOOD-GUSH

Brett is Principal Urban Designer/Associate at TPG Town Planning and Urban Design, a firm that is committed to improving the quality of the built environment and promoting professional development. Brett Wood-Gush has qualifications in architecture and town planning and a masters degree in urban design. He is also a Fellow of Leadership Western Australia. He was lead urban designer on the Wungong Urban Water Masterplanning Project. He publishes regularly and frequently advises on policies and speaks on a wide range of planning topics at conferences and seminars, as well as on radio and television.

### ASHTON RAGGATT MCDOUGALL

The architects ARM began in Melbourne, Australia in 1988 as a collaboration between Steve Ashton, Howard Raggatt and Ian McDougall. Since then, ARM has produced designs and analytic projects in architecture, urbanism, landscape and interior design. Their work has been awarded a number of national and international prizes and has featured in international exhibitions including the Venice Biennale and Royal College of the Arts, London. Their projects have become known worldwide through publications such as Charles Jencks' *Architecture of the Jumping Universe*, *Blueprint UK* (Best Public Building 2001), *10x10*, and *The Phaidon Atlas of Contemporary World Architecture*.

### WOHA

Formed in 1994 by Singaporean Wong Mun Summ and Australian Richard Hassell, WOHA is based on the model of the creative industries, rather than traditional construction services. With a mix of designers from diverse backgrounds, WOHA explores integrated design for the built environment, moving between masterplanning, architectural, landscape, interior and lighting and furniture design. WOHA has received numerous local and international awards for excellence in design such as the 2007 Aga Khan Award for Architecture, MIPIM AR Future Project Awards 2007, AR Awards for Emerging Architecture 2006 and RAIA International Award. WOHA has offices in Singapore and Thailand.

### IREDALE PEDERSEN HOOK

Iredale Pedersen Hook is an emerging Australian architecture practice with offices in Perth and Melbourne and a rapidly expanding diverse body of work scattered throughout Australia. The firm is dedicated to the pursuit of sustainable buildings with a responsible environmental and social agenda. Iph have exhibited in Tokyo, Barcelona, Berlin, Brno, Patras, London, Vancouver, Melbourne and Perth and received numerous international, national and state awards.

# CONTRIBUTORS

**SIMON ANDERSON**

Professor Simon Anderson has taught and practised architecture at The University of Western Australia since 1989. In that time has been Head and Dean of Architecture, won university and national awards and citations for excellence in teaching and championed the practice of architecture as a legitimate research activity for academics involved in the teaching of architecture. His residential, institutional and commercial buildings and designs have won awards from the Australian Institute of Architects and industry, been published in books and professional journals, and been widely exhibited, most notably at the 2006 Venice Biennale. Most recently, in 2007 he won the architectural competition for a world's best practice eco-resort at Ningaloo, and in January 2008 he was Artist in Residence at the Arthur & Yvonne Boyd Centre for Australian Art at Bundanon.

**DALE ALCOCK**

Dale Alcock Homes was established in 1987 and has become one of Australia's leading volume home builders.
The company has a history of innovation and has always strived to remain contemporary and relevant, whilst at the same time understanding that it is a retailer and its success is driven by meeting its customers demands and providing an affordable product to a consumer.

**JON TARRY**

Jon Tarry is a prominent Australian artist with a practice that combines sculpture, painting, film and architecture. Jon is represented in significant private and public collections including works in Parliament House, Canberra, the National Gallery of Australia, the Australian Embassy in Berlin, Fusina in Venice, Italy, and The Chrysler Building, New York. Jon Tarry is currently Lecturing at The University of Western Australia Faculty of Architecture, Landscape and Visual Arts.

**DARRYN ANSTED**

Darryn Ansted is currently completing a PhD on Gerhard Richter through The University of Western Australia.

**ANTHONY DUCKWORTH-SMITH**

Anthony Duckworth-Smith (BE BArch) is currently undertaking postgraduate studies in architecture at The University of Western Australia. He initially worked as a transport planning and design engineer before pursuing a career in architecture. By combining his research into housing and knowledge of infrastructure design and the operation of transport systems Anthony is currently exploring possibilities for higher density dwelling adjacent to arterial roadways.

**JULIAN BOLLETER**

Julian Bolleter is currently completing a PhD concerning and the potential application of landscape urbanism to Dubai, at the University of Western Australia. He has worked extensively in the middle-east and for Martha Schwartz Partners on a series of projects in Qatar, the United Kingdom and Monaco. Since returning to Perth in 2008 Julian has been teaching at the University of Western Australia and working part time with OCULUS Landscape Architects on projects in both Australia and China.

**CHARLES WALDHEIM**

Charles Waldheim is Associate Dean and Director of the Landscape Architecture program of the John H. Daniels Faculty of Architecture, Landscape, and Design at the University of Toronto. He coined the term "landscape urbanism" to describe emerging design practices in the context of North American urbanism and has written extensively on the positions, practices, and precedents of the topic. He has taught at Harvard University, the University of Pennsylvania, the University of Michigan, the Swiss Federal Institute (ETH) Zurich, the Royal Institute of Technology Stockholm, and the Technical University (TU) Vienna. He has been named recipient of the Rome Prize from the American Academy in Rome and Research Fellow at the Canadian Centre for Architecture (CCA). He was elected Fellow of the Institute for Urban Design, and Honorary Member of the Ontario Association of Landscape Architects (OALA). He currently serves as a member of the Toronto Waterfront Redevelopment Corporation Design Review Panel and sits on the editorial board of *Canadian Architect*.

UWAP is an imprint of UWA Publishing
a division of The University of Western Australia.

THE UNIVERSITY OF
WESTERN AUSTRALIA
*Achieving International Excellence*

UWA Publishing
Crawley, Western Australia 6009
www.uwap.uwa.edu.au

This book is copyright. Apart from any fair dealing for
the purpose private study, research, criticism or review,
as permitted under the Copyright Act 1968, no part may
be reproduced by any process without written permission.
Enquiries should be made to the publisher.

Copyright © Richard Weller 2009.

The moral right of the author has been asserted.

A full CIP record for this book is available from the
National Library of Australia.

Printed by 1010 Printing International Limited.

**ADDITIONAL PHOTOGRAPHY CREDITS**

Photograph on page 131 by Bartlomiej Stroinski.

The composite image on pages 294-295 uses images
reproduced with kind permission from Jenkins, E., *To Scale:
One Hundred Urban Plans*, Routledge, New York, 2008, pp.
9, 5, 17, 31, 41, 43, 59, 75, 99, 135, 139, 147, 151, 159,
171, 187, 189, 195.

Photograph on page 309 by Dez Pain.

# INDEX

**Aboriginal** people, 53, 56, 98
    heritage sites at Wungong, 243, 247, 251, 254
    Native Title claims, 155
agricultural lands, 19, 95, 118-21, 145
    area to support a city, 275-77, 279
    degraded, 171
    global availability, 97, 112
    market gardens, 145
    subdivision of, 116, 121-22, 128
    urban, 113-17, 119, 122, 181, 272
air pollution *see* greenhouse gas emissions; *and under* pollution
Armadale Redevelopment Authority, 239
Australian Bureau of Statistics, 35, 55
Avon catchment, 305-07

**BAU** City, xii, 37, 42, 179–85, 199–31
    alternatives to, 17–19, 42, 191, 258–59, 262, 389–93, 395
    innovations within, 187, 191, 254, 258
Beihai, China, 53
Birrell, Bob, 53
Boyd, Robin, 27
Bruegmann, Robert, 39–40
building materials, recycling, 420–23
building techniques, 402-03, 405, 412, 417, 419-25
bushland, 24, 124, 128
    houses in, 21, 23
    clearing of, 25, 128-29, 135
    linked, 124, 126, 162, 267
    preservation of, 29, 124, 129, 154-56

Business as Usual approach *see* BAU City

**Calthorpe**, Peter, 40
Canning Highway high rise zone, 361, 364, 371
Canning Road, 18
carbon sinks, 73, 84, 137
    reforestation of Avon catchment, 305-07
Car Free City, 291-96
cars, 78, 98, 134
    CBD parking, 78
    emissions, 80-2
    ownership, 30, 78-9, 83, 93, 133
    tyres in landfill, 62, 80
cities
    adaptability of, 17
    sustainability of, v
    sustenance for *see* ecological footprint
CityVision, 139, 143
climate change, 17, 67
    refugees, 134
    *see also* sea level
coastal development, 52-3, 124, 135, 137, 419
    high rise, 374–85
    Sea Change City, 298
Cribb, Julian, 113, 288–89
*The Cutting Edge*, 201-33

**Dale** Alcock Homes, 32–3
deforestation, 124
Denmark
    bicycle use, 79
    wind energy, 74

developers, 140, 187, 190, 201–33
    at Wungong, 253–54
    *see also* project homes
dwellings *see* housing

**East** Perth, 409–10
ecological footprint, v, 30, 80, 94
    predicted, 94, 95, 438–41
electricity supplies, 60, 72-3, 158
    green power participation, 72, 74
    for water supply, 71
employment, 56, 81, 93, 96, 100
    demand for workers, 134
    fly-in fly-out, 56, 297
    wages, 140
energy consumption, 72-4, 77
    residential, 75-6
energy efficiency, 75
energy supplies, 72–6
    biofuels, 137
    carbon dioxide emissions, 74
    fossil fuels, 75-77
    nuclear, 137
    renewable, 72-4, 76-7, 85, 102, 137
    solar, large scale, 137
    for transport, 72, 77
Environment Protection Authority, 53
exports *see under* trade

**Faust's** tower, 15, 17
Flannery, Dr Tim, 43, 44
Florence, 341
Florida, Richard, 30
food, 118
    consumption per capita, 112

  prices, 140, 145
  wasted, 62
Food City, 275–89
  agricultural land required, 275, 277, 278
  at Wungong, 277, 285
food production, 95
  Chinese cities, 120-22
  hydroponic, 114, 121
  integrated approach, 280
  increase needed, 282-3
  irrigation for, 116
  land for *see* agricultural land
  peri urban, 120
  within cities, 112, 115, 119, 122, 275
  within Perth, 114, 116, 120, 122, 123, 145
forests, 41, 50, 127-28, 154, 181, 305, 312
Freestone, Robert, 24, 265
Fremantle, 19
  high density housing sites, 343, 345, 352

**GDP**, 57, 88
Gans, Herbert, 27
Garden City concept, 265, 268
  density, 266-67
Geddes, Patrick, 43
Glenn, John, ii
Gnangara Mound aquifer, 67
Gold Rush, 19
  urban slums, 19, 21
*Gone With The Wind* (film), 428
Grace, William, 75
greenbelts, 265
Greenhouse and Energy Taskforce, 83, 291

greenhouse gas emissions, 72, 74, 80, 84-7
  per capita, 85, 87, 137, 305
  reduction targets, 137
  *see also* air *under* pollution
Greenwich Village, Manhattan, 341
Guildford, 19

**Hancock**, Lang, 428
homeless, 101, 109, 133
homes *see* housing
Hong Kong, food production, 122
households, 54, 96, 108, 128
  home ownership, 107, 108
housing, 30, 128
  affordability, 107-09, 133, 135, 140, 419–20
  air conditioning, 74-75, 102
  annual construction rate, 185
  apartments, 138
  on arterial roads, 333, 361, 371, 375, 378-9
  demand for, vi, 35, 37, 52
  density *see* housing density
  design, 139-40, 399, 402–05, 409
  in early suburbs, 21–5
  energy efficiency, 75, 135, 243, 253-54
  garage as feature, 30, 32-3
  gardens, 21, 22-3, 144, 280
  greenhouse gases, 83
  infrastructure for, ix, 19, 25, 35, 103
  inner-city *see under* Perth
  innovations *see* housing, innovative
  land for *see* suburban land
  lot sizes, 23, 25, 111, 138
  mortgaged, 98

# INDEX

prices, 104-7, 419
regulation, 25, 187, 371
sustainability, 135, 402
variety, 138, 372, 419-5
*see also* project homes; suburbs
housing, innovative, xii, 187, 402-17
    block, 406-7, 413, 417
    construction techniques, 419
    string, 412-16
    terrace, 407-11, 413
housing density, 29-30, 138-9, 181, 185, 384-85
    amenity for, 341, 343, 375
    high density, 313-15, 341-43, 361, 371-73, 375-77
    high-rise, 138-39, 316-17
    optimum, 343, 345
    vertical sprawl, 350-1, 372
Howard, Ebenezer, 265

**Jacobs**, Jane, 341

**Kunstler**, James Howard, 38, 40

**land** clearing *see under* suburbs
landscape,
    as basis for planning, 42-3, 165, 167, 171, 258
    suburban, 21, 181-83, 192-99
Landscape Structure Plan, 172, 263
    for Wungong Urban Water, 239, 245, 255
landscape urbanism, x, 166, 176
Le Corbusier, 341
Liveable Neighbourhoods, 243

**MVRDV,** 166, 171, 176

MacTiernan, Alannah, 134, 136-7, 138-39, 143
mapping *see* sieve mapping
Maylands, 21
McHarg, Ian, 166-67, 171, 176
Metropolitan Region Scheme, 28-9, 123
Metropolitan Improvement Tax, 29
migrants *see* immigrant *under* population
minerals boom, 133, 134
Morrison, Sean, 139, 143
Mumford, Lewis, 43, 167

**native** fauna, 125
    *see also* Perth Habitat Matrix
native vegetation *see* bushland
Network City, 40-2, 82, 138-39, 143, 239, 254, 259, 313
    activity centres, 40, 42, 313, 330-39
New Perth Waterfront, x, 139, 142-43, 355-59
New York, vertical farm, 121

**Ord** River irrigation scheme, 145

**POD** Cities, 263, 265-74
POS *see* public open space
Paris, 319-20
parks and reserves *see* public open space
Performance Oriented Development *see* POD Cities
Perth, 19, 43, 316-17
    economic vulnerability, 30, 35
    inner city development, 111, 142-43, 355, 409-10
        *see also* New Perth Waterfront
    isolation of, 30, 48, 73, 89, 93

original land grants, 16
population density, 111
Waterfront proposal *see* New Perth Waterfront
Perth Biodiversity Project, 124, 263, 375
Perth Habitat Matrix, 124, 162, 171, 263
Perth region, iv, vi-vii, 49, 172
    car travel within, 78-80, 82
    early settlement, 19
    environmental stress, 53
    future development of *see* alternatives to *under* BAU City
    infrastructure, 58-59
    land usage, 181
    lights from space, ii
    population density, 54, 97, 181
    urban area, 26, 30, 52, 181
    zoning, 41, 48, 163, 185, 314, 373
planning *see* urban planning
pollution, 17
    air, 80, 82
    water *see under* water run-off
    *see also* greenhouse gas emissions
population, 50-1, 54-7
    immigrant, 54-7, 134, 140
    sustainable, 134
population densities, 54, 97
    inner city, 111
    for urban infill, 316-17
    *see also* housing density
population growth, 54, 57, 96
    Australia, 50-1, 55
    with gold discoveries, 19
    predictions, viii, x, 35-7, 40, 52, 134, 185
post-war period, 27

power supplies *see* electricity supplies
*Prix D'Amour,* 428–37
    demolition, 433, 434–39
project homes, 27, 180, 202–35,
    398–412, 438–40
    energy efficiency, 75
    *see also* housing
public open space, 21, 24, 29, 155, 171
    regional, 29
    at Wungong, 242–45, 250–55
public opinions, 131–45
public transport, 77-81
    for BAU city, 185–87
    for car Free City, 291-5
    for Food City, 277, 280
    for Seachange City, 297, 314
public works, early, 19

Radiant City, 347
rail services, 78, 80, 82-3, 159
rainfall, 66
    water tanks, 69, 102
reforestation, 135, 270, 305
refugees, environmental, 134
Regional Ecological Linkages *see* Perth
    Habitat Matrix
research method, x, 42–3, 167
reserves, 150, 153–55, 163, 172
Residential Planning Codes, 371–72
residential sector *see* housing
River City, 360–70
Road Boards, 23
roads, 30, 48, 59, 78, 96, 159, 326-7,
    360, 193
    arterial, 326-27, 360, 378
    for Car Free City, 294-5
    congested, 78

    grid layout, 253-4
    suburban, 23-5
    at Wungong, 251, 253
Rockingham, high density site, 343
Rome, Adam, 40

**sanitation**, 19, 21, 59, 111
    *see also* wastewater
Saudi Arabia, 30
sea levels, 126, 134, 137, 297
    *see also* climate change
Seddon, George, 43
sewerage infrastructure, 66
Shanghai, 120
sieve mapping, 167, 168-9, 173, 181
Singapore, 30, 346-7
    food production, 122
    transport emissions, 80
Sky City, 341-54
    potential population, 343, 361
    *see also* New Perth Waterfront
South West Interconnected System *see*
    electricity supplies
South Western Australia Biodiversity
    HotSpot, 42, 48, 53, 124
sports fields *see* public open space
Steiner, Frederick, 40
Stephenson and Hepburn *see* Metropolitan
    Region Scheme
Stirling Highway, high rise zone, 361,
    365-66, 371
Subi Centro, 78, 138, 409
suburban land
    availability, 37, 140, 149, 171,
    173–75, 181, 184–85,
    265, 317
    clearing, 25–7, 124–26

water tables, 173, 183, 186-87,
    241-45, 264
suburbs, 63, 188
    costs, infill v greenfields, 42
    dependence on cars, 79, 98
    development of, 19, 21, 23, 130
    eco-villages, 137
    infill, 141, 178, 264, 315-17,
        322-26, 374, 184-85
    infrastructure for, 23, 25, 59, 62,
        187, 422
    redevelopment of, 422
    road areas, 293-97
    sustainability, 183-85, 245, 277,
        283, 373
    see also housing
Surf City, 377-83
Swan Coastal Plain, 44, 45, 126, 128,
    130-31, 279, 377
    see also Perth region
Swan River, 32, 128, 362-72
    amenity, 357
    foreshore reclamations, 128, 357
    residential bridges and wharves,
        363, 368-72

**town** planning *see* urban planning
Town Planning Board, 27
trade, vii, 90
    exports, 32, 36, 90, 92-3, 95
    food exports, 125
    imports, 90, 92-3
    interstate, 94
trains *see* rail services
Transit Oriented Development, 42, 84-5,
    293, 317
transport

    long-distance, 91, 95
    *see also* cars; public transport;
        roads; trains
Treechange City, 307-09

**urban** farming *see under* food production
urban planning, 17
    holistic approach, 261, 315
    legislation, 27
    place based, 249, 256
    social considerations, 98-9,
        259, 343, 345
    zoning *see under* Perth Region
    *see also* Metropolitan Region
        Scheme; Network City
urban sprawl, 29-31, 38-41, 98, 176,
    182-92

**Vancouver**, ecological footprint, 82

**Warnbro**, 54
waste, 64-6
    building materials, 64-5
    per capita, 64, 66-7
    in landfill, 64-7
    organic, 64-7
    recycled, 64, 66
    tyres, 64
wastewater, 70, 71
    recycling, 68, 69, 70, 104, 146
    *see also* sanitation
Water for a Healthy Nation, 241
water quality, 70
water run-off, 39, 146
    management at Wungong,
        256-57, 259, 260
    pollution from, 32, 128, 131, 146

water supplies, 19, 25, 45, 61, 68, 163
    desalination, 46, 69, 146
    groundwater, 68-9, 146, 154, 155
    land reserved for, 150
    reticulation, 67
    surface water, 69
water usage, 32, 68-73, 104
    for gardens, 146
waterbirds, 128
West Australian Planning Commission, 42
wetlands, 69, 126, 128, 183, 265
    for development, 153, 170, 183-7
    protected, 152
workforce *see* employment
Wright, Frank Lloyd, 277, 279
Wright, Shane, 59
Wright and Palassis, 430
Wungong Urban Water project, xii,
    240-57, 269
    Food City scenario, 279, 286
    Garden City comparison, 269, 277
    habitat linkage, 265